THE NEW YORK

PUBLIC LIBRARY

LITERATURE

COMPANION

EDITED BY ANNE SKILLION

THE FREE PRESS

NEW YORK   LONDON   TORONTO   SYDNEY   SINGAPORE

*f*P

THE FREE PRESS

A Division of Simon & Schuster, Inc.
Rockefeller Center
1230 Avenue of the Americas
New York, NY 10020

A STONESONG PRESS BOOK

For information regarding special discounts
for bulk purchases, please contact Simon &
Schuster Special Sales at 1-800-456-6798

Designed by Martin Lubin Graphic Design

Additional typesetting by Brad Walrod/High
Text Graphics, Inc.

Manufactured in the United States of America

10 9 8 7 6 5 4 3 2 1

LIBRARY OF CONGRESS
CATALOGING-IN-PUBLICATION DATA

New York Public Library.
  The New York Public Library literature
companion/by the staff of the New York Public
Library; edited by Anne Skillion.
    p. cm.
  Includes bibliographical references and
index.
  1. Literature—Dictionaries. 2. Literature—
Bio-bibliography. 3. Characters and character-
istics in literature—Dictionaries. I. Skillion,
Anne. II. Title

PN41.N49 2001   2001034219
803—cd21

ISBN 0-684-86890-3

PERMISSIONS

"Still I Rise" by Maya Angelou, from *And Still I Rise* by
Maya Angelou, copyright © 1978 by Maya Angelou. Used
by permission of Random House, Inc.

"The More Loving One," copyright © 1957 by W. H.
Auden, from *W. H. Auden: Collected Poems* by W. H.
Auden. Used by permission of Random House, Inc.

"A Song in the Front Yard" from *Blacks* by Gwendolyn
Brooks, copyright 1987 by Gwendolyn Brooks, reprinted by
permission of Third World Press, Inc., Chicago, Illinois.

The lines from "i sing of Olaf glad and big" Copyright
1931, © 1959, 1991 by the Trustees for the E. E. Cummings
Trust. Copyright © 1979 by George James Firmage, from
Complete Poems: 1904–1962 by E. E. Cummings, edited by
George J. Firmage. Used by permission of Liveright
Publishing Corporation.

"The Love Song of J. Alfred Prufrock," from *Collected Poems
1909–1962* by T. S. Eliot. Published by Harcourt, Inc.

"Howl" from *Collected Poems 1947–1980* by Allen
Ginsberg, copyright © 1955 by Allen Ginsberg. Used by
permission of HarperCollins Publishers.

"Resume," copyright 1926, 1928, renewed 1954, © 1956
by Dorothy Parker, from *The Portable Dorothy Parker* by
Dorothy Parker. Used by permission of Viking Penguin, a
division of Penguin Putnam Inc.

THE NEW YORK PUBLIC LIBRARY LITERATURE COMPANION

EDITOR-IN-CHIEF
Anne Skillion

ASSOCIATE EDITOR
Barbara Bergeron

NYPL PROJECT MANAGER
Kenneth Benson

SENIOR WRITERS

Michelle Alpern	Ruth Greenstein
Kenneth Benson	Jeff Hacker
Barbara Bergeron	Lara Merlin
Kathie Coblentz	George Ochoa
Melinda Corey	Anne Skillion
Justin Cronin	Amy Stoller

OTHER CONTRIBUTORS

Kerry Acker	Warren Platt
Bill Bennett	Marshall Robinson
Celia Bland	Jack Rummel
Liz Denlinger	Sarah Scheffel
Bonnie Fetterman	Nina Sonenberg
Kathryn Hilt	Tom Wiloch
Brendan January	Jennifer Woolf
Sarah Parvis	Robert Workoff
Rodney Phillips	

Special thanks to the many NYPL staff members who offered their review, information, and suggestions, including Fernando Acosta-Rodriguez, Robert Armitage, Usha Bhasker, Robert Davis, Elizabeth Diefendorf, Denise Hibay, Robert Kent, Chungsoo Kim, Wojciech Siemaszkiewicz, Michael Terry, Todd Thompson, and Qi Xie.

Contents

III   LITERARY FACTS AND RESOURCES

Foreword

For over one hundred years The New York Public Library has collected, preserved, and made accessible the written records of the world's literary heritage. Through its vast collections and myriad programs and initiatives, in its four research centers and its extensive system of neighborhood branches, the Library has served the world of literary scholarship and nurtured the love of literature for generations of readers.

From the beginning, writers and scholars have mined the Library's magisterial holdings in literature, which are both breathtaking in scope and brilliant in detail. The collections have long featured some of the rarest and most precious monuments of world literature, from beautiful illuminated medieval works to the first three folio editions of Shakespeare, as well as significant literary manuscripts by Nathaniel Hawthorne, William Makepeace Thackeray, Virginia Woolf, Langston Hughes, and many others. The continued generosity of donors has dramatically enriched the Library's literature collections, which now encompass rare books, critical works, manuscripts, notebooks, letters, and personal effects of authors from virtually all historical periods and in hundreds of languages.

All of those associated with the Library, either as users or staff members, have their favorites within this huge universe—perhaps the original manuscript of T. S. Eliot's *The Waste Land*, the autograph poems of Elizabeth Barrett Browning, the archives of *The New Yorker* magazine, or some other item from the many special caches of manuscripts, diaries, and letters of writers as various as Charles Dickens, Jack Kerouac, and Zora Neale Hurston.

The Library's dynamic relationship with literature and the writing life extends well beyond its famous collections and expert staff of librarians and curators, however. Its active publishing program produces books related to literature for both scholarly and general audiences, including volumes inspired by the Library's exhibitions, such as *Books of the Century* and *The Hand of the Poet*, and lists of recommended reading, such as *Books to Remember*, a popular annual selection that has been published for more than 40 years.

This splendid new reference work, *The New York Public Library Literature Companion*, is the latest embodiment of the Library's longtime and passionate commitment to the world of literature. Indeed, when it comes to its manifold contributions to literature and the literary life, one might with justification say that The New York Public Library is, to paraphrase Voltaire, the best of all possible libraries.

PAUL LeClerc

President, The New York Public Library

Editor's Note

This one-volume companion to literature is organized both for ease of use and to enhance the reader's opportunities for browsing, discovery, and pleasure. The book is divided into three major parts — Creators, Works of Literature, and Literary Facts and Resources — each with a number of sections and special features.

Wide-ranging in scope, *The New York Public Library Literature Companion* covers major figures and works of literature from around the world and all historical periods. English-language literature predominates, but the coverage of literature in other languages is significant, although in general focusing on authors and works currently available in English translation or whose historical importance mandated inclusion.

Authors and **Other Influential Figures:** Many of the writers listed in the Authors section have played multiple literary roles, just as many of the biographers, critics, editors, publishers, thinkers, and translators found in the section headed Other Influential Figures are or were also literary authors — that is, poets, playwrights, novelists, or writers of stories. The decision to place the entry for a given individual in one section or the other was based on a sense of where his or her greatest reputation and influence seem to reside today, without implying any judgment of that person's work in other genres.

Essays and Other Diversions: A unique feature of the book is the array of short historical and anecdotal essays, gatherings of quotations and excerpts, matching quizzes, and lists scattered throughout the book (set off by background shading), whose main purpose is to amuse and intrigue, but which may also sometimes have the effect of increasing awareness of the presence of literature in unsuspected places. These features are listed at the end of the index.

Pointers to Additional Resources: Readers who would like to delve more deeply into the lives of their favorite authors, the plot of a favorite book, or the critics' assessments of a poem or story will find guidance, based on the extensive experience of New York Public Library librarians, toward the best sources for further research on these and myriad other matters in the bibliographies included in each section. The bibliography of Websites for Literature lists some of the best and most authoritative literary sites on the Web (admittedly a constantly growing and fluctuating universe) as this book went to press.

Reading Lists: Those in search of suggestions to guide their own reading will find them not only in the section titled Recommended Reading, but also in the bibliography of Notable Biographical Works included in Sources in Literary Biography in Part I; in the Authors' and Book Awards lists; and in several of the essays and other diversions.

Editorial Practices

Alphabetization is letter-by-letter, not word-by-word.

Cross-references: The sections for **Authors, Other Influential Figures,** and **Works of Literature** include cross-references (in SMALL

CAPITAL LETTERS) to persons who have their own entries in the Authors or Other Influential Figures sections, to works with separate entries in the Works of Literature section, to periodicals included in the Influential Literary Periodicals section, and to literary characters with individual entries in the Characters section.

Dates: Dates after a title refer in all cases except plays to first publication; in the case of plays, dates refer to the first staged production unless otherwise stated. In the case of works first published in a language other than English, the date refers to first publication in the original language. Novels first published serially are cited by the date of first complete book publication. In entries for Russian individuals or titles, New Style dates only are given.

Personal Names: The boldface entry name is that under which the figure is most commonly known. Additional elements — the spelling out of a full name represented by an initial, official first names, titles (e.g., Sir, Comte), etc. — are supplied between brackets. Middle and other names that do not form a part of the commonly known name are not supplied. Further information about personal names is preceded by the following italicized notes: *pen name, original name, known as, in full,* etc.

Prizes: Major prizes (including the Nobel Prize in Literature, the Pulitzer Prize, the National Book Award, the Booker Prize, and the Prix Goncourt) are generally noted within entries in the Authors, Other Influential Figures, and Works sections. But the reader should consult the sections on Authors' Awards and on Book Awards for more extensive coverage of awards and prizes.

Titles of Works: Titles in the Works of Literature section are usually given in conventional shortened form (e.g., *Tristram Shandy*, rather than *The Life and Opinions of Tristram Shandy, Gentleman*), and, for multipart works, under the collective title, e.g., *Remembrance of Things Past*; more detailed information is provided within the entry. For non-English-language works, the title of the standard English-language translation is given first, followed in parentheses by the title in its original language, and by alternate published translated titles where appropriate. For works never to our knowledge published separately in English, the original title is followed in parentheses by a literal translation of the title in roman type.

CREATORS

Authors

Abbey, Edward (January 29, 1927–March 14, 1989). American essayist and novelist. Born and raised on a Pennsylvania farm, Abbey studied at the University of New Mexico before joining the National Park Service full time. His best-known work, *Desert Solitaire* (1968), a nonfiction account of his experiences as a ranger in Utah, is a meditation on the beauty of the Southwestern desert and the human practices that threaten it. This book and *The Monkey Wrench Gang* (1975), a novel about a band of radical environmentalists, quickly became revered guides for the environmental movement. Other novels include *The Brave Cowboy* (1958), *Fire on the Mountain* (1962), *The Fool's Progress* (1988), and *Hayduke Lives!* (1990), a sequel to *The Monkey Wrench Gang*.

Abbott, George (June 25, 1887–January 31, 1995). American playwright and screenwriter. Over the course of an exceptionally long career on Broadway (he worked well into his 90s and lived to be 107), Abbott coauthored and staged many popular farces and musical comedies. Born in Forestville, New York, Abbott studied at the University of Rochester and began his theater career as an actor. His productions — often collaborations — include such hits as *Broadway* (1926, cowritten with Philip Dunning), *Three Men on a Horse* (1935, cowritten with John Cecil Holm), and the musicals *The Pajama Game* (1954, cowritten with Richard Bissell), *Damn Yankees* (1955, cowritten with Douglas Wallop), and the Pulitzer Prize–winning *Fiorello!* (1959, cowritten with Jerome Weidman). Revivals of Abbott's musicals *On Your* *Toes* (1936, cowritten with Richard Rodgers and Lorenz Hart) and *Damn Yankees* in recent decades reveal the popular appeal and staying power of this artist's comic vision. In the 1920s and 1930s he wrote a number of screenplays, including the Academy Award–nominated *All Quiet on the Western Front* (1930), cowritten with Maxwell Anderson and Del Andrews. *Mister Abbott* (1963) is his autobiography.

Abe, Kōbō, *pen name of* Abe Kimifusa (March 7, 1924–January 22, 1993). Japanese novelist and playwright. One of the few Japanese writers to achieve international popularity, Abe created works detached from place and distinguished by a surrealist and absurdist sensibility. Their recurrent themes of isolation and alienation in modern urban life give them universal relevance. Abe grew up in Japanese-occupied Manchuria, and trained as a doctor in Tokyo, although he never practiced. In the late 1940s, he established a reputation as a writer of experimental allegories. His best-known work, THE WOMAN IN THE DUNES (*Suna no Onna*, 1962), is often cited as one of the finest Japanese novels of the post–World War II period. Other notable works include the novels *The Face of Another* (*Tanin no Kao*, 1964), *The Ruined Map* (*Moetsukita Chizu*, 1967), THE BOX MAN (*Hakootoko*, 1973), *The Secret Rendezvous* (*Mikkai*, 1977), *The Ark Sakura* (*Hakobune Sakura Maru*, 1984), and *The Kangaroo Note-book* (*Kangarū Nōto*, 1991). Many of Abe's works, including *The Woman in the Dunes*, have been made into films. A collection of his stories in English translation, *Beyond the Curve*, appeared in 1991.

Achebe, Chinua, *in full* Albert Chinualumogu Achebe (November 16, 1930–). Nigerian novelist, short-story writer, essayist, poet, and editor. One of Africa's best-known English-language writers, Achebe explores the impact of colonialism on traditional African life; his works reflect his firm belief that the writer should serve as both critic and conscience of his community. Educated at the University of Ibadan, Achebe worked at the Nigerian Broadcasting Corporation, cofounded a publishing company, and has held professorships at the University of Nigeria and at several American universities. As an editor and publisher, he has played an important role in bringing contemporary African literature to the West. Achebe came to international prominence after the publication of his enormously popular first novel, *THINGS FALL APART* (1958). His other novels include *No Longer at Ease* (1960), *Arrow of God* (1964), *A Man of the People* (1966), and *Anthills of the Savannah* (1987). He has also published collections of essays, stories, poems, and several children's books based on Igbo folktales.

Aciman, André (January 2, 1951–). American memoirist, essayist, and critic. Born and raised in Alexandria, Egypt, Aciman also lived in Italy and France before settling in the United States in 1968. He took a doctorate from Harvard, and has taught French and comparative literature at several colleges and universities, including Harvard, Princeton, New York University, and Bard. His much-acclaimed memoir, *Out of Egypt* (1995), tells the story of his cultured, urbane Jewish family's 60-year sojourn in Egypt, from their arrival in Alexandria in 1905 to their final expulsion in 1965, just before he turned 15. Aciman's lyrical, witty reflections on place, time, and memory have appeared in many publications, including *The New York Times* and *THE NEW YORKER*, and were collected in *False Papers: Essays on Exile and Memory* (2000), a book that led one critic to call him "our contemporary Proust." He also contributed to and edited the collection of essays *Letters of Transit:*

Reflections on Exile, Identity, and Loss (1999). Aciman's literary criticism has appeared in *PARTISAN REVIEW, THE NEW YORK REVIEW OF BOOKS,* and *THE NEW REPUBLIC,* among other journals.

"Writing has become my way of finding a space and of building a home for myself, my way of taking a shapeless, marshy world and firming it up with paper, the way the Venetians firm up eroded land by driving wooden piles into it."

André Aciman, "A Literary Pilgrim Progresses to the Past," *The New York Times* (August 28, 2000)

Ackroyd, Peter (October 5, 1949–). English novelist, biographer, and critic. Blurring the boundaries between past and present, fact and fiction, Ackroyd's innovative novels are marked by his idiosyncratic conception of history and the nature of time. Ackroyd was born in London and educated at Cambridge and Yale, returning in 1973 to London, where he began a career in literary journalism. Among his novels are *The Great Fire of London* (1982), *The Last Testament of Oscar Wilde* (1983), the popular and award-winning *Hawksmoor* (1985), *Chatterton* (1987), *English Music* (1992), and *The Trial of Elizabeth Cree: A Novel of the Limehouse Murders* (1994). Ackroyd's distinguished biographies include *Ezra Pound and His World* (1980), *T. S. Eliot: A Life* (1984), *Dickens* (1990), *Blake* (1995), and *The Life of Thomas More* (1998). *London: The Biography* appeared to critical acclaim in 2000.

Adams, Henry (February 16, 1838–March 27, 1918). American biographer, historian, and editor. The great-grandson of John Adams and the grandson of John Quincy Adams, both U.S. presidents, Adams chose the life of a reform-minded scholar instead of that of a statesman. His autobiography, *THE EDUCATION OF HENRY ADAMS* (1907), is one of the great works of American letters. Adams was born in Boston and educated at Harvard. During the Civil War, he worked in London as a secretary to his father, who was an ambassador to Britain. Back in the United States he worked for political reform as a journalist and, from 1870 to 1876, as editor of THE NORTH AMERICAN REVIEW. At the same time, he accepted a professorship in medieval history at Harvard. A remarkably productive scholar, Adams published two biographies and two novels—*Democracy, an American Novel* (1880), published anonymously, and *Esther* (1884), published pseudonymously—before turning to his monumental nine-volume *History of the United States of America During the Administrations of Thomas Jefferson and James Madison* (1889–91). Adams's exploration of the medieval worldview, MONT-SAINT-MICHEL AND CHARTRES (1904), also stands among his finest achievements.

Æ, *pen name of* George William Russell (April 10, 1867–July 17, 1935). Irish poet. An ardent nationalist, Russell led the early 20th-century Irish Literary Renaissance along with poet W. B. YEATS and playwright John Millington SYNGE, contributing to a revitalization of Irish literature and culture. Russell's mystical poetry, incorporating visions and magical themes, was first published in *Homeward: Songs by the Way* in 1894. He followed with *The Earth Breath* (1897), *The Divine Vision* (1904), *Gods of War* (1915), *Midsummer Eve* (1928), and the Celtic-themed *The House of the Titans* (1934). Russell edited the magazine *The Irish Homestead* from 1904 to 1923 and the more political journal, *The Irish Statesman*, from 1923 to 1930. Russell also wrote prolifically on political, economic, and social issues, including agricultural reform, cooperative societies, and the Irish question, as well as on mysticism. *The Living Torch* (1937) collects "A.E.'s table-talk," reprinted primarily from his columns in *The Irish Statesman*; an autobiography, *The Candle of Vision*, narrates the poet's efforts "to relate his own vision to the vision of the seers and writers of the sacred books." Russell received his unusual pen name by accident: in 1888, he wrote a letter to the editor of *Lucifer* signed "Aeon" (Latin, meaning age or lifetime; from the Greek *aion*), and the

printer could decipher only the first two letters—thus "Æ" was born.

Aeschylus, *in Greek* Aischylos (525 B.C.–456 B.C.). Greek playwright. The first distinguished playwright of ancient Athens, Aeschylus markedly changed the dramatic form of tragedy by increasing the number of actors to two and diminishing the role of the chorus, thereby making possible true dialogue and action. Born to an aristocratic family in Eleusis, northwest of Athens, Aeschylus was wounded at the battle of Marathon (490 B.C.) and probably fought the Persians again at Salamis in 480 B.C. He was a major competitor in the Dionysia, Athens's premier dramatic contest, which he first won in 484 B.C. after more than a decade of competing. His plays were noted for their august and lyrical language, moral and religious themes, and spectacular costumes and effects. He lost the Dionysia to Sophocles in 468 B.C., but had a final grand victory in 458 B.C. with his masterpiece, the ORESTEIA, a trilogy composed of *Agamemnōn, The Libation Bearers* (*Choēphoroi*), and *The Furies* (*Eumenides*). Only seven of his plays out of some 80 or 90 are extant; the others are *The Suppliants* (*Hiketides*, c. 423 B.C.), THE PERSIANS (*Persai*, 472 B.C.), SEVEN AGAINST THEBES (*Hepta epi Thēbas*, 467 B.C.), and PROMETHEUS BOUND (*Promētheus Desmōtēs*, date unknown). According to a popular story, Aeschylus died in Sicily when an eagle dropped a tortoise on his bald head, fulfilling a prophecy that he would be killed by a blow from heaven.

Aesop, *in Greek* Aisōpos. Greek fabulist. The Western tradition of fables, or moral tales with animal characters, began with the stories we now attribute to Aesop, some 200 of which—including "The Fox and the Grapes" and "The Tortoise and the Hare"—are collected in modern editions. There has been considerable speculation as to Aesop's identity and whether in fact he existed at all, but many scholars today believe that Aesop was simply a name invented to provide an author for an accumulating body of fables. The earliest surviving collections were gathered by Greek poets and Latin translators, who added Oriental and other ancient stories to form *AESOP'S FABLES*. The collection made by Phaedrus in the 1st century A.D. greatly influenced Jean de LA FONTAINE and other later fable writers.

Agee, James (November 27, 1909–May 16, 1955). American novelist, film critic, and screenwriter. Agee is remembered for his influential film criticism, his sensitive and lyrical autobiographical fiction, and his insights into the plight of America's poor. Agee grew up in Tennessee's Cumberland Mountains region and was educated at Harvard. His first book, *Permit Me Voyage*, a collection of poetry, was published in the Yale Series of Younger Poets in 1934. Two years later, he and photographer Walker Evans lived among sharecroppers in Alabama for a *Fortune* magazine piece; out of this experience came not an article, but the book *Let Us Now Praise Famous Men* (1941). In 1957, his posthumously published novel, *A DEATH IN THE FAMILY* (1957), won the Pulitzer Prize. After 1948, Agee concentrated on film reviewing and screenwriting, producing scripts for *The African Queen* (1951), *The Night of the Hunter* (1955), and other films. His film criticism and several screenplays are collected in the two-volume *Agee on Film* (1958, 1960).

Agnon, S. Y., *pen name of* Shmuel Yosef Halevi Czaczkes (July 17, 1888–February 17, 1970). Israeli novelist and short-story writer. Celebrated for reintroducing traditional Hebrew literary styles and considered by many to be modern Hebrew fiction's greatest virtuoso, Agnon became the first Hebrew-language writer to win the Nobel Prize (shared with Nelly Sachs, in 1966). Born in Galicia, where he received a traditional Jewish education, Agnon initially wrote in both Yiddish and Hebrew, but when he immigrated to Palestine in 1907, he adopted the surname Agnon and began to write exclusively in Hebrew. Among his best-known works are *The Bridal Canopy* (*Hakhnasat Kallah*, 1931), a story featuring a Hasidic wanderer in the Old World ghettos of Russia and Eastern Europe; *Days of Awe* (*Yamim Noraim*, 1937), an anthology of folktales inspired by the High Holy Days; *A Guest for the Night* (*Ore'ah Natah Lalun*, 1939), about the dissolution of European Jewish life after World War I; and *Only Yesterday* (*Tmol Shilshom*, 1945), an epic about Israel's early immigrant pioneers.

Aiken, Conrad (August 5, 1889–August 17, 1973). American poet, short-story writer, novelist, and critic. Aiken was born in Savannah, Georgia, and suffered a childhood trauma that had an undeniable impact on his life and work: the loss of his parents by a murder-suicide perpetrated by his father, the 11-year-old discovering their bodies. A later interest in psychoanalytic theory may be traced in part to this event. Aiken attended Harvard, along with his friend and fellow poet T. S. ELIOT, and began publishing soon after graduating in 1911. His *Selected Poems* (1929) won a Pulitzer Prize. Some of his finest poems, including "Preludes to Definition" and "Morning Song of Senlin," are gathered in *Collected Poems* (1953). Short-story collections include *Bring! Bring!* (1925) and *Among the Lost People* (1934). *Ushant* (1952), an autobiography, and *The Selected Letters of Conrad Aiken* (1978) shed light on Aiken's life and the literary figures he knew, including E. E. CUMMINGS, Wallace STEVENS, and EDMUND WILSON. As editor of Emily DICKINSON's *Selected Poems* (1924), Aiken played a key role in establishing her reputation.

Akhmatova, Anna, *pen name of* Anna Andreyevna Gorenko (June 23, 1889–March 5, 1966). Russian poet. A poet whose work is deeply informed by the textures and traditions of European, English, and of course her native Russian poetry, and whose life has become emblematic of the intellectual unbowed before the forces of totalitarianism, Akhmatova is now ranked as one of the greatest poets of the 20th century. Born near Odessa, Akhmatova became a key member, along with her first husband, Nikolay Gumilyov, and the poet Osip MANDELSHTAM, of the Acmeist school of poets, which championed precision, clarity, and a style of concrete realism in reaction to the Symbolist mysticism that prevailed in contemporary Russian poetry. The lyrical love poems in *Evening* (*Vecher*, 1912) formed her first book;

her second collection, *Rosary* (*Chetki*, 1914), made her famous. Although she included poems with patriotic themes in her next three volumes—*White Flock* (*Belaya Staya*, 1917), *Plantain* (*Podorozhnik*, 1921), and *Anno Domini MCMXXI* (1922)—Stalinist officials judged her work to be too preoccupied with love and God. From 1923 to 1940, no volume of her work was published in the Soviet Union, but she continued to write, including the long poem *REQUIEM* (*REKVIEM*, completed 1940, published 1963), written in response to her husband's execution and her son's 1937 imprisonment. (She later discovered at public readings that many in the audience could recite her clandestinely circulated poem from memory.) In 1946 she was expelled from the Writers' Union, but in the following decade, under Khrushchev's less restrictive regime, she was able to publish again. Her longest work, *Poem Without a Hero* (*Poema bez Geroya*, 1965), is widely regarded as a masterpiece. A landmark edition, *The Complete Poems of Anna Akhmatova*, with facing English and Russian texts, was published in 1990.

Aksyonov, Vasily *or* **Vassily** (August 20, 1932–). Russian novelist and short-story writer. A leader among the post–World War II generation of Soviet writers, Aksyonov has led a life deeply marked by the ravages of Soviet history. His parents spent years in Stalin's labor camps and he lived part of his childhood in exile in Siberia, an experience he later fictionalized in *The Burn* (*Ozhog*, 1980). After briefly practicing medicine, Aksyonov began writing full time, publishing three novels during the more lenient "thaw" era, including *A Ticket to the Stars* (*Zvezdnyĭ Bilet*, 1961), a notorious slang-filled account of the adventures of rebellious Soviet youth. But he eventually met with difficulties in publishing his ever-more avant-garde and satirical work. He resigned from the Writers' Union in 1979 and was soon forced into exile, returning to his homeland for the first time only in 1990. Aksyonov, who had previously taught at Johns Hopkins University and Goucher College, became professor of Russian literature and writing at George Mason University in 1988. His later

works include *The Island of Crimea* (*Ostrov Krym*, 1981); *Generations of Winter* (vols. 1 and 2 of the trilogy *Moskovskaya Saga*, 1993), a sprawling saga of a Moscow family during the Stalinist era; and the comic novel *The New Sweet Style* (*Novyĭ Sladostnyĭ Stil'*), chronicling the picaresque adventures of a Russian émigré, a singer/composer/playwright reviled by the Communist powers-that-be, who comes to America to make a fresh start in life.

Albee, Edward (March 12, 1928–). American playwright. Appearance versus reality, domination versus submission, and violence as an undeniable component of love are some of the dualities explored in Albee's dramas. Born somewhere in Virginia, Albee was adopted in Washington, D.C., at the age of two weeks by Reed and Frances Albee; his father was part-owner of the Keith-Albee circuit of vaudeville theaters. He graduated from Choate School and spent one year at Trinity College in Connecticut, then began writing plays in the late 1950s. Albee became closely identified with the Theater of the Absurd through his experimental, often bleak one-acts, including *THE ZOO STORY* (1959), *The Sandbox* (1960), and *THE AMERICAN DREAM* (1961). His first full-length play, *WHO'S AFRAID OF VIRGINIA WOOLF?* (1962), a harrowing portrayal of married life, is his best-known work. Other important works include three Pulitzer Prize winners, *A Delicate Balance* (1966), *Seascape* (1975), and *THREE TALL WOMEN* (1991); and *Tiny Alice* (1964) and *The Play About the Baby* (1998). Albee has also adapted for the stage the works of several other writers, including *THE BALLAD OF THE SAD CAFÉ* (1963), from the Carson MCCULLERS novella.

Alcott, Louisa May (November 29, 1832– March 6, 1888). American novelist, short-story writer, and children's author. Alcott is most famous for her novel *Little Women* (1868), a loving but realistic portrait of a family very much like her own. She spent most of her life in Massachusetts and is especially associated with Concord, where her father, the radical Transcendentalist philosopher Bronson Alcott, moved his family in 1840 after the failure of his experimental school in Boston. Alcott received a haphazard education, but she read voraciously and was strongly influenced by her father's friends Ralph Waldo EMERSON and Henry David THOREAU. She first achieved literary success with her lively *Hospital Sketches* (1863), cast from the letters she wrote home from Washington, D.C., while serving as a volunteer nurse during the Civil War. (Her tour of duty was cut short when she contracted typhoid fever, and she never fully recovered her health.) Throughout the 1860s, Alcott churned out sensationalistic potboilers for the money, all published either anonymously or pseudonymously. The enormous financial success of *Little Women* guaranteed that Alcott (and her family) would thereafter live comfortably. From 1870 onward, Alcott produced a steady succession of "healthy and hearty" tales, novels, and sketches for young readers, including *Little Men* (1871) and *Rose in Bloom* (1876). Her adult fiction includes *Moods* (1864), a study of marriage; *Work: A Story of Experience* (1874), based on her struggles to support herself; and *A Modern Mephistopheles* (1877), a steamy psychological thriller that was published anonymously.

Algren, Nelson, *original name* Nelson Ahlgren Abraham (March 28, 1909–May 9, 1981). American novelist and short-story writer. Algren's fiction is noted for its brutally honest depiction of the lives of the poor, especially in Chicago's slums. Born to a working-class family in Detroit, Algren was raised in Chicago and took a degree in journalism at the University of Illinois. His first novel, *Somebody in Boots* (1935), tells of a young Texas drifter in Depression-era Chicago. While his second novel, *Never Come Morning* (1942), the story of a criminal who aspires to be a prize-fighter, garnered some attention, his next, THE MAN WITH THE GOLDEN ARM (1949), dealing with drug addiction, won him the National Book Award and international acclaim. Algren's work caught the interest of Ernest HEMINGWAY as well as the French Existentialists, notably Simone de BEAUVOIR, who became his lover. *The Neon Wilderness* (1947) is a story collection

based on Algren's World War II service. A WALK ON THE WILD SIDE (1956), his final novel, is set in the bohemian enclaves of New Orleans.

Allende, Isabel (August 2, 1942–). Chilean novelist and short-story writer. One of Latin America's best-known and bestselling contemporary writers, Allende utilizes magic realism and women storytellers to explore political and emotional concerns. Born in Lima, Peru, Allende was raised in Chile and worked as a journalist there until she was forced into exile after the 1973 assassination of her uncle, President Salvador Allende. Her first novel, *The House of the Spirits* (*La Casa de los Espíritus*, 1982), was an international bestseller and drew comparisons to the work of Gabriel GARCÍA MÁRQUEZ. Other notable works include the novels *Of Love and Shadows* (*De Amor y de Sombra*, 1984), *Eva Luna* (1987), and *Daughter of Fortune* (*Hija de la Fortuna*, 1998); the story collection *The Stories of Eva Luna* (*Cuentos de Eva Luna*, 1990); and the memoir *Paula* (1994), an account of her daughter's fatal illness.

Almqvist *or* **Almquist, C**[arl] **J**[onas] **L**[ove] (November 28, 1793–September 26, 1866). Swedish novelist, poet, essayist, and playwright. An influential figure in the history of Swedish literature and a precursor to August STRINDBERG, the prolific Almqvist is especially noted today for his then unconventional feminist views about sex roles. While making his living at a series of jobs as a civil servant, farmer, teacher, and clergyman, he began to write, producing his first major literary work, *Amorina*, a novel about a young woman's incestuous love for her minister father, in 1821. In 1834, he wrote *The Queen's Diadem* (*Drottningens Juvelsmycke*), his greatest book, whose androgynous heroine, Tintomara, is the central symbolic figure in his work. In the later 1830s, he published *Sara Videbeck* (*Det Går An*, 1839), a novel that presented the author's radical views on love and marriage and effectively made him *persona non grata* in Sweden. Accused of forgery and murder, he went into exile in the United States and later Germany, where he died. Most of his novels, stories, plays, and poems are collected in the multivolume *Törnrosens Bok* (1832–51; The Book of the Thorn Rose).

Amado, Jorge (August 10, 1912–August 6, 2001). Brazilian novelist. Amado's influential and widely translated novels portray both the injustice of poverty and the vibrancy of life in Brazil. After a childhood spent on a cocoa plantation and in school in Salvador, Amado published his first novel at the age of 20. His early works include two sagas about the greed of landowners, *The Violent Land* (*Terras do Sem Fim*, 1942) and *The Golden Harvest* (*Saõ Jorge des Ilhéus*, 1944). His novels of the 1950s and 1960s, such as *Gabriela, Clove and Cinnamon* (*Gabriela, Cravo e Canela*, 1958) and *Dona Flor and Her Two Husbands* (*Dona Flor e Seus Dois Maridos*, 1966), are satirical in tone and feature self-made women who have risen above their impoverished upbringings. Amado's radical politics brought him, variously, imprisonment, exile, and election to the national Constituent Assembly. Later novels include *Showdown* (*Tocaia Grande*, 1984) and *The War of the Saints* (*Sumiço da Santa*, 1993).

Amis, [Sir] Kingsley (April 16, 1922–October 22, 1995). English novelist, poet, and critic. Best known for his popular first novel, *LUCKY JIM* (1954), Kingsley Amis wrote more than 20 novels noted for their sharp satire, clever dialogue, and eccentric antiheroes. Amis was born in South London and graduated from St. John's College, Oxford, in 1949, after serving in the Royal Corps of Signals during World War II. During his early career in academia, as a lecturer at the University College of Swansea and then at Cambridge, he decided to commit himself to writing. Amis published widely in several genres, including poetry and essays, but it was his novels that won him instant attention, a loyal following, and a reputation as one of Britain's Angry Young Men. Notable among them are *That Uncertain Feeling* (1955), *The Green Man* (1969), *Jake's Thing* (1978), the Booker Prize–winning *The Old Devils* (1986), and *The Russian Girl* (1992). His nonfiction includes *The King's English: A Guide to Modern Usage* (1998). The father of writer MARTIN AMIS, the senior Amis published his *Memoirs* in 1991; his *Letters* appeared in 2000.

Amis, Martin (August 25, 1949–). English novelist, journalist, and essayist. The son of writer KINGSLEY AMIS, Martin Amis is known for his inventive wordplay and his cynical satires exploring human cruelty and contemporary urban life. Amis was born in Oxford and graduated from Oxford University in 1971. He then worked as a journalist for the *TIMES LITERARY SUPPLEMENT* (1972–75) and *THE NEW STATESMAN* (1975–79). His first novel, *The Rachel Papers* (1973), announced a young writer of

---

"Literature is the great garden that is always there and is open to everyone 24 hours a day. Who tends it? The old tour guides and sylviculturists, the wardens, the fuming parkies in their sweat-soaked serge: these have died off. If you do see an official, a professional, these days, then he's likely to be a scowl in a labcoat, come to flatten a forest or decapitate a peak. The public wanders, with its oohs and ahs, its groans and jeers, its million opinions. The wanderers feed the animals, they walk on the grass, they step in the flowerbeds. But the garden never suffers. It is, of course, Eden; it is unfallen and needs no care."

Martin Amis, "Battling Banality," *The Guardian* (March 24, 2001)

---

great promise. His reputation was confirmed with *Success* (1978), *Money: A Suicide Note* (1984), *LONDON FIELDS* (1989), and *Time's Arrow* (1991), which documents in reverse chronology the life of a physician and Nazi war criminal. More recent works include the novels *The Information* (1995) and *Night Train* (1997), the story collection *Heavy Water and Other Stories* (1998), the memoir *Experience* (2000), and a collection of critical essays, *The War Against Cliché* (2001).

Anderson, Sherwood (September 13, 1876–March 8, 1941). American short-story writer and novelist. Celebrated for his masterwork, WINESBURG, OHIO (1919), Anderson had a marked impact on Ernest HEMINGWAY, William FAULKNER, and other American writers of his time. Anderson, who was born in Ohio, was largely self-educated and held a variety of jobs while writing for small magazines. In 1912, he abruptly left his wife and job and went to Chicago, where he met other Midwestern writers, including Theodore DREISER, and determined to pursue a literary career. His first two works were novels, *Windy McPherson's Son* (1916) and *Marching Man* (1917), but it was *Winesburg, Ohio* that established Anderson's reputation as an original voice. In a style drawn from everyday speech, *Winesburg* offers a series of related sketches about life in a small Midwestern town. Anderson's stories are collected in *The Triumph of the Egg* (1921), *Horses and Men* (1923), and *Death in the Woods* (1933). *The Memoirs of Sherwood Anderson* (1969) was published posthumously.

Angelou, Maya, *original name* Marguerite Johnson (April 4, 1928–). American poet and memoirist. Born in St. Louis and raised by her grandmother in segregated rural Arkansas, Angelou in much of her work tries to come to terms with some harrowing life events: at age eight she was raped by her mother's boyfriend and was mute for a period thereafter; at age 16 she gave birth to a son. Over the following decades she worked as an actress, singer, and dancer; a civil rights activist; an editor and lecturer in Ghana; and a professor and author. Her autobiographical works include *I Know Why the Caged Bird Sings* (1970), *Singin' and Swingin' and Gettin' Merry Like Christmas* (1976), *The Heart of a Woman* (1981), and *All God's Children Need Traveling Shoes* (1986). Her poetry collections include *Just Give Me a Cool Drink of Water 'fore I Diiie* (1971) and *And Still I Rise* (1987). In 1993, Angelou was invited to write and present a poem at the inauguration of President Clinton. Her powerful voice and presence have made her a popular public figure. Recent publications include *The Complete Collected Poems of Maya Angelou* (1994) and *Phenomenal Woman* (2000).

Anouilh, Jean (June 23, 1910–October 3, 1987). French playwright and screenwriter. A major force in French theater from the late 1930s through the 1950s, Anouilh drew international acclaim for complex, well-crafted dramas that stress imagination and poetry over realism. Anouilh was born in Bordeaux, briefly studied law at the Sorbonne, and worked as an advertising copywriter before devoting himself to theater. His first major success was a play about an amnesiac, *Traveller Without Luggage* (*Le Voyageur sans Bagage*, 1937). From then on, the prolific dramatist had a new play produced nearly every season. Anouilh employed a great range of moods and worked in many genres, from Greek myth to modern comedy. Among his best-known works are *Antigone* (1944), *The Rehearsal* (*La Répétition; ou, L'Amour Puni*, 1950), *The Waltz of the Toreadors* (*La Valse des Toréadors*, 1952), *The Lark* (*L'Alouette*, 1953), and *Becket, or, The Honor of God* (*Becket ou L'Honneur de Dieu*, 1959), which was made into a film starring Richard Burton and Peter O'Toole. His screenwriting credits include *Monsieur Vincent* (1947) and *La Ronde* (1964).

Anthony, Peter. *See* **Shaffer, Peter**

Apollinaire, Guillaume, *pen name of* Wilhelm Apollinaris de Kostrowitsky *or* Kostrowitzki (August 26, 1880–November 9, 1918). Italian-born French poet, short-story writer, critic, and playwright. His innovative writings influenced turn-of-the-century Paris's thriving avant-garde, and paved the way for many of the modernist literary styles of the 20th century. Arriving in Paris at the age of 20, he befriended writers and artists and began to establish a literary reputation. The publication of his *Cubist Painters* (*Les Peintres Cubistes*, 1913) broke new ground by defining the cubist style of his friends Picasso and Braque as a school of art. His poetic masterpiece, the collection *Alcools* (1913), uses traditional verse forms, images of a modernizing world, and snatches of street conversations, all without punctuation. Other notable works include *Heresiarch and Co.* (*L'Hérésiarque et*

Cie, 1910), a fantastical collection of stories, and *Calligrammes* (1918), a volume of "visual poetry" noted for its experimental use of typography. Apollinaire is credited as the creator of the term "Surrealist," and he called his play *The Breasts of Tiresias* (*Les Mamelles de Tirésias,* 1917) "a Surrealist drama"; the play was made into an opera by Francis Poulenc in 1947.

Apollonius of Rhodes, *in Greek* Apollōnios Rhodios (c. 295 B.C.–c. 215 B.C.). Greek poet. Apollonius was a pupil of the poet and scholar CALLIMACHUS and served as the chief librarian in Alexandria, spending the latter part of his life in Rhodes. His chief work, the four-volume *Argonautika,* introduced new elements into the epic form, including the treatment of love as a central theme. Tracing the mythological voyage of Jason and the Argonauts in search of the Golden Fleece, as well as Medea's love for Jason, it is narrated from a more personal, sympathetic, and psychological viewpoint than had been used in earlier epics, and marks him as a worthy successor to HOMER and a predecessor of VIRGIL in his mastery of the form.

Appelfeld, Aharon *or* **Aron** (February 16, 1932–). Israeli novelist and short-story writer. Appelfeld's spare, modern, allegorical fiction reflects his belief that "the Holocaust [is] a metaphor for our century. There cannot be an end to speaking and writing about it." Born in Czernovitz, Romania (now part of Ukraine), Appelfeld was captured with his parents by Nazi troops when he was eight years old. After killing his mother, the Nazis sent the boy to a labor camp with his father, which Appelfeld eventually escaped, only to wander the countryside for two years. In the late 1940s, he managed to immigrate to Palestine, where he served in the Israeli army, finished his education, and taught Hebrew literature at several universities. He began publishing in the 1960s, and by the 1970s had established an international reputation. His widely translated works, all composed in Hebrew, include *The Age of Wonders* (*Tor ha-Pela'ot,* 1978), *Badenheim 1939* (*Badenheim, 'ir Nofesh,* 1979), *Tzili: The Story of a Life* (*Ha-kutonet Veha-Pasim,* 1983), *The Iron Tracks* (*Mesilat Barzel,* 1991), *The Conversion* (*Timyon,* 1993), and *Beyond Despair: Three Lectures and a Conversation with Philip Roth* (1994).

Apuleius, *in full* Lucius Apuleius (c. 124–after c. 170). North African–born Roman writer, philosopher, and rhetorician. Apuleius is remembered for his influential 11-volume prose romance THE GOLDEN ASS (or *Metamorphoses*), a fanciful account of a young man who turns into a donkey. It is the only Latin novel that survives in its entirety, and includes the most thorough extant account of the myth of Cupid and Psyche. The primary source for Apuleius's life story is his *Apologia,* a speech written to disprove the claim by his rich wife's family that he had used magic to woo her. Apuleius was born in North Africa and educated in Carthage and Athens. He traveled widely, pursuing his interests in magic and religion, then worked for a time in Rome before settling in Carthage.

Archilochus, *in Greek* Archilochos (c. 675 B.C.– c. 635 B.C.?). Greek poet. Admired by later poets, including HORACE, and considered by some to be the greatest Greek poet after HOMER, Archilochus wrote short poems in a variety of meters, only fragments of which are extant. Although the details of his life remain uncertain, it is known that he was born in Paros and fought in Thasos and elsewhere; he reputedly died in battle. Archilochus was a master of iambic meter and was noted for verse that ranged from the melancholic to the bitingly satiric. His personal writing style and antiheroic stance are unique among the surviving works by early Greek poets.

Arenas, Reinaldo (July 16, 1943–December 7, 1990). Cuban novelist. Arenas is remembered for his imaginative, unconventional, poetic fiction as well as for the difficult life from which it sprang. He was raised in poverty in rural Cuba and, as a teenager, participated in the revolution that brought Fidel Castro to power. He then moved to Havana, where he worked as a library researcher, journalist, and editor. His first novel, *Singing from the Well* (*Celestino Antes del Alba,* 1967), was published in Cuba;

his second, *Hallucinations* (*El Mundo Alucinante*, 1969), was smuggled out of the country and published in France. Accusations of political dissent and "ideological deviation" (he was openly homosexual) led to his imprisonment. In 1980, he illegally immigrated to the United States (during the Mariel boatlift), where he continued to write novels, including *Farewell to the Sea* (*Otra Vez el Mar*, 1982), *Old Rosa* (*La Vieja Rosa*, 1980), and *The Doorman* (*El Portero*, 1988). Suffering from AIDS, Arenas committed suicide in 1990, leaving behind his autobiography, *Before Night Falls* (*Antes que Anochezca: Autobiografía*, 1992), and other works.

Aretino, Pietro (April 20, 1492–October 21, 1556). Italian prose writer, poet, and playwright. A self-declared "scourge of princes," Aretino earned considerable wealth and notoriety for his literary attacks on the rich and powerful. Born the son of a cobbler, he adopted the name "Aretino" (from the name of his native city, Arezzo), and claimed that he was the bastard son of a nobleman. In 1517, he moved to Rome, where his actions, including posting vicious political lampoons on a statue in the public square, outraged the citizens. His behavior, coupled with the publication of his *Lewd Sonnets* (*Sonetti Lussuriosi*, 1524), forced him to flee Rome several times. In 1527, Aretino settled in Venice, where he prospered. Among his notable extant works are the ribald *Discussions* (*Ragionamenti*, 1584), in which Roman prostitutes gossip about their well-known clients; several comedic dramas, including *The Courtesans* (*La Cortigiana*, 1534); and some 3,000 letters, collected and translated as *The Letters of Pietro Aretino* (1967) and *Selected Letters* (1976).

Ariosto, Ludovico (September 8, 1474–July 6, 1533). Italian poet and playwright. Ariosto's ORLANDO FURIOSO (1516), or "Mad Roland," an epic poem about the adventures of a hero of the Charlemagne epics, is widely regarded as the highest literary achievement of the Italian Renaissance. Born in Reggio, Ariosto showed writing talent at an early age; he spent several years studying law before returning to literature. But upon his father's death in 1500, Ariosto, as eldest son, faced the responsibility of supporting his large family; for most of the rest of his life, he served Cardinal Ippolito d'Este of Ferrara and his family, whom he exalted in his epic masterpiece, which was a continuation of Matteo Maria Boiardo's unfinished work *Orlando Innamorato* (written c. 1476–94), or "Roland in Love." *Orlando Furioso* was first published in 1516, but Ariosto continued to refine it until the end of his life, publishing a final version in 1532. He also wrote several comic dramas and seven satires modeled after HORACE's *Sermones*.

Aristophanes, *in Greek* Aristophanēs (c. 450 B.C.–388 B.C.). Greek playwright. Aristophanes' reputation as the comedic master of ancient Greece rests on plays noted for their witty dialogue, poetic choral lyrics, brilliant parodies, and pointed topical allusions. The few facts known about his life have been gleaned from his works. A citizen of Athens, Aristophanes launched his dramatic career in 427 B.C. and wrote an estimated 40 plays. His works are the only surviving examples of the outrageous form of social satire known as Old Comedy, which combines chorus, mime, and burlesque with fantasy and licentious humor to satirize public figures, institutions, and the gods alike. Although not all of his references are accessible to today's theatergoers, Aristophanes' comic brilliance still shines in contemporary productions of his work. Eleven of his plays survive in full. The best known among them are THE CLOUDS (*Nephelai*, 423 B.C.), a satire about Socrates; THE WASPS (*Sphēkes*, 422 B.C.), a satire on litigation; THE BIRDS (*Ornithes*, 414 B.C.), Aristophanes' masterwork, about the fantastical utopia Cloud-Cuckoo-land; LYSISTRATA (*Lysistratē*, 411 B.C.), about a clever women's peace organization; and THE FROGS (*Batrachoi*, 405 B.C.), which lampoons Euripides.

Arnim, Achim von, *original name* Ludwig Joachim von Arnim (January 26, 1781–January 21, 1831) and **Arnim, Bettina von,** *original name* Elisabeth Brentano (April 4, 1785–January 20, 1859). German authors. Part of the literary circle that included GOETHE and the brothers GRIMM, the Arnims contributed greatly to the second wave of German Romanticism. The two met through Bettina's brother, Clemens Brentano, with whom Achim edited *Youth's Magic Horn* (*Des Knaben Wunderhorn*, 1805–8), a popular collection of German folksongs. Bettina and Achim were married in 1811 and had seven children. Both wrote in hybrid prose styles that freely mixed fact and fiction. Achim authored plays, stories, and novels, including the historical romance *Isabella of Egypt* (*Isabella von Ägypten*, 1812) and an unfinished work about Germany during the Reformation, *Guardians of the Crown* (*Die Kronenwächter*, 1817). Bettina's best-known books include the epistolary novel *Goethe's Correspondence with a Child* (*Goethes Briefwechsel mit einem Kinde*, 1835) and her bold plea for the King of Prussia's assistance to the underprivileged, *This Book Belongs to the King* (*Dies Buch Gehört dem König*, 1843). Her unconventional personality and progressive views, reflected in her work, earned her a reputation as one of modern German literature's most striking figures.

Arnold, **Matthew** (December 24, 1822–April 15, 1888). English critic and poet. A key influence on the development of American and European criticism and an important figure of the Victorian age, Arnold was an accomplished poet who argued that in order to build a morally and spiritually sound society, the public must be educated in literature and culture. Born in Middlesex, the son of Thomas Arnold, the renowned headmaster of Rugby School, Arnold was educated at Oxford. In 1851, he became an inspector of schools, a position he held for most of his life and one that provided the inspiration for many of the critical writings of his later years. Arnold's first love, however, was poetry, in six volumes of which, beginning with *The Strayed Reveller and Other Poems* (1849) and ending with *New Poems* (1867), he published verses that range from lyrics and narratives to dramas and elegies. Many of these evoke alienation, melancholy, and despair. Among his best-known poems are "The

Scholar-Gipsy" (1853), "Sohrab and Rustum" (1853), "DOVER BEACH" (1867), and "Thyrsis" (1867). In 1857, he became a professor of poetry at Oxford, a position he held for ten years. His lectures from this time formed the basis for many of his influential essays on literature, education, social issues, and religion. These were published in several volumes, notably *Essays in Criticism* (First Series, 1865; Second Series, 1888) and *Culture and Anarchy* (1869).

Asch *or* **Ash, Sholem** *or* **Shalom** *or* **Sholom** (November 1, 1880–August 10, 1957). Polish-born American novelist and playwright, writing in Yiddish. The prolific Asch, whose work has been translated into many languages, is probably best known for his biblical novels, *The Nazarene* (*Der Man vun Notzeres*, 1939), *The Apostle* (*Paulus*, 1943), and *Mary* (*Maria*, 1949), which depict the formative years of Christianity and its evolution from Judaism. Born in Kutno, Poland, and educated at the town's Hebrew school, Asch moved to Warsaw in 1899, where he began his writing career. His early works, such as the play *The God of Vengeance* (*Got vun Nekome*, 1907), portray life in the Eastern European Jewish shtetl (or village). In 1910, Asch visited the United States, immigrating in 1914 and becoming a U.S. citizen in 1920. Other novels, frequently focusing on the Jewish-American immigrant experience, include *Chaim Lederer's Return* (*Khayim Lederers Tsurikkumen*, 1927), *East River* (*Ist River*, 1946), and *A Passage in the Night* (*Grosman un Zun*, 1953).

Ashbery, **John** (July 28, 1927–). American poet and art critic. Ashbery's poetry is noted for its elegant and demanding style, featuring intricate linguistic play and musical prosody. Thematically, it echoes the Transcendentalism of 19th-century American poetry; like WHITMAN and EMERSON, Ashbery explores the nature of the self and subjective consciousness with an open-ended, expansive vision. Educated at Harvard and Columbia, Ashbery worked as an art critic in Paris (1955–65), as executive editor of *Art News* in New York (1965–72), and then as a professor at Brooklyn College and Bard College. He first gained prominence as a poet in association with the New York School, the innovative circle of poets and Abstract Expressionist artists who emerged in the 1950s and is perhaps most widely celebrated for his long poem *Self-Portrait in a Convex Mirror* (1975; Pulitzer Prize and National Book Award). Among his other books are *Some Trees* (1956), *The Tennis Court Oath* (1962), *The Double Dream of Spring* (1970), *A Wave* (1984), *April Galleons* (1987), *Flow Chart* (1991), and *Girls on the Run* (1999). His art criticism is collected in *Reported Sightings: Art Chronicles, 1957–1987* (1989). The collection of essays *Other Traditions* (2000) emerged from the Charles Eliot Norton Lectures that Ashbery delivered at Harvard University in 1989–90.

Asimov, Isaac (January 2, 1920–April 6, 1992). Russian-born American science fiction writer. A prolific author of both popular science writing and science fiction, Asimov published more than 300 volumes in his lifetime. Born in Russia, he immigrated as a child with his parents to Brooklyn. After earning a Ph.D. from Columbia University in 1948, he joined the biochemistry faculty of Boston University, an association that lasted a lifetime. His early short story "Night Fall" (1941), about a planet where night falls only once every 2,000 years, is considered a masterpiece of science fiction. Among his works of fiction are the "Robot" series, beginning with the short-story collection *I, Robot* (1950), and his "Foundation" series about a galactic empire, beginning with the trilogy *Foundation, Foundation and Empire*, and *Second Foundation* (1951–53). Asimov's final novels, including *The Robots of Dawn* (1983) and *Forward the Foundation* (1993), merge the two series. Some of Asimov's works about science for a general audience are *Inside the Atom* (1956), *Until the Sun Dies* (1977), and *Asimov's Guide to Earth and Space* (1991).

Asturias, Miguel Ángel (October 19, 1899–June 9, 1974). Guatemalan novelist and poet. A committed opponent of the Cabrera and Ubico dictatorships of Guatemala, Asturias served as a diplomat under the more democratic regimes that followed. His political and social convictions, alongside his profound interest in the myths and history of Mayan culture, are interwoven throughout his literary works. Asturias received a degree in law in 1923 and then studied anthropology in Paris, where he published his first important work, the study *Legends of Guatemala* (*Leyendas de Guatemala*, 1930). Returning to Guatemala, he published poetry, including *Sonnets* (*Sonetos*, 1936), and novels, among them *The President* (*El Señor Presidente*, 1946), a scathing depiction of Cabrera's rule, and *Men of Maize* (*Hombres de Maíz*, 1949), which combines social criticism and lyrical mysticism in an account of indigenous peasant life. Asturias's other novels include the trilogy comprising *Strong Wind* (*Viento Fuerte*, 1950), *The Green Pope* (*El Papa Verde*, 1954), and *The Eyes of the Interred* (*Los Ojos de los Enterrados*, 1960). He was awarded the Nobel Prize in Literature in 1967.

'Aṭṭār, Farīd od-Dīn, *also called* Moḥammad ebn Ebrāhīm, *or* Farīd od-Dīn Abū Ḥamīd Moḥammad (c. 1142–c. 1220). Persian poet and prose writer. A major Muslim writer in the mystical Sūfī tradition, 'Aṭṭār profoundly influenced Persian and other Islamic literatures. Born in Nīshāpūr, in northeastern Persia (now Iran), 'Aṭṭār traveled extensively throughout the East as a young man. Once returned to Nīshāpūr, he practiced as a pharmacist while collecting the verses and other wisdom of celebrated Sūfīs. His best-known work, *The Conference of the Birds* (*Manṭeq oṭ-Ṭayr*), is an allegorical epic chronicling the journey of birds to the mythical Sīmorgh, or Phoenix, in which they discover their oneness with God. The poem is noted for its vibrant storytelling and expression of the spiritual unity of beings, as are 'Aṭṭār's other allegorical poetic works, including *Book of God* (*Elāhī-nāma*) and *Book of Affliction* (*Moṣībat-nāma*). *Muslim Saints and Mystics* is an abridged translation of *Tazkerat ol-Awlīyā*, 'Aṭṭār's seminal prose account of the lives of early Sūfī saints.

Atwood, Margaret (November 18, 1939–). Canadian poet, novelist, and critic. First known as a poet and later as a popular and critically acclaimed feminist novelist, Atwood casts a keen eye on women's changing lives and social roles. Born in Ottawa, she was educated at the University of Toronto, Radcliffe College, and Harvard University, and she has taught literature at several Canadian universities. Among her volumes of poetry are *The Circle Game* (1964), *The Journals of Susanna Moodie* (1970), based on the writings of an early 19th-century Canadian immigrant, and *Power Politics* (1971). Atwood's novels include *Surfacing* (1972), *Lady Oracle* (1976), *Life Before Man* (1979), *Bodily Harm* (1981), *The Handmaid's Tale* (1984), *Cat's Eye* (1988), *Alias Grace* (1996), and *The Blind Assassin* (2000; Booker Prize). Atwood has also published short-story collections, notably *Bluebeard's Egg* (1983), and critical writings, including *Survival* (1972), a survey of Canadian literature.

Auden, W[ystan] **H**[ugh] (February 21, 1907–September 29, 1973). English-born poet, playwright, critic, editor, translator, and librettist. One of the most important 20th-century poets, Auden is distinguished, both as a poet and as an astonishingly prolific man of letters, by his great technical virtuosity and erudition, his intellectual openness and range of interests, and his deep engagement with the sociopolitical, psychological, and — especially as he matured — spiritual concerns of his times. He first came to prominence in the 1930s as a leader of a left-leaning, politically engaged circle of Oxford-educated poets that included Stephen SPENDER and C. DAY-LEWIS. His early work, which is strongly marked by his reading of Karl Marx and Sigmund FREUD, includes *Poems* (1930), *The Orators* (1932), and *Look, Stranger!* (1936; U.S. title, *On This Island*), as well as experimental verse dramas, such as *The Dog Beneath the Skin* (1935) and *The Ascent of F6* (1936), both written with his friend Christopher ISHERWOOD. In 1939, Auden moved to the United States (he would become a citizen in 1946), where he taught and lectured widely, while continuing to produce poems celebrated for

their musicality, wit, and moral depth, as well as for their inventive use of the rhythms and phrases of colloquial speech. Major collections of the American years include *Another Time* (1940), *The Double Man* (1941; U.K. title, *New Year Letter*), *For the Time Being* (1944), THE AGE OF ANXIETY (1947; Pulitzer Prize), *Nones* (1951), and THE SHIELD OF ACHILLES (1955; National Book Award). An opera librettist of the highest order, Auden worked with such composers as Benjamin Britten, Igor Stravinsky (*The Rake's Progress*, on which he collaborated with his lifelong companion, the American poet Chester Kallman), and Hans Werner Henze. Important later collections of Auden's verse include *Homage to Clio* (1960), *City Without Walls* (1969), and *Epistle to a Godson* (1972). His critical prose is collected in *The Dyer's Hand* (1962) and *Forewords and Afterwords* (1973), while his *Lectures on Shakespeare* (based on class notes taken by Alan Ansen) appeared in 2000.

Austen, Jane (December 16, 1775–July 18, 1817). English novelist. For nearly two centuries, the inimitable Austen has achieved the rare feat of commanding the respect of literary scholars while entrancing a wide popular readership. Considered a founder of the modern novel, she is also one of the few writers of her time who are still read for pleasure, despite the narrow scope of her subject matter: with ironic wit, acute perception, and masterly style, she chronicled what she knew best, the everyday life of the English provincial gentry at the turn of the 19th century. The sixth child of the village rector in Steventon, Hampshire, Austen was educated mainly at home. As a teenager, she entertained her family with high-spirited sketches satirizing contemporary sentimental literature. In the late 1790s, she turned to the novel, completing the first versions of *Northanger Abbey*, which parodies Gothic romances, and the great novels of courtship *Sense and Sensibility* and *Pride and Prejudice*. They remained unpublished for more than a decade, while she sojourned with her family in the popular spa Bath (1801–5) and elsewhere. Not until 1809, when she settled back into a cottage in Chawton, Hampshire, with her widowed mother and sister, did she return to novel writing. This time she found a publisher for SENSE AND SENSIBILITY (1811) and PRIDE AND PREJUDICE (1813), and followed their success with MANSFIELD PARK (1814) and EMMA (1816). NORTHANGER ABBEY was finally published posthumously, with her last novel, PERSUASION, in 1817 (dated 1818). Working, as she put it, on a "little bit (two inches wide) of ivory... with so fine a brush, as produces little effect after much labour," Austen meticulously plotted the changing tensions of complex networks of relationships against an intricate background of contemporary social mores and insuperable economic realities. Her novels, graceful marvels of formal perfection, were all published anonymously; only in the "biographical notice" accompanying the final two did her brother Henry acknowledge her authorship.

Auster, Paul (February 3, 1947–). American novelist and essayist. Auster's novels, which often depict human isolation in urban landscapes, explore the enigmas of identity. Born in Newark, New Jersey, Auster was educated at Columbia University and then lived in France for several years. There he began to establish his reputation as a translator and published his own work in American journals. He came to prominence as a novelist with the innovative detective stories published collectively as *The New York Trilogy* (1987). Made up of *City of Glass* (1985), *Ghosts* (1986), and *The Locked Room* (1986), the trilogy merges elements of noir detective fiction with epistemological themes. Auster's other novels include *Moon Palace* (1989), *The Music of Chance* (1990), *Leviathan* (1992), *Mr. Vertigo* (1994), and *Timbuktu* (1999). He has also published the poetry collections *Unearth* (1974) and *Wall Writing* (1976), as well as essays on the nature of writing, such as *The Art of Hunger* (1982), and autobiographical reflections, including *The Invention of Solitude* (1982) and *Hand to Mouth* (1997).

Awoonor, Kofi, *original name* George Kofi Awoonor-Williams (March 13, 1935–). Ghanaian poet and novelist. Established as an impor-

tant African poet with the publication of his first volume, *Rediscovery* (1964), Awoonor integrates modern poetic form and the vernacular traditions of his native Ewe culture. Educated at the University College of Ghana, he later spent many years abroad, studying at the University of London and the State University of New York at Stony Brook, where he also taught in the early 1970s. Returning to his home country, he edited the literary journal *Okeyame* and taught at the University of Ghana. Awoonor's poems as well as his novel, *This Earth, My Brother* (1971), reflect insightfully on contemporary Ghanaian society from the perspective of traditional African values, myths, and rituals. His other volumes of poetry include *Night of My Blood* (1971), *Ride Me, Memory* (1973), *The House by the Sea* (1978), and *Until the Morning After* (1987). In the 1980s, he held ambassadorships in Brazil and Cuba, an experience he examined in *The Latin American and Caribbean Notebook* (1992).

Babel, Isaac *or* **Isaak** (July 13, 1894–1940). Russian short-story writer. Born into a middle-class Jewish family in Odessa, Babel drew his best-known fiction from his experience of daily life and persecution in the Jewish ghetto. His first stories were published in 1916 in a journal edited by Maxim GORKY, who became his mentor. Babel drew critical attention with his collection *Red Cavalry* (*Konarmiya*, 1926), complex, ironic stories inspired by his experiences in the Bolshevik army during its campaign in Poland, as well as by the violence and bigotry he witnessed among the Cossack soldiers. Babel's *Odessa Tales* (*Odesskie Rasskazy*, 1931) recreates his native ghetto with picaresque stories of Jewish gangsters alongside haunting recollections of pogroms. Perhaps the greatest short-story writer since CHEKHOV, Babel was an artful observer of social life who wrote with moral insight and with what Cynthia OZICK has called "burnished brevity." During the Stalinist purges of the 1930s, Babel's work came under fire from the Soviet authorities. Arrested in 1939, he was executed in the basement of a Moscow prison the next year. A landmark English translation, *The Complete Works of Isaac Babel*, including in one volume the complete short stories, plays, diaries, and screenplays, was published in 2001.

Bachman, Richard. *See* **King, Stephen**

Bacon, Francis, Viscount St. Albans, Baron Verulam (January 22, 1561–April 9, 1626). English essayist and philosopher. Known for his influential writings on science and scientific inquiry, the London-born Bacon studied law at Cambridge and began his turbulent political career in 1584, when he assumed the first of several seats he would occupy in Parliament. His influence increased markedly when he won the patronage of Robert Devereux, 2nd Earl of Essex, whom he ultimately denounced as a traitor. Under James I, he served as solicitor general and was named lord chancellor and Baron Verulam in 1618; in 1621 he was created Viscount St. Albans, but later that year he was charged with bribery and barred from Parliament. The ignoble conclusion of his public life did not, however, extinguish Bacon's enthusiasm for his great philosophical project, the *Instauratio Magna*, a sweeping refutation of Renaissance and medieval scholasticism that offered, in its place, a method of scientific investigation rooted in empirical observation and classification. Of the six volumes Bacon planned to write, he completed only two: *The Advancement of Learning* (1605) and *Novum Organum* (1620). Two other volumes of natural history—*Historia Ventorum* (1622; History of the Winds) and *Historia Vitae et Mortis* (1623; History of Life and Death)—expound on his system of scientific knowledge. Bacon also wrote extensively on English history, law, and society. His *Essays*, published in 1597 and enlarged in 1612, employ a highly aphoristic style to address a range of subjects in the sphere of human behavior and custom; *New Atlantis* (1627), one of his best-known works, explores Bacon's vision of utopia.

Bagnold, Enid (October 27, 1889–March 31, 1981). English novelist, playwright, and children's writer. Born in Rochester, England, Bagnold lived as a child in Jamaica before returning to England to attend school. Her experiences during World War I as an ambulance driver and nurse with the British Women's Services inspired her first two books, *Diary Without Dates* (1917) and *The Happy Foreigner* (1920). After the war she continued to write, enjoying moderate commercial and critical success with adult readers. Her most successful book by far, however, was the beloved children's classic *National Velvet* (1935), the story of a plucky English girl who wins Britain's Grand National horse race. Bagnold's other works include the novels *The Squire* (1938) and *The Loved and Envied* (1951), both with strong domestic themes, and a play, *The Chalk Garden* (1955).

Bainbridge, [Dame] Beryl (November 21, 1934–). English novelist and short-story writer. Bainbridge, who grew up in World War II Liverpool and trained as an actress before turning to writing, is known for her darkly comic portrayals of working-class English life. Several novels preceded a string of successes, beginning with *Harriet Said* (1972), a psychological thriller focusing on two English girls who become murderers. Her other novels include *Another Part of the* Wood (1968), *The Dressmaker* (1973), *Injury Time* (1977), *Young Adolf* (1978), *Winter Garden* (1980), *Filthy Lucre* (1986), *An Awfully Big Adventure* (1989), *The Birthday Boys* (1991), and *Every Man for Himself* (1996).

Baldwin, James (August 2, 1924–December 1, 1987). American novelist, playwright, and essayist. The son of a storefront preacher, Baldwin established his reputation as a leading black author of his generation with his first novel, the autobiographical GO TELL IT ON THE MOUNTAIN (1953), about a teenage boy's coming of age in Harlem. Disillusioned with the state of race relations in the United States, Baldwin spent much of his life, from age 24, living in France. His other novels, including GIOVANNI'S ROOM (1956), *Another Country* (1962), *Tell Me How Long the Train's Been Gone* (1968), and *Just Above My Head* (1979), all deal, in varying degrees, with the themes of intolerance and the struggle for individuality and free expression. His involvement with the civil rights movement and his own experiences with racism in America inspired a number of essays, including those collected in *Notes of a Native Son* (1955), *Nobody Knows My Name* (1961), and *The Fire Next Time* (1963), and several plays, the most important of which is *Blues for Mister Charlie* (1964). In the last years of his life he also published *The Price of the Ticket: Collected Non-Fiction, 1948–1985* (1985) and *Evidence of Things Not Seen* (1986), about the Atlanta child murders.

Ballard, J[ames] **G**[raham] (November 15, 1930–). English science-fiction writer, novelist, and screenwriter. Raised in Shanghai by English parents, Ballard spent four years as a boy in a Japanese prison camp during World War II, an experience that informed much of his fiction—directly in his most successful novel, the autobiographical *Empire of the Sun* (1984), and indirectly in much of his speculative fiction, which is characterized by apocalyptic imagery and a generally surreal tone. Educated at Cambridge (although he did not graduate), Ballard began to publish short stories in science-fiction magazines in the 1950s and quickly excited attention as a leading figure of the New Wave movement among British science-fiction writers. His first novel, *The Drowned World* (1962), about a world that has been transformed into a giant swamp, set the tone for many of his later novels. Running through Ballard's work are the dual themes of ecological catastrophe and the destructive influence of technology, dramatized variously in such novels as *The Terminal Beach* (1964), *The Disaster Area* (1967), *Crash* (1973), *High Rise* (1975), and, more recently, *Running Wild* (1988) and *Cocaine Nights* (1999).

Balzac, Honoré de (May 20, 1799–August 18, 1850). French novelist. Balzac's massive body of work—some 90 novels and tales that, together, he christened THE HUMAN COMEDY (*La Comédie Humaine*)—offers a sweeping panorama of 19th-century French society and provides the basis for his standing as the father of modern realism in the novel. Born in Tours and educated in Paris, the fame-hungry Balzac spent his 20s trying his hand at writing sensa-

tionalistic novels and plays pseudonymously, with no success, and a brief stint in business left him with debts that would torment him for life. The first novel he wrote under his own name, *Les Chouans* (1829), was also his first success. This was followed, in the same year, by *The Physiology of Marriage* (*La Physiologie du Mariage*) and then by *Scenes from Private Life* (*Scènes de la Vie Privée*, 1830), which, together, cemented his reputation as a superlatively gifted portraitist of contemporary social manners. A writer of prodigious energy, sometimes working around the clock, Balzac produced more than two dozen major works of fiction over the next decade, including the masterpieces *Eugénie Grandet* (1833), *The Quest of the Absolute* (*La Recherche de l'Absolu*, 1834), *Le Père Goriot* (1835), and *César Birotteau* (1837), as well as several volumes of shorter tales. Written between 1837 and 1843, *Lost Illusions* (*Illusions Perdues*), the story of Lucien de Rubempré, a naive and easily corrupted young poet who comes to Paris from the provinces in search of fame, remains for many critics Balzac's greatest achievement. Through the 1840s his productivity continued unabated; some of his finest works from this period are *The Black Sheep* (*La Rabouilleuse*, 1841–42), *A Harlot High and Low* (*Splendeurs et Misères des Courtisanes*, 1843–47), and *Cousin Bette* (*La Cousine Bette*, 1846). Combining a mountainous quantity of sharply observed physical detail with energetic (at times, melodramatic) plotting and a rich cast of characters from all walks of French life, Balzac's body of work is one of the greatest individual achievements in world literature and has exerted a profound influence on the subsequent development of the novel.

Bambara, Toni Cade, *original name* Miltona Mirkin Cade (March 25, 1939–December 9, 1995). American short-story writer and novelist. Born and raised in New York City, Bambara was educated at Queens College and the City College of the City University of New York, where she took an M.A. in American literature. Known both for her social activism and her writings about the lives of African Americans, she claimed that she never thought of herself as a writer, but as "a community person who writes." (Pregnant in 1970 and searching for a name for her daughter, she adopted the name "Bambara," after the African ethnolinguistic group, whose ceremonial art she admired.) Her first collection of stories, *Gorilla, My Love*, was published in 1972; frequently anthologized, the stories in that volume focus on black urban life in a vernacular and celebratory style. A second collection, *The Sea Birds Are Still Alive: Collected Stories* (1977), is more international in scope, the stories somewhat darker and less optimistic than Bambara's earlier work, reflecting her growing awareness of the difficulty of bringing about positive change in society. *The Salt Eaters*, her first novel, was published in 1980. Bambara was diagnosed with cancer in early 1993, and, after a brief remission, died two years later. Important posthumous publications, both edited by Bambara's lifelong friend and editor, Toni MORRISON, include *Deep Sightings and Rescue Missions* (1996), a collection of essays, stories, and interviews, and *Those Bones Are Not My Child* (1999), a novel inspired by the shocking spate of killings of young black children that terrorized Atlanta in the late 1970s and early 1980s.

Banks, Russell (March 28, 1940–). American novelist and short-story writer. An acclaimed chronicler of the American class system and working-class life, Banks was born in Newton, Massachusetts, and was educated at Colgate University and the University of North Carolina. In his work, he draws on his own bleak New England upbringing for inspiration, creating deeply flawed characters who are searching for something new, something better. Short-story collections include *Trailerpark* (1981), set in rural New Hampshire, where he was raised, the similarly set *Success Stories* (1986), and *The Angel on the Roof* (2000). Two of his novels, *The Book of Jamaica* (1980) and the highly regarded CONTINENTAL DRIFT (1985), grew out of his interest in Jamaica, where he lived for a time. Interest in Banks's work accelerated in 1997 with the release of film adaptations of his novels *Affliction* (1990) and *The Sweet Hereafter* (1992), the latter using four narrators to detail the effects of a fatal schoolbus crash on a small community. Other novels include *Rule of the Bone* (1996) and *Cloudsplitter* (1998), a historical novel based on the life of the abolitionist John Brown.

Banville, John (December 8, 1945–). Irish novelist and critic. Banville was born in Wexford, Ireland, and was educated at St. Peter's College there. His playful, at times highly experimental narrations tend to focus on questions of art and reality, often deploying fictionalized versions of historical figures to explore his themes. His first book was *Long Lankin* (1970), a collection of stories of suburban Dublin life. This was followed by *Nightspawn* (1971), *Birchwood* (1973), and a trilogy of novels exploring the lives of three major scientific figures: *Doctor Copernicus* (1976), *Kepler* (1981), and *The Newton Letter: An Interlude* (1982). Later novels include *Mefisto* (1986), *The Book of Evidence* (1989), *Ghosts* (1993), *Athena* (1994), *The Untouchable* (1997), and *Eclipse* (2000). In 1989 Banville became literary editor of *The Irish Times*.

Baraka, [Imamu] **Amiri,** *original name* [Everett] LeRoi Jones (October 7, 1934–). American poet, playwright, novelist, and essayist. Raised in a middle-class New Jersey household, Jones was educated at Howard and Rutgers universities, served for three years in the Air Force, lived in Greenwich Village while studying literature at Columbia, and published his first volume of poems, *Preface to a Twenty Volume Suicide Note*, in 1961. His early work is deeply personal and impressionistic, much in the style of the Beats, with whom he was associated. *The Toilet, The Slave,* and DUTCHMAN (all 1964), one-act plays, are strikingly different, adopting a highly confrontational tone in their explorations of racial tensions in the United States. By 1968, he had adopted the name Amiri Baraka to affirm his connection to the Black Nationalist movement (the name is an adaptation of "Ameer Baraka," meaning "blessed prince"; "Imamu" means "spiritual leader") and left his interracial first marriage. Enormously prolific, he has written many plays as well as volumes of poetry, essays, and stories, and a novel, *The System of Dante's Hell* (1965), which employs the Newark slums as a metaphor for the underworld. He has also written extensively about jazz, in *Blues People* (1963) and *Black Music* (1967), among other volumes. His memoir, *The Autobiography of LeRoi Jones*, first published in 1984, was reissued in an unexpurgated edition in 1997. Recent collections of his work include *The LeRoi Jones/Amiri Baraka Reader* (1999), *Transbluesency: The Selected Poems of Amiri Baraka/LeRoi Jones (1961–1995)* (1995), *Funk Lore: New Poems, 1984–1995* (1996), and *Eulogies* (1996), which gathers 42 tributes Baraka has written and spoken, in both poetry and prose, over the course of 30 years, honoring people who were important to him, from Malcolm X to Toni Cade BAMBARA.

Barker, Pat[ricia] (May 8, 1943–). English novelist. Raised in England's industrial northeast and educated at the London School of Economics, Barker used her childhood experiences as the basis for her first novel, *Union Street* (1982), an examination of women's lives in a gritty English city beset by unemployment and other social ills. Barker continued to explore the lives of contemporary working-class women in three subsequent novels, *Blow Your House Down* (1984), *The Century's Daughter* (1986), and *The Man Who Wasn't There* (1989), all well received. In the 1990s Barker turned to World War I as her subject, writing the REGENERATION TRILOGY (*Regeneration*, 1991; *The Eye in the Door*, 1993; and the Booker Prize–winning *The Ghost Road*, 1995), which explores the psychological and emotional devastation of that conflict. *Another World* (1999) weaves images of contemporary Britain with memories of trench warfare, recalled through the eyes of a grieving veteran. *Border Crossing* (2001) portrays the encounter of a psychiatrist with a child murderer.

Barnes, Djuna (June 12, 1892–June 18, 1982). American poet, playwright, and novelist. A writer associated with the "lost generation" and the Paris avant-garde, Barnes produced lyrical, ironic, and experimental works that often challenged prevailing views on women's roles and sexuality. Born in New York, Barnes worked as a journalist and graphic artist there before moving to Paris in 1920, where she was influenced by Gertrude STEIN, F. SCOTT FITZGERALD, and other members of the expatriate literary milieu. *A Book* (1923), her first major work, is a collection of short stories, poems, and plays, which she later expanded and republished as *A Night Among the Horses* (1929, revised as *Spillway*, 1962). *Ryder* (1928), rendered in a stream-of-consciousness style, is a satirical novel about family relationships. *NIGHTWOOD* (1936), considered her greatest achievement, is a dreamlike evocation of the relationships among five people in the Parisian artistic scene. Barnes also published fiction under a pseudonym, Lydia Steptoes.

Barnes, Julian (January 19, 1946–). English novelist, essayist, and literary critic. Born in Leicester and educated at Oxford, Barnes worked for many years as a critic (for THE NEW STATESMAN and the *Observer*, among other publications). His fiction, beginning with the novel *Metroland* (1980), is notable for its dexterity of form, combining elements of biography and scholarship with literary realism. His first major success came with his third novel, *Flaubert's Parrot* (1984), about a scholar's obsession with the French novelist. Barnes's habit of merging the techniques of literary analysis with fictional structures — often quite humorously — continues in his other works, including the novels *Staring at the Sun* (1986) and *The Porcupine* (1992), and the collection of essays and stories *A History of the World in 10½ Chapters* (1989). Other novels include *Before She Met Me* (1982); *Talking It Over* (1991) and its sequel, *Love, etc.* (2001); and the satirical *England, England* (1999). He has also published several detective novels under the name Dan Kavanagh (Barnes is married to the literary agent Pat Kavanagh). His writings for THE NEW YORKER magazine, for which he wrote a regular column, appear in *Letters from London 1990–1995* (1995).

Barrie, [Sir] **James M**[atthew] [bart.] (May 9, 1860–June 19, 1937). Scottish playwright, novelist, and screenwriter. Born in Kirriemuir, Scotland, and educated at the University of Edinburgh, Barrie worked as a journalist for the *Nottingham Journal* for several years before moving to London in the mid-1880s to pursue a career as a freelance writer. Although he wrote more than 40 plays and several commercially successful novels, Barrie's reputation rests almost entirely on one work: the play *Peter Pan* (1904). Inspired by stories he concocted for the sons of his friends Arthur and Sylvia Llewelyn Davies, Barrie's whimsical tale of a boy who won't grow up has become a classic on stage and in print. Much of Barrie's early work, such as the novel *The Little Minister* (1891), is frankly sentimental, but a number of his later works, especially the plays *The Admirable Crichton* (1902) and *What Every Woman Knows* (1908), show a more serious side to the writer and enjoyed both critical and popular success in their day.

Barth, John (May 27, 1930–). American short-story writer and novelist. Born in Cambridge, Maryland, Barth received an M.A. from Johns Hopkins University in 1952 and began a long teaching career at Penn State the next year. An influential postmodern prose stylist, he is known for his darkly comic vision and unconventional narrative structures, which frequently comment on the contingent relationship between language and reality. This approach, known as metafiction — fiction that expresses an awareness of itself as fiction — became Barth's stock-in-trade with his first novel, *The Floating Opera* (1956; rev. ed. 1967). It also brought this style, heretofore the subject of academic interest but little read otherwise, to a wider audience. Barth's other notable works in this vein include THE SOT-WEED FACTOR (1960), GILES GOAT-BOY (1966), and the stories in *Lost in the Funhouse* (1968), many of which have been widely anthologized. His later work includes the more conventional novels *Sabbatical: A Romance* (1982) and *The Tidewater Tales* (1987).

Barthelme, Donald (April 7, 1931–July 23, 1989). American novelist and short-story writer. A leading figure of the metafiction movement of the 1960s and 1970s, Barthelme produced works, especially short stories, distinctive for their use of fragmented narrative, pop-culture references, and collage-like points of view in their comic rendering of contemporary life. Born in Philadelphia and educated at the University of Houston (he dropped out in his junior year), Barthelme began to publish stories in THE NEW YORKER in the 1960s — a distinct break from that magazine's habit of publishing quiet, realistic stories. His first collection, *Come Back, Dr. Caligari* (1964), was followed by *Unspeakable Practices, Unnatural Acts* (1968), *City Life* (1970), *Guilty Pleasures* (1974), *Sixty Stories* (1981), and *Paradise* (1986), among others. His novels follow in much the same stylistic vein and have been called antinovels for their assault on traditional narrative shapes. These include *Snow White* (1967), a modern take on the classic fairy tale; *The Dead Father* (1975); and *The King,* published posthumously in 1990.

Barthelme, Frederick (October 10, 1943–). American novelist and short-story writer. The brother of writer DONALD BARTHELME, Frederick Barthelme is highly regarded for his satires of the contemporary suburban landscape of shopping malls, fast-food chains, and brand names. Born in Houston, Barthelme studied as an undergraduate at Tulane and Houston universities and received an M.A. from Johns Hopkins University in 1977. He originally intended to become an artist, and worked as an architectural draftsman and as a creative director for an advertising agency before turning to writing full time. His first book was *Rangoon* (1970), which brought together short stories, photographs, and drawings. Other works of note include the short-story collections *Moon Deluxe* (1983) and *Chroma* (1987), and the novels *Second Marriage* (1984), *Painted Desert* (1995), and *Bob the Gambler* (1997). Barthelme cowrote, with another brother, the writer-academic Steven Barthelme, *Double Down: Reflections on Gambling and Loss* (2000), a candid memoir (written in the third person) about how the two brothers, both compulsive gamblers, squandered a quarter-million-dollar inheritance in Mississippi riverboat casinos. *The Law of Averages: New & Selected Stories* also appeared in 2000.

Bashō, Matsuo, *pen name of* Matsuo Munefusa (1644–November 28, 1694). Japanese poet, essayist, and travel writer. Considered Japan's greatest writer of haiku, Bashō devoted much of his life to refining this traditional form, transforming it into a vehicle of great power and expressiveness. The son of a poor warrior, Bashō studied haikai (a long-poem form from which haiku derives), read Japanese and Chinese classics, studied Zen teachings, served for a time as a samurai in service to a local feudal lord, and embarked on long pilgrimages around Japan. He lived a spartan existence, owned almost nothing, and became a wandering poet-teacher. *The Narrow Road to the Deep North* (*Oku no Hosomichi*, 1689), his greatest achievement, collects the musings from his journey west over the mountains of Japan to the coast of the Japanese Sea. Through the simplest language, Bashō's haiku evokes a love for the simple, uncluttered life and an intense feeling for the harmonies of the natural world. Other works include *The Seashell Game* (*Kaiōi*, 1672), *In the Face of Wind and Rain* (*Nozarashi Kiko*, 1685), and *Diary at Saga* (*Saga Nikki*, 1691).

Baudelaire, Charles (April 9, 1821–August 31, 1867). French poet, essayist, art critic, and translator. Although Baudelaire published only one volume of poetry before his death from syphilis at age 46, that book — THE FLOWERS OF EVIL (*Les Fleurs du Mal*, 1857) — firmly established his reputation as one of the greatest French poets of the 19th century and a writer of uncommon daring. His poems were decried by many of his contemporaries as immoral and obscene. To the contemporary ear, however, the qualities that emerge most distinctly are an unabashed sensuality and a powerful eroticism, particularly in the cycle of love poems known as "Black Venus," inspired by the poet's relationship with a woman of mixed race, Jeanne Duval. Baudelaire himself lived a life of dazzling eccentricity and personal tragedy. Born to a relatively wealthy family, he studied law but announced early on that he intended to live by writing; when he came into his inheritance in 1842, he briefly lived the life of a profligate dandy in Paris, spending most of his money in just two years. It was also during this period that he began his association with such artists as Delacroix, Manet, and Courbet, and experimented with opium and other drugs, to which he became addicted. Thereafter he lived in considerably reduced circumstances, hounded by debts that would, in the last years of his life, drive him into poverty. His translations of the works of Edgar Allan POE, undertaken between 1852 and 1865, are considered superb examples of French prose, as are his many critical writings on literature and art. With the publication of *The Flowers of Evil*, Baudelaire's poetry became virtually synonymous with depravity in the public mind; six of the poems were banned from later editions, and Baudelaire himself (as well as his publisher) was prosecuted for obscenity and fined. Although he placed a few more poems in obscure journals, he was to publish no more books during his lifetime and died virtually forgotten. Other works, published posthumously, include *Paris Spleen* (*Le Spleen de Paris: Petits Poèmes en Prose*, 1869), several volumes of essays and critical writings, and his journals (*Journaux Intimes*, 1887).

Beattie, Ann (September 8, 1947–). American novelist and short-story writer. Born in Washington, D.C., Beattie attended American University and the University of Connecticut and began publishing her first short stories in the mid-1970s. With her contemporary Raymond CARVER, Beattie is a leading minimalist and a seminal figure in the popular revival of the short-story form in the 1970s and 1980s. Many of her stories have appeared in THE NEW YORKER, with which she has enjoyed a long association, and tend to focus on the feelings of rootlessness and alienation among the generation of Americans that came of age in the 1960s. Her first novel, *Chilly Scenes of Winter*, appeared in 1976, as did her first short-story collection, *Distortions*. Other novels include *Falling in Place* (1980), *Picturing Will* (1989), and *Another You* (1995). Notable among her collections are *Secrets and Surprises* (1978), *The Burning House* (1982), *Where You'll Find Me and Other Stories* (1986), and *Perfect Recall: New Stories* (2001).

Beaumarchais, Pierre-Augustin Caron de (January 24, 1732–May 18, 1799). French playwright. Inventor, entrepreneur, courtier, polemicist, music instructor to Louis XV's daughters, supplier of French arms to the American Revolution, and publisher of VOLTAIRE (among other activities), Beaumarchais is remembered for two ebullient comedies starring the wily FIGARO, the epitome of the servant who outsmarts his master: THE BARBER OF SEVILLE (*Le Barbier de Séville*, 1775), in which Figaro helps a nobleman win a wife, and THE MARRIAGE OF FIGARO (*Le Mariage de Figaro*, 1784), in which he thwarts the same nobleman's designs on his own intended. Rich in intrigues, memorable characters, and trenchant social observations, they are among the few 18th-century French comedies to hold the modern stage, but they are probably best know today in their operatic adaptations by, respectively, Rossini and Mozart.

Beauvoir, Simone de (January 9, 1908–April 14, 1986). French novelist, philosopher, and memoirist. Beauvoir was a major intellectual figure of the post–World War II era. Born in Montparnasse in Paris, she was educated at the Sorbonne, where in 1929 she met Jean-Paul SARTRE, with whom she formed a lifelong personal and professional partnership. Influenced by Sartre's existentialist philosophy, she explored its concerns with individual moral freedom and responsibility, focusing on relations between the sexes and between the self and society. Beauvoir's first novel, *She Came to Stay* (*L'Invitée*, 1943), dissects the psychological and moral dynamics of a triangular love affair. Among her other novels, the best known is THE MANDARINS (*Les Mandarins*, 1954; Prix Goncourt), which indelibly depicts her own milieu in 1940s Paris and the struggles of intellectuals with the historical realities of the Vichy regime and Stalinist repression. *The Second Sex* (*Le Deuxième Sexe*, 1949), a pioneering, now-classic feminist analysis of women's secondary status, from childhood to marriage, motherhood, and old age, is her most significant philosophical work. Beauvoir also wrote several important autobiographical works, including *Memoirs of a Dutiful Daughter* (*Mémoires d'une Jeune Fille Rangée*, 1958), *The Prime of Life* (*La Force de l'Âge*, 1960), *The Force of Circumstance* (*La Force des Choses*, 1963), and *All Said and Done* (*Tout Compte Fait*, 1972), as well as her late *Adieux: A Farewell to Sartre* (*La Cérémonie des Adieux*, 1981).

Beckett, Samuel (April 13? 1906–December 22, 1989). Irish-French novelist, playwright, short-story writer, and poet, writing in English and French. Beckett, for many the successor to Marcel PROUST, James JOYCE, and Franz KAFKA, was awarded the Nobel Prize in Literature in 1969, cited by the Swedish Academy for writing "in which . . . the destitution of modern man acquires its elevation." His best-known and most important play, *Waiting for Godot* (*En Attendant Godot*, 1953), focuses, like much of his dramatic work, on the essential absurdity and mystery of human existence, plumbing the depths of existential uncertainty; there is little action, and meaning resides instead in the words and wordplay (and even silences) of its characters, often to disturbingly comic effect. After graduating from Trinity College, Dublin, in 1927, Beckett settled in Paris, where he befriended Joyce (and worked as the novelist's amanuensis) and began to write; early works include the short stories collected in *More Pricks Than Kicks* (1934) and the novel MURPHY (1938). During the war, he joined the French Resistance and eventually was forced to flee to unoccupied France, returning to Paris in 1945. The period that followed was a time of intense activity and artistic growth, during which he began writing in French and produced the prose trilogy MOLLOY (1951), *MALONE DIES* (*Malone Meurt*, 1951), and THE UNNAMABLE (*L'Innommable*, 1953), as well as *Godot*. Other plays include ENDGAME (*Fin de Partie*, 1957),

KRAPP'S LAST TAPE (1958), *Happy Days* (1961), *Not I* (1972), and *Footfalls* (1976). Beckett's works have been gathered in numerous editions, including *Disjecta: Miscellaneous Writings and a Dramatic Fragment* (1983), *As the Story Was Told: Uncollected Late Prose* (1990), and the 12-volume *Beckett Short* (1999), which collects shorter works.

Behan, Brendan (February 9, 1923–March 20, 1964). Irish novelist, playwright, and poet. One of the great gallows satirists of 20th-century Irish letters, Behan was born to a working-class Dublin family with a long connection to the Irish Republican Army. Behan himself was arrested for terrorist activities at age 17 and was sentenced to two years in a reform school, the basis for his autobiographical novel *BORSTAL BOY* (1958). Shortly after his release, he was arrested a second time and served four years of a 14-year sentence for his involvement in the shooting of a policeman. In addition to *Borstal Boy*, his major works include the plays *The Quare Fellow* (1954), set in Dublin's Mountjoy Prison (where he served most of his second prison term) and *THE HOSTAGE* (1958); and *Hold Your Hour and Have Another* (1964), a compendium of his shorter comic pieces. A lifelong alcoholic, Behan was known for his drunken binges, which won him considerable notoriety on both sides of the Atlantic, often overshadowing his achievements as a writer.

Behn, Aphra (July 1640–April 16, 1689). English novelist, playwright, and poet. Behn was the first professional woman writer in the English language and the author of a number of accomplished works. Although little is known of her early life, Behn spent some time in Surinam (Dutch Guyana), which provided the basis for her best-known work, the adventure novel *Oroonoko, or The History of the Royal Slave* (1678). Widowed in the 1660s, she turned to writing to support herself and briefly served as a spy for King Charles II against the Dutch. Her first play, *The Forc'd Marriage* (1670), a domestic comedy, revealed that she was unafraid to tackle topics considered "unladylike" and established her reputation. Her wit and powers of characterization are particularly well represented in such comedies as *The City Heiress* (1682) and *The Rover* (1677), her best-known play. She also wrote many poems and a number of popular novels, which, as critics have only recently acknowledged, exerted an important influence on the development of the novel in English.

Belloc, [Joseph] Hilaire (July 27, 1870–July 16, 1953). English novelist, essayist, poet, children's writer, and critic. Best known for his light poetry for children and philosophically infused travel writings, the prolific Belloc was also a controversial figure because of his adamant Roman Catholicism and antimodernist beliefs. Born in France to an English mother and French father, Belloc escaped with his family to England when the Franco-Prussian war began. His first published book was *Verses and Sonnets* (1896), followed by the very popular *The Bad Child's Book of Beasts* (1896), a book of whimsical and satirical nonsense verse. Other writings for younger readers include *More Beasts (For Worse Children)* (1897) and *Cautionary Tales for Children* (1907). A brief political career as a

---

"When I am dead, I hope it may be said: 'His sins were scarlet, but his books were read.'"

Hilaire Belloc, "Epigrams," in "A Page of Recent Verse," *The Independent* (December 23, 1922)

---

liberal member of Parliament (1906–10) was set aside in favor of a life devoted to writing, journalism, and editing. His most famous work is probably *The Path to Rome* (1902), a travel book filled with humor, poetry, and musings on the natural beauty he encountered during a walking pilgrimage from France to Rome. Belloc adamantly maintained that Europe should return to a "Catholic society," a belief that colored much of his critical and historical writing, including the four-volume *A History of England* (1925–31), *Europe and Faith* (1920), and a number of biographies of prominent figures, such as Marie Antoinette and Charles II.

Bellow, Saul (June 10, 1915–). Canadian-born American novelist. The son of Russian-Jewish émigrés, Bellow was born in Montreal, grew up in Chicago, and studied anthropology before working for the WPA Writers Project, where he met such writers as the poet Delmore SCHWARTZ, with whom he became friends. His first novels, *The Dangling Man* (1944) and *The Victim* (1947), while not commercially successful, drew critical praise for their ethical intensity and Bellow's honest handling of urban themes, especially as they pertained to the experiences of urban Jews. THE *ADVENTURES OF AUGIE MARCH* (1953) and HENDERSON, *THE RAIN KING* (1959), both employing the energetic style and structure of the picaresque novel, marked Bellow as a writer of great originality and sophistication and met with a combination of critical and popular success that placed him in the forefront of writers of fiction in America. A trio of prize-winning novels followed: HERZOG (1964; National Book Award), MR. *SAMMLER'S PLANET* (1970; National Book Award), and HUMBOLDT'S GIFT (1975; Pulitzer Prize), the last inspired by his friendship with Schwartz. Although Bellow's work demonstrates a sweeping range of interests, his best-known novels tend to focus on a single figure loosely describable as an existential antihero, whose struggles to achieve a sense of self in the contemporary world have broader, even allegorical, implications. His long and vigorous career includes many novels, short-story collections, and volumes of critical writing, most recently *The Dean's December* (1982), *Him with His Foot in His Mouth and Other Stories* (1984), *More Die of Heartbreak* (1987), *A Theft* (1989), *It All Adds Up* (1994), a collection of nonfiction writings, *The Actual* (1997), and *Ravelstein* (2000). Bellow received the Nobel Prize in Literature in 1976.

Benét, Stephen Vincent (July 22, 1898–March 13, 1943). American poet, novelist, and short-story writer. The son of a career military man, Benét was born in Pennsylvania and grew up on a series of army bases in New York, Illinois, California, and Georgia before entering Yale University, where he received an M.A. in English in 1920. Benét was an exceptionally popular author in his time, embraced by the public and respected by critics for works that championed cardinal American virtues and brought the story of America's past to life. His most famous work, the long poem on the Civil War, JOHN BROWN'S BODY (1928), won the Pulitzer Prize in 1929, and *Western Star* (1943), an unfinished epic, earned him another Pulitzer posthumously. Benét's best-known short story, "The Devil and Daniel Webster" (1936), was made into a play, an opera, and a movie. A *Book of Americans* (1933), coauthored with his wife, told in verse the stories of many important Americans for a young audience.

Benn, Gottfried (May 2, 1886–July 7, 1956). German poet and essayist. Benn's Expressionistic writings created considerable controversy in their day, not least because of the right-wing political views they often expressed. The son of a Lutheran clergyman, Benn trained to be a physician, a choice that had a profound effect on his choice of subject matter and the sensibility he brought to bear upon it. His two most famous (and controversial) volumes, the notorious *Morgue und Andere Gedichte* (1912; Morgue and Other Poems) and *Fleisch* (1917; Flesh), are macabre studies of human mortality and bodily decay, executed with an icy exactitude that some critics found troublingly detached. Benn went on to publish many highly detailed and complex poems, filled with technical and scientific references. He initially embraced Nazism but eventually denounced it and was forced to write secretly during Hitler's reign. His later poems as well as his autobiography *Double Life* (*Doppelleben*, 1950) reveal a considerable softening of his earlier views. Collections of Benn's works in English translation include *Primal Vision: Selected Writings* (1960), *Selected Poems* (1970), and *Prose, Essays, Poems* (1987).

Bennett, Arnold (May 27, 1867–March 27, 1931). English novelist and critic. Born in the provincial Midlands of England, Bennett trained as a solicitor's clerk and went to London at 21. He abandoned the law and became a notable critic of theater and fiction before publishing the autobiographical novel *A Man from the North* (1898). In London he wrote for several periodicals and eventually edited *Woman* magazine while continuing to develop his skills as a novelist. Bennett set much of his work in the "Five Towns" region, a fictional recreation of the Midlands countryside of his youth, populating it with carefully drawn characters in the tradition of the French realist writers he admired. A number of his novels were extremely popular in their day, among them ANNA OF THE FIVE TOWNS (1902), *The Old Wives' Tale* (1908), and *Clayhanger* (1910), all set in the Five Towns. Other major novels include *Hilda Lessways* (1911) and *Riceyman Steps* (1923), chronicling life in an East London slum. His more than 30 works also include collections of short stories and a handful of plays.

Berberova, Nina (August 8, 1901–September 26, 1993). Russian-born émigré short-story writer, novelist, biographer, and translator. An art student in her home city of St. Petersburg, Berberova also wrote poetry as a young woman; she left Russia with her companion, the poet Vladislav Khodasevich, in 1922. Settling in Paris in 1925, Berberova worked as an editor for the journals *Novyĭ Dom* (1926; New House) and *Russkaya Mysl'* (1948–50; Russian Thought), and wrote short fiction. After moving to the United States in 1950, she became a citizen and taught literature at several universities, notably Yale and Princeton. Translations of her stories and novels, written during her years in Paris and focusing on the émigré experience, began to appear in English in the 1980s and 1990s to great critical acclaim, including *The Accompanist* (1988), *The Tattered Cloak* (1991), *The Ladies from St. Petersburg* (1998), *The Book of Happiness* (1999), and *Cape of Storms* (1999), among others. Her biography of Russian Symbolist poet Aleksandr BLOK appeared in English in 1996. *The Italics are Mine* (1969; reprinted in 1992), her autobiography, was later published in Russian as *Kursiv Moĭ* (1972).

Bernanos, Georges (February 20, 1888–July 5, 1948). French novelist and essayist. Known for his Roman Catholic subject matter and themes, Bernanos worked as a journalist and insurance inspector before publishing *The Star of Satan* (*Sous le Soleil de Satan*, 1926), his first novel and the first of his many literary explorations into the struggle between the elemental forces of good and evil. His most famous work is THE DIARY OF A COUNTRY PRIEST (*Journal d'un Curé de Campagne*, 1937), the tale of a young cleric's valiant struggle against sin. Bernanos also wrote *Joy* (*La Joie*, 1929), *Night Is Darkest* (*Un Mauvais Rêve*, 1935), and a character study of a self-loathing misanthrope, *The Open Mind* (*Monsieur Ouine*, 1943). Bernanos was an ardent Royalist whose Roman Catholic ideology found political expression in his belief that the restoration of monarchal institutions would bring about a moral reawakening in Europe. His Royalist sympathies modified, however, in light of atrocities he witnessed during the Spanish Civil War, an experience he recounted in a fiery antifascist polemic, *A Diary of My Times* (*Les Grands Cimetières sous la Lune*, 1938). His last work, the screenplay *Dialogues of the Carmelites* (*Dialogues des Carmélites*, 1949), was adapted for the opera by Francis Poulenc in 1957. Bernanos took his family into exile in Brazil from 1938 to 1945, during which time he wrote a number of anti-Vichy political tracts; after the war, he returned to France but quickly grew distressed by the war's failure to inspire a spiritual rebirth and spent the final years of his life in Tunis.

Bernhard, Thomas (September 11 or February 9/10, 1931–February 12, 1989). Austrian novelist and playwright. Bernhard's deeply pessimistic works incited controversy throughout his life. Born in a Dutch convent to an unwed mother, he spent much of his youth suffering from a variety of illnesses, including tuberculosis. As a writer, he tried his hand first at poetry before finding more success as a novelist, initially with *Frost* (1963). Bernhard's characteristically bleak tales explore injustice and hypocrisy through intellectual and artistic protagonists, and, as his work evolved, were increasingly built around extended, bitter, solipsistic monologues. Notable among his other novels are *Gargoyles*

(*Verstörung*, 1967), *The Lime Works* (*Das Kalkwerk*, 1970), *Correction* (*Korrektur*, 1975), *Concrete* (*Beton*, 1982), and *Woodcutters* (*Holzfällen*, 1984). The novels *Wittgenstein's Nephew* (*Wittgensteins Neffe*, 1982) and *The Loser* (*Der Untergeher*, 1983) both model their protagonists on real people—Austrian philosopher Ludwig Wittgenstein's nephew Paul and the Canadian pianist Glenn Gould, respectively. Bernhard's plays include *Ein Fest für Boris* (1970; A Party for Boris), *Die Jagdgesellschaft* (1974; The Hunting Party), and *Der Schein Trügt* (1984; Appearances Are Deceiving). A late play, *Heldenplatz* (1988; Heroes' Square), was a scathing indictment of Austrian anti-Semitism. Five volumes of autobiography have been collected and translated into English in *Gathering Evidence: A Memoir* (1985).

Berry, Wendell (August 5, 1934–). American poet, novelist, short-story writer, and essayist. Writing from his farm in Henry County, Kentucky, Berry brings to his work both a deep sense of connection to the land and an informed appraisal of the realities of modern country life. Educated at the University of Kentucky, Berry taught at Stanford and New York universities before returning to teach at his alma mater, a post he left in 1977 to devote himself to farming and writing. His poems, essays, and stories offer lyrical explorations of the purity and simplicity of the farming life, threaded with a concern for ecology and a profound respect for traditional values of family, home, and community. Some works include the poetry collections *Farming: A Handbook* (1970) and *The Collected Poems: 1957–1982* (1985); essay collections *The Long-Legged House* (1969) and *The Gift of Good Land* (1981); and the novels *Nathan Coulter* (1960; rev. 1985), *A Place on Earth* (1967; rev. 1983), and *The Memory of Old Jack* (1974). More recent works from this prolific author include the novels *Remembering* (1988), *A World Lost* (1996), and *Jayber Crow* (2000), as well as the short-fiction collections *The Wild Birds* (1986), *Fidelity* (1992), and *Watch with Me* (1994), all set, like most of Berry's fiction, in the sleepy river town of Port William, Kentucky; and such

collections of essays as *Home Economics* (1987), *What Are People For?* (1990), *Sex, Economy, Freedom & Community* (1993), and *Life Is a Miracle: An Essay Against Modern Superstition* (2000), a scathing rebuttal of *Consilience* (1998), E. O. Wilson's ambitious attempt to unify all the major branches of knowledge, including the arts and religion, under the banner of science.

Berryman, John (October 25, 1914–January 7, 1972). American poet. Berryman is grouped, along with his friend and associate ROBERT LOWELL, with the confessional poets, whose work typically addressed matters of deep personal importance. Educated at Columbia and Cambridge universities, Berryman assumed his first teaching post at Wayne State University in Detroit, eventually moving on to Harvard, Princeton, and the University of Minnesota. Although much of his early work—collected in the volumes *Poems* (1942) and *The Dispossessed* (1948), among others—shows great technical skill and depth of feeling, it was his later work, beginning with *Homage to Mistress Bradstreet* (1956, in which Berryman employed the colonial-era poet Anne Bradstreet as a poetic

---

"My idea is this: the artist is extremely lucky who is presented with the worst possible ordeal which will not actually kill him."

John Berryman, in an interview in *The Paris Review* (Winter 1972)

---

alter ego), that distinguished him as a stylistic innovator. His greatest achievement was the "Dream Songs," a series of 365 18-line monologues in the vernacular voice of a poet-persona called Henry, who speaks of himself in the third person. The first of the series appeared in *77 Dream Songs* (1964), which won the Pulitzer Prize; the sequence was continued in *His Toy, His Dream, His Rest* (1968) and gathered in its entirety in *The Dream Songs* (1969). An able formalist, Berryman also published a long sequence of Petrarchan sonnets, *Berryman's*

Sonnets, in 1967. The son of a suicide and a life-long alcoholic, in 1972 Berryman took his own life in Minneapolis by jumping from a bridge onto the ice of the frozen Mississippi River. Several posthumous volumes of prose and verse were published, including an unfinished novel, *Recovery* (1973), an autobiographical account of the poet's struggle with alcoholism.

Betjeman, [Sir] John (August 28, 1906–May 19, 1984). English poet and essayist. A writer of light, clever verse, Betjeman was highly popular in his day, much of his work infused with a deep nostalgia for a fading England of Victorian values and manners. He often used traditional poetic schemes to satirize suburban English life, usually of the upper-middle classes. Educated at Oxford, Betjeman never received a degree, but he formed important friendships with EVELYN WAUGH and W. H. AUDEN, who became an ardent supporter of his work. His first collection of verse was *Mount Zion* (1933). Other significant volumes include *Continual Dew* (1937), *New Bats in Old Belfries* (1945), and *Collected Poems* (1958), which was a best-seller. Betjeman also wrote extensively about architecture and published a number of guidebooks to the English countryside. Knighted in 1969, he was named Poet Laureate of England in 1972.

Bidart, Frank (1939–). American poet. A writer of complex, difficult poetry that employs, among other stylistic tropes, the use of unusual typography, Bidart is often cited for his mastery of dramatic monologue, his intensity as a storyteller, and his unsparing insights into the complexities of guilt and family relationships. Bidart, who was educated at the University of California at Riverside and at Harvard, first gained recognition with *The Golden State* (1973), a collection of verse executed with spare language that explored, among other themes, the child/parent relationship. Bidart won much praise for *The Sacrifice* (1983), which contained his most widely known poem, "The War of Vaslav Nijinsky." Other collections include *The Book of the Body* (1977), *In the Western Night:*

Collected Poems, 1965–1990 (1990), and *Desire* (1997).

Bierce, Ambrose (June 24, 1842–1914?). American short-story writer, essayist, and journalist. One of the best-known journalists of his generation, the versatile Bierce left his imprint on American letters with his intensely atmospheric tales of Gothic horror, his gritty tales of war, and his witty satires. Born to a poor religious family in Ohio, Bierce fought in several battles of the Civil War, was badly wounded, and at war's end moved to California, where he established his reputation as a satirist working for the San Francisco *News Letter*, among other publications. He assumed the post of editor of the *News Letter* in 1868, published his first story ("The Haunted Valley") in 1871, then moved to London, where he spent three years dividing his time between journalism and fiction and published three collections of sketches and tales, including *Cobwebs from an Empty Skull* (1874). In 1875 he returned to San Francisco, where he forged a national reputation with his satirical column, "The Prattler" (1887–1906). His major books include *Tales of Soldiers and Civilians* (1891; reprinted as *In the Midst of Life*), which includes his best-known story, "An Occurrence at Owl Creek Bridge"; *Can Such Things Be?* (1893), a mixed collection of humorous and supernatural stories; and *The Cynic's Word Book* (1906; reprinted as *The Devil's Dictionary*, 1911), a compendium of satirical definitions. He vanished without a trace during a trip to Mexico in late 1913 or early 1914.

Bishop, Elizabeth (February 8, 1911–October 6, 1979). American poet and essayist. Bishop was raised in Canada by her maternal grandparents. After graduating from Vassar College, she traveled extensively in Florida, Mexico, and South America, finally settling in Brazil, where she lived for almost 20 years. Her poetry, first published in *North & South* (1946), captures the contrast between Yankee sensibilities and tropical climes in a vivid and sophisticated style. Her collections *Poems: North and South. A Cold Spring* (1955; Pulitzer Prize) and *Geogra-*

phy III (1976) are among her best known; *The Complete Poems* (1969) won the National Book Award in 1970. After returning to the United States from Brazil, she lived in San Francisco and then in Cambridge, Massachusetts, where she taught at Harvard University. She also wrote a number of travel books and translated several major Brazilian works from the Portuguese, including the poems in *An Anthology of Twentieth-century Brazilian Poetry* (1972), which she also edited.

Blair, Eric. *See* **Orwell, George**

Blake, Nicholas. *See* **Day-Lewis, C.**

Blake, William (November 28, 1757–August 12, 1827). English poet and illustrator. Blake was a leading figure of the Romantic movement in England whose art and poetry, inextricably linked, are characterized by intense emotion, potent symbolism, elements of mysticism, and a highly idiosyncratic vision. Alexander Gilchrist, the poet's biographer, described Blake as "a divine child, whose playthings were sun, moon, and stars, the heavens and the Earth." Born to a family of moderate means, Blake was an imaginative and singular child, given to visions of angels, poets, and prophets. These visions were to continue throughout his adult life, informing his spirituality and permeating his poetry and art. Although he had no formal education, he studied drawing at a young age and was then apprenticed to an engraver. Using copperplate engravings, Blake went on to illustrate such works as Dante's DIVINE COMEDY as well as his own poetry and prose, which he published himself in tiny editions, the pages and illustrations colored by hand, either by the poet or his wife. His first publication was *Poetical Sketches* (1783), followed by *Songs of Innocence* (1789), which revealed his supremely distinctive voice. THE MARRIAGE OF HEAVEN AND HELL (c. 1790), Blake's most significant work in prose, advances an attack on 18th-century rationalism and espouses a mystical faith in "Contraries" — the dualities of "attraction and repulsion, reason and energy, love and hate" which he claims are "necessary to human existence." SONGS OF INNOCENCE AND OF EXPERIENCE, his master-

piece, appeared in 1794. In the works that followed, Blake developed his mythic system in the so-called "prophetic books": *America, A Prophecy* (1793), *Europe, A Prophecy* (1794), *The First Book of Urizen* (1794), and *The Book of Ahania, The Book of Los,* and *The Song of Los* (all 1795). His later works include *Milton* (1804–8) and the epic poem JERUSALEM (1804–20), in which he connects the imagination to an extracorporeal existence after death. A profound influence on later generations of English writers and thinkers, Blake endured the skepticism and censure of his contemporaries, many of whom thought him mad.

Blixen, Karen. *See* **Dinesen, Isak**

Blok, Aleksandr (November 28, 1880–August 7, 1921). Russian poet and playwright. Blok was one of the most important Russian writers of his age, and the preeminent Symbolist of Russian poetry. Born to intellectual parents — a professor of law and a literary translator — Blok grew up in the house of his maternal grandfather, who was rector at the University of St. Petersburg, where he eventually studied law and philology. In his first collection of poems, *Stikhi o Prekrasnoï Dame* (1905; Verses About a Beautiful Lady), he used the image of a woman he had once seen crushed under the wheels of a train as a symbol for his suffering homeland. This work established his reputation, and was followed by the play *The Puppet Show* (*Balaganchik,* 1906), the poem cycle *Gorod* (1904–8; The City), and the collection *Snezhnaya Maska* (1907; The Snow Mask), among others, which show an increasingly bitter and cynical outlook. Later poems, including *Rodina* (1907–16; Native Land), express his affection for Russia and his embrace of Bolshevism. His greatest work, the long poem *The Twelve* (*Dvenadtsat',* 1918), portrays the Russian Revolution of 1917 as a cosmic event and a form of historical retribution. But the ensuing chaos — and the dismissal of his work by the Bolsheviks — ultimately led Blok to stop writing. His poems in English translation have appeared in several collections.

Bly, Robert (December 12, 1926–). American poet, prose writer, and translator. Although highly regarded for his poetry, by many Bly is best known for his prose study of masculinity, *Iron John* (1990), which explores the idea of masculine identity in a mythic context and became a bestseller. Raised on a Minnesota farm and educated at St. Olaf College in Northfield, Minnesota, Harvard University, and the University of Iowa, Bly writes about rural life with a lively, surrealistic style that emphasizes an "antirationalist" philosophy of the unconscious; in the best of his work, meaning is deposited in so-called "deep images" that recall Jungian archetypes, fairy tales, and classical mythology. A distinguished translator, he established a magazine devoted specifically to poetry in translation, *The Fifties* (founded in 1958), which was renamed *The Sixties* and *The Seventies* in each succeeding decade. Among his most significant collections of poetry are *Sleepers Joining Hands* (1973) and *The Light Around the Body* (1967), for which he received the National Book Award in 1968. An outspoken antiwar activist and founder of American Writers against the Vietnam War, Bly donated the proceeds from that award to a draft resistance organization. Among his more recent books are *The Rag and Bone Shop of the Heart* (1992), an anthology of poems about men, *Morning Poems* (1997), and *Eating the Honey of Words: New and Selected Poems* (1999).

Boccaccio, Giovanni (1313–December 21, 1375). Italian poet and prose writer. One of the leading figures of the Italian Renaissance, Boccaccio was a seminal force in the revival of classical scholarship that marked Renaissance humanism, and one of the first great writers of prose in a modern language. His most celebrated work, THE DECAMERON (*Decamerone*, 1349–53), a collection of folktales and fairy tales written in vernacular Italian, stands beside DANTE's *DIVINE COMEDY* as one of the supreme literary achievements of the age. Born in Naples, Boccaccio spent most of his life in Florence, where he formed important friendships with the city's leading scholars and literary figures, including the poet PETRARCH. Other works in Italian include the five-book prose romance *Il Filocolo* (1336; The Love Afflicted);

the ottava rima poem *Il Filostrato* (1338; The Love Struck); *Fiammetta* (1343–44), an epistolary tale of love; and *Il Ninfale Fiesolano* (1346; The Fiesole Nymph), the first idyll, or poem about country life, written in Italian. In his later years, Boccaccio concentrated on scholarly studies, which he wrote in Latin, including the unusual *On Famous Women* (*De Claris Mulieribus*, 1360–74), which contains accounts of the admirable lives of 100 notable women. He was also the author of a eulogy of Dante and in the last years of his life delivered numerous public readings of *The Divine Comedy* and lectured on Dante's work.

Böll, Heinrich (December 21, 1917–July 16, 1985). German novelist and short-story writer. Böll's wartime experiences in the German army led to his outspoken rejection of militarism and war, and to an ironic, disillusioned view of his compatriots. These attitudes and themes, along with his country's postwar feelings of shame about the past, formed the basis for his best-known works, including BILLIARDS AT HALF-PAST NINE (*Billard um Halb Zehn*, 1959), *The Clown* (*Ansichten eines Clowns*, 1963), and his longest novel, GROUP PORTRAIT WITH LADY (*Gruppenbild mit Dame*, 1971). Other works that gained an international audience are *Acquainted with the Night* (*Und Sagte kein Einziges Wort*, 1953), THE LOST HONOR OF KATHARINA BLUM (*Die Verlorene Ehre der Katharina Blum*, 1974), and the posthumously published *Stories of Heinrich Böll* (1986). Böll was awarded the Nobel Prize in Literature in 1972.

Borges, Jorge Luis (August 24, 1899–June 14, 1986). Argentinean poet, essayist, and short-story writer. Borges's writings, both in poetry and prose, blend fantasy, myth, and philosophy with the textures of everyday life to produce a highly original body of work that most critics acknowledge as a singular contribution to world literature. Born in Argentina, Borges learned both English and Spanish as a youth, and as a teenager spent several years abroad in Spain and Switzerland, adding French and German to the list of languages at his command. He took his degree at the Collège de Genève and returned to Argentina in 1921; his first published book was a volume of poems, *Fervor of Buenos Aires, Poems* (*Fervour de Buenos Aires, Poemas*, 1923), a celebration of his homeland precipitated by his return. In 1938, his father died and Borges himself became gravely ill. These trials inspired a highly creative period during which he assembled his vision of a systematic alternate reality, which he explored in the stories eventually collected in FICTIONS (*Ficciones*, 1944). A volume of essays, *Other Inquisitions, 1937–1952* (*Otras Inquisiciones*, 1952), dates from the same period of his career and expounds the writer's ironic and paradoxical conceptions of art and existence. In 1955, after the end of the dictatorship of Juan Perón, of which he was openly critical, Borges was appointed director of the National Library of Argentina in Buenos Aires. In the 1950s, a congenital condition began to destroy his eyesight, leaving him virtually blind by 1970, and he wrote his later works by dictation. These include *The Book of Imaginary Beings* (*El Libro de los Seres Imaginarios*, 1967), a work blending poetry and prose; *The Book of Sand* (*El Libro de Arena*, 1975), a collection of stories; and *The Conspirators* (*Los Conjurados*, 1985). His poetry is collected in an English translation, *Selected Poems: 1923–1967* (1972).

Boswell, James (October 29, 1740–May 19, 1795). Scottish diarist, biographer, and essayist. Boswell's two-volume THE LIFE OF SAMUEL JOHNSON (1791), the work for which he is best known, is widely regarded as one of the great biographies in the English language. Boswell was born into a prominent Edinburgh family and went on to practice law. After meeting Johnson in London in 1763, Boswell embarked on a study of the English critic's life, traveling to see him and taking journeys with him over the next three decades, while his law practice languished. His association with Johnson is often thought of as one of the most interesting literary friendships in history, resulting in a work of spectacular detail and insight into the workings of two exceptionally erudite minds. Boswell's other works include *An Account of Corsica* (1768), his first book, chronicling that

island's failed attempts to win independence from Genoa, and his extensive diaries, which were published posthumously.

Bowen, Elizabeth (June 7, 1899–February 22, 1973). British novelist, short-story writer, and essayist. The author of a number of critically successful novels detailing unhappy relationships among the upper-middle class, Bowen was born to well-off Anglo-Irish parents in Dublin, and lived her early life both there and at her family's country home in County Cork. A prolific writer, Bowen worked steadily from 1923, when her first book, a short-story volume entitled *Encounters*, was published. THE DEATH OF THE HEART (1938), a coming-of-age story, is considered her best novel, although *The Hotel* (1927), THE HOUSE IN PARIS (1935), and *The Heat of the Day* (1949) are also much admired. Bowen also published several volumes of essays and critical writings.

"...the characters who came out of my childish reading to obsess me were the incalculable ones, who always moved in a blur of potentialities. It appeared that nobody who mattered was capable of being explained. Thus was inculcated a feeling for the dark horse. I can trace in all people whom I have loved a succession from book characters—not from one only, from a fusion of many. 'Millions of strange shadows on you tend.'"

Elizabeth Bowen, "Out of a Book," *Collected Impressions* (1950)

Bowles, Jane, *original name* Jane Sydney Auer (February 22, 1917–May 4, 1973). American novelist, playwright, and short-story writer. Bowles's idiosyncratic writing style left her outside the literary mainstream, but her one novel, two plays, and the seven short stories she published during her lifetime have long enjoyed something of a cult following. Along with her husband, the American writer and composer PAUL BOWLES, she spent most of her life as an expatriate, settling permanently in Tangier, Morocco, in 1952. *Two Serious Ladies* (1943), her novel, presents the separate lives of two women whose paths cross only twice in the book, and is told without any formal plot structure. Her play, *In the Summer House*, was produced in New York in 1954 starring Dame Judith Anderson. Bowles's small body of work also includes a collection of stories, *Plain Pleasures* (1966). A collected edition of Bowles's work, with an introduction by Truman CAPOTE, was published in 1966; an expanded edition appeared in 1978 as *My Sister's Hand in Mine*.

Bowles, Paul (December 30, 1910–November 18, 1999). American novelist and short-story writer. Bowles began his artistic career as a composer, training with American composer Aaron Copland and eventually composing music for some 30 ballets, stage plays, and movies, as well as an opera, *The Wind Remains* (1943). The husband of writer JANE BOWLES, he traveled in bohemian circles in Europe and North Africa, eventually settling in Tangier, Morocco, where he wrote his first novel, THE SHELTERING SKY (1949), an existential tale of sexual obsession set in North Africa after World War II in which the unforgiving Sahara figures prominently. This was followed by a collection, *The Delicate Prey and Other Stories* (1950), in which Bowles pursued his preoccupations with the collision between Oriental and Occidental cultures and the transforming power of nature over the human spirit. Among his later works are the novels *Let It Come Down* (1952), *The Spider's House* (1955), *Up Above the World* (1966), and *Points in Time* (1982); several collections of stories; translations of North African folktales; and two volumes of autobiography.

Box, Edgar. *See* **Vidal, Gore**

Bradbury, Ray (August 22, 1920–). American novelist, short-story writer, playwright, and poet. Although Bradbury is known primarily as a writer of fantasy and science fiction, his body of work ranges widely in both form and genre. An astute social critic, Bradbury writes fantastic narratives that are freighted with deeper concerns about the dangers of technological progress, and his best work, such as the 1953 novel FAHRENHEIT 451 (about a future in which all books are banned), is in the tradition of such anti-utopian writers as George ORWELL. Born in Illinois, Bradbury moved west with his family during the Depression and began his career writing stories for pulp fiction and fantasy magazines. His first book of stories was *Dark Carnival* (1947), which was followed by *The Martian Chronicles* (1950), a collection of linked stories about the human settlement of Mars that has remained immensely popular, a classic of speculative fiction. In a long and vigorous career, Bradbury has produced the collections *The Illustrated Man* (1951), *The Golden Apples of the Sun* (1953), *The October Country* (1955), and *I Sing the Body Electric!* (1969), as well as the novels *Something Wicked This Way Comes* (1962) and *Green Shadows, White Whale* (1992), among many other volumes. He has also written children's books, plays, several volumes of poetry, and a number of television and film screenplays, including *Moby Dick* (1956), which he coauthored with John Huston.

Brautigan, Richard (January 30, 1933–October 25, 1984). American novelist, short-story writer, and poet. Born in Tacoma, Washington, Brautigan is best known for his second novel, *Trout Fishing in America* (1967), a satirical examination of the condition of the environment that became both a bestseller and a literary manifesto for the 1960s counterculture and ecology movements. Surreal, humorous, and iconoclastic, Brautigan's novels and stories champion the virtues of the Beats and the hippies with whom he associated, and often employing highly whimsical, collage-like structures. Other works include the novels *A Confederate General from Big Sur* (1964), *In Watermelon Sugar* (1968), *The Abortion: An Historical Romance, 1966* (1971), and *So the Wind Won't Blow It All Away* (1982); a short-story collection, *Revenge of the Lawn: Stories, 1962–1970* (1971); and four volumes of poetry. Brautigan committed suicide in 1984.

Brecht, Bertolt, *original name* Eugen Berthold Friedrich Brecht (February 10, 1898–August

14, 1956). German playwright and poet. Brecht's singular contribution to the modern theater lay in his use of the stage as a platform for political and social commentary, an approach he eventually refined and encapsulated in his theory of "epic theater" — a vision of the stage not as an illusion of reality but as a highly stylized forum for presenting patterns of human behavior. Born in Augsburg, Brecht went on to study medicine and while working in an army hospital wrote his first plays, including *Baal* (1923), *Drums in the Night* (*Trommeln in der Nacht*, 1927), and *Edward II: A Chronicle Play* (*Leben Eduards des Zweiten von England*, 1924), based on the English poet Christopher MARLOWE's EDWARD II. Although well received, these works did not yet exhibit the technical daring and theoretical adventurousness of his later work, which began with *The Threepenny Opera* (*Die Dreigroschenoper*, 1928), a ballad opera written in collaboration with composer Kurt Weill. Offering a biting, satirical look at bourgeois society, the play also announced Brecht's embrace of Marxism. The rise of Nazism forced him into exile in 1933, and Brecht spent the next 14 years in Denmark, Sweden, Finland, and the United States. His plays from this period include much of his most daring and innovative work, including MOTHER COURAGE AND HER CHILDREN (*Mutter Courage und Ihre Kinder*, 1941), *The Life of Galileo* (*Leben des Galilei*, 1943), and THE CAUCASIAN CHALK CIRCLE (*Der Kaukasische Kreidekreis*, 1948). He returned to East Germany in 1949, where he formed his own company, the Berliner Ensemble, and remained there for the rest of his life. A large collection in English translation, *Bertolt Brecht Poems 1913–1956*, was published in 1979 (rev. 1987).

Breton, André (February 18, 1896–September 28, 1966). French poet, novelist, critic, and essayist. The father of the Surrealist literary movement in France, Breton was born in Tinchebray, France, and studied medicine and psychiatry in Paris before working as a medical assistant in army psychiatric centers during World War I. His studies in Freudian psychology and the Symbolist poets influenced him to explore in his writings the line between conscious and unconscious expression. He briefly joined the Dadaist movement, but left to explore "pure psychic automatism," as posited in the essay "Magnetic Fields" ("Les Champs Magnétiques," 1921), which he coauthored with Philippe Soupault. This experiment in automatic writing inspired Breton to formally found Surrealism in 1924 with the first of three major manifestoes. He also produced several collections of poetry, as well as the novel *Nadja* (1928); an analysis of how the practice of Surrealism can transform the experience of despair, *The Communicating Vessels* (*Les Vases Communicants*, 1932); and the autobiographical novel/manifesto, *Mad Love* (*L'Amour Fou*, 1937), among many other works. Breton spent World War II in the United States during the German occupation, but returned to France in 1946. Among the numerous editions of Breton's work in English are *Manifestoes of Surrealism* (1969), *What Is Surrealism: Selected Writings* (1978), and *The Automatic Message; The Magnetic Fields; The Immaculate Conception* (1997), as well as several collections of his poetry .

Breytenbach, Breyten (September 16, 1939–). South African memoirist, poet, and novelist, writing in Afrikaans and English. Life in exile and the political turbulence in his native country provide the themes for much of Breytenbach's best-known poetry and prose. Born and educated in South Africa, he left his homeland to travel in Europe, settling in Paris in 1961. His first books, written in Afrikaans, were a collection of poetry, *The Iron Cow Must Sweat* (*Die Ysterkoei Moet Sweet*, 1964), and a book of prose, *Catastrophes* (*Katastrophes*, 1964). During a 1975 visit to his homeland, Breytenbach, long a vocal critic of apartheid, was arrested for terrorism and was imprisoned for seven years. *The True Confessions of an Albino Terrorist* (1984), an account of his arrest and incarceration, brought him international recognition. Among his recent works are *The Memory of Birds in Times of Revolution*, a collection of essays on South Africa, and *Dog Heart: A Memoir* (1999).

Broch, Hermann (November 1, 1886–May 30, 1951). Austrian novelist. The ambitious and innovative fiction of this Vienna native earned him a place as one of the 20th century's notable German-language writers. Broch turned away from his family's textile business in midlife in order to study philosophy and mathematics at the University of Vienna. His best-known early work is a trilogy collectively titled THE SLEEP-WALKERS (*Die Schlafwandler*, 1930–32), a complex epic set in turn-of-the-century Europe that mixes a variety of styles and forms. In 1938 Broch was imprisoned by the Nazis and was released only after the intercession of others, including James JOYCE, with whose writing Broch's has been compared. He immigrated to the United States in 1940 and in 1945 published his greatest work, THE DEATH OF VIRGIL (*Der Tod des Vergil*), a lyrical evocation, part historical novel and part prose poem, of the ailing poet's last hours and the final stirrings of his consciousness.

"Reading a good book is not much different from a love affair, from love, complete with shyness and odd assertions of power and of independence and with many sorts of incompleteness in the experience. One can marry the book: reread it, add it to one's life, lie with it. Or it might be compared to pregnancy—serious reading even if you're reading trash: one is inside the experience and is about to be born; and one is carrying something, a sort of self inside oneself that one is about to give birth to, perhaps a monster."

Harold Brodkey, "Reading: The Most Dangerous Game," *The New York Times Book Review* (November 11, 1985)

Brodkey, Harold, *original name* Aaron Roy Weintraub (October 25, 1930–January 26, 1996). American short-story writer and novelist. Brodkey's prose incorporates microscopically focused autobiographical details and impres-

sions. He was born in Illinois and educated at Harvard. His early stories, many of which first appeared in THE NEW YORKER and *Esquire*, were collected in *First Love and Other Sorrows* (1957). This much-hailed debut was followed by a decades-long writer's block, for which the frustrated writer became famous. Nearly 30 years after his first book, Brodkey published a second collection, *Women and Angels* (1985), which was followed by *Stories in an Almost Classical Mode* (1988). His long-awaited autobiographical novel, *The Runaway Soul* (1991), met with mixed reviews. In the June 21, 1993, issue of *The New Yorker*, Brodkey announced he had AIDS, and chronicled his battle with the disease in *This Wild Darkness: The Story of My Death* (1996). Posthumous volumes include *My Venice* (1998), a tribute to a city Brodkey greatly loved, combining passages from several of his works with previously unpublished notes and essays; *The World Is the Home of Love and Death* (1998), a final volume of short stories; and *Sea Battles on Dry Land* (1999), a collection of his best essays.

Brodsky, Joseph, *original name* Iosif Aleksandrovich Brodsky (May 24, 1940–January 28, 1996). Russian-born American poet. Born and raised in Leningrad (now St. Petersburg), Brodsky was forced into exile in 1972, became a U.S. citizen in 1977, wrote essays and poems in English, and was appointed U.S. Poet Laureate in 1991. Four years earlier, Brodsky had become, at 47, one of the youngest writers ever to win the Nobel Prize in Literature. But despite his heroic embrace of a literary life outside of his native land, he would write, "A language is a much more ancient and inevitable thing than a state. I belong to the Russian language." At the age of 15, Brodsky left school to study on his own. As he began to attract attention as a promising young poet, he was arrested and convicted for "social parasitism" and was sentenced first to a mental hospital and then to five years' hard labor near the Arctic Circle. He was released after 18 months, following the protests of such early supporters as Anna AKHMATOVA, and immigrated to the United States. There Brodsky found a teaching position at the University of Michigan, and later taught at Columbia University and Mount Holyoke College. As Poet Laureate, he promoted the idea of providing poetry in airports, supermarkets, and hotel rooms, saying in a speech at the Library of

---

"...there is no doubt in my mind that, had we been choosing our leaders on the basis of their reading experience and not their political programs, there would be much less grief on earth. It seems to me that a potential master of our fates should be asked, first of all, not about how he imagines the course of his foreign policy, but about his attitude toward Stendhal, Dickens, Dostoevsky."

Joseph Brodsky, "Uncommon Visage: The Nobel Lecture," in *On Grief and Reason: Essays* (1995)

Congress that poetry "should be...as ubiquitous as gas stations, if not as cars themselves." His published work includes the collections of poems A PART OF SPEECH (1980; *Chost' Pechi*, 1977), *To Urania: Selected Poems, 1965–1985* (1984; *Uraniya*, 1984), and *So Forth: Poems* (1996). Essays written in English were collected in *Less Than One* (1986), which includes two memoirs of his childhood, and *On Grief and Reason* (1995). *Watermark* (1992) is a short book on Venice, Italy, where he spent several winters. Brodsky died of a heart attack in New York City, and was buried in Venice. *Collected Poems in English* was published posthumously in 2000.

Brontë, Charlotte (April 21, 1816–March 31, 1855). English novelist and poet. The author of the beloved *JANE EYRE* (1847), Brontë wrote novels remarkable for their intensely personal voice and their portrayal of independent women struggling to find a balance between love and self-development. The daughter of a Yorkshire clergyman and a mother who died early on, Charlotte and her sister Emily were sent to a boarding school with harsh rules and terrible conditions—later recast as Lowood

School in *Jane Eyre*. Charlotte worked as a teacher and a governess and, in 1842, went to Brussels with Emily to learn foreign languages with the intention of starting their own school back home. Charlotte's first novel, *The Professor* (published posthumously in 1857), was rejected by several houses, but her next effort, *Jane Eyre*, was an immediate success. Sadly, the untimely deaths of her three siblings, Emily, Anne, and Patrick Branwell, in quick succession did not enable her to enjoy her success. Her other fiction includes *SHIRLEY* (1849), a historical novel whose protagonist is based in part on EMILY BRONTË, and *Villette* (1853), a novel inspired by Charlotte's experiences in Brussels.

Brontë, Emily (July 30, 1818–December 19, 1848). English novelist and poet. Perhaps the most gifted of the Brontë sisters, Emily produced just one novel in her short lifetime, the extraordinary *WUTHERING HEIGHTS* (1847). This enigmatic and mystically inclined Brontë had no close friends, apart from her younger sister, Anne, with whom she created Gondal, an imaginary world that figures prominently in her poetry. In CHARLOTTE BRONTË's words, Emily was "stronger than a man, simpler than a child," with a nature that "stood apart." Emily's poetry appeared jointly and pseudonymously with that of her sisters in *Poems by Currer, Ellis, and Acton Bell* (1846), a volume that features such verses as "The Prisoner," "Remembrance," and "The Visionary." When *Wuthering Heights* first appeared—in the same year as *JANE EYRE*—it was viewed as excessively violent; decades passed before the novel was justly appreciated. Emily died of tuberculosis the year after its publication.

Brooke, Rupert (August 3, 1887–April 23, 1915). English poet. Brooke was educated at Rugby School and at King's College, Cambridge, where he excelled as an athlete, scholar, and promising poet. After graduation, he settled in the village of Grantchester, near Cambridge, which he celebrated in one of his most popular poems, "The Old Vicarage, Grantchester." In the following years, he traveled widely and began to publish his poems, all the while maintaining a distinguished circle of friends, whom he dazzled with his great personal beauty, charm, and literary gifts. His first collection, *Poems* (1911), received mixed reviews, but it marked the beginning of his public ascendance as the "golden young Apollo" of English poetry. With the coming of World War I, Brooke obtained a commission in the Royal Naval Division and was shipped off to Antwerp, Belgium. *1914* (1914), a sequence of five sonnets depicting a patriotic soldier's willing embrace of death, made Brooke a national hero overnight. Brooke's lyric idealism contrasts sharply with the grimness and despair found in the work of the later war poets, including Siegfried SASSOON and Wilfred OWEN, who experienced the full horrors of warfare, which Brooke in fact never saw. In April 1915, he died on a hospital ship off the coast of the Greek island of Skyros, from blood poisoning following a mosquito bite. Brooke quickly became a near-legendary figure, the model soldier-martyr. The posthumously published *Collected Poems* (1915) only burnished the reputation of the poet eulogized by Winston Churchill in the London *Times* as "all that one would wish England's noblest sons to be."

Brookner, Anita (July 16, 1928–). English novelist and critic. Brookner's novels are noted for their characteristic protagonists—lonely, dissatisfied women in their middle years—and admired for their acute irony, psychological and social insights, and precise visual and emotional detail. Born in London, Brookner studied art history at King's College and went on to enjoy a distinguished career as an art historian, becoming the first woman named Professor of Art at Cambridge University. Her art historical works include *The Genius of the Future: Studies in French Art Criticism* (1971), *Soundings: Studies in Art and Literature* (1997), and *Romanticism and Its Discontents* (2000), as well as works on Watteau, Ingres, Greuze, and David. Brookner did not begin writing fiction until she was in her 50s, but since the publication of her first novel, *A Start in Life* (1981), she has produced a new work nearly every year. Her novels include, among others, *Providence* (1982), *Look*

at Me (1983), the Booker Prize–winning *HOTEL DU LAC* (1984), *A Friend from England* (1987), *Fraud* (1992), *Incident in the Rue Laugier* (1996), *Falling Slowly* (1998), and *Undue Influence* (2000).

Brooks, Gwendolyn (June 7, 1917–December 3, 2000). American poet. A prominent voice of urban black life and a major poet of the mid-20th century, Brooks was the first African-American poet to receive the Pulitzer Prize. Born in Topeka, Kansas, and raised in Chicago's slums, Brooks first received recognition for her remarkable depictions of ordinary characters in *A Street in Bronzeville* (1945). Her Pulitzer Prize–winning second book, *Annie Allen* (1949), is a verse narrative centered around a young girl's coming of age during World War II. *The Bean Eaters* (1960) contains some of her finest poetry. Brooks's later work was more overtly political, reflecting the influence of such writers as James BALDWIN and Amiri BARAKA in such volumes as *In the Mecca* (1968), *Family Pictures* (1970), and *Children Coming Home* (1991). Brooks was also the author of the novel *Maud Martha* (1953).

Browning, Elizabeth Barrett (March 6, 1806–June 29, 1861). English poet. A much-loved poet of Victorian England, Browning is best known for her lyrics of love ("How do I love thee? Let me count the ways") published in *SONNETS FROM THE PORTUGUESE* (1850). Born to a large and wealthy family and raised in Herefordshire, Elizabeth Barrett was cloistered at home by her fiercely protective father. The studious young writer suffered from poor health, and spent her days composing poetry and letters in solitude. Her simply titled *Poems* (1844) was very well received, attracting the attention of many, including the poet ROBERT BROWNING. The two first met in 1845 and were secretly married the next year. They then moved to Italy, where her health and spirits improved considerably. In addition to her great poems of love, Browning's verse evokes the lands of Italy and England and expresses her concern for social and political justice. Her other major works include *AURORA LEIGH*

(1857) — a novel in verse about the life of a woman writer — and *Last Poems* (1862).

Browning, Robert (May 7, 1812–December 12, 1889). English poet. A major Victorian poet, Browning is acclaimed for his mastery of the dramatic monologue, his innovative use of conversational language, and his penetrating psychological insights. He was born and raised in a London suburb and educated largely through reading the books in his father's extraordinary library. Browning achieved fame relatively late in his career. His early writings — notably *Sordello* (1840) — were not well received by the general public, but were noticed by such writers as Charles DICKENS and Alfred, Lord TENNYSON. The books of his middle period include *Dramatic Lyrics* (1842), which contains the famous "MY LAST DUCHESS," and *Men and Women* (1855), which contains "FRA LIPPO LIPPI" and many other well-known poems. In 1845, Browning initiated a correspondence with the poet ELIZABETH BARRETT (BROWNING) that blossomed into one of the great literary romances. His 1864 collection, *Dramatis Personae*, at last won him popular acclaim, while his ambitious work THE RING AND THE BOOK (1868–69) — 12 poetic monologues about a murder trial in 17th-century Rome — cemented his reputation.

Bryant, William Cullen (November 3, 1794– June 12, 1878). American poet, critic, and editor. An important figure in early American literature as a poet and critic, Bryant is also renowned as the longtime editor in chief (1829–78) of the New York *Evening Post*, a leading liberal newspaper that supported workers' rights and abolition. Bryant first earned prominence for his famous poem "THANATOPSIS" (1817), a meditation on death and nature, and he continued to publish poems, including "To a Waterfowl" (1821), that remain significant as early American Romantic lyrics, sensitively reflecting on the guiding value of nature. Bryant's critical writings, including "Early American Verse" (1819), also represent notable early attempts to establish an American literary tradition. Born in Massachusetts, Bryant worked as an attorney until moving to New York City in 1825 to embark on a career in publishing.

Buck, Pearl S[ydenstricker] (June 26, 1892– March 6, 1973). American novelist, biographer, short-story writer, and playwright. Widely known for her novels of life in China, especially THE GOOD EARTH (1931; Pulitzer Prize), Buck contributed greatly to the West's understanding of that country. Born in West Virginia to missionary parents, Buck spent the first half of her life in China, with the exception of her years at Randolph-Macon Woman's College and Cornell University. She was married twice, first to a missionary and, later, to her publisher; raised nine children, eight of whom were adopted; and founded several humanitarian organizations. An exceptionally prolific and versatile writer, Buck published more than 80 works of fiction alone. *The Good Earth*, her second, and best-known, novel, is part of a trilogy entitled *The House of Earth*, which also includes *Sons* (1932) and *A House Divided* (1935). Buck's works were enormously successful with the public, but less so among critics. Nevertheless, her work was recognized in 1938 with the Nobel Prize in Literature. Other notable works include *The Mother* (1934); *Dragon Seed* (1942); *The Spirit and the Flesh* (1944), which contains biographies of her parents; *My Several Worlds* (1954), an autobiography; *Imperial Woman* (1956); and five novels set in America and written under the pseudonym John Sedges.

Bukowski, Charles (August 16, 1920–March 9, 1994). American poet, novelist, and short-story writer. Bukowski is known for his graphically violent, sexually explicit, often comic depictions of life among prostitutes, drunks, and other outsiders. Born in Germany, Bukowski moved to the United States at a young age. He lived mostly in Los Angeles, holding a variety of odd jobs as he began publishing his short stories in the 1940s. His first full-length poetry collection was *It Catches My Heart in Its Hands* (1963). In 1970 Bukowski accepted his publisher's offer of $100 a month to write full time. His better-known fiction includes the autobiographical novels *Post Office* (1971) and *Ham on Rye*

(1982), and the story collection *Hot Water Music* (1983). Bukowski's international cult following burgeoned in his later years, especially after he wrote the screenplay for the 1987 movie *Barfly*. *Run with the Hunted: A Charles Bukowski Reader* (1993) contains a selection of his poetry and prose.

Buntline, Ned, *pen name of* E[dward] Z[ane] C[arroll] Judson (March 20, 1823–July 16, 1886). American novelist. Buntline almost singlehandedly originated the dime, or pulp, novel in the United States. He began publishing his sensational adventure fiction in THE KNICKER-BOCKER MAGAZINE, but in 1844 he founded *Ned Buntline's Magazine* and, later, *Ned Buntline's Own*, a scandal sheet in which he also serialized his novels. He also led a boisterous life outside the realm of publishing. In the mid-1840s he was lynched for murdering his mistress's husband, but was cut down before he strangled to death. In 1849 he incited a famous riot at the Astor Place opera house in New York against the British actor William Macready, and in 1864 he was dishonorably discharged from the Union Army for drunkenness. Later, he befriended the frontiersman William F. Cody, whom Buntline transformed into the legendary "Buffalo Bill" in numerous novels. His works include *Magdalena, the Beautiful Mexican Maid* (1847), *The Mysteries and Miseries of New York* (1848), and *Red Ralph: The Ranger* (1870).

Bunyan, John (November? 1628–August 31, 1688). English writer. Through the 19th century, Bunyan's renowned religious allegory THE PILGRIM'S PROGRESS (1678–84) was nearly as popular as the BIBLE with readers in the English-speaking world. Bunyan was born and raised near Bedford, and served two years in the parliamentary army. In 1653, after reading his wife's devotional books, he joined a nonconformist church and began to preach there. His first books, *Some Gospel Truths Opened* (1656) and *A Vindication* (1657), expressed his objections to Quakerism. In 1660 he was arrested for preaching without a license and spent 12 years in jail. Bunyan wrote prodigiously during his

internment, composing his fervent spiritual history, *Grace Abounding to the Chief of Sinners* (1666); the beginning of his masterpiece, *The Pilgrim's Progress*; and many other works, including *The Life and Death of Mister Badman* (1680) and *The Holy War* (1682).

Burgess, Anthony, *pen name of* John Anthony Burgess Wilson (February 25, 1917–November 22, 1993). English novelist and critic. Burgess, the author of A CLOCKWORK ORANGE (1962), his famous dystopian novel about a state terrorized by teenage gangs, is much admired for his verbal inventiveness, biting wit, erudition, and prolific output. Born to a Catholic family in Manchester and educated at the university there, Burgess initially intended to pursue a career in music — an interest reflected in his fiction. His first three novels, set in the Far East, were written while he was in the colonial service in Malaya and Borneo. In 1958, after doctors erroneously predicted that he had only one year to live, Burgess devoted himself furiously to writing, completing five novels, including *Inside Mr. Enderby* (1963), which with its companion, *Enderby Outside* (1968), would be published in the United States as *Enderby* (1968). Other works include *Earthly Powers* (1980), a sprawling novel of the 20th century narrated by an elderly homosexual writer. Burgess also produced many musical works, film and television scripts, literary studies, reviews, stories, two volumes of memoirs, and novels about SHAKE-SPEARE, KEATS, MARLOWE, and JESUS.

Burney, Fanny, *in full* Frances Burney, Madame D'Arblay (June 13, 1752–January 6, 1840). English novelist and playwright. An accomplished and commercially successful novelist of manners, Burney is noted for her ear for dialogue and satire and her treatment of a subject that was relatively unexplored in her time: young women coming into their own in the world of society. The daughter of Dr. Charles Burney, a prominent musician and composer, she spent her youth surrounded by London society. Burney's first novel, *Evelina* (1778), about a naive young girl's development into a young woman, was published anonymously, but when the author's identity was uncovered, Burney's reputation with the public and other writers (Jane AUSTEN was among her many admirers) quickly spread. Her next novel, *Cecilia* (1782), a social satire, was followed by *Camilla* (1796), the story of a love affair. Burney's astute and lively journals and letters were published in two collections and later as an eight-volume set.

Burns, Robert (January 25, 1759–July 21, 1796). Scottish poet. Scotland's national poet shaped his native dialect into such enduring lyrics as "Auld Lang Syne" and "A Red, Red Rose," thus transforming—in the words of Ralph Waldo EMERSON—a *"patois* unintelligible to all but natives [into] a Doric dialect of fame." Born to a struggling farming family, Burns devoted much of his short life to farm labor, but still found the time to become well educated. As a young man, he was known for his rebellious streak and his democratic convictions (he was an early advocate of the French Revolution). His first collection, *Poems, Chiefly in the Scottish Dialect* (1786), was an overwhelming success. Later, Burns focused his energies on collecting and editing traditional Scottish airs. Among his well-known poems and lyrics are "The Cotter's Saturday Night," "To a Mouse," and "Scots, Wha Hae." He also wrote verse letters, satires ("Holy Willie's Prayer"), and the long narrative poem "Tam o' Shanter" (1791).

Burroughs, Edgar Rice (September 1, 1875–March 19, 1950). American novelist. Burroughs is the creator of the fictional adventure hero Tarzan. Born in Chicago, he tried his hand at several trades before turning to writing, with immediate success. In 1912, the character of Tarzan was introduced to the world in the magazine *All-Story*. The son of an English nobleman, Tarzan was abandoned in the African jungle and raised there by apes. The courage and strength of this "King of the Jungle" captured the popular imagination in books and in comics, as well as on radio, television, and in film. The first Tarzan novel, *Tarzan of the Apes* (1914), was followed by more than 20 others.

Burroughs also wrote numerous works of science fiction, and was a correspondent in the South Pacific during World War II.

Burroughs, William S[eward] (February 5, 1914–August 2, 1997). American novelist. Burroughs's unconventional and irreverent writing, coupled with his equally unconventional and irreverent life, turned this quintessential outsider artist into a countercultural hero. Burroughs came from a notable St. Louis family (his mother descended from Robert E. Lee and his grandfather invented the adding machine, the origin of the Burroughs Corporation) and studied English at Harvard. In the mid-1940s, he met the writers Jack KEROUAC and Allen GINSBERG in New York City. Although Burroughs was older and did not yet consider writing his vocation, he nonetheless became an integral part of the Beat movement. Burroughs traveled the globe in search of drugs and a lifestyle that would suit him, spending time in New York, New Orleans, Texas, Mexico City, South America, Tangier, Paris, and London before settling permanently in Lawrence, Kansas, in 1981. His idiosyncratic novels make use of black humor, stream of consciousness, and experimental structures. The first of these, *Junkie: Confessions of an Unredeemed Drug Addict* (1953, abridged version; 1977 unexpurgated), first published under the pen name William Lee, is a surrealistic chronicle of the author's addiction to morphine. Burroughs's best-known work, NAKED LUNCH (1959), also depicts the addict's world, employing what he called a "cut up" (or collage) technique. His other novels include *The Ticket That Exploded* (1962), *Cities of the Red Night* (1981), and *Queer* (1985).

Burton, Robert (February 8, 1577–January 25, 1640). English prose writer and scholar. Burton's extraordinary compendium, THE ANATOMY OF MELANCHOLY (1621), is the first extensive study of psychology in the English language. Born to a genteel family in Leicester, Burton studied at Oxford, where he stayed on as a vicar and keeper of his college's library. He was an exceptional scholar, with a wide-ranging store of knowledge amply reflected in his master-work. *The Anatomy of Melancholy* was exhaustively researched, citing more than 1,300 sources. Burton's choice of subject is not surprising, as he appears to have suffered from depression for most of his life.

Butler, Samuel (December 4, 1835–June 18, 1902). English novelist, essayist, and critic. A notorious iconoclast and satirist, Butler wrote eloquent critical works on Darwin's theories and didactic novels indicting many aspects of English society. Butler was born in Nottinghamshire and educated at Cambridge. His uncertainties about religion prompted him to eschew the family tradition of a career in the church. Instead, he headed to New Zealand where he set up as a sheep farmer and published articles on Darwinian themes, two of which he would later incorporate into his first major work, EREWHON (1872), a satirical assault on his society's illusory confidence in universal progress. Published anonymously, the novel was an immediate success. His next works of fiction were *The Fair Haven* (1873) and a sequel to his debut, *Erewhon Revisited* (1901). His much-admired final novel, THE WAY OF ALL FLESH (1903), is an autobiographical critique of middle-class Victorian family life.

Byatt, [Dame] **A**[ntonia] **S**[usan], *original surname* Drabble (August 24, 1936–). English novelist, short-story writer, and critic. Born in Sheffield, Byatt studied at Cambridge (as did her younger sister, the writer Margaret DRABBLE), Bryn Mawr College, and Oxford, and held teaching posts at several universities before deciding to devote herself to writing. Her first novels, *The Shadow of the Sun* (1964) and *The Game* (1967), explore the relationship between art and life as well as women's struggles for identity. Her highly regarded third novel, *The Virgin in the Garden* (1978), is set in 1953 during the coronation of Queen Elizabeth II. *Possession* (1990), Byatt's Booker Prize–winning romance, brought her international popularity and acclaim. Recent works of fiction include *Angels and Insects* (1992), *Babel Tower* (1996), *Elementals: Stories of Fire and Ice* (1998), and

The Biographer's Tale (2000). She has also written critical works on Iris MURDOCH, William WORDSWORTH, and Samuel Taylor COLERIDGE. *On Histories and Stories*, a collection of essays, appeared in 2000.

Byron, George Gordon, 6th Baron Byron of Rochdale, *called* **Lord Byron** (January 22, 1788–April 19, 1824). English poet. The embodiment of the Romantic hero, Lord Byron was lionized in his time and remains so today for the flamboyance, defiance, and ardor with which he lived and wrote. Born in London, the beautiful club-footed boy was raised by his mother in Scotland and educated at Cambridge. When his first book of poems, *Hours of Idleness* (1807), was scathingly criticized by the EDINBURGH REVIEW, Byron responded with the equally scabrous satire *English Bards and Scotch Reviewers* (1809). That year, Byron took his seat in the House of Lords and left England to travel the Mediterranean. Out of this trip emerged CHILDE HAROLD'S PILGRIMAGE (1812–18), a fictionalized travelogue that brought him overwhelming fame. After a failed marriage, Byron left England for good in 1816, spending the rest of his short life in Switzerland, Italy, and Greece. The restless poet engaged in intense and fleeting love affairs, worked on behalf of Italian nationalism, and fought for Greek independence, all the while continuing to write prolifically. The major works of these years include *The Prisoner of Chillon and Other Poems* (1816), the poetic drama *Manfred* (1817), and the satirical poem *Beppo* (1818). His masterpiece, the vast epic satire DON JUAN (1819–24), is a 16,000-line poem that traces the adventures of a character loosely modeled on the Spanish legend but really based on Byron himself. Byron died of a fever in Missolonghi, Greece, where he was given full military honors before being sent back to England for burial.

Cain, James M[allahan] (July 1, 1892–October 27, 1977). American novelist. Cain's novels exemplify the hard-boiled fiction that thrived in the United States during the 1930s and 1940s; his fast-paced, unsentimental crime stories feature tough, violence-prone protagonists in an amoral and desperate world. Born in Maryland, Cain worked as a coal miner and a journalist before moving in 1932 to Hollywood, where he worked as a screenwriter. His first novel, THE POSTMAN ALWAYS RINGS TWICE (1934), a tautly constructed story about a hobo who plots with his married lover to murder her husband, was a huge popular success. Other novels, the most successful of which appeared before World War II, include *Serenade* (1937), *Mildred Pierce* (1941), *Double Indemnity* (1943), *The Embezzler* (1943), *The Butterfly* (1947), *The Root of His Evil* (1951), and *Rainbow's End* (1975). The film adaptations of three of Cain's novels, *The Postman Always Rings Twice*, *Double Indemnity*, and *Mildred Pierce*, are classics of American film noir.

Calasso, Roberto (May 30, 1941–). Italian writer and editor. Calasso is most widely known for *The Marriage of Cadmus and Harmony* (*Le Nozze di Cadmo e Armonia*, 1988), his erudite and expansive retelling of classical Greek myths. Born in Florence, he studied English literature at the University of Rome. While still a student, he began working for Adelphi Edizioni, a major Italian publisher of classic and modern literature, eventually becoming editorial director of that distinguished house. Calasso's fiction challenges easy categorization, combining vivid narrative, philosophical rumination, and profuse cultural and literary allusions. *The Ruins of Kasch* (*La Rovina di Kasch*, 1983) uses an ancient African legend about a kingdom's deterioration as a central metaphor as it explores the history of the French Revolution. Calasso has continued his reexamination of mythology in *Ka* (1996) and *Literature and the Gods* (2001).

Calderón de la Barca, Pedro (January 17, 1600–May 25, 1681). Spanish playwright. One of the greatest playwrights of Spain's Golden Age, Calderón wrote more than 120 secular dramas and 74 *autos sacramentales*, or one-act morality plays. Born into an aristocratic family in Madrid, he was educated at a Jesuit college and the University of Salamanca, where he planned an ecclesiastical career. Instead, he served as a soldier and, from 1623, as a play-wright for the court of King Philip IV. In 1651, he was ordained a priest, after which he wrote primarily *autos sacramentales*. Throughout his work, Calderón wrote in a skillful Baroque style infused with complex, layered symbolism, rich poetry, and an intellectual outlook. His diverse secular output embraces cloak-and-dagger comedies (about aristocratic intrigue); tragedies exploring morality and honor, including *The Surgeon of His Honor* (*El Médico de su Honra*, 1635) and *The Mayor of Zalamea* (*El Alcalde de Zalamea*, c. 1636); and metaphysical inquiries into human existence and destiny, as in his masterpiece, *Life Is a Dream* (*La Vida es Sueño*, 1635). Calderón's religious-themed dramas include *The Constant Prince* (*El Príncipe Constante*, 1629) and *The Wonder-Working Magician* (*El Mágico Prodigioso*, 1637). His *autos sacramentales*, consummate achievements of the form, include *The Great Theater of the World* (*El Gran Teatro del Mundo*, c. 1649).

Caldwell, Erskine (December 17, 1903–April 11, 1987). American novelist and short-story writer. Caldwell's reputation is based primarily on the novels TOBACCO ROAD (1932) and GOD'S LITTLE ACRE (1933), both plain-spoken tragedies about the rural poor of his native Georgia. The controversial *Tobacco Road* portrays degraded sexual relationships among sharecroppers trapped by poverty; the novel gained a wide readership after it was successfully dramatized for Broadway by Jack Kirkland in 1933. After weathering an obscenity trial, *God's Little Acre* similarly became an international bestseller. Caldwell was born in Coweta County, Georgia, where his father, a traveling home missionary, ministered to sharecroppers. After attending colleges in South Carolina and Virginia, Caldwell worked as a menial laborer and a professional football player before he began publishing short stories, notably "Country Full of Swedes" (1933). Other publications include a documentary book on the rural South, *You Have Seen Their Faces* (1937), featuring photographs by Margaret Bourke-White, to whom Caldwell was married for three years, and the novel *Trouble in July* (1940), on Southern race relations.

Calisher, Hortense (December 20, 1911–). American novelist and short-story writer. Calisher was raised in a middle-class Jewish family in New York City and was educated at Barnard College, where she later taught. Her early short stories, many of which first appeared in THE NEW YORKER, are gathered in *Collected Stories* (1975) and include works featuring her alter ego Hester Elkin and her Jewish family in New York City. Calisher's novels, beginning with the interrelated *False Entry* (1961) and *The New Yorkers* (1969), are noted for their subtleties of language and character as well as their range of style and subject matter, from the comedy of sexual mores *Queenie* (1971), to *Mysteries of Motion* (1983), a science-fiction–inflected story of passengers on a space shuttle, and *In the Palace of the Movie King* (1993), a saga of an immigrant filmmaker. Calisher's acclaimed memoirs include *Herself* (1972) and *Kissing Cousins* (1988).

Callimachus, *in Greek* Kallimachos (c. 305 B.C.–240 B.C.). Greek poet and scholar. Callimachus was a leading poet of the Alexandrian school, which sought to revitalize Greek poetry, favoring concise, polished, erudite compositions over the then popular imitations of Homeric epics. Born in Cyrene, North Africa, Callimachus moved to Alexandria to work at the great Library of Alexandria. Of the fragments of his voluminous writings that survive, many were not found until the 20th century. His best-known poem is the sophisticated, four-book elegy *Causes* (*Aitia*, c. 270 B.C.), which recounts the legendary origins of ancient Greek customs and rites. Callimachus's other poetic works include the *Iamboi*, a group of short poems; *Hecale* (*Hekalē*) a short epic about Theseus; and *Epigrams* (*Epigrammata*), which treats intimate themes. Callimachus is also noted for his prose work *Tablets* (*Pinakes*), a 120-volume bibliography of the works in the Library of Alexandria.

Calvino, Italo (October 15, 1923–September 19, 1985). Cuban-born Italian novelist, short-story writer, and editor. Often described as a fabulist who successfully combines reality and fantasy, Calvino has attracted both critical admiration and a wide international readership. Born in Cuba to Italian parents, as a child he immigrated with his family to Italy. A member of the Resistance during World War II, after the war he graduated from the University of Turin, where he studied literature. As a student and after, Calvino worked as an editor and journalist at Einaudi, the great Italian publishing house; at the Italian Communist Party newspaper *L'Unità*; and, as co-editor, with novelist and

---

"The world's reality presents itself to our eyes as multiple, prickly, and as densely superimposed layers. Like an artichoke. What counts for us in a work of literature is the possibility of being able to continue to unpeel it like a never-ending artichoke, discovering more and more new dimensions in reading."

Italo Calvino, "The World Is an Artichoke" (1963), in *Why Read the Classics?* (1999)

---

critic Elio Vittorini, of the annual periodical *Il Menabò di Letteratura*. His first novel, *The Path to the Nest of Spiders* (*Il Sentiero dei Nidi di Ragno*, 1947), inspired by his war experiences, displayed the playful, fanciful style that would characterize all of his subsequent fiction. This includes the trilogy *Our Ancestors* (*I Nostri Antenati*, 1960; also translated in two volumes as *The Baron in the Trees* and *The Nonexistent Knight and the Cloven Viscount*), *Cosmicomics* (*Le Cosmicomiche*, 1965), *Invisible Cities* (*Le Città Invisibili*, 1972), *The Castle of Crossed Destinies* (*Il Castello dei Destini Incrociati*, 1973), IF ON A WINTER'S NIGHT A TRAVELER (*Se una Notte d'Inverno un Viaggiatore*, 1979), and *Mr. Palomar* (*Palomar*, 1983). In *Italian Folktales* (*Fiabe Italiane*, 1956), he retells Italian fables in a number of regional dialects. Calvino's critical works include *The Uses of Literature* (*Una Pietra Sopra*, 1980) and *Why Read the Classics?* (*Perché Leggere i Classici*, 1991). *The Road to San Giovanni* (*La Strada di San Giovanni*, 1990), a collection of his autobiographical essays gathered by his widow, was published posthumously.

Camões *or* **Camoëns, Luís** [Vaz] **de** (c. 1524–June 10, 1580). Portuguese poet. One of Portugal's greatest lyric poets, Camões is also renowned for his epic poem *THE LUSIADS* (*Os Lusíadas*, 1572), which recounts Portuguese explorer Vasco de Gama's discovery of a sea route to India. The classic poem blends mythical and historical elements and explores moral, religious, and nationalistic themes. Although many legends have arisen about Camões's adventures and hardships, it is known that he was born in Lisbon to an old but poor aristocratic family, traveled to Portuguese territory in North Africa, and spent 17 years in India, returning to Lisbon in 1570 and publishing *The Lusiads* two years later. Camões also composed sonnets and *canções*, many collected in *Rimas* (1595), that are noted for their treatment of loss and yearning.

Campbell, John W[ood], [Jr.] (June 8, 1910–July 11, 1971). American science-fiction writer and editor. Recognized by many as the originator of modern science fiction, Campbell published his first story, "When the Atoms Failed" (1930), while a student at the Massachusetts Institute of Technology. The story featured one of the earliest sci-fi portrayals of computers. Campbell continued to publish stories about outer space, and, under the pseudonym Don Stuart, he also wrote works, beginning with the story "Twilight" (1934), that shifted conventional science fiction's emphasis from technology to characterization and mood. His best-known short story, under the Stuart name, is "Who Goes There?" (1938), a haunting depiction of an Antarctic research facility beset by an alien presence; it served as the basis for the now-classic science-fiction film *The Thing from Another World* (1951), better known as *The Thing*. In 1937, Campbell began editing the magazine *Astounding Stories*, later renamed *Astounding Science Fiction*, then *Analog*, where he significantly influenced mid-20th-century science fiction, publishing such important practitioners of the genre as Isaac ASIMOV and Robert A. HEINLEIN.

Camus, Albert (November 7, 1913–January 4, 1960). French novelist, playwright, and philosophical essayist. A major mid-20th-century French writer, Camus explored the philosophy of the "absurd"; his works concern humanity's plight in an indifferent universe and the need for humanistic moral and ethical values to transcend this condition. Camus was born into a European family in a working-class section of Algiers and studied philosophy at the University of Algiers. In the late 1930s he worked as a journalist in North Africa and Paris. During the occupation of France in World War II, he became an intellectual leader in the French Resistance; he worked closely with Jean-Paul SARTRE and his circle (although he refuted existentialism on ethical grounds) and served as chief editor of the underground newspaper *Combat*. Camus gained international renown with his enigmatic novel *THE STRANGER* (*L'Étranger*, 1942) and his philosophical essay *The Myth of Sisyphus* (*Le Mythe de Sisyphe*, 1942), both compelling reflections on the absurd. Further works include the novels *THE PLAGUE* (*La Peste*, 1947) and *THE FALL* (*La Chute*, 1956), the essay *The Rebel* (*L'Homme Révolté*, 1951), the play *Caligula* (1944), and stage adaptations of FAULKNER's *Requiem for a Nun* (*Requiem pour une Nonne*, 1956) and DOSTOYEVSKY's *THE POSSESSED* (*Les Possédés*, 1959). The autobiographical novel *The First Man* (*Le Premier Homme*, 1994) was discovered unfinished after his death and edited for publication by his daughter Catherine. Camus was awarded the Nobel Prize in Literature in 1957; three years later, he was killed in an automobile accident.

Canetti, Elias (July 25, 1905–August 13, 1994). Bulgarian-born novelist, playwright, and essayist, writing in German. Born a Sephardic Jew in Bulgaria, Canetti moved with his family around Europe and was educated in Switzerland, Germany, and Austria, earning a doctorate in chemistry at the University of Vienna in 1929. In Vienna, he planned an eight-volume series documenting monomaniacs, but completed only one volume, his sole novel, *AUTO-DA-FÉ* (*Die Blendung*, 1935), a highly original portrayal of a misanthropic, book-obsessed scholar who marries his predatory housekeeper with disastrous consequences. Just before World War II, Canetti immigrated to London, where he began the 25 years of study that led to his masterwork, *Crowds and Power* (*Masse und Macht*, 1960), a unique, multidisciplinary study of the psycho-pathology of the mass mind. Canetti also published three plays, *The Wedding* (*Hochzeit*, 1932), *Comedy of Vanity* (*Komödie der Eitelkeit*, 1950), and *Life-Terms* (*Die Befristeten*, 1964). His other works include 50 studies of mono-mania collected in *The Earwitness* (*Der Ohr-enzeuge*, 1974), and three volumes of autobiography: *The Tongue Set Free* (*Die Gerettete Zunge*, 1977), *The Torch in My Ear* (*Die Fackel im Ohr*, 1980), and *The Play of the Eyes* (*Das Augenspiel*, 1985). Canetti was awarded the Nobel Prize in Literature in 1981.

Cao Zhan, *also* Ts'ao Chan *or* Ts'ao Hsüeh-ch'in (c. 1715–February 12, 1763). Chinese novelist. Cao is the author of THE DREAM OF THE RED CHAMBER (*Honglou Meng*), also known as *The Story of Stone* (*Shi tou Ji*), considered one of the greatest traditional Chinese narratives and the inspiration for innumerable imitations, adaptations, and scholarly studies. The autobiographical novel portrays the decline of the powerful Chia family with psychological insight and a rich blend of realistic and supernatural elements. Cao's own family also suffered a reversal of fortune. Born in Jiangning, the grandson of the affluent director of imperial textiles, Cao Yin, Cao Zhan moved with his family to Beijing in 1728 upon encountering the first of several financial setbacks. Cao worked on *The Dream of the Red Chamber* for more than 20 years, beginning around 1742. The work was at least two-thirds complete at his death; the remaining chapters were written by Gao E, about whom little is known.

Čapek, Karel (January 9, 1890–December 25, 1938). Czech playwright, novelist, and essayist. The most-admired writer of the first Czech republic, Čapek is best known today for his science-fiction fantasies, which examine the dangers of a technological society and the quest for power. Born in Bohemia, he studied philoso-phy abroad before settling in Prague in 1917. He wrote many of his early plays, notably *The Insect Play* (*Ze Života Hmyzu*, 1922), and stories in collaboration with his brother Josef, an avant-garde painter. Čapek's drama *R.U.R.: Rossum's Universal Robots* (1920), which introduced the word "robot" to the world, earned international attention for its dark vision of a revolt of robots who were designed to serve humans. His novel *War with the Newts* (*Válka s Mloky*, 1936) and play *Power and Glory* (*Bílá Nemoc*, 1937) are complex fantasies that critique totalitarianism. Čapek also wrote a trilogy of poetic novels that investigate the mysteries of inner identity: *Hordubal* (1933), *Meteor* (*Povětroň*, 1934), and *An Ordinary Life* (*Obyčejný Život*, 1934). His late short stories, inventive detective tales, are collected in translation as *Tales from Two Pockets* (1932).

Capote, Truman, *original name* Truman Streckfus Persons (September 30, 1924–August 25, 1984). American novelist, short-story writer, screenwriter, and journalist. The perpetual *enfant terrible* of the New York glitterati, Capote had a penchant for celebrity that often over-shadowed his reputation as a writer of stature. New Orleans–born (he was the model for "Dill" in his friend HARPER LEE's TO KILL A MOCKINGBIRD), he made his first real impact with the coming-of-age novel *Other Voices, Other Rooms* (1948). His most enduring fictional creation is Holly GOLIGHTLY, the free-spirited heroine of the novella BREAKFAST AT TIFFANY'S (1958). Capote set a new standard and style for reportorial writing with his "non-fiction novel" IN COLD BLOOD (1965), about the murder of a family in rural Kansas. He then lost the approval and friendship of many of his jet-set confreres in the 1970s when he turned his reporter's eye on them in a work-in-progress that appeared serially in *Esquire* (published posthumously, in 1987, as *Answered Prayers: The Unfinished Novel*). Other works include the novel *The Grass Harp* (1951), the short story "A Christmas Memory" (1956), and the screenplay, cowritten with the director, for John Huston's *Beat the Devil* (1953).

Cardenal [Martínez], **Ernesto** (January 20, 1925–). Nicaraguan poet. Educated in Nicaragua, Mexico, and at Columbia University in New York, Cardenal converted to Roman Catholicism in 1957 and became a proponent of liberation theology. He was ordained as a priest in 1965, after studying with the American Roman Catholic monk and poet Thomas Merton at the Trappist Abbey of Gethsemani in Kentucky. A trip to Cuba in 1970 provoked a "second conversion" to Marxism. Not long after, he published his *Zero Hour and Other Documentary Poems* (*La Hora Cero*, 1971), which rages against American support of Anastasio Somoza's repressive regime. Some of his most accomplished poems are found in the collections *Homage to the American Indians* (*Homenaje a los Indios Americanos*, 1969), *Cosmic Canticle* (*Cántico Cósmico*, 1989), and *Golden UFOs: The Indian Poems* (*Los Ovnis de Oro: Poemas Indios*, 1988). The first volume of his memoirs, *Viva Perdida* (Lost Life), appeared in 1999. He was Nicaragua's minister of culture from 1979 to 1988.

Carpentier [y Valmont], **Alejo** (December 26, 1904–April 24, 1980). Cuban novelist and journalist. A major Latin-American novelist, Carpentier was the first to use the term "magic realism" to indicate the literary juxtaposition of ordinary life with fabulous events. He grew up in a vivid mix of cultures in Havana and studied at the University of Havana. After spending years abroad for political reasons, Carpentier returned to Cuba after the Revolution in 1959, and in 1970 became the Cuban cultural attaché in Paris. The effects of European conquest in South America and the West Indies inform some of his best-known and most critically acclaimed novels: *The Lost Steps* (*Los Pasos Perdidos*, 1953), in which a composer traces the upper reaches of the Orinoco River in South America; *Explosion in a Cathedral* (*El Siglo de las Luces*, 1962), set on Guadeloupe at the time of the French Revolution; and *The Harp and the Shadow* (*El Arpa y la Sombra*, 1979), a powerful retelling of Columbus's journey. Other works include the novels *The Kingdom of This World* (*El Reino de Este Mundo*,

1949), about the Haitian leader Henri Christophe, and *Reasons of State* (*El Recurso del Método*, 1974), about the Cuban dictator Machado; and a history of Cuban music.

Carroll, Lewis, *pen name of* Charles Lutwidge Dodgson (January 27, 1832–January 14, 1898). English writer. Carroll is the author of ALICE'S ADVENTURES IN WONDERLAND (1865) and its sequel, *THROUGH THE LOOKING-GLASS AND WHAT ALICE FOUND THERE* (1871), for which he is remembered and loved throughout the world. "Lewis Carroll" was a pseudonym that Dodgson, a deacon of the Church of England, a mathematics lecturer, and a Student (resident scholar) of Christ Church, Oxford, from 1852 until his death, assumed to protect his privacy and reputation as a serious scholar when the first of the "Alice" books was published. Their genesis was a story made up for his favorite child-friend, Alice Liddell, and her two sisters, daughters of the Dean of Christ Church, one summer afternoon in 1862. It was such a success that he wrote it down, illustrating it himself. Published three years later with illustrations by John Tenniel, it brought him instant celebrity, leading to friendships and correspondence with many notables of Victorian society. Carroll's other works include *The Hunting of the Snark* (1876), *A Tangled Tale* (1885), and *Sylvie and Bruno* (1889). Under his real name, Dodgson published several important works on mathematics and logic, and he was also an accomplished photographer.

Carver, Raymond (May 25, 1938–August 2, 1988). American short-story writer and poet. Depicting people menaced by ordinary problems that snowball out of control, Carver is credited with returning realism to American fiction, rejecting the Surrealist tendencies of postmodernism. The backgrounds of his characters generally resemble the blue-collar environment in which Carver himself was raised; their weakness for alcohol reflects his own. Although he disapproved of the term *minimalist*, Carver's deliberately plain style deeply influenced younger fiction writers. After publishing stories for years, he finally gained widespread attention when "Neighbors" appeared in *Esquire* in 1971. Among Carver's several story collections are *Will You Please Be Quiet, Please?* (1976), WHAT WE TALK ABOUT WHEN WE TALK ABOUT LOVE (1981), and *Cathedral* (1983). The best known of his poetry collections is the posthumous *A New Path to the Waterfall* (1989), written during his terminal bout with lung cancer. *Call If You Need Me: The Uncollected Fiction and Other Prose* appeared in 2001.

Cary, [Arthur] Joyce (December 7, 1888–March 29, 1957). British novelist. After a sickly childhood in Ireland, Cary studied law at Oxford, then enlisted with the colonial service in Nigeria and worked there for a decade, until 1920. His first novel, *Aissa Saved* (1932), examines British colonialism in Africa, an important focus in several of his other novels, including the accomplished *Mister Johnson* (1939). He is best known for his two trilogies, the first consisting of *Herself Surprised* (1941), *To Be a Pilgrim* (1942), and THE HORSE'S MOUTH (1944), which explore personal freedom and artistic creativity. The second, *Prisoner of Grace* (1952), *Except the Lord* (1953), and *Not Honour More* (1955), centers on politics. Cary also wrote essays, stories, and poetry.

Castiglione, Baldesar *or* **Baldassare,** [Conte] (December 6, 1478–February 2, 1529). Italian man of letters. Born into the nobility, in 1504 Castiglione entered the service of Guidobaldo da Montefeltro, Duke of Urbino, in whose court he wrote his masterpiece, *The Book of the Courtier* (*Il Libro del Cortegiano*, written 1513–18, published 1528). Fashioned as a dialogue among a group of his friends, it can be read as a manual for courtly etiquette, but its primary purpose is to develop, in the perfect Courtier and Court Lady, a humanist ideal of society and the individual. It was quickly recognized as a classic across Renaissance Europe. Other works, much admired and imitated, include a dramatic eclogue, *Thyrsis* (*Tirsi*, 1506), cowritten with one of his cousins; a Latin pastoral elegy, *Alcon* (c. 1506); and numerous Petrarchan sonnets in Italian. Castiglione served Guidobaldo and his successors until 1524, when Pope Clement VII appointed him papal nuncio to the court of Emperor Charles V in Spain. He retained the favor of both Clement and Charles even after the emperor's 1527 sack of Rome, and was awarded the bishopric of Ávila, which he held until his death.

Cather, Willa, *original name* Wilella Cather (December 7, 1873–April 24, 1947). American novelist, short-story writer, and essayist. Cather celebrated America's pioneers in such enduring novels as O PIONEERS! (1913) and MY ÁNTONIA (1918). Born in Virginia, she moved with her family to the frontier town of Red Cloud, Nebraska, when she was ten. Cather won notice for her first short-story collection, *The Troll Garden* (1905), and first novel, *Alexander's Bridge* (1912), but she found her true subject with her second novel, *O Pioneers!*, which drew upon her childhood observations of European immigrants to chronicle one Swedish family's efforts to tame the western plains. *My Ántonia* followed, tracing Bohemian immigrant Ántonia SHIMERDA's life of struggle and eventual joy on the prairie. In 1923, Cather won the Pulitzer Prize for *One of Ours* (1922), the story of a Nebraska boy fighting in World War I. In later works, Cather turned to history to capture the pioneering spirit that she believed was disappearing from America—19th-century New Mexico in DEATH COMES FOR THE ARCHBISHOP (1927), 17th-century Quebec in SHADOWS ON THE ROCK (1931), and the U.S. Civil War in *Sapphira and the Slave Girl* (1940). In other major works Cather explored art and disillusionment; they include A LOST LADY (1923), THE PROFESSOR'S HOUSE (1925), and the essay collection *Not Under Forty* (1936).

Catullus, *in full* Gaius Valerius Catullus (c. 84 B.C.–c. 54 B.C.). Roman poet. Preserved in a single copy discovered in the 14th century, the 116 extant poems of Catullus include some of the most admired lyric verses of ancient Rome. The 25 love poems to Lesbia—believed to be modeled after his mistress, Clodia Pulchra, the wife of a consul—were widely imitated by later European poets. Among the others are elegies, marriage hymns, a short epic ("The Marriage of

Peleus and Thetis"), and a series of satirical epigrams attacking Julius Caesar. Catullus was one of the first Roman poets to employ the lyric rhythms and learned manner of the classical Greek school. The little that is known of his life has been deduced from his poetry: he was born in Verona and went to Rome in his early 20s. His relationship with the older, aristocratic Clodia ended badly and, about 57 B.C., he escaped to the province of Bithynia in Asia Minor. On the trip back to Rome, he visited his brother's grave near Troy, where he likely wrote the famous ode "Hail and Farewell ("Ave atque Vale").

Cavafy, Constantine, *or* C. P. Cavafy *or* K[ōnstantinos] P[etrou] Kavaphēs (April 17, 1863–April 29, 1933). Egyptian-born Greek poet. Cavafy's verse is considered among the finest in modern Greek, although he wrote fewer than 300 poems. Born in Alexandria, Cavafy was educated in England. After returning to Alexandria, he lived a quiet life as a civil servant, his poetry eventually attracting the attention and support of more established writers, including E. M. FORSTER, a personal friend, T. S. ELIOT, and W. H. AUDEN. Lawrence DURRELL, whose ALEXANDRIA QUARTET makes many references to Cavafy, was also a champion. Cavafy's ironic, skeptical worldview, his mix of formal and plain language, his frankness about his homosexuality, and his frequent references to the lessons of ancient history create a poetry that is readily recognizable, even in translation. Among his best-known poems are "Waiting for the Barbarians" ("Perimenontas tous Varvarous," 1898), "Thermopylae" ("Thermopyles," 1903), and "Ithaca" ("Ithakē," 1910). Notable English translations of his work include *The Complete Poems of Cavafy* (1961; expanded ed. 1976), translated by Rae Dalven; *Collected Poems* (1992), translated by Edmund Keeley and Philip Sherrard; and *Before Time Could Change Them: The Complete Poems of Constantine P. Cavafy* (2001), translated by Theoharis Constantine Theoharis.

Cela [y Trulock], **Camilo José** (May 11, 1916–). Spanish novelist and essayist. Cela's uncon-ventional, often formally experimental novels reinvigorated Spanish fiction and earned him the Nobel Prize in 1989. Born in Iria Flavia in northwestern Spain, Cela moved with his family to Madrid in 1925. He entered the University of Madrid as a medical student, but soon began to devote himself to literature—until he was drafted into Franco's army during the Spanish Civil War. Returning to Madrid in 1940, he studied law and wrote a successful first novel, *The Family of Pascual Duarte* (*La Familia de Pascual Duarte*, 1942), in which a multiple murderer recounts his brutal life. *The Hive* (*La Colmena*, 1951) is a grim examination of postwar Madrid. Other novels are *Mrs. Caldwell Speaks to Her Son* (*Mrs. Caldwell Habla con Su Hijo*, 1953), which recalls the speech of Cela's English mother; the long, bitter interior monologue *San Camilo, 1936* (*Vísperas, Festividad y Octava de San Camilio del Año 1936 en Madrid*, 1969); and the autobiographical *Mazurka for Two Dead Men* (*Mazurca para Dos Muertos*, 1983). Cela is considered a practitioner, if not the inventor, of "tremendismo," fiction that focuses on the dark, grotesque, and vulgar.

Celan, Paul, *pen name of* Paul Antschel (November 23, 1920–April 1970). Romanian-born poet, essayist, and translator, writing in German. George STEINER has called Celan "almost certainly the major European poet of the period after 1945." Born into a community of German-speaking Jews, Celan lost his parents in the Holocaust, and his Bukovinan homeland (now in Ukraine) after the war, when he chose to live in France. His mother tongue had become the tongue of his mother's murderers. Yet, declaring that "only in the mother tongue can one speak one's own truth," he persisted in defying Theodor Adorno's dictum that "to write poetry after Auschwitz is barbaric," publishing eight collections of verse in his last 20 years. They include *Poppy and Memory* (*Mohn und Gedächtnis*, 1952), *Speech-Grille* (*Sprachgitter*, 1959), and *Breathturn* (*Atemwende*, 1967). His best-known poem is "Death Fugue" ("Todesfuge," 1948), written in the voice of the victims of the camps. His brief, cryptic late poems make extensive use of powerfully evocative coinages and plays on words. His last years were darkened by mental illness; in April 1970, he drowned himself in the Seine.

Céline, Louis-Ferdinand, *pen name of* Louis-Ferdinand Destouches (May 27, 1894–July 1, 1961). French novelist. A practicing physician who wrote in his spare time, Céline produced several novels whose nihilistic vision, black humor, and anarchic writing style prefigured the literature of the absurd. The first two— JOURNEY TO THE END OF THE NIGHT (*Voyage au Bout de la Nuit*, 1932) and DEATH ON THE INSTALLMENT PLAN (*Mort à Crédit*, 1936), stark evocations of human suffering in a decaying world—attracted attention for their powerful imagery and stylistic innovation. Céline aired a rabid anti-Semitism in three pamphlets published in the late 1930s and early 1940s, and was suspected of Nazi collaboration during the occupation of France. He fled to Germany in 1944 and then moved to Denmark, where he was imprisoned for one year after condemnation in absentia by a French tribunal. Granted amnesty in 1951, he returned to France and worked as a doctor for the poor. Continuing to write, he produced a trilogy of novels based on his wartime experiences: *Castle to Castle* (*D'un Château l'Autre*, 1957), *North* (*Nord*, 1960), and the posthumous *Rigadoon* (*Rigodon*, 1969).

Cervantes [y Saavedra], **Miguel de** (September 29?, 1547–April 23, 1616). Spanish novelist, short-story writer, playwright, and poet. A towering figure in Western literary history, Cervantes is celebrated as the author of DON QUIXOTE (*El Ingenioso Hidalgo Don Quixote de la Mancha*, Part I, 1605; Part II, 1615), an early masterpiece of prose fiction. If not strictly the inventor of the modern novel, as some have called him, he demonstrated the possibilities of fictional realism and satiric narrative in a manner that has inspired novelists ever since. Modern critics continue to plumb the depths of his landmark experiment. Born into the impoverished family of a barber-surgeon in Alcalá de Henares outside Madrid, he published his first poems in his early 20s. He became a soldier in 1569 and lost the use of his arm in the Battle of Lepanto two years later. Captured by Algerian pirates on the voyage home, he was enslaved for five years until ransomed by Trinitarian friars. His first serious literary efforts, several plays and the pastoral romance *Galatea* (1585), were largely unsuccessful, and he found employment in Andalusia as a navy purchasing agent. He was jailed at least twice for bad debts, but the success of *Don Quixote, Part I* enabled him to devote his remaining years to writing. Memorable last works include *Exemplary Stories* (*Novelas Ejemplares*, 1613), 12 diverse narratives, and *The Trials of Persiles and Sigismunda* (*Los Trabajos de Persiles y Sigismunda*, 1617), an epic romance completed three days before his death. He is believed to have written at least 30 plays, of which about half survive.

Césaire, Aimé (June 25, 1913–). Martinican poet and playwright. Césaire is known for his complex, surrealistic writings and his passionate political commitments. He was born on the island of Martinique and educated in Paris. With Léopold SENGHOR and Léon Damas, he was a founder and a principal exponent of Négritude, an anticolonialist movement in support of black culture and identity. Returning to the Caribbean in the early 1940s, he began a career in government, serving as mayor of Martinique's capital, Fort-de-France, and deputy in the French National Assembly. His poetry collections include his widely known first book, *Notebook of a Return to My Native Land* (*Cahier d'un Retour au Pays Natal*, 1947), and *Aimé Césaire: The Collected Poetry* (1983). Among his plays are *The Tragedy of King Christophe* (*La Tragédie du Roi Christophe*, 1963), *A Season in the Congo* (*Une Saison au Congo*, 1966), and *A Tempest* (*Une Tempête*, 1969). Césaire's influential essays include, in particular, his *Discourse on Colonialism* (*Discours sur le Colonialisme*, 1950). The three-volume *Oeuvres Complètes* appeared in 1976.

Chandler, Raymond (July 23, 1888–March 26, 1959). American novelist. A master of the quintessentially American genre of hard-boiled detective fiction, Chandler was born in

Chicago and moved to England with his newly divorced mother when he was seven. Educated there and in Germany and France, he became a civil servant for the British Admiralty, but soon turned to work as a reporter for newspapers in London and Bristol. In 1912, Chandler sailed for America, eventually enjoying great success as an oil executive before his alcoholism—a lifelong affliction—and the Great Depression wrecked his career. He then turned to his first love, writing, beginning his mystery writing career, at age 45, with the 1933 publication of a story in the pulp magazine *Black Mask*. Among his seven novels were *The Big Sleep* (1939), *Farewell, My Lovely* (1940), *The High Window* (1942), and *The Long Goodbye* (1953). In each, the tough but compassionate private eye Philip MARLOWE becomes entangled in a web of murder, corruption, and sleaze as he attempts simultaneously to serve his client and maintain his integrity. Transferred to the screen, the Marlowe novels became classics of film noir, a genre to which Chandler also contributed through such screenplays as *Double Indemnity* (1944) and *Strangers on a Train* (1951). His short stories have been collected in such volumes as *The Midnight Raymond Chandler* (1971). The novel *Poodle Springs* (1989), left unfinished at Chandler's death, was completed by Robert B. Parker.

Chateaubriand, François-René, Vicomte de (September 4, 1768–July 4, 1848). French novelist and essayist. A forerunner of the French Romantic movement and a leading French writer of his day, Chateaubriand reflected in his work his passions for history, religion, politics, and the exotic. He was born in Saint-Malo and served as a cavalry officer in the early days of the French Revolution. In 1791, after refusing to join the Royalist army, he sailed for America, the land that became, after his return to Paris in 1800, the setting of his most popular novels, *ATALA* (1801) and *René* (1805). In the work that established his contemporary reputation, *The Genius of Christianity* (*Le Génie du Christianisme*, 1802), Chateaubriand extols the virtues and creative freedom his religion affords. Despite a political career that was rocked by

his support of the Bourbons and the upheavals of the times, Chateaubriand served in several prominent posts, including as an ambassador under Louis XVIII. His memoir from "beyond the tomb" (*Mémoires d'Outre-tombe*), written for posthumous publication, appeared in 1849–50.

Chatterji, Bankim Chandra (June 26/27, 1838–April 8, 1894). Indian novelist. Considered the greatest Bengali novelist, Chatterji occupies a position of prominence in his national literature equivalent to Tolstoy's or Dickens's in theirs. Known primarily for his panoramic tales of India's past, he was also revered by Hindu nationalists for the patriotic values his work expressed. Educated at the University of Calcutta, the bilingual Chatterji, who worked for many years as a civil servant, made his debut with the novel *Rajmohan's Wife* (1864), his only major work in English. Thereafter, he wrote in Bengali, beginning with *Durgesa Nandini, or, The Chieftain's Daughter, A Bengali Romance* (*Durgeśanandinī*, 1865). Other novels exploring and promoting India's Hindu culture include *The Poison Tree: A Tale of Hindu Life in Bengal* (*Bishabriksha*, 1873), *Krishna Kanta's Will* (*Krichnakanter Uil*, 1878), and *The Abbey of Bliss* (*Ananda Math*, 1882), which contains the patriotic hymn "Bande Mātaram" ("Hail to Thee, Mother India"), a rallying song embraced by Hindu nationalists fighting against their British occupiers.

Chatwin, [Charles] Bruce (May 13, 1940–January 18, 1989). English novelist and travel writer. Chatwin prepared for his eclectic career as a professional wanderer at the University of Edinburgh, where he studied archaeology; at Sotheby's, the auction house, where he eventually served as a director; and at various newspapers, for which he worked as a traveling correspondent. *In Patagonia* (1977), a nonfiction account of his travels in South America and his first major work, won wide acclaim in both Europe and America. *Songlines* (1987) is a sensitive anthropological study of Australia's aborigines. Other notable works include the novels *The Viceroy of Ouidah* (1980), *On the*

Black Hill (1982), and *Utz* (1988); *What Am I Doing Here?* (1989), a collection of essays; and *Far Journeys: Photographs and Notebooks* (1993), a posthumously published volume of Chatwin's travel writings and photographs. *Anatomy of Restlessness: Uncollected Writings* appeared in 1996.

Chaucer, Geoffrey (c. 1343–October 25, 1400). English poet. The greatest Middle English writer, Chaucer wrote works of narrative poetry, including THE CANTERBURY TALES (1387–1400), that are among the major achievements of world literature. Born to a family of the mercantile middle class, Chaucer entered royal service as a page in his teens. In 1359, he served during the military invasion of France, and from 1367 onward, he held numerous government and diplomatic posts. His first major poem, *Book of the Duchesse* (c. 1369–70), is an accomplished elegy in the manner of the French romance. In several works, *Hous of Fame* (c. 1380), *The Parlement of Foules* (c. 1382), and the collection of tales *Legend of Good Women* (c. 1386), Chaucer drew his style from Italian sources, including DANTE and BOCCACCIO, whose influence he absorbed on diplomatic trips to Italy in the 1370s. His romance TROILUS AND CRISEYDE (c. 1383), one of the finest works of medieval poetry, draws from Boccaccio's retelling of a classical myth. Chaucer increasingly expanded the scope of Middle English literature beyond conventional, aristocratic ideals and moral didacticism. His last and best-known work, the classic *Canterbury Tales*, presents 24 stories told by a diverse group of pilgrims on their way to Canterbury, organized by the framing conceit of a storytelling contest among them. As the tales, which range from romance to sermon to bawdy verses, reflect on their tellers, the work illuminates a panorama of characters and social life with boundless insight, rich humor, and masterful craft.

Chayefsky, Paddy, *original name* Sidney Chayefsky (January 29, 1923–August 1, 1981). American playwright, screenwriter, and novelist. Chayefsky, arguably the most important single writer associated with the Golden Age of live television drama, also achieved success as a playwright and screenwriter. Born in New York City, he was educated at the City College of New York and began writing for television and radio in his late 20s. His first major success was *Marty*, broadcast live on "Goodyear TV Playhouse" in 1953. This tale of a lonely Bronx butcher who finds love was memorably adapted for the screen in 1955; for his screenplay, Chayefsky received the first of his three Academy Awards (the others were for *The Hospital*, 1971, and *Network*, 1976). Other teleplays adapted for film include *The Bachelor Party* (TV, 1953; film, 1957) and *The Catered Affair* (TV, 1955; film, 1956, with a screenplay by Gore VIDAL). Chayefsky made his debut as a Broadway playwright in 1956 with *Middle of the Night*, which was followed by *The Tenth Man* (1959), *Gideon* (1961), and *The Passion of Josef D.* (1964). His novel, *Altered States* (1978), a contemporary reworking of Robert Louis STEVENSON's DR. JEKYLL AND MR. HYDE, is about a scientist who experiments with psychotropic drugs.

Cheever, John (May 27, 1912–June 18, 1982). American short-story writer and novelist. One of the most influential short-story writers of the 20th century, Cheever is remembered for his subtle, elegiac portraits of postwar suburban life in America. Born into a New England family of failing fortune, he attended Thayer Academy in Massachusetts but was expelled at age 17, an experience he transformed into fiction for his first published story ("Expelled"), which appeared in THE NEW REPUBLIC (October 1, 1930). From the mid-1940s onward, his stories appeared regularly in THE NEW YORKER and helped to define that magazine's elegant, urbane style. His first collection, *The Way Some People Live*, appeared in 1943, and was followed by *The Enormous Radio and Other Stories* (1953), *The Housebreaker of Shady Hill* (1958), *The Brigadier and the Golf Widow* (1964), and *The World of Apples* (1973). Many of his stories (e.g., "THE SWIMMER") are set in the affluent suburbs north of New York City, where Cheever lived for many years, and express a complex moral sympathy for the lives of his characters. Themes of adultery, alcoholism, isolation, and fratricide also appear frequently in his work. A collected edition, *The Stories of John Cheever* (1978), won both the Pulitzer Prize and the National Book Critics Circle Award. Cheever's first novel, THE WAPSHOT CHRONICLE (1957), won the National Book Award, but a sequel, *The Wapshot Scandal* (1964), and his next novel, *Bullet Park* (1969), failed to meet expectations. *Falconer* (1977), about a heroin addict jailed for killing his brother, is regarded by many as his finest novel. *Oh What a Paradise It Seems* (1982), published shortly before his death, is a wistful tale of an elderly man's efforts to save a favorite skating pond. *The Letters of John Cheever* (1988) and *The Journals of John Cheever* (1991), both edited by his son Benjamin, appeared posthumously.

Chekhov, Anton (January 29, 1860–July 14, 1904). Russian playwright and short-story writer. One of the great Russian writers of the 19th century, Chekhov is distinguished for understated works that explore the subtleties of human emotions and relationships. Chekhov was born in southern Russia, the son of a struggling grocer, and studied medicine at Moscow University. While still a student, he supported himself and his family by publishing hundreds of comic stories and sketches in newspapers and commercial magazines. After graduation in 1884, he began to write more substantial stories as well as plays, and once established on an estate outside Moscow in 1892, he devoted himself to his literary vocation while occasionally practicing medicine. His masterful short stories, among them "A DREARY STORY" ("Skuchnaya Istoriya," 1889), "WARD NUMBER SIX" ("Palata No. 6," 1892), and "The Black Monk" ("Chernyĭ Monakh," 1894), were followed by his first great plays, UNCLE VANYA (*Dyadya Vanya*, 1897) and THE SEAGULL (*Chaĭka*, 1897). In 1898 Chekhov moved to the Crimea in an attempt to cope with his long-standing tuberculosis, and there he wrote two final plays, THE THREE SISTERS (*Tri Sestry*, 1901) and THE CHERRY ORCHARD (*Vishnevyĭ Sad*, 1904), before his death from the disease. Chekhov, whose works are set amid the declining Russian feudal

> "Medicine is my lawful wife and literature is my mistress. When I get tired of one I spend the night with the other."
>
> Anton Chekhov, letter to A. S. Suvorin, September 11, 1888, in *Anton Chekhov and His Times*, edited by Andrei Turkov (1995)

society of his time, paints social atmosphere and character with a lucid and compassionate gaze, exploring with particular suggestiveness states of human uncertainty and the difficulties of connection and communication. Tragicomic or gently melancholy in tone, his works express the complexities of the inner life with economy, subtle lyricism, and precise, illuminating detail.

Chénier, André de (October 30, 1762–July 25, 1794). French poet and political writer. Chénier's standing as the preeminent poet of 18th-century France is augmented by his legacy as a voice of moderation during the political and social turmoil of the French Revolution. Educated at the Collège de Navarre, Chénier was working in London at the French embassy when the political crisis at home inspired his return to Paris in 1789. His political journalism initially supported the revolution, but a series of pamphlets critical of Jacobin atrocities caused him to be arrested and guillotined in 1794. The vast majority of his works in verse were published after his death; his collected poems, published in 1819, included his *Bucoliques*, *Élégies*, and *Ïambes*, the last written during his four-month captivity prior to his execution. These final works, secreted out of Saint-Lazare prison, include the well-known ode *La Jeune Captive* (The Young Prisoner). His heroic life is honored in a number of works, including *Andrea Chénier* (1896), an opera by Italian composer Umberto Giordano.

Chesnutt, Charles W[addell] (June 20, 1858–November 15, 1932). American novelist, short-story writer, and biographer. The author of trailblazing novels and stories of the African-American experience in the pre– and post–Civil War South, Chesnutt is widely regarded as America's first important black novelist. The son of freed slaves from North Carolina, Chesnutt was born in Cleveland and had careers as a lawyer, reporter, and educator. "The Goophered Grapevine," his realistic tale of plantation life, was the first story by a black writer published in THE ATLANTIC MONTHLY (August 1887). Many of his published stories can be found in the collections *The Conjure Woman* (1899), a series of linked narratives set in North Carolina, where he lived for a number of years after the civil war, before returning to Cleveland, and *The Wife of His Youth and Other Stories of the Color Line* (1899). His other works include *The Marrow of Tradition* (1901) and *The Colonel's Dream* (1905), novels; and a biography of black leader Frederick Douglass. Recent publications of importance include three novels for which Chesnutt was unable to find publishers during his lifetime: *Mandy Oxendine* (1997; completed late 1890s), a romance-mystery centering on two racially mixed lovers who choose to live on opposite sides of the color line; *Paul Marchand, F.M.C.* (1998; completed 1921), about a "Free Man of Color" who can pass for white, and who will come into an inheritance only if he renounces his mixed-race wife and children; and *The Quarry* (1999; completed 1928), about a distinguished man of letters, a light-skinned Negro, and the social and intellectual temptations he confronts and overcomes. Major editions of nonfiction include *The Short Fiction of Charles W. Chesnutt* (1974), *The Journals of Charles W. Chesnutt* (1993), *"To Be an Author": Letters of Charles W. Chesnutt, 1889–1905* (1997), and *Charles W. Chesnutt: Essays and Speeches* (1999).

Chikamatsu, Monzaemon, *original name* Sugimori Nobumori (1653–January 6, 1725). Japanese playwright. Chikamatsu was Japan's greatest innovator of the bunraku, or puppet theater. For many years he was associated with Takemoto Gidayu, a bunraku chanter, for whom he wrote most of his major works. His plays, which complement the artistry of the puppeteer with strong narrative lines exploring themes of love, honor, and duty, include such works as *The Love Suicides at Sonezaki* (*Sonezaki Shinjū*, 1703), *The Battles of Coxinga* (*Kokusen'ya Kassen*, 1715), and *The Love Suicide at Amijima* (*Shinju Ten no Amijima*, 1721). He also wrote for the Kabuki theater.

Chopin, Kate, *original name* Katherine O'Flaherty (February 8, 1851–August 22, 1904). American short-story writer and novelist. Chopin's best-known work is the novel THE AWAKENING (1899), a tragic portrait of a wealthy Louisiana woman's struggle to achieve independence. The novel's frank handling of sexual themes, including the protagonist's extramarital affair, aroused violent critical censure that virtually put an end to the writer's career, but the book, rediscovered in the 1960s, is now greatly admired for its exceptional artistry and Chopin's progressive inquiry into matters of female identity. Chopin, who was born in St. Louis, moved to New Orleans with her husband, Oscar Chopin, a planter, following their marriage in 1870. His death 12 years later left her in debt, but also free to write. In addition to *The Awakening*, she wrote many stories of Cajun and Creole life, collected in *Bayou Folk* (1894) and *A Night in Acadie* (1897).

Chrétien de Troyes (fl. 1160–90). French poet. A seminal figure in the Arthurian tradition in literature, Chrétien was probably a poet at the court of Marie de Champagne and Philip of Flanders. Five romances concerning King ARTHUR and the Knights of the Round Table can be confidently ascribed to him, including *Lancelot, or The Knight of the Cart* (*Lancelot, ou Le Chevalier de la Charrette*), about the knight LANCELOT and his love for GUINEVERE; and the unfinished *Perceval, or The Story of the Grail* (*Perceval le Gallois*, also translated under variant titles), which ranks as the first narrative to attach Arthur to the legend of the Holy Grail. Chrétien's works were probably informed by the publication of a French translation of Geoffrey of Monmouth's *Historia Regnum Britanniae*, the source of the Arthurian legend, and did much to further the Arthurian tradition in England and on the Continent.

Christie, [Dame] Agatha (September 15, 1890–January 12, 1976). English novelist and playwright. The author of more than 80 detective novels, translated into some 100 languages, Christie is one of the most popular and successful writers of all time, with more than two billion copies of her work sold worldwide. Born and reared in Torquay, Devon, she served as a nurse and chemist's assistant in World War I, an experience that gave her intimate knowledge of poisons, which would eventually figure so prominently in her writing. Her mysteries usually feature one of her two famous sleuths: the eccentric Belgian Hercule Poirot, introduced in her first novel, *The Mysterious Affair at Styles* (1920), and featured in her first great popular success, *The Murder of Roger Ackroyd* (1926); or the elderly spinster, Miss Jane Marple, who first appeared in *Murder at the Vicarage* (1930). Christie also wrote and adapted many works for the stage; her most successful play, *The Mousetrap*, opened in 1952 and is still running in London's West End, making it the longest-running play in theater history. Many of her books have been adapted successfully for film and television; these include *Murder on the Orient Express* (1933; filmed in 1974) and *Death on the Nile* (1937; filmed in 1978). She is the author of a volume of autobiography, published in 1977, and, under the pen name Mary Westmacott, of a number of romantic novels.

Christine de Pisan (c. 1365–c. 1431). Italian-born French poet and prose writer. As a young girl, the Venice-born Christine moved from Italy to France when her father was appointed court astrologer to Charles V. Married at age 15, she began writing poems when, ten years later, she was left a widow with three young children and considerable debts. In her poetry as well as her prose, Christine wrote extensively of women's experience in medieval France, refuting the misogyny in Jean de Meun's ROMANCE OF THE ROSE in her *L'Épistre au Dieu d'Amours* (1399; Letters to the God of Loves), describing heroic women's lives in *The Book of the City of Ladies* (*Le Livre de la Cité des Dames*, 1405), and classifying women's roles in *The Book of Three Virtues* (*Le Livre des Trois Vertus*, 1405). *Le Ditié de Jehanne d'Arc* (1429), her final work, is the only known account in French of the life of Joan of Arc written during the saint's lifetime. Christine earned the support of important nobles, including Charles V, and after his death she was commissioned to write his biography, *Book of the Deeds and Good Morals of the Wise King Charles V* (*Le Livre des Fais et Bonnes Meurs du Sage Roy Charles V*, 1404).

Churchill, Caryl (September 3, 1938–). English playwright. One of the most innovative dramatists to come out of England in the 1970s, Churchill was born in London, educated at Oxford University, and began writing radio and stage plays in the 1960s. Her first critical and popular success, *Cloud Nine* (1979), set in both British colonial Africa and contemporary London, uses experimental techniques—fractured chronology, gender role reversal—to explore sexual and racial identities. Her next major work, *Top Girls* (1982), incorporates historical characters, including the legendary Pope Joan, in its examination of women and financial success. *Serious Money* (1987) is set in the world of London's stock exchange, while *Mad Forest* (1990) concerns the effects of totalitarianism on two families in Ceausescu's Romania. Other works include *Fen* (1983), *The Skriker* (1994), *Blue Heart* (1997), which is made up of two short plays, *Heart's Desire* and *Blue Kettle*, and *Far Away* (2000).

Cicero, [Marcus Tullius] (106 B.C.–43 B.C.). Roman orator, philosopher, and man of letters. One of the greatest orators of the ancient world, Cicero led a life of political intrigue that placed him at the center of some of the most important events in the history of the Roman Republic. Born to a wealthy family, he studied law and rhetoric and became known as a lawyer of uncommon ability. He entered public life in 76 B.C. and rose steadily through the ranks, winning election as consul of Rome in 64 B.C. as a member of the aristocratic party. His four orations against the conspirator Cataline in 63 B.C. (*In Catilinam*), among his greatest achievements, demonstrated his mastery of rhetoric and the political moment, although by 58 B.C. his fortunes had fallen and he spent a year and a half in exile in Greece. In the turbulent years that followed, he produced some of his greatest writings, including the six-volume *On the Commonwealth* (*De Republica*, 52 B.C.; also translated under the title *The Republic*), a comprehensive statement of political philosophy; and his great discourse *On Oratory and Orators* (*De Oratore*, 55 B.C.). In the aftermath of Julius Caesar's assassination, Cicero supported Octavius (Augustus) against Mark Antony, but Octavius betrayed him and Cicero was killed by a mob of bounty hunters in 43 B.C. Other important works include *On the Laws* (*De Legibus*, 52 B.C.), *On Stoic Good and Evil* (*De Finibus Bonorum et Malorum*, 45 B.C.), *Of Old Age* (*De Senectute*, 44 B.C.), and *The Nature of the Gods* (*De Natura Deorum*, 44 B.C.). His rhetorical style and his rich use of Latin remained in vogue until the Augustine Empire. Some 58 of his public speeches are extant, as are more than 900 of his letters.

Clarke, [Sir] Arthur C[harles] (December 6, 1917–). English science-fiction writer. In nearly all his novels and stories, the prolific Clarke presented futuristic scenarios that, although fanciful and richly imagined, were based on scientific knowledge. This disciplined approach set him apart from the vast majority of science-fiction writers and became the source of his lasting popularity. Clarke studied mathematics and physics at Kings College, London, after serving in the Royal Air Force from 1941 to 1946 as a radar instructor. His scientific training informs such popular novels of space and sea exploration as *Childhood's End* (1953), *The City and the Stars* (1956), *Tales from the White Hart* (1957), *The Deep Range* (1957), *A Fall of Moondust* (1961), *Rendezvous with Rama* (1973), *The Garden of Rama* (1991), and *The Hammer of God* (1993). Outside of science-fiction circles, he is best known for his collaboration with director Stanley Kubrick on the screenplay *2001: A Space Odyssey* (1968), based on his earlier story, "The Sentinel." *2001: A*

SPACE ODYSSEY was also developed into a novel and became the basis for a trilogy of popular sequels, including *2010: Odyssey Two* (1982), *2061: Odyssey Three* (1988), and *3001: The Final Odyssey* (1997). His nonfiction writings on such topics as artificial intelligence, communications satellites, and deep-sea exploration are well respected and can be found in such volumes as *Voices from the Sky* (1965), *The View from Serendip* (1977), *Ascent to Orbit: A Scientific Autobiography* (1984), *Astounding Days: A Science Fictional Autobiography* (1989), and *Greetings, Carbon-based Bipeds!: Collected Essays, 1934–1998* (1999). He has lived since the 1950s in Sri Lanka.

Clemens, Samuel Langhorne. *See* **Twain, Mark**

Cocteau, Jean (July 5, 1889–October 11, 1963). French poet, playwright, novelist, screenwriter, and librettist. Born in Maisons-Laffitte, an elegant resort town outside of Paris, into a well-to-do and cultivated family that encouraged his artistic aspirations, Cocteau was a virtuoso in an impressive range of creative endeavors. Although he considered himself first and foremost a poet, he was also a novelist and belle-lettrist, as well as an illustrator, filmmaker, actor, producer, and opera and ballet librettist, and in these latter roles collaborated with some of the 20th century's greatest artists, including Pablo Picasso, Sergei Diaghilev, Francis Poulenc, and Jean GENET. Cocteau published a book of poetry, *La Lampe d'Aladin* (1909; Aladdin's Lamp), before his 20th birthday, but his first great success came with his scenario for the ballet *Parade* (first staged in Paris in 1917, with sets by Picasso and music by Eric Satie). In his program notes for the premiere, APOLLINAIRE used the word *surrealism* for the first time, hailing *Parade*'s "alliance of painting and dance, of music and the plastic arts.... From this new alliance has resulted something beyond realism ... surrealism." With *Parade*, Cocteau became a key member of the artistic generation whose daring gave birth to the avant-garde. Other major works for the stage include the ballet *Le Boeuf sur le Toit; ou, The Nothing*

Doing Bar (1920; The Ox on the Roof; with scenario by Cocteau and music by Darius Milhaud); the plays *Antigone* (1922, after Sophocles, with music by Arthur Honegger), *Orpheus* (*Orphée*, 1926), *The Human Voice* (*La Voix Humaine*, 1930; adapted as a one-act opera by Poulenc in 1959), *The Infernal Machine* (*La Machine Infernale*, 1934), and *Les Parents Terribles* (1938; the French title is used for most English translations, but the play has also been translated as *Intimate Relations*, *The Awful Parents*, and *Indiscretions*); and the great opera-oratorio after Sophocles, *Oedipus-Rex* (1928, with libretto by Cocteau and music by Igor Stravinsky). Among Cocteau's most important novels are *The Impostor* (*Thomas l'Imposteur*, 1923; also translated as *Thomas the Imposter*), a "hymn to the cult of youth" set during World War I; the autobiographical tale of youthful love and loss, *The Grand Écart* (*Le Grand Écart*, 1923; The Big Split; also translated as *The Miscreant*); and the study of adolescent alienation and the lost paradise of childhood, *Les Enfants Terribles* (1929; also translated as *The Holy Terrors* and *The Children of the Game*). Important English-language collections of Cocteau's work include *Tempest of Stars*, selected poems with parallel French/English texts; *The Art of Cinema* (1992), gathering his writings on film; and *Past Tense*, the diaries (2 vols.; 1987–88). *Souvenir Portraits: Paris in the Belle Epoque* (*Portraits-Souvenir, 1900–1914*, 1935), with the author's own line drawings, gathers sketches of Cocteau's childhood and youth in which COLETTE, Sarah Bernhardt, Mistinguett, and many other famous figures make cameo appearances.

Coetzee, J[ohn] M[ichael] (February 9, 1940–). South African novelist. The first writer to win the Booker Prize twice — in 1983 for *The Life and Times of Michael K*, and in 1999 for *Disgrace* — Coetzee writes novels admired for their compact power and nuanced presentation of the complexities of life in contemporary South Africa. His critique of apartheid and the legacy of colonialism is often presented obliquely, through the study of individual lives caught up in an oppressive system. Coetzee grew up in Cape Town, earned his Ph.D. at the University of Texas, worked in England as a computer programmer, and taught at the State University of New York at Buffalo before returning to Cape Town to write and teach. His other fiction includes *Dusklands* (1974), a pair of novellas; and the novels *In the Heart of the Country* (1977), *Waiting for the Barbarians* (1980), and *Age of Iron* (1990). Other works include an adaptation of *Robinson Crusoe* entitled *Foe* (1986) and an autobiographical narrative, *Boyhood: Scenes from Provincial Life* (1997).

Coleridge, Samuel Taylor (October 21, 1772– July 25, 1834). English poet and critic. One of the founding figures of English Romanticism, Coleridge was the son of a Devon cleric, and from an early age exhibited the introspective and mystical tendencies that would color his career. He attended Cambridge but did not graduate, and with poet Robert Southey embarked on a plan to found a utopian community in Pennsylvania, which ended in failure. He married a schoolteacher, Sara Fricker, but from the start the union was an unhappy one. In 1795 a propitious meeting with William WORDSWORTH led to a creative partnership that changed English poetry. The poems that Coleridge wrote during the next few years — including "THE RIME OF THE ANCIENT MARINER" and "Frost at Midnight" — were highly experimental for their day, and their publication in *LYRICAL BALLADS* (1798; rev. and expanded ed. 1800) along with poems by Wordsworth is generally identified by scholars as the dawn of the Romantic movement. Other poems produced during this period include the unfinished "KUBLA KHAN" and the first part of "Christabel." Wordsworth and Coleridge traveled together to Germany, and after a brief period apart, Coleridge settled in the Lake District to be near his friend. It was during this period that he became badly addicted to opium. His marriage also failed, in large part because he had fallen in love with Sara Hutchinson, the sister of Wordsworth's fiancée. Thereafter, he wrote very little poetry. Although his body of creative work is comparatively slender, Coleridge's theories of organic form, and the visionary, highly personal quality of his writings, secured his legacy as a poet and thinker of immense importance. Verse collections include *Christabel and Other Poems* (1816) and *Sibylline Leaves* (1817). *Biographia Literaria* (1817), a volume of criticism and autobiography, is highly regarded, particularly for its insights into Wordsworth's work.

Colette, *original name* Sidonie-Gabriele Colette (January 28, 1873–August 3, 1954). French novelist. Known for her uninhibited explorations of the stages of womanhood and her precise, sensually evocative prose style, Colette grew up in a small village in Burgundy and was educated in the ways of Parisian society by her first husband, Henri Gauthier-Villars, with whom she collaborated on the four novels of the *Claudine* series (1900–1903), published under her husband's pen name, Willy. After the two separated in 1906, Colette worked as a dance-hall performer and began publishing, under her own name, novels including *The Vagabond* (*La Vagabonde,* 1910), *Music-hall Sidelights* (*L'Envers du Music-hall,* 1913), and *Mitsou* (1919), in which she explored sensuality and female liberty. With the novels *CHÉRI* (1920) and *The Last of Chéri* (*La Fin de Chéri,* 1926), about the love affair of a young man and his older mistress in the aftermath of World War I, Colette established herself as a major figure in French letters. Other important works include *Ripening Seed* (*La Blé en Herbe,* 1923), *The Cat* (*La Chatte,* 1933), *Duo* (1934), *My Mother's House* (*La Maison de Claudine,* 1922), and *Sido* (1930). One of her best-known works, *Gigi* (1944), about a courtesan, was adapted for both stage and screen.

Collins, [William] **Wilkie** (January 8, 1824–September 23, 1889). English novelist. Considered the first English writer of detective fiction, the London-born Collins studied law and was admitted to the bar, but soon abandoned a legal career for writing. His first novels were *Antonina: or, The Fall of Rome* (1850) and *Basil* (1852), his first foray into mystery and suspense.

Thereafter, Collins's career was greatly influenced by his friendship with Charles DICKENS, who published his work serially in his magazines *Household Words* and *All the Year Round.* *THE WOMAN IN WHITE* (1860) and *THE MOONSTONE* (1868) are Collins's best-known and most-respected works. Others include *Armadale* (1866), *The New Magdalen* (1873), *The Haunted Hotel* (1879), and *Heart and Science* (1883).

Compton-Burnett, [Dame] **Ivy** (June 5, 1884–August 27, 1969). English novelist. Except for her first novel, the conventional *Dolores* (1911), Compton-Burnett wrote her eccentric major works almost entirely in dialogue. The typical setting of her novels is an Edwardian household, lorded over by a bullying parental figure, and the action unfolds through oblique, often tantalizingly elusive exchanges that lead to psychological damage and even cataclysmic violence. Her work was informed by her interest

---

"At a certain point my novels set. They set just as hard as that jam jar. And then I know they are finished."

Ivy Compton-Burnett, quoted by Joyce Cary in *Art and Reality* (1958)

---

in Greek tragedy and the terrible losses she incurred in the 14 years between her first and second novels—including the deaths of her parents, her brother (who was killed in the war), and two sisters, in a joint suicide. *Pastors and Masters* (1925), written after she recovered from a breakdown, is the first of her dialogue-driven novels. Eighteen novels followed, notably *Brothers and Sisters* (1929), *More Women Than Men* (1933), *A Family and a Fortune* (1939), *Manservant and Maidservant* (1947)—thought to be her most accomplished work—and *Mother and Son* (1955). After Compton-Burnett settled into her career as a steadily productive novelist, her life was for the most part uneventful. When asked about herself by *The Times*

(London) in 1969, she replied, "There's not much to say. I haven't been at all deedy."

Congreve, William (January 24, 1670–January 19, 1729). English playwright. A major figure of the Restoration theater, Congreve began writing plays at age 23 and wrote his last play before his 30th birthday. In that brief time, however, in such plays as the masterfully satirical THE WAY OF THE WORLD (1700), Congreve established himself as a preeminent writer of the Neoclassical comedy of manners, second only to the French playwright MOLIÈRE. His work was also enormously popular. The son of an army officer stationed in Dublin, he attended school with Jonathan SWIFT and completed his education at Trinity College before writing his first play, *The Old Bachelour* (1693), which his friend and mentor John DRYDEN declared "the best play he had ever seen." His second play, *The Double-Dealer* (1693), was less popular with audiences, but *Love for Love* (1695) returned him to his standing with the public. *The Mourning Bride* (1697), a sentimental tragedy, was his most popular play, although today it is remembered in the main for originating the adages "Hell hath no fury like a woman scorned" and "Music hath charms to soothe the savage breast." Although *The Way of the World* was his least successful major production, it remains the work most respected by critics and is frequently revived. Congreve's public dispute with the Reverend Jeremy Collier, a vocal critic of the English stage, led to Congreve's early retirement from the theater in 1700. He spent the last 29 years of his life writing poems and living the life of a celebrity writer, hobnobbing with such figures as Swift, POPE, and VOLTAIRE.

Conrad, Joseph, *original name* Józef Teodor Konrad Korzeniowski (December 3, 1857–August 3, 1924). Polish-born English novelist and short-story writer. Known first as a writer of exotic sea adventures, Conrad came to enjoy great critical respect for the probing moral seriousness of his work and his masterful prose — despite the fact that he did not learn English until his early 20s. Born in Poland, he moved to Volgda, Russia, after his father, a Polish nationalist, was exiled. His parents died of tuberculosis before he was a teenager and Conrad was sent to live with a relative in Switzerland. At 17 he joined the French Merchant Marine as a deckhand and set sail for the West Indies; four years later he joined the British Merchant navy and rose steadily through the ranks, eventually securing a command of his own. These voyages around the world informed the vast body of his fiction, first in the novel *Almayer's Folly* (1895) and subsequently in such works as *An Outcast of the Islands* (1896), THE NIGGER OF THE "NARCISSUS" (1897), LORD JIM (1900), *Typhoon* (1903), NOSTROMO (1904), and *Under Western Eyes* (1911). *Chance* (1914), serialized in *The New York Herald*, was the work that made him famous, but HEART OF DARKNESS (1902), inspired by a trip on a Congo River steamboat, and THE SECRET AGENT (1907), a psychological thriller set in London, are probably his most highly regarded works. Conrad became a British subject in 1886 and lived out his life from 1895 in London.

Cooper, James Fenimore (September 15, 1789–September 14, 1851). American novelist. Widely regarded as the first bona-fide American novelist, Cooper wrote tales of frontier adventure that helped to create a uniquely American literary tradition. He is best known for THE LEATHERSTOCKING TALES, comprising *The Pioneers* (1823), *The Last of the Mohicans* (1826), *The Prairie* (1827), *The Pathfinder* (1840), and *The Deerslayer* (1841), and featuring the memorable frontier scout Natty BUMPPO, alias Leatherstocking. The son of a wealthy New York landowner (who founded Cooperstown, New York), Cooper entered Yale at age 13 but was expelled in his junior year for being a prankster. An eight-year tour of duty in the navy followed, but Cooper left the service early when his father died in 1809, leaving him a substantial inheritance. His first novel, *Precaution* (1820), was a critical failure and attracted few readers, but his second, *The Spy* (1821), won wide attention for its use of an American setting and characters. Besides *The Leatherstocking Tales*, which were enormously popular, Cooper also wrote several novels of seafaring life, beginning with *The Pilot* (1823), which did much to establish the genre. In his later years Cooper became an outspoken critic of "mobocracy"; his increasingly strident critique of American democracy, and the unflattering response he received in the Whig press, embroiled him in numerous lawsuits, many of which he won. *A Letter to His Countrymen* (1834) and *The American Democrat* (1838) are works of social criticism in which he expounds on his aristocratic political philosophy. Other important works include *Red Rover* (1827), *The Water-Witch* (1830), and *The Sea Lions* (1849), novels of the sea; and the three novels of *The Littlepage Manuscripts*, including *Satanstoe* (1845), *The Chainbearer* (1845), and *The Redskins* (1846), based on the New York antirent controversy.

Corneille, Pierre (June 6, 1606–October 1, 1684). French playwright. Of Corneille's some 33 major plays, the masterpiece is LE CID (1637), generally acknowledged as the first classical tragedy of the French theater despite its disregard for the Aristotelian unities, for which it was censured by the Académie Française. Corneille was born in Rouen, educated by the Jesuits, and practiced law there as king's advocate. Turning to the theater, he began by writing comedies; his first play, *Melite* (*Mélite*, 1630), was followed by *The Widow* (*La Veuve*, 1632), *The Maidservant* (*La Suivante*, 1634), *The Illusion* (*L'Illusion Comique*, 1636; also translated as *The Theatrical Illusion*), and *The Liar* (*Le Menteur*, 1644), among others. His first tragedy, *Medea* (*Médée*, 1635), was an adaptation of Seneca's version of the legend. *Horace* (1641), *Cinna* (1641) and *Polyeucte* (1643), all in the classical tragic mode, form with *Le Cid* a tetralogy that represents one of the singular achievements in French literature. Corneille produced plays regularly for the theater over the next decades; these later dramas include *Psyché* (1671), written with MOLIÈRE, and *Surenas* (*Suréna, Général des Parthes*, 1674), his final work for the stage. Even in his lesser plays, Corneille proved himself a writer of uncommon artistry and psychological insight, able to produce entirely new effects in his presentation of passionate heroes caught between elemental forces of desire, duty, and destiny.

Corso, Gregory (March 26, 1930–January 17, 2001). American poet. An associate of Allen GINSBERG, Corso lived the kind of adventurous, marginal existence celebrated and explored by writers of the Beat movement. Born in New York City to an Italian immigrant family, he had stints in several foster homes and a number of brushes with the law, culminating in a three-year imprisonment for theft. Released at age 20, he met Ginsberg in New York City's Greenwich Village and moved in 1956 to San Francisco to be near his friend and mentor, around whom the Beats had coalesced. His first collection, *The Vestal Lady on Brattle* (1955), was followed by *Gasoline* (1958), *The Happy Birthday of Death* (1960), *Long Live Man* (1962), *The Mutation of the Spirit* (1964), *Elegiac Feelings American* (1970), *Earthegg* (1974), *Herald of the Autochthonic Spirit* (1981), and *Mindfield* (1989). As was typical of the Beat poets, Corso wrote in a tradition descended from the works of 19th-century poet Walt WHITMAN, informal in tone and utilizing the rough energy of spoken speech to express powerful feelings about American life. Many of his poems, such as the well-known "Bomb" (1958), written in the shape of a mushroom cloud, express great ironic sadness and rage. In addition to his verse, Corso wrote a novel, *The American Express* (1961), and a play, *This Hung-Up Age* (1955).

Cortázar, Julio (August 26, 1914–February 12, 1984). Belgian-born Argentinean short-story writer, novelist, and critic. Cortázar is known for his political radicalism, his bold experiments with narrative structure, and the philosophical seriousness of his writings. Born in Brussels, he returned with his family to Argentina as a youth and lived there until his late 30s, when he moved to France in protest of the right-wing Perón regime. His short fiction is highly achieved, incorporating elements of fantasy and myth in a fashion reminiscent of BORGES. Philosophical questions about the texture of time and existence, and the meaning of life and creativity, dominate his work, although he is often whimsical and ironic despite the gravity of his themes. Collections include *Bestiary* (*Bestiaro*, 1951), *End of the Game* (*Final del Juego*, 1956), *Secret Weapons* (*Las Armas Secretas*, 1958), and *Cronopios and Famas* (*Historias de Cronopios y de Fama*, 1962). Of his six novels, the greatest is HOPSCOTCH (*Rayuela*, 1963), a tour-de-force of structural innovation; arranged in sections, the book can be read in a variety of orders to achieve different meanings and effects. An outspoken leftist, Cortázar supported socialist movements in several Central and Latin American countries, including Nicaragua's Sandinistas, about whom he wrote in *Nicaraguan Sketches* (*Nicaragua Tan Violentemente Dulce*, 1984). Other novels include *The Winners* (*Los Premios*, 1960) and *A Manual for Manuel* (*Libro de Manuel*, 1973). *Obra Crítica* (1994) is a three-volume work of criticism.

Coward, [Sir] **Noël** (December 16, 1899–March 26, 1973). English playwright and songwriter. A remarkably versatile and prolific man of the stage, Coward is best remembered for his daring and sophisticated comedies of manners and his unforgettable popular songs (for which he wrote both words and music). Coward was born in Teddington, Middlesex. His acting debut at age 12 marked the beginning of a professional life that embraced virtually every aspect of the theater. By the mid-1920s, with the success of *The Vortex* (1924), a serious drama in which Coward played the lead, and *Hay Fever* (1925), a comedy, his career as a playwright was firmly established. In the popular comedies that followed — PRIVATE LIVES (1930), DESIGN FOR LIVING (1933), and BLITHE SPIRIT (1941), to name a few — Coward refined the trademark wit that he often used to poke fun at the immorality and hypocrisy of the English bourgeoisie. The seemingly tireless writer also composed popular musicals (*Bitter Sweet*, 1929) and patriotic dramas (*Cavalcade*, 1931), adapted several of his plays for the screen (including *Brief Encounter*, 1946, from his *Still Life*, 1936), excelled as a songwriter ("Mad Dogs and Englishmen," "I'll See You Again"), published fiction (*Pomp and Circumstance*, 1960), and wrote volumes of autobiography:

Present Indicative (1937), *Future Indefinite* (1954), and the unfinished *Past Conditional* (1986).

Crane, [Harold] **Hart** (July 21, 1899–April 27, 1932). American poet. A suicide at age 32, Crane left behind a poem — THE BRIDGE (1930) — that for its technical mastery, bold imagery, and sweeping American themes remains a lasting achievement of 20th-century American writing. Although uneven, Crane's 15-part epic poem, inspired by the Brooklyn Bridge, is regarded by scholars as a spiritual counterpart to T. S. ELIOT's THE WASTE LAND, grappling with many of the same questions but rebuffing its saturnine view of the modern industrial landscape in favor of a muscular, Whitmanesque vision of American achievement and strength. Born in Ohio, Crane lived in New York and Cleveland and worked in a munitions plant during World War I. His poems began appearing in literary reviews in the early 1920s, and his first collection, *White Buildings*, appeared in 1926. In 1932, suffering from depression, Crane took his own life by jumping from a ship that was returning from Mexico. *Collected Poems* (1933) included works from an unpublished manuscript found after his death; *The Complete Poems and Selected Letters and Prose* appeared in 1966.

Crane, Stephen (November 1, 1871–June 5, 1900). American novelist, poet, short-story writer, and journalist. In his short life Crane produced a number of lasting works, particularly THE RED BADGE OF COURAGE (1895), a slender, insightful portrait of a young Civil War soldier. Born in Newark, New Jersey, Crane became a journalist in New York City, where his investigations into the lives of the city's poor inspired his first novel, *Maggie: A Girl of the Streets* (1893), a grimly realistic study of a slum prostitute. Although self-published under a pseudonym, the book won him the attention and friendship of William Dean HOWELLS, who championed his work. Two years later, the publication of *The Red Badge of Courage* and of Crane's first collection of poems, *The Black Rider and Other Lines*, catapulted him to international fame. Crane continued to work as a journalist, and on New Year's day 1897, en route to Cuba as a war correspondent, he was aboard the steamship *Commodore* when it sank off the coast of Florida, an experience he recounted in one of his best-known short stories, "THE OPEN BOAT." He later traveled to Greece to cover the Greco-Turkish War, and eventually settled in Sussex, England, where he associated with a number of leading literary figures, including Joseph CONRAD; he died of tuberculosis at age 28 while on a trip to Germany. Crane's legacy as the first modernist American writer is supported by a number of works, in particular his highly realistic short stories, which are widely anthologized. The finest of these include "The Blue Hotel" and "The Bride Comes to Yellow Sky." His poems, although less distinguished than his fiction, are finely wrought examples of epigrammatic free verse. *George's Mother* (1896), *The Little Regiment* (1896), *The Monster and Other Stories* (1899), and *Whilomville Stories* (1900) are notable short-story collections.

Creeley, Robert (May 21, 1926–). American poet. Creeley was an early editor of THE BLACK MOUNTAIN REVIEW and a leader among the Black Mountain poets, a group centered around Black Mountain College in North Carolina, where he was on the faculty during the 1950s. With his colleagues Charles OLSON and Robert Duncan, he made the college and its literary magazine an important forum for antiformalist, experimental verse, publishing the work of such poets as WILLIAM CARLOS WILLIAMS, Gary SNYDER, and Denise LEVERTOV. Creeley himself is a poet of considerable accomplishment, whose spare, conversational idiom masks complex interior structures of sound and meaning. *For Love: Poems 1950–1960* (1962), his first major collection, was followed by such volumes as *Words* (1967), *Pieces* (1969), *The Finger* (1970), *St. Martin's* (1971), *A Day Book* (1972), *Later* (1978), *Collected Poems* (1982), *Memory Gardens* (1986), *Windows* (1990), *Selected Poems* (1991), *Echoes* (1994), and *Life and Death* (1998). A *Quick*

Graph (1970) and *Was That a Real Poem and Other Essays* (1979) are critical writings.

Cross, Amanda. *See* **Heilbrun, Carolyn** [in Other Influential Figures]

Cullen, Countee (May 30, 1903–January 9, 1946). American poet. A leading poet of the Harlem Renaissance, Cullen, unlike many of his contemporaries, eschewed the blues- and jazz-influenced style associated with that movement in favor of highly crafted, traditional verse forms. He was a controversial figure among black critics and readers, but his poems also won a wide readership among mainstream audiences. Questions remain about his early life, but as a teenager he was taken in by the Reverend Frederick Cullen, the leader of one of Harlem's largest churches. He attended New York and Harvard universities, and his first collection, *Color* (1925), was published to broad acclaim while he was still a student. "Yet Do I Marvel," perhaps his best-known poem, appears in that volume. Subsequent volumes include *Copper Sun* (1927), *The Ballad of the Brown Girl* (1927), *The Black Christ and Other Poems* (1929), and *The Medea and Some Poems* (1935). Cullen also worked as an editor at *Opportunities* magazine and as a teacher in the New York City public schools. Both a New York City public school and a branch of The New York Public Library have been named in his honor.

Cummings, E[dward] **E**[stlin] (October 14, 1894–September 3, 1962). American poet and novelist. Cummings's highly unconventional writing style—marked by quirky punctuation and typography, uninhibited word play, and a sometimes whimsical tone—placed him at the forefront of modernism. The Harvard-educated Cummings served as an ambulance driver in France during World War I and, through a complicated series of events, found himself detained in a French concentration camp for several months on unfounded charges of treasonable correspondence. This experience awakened his skepticism about bureaucratic institutions and found a place in his first book and only novel, THE ENORMOUS ROOM (1922).

Although Cummings worked as both a painter and a poet, it was as the latter that he made his mark. His best-known lyrics outwardly express an almost childlike lightheartedness and joy in living, but his work is highly complex, containing layers of feeling and irony. His major volumes include *Tulips and Chimneys* (1923), *XLI Poems* (1925), *&* (1925), *is 5* (1926), *ViVa* (1931), *50 Poems* (1940), *1x1* (1944), *Ninety-five Poems* (1958), and *73 Poems* (1962), which was published posthumously. Cummings also published the prose work *Eimi* (1933) after traveling to the USSR, and *i: six nonlectures* (1953), the Charles Eliot Norton Lectures on poetry that he delivered at his alma mater, Harvard. The play *him* was produced in 1927.

Dahl, Roald (September 13, 1916–November 23, 1990). British novelist, short-story writer, children's writer, and screenwriter. Author of the childhood classic *Charlie and the Chocolate Factory* (1964), Dahl, whether writing for children or adults, exhibits a macabre sensibility and sly humor. Born in Wales, Dahl did not attend college and served in the Royal Air Force in World War II. He was eventually assigned to a post in Washington, D.C. (1942–43), where he began to write and publish stories of his experiences as an aviator. His works for adults include the story collections *Over to You* (1946), *Someone Like You* (1953), *Kiss Kiss* (1960), and *Switch Bitch* (1974) as well as the novel *My Uncle Oswald* (1979). His popular works for young readers include *James and the Giant Peach* (1961), *The Witches* (1983), *Matilda* (1988), and *The Enormous Crocodile* (1993). Dahl, whose first wife was actress Patricia Neal, also worked extensively in film, writing the screenplays for, among others, *You Only Live Twice* (1967) and *Chitty Chitty Bang Bang* (1968), both based on novels by Ian FLEMING, and for *Willie Wonka and the Chocolate Factory* (1971), adapted from his own *Charlie and the Chocolate Factory*.

Dana, Richard Henry, Jr. (August 1, 1815–January 6, 1882). American writer. Dana's literary reputation rests on TWO YEARS BEFORE THE MAST (1840), an autobiographical narrative shaped from journals he kept during a two-year working sea voyage around Cape Horn. The voyage was undertaken after Dana, then a sophomore at Harvard University, suffered serious eye problems that forced him to leave school. He put to sea in 1834 and arrived two years later in California, where he worked a year in the fur trade before returning to complete his education, eventually taking a degree from Harvard Law School. Dana's sympathetic and frank account of his time aboard the *Pilgrim*, and in particular of the brutality suffered by the common sailors with whom he worked, set a new standard of realism for writing about the sea. *The Seaman's Friend* (1841), which Dana wrote in his capacity as a practicing attorney specializing in the law of the sea, is a manual advising sailors on their legal rights and duties. Dana eventually became the U.S. Attorney for the district of Massachusetts, but his further political ambitions were thwarted by charges of plagiarism surrounding his edition of Henry Wheaton's *Elements of International Law* (1866).

D'Annunzio, Gabriele (March 12, 1863–March 1, 1938). Italian novelist, poet, and playwright. In both his life and his art, D'Annunzio embodied turn-of-the-century European decadence. His fiction often featured an egocentric, Nietzschean hero devoid of moral consideration and completely consumed by life's sensual offerings, as in the novels *Child of Pleasure* (*Il Piacere*, 1889), *The Intruder* (*L'Innocente*, 1892), *The Triumph of Death* (*Il Trionfo della Morte*, 1894), and *Flame of Life* (*Il Fuoco*, 1900), an autobiographical work based on his love affair with the famous actress Eleanora Duse. His poetry is similarly marked by sensory extravagance; collections include *Early Spring* (*Primo Vere*, 1879), *New Song* (*Canto Novo*, 1882), and *Alcyone* (1904), the last a richly rendered meditation on the pleasures of a Tuscan summer. He wrote a number of plays as well, many of them as vehicles for Duse, but his best work for the stage was *The Daughter of Jorio* (*La Figlia di Iorio*, 1904), written after their separation. D'Annunzio's fame as a writer helped to win him a spot as a parliamentary deputy from

1897 to 1900. Debts incurred through prodigal living forced him to flee to France in 1910, but he returned to Italy at the start of World War I to fight in the conflict. In 1919, D'Annunzio and his nationalist supporters violated the Versailles Treaty by occupying the disputed port of Fiume in present-day Croatia; D'Annunzio ruled the port as dictator until the Italian army forced him to stand aside.

Dante, *in full* Dante Alighieri (between May 15 and June 15, 1265–September 13/14, 1321). Italian poet. A giant of world literature, the greatest of Italian poets, and the original genius at the center of the Renaissance's great flowering of human creativity, Dante was both a man very much of his time and a figure for the ages. His epic masterpiece, THE DIVINE COMEDY (*La Divina Commedia*, c. 1314–21), stands as one of the singular achievements in all literature, providing a sweeping vision of humanity and its place in the cosmos. Born in Florence to an aristocratic family, Dante came of age at a time when two rival parties, the Guelphs and Ghibbelines, warred for control of the city. His allegiance to one faction of the Guelph party, the Bianchi (or "Whites"), led him, with many others, to be banished from Florence in 1302. Thereafter, he lived in several Italian cities, finally settling in Ravenna, near the Adriatic. His early works are found in two collections of verse and prose: *The New Life* (*La Vita Nuova*, 1293), written before his banishment, and *The Banquet* (*Il Convivio*, 1304–7). All of his later writings are highly distinguished. These include *Concerning Vernacular Eloquence* (*De Vulgari Eloquentia*, 1304–7), a treatise, written in Latin, on the uses of the Italian language; and *On Monarchy* (*De Monarchia*, 1313), a work of Christian political philosophy advocating a universal government headed by the Pope. *The Divine Comedy* (which Dante originally entitled simply *Commedia*) was, however, the centerpiece and great project of Dante's years in exile. Describing a man's journey through the three divine realms of Hell, Purgatory, and Paradise, the poem is at once a deeply Christian work in the tradition of St. Thomas Aquinas and a sophisticated commentary on worldly matters, including the political machinations that led to the author's banishment. Along the way, Dante's traveler is assisted first by the Latin poet VIRGIL, and then by the woman BEATRICE, a figure of divine love inspired by Beatrice Portinari (d. 1290), whom Dante had first glimpsed when he was a boy of nine and for whom he maintained a lifelong devotion. Dante's masterwork made him famous, and its use of Dante's Tuscan dialect paved the way for modern Italian.

Darío, Rubén, *pen name of* Félix Rubén García y Sarmiento (January 18, 1867–February 6, 1916). Nicaraguan poet. The founder of the Modernismo movement in Spanish-language poetry, Darío was born in Metapa, Nicaragua, where he published his first poem at age 13. The peripatetic Darío worked as a journalist for newspapers in Valparaiso, Chile, and Buenos Aires, Argentina, founded newspapers in El Salvador and Guatemala, lived for a time in Costa Rica, and made his first visits to Europe in the 1890s. In Buenos Aires, the new literary movement—less an organized aesthetic school than an eclectic, Symbolist-inspired response to the sentimental writing then popular in Latin America—coalesced around him on the basis of his early collections *Azul* (1888; Blue) and *Prosas Profanas y Otros Poemas* (1896; Profane Hymns and Other Poems), both marked by lush imagery and experimentation with form. He remained in Argentina until 1898, when *La Nación* sent him to Europe as a correspondent, first to Spain and then to Paris, where he lived for nearly five years. He left Europe on the outbreak of World War I. His later works reflect Darío's deepening political consciousness, particularly his concerns about the impact of U.S. foreign policy on Latin American cultures following the Spanish-American War. *Cantos de Vida y Esperanza* (1905; Songs of Life and Hope) is both his most technically achieved work and his most socially minded, addressing themes of Latin American cultural solidarity. During a lecture tour of North America, Darío became ill with pneumonia in New York and returned to Nicaragua, where he died. *Selected Poems of Rubén Darío* (1965), with a prologue by Octavio PAZ, and a bilingual edition, *Selected Poems of Rubén Darío* (2001), are collections in English translation.

Davies, Robertson (August 28, 1913–December 2, 1995). Canadian novelist, playwright, and essayist. Best known for his Deptford trilogy of novels—*Fifth Business* (1970), *The Manticore* (1972), and *World of Wonders* (1975)—Davies was both a tremendously popular novelist and a writer of great erudition, whose books reveal his widely ranging interests, from the lore of his native Ontario to the principles of Jungian analysis. Educated at Oxford, Davies worked in the theater for many years, was a journalist and theater critic, and a professor of English at the University of Toronto for more than 20 years (1960–81). His novels are conventionally structured and formally told, but abound in imaginative qualities, playful humor, and subtlety. In addition to the Deptford Trilogy, they include the three novels of the Salterton Trilogy—*Tempest-Tost* (1951), *Leaven of Malice* (1954), and *A Mixture of Frailties* (1958)—as well as THE REBEL ANGELS (1981), WHAT'S BRED IN THE BONE (1985), THE LYRE OF ORPHEUS (1988), *Murther and Walking Spirits* (1991), and *The Cunning Man* (1994). His daily humorous columns for the Peterborough *Examiner* are collected in *The Diary of Samuel Marchbanks* (1947) and *Samuel Marchbanks' Almanack* (1967). *The Merry Heart* (1998) and *Happy Alchemy* (1999) are collections of essays published after his death.

Day-Lewis, C[ecil] (April 27, 1904–May 22, 1972). Irish-born English poet, critic, translator, and novelist. Poet Laureate of England from 1968 until his death, Day-Lewis began as a writer of leftist political poetry, much in the vein of his friends Stephen SPENDER and W. H. AUDEN, during the 1930s. Eventually, however, these didactic tendencies gave way to a more lyrical and personal verse style. Brought to England as an infant, Day-Lewis was raised in a traditional Anglo-Irish household and educated at Oxford. He abandoned a teaching career in 1935 and thereafter devoted himself full time to writing, including a number of detective novels under the pseudonym Nicholas Blake. His collections of poetry include *Transitional Poems* (1929), *From Feathers to Iron* (1931), *The Magnetic Mountain* (1933), *The Gate* (1962), *The Room and Other Poems* (1965), and *Whispering Roots* (1970). Among his major works of criticism are *A Hope for Poetry* (1934), *The Poetic Image* (1947), and *The Poetic Impulse* (1965). He published his autobiography, *The Buried Day*, in 1960. His translations of VIRGIL's *Georgics* (1940), AENEID (1952), and *Eclogues* (1963) are well respected.

Defoe, Daniel, *original name* Daniel Foe (1600–April 24, 1731). English novelist, pamphleteer, and journalist. Often described as the first true English novelist, Defoe had an intensely varied career. Enormously prolific, he produced more than 500 books, although the precise number will never be known, as many were anonymous. The greatest of these were his vigorous novels of personality ROBINSON CRUSOE (1719) and MOLL FLANDERS (1722), in which he displayed to great advantage the same powers of observation that distinguished the best of his journalism. The son of a London butcher, Defoe was educated for the ministry but chose instead a life in business, initially as a purveyor of hosiery. He traveled widely—a lifelong pursuit—and became involved in politics as a vehement supporter of William of Orange. This led to his first major work, *The True-Born Englishman* (1701), a satirical poem defending the foreign king. A year later, his pamphlet *The Shortest Way with Dissenters* (1702), a withering, skillful parody of High Church fanaticism, resulted in Defoe's punishment in the pillory and a prison sentence for libel. The intercession of Tory politician Robert Harley secured his release on the condition that Defoe work for him as a pamphleteer and intelligence agent. Between 1704 and 1713 Defoe edited the *Review*, writing nearly all the articles and securing his legacy as the greatest journalist of his age. His other major works include the fictional *A JOURNAL OF THE PLAGUE YEAR* (1722), *Colonel Jack* (1722), *Memoirs of a Cavalier* (1720), *Captain Singleton* (1720), and *Roxana* (1724), and the nonfictional *The Family Instructor*

(1715), *A Tour Through the Whole Island of Great Britain* (1724–26), *The Complete English Tradesman* (1726), and *A Plan of the English Commerce* (1728).

De La Mare, Walter (April 25, 1873–June 22, 1956). English poet, novelist, and anthologist. As a writer for both adults and children, De La Mare paid close attention to the disquieting and eerie qualities of human experience. In his fanciful stories, novels, and poems, ordinary life is frequently disrupted by occurrences that range from the bizarre to the supernatural. Born and educated in London, he worked for nearly 20 years for Standard Oil Company until a pension made it possible for him to concentrate on writing. *Songs of Childhood* (1902), his first collection, was published under the pseudonym Walter Ramal while he was still working for Standard Oil. This was followed by a novel, *Henry Brocken* (1904), a second collection of verse, *Poems*, in 1906, and *The Listeners* (1912), with its memorable title poem. *Peacock Pie* (1913) is his finest collection of verse for children. He also published *Collected Poems* (1920, 1935, 1942), *Collected Rhymes and Verses* (1944), and *Collected Stories for Children* (1947) as well as the anthologies *Come Hither* (1923), *Early One Morning* (1935), *Behold, This Dreamer!* (1939), and *Love* (1943). *Memoirs of a Midget* (1921) is considered his best novel.

Delany, Samuel R[ay] (April 1, 1942–). American science-fiction novelist and critic. Born in New York City, Delany attended the City University of New York for one semester in the early 1960s and then worked as a singer and musician in Greenwich Village while he began to establish himself as a writer. His highly acclaimed novels provocatively explore themes of race, class, gender, and sexual identity in futuristic settings; as science-fiction scholar John Clute observed, "As a black gay New Yorker much too well educated for his own good, Delany…illuminate[s] the world the way a torch might cast light in a cellar." *Dhalgren* (1975), about a bisexual youth living in an apocalyptic future, is typical of his work and is his best-regarded novel. Other important books include his debut, *The Jewels of Aptor* (1962), as well as *Babel-17* (1966), *The Einstein Intersection* (1967), *Nova* (1969), *Triton* (1976), and *Stars in My Pocket Like Grains of Sand* (1984). The four novels of his Nevèrÿon series (1979–87) explore human communities in a prehistoric setting. Delany's critical works include *The Jewel-Hinged Jaw: Notes on the Language of Science Fiction* (1977) and *Shorter Views: Queer Thoughts and the Politics of the Paraliterary* (1999). *The Motion of Light in Water: Sex and Science Fiction Writing in the East Village, 1957–1965* (1988) is a memoir of Delany's early days as a writer and of his sexual experimentation and eventual acceptance of his homosexuality. The two essays in *Times Square Red, Times Square Blue (Sexual Culture)* (1999) offer personal reminiscences of the peep shows and pornographic movie houses of New York City's Times Square and argue for the value of the sexual culture that has been largely obliterated by the gentrification of that once seamy neighborhood.

DeLillo, Don (November 20, 1936–). American novelist. Both a bestselling writer and an astute social critic, DeLillo has won a devoted following with such darkly comic novels as the American Book Award–winning WHITE NOISE (1985), a wry sendup of postmodern pop culture set on a college campus. Raised by Italian immigrants in the Bronx, New York, DeLillo attended Fordham University and spent several years working in advertising before writing his first novel, *Americana* (1971), followed by *End Zone* (1972), *Great Jones Street* (1973), *Ranter's Star* (1976), *Running Dog* (1978), and *The Names* (1982). Among his most commercially successful and artistically achieved works are the novels LIBRA (1988), a fictional portrait of presidential assassin Lee Harvey Oswald; *Mao II* (1991), about terrorism and a disillusioned artist; and *Underworld* (1999), a highly original narrative of the Cold War featuring such characters as J. Edgar Hoover, Jackie Gleason, Frank Sinatra, and baseball great Bobby Thompson.

De Quincey, Thomas, *original name* Thomas Quincey (August 15, 1785–December 8, 1859). English essayist and critic. One of the great English prose writers of the 19th century, De Quincey is best known for his *Confessions of an English Opium-Eater* (1822), a haunting account of his addiction, and even more importantly a meditation on the nature of the imagination and a probing examination of the process whereby experiences are transmuted into the symbolic imagery of dreams. Born in Manchester into a prosperous family, De Quincey seems to have been permanently marked as a young boy by the death of both a beloved sister and, soon after that, his father; he would later write of the "perpetual sense of desertion" and the "chronic passion of anxiety" that plagued him. A brilliant but often wayward student, in 1802 he ran away from the famous Manchester Grammar School to wander about Wales and London aimlessly (often in desperate straits) until reconciling with his family. It was as a student at Oxford (1803–8) that De Quincey began to take opium, then a commonly prescribed painkiller, although he did not become seriously addicted for another decade. After Oxford, he embarked on a literary career, forging close relationships with William WORDSWORTH and Samuel Taylor COLERIDGE, and contributing essays and literary journalism on a prodigiously wide range of subjects to such periodicals as BLACKWOOD's and *Tait's Edinburgh Magazine.* After the publication of the *Confessions,* his reputation was secure, but it was not until the last years of his life that he lived in relative comfort and financial security, as he was frequently dilatory about deadlines, had no head for business, and was hopeless with money. De Quincey practiced what he called "impassioned prose"; among the most famous examples, aside from his masterpiece, the *Confessions,* are the essays "On the Knocking at the Gate in *Macbeth*" (1823), a subtle analysis from a writer who wrote surprisingly little "pure" literary criticism (his interest in writers was primarily biographical); "On Murder Considered as One of the Fine Arts" (1827), an early classic of crime writing; "Suspiria de Profundis" (1845), the fragmentary "sequel" to the *Confessions;* and "The English Mail-Coach" (1849), an elegiac celebration of animal velocity and a then vanishing mode of transportation. A new critical edition, the 21-volume *The Works of Thomas De Quincey,* began publication in 2000.

Desai, Anita (June 24, 1937–). Indian novelist. One of India's leading writers, Desai is noted for the poetic sensuality of her prose. Her major works are set in contemporary India, and quietly explore issues of identity, especially among women and within families. Desai's father was Bengali, her mother a German Jew; she learned English as a child and adopted it as the language for all her writings, beginning with *Cry, the Peacock* (1963). Notable novels by Desai include *Bye, Bye, Blackbird* (1968), *Where Shall We Go This Summer?* (1975), *Fire on the Mountain* (1977), *In Custody* (1984), *Baumgartner's Bombay* (1989), *Journey to Ithaca* (1995), and *Fasting, Feasting* (1999).

Dick, Philip K[indred] (December 16, 1928–March 2, 1982). American science-fiction writer. Dick's best-known work, *Do Androids Dream of Electric Sheep?* (1968), imagines a future in which humanlike robots pass easily as human beings. Adapted for film as *Blade Runner* (1982), Dick's tale is typical of much of his work, applying the futuristic tropes of science fiction to investigate broader questions about the nature of consciousness and perception, and the relationship between technology and the mind. Born in Chicago, Dick lived most of his life in the San Francisco Bay area of California. From an early age he battled mental illness and drug addiction, an influence on the themes of his work. He wrote more than 30 novels and five collections of short stories, including, notably, *A Handful of Darkness* (1955), *Flow My Tears, the Policeman Said* (1974), *A Scanner Darkly* (1977), and a trilogy formed by VALIS (1981), *The Divine Invasion* (1981), and *The Transmigration of Timothy Archer* (1982). *The Man in the High Castle* (1962) won science fiction's Hugo Award. A number of his other works were adapted for film, including the story "We Can Remember It for You Wholesale," which became *Total Recall* (1990).

Dickens, Charles (February 7, 1812–June 9, 1870). English novelist. Dickens was beloved in his lifetime on both sides of the Atlantic, and many scholars consider him the single greatest novelist that England has ever produced. Like many of his characters, Dickens endured great hardship in his youth; his father, a clerk, was jailed for his debts, and Dickens at age 12 went to work in a blacking factory, where he suffered grueling abuse. Although he had little education, the resourceful Dickens steadily improved his station, working first as a clerk in a law office, and later as a reporter in Parliament and for several London newspapers. He began to publish his fiction in periodicals in the 1830s, satirical works gathered in his first book, *Sketches by "Boz"* (1836); a year later, THE PICK-WICK PAPERS (1837), a serialized comic novel, launched his literary career in earnest. This was followed in quick succession by OLIVER TWIST (1838), NICHOLAS NICKLEBY (1839), *Barnaby Rudge* (1841), and *The Old Curiosity Shop* (1841). After a brief tour of the United States, the inspiration for *American Notes* (1842) and MARTIN CHUZZLEWIT (1844), Dickens wrote A CHRISTMAS CAROL (1843), one of his most beloved tales, followed by such well-known novels as DAVID COPPERFIELD (1850), BLEAK HOUSE (1853), HARD TIMES (1854), LITTLE DORRIT (1857), A TALE OF TWO CITIES (1859), GREAT EXPECTATIONS (1861), and OUR MUTUAL FRIEND (1865). Dickens's work from the 1850s and 1860s is generally regarded as his most accomplished and serious; although often satirical, his writings exhibit a strong moral undercurrent, reflecting his memories of his own youthful difficulties and his deep concerns about the gross inequities of industrial Victorian society. The social pageantry of his novels is without peer, as is his gift for creating memorable characters. Dickens also founded and edited the successful weekly magazines *Household Words* and *All the Year Round,* which showcased many of his own works and launched the careers of a number of notable contemporaries, including his friend Wilkie COLLINS. Dickens's reading tours, in both Europe and the United States, drew enormous crowds, and he is considered by many to have been the first celebrity author of the industrial age. The father of nine children, Dickens separated from his wife, the former Catherine Hogarth, in 1858, and for many years was associated with Ellen Ternan, an actress many years his junior. He was buried in Westminster Abbey.

Dickey, James (February 2, 1923–January 19, 1997). American poet and novelist. Dickey is best known for his popular wilderness adventure novel *Deliverance* (1970). The theme of that work—the transforming, often violent power of nature—also figures prominently in his many accomplished works of poetry, collected in such volumes as *Into the Stone* (1960), *Drowning with Others* (1962), *Helmets* (1964), *Buck-dancer's Choice* (1965; National Book Award), *The Zodiac* (1976), *The Strength of Fields* (1979), *Puella* (1982), and *The Whole Motion* (1992). Born in Georgia, Dickey served as a fighter-bomber pilot in World War II and the Korean War, earned bachelor's and master's degrees from Vanderbilt University, and later taught at the University of South Carolina. He also served for two years as poetry consultant to the Library of Congress (1966–68). *Self-Interviews* (1970) and *Jericho: The South Beheld* (1974) are autobiographical works of prose. *Crux: The Letters of James Dickey* appeared in 1999, as did *Summer of Deliverance: A Memoir of Father and Son*, written by Christopher Dickey, the writer's son and a noted journalist.

Dickinson, Emily (December 10, 1830–May 15, 1886). American poet. Although Dickinson was largely unknown during her lifetime, her highly original poems are today regarded as among the great achievements of American writing, as important as Walt WHITMAN's in their lasting influence on the making of verse in America. Unlike Whitman's robust, vernacular free verse, however, Dickinson's poems are highly formal, marked by a precise delicacy of expression, and reflect the poet's solitary life and New England Calvinist upbringing. Born to a prominent family in Amherst, Massachusetts, Dickinson was educated at Amherst Academy and nearby Mount Holyoke Female Seminary. Of her almost 1,800 poems, most date from the period 1858 to 1865, but only ten are known to have been published in her lifetime. By 1860 she had secluded herself in her room at her parents' Amherst home; thereafter, she left the property only rarely, and received few visitors. On the advice of her friend Thomas Wentworth Higginson, a literary admirer with whom she maintained a correspondence, she made no attempt to publish after 1862, devoting herself instead to the pure expression of her artistry. Despite her social

---

"If I read a book and it makes my whole body so cold no fire can ever warm me, I know that is poetry. If I feel physically as if the top of my head were taken off, I know that is poetry. These are the only ways I know it. Is there any other way?"

Emily Dickinson, quoted in Thomas Wentworth Higginson, "Emily Dickinson's Letters," *The Atlantic Monthly* (October 1891)

---

isolation, Dickinson's poems display a mind uniquely alive to the world and its experiences. Written for the most part in quatrains of iambic trimeter, often employing unusual typographical devices (she is known for her use of the dash) and melodiously suggestive off-rhymes to organize her thoughts, Dickinson's poems capture the surface of life with striking precision, while linking it to a broader consideration of such matters as death, immortality, and the nature of art. Her reputation grew steadily after her death. A number of editions of her work were published posthumously, but most took substantial liberties with her presentation. In the 1950s, the work of editor Thomas H. Johnson, compiled in *The Complete Poems of Emily Dickinson* (1955), restored her work to its original design. Johnson's pioneering edition has

now been superseded by R. W. Franklin's three-volume edition of *The Poems of Emily Dickinson* (1998).

Diderot, Denis (October 5, 1713–July 31, 1784). French philosopher, encyclopedist, critic, novelist, and playwright. An intellectual polymath and prolific man of letters, Diderot is best known as the chief editor of the *Encyclopédie* (28 vols., 1751–72), a monument of the French Enlightenment. Intended to induce "a revolution in men's minds," the *Encyclopédie*, like many of his own writings, was an instrument of radical opinion, scientific knowledge, and materialist philosophy. Of pious religious upbringing, Diderot attended a Jesuit university in his hometown of Langres but renounced his faith after studying at the University of Paris. In *Philosophical Thoughts* (*Pensées Philosophiques*, 1746), published anonymously, he advocated a natural morality independent of church doctrine. His most acclaimed novels, each experimental in form, were not published until after his death: *The Nun* (*La Religieuse*, 1796), a criticism of convent life; *Jacques the Fatalist and His Master* (*Jacques le Fataliste et Son Maître*, 1796), a philosophical satire on free will and determinism; and *Rameau's Nephew* (*Le Neveu de Rameau*, 1805), a moral satire in dialogue form. *Salons* (1759–81), essays for the journal *Correspondance Littéraire*, is considered a seminal work in modern art criticism. His breadth of intellect is further evidenced by writings on nature, biology, the scientific method, linguistics, aesthetics, the deaf, the blind, and French industries and crafts, among other subjects.

Didion, Joan (December 5, 1934–). American novelist and essayist. In both her fiction and nonfiction, Didion captures the fragmentation of modern American culture. A native Californian, she has frequently used that state as a setting for her work and a laboratory for her themes. Educated at the University of California at Berkeley, in the late 1950s and early 1960s Didion worked for *Vogue* magazine, as a reporter and editor. Her first novel, *Run River* (1963), was followed by two highly successful

WRITERS ON WRITERS

JAMES JOYCE ON GEOFFREY CHAUCER

"Of all English writers Chaucer is the clearest. He is as precise and slick as a Frenchman."

WILLIAM HAZLITT ON MICHEL DE MONTAIGNE

"[Montaigne] does not converse with us like a pedagogue with his pupil, whom he wishes to make as great a blockhead as himself, but like a philosopher and friend who has passed through life with thought and observation, and is willing to enable others to pass through it with pleasure and profit. A writer of this stamp, I confess, appears to me as much superior to a common bookworm, as a library of real books is superior to a mere book-case."

THOMAS CARLYLE ON CHARLES LAMB

"Charles Lamb I sincerely believe to be in some considerable degree insane. A more pitiful, rickety, gasping, staggering Tomfool I do not know."

DYLAN THOMAS ON WILLIAM WORDSWORTH

"Wordsworth was a tea-time bore, the great Frost of literature, the verbose, the humourless, the platitudinary reporter of Nature in her dullest moods. Open him at any page: and there lies the English language not, as George Moore said of Pater, in a glass coffin, but in a large, sultry, and unhygienic box."

VIRGINIA WOOLF ON JANE AUSTEN

"Anybody who has had the temerity to write about Jane Austen is aware of two facts: first, that of all great writers she is the most difficult to catch in the act of greatness; second, that there are twenty-five elderly gentlemen living in the neighborhood of London who resent any slight upon her genius as if it were an insult offered to the chastity of their Aunts."

V. S. PRITCHETT ON CHARLES DICKENS

"Dickens is a city."

OSCAR WILDE ON CHARLES DICKENS'S THE OLD CURIOSITY SHOP

"One must have a heart of stone to read the death of Little Nell without laughing."

HENRY JAMES ON GEORGE ELIOT

"She is magnificently ugly—deliciously hideous. She has a low forehead, a dull grey eye, a vast pendulous nose.... Now in this vast ugliness resides a most powerful beauty which, in a very few minutes steals forth and charms the mind, so that you end as I ended, in falling in love with her. Yes, behold me literally in love with this great horse-faced blue-stocking."

JORGE LUIS BORGES ON FYODOR DOSTOYEVSKY

"Like the discovery of love, like the discovery of the sea, the discovery of Dostoyevsky marks an important date in one's life. This usually occurs in adolescence; maturity seeks out more serene writers."

ANTON CHEKHOV ON HENRIK IBSEN

"But listen, Ibsen is no playwright!...Ibsen just doesn't know life. In life it simply isn't like that."

OLIVER WENDELL HOLMES ON
RALPH WALDO EMERSON

"Emerson is a citizen of the universe....This little planet could not provincialize such a man."

WILLIAM DEAN HOWELLS ON MARK TWAIN

"Sole, incomparable, the Lincoln of our literature."

ROBERT LOUIS STEVENSON ON
WALT WHITMAN

"Whitman, like a large shaggy dog, just unchained, scouring the beaches of the world and baying at the moon."

RANDALL JARRELL ON WALT WHITMAN

"They might have put on his tombstone WALT WHITMAN: HE HAD HIS NERVE. He is the rashest, the most inexplicable and unlikely—the most impossible, one wants to say—of poets. He somehow is in a class by himself...."

H. L. MENCKEN ON HENRY JAMES

"...an idiot, and a Boston idiot, to boot, than which there is nothing lower in the world."

JAMES THURBER ON HENRY JAMES

"He would have been most unhappy now, I'm sure, in an age when the male sometimes even takes off his hat, or the woman her overcoat. (In bed, of course, I mean.)"

P. G. WODEHOUSE ON A. A. MILNE

"My personal animosity against a writer never affects my opinion of what he writes. Nobody could be more anxious than myself, for instance, that Alan Alexander Milne should trip over a bootlace and break his bloody neck, yet I reread his early stuff at regular intervals with all the old enjoyment."

ROBERT FROST ON WILLA CATHER

"With Carl Sandburg, it was 'the people, yes.' With Willa Cather, it was 'the people, no.'"

H. G. WELLS ON GEORGE BERNARD SHAW

"Mr. Shaw objects to my calling him muddleheaded. But I have always considered him muddleheaded. If I have not called him that in public before it is simply because I thought the thing too obvious to need pointing out."

ELIZABETH BOWEN ON EDITH SITWELL

"A high altar on the move."

CYRIL CONNOLLY ON GEORGE ORWELL

"He could not blow his nose without moralizing on the state of the handkerchief industry."

(Writers on Writers, continued)

GERTRUDE STEIN ON EZRA POUND

"A village explainer, excellent if you were a village, but if you were not, not."

GERTRUDE STEIN ON JAMES JOYCE

"Joyce is *good*. He is a *good* writer. People like him because he is incomprehensible and anybody can understand him. But who came first, Gertrude Stein or James Joyce? Do not forget that my first great book, *Three Lives*, was published in 1908. That was long before *Ulysses*. But Joyce *has* done *something*. His influence, however, is local."

EVELYN WAUGH ON HILAIRE BELLOC

"Poor Mr. Belloc looked as though the grave were the only place for him....He lost and stole and whatever went into his pockets, toast, cigarettes, books never appeared, like the reverse of a conjuror's hat."

ALAN BENNETT ON FRANZ KAFKA

"Kafka could never have written as he did had he lived in a house. His writing is that of someone whose whole life was spent in apartments, with lifts, stairwells, muffled voices behind closed doors, and sounds through walls. Put in a nice detached villa and he'd never have written a word."

ELIZABETH BISHOP ON MARIANNE MOORE

"If she speaks of a chair you can practically sit on it."

TRUMAN CAPOTE ON MARIANNE MOORE

"Adorned with cape, with tricorn, saintly soul singing in librarian tones an enameled song that coolly celebrates her chewing-gum enthusiasms."

SEAN O'CASEY ON P. G. WODEHOUSE

"English literature's performing flea."

---

collections of essays, *Slouching Towards Bethlehem* (1968) and *The White Album* (1979), both of which offer astute analyses of cultural change in the 1960s. Other notable works of nonfiction include *Salvador* (1983), about political unrest in Latin America; *Miami* (1987), a study of that city; and *After Henry* (1992), essays. *PLAY IT AS IT LAYS* (1970), *A Book of Common Prayer* (1977), *Democracy* (1984), and *The Last Thing He Wanted* (1996) are novels. Didion has also collaborated with her husband, writer John Gregory Dunne, on a number of projects, including screenplays.

Dinesen, Isak, *pen name of* Karen Dinesen, Baroness Blixen-Finecke (April 17, 1885–September 7, 1962). Danish short-story writer and memoirist, writing in English. Dinesen is best known for *OUT OF AFRICA* (1937), a sympathetic memoir of her life on a Kenyan coffee plantation. After attending the Academy of Fine Arts in Copenhagen, Dinesen moved to Africa with her husband, her cousin Baron Brør Blixen-Finecke, shortly after their marriage in 1914; although the marriage ended seven years later (after Dinesen contracted syphilis from her husband), she remained in Kenya for another decade, until the failure of her plantation finally forced her to return to Denmark. Her many fanciful short stories, told in the vein of fairy tales, can be found in such collections as

SEAMUS HEANEY ON W. H. AUDEN

"Auden of the last years, when he had begun to resemble in his own person an ample, flopping, ambulatory volume of the OED in carpet slippers."

MARY MCCARTHY ON LILLIAN HELLMAN

"Every word she writes is a lie, including 'and' and 'the.'"

JEAN GOYTISOLO ON JEAN GENET

"He was alien to all kinds of vanity. Because of him, I discovered I was interested in literature, not in literary life."

MARY MCCARTHY ON EUGENE O'NEILL

"O'Neill belongs to that group of American authors, which includes Farrell and Dreiser, whose choice of vocation was a kind of triumphant catastrophe; none of these men possessed the slightest ear for the word, the sentence, the speech, the paragraph...how is one to judge the great, logical symphony of a tone-deaf musician?"

TRUMAN CAPOTE ON JACK KEROUAC

"That's not writing, that's typing."

GORE VIDAL ON HERMAN WOUK'S *THE WINDS OF WAR*

"This is not at all bad, except as prose."

JOHN UPDIKE ON MURIEL SPARK

"Her sentences march under a harsh sun that bleaches color from them but bestows a peculiar, invigorating, Pascalian clarity."

MARTIN AMIS ON SAUL BELLOW

"...in the novels, as they unfold, we see a man (we see a consciousness) heading towards death with his eyes open and his head high...."

SEVEN GOTHIC TALES (1934), *WINTER'S TALES* (1942), and *Last Tales* (1957). Dinesen wrote in English but also translated her work into Danish. *The Angelic Avengers* (1942), an allegorical tale of life in Denmark under the Nazi regime, is her only novel.

Doctorow, E[dgar] L[awrence] (January 6, 1931–). American novelist. Doctorow's socially minded novels about America's past skillfully integrate fictional characters with prominent historical figures, from magician Harry Houdini to financier J. P. Morgan to mobster Dutch Schultz. The author's native New York City is also a dominant presence in his works. These include *Ragtime* (1975), a richly imagined portrait of turn-of-the-20th-century New York City; *The Book of Daniel* (1971), based on the 1953 espionage trial of Julius and Ethel Rosenberg; *Billy Bathgate* (1989), about organized crime in the 1930s; *World's Fair* (1985; National Book Award), a coming-of-age story set at the time of the 1939 New York World's Fair; *The Waterworks* (1994), a mystery set in the aftermath of the Civil War; and *City of God* (2000), an investigation into a contemporary act of religious desecration that becomes a quest for authentic spirituality, with a title echoing the masterwork by St. Augustine. Born in the Bronx, Doctorow was educated at Ohio's Kenyon College and Columbia University in New York. For a number of years he worked in publishing, eventually becoming editor-in-chief at The Dial Press. He later taught at Sarah Lawrence College and Columbia. Other works include the novels *Welcome to Hard Times* (1960), *Big as Life* (1966), and *Loon Lake* (1980); and *Lives of the Poets* (1984), a novella and stories. Doctorow edited the 2000 edition of the annual anthology *The Best American Short Stories.*

Dodgson, Charles Lutwidge. *See* **Carroll, Lewis**

Donleavy, J[ames] **P**[atrick] (April 23, 1926–). American-born Irish novelist, short-story writer, and playwright. Of Donleavy's many comic works, the best known is THE GINGER MAN (France, 1955; U.S. 1958, 1965), featuring the uncouth antihero Sebastian Dangerfield, an American student at Dublin's Trinity College, the author's alma mater. Rich in wordplay and bawdy high jinks, that novel established Donleavy's reputation as a master of colorful farce and a spirited interlocutor of life's absurdities. Born in Brooklyn to Irish parents, Donleavy served in the U.S. Navy during World War II and returned to Ireland to complete his education at Trinity; he became an Irish citizen in 1967. Other novels, much in the same vein, include *A Singular Man* (1963), *The Saddest Summer of Samuel S.* (1966), *The Beastly Beatitudes of Balthazar B.* (1968), *The Onion Eaters* (1971), *A Fairy Tale of New York* (1973), *The Destinies of Darcy Dancer, Gentleman* (1977), *Schultz* (1979), *The Lady Who Liked Clean Restrooms* (1997), and *Wrong Information Is Being Given Out at Princeton* (1998). Donleavy also adapted a number of his works for the stage, including *The Ginger Man* (1959, 1963). *The History of the Ginger Man* (1993) is an autobiography.

Donne, John (between January 24 and June 19, 1572–March 31, 1631). English poet. The greatest of the Metaphysical poets, Donne produced highly original verses on religious topics as well as love poems of great spiritual and physical intensity. Born to a staunchly Roman Catholic family, Donne later experienced a crisis of faith that led to his conversion to Anglicanism in 1614. His secret marriage in 1601 to Anne More, the 17-year-old niece of Sir Thomas Egerton, whom Donne served as secretary, aroused a scandal. Donne wed More without her father's consent, and for this crime he was dismissed from his post and served a short prison sentence, which put an end to his hopes for a career in government. A majority of his love verses and most of his secular poetry date from the 1590s, especially the years immediately prior to his marriage. These include such well-known lyrics as "The Good Morrow," "The Canonization," "The Bait," "The Sunne Rising," "To His Mistress Going to Bed," and "GO AND CATCH A FALLING STAR." The decade of his most profound religious questioning (1607–17) produced the poems known as THE HOLY SONNETS, on which his reputation as a religious poet largely rests. Of these, "DEATH BE NOT PROUD" and "BATTER MY HEART" are among the best known. In later life, Donne continued to write poems on both secular and spiritual topics, while also establishing himself as an Anglican preacher of formidable eloquence during his tenure (1621–31) as dean of London's St. Paul's Cathedral. During Donne's lifetime, his verse circulated only in manuscript copies; the first print edition, the *Songs and Sonnets,* was published in 1633, two years after his death. Donne's prose works include *Biathanatos* (1607), a treatise on Christianity and suicide dating from the darkest years of his life; *Devotions upon Emergent Occasions* (1624), a book of prayers and meditations inspired by a period of illness; and some 160 sermons, including his own funeral sermon, *Deaths Duell (1630).*

Doolittle, Hilda. *See* **H. D.**

Dos Passos, John (January 14, 1896–September 28, 1970). American novelist. Dos Passos's reputation rests on a large body of work, both fiction and nonfiction, that depicts a nation in spiritual and social decline. His greatest achievement is a trilogy of novels, *The 42nd Parallel* (1930), *1919* (1932), and *The Big Money* (1936), published together as U.S.A. in 1937. A writer of the "lost generation," Dos Passos was born to an affluent Chicago family, educated at Harvard, and served with Ernest HEMINGWAY as an ambulance driver in France during World War I. His bleak outlook on the American national character was formed initially by his work as a journalist, through which he came to view America as a nation deeply divided by class and corrupted by commercialism. These beliefs found their expression in several early novels, notably *Manhattan Transfer* (1925), a portrait of New York City life presented in a highly eclectic, stream-of-consciousness style that Dos Passos refined and expanded for the novels of the *U.S.A.* trilogy. *Adventures of a Young Man* (1939), *Number One* (1943), and *The Grand Design* (1949) make up a second trilogy, *District of Columbia*, a family chronicle that offers a pessimistic critique of the failures of various liberal movements in the United States. Other works of note include the novels *The Prospect Before Us* (1950), *Most Likely to Succeed* (1954), and *The Great Days* (1958); several works of history and biography; and *The Best Times* (1966), a memoir.

Dostoyevsky, Fyodor (November 11, 1821–February 9, 1881). Russian novelist, short-story writer, and journalist. Dostoyevsky was a master of the psychological portrait and a prose stylist of great invention and prodigious energy. The son of a Moscow doctor, he was raised in a family of nine children and prepared for a career as a military engineer, although he abandoned those plans, choosing instead to become a writer. His father was murdered by serfs in 1839, an event that many scholars identify as the source of Dostoyevsky's fascination with murder and guilt. Other shaping influences include his epilepsy, which was at times deeply debilitating, and a gambling habit that frequently left him in dire financial straits. His early writings include stories, sketches, and the short novel *The Double* (*Dvoĭnik*, 1846), his first foray into the theme of the divided personality. His career was interrupted in 1849 when he was arrested and charged with subversion for his participation in the Petrashevsky Circle, a left-wing reading group. Dostoyevsky and his associates were given a sentence of death, but at the

last minute this was commuted, and Dostoyevsky spent four years at hard labor and another four as a soldier in Siberia before winning his liberty. He returned to St. Petersburg and resumed his literary career, publishing a number of stories, including *NOTES FROM THE UNDERGROUND* (*Zapiski iz Podpol'ya*, 1864), before writing *CRIME AND PUNISHMENT* (*Prestuplenie i Nakazanie*, 1867), his first major novel. This was followed by a string of important works, including *THE IDIOT* (*Idiot*, 1874), *THE POSSESSED* (*Besy*, 1872), and *THE BROTHERS KARAMAZOV* (*Bratya Karamazovy*, 1880), generally regarded as his greatest achievement. In these novels, as in nearly all his writings, Dostoyevsky concerned himself with the darkest of human emotions and deeds, offering an incisive portrait of the criminal mind and the yearnings of the human spirit for redemption. His work had a profound influence on later generations of novelists and ranks beside TOLSTOY's as Russia's greatest contribution to world literature.

Dove, Rita (August 28, 1952–). American poet. Dove is the author of several accomplished collections of verse, including *Thomas and Beulah* (1986; Pulitzer Prize), a cycle of poems inspired by the lives of her maternal grandparents in the Deep South at the turn of the 20th century; her quiet, lyrical verse generally deals with domestic and family themes, using private experience as a window on public contexts, including questions of race. Educated at Miami University of Ohio and the University of Iowa, Dove published her first book-length collection, *The Yellow House on the Corner*, in 1980. Her other collections of verse include *Museum* (1983), *The Other Side of the House* (1988), *Grace Notes* (1989), *Mother Love* (1995), and *On the Bus with Rosa Parks* (1999). *Fifth Sunday* (1985) is a collection of her short fiction; *Through the Ivory Gate* (1992) is a novel. From 1993 to 1995, she served as Poet Laureate of the United States, making her both the youngest person and the first African American to hold that post.

Dowson, Ernest (August 2, 1867–February 23, 1900). English poet. Dowson's literary reputation rests on a slender body of work noted for its expert craftsmanship and delicate imagery. The son of a London businessman, Dowson attended Oxford but was forced to leave school to work in his father's failing shipping business. In the 1890s he became associated with a group of London poets and writers, known as the Decadents, that included such figures as Oscar WILDE and Aubrey Beardsley. It was also during this time that Dowson fell in love with Adelaide Foltinowicz, a waitress who was 12 years old. His unrequited love for her became the inspiration for much of his writing, including his best-known poem, "Non Sum Qualis Eram Bonae sub Regno Cynarae," with its oft-quoted refrain of devotion ("I have been faithful to thee, Cynara, in my fashion"). In 1897 he moved to France, where he became addicted to absinthe and was reduced to wretched poverty. He was found there by a friend, R. H. Sherard, who returned him to London, but he died soon after. His highly musical poetry, expressing a love of nature, feelings of religious devotion, and the pangs of unrequited love, can be found in *Verses* (1896) and *Decorations* (1899). His short stories are collected in *Dilemmas* (1895).

Doyle, [Sir] **Arthur Conan** (May 22, 1859–July 7, 1930). English novelist. Doyle's lasting creation was Sherlock HOLMES, the masterful sleuth known for his triumphs of deductive reasoning. Holmes, said to have been based on one of Doyle's teachers at the University of Edinburgh, made his debut in *A Study in Scarlet* (1887), which Doyle wrote in part to shore up the finances of his struggling Southsea medical practice. More tales of the amateur crimehound subsequently appeared in the *Strand Magazine* and were gathered in such collections as THE ADVENTURES OF SHERLOCK HOLMES (1892), *The Memoirs of Sherlock Holmes* (1894), *The Return of Sherlock Holmes* (1905), and *The Case-Book of Sherlock Holmes* (1927). *The Sign of Four* (1890), *The Hound of the Baskervilles* (1902), and *The Valley of Fear* (1915) are among the most popular of the Holmes novels. So beloved was Doyle's creation that when he attempted to kill him off in the story "The Final Problem" (1893), objections from the public and significant financial offers from several magazines convinced the writer to resurrect him in "The Empty House" (1903).

Drabble, Margaret (June 5, 1939–). English novelist, biographer, and editor. The prolific and versatile Drabble is best known for her novels exploring women's issues, especially the conflict between motherhood and career. The daughter of a lawyer, she was educated at Cambridge University and made her debut with *A Summer Birdcage* (1963), about the coming-of-age of two young women. This was followed by such works as *The Garrick Year* (1964), *Jerusalem the Golden* (1967), *The Waterfall* (1969), *The Needle's Eye* (1972), *The Ice Age* (1977), *The Witch of Exmoor* (1996), and *The Peppered Moth* (2001). *The Radiant Way* (1987), *A Natural Curiosity* (1989), and *The Gates of Ivory* (1991) form a trilogy examining the turbulent cultural climate of 1980s Britain through the lives of three women friends. She has also written biographies of Arnold BENNETT, William WORDSWORTH, and ANGUS WILSON, is a recognized authority on Jane AUSTEN, and edited the fifth edition of *The Oxford Companion to English Literature* (1985). She is the sister of novelist A. S. BYATT.

Dreiser, Theodore (August 27, 1871–December 28, 1945). American novelist. Dreiser's deeply American novels of class and culture are considered major works of naturalism, a literary approach that aims for an objective, unjudgmental, unselective presentation of the world. Born poor, in a large Catholic family, Dreiser briefly attended Indiana University before embarking on a career as a newspaper journalist, an experience that sharpened his powers of observation and fueled his feeling that impersonal forces shape human destiny. His first novel—considered by many to be his finest—was SISTER CARRIE (1900), about a resourceful small-town girl who becomes a successful Broadway actress. Dreiser's presentation of his heroine's transgressions against conventional codes of morality so disturbed his publishers that they insisted on substantial revisions in the text and then agreed to publish the book but not to promote it, withdrawing it quickly after it sold fewer than 500 copies. This experience led to a period of depression for Dreiser, although he did succeed as editor of several women's magazines before publishing his next novel, *Jennie Gerhardt* (1911). The success of that book inspired his publisher, Doubleday, Page and Co., to reissue *Sister Carrie*. Then followed a pair of novels, the first two in a trilogy based on the life of industrialist Charles Yerkes, *The Financier* (1912) and *The Titan* (1914); the third novel, *The Stoic* (1947), was completed shortly before his death. *The "Genius"* (1915), a candid autobiographical portrait of an American artist and his romantic escapades, was both popular and scandalous. Dreiser's last great achievement was AN AMERICAN TRAGEDY (1925), based on the widely publicized trial and execution of a New York man who murdered his pregnant mistress. Although many critics have derided Dreiser for his contorted prose, his body of work, and in particular his robust, unmannered presentation of urban life in the first decades of the 20th century, changed the way novels were written in America. He also wrote stories, sketches, a number of plays, and several volumes of autobiographical reflections and commentary, notably *A Book About Myself* (1922), *Tragic America* (1931), and *America Is Worth Saving* (1941). In 1981, the University of Pennsylvania Press issued the first unexpurgated version of *Sister Carrie*, based upon the original manuscript.

Dryden, John (August 19, 1631–May 1, 1700). English poet, playwright, and literary critic. As both author and critic, Dryden occupied a place in the competitive literary culture of the Restoration period that was contested but never equaled. Raised in the country, he moved to London in his 20s. His wit and literary skill gained him many admirers, and he won royal attention with a poem celebrating Charles II's restoration to the throne ("To His Sacred Majesty," 1661). The reopening of the theaters, closed for nearly 20 years under the Protectorate, initiated his distinguished career as a playwright, beginning with a broad farce, *The Wild Gallant* (1663). A series of successes followed, including *The Indian Queen* (coauthored with Robert Howard, 1665), *Secret Love, or The Maiden Queen* (1667), *The Conquest of Granada* (1670), *Marriage à-la-Mode* (1672), *Aureng-Zebe* (1675), and *All for Love* (1677), based on SHAKESPEARE's ANTONY AND CLEOPATRA. *Of Dramatic Poesie, An Essay* (1668) is his highly influential treatise on the English stage and its conventions. His verse satires were equally important in their day, in terms of both his artistry and the long reach of his critical and personal authority; the lengthy *Absalom and Achitophel* (1681), a political satire, and *Mac Flecknoe* (1682), which mocks playwright Thomas Shadwell, are admired examples of his polished style and penetrating intelligence. Dryden served as Poet Laureate (1668–88) and royal historiographer (appointed 1670) under Charles II, positions that both acknowledged and extended his influence. In the 1680s, under James II, he converted to Catholicism. In the last years of his career, he devoted himself to translating the works of several ancient writers, including JUVENAL, Persius, and VIRGIL.

Dumas, Alexandre, *known as* **Alexandre Dumas** *fils* (son) (July 27, 1824–November 27, 1895). French playwright and novelist. The son of the well-known novelist whose name he shares, Dumas *fils* was one of the most successful playwrights of his day, although today he is remembered solely for the novel *Camille* and its stage adaptation, which were the basis of Giuseppe Verdi's opera *La Traviata*. Dumas was born out of wedlock in Paris, but his father legally recognized him and took charge of his care. At 21, he dropped out of school to pursue writing and to clear up his mounting debts. He had his first great success with his second novel, *Camille* (*La Dame aux Camélias*, 1848; also translated as *The Lady of the Camellias*), about a reformed courtesan and her doomed love affair. He produced more than a dozen novels between 1848 and 1856, but the phenomenal success in 1852 of his adaptation of *Camille* convinced him to devote himself to the theater. Dumas went on to write many popular realistic dramas concerning the moral and social dilemmas of the upper classes, including *The "Demi-Monde"* (*Le Demi-monde*, 1855), *Claude's Wife* (*La Femme de Claude*, 1873), and *The Foreigner* (*L'Etrangère*, 1876).

Dumas, Alexandre, *known as* **Alexandre Dumas** *père* (father) (July 24, 1802–December 5, 1870). French novelist, playwright, and memoirist. A hugely prolific and popular 19th-century writer—"No popularity of this century has surpassed that of Alexandre Dumas," remarked Victor HUGO—Dumas *père* is best remembered for his exciting historical adventure novels THE THREE MUSKETEERS (*Les Trois Mousquetaires*, 1844) and THE COUNT OF MONTE CRISTO (*Le Comte de Monte-Cristo*, 1844–45). The son of a celebrated mulatto general in Napoleon's army, Dumas initially made his name in Paris with such plays as *Henri III et Sa Cour* (1829), *Napoléon Bonaparte* (1831), and *Antony* (1831). He then turned to writing historical fiction—often with collaborators, whose contribution is the subject of some critical dispute—even as he continued to write for the theater, sometimes adapting his popular novels as stage melodramas. These daring romantic adventure novels, with their swashbuckling heroes and colorful plots, began with *The Three Musketeers* and continued with its sequels *Twenty Years After* (*Vingt Ans Après*, 1845) and *The Viscount of Bragelonne; or, Ten Years Later* (*Le Vicomte de Bragelonne; ou, Dix Ans Plus Tard*, 1848–50); the second and third volumes of the latter work are often published separately, as, respectively, *Louise de la Vallière* and *The Man in the Iron Mask*. His many other novels include *The Black Tulip* (*La Tulipe Noir*, 1850), a tale of murder and romance set in 17th-century Holland. Dumas lived flamboyantly, winning and losing fortunes and enjoying the company of many mistresses. He documented his exuberant life in several volumes of memoirs.

du Maurier, [Dame] Daphne (May 13, 1907–April 19, 1989). English novelist, short-story writer, and biographer. Du Maurier, the prolific and enormously popular author of the Gothic classic REBECCA (1938), earned a wide readership with her compelling evocations of history and atmosphere, and her mastery of adventure, romance, psychological drama, and suspense. Du Maurier was born in London to a privileged artistic family—her father was the actor Gerald du Maurier and her grandfather the artist and writer George du Maurier. She attended a finishing school in Paris before moving to Cornwall, where many of her works are set. Her first novel, *The Loving Spirit* (1931), was followed by a long succession of popular books, including *Jamaica Inn* (1936), *The Scapegoat* (1957), and *The House on the Strand* (1969). Filmmakers quickly recognized the dramatic power of her work, among them Alfred Hitchcock, who adapted her story "The Birds" (1952) as well as her novels *Jamaica Inn* and *Rebecca* for the screen. Du Maurier also published several volumes of family history and biography, including the memoir *Growing Pains: The Shaping of a Writer* (1977), published in the United States as *Myself When Young*.

Dunbar, Paul Laurence (June 27, 1872–February 9, 1906). American poet, short-story writer, and novelist. Dunbar, who was hailed by Booker T. Washington as the "Poet Laureate of the Negro Race," was one of the first African-American authors to achieve nationwide fame. Dunbar was born to two former slaves who raised him in Dayton, Ohio. He was a top student and a leader at his otherwise all-white high school, but, upon graduation, he found few jobs open to him. While working as an elevator operator, he published his first book of poems, *Oak and Ivy* (1893), at his own expense. Critic William Dean HOWELLS helped to make Dunbar's reputation by praising his second collection, *Majors and Minors* (1895), and writing the introduction to his third and best-known work, *Lyrics of Lowly Life* (1896). Although Dunbar has been accused of depicting the black experience uncritically for the benefit of white audiences, he did tackle the subject of racial injustice and was widely admired by readers and opinion-makers of both races. Dunbar published more than 20 books in his short life—he died of tuberculosis at the age of 33. His fiction includes *The Sport of the Gods*

(1903), a novel about a Southern family's struggle to make it in Harlem.

Duras, Marguerite, *pen name of* Marguerite Donnadieu (April 4, 1914–March 3, 1996). French novelist, screenwriter, and playwright. Duras's provocative, unsentimental writings on love, death, and desire, along with her unconventional approach to form, earned her an international literary reputation. Duras grew up in French Indochina in a town near Saigon, and studied law and political science at the Sorbonne. She was active in the French Resistance during World War II, and for a time was a member of the Communist Party. She began publishing fiction in 1943, and by 1950, when her third novel, *The Sea Wall* (*Un Barrage Contre le Pacifique*), appeared, she had established a solid reputation. Director Alain Resnais asked Duras to write the screenplay for *Hiroshima Mon Amour* (1959). She continued to write in several genres, but was not widely known until *The Lover* (*L'Amant*, 1984), her autobiographical novel about a teenage girl and her older Chinese lover, won the Prix Goncourt. Among her other works are the novels *Moderato Cantabile* (1958), *The Ravishing of Lol Stein* (*Le Ravissement de Lol V. Stein*, 1964), *Destroy, She Said* (*Détruire, Dit-Elle*, 1969), and *The North China Lover* (*L'Amant de la Chine du Nord*, 1991); the play *India Song* (1973), which she adapted and directed for the screen two years later; and her brief literary farewell, *No More* (*C'est Tout*, 1995).

Durrell, Lawrence (February 27, 1912–November 7, 1990). English novelist, poet, and travel writer. Durrell's acknowledged masterwork is THE ALEXANDRIA QUARTET (1957–60), a tetralogy of interconnected novels that traces the lives and fortunes of several characters in Egypt during the 1940s. These novels—*Justine* (1957), *Balthazar* (1958), *Mountolive* (1958), and *Clea* (1960)—are esteemed not only for their sophisticated handling of character and point of view, but also for their sumptuous recreation of Alexandria and its denizens. Although English by birth, Durrell spent little time in England; born in India and raised both

there and on the Greek island of Corfu, he served during World War II as a press attaché to the British embassies in Cairo and Alexandria. He spent subsequent years in the employment of the British Foreign Office in Cyprus, Greece, and the south of France, where he lived until his death in 1990. His poems are highly regarded and can be found in such collections as *A Private Country* (1943), *Cities, Plains and People* (1946), *Collected Poems* (1956), *Vega and Other Poems* (1973), and *Collected Poems, 1931–1974* (1980). His travels are recorded in a variety of nonfiction works, including *Prospero's Cell* (1945), about the island of Corfu, *Reflections on a Marine Venus: A Companion to the Landscape of Rhodes* (1953), and *Bitter Lemons* (1957), about the contest for the island of Cyprus by Greek, Turkish, and British interests. *Spirit of Place: Letters and Essays on Travel* (1969) is a collection of his shorter works. A final cycle of novels—*The Avignon Quintet*—appeared posthumously in 1992.

Dürrenmatt, Friedrich (January 5, 1921–December 14, 1990). Swiss playwright and novelist, writing in German. A dominant figure in postwar German theater whose grotesque tragicomedies are staged around the world, Dürrenmatt was a pastor's son who came of age in neutral Switzerland during World War II, an experience that colored his ironic, pessimistic worldview. Though he declared comedy to be the only possible dramatic form in the modern world, he also asserted that "The tragic is still possible....We can achieve the tragic out of comedy. We can bring it forth as a frightening moment, an abyss that opens suddenly." His best-known plays are THE VISIT (*Der Besuch der Alten Dame*, 1956), about a wealthy woman's bizarre revenge on a treacherous lover from her past, and THE PHYSICISTS (*Die Physiker*, 1962), a farce set in an insane asylum, which addresses the responsibilities of scientists in the nuclear age. Dürrenmatt also wrote a series of critically acclaimed popular mystery novels, beginning with *The Judge and His Hangman* (*Der Richter und Sein Henker*, 1952).

Eberhart, Richard (April 5, 1904–). American poet. In more than 30 collections of poetry—generally lyrical and often praised for forthrightness—Eberhart has embodied his philosophy, articulated in the critical volume *Of Poetry and Poets* (1979), that "poetry is a confrontation of the whole being with reality." Born in Austin, Minnesota, he was educated at the University of Minnesota, Dartmouth College, St. John's College, Cambridge, and Harvard University; he interrupted his education in 1930–31 to serve as tutor to the son of King Prajadhipok of Siam. He later taught at a number of colleges and universities in the United States, including Dartmouth, where he is professor emeritus. His first volume of poetry, *A Bravery of Earth*, appeared in 1930, and he continued to publish steadily through the 1980s. His collections and chapbooks include *Collected Poems* (1976), *Ways of Light* (1980), *The Long Reach* (1984), *Collected Poems 1930–1986* (1988), *Maine Poems* (1989), and *New and Selected Poems, 1930–1990* (1990). His work received the Pulitzer Prize for Poetry (for his 1965 publication *Selected Poems, 1930–1965*), the Bollingen Prize (with John Hall Wheelock, 1962), and the National Book Award for Poetry (1977), and he was Poetry Consultant to the Library of Congress from 1959 to 1961. He founded the Poets' Theatre in Cambridge, Massachusetts, in 1950, and his *Collected Verse Plays* appeared in 1962.

Eça de Queiroz [or Queirós], José Maria de (November 25, 1845–August 16, 1900). Portuguese novelist. Portugal's preeminent 19th-century novelist and a brilliant social satirist, Eça de Queiroz was one of the Generation of '70, a salon of reformist Portuguese artists, writers, and intellectuals. Born in Póvoa do Varzim and educated in the law, he later served as a municipal official and diplomat. These experiences found expression in his best-known works, the socially minded novels of class and culture *The Sin of Father Amaro* (*O Crime do Padre Amaro*, 1876), a portrait of a corrupt churchman; *Cousin Bazilio* (*O Primo Basílio*, 1878), a satiric portrayal of the Portuguese bourgeoisie; and *The Maias* (*Os Maias*, 1880), the chronicle of a wealthy family and its amoral

excesses. He served as a diplomat to the French government in Paris for the last 12 years of his life.

Eco, Umberto (January 5, 1932–). Italian novelist, historian, critic, and philosopher. Eco is best known outside academia for his bestselling novels, especially THE NAME OF THE ROSE (*Il Nome della Rosa*, 1980), an erudite mystery set in a medieval monastery and inspired by an interesting compulsion: "I felt like poisoning a monk." His first important book, however, was *Art and Beauty in the Middle Ages* (*Sviluppo dell'Estetica Medievale*), published in 1959. The same year, he started writing for the avant-garde magazine *Il Verri* and began working as an editor at the publisher Bompiani in Milan. He taught at several Italian universities before becoming, in 1971, professor of semiotics at the University of Bologna. He has written extensively in Italian and English on aesthetics, semiotics, and language; among his many publications are *The Open Work* (*Opera Aperta*, 1962; rev. 1972, 1976), *A Theory of Semiotics* (1976), *Semiotics and the Philosophy of Language* (1984), *The Limits of Interpretation* (*I Limiti dell'Interpretazione*, 1990), *Six Walks in the Fictional Woods* (1994, written in English), and the children's book *The Three Astronauts* (*I Tre Cosmonauti*, 1966). His other novels are *Foucault's Pendulum* (*Il Pendolo di Foucault*, 1988), *The Island of the Day Before* (*L'Isola del Giorno Prima*, 1994), and *Baudolino* (2000).

Edgeworth, Maria (January 1, 1767–May 22, 1849). Anglo-Irish novelist. Edgeworth's novels portraying the history and culture of Irish country life, especially her first novel, *Castle Rackrent* (1800), prefigured the works of other regionalist writers in English, especially SIR WALTER SCOTT. The eldest daughter of Richard Lovell Edgeworth, Maria Edgeworth lived in England until age 15, when she moved to her father's large estate in County Longford, Ireland. Her father had 22 children by his four marriages, and Edgeworth's early stories, published as *The Parent's Assistant* (1796), are notable for their honest and energetic portrayal of children. Following the publication of *Castle*

Rackrent, she continued to win admirers with the novels *Belinda* (1801), *The Absentee* (1812), *Vivian* (1812), *Patronage* (1814), and *Ormond* (1817). Although the majority of Edgeworth's writings are set in fashionable society, her works are also fortified by strong social themes, especially her deep concern for the welfare of the Irish peasantry. A number of them reflect the influence of her father, whose *Memoirs* (1820) she completed after his death in 1817. Her other works include a number of volumes of tales for children, including *Moral Tales* (1801) and *Popular Tales* (1804). Among the writers who acknowledged a debt to Edgeworth were Scott, Jane AUSTEN, William Makepeace THACKERAY, and Ivan TURGENEV.

Eliot, George, *original name* Marian *or* Mary Ann Evans (November 22, 1819–December 22, 1880). English novelist and essayist. Eliot contributed a new intellectual power to the 19th-century English novel, above all in her masterpiece, *MIDDLEMARCH* (1872), a luminous portrait of life in a provincial town and one of the greatest of Victorian novels. Among Eliot's many accomplishments as a novelist are her sure historical grasp, her probing delineation of individual character, and her moral seriousness; in her unflinching but deeply compassionate analysis of human character, she achieves what F. R. LEAVIS called "a Tolstoyan depth and reality." Born in rural Warwickshire, Eliot attended boarding schools until her mother's death in 1836, when she was charged with managing her father's household. She continued her education on her own, and after her father's death moved to London, where she served from 1851 to 1854 as assistant editor of *The Westminster Review*, a leading cultural and philosophical journal. A freethinker, Eliot scandalized polite society when she became the lifelong companion of the English man of letters George Henry Lewes, who was unable to divorce his wife. Her first book, the three tales that make up *Scenes of Clerical Life*, was published in 1858. Eliot's most ambitious novel, the magisterial *Middlemarch*, is a multilayered narrative tracing the interweaving lives of a huge, and brilliantly drawn, cast of characters, centering on Doro-

thea BROOKE, whose ardent and intellectual nature is hemmed in both by her provincial society and by her marriage to the Rev. Edward CAUSABON, a cold and pedantic scholar; it is, said VIRGINIA WOOLF, "one of the few English novels written for adult people." Eliot's other novels include *ADAM BEDE* (1859), *SILAS MARNER* (1861), *Felix Holt* (1866), *DANIEL DERONDA* (1876), and the autobiographical *THE MILL ON THE FLOSS* (1860), which concerns a woman's profound struggle with her family over her pursuit of intellectual and creative fulfillment.

Eliot, T[homas] **S**[tearns] (September 26, 1888–January 4, 1965). American-English poet, playwright, and critic. A dominant figure in modernist English poetry, Eliot was awarded the Nobel Prize in Literature in 1948. Born in St. Louis to a well-to-do family, he was educated at Harvard and did graduate work at Oxford University. Eliot moved to London in 1915 and worked as a clerk at Lloyd's Bank for several years before becoming an editor at Faber & Faber in 1925, a position he would hold to the end of his life. His first major poem, "THE LOVE SONG OF J. ALFRED PRUFROCK," was published in the little magazine *POETRY* in 1915 and subsequently in his first volume, *Prufrock and Other Observations* (1917). Eliot immediately attracted attention for his innovative poetic diction, which he continued to develop in *THE WASTE LAND* (1922), now recognized as a central work of literary modernism and arguably the most influential poem of 20th-century English literature. In *The Waste Land*, Eliot expressed his despair with the instability, amorality, and spiritual barrenness of his age, which he contrasts with the rootedness and fertility of ancient cultures. He also advanced the formal means to explore his epoch, incorporating vernacular speech and weaving a dense web of erudite allusions, ranging from ancient myth to DANTE and SHAKESPEARE. In 1927, Eliot converted to the Anglican church and also became a British subject. Among his later works are "ASH WEDNESDAY" (1930) and *FOUR QUARTETS* (1943), an elaborate series of poems, quietly meditative in tone, contemplating the need for transcendent, timeless states of being amid the disruptions of history. Eliot also wrote several plays in verse, including MURDER IN THE CATHE-DRAL (1935), on St. Thomas Becket, and THE COCKTAIL PARTY (1950), which explores themes of moral redemption. Throughout most of his career, Eliot wielded immense influence as both a literary and social critic. He edited the cultural journal THE CRITERION from 1922 to 1939, and his critical writings, notably the essay collections *The Sacred Wood* (1920) and *The Use of Poetry and the Use of Criticism* (1933), significantly shaped Anglo-American discourse on poetry, particularly that of the New Critics. Emphasizing formal discipline, Eliot rejected the romantic creed of individual expressiveness as well as Victorian sentimentality, and moved critics to pay renewed attention to literature's aesthetic properties.

Elkin, Stanley (May 11, 1930–May 31, 1995). American novelist and short-story writer. Elkin's tragicomic novels are notable for their linguistic playfulness and narrative complexity. These qualities are displayed to great effect in such works as *Boswell, A Modern Comedy* (1964), about a man who schemes to win personal glory through his association with famous people; *The Franchiser* (1976), a satiric portrait of America presented through the eyes of a chain-motel developer; and *The MacGuffin* (1991), about a paranoid city official. Many of his works concern Jewish life and explore religious themes, as in *The Living End* (1979), a collection of novellas about the afterlife, and *George Mills* (1982), a novel concerning reincarnation. Elkin was born in Chicago, educated at the University of Illinois at Urbana-Champaign, and taught for many years at Washington University in St. Louis, Missouri. His other major works include the novels *A Bad Man* (1967), *The Magic Kingdom* (1985), and *The Rabbi of Lud* (1987); and the short-story collections *Criers and Kibitzers, Kibitzers and Criers* (1966) and *Searches and Seizures* (1973). *Pieces of Soap* (1992) is a nonfiction collection.

Ellison, Harlan (May 27, 1934–). American short-story writer, novelist, and screenwriter.

Widely known as a writer of science fiction and fantasy, Ellison is particularly acclaimed for his shorter works. These can be found in such collections as *I Have No Mouth and I Must Scream* (1967), *The Beast That Shouted Love at the Heart of the World* (1969), *Over the Edge* (1970), *Deathbird Stories: A Pantheon of Modern Gods* (1975), *Shatterday* (1980), *Stalking the Nightmare* (1982), and *Slippage: Precariously Poised, Previously Uncollected Stories* (1997), among many others. Educated at Ohio State University, Ellison began his strikingly varied and prolific career by publishing crime fiction, horror, and erotica in pulp magazines in the 1950s. Other works include the novellas *All the Lies That Are My Life* (1980) and *Mefisto in Onyx* (1993), and *The Harlan Ellison Hornbook* (1990), a book of essays. Ellison was also a writer for a number of popular and successful television shows, including *The Outer Limits*, *The Twilight Zone*, and *Star Trek*, to which he contributed the award-winning episode "The City on the Edge of Forever."

Ellison, Ralph (March 1, 1914–April 16, 1994). American novelist and essayist. Ellison's first novel, the only one published in his lifetime, was INVISIBLE MAN (1952; National Book Award), a groundbreaking examination of race relations in the United States. Born in Oklahoma, Ellison originally trained as a musician but put this pursuit aside to join the Federal Writers' Project in New York City in 1936. There he won the friendship of RICHARD WRIGHT, and began to publish the essays and reviews gathered in his second book, *Shadow and Act* (1964). A second volume of nonfiction, *Going to the Territory*, appeared in 1986. For 40 years Ellison labored to produce a second novel, leaving a 1,400-page manuscript unfinished at his death. A much pared-down version was published under the title *Juneteenth* in 1999; *Flying Home and Other Stories* also appeared posthumously, in 1996. Although he traveled and lectured widely, Ellison lived most of his adult life in New York City, where he was the Albert Schweitzer Professor of Humanities at New York University (1970–79).

Éluard, Paul, *pen name of* Eugène Grindel (December 14, 1895–November 18, 1952). French poet. A pioneer of Surrealism, Éluard wrote poems exploring the relationship between the conscious and unconscious mind. The association of Éluard and fellow poets André BRETON, Philippe Soupault, and Louis Aragon is generally considered the cradle of the Surrealist movement, which was founded in Paris in 1924 and lasted into the late 1930s. Éluard's collections from this period include *Capital of Pain* (*Capitale de la Douleur*, 1926), *La Rose Publique* (1934; The Public Rose), and *Les Yeux Fertiles* (1936; The Fertile Eyes), containing poems notable for their deft lyricism and dreamlike images of startling intensity. Themes of love and spiritual union abound in these works, arguably the most accomplished to come from the Surrealist movement. His later works are more political, inspired in part by his horror at the Spanish Civil War and World War II. Themes of universal fellowship and solidarity reflect Éluard's involvement with the French Communist Party, which he joined in 1942, and his association with the French Resistance movement. These later volumes include *Poésie et Vérité* (1942; Poetry and Truth), *Au Rendezvous Allemand* (1944; To the German Rendezvous), and *Dignes de Vivre* (1944; Worthy of Living). His two-volume *Oeuvres Complètes* was published in 1968.

Elytis, Odysseus, *or* Odysseas Elytēs, *original name* Odysseus Alepoudhelis *or* Alepoudelēs (November 2, 1911–March 18, 1996). Greek poet. Elytis, the recipient of the 1979 Nobel Prize in Literature, is the most honored Greek poet of the modern era. Alhough his early work was influenced by the Surrealists, especially Paul ÉLUARD and Andreas Embirikos, it also displayed the distinctive personal idiom and awareness of the larger Greek humanistic tradition for which he would later be celebrated. Born to a wealthy Crete family named Alepoudhelis, he changed his name to Elytis in his 20s, when he abandoned his preparation for a career in law and began to publish the poems gathered in his first collection, *Orientations* (*Prosanatolismoi*, 1939). During World War II, Elytis fought with the resistance in Albania; his poem based on his wartime experiences, "Song Heroic and Mourning for the Lost Second Lieutenant of the Albanian Campaign" ("Asma Hērōiko kai Penthimo gia ton Chameno Anthypolochago tēs Alvanias," 1945), was widely circulated and won him great fame. For more than a decade after the war he published very little poetry, devoting himself to a variety of pursuits, including the writing of his masterwork, the long poem cycle *The Axion Esti* (*To Axion Esti*, 1959; the title is a phrase from the Greek Orthodox liturgy meaning "Worthy It Is"). Following the Greek military coup in 1967, he moved to Paris, forming friendships with a number of leading artists, including Picasso and Matisse, who illustrated some of his later works. Other notable collections include *Six and One Remorses for the Sky* (*Hexē kai Mai Typseis gia ton Ourano*, 1960), "The Monogram" ("To Monogramma," 1972), *The Stepchildren* (*Ta Heterothalē*, 1974), and *The Little Seafarer* (*Ho Mikros Nautilos*, 1986; also translated as *The Little Mariner*). *Open Papers* (*Anoichta Chartia*, 1974; updated 1987) is one of several volumes of his critical writings. Elytis's *Collected Poems* were published in English in 1997.

Emerson, Ralph Waldo (May 25, 1803–April 27, 1882). American poet and philosopher. The intellectual leader of the school of thought and writing known as Transcendentalism, Emerson, the scion of an old New England family, was educated at Harvard University and was ordained as a Unitarian minister in 1829. His career in the pulpit of Boston's Second Church was cut short, however, when the young preacher found himself increasingly dissatisfied with the rigidity of orthodox Christian teachings. These misgivings were exacerbated by the death of his wife, Ellen Tucker, in 1831, and a year later he resigned from the ministry and left for Europe, where he spent the next two years. In England he spent time with Thomas CARLYLE, William WORDSWORTH, and Samuel Taylor COLERIDGE, whose influence guided Emerson in the writing of his first major philosophical treatise, "NATURE" (1836), in which he advanced his core beliefs in the harmony of the universe, the limitless potential of the human mind, and the preeminent function of private intuition in the apprehension of divinity. Although published anonymously, Emerson's pamphlet won him many followers; resettled in his native Concord, outside Boston, he became the center of a coterie of like-minded writers and thinkers, including such leading figures of the Transcendentalist movement as Henry David THOREAU, Louisa May ALCOTT, and Margaret FULLER. His extensive philosophical writings include his two-volume ESSAYS (1841, 1844), which features such well-known pieces as "Self-Reliance," "The Over-Soul," "Love," "Friendship," and "Spiritual

---

"The three practical rules, then, which I have to offer, are—(1) Never read any book that is not a year old. (2) Never read any but famed books. (3) Never read any but what you like...."

Ralph Waldo Emerson, "Books," in *Essays: First Series* (1841)

Laws," all based on lyceum talks he first delivered in the 1830s; "The American Scholar" (1837), a lecture exploring the relationship between Transcendentalist ideas and the politics of his day; *Addresses and Lectures* (1849); *Representative Men* (1850); *The Conduct of Life* (1860); *Letters and Social Aims* (1876); and *Natural History of Intellect* (1893). In 1840, he and Fuller cofounded THE DIAL, an outlet for Transcendentalist writings, and he served as its editor from 1842 to 1844. *Poems* (1847) and *May-Day* (1867) are volumes of verse. Emerson's eclectic incorporation of various philosophical strains—from German and English Romanticism to neo-Platonism and Eastern mysticism—into a highly original vision of creation and human potential marks him as one of the most important and influential of all American thinkers.

Erdrich, [Karen] Louise (June 7, 1954–). American novelist, short-story writer, and poet. Although she began her writing career as a poet, Erdrich is best known for her stories and novels of Native-American life in the Upper Midwest, based on her experiences growing up in Wahpeton, North Dakota, where her parents were teachers at a boarding school for Indian youth. Educated at Dartmouth College and Johns Hopkins University, Erdrich won wide praise for her first book of fiction, *Love Medicine* (1984), a series of linked stories about a Chippewa community. She revisited these characters in several subsequent works, including *The Beet Queen* (1986), *Tracks* (1988), and *The Bingo Palace* (1994), all notable for their narrative artistry and sensitive exploration of contemporary Native-American life. She collaborated with her husband, teacher and writer Michael Dorris (1945–1997), on many works, including the bestselling novel *Crown of Columbus* (1991). Other books by Erdrich include the novels *Tales of Burning Love* (1996), *The Antelope Wife* (1998), and *The Last Report on the Miracles at Little No Horse* (2001); several works for children, including *Grandmother's Pigeon* (1996) and *The Birchbark House* (1999); and *The Blue Jay's Dance: A Birth Year* (1995), an impressionistic record of the birth of one of her children.

Etherege, [Sir] George (c. 1635–c. May 10, 1692). English playwright. Etherege's works for the stage include several plays notable for their spirited tone, romantic high-jinks, and expert craftsmanship, and many scholars identify Etherege's second major play, *She Wou'd if She Cou'd* (1668) as the first true Restoration comedy of manners. His early life was spent in France, where he was exposed to the French stage of MOLIÈRE, an important influence on his work. His first play, *The Comical Revenge; or, Love in a Tub*, which premiered in 1664, won him many admirers and secured his entrée into the fashionable London society he burlesqued on stage. *The Man of Mode; or, Sir Fopling Flutter* (1676) is considered his most clever creation. Knighted in 1680, Etherege, a Jacobite, followed the exiled King James II to

Paris after the "Glorious Revolution" of 1688, and lived there for the remainder of his life. After his death, Etherege's work fell from favor, in part because a number of 18th-century critics castigated him for moral looseness, but today his plays, particularly *The Man of Mode*, are still revived.

Euripides, *in Greek* Euripidēs (c. 484 B.C.–406 B.C.). Greek playwright. One of the great playwrights of antiquity, Euripides wrote some 92 plays, of which 19 survive. Of these, MEDEA (*Mēdeia*, 431 B.C.), *Hippolytus* (*Hippolytos*, 428 B.C.), ELECTRA (*Ēlektra*, 418 B.C.), and THE BAC-CHAE (*Bakchai*, 406 B.C.) are the most highly regarded. Little is known of his early life, but like most playwrights of the period, he built his reputation by competing in the annual dramatic festival of Dionysus, which he won 22 times. Of the three major Greek tragedians of the ancient period (the others being SOPHOCLES and AESCHYLUS), Euripides was notable for creating characters, particularly women, with complex personalities and rich emotional contours. The gods appear as generally indifferent to earthly affairs; human weakness is the cause of great, unanswered suffering, and a number of plays reflect Euripides' deep dislike of war. The challenges in his work to prevailing beliefs on such matters as the role of women in society frequently irritated his Athenian audiences, and his personal reputation as a pedant inspired two bitter stage parodies by ARISTOPHANES, a rival. Stung by this criticism, Euripides left Athens in 408 and lived the last two years of his life in the Macedonian court of King Archelaus, who favored his work.

Fair, A. A. *See* **Gardner, Erle Stanley**

Farrell, James T[homas] (February 27, 1904–August 22, 1979). American novelist and short-story writer. Farrell, a writer of prodigious energy, is best known for the three novels of the STUDS LONIGAN trilogy — including *Young Lonigan* (1932), *The Young Manhood of Studs Lonigan* (1934), and *Judgment Day* (1935) — a comprehensive portrait of life in the Irish ghettos of Chicago's South Side, where Farrell grew up. Educated at the University of Chicago, Far-

rell moved to New York City in 1932. Critics disagree about his work; while some have argued that his portrayals of slum life and the struggles of the working poor are compromised by a didactic tone and obsessive bleakness, others have praised his work as an example of socially inspired naturalism. Farrell's tremendous output included more than 50 books, including 25 novels and 17 collections of short fiction. Other notable works include the novel *The Face of Time* (1953), part of his ten-volume cycle *The Universe of Time*; *Olive and Mary Anne* (1977), short stories; and *Notes on Literary Criticism* (1936), a nonfiction work in which Farrell articulates his reform-minded political and literary philosophy.

Faulkner, William (September 25, 1897–July 6, 1962). American novelist and short-story writer. Winner of the Nobel Prize in Literature (1949), Faulkner concerned himself in his short stories and novels with "the tragic fable of southern history," creating a body of work that stands as one of the greatest achievements in 20th-century world literature. He is most widely known as the creator of the fictional Yoknapatawpha County, Mississippi, a microcosm of Southern society, where many of his works are set. Born to an old Mississippi family in the rural town of New Albany, Faulkner dropped out of high school, briefly attended the University of Mississippi, and lived most of his life in the town of Oxford. Much of his work was based on his own colorful family history, in particular the life of his great-grandfather, a Confederate colonel whose violent death he reimagined in his third novel, *Sartoris* (1929), and whose descendants populate many of his tales, including such major works as THE SOUND AND THE FURY (1929), AS I LAY DYING (1930), SANCTUARY (1931), LIGHT IN AUGUST (1932), ABSALOM, ABSALOM! (1936), and GO DOWN, MOSES (1942). Faulkner's great, binding themes — the struggles of the Southern aristocracy to come to terms with the realities of the modern world, the inequalities of race in Southern society, and the haunting legacies of slavery and the Civil War — are articulated in his work with great moral force and aesthetic originality;

MAIDEN VOYAGES:
FIRST BOOKS BY TEN AMERICAN WRITERS

JAMES BALDWIN. After ten years of struggling with it, James Baldwin finished his first novel, *Go Tell It on the Mountain*, above the Café Flore in Paris and on a Swiss mountainside where "no black man had ever set foot." About the birth of his first book, Baldwin explained, "I remember playing Bessie Smith all the time while I was in the mountains, and playing her till I fell asleep. The book was very hard to write because I was too young when I started, seventeen; it was really about me and my father. There were things I couldn't deal with technically at first. Most of all, I couldn't deal with me." The book was accepted by the publisher Alfred A. Knopf, who published it in 1953.

WILLIAM S. BURROUGHS. About his first book, William S. Burroughs recorded, "I began writing...at the age of thirty-five, in Mexico City after the war. Encouraged by Allen Ginsberg, I set down my experiences from five years of addiction to opiates, sticking close to the facts and using, as Wordsworth put it, 'the language actually used by men.'" *Junkie* was first published in 1953 by the firm of A. A. Wyn, whose paperback line was Ace Books. The book was published in the Ace Double format (used mainly at the time for science-fiction novelettes), back to back with *Narcotics Agent* by one Maurice Helbrant, a strategy to make a detailed look at such a taboo subject seem a little more acceptable.

HART CRANE. When he was 19, Hart Crane worked at the Crane's Candy Company counter in the Portage Drug Store in Akron, Ohio. He also took the time to read the current issue of *The Little Review*, Eliot's *Prufrock*, and Pound's *Pavannes and Divigations*, and to finish his own poem "My Grandmother's Love Letters," which later appeared in his first book, *White Buildings*. When he was interviewed about his poetry for a local newspaper, the headline on the story, which barely mentioned poetry, read, "Millionaire's Son Is Clerk in an Akron Drug Store." His book was published in 1926 by Boni and Liveright. The foreword was by Allen Tate, who had offered to have it printed under Eugene O'Neill's name, since the publishers had agreed to accept the book only if O'Neill would write a preface (they published it anyway).

WILLIAM FAULKNER. Faulkner often referred to himself as a "failed poet." At the beginning of his career, he pursued his failure with a single-minded dedication that alarmed some of his relatives, who shook their heads as he padded about Oxford, Mississippi, in bare feet and drifted from job to job. From his teens until well into his 20s, Faulkner wrote hundreds of poems, laboriously reworking many of them. His first appearance in print was in the August 6, 1919, issue of *The New Republic*, which paid $15 for "L'Après-midi d'un Faune." The magazine rejected another handful of his poems, so Faulkner, as a joke, typed up Coleridge's "Kubla Khan" and submitted it. The editor wrote, "We like your poem, Mr. Coleridge, but we don't think it gets anywhere much." His first book of poems, *The Marble Faun*, a pastoral fantasy in the voices of nymphs and shepherds, was published in 1924 by the Four Seas Company, a vanity book publisher.

H. D. (HILDA DOOLITTLE). The poet H. D. was obsessed throughout her life with ancient Greek civilization. After moving to London in 1911, she frequented the British Museum, where she studied the classics in the *Greek Anthology* along with friends Ezra Pound and Richard Aldington. Her first book, a translation from the Greek of the Choruses from Euripides' *Iphigeneia in Aulis*, was published in 1916 as number three in the Poets Translation Series. Reviewing the volume in *Poetry* (November 1916), T. S. Eliot observed, "She has turned Euripides into English verse which can be taken seriously, verse of our own time, as modern as Swinburne's when it appeared." H. D. died in 1961; for her gravestone she chose the epigram "Greek Flower, Greek Ecstasy."

ERNEST HEMINGWAY. Hemingway came to Paris with his new wife, Hadley Richardson, in December 1921, and quickly made friends with Gertrude Stein, who later reviewed his first book, *Three Stories and Ten Poems*, in the Paris *Tribune* of November 27, 1923: "I may say of Ernest Hemingway that as he sticks to poetry and intelligence it is both poetry and intelligent....I should say that Hemingway should stick to poetry and intelligence and eschew the hotter emotions and the more turgid vision. Intelligence and a great deal of it is a good thing to use when you have it, it's all for the best." In July 1923, three hundred copies of the book were printed in Dijon by Maurice Darantière, who had the previous year printed James Joyce's *Ulysses*. The publisher was the American émigré Robert McAlmon.

JACK LONDON. London had gone to the Klondike in the gold rush of 1897, and nearly died of scurvy. Unable to find work on his return to California, he turned to writing about his Alaskan experiences. *The Overland Monthly*, Bret Harte's San Francisco periodical, gave him his start, accepting "To the Man on Trial" in 1898. The eight stories ultimately published there, plus "An Odyssey of the North," published in *The Atlantic Monthly*, made up London's first book, *The Son of the Wolf: Tales of the Far North* (1900). Thereafter he had no trouble selling as much as he could write—50 volumes in 18 years. During his lifetime, he is said to have earned over a million dollars, all of which he spent.

EDNA ST. VINCENT MILLAY. "Renascence," a long meditative poem concerned with the author's near-death experience as a child, changed the life of its young author, who was to become in the public's eye, for a time, the absolute epitome of the poet. Millay had been pushed by her mother to enter a national poetry contest. When she recited "Renascence" in public a few months later, the poet, identified only as "E. Vincent Millay, Esq.," turned out to be an ethereal, low-voiced 20-year-old woman with flowing red hair. An

(Maiden Voyages: First Books by Ten American Writers, continued)

astounded stranger in the audience offered her a college scholarship. She entered Vassar College and became its most famous graduate. Her first book, *Renascence and Other Poems*, was published in 1917 by Mitchell Kennerley.

HENRY MILLER. "This is not a book, in the ordinary sense of the word. No, this is a prolonged insult, a gob of spit in the face of art, a kick in the pants to God, Man, Destiny, Time, Love, Beauty...." So begins *Tropic of Cancer*, one of the most famous books of the 20th century, written and rewritten in Paris, where the Brooklyn-born author found it was cheaper to live and write. The book, Miller's first, was published in 1934, when he was 43 years old, by Jack Kahane, a British émigré who owned the Obelisk Press (and had published Frank Harris's *My Life and Loves* and Radclyffe Hall's *The Well of Loneliness*). It was financed largely by Miller's friend, the novelist and

his use of stream-of-consciousness narration, for example, in *The Sound and the Fury*, led many critics to compare him to James JOYCE, although elsewhere his writing took a more conventional, if highly achieved, approach. In the mid-1940s Faulkner's career stalled, and he briefly worked as a contract screenwriter in Hollywood; however, the publication in 1946 of *The Portable Faulkner*, introduced by the critic Malcolm COWLEY, revived interest in his work and afforded the writer a level of critical respect that has not since waned. In addition to the Nobel, Faulkner won the Pulitzer Prize twice, for *A Fable* (1954) and *The Reivers* (1962), and the National Book Award in 1950 for *Collected Stories*. Other important works include *The Wild Palms* (1939); INTRUDER IN THE DUST (1948); and the powerful "SNOPES" trilogy, about the rapacious and clever Flem Snopes and his "poor white" kin: THE HAMLET (1940), THE TOWN (1957), and THE MANSION (1958).

Ferber, Edna (August 15, 1885–April 16, 1968). American novelist, playwright, and short-story writer. An entertaining chronicler of America's middle class, Ferber enjoyed great popularity in her day. She was born in Kalamazoo, Michigan, and, without money to attend college, went to work as a journalist. In 1911, she began to write stories featuring the character Emma McChesney, a divorced petticoat saleswoman who became the first businesswoman-heroine of ladies' magazines. Those stories were collected in *Roast Beef, Medium* (1913), *Personality Plus* (1914), and *Emma McChesney & Co.* (1915) and were adapted successfully for the stage as *Our Mrs. McChesney* (1915), by Ferber and George V. Hobart. Ferber's literary stature grew as she began to write novels set throughout the country, especially when *So Big* (1924), whose heroine, Selina DeJong, rescues her farming family from debt, won the Pulitzer Prize. Other well-received novels include *The Girls* (1921), *Show Boat* (1926), *Cimarron* (1930), *Saratoga Trunk* (1941), and GIANT (1952). Ferber's popularity declined in subsequent decades as critics noted her emphasis on surface rather than depth, but her portraits of contemporary manners endure. Among her plays are three notable collaborations with George S. KAUFMAN: *The Royal Family* (1927), *Dinner at Eight* (1932), and *Stage Door* (1936). Two autobiographies, *A Peculiar Treasure* (1939) and *A Kind of Magic* (1963), celebrated her Jewish heritage and American pride.

diarist Anaïs Nin, who also helped Miller to edit the book, changing sequence and removing some of the more outrageous and offensive material.

GERTRUDE STEIN. *Three Lives: Stories of the Good Anna, Melanctha and the Gentle Lena* (1909), Gertrude Stein's first book, does not look much like anything else she wrote. She financed its publication herself, and it was very much just the beginning. In writing it, Stein said she was influenced by Flaubert a little,

"Because the realism of the people who did realism before was a realism of trying to make people real. I was not interested in making people real, but in the essence, or as a painter would call it value. One cannot live without the other ... the Cézanne thing I put into words came in *Three Lives*."

This text was adapted from a 1997 exhibition of the first books of more than one hundred American authors at The New York Public Library's Berg Collection.

Ferlinghetti, Lawrence (March 24, 1920–). American poet, publisher, and bookseller. A leading Beat poet in the 1950s, Ferlinghetti established San Francisco's City Lights bookstore and the publishing imprint City Lights Books, two venerable institutions of Beat literary culture. The first volume printed by the press was Ferlinghetti's own book of poems, *Pictures of the Gone World* (1955); the second was Allen GINSBERG's *HOWL* (1956), widely considered the most significant work of Beat poetry. Raised in France and New York, Ferlinghetti served in the Navy during World War II and attended the University of North Carolina, Columbia University, and the Sorbonne. His verse, written in the rhythmic, oral style of the Beats, explores political and social topics with an ironic tone that found a following among young people on the coffeehouse circuit. Among his many collections are *A Coney Island of the Mind* (1958), *An Eye on the World* (1967), *Landscapes of Living and Dying* (1979), *Love in the Days of Rage* (1988), and *How to Paint Sunlight: Lyric Poems and Others* (1997–2000) (2001). In addition to operating City Lights Books, Ferlinghetti published the works of many of his fellow Beats in *City Lights Journal*.

Fielding, Henry (April 22, 1707–October 8, 1754). English novelist and playwright. One of the founding figures of the English novel, Fielding began his literary career as a playwright, writing some 25 stage dramas before turning to fiction. His first novel was a ruthless parody of SAMUEL RICHARDSON's sentimental novel *PAMELA* (1740), entitled *Shamela* (1741). Although published under a pseudonym, the book is generally accepted as Fielding's creation, in part because of its resemblance to two later novels, *JOSEPH ANDREWS* (1742, also inspired in part by *Pamela*) and *TOM JONES* (1749), both picaresque tales. In the latter especially, Fielding displayed his superb gifts for comedy and social satire, and both works stand as durable examples of the English novel in its earliest form. Anti-Jacobite writings won Fielding political favor in his later life, and he served for many years as a London judge. He also published a newspaper, *Champion; or, British Mercury* (1739–41). His other novels are *Amelia* (1751) and *The Life of Mr. Jonathan Wild the Great* (1743).

FitzGerald, Edward. *See* 'Omar Khayyám

Fitzgerald, F[rancis] **Scott** (September 24, 1896–December 21, 1940). American novelist and short-story writer. Celebrated first for his stories of the Jazz Age, Fitzgerald is now recognized as one of the 20th century's great novelists. Born in St. Paul, Minnesota, he began *THIS SIDE OF PARADISE* (1920) as a student at Princeton University, tracking its social rituals as the hero, Amory Blaine, pursues a girl too rich and too beautiful for him. The novel was a bestseller, and for the next decade Fitzgerald's short stories appeared in *Scribner's* and *The Saturday Evening Post*; many were collected in *Flappers*

"Begin with an individual, and before you know it you find that you have created a type; begin with a type, and you find that you have created—nothing."

F. Scott Fitzgerald, "The Rich Boy," in *All the Sad Young Men* (1926)

---

and Philosophers (1920); *Tales of the Jazz Age* (1922); and *All the Sad Young Men* (1926). His second novel, *THE BEAUTIFUL AND DAMNED* (1922), recounts the rise and fall of a glittering, reckless couple who revel in excess, evoking the hedonistic social whirl that was relished—notoriously—by both Fitzgerald and his wife, Zelda. In 1924, Fitzgerald joined other American writers in France, where he finished his masterpiece, *THE GREAT GATSBY* (1925). The story of Jay GATSBY, a bootlegger who reinvents himself to win back his lost love, Daisy BUCHANAN, has proved to be a lasting tribute to the American dream of new beginnings. Later works spoke of loss as Fitzgerald battled alcoholism and a fading reputation. *TENDER IS THE NIGHT* (1933) follows a psychiatrist's efforts to save his wife from madness—written as Zelda entered a sanitarium. Fitzgerald had half-finished *THE LAST TYCOON* (1941), drawing on his experiences as a screenwriter in Hollywood, when he suffered a fatal heart attack. His reputation grew with posthumous publications, including his notebooks in *THE CRACK-UP* (1945), reissues of his stories and novels, and admiring critical studies.

Fitzgerald, Penelope, *original surname* Knox (December 17, 1916–April 28, 2000). English novelist, critic, and biographer. This Booker Prize–winning novelist, whose fiction was first published when she was in her 60s, is admired for her economical style, her keen characterizations, and her evocations of human absurdities. Fitzgerald was born into a literary family: her uncle was a novelist and translator, and her father edited the humor magazine *Punch*. After graduating from Oxford, she enjoyed varied careers as a journalist, bookseller, and teacher. During World War II, she worked for the BBC, an experience satirized in her 1980 novel, *Human Voices*. Fitzgerald wrote two biographies before publishing her first novel, *The Golden Child* (1977), a satirical murder mystery set in a museum. *Offshore* (1979; Booker Prize) is the story of houseboat dwellers on the Thames. Her later works include the highly regarded historical novels *The Beginning of Spring* (1988), set in prerevolutionary Moscow; *The Gate of Angels* (1990), concerning a Cambridge college in Edwardian England; and *THE BLUE FLOWER* (1995), based on the life of the 18th-century German poet NOVALIS.

Flaubert, Gustave (December 12, 1821–May 8, 1880). French novelist and short-story writer. After Flaubert's sudden death at home at Croisset, a press clipping found on his writing table described him as "one of the uncontested masters of the contemporary novel, perhaps the only one who owes nothing to anyone, and whom everyone else has more or less imitated." Born in Rouen to a respected surgeon, Flaubert was a precocious child who began writing fiction in his youth. He enrolled in law school in Paris, but in 1844 he suffered a nervous breakdown and abandoned, without regret, the "flatly bourgeois...wooden benches of the Law School," and retired to a small 18th-century château at Croisset, a village on the Seine a few miles below Rouen. With an almost monastic commitment, he began to devote his life to writing. He completed a draft of the novel *The Temptation of Saint Anthony* (*La Tentation de Saint Antoine*, 1874) in 1849 and then worked for five years on his first mature novel, the masterpiece *MADAME BOVARY* (1857). This portrait of the life of a dissatisfied, romantic, middle-class provincial woman and her adulterous affairs, painted with striking objectivity and a meticulously shaped, sonorous, impersonal style, revolutionized the novel. Charles-Augustin SAINTE-BEUVE, the preeminent French literary critic of the day, while acknowledging the novel's remarkable power, complained that Flaubert the artist asked himself but one thing: "Is it true?" Indeed, Flaubert believed that poetry was as precise a science as geometry, and his gaze was dispassionate, an artistic sensibility that came to define later modernist literature. After Flaubert and his publisher were unsuccessfully prosecuted for the book's supposed offenses to morality, it found immediate success. His fiction also includes *Salammbô* (1862), a lushly decadent historical novel set in Carthage during the Punic Wars; A SENTIMENTAL EDUCATION (*L'Éducation Sentimentale*, 1869), a cool but deeply moving Bildungsroman that EDMUND WILSON compared to "listening to a muted symphony of … varied instrumentation and … melancholy sonorities";

"The artist in his work must be like God in his creation—invisible and all-powerful: he must be everywhere felt, but never seen."

Gustave Flaubert, letter to Mademoiselle Leroyer de Chantepie, March 18, 1857, translated by Francis Steegmuller, in *The Letters of Gustave Flaubert, 1830–1857* (1980)

Three Tales (*Trois Contes*, 1877), which includes the celebrated story "A Simple Heart" ("Un Coeur Simple"), the poignant tale of the day-to-day life of an unassuming housemaid and the inspiration for JULIAN BARNES's *Flaubert's Parrot*; and *Bouvard et Pécuchet* (1881), an unfinished novel into which Flaubert poured a lifetime's worth of scorn for the bourgeoisie and for human stupidity in general, "a kind of encyclopedia made into farce." Although his later novels were either misunderstood or dismissed by most critics, Flaubert was revered by other writers. HENRY JAMES called

him a "novelist's novelist," and his impact on the literary culture that followed him was profound. NABOKOV wrote, "Without Flaubert there would have been no Marcel PROUST in France, no James JOYCE in Ireland. CHEKHOV in Russia would not have been quite Chekhov. So much for Flaubert's literary influence."

Fleming, Ian (May 28, 1908–August 12, 1964). English novelist. The creator of the debonair British secret agent 007, Fleming worked as an international journalist, a banker, and a British Intelligence officer during World War II before turning to fiction with the first of his 12 James BOND novels, *Casino Royale* (1953). Other titles in the series, all international bestsellers, include *From Russia, with Love* (1957), *Dr. No* (1958), *Goldfinger* (1959), *On Her Majesty's Secret Service* (1963), and *You Only Live Twice* (1964). All of Fleming's novels were made into popular films, as were a number of James Bond titles written by other writers after Fleming's death. Fleming was also the author of the children's book *Chitty Chitty Bang Bang* (1964), about a magical car.

Fo, Dario (March 24, 1926–). Italian playwright. Fo's collaboration with actress Franca Rame (from whom he was divorced in 1988) produced a prodigious body of highly original theater, influenced by commedia dell'arte as well as by the circus and slapstick. With Rame, Fo founded and operated three theater companies—La Compagnia Dario Fo–Franca Rame (founded 1959), Nuova Scena (founded 1968), and Collettivo Teatrale la Comune (founded 1970)—all known for their eclectic comic productions and leftist politics. Of his numerous plays, the best known include *Archangels Don't Play Pinball* (*Gli Arcangeli Non Giocano a Flipper*, 1959), *Accidental Death of an Anarchist* (*Morte Accidentale di un Anarchico*, 1970), *We Can't Pay? We Won't Pay!* (*Non Si Paga, Non Si Paga*, 1974), and *One Was Nude and One Wore Tails* (*L'Uomo Nudo e l'Uomo in Frak*, 1985). Collaborations with Rame include *Orgasmo Adulto Escapes from the Zoo* (*Tutta Casa, Letto e Chiesa*, 1978) and *The Open Couple* (*Coppia Aperta*, 1983). Fo was awarded the

Nobel Prize in Literature in 1997, the Swedish Academy describing him as one "who emulates the jesters of the Middle Ages in scourging authority and upholding the dignity of the downtrodden."

Fontane, [Henri] Theodor (December 30, 1819–September 20, 1898). German novelist, journalist, travel writer, and poet. Of middle-class background (his ancestors were Huguenot refugees in Prussia), Fontane is noted for his affectionate portraits of aristocratic Prussian society, which he created as the rise of industrialism in Bismarck's German empire was beginning to undermine the aristocracy's traditional status as Prussia's military and governing caste. After a long career as a journalist, he was nearly 60 when he published his first novel, *Before the Storm* (*Vor dem Sturm*, 1878), set in the Napoleonic era. Although he wrote other historical novels, notably *A Man of Honor* (*Schach von Wuthenow*, 1883), his strength was the modern novel, which he said "should be a picture of the age, of *its* age." He wrote about social issues, such as the plight of women trapped by the rigid codes of a male-dominated society, as in his best-known work, EFFI BRIEST (1895), or love between the classes, as in *Delusions, Confusions* (*Irrungen, Wirrungen*, 1888); but in many of his finest works, like *The Poggenpuhl Family* (*Die Poggenpuhls*, 1896) and *The Stechlin* (*Der Stechlin*, 1899), the main point seems to be the sparkling conversations and the characters' nuanced charm. He is commonly regarded as Germany's greatest 19th-century novelist and one of its greatest writers in the realist tradition.

Forché, Carolyn (April 28, 1950–). American poet and journalist. Forché's socially conscious poems, as well as her long association with the human rights group Amnesty International, place her among the leading political poets of her generation. Educated at Michigan State and Bowling Green State universities, Forché published her first collection, *Gathering the Tribes* (1976), in the Yale Younger Poets Series. Although the poems in that volume focus primarily on private, domestic experiences, her second collection, *The Country Between Us* (1982), inspired by the author's two-year stint in El Salvador as a journalist and human rights worker, established her reputation as a forceful voice against oppression. *The Angel of History* (1994), a book-length poem in five parts, ranges over a broader historical and geographical ground, ruminating on the 20th century's moral disasters (genocide, the Holocaust, war, the atom bomb). Forché has also translated a number of El Salvadoran and Latin-American poets, including Claribel Alegría, and she edited the anthology *Against Forgetting: The Poetry of Witness* (1993).

Ford, Ford Madox, *original name* Ford Hermann Hueffer (December 17, 1873–June 26, 1939). English novelist and critic. Of the more than 80 books Ford published in his lifetime, his novel THE GOOD SOLDIER (1915), a tragic study of a failing marriage among the reserved English upper class, has come to be considered his best, and one of the great novels of the 20th century. The scion of an artistic family—he was the grandson of the Pre-Raphaelite painter Ford Madox Brown and the son of Dr. Francis Hueffer, a respected music critic—Ford published his first stories when he was just 19. A collaborative friendship with novelist Joseph CONRAD produced two novels, *The Inheritors* (1901) and *Romance* (1903), and although their personal relationship later suffered, Conrad remained an ardent supporter of his work, especially of Ford's *Fifth Queen* trilogy of novels (1907–8), a historical chronicle about Catherine Howard, the fifth wife of Henry VIII. Ford served two years in the army during World War I, and after the war settled in Paris, where he traveled in literary circles and produced his other major work of fiction, the tetralogy of novels known as PARADE'S END (1924–28). In France, Ford also founded and edited THE TRANSATLANTIC REVIEW (1924), publishing the work of such writers as James JOYCE, Ezra POUND, and Gertrude STEIN. He lived the remainder of his life both in France and in the United States. *Return to Yesterday* (1931) and *It Was the Nightingale* (1933) are memoirs; *The March of Literature: From Confucius to Modern Times* (1938) is a lively survey of world literature, written for the general reader, and was Ford's last book. Since his death, Ford's critical reputation has grown; today he is widely respected as a prose stylist of uncommon precision and one of his country's most thoughtful observers of the decline of the English aristocracy in the post-Victorian period.

Ford, Richard (February 16, 1944–). American novelist, short-story writer, and sportswriter. Winner of the 1995 Pulitzer Prize for his novel INDEPENDENCE DAY, about a New Jersey real estate agent's search for meaning, Ford is known for his portraits of contemporary American men and their struggles to come to terms with a changing culture. Educated at Michigan State University and the University of California at Irvine, Ford won considerable attention for his first novel, *A Piece of My Heart* (1981), as well as for his short stories, which began appearing in the early 1980s in such magazines as *Esquire*, *GQ*, and THE PARIS REVIEW. Fame came with the publication of an acclaimed collection, *Rock Springs* (1987), and a novel, *The Sportswriter* (1986), in which he introduced the character Frank BASCOMBE, a divorced ex-writer turned sports journalist who would later also serve as the protagonist of *Independence Day*. Other works include *The Ultimate Good Luck* (1981), a novel set in Mexico; *Wildlife* (1990), about a young man's coming-of-age in Montana; and *Women with Men: Three Stories* (1997). Ford has also edited or coedited a number of volumes, including *The Granta Book of the American Short Story* (1998).

Forester, C[ecil] S[cott] (August 27, 1899–April 2, 1966). English novelist. Born in Cairo and educated in England, Forester abandoned his medical studies in 1921 when he determined to become a full-time writer. Highly prolific in a variety of genres, he is best remembered as the creator of British naval officer Horatio HORNBLOWER, the protagonist of a series of novels set during the Napoleonic Wars. Hornblower, who made his debut as a midshipman in *The Happy Return* (1937), eventually appeared in some 12 books, rising to the rank of admiral. Of Forester's other novels, *The African Queen*

(1935) remains the best known, its lasting popularity owed in part to the 1951 film adaptation directed by John Huston. Forester published a number of historical works about the sea, including *The Age of Fighting Sail: The Story of the Naval War of 1812* (1956) and *The Last Nine Days of the Bismarck* (1959). *The Hornblower Companion* (1964) and *Long Before Forty* (1967) are autobiographical works.

Forster, E[dward] M[organ] (January 1, 1879– June 7, 1970). English novelist, essayist, and critic. A distinguished modernist, Forster, whose father died when he was just a year old, was raised by his mother in an upper-middle-class Edwardian household. His years at King's College, Cambridge, where he moved in literary circles, were followed by a year-long sojourn with his mother on the Continent, an experience that would inform his shrewdly observant novels of English tourists abroad. Upon his return to England, he began to write for the *Independent Review*, then turned to fiction, producing four novels in just six years: *Where Angels Fear to Tread* (1905), *The Longest Journey* (1907), A ROOM WITH A VIEW (1908), and HOWARDS END (1910). In these works, Forster distinguished himself not only by his unmannered craftsmanship but also by the philosophical urgency with which he explored such themes as the contest between materialism and spirituality, the nature of economic and social injustice, and the dissolution of the English upper classes. A PASSAGE TO INDIA (1924), a novel inspired by several trips to India and Forster's four years of service with the Red Cross in Alexandria, Egypt, during World War I, is thought to be his crowning achievement. As a literary and social critic, he was also highly influential. *Aspects of the Novel* (1927) stands as one of the most thoughtful considerations of narrative aesthetics produced during the 20th century. The novel *Maurice*, written before World War I but published posthumously in 1971, explores homosexual themes. Volumes of essays and criticism include *Abinger Harvest* (1936) and *Two Cheers for Democracy* (1951).

Forsyth, Frederick (August 25, 1938–). English novelist. Born in Ashford, Kent, Forsyth studied at the University of Granada in Spain and served in the Royal Air Force for two years before embarking on a career as a journalist in 1958. His first novel was the thriller *The Day of the Jackal* (1971), about a plot to assassinate French President Charles de Gaulle. Written with vigor and intelligence, and informed by the author's long tenure as a foreign correspondent for Reuters and the BBC, it became an international bestseller and was made into a successful film. Forsyth's popularity grew with subsequent works, including *The Odessa File* (1972), *The Dogs of War* (1974), *The Fourth Protocol* (1984), *The Negotiator* (1989), and *The Fist of God* (1994), all international spy thrillers; and *The Phantom of Manhattan* (1999), a historical novel inspired by Gaston Leroux's *The Phantom of the Opera*.

Foscolo, Ugo, *original name* Niccolò Foscolo (February 6, 1778–September 10, 1827). Italian poet and novelist. The son of a Greek mother and an Italian father, Foscolo was born on the Ionian island of Zacynthus (then part of the Venetian Republic; now Zákinthos, Greece), where he spent most of his early years. At 14 he joined his mother in Venice, where he soon attracted attention in literary circles, scoring a triumph with his tragedy *Tieste* (1797; Thyestes) when he was not yet 20. Foscolo's epistolary narrative *The Last Letters of Jacopo Ortis* (*Ultime Lettere di Jacopo Ortis*, 1802) is widely regarded as the first modern Italian novel. Inspired by Foscolo's own disappointment at Napoleon's cession of Venice to Austria under the Treaty of Campoformio (1797), it tells the tragic story of a young man's thwarted passion for a married woman, which ends in suicide. Foscolo's feelings of betrayal did not deter him, however, from fighting for Napoleon against the Austrians in northern Italy, and he was eventually forced to flee his country, first to Switzerland (1814) and later to London (1816), where he lived the last decade of his life. He is equally renowned as a poet, particularly for his many sonnets and his long poem *Dei Sepolcri* (1807; On Sepulchres), a meditation on history written

in a measured, neoclassical style. In exile he turned his energies to translation and critical scholarship, writing studies of such figures as DANTE and PETRARCH.

Fowles, John (March 31, 1926–). English novelist, short-story writer, poet, essayist, and translator. A popular novelist who combines skillful storytelling with formal experimentation, Fowles was educated at Oxford University and taught for a number of years in France, Greece, and England before beginning to write. His major works include the thriller *The Collector* (1958); a philosophical novel, THE MAGUS (1966; rev. ed. 1977), based in part on his years in Greece; a historical novel, THE FRENCH LIEUTENANT'S WOMAN (1969); *The Ebony Tower* (1974), a collection of interconnected short stories; *Daniel Martin* (1977), a portrait of a middle-aged writer's search for meaning; *Mantissa* (1982), a parody of contemporary poststructuralists; and a historical detective story, *A Maggot* (1985). *Wormholes: Essays and Occasional Writings* appeared in 1998.

France, Anatole, *pen name of* Jacques-Anatole-François Thibault (April 16, 1844–October 12, 1924). French writer and critic. Recipient of the Nobel Prize in Literature in 1921, France was the son of a Paris bookseller and began his career as a poet. It was in his novels and critical writings, however, that his urbane intelligence and the unmannered felicity of his style reached their highest levels of achievement, bringing him fame and fortune. A cluster of works produced over the last two decades of the 19th century secured his position in the top rank of French writers: *The Crime of Sylvestre Bonnard* (*Le Crime de Sylvestre Bonnard*, 1881), his first great novel; *Thaïs* (1890); *At the Sign of the Reine Pedauque* (*La Rôtissserie de la Reine Pédauque*, 1893); *The Red Lily* (*Le Lys Rouge*, 1894); and a quartet of satirical novels known as *Histoire Contemporaine* (1897–1901), featuring one of his most memorable characters, the skeptical Professor Bergeret, whose voice was France's own. France was elected to the Académie Française in 1896, and his influence as a critic was unparalleled in his day. His shorter works of fiction are gathered in *Mother of Pearl* (*L'Étui de Nacre*, 1892), and *Crainquebille* (1901), among others. Later works include the novels *Penguin Island* (*L'Île des Pingouins*, 1908), a ferocious satire of French history, and *The Gods Are Athirst* (*Les Dieux Ont Soif*, 1912; also translated as *The Gods Will Have Blood*), an exposé of the excesses committed in the name of the French Revolution and often recalled as his finest novel. France was the primary model for the writer Bergotte in Marcel PROUST's *REMEMBRANCE OF THINGS PAST*.

Friel, Brian (January 29, 1929–). Irish playwright. A Catholic raised in Northern Ireland, Friel made his mark first as a writer of short stories, his work appearing in *THE NEW YORKER* and elsewhere. *Philadelphia, Here I Come* (1964), about an Irish youth about to immigrate to America, was his first stage success and the first of many plays exploring Irish life, which are often set in the fictional town of Ballybeg. Some of Friel's plays, such as *The Freedom of the City* (1973), *Translations* (1981), and *Making History* (1988), wrestle overtly with public questions of Irish independence and Protestant-Catholic conflict in Northern Ireland; others, such as *Aristocrats* (1979) and *Molly Sweeney* (1994), concern themselves primarily with private experience in the context of family and community. Perhaps his best-known play, the bittersweet *Dancing at Lughnasa* (1990), depicts two days in the lives of five unmarried sisters who live together in a house just outside Ballybeg.

Frisch, Max (May 15, 1911–April 4, 1991). Swiss playwright, novelist, and diarist. Frisch, whose early career included stints as a newspaper journalist and architect, began writing plays in the last years of World War II. Much of his early work for the stage concerns the war directly or indirectly, examining its corrosive effects on the human spirit and frequently employing surrealistic effects to broadcast these interests. His plays include *Santa Cruz* (1946), *The Chinese Wall* (*Die Chinesische Mauer*, 1946; also translated as *The Great Wall of China*), *When the War Was Over* (*Als der Krieg*

zu Ende War, 1949), and *Count Oederland* (*Graf Öderland*, 1951). *Don Juan, or, The Love of Geometry* (*Don Juan; oder, Die Liebe zur Geometrie*, 1953), one of his best-known works for the stage, revisits the legend of Don JUAN. Later plays include *The Firebugs* (*Herr Biedermann und die Brandstifter*, 1958; also translated as *The Fire Raisers*), *Andorra* (1961), and *Biography* (*Biographie*, 1968). Novels by Frisch include *I'M NOT STILLER* (*Stiller*, 1954), *Homo Faber* (1957), *A Wilderness of Mirrors* (*Mein Name sei Gantenbein*, 1964), *Montauk* (1975), *Man in the Holocene* (*Der Mensch Erscheint im Holozän*, 1979), and *Bluebeard* (*Blaubart*, 1982). Addressing a variety of subjects, they are bound to some degree by themes of human baseness and the struggle for identity. Two volumes of Frisch's diaries were published in 1950 and 1972.

Frost, Robert (March 26, 1874–January 29, 1963). American poet. Although born in California, Frost is known as a poet of New England, and as one of the greatest poets America has ever produced. His work is distinguished by its use of familiar diction, melodious patterns of rhyme and meter, and a profound affection for the landscape of New England, particularly the rural countryside around Franconia, New Hampshire, where Frost lived most of his life. In such deceptively simple and oft-quoted poems as "THE ROAD NOT TAKEN" (in *Mountain Interval*, 1916) and "STOPPING BY WOODS ON A SNOWY EVENING" (in *New Hampshire*, 1923), Frost's vision of the natural world is colored by a mystical reverence that links his work to the writings of the New England Transcendentalists and the poetic tradition of Emily DICKINSON, who is often considered a forebear. Educated at Dartmouth College and Harvard, Frost, who never completed his undergraduate studies, began to publish his poems while living in England before World War I, producing two collections for British publishers: *A Boy's Will* (1913) and *North of Boston* (1914), which includes the famous poem "MENDING WALL." Upon his return to the United States in 1915, Frost took up residence at his isolated Franconia farm and wrote steadily, and his reputation with American readers blossomed swiftly. Other notable collections include *West Running Brook* (1928), *A Further Range* (1936), *A Witness Tree* (1942), *Complete Poems* (1945), and *In the Clearing* (1962). Frost received the Pulitzer Prize four times, and read his poem "The Gift Outright" in 1961 at the inauguration of President John F. Kennedy.

Fuentes, Carlos (November 11, 1928–). Mexican novelist and short-story writer. One of Mexico's greatest writers, Fuentes was born to a wealthy family and worked as a lawyer and diplomat (following in his father's footsteps) before achieving fame as a novelist. His fiction is characterized by strong populist themes and the blending of dream and myth with conventional narration, much in the manner of fellow Latin American writers Gabriel GARCÍA MÁRQUEZ and Jorge Luis BORGES. Fuentes's concern for social justice was expressed in his first novel, *Where the Air Is Clear* (*La Región Más Transparente*, 1958), an examination of the failures of the Mexican revolution. This was followed by the novels *The Good Conscience* (*Las Buenas Conciencias*, 1959), *Aura* (1962), and *THE DEATH OF ARTEMIO CRUZ* (*La Muerte de Artemio Cruz*, 1962), a densely philosophical work about the last, regretful hours of a dying political leader. This work, more than any other, secured Fuentes's stature as Mexico's preeminent writer and won him a worldwide following. Other works include *The Masked Days* (*Los Días Enmascarados*, 1954) and *Burnt Water* (1980), both story collections; and the novels *Our Land* (*Terra Nostra*, 1975), *Distant Relations* (*Una Familia Lejana*, 1980), *The Old Gringo* (*Gringo Viejo*, 1985), and *The Years with Laura Diaz* (*Los Años con Laura Díaz*, 1999). Fuentes, who learned English at the age of four, lives in the United States, where he has taught at several universities, including Harvard. His literary and cultural criticism appears in such volumes as *The Buried Mirror: Reflections on Spain and the New World* (1992), published simultaneously in Spanish as *El Espejo Enterrado*; and *Myself with Others: Selected Essays* (1998), published in English.

Fugard, [Harold] **Athol** (June 11, 1932–). South African playwright. One of modern South Africa's most important playwrights, Fugard is known for works that address both the specific evils of apartheid and larger questions of human liberty in the face of oppressive social institutions. *The Blood Knot* (1961) established his reputation, both in South Africa and, later, in London and New York. The play, about brothers torn apart by racism, premiered in Port Elizabeth, South Africa, at Fugard's theater company, where it was the first production in apartheid South Africa to have a mixed-race cast (the white Fugard played the brother who passes for white). He followed *The Blood Knot* with *Hello and Goodbye* (1966) and *Boesman and Lena* (1969), one of his most important works; the three plays were published together as *Three Port Elizabeth Plays* (1974). Other works (in many of which Fugard also acted) include *Sizwe Bansi Is Dead* (1974), *A Lesson from Aloes* (1978), the autobiographical "*Master Harold*"... *and the Boys* (1982), *The Road to Mecca* (1984), *My Children! My Africa!* (1989), *Playland* (1992; his first postapartheid work), *Valley Song* (1995), the autobiographical *The Captain's Tiger* (1999), and *Sorrows and Rejoicings* (2001), which again deals with apartheid. *Tsotsi* (1980) is a novel.

Fujiwara, Toshinari, *also called* Shunzei (1114–December 22, 1204). Japanese poet and critic. An early practitioner of the classical court verse known as *waka* (alternating five- and seven-syllable lines, with a final line of seven syllables), Fujiwara is one of Imperial Japan's most important poets. Guiding his writings was the notion of *yugen*, a mystical transmission of feeling for the natural world achieved through the nuances of language. His achievements as a poet were formally recognized in 1187, when he was charged with assembling the seventh Imperial anthology, *Collection of a Thousand Years* (*Senzaishu*). His critical writings are instructive, sympathetic, and subtle. The most notable of these are found in "Notes on Poetic Style Through the Ages" (*Korai Futeisho*, 1197). Toshinari Fujiwara was the father of the critic SADAIE FUJIWARA, whom he trained in the *waka* form.

Fukuzawa, Yukichi (January 10, 1835–February 3, 1901). Japanese intellectual and memoirist. Although born to the samurai class, one of the most privileged groups in feudal Japan, Fukuzawa spent much of his life trying to bring Western-style reforms to his country. A journalist, teacher, and university founder, he summarized his beliefs in his essay *Gakumon no Susume* (1876; An Encouragement of Learning), a deeply felt entreaty on behalf of social and educational reform. His great contribution to the literature of his country, *Fukuō Jiden* (1899; The Autobiography of Fukuzawa Yukichi) is the first autobiography by a Japanese writer of the modern era.

Gaddis, William (December 29, 1922–December 16, 1998). American novelist. Gaddis was a leading experimental novelist, preoccupied with the deceptiveness, amorality, and materialist values of contemporary society; his work influenced such authors as Thomas PYNCHON and Don DELILLO. Raised on Long Island and educated at Harvard, Gaddis published his first novel, *THE RECOGNITIONS*, in 1955. Minimally plotted and heavily allusive, the novel treats problems of imitation and authenticity in its portrayal of an artist who forges Old Master paintings. After a 20-year silence, Gaddis published a second novel, *JR* (1975), a dark comedy composed in uninterrupted dialogue and concerning a young boy who becomes a fantastically successful stock speculator. Gaddis's later novels are *Carpenter's Gothic* (1985) and *A Frolic of His Own* (1994).

Gallant, Mavis, *original name* Mavis Young (August 11, 1922–). Canadian short-story writer and novelist. Born in Montreal, as a child Gallant was sent away to be educated in a number of schools in Canada and the United States, graduating from high school in New York City. She later worked for the Montreal *Standard* until moving to Europe in 1950, eventually settling in Paris, where she pursued a career as a writer. She has published many of her stories in *THE NEW YORKER*, earning high regard for her ironic, sensitively observed fiction, which frequently concerns dislocated characters, among them expatriates, isolated children, and Europeans struggling in the aftermath of World War II. Gallant's short-story collections include *The Other Paris* (1956), *My Heart Is Broken* (1964), *The Pegnitz Junction* (1973), *From the Fifteenth District* (1979), *Home Truths: Selected Canadian Stories* (1981), *In Transit* (1988), *Across the Bridge* (1993), *The Moslem Wife and Other Stories* (1996), and others. A compilation of her stories, selected by the author, was published as *The Collected Stories of Mavis Gallant* in 1996. Gallant has also published the novels *Green Water, Green Sky* (1959) and *A Fairly Good Time* (1970), and the acclaimed *Paris Notebooks: Essays & Reviews* (1986).

Galsworthy, John (August 14, 1867–January 31, 1933). English novelist, playwright, and essayist. Son of a respected solicitor, Galsworthy also studied law but practiced only briefly, turning instead to writing. After his first play, *The Silver Box* (1906), was produced, he developed a reputation for finely crafted dramas about middle-class hypocrisies and social injustice. In the same year, Galsworthy also published the novel *The Man of Property*, the first volume in a sequence of novels and stories that would become *THE FORSYTE SAGA*, chronicling the lives of an upper-middle-class Edwardian family. Acclaimed for its perceptive characterization and acutely observed social history, the series continued with "Indian Summer of a Forsyte" (1918), *In Chancery* (1920), "Awakening" (1920), and *To Let* (1921). Subsequent novels about the Forsytes, including *The White Monkey* (1924), *The Silver Spoon* (1926), and *Swan Song* (1928), comprise, with *The Forsyte Saga*, the larger entity known as *The Forsyte Chronicles*. Among Galsworthy's plays are *Strife* (1909), *Justice* (1910), and *The Skin Game* (1920). Galsworthy was awarded the Nobel Prize in Literature in 1932. He is also noted as the founder in 1921 of PEN, the organization of writers.

Gao Xingjian (January 4, 1940–). Chinese-French playwright, novelist, and critic, writing in Chinese and French. Awarded the Nobel Prize in Literature in 2000, Gao is a major experimental writer and a Chinese political dissident. Born in Eastern China, he studied French at the Beijing Foreign Languages Institute. With the advent of the Cultural Revolution, he was compelled to burn his early writings and was sent to a re-education camp. Permitted to publish in the 1980s, he issued controversial critical writings advocating modernism, and plays, such as *Bus Stop* (*Chezhan*, 1983), that were equally controversial. Gao moved to France in 1987 and became a French citizen. Since writing *Fugitives* (1989; original title unavailable), a play critical of the Tiananmen Square massacre, he has been prohibited from publishing in China. Gao's plays combine political observations with highly personal themes and draw from modern European playwrights such as BECKETT and ARTAUD as well as traditional Chinese theatrical forms. His best-known novel, *Soul Mountain* (*Lingshan*, 1990), is an autobiographical narrative about a journey through the Hunan countryside that reflects on complex issues related to love, storytelling, and Chinese society. *The Other Shore: Plays by Gao Xingjian* (1999) is a collection of five plays in English translation.

García Lorca, Federico (June 5, 1898–August 9, 1936). Spanish poet and playwright. One of the greatest 20th-century poets, García Lorca plumbed love and lust, life and death, and what he called "the dark root of the scream" with lyrical, surrealistic intensity. He wrote prolifically in a number of genres, while simultaneously pursuing his passions for theater and music as a producer, director, composer, and performer. Born in the village of Fuentevaqueros, near Granada, García Lorca was educated at the university there, and then at the University of Madrid, where he rarely attended lectures, instead immersing himself in modernist writers and striking up friendships with such gifted iconoclasts as Savador Dalí and Luis Buñuel, with both of whom he would eventually collaborate. In Madrid he began to gain fame as a modern-day troubadour whose knowledge of Spanish folksong was all-embracing. International acclaim came with his third book of poetry, *GYPSY BALLADS* (*Primer Romancero*

Gitano, 1928), which revitalized the traditional Spanish *romance* with startling metaphors, sensuous language, and heightened emotionality. He had already begun to write plays, scoring his first commercial success with *Mariana Pineda* (1927), a historical verse drama. García Lorca spent 1929–30 in New York City, a miserable sojourn that inspired the anguished poem sequence published posthumously as *The Poet in New York* (*Poeta en Nueva York*, 1940). The great plays of the so-called "Rural Trilogy"— BLOOD WEDDING (*Bodas de Sangre*, 1933), YERMA (1934), and THE HOUSE OF BERNARDA ALBA (*La Casa de Bernarda Alba*, completed 1936; first produced 1945)—are tragic studies of the destructiveness of repressive tradition and societal constraints. "LAMENT FOR THE DEATH OF A BULLFIGHTER" ("Llanto por Ignacio Sánchez Mejías," 1935), one of world literature's greatest elegies, was inspired by the death of a dear friend, a famous bullfighter who died in the ring. Although García Lorca was not political, he was a radical who always took the side of the oppressed in his work ("I damn all the people / Who ignore the other half... I spit in your face, I say"), and he made enemies. One early August morning, shortly after the start of the Spanish Civil War, he was dragged from a friend's house by thugs associated with the ultra-nationalist Acción Popular and was shot dead in the street. García Lorca's poetry has attracted many distinguished poet-translators, including Stephen SPENDER and LANGSTON HUGHES; a comprehensive three-volume English translation, with facing Spanish text, *The Poetical Works of Federico García Lorca*, appeared in 1988–95.

García Márquez, Gabriel (March 6, 1928–). Colombian novelist, short-story writer, and essayist. One of the most widely recognized writers in contemporary world literature, García Márquez emerged as a leading proponent of the Latin-American fictional style known as magic realism, which blends dreamlike fantasy with realistic narrative. García Márquez was raised in the Colombian coastal town of Aractaca and studied law and journalism at universities in Bogotá and Cartagena. He worked as a journalist in Latin America and Europe in the 1950s and began to publish fiction, gaining a world-wide reputation in 1967 with the publication of his novel ONE HUNDRED YEARS OF SOLITUDE (*Cien Años de Soledad*). Characteristic of his work, this teeming novel combines a historical saga of Colombian life with elements of myth and imaginative fantasy. Among his other novels are *The Autumn of the Patriarch* (*El Otoño del Patriarca*, 1975), *Chronicle of a Death Foretold* (*Crónica de una Muerte Anuncida*, 1981), LOVE IN THE TIME OF CHOLERA (*El Amor en los Tiempos del Cólera*, 1985), *The General in His Labyrinth* (*El General en Su Laberinto*, 1989), *Of Love and Other Demons* (*Del Amor y Otros Demonios*, 1994), and *News of a Kidnapping* (*Noticia de un Secuestro*, 1996). Short-story collections in English translation include *No One Writes to the Colonel, and Other Stories* (1968), *Leaf Storm, and Other Stories* (1972), *Innocent Eréndira, and Other Stories* (1978), and *Strange Pilgrims: Twelve Stories* (1993), as well as two *Collected Stories* (1984 and 1999). García Márquez was awarded the Nobel Prize in Literature in 1982.

Gardner, Erle Stanley (July 17, 1889–March 11, 1970). American novelist. Gardner, the creator of defense attorney Perry MASON, was one of the bestselling detective novelists in American publishing history. Born in Massachusetts, he began his professional life as a lawyer in California, writing in his spare time until the success of the Mason books allowed him to devote himself full time to fiction. Incredibly productive, he often needed only a few days to write an entire book. His best-known protagonists are Mason and Douglas Selby, a district attorney. Gardner's Perry Mason books include *The Case of the Velvet Claws* (1933), *The Case of the Perjured Parrot* (1939), and some 80 others; *The D.A. Calls It Murder* (1937) is the first of his Selby books. He also published under several pseudonyms, notably A. A. Fair. Gardner's own Paisano Productions produced the long-running television series (1957–66) featuring Raymond Burr as Perry Mason, which earned Gardner millions of dollars.

Gardner, John (July 21, 1933–September 14, 1982). American novelist and critic. Born in Pennsylvania and educated at Washington University in St. Louis and the University of Iowa, Gardner was a scholar of medieval literature who taught at a number of American colleges and universities, and a versatile and prolific writer. His third novel, *Grendel* (1971) — the BEOWULF legend told from the monster's point of view — gained him literary attention. Other significant novels are *The Sunlight Dialogues* (1972), *October Light* (1976; National Book Critics Circle Award), and *Mickellson's Ghost* (1982). In addition to novels, Gardner wrote short stories, children's fiction, poetry, opera libretti, commentaries on the craft of writing, and literary criticism. He also made translations of and even wrote Cliffs Notes for medieval classics. Believing that contemporary writers accentuated the negative and trumpeted despair, Gardner reproached them in *On Moral Fiction* (1978). Gardner was killed in a motorcycle accident; two more works of criticism, *On Becoming a Novelist* and *The Art of Fiction: Notes on Craft for Young Writers*, were published posthumously, in 1983 and 1984, respectively.

Garland, [Hannibal] Hamlin (September 14, 1860–March 4, 1940). American short-story writer, novelist, and memoirist. Garland's popular, realistic novels depicting Midwestern farm life made him one of the most important regional writers of his day. Garland was born in Wisconsin and helped his parents homestead farms there and in Iowa and South Dakota. After his education at the Cedar Valley Seminary in Iowa, he went to Boston, came under the influence of William Dean HOWELLS, and began teaching and writing bleak, often bitterly realistic tales of the hardships of rural life. Among his best-known books in this style are the story collection *Main-Travelled Roads* (1891) and the novel *Rose of Dutcher's Cooly* (1895). Influenced by the Populist movement, Garland also wrote novels with topical political themes and published several autobiographical works, including *A Son of the Middle Border*

(1917) and *A Daughter of the Middle Border* (1921), which won the Pulitzer Prize.

Garrett, João, *in full* João Baptista da Silva Leitão de Almeida, Viscount (Visconde) de Almeida Garrett (February 4, 1799–December 9, 1854). Portuguese playwright and poet. Garrett was a leader of the Romantic movement in his country and one of the greatest writers of the century there. A law graduate, Garrett had already written a few plays when he began an impassioned struggle for liberal democracy. In 1823 he was exiled for his liberal politics, first to England, then France, where he absorbed the sensibility of Romanticism. He returned to Portugal in 1832 and almost singlehandedly restored his country's theater tradition with a series of plays, including *Um Auto de Gil Vicente* (1838; A Short Play of Gil Vicente), *O Alfageme de Santerém* (1841; The Armorer of Santerém), and *Frei Luís de Sousa* (1843; Brother Luís de Sousa). Among his much-admired verse is the long poem *Camões* (1825) and the love poems in *Folhas Caídas* (1853; Fallen Leaves). He is also the author of a brilliant travel memoir, *Travels in My Homeland* (*Viagens na Minha Terra*, 1846).

Gaskell, Elizabeth Cleghorn, *original surname* Stevenson, *known as* **Mrs. Gaskell** (September 29, 1810–November 12, 1865). English novelist, short-story writer, and biographer. One of the most popular of all Victorian writers, Gaskell realistically examined women's roles and the social issues posed by industrialism in 19th-century England. Raised in Cheshire, she spent most of her life in Manchester with her husband, a Unitarian minister, with whom she raised four daughters. Her first novel, *Mary Barton* (1848), chronicles the struggles of a working-class family. *Cranford* (1853) draws on her childhood memories of small-town life in Cheshire. Other novels include *North and South* (1858), an examination of the cotton-mill industry, and the work that some regard as her best, the long, unfinished *Wives and Daughters* (1864–66). *The Life of Charlotte Brontë* (1857), a portrait of her friend, was the first biography of the writer.

Gass, William H[oward] (July 30, 1924–). American novelist and essayist. Gass, who spent most of his career as a professor of philosophy at Washington University in St. Louis, is noted for his compelling experiments with novelistic structure and his philosophical reflections on language and communication. His first novel, *Omensetter's Luck* (1966), blends different voices and perspectives in a fragmented, tenuous tale about good and evil in a 19th-century Midwestern town. *Willie Masters' Lonesome Wife* (1971) is a pastiche of fiction, nonfiction, photography, and experimental typography, and *The Tunnel* (1994), which presents the reflections of a historian, similarly combines disparate forms, genres, and media. Gass's collections of short fiction include *In the Heart of the Heart of the Country* (1968) and *Cartesian Sonata and Other Novellas* (1998). His critical writings on literature, art, and philosophy include *Fiction and the Figures of Life* (1970), *On Being Blue* (1975), *The World Within the Word* (1978), *Habitations of the Word* (1985), *Finding a Form: Essays* (1996), and *Reading Rilke: Reflections on the Problems of Translation* (1999).

Gautier, Théophile (August 31, 1811–October 23, 1872). French poet, novelist, journalist, and critic. A key participant in the Romantic movement in France and later a proponent of "art for art's sake," Gautier, in his poetic masterwork *Enamels and Cameos* (*Émaux et Camées*, 1852), introduced the process of "transposing art," or describing with precision his experience of art in poetry. As a popular journalist, he served as art critic for *La Presse* and wrote for such other magazines as *Le Moniteur Universel* and *La Revue de Paris*, using the byline "Le Bon Théo." His ideas greatly influenced the Parnassians and writers such as BAUDELAIRE, who dedicated *FLOWERS OF EVIL* to him. His works of criticism include *Les Beaux-Arts en Europe* (1855) and *Histoire de l'Art Dramatique en France depuis Vingt-cinq Ans* (1858–59; History of Drama in France for Twenty-five Years). Gautier's first full-length, and perhaps his best-known, novel is *Mademoiselle de Maupin* (*Mademoiselle de Maupin, Double Amour*, 1835); in the polemical preface to that once rather racy tale he broadly laid out his theories about "l'art pour l'art," asserting categorically that all useful things are ugly, that beauty must be "useless."

Genet, Jean (December 19, 1910–April 15, 1986). French novelist and playwright. Influenced by the existentialism of Jean-Paul SARTRE as well as by the erotic and violent works of the Marquis de SADE, Genet is renowned for his haunting novels of criminal life and his absurdist, avant-garde plays. An illegitimate child, Genet was abandoned by his mother at birth, and spent his childhood successively in an orphanage, a foster home, and a reformatory, running away from the latter to join the Foreign Legion, which he deserted. He then turned to a career as a drifter, thief, and male prostitute, writing his first novel, OUR LADY OF THE FLOWERS (Notre-Dame des Fleurs, 1943), in prison, where he was serving a life sentence. On its strength, several major French writers, among them Sartre and Jean COCTEAU (who called him the "Black Prince of Letters"), successfully campaigned for Genet's pardon and continued to support his writing after his release. The novels that followed, including *Miracle of the Rose* (*Miracle de la Rose*, 1946), offer tours—at once rapturous and shocking—of the criminal underground, mixing lyrical, mystical prose, graphic eroticism, and acute criticism of bourgeois values. Genet published the celebrated memoir *The Thief's Journal* (*Journal du Voleur*) in 1949 and then turned increasingly to drama. With challenging, self-conscious dramaturgy, his plays reflect on complex issues of identity, illusion, and the social dynamics of power. His plays, among them *The Maids* (*Les Bonnes*, 1947), THE BALCONY (*Le Balcon*, 1956), and *The Blacks* (*Les Nègres*, 1958), have greatly influenced later developments in the avant-garde theater.

Gibran, Kahlil, *original name* Jubrān Khalīl Jubrān (January 6, 1883–April 10, 1931). Lebanese-American poet, novelist, and essayist. Gibran's lyrical writings—including his perennially popular volume THE PROPHET (1923)—offer a blend of philosophy, religion, mysticism, and parable. Born in Lebanon, Gibran immigrated with his family to the United States in 1895. He returned to Beirut for his education, went to Paris to study art, and then returned to the United States, later settling in 1912 in New York City, where he spent the rest of his life. Gibran wrote in both English and Arabic, and was influenced by William BLAKE and the BIBLE. His other works include *The Madman* (1918), *The Broken Wings* (*Al-Ajniḥah al-Mutakassirah*, 1922), *The Procession* (*Al-Mawākib*, 1923), and *Jesus, the Son of Man* (1928).

Gibson, William (March 17, 1948–). American novelist and short-story writer. Following the publication of his groundbreaking first novel, *Neuromancer* (1984), Gibson emerged as a leader of the cyberpunk science-fiction movement and a prescient futurist who envisioned the direction of computer technology, corporate conglomerates, and the information revolution. Gibson was born in Conway, South Carolina, and studied literature at the University of British Columbia. He began his writing career by publishing science fiction in magazines such as *Omni*; many of his short works are collected in *Burning Chrome* (1986). *Neuromancer*, in which he introduced the term "cyberspace," is part of a trilogy that also includes *Count Zero* (1986) and *Mona Lisa Overdrive* (1988). Gibson's other novels include *Virtual Light* (1993), *Idoru* (1997), and *All Tomorrow's Parties* (1999).

Gide, André (November 22, 1869–February 19, 1951). French novelist, playwright, and essayist. The recipient of the Nobel Prize in Literature in 1947, Gide was a leading figure in French intellectual life during the first half of the 20th century. As he recalled in his autobiography *If It Die* (*Si le Grain ne Meurt*, 1926), he was raised in a strict Calvinist household and at an early age experienced conflict between traditional religious and moral conventions and his need for sensuality and moral independence. This internal conflict became the central concern of his writing. In the 1890s Gide took several trips to North Africa, where he witnessed a society with a radically different approach to sex and morality, acknowledged his own homosexuality, and began to publish a number of works, including *The Fruits of the Earth* (*Les Nourritures Terrestres*, 1897), a poetic prose work influenced by Symbolism. He attained major stature with THE IMMORALIST (*L'Immoraliste*, 1902), an autobiographical novel of rich psychological complexity. Gide's other novels include *Strait Is the Gate* (*La Porte Étroite*, 1909), LAFCADIO'S ADVENTURES (*Les Caves du Vatican*, 1914; also translated as *The Vatican Swindle*), *The Pastoral Symphony* (*La Symphonie Pastorale*, 1919), and THE COUNTERFEITERS (*Les Faux-Monnayeurs*, 1926). He cofounded the journal LA NOUVELLE REVUE FRANÇAISE in 1908, and his significant nonfiction works include the long essay *Corydon* (1924), a defense of homosexuality, and his inimitable journal, available, in a four-volume English translation overseen by Gide himself, as *The Journals of André Gide* (1947–51; repr. 2000 as *Journals*).

Gilbert, [Sir] **W**[illiam] **S**[chwenk] (November 18, 1836–May 29, 1911). English playwright and verse humorist. The literary half of the famed Gilbert and Sullivan duo and self-proclaimed "doggerel bard" made his name as a master of light verse and comic opera. Gilbert was born in London and educated at King's College there. He began his writing career in 1861, with a humorous verse series for *Fun* magazine, published under his childhood nickname, "Bab," and collected in several volumes, beginning with *The Bab Ballads: Much Sound and Little Sense* (1869). In 1866, when he was asked to turn out a quick Christmas play, he made his entrée into the world of theater: less than two weeks later, *Dulcamara*, his first production, was on the boards. In 1870, Gilbert met composer Arthur Seymour Sullivan, and began the 20-year partnership that resulted in a string of classic comic operas, the best known of which were originally staged by Richard D'Oyly Carte at the Savoy Theatre; these include *H.M.S. Pinafore* (1878), *The Pirates of Penzance* (1879), *Iolanthe* (1882), *Princess Ida* (1884), *The Mikado* (1884), and *The Yeoman of the Guard* (1888), among others. *Plays and Poems of W. S. Gilbert* (1932) includes the complete text of 14 operettas, three additional plays, and all of the "Bab" ballads.

Gilman, Charlotte Perkins (July 3, 1860–August 17, 1935). American novelist, short-story writer, essayist, journalist, and poet. A leading figure in the women's movement at the turn of the 20th century, Gilman boldly challenged conventional gender roles in her fiction and nonfiction. Born to a prominent family in Hartford, Connecticut (her relatives included the Congregationalist minister Lyman Beecher and the writer Harriet Beecher STOWE), she suffered a difficult childhood and an unhappy first marriage. Stifled by domestic life and suffering from a severe bout of depression, she divorced her husband, gave him custody of their daughter, and moved to California. Among her most important writings are the story "THE YELLOW WALLPAPER" (1892), the feminist classic *Women and Economics* (1898), and the utopian novel *Herland* (1915). In 1935 she committed suicide to avoid an extended battle with breast cancer. Her autobiography, *The Living of Charlotte Perkins Gilman*, was published that year.

Ginsberg, Allen (June 3, 1926–April 5, 1997). American poet. A guiding light of the Beat movement, Ginsberg was raised in working-class Paterson, New Jersey, the son of a poet-teacher father and a mother who was active in left-wing causes and suffered from severe mental illness. After graduating from Columbia University in 1948, Ginsberg began to work at odd jobs and write poetry in New York and San Francisco. He and fellow Beat writers William S. BURROUGHS and Jack KEROUAC became notorious for opposing conformist 1950s American society both in their compelling, free-form writings and in their bohemian lifestyles. After weathering an obscenity trial, Ginsberg's epic poem HOWL (1956) became an anthem for countercultural rebellion. Ginsberg's poetry, which draws from the traditions of Walt WHITMAN and WILLIAM CARLOS WILLIAMS, is both deeply personal and socially and politically engaged, expansive in form, prophetic in tone, and replete with American vernacular imagery. His later poems increasingly reveal his interest in Zen Buddhism. Ginsberg's major collections include *KADDISH and Other Poems* (1961), which features the moving and anguished title poem, an elegy to his mother; *Reality Sandwiches* (1966); *The Fall of America* (1973); *Collected Poems 1947–1980* (1984); and *Cosmopolitan Greetings: Poems, 1986–1992* (1993).

Ginzburg, Natalia, *original name* Natalia Levi (July 14, 1916–October 7, 1991). Italian novelist, playwright, and essayist. One of Italy's most acclaimed post–World War II writers, Ginzburg was born in Palermo and raised in Turin. The daughter of a Jewish father and a Catholic mother, she grew up in an intellectual, agnostic household. Her first husband, anti-Fascist activist Leone Ginzburg, died in a Nazi prison in 1944, and she wrote her first novella, *The Road to the City* (*La Strada Che Va in Città*, 1942), while confined to a ghetto by the Fascists. Several of Ginzburg's novels, including *All Our Yesterdays* (*Tutti i Nostri Ieri*, 1952; also translated under the titles *Light for Fools* and *Dead Yesterdays*) and *Voices in the Evening* (*Le Voci della Sera*, 1961), concern life during World War II. Her fiction, often autobiographical, focuses on the subtleties of intimate relationships in a spare, understated, deceptively simple style. Among her works are the novels *Family Sayings* (*Lessico Famigliare*, 1963; also translated under the title *The Things We Used to Say*) and *The City and the House* (*La Città e la Casa*, 1985); the essay collections *The Little Virtues* (*Le Piccole Virtú*, 1962) and *Never Must You Ask Me* (*Mai Devi Domandarmi*, 1970); several plays; and an acclaimed biography of Alessandro MANZONI.

Giovanni, Nikki, *original name* Yolande Cornelia Giovanni, Jr. (June 7, 1943–). American poet. Born in Tennessee, Giovanni was educated at Fisk and Columbia universities. She came of age at the height of the civil rights movement and became one of the leading poets of the movement's Black Power wing. Noted for poems employing intricate rhythms and imagery drawn from African-American vernacular culture, Giovanni expressed militant black

messages in her early books of poetry, *Black Feeling, Black Talk* (1968), *Black Judgment* (1968), and *Re:Creation* (1970). Her later poems focus on the concerns of daily life, including families and relationships. Other works include *My House* (1972), *The Women and the Men* (1975), *Those Who Ride the Night Wind* (1983), *Love Poems* (1997), and *Blues: For All the Changes* (1999). Giovanni has also taught at several universities, including Virginia Polytechnic Institute.

Giraudoux, [Hippolyte-]**Jean** (October 29, 1882–January 31, 1944). French novelist and playwright. Born in the provincial French town of Bellac, Giraudoux served for 30 years in France's diplomatic corps while building a literary reputation, first for poetic novels such as *Suzanne and the Pacific* (*Suzanne et le Pacifique*, 1922), and then for distinguished dramas. Giraudoux's plays, which range from *Siegfried* (1928) to *The Madwoman of Chaillot* (*La Folle de Chaillot*; produced posthumously 1945), feature elements of magical fantasy and a witty and graceful prose style, as they explore themes of love, war, and death. His plays frequently revisit classical stories, as in *Tiger at the Gates* (*La Guerre de Troie n'aura pas Lieu*, 1935; literally, "The Trojan War Will Not Take Place") and *Electra* (*Électre*, 1937); biblical tales, as in *Judith* (1931); and folk legends, as in *Ondine* (1939). Giraudoux's play *Intermezzo* (1933) tells the story of a woman who must choose for a mate either a ghost, who can impart the secrets of the dead, or a living man, who promises to reveal the beauty of everyday life.

Gissing, George (November 22, 1857–December 28, 1903). English novelist. Gissing's uncompromisingly realistic novels focus on poverty, social injustice, and the plight of women. Born in Yorkshire, Gissing was a brilliant classics student at Owens College in Manchester, but his personal life was a disaster. He was expelled from college for stealing, married a young woman reputed to be a prostitute, and lived in poverty; a second marriage was equally unhappy. He drew from his own life in his best-known work, the three-volume novel *New Grub*

Street (1891), and in *The Private Papers of Henry Ryecroft* (1903). Highly productive, Gissing published a new work (and sometimes two or three) nearly every year. Among these are *Workers in the Dawn* (1880), his first novel; *Born into Exile* (1892); and *The Odd Women* (1893). He also wrote a well-regarded critical study of Charles DICKENS.

Glasgow, Ellen (April 22, 1873–November 21, 1945). American novelist. Born into a wealthy Virginia family, Glasgow lived the life of privilege that she depicts in her novels. Considered by many to have initiated a renaissance in Southern fiction, Glasgow revised romanticized notions of the genteel Old South through the realistic and acute insights she called "blood and irony." In novels such as *The Romantic Comedians* (1926), *They Stooped to Folly* (1929), and *The Sheltered Life* (1932), she used wit and satire to critique the relationships between Virginian men and women. Other novels are remarkable for their depiction of independent, persevering women; among these are *Barren Ground* (1925) and *Vein of Iron* (1935). Her posthumously published autobiography, *The Woman Within* (1954), chronicles her life and development as a writer. Glasgow received the Pulitzer Prize for the novel *In This Our Life* (1941).

Glissant, Édouard (September 21, 1928–). Martinican poet, novelist, essayist, and critic. Glissant draws upon Creole and formal French influences to examine history and identity in a hybrid Caribbean culture. Born on the island of Martinique and educated in France, Glissant was active in the Négritude movement founded by Aimé CÉSAIRE and others, which sought to foster a pure expression of black experience free of colonial influences. In poetry collections such as *The Indies* (*Les Indes*, 1956), Glissant celebrates the victories of blacks over their colonial masters. His novels include *The Ripening* (*La Lézarde*, 1958) and *The Fourth Century* (*Le Quatrième Siècle*, 1962). His essays and critical writings can be found in *Caribbean Discourse* (*Le Discours Antillais*, 1981), *Poetics of Relation* (*Poétique de la Relation*, 1990), and *Faulkner,*

Mississippi (1996), a study of William FAULKNER.

Goethe, Johann Wolfgang von (August 28, 1749–March 27, 1832). German poet, novelist, and playwright. A towering figure in German and world literature, Goethe first became prominent as a leading writer of the *Sturm und Drang* (Storm and Stress) movement, which initiated German Romanticism. His closet drama *Götz von Berlichingen* (1773), about political conflict in the Middle Ages, and his sensationally popular novel THE SORROWS OF YOUNG WERTHER (*Die Leiden des Jungen Werthers*, 1774), about the frustrations of a sensitive hero, were major works of the movement, which rejected Enlightenment rationalism in favor of emotional passion and open form. In 1775, Goethe moved from his native Frankfurt to the duchy of Weimar, which was becoming Germany's cultural capital at this time, and then served as a government official for the duke for ten years. In 1786, he made an important trip to Italy, where he absorbed classical influences and developed a more objective approach in his writing. Upon his return to Weimar, he developed a mutually influential friendship with the poet and playwright Friedrich von SCHILLER, who similarly bridged classical, Enlightenment, and Romantic themes. Goethe's mature works include lyric poems; the epic poem *Hermann und Dorothea* (1798); the first major Bildungsroman, WILHELM MEISTER'S APPRENTICESHIP (*Wilhelm Meisters Lehrjahre*, 1795–96); and the dramas *Egmont* (1788) and *Torquato Tasso* (1790), about the life of the Italian Renaissance poet. His greatest achievement, the drama FAUST (Part I, 1808; Part II, 1832), expands the legend of a scholar who promises his soul to the devil in return for knowledge and experience; Goethe's richly layered version explores complex themes of desire, ambition, reason, and sensation. Goethe's other works include treatises on botany and physiology and the autobiography *Poetry and Truth* (*Dichtung und Wahrheit*, 1811–33).

Gogol, Nikolai (March 31, 1809–March 4, 1852). Russian novelist, short-story writer, and playwright. A seminal Russian writer of the 19th century, Gogol wrote of his society with biting satire and sharp-edged realism in an imaginative prose style. Born in Ukraine, Gogol moved to the Russian capital, St. Petersburg, in 1828, where he tried his hand at civil service and teaching while beginning to write. Two collections of his short stories—*Mirgorod* and *Arabesques* (*Arabeski*), which include "TARAS BULBA" ("Taras Bul′ba"), a fierce tale about the Cossacks, and "DIARY OF A MADMAN" ("Zapiski Sumasshedshego"), an account of a civil servant's descent into insanity—appeared in 1835. Gogol turned to drama with THE INSPECTOR GENERAL (*Revizor*, 1836; also translated as *The Government Inspector*), an acid satire of greed and corruption in a provincial town. Following its production, Gogol traveled through Europe, living mostly in Rome, where he wrote his best-known work, the novel DEAD SOULS (*Mertvye Dushi*, 1842). With sly humor, it tells the story of a silver-tongued rogue who schemes to purchase dead serfs whose papers he can turn to profit, a sardonic commentary on Russian feudal society. At this time Gogol also published the classic story "THE OVERCOAT" ("Shinel′," 1842), a fable about a meek government clerk beset by a hostile society. In 1847 he published a didactic work asserting conservative political ideals, for which he was roundly criticized by the liberal intelligentsia, inspiring, for example, the eminent critic Vissarion BELINSKY's famous rebuttal in his "Letter to Gogol" (1847). Beginning in the mid-1840s, Gogol began to experience profound bouts of anxiety and depression and became increasingly preoccupied with thoughts of sin and damnation. After a trip to the Holy Land in 1848, he returned to Russia, settling in Moscow, where he eventually fell under the sway of a fanatical priest who ordered him to destroy the manuscript, apparently complete, of the second part of *Dead Souls* to atone for the sin of having written the first part. Although Gogol had been laboring on the second part for seven years, on February 24, 1852, in a fit of religious mania, he consigned the manuscript to the flames; nine days later he was dead, having refused any food since the conflagration. All that remains of the second part of *Dead Souls* are fragments of a handful of chapters, apparently from an earlier draft of the novel.

Golding, [Sir] William (September 19, 1911–June 19, 1993). English novelist. An Oxford graduate, Golding worked in a London theater during his youth, served in the Navy in World War II, and was for many years a school headmaster. He published his first book, LORD OF THE FLIES (1954), in his early 40s, and the novel immediately established his literary reputation. Conceived as an attack on the notion of innate human goodness, the novel depicts a group of English schoolboys who are marooned on a deserted island, and who eventually degenerate into savage war bands. Golding's next novel, *The Inheritors* (1955), portrays the fatal encounter between a peaceful tribe of eight Neanderthals (the last surviving members of their race) and an ascendant, violent race with weapon-making skills, whose descendants would name their species Homo sapiens. Golding continued to craft allegories about the brutal nature of man in novels such as *Free Fall* (1959), *The Spire* (1964), *Darkness Visible* (1979), *Rites of Passage* (1980; Booker Prize), and *Close Quarters* (1987). He was awarded the Nobel Prize in Literature in 1983.

Goldoni, Carlo (February 25, 1707–February 6, 1793). Italian playwright and librettist. A native of Venice, Goldoni practiced law until 1747, when he abandoned that career for the theater. From 1748 to 1762, he worked for the Teatro Sant'Angelo and the Teatro San Luca in Venice. As a playwright, he began in the conventional commedia dell'arte style, but soon revolutionized Italian theater by abandoning the use of masks, writing more completely conceived characters, and emphasizing written texts over improvisation. These innovations and Goldoni's ironic treatment of contemporary society have earned him recognition as the founder of modern Italian comedy. Admiring the tradition of MOLIÈRE, Goldoni left Italy in

1762 for France, where he directed the Comédie-Italienne and wrote plays in French. His last years were spent teaching Italian at Versailles and composing his acclaimed *Mémoires* (1787). Goldoni wrote more than 150 plays and opera libretti, including *The Mistress of the Inn* (*La Locandiera*, 1753; also translated under the title *Mine Hostess*), *The Boors* (*I Rusteghi*, 1760), *The Squabbles of Chiaggio* (*Le Baruffe Chiozzote*, 1762), and *The Fan* (*Il Ventaglio*, 1764).

Goldsmith, Oliver (November 10, 1730–April 4, 1774). Irish-born English novelist, playwright, poet, and essayist. The son of an Anglican minister who had immigrated to Ireland, Goldsmith was educated at Trinity College in Dublin. He briefly studied medicine in Edinburgh (later he would claim to be an M.D.), before ultimately settling in London, where he wrote stories and essays for periodicals. He was befriended by SAMUEL JOHNSON and became known in literary circles as an eccentric wit. Notorious for his improvidence, Goldsmith was forced to take on hack work until his novel THE VICAR OF WAKEFIELD (1766), a humorous story about English country life, made him famous. The novel's slyly ironic characterizations and regional flavor were greatly esteemed by 19th-century novelists, and Goldsmith's popular, long pastoral poem *The Deserted Village* (1770), contributed to Romantic interest in the genre. Goldsmith is also noted for his comic dramas *The Good Natur'd Man* (1768) and SHE STOOPS TO CONQUER (1773), satires on contemporary English manners, and the essays in *The Citizen of the World; or, Letters from a Chinese Philosopher, Residing in London, to His Friends in the East* (1762).

Goncharov, Ivan (June 18, 1812–September 27, 1891). Russian novelist. Goncharov made his name as the author of OBLOMOV, a masterpiece of Russian realism. The son of a wealthy merchant in Simbirsk, Goncharov was educated at Moscow University and made a smooth transition into a secure career in the Russian state bureaucracy, rising through the Ministry of Finance to the Admiralty. While his first novel,

A Common Story (*Obyknovennaya Istoriya*, 1847), won critical recognition, his next novel, *Oblomov* (1859), the story of a wealthy and self-satisfied provincial family, whose eponymous hero spends his days lying on the couch, mired in mental and physical sloth, was a popular success and created a huge stir of self-recognition among Russians. As one critic put it, "Something of OBLOMOV is to be found in every one of us." Goncharov also wrote a travelogue, *The Frigate "Pallada"* (*Fregat Pallada*, 1858) and another novel, *The Precipice* (*Obryv*, 1869).

Gopaleen, Myles na. *See* O'Brien, Flann

Gordimer, Nadine (November 20, 1923–). South African novelist and short-story writer. For her profound fictional examinations of the consequences of apartheid, Gordimer was awarded the Nobel Prize in Literature in 1991. Born to an English mother and a Lithuanian father in Springs, Transvaal, near Johannesburg, Gordimer took up writing at an early age and began publishing her stories as a teenager. Coming into adulthood in the early years of apartheid, Gordimer felt obliged to confront its effects on her homeland. She became a strong critic of the ruling party and used her fiction to explore how people compromise their ideals in order to find a place in society. Many of her stories have appeared in THE NEW YORKER, and have been collected in *The Soft Voice of the Serpent* (1952), *Selected Stories* (1975), and *Jump and Other Stories* (1991). Among her novels are *A Guest of Honour* (1970), *The Conservationist* (1974; Booker Prize), BURGER'S DAUGHTER (1979), *July's People* (1981), *A Sport of Nature* (1987), *My Son's Story* (1990), *None to Accompany Me* (1994), and *The House Gun* (1998).

Gorky, Maxim or **Maksim**, *pen name of* Aleksey Maksimovich Peshkov (March 28, 1868–June 14, 1936). Russian novelist, playwright, and short-story writer. Born into a poor family, Gorky began working while still a young boy. After years of vagabond living, his story "Chelkash" (1895) was published in a St. Petersburg journal, winning the admiration of Anton CHEKHOV, among others, and, along with his first two collections, both published in 1898, bringing him renown. His 1902 play THE LOWER DEPTHS (*Na Dne*), one of his best-known works, reflects an increasingly angry outlook about people at the bottom of society. Gorky took part in the 1905 revolution against the tsar, then spent seven years in political exile in Capri. He returned in time to agitate against Russia's entry into World War I, but a falling-out with the Communist leader V.I. Lenin, coupled with health problems, led to another period of exile in Italy. He finally returned permanently to the Soviet Union and became president of the Union of Soviet Writers. Gorky's esteemed autobiographical trilogy includes *My Childhood* (*Detstvo*, 1913–14), *In the World* (*V Lyudyakh*, 1915–16), and *My Universities* (*Moi Universitety*, 1923). Other works include his first novel, *Foma Gordeev* (1899), his revolutionary novel *Mother* (*Mat'*, 1906), and his highly regarded *Reminiscences of Leo Nikolaevich Tolstoy* (*Vospominaniya o L've Nikolaeviche Tolstom*, 1919).

Goytisolo, Juan (January 5, 1931–). Spanish novelist, short-story writer, and essayist. Hailed by Carlos FUENTES as "undoubtedly, the greatest living Spanish novelist," Goytisolo was born in Barcelona and educated at universities there and in Madrid. His first novel, *The Young Assassins* (*Juegos de Manos*, 1954), was highly praised, but, as his autobiography *Forbidden Territory* (*Coto Vedado*, 1985) reveals, he was deeply alienated by the repressive atmosphere of Franco's Spain. In the mid-1950s, he moved to Paris, where his life and writing changed radically, as he rejected the social realism of his first books and eventually learned to accept his homosexuality. Goytisolo divides his time between Paris and Morocco, and the relations between Islam and the West and modern Spain's suppressed Moorish roots are among his frequent subjects. He first notably experimented with language and narrative form in the trilogy *Marks of Identity* (*Senas de Identidad*, 1966), *Count Julian* (*Reivindicación del Conde don Julián*, 1970), for many his masterpiece, and *Juan the Landless* (*Juan sin Tierra*, 1975), novels excoriating what he saw as the wasteland of Spanish culture and celebrating the author's identification with society's "deviants." His writ-

ing has since become still more experimental, even "flamboyantly eccentric," as *The New York Times* said of *Landscapes After the Battle* (*Paisajes Después de la Batalla*, 1982), in which Goytisolo turned his alienated, scorching vision to contemporary Paris. More recent works appearing in English translation include a second volume of autobiography, *Realms of Strife* (*En los Reinos de Taifa*, 1986), a collection of literary essays, *Saracen Chronicles* (1992), and the novels *Quarantine* (*La Cuarentena*, 1991), a surrealistic journey to the "frontiers between reality and dream"; *The Marx Family Saga* (*La Saga de los Marx*, 1993), in which a resurrected Karl Marx investigates the New World Order; and *The Garden of Secrets* (*Semanas del Jardín*, 1997), in which 28 storytellers recount the life of Eusebio, a homosexual dissident poet who was a contemporary of Federico GARCÍA LORCA. The essays collected in *Landscapes of War* (2000), which originated in Goytisolo's travels in the late 1990s, mix historical analysis and first-person reportage of life in four warzones: Sarajevo, Algeria, the West Bank and Gaza, and Chechnya.

Grass, Günter (October 16, 1927–). German novelist, poet, and playwright. Grass has described himself as a "Spätaufklärer," a belated apostle of enlightenment in an era that has grown tired of reason. He established his reputation with his extraordinary allegorical novel, THE TIN DRUM (1959), and in 1999, for his "frolicsome black fables [that] portray the forgotten face of history," he was awarded the Nobel Prize in Literature. In its citation, the Nobel Prize committee wrote, "When Günter Grass published *The Tin Drum* in 1959 it was as if German literature had been granted a new beginning after decades of linguistic and moral destruction." Born in Danzig (now Gdansk), Grass was wounded while serving in World War II and taken prisoner of war. After the war he began writing poetry and plays chronicling the experiences of the generation that came of age during the Third Reich. *The Tin Drum* (*Die Blechtrommel*, 1959), an immediate international success, was the first in a trilogy of novels set in Danzig, which also includes *Cat and*

Mouse (*Katz und Maus*, 1961) and *Dog Years* (*Hundejahre*, 1963). Grass's more overtly political later works include *The Flounder* (*Der Butt*, 1977), *The Call of the Toad* (*Unkenrufe*, 1992), *A Broad Field* (*Ein Weites Feld*, 1995), and *My Century* (*Mein Jahrhundert*, 1999).

Graves, Robert (July 24/26, 1895–December 7, 1985). English poet, novelist, and critic. For his lucid verse meditations on nature, love, and myth, Graves has been called "the last English Romantic," but his historical fiction and unorthodox nonfiction have been equally influential. Born in Wimbledon and educated at Oxford, Graves volunteered in the Royal Welsh Fusiliers at the outbreak of World War I. He wrote about his early years and war experiences in *Good-Bye to All That* (1929), one of the liveliest and most scathing memoirs of its time. After the war Graves began a close association with the poet Laura Riding and moved to the island of Majorca, where he eventually settled. Graves professed to worship a muse he called "the White Goddess," and published his theories on the subject in *The White Goddess* (1948). His *Collected Poems* have appeared in several editions, most recently in 1975; the *Complete Poems*, edited by Beryl Graves and Dunstan Ward, appeared in three volumes (1995–2000). Graves also published a number of acclaimed historical novels, including *I, CLAUDIUS* and *Claudius the God* (both 1934); critical works such as *A Survey of Modernist Poetry* (1927); translations from the classics; and scholarly writings on mythology and religion.

Gray, Thomas (December 26, 1716–July 30, 1771). English poet. Educated at Cambridge University, Gray lived, studied, and worked in the town of Cambridge for most of his life. He achieved widespread fame with "AN ELEGY WRITTEN IN A COUNTRY CHURCHYARD" (1751), a poem inspired by the death of his friend Richard West, which remains one of the best-known 18th-century English verse works. Gray's melancholy, introspective tone and his concern with nature prefigured Romantic poetry, although WORDSWORTH would later quarrel with Gray's elevated language; Gray dismissed this,

writing that "the language of the age is never the language of poetry." In his last years, Gray taught history at Cambridge and studied Old Welsh and Norse verse, drawing from these traditions in poems such as "The Descent of Odin" (1761). Other notable poems include "Ode on a Distant Prospect of Eton College" (1742), "The Bard" (1757), and "The Progress of Poesy" (1757).

Green, Henry, *pen name of* Henry Vincent Yorke (October 29, 1905–December 13, 1973). English novelist. Sometimes called "a writer's writer," Green has attracted wider recognition in recent years for his subtle, eccentric modernist novels about the English upper and lower classes. Born to an aristocratic mother and a wealthy industrialist father, he was educated at Eton and published his first novel, *Blindness* (1926), while still a student at Oxford. For most of his life, he led a dual existence as an executive at his family's manufacturing company (where he began as a foundry laborer) and as a pseudonymous novelist. His narratives are marked by an extraordinarily attentive rendering of speech, especially dialects and inflections, and some of his novels are written almost entirely in dialogue. The novels *Party Going* (1939) and *Loving* (1945) and the memoir *Pack My Bag: A Self-Portrait* (1940) are usually considered his finest achievements. His other novels include *Living* (1929), *Caught* (1943), *Concluding* (1948), *Nothing* (1950), and *Doting* (1952).

Greene, [Henry] **Graham** (October 2, 1904–April 3, 1991). English novelist, short-story writer, journalist, playwright, and screenwriter. By imbuing his suspenseful, entertaining novels with an unusual moral and intellectual depth, Greene became—over the course of a long and prolific career—one of the most popular and acclaimed English writers of the 20th century. Greene was born in Berkhamsted, near London, and educated at Oxford. In 1926 he converted to Roman Catholicism, an influence in many of his works, and embarked on a career in journalism. His early novels, such as *Stamboul Train* (1932, also called *Orient Express*), were conventional suspense stories—"entertainments," Greene called them. But by the late 1930s, he had begun publishing the weightier works for which he is best known, many of which carry religious themes. These include BRIGHTON ROCK (1938), THE POWER AND THE GLORY (1940), THE HEART OF THE MATTER (1948), and THE END OF THE AFFAIR (1951). Greene traveled widely as a journalist, and set many of his novels in far-flung locales, often against backdrops of political unrest. Among these are OUR MAN IN HAVANA (1958), a spy novel set in Cuba, and A BURNT-OUT CASE (1961), set in a Congolese leper colony.

" ... every creative writer worth our consideration, every writer who can be called in the wise use of the term a poet, is a victim: a man given over to an obsession."

Graham Greene, quoted by Philip Rahv in his introduction to *Selected Short Stories of Franz Kafka* (1952)

Greene's vast and varied output also includes dramas, screenplays, stories, essays, literary and film criticism, travel writings, and two volumes of memoir. Most of his novels have been adapted for the screen.

Gregory, Lady [Isabella] **Augusta,** *original surname* Persse, known as **Lady Gregory** (March 5, 1852–May 22, 1932). Irish playwright and translator. Through her writings and her affiliations with W. B. YEATS and the renowned Abbey Theatre, Lady Gregory played a vital role in the late 19th-century Irish Literary Renaissance. Born to a wealthy landowner in County Galway and married to a member of Parliament, she did not begin writing until the second half of her life, after her husband's death. In the late 1890s she met Yeats, and with him and J. M. SYNGE she founded the Irish Literary Theatre, which evolved into the Abbey Theatre, where she also served as a director. Lady Gregory's forte was the one-act comedy; her most popular plays include *Spreading the News* (1904), *The Rising*

of the Moon (1907), and *The Workhouse Ward* (1908). Her compilations and translations of Irish folklore can be found in *Poets and Dreamers* (1903), *Gods and Fighting Men* (1904), *A Book of Saints and Wonders* (1906), and *Beliefs in the West of Ireland* (1920).

Grey, [Pearl] **Zane** (January 31, 1872–October 23, 1939). American novelist. Grey is chiefly known as one of the earliest writers of the western. Born in Zanesville, Ohio, and educated at the University of Pennsylvania, Grey began his professional life as a dentist in New York, but decided in 1904 to turn his attention to writing. He published *The Last of the Plainsmen* in 1908, but his big break came with *Riders of the Purple Sage* (1912), one of the most famous novels of the American West. *Riders* initiated a string of bestsellers, including *Desert Gold* (1913), *The Mysterious Rider* (1921), and *Code of the West* (1934). Grey also wrote several nonfiction books about the outdoors, including *Tales of Fishing* (1925).

Guare, John (February 5, 1938–). American playwright. Guare's popular black comedies explore family relationships and society's obsession with celebrity and success. Guare was born in New York City and educated at Georgetown and the Yale School of Drama. He scored an early success with his Obie Award–winning one-act, *Muzeeka* (1968). This was followed by *The House of Blue Leaves* (1971), an award-winning farce about a failed songwriter who murders his wife. His best-known play is *Six Degrees of Separation* (1990), the story of a young black hustler who wheedles his way into the lives of a wealthy white couple. Among Guare's other works are *Rich and Famous* (1976), *Landscape of the Body* (1977), *Bosoms and Neglect* (1979), *Lydie Breeze* (1982), *Four Baboons Adoring the Sun* (1992), and *Chaucer in Rome* (2001), as well as several screenplays, among them *Atlantic City* (1981). Guare also cowrote (with Mel Shapiro) the book and lyrics for Galt MacDermot's 1971 rock musical adaptation of SHAKESPEARE'S TWO GENTLEMEN OF VERONA.

Ḥāfiz or **Ḥāfez,** *in full* Moḥammad Shams od-Dīn Ḥāfeẓ (c. 1327–c. 1389). Persian poet. A member of the ecstatic Sūfī sect of Islam, Ḥāfiz is renowned for his lyric poetry, which reflects on the transitory nature of life and the divine found within the earthly. He was given the honorary title "Ḥāfiz" after his death; the title, meaning "one who remembers," was customarily given to those who knew the KORAN by heart. Ḥāfiz's poems combine Sūfī mysticism with a celebration of sensual life. Many of them are frankly erotic, as in "Thy rosy limbs, unless I may embrace, / Lose for my longing eyes full half their grace, / Nor does the scarlet mouth with honey drip / Unless I taste its honey lip to lip." The eroticism of Ḥāfiz's poetry has often been interpreted as having a double meaning, extolling both a particular woman and the god or goddess that lies within the individual.

Haggard, [Sir] H[enry] Rider, (June 22, 1856–May 14, 1925). English novelist. Born in Norfolk, Haggard was an indifferent student. At age 19, he went to South Africa to work for the British commissioner for the Transvaal, staying until 1881. After returning to England he incorporated his experiences in Africa into a series of romantic and often fantastic tales drawing on ancient myths and legends. The best known of these are the adventure novels *King Solomon's Mines* (1885), based on folk tales about an ancient city in Zimbabwe, and *SHE* (1887), about two explorers who search for Ayesha, or "She-Who-Must-Be-Obeyed," the white queen of a lost African city. Haggard's other stories of Africa include *Allan Quatermain* (1887), *Queen Sheba's Ring* (1910), and *The Ivory Child* (1916). After gaining literary success, Haggard moved to an estate in the English countryside and wrote agricultural studies, including the influential *Rural England* (1902).

Haley, Alex (August 11, 1921–February 10, 1992). American journalist, novelist, and biographer. Haley came relatively late to writing, after serving in the Coast Guard for 20 years. After contributing articles and interviews to such magazines as *Playboy*, he wrote his first book, *The Autobiography of Malcolm X* (1965), in collaboration with the black Muslim leader,

a work now considered a classic of African-American autobiography. Haley then turned to his own family, tracing his ancestors' journey from Africa to America, from freedom to slavery to emancipation, in the bestselling *ROOTS: THE SAGA OF AN AMERICAN FAMILY* (1976; special Pulitzer Prize). Although *Roots* was subsequently criticized for some factual inaccuracies, the book, and the phenomenally successful 1977 television miniseries based on it, spiked popular interest in African-American history. Haley's later books include the novella *A Different Kind of Christmas* (1988); the memoir *Henning, Tennessee* (1989), and the posthumously published *Alex Haley's Queen: The Story of an American Family* (1993), completed by David Stevens after Haley's death.

Hall, Donald (September 20, 1928–). American poet. Born in New Haven, Connecticut and educated at Harvard and Oxford, Hall taught poetry at the University of Michigan and, from 1953 to 1962, served as poetry editor of *THE PARIS REVIEW*. He won praise for his first volume, *Exiles and Marriages* (1955), a collection of finely crafted poems that are traditional in form. His subsequent poetry, more open in form, eloquently treats themes of mortality, spirituality, and nature. Among his collections are *A Roof of Tiger Lilies* (1964), *The Alligator Bride* (1969), *Kicking the Leaves* (1978), *The Twelve Seasons* (1983), *Old and New Poems* (1990), and *Without* (1998). He has also published literary criticism, including *Marianne Moore* (1970); *Henry Moore* (1966), a biography of the sculptor; and *Life Work* (1993), a memoir about his struggles with cancer.

Hammett, [Samuel] Dashiell (May 27, 1894–January 10, 1961). American novelist. Born in Maryland and raised in Philadelphia and Baltimore, Hammett quit school at age 14 and began working at a succession of blue-collar jobs. After stints as a messenger boy, clerk, railroad yardman, and machine operator, he took a job in San Francisco with the Pinkerton Detective Agency, the largest private investigation company in the United States. During his spare time, Hammett began writing stories about detectives and virtually invented the "hard-boiled" detective style. With the success of *Red Harvest* (1929), *The Dain Curse* (1929), and THE MALTESE FALCON (1930), Hammett turned to writing full time and began working in Hollywood as a scriptwriter. His final novel, THE THIN MAN (1934), was adapted into a successful film. Hammett wrote no fiction thereafter; his later publications were anthologies of stories written before 1934. The only screenplay for which he received credit was the 1943 adaptation of Lillian HELLMAN's play *Watch on the Rhine*. Along with Hellman, his lover, Hammett resisted the McCarthy-era purges of Hollywood, for which he served a six-month jail sentence.

Hamsun, Knut, *pen name of* Knut Pederson Hamsund (August 4, 1859–February 19, 1952). Norwegian novelist and poet. One of Norway's finest novelists, Hamsun grew up in poverty on a farm in an austere northern region of the country. He held a series of odd jobs and twice traveled to the United States, where he worked as a streetcar conductor in Chicago and a farmer in North Dakota. Hamsun achieved prominence with the publication of *HUNGER* (*Sult*, 1899), a stream-of-consciousness novel about an impoverished writer. An immediate success in Norway, *Hunger* expressed Hamsun's profound mistrust of modern, industrialized society, as did *Mysteries* (*Mysterier*, 1892) and *Pan* (1894). *Growth of the Soil* (*Markens Grøde*, 1917) reflects his longing for a return to agrarian life. Hamsun was awarded the Nobel Prize in Literature in 1920, but subsequently became a controversial figure for his support of the Nazis and the Nazi puppet government in Norway during World War II.

Handke, Peter (December 6, 1942–). Austrian novelist and playwright. An experimental, postmodern writer, in his work Handke focuses on irrational behavior and the stifling effects of social conventions. He studied law from 1961 to 1965, but soon after began his career as a playwright with *Offending the Audience* (*Publikumsbeschimpfung*, 1966), in which four actors provocatively discuss the nature of theater. His

best-known play, *Kaspar* (1968), portrays the real-life foundling Kaspar Hauser, an unschooled, speechless boy who wanders into a staid German town in the early 1800s and is nearly destroyed. Handke also achieved renown as a novelist, especially with *The Goalie's Anxiety at the Penalty Kick* (*Die Angst des Tormanns beim Elfmeter*, 1970), the story of an athlete turned manual laborer who commits murder. Handke's other works include the novels *Short Letter, Long Farewell* (*Der kurze Brief Zum Langen Abschied*, 1972), *My Year in the No-Man's Bay* (*Mein Jahr in der Niemandsbucht*, 1994), and *On a Dark Night I Left My Silent House* (*In einer Dunklen Nacht Ging Ich aus Meinem Stillen Haus*, 1997). *A Sorrow Beyond Dreams* (*Wunschloses Unglück*, 1972) is a memoir about his mother's suicide.

Hansberry, Lorraine (May 19, 1930–January 12, 1965). American playwright. Hansberry grew up in Chicago in a middle-class African-American family. After attending the University of Wisconsin and studying painting at the Art Institute of Chicago, she moved to New York City to pursue a writing career, beginning with a job at Paul Robeson's newspaper, *Freedom*. Hansberry drew from her childhood experience for her first play, A RAISIN IN THE SUN (1959), about the emotional toll on a black family that attempts to move into a white neighborhood. A critical and commercial success, *Raisin* was the first play written by an African-American woman to be produced on Broadway and won the Drama Critics' Circle Award; Hansberry also adapted it for the screen. Hansberry's second play, *The Sign in Sidney Brustein's Window* (1964), portrays a group of intellectual and political activists in the mixed racial and ethnic community of Greenwich Village. Hansberry died of cancer on the same night that the play ended its modest Broadway run. In 1969, Robert Nemiroff, Hansberry's literary executor and ex-husband, created *To Be Young, Gifted and Black*, a stage autobiography compiled from Hansberry's letters, journals, memoirs, and poetry. Following its off-Broadway production, the text was issued in book form in 1970. *The*

Collected Last Plays of Lorraine Hansberry, edited by Nemiroff, appeared in 1972.

Hardy, Thomas (June 2, 1840–January 11, 1928). English novelist, short-story writer, and poet. For VIRGINIA WOOLF, Hardy was "the greatest tragic writer among English novelists." But today he is at least as highly admired for his poetry, to which he devoted himself exclusively after the hysterical critical assault on his last novel, the dark and wrenching *JUDE THE OBSCURE* (1895); indeed, in 1970, Ezra POUND asked pertinently: "When we, if we live long enough, come to estimate the 'poetry of the period,' against Hardy's 600 pages we will put what?" Hardy was born in a thatch-roofed cottage in a tiny hamlet near the county-town of Dorchester in Dorset in England's southwest; it was a beautiful and magical landscape that he would make world famous as Wessex, the "partly real, partly dream-country" of his novels and verse. In January 1874, Hardy, an architect by profession with three modestly successful novels and scores of (rejected) poems behind him, enjoyed his first critical triumph when *THE CORNHILL MAGAZINE* published his first masterpiece, *FAR FROM THE MADDING CROWD*, a tragi-comic tale of a beautiful, willful woman and her three suitors. Emboldened by the success of the novel, Hardy married, convinced now that authorship would enable him to support a wife. It was during one of the happier periods of his generally miserable marriage that Hardy wrote *THE RETURN OF THE NATIVE* (1878), one of his greatest novels, powered by two of the novelist's master obsessions: the diabolical role of chance in determining the course of one's life and the indifference, even hosility, of nature to man. Hardy's fame continued to grow steadily with the tragedy of *THE MAYOR OF CASTERBRIDGE* (1886), subtitled "The Life and Death of a Man of Character," and *The Woodlanders* (1887), a powerful study of "matrimonial divergence." The succession of novels appearing every year or two, almost every one a masterpiece of its kind, culminated in 1891 in *TESS OF THE D'URBERVILLES*, a shattering, extremely bleak tale of a "pure woman" who is destroyed by society and its hypocrisies;

the novel was widely denounced as coarse, immoral, and impious, and of course became a bestseller. When the unrelievedly pessimistic *Jude* was similarly abused by critics as, for example, a "shameful nightmare," Hardy abandoned novel-writing and turned to poetry, which he claimed had always been more "instinctive" with him. When his wife died suddenly in 1912, Hardy was overcome with remorse over her silent anger and his neglect, and he poured his grief into poetry. The flowering of lyric masterpieces inspired by her loss, the sequence "Poems of 1912–13," is now recognized as one of the signal achievements of 20th-century verse. (However, as the poems continued to flow, by the hundreds, most contemporary critics responded with lukewarm enthusiasm, at best.) In 1914, Hardy married again, this time happily; his widow would be the "author" of a posthumously published two-volume biography of her husband, which in fact was written by the great man himself to frustrate "the post-mortem exploiters." A critical edition of *The Life and Work of Thomas Hardy*, restoring the cuts the second Mrs. Hardy had made to the manuscript and excising her alterations, appeared in 1985.

Hart, Moss (October 24, 1904–December 20, 1961). American playwright, librettist, and screenwriter. One of the finest American librettists of the 20th century and a witty playwright who humorously explored modern, urban American life, Hart was born in the Bronx, New York, to poor working-class parents who took in boarders to make ends meet. With only a seventh-grade education, he worked at a series of jobs before going to work for a theatrical manager and then writing and directing plays for the Borscht Circuit in the Catskills. After reading the first version of Hart's script for the Hollywood satire *Once in a Lifetime*, producer Sam Harris suggested that Hart collaborate on the revisions with playwright George S. KAUFMAN. The result, in 1930, was Hart's first hit, and the first of a string of popular comedies that the pair would produce in the 1930s, including *YOU CAN'T TAKE IT WITH YOU* (1937; Pulitzer Prize), about a gleefully eccentric family, and *The Man Who Came to Dinner* (1939). Hart's solo efforts for the theater include *Winged Victory* (1943) and *Light Up the Sky* (1949). He collaborated with composer and lyricist Irving Berlin on the musical revues *Face the Music* (1932) and *As Thousands Cheer* (1933), and he teamed with composer Kurt Weill and lyricist Ira Gershwin for *Lady in the Dark* (1941). Also a noted director, he staged the original Broadway production of *My Fair Lady* (1956). His screenplays include *Gentleman's Agreement* (1947) and *A Star Is Born* (1954). *Act One: An Autobiography* (1959) recounts his early life.

Harte, [Francis] **Bret**[t] (August 25, 1836–May 5, 1902). American short-story writer, novelist, and poet. Born in New York State, Harte went to California in 1854. There he unsuccessfully worked a gold stake on the Stanislaus River and began writing and editing stories for magazines in San Francisco. He achieved success with the publication of *The Luck of Roaring Camp and Other Sketches* (1868), a collection of short stories about gold-mining camps and frontier life, which includes "THE LUCK OF ROARING CAMP" and "THE OUTCASTS OF POKER FLAT." The collection, and Harte's ballad "Plain Language from Truthful James" (1870), are prominent examples of local color writing, a type of regional fiction popular in the United States in the late 19th century. In the early 1870s, Harte moved to Boston, where he wrote stories for *THE ATLANTIC MONTHLY* and a novel, *Gabriel Conroy* (1875). He also collaborated with Mark TWAIN on a play, *Ah, Sin* (1877). By the late 1870s, his writing had fallen out of favor with the public, and he spent his last years in Germany and England.

Hašek, Jaroslav (April 30, 1883–January 3, 1923). Czech journalist, short-story writer, and novelist. Born in the fertile literary ground of turn-of-the-20th-century Prague (which also produced Franz KAFKA), Hašek explored in his satirical fictions the clashes of tradition and modernity in the crumbling Austro-Hungarian Empire. Before World War I, he worked as a journalist and wrote numer-ous short stories, several of which featured his most famous character, Good Soldier Schweik. Hašek was captured by the Russian Army during the war and, after the war ended, wrote the novel for which he is best known, *THE GOOD SOLDIER SCHWEIK* (*Osudy Dobrého Vojáka Švejka za Světové Války*, 1921–23) in four volumes (Hašek had planned a six-volume work; the fourth was completed by Karel Vanek from the unfinished manuscript after Hašek's death). Hailed as a brilliant satire on modern society, the work relates the misadventures of Schweik, a canny simpleton grappling with an absurdly dehumanized military bureaucracy. This classic antiwar novel, a picaresque salute to what Martin Esslin has called "unheroic irony and subservient resistance" and a direct ancestor of Joseph HELLER's *CATCH-22*, has been translated into more than 50 languages, and has inspired numerous adaptations, including a stage production by Bertolt BRECHT (in collaboration with Erwin Piscator) in 1928.

Hauptmann, Gerhart (November 15, 1862–June 6, 1946). German playwright, poet, and novelist. The most influential German playwright of the late 19th century, Hauptmann dramatized the social changes occurring in an industrializing Germany. With naturalistic observation, his plays explore the effects of repressive economic and social conditions on the lives of ordinary people. Hauptmann's first play, *Before Dawn* (*Vor Sonnenaufgang*, 1889), was controversial for its acutely realistic portrayal of a peasant and an idealistic socialist. His other plays include *The Weavers* (*Die Weber*, 1892), his best-known work, which depicts a weaver's strike in 1844, *Lonely Lives* (*Einsame Menschen*, 1891), and *Drayman Henschel* (*Fuhrmann Henschel*, 1899). A current of mystical faith runs through Hauptmann's later writings, such as the novel *The Fool in Christ: Emmanuel Quint* (*Der Narr in Christo: Emmanuel Quint*, 1911), about a peasant who imitates the life of Christ. Hauptmann considered his finest work to be the long poem *The Great Dream* (*Der Grosse Traum*, 1942), which he modeled on DANTE's *DIVINE COMEDY* and in which he reflects on his epoch. Hauptmann was awarded the Nobel Prize in Literature in 1912.

Havel, Václav (October 5, 1936–). Czech playwright. A pivotal figure in 20th-century Czech theater and politics, Havel was influenced by the American Beat movement, jazz, and rock music as well as the Czech literary tradition. Beginning as a stagehand at Prague's Divadlo Na Zábradli (Theater on the Balustrade), Havel wrote for the company from 1962 to 1968. He attained prominence for plays such as *The Garden Party* (*Zahradní Slavnost*, 1963), *The Memorandum* (*Vyrozumění*, 1965), and *The Increased Difficulty of Concentration* (*Ztížená Možnost Soustředění* 1968), which satirize life under Communist rule, portraying an absurdly dehumanized, bureaucratic culture unable to accommodate feeling and spirit. After the Soviets crushed the "Prague Spring" reform movement in 1968, Havel became increasingly involved in opposition to the Soviet-dominated Communist government. He was restrained from producing his later plays, psychological studies of totalitarianism, including *The Conspirators* (*Spiklenci*, 1970), *Audience* (1976), and *Largo Desolato* (1986), and was jailed on charges of subversion from 1979 to 1983. When the Czech Communist government fell in 1989, Havel was elected president of Czechoslovakia. He then presided over the division of Czechoslovakia into the Czech Republic and Slovakia in 1992, becoming president of the Czech Republic in 1993.

Hawkes, John (August 17, 1925–May 15, 1998). American novelist and short-story writer. An avant-garde writer who favored mood and literary style over conventional plot, Hawkes was concerned with human frailties in bleak, often surreally nightmarish conditions. His early novels are often set in Europe just after World War II: *The Cannibal* (1950) is set in Germany, the novellas *The Owl* and *The Goose on the Grave* (published together in 1954) take place in Italy, and *The Lime Twig* (1961) explores the criminal underworld of postwar England. The novel *Second Skin* (1964), the confession of a retired military officer, exposes a man's sensitive and vulnerable internal life. Hawkes turned his attention to darkly troubled marital and sexual relationships in such novels as *The Blood Oranges* (1970), *Travesty* (1976), and *The Passion Artist* (1979). His later novels include *Adventures in the Alaskan Skin Trade* (1985), *Whistlejacket* (1989), and *An Irish Eye* (1997). Educated at Harvard, Hawkes was a professor of English at Brown University.

Hawthorne, Nathaniel, *original name* Nathaniel Hathorne (July 4, 1804–May 19, 1864). American novelist and short-story writer. In 1850, Herman MELVILLE, a thunderstruck admirer, wrote of Hawthorne that "this great power of blackness in him derives its force from its appeals to that Calvinistic sense of Innate Depravity and Original Sin. . . . Perhaps no writer has ever wielded this terrific thought with greater terror." As Melville, who also rejected Emersonian optimism, recognized, Hawthorne's work is marked by a tragic vision of life and a comprehension of human complexity that directly confronted, for the first time in his nation's literature, the awful truth that man is irremediably imperfect, an ever-fluctuating mixture of evil and good. Born in Salem, Massachusetts, Hawthorne never really knew his father, a ship's captain, who died of typhoid fever while at sea when his son was not yet four years old, and whose ancestors could be traced back to the earliest days of the Puritan colony of Salem (one Hathorne forebear, in fact, was a judge at the Salem witch trials); Hawthorne's mother's family were prosperous merchants. A dreamy and bookish child, Hawthorne was raised in both Salem and Maine, where his mother's family had property. After graduating from Bowdoin College in 1825, he lived in relative seclusion with his mother and sisters in Salem, having sworn to devote his life to literature and remaining, as he would write of one of his characters, "aloof from the regular business of life." Thus began a 12-year literary apprenticeship, which culminated in the 1837 publication of TWICE-TOLD TALES, a collection of 18 previously published stories, including such classics as "The May-

Pole of Merry Mount," an allegory of Puritan repression. In 1839 Hawthorne secured a position at the Boston Custom House, but soon resigned due to the tedium of the position; he then joined the band of utopian reformers at Brook Farm, a folly for a man of such solitary, brooding temperament, and an experience he would later memorably mine in his satirical novel *The Blithedale Romance* (1852). In the summer of 1842, Hawthorne and his wife began a three-year sublet of the Emerson family home, the Old Manse, in Concord, Massachusetts, where he wrote the tales and sketches collected in *Mosses from an Old Manse* (1846), which includes one of his greatest studies of monomania, "RAPPACCINI'S DAUGHTER." But it was not until THE SCARLET LETTER (1850), a "hell-fired" story of adultery in Puritan New England, that Hawthorne gained widespread contemporary fame. He followed this masterpiece almost immediately with another, THE HOUSE OF THE SEVEN GABLES (1851), which explores the poisonous legacy of human guilt by tracing the history of a house and a family cursed by a "mysterious and terrible past." In 1853 Hawthorne was appointed American consul in Liverpool, and after his appointment expired he and his family traveled on the Continent; his impressions from these years were collected and published posthumously in various editions of his so-called English, French, and Italian *Notebooks*. *The Marble Faun* (1860), Hawthorne's last and most neglected novel, follows the adventures of two American artists in Rome, innocents abroad in the beautiful but somehow treacherous and corrupt "home of art," Rome.

Hazzard, Shirley (January 30, 1931–). Australian-born American novelist and short-story writer. Born in Sydney, Hazzard, whose father was a government official, traveled widely with her family, eventually settling in New York City and obtaining U.S. citizenship. She worked at United Nations headquarters for ten years (her 1967 *People in Glass Houses: Portraits from Organization Life* is a collection of satirical sketches about life at the UN) and began publishing short stories in THE NEW YORKER,

which were collected in her first book, *Cliffs of Fall* (1963). Hazzard's novels include *The Evening of the Holiday* (1966), *The Bay of Noon* (1970), and the highly acclaimed *The Transit of Venus* (1980), which portrays two Australian sisters' immigration to America. Her *Greene on Capri* (2000) is a memoir about her years on the Isle of Capri with her husband, the American writer and translator Francis STEEGMULLER, and their friendship with the English novelist Graham GREENE.

H. D., *pen name of* Hilda Doolittle (September 10, 1886–September 27, 1961). American poet. H. D. was a prominent Imagist poet, whose association with Ezra POUND and English poet Richard Aldington originated that movement. Raised in a Moravian community in Bethlehem, Pennsylvania, Hilda Doolittle was educated at Bryn Mawr College, where as an undergraduate in 1905 she met Pound (to whom she was briefly engaged), who was studying at the University of Pennsylvania. She then lived in New York's Greenwich Village before moving to Europe in 1911. There she fell in with a circle of writers that included T. S. ELIOT, D. H. LAWRENCE, MARIANNE MOORE, the novelist Bryher (Annie Winifred Ellerman), and Aldington, whom she married in 1913. She made her literary debut that year in POETRY magazine, publishing for the first time as H. D. Her first collection, *Sea Garden*, appeared in 1916; other collections include *Hymen* (1921), *Heliodora and Other Poems* (1924), and a trilogy inspired by classical mythology: *The Walls Do Not Fall* (1944), *Tribute to Angels* (1945), and *Flowering of the Rod* (1946). Her sessions in the 1930s with Sigmund FREUD inspired the nonfiction work *Tribute to Freud* (1956). The posthumously published *End to Torment* (1979) recounts her friendship with Pound, and the autobiographical novel *HERmione* (1981) has a lesbian theme (H. D. and Bryher had a long-term relationship.) Her *Collected Poems 1912–1944* was published in 1983.

Heaney, Seamus (April 13, 1939–). Irish poet and essayist. The 1995 recipient of the Nobel Prize in Literature, Heaney writes of the intimacies of daily life in his native Northern Ireland, as well as the political conflicts that have torn the country. His poetry draws upon Irish history and mythology and is marked by a clear, musical style and sensory language. Educated at Queen's University in Belfast, Heaney taught at Harvard and Oxford. His first volume, *Death of a Naturalist* (1966), offered rich evocations of childhood experiences in the countryside. He more overtly reflected on Northern Irish politics in such works as *Wintering Out* (1972), *North* (1975), *Field Work* (1979), and *The Haw Lantern* (1987). Subsequent volumes include *Seeing Things* (1991), *The Spirit Level* (1996), and *Opened Ground* (1998). He has also published numerous critical studies and won the Whitbread Award for his bestselling translation of *BEOWULF* (1999).

Hecht, Anthony (January 16, 1923–). American poet. After graduating from Bard College, Hecht fought in both Japan and Europe during World War II and witnessed the liberation of concentration camps at the end of the war; the cruelties of modern history, particularly the Holocaust, are recurrent concerns in his writing. Upon returning to the United States, Hecht received a master's degree from Columbia University and taught at a number of colleges, most extensively at Georgetown University. His poetry, beginning with *A Summoning of Stones* (1954), is highly formally crafted and weaves allusions to theology and classical mythology into cultural and personal contexts. Among his other volumes are *The Seven Deadly Sins* (1958), *The Hard Hours* (1967; Pulitzer Prize), *Millions of Strange Shadows* (1977), *The Transparent Man* (1990), and *Flight Among the Tombs* (1996). Hecht also published with John Hollander *Jiggery-Pokery* (1967), a collection that introduced the "double dactyl," a form of light, comic verse.

Hecht, Ben (February 28, 1894–April 18, 1964). American journalist, playwright, screenwriter, and novelist. Hecht collaborated with playwright Charles MacArthur on acclaimed comedic plays, including *The Front Page* (1928), about the fast-paced, treacherous world

of newspaper reporting, and *Twentieth Century* (1932), a satire of Hollywood; both plays were successfully adapted to the screen. The child of Russian-Jewish immigrants, Hecht learned the details of the newspaper business while reporting for the *Chicago Journal* and the *Chicago Daily News* and by founding and editing the *Chicago Literary Times*. He based his novel *Erik Dorn* (1921) on the year he spent reporting in Berlin. Hecht's energetic, vivid treatment of modern life is also featured in such short-story collections as *A Thousand and One Afternoons in Chicago* (1922). He wrote numerous screenplays with MacArthur, including *Nothing Sacred* (1937) and *Notorious* (1946). His autobiography, *A Child of the Century*, appeared in 1954.

Heine, [Christian Johann] **Heinrich**, *original name* Harry Heine (December 13, 1797–February 17, 1856). German poet. One of Germany's greatest poets of the post-Romantic era, Heine resided in Paris for much of his life. Born in Düsseldorf to a Jewish family, he studied law to please a wealthy uncle and reluctantly converted to Protestantism with a view to entering the civil service, an occupation then closed to Jews. While a student, he began to write evocative lyrics about love and longing, often concluding with an ironic sting; they were published in his first collection, *The Book of Songs* (*Buch der Lieder*, 1827). Impressed by the French July Revolution, he moved to Paris in 1831. There he wrote for newspapers and published witty and impudent essays on social and cultural issues; his verse, too, was by then often overtly political, as in *Germany, a Winter's Tale* (*Deutschland, Ein Wintermärchen*, 1844), a long verse satire on Germany in the reactionary Metternich era. From 1835 onward, Heine's works were banned in Germany, and his stay in Paris became exile. Bedridden for his last seven years, he confronted his physical and spiritual suffering in his final verse collection, *Romanzero* (1851). Controversial in Germany for his political views and at times despised for his Jewish background, Heine is perhaps the best known and most beloved of all German poets internationally. His poems have been translated into most of the world's major languages, and hundreds of them have been set to music by prominent composers, including Schubert and Schumann.

Heinlein, Robert A[nson] (July 7, 1907–May 8, 1988). American science-fiction writer. Heinlein won Hugo Awards for his best-known novels, *Starship Troopers* (1960) and *STRANGER IN A STRANGE LAND* (1962), as well as for *The Star Kings* (1947) and *The Moon Is a Harsh Mistress* (1966). He was educated at the United States Naval Academy and served as a naval officer for four years, until his retirement in 1934 owing to poor health. He began writing short stories for the magazine *Astounding Science Fiction* in 1939. Many of Heinlein's novels concern the conquest of space and eugenic breeding and are marked by mysticism and eroticism. Popular as well as controversial, they have often been charged with promoting militaristic heroism and rightist libertarian politics. *Stranger in a Strange Land*, which portrays a messianic hero from Mars, attracted a cult following in the 1960s. Among Heinlein's other novels are *Double Star* (1956) and *I Will Fear No Evil* (1970).

Heller, Joseph (May 1, 1923–December 12, 1999). American novelist. Heller's first book, *CATCH-22* (1961), was a critical and popular success that introduced to the vernacular lexicon the term "Catch-22," meaning an impossibly frustrating, no-win situation. Flying 60 missions as a B-25 bombardier in World War II provided Heller with ample material for the book, a satire on the absurdity of war. Under the GI Bill, he studied English at the University of Southern California, New York University, and Columbia University. After a year as a Fulbright scholar at Oxford, he taught and worked for *Time* and *Look* magazines. The phenomenal reception of *Catch-22* earned him prominence as a black humorist. Heller's later novels include *Something Happened* (1974), *Good as Gold* (1979), *God Knows* (1984), and *Closing Time* (1994), a sequel to *Catch-22*. He also wrote the play *We Bombed in New Haven* (1967) and cowrote the screenplays *Sex and the Single Girl* (1964) and *Dirty Dingus Magee* (1970), among others.

Hellman, Lillian (June 20, 1905–June 30, 1984). American playwright and memoirist. Born to a Jewish family in New Orleans, Hellman grew up in New York and moved to Hollywood in 1930 to work as a script reader. She became one of the most celebrated playwrights of the 1930s with *THE CHILDREN'S HOUR* (1934), a daring play about two schoolteachers accused of lesbianism by a student. Hellman drew on her memories of the South for *THE LITTLE FOXES* (1939), a searing portrait of a ruthless, wealthy Southern family, and its prequel, *Another Part of the Forest* (1946). Politically active, along with her longtime lover, novelist Dashiell HAMMETT, in leftist and antifascist movements, Hellman was blacklisted during the anti-Communist witch-hunts of the 1950s. She published several volumes of autobiography, including *An Unfinished Woman* (1969), *Pentimento* (1973), and *Scoundrel Time* (1976), which are acclaimed for their eloquence, although controversial for some factual inaccuracies. Her other plays include the anti-Nazi *Watch on the Rhine* (1941) and *Toys in the Attic* (1960).

Hemingway, Ernest (July 21, 1899–July 2, 1961). American novelist and short-story writer. A modernist master who enjoyed worldwide fame and critical esteem for most of his career, Hemingway was awarded the Nobel Prize in Literature in 1954, the Swedish Academy citing his "mastery of the art of narrative," as well as his profound influence on "contemporary style." Raised in the Midwest, he served in World War I as an ambulance driver in France and an infantryman in Italy, where he was seriously wounded. In the 1920s, he lived in Paris among other expatriate writers, including Gertrude STEIN, F. Scott FITZGERALD, and Ezra POUND. He first achieved prominence with the novel *THE SUN ALSO RISES* (1926), which captures his generation's disillusionment and displays his characteristically terse, understated style. Hemingway's writing frequently reflects his interest in primitive, violent activity, such as bullfighting in his study of the sport, *Death in the Afternoon* (1932), and big game hunting in his story "THE SNOWS OF KILIMANJARO" (1936). War

"All good books are alike in that they are truer than if they had really happened and after you are finished reading one you will feel that all that happened to you and afterwards it all belongs to you: the good and the bad, the ecstasy, the remorse and sorrow, the people and the places and how the weather was."

Ernest Hemingway, "Old Newsman Writes," *Esquire* (December 1934)

---

serves as the setting for the novels *A FAREWELL TO ARMS* (1929), based on his own war experiences, and the bestselling *FOR WHOM THE BELL TOLLS* (1940), on the Spanish Civil War. Hemingway moved to Cuba in the 1940s and wrote the novella *THE OLD MAN AND THE SEA* (1952; Pulitzer Prize), about a Cuban fisherman. His short stories, including such significant examples of the genre as "HILLS LIKE WHITE ELEPHANTS," "A CLEAN, WELL-LIGHTED PLACE," and "THE SHORT HAPPY LIFE OF FRANCIS MACOMBER," appeared in such collections as *In Our Time* (1925) and *Men Without Women* (1927). Hemingway committed suicide in Idaho in 1961. A memoir, *A Moveable Feast* (1964), was published posthumously.

Henry, O., *pen name of* William Sydney Porter (September 11, 1862–June 5, 1910). American short-story writer. The popularity of O. Henry's closely detailed, cleverly plotted stories led to the use of his name for a major annual short-story award. Raised in North Carolina, he moved to Texas, where he wrote comic sketches for newspapers and worked as a bank teller. In 1898, he was convicted of embezzling from the bank, and while serving three years in Ohio State Penitentiary, he began to write under the name O. Henry. After his release, he moved to New York City and published frequently in magazines and anthologies. O. Henry's stories, many of which depict the everyday lives of New Yorkers, are humorous and sentimental, and are noted for their ironic, surprise endings. His best-known stories include "THE GIFT OF THE MAGI" and "The Furnished Room," published in *THE FOUR MILLION* (1906), "The Last Leaf" from *The Trimmed Lamp* (1907), and "THE RANSOM OF RED CHIEF" from *Whirligigs* (1910).

Herbert, Frank (October 8, 1920–February 11, 1986). American science-fiction writer. Herbert was educated at the University of Washington in Seattle and reported for newspapers on the West Coast before publishing fiction. Along with ecological concerns, he examined complex issues related to intelligence, evolutionary biology, religion, and politics in his works. His second novel, *DUNE* (1965), an epic story of life on a desert planet, is recognized as one of the finest achievements of science fiction. It was followed by five sequels: *Dune Messiah* (1969), *Children of Dune* (1976), *God Emperor of Dune* (1981), *Heretics of Dune* (1981), and *Chapterhouse: Dune* (1985). His other novels include *The Dosadi Experiment* (1977), *Hellstrom's Hive* (1975), *The Jesus Incident* (1979), *The White Plague* (1982), and *The Lazarus Effect* (1983).

Herbert, George (April 3, 1593–March 1, 1633). English poet. Herbert was born in Wales and educated at Trinity College, Cambridge. As the University Orator of Cambridge, he frequently attended James I's court, but he ultimately pursued a vocation in the Church. He never published his metaphysical poetry during his lifetime, but on his deathbed he sent a collection to his friend and fellow clergyman, Nicholas Ferrar, instructing him to publish the poems if they might inspire "any dejected poor soul"; otherwise, Ferrar was to destroy them. Ferrar published them as *The Temple* (1633). Herbert's poems treat religious devotional themes with a movingly introspective tone. Like the works of his contemporary John DONNE, they are marked by intricate meters and striking visual conceits. Herbert also experimented with pattern poetry, as in "Easter Wings," in which the lines are visually designed to represent the poem's subject. He left an enlightening memoir, *A Priest to the Temple: or The Country Parson* (1652).

Herrick, Robert (baptized August 24, 1591–October 1674). English poet. Herrick spent six years as an apprentice to his uncle, a prominent goldsmith, before attending Cambridge University. Moving to London, he met the eminent poet Ben JONSON and began writing his own glittering, clever poems. Herrick was ordained in 1623 and spent most of his life as a clergyman in rural Devonshire, although he lost his post for 16 years during the English Civil War because of his royalist sympathies. His verse portrays the rustic English countryside as well as the sophisticated London court. He also wrote frankly erotic love poems. Herrick's major collection, *Hesperides* (1648), comprises more than 1,400 short poems, including epigrams, songs, elegies, and a section of religious verse, *Noble Numbers*. His lyric "To the Virgins to Make Much of Time" opens with one of his best-known lines, "Gather ye rosebuds while ye may."

Hersey, John (June 17, 1914–March 24, 1993). American novelist and journalist. Hersey was born in China to missionary parents and came to the United States at age ten. Educated at Yale University, he began writing as a foreign correspondent for *Time* and *Life* magazines, traveling widely in Asia. Acclaimed for his books examining the effects of World War II on individual lives, Hersey won the Pulitzer Prize for his novel *A Bell for Adano* (1944), which depicts the Allied occupation of a town in Sicily. His other war novels include *Into the Valley* (1943) and *The Wall* (1950), which takes the reader inside the Warsaw ghetto during an unsuccessful rebellion against the Nazis. Hersey's best-known work, *Hiroshima* (1946), is a nonfiction narrative about six survivors of the atomic blast. First published in THE NEW YORKER, which devoted an entire issue to the work, and then issued in book form three months later, it inspired public opposition to nuclear weapons. He displayed an eloquent journalistic style and narrative skill in both his fiction and documentary studies, which include such later works as the nonfiction *The Algiers Motel Incident* (1968) and the novel *The Call* (1985).

Hesiod, in Greek Hēsiodos (fl. c. 700 B.C.). Greek poet. The didactic epics *Theogony* (*Theogonía*) and *Works and Days* (*Erga kai Hēmerai*) are attributed to Hesiod; his authorship of other works that have sometimes been attributed to him is generally doubted. Little is known of his life, except that he was a farmer from Boeotia. He wrote in *Theogony* that he was inspired to write by a visit from the Muses while he tended his sheep on Mount Helicon. *Theogony* recounts the mythical origins of the earth and the genealogy and relationships of the Greek gods, and remains a principal source of Greek mythology. *Works and Days* colorfully depicts peasant life, incorporating myths, fables, and agricultural advice, and promotes the value of honest labor.

Hesse, Hermann (July 2, 1877–August 9, 1962). German-Swiss novelist and poet. Hesse's work is rooted in the German Romantic tradition and reflects his interest in Eastern religious philosophy and Jungian psychoanalysis. His

---

"Poets live and die, known by few or none, and we see their work after their death, often decades after their death, suddenly rise resplendent from the grave as though time did not exist."

Hermann Hesse, "The Magic of the Book" (1930), in *My Belief: Essays on Life and Art*, translated by Denver Lindley (1974)

---

novels characteristically portray the individual's search for self-awareness and spiritual purpose. Born to missionary parents in Germany, Hesse attended a Protestant seminary but left after six months and worked at a variety of jobs, including in a bookshop and as an apprentice mechanic, before joining a publishing firm. He turned to writing full time with the success of his first novel, *Peter Camenzind* (1904). Hesse made a trip to India in 1911, from which he drew for his novel SIDDHARTHA (1922), a chronicle of the life of Buddha. A pacifist, he moved to Switzerland during World War I and became a Swiss citizen in 1923. His major novels *STEPPENWOLF* (*Der Steppenwolf*, 1927) and *The Glass Bead Game*, or *MAGISTER LUDI* (*Das Glasperlenspiel*, 1943), explore the conflict between spiritual devotion and the demands of worldly life. Hesse won the Nobel Prize in Literature in 1946.

Highsmith, Patricia, *original name* Mary Patricia Plangman (January 19, 1921–February 5, 1995). American novelist and short-story writer. Born in Texas, Highsmith was raised in Manhattan and educated at Barnard College. Increasingly reclusive, she lived much of her life alone in England, France, and Switzerland. Her first novel, *Strangers on a Train*, met with immediate success on its publication in 1950 and was filmed by Alfred Hitchcock a year later. Highsmith's crime novels examine the often permeable boundaries between good and evil, portraying the ease with which a moral person can commit a crime, or a sane person cross the line into insanity. Highsmith is best known for her novels featuring the charming but cunning Tom Ripley, who appeared in *The Talented Mr. Ripley* (1955) and in four sequels. Her other works include the lesbian love story *The Price of Salt* (1953, published under the pseudonym Claire Morgan), the thriller *The Tremor of Forgery* (1969), and the short-story collection *The Black House* (1981).

Hijuelos, Oscar (August 24, 1951–). American novelist. Hijuelos's novels explore the experiences and struggles of Cuban immigrants in the United States and questions of cultural identity. They are noted for their historical and social detail and their expansive, colorful prose. Hijuelos's parents immigrated to New York from Cuba in the 1940s. After receiving bachelor's and master's degrees in English from the City College of the City University of New York, where one of his instructors was DONALD BARTHELME, he worked as an advertising media traffic manager and began publishing short fiction, including the Pushcart Prize-winning "Columbus Discovers America." His first novel, *Our House in the Last World* (1983), employs elements of magic realism to tell the story of Cuban immigrants and their family in New York City. His second novel, *THE MAMBO KINGS PLAY SONGS OF LOVE* (1989), won the Pulitzer Prize. His other novels include *The Fourteen Sisters of Emilio Montez O'Brien* (1993), *Mr Ives' Christmas* (1995), and *Empress of the Splendid Season* (1999).

Hildegard von Bingen, *also known as* **Hildegard of Bingen** *and* **Saint Hildegard** (1098–September 17, 1179). German mystic and poet, writing in Latin. Widely revered as a prophet and healer in her own time, Hildegard von Bingen came to be regarded as a saint after her death, although she was never formally canonized. Of noble birth, Hildegard spent her early life at the Benedictine monastery of Disibodenberg, near Bad Kreuznach, becoming prioress of the small community of nuns there in 1136. Around 1150, she left to found a new convent at Rupertsberg, near Bingen. Having experienced visions since childhood, she eventually received papal sanction to preserve in writing what contemporaries saw as divinely inspired prophecies. Twenty-six were recorded and glossed between 1141 and 1151 under the title *Scivias* (first published 1513; Know the Ways [of God]). Among her many other surviving works are perhaps the earliest morality play, the *Play of Virtues* (*Ordo Virtutum*, probably 1150s); treatises on medicine and natural history; and letters advising and admonishing bishops, popes, and the Emperor Frederick Barbarossa. Hildegard was also a composer of great originality, providing for the needs of her own and other sacred communities with such liturgical compositions as the *Symphonia Armoniae Celestium Revelationum* (c. 1150s; Symphony of the Harmony of Celestial Revelations), for which she composed both the words and the music. Only recently have scholars, musicians, and audiences begun to rediscover the musical genius of the "Sybil of the Rhine."

Himes, Chester (July 29, 1909–November 12, 1984). American novelist. Himes's novels angrily explore racial oppression and hatred in American life. After his expulsion from Ohio State University, he began writing while serving a sentence for armed robbery in the Ohio State Penitentiary, publishing his first story, "Crazy in the Stir," in *Esquire* (1934) while he was still incarcerated. Released after serving seven years of his 25-year sentence, Himes published several novels on social issues, such as *If He Hollers Let Him Go* (1945) and *Lonely Crusade* (1947), which examine the prejudices faced by black men in employment. He also published the autobiographical novels *Cast the First Stone* (1952), on prison life, and *The Third Generation* (1954), which depicts several generations of a black family. Himes moved to France in 1953, where he began to write a series of detective novels set in Harlem and featuring two hard-edged black police detectives, Grave Digger Jones and Coffin Ed Johnson. Internationally popular, the series includes *For Love of Imabelle* (1957, now better known as *The Rage in Harlem*), *The Crazy Kill* (1959), and *Cotton Comes to Harlem* (1965). Himes's autobiographies are *The Quality of Hurt* (1972) and *My Life of Absurdity* (1976).

Hobson, Laura Z[ametkin] (June 19, 1900–February 28, 1986). American novelist and short-story writer. Born in New York City and raised on Long Island, Hobson grew up, as she recalled, "in an agnostic broad-minded family"; her father was editor of the *Jewish Daily Forward* and a labor organizer and both parents were Socialists. After graduating from Cornell University, Hobson worked successively as an advertising copywriter, a reporter for the *New York Evening Post*, and a writer for *Time*, eventually rising to promotion director for the magazine. In the mid-1930s her writing career began to take off steadily as she placed short stories in *Cosmopolitan* and other magazines. But it was only with her 1947 novel, *Gentleman's Agreement*, a searing exposé of all-pervasive anti-Semitism in postwar American society, particularly its more genteel forms of social and business exclusion, that Hobson scored a commercial triumph. It was perhaps the most talked-about book of the year, and the screen adaptation, directed by Elia Kazan, won the Academy Award for Best Picture of 1947. Hobson candidly admitted that the "biggest chunks"

of her life appeared in her many short stories and nine novels, which frequently address the social issues and liberal causes that concerned her, such as combating prejudice and the promotion of equal justice for all citizens. Of her other novels, the pathbreaking bestseller *Consenting Adult* (1975) is one of her most notable; it narrates a mother's difficult coming to terms with her son's homosexuality (one of Hobson's sons was, in fact, gay). *Laura Z: A Life* (1983) is the first volume of her autobiography; at the time of her death she was at work on the second volume, which was published posthumously as *Laura Z: A Life: Years of Fulfillment* (1986).

Hoffmann, E[rnst] **T**[heodor] **A**[madeus] (January 24, 1776–June 25, 1822). German short-story writer and novelist. A specialist in the fantastic, bizarre, and grotesque, Hoffmann was also a composer, conductor, artist, and architect, becoming a writer only late in life, but for much of his career he earned his living as a civil servant. He changed his third given name (originally Wilhelm) in honor of his idol, Mozart, and his stories often deal with musical subjects. His best-known tales include "Don Juan" (1813), about a strangely powerful performance of Mozart's opera, and "The Golden Pot" ("Der Goldene Topf," 1814), in which a student is torn between a human love and a supernatural "serpent-girl." His novel *The Devil's Elixir* (*Die Elixiere des Teufels*, 1815–16) describes a monk's commerce with evil spirits, while *The Life and Opinions of the Tomcat Murr* (*Lebensansichten des Katers Murr*, 1820–22) is an eccentric satire in which the cat-philosopher's views alternate with leaves from a fictional musician's biography. Jacques Offenbach's opera *Les Contes d'Hoffmann* (1881) adapts several of Hoffmann's fantastic tales, with the writer himself in the central role of a poet whose romantic adventures all end in disaster; other tales inspired the classic ballets *The Nutcracker* and *Coppélia*.

Hölderlin, [Johann Christian] **Friedrich** (March 20, 1770–June 7, 1843). German poet. An ex-seminarian, Hölderlin pursued his poet's vocation with a priestlike fervor, striving to mediate between humanity and his vision of the divine. In 1796, while serving as a tutor in a Frankfurt banker's household, he met his great love and muse, his employer's wife, Susette Gontard. She became the "Diotima" of his poems and his novel *Hyperion* (1797–99), about a modern Greek's quest to recapture the state of universal harmony Hölderlin ascribed to ancient Athenian culture; its absence in the modern world is a recurring theme in his verse. Hölderlin's enforced separation from Susette and her early death were blows that may have contributed to the mental illness that increasingly claimed him after 1802; he spent his last decades in semiconfinement in Tübingen. His collected poems were first published in 1826. His renown as one of Germany's foremost lyric poets rests largely on his visionary late hymns and fragments, such as "Patmos," and his odes and elegies in classical meters, like "Bread and Wine" ("Brot und Wein"), in which rhythms from ancient verse traditions are imposed on the very differently structured German language in a masterly fashion, yielding poetry of haunting beauty and emotional power.

Homer, *in Greek* Homēros (8th century B.C.). Ionian Greek poet. A largely unknown figure traditionally credited with composing the ILIAD (*Ilias*) and the ODYSSEY (*Odysseia*), Homer is thereby recognized as the earliest and greatest of the Greek epic poets and a literary inventor of immeasurable influence on Western culture. The authorship of both works and the means of composition remain matters of scholarly disagreement, and virtually nothing is known of the poet other than that he probably was blind. Seven cities in Ionia (on the western coast of modern Turkey) claimed to have been his birthplace. Archaeological and textual evidence now places him firmly in the latter part of the 8th century B.C., more than four centuries after the Trojan War, around which the two epics revolved. Both works are clearly based on oral tradition, and some historians have contended that they were not written down until long after Homer, by this theory a bardic singer, had died. Ancient Greeks from the 6th or 5th century B.C. ascribed both epics to Homer, whom they considered divinely inspired. So admired were the poems that they were central to elementary education in classical Greece and Rome, and they remain at the core of liberal arts education to the present day. Also attributed to Homer are the comic poem *Battle of the Frogs and Mice* (*Batrachomyomachia*), the Homeric Hymns, and several poems of the so-called Epic Cycle.

Hopkins, Gerard Manley (June 11, 1844–June 8, 1889). English poet. Although he wrote in the Victorian era, Hopkins is generally grouped with 20th-century poets because of his innovative poetic language. Born in Stratford, Essex, Hopkins studied classics and wrote poetry at Oxford. Upon his decision to convert to Roman Catholicism and become a Jesuit priest, he burned his early verses and stopped writing for seven years while he studied theology. Moved by the shipwreck and drowning death of five Franciscan nuns in 1875, Hopkins wrote "THE WRECK OF THE DEUTSCHLAND," followed by a series of sonnets including "The Windhover," "Pied Beauty," and "God's Grandeur." His later poems, such as "Carrion Comfort," were written in a period of personal desolation and religious struggle while living in Dublin. His poems are distinguished by tightly compressed images and an original style that he called "sprung rhythm," which, unlike iambic verse, emulates the stresses of spoken speech. The first collection of his work, *Poems* (1918), edited by Poet Laureate Robert Bridges, was published almost 30 years after his death. It received little attention, but a second edition in 1930 had a profound influence on such modern poets as T. S. ELIOT, Dylan THOMAS, and W. H. AUDEN.

Horace, *in Latin* Quintus Horatius Flaccus (65 B.C.–8 B.C.). Roman poet. One of the leading poets of the Augustan age, Horace is best known as the stylist who applied Greek lyric traditions to Latin poetry. The son of a freed slave, he was educated in Rome and Athens and fought with the army of Brutus in the civil war following Julius Caesar's death. Returning to Rome, he befriended the poet VIRGIL and acquired a powerful patron in Maecenas, an adviser to Octavian (styled Augustus in 27 B.C.). His early books—the first multivolume works—*Satires* (*Satirae*, 35 B.C.) and *Epodes* (c. 30 B.C.), aimed satirical barbs at contemporary Roman society; *Odes* (c. 24 B.C.) contains his finest lyric poems. Reflecting the peaceful era of Augustus, Horace's good-natured aphorisms, ironic wit, and devotion to art found a ready audience in his contemporaries. His odes and literary essays, especially those in *Ars Poetica* (19–18 B.C.), were studied by Renaissance scholars and Neo-classical English poets of the 17th–19th centuries.

Housman, A[lfred] **E**[dward] (March 26, 1859–April 30, 1936). English poet. For his romantic and deeply pessimistic poems, Hous-man created a simple, lyrical style influenced by the Scottish ballad, the musicality of HEINE's verse, and the precise, epigrammatic quality of classical Latin poetry. His best-known poems, "TO AN ATHLETE DYING YOUNG" and "When I Was One-and-Twenty," contain some of his central themes: unrequited love, the brevity of life, and the finality of death. Housman studied classics at Oxford, but failed to graduate and spent the next ten years working as a clerk in a government patent office in London. During this time, he published several scholarly studies that earned him, in 1892, an appointment as professor of Latin at University College, London. His first poetry collection, *A SHROPSHIRE LAD* (1896), gradually gained recognition, becoming popular during World War I; his second volume, *Last Poems* (1922), was also well received. *More Poems* (1936) was published posthumously. From 1911 until his death he was Kennedy Professor of Latin at Trinity College, Cambridge. Housman is the subject of Tom STOPPARD's play *The Invention of Love* (1997).

Hughes, [James Mercer] **Langston** (February 1, 1902–May 22, 1967). American poet, playwright, and short-story writer. A leading figure in the Harlem Renaissance in the 1920s and 30s, Hughes celebrated the vitality of African-American culture in many genres. He is best known for "jazz poetry," a new poetic form that incorporated the musical rhythms of jazz and blues as well as black "street talk." Born in Joplin, Missouri, Hughes attended Columbia University and took a degree from Lincoln University in Pennsylvania in 1929. But he had already gained recognition for his first poem, published in *Crisis* magazine in 1921, "THE NEGRO SPEAKS OF RIVERS," and through the early support of poet Vachel Lindsay. His first collections, *THE WEARY BLUES* (1926) and *Fine Clothes to the Jew* (1927), established his reputation. Hughes's literary output is distinguished by its versatility: he wrote plays, including *Mulatto* (1935) and, with Zora Neale HURSTON, *Mule Bone* (written 1931; published 1990); librettos and lyrics for operas and musicals; short stories, collected in *The Ways of White Folks* (1934); memoirs, *The Big Sea* (1940) and *I Wonder As I Wander* (1956); and newspaper sketches, collected in *Simple Speaks His Mind* (1950) and other volumes. His later poetic works include *Shakespeare in Harlem* (1942), *Montage of a Dream Deferred* (1951), *Selected Poems* (1959), *Ask Your Mama* (1961), and the posthumous *Collected Poems* (1994).

Hughes, Ted, *in full* Edward James Hughes (August 16, 1930–October 28, 1998). English poet. Reflecting his passion for the Yorkshire countryside, Hughes's daring and disjunctive poems present a dramatic, brutal, unsentimentalized view of nature and animal life in the controlled diction of a keen observer. Born in Mytholmroyd in West Yorkshire, Hughes studied anthropology and mythology at Pembroke College, Cambridge, where he met his future wife, poet Sylvia PLATH. His first collection, *The Hawk in the Rain* (1957), followed by *Lupercal* (1960), brought him acclaim. His other works include the poetry collections *Wodwo* (1967), *Crow* (1970), *Moortown* (1979), and *Wolfwatching* (1989); the children's book *Under the North Star* (1981); and a translation, *Tales from Ovid* (1997). Hughes's marriage to Plath ended in separation, followed by her suicide in 1963. He edited and published her *Collected Poems* (1981) after her death. His last book, *Birthday Letters* (1998), is a collection of poems about Plath, breaking his 35-year silence about their relationship. Hughes was Britain's Poet Laureate from 1984 to 1998.

Hugo, Victor (February 26, 1802–May 22, 1885). French poet, playwright, and novelist. One of France's greatest poets, Hugo led the Romantic revolution in French poetry, drama, and fiction. Born in Besançon the son of an army officer, he began his literary career at the age of 17 by founding the journal *Conservateur Littéraire* (1819–21). His first full-scale works, a volume of poems, *Odes et Poésies Diverses* (1822), and a novel, *Hans of Iceland* (*Han d'Islande*, 1823), were followed by numerous poetry collections, including *Nouvelles Odes* (1824), *Les Orientales* (1829), and *Feuilles d'Automne* (1831; Autumn Leaves). National recognition came with the publication of his play *Cromwell* (1827); its preface was adopted by the Romantics as a manifesto of liberation from the classical conventions of French theater. Other verse plays include *Hernani* (1830) and *Ruy Blas* (1838). His great historical novels, *THE HUNCHBACK OF NOTRE-DAME* (*Nôtre-Dame de Paris*, 1831) and *LES MISÉRABLES* (1862), for which he is best known in English, brought him enormous popularity in his own time and remain classics. Hugo was regarded as a national hero for his advocacy of republican causes, his voluntary exile from France after the coup d'état of Napoleon III in 1851, and his triumphant return to Paris in 1870 with the proclamation of the Third French Republic. Other notable works include *Les Châtiments* (1853; The Punishments), satirical poems; *Les Contemplations* (1856), poems mourning the death of his daughter by drowning; and novels such as *Toilers of the Sea* (*Les Travailleurs de la Mer*, 1866).

Hurston, Zora Neale (January 7, 1903–January 28, 1960). American novelist and playwright. With her groundbreaking work steeped in Southern black culture and folklore, Hurston played a pivotal role in African-American literature. Born in the all-black town of Eatonville, Florida, Hurston attended Howard University and studied anthropology with Franz Boas at Barnard College. She was the leading black woman writer in the 1930s during the Harlem Renaissance, but her works drew criticism from RICHARD WRIGHT and other black writers for not dealing with issues of racism and black victimization, and for using black dialect, which they felt perpetuated stereotypes. Forgotten in the 1950s, she died in poverty. Her writings were rediscovered in the 1970s with the emergence of African-American and women's studies, and the support of writers such as Alice WALKER, who edited a Hurston reader, *I Love Myself When I Am Laughing . . .* (1979). Her writings include the novels *Jonah's Gourd Vine* (1934), *THEIR EYES WERE WATCHING GOD* (1937), and *Moses, Man of the Mountain* (1939); the play *MULE BONE* (written 1931; published 1990), with LANGSTON HUGHES; the folklore studies *Mules and Men* (1935) and *Tell My Horse* (1938); and an autobiography, *Dust Tracks on a Road* (1942).

Huxley, Aldous (July 26, 1894–November 22, 1963). English novelist and social critic. Huxley's *BRAVE NEW WORLD* (1932), a nightmarish vision of a society based on science, technology, and social control, became a symbol for a generation's fears for the future. Born in Surrey, England, Huxley was educated at Eton and graduated from Oxford, despite an eye ailment that left him partially blind. His early novels, *CROME YELLOW* (1921), *ANTIC HAY* (1923), *Those Barren Leaves* (1925), and *POINT COUNTER POINT* (1928), are biting works of social satire and criticism, as is *EYELESS IN GAZA* (1936). Discouraged by the failure of pacifist politics in Europe, Huxley came to America in 1937. His later works, including the novels *After Many a Summer Dies the Swan* (1939) and *Ape and Essence* (1948), reflect his growing distrust of political and social trends; *Island* (1962) reflects in addition his passionate belief in Eastern religions and mysticism as panaceas. Among the prolific Huxley's many nonfiction works are *Devils of Loudon* (1952); two works recording his experiments with hallucinogenic drugs, *The Doors of Perception* (1954) and *Heaven and Hell* (1956); and a retrospective essay on his most famous work, *Brave New World Revisited* (1958).

Huysmans, Joris-Karl, *original name* Charles-Marie-Georges Huysmans (February 5, 1848–May 12, 1907). French novelist. A leading figure in the Decadent movement in late 19th-century France, Huysmans gave emblematic expression to the spiritual discontent and aesthetic tastes of the *fin-de-siècle* generation. Born in Paris, the son of a French mother and Dutch father, Huysmans had a long career at the Ministry of the Interior. His first novel, *Marthe* (*Marthe, Histoire d'une Fille*, 1876), was written in the naturalistic style of Émile ZOLA and his circle, but later works—notably AGAINST THE GRAIN (*À Rebours*, 1884), a novel praised by Oscar WILDE and mentioned in THE PICTURE OF DORIAN GRAY—are characterized by his increasing disillusionment with society and interest in mysticism. His spiritual journeys are depicted in a series of novels: *En Route* (1895), *The Cathedral* (*La Cathédrale*, 1898), and *The Oblate* (*L'Oblat*, 1903). Other novels include *Down Stream* (*À Vau-l'eau*, 1882) and *Down There* (*Là-bas*, 1891), a portrait of a Satanic cult. Huysmans was one of the founders and the first president of the Académie Goncourt.

Ibsen, Henrik (March 20, 1828–May 23, 1906). Norwegian playwright and poet. Often called the father of modern drama, Ibsen was born near Christiania (now Oslo) to wealthy parents, but when he was six years old his father's business failed and the family lost its money. He left school at 15 and served for several years as a pharmacist's assistant before moving to Christiania and writing his first play, *Catiline* (*Catalina*), in 1850. Ibsen then worked as a manager and director for theatrical companies in Bergen and Christiania until 1864, when, with the help of a government grant, he traveled abroad, where he found his voice as a playwright with the verse dramas *Brand* (published 1866, produced 1885) and PEER GYNT (published 1867, produced 1876). The latter, blending folklore and satire in the saga of a resourceful scoundrel, is sometimes called his masterpiece, but it was the dozen realist dramas he wrote after 1877, in which he grappled with contemporary social problems and psychological quandaries, that revolutionized international theater and established his lasting renown. They include A DOLL'S HOUSE (*Et Dukkehjem*, 1879), in which a woman slams the door on a marriage compromised by patriarchalism; GHOSTS (*Gengangere*, 1882), about the fatal consequences of hypocrisy; AN ENEMY OF THE PEOPLE (*En Folkefiende*, 1883) and THE WILD DUCK (*Vildanden*, 1885), which deal with the good and harm done by uncompromising idealists; and two plays whose complex, troubled heroines face their problems in drastically different ways, *The Lady from the Sea* (*Fruen fra Havet*, 1889) and HEDDA GABLER (1891). In 1891, after 27 years in Italy and Germany, Ibsen returned to his homeland. In the mid-1880s, a Symbolist strain began to color his realism. His last works, such as THE MASTER BUILDER (*Bygmester Solness*, 1893), contain clearly autobiographical elements; his final play, *When We Dead Awaken* (*Når Vi Døde Vågner*, 1900), is a difficult parable about art and life. Ibsen died beloved and revered as Norway's greatest writer.

Ignatow, David, *original name* David Ignatowsky (February 7, 1914–November 17, 1997). American poet. For his down-to-earth realism and everyday themes, fellow poet Robert BLY called Ignatow "a poet of the community, of people who work for a living." Winner of the Bollingen Prize in 1977, Ignatow wrote free verse poems reflecting on urban life and personal realities such as marriage, love, family, and death. Born in Brooklyn to Russian-Jewish immigrant parents, he worked for the WPA Federal Writers' Project during the Depression and held low-paying jobs until he began to teach at various colleges. WILLIAM CARLOS WILLIAMS hailed his first collection, *Poems* (1948), as "poems for the millions." His other collections include *The Gentle Weight Lifter* (1955), *Figures of the Human* (1964), *Rescue the Dead* (1968), *Tread the Dark* (1978), *Whisper to the Earth* (1981), and *Against the Evidence: Selected Poems 1934–1994* (1993). *The One in the Many: A Poet's Memoirs* appeared in 1988.

Imru' al-Qays, *in full* Imru' al-Qays ibn Ḥujr (497–545). Arab poet. One of the earliest and most distinguished of the pre-Islamic poets,

Imru' al-Qays is credited with the invention of a fixed form of ode called a *qasida*. His work is included, along with that of six other poets, in the *al-Mu'allaqāt*, an 8th-century compilation of orally transmitted odes from the pre-Islamic period. Imru' al-Qays's highly erotic love poems feature imagery from Bedouin life and the landscape of the Arabian desert. According to legend, he was the son of the king of Kindah. Twice expelled from his father's court for his erotic poetry, he waged war against rival Bedouin tribes after his father's murder and was probably assassinated by the Byzantine emperor Justinian I. As many as 68 poems were attributed to him by medieval Arab scholars. Among several English translations of the *al-Mu'allaqāt* are *The Seven Golden Odes of Pagan Arabia* (1903) and *The Seven Odes* (1957).

Inge, William (May 3, 1913–June 10, 1973). American playwright. Exploring the malaise and hidden disappointments of small-town Midwestern life in the 1950s and 1960s, Inge's plays, many adapted for film, captured the underlying anxiety of an era. Inge was born in Independence, Kansas, and worked as a teacher and newspaper drama critic. With the support of TENNESSEE WILLIAMS, his first play, *Farther Off from Heaven* (1947), was produced in Dallas; a decade later, he revised it for Broadway as *The Dark at the Top of the Stairs* (1957). COME BACK, LITTLE SHEBA (1950) established his reputation. Inge won a Pulitzer Prize for PICNIC (1953), and an Academy Award for his original screenplay, *Splendor in the Grass* (1961). His other plays include *Bus Stop* (1955) and *A Loss of Roses* (1960). Discouraged by several failed productions in the late 1960s, Inge turned to writing novels. His death in 1973 was an apparent suicide.

Ionesco, Eugène (November 26, 1909–March 28, 1994). Romanian-born French playwright. One of the originators, along with Samuel BECKETT and Jean GENET, of the Theater of the Absurd, Ionesco used unconventional dramatic techniques such as illogical dialogue and bizarrely comic situations to underscore the human search for meaning in a meaningless universe. Like other postwar Existentialist writings, his plays give expression to the individual's sense of alienation and isolation in modern society. As a student in his native Romania, Ionesco saw many of his academic colleagues join the fascist Iron Guard. He lived in Paris and Bucharest, settling permanently in France after 1942. His first play, THE BALD SOPRANO (*La Cantatrice Chauve*, 1950), was followed by *The Lesson* (*La Leçon*, 1951), *The Chairs* (*Les Chaises*, 1952) and *Amédée* (1954). His best-known play, RHINOCEROS (*Le Rhinocéros*, 1959), is an allegorical depiction of the Nazi era. His later plays include *Exit the King* (*Le Roi se Meurt*, 1962), *A Stroll in the Air* (*Le Piéton de l'Air*, 1963), and *Macbett* (1972). *Present Past, Past Present* (*Présent Passé, Passé Présent*, 1968) is a memoir. Ionesco was elected to the Académie Française in 1970.

Irving, John (March 2, 1942–). American novelist. Known for its individualistic zany, dark humor, Irving's fiction weaves bizarre and incomprehensible events, both comic and tragic, into the fabric of seemingly normal, everyday life. In the words of his best-known fictional character, T. S. Garp, a novelist who comments on contemporary society, "Life is an X-rated soap opera." THE WORLD ACCORDING TO GARP (1978), his fourth novel, became a runaway bestseller. Born in Exeter, New Hampshire, Irving had already displayed his sense of the absurd in *Setting Free the Bears* (1969), *The Water-Method Man* (1972), and *The 158-Pound Marriage* (1974). His later works include the novels *The Hotel New Hampshire* (1981), *The Cider House Rules* (1985), *A Prayer for Owen Meany* (1989), *A Son of the Circus* (1994), and *A Widow for One Year* (1998); a story collection, *Nowhere Man* (1992); and the memoirs *The Imaginary Girlfriend* (1996) and *My Movie Business* (1999). For his screenplay adaptation of *The Cider House Rules*, Irving won a 1999 Academy Award.

Irving, Washington (April 3, 1783–November 28, 1859). American essayist, short-story writer, and biographer. Called "the first American man of letters," Irving is known for his satirical essays, travel sketches, and contributions to

American folklore, such as the stories "The Legend of Sleepy Hollow" and "RIP VAN WINKLE." The son of a wealthy British merchant who had sided with the rebels in the Revolutionary War, Irving grew up in New York and began his literary career with whimsical essays for the literary journal *Salmagundi* (1808), of which he was a co-publisher. His burlesque *History of New York . . .* (1809), published under the pseudonym Diedrich Knickerbocker, was to make "Knickerbocker" a byword for New Yorkers of Dutch ancestry. *The Sketch Book of Geoffrey Crayon, Gent.* (1819–20) contains his best-known stories and established his international reputation. Irving lived abroad for 17 years, including three years as a diplomatic attaché in Spain (1826–29). His works from this period include *Christopher Columbus* (1828), *The Conquest of Granada* (1829), and *Legends of the Alhambra* (1832). Irving also made several trips to the American West, recording his impressions in *A Tour of the Prairies* (1835) and *Astoria* (1836). He served as U.S. Minister to Spain from 1842 to 1846. His biographical works include *Mohammed* (1849) and the five-volume *George Washington* (1855–59).

Isherwood, Christopher (August 26, 1904–January 4, 1986). English-born novelist and playwright. As a British expatriate living in Germany in the 1930s, Isherwood was a close observer of the rise to power of the Nazis. His best-known novels, *Mr. Norris Changes Trains* (1935) and *Goodbye to Berlin* (1939), reissued together as THE BERLIN STORIES (1946), became the basis for a play by John Van Druten, *I Am a Camera* (1952), and a Broadway musical, *Cabaret* (1966). Isherwood also collaborated with W. H. AUDEN on several verse plays, including *The Ascent of F6* (1936). In 1939, Isherwood immigrated to the United States and settled in southern California, where he became a film scenarist; he became an American citizen in 1976. Influenced by Aldous HUXLEY, Isherwood became a devotee of Hinduism; he translated the BHAGAVADGĪTĀ (1944, with Swami Prabhavananda) and edited several works on Vedanta. His later novels include *Prater Violet* (1945), on life in Hollywood, and

A Single Man (1964), on homosexuality. Among his autobiographical works are *Kathleen and Frank* (1971), *Christopher and His Kind* (1976), and *My Guru and His Disciple* (1980).

Ishiguro, Kazuo (November 8, 1954–). Japanese-born English novelist. Part of a new generation of British writers with multicultural roots, the Nagasaki-born Ishiguro, who moved to England with his parents at the age of five, describes himself as a writer of "international novels" or, as he explains it, fiction that imparts "a vision of life that is of importance to people of varied backgrounds around the world." His novels often feature subtle portraits of characters whose personal losses and past mistakes reflect on the history, politics, and culture of an era. He is best known for his novel THE REMAINS OF THE DAY (1989; Booker Prize), a study of a perfect English butler whose lifelong devotion to his employer stunts his own emotional life. His first novels, *A Pale View of Hills* (1982) and *An Artist of the Floating World* (1986; Whitbread Book of the Year), treat themes related to the war years in Japan. His later works include *The Unconsoled* (1995) and *When We Were Orphans* (2000).

Jackson, Helen Hunt, *original name* Maria Fiske (October 15, 1830–August 12, 1885). American essayist, novelist, and poet. Adopting as her cause the mistreatment of Native Americans, in her nonfiction and fictional works Jackson campaigned for the reform of government policies. Born in Amherst, Massachusetts, she turned to writing after the deaths of her husband, Captain Edward Hunt, and their two sons. She moved to Colorado with her second husband, William Jackson, in 1875. *A Century of Dishonor* (1881), a historical indictment of federal policies concerning Native Americans, led to her appointment as a federal investigator of the California Mission. Her novel *Ramona* (1884) provides insight into the plight of Native Americans as well as a portrait of old California. An earlier novel, *Mercy Philbrick's Choice* (1876), is thought to be based in part on the life of her friend Emily DICKINSON. Her other works include poetry, travel sketches, and children's books.

Jackson, Shirley (December 14, 1919–August 8, 1965). American novelist and short-story writer. A master of horror and the occult, Jackson relied on realistic details and gradual twists to build a mounting sense of terror in her protagonists as well as her readers. Her best-known story, "THE LOTTERY" (published in THE NEW YORKER in 1948), draws the reader into the life of an ordinary small town as it prepares for a bizarre and chilling annual rite. Jackson's fiction often features female protagonists caught in the web of a nightmarish reality, as in "The Daemon Lover," "The Visit," and "Pillar of Salt." Born in San Francisco, Jackson moved with her family to Rochester, New York, in her mid-teens, and attended the University of Rochester and Syracuse University, from which she received her B.A. in 1940. That same year she married a classmate, Stanley Edgar Hyman, who became a distinguished literary critic. Jackson battled her own demons in the form of depression and agoraphobia. Her other work includes novels (*The Bird's Nest*, 1954; *The Haunting of Hill House*, 1959; and *We Have Always Lived in the Castle*, 1962), a memoir (*Life Among the Savages*, 1953), and children's books. Her stories are collected in the posthumously published *Come Along with Me* (1968).

Jacob, [Cyprien-]**Max** (July 12, 1876–March 5, 1944). French poet and novelist. An intimate of Picasso and APOLLINAIRE, Jacob explored progressive modernist techniques as a poet and painter. In 1915, he converted from Judaism to Catholicism and from 1921 onward lived in monastic seclusion. Jacob's poetry, most notably the prose poetry collection *The Dice Cup* (*Le Cornet à Dés*, 1917), is associated with Cubism and Surrealism and is celebrated for its verbal playfulness and shifting perspectives. His voluminous body of work also includes *Saint Matorel* (1909), *Oeuvres Burlesques et Mystiques de Frère Matorel* (1911; The Burlesque and Mystical Works of Brother Matorel), *La Défense de Tartufe* (1919; The Defense of Tartufe), and *Le Laboratoire Central* (1921;

The Central Laboratory). Collections of his works in English translation include *Drawings and Poems* (1951), *Hesitant Fire: Selected Prose of Max Jacob* (1991), and *Selected Poems of Max Jacob* (1999). Jacob was arrested by the Nazis in 1944 and died in a concentration camp.

James, Henry (April 15, 1843–February 28, 1916). American novelist, short-story writer, playwright, and essayist. A progenitor of the modernist novel, James grew up in a prosperous New York City family of formidable intellect; his father, Henry, Sr., was a philosopher, and his elder brother, William, a pioneering psychologist and philosopher. Seeking to escape American provincialism, he spent an increasing amount of time in Europe, and from 1876 onward he lived in London, becoming a British subject in 1915. His mature work frequently portrays American expatriates in Europe and reflects on cultural differences between the Old World and the New. Beginning with the novel *Roderick Hudson* (1876), James's early mature fiction includes THE AMERICAN (1877), *The Europeans* (1879), DAISY MILLER (1879), WASHINGTON SQUARE (1880), and THE PORTRAIT OF A LADY (1881). His so-called "middle period" of stylistic transition includes novels about social reform, such as THE BOSTONIANS (1886) and *The Princess Casamassima* (1886), and artists, as in THE ASPERN PAPERS (1888). His late period began with a series of works set in England, including *The Spoils of Poynton* (1897), WHAT MAISIE KNEW (1897), THE TURN OF THE SCREW (1898), and *The Awkward Age* (1899). In these works, James developed the innovative technique of presenting events through characters' limited points of view, a method powerfully employed in his final masterworks, THE WINGS OF THE DOVE (1902), THE AMBASSADORS (1903), and THE GOLDEN BOWL (1904), novels that returned to his motif of Americans in Europe. The prolific James is also renowned for his literary and art criticism, including the highly regarded critical prefaces he wrote for the New York edition of his own selected work (1907–9).

James, P[hyllis] **D**[orothy] [Baroness James of Holland Park] (August 3, 1920–). English detective novelist. A distinguished practitioner of the mystery fiction genre who began writing only after she was 40, James is acclaimed for her complex characters and discerning treatment of themes of truth and deception. After many years working in nursing and hospital administration, during the 1960s and 1970s she worked in the criminal section of the government Department of Home Affairs, where her involvement in forensics and criminal justice stimulated her interest in writing about crime. After publishing her first book, *Cover Her Face* (1962), she wrote *A Mind to Murder* (1963), the novel that initiated her popular Adam Dalgliesh series, about a detective who is also a poet. Other Dalgliesh books include *Unnatural Causes* (1967), *Shroud for a Nightingale* (1971), *The Black Tower* (1975), *Death of an Expert Witness* (1977), *Devices and Desires* (1989), *Original Sin* (1994), and *Death in Holy Orders* (2001). *An Unsuitable Job for a Woman* (1972) began a second cycle, about female investigator Cornelia Gray. James's nonseries books include *Innocent Blood* (1980) and *The Children of Men* (1992).

Jarrell, Randall (May 6, 1914–October 14, 1965). American poet and critic. Widely known for his resonant poetry about World War II, Jarrell is also noted for his eloquent, generous critical writing. Born in Tennessee and educated at Vanderbilt University, Jarrell served in the Air Force from 1942 to 1946, during which time he wrote poems, including "The Death of the Ball-Turret Gunner," published in *Little Friend, Little Friend* (1945), portraying the inner struggles of ordinary soldiers. From 1946 to 1947, he taught at Sarah Lawrence College, drawing upon the experience for his only novel, the satirical *Pictures from an Institution* (1954). While teaching at the University of North Carolina from 1947 to 1965, Jarrell wrote insightful essays on such poets as Robert FROST, Walt WHITMAN, Elizabeth BISHOP, and ROBERT LOWELL, significantly contributing to their critical recognition. His further volumes of poetry include *Losses* (1948), *The Woman at the Wash-*

ington Zoo (1960), and *The Lost World* (1965). Collections of his criticism include *Poetry and the Age* (1953), *A Sad Heart at the Supermarket* (1962), and *The Third Book of Criticism* (1969). A collection of his essays over three decades, *No Other Books*, appeared in 2000.

Jarry, Alfred (September 8, 1873–November 1, 1907). French playwright, poet, and novelist. As a student in Rennes, Jarry developed his best-known creation, the character Père Ubu, a grotesque parody of a crass bourgeois who lusts for power and wealth. His play UBU ROI, a scatological satire in which Ubu becomes King of Poland, had a sensational debut in Paris in 1896, generating much controversy. Jarry became an important avant-garde figure, known for his eccentric manner as well as his plays, poems, and novels written in accordance with his method of "pataphysics," the cultivation of dream states, playfulness, and irrationality. Jarry's other Ubu dramas include *Ubu Enchained* (*Ubu Enchaîné*, 1900) and *Ubu Cuckolded* (*Ubu Cocu*, published posthumously in 1944). The fantasy *Exploits and Opinions of Doctor Faustroll, Pataphysician* (*Gestes et Opinions du Docteur Faustroll, 'Pataphysicien,'* 1911), about the "science of imaginary solutions," was published after his death from acute alcoholism.

Jeffers, [John] **Robinson** (January 10, 1887–January 20, 1962). American poet and playwright. "It would not have been written at all," Jeffers said of his poetry, "except for certain accidents that changed and directed my life." Born in Pittsburgh, he learned Latin and Greek before he was 12 from his father, a Presbyterian minister, who then sent his son to Switzerland for more rigorous schooling. Returning to the United States at age 15, Jeffers finished college in two years, began graduate work in philosophy and comparative literature, switched to medicine, and then to forestry. With the help of an inheritance, he made a final change, devoting himself to poetry and settling, with his wife and children, in the Monterey region of California—the setting of most of his poems. With his first major volume, *Tamar and Other Poems* (1924), he gained attention for seeking to reinvest poetry with the tragic sensibility and violent emotion found in classical myth. Jeffers opposed the delicate suggestiveness of Symbolist poetry, asserting instead that "the poet / ... wishes not to play games with words, / His affair being to awake dangerous images." When his antiwar collection *The Double Axe* appeared in 1948, its publisher, Random House, added a note expressing "disagreement over some of the political views" expressed by the poet. His poetry presents allegorical scenarios of fury and lust, often revisions of biblical and ancient Greek stories, and remains controversial for emphasizing the corrupt, dark side of human nature. Jeffers's other works include "Roan Stallion" (1925), the volumes *The Women of Point Sur* (1927), *Be Angry at the Sun* (1941), and *The Beginning and the End and Other Poems* (1963). The multivolume *Collected Poems of Robinson Jeffers* began publication in 1988. His interest in Greek tragedy is reflected in his 1946 adaptation of EURIPIDES' *MEDEA*, which remains the most-produced English-language version of the play, and *Tower Beyond Tragedy* (1950), based on Aeschylus's *ORESTEIA*.

Jewett, Sarah Orne (September 3, 1849–June 24, 1909). American novelist and short-story writer. Her lyrical, subtle fiction about ordinary lives in her native Maine shows Jewett to be a master of American regional writing. As a child, she frequently accompanied her father, a physician, on his rounds in the impoverished local countryside, and at age 19 she began publishing closely observed stories about Maine's rural life, collected in *Deephaven* (1877). From 1881 onward, Jewett divided her time between Maine and Boston, living with her companion, Annie Adams Fields, the widow of a prominent Boston publisher. She also became a mentor to other women writers, including Willa CATHER. Her books include the novel *A Country Doctor* (1884), the short-story collection *White Heron* (1886), and her most celebrated work, *THE COUNTRY OF THE POINTED FIRS* (1896), a finely crafted, quietly reflective series of connected stories about women in small-town Maine.

Jhabvala, Ruth Prawer (May 7, 1927–). American novelist, short-story writer, and screenwriter. Born of Polish-Jewish parents in Germany, Jhabvala immigrated with her family to England just before World War II. After graduating from the University of London in the early 1950s, she married an Indian architect and moved to Delhi, where she lived until 1975, when she moved to New York. Jhabvala's best-known novels explore India from an outsider's viewpoint and examine the lives and culture of both expatriate Europeans and native Indians. Her works include the novels *To Whom She Will* (1955), *The Householder* (1960), *HEAT AND DUST* (1975; Booker Prize), *Three Continents* (1987), *Shards of Memory* (1995), and *In Search of Love and Beauty* (1999), and the short-story collections *Out of India* (1986) and *East into Upper East: Plain Tales from New York and New Delhi* (1998). She has also written screenplays for the filmmaking team of James Ivory and Ismail Merchant, winning Academy Awards for her adaptations of E. M. FORSTER's *A ROOM WITH A VIEW* (1986) and *HOWARDS END* (1992).

Jiménez [Mantecon], **Juan Ramón** (December 24, 1881–May 29, 1958). Spanish poet. Awarded the Nobel Prize in Literature in 1956, Jiménez was a major figure in modern Spanish literature. Born in Andalusia, he studied law in Seville but soon abandoned that career, instead moving to Madrid in 1900 to write poetry. His early verse, published in collections including *Jardines Lejanos* (1904; Distant Gardens) and *Elejías Puras* (1908; Pure Elegies), was influenced by the French Symbolists as well as the Modernismo of Rubén DARÍO and is marked by delicate, musical form and a melancholy tone. Beginning with *Diario de un Poeta Recién-casado* (1917; Diary of a Recently Married Poet), Jiménez developed the technique of "La Poesía Desnuda," or "naked poetry," a style of finely concentrated, pared-down composition. During the Spanish Civil War, Jiménez moved to Puerto Rico, where he remained for the rest of his life. His late volumes, including *Animal de Fondo* (1947; Animal at Bottom), offer accomplished free-verse explorations of the human condition. Jiménez is best known in the United States for *Platero and I* (*Platero y Yo*, 1917), a poetic prose work about the travels of a poet and his donkey through Andalusia. *Forty Poems* (1967) is an anthology of his poems in English translation by the American poet Robert BLY.

John of the Cross, [Saint], *in Spanish* [San] Juan de la Cruz, *original name* Juan de Yepes y Álvarez (June 24, 1542–December 14, 1591). Spanish poet and mystic. A major Spanish lyricist, John was a member of the Catholic Carmelite order. He supported Saint Teresa's reform of the group, asking for a return to its original, stricter rules of silence, seclusion, and austerity, but was opposed by his superiors, who imprisoned him in 1577. His best-known works were written in prison or shortly after he managed to escape in 1578. They include the exquisite verses beginning "In a Dark Night" ("En una Noche Oscura") and "O Living Flame of Love" ("Oh Llama de Amor Viva") and some 20 other poems, and four impassioned mystical treatises composed in their explanation. With vivid emotion and visionary imagery, John describes the ecstasy achieved by the soul that transcends human suffering and worldly concerns to achieve spiritual union with God. John's works were first published in 1616. He was canonized in 1726.

Johnson, Diane (April 28, 1934–). American novelist and essayist. A Californian transplanted from the Midwest, Johnson received a Ph.D. from UCLA and became a professor of English at the University of California at Davis; in recent years, she has divided her time between San Francisco and Paris. Johnson began her writing career with unsettling novels about life in contemporary California, portraying women's struggles with the instabilities and uncertainties of modern society in such novels as *Fair Game* (1965), *The Shadow Knows* (1974), and *Lying Low* (1978). Her later novels often examine cross-cultural encounters, as in *Persian Nights* (1987), about an American woman in Iran, and *Le Divorce* (1997) and *Le Mariage* (2000), astute social satires about rela-

tions among Americans and Europeans in Paris. Johnson has also written biographies, including *Lesser Lives: The True History of the First Mrs. Meredith* (1973) and *Dashiell Hammett* (1983); a book of travel essays, *Natural Opium* (1993); a book of essays and reviews, *Terrorists and Novelists* (1982); and the screenplay for Stanley Kubrick's film of Stephen King's *The Shining* (1980).

Johnson, James Weldon (June 17, 1871–June 26, 1938). American poet, novelist, and editor. Born in Jacksonville, Florida, Johnson studied law and was the first African-American admitted to the Florida bar. He moved to New York to write songs for the stage with his brother, John Rosamond Johnson, with whom he also composed gospel songs, including "Lift Every Voice and Sing" (1899). He then served as a consul in the U.S. Foreign Service from 1908 to 1912 and, on his return to New York, worked for the National Association for the Advancement of Colored People, serving as executive secretary from 1920 to 1930. An important literary figure of the Harlem Renaissance, Johnson edited the landmark anthology *The Book of American Negro Poetry* (1922). His major writings include the fictional THE AUTOBIOGRAPHY OF AN EX-COLORED MAN (1912), about a black man who passes for white, and GOD'S TROMBONES (1927), a volume of verses modeled on sermons and steeped in rural black culture.

Johnson, Samuel (September 18, 1709–December 13, 1784). English lexicographer, biographer, poet, and essayist. "If I had no duties, and no reference to futurity, I would spend my life in driving briskly in a post-chaise with a pretty woman." This observation, quoted by James BOSWELL in THE LIFE OF SAMUEL JOHNSON (1791), appears indeed to have been wishful thinking on the part of the speaker, who so dominated the mid-18th-century English literary world that it is now known as the Age of Johnson. The son of a bookseller, Johnson attended Oxford and worked in his native Lichfield as a schoolmaster. Determined to become a writer, he moved in 1737 to London, where he wrote for *The Gentleman's Magazine* and other periodicals; produced his greatest poem, *The Vanity of Human Wishes. The Tenth Satire of Juvenal, Imitated* (1749), expressing his characteristic moral concern with the folly of hubris; and one month later saw his verse

---

"No man but a blockhead ever wrote, except for money."

Samuel Johnson, quoted in James Boswell, *The Life of Samuel Johnson* (1791)

---

tragedy, *Irene*, produced by the great actor-manager David Garrick (a former pupil). He also, in 1746, began singlehandedly to compile the first scholarly, historical dictionary of the English language; upon its completion in 1755, it was immediately recognized as England's greatest contribution to date to lexicography and established Johnson's reputation as a major scholar and man of letters. Johnson's essays, including those published twice weekly as *The Rambler* (1750–52) and those that made up his weekly column "The Idler" (1758–60) for the *Universal Chronicle*, were admired for their learned, measured commentary and acute observations on morals and manners. His other works include *RASSELAS: The Prince of Abyssinia* (1759), an allegorical romance that critiques Enlightenment optimism, and *Prefaces, Biographical and Critical, to the Works of the English Poets*, better known as *Lives of the Poets* (10 vols.; 1779–81), a prodigious biographical and critical work. In 1763, Johnson met James Boswell, the young son of a Scottish judge, who became his boon companion and immortalized Johnson's distinctive conversational wit in his *Life of Samuel Johnson*, perhaps the greatest literary biography of all time. Their 1773 tour of Scotland is recollected in Johnson's *A Journey to the Western Islands of Scotland* (1775) and in Boswell's journal.

Jones, James (November 6, 1921–May 9, 1977). American novelist. Jones earned literary prominence with his first novel, *FROM HERE TO ETERNITY* (1951; National Book Award), a vivid account of peacetime life at a Hawaii Army base in the months before the Pearl Harbor attack. A bestseller, the novel was adapted into an Academy Award–winning film. Born in Illinois, Jones attended the University of Hawaii until, struggling financially, he enlisted in the Army, in which he served from 1939 to 1945. His other World War II novels are *The Thin Red Line* (1962), based on his experiences as an infantryman at Guadalcanal, and *Whistle* (1978), which depicts the war's psychological effect on returned soldiers. His Army trilogy remains widely read for its revealing observation of ordinary servicemen. His other novels include *Some Came Running* (1957) and *Go to the Widow Maker* (1967).

Jones, LeRoi. *See* **Baraka, Amiri**

Jonson, Ben (c. June 11, 1572–August 6, 1637). English playwright, poet, and critic. A commanding figure in Jacobean letters, Jonson is renowned for his satirical wit, learned convictions, and elegant, classicist verse. The adopted son of a bricklayer, he received little formal education, and briefly worked in the family trade before joining the fight against the Spanish in Flanders. He returned to England around 1595 and settled in London, where he began working first as an actor and then as a playwright. His first play, *Every Man in His Humour*, debuted in 1598 and featured William SHAKESPEARE as a member of the cast. He followed its success with *Every Man Out of His Humour* in 1599. In the early 1600s, he became one of the leading writers of masques, a contemporary form of court society theater that combined glittering spectacle, music, and poetry. Jonson was recognized as a major writer with his comedies *VOLPONE* (1607), *Epicene* (1609), and *The Alchemist* (1612), brilliant satires of human folly and corruption. His classical, formally controlled style, also displayed in his lyric poems, including the well-known "Song to Celia," was widely influential in the Restoration and Augustan periods. He published his collected *Works* in 1616 and was appointed Poet Laureate the same year. An outspoken intellectual figure, Jonson was second only to Shakespeare in importance among his contemporaries, and his followers, including poet Robert HERRICK, were commonly dubbed the "Sons of Ben."

Joyce, James (February 2, 1882–January 13, 1941). Irish novelist and short-story writer. A towering figure in 20th-century literature, Joyce developed innovative narrative and linguistic techniques that had a profound influence on modernist literature. Born in Dublin, James used his native city as the central setting for his fiction, although he spent most of his adult life in exile, seeking to escape the provincialism and repressive social conventions he found in Irish Catholic culture. With his wife, Nora Barnacle, he left for the Continent in 1904. They lived at various times in Trieste, Zurich, and Paris, struggling with poverty and Joyce's lifelong eye troubles, which ultimately resulted in near blindness. His first major work, *DUBLINERS* (1914), a collection of short stories including "THE DEAD," was followed by the autobiographical novel *A PORTRAIT OF THE ARTIST AS A YOUNG MAN* (1916) and a play, *Exiles* (1918). But Joyce was relatively unknown to the public until the publication of *ULYSSES*, a novel that chronicles a single day in the lives of three Dubliners. Banned in the United States for its frank sexuality and irreverence when excerpts from it were published in *THE LITTLE REVIEW* in 1918, the novel aroused great interest and controversy when Sylvia BEACH published it in book form in Paris in 1922. For the next 17 years, Joyce worked on a single novel, *FINNEGANS WAKE* (1939), a labyrinthine work that recounts the dream of an ordinary Irishman in opaque, experimental language. Joyce's work advanced the major modernist technique of the interior monologue, presenting the internal, often associative and fragmented thoughts and emotions of his characters. His writing employs musical, rhythmic language, shifting perspectives and temporalities, and symbolic allusions to myth, history, and literature, creating powerful literary explorations of modern life and consciousness.

Juana Inés de la Cruz, [Sor], *original name* Juana Inés de Asbaje (November 12, 1651–April 17, 1695). Mexican poet. Hailed as "the tenth muse" during her lifetime, Sor Juana has received renewed critical attention from recent scholars and poets such as Octavio PAZ. Raised outside Mexico City, she was an intellectual prodigy and earned a position at court. At 17, she entered a convent, where she amassed more than 4,000 books and collected scientific and musical instruments. Although primarily a poet, Sor Juana's most recognized work may be her "Reply to Sister Philotea" ("Respuesta a Sor Filotea," 1691), written after she was admonished for her secular intellectual activities. Sor Juana's letter pleads for women to be accepted as scholars on equal terms with men and affirms her religious devotion. Shortly thereafter, however, she stopped writing and withdrew into the religious life of the convent. Sor Juana's poetry, including the major philosophical poem "Dream" ("El Sueño," 1692), was first published in Spain in three volumes between 1689 and 1700.

Judson, E. Z. C. *See* **Buntline, Ned**

Justice, Donald (August 12, 1925–). American poet. Justice originally planned a career in music, but suspected that he "might have more talent as a writer," and so turned to poetry, publishing his first collection at age 35. In his poetry, characterized by skilled formal craft, musical rhythm, and a wry, restrained tone, he has used the elegy form to evoke the past, and incorporated striking images of skewed perception to meditate on madness. Born in Miami, he studied at the University of Miami, University of North Carolina, and the University of Iowa and taught poetry at the Iowa Writers' Workshop and elsewhere. His books include *The Summer Anniversaries* (1960), *Night Light* (1967), *Selected Poems* (1979; Pulitzer Prize), *The Sunset Maker: Poems, Stories, a Memoir* (1987), and *Orpheus Hesitated Beside the Black River: Poems, 1957–1997* (1998). In 1991, he received the Bollingen Prize. Justice also wrote the libretto for *The Death of Lincoln* (1988), with music by A. Thomas Taylor.

Juvenal, *Latin in full* Decimus Junius Juvenalis (c. 55–c. 130). Roman poet. Born at a time of corruption and stagnation in the Roman Empire, from about A.D. 100 to 128 Juvenal turned his pen to writing satirical verses about Roman life and society, collected in the classic SATIRES (Satirae). His verse is marked by a fierce, biting tone and oratorical style that scholars often contrast with the gentle, conversational poetry of HORACE, the other major satirist of classical Rome. With searing rhetoric, Juvenal derides a contemporary Rome overrun by vice and degradation. "Why do I write satire?" Juvenal asks in one famous verse. "Say, rather, how could I help it." His most passionate criticism is directed at wealthy society, but he also expresses misogynist sentiments ("Why marry," he asks, "as long as there is still rope to hang oneself with?"). Little is known of Juvenal's life, but it is believed that he was exiled to Egypt for a time by the emperor Domitian and later returned to Rome, where he was supported by patrons. His verse was germinal to the satiric form and was subsequently praised and imitated by such writers as John DRYDEN, Jonathan SWIFT, and Lord BYRON.

Kafka, Franz (July 3, 1883–June 3, 1924). Prague-born novelist and short-story writer, writing in German. Kafka's fiction expressed the anxieties and alienation of life in the early 20th century with singular symbolic depth and power. Kafka was born in Prague to a middle-class German-Jewish family with whom he lived for most of his life, despite his feelings of domination by his father. Educated in the law, he worked as an accident insurance company official throughout his career. His ambivalence about his family, bureaucratic occupation, and uncertain social position influenced his fiction, which, in objective, detached prose, portrays the guilt and insecurity of individuals caught in a nightmarish world governed by incomprehensible authority. The works published during his lifetime include the story "Before the Law" ("Vor dem Gesetz," 1914), the novellas THE METAMORPHOSIS (Die Verwandlung, 1915) and In the Penal Colony (In der Strafkolonie, 1919), and the collection A Hunger Artist (Ein Hungerkünstler, 1924). Doubting the value of his work, he instructed his friend, literary

executor, and later biographer Max BROD to destroy his remaining manuscripts upon his

---

"I think we ought to read only the kind of books that wound and stab us. If the book we're reading doesn't wake us up with a blow on the head, what are we reading it for? ... But we need the books that affect us like a disaster, that grieve us deeply, like the death of someone we loved more than ourselves, like being banished into forests far from everyone, like a suicide. A book must be the axe for the frozen sea inside us. That is my belief."

Franz Kafka, letter to Oskar Pollak, January 27, 1904, in Letters to Friends, Family, and Editors, translated by Richard and Clara Winston (1977)

---

death; Brod nonetheless published the works, including the great novels THE TRIAL (Der Prozess, 1925), THE CASTLE (Das Schloss, 1926), and Amerika (1927).

Kālidāsa (c. 5th century A.D.). Indian poet and playwright. One of the greatest Sanskrit poets, Kālidāsa was called the Indian SHAKESPEARE by his first English translator, Sir William Jones. Concrete details of Kālidāsa's life are few and disputed, although some critics have deduced from his poems that he may have been a priest. His poetry is remarkable for its interlocking meter and striking imagery, particularly of nature. His works elaborate the classical tradition of the MAHĀBHĀRATA and the RĀMĀYAṆA and reflect on love, ideals of conduct, and the relationship between mortals and gods. Kālidāsa's best-known work is his consummate drama in verse, The Recognition of Śakuntala (Abhijñānaśākuntala). He also wrote the verse dramas Urvaśī Won by Valor (Vikramorvaśī) and Mālavikā and Agnimitra (Mālavikāgnimitra), the epic poems Dynasty of Raghu (Raghuvamśa) and Birth of the War God (Kumārasambhava) and the extended lyric The Cloud Messenger (Meghadūta).

Kantor, MacKinlay, *original name* Benjamin McKinlay Kantor (February 4, 1904–October 4, 1977). American novelist, short-story writer, and poet. Kantor's vivid stories and novels explore episodes in American history, ranging widely from the Civil War to the Chicago gangland of the 1920s. Born in Iowa, he began writing for local newspapers after graduating from high school. He turned to freelance writing and won acclaim for his first novel, *Long Remember* (1934), on life in Gettysburg during the Civil War battle. His verse novel *Glory for Me* (1945), based on his World War II experiences, served as the basis for the Academy Award–winning film *The Best Years of Our Lives.* ANDERSON-VILLE (1955; Pulitzer Prize) is a novel about the eponymous Civil War prison camp. Among his other novels are *The Voice of Bugle Ann* (1935), *Spirit Lake* (1961), and *Valley Forge* (1975).

Kaufman, George S[imon] (November 16, 1889–June 2, 1961). American playwright, columnist, and critic. Noted for his caustic wit, Kaufman was a poker-playing member of the famed Algonquin Round Table and one of the most successful playwrights of his generation. Born in Pittsburgh, Pennsylvania, he held a variety of jobs before embarking on a journalism career in 1912 at the *Washington Times*; by 1917 he was at *The New York Times*, where he served as reporter, critic, and drama editor, staying on until 1930 even while scoring a string of Broadway hits, usually in collaboration with others. Among his plays are *The Butter and Egg Man* (1925); *Dulcy* (1921) and *Beggar on Horseback* (1924), with Marc Connelly; *June Moon* (1930), with Ring LARDNER; *The Royal Family* (1928), *Dinner at Eight* (1932), and *Stage Door* (1936), with Edna FERBER; and YOU CAN'T TAKE IT WITH YOU (1936; Pulitzer Prize) and *The Man Who Came to Dinner* (1939), with Moss HART. Kaufman also wrote the books for many musical comedies, including *The Cocoanuts* (1925; music and lyrics by Irving Berlin) and, with Leueen McGrath (his second wife) and Abe Burrows, *Silk Stockings* (1955; music and lyrics by Cole Porter). Collaborations with writer Morrie Ryskind include the books for *Animal Crackers* (1928; music and lyrics by Bert Kalmar and Harry Ruby) and several shows with songs by George and Ira Gershwin, notably *Of Thee I Sing* (1931), the first musical to be awarded the Pulitzer Prize for Drama (the award citation neglecting to acknowledge the composer). His screenplays include *A Night at the Opera* (1935), with Ryskind, for the Marx Brothers.

Kavanagh, Dan. *See* **Barnes, Julian**

Kawabata, Yasunari (June 11, 1899–April 16, 1972). Japanese novelist, short-story writer, and critic. One of the most distinguished novelists of modern Japan, Kawabata explored loneliness, loss, and desire in his poetic fiction. The melancholy tenor of his writings was admittedly inspired by his own lonely childhood; orphaned at the age of three, he boarded with various relatives in his youth. After studying literature at Tokyo Imperial University, Kawabata founded the avant-garde journal *Bungei Jidai* (1924–27) and earned wide acclaim for his first novel, *The Izu Dancer (Izu no Odoriko,* 1926). His fiction, which often combines techniques from both European modernism and traditional Japanese literature, examines erotic relationships, the sensory world of nature, and the transience of life. In 1968, he became the first Japanese writer to win the Nobel Prize in Literature. Kawabata ended his own life shortly after the suicide of his friend Yukio MISHIMA. Kawabata's best-known novels include SNOW COUNTRY (*Yukiguni,* 1948), THOUSAND CRANES (*Senbazuru,* 1952), and *The Sound of the Mountain (Yama no Oto,* 1952).

Kazantzakis *or* **Kazantzakēs, Nikos** (February 18, 1883–October 26, 1957). Greek novelist, philosopher, and poet. A major figure in modern Greek literature, Kazantzakis produced works in a wide variety of genres, including essays, novels, poems, travelogues, and translations, but he is best known outside of Greece for his novels. Born in Crete, he studied law at the University of Athens and philosophy with Henri BERGSON in Paris. The philosophical preoccupations of his novels were also influenced by the writings of Friedrich NIETZSCHE, and by Buddhist and Christian ideas, and often explore the conflict between spirituality and worldly desires. His best-known work, ZORBA THE GREEK (*Vios kai Politeia tou Alexē Zormpa*, 1946), was made into a popular film starring Anthony Quinn. Other works include the novels *The Greek Passion* (*Ho Christos Xanastaurōnetai*, 1954), which explores the plight of Greek refugees in Turkey with intricate Christian symbolism, and the controversial *The Last Temptation of Christ* (*Ho Teleutaios Peirasmos*, 1955), as well as a long poem, *The Odyssey* (*Odysseia*, 1938), a 33,333-verse modern sequel to HOMER'S ODYSSEY.

Keats, John (October 31, 1795–February 23, 1821). English poet. Keats's passionate and sensual Romantic poetry is among the most beloved in the English language. Born in London, he was apprenticed to a surgeon and, in 1815, began to study medicine, but by 1817 he had turned to poetry. He was encouraged in his vocation by the poet, journalist, and political

---

"**We hate poetry that has a palpable design upon us.... Poetry should be great and unobtrusive, a thing which enters into one's soul, and does not startle or amaze it with itself but with its subject.—How beautiful are the retired flowers! how would they lose their beauty were they to throng into the highway crying out, 'admire me I am a violet!—dote upon me I am a primrose!'**"

John Keats, letter to J. H. Reynolds, February 3, 1818, in *The Letters of John Keats* (1952)

---

radical Leigh HUNT, who sponsored Keats's first volume, *Poems* (1817), which includes "ON FIRST LOOKING INTO CHAPMAN'S HOMER." In 1818, he published ENDYMION, an ambitious, 4,000-line poem based on the Greek myth of a mortal shepherd's love for a goddess, but also endured a series of personal crises: he noticed his first symptoms of tuberculosis, and nursed his dying brother, also suffering from tuberculosis; his poetry was attacked by conservative crit-

ics; and he fell in love with Fanny Brawne, becoming engaged to her the following year, despite his poverty. (He would later break off the engagement because of his failing health.) Keats met the emotional upheaval in his life with spectacular creativity. In 1819, he wrote "Lamia," "THE EVE OF SAINT AGNES," "LA BELLE DAME SANS MERCI," the unfinished epic *Hyperion*, and six brilliant odes ("Ode on Indolence," "ODE ON A GRECIAN URN," "Ode to Psyche," "ODE TO A NIGHTINGALE," "Ode on Melancholy," and "To Autumn"). With evocative imagery and subtle musicality, the poems reflect on the flux and impermanence of life and the abiding power of the imagination, and are among the finest achievements of English poetry. In 1820, with his tuberculosis advancing, Keats moved to Rome in a last bid for health, but died the next February at age 25.

Keith, David. *See* **Steegmuller, Francis** [in Other Influential Figures]

Kempe, Margery (c. 1373–c. 1440). English mystic. Kempe was born into a prominent bourgeois family in Bishop's Lynn. She married a local businessman, but the birth of her first child precipitated a nervous breakdown. She was confined for several months, until she was cured by what she believed to be a visitation by Christ. Although she was to bear 14 children, her return to the world proved unfulfilling, and another vision convinced her to devote her life to God. Presumably because she was illiterate, she dictated her autobiography, *The Book of Margery Kempe* (c. 1438; published in a modernized version, 1936; in Middle English, 1940), which tells of her conversations with Jesus and Mary, her agonies of self-doubt, and her struggles against repeated charges of hypocrisy and heresy. It also describes her pilgrimages in England and abroad, and her consultations with clergy and with other mystics. It is considered by many to be the first English autobiography, although written in the third person, and organized not as a journal of Kempe's everyday life but as a record of her spiritual awakening and the revelation of God's love.

Keneally, Thomas (October 7, 1935–). Australian novelist. In his historical novels Keneally examines the effects of social forces on individual lives and of the past on the present. Keneally was trained at a Roman Catholic seminary but was not ordained; he based his first novel, *The Place at Whitton* (1964), on the experience. In 1967, he won national fame for his historical novel *Bring Larks and Heroes*, set in a penal colony in 1790s Australia. He subsequently explored such subjects as 19th-century aborigines in *The Chant of Jimmie Blacksmith* (1972) and the American Civil War in *Confederates* (1979). Keneally earned international acclaim for *Schindler's Ark* (1982; U.S. title, SCHINDLER'S LIST; Booker Prize), a fictionalized history of Oskar Schindler, the German industrialist who saved 1,300 Jews during World War II. The book was later adapted into an Academy Award–winning film. Keneally's later novels include *A Family Madness* (1985), *Women of the Inner Sea* (1992), and *The Great Shame* (1998), which imaginatively chronicles his own Irish family history in Australia.

Kennedy, William (January 16, 1928–). American novelist. Kennedy was born in Albany, New York, where his novels are set. After graduating from Siena College in 1949, he worked as a journalist in Albany and San Juan, Puerto Rico, where he met novelist Saul BELLOW, who became his mentor. Kennedy returned to his native city in the 1960s and embarked on a series of lyrical novels that depict the lives of an Irish-American extended family in Albany, spanning the 19th through the 20th centuries and portraying love and survival in an atmosphere of contentious local politics and economic impoverishment. Kennedy won the Pulitzer Prize in 1984 for one of the novels in the series, IRONWEED (1983), set during the Depression, and wrote the screenplay for the film adaptation in 1987. His other Albany novels are *Legs* (1975), *Billy Phelan's Greatest Game* (1978), *Quinn's Book* (1988), *Very Old Bones* (1992), and *The Flaming Corsage* (1996).

Kerouac, Jack, *original name* Jean-Louis Lebris de Kerouac (March 12, 1922–October 21, 1969). American novelist and poet. Kerouac's spontaneous, improvisatory prose and poetry defined the spirit of the Beat movement. Born into a French-Canadian family in Lowell, Massachusetts, Kerouac attended Columbia University from 1940 to 1942, interrupted by a stint in the Merchant Marine. He then enlisted in the Navy, from which he was discharged as a "schizoid personality." Back in New York, Kerouac formed three friendships that would change his life, with writers Allen GINSBERG and WILLIAM S. BURROUGHS, and with the charismatic Neal Cassady. During this period, Kerouac also wandered through the United States and Mexico and published his first novel, the autobiographical *The Town and the City* (1950). Dissatisfied with its conventional form, with his next novel, ON THE ROAD (1957), typed on a 120-foot scroll in a 20-day marathon, he used loose, free-form structure and syntax. A portrayal of the Beat milieu and of his travels with Cassady, it became a cult classic and alerted mainstream America to the bohemian Beat subculture. Kerouac's subsequent novels, including THE DHARMA BUMS (1958), *The Subterraneans* (1958), and *Desolation Angels* (1965), further depict his circle's rejection of materialistic values and search for meaningful experience, explorations of sex, drugs, and jazz, and roamings through the American landscape. Kerouac's other writings include the poetry volume *Mexico City Blues* (1959) and *Visions of Cody* (1972), sketches composed during the writing of *On the Road*.

Kesey, Ken (September 17, 1935–). American novelist and essayist. A darkly comic novelist, Kesey is renowned for chronicling his participation in the 1960s counterculture revolution. After studying at the University of Oregon and Stanford University, Kesey worked at a California hospital as a paid experimental subject, taking mind-altering drugs and reporting on their effects. The experience inspired his first novel, the widely successful ONE FLEW OVER THE CUCKOO'S NEST (1962), a black comedy about patients in a psychiatric hospital. Like Kesey's subsequent novels, *Sometimes a Great Notion*

(1964) and *Sailor Song* (1992), it explored themes of freedom and social constraint, irrational spontaneity, and cultural repression. Kesey has also written essays centering on his travels with the "Merry Pranksters," a group of revelers in the 1960s who roamed the country in a bus, experimenting with free love and psychedelic drugs. His works reflecting on the experience include *Kesey's Garage Sale* (1973) and *Demon Box* (1986). The "Merry Pranksters" are also the subject of TOM WOLFE's *The Electric Kool-Aid Acid Test* (1968).

Kincaid, Jamaica, *original name* Elaine Potter Richardson (May 25, 1949–). Antiguan novelist, short-story writer, and essayist. Kincaid was educated at elite private schools in her native Antigua, which she later described as so "Empire" that "I thought all great writing was done before 1900." At age 16, she left Antigua and moved to New York City, where she worked as an au pair, an experience she examined in her novel *Lucy* (1990). She first published her fiction in THE NEW YORKER and gathered her early short stories in *At the Bottom of the River* (1983). Her first novel, *Annie John* (1985), is about a young girl's coming-of-age in Antigua. Other works include the novel *The Autobiography of My Mother* (1995); *My Brother* (1997), an account of her brother's death from AIDS; and a book-length essay on the destructiveness of colonialism, *A Small Place* (1988).

King, Stephen (September 21, 1947–). American novelist and short-story writer. A prolific author who has achieved extraordinary popular success, King combines elements of horror, science fiction, and fantasy in vivid, accessible narratives set in small-town America. King was born and raised in Maine and graduated from the University of Maine in 1970. His first novel, CARRIE (1974), about an outcast girl who uses her telekinetic powers to take revenge on her tormentors, began his string of bestsellers, many of which have been adapted for film and television. His novels include *Salem's Lot* (1975), *The Shining* (1977), *The Dead Zone* (1979), *Firestarter* (1980), *Cujo* (1981), *Christine* (1983), *Misery* (1987), *Bag of Bones* (1998), and

The Girl Who Loved Tom Gordon (1999). He also published several novels under the pen name Richard Bachman, including *Rage* (1977) and *The Running Man* (1982), and, more recently, *The Regulators* (1996). In the 1990s King began to experiment with methods of publishing, issuing *The Green Mile* in installments (March–August 1996) and in July 2000 beginning the Internet-first publication of *The Plant* in monthly installments. The latter venture proved commercially unsuccessful, and publication was suspended after the November installment. *On Writing: A Memoir of the Craft* (2000) is both an exploration, with examples, of the art and craft of writing and a memoir of King's early life and the sources of his work, including reflections on the 1999 automobile accident that nearly ended his life.

Kingsolver, Barbara (April 8, 1955–). American novelist, essayist, and journalist. Raised mostly in rural Kentucky, Kingsolver developed a social and political consciousness while studying at DePauw University in the final years of the anti–Vietnam War protest movement. She began her career writing scientific articles, then moved into freelance journalism. Her first novel was *The Bean Trees* (1988), about a Caucasian woman who adopts a Cherokee girl; the story continues in a sequel, *Pigs in Heaven* (1993). Her highly acclaimed *The Poisonwood Bible* (1998), about the experiences of the family of an evangelical missionary during the Congo's struggle for independence from Belgium, is narrated by the minister's wife and four daughters, who reveal redemption as a process fraught with both joy and error. Kingsolver's other works include the novels *Animal Dreams* (1990) and *Prodigal Summer* (2000), the essay collection *High Tide in Tucson* (1995), a volume of poetry, *Another America: Otra America* (1992), and the historical work *Holding the Line: Women in the Great Arizona Mine Strike of 1983* (1989; rev. ed. 1996).

Kingston, Maxine Hong (October 22, 1940–). American novelist and memoirist. Kingston's lyrical autobiographical narratives explore Chinese-American life, examining issues of identity amid cross-cultural legacies and probing the role of gender in Chinese and American societies. Born in Stockton, California, to parents who had emigrated from China, she was educated at Berkeley and settled in Hawaii, where she taught at the University of Hawaii. Her first book, the highly praised *The Woman Warrior: Memoirs of a Girlhood Among Ghosts* (1976), focuses on her family's women and combines autobiography with elements of fantasy and Chinese legends. Kingston portrayed her father and the compromises he made to live in America in *China Men* (1980). Her other works include *Tripmaster Monkey: His Fake Book* (1988), a picaresque novel about a Chinese-American youth in search of himself, and *Hawai'i One Summer* (1987), a collection of essays.

Kinnell, Galway (February 1, 1927–). American poet. In poems marked by stark, powerful emotion, concrete detail, and supple, free form, Kinnell explores the individual's encounters with the primal forces of birth, death, nature, and violence. Kinnell was born and raised in Rhode Island, studied at Princeton and the University of Rochester, and has taught at several universities. His first collection of poems, *What a Kingdom It Was*, appeared in 1960; *Selected Poems* (1982) won the National Book Award and a Pulitzer Prize. His other volumes include *Body Rags* (1967), *The Book of Nightmares* (1971), *The Avenue Bearing the Initial of Christ into the New World* (1974), *Mortal Acts, Mortal Words* (1980), and *When One Has Lived a Long Time Alone* (1990). A *New Selected Poems* was issued in 2000. He has also published a novel, *Black Light* (1966, rev. 1980), and *Walking Down the Stairs: Selections from Interviews* (1992).

Kipling, [Joseph] **Rudyard** (December 30, 1865–January 18, 1936). English short-story writer, poet, and novelist. The first English writer to win the Nobel Prize in Literature (1907), Kipling gained a vast and enduring readership with his story collections for children — *The Jungle Book* (1894), *The Second Jungle Book* (1895), and *Just So Stories* (1902)

among them — and his writings on British imperialism and life in India, including the novel *KIM* (1901) and such poems as "Gunga Din," "Mandalay," "The White Man's Burden," and "Danny Deever." The son of an artist and scholar, he was born in Bombay and lived there to the age of six. Taken to England for his education, he lived at a foster home in Southsea, a time grimly recalled in the story "Baa, Baa, Black Sheep" (1888) and the autobiographical fragment *Something of Myself* (1937). Returning to India in 1882, he spent seven years as a journalist, publishing his first sketches and verse. Back in England after 1889, he attained rapid celebrity with several collections. The years 1890–1902, including four in Vermont, were his most productive. His vast output includes such other well-known works as the novel *CAPTAINS COURAGEOUS* (1897) and the adventure story "THE MAN WHO WOULD BE KING" (1888).

Kiš, Danilo (February 22, 1935–October 15, 1989). Serbian novelist and short-story writer. Born into a Jewish family in a small Yugoslavian village, Kiš grew up amid the violence of World War II, losing many of his relatives in the Holocaust. He was educated at the University of Belgrade and ultimately settled in France, where he taught at the university level and gradually developed an international reputation for his fiction. He is best known for his autobiographical novel trilogy — *Garden, Ashes* (*Bašta, Pepeo*, 1965), *Early Sorrows* (*Rani Jadi*, 1969), and *Hourglass* (*Peščanik*, 1972) — which centers on his father's death in Auschwitz. His other works include the short-story collections *A Tomb for Boris Davidovich* (*Grobnica za Borisa Davidoviča*, 1976), on Stalinist prison camps, and *The Encyclopedia of the Dead* (*Enciklopedija Mrtvih*, 1983). *Homo Poeticus* (1995) is a collection of essays and interviews edited by Susan SONTAG.

Kleist, [Bernd] **Heinrich** [Wilhelm] **von** (October 18, 1777–November 21, 1811). German playwright and short-story writer. Abandoning a military career, Kleist spent the last dozen years of his life in restless travels, composing eight verse dramas and eight tales that would assure his renown, although only long after his death. Tight formal control and intense emotional dilemmas are the hallmarks of all his works. They include *Penthesilea* (published 1808, performed 1876), an extravagant tragedy; *The Broken Jug* (*Der Zerbrochene Krug*, 1808), one of the most frequently staged German comedies; novellas and stories such as *Michael Kohlhaas* (1810), about a just man's private war against an unjust ruler, and "THE MARQUISE OF O..." ("Die Marquise von O...," 1810); and a much-admired essay about consciousness and grace, "On the Puppet Theater" ("Über das Marionettentheater," 1810). Isolated and impoverished, his achievements all but unrecognized, Kleist took his own life. It would be ten years before his masterpiece, the lyrical drama *Prince Friedrich of Homburg* (*Prinz Friedrich von Homburg*, 1821), was published and performed. Its hero is an impetuous young officer whose ambition is tamed by a confrontation with imminent death, and who then embraces that death with such fervor that he paradoxically becomes worthy of life. Many modernist authors acknowledge his influence.

Klíma, Ivan (September 14, 1931–). Czech playwright, novelist, and short-story writer. Klíma explores spiritual alienation, the collapse of morality and ethics under Communist rule, and the turbulence of the post-Communist period. A Jew, he spent three years in a Nazi concentration camp during World War II, and his first published writing records the experience. He gained prominence in the 1960s for his dramas condemning Communist ethics, and his works were banned in his native country from 1969 to 1988. His plays, including *The Castle* (*Zámek*, 1964), *The Jury* (*Porota*, 1969), and *The Pastry Shop Miriam* (*Cukrárna Myriam*, 1971), are Kafkaesque tragicomedies linked with the Theater of the Absurd. Klíma has also examined the deep strains in Czech society in perceptive novels, among them *A Ship Named Hope* (*Loď Jménem Naděje*, 1969), *Judge on Trial* (*Soudce z Milosti*, 1986), *Love and Garbage* (*Láska a Smetí*, 1988), and

Waiting for the Dark, Waiting for the Light (*Čekání na Tmu, Čekání na Světlo*, 1993).

Koestler, Arthur (September 5, 1905–c. March 3, 1983). Hungarian-born English novelist and essayist. Best known for the novel DARKNESS AT NOON (1940), Koestler was an important modern writer on politics and philosophical ethics who examined fascist and Stalinist ideologies. Born in Budapest, Koestler was taken by his parents to Vienna on the outbreak of World War I, and worked as a journalist for several European newspapers in the 1920s and 1930s. He joined the Communist Party in 1932 and was imprisoned by the Fascists while covering the Spanish Civil War in the late 1930s. Narrowly escaping death, he ultimately settled in England. He explored the experience in memoirs, including *Spanish Testament* (1937) and *The Scum of the Earth* (1941). Koestler's break with Communism over Stalinist ideology inspired such essay collections as *The Yogi and the Commissar* (1945) and the novels *The Gladiators* (1939) and *Darkness at Noon*, in which an aging Bolshevik must face the horrors of Stalinist crimes. Koestler's later writings include a historical study of the Jews in Palestine, *Promise and Fulfillment* (1949), and a philosophical investigation of science and art, *The Act of Creation* (1964). *Bricks to Babel* (1981) is a selection of writings from his 50-year career. Koestler and his third wife, Cynthia, died in a double suicide; their bodies were discovered on March 3, 1983.

Kosinski, Jerzy (June 14, 1933–May 3, 1991). Polish-born American novelist. Kosinski is best known for his first, highly successful, purportedly autobiographical novel, THE PAINTED BIRD (1965). The novel's strictly autobiographical veracity was disputed in the 1980s, but it remains a major work of Holocaust literature, telling the haunting story of a young boy suffering brutality as he wanders alone through Eastern Europe, attempting to escape the Germans. As a Jewish child in Poland, Kosinski was hidden during World War II. He later studied at the University of Lodz and became a professor of sociology at the Polish Academy of Sciences.

He immigrated to the United States in 1957 and earned prominence with two sociological essays on Soviet communism, *The Future Is Ours, Comrade* (1960) and *No Third Path* (1962), published under the pseudonym Joseph Novak. Kosinski's later novels include *Steps* (1968; National Book Award), *Being There* (1970), *The Devil Tree* (1973), *Cockpit* (1975), and *The Hermit of 69th Street* (1988). Kosinski took his own life in 1991.

Kundera, Milan (April 1, 1929–). Czech novelist, playwright, poet, and short-story writer, writing in Czech and French. Kundera's first works—poetry collections published in the 1950s—gained attention for their eroticism and ironic social commentary, attributes for which they were also condemned by Czech authorities. After the Soviet invasion in 1968, Kundera's works were banned, and in 1975 he left Czechoslovakia, settling in France. His books were prohibited in his native country until 1989. Kundera earned international acclaim for his novels, which focus on contemporary love relationships and are marked by reflective speculation on the nature of modern culture and society. He is noted for his ironic tone and polyphonic, musical structures, interweaving multiple voices and points of view. Among his best-known novels are *The Joke* (*Žert*, 1967), *Life Is Elsewhere* (*Život Je Jinde*, 1969), THE BOOK OF LAUGHTER AND FORGETTING (*Kniha Smíchu a Zapomnění*, 1979), and THE UNBEARABLE LIGHTNESS OF BEING (*Nesnesitelná Lehkost Bytí*, 1984). Kundera's recent novels, written in French, include *Slowness* (*La Lenteur*, 1997) and *Identity* (*L'Identité*, 1998).

Kunitz, Stanley J[asspon] (July 29, 1905–). American poet. A master of rhythm and diction, Kunitz is among the most esteemed of modern American metaphysical poets. After studying at Harvard, he worked as an editor and published his first collection of poetry, *Intellectual Things*, in 1930. His early poetry, gathered in *Selected Poems: 1928–1958* (1958; Pulitzer Prize), is intricately crafted in form and intellectual in tone. Beginning with *The Testing Tree* (1971), he developed a more personal, open, and ver-

nacular style that nonetheless retains the precise craftsmanship that has made him a "poet's poet." Kunitz's later volumes include *The Coat Without a Seam* (1974), *The Terrible Threshold* (1974), *Next-to-Last Things* (1985), *Passing Through* (1995; National Book Award), and *Collected Poems* (2000). He taught poetry for many years at Columbia University and edited a number of literary reference books. He was named U.S. Poet Laureate for the term 1974–76, and again for 2000–2001.

Kureishi, Hanif (December 5, 1954–). English playwright, novelist, and screenwriter. With its irreverent humor and vivid urban atmosphere, Kureishi's work portrays the multicultural lives of South Asians in England, examining with a satirical edge English racism, Muslim narrowness, and sexual prejudice. The son of an Indian immigrant father and an English mother, he was raised in a suburb of London and educated at King's College. Kureishi first gained wide acclaim with his screenplays for the films *My Beautiful Laundrette* (1985), *Sammy and Rosie Get Laid* (1987), and *London Kills Me* (1991), the last of which he also directed. His other works include the novels *The Buddha of Suburbia* (1989), *The Black Album* (1995), and *Intimacy* (1998); the short-story collection *Midnight All Day* (1999); and the play *Sleep with Me* (1999).

Kushner, Tony (July 16, 1956–). American playwright. Kushner emerged as a leading American playwright with his two-part, seven-hour play on the AIDS epidemic, ANGELS IN AMERICA: *A Gay Fantasia on National Themes* (1991), comprising *Millennium Approaches* (Pulitzer Prize) and *Perestroika*. Born in New York City, Kushner grew up in Louisiana and returned to New York to study at Columbia University and New York University. His first play produced in New York, *A Bright Room Called Day* (1985), is set in Berlin in the 1930s. Kushner's dramas explore social ethics in repressive political climates, focusing on such issues as sexuality, religion, socialist politics, and gay rights. His plays frequently incorporate fantasy and symbolism and draw conceptually from the work of Marx, FREUD, and BRECHT. Other plays include *Slavs! (Thinking About the Longstanding Problems of Virtue and Happiness)* (1994), which concerns the collapse of the Soviet Union, and free adaptations of CORNEILLE's *The Illusion* (1994) and S. Ansky's *THE DYBBUK* (1998).

Kyd, Thomas (c. November 1558–c. December 1594). English playwright. Kyd is remembered today for only one work, *The Spanish Tragedie* (c. 1582–92), one of the most popular plays of Elizabethan England. A compelling story of revenge, it introduced to England the genre of the revenge tragedy and was subsequently widely imitated by other contemporary playwrights. Indeed, the play's plot and leading character, Hieronimo, were sources for SHAKE-SPEARE's *HAMLET*; some scholars have even speculated that Kyd wrote an earlier (now lost) version of *Hamlet*. Little is known of Kyd's life, except that he worked as a scribe before turning to the theater and that he was arrested for heresy in 1593, possibly in connection with his friend, playwright and atheist Christopher MARLOWE. Kyd also wrote the play *Cornelia* (1594); scholars disagree on which other works may be attributed to him.

Laclos, [Pierre-Ambroise-François] Choderlos de (October 18, 1741–November 5, 1803). French novelist. Although Laclos wrote poetry, pamphlets, and essays, including an admiring critique of Fanny BURNEY's *Cecilia*, he is remembered solely for his only novel, *LES LIAISONS DANGEREUSES*, which created an international sensation when it was published in the spring of 1782. Told entirely in letters, the novel depicts, with pitiless detachment and great artistry, the schemes of a pair of unscrupulous aristocrats whose licentiousness and moral depravity is so shocking that even so subtle a reader as André GIDE declared that Laclos was "hand in glove with the devil." He was in fact a rather conventional man, a loving husband and doting father, who planned to write a second novel to prove his thesis that "there is no happiness to be found except within the family," but this project was never realized. Born in Amiens

to a family of minor nobility, Laclos received a commission in the Royal Artillery Corps in 1761, and spent his entire career as a highly respected professional soldier, with particular expertise in fortifications, eventually rising to the rank of general under Napoleon. In 1803, he died in Italy, where he had been posted as Artillery Commander of the French Army of the Kingdom of Naples.

La Fontaine, Jean de (c. July 8, 1621–April 13, 1695). French poet. La Fontaine's verse *FABLES* (1668–94) are counted among the masterpieces of French literature. Although he became a productive poet relatively late in life—he wrote his first significant poem when he was 37— La Fontaine went on to create a body of work whose popularity has never waned. Born into a respectable provincial family in Château-Thierry, a town about 50 miles from Paris, he had an unexceptional academic career: Latin and Greek at the local *collège* were followed by a few years of theology and law in Paris, where he began to frequent literary circles and to think of himself as a poet. In time, he gained the respect and support of several well-placed patrons, including the Duchesse de Bouillon and Madame de la Sablière. The *Fables* were published in 12 books over the last 25 years of his life and comprise more than 240 poems. Inspired by the Greek AESOP, the Roman Phaedrus, and the Indian storyteller Bidpai, they transcend the form's didactic idealism, retelling the simple stories with a worldly tone, exploring human vanity and moral dilemmas with generous warmth and ironic wit. La Fontaine was elected to the Académie Française in 1684.

Lagerkvist, Pär (May 23, 1891–July 11, 1974). Swedish novelist, playwright, and poet. Lagerkvist's work characteristically explores the need to reconcile spiritual values and faith with the skepticism and turmoil of the 20th century. His early plays and poems as well as his novel *The Eternal Smile* (*Det Eviga Leendet*, 1920) are composed in an Expressionist mode influenced by STRINDBERG, while his works of the 1930s, among them the novel *The Hangman* (*Bödeln*, 1933) and the play *The Man Without a Soul*

(*Mannen utan Själ*, 1936), examine human brutality in the context of totalitarianism. Lagerkvist gained international recognition with his symbolic novels *The Dwarf* (*Dvärgen*, 1944), about a Renaissance court retainer disfigured by hate, and BARABBAS (1950), drawn from the New Testament story about a man who was released from prison in place of JESUS. Other major works include the autobiographical novel *Guest of Reality* (*Gäst hos Verkligheten*, 1925) and the late novel *The Sibyl* (*Sibyllen*, 1956). Lagerkvist's stature was acknowledged when he was awarded the Nobel Prize in Literature in 1951.

Lagerlöf, Selma (November 20, 1858–March 16, 1940). Swedish novelist and short-story writer. Lagerlöf lived most of her life in the Swedish countryside and drew her fiction from folk tales and the ancient Icelandic sagas. Her work extends the tradition of Romanticism, spinning, in lyrical, simple language, folkloric legends in vivid rural settings. Her first novel, *Gösta Berling's Saga* (*Gösta Berlings Saga*, 1891), remains her best known. *The Miracles of Antichrist* (*Antikrists Mirakler*, 1897) and *Jerusalem* (1901–2) reflect her travels to Sicily and Palestine, respectively. Other works include the novella *The Tale of a Manor* (*En Herrgårdssägen*, 1899), the novel trilogy published as *The Ring of the Löwenskölds* (*Löwensköldska Ringen*, 1925–28), and the memoirs *Mårbacka* (1922), named after her country estate, and *Memories of My Childhood* (*Ett Barns Memoarer*, 1930). Lagerlöf also wrote an acclaimed two-volume children's book, *The Wonderful Adventures of Nils* (*Nils Holgerssons Underbara Resa genom Sverige*, 1906–7). In 1909 she became the first woman and the first Swede to win the Nobel Prize in Literature.

Lampedusa, Giuseppe Tomasi di (December 23, 1896–July 23, 1957). Italian novelist. Lampedusa's international reputation rests on his sole novel, THE LEOPARD (*Il Gattopardo*, 1958), a rich historical and psychological portrait of a 19th-century Sicilian aristocratic family, who witness the decline of the old nobility and the rise of the bourgeoisie. Born to the Sicilian nobility, he was the duke of Palma and the prince of Lampedusa. He planned a diplomatic career, but abandoned that path after serving as an artillery officer in World War I, during which he was held prisoner of war. After the war, he retreated into a private life of intellectual study, and began to write only during the last years of his life. His novel *The Leopard* and collection *Two Stories and a Memory* (*Racconti*, 1961) were published posthumously. *The Leopard* was adapted into an acclaimed film by Luchino Visconti in 1963.

Lardner, Ring[gold] (March 6, 1885–September 25, 1933). American short-story writer. Lardner's stories are praised for their sharp, satirical treatment of contemporary American life and follies, as well as for their deftly drawn characters and narrative voices. Raised in the Midwest, he began his writing career in sports journalism and eventually wrote a syndicated weekly humor column for the *Chicago Tribune*. His first volume, *You Know Me Al* (1916), is a collection of mordantly witty short stories written in the guise of letters from a rookie baseball player. Lardner moved to New York City in 1919 and won wide recognition with his collection *How to Write Short Stories* (1924), which parodies familiar short fiction styles and includes the well-known story "Champion." His other works include the collections *Gullible's Travels* (1917) and *The Love Nest* (1926) and the play *June Moon* (1929), cowritten with George S. KAUFMAN.

Larkin, Philip (August 9, 1922–December 2, 1985). English poet and novelist. A writer of spare, often cynical and pessimistic verse, Larkin was the chief figure in an anti-Romantic movement in English poetry during the 1950s. Born into a working-class family in the north of England, Larkin was educated at Oxford and worked as a librarian throughout his career, including 30 years as head librarian at the University of Hull. His first published works were the poetry collection *The North Ship* (1945) and the lyrical novels *Jill* (1946) and *A Girl in Winter* (1947), but he established his mature style with the acclaimed volume of poetry *The*

Less Deceived (1955). Larkin was loosely associated with the antimodernist, anti-experimental group of poets called The Movement, which embraced precision and clarity through a return to traditional techniques. But his style was original, using colloquial language to write exclusively about the realities of modern life, especially about its mundane disillusionments and disappointments, with a wry, bleak, mordant lucidity. He once told the *Observer*, "I think writing about unhappiness is probably the source of my popularity.... Deprivation is for me what daffodils were for Wordsworth." His later collections of poetry include *The Whitsun Windows* (1964), *High Windows* (1974), and *Aubade* (1980). Larkin's jazz criticism is collected in the anthology *All What Jazz?: A Record Diary 1961–68* (1970) and his other criticism in *Required Writing* (1982).

La Rochefoucauld, [François VI, Duc de] (September 15, 1613–March 16, 1680). French prose writer. A singular figure of the French classical period, La Rochefoucauld shaped his biting, satirical observations of human nature into spare, elegant epigrams. He was involved with the Fronde, an insurrectionist movement against the excesses of royal power, but eventually regained the court's tolerance. He and his circle of intellectual intimates often played a game in which they tried to summarize human manners and behavior in brief, witty *aperçus*. His notes reflecting on the game led to the writing of his famous MAXIMS (*Maximes*, 1665–78), in which he powerfully dissects human pretenses, conceits, and motives, revealing the self-interest at their core. His epigrams widely influenced later writings in the form. La Rochefoucauld's only other publication is his *Memoirs* (*Mémoires*, 1662).

Lautréamont, [Comte de], *pen name of* Lucien Ducasse (April 4, 1846–November 24, 1870). French poet. Born and raised in Montevideo, Uruguay, the son of a French consular official, Lautréamont was educated from about age 13 in France, at Tarbes and Pau. In 1867 he moved to Paris, where, supported by his father, he began writing his six-part prose

poem, *The Songs of Maldoror* (*Les Chants de Maldoror*). The first stanza was published anonymously in 1868 and the complete text printed in 1869, but the work, inspired by BAUDELAIRE and popular Gothic novels, was so disturbing that its publisher, Albert Lacroix, refused to distribute it until 1874. *Maldoror* remained little known until 1927, when the French Surrealist movement adopted it as a seminal text. Lautréamont's only complete publication in his lifetime was a collection of poems, *Poésies* (1870). That same year he was found dead at age 24, the cause unknown; it is thought by some that he was assassinated by police during the siege of Paris. Lautréamont took his pseudonym (varying the spelling) from the eponymous hero of Eugène Sue's historical novel *Latréaumont* (1837).

Lawrence, D[avid] **H**[erbert] (September 11, 1885–March 2, 1930). English novelist, poet, short-story writer, and essayist. Believing that "nothing that comes from the deep passional soul is bad, or can be bad," Lawrence lived and wrote with a violent intensity that shocked his contemporaries. Born to a coal miner in the Midlands region of England, he grew up in a household rife with hostility between his father and more genteel mother, an atmosphere he explored in his autobiographical novel, *SONS AND LOVERS* (1913). Lawrence attended University College in Nottingham and taught school before devoting himself to writing; his first

---

"Never trust the artist. Trust the tale. The proper function of a critic is to save the tale from the artist who created it."

D. H. Lawrence, *Studies in Classic American Literature* (1923)

---

novel, *The White Peacock*, was published in 1911. His marriage in 1914 to Frieda von Richthofen Weekley—which proved to be as much battlefield and struggle as mutually rewarding compact—inspired his greatest novels, *THE RAINBOW* (1915) and its sequel, *WOMEN IN LOVE* (1921), which teem with preoccupations that pervade all his work—sexuality, class, the damaging constraints of social convention, and the tumultuous relationship between man and woman. In 1915, Lawrence and his wife left England and traveled widely until his death from tuberculosis in 1930. His other novels include *The Lost Girl* (1920), AARON'S ROD (1922), *Kangaroo* (1923), *The Plumed Serpent* (1926), and the notorious LADY CHATTERLEY'S LOVER, completed in 1928 but banned in the United States and England for the next 30 years. His *Studies in Classic American Literature* (1923) is a distinguished work of criticism. *The Complete Poems of D. H. Lawrence* (1964) is a definitive collection that also includes Lawrence's critical introductions to his poems. "Not I, But the Wind..." (1934) is Frieda's spirited, if not entirely candid, account of her life with Lawrence.

Lawrence, T[homas] **E**[dward] (August 15, 1888–May 19, 1935). English writer. Commonly known as "Lawrence of Arabia," Lawrence wrote of his role in the Arab revolt against Turkey during World War I. He was educated at Oxford and went to the Middle East as an archaeologist in 1911. At the beginning of the war, he worked with British intelligence to organize an Arab rebellion against Turkey, an ally of Germany. As a result of his strategies, he became a legendary figure and a hero among the Arabs, whom he represented at the Paris Peace Conference in Versailles in 1919. Lawrence's account of his experience, *The Seven Pillars of Wisdom* (1926), abridged as *Revolt in the Desert* (1927), was widely admired for its vigorous depiction of his military campaign, although it has been described as overwritten. In his later years, Lawrence withdrew from the public eye, serving in the Air Force under aliases. His other writings include a prose translation of HOMER'S ODYSSEY (1932) and the memoir *The Mint* (1938).

Laxness, Halldór, *pen name of* Halldór Kiljan Gudjónsson (April 23, 1902–February 8, 1998). Icelandic novelist. The son of a farmer, Laxness learned many lines of Old Icelandic poetry at his grandmother's knee before he could even read. In his youth he traveled extensively, adopting and then rejecting Catholicism, then embracing Socialism during a stay in the United States. He returned to Iceland in 1930, and for two decades his principal subject was the plight of Iceland's poor farmers and fishermen, as in *Salka Valka* (*Þú Vínviður Hreini*, 1931, and *Fuglinn í Fjörunni*, 1932), INDEPENDENT PEOPLE (*Sjálfstætt Fólk*, 1934–35), and *The Light of the World* (*Ljós Heimsins*, 1937–40). From the late 1940s onward, he turned for inspiration to the saga tradition and the Icelandic past, as in *The Bell of Iceland* (*Íslandsklukkan*, 1943–46), while also producing works with a satirical edge, like *The Atom Station* (*Atómstöðin*, 1948). He published several volumes of memoirs in his 70s and 80s. Laxness was awarded the Nobel Prize in Literature in 1955; in the presentation, he was extolled for having "renewed the Icelandic language as an artistic means of expression."

Lazarus, Emma (July 22, 1849–November 19, 1887). American poet and essayist. Although her fame today rests mainly on one poem, New York–native Lazarus published several books and elicited admiration from such contemporaries as Ralph Waldo EMERSON. While still in her teens she published *Poems and Translations* (1866); subsequent works include *Admetus and Other Poems* (1871), *Alide: An Episode of Goethe's Life* (1874), and *The Spagnoletto: A Drama in Verse* (1876). In 1882 her life changed drastically when she reacted with outrage to news of Russian pogroms; from that point on, she was consciously a Jewish writer and a spokeswoman for Jewish causes. *Songs of a Semite* (1882) reflects her new passion. In 1883, while working with Jewish immigrants, she wrote a sonnet, "The New Colossus," as a contribution to the fundraising campaign for the Statue of Liberty. It hails the United States as a haven for the world's unwanted: "Give me your tired, your poor, / Your huddled masses yearning to breathe free, / The wretched refuse of your teeming shore." In 1903, the poem was inscribed on the Statue's pedestal.

Lear, Edward (May 12, 1812–January 29, 1888). English humorist, poet, and travel writer. Famous in his time also as a landscape artist, illustrator, and travel writer, Lear is remembered today chiefly for his books of nonsense verse and limericks. The 20th of 21 children, Lear was a sickly child, and suffered all his life from epilepsy, asthma, and bronchitis. He began earning his living as an artist, his first love, while in his teens; among his most significant achievements was *Illustrations of the Family of Psittacidae, or Parrots* (1832), the first illustrated work devoted to a single family of birds, for which he created both the hand-colored lithographs and the text. A commission to draw the animals on the estate of the Earl of Derby brought him into contact from 1832 to 1837 with the Earl's children, for whom he began writing the limericks (a form he popularized) that he would eventually publish, under the pseudonym Derry Down Derry, as *The Book of Nonsense* (1846; expanded 1861, 1863). From 1837 onward, prompted by ill health and failing eyesight, he concentrated on landscape painting, traveling extensively in southern Europe, North Africa, the Near East, Ceylon, and India, and publishing several well-regarded illustrated travel books, including *Views in Rome and Its Environs* (1841) and *Journals of a Landscape Painter in Albania, etc.* (1851). But it is his collections of self-illustrated verse, prose, and songs (some of which he set to music himself) that have ensured his fame; although written ostensibly for children, they are much treasured by adults as well, for as T. S. ELIOT noted, "His non-sense is not vacuity of sense: it is a parody of sense, and that is the sense of it." "The Owl and the Pussycat" (1871), "The Jumblies" (1871), and "The Dong with a Luminous Nose" (1877) are among his best-known longer poems. He died in San Remo, Italy, at "Villa Emily" (named for his good friend Emily Tennyson, the wife of Alfred, Lord TENNYSON), where—grown weary of traveling—he had made his main home since 1871; his tombstone is inscribed, "A landscape painter in many lands."

Le Carré, John, *pen name of* David Cornwell (October 19, 1931–). English novelist. Based on firsthand experience in diplomatic intelligence, Le Carré's novels feature byzantine plots, subtly drawn characters, and realistic portrayals of international intrigue. Educated at Oxford, Le Carré taught briefly at Eton before joining the British Foreign Office in 1960. He began writing thrillers while stationed in West Germany and ended his diplomatic career after the enormous success of his third novel, the bestselling Cold War thriller *The Spy Who Came In from the Cold* (1963), which brought him acclaim as a master of the contemporary spy novel. His next works, *The Looking Glass War* (1965) and *A Small Town in Germany* (1968), were also bestsellers. The trilogy consisting of *Tinker, Tailor, Soldier, Spy* (1974), *The Honourable Schoolboy* (1977), and *Smiley's People* (1980) centers on his best-known character, the retiring but ever-resourceful secret agent George Smiley. Later titles include *The Little Drummer Girl* (1983), *A Perfect Spy* (1986), *The Russia House* (1989), *The Secret Pilgrim* (1991), *The Night Manager* (1993), *The Tailor of Panama* (1996), and *The Constant Gardener* (2000).

Lee, [Nelle] Harper (April 28, 1926–). American novelist. Since winning the Pulitzer Prize for her first novel, TO KILL A MOCKINGBIRD (1960), Lee has published only a few essays. Nevertheless, the novel—a treatment of intolerance and nobility, told from the point of view of a six-year-old girl—assures her place in American literature. A childhood friend of Truman CAPOTE in Monroeville, Alabama, Lee shares with him a gift for evoking a child's view of life in a small southern town of the 1930s. In 1959 she traveled to Holcomb, Kansas, to assist Capote in his research for IN COLD BLOOD (1966).

Le Guin, Ursula K[roeber] (October 21, 1929–). American science-fiction and fantasy writer. Berkeley-born and Radcliffe-educated, Le Guin is the daughter of renowned anthropologist Alfred L. Kroeber and anthropologist-writer Theodora Kroeber. The lessons she learned from them served her in creating the realistically described worlds of her novels, in which she joins fantastic plots to serious concerns—the need for tolerance, the fragmentation of the human psyche, the limitations of partriarchy. The first world Le Guin created was the planet Hain, whose inhabitants spread throughout the universe to colonize the other planets. The three early Hainish novels—*Rocannon's World* (1966), *Planet of Exile* (1966), *City of Illusions* (1967)—were joined three decades later by a fourth, *The Telling* (2000). Another cycle, the four Earthsea novels (1968–90), was intended for young adults. Among Le Guin's most highly regarded works are THE LEFT HAND OF DARKNESS (1969) and *The Dispossessed* (1974), each of which won both the Nebula and Hugo awards. Her essays are collected in *The Language of Night* (1979) and *Dancing at the Edge of the World* (1989).

Lem, Stanisław (September 12, 1921–). Polish science-fiction writer, memoirist, and essayist. Born and raised in Lwów, Poland, Lem resettled with his family in Krakow in 1946, when his hometown became Lvov, Ukraine. He had studied medicine, but gave up the profession to avoid serving as an army doctor for Poland's new Communist government, and instead began writing realistic stories and lyric poetry. By the 1950s he had turned to the science fiction for which he is world famous, with novels such as *Astronauts* (*Astronauci*, 1951) and *Eden* (1959). Lem's concentration on an "unimportant" genre permitted him to use his stories (written in an impressive variety of styles) as vehicles for risky sociopolitical commentary. Among his best-known works are *Solaris* (1961), about a sentient ocean that creates disturbing visions in the scientists who attempt to study it; *The Cyberiad* (*Cyberiada*, 1965); *Tales of Pirx the Pilot* (*Opowieści o Pilocie Pirxie*, 1968); and *Imaginary Magnitude* (*Wielkość Urojona*, 1973), an homage to Jorge Luis BORGES, to whom Lem has sometimes been compared. Other works include his memoir, *Highcastle: A Remembrance* (*Wysoki Zamek*, 1966). A recent novel, after a long, self-imposed retirement

from fiction, is *Okamgnienie* (2000; Twinkling of an Eye).

Leonard, Elmore (October 11, 1925–). American novelist. Transcending mere entertainment, Leonard's crime novels and westerns are admired for their brilliant dialogue and black humor, and for conveying a sense of place, whether it be New Mexico, Detroit, or South Beach, Florida. Although his plots appear to be tightly constructed, his characters—grifters, crime bosses, amiable losers, psychopaths, women with a mission—act out a chain of events that Leonard creates as he goes along. Born in New Orleans, Leonard served in the Naval Reserve and then attended the University of Detroit. In the 1950s, he began writing westerns, including *Hombre* (1961) and *Valdez Is Coming* (1970), both of which were made into films. However, it was his gripping crime novels, many of which have been filmed, that gained him a wide readership. *Fifty-Two Pickup* (1974) brought recognition; with *Stick* (1983) he became a consistently bestselling author. Other popular suspense novels include *La Brava* (1983; Edgar Award), *Glitz* (1985), *Get Shorty* (1990), *Rum Punch* (1992), *Out of Sight* (1996), and *Pagan Babies* (2000). At times Leonard merges genres, as in *Cuba Libre* (1998), where a bank-robbing cowboy with a scheme for gunrunning is plopped into the Spanish-American War. Leonard is also the author of an e-book, *Fire in the Hole* (2001).

Leopardi, Giacomo (June 29, 1798–June 14, 1837). Italian poet. Considered Italy's greatest poet of the modern era, Leopardi was a child prodigy who acquired vast learning while still in his teens, but physical deformity (curvature of the spine) and poor health plagued him all his life, perhaps contributing to his fundamental and profound pessimism. His 41 poems, known as *I Canti* from two collections published in his lifetime (1831, 1835), are notable for their limpid musicality and "grace and force of words" (W. M. Rossetti). Among the best known are "The Infinite" ("L'Infinito," written 1819), "To Silvia" ("A Silvia," written 1828), addressed to a young girl who has just died, and "The

Broom Flower" ("La Ginestra," written 1836, published 1845). The last, a piercing indictment of 19th-century religiosity and progressivism, proclaims his mature philosophy: mankind should follow the example of the humble broom, flowering sweetly on the slopes of Vesuvius, rather than cherish illusions of divine favor in the face of "stepmother nature's" indifference and devastation. Leopardi's prose works, especially the *Moral Essays* (*Operette Morali*, 1827; also translated as *Essays and Dialogues*) and the posthumously published *Notebook* or *Thoughts* (*Zibaldone di Pensieri*, published as *Pensieri di Varia Filosofia e di Bella Letteratura*, 1898–1900), are also highly regarded.

Lermontov, Mikhail (October 15, 1814–July 27, 1841). Russian poet, novelist, and playwright. Lermontov is considered Russia's greatest poet after PUSHKIN. Although BYRON was a lifelong inspiration to him, Lermontov's Byronism was not affectation; it derived from his background and temperament. After a privileged but isolated childhood, he was commissioned an officer of hussars in St. Petersburg. An 1837 poem, "The Death of a Poet" ("Smert' Poèta," published 1856), in which he accused the aristocracy of complicity in Pushkin's death, circulated like wildfire in manuscript, turning him overnight into a national celebrity, but also sending him into temporary exile in the Caucasus. The region's magnificent landscapes and unsubdued indigenous peoples inspired much of his finest poetry, beloved lyrics as well as narrative poems like "The Novice" ("Mtsyri," 1840) and *The Demon* (*Demon*, first complete publication 1856). During another period of exile following a duel, Lermontov distinguished himself in combat in Chechnya, only to be killed in another duel at the age of 26. His best-known work outside Russia is his only novel, the structurally complex, innovative *A HERO OF OUR TIME* (*Geroĭ Nashego Vremeni*, 1840; one translation is by Vladimir NABOKOV), the first Russian psychological novel. Its antihero is one of the first "superfluous men" (in TURGENEV's phrase) haunting 19th-century Russian literature. Somewhat like Lermontov himself, such

men possess the capacity for heroic action, but lack meaningful scope for it in an age of mediocrity and repression.

Lessing, Doris, *original name* Doris Tayler (October 22, 1919–). English novelist and short-story writer. Born in Kermanshah, Persia (now Iran), and raised on a farm in Southern Rhodesia (now Zimbabwe), Lessing has brought a penetrating and inventive narrative style to weighty contemporary themes: political upheaval, racial injustice, feminine identity, and the quest for self-knowledge in a chaotic world. Her first two books—*The Grass Is Singing* (1950) and the story collection *This Was the Old Chief's Country* (1951), both set in Africa—appeared shortly after she settled in England in 1949. From 1952 to 1969, Lessing produced a series of five novels, collectively entitled *The Children of Violence*, which follow an autobiographical character named Martha Quest. *THE GOLDEN NOTEBOOK* (1962), her most acclaimed work, is a complex novel of ideas hailed as a landmark by the feminist movement. After a foray into "inner space fiction," in which she explored the depths of personal and societal breakdown, Lessing abandoned the realistic mode for an imaginative flight of "space fiction" in the five-novel series *Canopus in Argos: Archives* (1979–83). *Under My Skin* (1994) is the first volume of her autobiography; *Walking in the Shade* (1997) is the second.

Lessing, Gotthold Ephraim (January 22, 1729–February 15, 1781). German playwright and critic. A central figure in the German Enlightenment and perhaps the first modern German writer of European stature, Lessing owes his place in German literature equally to his well-crafted and accessible dramas, which still hold the stage, and to his lucid and penetratingly intelligent theoretical writings on theater, aesthetics, and religion. Lessing worked most of his life as a journalist and freelance author in Berlin, Leipzig, and elsewhere in Germany. After participating in an unsuccessful attempt to create a German national theater at Hamburg, he published the *Hamburg Dra-*

maturgy (*Hamburgische Dramaturgie*, 1767–69), rejecting French dramatic models in favor of English and reinterpreting ARISTOTLE's *Poetics* in the light of SHAKESPEARE. His treatise *Laocoön, or On the Limits of Painting and Poetry* (*Laokoon, oder Über die Grenzen der Malerei und Poesie*, 1766) distinguished between the aesthetic tasks of visual art and poetry. Lessing's major plays are *Miss Sara Sampson* (1755), the first German domestic tragedy; the comedy *Minna von Barnhelm* (1767), in which a resolute woman's love prevails over a man's unbending principles; the tragedy *Emilia Galotti* (1772), a variant on the ancient theme of death before dishonor; and the "dramatic poem" *Nathan the Wise* (*Nathan der Weise*, 1779), an eloquent plea for religious tolerance and the first important German drama in blank verse. Lessing spent his final years as the librarian at Wolfenbüttel.

Levertov, Denise, *original surname* Levertoff (October 24, 1923–December 20, 1997). English-born American poet and essayist. The daughter of a Welsh mother and a Russian-Jewish father who became an Anglican priest, Levertov was educated at home and began writing poetry as a child. After marrying the American poet Mitchell Goodman in 1947, she settled in the United States, where she came under the influence of WILLIAM CARLOS WILLIAMS and the Black Mountain poets. Such early collections as *With Eyes at the Back of Our Heads* (1959), *The Jacob's Ladder* (1961), and *O Taste and See* (1964) forged the idiomatic style, imagistic clarity, and emotional immediacy for which her poetry became known. Her passionate opposition to the Vietnam War found expression in *The Sorrow Dance* (1967) and *Relearning the Alphabet* (1970); her concern for feminist, Third World, and other political causes is a recurring theme in her work. Experiences of the everyday, the political, and the mystical come together in such later volumes as *Footprints* (1972), *Candles in Babylon* (1982), *Breathing the Water* (1987), *A Door in the Hive* (1989), and *Sands of the Well* (1996). Her essays appear in *The Poet in the World* (1973).

Levi, Primo (July 31, 1919–April 11, 1987). Italian memoirist, short-story writer, essayist, and poet. Levi's mission as a survivor of Auschwitz was to record, describe, and analyze the world inside the concentration camps. Born in Turin, he grew up in an Italian-Jewish family and earned a doctorate in chemistry. In 1943, he was arrested as a member of the anti-Fascist resistance and deported to Auschwitz. After liberation, he returned to Turin, where he resumed his career as a chemist and published his two major works of witness: *Survival in Auschwitz* (*Se Questo È un Uomo*, 1947; U.K. title, *If This Is a Man*) and *The Reawakening* (*La Tregua*, 1963; U.K. title, *The Truce*). Levi acquired international recognition in 1984 with the English-language publication of THE PERIODIC TABLE (*Il Sistema Periodico*, 1975), a memoir combining insights from chemistry with personal reminiscences. His last work, *The Drowned and the Saved* (*I Sommersi e i Salvati*, 1986), is a penetrating analysis of the legacy of the Holocaust. He died in 1987, an apparent suicide.

Lewis, C[live] S[taples] (November 29, 1898–November 22, 1963). English novelist, critic, and essayist. Widely known for his imaginative and apologetic writings on Christian belief and morality—notably THE SCREWTAPE LETTERS (1942) and *The Problem of Pain* (1940)—and for the *Perelandra* science-fiction trilogy and the *Chronicles of Narnia* fantasy series for children, Lewis was equally successful as a literary scholar. A fellow at Magdalen College, Oxford, from 1925 to 1954, he established his reputation with several critical studies: *The Allegory of Love* (1936), a standard text on medieval literary tradition; *A Preface to Paradise Lost* (1942); and *English Literature in the 16th Century* (1954). He began writing on religious themes after a Christian reawakening in 1931, recounted in *Surprised by Joy* (1955). *Out of the Silent Planet* (1938) was the first of his science-fiction allegories about the conflict between good and evil; *Perelandra* (1943) and *That Hideous Strength* (1945) completed the trilogy. *The Lion, the Witch and the Wardrobe* (1950) began his popular seven-volume series about the kingdom of

Narnia. Lewis taught medieval and Renaissance literature at Cambridge from 1954 to 1963.

Lewis, [Harry] Sinclair (February 7, 1885–January 10, 1951). American novelist. His five popular novels of the 1920s, sharply satiric portrayals of middle-class values and small-town manners in the American Midwest, earned Lewis the Nobel Prize in Literature in 1930 — the first awarded to an American writer. Lewis was born in the village of Sauk Centre, Minnesota, which served as a model for Gopher Prairie, the setting of his first important work, MAIN STREET (1920). After graduating from Yale in 1908, he worked as a journalist and editor for several years and wrote five unsuccessful novels before the sensation of *Main Street*. He continued his satire of Middle American provincialism with BABBITT (1922), about a smug, self-satisfied small businessman; ARROWSMITH (1925; Pulitzer Prize), a jaundiced look at the medical profession and the thwarting of scientific ideals; ELMER GANTRY (1927), attacking hypocrisy in the evangelical revivalist movement; and *Dodsworth* (1929), the portrait of a middle-aged American industrialist traveling in Europe. Lewis published ten less successful novels after his Nobel Prize, including *It Can't Happen Here* (1935), a warning about Fascism in America, and *Kingsblood Royal* (1947), on racial bigotry. His second wife, from 1928 to 1942, was the journalist Dorothy Thompson.

Lewis, [Percy] Wyndham (November 18, 1882–March 7, 1957). Canadian-born English novelist, poet, and critic. A founder of Vorticism (an artistic/literary movement related to Futurism), Lewis, who was also an artist, edited the short-lived but influential Vorticist magazine, BLAST (1914–15). His paintings, some held in important museum collections, include both Vorticist and realistic works. As a writer he affected an outsider, contrarian stance, at one time adopting the sobriquet "The Enemy"; he reached his nadir with the pro-Nazi *Hitler* (1931), which dismissed its subject's anti-Semitism as a passing nonissue. Lewis's reputation never fully recovered from this fascist *apologia* and from the two pro-fascist pamphlets he produced in the mid-1930s, despite his later retractions in *The Jews, Are They Human?* (1939) and *The Hitler Cult and How It Will End* (1939). His fiction includes the novels *The Childermass* (1928; rev. and expanded as *The Human Age*, 1955–56); *The Apes of God* (1930), a merciless satire of the Bloomsbury Group and other modernists, including JOYCE, POUND, T. S. ELIOT, and STEIN; and the stories collected in *Rotting Hill* (1951). Nonfiction works include *The Art of Being Ruled* (1926), *Time and Western Man* (1927), *The Writer and the Absolute* (1952), and the memoirs *Blasting and Bombardiering* (1937) and *Rude Assignment* (1950).

Li Bo, *also known as* Li T'ai-po, Li Po, *or* Li Bai (701–762). Chinese poet. Referred to as the "Angel of Verse," Li Bo is considered one of China's greatest lyric poets. Widely admired in its day, his verse celebrates the majesty of mountain scenery, the philosophy of Taoism, and the exhilarating pleasures of wine, moonlight, and feminine beauty. A native of Szechwan (Sichuan) Province, he left home at age 20 to wander the landscapes of northern and central China. He spent the years 742–744 as a court poet of the Tang emperor in Chang'an (now X'ian) before resuming his travels. He served the rebellious Prince Lin beginning in 756 and was imprisoned the following year for complicity in a revolt, then banished to the remote southwest. Granted amnesty in 758, he returned to central China, where he continued to roam and compose poetry. According to legend (likely untrue), he died while drunkenly attempting to grasp the moonlight reflected on a river.

Lively, Penelope (March 17, 1933–). English novelist and children's writer. The central preoccupation of Lively's fiction is the interplay of history and memory, or what she terms "the jigsaw of time and reference." Her protagonists — historians, anthropologists, and architects — are often obsessed with time and with the presence of the past in the present. Lively grew up in Cairo, the child of English parents, and was educated at St. Anne's College, Oxford. She began her career writing children's books, which include *Astercote* (1970), *The Ghost of Thomas Kempe* (1973), and *A Stitch in Time* (1976). Her adult novels include *The Road to Lichfield* (1977), *Treasures of Time* (1979), *Moon Tiger* (1987; Booker Prize), *City of the Mind* (1991), *Heat Wave* (1996), and *Spiderweb* (1998). Her works also include a short-story collection, *Pack of Cards* (1986), and a memoir of her childhood in Egypt, *Oleander, Jacaranda* (1994).

Lodge, David (January 28, 1935–). English novelist, critic, and playwright. In fiction satirizing British academic life, Lodge enters his stories as an "intrusive narrator" who comments with detached wit on the unfolding plots. His best-known novels about academia, *Changing Places* (1975) and *Small World* (1984), are about two British and American professors who, in the first novel, trade places at their respective universities; the characters reappear in the later novel. Lodge grew up in a Roman Catholic family in London, and several of his novels are coming-of-age stories about British Catholic youth: *The Picturegoers* (1960), *The British Museum Is Falling Down* (1965), *Out of the Shelter* (1970), and *How Far Can You Go?* (1980; U.S. title, *Souls & Bodies*). He has also published literary studies such as *Language of Fiction* (1966), *The Novelist at the Crossroads* (1971), and *The Art of Fiction* (1992), and coauthored two plays, *Between These Four Walls* (1963) and *Slap in the Middle* (1965). His later novels include *Nice Work* (1988), *Paradise News* (1991), *Therapy* (1995), *Home Truths* (2000), and *Thinks* (2001).

London, Jack, *original name* John Griffith London (January 12, 1876–November 22, 1916). American novelist, short-story writer, and essayist. Raised in poverty, London rose from the slums of Oakland, California—and teenage experiences as a cannery worker, oyster pirate, seaman, and hobo—to become one of the most widely read American authors of the early 20th century. Almost entirely self-educated, London began his writing career after returning from a failed expedition in the Klondike Gold Rush of 1897. His rugged tales of freedom and survival

in the Alaskan wilderness, collected in *The Son of the Wolf* (1900), gained a wide following, and THE CALL OF THE WILD (1903), a novel about a tame sled-dog who becomes leader of a wolf pack, brought celebrity and fortune. Notable among London's other novels are THE SEA-WOLF (1904), about a tyrannical ship's captain; WHITE FANG (1906), another allegory of a dog's struggle to survive; and the largely autobiographical *Martin Eden* (1909). An ardent socialist, London considered his more ideological works, such as *The People of the Abyss* (1903) and *The Iron Heel* (1907), to be his most important. Destitute and ravaged by alcoholism, he committed suicide at age 40.

Longfellow, Henry Wadsworth (February 27, 1807–March 24, 1882). American poet. Longfellow created some of the most popular poetry of his day and gave a respected voice to uniquely American subject matter. Born in Maine to an old New England family, he studied in Europe for three years before returning to teach languages at his alma mater, Bowdoin College, and later Harvard. His first book, travel sketches entitled *Outre-Mer: A Pilgrimage Beyond the Sea* (1835), was followed by *Hyperion* (1839), a romantic novel; *Voices of the Night* (1839), his first book of verse; and *Ballads and Other Poems* (1842). Longfellow achieved enduring fame with the long narrative poems EVANGELINE (1847), *The Song of* HIAWATHA (1855), and *The Courtship of Miles Standish* (1858), and with *Tales of the Wayside Inn* (1863), which included "PAUL REVERE'S RIDE," familiar to generations of schoolchildren. Among the best known of his shorter poems are "The Village Blacksmith," "The Wreck of the Hesperus," "A Psalm of Life," and "The Arsenal at Springfield." His works also include a major translation of DANTE'S *DIVINE COMEDY* (1865–67) and the critical essay "Defense of Poetry" (1832).

Loos, Anita (April 26, 1893–August 18, 1981). American novelist, screenwriter, and playwright. A child actress and silent-screen writer in her native California, Loos earned instant celebrity with her novel *Gentlemen Prefer*

Blondes (1925), later adapted as a play, two musicals, and two films. The story of Lorelei LEE, a flighty blonde flapper and inveterate lover of diamonds, *Gentlemen* gave American popular culture one of its most endearing and familiar figures. Loos's work also includes the 1926 stage adaptation of *Gentlemen;* the novels *But Gentlemen Marry Brunettes* (1928), a largely unsuccessful sequel, and *No Mother to Guide Her* (1961); the plays *Happy Birthday* (1946), *A Mouse Is Born* (1951), and *Gigi* (1951, based on the novel by COLETTE); more than 60 screenplays and scenarios; and the autobiographical *A Girl Like I* (1966), *Kiss Hollywood Good-by* (1974), and *Cast of Thousands* (1977).

Lorde, Audre (February 18, 1934–November 17, 1992). American poet, novelist, essayist, and memoirist. Born in New York City to West Indian parents, Lorde began writing poetry in her teens. Her works, in collections that include *Cables to Rage* (1970), *The New York Head Shop and Museum* (1974), *Coal* (1976), *The Black Unicorn* (1978), and *Undersong: Chosen Poems Old and New* (1992), explore such personal/political themes as parent-child relationships, lesbian love, feminist politics, and rage against racial and other social discrimination. Her battles with the medical establishment over the treatment of her breast cancer are detailed in her prose works *The Cancer Journals* (1980) and *A Burst of Light* (1988). Other books include the novel *Zami: A New Spelling of My Name* (1982), which deals with the troubled relationship of a mother and daughter. In the late 1980s, Lorde cofounded the Women of Color Press to support the efforts of black feminist writers. In 1991, she was named Poet Laureate of the State of New York. She succumbed to cancer the following year. *The Collected Poems of Audre Lorde* appeared in 1997, *The Audre Lorde Compendium: Essays, Speeches, and Journals* in 1996.

Lowell, Robert (March 1, 1917–September 12, 1977). American poet, playwright, and translator. Born into a prominent Boston family, Lowell was one of the most accomplished American poets of the post–World War II period, distinguished for his technical virtuosity, use of dense symbolism, and "confessional" voice. Lowell attended Harvard for two years before transferring to Kenyon College to study under John Crowe RANSOM. After graduating in 1940, he married the fiction writer Jean Stafford and converted to Roman Catholicism. During World War II, he served five months in prison as a conscientious objector. Divorced from Stafford in 1948, he married novelist and essayist Elizabeth HARDWICK the following year. In 1972, after his divorce from Hardwick, Lady Caroline Blackwell became his third wife. Lowell's first poetry collection, *Land of Unlikeness* (1944), went unnoticed, but the second, *Lord Weary's Castle* (1946), won the Pulitzer Prize. *LIFE STUDIES* (1959; National Book Award) introduced the highly personal tone for which he became known. *For the Union Dead* (1964), *Near the Ocean* (1967), and *Notebook 1967–68* (1969) reflect a profound social conscience and the politics of the times. Later volumes, such as *The Dolphin* (1973; Pulitzer Prize) and *Day by Day* (1977), are more subdued in tone and autobiographical in content. Other works include a trilogy of plays, *The Old Glory* (1965), and translations of AESCHYLUS, RACINE, and European poets.

Lowry, Malcolm (July 28, 1909–June 27, 1957). English novelist and short-story writer. A writer of difficult, experimental prose who went largely unrecognized during his lifetime, Lowry is best known for his novel *Under the Volcano* (1947), the autobiographical story of an alcoholic expatriate in Mexico. As a young man, Lowry traveled to Asia and the Americas, returning to England to attend Cambridge. At 24, he published *Ultramarine* (1933), an impressionistic novel of the sea inspired by his travels. He lived in the United States, Mexico, and Canada before eventually returning to England, where he committed suicide. Lowry wrote of his alcoholism with often harrowing forthrightness, as in the novella *Lunar Caustic* (1958), based on his experience in a detoxification program at New York's Bellevue Hospital. Lowry's posthumous publications include *Hear*

Us O Lord from Heaven Thy Dwelling Place (1961) and *Dark As the Grave Wherein My Friend Is Laid* (1968), both collections of short stories; and the unfinished novel *October Ferry to Gabriola* (1970).

Lucian, *in Greek* Loukianos (c. A.D. 120–c. A.D. 180). Greek satirist. Born at Samosata on the Euphrates River (now part of modern-day Syria), Lucian traveled widely throughout Asia Minor, becoming a lecturer and writer of substantial reputation. Although his native language was Aramaic, he wrote exclusively in Greek, and some 70 extant works are attributed to him, including prose, dialogues, poetry, and criticism. In nearly all his writings, Lucian points a singularly irreverent and penetrating wit at the follies of his day, and his work exerted a profound influence on later generations of satirists, including VOLTAIRE and SWIFT. Especially open to Lucian's ridicule are excesses of religious devotion and practice, as well as various forms of intellectual dishonesty and hypocrisy. Among the best known of his works are *Dialogues of the Dead* (*Nekrikoi Dialogoi*), *Timon* (*Timōn*), *Charon* (*Charōn*), *Nigrinus* (*Nigrinos*), and a novel, *Lucius, or The Ass* (*Loukios, ē Onos*). His *Veracious History* (*Alēthōn Diēgēmatōn*, also translated as *True History* and *True Story*), a series of fictional journeys, is believed to have served as a model for Swift's GULLIVER'S TRAVELS. Lucian's popularity and visibility in Roman circles of power briefly won him a government post at Alexandria, although he later returned to Athens to live out his life.

Lucretius, *in full* Titus Lucretius Carus (c. 94 B.C.–c. 55 B.C.). Roman poet. Little is known of Lucretius's life, and the only work that can be confidently ascribed to him is the ambitious pedagogical poem *On the Nature of Things* (*De Rerum Naturum*). In it, the poet presents a comprehensive world view, based upon the writings of Epicurus and other ancient thinkers, that explains all earthly phenomena as derived from a system of natural laws. The aggregate effect is a philosophy that seeks to supplant superstition with science and offers a reasoned alternative to classical polytheism. Written in dactylic hexameter, this six-volume work is also notable for its forceful eloquence and artistic achievement. Lore has it that Lucretius committed suicide after drinking a love potion given to him by his wife, a legend that inspired TENNYSON's ode "Lucretius."

Lurie, Alison (September 3, 1926–). American novelist and children's writer. An author of mordant social and domestic satire, often set in the academic world, Lurie was educated at Radcliffe and taught for many years at Cornell University—the latter serving as a blueprint for the fictional Corinth University, where many of her works take place. Her best-known novels are *The War Between the Tates* (1974), the story of a political science professor's failing marriage, set against the backdrop of the Vietnam War; and *Foreign Affairs* (1984; Pulitzer Prize), the story of a pair of married academics and their romantic misadventures on sabbatical. Other popular and critical successes include the novels *Love and Friendship* (1962), *Imaginary Friends* (1967), *The Truth About Lorin Jones* (1988), and *The Last Resort* (1998). Lurie also writes children's books and criticism of children's literature, the latter collected in *Don't Tell the Grown-Ups: Subversive Children's Literature* (1990), and she is the editor of *The Oxford Book of Modern Fairy Tales* (1993). Works of nonfiction include *The Language of Clothes* (1981) and *Familiar Spirits: A Memoir of James Merrill and David Jackson* (2001).

Macdonald, Ross, *pen name of* Kenneth Millar (December 13, 1915–July 11, 1983). American novelist. Macdonald's literate, stylish crime novels set him apart from the vast majority of writers of detective fiction, and brought a new measure of respectability to that genre. Best known among his works is the series of novels featuring Lew Archer, a hardboiled detective who abhors violence. After debuting in *The Moving Target* (1949), Archer went on to appear in numerous other novels, including *The Way Some People Die* (1951), *Find a Victim* (1954), *The Name Is Archer* (1955), *The Goodbye Look* (1969), *The Under-*

ground Man (1971), *Sleeping Beauty* (1973), and *The Blue Hammer* (1976). These vigorously executed thrillers made Macdonald both a bestselling author and a favorite of the critics, who praised his vivid characterization and intense, morally charged atmospheres. A lifelong Californian, Macdonald became passionately concerned with environmental conservation, a theme that appears in a number of his books.

Machado de Assis, Joachim Maria (June 21, 1839–September 29, 1908). Brazilian poet, short-story writer, novelist, and essayist. A central figure in Brazilian literature and a modernist master, Machado de Assis grew up poor in Rio de Janeiro and suffered from both epilepsy and a speech impediment. He began to write while working as a printer's apprentice, and quickly won acclaim for his earliest published poetry. He then wrote several novels in the prevailing style of Brazilian Romanticism, but his greatest achievements began with the playful and iconoclastic novel *Epitaph of a Small Winner* (*Memorias Posthumas de Braz Cubas*, 1891), the autobiography of a dead writer ("I am a deceased writer not in the sense of one who has written and is now deceased, but in the sense of one who has died and is now writing"). Through his amused narrator, Machado explores the absurdities of life and death, including especially the primacy of self-love in human nature. Susan SONTAG described it as a "thrillingly original, radically skeptical book." Other works include the novels *Philosopher or Dog?* (*Quincas Borba*, 1891) and *Dom Casmurro* (1899), a tale of deception and ambiguity generally considered his masterpiece, as well as some 200 short stories, only a small number of which have been translated into English; collections include *The Psychiatrist and Other Stories* (1963) and *The Devil's Church and Other Stories* (1977). Machado had a long career in the Brazilian civil service, ultimately becoming the Minister of Agriculture. In 1896, he founded the Brazilian Academy of Arts and Letters.

MacLeish, Archibald (June 7, 1892–April 20, 1982). American poet and playwright. A poet whose political beliefs frequently inspired and colored his writing, MacLeish was educated at Yale and published two volumes of poems in his early 20s, *Summer Day* (1915) and *Tower of Ivory* (1917). He then moved to Paris, where he traveled in British and American expatriate circles and came under the influence of T. S. ELIOT and Ezra POUND. The work from that period, including the collections *The Happy Marriage* (1924), *The Pot of Earth* (1925), *Streets in the Moon* (1926), and the verse play *Nobodaddy* (1926), shows his growth as a poet and his development of a lyrical, uncluttered style. His long narrative poem *Conquistador* (1932; Pulitzer Prize), about the history of Mexico, was the first of many "public" poems motivated by MacLeish's deep concerns about the rise of fascism. Thereafter, much of his work was openly political, and a number of his verse plays were written for radio broadcast, including *The Fall of the City* (1937) and *Air Raid* (1938). MacLeish served as Librarian of Congress (1939–44) and Assistant Secretary of State during World War II, and later taught at Harvard University. He won the Pulitzer Prize twice more, for *Collected Poems 1917–1952* (1952) and *J.B.* (1958), a verse drama based on the biblical story of Job. *New and Collected Poems, 1917–1984* (1985) showcases the great range of his varied career; *Riders on the Earth* (1978) collects many of his finest essays.

MacNeice, [Frederick] Louis (September 12, 1907–September 3, 1963). Irish-born English poet and playwright. The son of a prominent Irish churchman, MacNeice was raised in Ulster and educated at Oxford, where he associated with W. H. AUDEN and Stephen SPENDER and wrote the poems that became his first collection, *Blind Fireworks* (1929). He worked for the British Broadcasting Corporation as a writer-producer during World War II, writing radio plays including *The Dark Tower* (1947), generally considered his finest. MacNeice made his greatest mark, however, with his technically precise but informal and often amusing poetry, collected in *Poems* (1935), *The Earth*

Compels (1938), *Autumn Journal* (1938), *Plant and Phantom* (1941), *Springboard* (1944), *Holes in the Sky* (1948), and *Autumn Sequel* (1954). His poetry synthesized the intermingling and randomness of life's patterns, what he called "the drunkenness of things being various." MacNeice also translated works by AESCHYLUS and GOETHE and wrote *Letters from Iceland* with Auden in 1937. His talent and importance were not fully appreciated until the 1966 publication of his *Collected Poems.*

Macpherson, James. *See Ossian*

Maeterlinck, Maurice (August 29, 1862–May 6, 1949). Belgian poet, playwright, and essayist. A leading Symbolist, Maeterlinck wrote poems steeped in the fanciful, otherworldly images of fairy tales and classical mythology, as in *Hothouses* (*Serres Chaudes*, 1889) and *Twelve Songs* (*Douze Chansons*, 1896), his first two collections. His most lasting fame, however, stems from his works for the stage, which were as ambitious as they were commercially popular. Among his many plays the best are *La Princesse Maleine* (1889) and *Pelleas and Melisande* (*Pelléas et Mélisande*, 1892), which was adapted into an opera by Claude Debussy in 1902. Maeterlinck's spiritual development and increasing interest in the natural world were reflected most pointedly in the play *The Blue Bird* (*L'Oiseau Bleu*, 1908) and in two volumes of philosophical writing, *The Life of the Bee* (*La Vie des Abeilles*, 1901) and *The Intelligence of Flowers* (*L'Intelligence des Fleurs*, 1907). Maeterlinck was awarded the Nobel Prize in Literature in 1911.

Mahfouz, Naguib (December 11, 1911–). Egyptian novelist and short-story writer. Mahfouz, whose work has won wide praise for its complex evocation of 20th-century Egyptian life, was the first Arabic writer to receive the Nobel Prize in Literature. The author of some 40 novels, Mahfouz is best known for the three volumes of his CAIRO TRILOGY (*al-Thulathiyya,* 1956–57), which follow the fortunes of a middle-class Cairo family from World War I to the end of the monarchy and the overthrow of King Farouk I. These works, like most of his writings, are distinguished not only by their finely rendered characters and richly textured plots, but also by their broad social canvas, offering readers a comprehensive portrait of Egyptian society and its difficult transition to the modern age. Many of his works are openly political; a number were either banned in Egypt or saw their publication delayed because of their provocative content, and in the mid-1990s Islamic fundamentalists condemned him for blasphemy. Besides *The Cairo Trilogy*, other notable works translated into English include *Midaq Alley* (*Zuqāq al-Midaqq*, 1947), *Children of Gelbewi* (*Awlād Hāritnā*, 1959), *The Thief and the Dogs* (*al-Liṣṣ wa-al-Kilāb*, 1961), and *Miramar* (1967). *Echoes of an Autobiography* (*Asdaa' al-sira al-Dhatiyya*) was published in 1995. Awarding him the Nobel Prize in 1988, the Nobel committee called his "evocatively ambiguous" work "an Arabic narrative art that applies to all mankind."

Mailer, Norman (January 31, 1923–). American novelist, journalist, and essayist. Drafted straight out of Harvard University to fight in World War II, Mailer drew on his experiences in the Pacific Theater for his first novel, THE NAKED AND THE DEAD (1948). The story of the invasion of a Japanese-held island, Mailer's novel was an instant commercial success, widely praised for its unflinching realism. Although his next novels, including *Barbary Shore* (1951), *The Deer Park* (1955), and AN AMERICAN DREAM (1965), were less well received, *Advertisements for Myself* (1959), a collection of nonfiction pieces including the widely read essay "The White Negro," established him as an iconoclastic social critic and celebrity man of letters. Apart from *The Naked and the Dead*, Mailer's reputation rests largely on his journalism, which melds personal narrative with conventional reportage in a style that has come to be known as New Journalism. His participation in an antiwar march on Washington in October 1967, for example, during which Mailer was arrested, led to *The Armies of the Night* (1968), which received the Pulitzer Prize, as did THE EXECUTIONER'S SONG (1979), his "true life novel" about condemned murderer Gary Gilmore. Other non-fiction books of note include *Miami and the Siege of Chicago* (1968), about that year's contentious political conventions; *Of a Fire on the Moon* (1970), concerning space exploration; and *Oswald's Tale: An American Mystery* (1995), an exploration of presidential assassin Lee Harvey Oswald's years in the Soviet Union. Among his later novels are *Ancient Evenings* (1983), *Tough Guys Don't Dance* (1984), *Harlot's Ghost* (1991), and *The Gospel According to the Son* (1997), about JESUS. Collected essays can be found in *The Presidential Papers* (1963) and *Cannibals and Christians* (1966). *The Time of Our Time* (1998) is Mailer's own selection from 50 years of his fiction and nonfiction.

Malamud, Bernard (April 26, 1914–March 18, 1986). American novelist and short-story writer. The creator of modern parables steeped in American Jewish culture, Malamud was also influenced by Russian and European Jewish literature, as well as by such American forebears as Nathaniel HAWTHORNE and HENRY JAMES. The son of Russian immigrants who settled in Brooklyn, he was educated at Columbia University and the City College of New York. His first novel, THE NATURAL (1952), concerning a supernaturally gifted baseball player's search for salvation (which was made into a film starring Robert Redford) remains his best-known work. This was followed by a novel that many critics consider his best: THE ASSISTANT (1957), about an elderly Jewish grocer and the young Italian-American petty criminal whom he hires as his assistant. THE FIXER (1966), a novel about a Jewish handyman falsely accused of murder in tsarist Russia, won both the Pulitzer Prize and the National Book Award. Malamud's stories—collected in such volumes as *The Magic Barrel* (1958; National Book Award), *Idiots First* (1963), and *Rembrandt's Hat* (1973)—have also won wide praise for their spare, lyrical style, metaphoric richness, and broad human sympathy. His other novels include *The Tenants* (1971), *Dubin's Lives* (1979), and *God's Grace* (1982). *The Complete Stories* appeared in 1997.

Mallarmé, Stéphane (March 18, 1842–September 9, 1898). French poet. A founding member of the Symbolist movement in French poetry, Mallarmé was an important thinker whose theories of aesthetics influenced generations of writers. In striking contrast to the prevailing conventions of his day, which favored traditional forms, Mallarmé's poems are characterized by great syntactical difficulty and the use of a single, central image, from which all other images in the poem descend. At the core of his work was his prevailing belief in the duty of the poet to penetrate an imperfect reality to reveal the perfect forms that lie beyond. His most

---

"**The world exists to end up in a book.**"

Stéphane Mallarmé, "Réponses à des Enquêtes: Sur l'Évolution Littéraire" (1891), in *Oeuvres Complètes* (1945)

---

noted work, *The Afternoon of a Faun* (*L'Après-Midi d'un Faune*, 1876), was set to music by Claude Debussy. Mallarmé's singular style is reflected in his other major work, "Hérodiade" (c. 1864), and in the works collected in *Poésies* (1887) and *Vers et Prose* (1893; Verse and Prose). He is also known for his elegies for, among other notable figures, fellow Symbolists Paul VERLAINE and Charles BAUDELAIRE, and Edgar Allan POE, as well as for a number of sonnets to his mistress.

Malory, [Sir] Thomas (c. 1408–c. 1471). English prose writer. The author of LE MORTE D'ARTHUR (1485), the collected prose tales of Arthurian legend, is thought to be Sir Thomas Malory of Newbold Revel, Warwickshire, although this attribution remains open to debate. The facts of his life are scant. Literary historians base this identification largely on the manuscript's colophon, in which the author indicates that it was completed in the ninth year of the reign of Henry V and asks for release from prison; Malory, a former knight and member of Parliament, was imprisoned at that time for crimes including rape and thievery. He died in jail, and his masterpiece was printed posthumously. Despite its shadowy and inauspicious origins, Malory's manuscript, the first complete collection of Arthurian tales, remains a rich and influential source of the myth of Camelot, King ARTHUR, and the Knights of the Round Table.

Malraux, [Georges] **André** (November 3, 1901–November 23, 1976). French novelist, essayist, and art critic. Trained as an archaeologist, Malraux ran afoul of French colonial authorities on a trip to Cambodia at age 21, an experience that profoundly altered his view of the world and inspired his passionate involvement in left-wing politics, first in China during the civil wars of the 1920s, and then in Spain, where he fought for the anti-Fascist Republicans during the Spanish Civil War. During World War II he served as a tank commander against the Nazis and was captured twice, escaping both times to join the Resistance. Malraux's novels follow in the same adventurous, politically inspired vein, all advancing revolutionary ideas and set during times of social upheaval. They include *The Conquerors* (*Les Conquérants*, 1928), based on his experiences in China, and *Man's Hope* (*L'Espoir*, 1937), set during the Spanish Civil War. *Man's Fate* (*La Condition Humaine*, 1933), inspired by the Shanghai insurrection of 1927, is generally considered his most accomplished novel. During his military service Malraux made the acquaintance of General Charles de Gaulle, who after the war appointed him the French Minister of Culture, a position he occupied for a decade (1958–68). Malraux's later writings are nearly all art criticism and history, collected in three volumes under the title *The Voices of Silence* (*Les Voix du Silence*, 1951). *Anti-Memoirs* (*Antimémoires*), his autobiography, was published in 1967.

Mamet, David (November 30, 1947–). American playwright and screenwriter. A Chicago native, Mamet began writing for the stage while still a student at Goddard College in Vermont and worked for several years in the blue-collar world that his plays frequently explore. His first notable works were *Duck Variations* (1972) and

Sexual Perversity in Chicago (1974), followed by AMERICAN BUFFALO (1976), which startled audiences with its liberal use of four-letter words and established Mamet as a force in American theater. Subsequent plays, including *Speed-the-Plow* (1987), *Oleanna* (1991), and *The Cryptogram* (1994), advanced his reputation for tackling controversial subjects with satiric energy and uncompromising realism. GLENGARRY GLEN ROSS (1983; Pulitzer Prize) is a scathing indictment of the world of commercial real estate. Mamet has also worked extensively in film, writing the screenplay for *The Postman Always Rings Twice* (1981) and both writing and directing *House of Games* (1987), *Homicide* (1991), *The Spanish Prisoner* (1998), and *The Winslow Boy* (1999, from the play by Terence RATTIGAN), among others. Mamet's essays on writing, film, and the theater are collected in *A Whore's Profession* (1994).

Mandelshtam, Osip (January 15, 1891–c. 1938). Russian poet. Born in Warsaw, Poland, and raised in St. Petersburg, Russia, Mandelshtam is today considered one of the 20th century's greatest Russian poets, although his work went largely unnoticed in the English-speaking world until long after his death, and much of it was suppressed during his lifetime. His concise, clear style is a hallmark of the Acmeist movement, to which he made significant contributions with *Stone* (*Kamen'*, 1913) and *Tristia* (1922). Subsequent works included a volume of new and collected works, *Stikhotvoreniya* (1928; Poems), and a volume of critical writings, *O Poèzii* (1928; On Poetry). Although his work did not deal directly with political matters, it came under increasing scrutiny by the Communist regime, and in 1934 he was arrested. He spent three years in internal exile, during which time he attempted suicide. He also completed the long cycle of poems *Voronezh Notebooks: Poems 1935–1937* (*Voronezhskie Tetradi*, 1980). He returned to Moscow in 1937 but was arrested again a year later and is thought to have died in a concentration camp near Vladivostok. It was not until the 1960s that efforts by Mandelshtam's widow, Nadezhda, led to publication of his work in the West (her memoirs are *Hope Against Hope*, 1970, and *Hope Abandoned*, 1974). His work is available in English in many editions, including *Fifty Poems* (1977), with an introduction by Joseph BRODSKY; *The Eyesight of Wasps* (1989), selected poems; *Poems from Mandelstam* (1990); *Critical Prose and Letters* (1979); and *The Noise of Time: The Prose of Osip Mandelstam* (1993).

Mann, [Paul] **Thomas** (June 6, 1875–August 12, 1955). German novelist and essayist. Winner of the Nobel Prize in Literature in 1929, Mann was a writer of formidable artistic power and philosophical richness. Central to nearly all his work are questions on the nature of art and the struggle of the artistic temperament to find spiritual nourishment in bourgeois European society. This conflict is dramatized in such early works as the story "TONIO KRÖGER" (1903), the novel *BUDDENBROOKS* (1903), and *DEATH IN VENICE* (*Der Tod in Venedig*, 1912), an exploration of artistic decadence that is considered one of the finest novellas ever written. As an essayist Mann frequently engaged political and social topics, but in his fiction he tended to subordinate politics to larger questions of the spirit; in the long allegorical novel *THE MAGIC MOUNTAIN* (*Der Zauberberg*, 1924), for example, life in a Swiss tuberculosis sanitarium on the eve of World War I comes to represent an unhealthful separation of the intellect from the workaday world. Mann was forced to emigrate from Germany in the 1930s for criticizing Hitler's government. He became a United States citizen in 1944 but remained concerned with the fate of his native country, returning to Europe often after the war and eventually dying in Switzerland. Of his many other works, the most noted include the novellas *Early Sorrow* (*Unordnung und Frühes Leid*, 1926) and *Mario and the Magician* (*Mario und der Zauberer*, 1930); *JOSEPH AND HIS BROTHERS* (*Joseph und Seine Brüder*, 1933–43), a tetralogy of novels about the biblical character Joseph; and the novel *DOCTOR FAUSTUS* (*Doktor Faustus*, 1947), an allegory about the decadence of German culture.

Mansfield, Katherine, *original name* Kathleen Mansfield Beauchamp (October 14, 1888–January 9, 1923). New Zealand-born short-story writer. Mansfield moved from her native New Zealand to England at age 19 to establish herself as a writer. The stories in her first collection, *In a German Pension* (1911), although less mature than her later work, possess a quiet precision reminiscent of CHEKHOV, whose writing she admired. Subsequent collections include *Prelude* (1918), *Bliss* (1920), and *THE GARDEN PARTY and Other Stories* (1922), the last containing many of the stories for which she remains best known; *The Doves' Nest* (1923) and *Something Childish* (1924; U.S. title, *The Little Girl*) were published posthumously. Although her life's work was not especially voluminous, her influence on the short-story form was substantial, inspiring many to emulate her use of small, seemingly inconsequential moments to uncover the ambiguity and psychological depths of her characters. With her husband, editor and critic John Middleton MURRY, she collaborated on a number of magazines, including *Rhythm* and *The Blue Review*. After her death, her husband edited her *Journal* (1927) and *Letters* (1928). *The Collected Letters of Katherine Mansfield* appeared, in two volumes, in 1984–87.

Manzoni, Alessandro (March 7, 1785–May 22, 1873). Italian novelist, essayist, and poet. Manzoni's foremost achievement was *THE BETROTHED* (*I Promessi Sposi*, 1825–26), his ambitious novel of love, religion, and political intrigue set during the Thirty Years War. Originally published in three volumes, Manzoni's tale became a patriotic anthem for Italian nationalists of the period and was the first major work of literature to appear in vernacular Florentine Italian. A devout Catholic, Manzoni began his career as a writer of religious poetry, but his work in verse (and later for the stage) also embraced political and historical themes of Italian identity. Among the most recognized of these are *The Sacred Hymns* (*Inni Sacri*, 1815), a series of religious poems, and two historical tragedies for the stage, *Il Conte di Carmagnola* (1820; The Count of Carmagnola) and *Adelchi*

(1822). He was admired by many of his Romantic contemporaries, including SIR WALTER SCOTT, and was honored in music with Giuseppe Verdi's *Manzoni Requiem* (1874).

Marlowe, Christopher (baptized February 26, 1564–May 30, 1593). English poet and playwright. Despite his short, violent life, Marlowe produced a large and complex body of work that won him critical acclaim in his time and established his reputation as the most important Elizabethan playwright prior to SHAKESPEARE. All his work for the stage was written in a six-year burst of creativity, beginning with *TAMBURLAINE THE GREAT* (1587) and continuing with *The Tragicall History of DOCTOR FAUSTUS* (c. 1588), *THE JEW OF MALTA* (1589), *EDWARD II* (1593), and *Dido, Queen of Carthage* (1593), cowritten with his friend and fellow playwright Thomas Nashe. Marlowe's drama is distinctive not only for its emphasis on a passionate central character, but also for the felicity and vigor of its verse, which earned it the sobriquet "mighty line." Although hard evidence is scant, some scholars still hypothesize that several of Shakespeare's plays, among them *TITUS ANDRONICUS* (c. 1593–94), were written in part by Marlowe. As a poet, Marlowe was no less accomplished; his long erotic poem *Hero and Leander*, unfinished at his death, is considered among the finest of the period. Other major works include translations of OVID's *Elegies* and the oft-quoted love poem that begins "Come live with me and be my love," published after his death in *The Passionate Pilgrim* (1599). Of humble origins—his father was a cobbler—Marlowe was educated at Cambridge and at various times was involved in criminal behavior, from forgery to street fighting to espionage. He was killed at age 29 in a dispute over a tavern bill.

Marquand, John P[hillips] (November 10, 1893–July 16, 1960). American novelist. Born in Delaware, Marquand was sent to Massachusetts to live with relatives after the failure of his family's business, a reversal that later informed his many satirical novels of class and culture among upper-crust New Englanders. Educated at Harvard, which he attended on scholarship, he first made a name for himself as the author of the Mr. Moto series of spy novels. With *The Late George Apley* (1937), Marquand began his wry commentaries on Yankee culture, which he continued in *Wickford Point* (1939) and *H. M. Pulham, Esquire* (1941). *Point of No Return* (1949), which most critics consider his best novel, is a more serious study of New England small-town life. *Women and Thomas Harrow* (1958) is his most autobiographical work. He also wrote a number of novels about life on the home front during World War II, including *So Little Time* (1943) and *Repent in Haste* (1945).

Marsh, [Dame] [Edith] **Ngaio** (April 23, 1899–February 18, 1982). New Zealand novelist. An artist and theatrical producer in New Zealand, Marsh wrote her first detective novel, *A Man Lay Dead* (1934), while living in England. Presented in a lithe, literary style, it introduced the character of Scotland Yard Inspector Roderick Alleyn, who eventually figured in many of her works. *Artists in Crime* (1938), *A Surfeit of Lampreys* (1941), *Final Curtain* (1947), *Opening Night* (1951), *Dead Water* (1963), and *Black as He's Painted* (1975) advanced her reputation as a mystery writer of unusual elegance and literary skill. Many of her novels were set in the world of art and theater, in which she remained active. Marsh's autobiography is *Black Beech and Honeydew* (1965).

Martial, *in full* Marcus Valerius Martialus (c. A.D. 38/41–c. A.D. 103). Roman epigrammatist. Born in Spain, as a young man Martial traveled to Rome, where his pithy, often racy epigrams (*Epigrammata*) eventually gained him admission to the highest circles of imperial society. Celebrating life's pleasures and mocking its excesses, these 1,500 verses, gathered in some 12 volumes, offer an unusually candid and penetrating portrait of life in 1st-century Rome. Martial's cleverness won him the friendship and patronage of several Roman emperors, including both Titus and Trajan, and he was acquainted with the major poets of his day, among them Lucan, whose widow gave him an estate near Rome. His other poetry is generally considered of a lesser quality.

Marvell, Andrew (March 31, 1621–August 18, 1678). English poet. A poet of considerable range and lasting influence, Marvell was educated at Cambridge and during the Protectorate became tutor to Oliver Cromwell's ward, William Dutton. He also served as an assistant to John MILTON in his duties as Latin secretary of the foreign office—a post he assumed himself when Milton became blind—and was elected to Parliament in 1659, continuing in office for the remainder of his life. His literary achievements were largely neglected after his death, but efforts in the modern era, particularly by T. S. ELIOT, have resuscitated his standing. He is primarily remembered as a secular metaphysical poet for such well-known lyrics as "TO HIS COY MISTRESS," "The Garden," and "A Dialogue Between the Soul and Body," although his satirical poems, such as "The Last Instructions to a Printer" (on the subject of the Dutch War), were much admired in their day. Other notable poems include "An Horatian Ode upon Cromwell's Return from Ireland," "Upon Appleton House," and "Upon the Death of His Late Highness the Lord Protector." Few of Marvell's poems were published during his lifetime; the first collected edition was published in 1681.

Masefield, John (June 1, 1878–May 12, 1967). English poet, novelist, and playwright. Poet Laureate of England from 1930 until his death, Masefield is best recalled for his poems of seafaring life. As a young man he traveled the world as a cadet in the Merchant Marine and lived for a time in the United States, paying his way through a series of odd jobs. *Salt Water Ballads*, based on his experiences at sea, appeared in 1902; *The Everlasting Mercy*, the first of his long narrative poems (1911), provoked both admiration and controversy for its use of a rough, unpolished idiom. Of his dozens of other works, *Dauber* (1913) and *Reynard the Fox* (1919), both long narrative poems, and the play *The Tragedy of Nan* (1908) are notable. He also wrote a number of adventure novels, stories for children, and three volumes of autobiography.

Mason, Bobbie Ann (May 1, 1940–). American novelist and short-story writer. Mason's understated, realistic stories of life in a changing rural South began appearing in such periodicals as THE NEW YORKER and THE ATLANTIC MONTHLY in the late 1970s, and her debut collection, *Shiloh and Other Stories* (1982), garnered much critical acclaim. A native of western Kentucky, Mason graduated from the University of Kentucky, did graduate work at the State University of New York and the University of Connecticut, and worked for many years in the publishing industry in New York City. Her stories and novels, many of them set in her native Kentucky, offer glimpses into the lives of contemporary working-class Southerners; their style has been described as "Shopping Mall Realism" for Mason's use of brand names to create a landscape under the sway of mass consumerism. Her novels include *Spence + Lila* (1988), *Feather Crowns* (1993), and *In Country* (1985), which was later made into a film. She published a second collection, *Midnight Magic*, in 1998, and the memoir *Clear Springs* in 1999.

Masters, Edgar Lee (August 23, 1869–March 5, 1950). American poet, novelist, and biographer. Masters's standing among 20th-century American poets rests almost entirely on the poems of SPOON RIVER ANTHOLOGY (1915), a series of monologic epitaphs in the voices of the inhabitants of the fictitious Midwestern town of Spoon River. Born in Kansas, Masters grew up on an Illinois farm and became a successful Chicago lawyer before his first poems were published. His early work, including the poems in his debut collection, *Book of Verses* (1898), is generally regarded as unremarkable. *Spoon River Anthology*, however, distinguished Masters as a highly original poet, a master of free verse, and a precise observer of Midwestern village life. Highly prolific, Masters went on to publish numerous other collections of verse, although none garnered the acclaim of *Spoon River Anthology; Domesday Book* (1920) and *Illinois Poems* (1941) are considered two of the best. He also wrote many novels as well as a number of biographies of literary and public figures, such as Mark TWAIN and Abraham Lincoln. His autobiography, *Across Spoon River*, was published in 1936.

Matthiessen, Peter (May 22, 1927–). American nature writer and novelist. Matthiessen's writings, both fiction and nonfiction, are unified by his abiding concern with the destructive effects of industrial technology on the natural world and on human societies. His many works of nonfiction include *Wildlife in America* (1959), a discussion of disappearing wildlife and its effects; *The Cloud Forest* (1961), based on his travels in the Amazon basin; *Blue Meridian: The Search for the Great White Shark* (1971); and *The Snow Leopard* (1978; National Book Award), a thoughtful account of his travels in Nepal. *In the Spirit of Crazy Horse* (1983), concerning a 1973 confrontation between federal agents and members of the American Indian Movement at Wounded Knee, South Dakota, stirred considerable controversy and, following its initial publication in 1983, was kept out of print by a libel suit; the suit's settlement in 1990 was followed by the book's reissue in 1991. Matthiessen explores similar issues in his novels, which include *At Play in the Fields of the Lord* (1965), the story of an American pilot lost in the South American jungle; *Far Tortuga* (1975), about turtle fishing in the Caribbean; and a trilogy of historical novels set in the Florida Everglades, *Killing Mr. Watson* (1990), *Lost Man's River* (1997), and *Bone by Bone* (1999). As a young man Matthiessen served in the Navy before attending Yale University and the Sorbonne; while living in France, he cofounded the influential literary journal THE PARIS REVIEW with George PLIMPTON.

Maugham, W[illiam] **Somerset** (January 25, 1874–December 16, 1965). English novelist, short-story writer, and playwright. Trained as a physician, Maugham abandoned medicine to pursue writing full time after the publication of his first novel, *Liza of Lambeth* (1897), based on his experiences at an obstetrics clinic in the slums of London. *Mrs. Craddock* (1902) and *The Magician* (1909) followed, but he achieved his first real fame with the play *Lady Frederick*

(1907). Succeeding plays, all lighthearted social comedies, were enormously popular, especially *The Circle* (1921) and *The Constant Wife* (1926). Today, Maugham is best known for several of his novels, especially OF HUMAN BONDAGE (1915), THE MOON AND SIXPENCE (1917), CAKES AND ALE (1930), and THE RAZOR'S EDGE (1944). He also published several short-story collections and a number of critical works, including *The Art of Fiction* (1955). His expertly crafted novels and stories enjoy an enduring popularity despite his own assertion, recorded in his autobiography, *The Summing Up* (1938), that he was "in the very first row of the second-raters."

Maupassant, [Henri-René-Albert-]**Guy de** (August 5, 1850–July 6, 1893). French short-story writer and novelist. A master of the short story, whose work takes a somber view of the greed, vanity, and bitter ironies that beset human life, Maupassant achieved success as a member of Émile ZOLA's naturalist group in the early 1880s. Many of his stories (300 in all) drew on peasant life in his native Normandy, the Franco-Prussian war, in which he served, the bureaucratic world he joined as a young civil servant, and the wealthy Parisian circles he entered as a writer. His best works — including such classics as "BOULE DE SUIF" (some translations are published under the titles "Ball of Fat" or "Ball of Tallow"), "The Necklace" ("La Parure"), "The House of Mme Tellier" ("La Maison Tellier"), and "The Umbrella" ("Le Parapluie") — are notable for their realism, simplicity of style, and attention to detail, qualities attributed to his apprenticeship with Gustave FLAUBERT. Maupassant's novels include *A Life* (*Une Vie*, 1883), *Bel-Ami* (1885), and *Pierre et Jean* (1888). His output was prodigious (16 story collections and six novels in 10 years) until the onset of insanity in the early 1890s. He died in a Paris asylum.

Mauriac, François (October 11, 1885–September 1, 1970). French novelist, essayist, and playwright. Winner of the Nobel Prize in Literature in 1952, Mauriac is regarded by some critics as the greatest French novelist since Marcel PROUST. His 23 novels, most of them set in and around his native Bordeaux, examine the struggle for redemption in modern life from the standpoint of a profound, if nonconformist, Roman Catholicism. His major works—including *The Kiss to the Leper* (*Le Baiser au Lépreux*, 1922), *The Desert of Love* (*Le Désert de l'Amour*, 1925), *THÉRÈSE DESQUEYROUX* (1927), *Vipers' Tangle* (*Le Noeud de Vipers*, 1932), *The Frontenac Mystery* (*Le Mystère Frontenac*, 1933), and *A Woman of the Pharisees* (*La Pharisienne*, 1941)—portray ordinary souls wrestling with their sinfulness, passion, and spiritual emptiness. Similar themes are addressed in his plays, the most acclaimed of which is *Asmodée* (1938). An ardent opponent of political repression, Mauriac wrote powerful polemics against the fascist movements in Italy and Spain, and worked with the French Resistance during World War II. His articles, essays, and reminiscences appear in *The Novelist and His Characters* (*Le Romancier et Ses Personages*, 1933), the five-volume *Journals* (1934–53), and the three-volume *Mémoires* (1959–67).

Maxwell, William (August 16, 1908–July 31, 2000). American novelist, short-story writer, essayist, and editor. Known for his fictional evocations of Midwestern life in the early 20th century, Maxwell established his reputation with his second novel, *They Came Like Swallows* (1937), describing the joys of his childhood and the ravages in his native Lincoln, Illinois, of the 1918–19 influenza epidemic. His best-known work, *The Folded Leaf* (1945), recounts the friendship of two young men. Other novels include *Time Will Darken It* (1949), *The Chateau* (1961), and *So Long, See You Tomorrow* (1980). His short stories are collected in *The Old Man at the Railroad Crossing* (1966), *Over by the River* (1977), *Billie Dyer* (1992), and *All the Days and Nights* (1995). *Ancestors* (1971) is a family history, and *The Outermost Dream* (1989) is a collection of reviews and essays from Maxwell's 40 years as a fiction editor at THE NEW YORKER magazine.

Mayakovsky, Vladimir (July 19, 1893–April 14, 1930). Russian poet and playwright. Mayakovsky captured the epoch-smashing spirit of the Rus-

sian Revolution in the startling imagery and exuberant rhythms of his verse, as well as in his striking graphic art for books and posters. Involved in radical politics as a teenager, he was imprisoned for political agitation in 1909. Upon his release, he went to art school and embraced Futurism, which offered an escape from the traditions of the past and the opportunity to create a poetry fit for the new century; in addition, he cosigned (with David Burliuk, Aleksandr Kruchenykh, and Victor Khlebnikov) the aesthetic movement's notorious manifesto, *A Slap in the Face of Public Taste* (*Poshchechina Obshchestvennomu Vkusu*, 1917). He created an irregular line based not upon syllables or accents but held together by strong stresses and outrageous rhymes. His poetic reputation rests largely on four long narrative poems written between 1914 and 1916, beginning with *A Cloud in Trousers* (*Oblako v Shtanakh*, 1915) and concluding with *Chelovek* (1918; Man), considered his finest work of this period. Mayakovsky ardently championed the Revolution of 1917 and dedicated himself to literary and propaganda work in the name of the new Soviet Union with such patriotic works as "Ode to the Revolution" ("Oda Revolyutsii," 1918) and *Vladimir Ilyich Lenin* (*Vladimir Il'ich Lenin*, 1924), which transformed the first Soviet leader into the stuff of myth. In his own life, a series of unrequited love affairs tormented the poet; in 1930, he shot himself to escape his romantic disappointments. His other notable works include *I* (*Ya*, 1913), his first collection of poetry; the plays *The Bedbug* (*Klop*, 1928) and *The Bathhouse* (*Banya*, 1929), satires on Soviet philistinism; and his final poem, "At the Top of My Voice" ("Vo Vez' Golos," unfinished at the author's death). Additional works in English include the collection *Listen!: Early Poems 1913–1918* (1987); *Love Is the Heart of Everything: Correspondence Between Vladimir Mayakovsky and Lili Brik, 1915–1930* (1986); and *For the Voice* (*Dlya Golosa*, 1923), a landmark Futurist book first issued in translation in 2000, which includes 13 poems by Mayakovsky and illustrations by El Lissitzky.

McCarthy, Cormac, *original name* Charles McCarthy, Jr. (July 30, 1933–). American novelist. In novels that penetrate "the violent heart of the Old West," McCarthy explores the brutality of human life in rural settings in the American South and Southwest. His best-known novel, *All the Pretty Horses* (1992; National Book Award), was followed by two more volumes in THE BORDER TRILOGY, *The Crossing* (1994) and *Cities of the Plain* (1998). Born in Providence, Rhode Island, McCarthy grew up in Knoxville, Tennessee, and later, in 1976, settled in El Paso, Texas. His novels, including *The Orchard Keeper* (1965), *Outer Dark* (1968), *Child of God* (1974), *Suttree* (1979), and *Blood Meridian* (1985), often feature drifters and outcasts pitted against nature and society. Esteemed for a dense and lyrical prose style reminiscent of FAULKNER, and praised by Saul BELLOW for his "absolutely overpowering use of language, his life-giving and death-dealing sentences," McCarthy was awarded a MacArthur Fellowship in 1981.

McCarthy, Mary (June 21, 1912–October 25, 1989). American critic and novelist. Her determination to expose the truth behind all facades made McCarthy one of the most potent American intellectuals of her day. Born in Seattle, she was orphaned at the age of six and raised by a great-aunt and uncle. After graduation from Vassar, she reviewed books and theater for THE NATION, THE NEW REPUBLIC, and PARTISAN REVIEW; her brilliant, severe drama criticism is collected in *Mary McCarthy's Theatre Chronicles, 1937–1962* (1963). She began to write fiction with the encouragement of her second husband, critic EDMUND WILSON (whom she later divorced), scoring a bestseller with the sexually frank novel THE GROUP (1963), which traces the lives of eight Vassar graduates over a seven-year period. Her other fiction includes the short-story collections *The Company She Keeps* (1942) and *Cast a Cold Eye* (1950), and the satirical novels *The Oasis* (1949), *The Groves of Academe* (1952), *A Charmed Life* (1955), and *Birds of America* (1971). Literary essays are collected in *The Writing on the Wall* (1970) and *Ideas and the Novel* (1980). Other

nonfiction includes *Venice Observed* (1956), *The Stones of Florence* (1959), *The Seventeenth Degree* (1974), in which she expressed her outrage over U.S. involvement in the Vietnam war, and *The Mask of State: Watergate Portraits* (1974). In her lively memoirs *Memories of a Catholic Girlhood* (1957), *How I Grew* (1957), and *Intellectual Memoirs: New York 1936–1938* (1992), she chronicled her coming of age as a young writer and intellectual, and her relationships with *Partisan Review* editor Philip RAHV and with Wilson.

McCourt, Frank (August 19, 1930–). Irish-American memoirist and playwright. In *Angela's Ashes* (1996; Pulitzer Prize, National Book Critics Circle Award), McCourt tells the story of his life from age 3 to 19: his family's departure from Brooklyn, where he was born, for Ireland, where the poverty, brutality, and institutional indifference rampant in the Limerick slums cannot quench the spark of inspiration he eventually finds in reading SHAKESPEARE. *'Tis* (1999) begins with McCourt's return to New York and recounts a series of menial jobs and social humiliations, until he is conscripted during the Korean War. After his tour of duty, the prospect of a dead-end life as a dockworker prompted him to take advantage of the GI Bill and he matriculated at New York University, where he prepared for what would be a 27-year career as an English teacher in New York City's public schools, including the prestigious Stuyvesant High School. Other works include the theatrical revues *A Couple of Blaguards* (1976–77), cowritten and performed with his actor-raconteur brother Malachy, and *The Irish . . . And How They Got That Way* (1997).

McCullers, Carson, *original name* Lula Carson Smith (February 19, 1917–September 29, 1967). American novelist. In McCullers's novels, set in the small Southern towns of her childhood, loneliness and spiritual isolation are perennial and inescapable features of the human condition. Her best-known novel, THE MEMBER OF THE WEDDING (1946), records the dreams of a lonely adolescent girl who hopes her brother's forthcoming marriage will also mean a new life for her; McCullers herself adapted it for the stage in 1952. Born in Columbus, Georgia, she came to New York to study music at Juilliard, but switched to Columbia to pursue a writing career. Her first novel, THE HEART IS A LONELY HUNTER (1940), established her literary reputation. Her other works include the novels REFLECTIONS IN A GOLDEN EYE (1941) and *Clock Without Hands* (1961); the novella THE BALLAD OF THE SAD CAFÉ (1951; dramatized by Edward ALBEE in 1963); a play, *The Square Root of Wonderful* (1958); and a posthumously published story collection, *The Mortgaged Heart* (1971), and unfinished autobiography, *Illumination and Night Glare* (1999). Besieged by health problems, McCullers was disabled by a series of strokes beginning in her 20s, leading to her early death at age 50.

McEwan, Ian (June 21, 1948–). English novelist, short-story writer, and screenwriter. From his first short-story collections, *First Love, Last Rites* (1975) and *In Between the Sheets* (1978), McEwan attracted notoriety for his disturbing portrayals of violence, depravity, and erotic obsession. His early novels—*The Cement Garden* (1978), about four siblings who bury their dead mother in the house, and *The Comfort of Strangers* (1981), the sadomasochistic nightmare of a young couple on honeymoon— established his reputation for the sensational. Later novels, such as *The Child in Time* (1987), *The Innocent* (1990), *Black Dogs* (1992), *The Daydreamer* (1994), and *Enduring Love* (1997) expanded the subject matter of his work without surrendering elements of the grotesque or his sharp, witty psychological exploration. *Amsterdam* (1998), a satire about a death-pact between a newspaper editor and a composer, was awarded the Booker Prize. McEwan's scriptwriting credits include *The Imitation Game: Three Plays for Television* (1981); screenplays for *The Ploughman's Lunch* (1983), *The Good Son* (1993), and *The Innocent* (1993); and the antinuclear oratorio *Or Shall We Die?* (1983).

McKay, Claude (September 15, 1890–May 22, 1948). Jamaican-American poet and novelist.

McKay's moving eloquence and uncommon militancy about racial injustice and the African-American experience are demonstrated in such works as HOME TO HARLEM (1928), the first bestselling novel by a black author, and the poem "If We Must Die," a response to the Harlem race riots of 1919. Born in Jamaica, he moved to the United States in 1912 and to Harlem two years later. His verse collections *Spring in New Hampshire* (1920) and *Harlem Shadows* (1922) were the first books published during the Harlem Renaissance. Attracted to communism as a young man, he lived for 12 years in the Soviet Union, France, and elsewhere abroad. He returned to the United States in 1934 and converted to Roman Catholicism in the 1940s. In addition to *Home to Harlem*, about a black soldier coming home from World War I, his novels include *Banjo* (1929), set in Marseille, and *Banana Bottom* (1933), set in Jamaica. A *Long Way from Home* (1937) is an autobiography.

McMurtry, Larry (June 3, 1936–). American novelist. In popular novels about contemporary small-town life in Texas, McMurtry challenges the myth of the heroic Old West and its legacy. "I'm a critic of the myth of the cowboy," he writes. "The idea that men are men and women are women and horses are best of all is not a myth that makes for the best sort of domestic life [or] cultural life." Yet for all its corrective realism, his Pulitzer Prize–winning novel, LONESOME DOVE (1985), emerged as a frontier epic in its own right as well as an elegy for a vanishing way of life. Born in Wichita Falls, Texas, McMurtry established his reputation with his first novel, *Horseman, Pass By* (1961; filmed as *Hud*, 1963), followed by *Leaving Cheyenne* (1963) and by *The Last Picture Show* (1966; filmed in 1971, with an Academy Award–winning screenplay by McMurtry) and its sequels, *Texasville* (1987) and *Duane's Depressed* (1999). Other works include *Terms of Endearment* (1975), *Buffalo Girls* (1990), *Streets of Laredo* (1993), *Boone's Lick* (2000), and a memoir, *Walter Benjamin at the Dairy Queen* (1999).

McNally, Terrence (November 3, 1939–). American playwright, librettist, and screenwriter. Difficult, seemingly impossible relationships—between artists and their art, stars and fans, gay men in an AIDS-harrowed world, lonely people of any sort—abound in McNally's works. While his plays of the 1960s and 1970s, including *Where Has Tommy Flowers Gone?* (1971) and *Bad Habits* (1974), were occasionally faulted by critics for displaying more wit than depth, his craftsmanship was always acknowledged. By the mid-1970s it had flowered in a hilarious farce set in a gay bathhouse, *The Ritz* (1975; also screenplay, 1976). In the early 1980s, the Manhattan Theatre Club became his artistic home, fostering such plays as *Frankie and Johnny in the Clair de Lune* (1987; also screenplay, 1991); *Lips Together, Teeth Apart* (1991); *Love! Valour! Compassion!* (1994; also screenplay, 1997); and the first of two plays connected in different ways to Maria Callas, *The Lisbon Traviata* (1985). The second Callas play, *Master Class* (1995), was produced on Broadway. He has also written the books for a number of Broadway musicals, including two with composer John Kander and lyricist Fred Ebb—*The Rink* (1984) and *Kiss of the Spider Woman* (1992; based on the novel by Manuel PUIG)—as well as *Ragtime* (1996; music by Stephen Flaherty, lyrics by Lynn Ahrens; based on the novel by E. L. DOCTOROW) and *The Full Monty* (2000; music and lyrics by David Yazbek; based on the 1997 film). Television work includes the Emmy Award–winning *Andre's Mother* (1990).

Mehta, Ved (March 21, 1934–). Indian-born American autobiographer, biographer, novelist, and essayist. Born in Lahore, now part of Pakistan, Mehta lost his vision at age four owing to meningitis. Determined that he should be educated, his parents sent him to America at 15 to attend the Arkansas School for the Blind. He proceeded to a brilliant academic career, first at Pomona College in California and then at Oxford University. Mehta's first autobiographical work, *Face to Face* (1957), was published to critical acclaim when he was only 23, and was followed by *Daddyji* (1972), *Mamaji* (1979),

Vedi (1982), *The Ledge Between the Streams* (1984), *Sound-Shadows of the New World* (1986), *The Stolen Light* (1989), and *Up at Oxford* (1993). Mehta has also written more broadly on India in, among other works, *Portrait of India* (1970), *The New India* (1978), and *Three Stories of the Raj* (1986). He was a longtime staff writer for THE NEW YORKER; *A Ved Mehta Reader: The Craft of the Essay*, a compilation of works first published in the magazine's pages, appeared in 1998. He recalled the magazine affectionately in *Remembering Mr. Shawn's New Yorker: The Invisible Art of Editing* (1998).

Melville, Herman (August 1, 1819–September 28, 1891). American novelist, short-story writer, and poet. Melville's masterpiece, MOBY-DICK (1851), a vast allegory about men, whales, and destiny, was initially dismissed by critics, who preferred his earlier adventure novels, *Typee* (1846) and *Omoo* (1847). Rediscovered in the 1920s, *Moby-Dick* is now often considered the greatest American novel. "If he were a religious man, he would be one of the most truly religious, better worth immortality than most of us," Nathaniel HAWTHORNE wrote of Melville. "He can neither believe, nor be comfortable in his unbelief; and he is too honest and courageous not to try to do one or the other." Born in New York City to a family of Dutch and Scottish ancestry, Melville was forced to quit school at age 15 and worked as a clerk before joining the crew of a seafaring vessel. He achieved fleeting literary fame in the 1840s with several novels based on his experiences at sea—*Typee* and *Omoo*, followed by *Redburn* (1849) and *White Jacket* (1850)—but his popularity declined with the appearance of his increasingly allegorical works, *Mardi* (1849), *Moby-Dick*, and PIERRE (1852). In 1866, Melville took a job as a customs inspector to support his family. Although he was demoralized by his commercial and critical failure as an author and by the deaths of two sons in 1867 and 1886, he continued to write. Among his later books are the short-story collection *The Piazza Tales* (1856), including "Benito Cereno" and "BARTLEBY THE SCRIVENER"; the long poem *Clarel* (1876) and the verse collection *Timoleon* (1891); and the novels *The Confidence Man* (1857) and BILLY BUDD (written 1888, published 1924).

Meredith, George (February 12, 1828–May 18, 1909). English novelist, poet, and critic. The last of the great Victorians, Meredith was England's most honored novelist at the turn of the 20th century. The son of an indigent tailor from Portsmouth, he supported himself as a journalist and publisher's reader until he was well into his 60s. Meredith began and ended his literary career as a poet, producing such works as *Modern Love* (1862), *Poems and Lyrics of the Joy of Earth* (1883), and *Ballads and Poems of Tragic Life* (1887), composed after the death of his second wife. But he is best remembered for his fiction, even if his oblique narrative style and subtle psychological insights mostly defied popular appeal. His first major novel, *The Ordeal of Richard Feverel* (1859), sold poorly, as did *Beauchamp's Career* (1875) and others. Not until THE EGOIST (1879), his comic masterpiece, and *Diana of the Crossways* (1885), about a woman struggling for emancipation, did Meredith win over the reading public. *The Idea of Comedy and the Uses of the Comic Spirit* (1877) is his celebrated essay on the moral and social virtues of comedy.

Merrill, James (March 3, 1926–February 6, 1995). American poet, novelist, and playwright. Born in New York City into a wealthy and socially prominent family (his father was a founder of the Merrill Lynch brokerage house) and educated at Amherst College, Merrill reaped the benefits, both cultural and educational, of his privileged position, cultivating passions for literature, opera, foreign languages, travel, and beautiful things and places, all of which would mark his work. His early lyrics—collected in *The Black Swan* (1946), *First Poems* (1951), *The Country of a Thousand Years of Peace* (1959), *Water Street* (1962), *Nights and Days* (1966; National Book Award), and *Braving the Elements* (1972), among other volumes—were admired for their wit, formal mastery, playfulness, and high polish. Far grander in scale, more personal, and certainly more eccentric is the three-part 17,000-line visionary epic that was first published separately as "The Book of Ephraim" (in *Divine Comedies*, 1976; Pulitzer Prize), *Mirabell: Books of Number* (1978; National Book Award), and *Scripts for the Pageant* (1980). Based on the revelations gleaned by Merrill and his partner David Jackson from more than 20 years of sessions at a Ouija board, all three were collected, together with the new *Coda: The Higher Keys*, as *The Changing Light at Sandover* (1982; National Book Critics Circle Award). Later collections include *Late Settings* (1985), *The Inner Room* (1988), and the posthumously published *A Scattering of Salts* (1995). *A Different Person* (1993) is a memoir. The immense *Collected Poems*, containing nearly all of Merrill's published work (excluding *Sandover*), as well as his many translations of poets writing in a wide range of languages, including his acclaimed versions of Constantine CAVAFY, appeared in 2001.

Merwin, W[illiam] S[tanley] (September 30, 1927–). American poet and translator. A prolific writer of spare poetic verse, Merwin has brought an increasingly honed and meditative quality to his work. Early collections, such as *A Mask for Janus* (1952), *The Dancing Bears* (1954), and *Green with Beasts* (1956), were relatively conventional lyrical narratives with themes from mythology, folk tales, and animal lore. Beginning in the 1960s, however, with *The Drunk in the Furnace* (1960), *The Moving Target* (1963), and especially *The Lice* (1967), his work became more muted in voice, surrealistic in style, and apocalyptic in vision. *The Carrier of Ladders* (1970) was awarded a Pulitzer Prize. Later poetic works include *The Compass Flower* (1977), *Opening the Hand* (1983), *The Rain in the Trees* (1988), *The Folding Cliffs* (1998), and *The River Sound* (1999). *The Miner's Pale Children* (1970) and *Houses and Travellers* (1977) are prose parable collections, and *Unframed Originals: Recollections* (1982) is a family memoir. Extensively trained in foreign languages, Merwin is also known for his translations of THE POEM OF THE CID (1959), THE SONG OF ROLAND (1963), and other classics.

Michener, James A[lbert] (February 3, 1907?– October 16, 1997). American novelist. Combining meticulous historical research with creative storytelling, Michener's sweeping multigenerational novels introduced postwar Americans to many cultures around the world. A foundling adopted by a poor Quaker widow in Doylestown, Pennsylvania, Michener won a scholarship to Swarthmore and worked as a teacher and book editor. His first book, *Tales of the South Pacific* (1947), based on stories he wrote while serving in the U.S. Navy during World War II, won a Pulitzer Prize; it became a bestseller two years later with the success of the Rodgers and Hammerstein musical adaptation, *South Pacific,* which also won a Pulitzer. Michener made publishing history both for popularizing the genre of "fictional documentaries" and for his uninterrupted string of bestsellers, including *Hawaii* (1959) and *The Source* (1965), a novel about ancient and modern Israel. Among his many other novels are *The Bridges at Toko-Ri* (1953), *Caravans* (1963), *Centennial* (1974), *Chesapeake* (1978), *Covenant* (1980), and *Mexico* (1992). Other works include an autobiographical novel, *The Fires of Spring* (1949), and a memoir, *The World Is My Home* (1992).

Millay, Edna St. Vincent (February 22, 1892– October 19, 1950). American poet. One of the most popular poets of the 1920s, Millay brought a distinctly feminine voice to the traditional sonnet while exemplifying the independence and emotional frankness of a modern woman. Born in Rockland, Maine, at age 20 she won a poetry award for what would become her best-known poem, "RENASCENCE"; her public recitation of the poem brought her a benefactor who enabled her to attend Vassar College. Upon graduation, she moved to Greenwich Village, supporting herself by writing columns for *Vanity Fair.* Among her works are *Renascence and Other Poems* (1917), *A Few Figs from Thistles* (1920), which won her national recognition, *Second April* (1921), *The Ballad of the Harp-Weaver* (1923; Pulitzer Prize), a libretto for Deems Taylor's opera *The King's Henchman* (1927), *Fatal Interview* (1931), *Wine from These Grapes* (1934), *Conversation at Midnight* (1937), and *Make Bright the Arrows* (1940). Her poems are gathered in the posthumously published *Mine the Harvest* (1954) and *Collected Poems* (1956).

Miller, Arthur (October 17, 1915–). American playwright. Tackling the moral issues at the heart of America's political and social life, Miller's plays established the "common man" as the new tragic hero of 20th-century American drama. Among his best-known plays, DEATH OF A SALESMAN (1949; Pulitzer Prize) and THE CRUCIBLE (1953) are regarded as American classics. Born in Harlem, the son of an immigrant Jewish businessman ruined in the Great Depression, after high school Miller worked in a warehouse while saving for college, eventually earning his bachelor's degree from the University of Michigan. He drew on his experience of the Depression years in developing his themes of the failure of the American Dream and the human costs of "making it," explored in his first important play, ALL MY SONS (1947), and notably in *Death of a Salesman*, whose title character has "dreamed the wrong dream." Miller continued to probe issues of personal and social morality in *The Crucible*, which used the Salem witch trials as a metaphor for McCarthyism in the 1950s, and such other works as A VIEW FROM THE BRIDGE (1955), AFTER THE FALL (1964), *Incident at Vichy* (1965), *The Price* (1968), *The American Clock* (1980, inspired by Studs Terkel's *Hard Times*), *The Last Yankee* (1991), *Broken Glass* (1994), and *Mr. Peters' Connections* (1998). *The Misfits* (1961), a screenplay, was written for his second wife, actress Marilyn Monroe. Miller has also written a novel, *Focus* (1945); a novella, *Homely Girl* (1995); short stories, collected in *I Don't Need You Anymore* (1967) and *"The Misfits" and Other Stories* (1987); the television drama *Playing for Time* (1980); and an autobiography, *Timebends* (1987). *The Theater Essays of Arthur Miller* (1978; revised ed. 1996) includes the influential "Tragedy and the Common Man." As president of PEN International (1965–69), Miller opened the organization to writers in the Soviet Union and offered support for dissident writers persecuted by totalitarian regimes.

Death of a Salesman was one of the first American plays to be produced in Beijing; Miller documented the production, which he directed, in *Salesman in Beijing* (1984), one of several collaborations with his third wife, photographer Inge Morath.

Miller, Henry (December 26, 1891–June 7, 1980). American novelist, short-story writer, and essayist. Celebrating freedom and a bohemian way of living, Miller's autobiographical writings were a major influence on the Beat generation of the 1950s. Miller is best known for two books initially banned in the United States, TROPIC OF CANCER (France, 1934; U.S., 1961) and *Tropic of Capricorn* (France, 1939; U.S., 1962), whose frank treatment of sex provoked a 30-year debate over censorship that ended in 1964 with a Supreme Court ruling in Miller's favor. Born in Brooklyn, New York, he lived in Paris in the 1930s and wrote *The Colossus of Maroussi* (1941), a paean to the Greek spirit, while sojourning in Greece. His works include stories and essays, collected in *Black Spring* (France, 1936; U.S., 1963), *The Cosmological Eye* (1939), and *Wisdom of the Heart* (1941). Returning to America in 1940, Miller settled in Big Sur, California, where he became a cult figure for younger writers. Later works include *The Air-Conditioned Nightmare* (1945); *Big Sur* (1957); an autobiographical trilogy, *The Rosy Crucifixion: Sexus* (1949), *Plexus* (1953), and *Nexus* (1960; U.S. edition, 1965); *My Life and Times* (1972); and *Genius and Lust* (1976), an anthology edited by Norman MAILER.

Miłosz, Czesław (June 30, 1911–). Lithuanian-born Polish-American poet, essayist, novelist, and translator. The recipient of the Nobel Prize in Literature in 1980, Miłosz is widely considered the greatest Polish-language poet of his time. He established his reputation with his first two collections, *Poemat o Czasie Zastygłym* (1933; Poem on Time Frozen) and *Trzy Zimy* (1936; Three Winters). He served as a Polish diplomat after World War II, but sought political asylum from the Communist regime in Paris in 1951 and later immigrated to the United States. His major writings include the anti-Communist essay collection *The Captive Mind* (*Zniewolony Umysł*, 1953), the autobiography *Native Realm* (*Rodzinna Europa*, 1959), and the novel *Seizure of Power* (first published in French as *La Prise du Pouvoir*, 1953). English translations of his poetry have appeared in *Bells in Winter* (1978), *Collected Poems, 1931–87* (1988), *Provinces: Poems, 1987–91* (1993), *Facing the River* (1995), and other volumes. *Road-Side Dog* (1998) is a collection of ruminations and reflections. He has also written a history of Polish literature and translated the BIBLE, SHAKESPEARE, and MILTON, among others, into Polish.

Milton, John (December 9, 1608–November 8, 1674). English poet and pamphleteer. To Byron "the prince of poets," to Wordsworth "that mighty orb of song," Milton wrote one of the masterpieces of the English language, the monumental Christian epic PARADISE LOST (1667). The son of a well-to-do scrivener and composer, he attended St. Paul's School and Cambridge before embarking on intensive

---

"A good book is the precious life-blood of a master spirit."

John Milton, *Areopagitica* (1644)

---

independent scholarship for seven years at home and overseas and, during this time, composed several of his best-known and greatest works: "L'Allegro" and "Il Penseroso" (both 1632), the masque COMUS (1634), and the pastoral elegy "Lycidas" (1637). A strong supporter of the Commonwealth and the Puritan cause, Milton spent the years 1641–60 writing in defense of religious and civil freedom and serving as a secretary in the Cromwell government. Notable works of the time include *Of Education* (1644); AREOPAGITICA (1644), his great attack on press censorship; and *Of the Tenure of Kings and Magistrates* (1649), a defense of republicanism. Blind from 1652 on, his dream of a republican England dashed by the Restoration in 1660, he took up his majestic account of "man's first disobedience." *Paradise Lost* was followed by the more austere "brief epic," *Paradise Regained* (1671), and the last of his great works, the verse drama SAMSON AGONISTES (1671).

Mishima, Yukio, *pen name of* Hiraoka Kimitake (January 14, 1925–November 25, 1970). Japanese novelist and playwright. The best-known and perhaps most influential of 20th-century Japanese writers, Mishima explored the pursuit of unattainable ideals—beauty, love, and a heroic destiny—in the modern world. Classically Japanese in their evocations of nature, his 40 novels—beginning with the autobiographical CONFESSIONS OF A MASK (*Kamen no Kokuhaku*, 1949), about a man who hides his homosexuality, and including such others as *The Sound of Waves* (*Shiosai*, 1954), THE TEMPLE OF THE GOLDEN PAVILION (*Kinkakuji*, 1956), and *The Sailor Who Fell from Grace with the Sea* (*Gogo no Eikō*, 1963)—also featured a dramatic vitality and depth of human understanding that moved KAWABATA to call him "the kind of genius that comes along perhaps once every three hundred years." Mishima's theatrical works include *Five Modern Nō Plays* (*Kindai Nōgakushū*, 1956) and *Madame de Sade* (*Sado Kōshaku Fujin*, 1965). His last works of fiction, a tetralogy of novels finished the day he died and collectively titled *The Sea of Fertility* (*Hōjō No Umi*, 1965–70), span 50 years of 20th-century Japanese life. Fascinated by death, imperial tradition, and the cult of the samurai, Mishima committed *seppuku* (ritual suicide) at age 45.

Mistral, Gabriela, *pen name of* Lucila Godoy y Alcayaga (April 7, 1889–January 10, 1957). Chilean poet. The first Latin American author to receive the Nobel Prize in Literature, in 1945, Mistral wrote passionately of love and sorrow, and addressed herself to the outcast and impoverished in poems that strove to reconcile suffering with the will of God. In 1914, she won a national writing contest with her "Sonetos de la Muerte" (Sonnets of Death), composed after her lover committed suicide, and very soon acquired a national reputation. Her major collections were *Desolación* (1922, later reworked; Desolation), *Tala* (1936; Felling Trees), *Lagar* (1954; The Wine Press), the posthumous *Poema de Chile* (1967; Poem of Chile), and *Ternura* (1924, 1945; Tenderness), which brought together from her other books poems about and for children. In awarding her the Nobel Prize, the Swedish Academy commended her lyric poetry, "which, inspired by powerful emotions, has made her name a symbol of the idealistic aspirations of the entire Latin American world." Mistral was also an educator in Chile and Mexico, as well as a diplomat, serving as Chilean consul in several cities, including New York. In 1957, her *Selected Poems* were published in LANGSTON HUGHES's translation. *A Gabriela Mistral Reader*, another selection of her works in English, appeared in 1997.

Mitchell, Joseph (July 27, 1908–May 24, 1996). American journalist. A master of the biographical sketch, Mitchell created warm and witty portraits of offbeat New Yorkers. Mitchell was born on a farm in Robeson County, North Carolina. In 1929, after attending college in his home state, he moved to New York City to pursue a career in journalism. He worked as a newspaper reporter and feature writer until 1938, when he joined the staff of THE NEW YORKER. He remained there for the rest of his life, even though he wrote little during his last three decades. Mitchell published six books, all of which are compendiums of his journalism. Best known among these are *McSorley's Wonderful Saloon* (1943), *Joe Gould's Secret* (1965), and *Up in the Old Hotel and Other Stories* (1992), a collection of pieces from four previous volumes.

Mitchell, Margaret (November 8, 1900–August 16, 1949). American novelist. Mitchell's enduring reputation rests on her sole book, the record-breaking bestseller GONE WITH THE WIND (1936; Pulitzer Prize). A native and lifelong resident of Atlanta, Georgia, Mitchell was educated at Smith College and worked for a time as a journalist. Her magnum opus, the sweeping romance and Civil War saga featuring the famed Southern belle Scarlett O'HARA, was written over a period of ten years and caused such a sensation that it changed Mitchell's life forever. The 1939 screen adaptation starring Clark Gable and Vivien Leigh is one of the most popular films of all time.

Mitford, Nancy (November 28, 1904–June 30, 1973). English novelist, biographer, and journalist. Endowed, according to one critic, with the "sane simplicity of Jane AUSTEN," Mitford made her name with hilarious satires of what she knew best: the eccentricities and foibles of the upper classes. She was born in London into a large aristocratic family that would provide the material for much of her writing. Her early novels included *Highland Fling* (1931), *Christmas Pudding* (1932), and *Wigs on the Green* (1935). In 1945, she moved to Paris and found her first real success with the novel *The Pursuit of Love* (1945), followed some years later by its companion, *Love in a Cold Climate* (1949); both are sophisticated, farcical portraits of her milieu and period, laced with the acerbic wit for which she became famous. Subsequent novels in the same vein include *The Blessing* (1951) and *Don't Tell Alfred* (1960). Her translation of Madame de Lafayette's THE PRINCESS OF CLEVES appeared in 1950. Mitford also wrote a series of historical biographies, including *Madame de Pompadour* (1954; revised 1968), *Voltaire in Love* (1957), *The Sun King* (1966), and *Frederick the Great* (1970). *Noblesse Oblige: An Enquiry into the Identifiable Characteristics of the English Aristocracy* (1956) is her humorous delineation of the distinctions between upper-class and non-upper-class uses of language, and *A Talent to Annoy: Essays, Articles and Reviews 1929–1968* (1986) is a collection of her journalism. Her voluminous, vivid correspondence with family members and notable literary friends has been collected in *Love from Nancy: The Letters of Nancy Mitford* (1993) and *The Letters of Nancy Mitford and Evelyn Waugh* (1997).

Molière, *original name* Jean-Baptiste Poquelin (January 15, 1622–February 17, 1673). French playwright. Molière's unrivaled dramatic gifts—his pitch-perfect ear for language, his incisive character portraits, his sophisticated depictions

of the human condition, and his ability to evoke the absurd as well as the profound—combined to create a new style of comedy and earned him a reputation as France's greatest comic writer. Born to a court furnisher in Paris, Molière gave up the promise of a secure future to devote his life to the theater. As an actor, director, producer, and writer, he toured France for more than a decade before finding favor with King Louis XIV in Paris, who invited him to use a theater at the Louvre. There, his popular comedies, including *The Affected Young Ladies* (*Les Précieuses Ridicules*, 1659), THE SCHOOL FOR WIVES (*L'École des Femmes*, 1662), THE MISANTHROPE (*Le Misanthrope*, 1666), THE MISER (*L'Avare*, 1668), and THE BOURGEOIS GENTLEMAN (*Le Bourgeois Gentilhomme*, 1670), met with increasing success, along with jealousy and ire. His satire of religious hypocrisy, TARTUFFE (*Le Tartuffe*, 1664), was banned for several years by the Church. Nevertheless, he continued undaunted until his final hours when, during a performance of his last play, THE IMAGINARY INVALID (*Le Malade Imaginaire*, 1673), he collapsed on stage. He died later that night.

Momaday, N[avarre] Scott (February 27, 1934–). American novelist and poet. Mining the rich vein of Native American culture, Momaday's writings are infused with insights from his Kiowa heritage. Commenting on the oral tradition that informs his art, he writes, "In the Indian world it is almost irrefutable. Man understands that he is obligated in certain ways to the landscape, that he is responsible for it, that he shares in the spirit of the place." Born in Lawton, Oklahoma, Momaday grew up in the Southwest, where his parents taught on reservations; he later earned a doctorate in literature at Stanford University. His first novel, *House Made of Dawn* (1968; Pulitzer Prize), tells of a young man's return from the U.S. Army to his Kiowa pueblo. His other works include poetry, collected in *Angle of Geese* (1974) and *The Gourd Dancer* (1976); a work on Kiowa folklore, *The Way to Rainy Mountain* (1969); *In the Presence of the Sun: Stories and Poems* (1992); *The Man Made of Words: Essays, Stories, Passages* (1997); a memoir, *The Names* (1976); and an autobiographical novel, *The Ancient Child* (1989).

Montaigne, Michel [Eyquem] **de** (February 28, 1533–September 13, 1592). French essayist. Montaigne's ESSAYS (*Essais*, 1580–88) introduced the modern essay to Western literature, and the French term "essai," or "attempt," was ultimately adopted for the new form. The son of a wealthy landowner in Montaigne, near Bordeaux, and a mother of Spanish Jewish descent, Montaigne received a rigorous classical education and studied law as a young man. He served as a counselor in Parliament from 1557 until 1571, when he retired to his family estate to devote himself to study and writing. During the turbulent civil wars of the Reformation period, Montaigne was several times drawn back to political affairs, serving as a mediator esteemed for his tolerant, Catholic stance and, from 1581 to 1585, as the mayor of Bordeaux. Steadily penning his *Essais*, Montaigne published the first two volumes in 1580 and a third in 1588. While he drew from established literary forms such as the religious confession and the treatise, his composition of brief observations in a personal, secular voice was remarkably innovative. Exploratory in tone, the essays reflect with striking candor and acuity on contemporary social affairs, as well as on fundamental human concerns ranging from friendship, sexuality, and death to digestion and sleep. Montaigne is particularly admired for his broad-minded insights into such major historical concerns as religious conflict and the European exploration of the New World.

Montale, Eugenio (October 12, 1896–September 12, 1981). Italian poet, critic, and translator. In hermetic, pessimistic poetry marked by brief moments of joy, Montale, who was awarded the Nobel Prize in Literature in 1975, grappled with modern political, historical, and existential dilemmas as well as problems of language and meaning. Montale was born in Genoa and served as an infantry officer in World War I. Although his opposition to the Mussolini regime hindered his early literary career, he managed to earn a living variously as a librar-

ian, translator, and critic. His first collection, *Cuttlefish Bones* (*Ossi di Seppia*, 1925), paved the way for a handful of others, including *The Occasions* (*Le Occasioni*, 1939), *The Storm and Other Things* (*La Bufera e Altro*, 1956), *Satura* (1962), and *Diario del '71 e del '72* (1973; *Diary of 1971 and 1972*). In them, Montale employs an unusual mix of vocabularies from all walks of life. Also noteworthy is *The Butterfly of Dinard* (*La Farfalla di Dinard*, 1956, 1960), a volume of cultural criticism. His complete poems are collected in *Eugenio Montale: L'Opera in Versi* (1980). Notable English translations of his poems include *Collected Poems 1920–1954* (1998), edited and translated by Jonathan Galassi.

Moore, Brian (August 25, 1921–January 11, 1999). Irish-born novelist. Whether writing about contemporary or historical subjects, immigrants or natives, honorable folks or criminals, men or women, Moore invoked large concerns and addressed them with economy, sympathy, and understatement. Born and educated in Belfast, Moore moved in 1948 to Canada, where he worked as a journalist, and eventually settled in California. He first found success with *The Lonely Passion of Judith Hearne* (1955), the story of a Belfast spinster who drowns her sorrows in alcohol. From there, he produced a steady stream of popular and critically acclaimed novels for more than 40 years, including *The Luck of Ginger Coffey* (1960), *I Am Mary Dunne* (1968), *Catholics* (1972), *The Doctor's Wife* (1976), *The Mangan Inheritance* (1979), *The Black Robe* (1985), *The Statement* (1996), and *The Magician's Wife* (1998).

Moore, Marianne (November 15, 1887–February 5, 1972). American poet and critic. One of the great originals of American modernism, whose poems overflow with precise observation, scintillating wit, intellectual play, and profound moral insight, Moore was one of the most popular and critically admired poets of her generation. "More than any modern poet," said John ASHBERY, "she gives us the feeling that life is softly exploding around us, within easy reach."

Moore was born near St. Louis, Missouri, and raised in Carlisle, Pennsylvania. While studying biology at Bryn Mawr College, she became friendly with the poet H. D., who would be instrumental in launching Moore's poetic career. After graduation, she returned to Carlisle, where she taught business courses at the United States Indian School from 1911 to 1915. She moved to New York City in 1918, settling in Brooklyn (late in life she would move to Manhattan's Greenwich Village), and began to move in bohemian and avant-garde artistic circles (although she herself was distinctly unbohemian in both her life and her political beliefs), forging close personal and/or working relationships with nearly all the significant poets of the time, including E. E. CUMMINGS, Wallace STEVENS, WILLIAM CARLOS WILLIAMS, and Ezra POUND, and, eventually, with such younger poets as Elizabeth BISHOP and Allen GINSBERG. From 1921 to 1925 she worked as a clerk at the Hudson Park Branch of The New York Public Library, before becoming editor, from 1925 to 1929, of the preeminent American literary journal THE DIAL. Her first collection, *Poems* (1921), was published, without her knowledge or permission, by friends in London and included her best-known poem, "Poetry" ("I, too, dislike it."). Her *Selected Poems*, with an introduction by T. S. ELIOT, appeared in 1935. While Moore was writing such great poems as "A Grave" (1924), "The Pangolin" (1936), and "What Are Years?" (1941), she remained primarily a "poet's poet," but wth her *Collected Poems* (1951), which won both the National Book Award and the Pulitzer Prize, she became something of a celebrity. Moore's passionate devotion to sports and sportsmen (especially baseball players) inspired such poems as "Hometown Piece for Messrs. Alston and Reese" (1959) and "Baseball and Writing" (1966) ("Fanaticism? No. Writing is exciting / and baseball is like writing."), and also resulted in many opportunities for the poet to pose (often wearing her signature cape and tricorne hat) for photographs with a variety of athletes, including Joe DiMaggio. Moore was a constant (and to some critics, notorious) reviser of her

work; *The Complete Poems of Marianne Moore* (1967) incorporates all the final revisions she made to her poems. *The Complete Prose of Marianne Moore* (1986) gathers Moore's alert and sensitive critical writings; *The Selected Letters of Marianne Moore* (1997) is a collection of her inimitable correspondence.

Moravia, Alberto, *pen name of* Alberto Pincherle (November 28, 1907–September 26, 1990). Italian novelist and short-story writer. A leading Neorealist writer in postwar Italy, Moravia is remembered for his stark depictions of a society in which alienation, moral corruption, and empty sexuality are the norm. Born in Rome, he contracted tuberculosis of the bone as a child, and spent much of his youth and adolescence in solitude, reading, writing, and studying languages. During the 1930s, he worked as a journalist and traveled widely; for a time he was married to novelist Elsa Morante. Moravia's first novel, *The Time of Indifference* (*Gli Indifferenti*, 1929), about a corrupt middle-class family during the rise of fascism, was a popular success and set the tone for his later works. Although his books were condemned by Mussolini and later by the Vatican, his reputation continued to grow with novels such as *The Woman of Rome* (*La Romana*, 1947), *The Conformist* (*Il Conformista*, 1951), and TWO WOMEN (*La Ciociara*, 1957). He also published popular story collections, including *Roman Tales* (*Racconti Romani*, 1954) and *Erotic Tales* (*La Cosa e Altri Racconti*, 1983). Numerous films have been adapted from his works; among the best known are Vittorio de Sica's *Two Women* (1961) and Bernardo Bertolucci's *The Conformist* (1970).

Morgan, Claire. *See* **Highsmith, Patricia**

Morrison, Toni, *original name* Chloe Anthony Wofford (February 18, 1931–). American novelist. Morrison's powerful and poetic novels of the black American experience and the lives of black women in particular have made her one of the most significant writers of her day, a status confirmed in 1993, when she became the first African-American writer to win the Nobel Prize in Literature. Born in Ohio, Morrison studied at Howard and Cornell universities. She then embarked on a distinguished career as a university professor and book editor. From her first novel, *The Bluest Eye* (1970), onward, Morrison's work has been characterized by a rich prose style that combines reality and fantasy, history and myth. *Sula* (1973) is the story of two friends whose paths diverge, and *Song of Solomon* (1977) is about a young black man's search for identity. In the 1980s, she continued to explore the lives of women in *Tar Baby* (1981) and BELOVED (1987; Pulitzer Prize). More recent novels include *Jazz* (1992), a story set in 1920s Harlem, and *Paradise* (1998), about an all-black town.

Mortimer, [Sir] John (April 21, 1923–). English novelist and playwright. The creator of the comically eccentric defense lawyer Horace RUMPOLE, Mortimer is admired for his comic sensibility and gift for satire and mystery. Born in London and educated at Oxford, he published his first novel, *Charade*, in 1947, then took the bar, and for many years carried on a double career as barrister and writer. In 1966, he was appointed Queen's Counsel, and subsequently argued several noted censorship cases. His reputation as a writer took off when his play *The Dock Brief* (1957) was broadcast on BBC radio and TV. Mortimer wrote many more popular dramas, including one of his best works, *A Voyage Round My Father* (1970), and a television adaptation of EVELYN WAUGH's *BRIDESHEAD REVISITED* (1981). In 1975, he introduced the cynical barrister Horace Rumpole in a television film, *Rumpole of the Bailey*, followed by a long-running BBC television series of the same name, as well as several collections of short stories, beginning in 1978. His other works include the autobiographies *Clinging to the Wreckage* (1982) and *The Summer of a Dormouse* (2001) and the novels *Paradise Postponed* (1985), *Summer's Lease* (1988), and *The Sound of Trumpets* (1998).

Mukherjee, Bharati (July 27, 1940–). Indian-born American novelist and short-story writer. Mukherjee's fictional explorations of the immigrant experience have contributed an Indian-American perspective to America's literary melting pot. Born in Calcutta to a wealthy Bengali family, she studied English in London and India, then earned a doctorate at the University of Iowa Writers' Workshop. She spent 14 years in Canada before immigrating in 1980 to America, where she has held several professorships. The self-proclaimed "Ellis Island writer" began to portray lives caught between East and West in the novels *The Tiger's Daughter* (1972) and *Wife* (1975), about a woman in an arranged marriage who goes mad in New York City. Similar themes appear in her later novels, *Jasmine* (1989), *The Holder of the World* (1993), and *Leave It to Me* (1997), as well as her story collections, *Darkness* (1985) and *The Middleman and Other Stories* (1988), a widely acclaimed volume that features immigrants from around the world. Mukherjee's travel journal, *Days and Nights in Calcutta* (1977), was cowritten with her husband, Canadian writer Clark Blaise.

Munro, Alice, *original name* Alice Anne Laidlaw (July 10, 1931–). Canadian short-story writer. For stories that depict everyday existence and its disturbing undercurrents with the depth and density of novels, Munro has won numerous awards, widespread popular acclaim, and a reputation as "the Canadian CHEKHOV." Munro was born and educated in southwestern Ontario, the setting of many of her finest stories. She began writing at an early age, influenced by women writers from the American South; although she did not publish her first book, *Dance of the Happy Shades*, until 1968, that work immediately established her reputation. Her other collections, often narrated by girls and women in search of truth, include *Something I've Been Meaning to Tell You* (1974); *The Beggar Maid* (1979; originally published in 1978 as *Who Do You Think You Are?*), a series of interlinking tales that is among her best-known works; THE MOONS OF JUPITER (1982); *The Progress of Love* (1986); *Open Secrets* (1994); and *The Love of a Good Woman* (1998; National Book Critics Circle Award).

Munro, H. H. *See* **Saki**

Murasaki, Shikibu (c. 978–? [between 1014 and 1030]). Japanese novelist and diarist. Little is known about the woman who wrote THE TALE OF GENJI (*Genji Monogatari*, c. 1004), a monument of Japanese literature and a work of enduring influence. Lady Murasaki, whose name is a pseudonym, was born in Kyoto and received an unusually fine education. She appears to have married an older nobleman and to have given birth to a daughter. After her husband died, she entered into the court of the empress as a lady-in-waiting. It was probably here that she wrote her epic masterpiece of imperial court life and princely romance. Murasaki's diary, *Murasaki Shikibu Nikki*, and poetry, *Murasaki Shikibu-shū*, appear in English as *Murasaki Shikibu: Her Diary and Poetic Memoirs* (1982).

Murdoch, [Dame] [Jean] **Iris** (July 15, 1919–February 8, 1999). Irish-born English novelist and philosopher. One of Britain's most important post–World War II novelists, Murdoch utilized psychological insight and philosophical inquiry to explore questions of free will, self-knowledge, and morality. Born in Dublin and educated at Oxford and Cambridge, she worked as a civil servant and a lecturer in philosophy at Oxford before devoting herself fully to writing. One year after the publication of her first book, a critical study of Jean-Paul SARTRE, her novel UNDER THE NET (1954) appeared, marking the beginning of an unusually successful and prolific fiction career. Murdoch proceeded to publish more than two dozen novels noted for their humor, expansiveness, and complexity, including *The Bell* (1958), *A Severed Head* (1961), *The Black Prince* (1973), *The Sacred and Profane Love Machine* (1974), and THE SEA, THE SEA (1978; Booker Prize). Her later works include *The Philosopher's Pupil* (1983), *The Book and the Brotherhood* (1987), *The Green Knight* (1993), and *Jackson's Dilemma* (1995). Murdoch also published plays, poetry, and numerous works of philosophy. In 1998, her husband, literary critic John BAYLEY, published a memoir about their marriage and Murdoch's long struggle with Alzheimer's disease, *Elegy for Iris*; after she died, a sequel, *Iris and Her Friends* (1999), appeared.

Musil, Robert (November 6, 1880–April 15, 1942). Austrian novelist. Musil's massive unfinished epic, THE MAN WITHOUT QUALITIES (*Der Mann ohne Eigenschaften*, 1930–43), with its wit, complexity, and intelligence, and its focus on ideas rather than action, often elicits comparisons to the works of JOYCE and PROUST, and is regarded as a modernist masterpiece. Born in Klagenfurt, Austria, Musil attended prestigious military academies as a youth, trained as a civil engineer, and took a doctorate in psychology and philosophy at the University of Berlin. After serving in World War I, he worked as a journalist and essayist and published fiction and drama, including his acclaimed first novel, *Young Törless* (*Die Verwirrungen des Zöglings Törless*, 1906), the play *The Enthusiasts* (*Die Schwärmer*, 1921), and the novella collection *Three Women* (*Drei Frauen*, 1924). During the 1930s, Musil lived in Vienna, but with the rise of Nazism, he and his Jewish wife immigrated to Switzerland. Musil had been working on his influential multivolume novel about the final decadent years of the Austro-Hungarian Empire for nearly two decades when a cerebral hemorrhage during his morning exercises abruptly terminated the project and his life. His stories, essays, and diaries appear in several collections.

Nabokov, Vladimir (April 23, 1899–July 2, 1977). Russian-born American novelist, critic, and translator. "*Lolita* is famous, not I," claimed Nabokov, whose imaginative, inventive, and erudite novels earned him a place as one of the 20th century's most important writers. Born to an aristocratic family in St. Petersburg, Nabokov began publishing poetry while still in his teens. He studied French and Russian literature at Cambridge, then moved to Berlin, where he wrote several novels in Russian under the pseudonym Vladimir Sirin, including *Mary* (*Mashen'ka*, 1926), *Glory* (*Podvig*, 1932), *Laughter in the Dark* (*Kamera Obskura*, 1933), *Despair* (*Otchayanie*, 1936), and *The Gift* (*Dar*, 1937). He moved to Paris in the late 1930s and then to the United States in 1940, where he taught at several universities. His first book written in English was THE REAL LIFE OF SEBASTIAN KNIGHT (1941). During his tenure at Cornell, he wrote the then-scandalous novel LOLITA (1955, published first in France and in the United States three years later); its phenomenal success enabled him to devote himself fully to writing thereafter. In 1959, he immigrated to Montreux, Switzerland, where he would reside for the rest of his life. Other acclaimed works written in English are the novels PNIN (1957), PALE FIRE (1962), and *Ada or Ardor: A Family Chronicle* (1969), and the memoir *Conclusive Evidence* (1951), revised as *Speak, Memory* (1966). Nabokov also published several volumes of stories, the critical study *Nikolai Gogol* (1944), and a renowned translation of PUSHKIN'S EUGENE ONEGIN (1964). Collections of his literary criticism, originally presented as lectures to his university students, were published as *Lectures on Literature* (1980), *Lectures on Russian Literature* (1981), and *Lectures on Don Quixote* (1983). Nabokov was also a lepidopterist of some renown whose discoveries added to the body of scientific knowledge about butterflies, especially the American varieties of the species known as blues.

Naipaul, [Sir] **V**[idiadhar] **S**[urajprasad] (August 17, 1932–). Trinidadian-born English novelist, essayist, and travel writer. Naipaul's work, often pessimistically ironic, focuses on the troubles of existence in emerging nations and life in exile. Born and raised in Trinidad to parents of Indian descent, Naipaul was educated at Oxford and remained in England thereafter. His early fiction, including his first book, *The Mystic Masseur* (1957), satirizes life in the West Indies. Naipaul developed a following with his acclaimed fourth book, A HOUSE FOR MR. BISWAS (1961). His subsequent works reflect an increasingly political, complex, and somber world view. Among his notable works of fiction are *In a Free State* (1971; Booker Prize); *Guerrillas* (1975), a portrait of political and sexual violence; A BEND IN THE RIVER (1979), a novel set in East Africa; and two autobiographically based books, *The Enigma of Arrival* (1987) and *A Way in the World* (1994). Naipaul's

extended travels in developing nations sparked several unsparingly honest and at times controversial volumes of nonfiction, including *An Area of Darkness* (1964), *India: A Wounded Civilization* (1977), *Among the Believers: An Islamic Journey* (1981), and *India: A Million Mutinies Now* (1990).

Narayan, R[asipuram] **K**[rishnaswami], *original surname* Narayanswami (October 10, 1906– May 13, 2001). Indian novelist and short-story writer. A series of tenderly ironic comedies about contemporary life in Southern India secured Narayan's international reputation as one of India's foremost English-language writers. Narayan was born in Madras and educated in Mysore. He worked briefly as a teacher and journalist before launching his literary career with the novel *Swami and Friends* (1935). Many of Narayan's books are set in the fictional town of Malgudi, where a diverse and realistic cast of characters are caught at the intersection of tradition and modernity. Graham GREENE was an early champion of Narayan's work, which he likened to CHEKHOV's, and helped to introduce it to Western readers. Among Narayan's popular novels are *The Bachelor of Arts* (1937), *The English Teacher* (1945), *The Financial Expert* (1952), *The Guide* (1958), *The Man-Eater of Malgudi* (1961), *The Vendor of Sweets* (1967), and *A Tiger for Malgudi* (1983). His story collections include *Malgudi Days* (1982), *Under the Banyan Tree* (1985), and *The Grandmother's Tale* (1993). Narayan also published modern retellings of the RĀMĀYANA and the MAHĀBHĀRATA as well as *My Days: A Memoir* (1974).

Nash, [Frederic] **Ogden** (August 19, 1902–May 19, 1971). American poet. Nash's witty and whimsical verse—"Candy / Is dandy / But liquor / Is quicker"—peppered with screwball rhymes and all-around wordplay, made him the most popular and quotable versifier of his day. Born in Rye, New York, Nash spent one year at Harvard, then worked as a teacher, bond salesman, and streetcar ad writer. As an early staff editor at THE NEW YORKER as well as a frequent contributor there, Nash helped to shape the

AUTHOR PSEUDONYMS: WHAT'S IN A NAME?

Ed McBain (the author of the 87th Precinct series), Ellery Queen (the mystery writer and editor), and Carolyn Keene (author of the Nancy Drew series of young adult mysteries) are three of the most-read writers of the 20th century, but you will not find birth certificates on file for them under any of these names. The reason: they are all pen names, or pseudonyms (Greek for "false names").

"McBain," for example, is the creation of Evan Hunter (born Salvatore Lombino), who as Evan Hunter publishes "serious" novels such as *The Blackboard Jungle* (1954); and he has also written under the names Richard Marsten, Curt Cannon, and Hunt Collins. Hunter has even "collaborated" with "McBain" on *Candyland* (2000), a novel whose first half is written in Hunter's style, with its second part in the style of "McBain." (Jacket photographs show the "two" authors dressed in their contrasting habiliment.) Hunter is only one of many writers who choose to keep separate in the public mind their work in different genres. Others who have taken this approach include Anne Rice, author of the Vampire Chronicles. Her other authorial identities, for erotic fiction, are "Anne Rampling," who wrote *Belinda* (1989) and *Last Exit to Eden* (1985), and "A. N. Roquelaure" (meaning "Anne under the cloak"), author of the Sleeping Beauty trilogy. Booker Prize–winning novelist Julian Barnes (*Flaubert's Parrot*, 1984) writes crime novels under the alias "Dan Kavanagh." Patricia

Highsmith, known for *Strangers on a Train* (1950) and the Ripley series, used the name "Claire Morgan" when she published the now classic lesbian novel *The Price of Salt* (1952). Even Louisa May Alcott, before she became famous as the author of *Little Women* (1868), used a pseudonym—A. M. Barnard—for the potboilers she wrote for ready cash.

"Ellery Queen," on the other hand, is a joint pseudonym for the team of Frederic Dannay and Manfred B. Lee, cousins who collaborated from 1929 until Lee's death in 1971; on a few of their works, they called themselves "Barnaby Ross." Other joint pseudonyms include "Lewis Padgett," for the science-fiction works produced by the husband-and-wife team of C. L. Moore and Henry Kuttner, both of whom also published works on their own (for some of his, Kuttner employed additional pseudonyms, including "Jack Vance" and "Will Garth"). "Emma Lathen," whom C. P. Snow once called "probably the best living American writer of detective stories," was actually two women, Mary J. Latsis, an economist, and Martha Hennissart, an attorney, who teamed up for a series of books featuring John Putnam Thatcher, a sleuthing Wall Street banker. Their pen name combined the first syllables of each of their surnames to make "Lathen"; "Emma" comes from the "M" in Mary and the "Ma" in Martha.

As for the creator of that teenaged detective Nancy Drew, "Carolyn Keene" was the brainchild of the Stratemeyer Syndicate, the publishing venture responsible for such children's and young adult series as Tom Swift, the Hardy Boys, and the Bobbsey Twins. When Nancy Drew solved her first mystery in *The Secret of the Old Clock* (1930), the book was written by Mildred Benson (who wrote many other books under an assortment of less-famous pseudonyms). Benson stayed with the series until the 1950s; since then Nancy's sleuthing has continued with the help of a multitude of "Carolyns."

Some writers use pen names to keep their private lives separate from their writing, or to avoid confusion. When William S. Burroughs, author of *Naked Lunch* (1959), published his first book, the autobiographical, first-person *Junkie: Confessions of an Unredeemed Drug Addict* (1953), he used the name "William Lee" ("Lee" was the maiden name of his mother, a descendant of Robert E. Lee). When the young Vladimir Nabokov began publishing poems and chess problems in a Russian periodical edited by his father, also named Vladimir, the son chose the name "V. Sirin," which he used on all his Russian-language works, even after his father's death.

Before the 20th century, women found that works submitted with a man's name attached were much more likely to be accepted for publication. As a result, Baroness Aurore Dudevant and Mary Ann Evans published, respectively, as "George Sand" and "George Eliot," and the Brontë sisters (Emily, Charlotte, and Anne) chose to call themselves, respectively, "Ellis, Currer, and Acton Bell" when they published their poems, and when Charlotte and Emily published novels. But the use of pseudonyms was not restricted to women: consider Mark Twain (for Samuel Langhorne Clemens), Lewis Carroll (Charles Lutwidge Dodgson), O. Henry (William Sydney Porter), and Saki (H. H. Munro).

A pen name can also be used to prove a point. In the 1980s, Doris Lessing, the critically acclaimed author of *The Golden Notebook* (1962), demonstrated the difficulties facing unknown writers when she submitted a manuscript to her publisher under the pen name "Jane Somers"—only to have it rejected as "too depressing." Two works by "Somers" were eventually published—*The Diary of a Good Neighbour* (1983) in the United States and *If the Old Could . . .* (1984) in England—but they were ignored by critics.

The most prolific author in literary history is, of course, the sometimes pseudonymous "Anonymous," whose name has appeared not only on works of uncertain authorship but on works whose authors wanted to keep their identities to themselves. Recently, "Anonymous" reared his head as the author of *Primary Colors* (1996), a satiric *roman à clef* about the 1992 presidential campaign. For weeks after the book's ballyhooed publication, tabloids and cocktail parties buzzed with speculation over the identity of the author, until *Newsweek* writer and editor Joe Klein stepped forward. "I didn't intend to be anonymous," he confessed in *The New York Times*. "I wanted to be pseudonymous."

magazine's character and style. His first poetry collections—*Free Wheeling* and *Hard Lines*—were published in 1931. Other popular volumes continued to appear steadily for 40 years and include *I'm a Stranger Here Myself* (1938), *Everyone But Thee and Me* (1962), *Bed Riddance* (1970), and *I Wouldn't Have Missed It: Selected Poems of Ogden Nash* (1975). Nash also wrote children's books and collaborated on several Broadway musicals, including *One Touch of Venus* (1943) and *Two's Company* (1952).

Naylor, Gloria (January 25, 1950–). American novelist. Naylor's popular and critically acclaimed novels explore the diversity of African-American experience and identity, and celebrate the lives of black women. Born and raised in New York City, Naylor worked as a missionary for the Jehovah's Witnesses for seven years before attending college. As an undergraduate at Brooklyn College, she was inspired by the work of Toni MORRISON and determined to follow in her footsteps. Naylor completed her successful first novel, THE WOMEN OF BREWSTER PLACE (1982), while she was a graduate student at Yale, and later adapted the book for television; *The Men of Brewster Place* (1998) gives the other side of the story. Her other novels include *Linden Hills* (1985), about an affluent black suburb that echoes DANTE's Hell; *Mama Day* (1988), a mythic tale set in the rural South; and *Bailey's Cafe* (1992), about eccentrics who find refuge at a Brooklyn diner.

Neruda, Pablo, *pen name of* Neftalí Ricardo Reyes Basoalto (July 12, 1904–September 23, 1973). Chilean poet. Whether writing about love, politics, or everyday objects, Neruda's passion, vision, and intimacy made him a national hero, one of the great Spanish-language poets, and, in 1971, the recipient of a Nobel Prize in Literature. Neruda was raised in southern Chile and began publishing his poetry at the age of 13. By age 20, with the encouragement of poet GABRIELA MISTRAL and the success of his passionate collection TWENTY LOVE POEMS AND A SONG OF DESPAIR (*Viente Poemas de Amor y una Canción Desesperada*, 1924), his reputation was

well established. Beginning in 1927, Neruda served as a diplomat in Southeast Asia and Spain. The publication during this time of the darkly surrealistic volume RESIDENCE ON EARTH (*Residencia en la Tierra*, 1933) marked a change in his voice and vision. The Spanish Civil War and the death of his friend Federico GARCÍA LORCA affected Neruda deeply, and his poetry became increasingly political. These sentiments are reflected in his epic of Spanish-American history, *Canto General* (1950), which features his celebrated long poem THE HEIGHTS OF MACCHU PICCHU (*Alturas de Macchu Picchu*, 1945). In the mid-1940s Neruda joined the Communist Party, and lived in exile for several years. He returned to Chile in 1952 and enjoyed two decades of fame, happiness, and great productivity, during which he published *Odes to Common Things* (*Odas Elementales*, 1954). President Salvador Allende appointed Neruda ambassador to France in 1970, but three years later the new government was overthrown and Allende was killed. Days later, Neruda passed away.

Nin, Anaïs (February 21, 1903–January 14, 1977). French-born American diarist, novelist, short-story writer, and critic. Nin's personal, poetic, psychological writings chronicle her self-exploration, reflect on female identity, and express her desire "to live life as a dream." Born in a Paris suburb to musician parents, Nin came to the United States at age 11, and returned to Paris ten years later, after her marriage. The publication of her first book, *D. H. Lawrence: An Unprofessional Study* (1932), drew her into the Surrealist and bohemian circles that, along with her forays into psychoanalysis, were to influence her life and work. Turning her attention to fiction, she wrote the prose poem *House of Incest* (1936), the novel *Winter of Artifice* (1939), the story collection *Under a Glass Bell* (1944), and the five-volume sequence *Cities of the Interior: A Continuous Novel* (1959), which contains *A Spy in the House of Love* (1954). Nin's literary reputation remains modest, although the publication of *The Diary of Anaïs Nin 1931–1966* (1966) thrust her, for a time, into the public eye and made her a heroine of the women's movement. These intimate journals, which eventually formed several volumes, reveal her love affair and long friendship with HENRY MILLER. Nin's erotica is collected in *Delta of Venus* (1977) and *Little Birds* (1979).

Nooteboom, Cees, *original name* Cornelis Johannes Jacobus Maria Nooteboom (July 31, 1933–). Dutch novelist, travel writer, and poet. A lifelong traveler whose journeys inform all his work, Nooteboom is one of Holland's most popular and frequently translated writers. He was born in The Hague and has worked as a travel journalist. His short, unconventional novels often experiment with perspective and identity. Notable among them are *Philip and the Others* (*Philip en de Anderen*, 1955), inspired by a hitchhiking trip through Europe, *Rituals* (*Rituelen*, 1980), *In the Dutch Mountains* (*In Nederland*, 1984), and *The Following Story* (*Het Volgende Verbaal*, 1991). His acclaimed volumes of travel essays include *A Night in Tunisia* (*Een Nacht in Tunesie*, 1965), *Berlin Notes* (*Berlijnse Notities*, 1990), and *Roads to Santiago: Detours and Riddles in the Lands and History of Spain* (*De Omweg naar Santiago*, 1992). *The Captain of the Butterflies* (1997) is a thematically arranged selection of four decades' worth of his verse.

Norris, [Benjamin] **Frank**[lin] (March 5, 1870– October 25, 1902). American novelist. "We don't want literature, we want life," declared Norris, who, in his own brief life, became one of America's first and foremost naturalistic writers. Born in Chicago, as a teenager Norris moved to San Francisco with his family. He was educated in Paris, at the University of California at Berkeley, and at Harvard, and worked abroad as a war correspondent. His fiction writing began with several romances; then, inspired by the naturalistic writings of Émile ZOLA, he produced his well-known crime novel, *MCTEAGUE* (1899), the story of a middle-class dentist who murders his wife. He then embarked upon an ambitious trilogy to be called The Epic of the Wheat, completing the acclaimed first volume, *THE OCTOPUS* (1901), about wheat cultivation in California, and the second, *The Pit* (1903), set

at the Chicago commodities exchange, but died while planning the third volume. His posthumously published works include *The Responsibilities of the Novelist* (1903), a collection of essays and articles; and *Vandover and the Brute* (1914), a novel.

Novalis, *pen name of* [Georg Philipp] Friedrich, Baron von Hardenberg (May 2, 1772–March 25, 1801). German poet and novelist. In his lyrical, mystical, religious writings, Novalis called for a return to nature and union with the universe. He was born to nobility in Wiederstedt, Prussian Saxony, and studied law and philosophy. The early death from tuberculosis of his beloved young fiancée inspired his poetic lamentation *Hymns to the Night* (*Hymnen an die Nacht*, 1800); their relationship became the stuff of legend, as in PENELOPE FITZGERALD's novel *THE BLUE FLOWER* (1995). The young author also wrote two novels — *Heinrich von Ofterdingen* (1802), about a medieval poet and his search for "the blue flower," a symbol for all of Romanticism, and *The Apprentices at Sais* (*Die Lehrlinge zu Sais*, 1802) — but these remained unfinished when he, too, lost his life to tuberculosis. Some of Novalis's ecclesiastical verse can be found in modern hymnals.

Oates, Joyce Carol (June 16, 1938–). American novelist, short-story writer, and essayist. Oates's vast body of work ranges from the naturalistic to the nightmarish; her characters are subject to extremes of passion and often find themselves caught in the capricious and violent grip of fate. Oates was born and raised in upstate New York and educated at Syracuse University and the University of Wisconsin. She started publishing stories in college, and in the early 1960s began her long career as an English professor. Her first book, the story collection *By the North Gate* (1963), was followed by the novel *With Shuddering Fall* (1964). In 1969, her novel *THEM* won a National Book Award. Other novels include *Bellefleur* (1980), *Because It Is Bitter, and Because It Is My Heart* (1990), *Foxfire: Confessions of a Girl Gang* (1993), and *We Were the Mulvaneys* (1996), which explores a family's reaction to a rape. Oates has also published criticism, poetry, and many story collections. Among her recent works are the novels *Broke Heart Blues* (1999) and *Blonde* (2000), based on the life of Marilyn Monroe.

O'Brian, Patrick, *original name* Richard Patrick Russ (December 12, 1914–January 2, 2000). English novelist and translator. O'Brian is best known for his 20-novel series of Napoleonic-era sea adventures featuring Captain Jack Aubrey and ship's surgeon/spy Stephen Maturin, beginning with *Master and Commander* (1969) and ending with the best-selling *Blue at the Mizzen* (1999). His most audacious creation, however, was himself. Born Richard Russ in England, and raised in reduced circumstances, he published his first book at age 15: *Caesar: The Life Story of a Panda Leopard* (1930), the highly imaginative tale of a mythical animal. In 1939, he deserted his wife and family when his second child was born with a fatal condition. He joined a volunteer ambulance brigade in London, where he met Mary, Countess Tolstoy Miloslavsky, who would become his second wife. They married in 1945, whereupon he changed his name legally to Patrick O'Brian, and the couple moved to Wales. There O'Brian constructed a fictional biography that varied in details over the years but consistently included these major false-hoods: that he was Irish gentry, university edu-cated, and an experienced seaman. In 1949, he and his wife (by now his unofficial editor) moved to France. In addition to his novels and two critically admired biographies, *Picasso* (1976) and *Joseph Banks* (1987), he translated the works of numerous French authors into English, most notably Simone de BEAUVOIR.

O'Brien, Edna (December 15, 1932–). Irish novelist and short-story writer. In her sophisticated and lyrical fiction, O'Brien explores the lives of women; her frank depictions of sex, love, religion, and the Irish led to the banning of some of her work in Ireland. O'Brien was born in County Clare in rural Ireland, and moved to London in 1959. She found success in the early 1960s with a trilogy of novels — *The Country Girls* (1960), *The Lonely Girl* (1962),

and *Girls in Their Married Bliss* (1964) — about two country girls who move to the city in search of a better life, later published in one volume as *THE COUNTRY GIRLS TRILOGY and Epilogue* (1986). Other novels include *Casualties of Peace* (1966), *Johnny I Hardly Knew You* (1977; published in the United States as *I Hardly Knew You*), *The High Road* (1988), *House of Splendid Isolation* (1994), *Down by the River* (1996), and *Wild Decembers* (2000). Among her several story collections are *A Fanatic Heart* (1984) and *Lantern Slides* (1990). O'Brien has also written plays, screenplays, and nonfiction. Her biography of James JOYCE was published in 1999.

O'Brien, Flann, *pen name of* Brian O'Nolan *or* O Nuallain (October 5, 1911–April 1, 1966). Irish novelist and journalist. O'Brien's delight-fully satirical writings probe and poke fun at Ireland and the Irish. Born in County Tyrone and educated in Dublin, O'Brien worked as a civil servant until 1953. He built a following as a writer through his long-running political column in the *Irish Times*, published under the pseudonym Myles na Gopaleen, but his fiction was slower to catch on. His inventive, multilay-ered first novel, *At Swim-Two-Birds* (1939), did not garner substantial attention until its reissue in 1960. O'Brien's other novels are *The Poor Mouth* (*An Béal Bocht*, 1941; written in Gaelic), *The Hard Life* (1961), *The Dalkey Archive* (1964), and *The Third Policeman* (1967). His newspaper columns were collected in 1968 in *The Best of Myles* and in 1977 in *The Hair of the Dogma*.

O'Casey, Sean, *original name* John Casey (March 30, 1880–September 18, 1964). Irish playwright and memoirist. A prominent figure in Ireland's Literary Renaissance, O'Casey wrote politically impassioned plays marked by provocative social themes. He was raised in the slums of Dublin. Largely self-educated, he worked from age 14 on as a railway laborer and union organizer. An enthusiasm for the theater led him to try his hand at writing plays; the first to reach the stage, *The Shadow of a Gunman* (1923), was produced by the renowned Abbey Theatre. Two popular yet controversial dramas followed, *JUNO AND THE PAYCOCK* (1924) and *THE PLOUGH AND THE STARS* (1926), the latter inciting rioting at the theater. O'Casey moved from realism toward Expressionism in his later works, which include *The Silver Tassie* (1929), *Within the Gates* (1934), *Red Roses for Me* (1943), and *The Bishop's Bonfire* (1955). In 1926 he settled permanently in London. His six-volume autobiography begins with *I Knock at the Door* (1939) and concludes with *Sunset and Evening Star* (1954).

O'Connor, [Mary] **Flannery** (March 25, 1925–August 3, 1964). American short-story writer and novelist. O'Connor's complex, lyrical tales combine violence, romance, grotesquerie, and religious fervor in a unique Southern Gothic style. Born in Savannah, Georgia, O'Connor was raised an ardent Roman Catholic in the largely Protestant South. She studied sociology and English at Georgia State College for Women, and was an early student at the University of Iowa's renowned Writers' Workshop. In 1946 she made her fiction debut with the story "The Geranium"; five years later, she was diagnosed with lupus erythematosus, a disease that had taken her father's life. Although only three books were published in her lifetime — the story collection *A GOOD MAN IS HARD TO FIND* (1955) and the novels *WISE BLOOD* (1952) and *THE VIOLENT BEAR IT AWAY* (1960) — her concerns with hubris and salvation and her uncanny blend of the brutal and the sublime gave her an unmistakable literary signature. A fourth volume, the collection *EVERYTHING THAT RISES MUST CONVERGE* (1965), was published posthumously; *The Complete Stories* (1971; National Book Award) confirmed her reputation as a master of the story form. *Mystery and Manners* (1969) is a collection of prose pieces; *The Habit of Being* (1979) is collected letters.

O'Connor, Frank, *pen name of* Michael Francis O'Donovan (September 17, 1903–March 10, 1966). Irish short-story writer, translator, and critic. A versatile and prolific contributor to the Irish Literary Renaissance, O'Connor "[did] for Ireland what CHEKHOV did for Russia," according to W. B. YEATS, namely, he captured the lives of his countrymen with realism, sensitivity, humor, and warmth. Born and raised in Cork, O'Connor had a youth shadowed by poverty. As a teenager he joined the Irish Republican Army, and later worked as a teacher and librarian. In the early 1930s, he became a member of the Abbey Theatre's board of directors and a prominent figure in Dublin's literary circles. He came to the United States in 1951, and taught at several universities. O'Connor's masterful stories appeared frequently in *THE NEW YORKER* and were collected in several volumes, including *Guests of the Nation* (1931), *Crab Apple Jelly* (1944), and *Domestic Relations* (1957). His notable nonfiction includes *The Big Fellow* (1937), a biography of Michael Collins; *The Lonely Voice: A Study of the Short Story* (1962); and two volumes of autobiography: *An Only Child* (1960) and *My Father's Son* (1968).

Odets, Clifford (July 18, 1906–August 14, 1963). American playwright. A major figure in the American theater of the 1930s, Odets became famous for his moving, effective use of social protest theater and naturalism. Born in Philadelphia and raised in New York, Odets began his career as an actor with the Theatre Guild. In 1931 he became a founding member (with Harold Clurman, Lee Strasberg, and Cheryl Crawford) of the Group Theater. Their production of *WAITING FOR LEFTY* (1935) made Odets an overnight success; that play and his *AWAKE AND SING!* (1935) powerfully dramatized issues of class struggle. Odets was also a successful Hollywood screenwriter and director, vacillating between Broadway and Hollywood, and between the political and commercial uses of theater. Briefly a member of the Communist Party, he was a cooperative witness before the House Committee on Un-American Activities. Among his other notable plays are *Golden Boy* (1937), about an Italian-American prizefighter; *The Big Knife* (1949), an indictment of Hollywood; and *The Country Girl* (1950), about an alcoholic actor's attempt at a comeback.

Ōe, Kenzaburō (January 31, 1935–). Japanese novelist, short-story writer, and essayist. The winner of the 1994 Nobel Prize in Literature, who found early notoriety for his unconventional subject matter and style as well as his leftist politics, Ōe explores Japan's postwar struggle with alienation and identity in a gritty, personal style. Ōe was born in a remote mountain village on the island of Shikoku. At 18 he moved to Tokyo, where he studied French literature at Tokyo University. He began his career with the award-winning novella *The Catch* (*Shiiku*, 1958), followed by the novel *Nip the Buds, Shoot the Kids* (*Memushiri Kouchi*, 1958). Ōe was profoundly affected by two events during the 1960s: the birth of a son with brain damage and a visit to Hiroshima. He dealt with the former in *A Personal Matter* (*Kojinteki-na Taiken*, 1964) and *Teach Us to Outgrow Our Madness* (*Warera no Kyōki o Ikinobiru Michi o Oshie yo*, 1969), and addressed the latter in *Hiroshima Notes* (*Hiroshima Nōto*, 1965). During this period, he also became a vocal antiwar activist. Considered one of his finest works, his second novel, THE SILENT CRY (*Man'en Gannen no Futtōbōru*, 1967), is an allegory that interweaves myth, history, and contemporary life. Among his many other books are the satirical nuclear war fantasy *The Pinch Runner Memorandum* (*Pinchi Rannā Chōsho*, 1976) and the autobiographical *A Quiet Life* (*Shizuka na Seikatsu*, 1990).

O'Faolain, Sean, *original name* John Francis Whelan (February 22, 1900–April 20, 1991). Irish short-story writer, novelist, and editor. The son of a Cork policeman, O'Faolain chose his Gaelic name to show support for the Irish cause and fought on the side of the Irish Republican Army during the insurrection of 1918–21. He was educated at the National University of Ireland and Harvard University and, after brief teaching stints in the United States, Britain, and Ireland, turned to writing full time. His first collection of stories, *Midsummer Night Madness and Other Stories* (1932), was followed a year later by a novel, *A Nest of Simple Folk* (1933), the pair establishing him as a significant new voice in Irish letters. In nearly all his writings, O'Faolain explores questions of Irish identity, the influence of Irish Roman Catholicism

(which he portrays as provincial and stifling), and the frustrated hopes of the nationalist movement. Other works include the novels *Bird Alone* (1936) and *Come Back to Erin* (1940); the story collections *The Man Who Invented Sin* (1947), *The Heat of the Sun* (1966), *Foreign Affairs* (1976), and *Selected Stories* (1978); two volumes of Irish history, *The Irish, A Character Study* (1949, revised 1969) and *An Irish Journey* (1940); and a memoir, *Vive Moi* (1964). O'Faolain also exerted influence on Irish literary culture as founding editor of THE BELL, a literary journal based in Dublin.

O'Hara, Frank (June 27, 1926–July 25, 1966). American poet, art critic, and playwright. O'Hara was at the center of New York's mid-20th-century avant-garde, and a leader among the group of poets known as the New York School. He was born in Baltimore and raised in Grafton, Massachusetts; did a stint in the Navy; and was educated at Harvard and the University of Michigan. O'Hara settled in New York in the early 1950s and found work at the Museum of Modern Art. From 1953 to 1955, he was an editor at *Art News* magazine, where much of his art criticism (collected in *Art Chronicles*, 1975) first appeared. O'Hara's close association with artists like Jackson Pollock and Willem de Kooning inspired much of the improvisational writing for which he is known. Poems such as his mock manifesto, "Personism"; his tribute to Billie Holiday, "The Day Lady Died"; and his longer poem "In Memory of My Feelings" as well as collections like *Meditations in an Emergency* (1956) and *Lunch Poems* (1964) exemplify his style. O'Hara's life was cut short in 1966 when he was struck by a dune buggy on New York's Fire Island at 3:00 a.m. *Selected Poems* (1973; National Book Award) was published posthumously.

O'Hara, John (January 31, 1905–April 11, 1970). American short-story writer and novelist. This bestselling author of more than 30 works chronicling the behavior and aspirations of the upwardly mobile tells us with frankness, wit, and precision "how people look and how they want to look...how they speak and how they think they ought to speak" (Lionel TRILLING). O'Hara hailed from the small town of Pottsville, Pennsylvania, the basis for the fictional town of Gibbsville that appears in many of his works. Although he never attended college, his career as a newspaperman gave him ample opportunity to hone his writing skills. His first book, the novel APPOINTMENT IN SAMARRA (1934), was an immediate success. O'Hara's stories frequently appeared in THE NEW YORKER, and in collections such as *The Doctor's Son* (1935) and *Hellbox* (1947). *Pal Joey* (1940), a story told through letters, was made into a popular Rodgers and Hart musical. Among O'Hara's other well-known novels—many of which were adapted for the screen—are *BUtterfield 8* (1935) and *Ten North Frederick* (1955; National Book Award).

Okri, Ben (March 15, 1959–). Nigerian novelist, short-story writer, and poet. Okri's writings address his country's need to reconcile African mysticism with Western modernism, and to forge a contemporary identity. Okri was raised in Lagos, Nigeria, and began writing as a teenager. His first novels, *Flowers and Shadows* (1980) and *The Landscapes Within* (1981), were published while he was a student at the University of Essex in England. During the mid-1980s, Okri worked as a broadcaster for the BBC and a poetry editor of *West Africa* magazine. He published two story collections—*Incidents at the Shrine* (1986) and *Stars of the New Curfew* (1988)—before winning the Booker Prize for *The Famished Road* (1991), a novel about a child-spirit searching for his identity. Okri continues this motif in *Songs of Enchantment* (1993) and *Infinite Riches* (1998). His other works include the novel *Astonishing the Gods* (1995) and the poetry collection *An African Elegy* (1992).

Olson, Charles (December 27, 1910–January 10, 1970). American poet and literary theorist. Olson's "projective" or open verse emphasizes a free style of writing shaped by sound rather than sense, which aims to transmit energy directly to the reader. Born in Worcester, Massachusetts, and educated at Wesleyan and Harvard, Olson earned a reputation as a literary theorist with works like *Call Me Ishmael* (1947), a study of the literary sources that influenced MELVILLE's *MOBY-DICK*. In the late 1940s he began teaching at North Carolina's Black Mountain College, and from 1951 to 1956 he served as rector there. Through his teaching, his editorship of *THE BLACK MOUNTAIN REVIEW*, and his manifesto, *Projective Verse* (1950), he helped to shape a generation of poets (among them Robert CREELEY, Denise LEVERTOV, and Robert Duncan) who would bring a new consciousness to postwar American poetry. Olson put his theories into play in his own work, in poems like "The Kingfisher," featured in his first collection, *In Cold Hell, in Thicket* (1953). During the final years of his life, Olson dedicated himself to his multivolume epic-length work, *The Maximus Poems*, published in its entirety in 1983.

'Omar Khayyám (May 18, 1048–December 4, 1131). Persian poet. 'Omar Khayyám's clever, memorable, oft-quoted verses ("A Jug of Wine, a Loaf of Bread—and Thou") extol the fleeting pleasures of the moment and reveal a metaphysical bent and a genial cynicism. 'Omar Khayyám spent most of his life in his native Nishapur, where he received a privileged education. Widely known in his time as an astronomer, mathematician, and scholar, he helped to standardize the calendar and published a wide range of prose works, although few of these survive. His famed quatrains, or *robá'iyat*, became popular only centuries after his death, when Edward FitzGerald (1809–1883) translated a selection into English and arranged them into a unified work entitled *THE RUBÁIYÁT OF 'OMAR KHAYYÁM* (1859). Hundreds of editions have appeared in the years since, and scholarly debate continues over the question of how many of the several hundred extant quatrains attributed to 'Omar Khayyám were actually written by him.

Ondaatje, [Philip] Michael (September 12, 1943–). Sri Lankan-born Canadian novelist and poet. The author of *The English Patient* (1992; Booker Prize), a novel about four intertwining lives at the end of World War II, Ondaatje creates lyrical, intimate, collage-like works that mix genres as they explore culture, nature, history, and art. Born in Ceylon (now Sri Lanka) of Dutch and Indian ancestry, Ondaatje was raised there and in England, and educated in London, Quebec, and Ontario. He moved permanently to Canada in 1962, where he has worked intermittently as an English professor, film director, and hog farmer. In the late 1960s, Ondaatje gained notice for his poetry, including his first collection, *The Dainty Monsters* (1967). But it was his celebrated third volume, *The Collected Works of Billy the Kid: Left-handed Poems* (1970), and later his fiction that catapulted him into the spotlight. In addition to *The English Patient*, Ondaatje's other prose works include *Coming Through Slaughter* (1976), *Running in the Family* (1982), *In the Skin of the Lion* (1987), and *Anil's Ghost* (2000).

O'Neill, Eugene (October 16, 1888–November 27, 1953). American playwright. An American theatrical pioneer and one of the most acclaimed playwrights of the 20th century, O'Neill experimented freely with form and brought European movements such as realism, naturalism, and Expressionism to the American stage. O'Neill was born in New York to a theatrical family; his father was the well-known melodramatic actor James O'Neill. After a year at Princeton, Eugene O'Neill held a series of odd jobs, including a stint as a seaman. A bout with tuberculosis in 1912 gave him a chance to start writing, and he did so furiously, honing his craft with the renowned drama teacher George Pierce Baker and then teaming up with the Provincetown Players, which produced many of his early one-acts. By 1920, O'Neill had a play on Broadway (*Beyond the Horizon*), a Pulitzer Prize, and a reputation as an unusually gifted playwright. O'Neill enjoyed enormous critical acclaim during his lifetime — he won three Pulitzer Prizes and, in 1936, the Nobel Prize in Literature — yet commercial success generally eluded him. Among his many esteemed works are THE EMPEROR JONES (1920), the first mainstream American drama to feature a black

actor in a leading role; ANNA CHRISTIE (1921; Pulitzer Prize); DESIRE UNDER THE ELMS (1924), his first Greek-style tragedy; STRANGE INTERLUDE (1928; Pulitzer Prize), a lengthy work that reflects the influence of FREUD; the epic tragedy MOURNING BECOMES ELECTRA (1931); the comedy AH, WILDERNESS! (1933); the complex drama THE ICEMAN COMETH (1946); and his greatest play, the autobiographical LONG DAY'S JOURNEY INTO NIGHT (written in 1941 but not produced until 1956), for which O'Neill was awarded a fourth, posthumous Pulitzer Prize.

Orton, Joe, *original name* John Kingsley Orton (January 1, 1933–August 10, 1967). English playwright. Orton's outrageous farces — in which characters gleefully pursue all forms of lust: for men, women, money, power, and fantasy — are brutal, corrupt, scandalous, and viciously entertaining. Born in Leicester, Orton trained briefly at Clark's College and later at the Royal Academy of Dramatic Art, where he met his lifelong companion and sometime literary collaborator, Kenneth Halliwell. His seven plays for radio, stage, and television owe a debt to Greek comedy and Oscar WILDE. His first full-length work, *Entertaining Mr. Sloane* (1964), is a story of murder, manipulation, and seduction; in *Loot* (1966), a thief hides stolen goods in his mother's coffin. In *The Erpingham Camp* (1967), his popular one-act, guests and staff at a seaside resort serve as sexual predator and prey. The posthumously produced *What the Butler Saw* (1969) is a scathing satire of psychiatry and of farce itself. At the height of Orton's career, in 1967, Halliwell, apparently in a fit of jealousy, bludgeoned the playwright to death in a notorious murder-suicide.

Orwell, George, *pen name of* Eric Arthur Blair (June 25, 1903–January 21, 1950). English novelist, essayist, and critic. The renowned author of two dark masterpieces of political satire and antitotalitarianism, ANIMAL FARM (1945) and NINETEEN EIGHTY-FOUR (1949), Orwell was born in Bengal, India, raised in England, and educated on scholarship at Eton, where Aldous HUXLEY was one of his teachers. Rather than continue his education at a university, he chose instead to join the Indian Imperial Police in Burma (now Myanmar). But five years of service left him deeply disillusioned with imperialism. He returned to Europe in 1927 and lived an impoverished life in its capital cities, struggles captured evocatively in his first book, DOWN AND OUT IN PARIS AND LONDON (1933). Orwell's semiautobiographical novel *Burmese Days* (1934), and his documentary-style book about working-class conditions in Britain, *The Road to Wigan Pier* (1937), reflect the passionately held sociopolitical liberalism that drove much of his writing. Orwell fought in the Spanish Civil War and reported on his experiences in *Homage to Catalonia* (1939). Among his important essay collections are *Inside the Whale* (1940) and *Shooting an Elephant* (1950). Orwell enjoyed a few brief years of fame and fortune before his death from tuberculosis in 1950. The four-volume *Collected Essays, Journalism and Letters of George Orwell* was published in 1968.

Osborne, John (December 12, 1929–December 24, 1994). English playwright. Through daringly realistic dramas such as LOOK BACK IN ANGER (1956), Osborne brought working-class discontent to the stage, led the way for a generation of writers known as the Angry Young Men, and became one of Britain's most important postwar playwrights. Osborne was born in London and educated at Belmont College in Devon. He worked as an actor-manager in provincial theaters until 1956, when the successful debut production of *Look Back in Anger* propelled him into the front ranks of England's contemporary dramatists. Osborne's plays all feature rebellious, individualistic heroes who fight back against apathy, triviality, and the uncaring modern world. Notable among them are THE ENTERTAINER (1957), about a declining vaudevillian; *Luther* (1961), about the Protestant reformer; and *Inadmissible Evidence* (1965), about a frustrated solicitor at a law firm. Osborne also wrote the Academy Award–winning screenplay for *Tom Jones* (1963), and two memoirs: *A Better Class of Person* (1981) and *Almost a Gentleman* (1991).

Ossian, *pen name of* James Macpherson (October 27, 1736–February 17, 1796). Scottish poet. The name Ossian is a corruption of Oisín, traditionally the son of the legendary Irish hero Finn MacCumhaill, and the presumed writer of the 3rd-century Irish Gaelic poems that were allegedly "discovered" and "translated" by Macpherson, including *Fragments of Ancient Poetry...* (1760) and the epics *Fingal* (1762) and *Temora* (1763). Macpherson, a Scot, had actually written them himself, basing them partly (and carelessly; he claimed indisputably Hibernian heroes as Caledonians) on historic Irish legends, as well as on poetry dating to the 15th century. Their authenticity was questioned almost immediately, notably by SAMUEL JOHNSON. Admirers included GOETHE, who incorporated selections in THE SORROWS OF YOUNG WERTHER; Napoleon, who under their influence had his godson (later king of Sweden) named Oscar; and Thomas Jefferson, who thought "Ossian" "the greatest poet that has ever existed." By the late 1800s the works were conclusively exposed as forgeries; the debate over what intrinsic merit they may possess continues to this day. There is similarly no consensus on the worth of the poetry Macpherson published in his own name, or on the several British histories he wrote as a government employee. The work of Macpherson's "Ossian" should not be confused with the genuine Scots-Irish Gaelic poetry known as the Ossianic ballads.

Ovid, *Latin in full* Publius Ovidius Naso (March 20, 43 B.C.–A.D. 17 or 18). Roman poet. From his own time down through the millennia, the passionate, witty, and technically adroit poetry of Ovid—especially METAMORPHOSES, his masterpiece on the theme of change and transformation in Greek and Roman myth—has profoundly influenced writers from around the world: in English literature alone, the works of CHAUCER, SPENSER, MILTON, SHAKESPEARE, and DRYDEN exhibit a debt to him. Ovid was born in Sulmo (now Sulmona) in the Apennines, east of Rome. Although his father intended him to pursue a career in law, Ovid's interest in poetry drew him in another direction. His love elegies, *Amores*; imaginary letters, *Heroines* (*Heroides*); and instructional volumes on *The Art of Love* (*Ars Amatoria*) established his position as a major writer. Ovid was held in high esteem by the court of Emperor Augustus until A.D. 8, when he was mysteriously exiled to the Black Sea. His entreaties to Augustus for pardon, published as *Sorrows* (*Tristia*) and *Letters from Pontus* (*Epistulae ex Ponto*), failed to achieve their intended purpose. Ovid's works were kept alive through the Middle Ages despite the Church's objections, and have been revered by writers (and composers and artists; Pablo Picasso illustrated an edition of the *Metamorphoses*) from the Renaissance onward. Interesting recent translations of *Metamorphoses* include Seamus HEANEY's selected translations in his *The Midnight Verdict* (1993); *After Ovid: New Metamorphoses* (1995), an anthology of versions by major contemporary poets, including Heaney, TED HUGHES, Amy Clampitt, and Charles SIMIC; and Hughes's free renditions of selected narratives, *Tales from Ovid* (1997).

Owen, Wilfred (March 18, 1893–November 4, 1918). English poet. Regarded as the finest poet of World War I, Owen offers a passionate treatise against war in his harrowingly realistic, stylistically innovative verse. Born in Shropshire and educated at Shrewsbury Technical College, Owen worked as a teacher until 1915, when he enlisted in the army. Owen had been writing since his youth, and in 1917, while mending from his battle wounds in a Scottish hospital, he was encouraged in his literary pursuits by poet and fellow soldier Siegfried SASSOON. The following year he returned to the front, only to be killed one week before the armistice. Only a handful of Owen's poems were published before his death, but his posthumous discovery after the publication of his *Poems* (with an introduction by Sassoon) in 1920 earned him a lasting legacy. Among his best-known poems are "Dulce et Decorum Est," "Strange Meeting," and "Anthem for Doomed Youth." Composer Benjamin Britten used Owen's verse for his *War Requiem*.

Oz, Amos, *original name* Amos Klausner (May 4, 1939–). Israeli novelist, short-story writer, and essayist. Among the most influential figures in the "New Wave" of Israeli writers that emerged in the 1960s, in his bold, lyrical fiction Oz gives expression to the existential dilemmas of younger generations of Israelis living with the legacy of their idealistic forebears. Entering the interior world of his characters, he uncovers "the hidden — or suppressed — emotional netherworld of Israeli national existence," according to critic Robert Alter. Born in Jerusalem, Oz joined Kibbutz Hulda in the Negev at the age of 15. *Where the Jackals Howl* (*Artsot Ha-tan*, 1965), a collection of stories about kibbutz life, and the early novels *Elsewhere Perhaps* (*Makom Aher*, 1966) and *My Michael* (*Mikha'el Sheli*, 1968) established his international reputation. His later writings include *A Perfect Peace* (*Menuhah Nekhonah*, 1982), *To Know a Woman* (*La-daa't Ishah*, 1989), and *Don't Call It Night* (*Al Tagidi Lailah*, 1994) as well as reportage, *In the Land of Israel* (*Poh ve-Sham be-Erets Yisrael bi-Setav*, 1982, 1983), and literary criticism.

Ozick, Cynthia (April 17, 1928–). American novelist, short-story writer, essayist, and playwright. A leading American literary stylist and a major figure in Jewish-American letters, in her fiction and essays Ozick explores the nature of the imaginative process, the writer's vocation, and themes of radical impersonation. Born in New York City to Russian immigrant parents, both of them pharmacists, Ozick grew up in Pelham Bay, the Bronx, and studied literature at New York University and Ohio State University. Her first novel, *Trust* (1966), was followed by several collections of award-winning stories: *The Pagan Rabbi* (1971), *Bloodshed* (1976), and *Levitation* (1982). Her later work includes the novels *The Cannibal Galaxy* (1983), THE MESSIAH OF STOCKHOLM (1987), *The Shawl* (1989), and *The Puttermesser Papers* (1997), and the essay collections *Art & Ardor* (1983), *Metaphor & Memory* (1989), *Fame & Folly* (1996), and *Quarrel & Quandary* (2000).

Paley, Grace (December 11, 1922–). American short-story writer and poet. In three acclaimed volumes of short stories — THE LITTLE DISTURBANCES OF MAN (1959), *Enormous Changes at the Last Minute* (1974), and *Later the Same Day* (1985) — Paley examined the lives of ordinary New Yorkers in a style that is tough, precise, colloquial, and funny. She grew up in a socialist family in the Bronx, New York, listening to stories in English, Russian, and Yiddish. She studied poetry with W. H. AUDEN and later taught at Sarah Lawrence College for more than 20 years. *The Collected Stories* appeared in 1994, a volume of nonfiction prose, *Just As I Thought*, in 1998, and a second edition of *Begin Again: Collected Poems* in 2000.

Parker, Dorothy, *original surname* Rothschild (August 22, 1893–June 7, 1967). American critic, journalist, short-story writer, poet, and screenwriter. Described by *Time* magazine as "the tongue heard round the world," Parker became legendary for her sardonic wit. Born in New Jersey and raised on 57th Street in Manhattan, she unleashed her quips first at *Vanity Fair* from 1917 to 1920, but was fired for panning several major plays. From 1927 to 1933, she wrote the "Constant Reader" book review column for THE NEW YORKER, winning renown for her anecdotal humor and literary insight; reviewing a Broadway play during this period she wrote that Katharine Hepburn "ran the gamut of emotions from A to B," a good example of her mordant style. She was also a leading member of the Algonquin Round Table, a regular gathering at the Algonquin Hotel in the 1920s of writers famed for their cutting humor. Her popular volumes of poetry, including *Enough Rope* (1926) and *Death and Taxes* (1931), and short stories, *Laments for the Living* (1930) and *After Such Pleasures* (1933), later collected in *Here Lies* (1939), satirize her sophisticated social circle as well as unsuccessful love relationships with an ironic, melancholy tone. Her *New Yorker* reviews are collected in *A Month of Sundays* (1971); *The Portable Dorothy Parker* (1973) reprints work in various genres. She also wrote numerous screenplays, including the 1937 version of *A Star Is Born* (cowritten with her second husband, Alan Parker). Blacklisted in the 1940s for her left-wing politics, she left her entire estate to Martin Luther King, Jr.

Pasternak, Boris (February 10, 1890–May 30, 1960). Russian poet, novelist, and translator. Born in Moscow to artist parents (his father was a famous painter and illustrator and his mother had been a concert pianist), and raised in a cultivated milieu in which he routinely encountered such major cultural figures as Leo TOLSTOY and Aleksandr Scriabin, Pasternak studied music and philosophy in Russia and Germany and began publishing poetry soon after. His reputation as an important young Soviet poet was made with his collections *My Sister — Life: Summer, 1917* (*Sestra Moya Zhizn'*, 1922) and *Themes and Variations* (*Temy i Variyatsi*, 1923). Over the next decade, he published several poems about the 1905 revolution, a collection of short fiction entitled *Aerial Ways* (*Vozdushnye Puti*, 1925), an autobiography, *Safe Conduct* (*Okhrannaya Gramota*, 1931), and several other works. But by 1933, Soviet censors had gained considerable control over literature, and Pasternak was not able to publish. For many years, he made his living translating SHAKESPEARE, GOETHE, PERCY BYSSHE SHELLEY, VERLAINE, and many others. Pasternak's masterpiece and only novel, DOCTOR ZHIVAGO (*Doktor Zhivago*, 1957) — a soaring romantic epic set during the Russian Revolution, affirming the value of individuality and critical of Marxism — so angered the Soviet government (which felt it demonstrated "nonacceptance of the socialist revolution") that, after at first accepting the 1958 Nobel Prize in Literature ("Immensely thankful, touched, proud, astonished, abashed," he telegraphed to the Swedish Academy), Pasternak ultimately felt compelled to reject the prize. First published in Italy (in Russian) and acclaimed worldwide, *Doctor Zhivago* was not published in Pasternak's native country until 1988. While some critics considered the novel technically awkward and more important as a social document than as a work of art, the critic Edmund WILSON wrote in THE NEW YORKER, "Nobody could have written it in a totalitarian state and turned it loose on the world who did not have the courage of genius.... [Pasternak's] book is a great act of faith in art and in the human spirit." *I Remember: Sketch for an Autobiography* (*Biografichesky Ocherk*) was first published in Italian in 1959.

Paton, Alan (January 11, 1903–April 12, 1988). South African novelist and biographer. Paton's first and most famous novel, CRY, THE BELOVED COUNTRY (1948), brought worldwide attention to South Africa's apartheid system. This white South African fought racism through his work as a leader of the Liberal Party, as a school teacher and principal, and in several other books, including the novels *Too Late the Phalarope* (1953) and *Ah But Your Land Is Beautiful* (1981). A memoir of the first half of his life, *Towards the Mountain*, was published in 1980 and its companion, *Journey Continued*, in 1988, the year he died.

Paz, Octavio (March 31, 1914–April 19, 1998). Mexican poet, essayist, editor, and critic. A major figure in Latin American literature, Paz imbues his richly lyrical writing with images of history and myth. Paz published his first poetry collection, *Luna Silvestre*, at 19, and founded and edited several literary journals during his long career. For 25 years he served as a diplomat, resigning in 1968 over a government crackdown on free speech. His major collections are *They Shall Not Pass!* (*No Pasaran!*, 1937), *Eagle or Sun?* (*Aguila o Sol?*, 1951), *Sun Stone* (*Piedra de Sol*, 1957), *Salamandra* (1962), and *Poemas 1935–1975* (1979). His prose works include *The Labyrinth of Solitude* (*El Laberinto de la Soledad*, 1950), an original and influential study of the Mexican character, and many essays on literature, writing, sex, history, religion, and politics. In 1990, he was awarded the Nobel Prize in Literature.

Peacock, Thomas Love (October 18, 1785–January 23, 1866). English novelist, poet, and essayist. Peacock can be said to have invented a species of novel of ideas, in which contemporary figures are caricatured and intellectual conversations predominate. His satirical novels—including *Headlong Hall* (1816), *Nightmare*

Abbey (1818), *Crotchet Castle* (1831), and *Gryll Grange* (1860–61)—feature extended philosophical discussions, often around a convivial dinner table, that skewer the culture and politics of the day. *Nightmare Abbey*, for example, satirizes Romantic melancholy with characters based upon PERCY BYSSHE SHELLEY, COLERIDGE, and BYRON, and other novels feature characters based on the philosophers and economists Jeremy Bentham, John Stuart Mill, and Thomas Malthus. The son of a London merchant, Peacock received a traditional classical education. His formal schooling ended before his 13th birthday, when he became a clerk, but he continued to pursue his Greek and Latin studies for the remainder of his long life. He had published three volumes of poetry by 1812, the year he met Shelley, who became a close friend and key influence. In *The Four Ages of Poetry* (1820), a mocking essay that inspired Shelley's impassioned rebuttal, A *Defence of Poetry* (written in 1821, but not published until 1840), Peacock argued that humanity would be better served if intellectuals directed their energies away from literature and toward commerce and the practical sciences. He himself had done precisely that when, in 1819, he accepted a position in the Examiners Office of the East India Company, where he would remain for the next three and a half decades. As he ascended to positions of increasing responsibility, his literary output declined proportionately. In the last decade of his life, however, he again took up his pen, writing his final comic novel, *Gryll Grange*, and summing up recollections of his friendship with Shelley in a restrained memoir, intended as an antidote to the lurid biographies of the poet by other contemporaries. *Memoirs of Shelley and Other Essays and Reviews* (1970) is a recent collection.

Peake, Mervyn (July 9, 1911–November 17, 1968). English novelist and poet. Peake is best known for his Gormenghast Trilogy, a Gothic fantasy featuring Titus, 77th Earl of Groan. Born in China, where his father was a missionary, Peake moved to England as a boy. After training as a painter, he taught art and began illustrating and writing children's books. During

World War II, he worked as a journalist and artist. *Titus Groan*, the first novel in his trilogy, was published in 1946, followed by *Gormenghast* (1950) and *Titus Alone* (1959). Peake illustrated many of his own novels as well as those of others, and wrote several volumes of poetry, including *The Glassblowers* (1950) and *The Rhyme of the Flying Bomb* (1962), a recollection of the London blitz, as well as *The Wit to Woo* (1957), a play.

Pepys, Samuel (February 23, 1633–May 26, 1703). English diarist. Pepys's *Diary*, kept between 1660 and 1669, provides an unusually candid portrait of 17th-century court life and the life of its author, and chronicles key events of the time, including the coronation of Charles II, the plague, and the great fire of London. The son of a London tailor, Pepys was educated at Cambridge and given entree to high society by his father's cousin Sir Edward Montagu, who was the Earl of Sandwich and Pepys's benefactor. Pepys served as a naval officer, a member of Parliament, and president of the Royal Society. His contribution to the literary world was not discovered until 1825, when his diary, written in a form of shorthand and stored at Cambridge, was deciphered.

Percy, Walker (May 28, 1916–May 10, 1990). American novelist and essayist. With THE MOVIEGOER (1961; National Book Award), his fiction debut, Percy set the tone for all of his novels: comical yet philosophically penetrating stories in which characters of the New South struggle against alienation and existential malaise. Born in Alabama and orphaned in his teens, Percy was subsequently raised by a well-to-do poet cousin in Mississippi. He studied chemistry at the University of North Carolina and medicine at Columbia University and worked at Bellevue Hospital in New York, but ended his short-lived medical career after contracting tuberculosis on the job. During his extended convalescence, Percy discovered Existentialism, Catholicism, and writing. He moved to New Orleans and later to Covington, Louisiana, and continued publishing fiction with *The Last Gentleman* (1966), *Love in*

the Ruins: The Adventures of a Bad Catholic at a Time Near the End of the World (1971), *Lancelot* (1977), *The Second Coming* (1980), and his quasi-thriller, *The Thanatos Syndrome* (1987). His nonfiction writings on philosophy, psychiatry, science, linguistics, literature, and the South are collected in several volumes, including *The Message in the Bottle* (1975) and *Signposts in a Strange Land* (1991).

Perec, Georges (March 7, 1936–March 3, 1982). French novelist. Perec was born in Paris to Polish-Jewish Yiddish-speaking parents and studied at the Sorbonne and in Tunisia. His lifelong fascination with puzzles and word games is reflected in his formally challenging and innovative fiction. His popular first novel, *Things: A Story of the Sixties* (*Les Choses: Une Histoire des Années Soixante*, 1965), launched his literary career. The experimental works that followed were influenced by Perec's association with the avant-garde literary group OuLiPo. *The Disappearance* (*La Disparition*, 1969; also translated as *A Void*) is a mystery written entirely without using the letter "e." His autobiography, *W, or The Memory of Childhood* (*W, ou Le Souvenir d'Enfance*, 1975), alternates between truth and fiction, while *Life: A User's Manual* (*La Vie, Mode d'Emploi*, 1978), Perec's most acclaimed work, features an apartment building with 100 rooms arranged in a "magic square." An unfinished intellectual thriller, *53 Days* (*53 Jours: Roman*), was published posthumously in 1989.

Perelman, S[idney] **J**[oseph] (February 1, 1904–October 17, 1979). American humorist, essayist, and screenwriter. One of the 20th century's funniest men of letters, Perelman made masterful use of mimicry, puns, cliché, absurdisms, non sequiturs, and all-around wordplay in his sendups of contemporary society and culture. He was born in Brooklyn and educated at Brown University. In 1929 he published his acclaimed first book, *Dawn Ginsbergh's Revenge*, and married NATHANAEL WEST's sister, Laura. Soon after, he headed to Hollywood, where he worked with the Marx Brothers on the screenplays for *Monkey Business* (1931) and

Horse Feathers (1932), and collaborated on the Academy Award–winning script for *Around the World in 80 Days* (1956). Many of Perelman's fleet-footed satires first appeared in the pages of THE NEW YORKER. His writings are collected in numerous volumes, including *Strictly from Hunger* (1937), *Westward Ha! or, Around the World in 80 Clichés* (1947), *The Swiss Family Perelman* (1950), *The Road to Miltown, or, Under the Spreading Atrophy* (1957), and *The Last Laugh* (1981). His selected letters were published as *Don't Tread on Me* (1987).

Pérez Galdós, Benito (May 10, 1843–January 24, 1920). Spanish novelist. Often compared to BALZAC and DICKENS and hailed as the greatest Spanish novelist since CERVANTES, Pérez Galdós wrote many novels capturing the life and history of 19th-century Spain. Born in the Canary Islands, Pérez Galdós moved to Madrid as a student and published his successful first novel, *The Golden Fountain Cafe* (*La Fontana de Oro*), in 1870. He meticulously evoked 70 years of Spanish history, from the battle of Trafalgar to the restoration of the monarchy, in a series of 46 novels now known as the Episodios Nacionales (1873–1912). Through the 1880s and 1890s, Pérez Galdós also wrote numerous novels set in contemporary Spain; among the most highly esteemed are the four-volume FORTUNATA AND JACINTA (*Fortunata y Jacinta*, 1886–87), *The Disinherited Lady* (*La Desheredada*, 1881), *Nazarín* (1895), and *Misericordia* (1897).

Pessoa, Fernando (June 13, 1888–November 30, 1935). Portuguese poet and man of letters. Although he did not achieve fame in his lifetime, this modernist writer helped to draw world interest to Portuguese literature. Pessoa was born in Lisbon and raised in South Africa, where his stepfather was the Portuguese consul. Fluent in English, he returned to Portugal as a young man, working as a translator and a contributor to the modernist journal ORPHEU. His earliest books of poetry were written and published in English, but in 1934 he published *Message* (*Mensagem*), his first book in Portuguese. Much of Pessoa's verse is written in the voice of heteronyms, or literary alter egos, able to express realities different from Pessoa's own. His major collections are *Poesias de Fernando Pessoa* (1942), *Poesias de Alvaro de Campos* (1944), *Poemas de Alberto Caeiro* (1946), and *Odes de Ricardo Reis* (1946). Pessoa came to the attention of the English-reading public in 1991 with the publication of the autobiographical prose work THE BOOK OF DISQUIET (*Livro do Desassossego*, 1961).

Petrarch, *in full* Francesco Petrarca (July 20, 1304–July 19, 1374). Italian poet and scholar. A giant of the Western European literary tradition, Petrarch was a founder of Renaissance humanism, one of the first great modern lyric poets, and a renowned scholar of ancient classical culture. Petrarch studied law as a young man, but in 1326 he moved to Avignon, France, and shifted his attention to classical literature, writing, and religion. In 1341 he was crowned Poet Laureate in Rome. Learned in classical Latin, he wrote a number of important humanist works in that language, including the biographical sketches in *On Illustrious Men* (*De Viris Illustribus*, begun c. 1337), the epic poem *Africa* (begun c. 1338), the autobiographical dialogue *Petrarch's Secret* (*Secretum Meum*, 1342–58), and treatises such as *On the Solitary Life* (*De Vita Solitaria*, 1345–47) and *On the Virtue of the Religious Life* (*De Otio Religioso*, 1345–47) as well as many letters. In Italian, he produced the work that gave him lasting fame — the poems collected in a *canzoniere* (songbook) often referred to as *Rime*. Many of Petrarch's poems address his chaste passion for "LAURA" — a woman who may or may not have existed — and the psychological conflicts that ensued. The *Rime* were tremendously important to the development of European poetry, and the Petrarchan sonnet form bears his name.

Petronius Arbiter, [Gaius] (birth date unknown–A.D. 66). Roman satirist. To Petronius is ascribed the authorship of the SATYRICON, a lengthy saga in prose and verse of 1st-century Roman life high and low, which survives only in fragments. In the broad, episodic comedy of the *Satyricon*, Petronius mocks the excesses of

Rome's new rich through the figure of Trimalchio and provides fascinating glimpses of Roman life in the sometimes bawdy adventures of the narrator Encolpius and his friends. Petronius's existence is chronicled in the *Annals* of Tacitus, where he is described as a courtier, public officer, pleasure seeker, and *arbiter elegantiae* ("arbiter of taste") in Emperor Nero's Rome. Petronius was arrested after a jealous rival falsely accused him of participating in a conspiracy to assassinate the emperor. He committed suicide to avoid execution.

Phillips, Caryl (March 13, 1958–). West Indian–born English novelist and playwright. Using shifting viewpoints and unusual narrative structures, Phillips writes about the dispossessed — most often, blacks of the African diaspora living in white-dominated societies. Phillips was born in St. Kitts, grew up in England, and was educated at Oxford, where he was active in theater. He began his career writing for the stage as well as for radio, television, and film. His first novel, *The Final Passage* (1985), tells the story of a young mulatto woman of the 1950s and her experiences with racial injustice. *Cambridge* (1991) describes a slave plantation from two very different points of view. Phillips's highly praised 1993 novel, *Crossing the River*, links four separate stories through the theme of slavery and its legacy. *The Nature of Blood* (1997) explores the post–World War II Jewish diaspora.

Pindar, *in Greek* Pindaros (c. 518 B.C.–c. 438 B.C.). Greek lyric poet. A master of the tripartite (strophe–antistrophe–epode), exalted ode form that bears his name, Pindar inspired some of the greatest poets in world literature: Ben JONSON wrote true Pindaric odes, while DRYDEN, WORDSWORTH, SHELLEY, KEATS, and TENNYSON all used the looser form known as Pindarics. Pindar was born and raised near Thebes, apparently in an aristocratic milieu. His choral lyrics, composed for various occasions, include mythic tales of heroism and hymns to the gods. Although 17 volumes of his choral lyrics are known to have existed in antiquity, only four books have survived complete, augmented by some fragments. Bold in imagery, varied in meter, and elaborate in structure, most of this surviving poetry consists of odes to victory (*epinikia*), celebrating the successes of athletes at the Panhellenic games at Olympia and elsewhere, as well as the triumphant victories of various rulers.

Pinsky, Robert (October 20, 1940–). American poet and critic. As critic Hugh KENNER observed, Pinsky's goal is "nothing less than the recovery for language of a whole domain of mute and familiar experience"; Pinsky himself explained, "I am from a lower middle-class family in a small town in New Jersey. My grandpa had a bar there. My family was nominally Orthodox Jewish. In my work I try to pull together as many of the different kinds and levels of American experience as I can." His first volume, *Sadness and Happiness* (1975), followed by the book-length poem *An Explanation of America* (1979) and the collection *History of My Heart* (1984), confirmed his place among contemporary American poets. *The Figured Wheel: New and Collected Poems, 1966–1996* (1997) includes all his work to that date; *Jersey Rain* (2000) is a recent collection. He is also noted as a translator of DANTE — *The Inferno of Dante: A New Verse Translation* appeared in 1994 — and of Czeslaw MILOSZ, Paul CELAN, and others. His influential critical works include *The Situation of Poetry: Contemporary Poetry and Its Traditions* (1976) and *The Sounds of Poetry: A Brief Guide* (1998), for the general reader. He has also written a critical study (1968) of the English writer Walter Savage Landor. As United States POET LAUREATE (1997–2000), Pinsky initiated the Favorite Poem Project, inviting Americans to write to him about the poems that mattered most to them; *Americans' Favorite Poems* (1999), edited by Pinsky and Maggie Dietz, is an anthology, with excerpts from the letters he received. Educated at Rutgers and Stanford universities, he has held professorships at several universities.

Pinter, Harold (October 10, 1930–). English playwright and screenwriter. In the playwright's own words, "I can sum up none of my plays. I can describe none of them, except to say: That is what happened. That is what they said. That is what they did." Resembling "a Hitchcock film with the last reel missing" (as one critic put it in 1958), a Pinter play is typically subtle and enigmatic, featuring menacing, unexplained situations and dialogue that is often punctuated with characteristic "Pinter pauses." The son of a tailor, and the grandson of Ashkenazic Jews who had fled pogroms in Russia and Poland, Pinter grew up working class in London. He studied

---

"You do have a leash, finally, as a writer. You're holding a dog. You let the dog run about. But you finally can pull him back. Finally, I'm in control. But the great excitement is to see what happens if you let the whole thing go. And the dog or the character really runs about, bites everyone in sight, jumps up trees, falls into lakes, gets wet, and you let that happen. That's the excitement of writing plays—to allow the thing to be free but still hold the final leash."

Harold Pinter, in an interview with Anne-Marie Cusac, *The Progressive* (March 2001)

---

acting briefly at the Royal Academy of Dramatic Art before joining a touring troupe, eventually trying his hand at writing plays (he had already written a great deal of poetry). His one-act plays *The Room* (1957) and *The Dumbwaiter* (1957) were followed by the London debut of the full-length play THE BIRTHDAY PARTY (1958), which was poorly received. With the success of THE CARETAKER (1960), he began an outpouring of dramas noted for their mordant humor and their bold and disturbing plot lines: the shocking sexual revelation in THE HOMECOMING (1965), the odd relationship between a wealthy alcoholic recluse and a poet in *No Man's Land* (1975), and the dissection of a marriage in *Betrayal* (1978), among others. More recent plays, starker and more imagistic than his earlier works, include *Moonlight* (1993) and *Ashes*

to Ashes (1996). Pinter's screenwriting credits include *The Servant* (1963), *Accident* (1967), *The Go-Between* (1971), *The Last Tycoon* (1974), *The French Lieutenant's Woman* (1981), and *The Comfort of Strangers* (1990). *Collected Poems and Prose* appeared in 1996; *Various Voices: Prose, Poetry, Politics 1948–1998* in 1998. He is married to the historian and fiction writer Antonia Fraser.

Pirandello, Luigi (June 28, 1867–December 10, 1936). Italian playwright, novelist, and short-story writer. A remarkable creative innovator who was lauded for turning psychological analysis into great theater, in his dramas Pirandello offered an alternative to naturalism and influenced many of the important playwrights who followed. Born in Sicily, Pirandello earned a doctorate at the University of Bonn, and then taught literature in Rome. His early writings set the stage for all of his work: explorations of madness, isolation, and the illusory nature of personality that are at once comic, pessimistic, and poignant. Notable among these are the story collections *Loves Without Love* (*Amori senza Amore*, 1894) and *The Jests of Life and Death* (*Beffe della Morte e della Vita*, 1902–3) and the acclaimed novel *The Late Mattia Pascal* (*Il Fu Mattia Pascal*, 1904). The essay *On Humor* (*L'Umorismo*, 1908) illuminates the psychological bases of his art. In 1917 Pirandello wrote one of his best-known plays, RIGHT YOU ARE—IF YOU THINK YOU ARE (*Così è Se Vi Pare*), and by the 1920s, with his masterpieces SIX CHARACTERS IN SEARCH OF AN AUTHOR (*Sei Personaggi in Cerce d'Autore,* 1921) and *Henry IV* (*Enrico IV*, 1922), his reputation as a major figure in modern theater was established. In 1934, he was awarded the Nobel Prize in Literature.

Plath, Sylvia (October 27, 1932–February 11, 1963). American poet. Plath's haunting, sometimes violent personal poetry, her prodigious output, and the story of her tragically short life have earned her a place in the contemporary pantheon of women poets. Born in Boston, Plath attended Smith College and then Cambridge University in England as a Fulbright

Scholar. In 1956 she married poet TED HUGHES. The two settled in England, where Plath wrote intensively, although her poetry was not widely known until a decade after her death. Her first collection, *The Colossus*, came out in 1960, followed by her sole novel, THE BELL JAR (1963), an autobiographical work which she first published under the pseudonym Marjorie Kellogg less than a month before her suicide in London. Her posthumous poetry collections include *ARIEL* (1965), *Crossing the Water* (1971), and *Winter Trees* (1972). *The Collected Poems* (1981; Pulitzer Prize) was edited by Hughes. *The Journals of Sylvia Plath* was published in 1982; *Letters Home: Correspondence, 1950–1963* appeared in 1975.

Plautus, [Titus Maccius] (c. 254 B.C.–184 B.C.). Roman comic playwright. Roman comedy had two masters: Plautus and TERENCE. Plautus adapted the popular style of the New Greek Comedy—masked, realistic, five-act plays featuring well-delineated characters from wealthy families—for the Latin-speaking world. Much is uncertain about Plautus, even his name, and his literary legacy is limited to 20 extant plays from approximately 130 original works. His surviving plays have been augmented and adapted through the centuries, and the original structure of some of them may never be ascertained. Nevertheless, his clever works, which ranged from bawdy and broad to nuanced and sly, and the character types he immortalized, influenced SHAKESPEARE, MOLIÈRE, and others. Among them are *Amphitryon* (*Amphitruo*), *Miles Gloriosus*, *The Pot of Gold* (*Aulularia*), *The Two Menaechmuses* (*Menaechmi*), and *Pseudolus*.

Plutarch, *in Greek* Ploutarchos (A.D. 46–c. A.D. 120). Greek biographer and philosopher. Although only two of his major works are extant, Plutarch's influence was great, especially during the Renaissance, and his intellectual legacy is far-reaching. Few facts about his life are certain, except that he was born and spent most of his days in Chaeronea, Boeotia in Greece. His best-known work, *Parallel Lives* (*Bioi Parallēloi*), first translated into English by

Sir Thomas North in 1579 (from the earlier French translation by Jacques Amyot) under the title *The Lives of the Noble Grecians and Romanes*, provided the basis for several of SHAKESPEARE's Roman plays, including *JULIUS CAESAR* and *ANTONY AND CLEOPATRA*. Plutarch's book of *Essays* (*Ēthika*), dialogues and treatises on subjects including philosophy, religion, science, education, politics, and literature, was first published in English in its entirety in 1603.

Poe, Edgar Allan (January 19, 1809–October 7, 1849). American poet, short-story writer, and critic. Poe's unforgettable poems and Gothic tales of horror have earned him a lasting place as one of America's best-loved writers. Born in Boston to actor parents and orphaned soon after, he was taken in by a wealthy Richmond merchant, John Allan (whence Poe's middle name). Poe studied briefly at the University of Virginia and West Point and spent a short time in the army. During this period, he self-published *Tamerlane and Other Poems* (1827), *Al Aaraaf* (1829), and *Poems* (1831). He then turned to writing stories, winning a contest for "MS. Found in a Bottle" (1833). Poe made his living as an editor and writer for various periodicals, and in 1836 he married a 13-year-old cousin. In 1840 he published *Tales of the Grotesque and Arabesque*, which contains the now classic "THE FALL OF THE HOUSE OF USHER," and achieved national fame in 1845 with *THE RAVEN and Other Poems*. But in two years his wife would pass away and, in two more, so would Poe, from the fatal combination of alcohol and epilepsy. Poe's renown grew after his death, and he was a major influence on BAUDELAIRE and the French Symbolists, among others. His most famous tales include the seminal detective story "THE MURDERS IN THE RUE MORGUE" (1841), as well as "THE GOLD BUG" (1843), "THE PIT AND THE PENDULUM" (1843), and "THE TELL-TALE HEART" (1843). His best-loved poems include "ULALUME" (1847), "ANNABEL LEE" (1849), and "The Bells" (1849).

Pope, Alexander (May 21, 1688–May 30, 1744). English poet and satirist. The foremost poet of his day and an important influence on fellow and future satirists, Pope demonstrated a command of the heroic couplet, a dazzling and fluid style of versification, and an audacious wit. Pope's achievements are all the more remarkable in light of his childhood disadvantages: he was raised a Roman Catholic when his country was anti-Catholic, his formal education was erratic (he was mostly self-taught), and at the age of 12 a severe illness wrecked his health and stunted his growth. Still, his literary gift was evident early on and was publicly noted when AN ESSAY ON CRITICISM (1711) — Pope's poem about writing — launched him onto the London literary scene. In 1712 he published "THE RAPE OF THE LOCK," the formidable satirical poem about a feud begun over a clipping of hair. In the 1720s he produced translations of HOMER's ILIAD (1720) and ODYSSEY (1725–26), and a controversial edition of SHAKESPEARE (1725). His other important works include "Verses to the Memory of an Unfortunate Lady" (1717), "Eloisa to Abelard" (1717), AN ESSAY ON MAN (1733–34), "An Epistle to Dr. Arbuthnot" (1735), and his "dunce-epic" THE DUNCIAD (1728; final revision 1743), a masterpiece of literary revenge.

Porter, Katherine Anne, *original name* Callie Russell Porter (May 15, 1890–September 18, 1980). American short-story writer and novelist. A master of the short story, Porter was born in Texas and raised by her grandmother. Her colorful life included several failed marriages as well as stints as a journalist, actress, singer, and art student in Mexico. Her work tackles morality, history, women's roles, and the South, and is highly regarded for its complex characterizations and psychological and social insight. Her most celebrated collections include FLOWERING JUDAS (1930), PALE HORSE, PALE RIDER (1939), and *The Collected Stories of Katherine Anne Porter* (1965; National Book Award). Her single novel is the allegorical epic SHIP OF FOOLS (1962), about a voyage from Mexico to Germany on the cusp of World War II. Most of her nonfiction work is contained in *The Collected Essays and Occasional Writings* (1970).

Porter, William Sydney. *See* **Henry, O.**

Potok, Chaim, *original name* Herman Harold Potok (February 17, 1929–). American novelist. Potok's popular novels portray the lives of modern American Jews and their struggle for identity. Born in New York City to Polish immigrant parents, Potok attended Yeshiva University and the Jewish Theological Seminary and was ordained a Conservative rabbi in 1954. He worked as an army chaplain during the Korean conflict, and has since held several editorial and teaching posts. His first and best-known novel, *The Chosen* (1967), charts the friendship between two young men, one Orthodox and the other Hasidic. This was followed by a sequel, *The Promise* (1969), and *My Name Is Asher Lev* (1972). Potok's notable nonfiction includes *Wanderings: Chaim Potok's History of the Jews* (1978) and *The Gates of November: Chronicles of the Slepak Family* (1996). His later fiction includes *The Gift of Asher Lev* (1990) and *I Am the Clay* (1992) as well as several books for children and young adults.

Pound, Ezra (October 30, 1885–November 1, 1972). American poet, critic, and editor. Although Pound's political and aesthetic positions remain controversial, his enormous influence on 20th-century literature — through his groundbreaking poetry as well as his support of many major writers — is unquestionable. Pound was born in Idaho, raised in Pennsylvania, and educated at Hamilton College and the University of Pennsylvania, where his friendships with WILLIAM CARLOS WILLIAMS and H. D. (Hilda Doolittle) began. After a brief teaching stint, Pound headed to Europe. He self-published his first book, *A Lume Spento* (1908), in Venice, then moved to London, where his multifaceted literary career developed. As a leading Imagist, he promoted the use of free meter and unfettered imagery and edited the anthology *Des Imagistes* (1914). As an influential journal editor, Pound championed the work of T. S. ELIOT, James JOYCE, W. B. YEATS, Ernest HEMINGWAY, Robert FROST, and others. At the same time, he published adaptations of Chinese poetry and several volumes of his own verse, including *Personae* (1909), and began his formidable lifelong work, THE CANTOS. In 1920, he moved to Paris, joining Gertrude STEIN's circle and publishing *HUGH SELWYN MAUBERLEY* (1920) before settling in Rapallo, Italy, in 1924. During World War II, Pound's association with Mussolini and his anti-American radio broadcasts led to his arrest in 1945. He was confined in Pisa, where he composed *The Pisan Cantos* (1948), and was then sent back to the United States and committed to a psychiatric hospital. Released after 12 years, he returned to Italy, where he spent the rest of his life.

Powell, Anthony (December 21, 1905–March 28, 2000). English novelist. Powell's 12-volume masterwork, *A DANCE TO THE MUSIC OF TIME*, stands as a major achievement among 20th-century novels. Powell was born in London, educated at Eton and Oxford, and worked in publishing and journalism. During the 1930s, he wrote a number of accomplished novels satirizing the British upper class, including *Afternoon Men* (1931), *From a View to a Death* (1933), and *What's Become of Waring?* (1939). After serving in World War II, Powell began the epic sequence that would be published over two-and-a-half decades, beginning in 1951 with *A Question of Upbringing* and concluding with *Hearing Secret Harmonies* in 1975. He followed with a four-volume memoir, collectively titled *To Keep the Ball Rolling* (1976–82, abridged version, 2001), which offers insights into his masterwork. His later works include *The Fisher King* (1986) as well as several dramas, collections of criticism, and journals.

Powell, Dawn (November 28, 1897–November 15, 1965). American novelist, short-story writer, and diarist. Admired by fellow writers Ernest HEMINGWAY and EDMUND WILSON, Powell's work was nonetheless underappreciated in her time, but, championed by Gore VIDAL and others, its reputation rose sharply in the late 20th century. Raised in rural Ohio, Powell moved at age 20 to New York's Greenwich Village and lived there for the rest of her life. Manhattan provides the setting for many of her novels, among them *Turn, Magic Wheel* (1936), *Angels on Toast* (1940), *My Home Is Far Away* (1944), *The Locusts Have No King* (1948), and *The Golden*

Spur (1962), which vividly and mercilessly evoke New Yorkers drinking, smoking, scheming, working, and falling in love and off barstools. Other novels, including *Dance Night* (1930) and *The Story of a Country Boy* (1934), are set in her native Midwest but are equally gritty, if less cosmopolitan. *The Diaries of Dawn Powell, 1931–1965* was published in 1995 to critical and popular acclaim.

Powys, John Cowper (October 8, 1872–June 17, 1963). English-born Welsh novelist, essayist, and poet. England's West Country, where Powys was raised, figures prominently in an idiosyncratic literary vision filled with themes from Celtic myth and country life. Powys hailed from a large family with considerable literary talent: his brothers Theodore Francis Powys and Llewellyn Powys also became noted writers and the poets William Cowper and John DONNE were among his antecedents. Powys was educated at Cambridge and began his literary career writing poetry. The prolific author found success with his third novel, *Wolf Solent* (1929), a love story of opposites. Powys lectured extensively in the United States before settling in Wales. His other novels include *A Glastonbury Romance* (1932), *Weymouth Sands* (1934), and *Owen Glendower* (1940). His *Autobiography* (1934) is revealing and highly regarded.

Price, [Edward] Reynolds (February 1, 1933–). American novelist and short-story writer. A leading contemporary writer of the South, Price is best known for his sharp portrayals of complex characters linked to the Carolina countryside. The lifelong North Carolinian attended Duke University and Oxford, returning to Duke as a professor of English. His first novel, *A Long and Happy Life* (1962), and first story collection, *The Names and Faces of Heroes* (1963), as well as many of his subsequent works, center on the Mustian family and the memorable heroine Rosacoke. The critically acclaimed coming-of-age novel *Kate Vaiden* (1986) is one of Price's best-loved books. His memoirs *Clear Pictures* (1989) and *A Whole New Life* (1994) were written following the spinal cancer that left him paralyzed. Price maintains his productive writing and teaching career, publishing poetry, plays, essays, and biblical translations in addition to fiction.

Priestley, J[ohn] **B**[oynton] (September 13, 1894–August 14, 1984). English novelist, playwright, essayist, and critic. While the wide-ranging work of this prolific author defies simple categorization, his popular novels and dramas made him one of the favorite British writers of his day. After serving in World War I, Priestley studied at Cambridge, then went to London as a journalist and critic. His first popular success was his novel of stage life, *The Good Companions* (1929). Other notable fiction includes *The Image Men* (1968), a long novel about the advertising world. Among his major plays are *An Inspector Calls* (1946), *I Have Been Here Before* (1937), and *Time and the Conways* (1937). Priestley was also known for his commitment to social and political causes, his popular wartime radio broadcasts, and his accomplished literary criticism, travel writing, and memoirs.

Pritchett, [Sir] **V**[ictor] **S**[awdon] (December 16, 1900–March 20, 1997). English short-story writer, critic, novelist, biographer, and travel essayist. A master at capturing irony and the idiosyncrasies of human nature in his dozens of stories, and a gifted, cosmopolitan critic and biographer, Pritchett was one of the century's

---

"I saw very little of England for seven years ... I became a foreigner. For myself that is what a writer is—a man living on the other side of a frontier."

V. S. Pritchett, *A Cab at the Door: A Memoir* (1968)

---

leading men of letters. He was born to a lower-middle-class family in Ipswich, and left school in his teens to work in the leather trade. By his early 20s, he had landed a job in Paris as a correspondent for the *Christian Science Monitor*, a position that took him to Ireland and Spain and provided material for his first books, the nonfic-

tion *Marching Spain* (1928) and the story collection *The Spanish Virgin and Other Stories* (1930). A steady stream of fiction was to follow, including the novel *Mr. Beluncle* (1951) and the story collections *When My Girl Comes Home* (1961), *The Camberwell Beauty* (1974), and *A Careless Widow and Other Stories* (1989). Pritchett's lucid and engaging critical voice can be found in several collections, including *The Myth Makers* (1979), *Man of Letters* (1985), and *Lasting Impressions* (1990), and biographies of BALZAC, TURGENEV, and CHEKHOV. His memoirs are *A Cab at the Door* (1968) and *Midnight Oil* (1971). A selection of his work appears in *The Pritchett Century* (1997), edited by his son Oliver.

Propertius, Sextus (c. 55 B.C.–after 16 B.C.). Roman poet. The elegiac verse of Propertius, considered among the greatest written in Latin, appeared in four books (the second of which some literary historians divide in two) dated from 29 B.C. to 16 B.C. His poems celebrate love—specifically for the heroine Cynthia, believed to have been modeled after the poet's lover, the courtesan Hostia—in all its vicissitudes. Little else is known of Propertius's life, other than that he was born in Umbria and settled in Rome, where he befriended OVID and VIRGIL and devoted himself to poetry. Ezra POUND revived interest in his elegies with 12 modern imitations in "Homage to Sextus Propertius" (1919).

Proulx, [Edna] **Annie** (August 22, 1935–). American novelist and short-story writer. With THE SHIPPING NEWS (1993), her novel of an odd family in Newfoundland, Proulx earned international regard as one of America's finest contemporary writers. Born in Connecticut and educated in Vermont and Canada, Proulx took up magazine writing to support her three sons. Her first book of fiction, *Heart Songs and Other Stories* (1988), introduced readers to her characteristically dense, tragicomic prose. Her highly praised first novel, *Postcards* (1992), traces change in America over 40 years. Her second, *The Shipping News*, won the National Book Award, the Pulitzer Prize, and wide acclaim. Proulx's recent works include the novel *Accordion Crimes* (1996), which follows the history of a musical instrument, and *Close Range: Wyoming Stories* (1999).

Proust, Marcel (July 10, 1871–November 18, 1922). French novelist. On the strength of his seven-part masterpiece, REMEMBRANCE OF THINGS PAST (*À la Recherche du Temps Perdu*, 1913–27), Proust is widely recognized as one of the greatest 20th-century novelists. Evoking the flux of time and consciousness, the transience of love and society, and the redemptive power of the imagination, the narrator's interior monologue relates his shifting associations in a struggle to find meaning and beauty in the chaos of experience. Proust was born in Paris to a prosperous Catholic doctor and a devoted Jewish mother, and was educated at the Lycée Condorcet. As a young man, he frequented the salons of fashionable Parisian society, a milieu he portrayed throughout his writings, beginning with the story and essay collection *Pleasures and Days* (*Les Plaisirs et les Jours*, 1896). Henri BERGSON's philosophy of subjective time and the aesthetic principle of "truth to nature" as articulated by John RUSKIN (whose *Bible of Amiens* and *Sesame and Lilies* Proust translated in his early 30s) inspired Proust's approach to the novel. After a worsening of his chronic asthma in 1902 and the death of his mother in 1905, he curtailed his social life and retreated to the corklined room in which his great novel gradually took shape. The first volume, *Swann's Way* (*Du Côté de Chez Swann*), was published in 1913 at his own expense and won scant recognition, but the second, *Within a Budding Grove* (*À l'Ombre des Jeunes Filles en Fleurs*), was awarded the Prix Goncourt in 1919. At the time of his death, from pneumonia, three volumes were still unpublished. Decades later, scholars discovered several additional, unpublished works by Proust, including the unfinished novel *Jean Santeuil* (1952) and the critical essay *Contre Sainte-Beuve* (1954), which attacks biographical approaches to literary interpretation.

Puig, Manuel (December 28, 1932–July 22, 1990). Argentinean novelist and screenwriter. Puig is best known for KISS OF THE SPIDER WOMAN (*El Beso de la Mujer Araña*, 1976), a novel of an unlikely friendship, which was successfully adapted for stage and screen. As a boy, Puig was obsessed with Hollywood films and learned English by watching them. He studied film in Rome and took up screenwriting, but soon turned his attention to writing novels, beginning with the autobiographical *Betrayed by Rita Hayworth* (*La Traición de Rita Hayworth*, 1968) and the parody *Heartbreak Tango* (*Boquitas Pintadas*, 1969). Puig developed themes of sexual and political repression in his thriller *The Buenos Aires Affair* (1973, in Spanish despite the title). His controversial works, often charged with sexuality and violence, include later novels such as *Angelic Pubis* (*Pubis Angelical*, 1979) and *Eternal Curse on the Reader of These Pages* (*Maldición Eterna a Quien Lea Estas Páginas*, 1980).

Purdy, James (July 17, 1923–). American novelist and short-story writer. Purdy's bleak, Gothic allegories probe identity, homosexuality, and the destructive forces within the family. Born in Ohio, he studied in Chicago and Mexico before finding work as an interpreter and teacher. His first books, the novella *63: Dream Palace* (1956) and the story collection *Don't Call Me by My Right Name* (1956), were initially self-published, then championed by Dame Edith SITWELL, who arranged for their publication in England. Among Purdy's better-known novels are *Malcolm* (1959), which was later dramatized by Edward ALBEE, *In a Shallow Grave* (1975), *Narrow Rooms* (1978), the trilogy *Sleepers in Moon-Crowned Valleys* (consisting of *Jeremy's Version*, 1970; *The House of the Solitary Maggot*, 1974; and *Mourners Below*, 1981), and *Gertrude of Stony Island Avenue* (1998). He has also published poetry and plays.

Pushkin, Aleksandr (June 6, 1799–February 10, 1837). Russian poet, playwright, and fiction writer. Regarded as the founding father of modern Russian literature, Pushkin wrote innovative and powerful works in a remarkable range of genres and holds the position in Russian letters that SHAKESPEARE has in the English-speaking world. Pushkin was born in Moscow to an aristocratic family of African ancestry on his mother's side. After studying at the elite Imperial Lyceum, he served in the foreign office in St. Petersburg, but was exiled to the south in 1820 for issuing poems criticizing the rule of Tsar Alexander I. During his "southern period," he emerged as a leading Romantic poet, publishing narrative poems that include *The Prisoner of the Caucasus* (*Kavkazskiĭ Plennik*, 1820–21), *The Fountain of Bakhchisarai* (*Bakhchisaraĭskiĭ Fontan*, 1823), and *The Gypsies* (*Tsygany*, 1824), which, influenced by BYRON, portray heroes in rebellion against social and political authority. In 1824, Pushkin was again sentenced to exile, now at his mother's country estate, where he wrote the historical verse tragedy BORIS GODUNOV (1831). Offered patronage by the new tsar, Nicholas I, in 1826, Pushkin was finally able to return to Moscow. In 1831, he married the 19-year-old Natalya Goncharova and, six years later, died in a duel with a man he believed to be her lover. Pushkin's late works, beginning in the mid-1820s, moved increasingly away from the dominant neoclassical style of polished rhetoric, experimenting instead with open form, spare, simplified diction, and complex narrative voice and characterization. Pushkin's best-known late work is the verse novel EUGENE ONEGIN (*Evgeniĭ Onegin*, 1833), a masterpiece begun in 1823 and reworked for nearly ten years. Centering on an unfulfilled love affair complicated by social conventions, it insightfully portrays contemporary Russian society. Among Pushkin's other major works are the short story "THE QUEEN OF SPADES" ("Pikovaya Dama," 1834), the novella *The Captain's Daughter* (*Kapitanskaya Dochka*, 1836), and the narrative poem THE BRONZE HORSEMAN (*Mednyĭ Vsadnik*, 1837).

Pym, Barbara (June 2, 1913–January 11, 1980). English novelist. Pym's genteel, understated heroines live solitary lives, quietly but penetratingly observing the world around them. Pym was educated at Oxford and worked as an editor of the anthropological journal *Africa*. Her first novel, *Some Tame Gazelle* (1950), was followed over the next decade by several well-regarded works, including *Excellent Women* (1952) and *A Glass of Blessings* (1958), but the shift in popular taste that occurred in the 1960s resulted in her virtual eclipse. She was ignored by both readers and publishers until 1977, when both Philip LARKIN and Lord David Cecil described her in the TIMES LITERARY SUPPLEMENT as one of the most underrated writers of her age. This "rediscovery" led to the 1977 publication of *Quartet in Autumn*. Two more volumes followed before her death and several after, including the novel *An Unsuitable Attachment* (1982) and the autobiographical compilation *A Very Private Eye* (1984).

Pynchon, Thomas (May 8, 1937–). American novelist. Integrating multilayered story lines, bizarre characters, labyrinthine quests, and arcana, Pynchon's quintessentially postmodern novels illustrate the chaos of life in the age of technology. Pynchon was born on Long Island, New York, and studied physics, engineering, and English at Cornell. He served in the Navy and worked briefly as a technical writer for Boeing. With his first novel, *v.* (1963), he introduced the dense, technical, black-comic nightmares of paranoia and conspiracy for which he is known. His second and most accessible work, THE CRYING OF LOT 49 (1966), was followed by his epic of apocalypse, GRAVITY'S RAINBOW (1973; National Book Award). The famously reclusive author's long-awaited fourth novel, *Vineland* (1990), did not live up to the expectations of his admirers, but his sprawling historical novel *Mason & Dixon* (1997) was praised as a worthy comeback. A selection of Pynchon's stories appear in *Slow Learner* (1984).

Rabe, David (March 10, 1940–). American playwright and screenwriter. Rabe made his name in the 1970s by translating his Vietnam War experience into drama. Born in Iowa, Rabe spent three years in the Army before finishing his theater education at Villanova University. His reputation was built on a trio of Vietnam plays: *The Basic Training of Pavlo Hummel* (1971), *Sticks and Bones* (1971) — Rabe's Broadway debut — and *Streamers* (1976), which he also adapted for film. Dark humor and social commentary weave through all of Rabe's dramas, including his sad portrait of a go-go dancer, *In the Boom Boom Room* (1975), and his scathing indictment of Hollywood life, *Hurlyburly* (1983). His screenwriting credits include *I'm Dancing as Fast as I Can* (1982), *Casualties of War* (1989), and *The Firm* (1993), while his recent dramas include *A Question of Mercy* (1998).

Rabelais, François (c. 1494–April 9, 1553). French writer. Rabelais's five-volume masterpiece, GARGANTUA AND PANTAGRUEL (1532–64) — an unusual combination of licentious comedy, humanist erudition, and biting satire of the institutions and mores of the day — was banned in France and placed on the Catholic Index Librorum Prohibitorum during his lifetime. A Benedictine monk and a doctor, Rabelais was also a teacher, translator, and writer on many subjects, with a reputation for encyclopedic knowledge in several fields — the quintessential Renaissance man. The distinctive quality we now call "Rabelaisian" is a mixture of coarse humor, extravagance, grotesqueries, ribaldry, and boisterousness. Rabelais influenced such later writers as VOLTAIRE, SWIFT, HUGO, JOYCE, and HENRY MILLER.

Racine, Jean (baptized December 22, 1639–April 21, 1699). French playwright. Racine's tragedies, on themes from classical history and myth, elegantly depict man's passionate struggle for the unobtainable. Orphaned early in life and sent by his grandmother to be educated by the Jansenists, Racine finished his studies at the University of Paris, where he discovered the theater. His first two plays, *The Thebaid* (*La Thébaïde*, 1664) and *Alexander the Great* (*Alexandre le Grand*, 1665), were produced by his friend MOLIÈRE. Overwhelming acclaim greeted the plays that followed, which included *Andromache* (*Andromaque*, 1667), *Britannicus* (1669), *Bérénice* (1670), *Bajazet* (1672), *Iphigenia* (*Iphigénie*, 1674), and PHAE-DRA (*Phèdre*, 1677). When Louis XIV appointed Racine a royal historian, the king's wife, Mme. de Maintenon, commissioned the playwright's final works, the biblically themed *Esther* (1689) and *Athalia* (*Athalie*, 1691).

Radcliffe, Ann, *original surname* Ward (July 9, 1764–February 7, 1823). English novelist. Suspenseful depictions of atmospheres both fearsome and romantic coupled with psychological explorations of madness and terror made this mistress of the Gothic novel the bestselling writer of her day. A London native, Radcliffe married a newspaperman and soon began publishing her popular novels. *The Castles of Athlin and Dunbayne* (1789), *A Sicilian Romance* (1790), and *The Romance of the Forest* (1791) preceded her most famous work, THE MYSTERIES OF UDOLPHO (1794). *Udolpho* commanded the largest publishing advance of its time for a novel, and was later satirized by Jane AUSTEN. Radcliffe's fifth novel, *The Italian* (1797), features the evil monk Schedoni. Her travel journals and the novel *Gaston de Blondeville* (1826) were published posthumously.

Raleigh, [Sir] **Walter,** *original spelling* Ralegh (c. 1554–October 29, 1618). English poet. After a series of successful campaigns, the soldier Raleigh became a favorite of Queen Elizabeth I. While at court, he supported the publication of SPENSER's THE FAERIE QUEENE, but lost favor after an affair with one of the queen's maids. He sought to regain the queen's good will by traveling to South America in search of gold — a journey embellished in *Discovery of Guiana* (1596) — but was welcomed back only to be imprisoned by James I in the Tower of London, where Raleigh wrote the ambitious *The History of the World* (1614). After 13 years there, Raleigh convinced the king to allow him to try his luck once again in Guiana (now Venezuela). But when his ill-fated expedition returned without gold, he was executed. Raleigh never published his poetry, but a few poems survive, including "Epitaph of Sir Philip Sidney" and the sonnet that begins "Methought I saw the grave where Laura lay," which prefaces *The Faerie Queene*. Also extant are "The Nymph's Reply to the

Shepherd" and a fragment of "Cynthia," his long ode to the queen.

Rand, Ayn, *original name* Alyssa, Alice, *or* Alysia Rosenbaum (February 2, 1905–March 6, 1982). Russian-born American novelist and playwright. Rand's work espouses her philosophy of objectivism, promoting the values of capitalism, personal achievement, and "rational self-interest." Born and educated in Russia, in 1926 she moved to the United States, changed her name from Rosenbaum to Rand (after the typewriter), and went to Hollywood to write for the screen. But it was her fiction, beginning with *We the Living* (1936), a historical novel set against the background of the Russian Revolution, that secured her fame. In the works that followed—the novella *Anthem* (1938) and the novels THE FOUNTAINHEAD (1943) and ATLAS SHRUGGED (1957)—uncompromising individualism and selfishness are lauded over altruism and the interests of "the State." Rand elaborates on objectivism in several nonfiction works, including *For the New Intellectual: The Philosophy of Ayn Rand* (1961) and *The Virtue of Selfishness: A New Concept of Egoism* (1964). She also wrote several plays, two of which were produced on Broadway.

Rattigan, [Sir] **Terence** (June 10, 1911–November 30, 1977). English playwright. With his traditional, accessible dramas, this master of the "well-made play" has enjoyed popularity with English-speaking audiences on both side of the Atlantic. Educated at Oxford, Rattigan found success as a young London writer with his comedy *French Without Tears* (1936). *Tears* was followed most notably by *The Winslow Boy* (1946), about a father defending his son from an accusation of theft, which was filmed memorably by David MAMET in 1999. Two years later came *The Browning Version* (1948), a psychological examination of the loveless life of a schoolmaster. His double one-act about loneliness, *Separate Tables*, was produced in 1954 and his biographical drama of T. E. LAWRENCE, *Ross*, came in 1960.

Rechy, John (March 10, 1934–). American novelist. Rechy's autobiographical novels pro-

voked controversy in the 1960s for their daring portrayal of homosexual life. Born to Mexican-American parents in El Paso and educated in Texas and New York, Rechy spent time in the Army before beginning his career as a novelist. His first book, the bestselling *City of Night* (1963), is a picaresque tale of the seamy side of the gay underground. Among the notable works that followed are *Numbers* (1967), *The Fourth Angel* (1972), and his "prose documentary," *The Sexual Outlaw* (1977). Recent novels include *The Miraculous Day of Amalia Gómez* (1991), *Our Lady of Babylon* (1996), and *The Coming of the Night* (1999).

Reed, Ishmael (February 22, 1938–). American novelist, essayist, and poet. Reed's experimental writings combine a variety of literary styles and linguistic approaches with racial and political commentary to invoke a cultural legacy that is distinctly African American. Born in Tennessee, Reed grew up in Buffalo, where he studied at the University of Buffalo. He cofounded the popular underground New York City newspaper *The East Village Other* in the 1960s before introducing his singular brand of parody with his first novel, *The Free-Lance Pallbearer* (1967). His biting, satirical fiction continued with *Yellow Back Radio Broke-Down* (1969), MUMBO JUMBO (1972), and other notable titles, including *Flight to Canada* (1976), *The Terrible Twos* (1982), *The Terrible Threes* (1989), and *Japanese by Spring* (1993). A selection of Reed's fiction, poetry, essays, and drama can be found in *The Reed Reader* (2000).

Remarque, Erich Maria, *pen name of* Erich Paul Remark (June 22, 1898–September 25, 1970). German novelist. Remarque was born in Osnabrück, a medieval town in northern Germany, and was drafted at 18. In 1917, the young soldier was wounded behind enemy lines. He immortalized his experience in his powerful first novel, the internationally acclaimed ALL QUIET ON THE WESTERN FRONT (*Im Westen Nichts Neues*, 1929), an important literary document of World War I. He followed with a sequel, *The Road Back* (*Der Weg Zurück*, 1931), and several more novels. Some were popular successes, but he never again achieved the critical esteem he enjoyed with his first book.

Renault, Mary, *pen name of* [Eileen] Mary Challans (September 4, 1905–December 13, 1983). English-born South African novelist. Renault's detailed, engaging fictions about ancient and postclassical Greek culture brought her international recognition. A native of London and the daughter of a physician, Renault received medical training at Oxford before serving as a nurse in World War II; her background in medicine is reflected in her early novels, notably *Promise of Love* (1939). Renault moved permanently to South Africa in 1947 and traveled throughout Africa and Greece. *The King Must Die* (1958) and *The Bull from the Sea* (1962) creatively retell the myth of Theseus and the Minotaur; her trilogy of novels about Alexander the Great, composed of *Fire from Heaven* (1970), *The Persian Boy* (1972), and *Funeral Games* (1981), vividly recreates the world of Alexander and his conquests. Her research for the trilogy was gathered in a well-received biography, *The Nature of Alexander* (1975).

Rexroth, Kenneth (December 22, 1905–June 6, 1982). American poet, essayist, and translator. An important influence on writers of the Beat movement (although never a member himself), Rexroth advocated a "poetry of responsibility" that addressed social issues in clear, colloquial, language. Primarily self-educated, he was a freethinker and iconoclast whose deep immersion in the philosophies and literatures of the Far East helped to shape his mature poetry, which is marked by a lyrical search for transcendence and a spare, imagist technique. Born in South Bend, Indiana, and orphaned at the age of 12, he became actively involved with anarchist and avant-garde circles during the second Chicago Renaissance before settling in San Francisco in 1927, where he became a central figure of the Bay Area's literary scene, a well-known columnist and radio personality who was as famous for his irascibility as for his erudition (Alfred KAZIN called him an "all-American sorehead").

Among his many poetry collections are the *Collected Shorter Poems* (1967) and the *Collected Longer Poems* (1968). His adept translations from several languages include *One Hundred Poems from the Japanese* (1955), *Poems from the Greek Anthology* (1962), and *The Orchid Boat: Women Poets of China* (1972). Among his essay collections are *Bird in the Bush* (1959), *Classics Revisited* (1968), and *The Alternative Society* (1970). *An Autobiographical Novel* was published in 1966; a revised and enlarged edition appeared in 1991.

Rhys, Jean, *original name* Ella Gwendolen Rees Williams (August 24, 1890–May 14, 1979). English novelist and short-story writer. Rhys's novels present stark narratives of unmoored, sensitive women struggling to escape from their dependence on men. Born in Dominica in the West Indies (her father was a Welsh doctor, her mother a third-generation Dominican Creole), Rhys traveled to England as a teenager and worked at jobs ranging from cook to chorus girl. After marrying the first of her three husbands, she moved to Paris, where she began writing fiction. *The Left Bank and Other Stories* (1927) was published with an enthusiastic introduction by her mentor and former lover FORD MADOX FORD. Several novels in Rhys's unsparing style followed: *Postures* (1928; U.S. title, *Quartet*), *After Leaving Mr. Mackenzie* (1930), and *Voyage in the Dark* (1934). A decades-long silence followed the publication of *Good Morning, Midnight* (1939), during which Rhys, who suffered from depression and alcoholism, "disappeared" so completely that many in the literary world assumed she was dead. She returned spectacularly with her novel *WIDE SARGASSO SEA* (1966), a richly imagined reconstruction of the early life of Antoinette Cosway, the haunted Mrs. Rochester in CHARLOTTE BRONTË's novel *JANE EYRE*. Among her later story collections is *Sleep It Off Lady* (1976). Rhys's fragmentary autobiography, *Smile Please*, on which she was working at her death, was published in 1979.

Rich, Adrienne (May 16, 1929–). American poet and critic. A feminist and activist, Rich writes highly personal, political poetry. Born in Baltimore and educated at Radcliffe College, Rich published her first verse collection, *A Change of World*, in 1951 after winning the Yale Younger Poets Award. Originally noted for its elegant, controlled form and intellectuality, her poetry evolved—beginning with the collection *Snapshots of a Daughter-in-Law* (1963)—into a free verse marked by loosely punctuated short lines and emotional candor. During the 1960s, Rich's increasing involvement in the civil rights, antiwar, and women's movements paralleled her increasing frustration with women's traditional roles in society, as well as with the politics of language. After the dissolution of her marriage in 1970, she committed herself fully to feminism, using poetry as a tool for change. Her personal evolution is reflected in the collections *Leaflets* (1969), *Diving into the Wreck* (1974; National Book Award), *The Dream of a Common Language* (1978), and *Midnight Salvage* (1999). Prose works include her study on motherhood, *Of Woman Born: Motherhood as Experience and Institution* (1976), *Blood, Bread, and Poetry* (1986), and *What Is Found There: Notebooks on Poetry and Politics* (1993).

Richardson, Dorothy (May 17, 1873–June 17, 1957). English novelist. A psychologically astute and intimate writer, Richardson pioneered stream-of-consciousness narration in her challenging 13-volume novel *PILGRIMAGE* (1915–67). Born in Abingdon, Berkshire, Richardson moved to Bloomsbury after her mother's suicide in 1895. Encouraged by friends, including her confidant H. G. WELLS, she began the two-thousand-page *Pilgrimage* with *Pointed Roofs* in 1915; the last volume, *March Moonlight*, was published posthumously in 1967. Richardson's partly autobiographical masterpiece relates the life and evolving consciousness of her heroine, Miriam, who shrugs off the constraints of Victorian conventions. Richardson's subtle, free-form style influenced VIRGINIA WOOLF, who wrote that she had created "the psychological sentence of the feminine gender."

Richardson, Samuel (baptized August 19, 1689–July 4, 1761). English novelist. Considered the progenitor of the modern novel, Richardson explored the psychologies of his characters with great insight and addressed changing social roles in his popular epistolary novels, a form he invented. Born near Derby, at 17 Richardson apprenticed with a printer, eventually establishing his own very prosperous printing and publishing business. But by 1732, his first wife and their six children had all died—a cumulative shock to which he attributed his subsequent nervous disorders. At age 50, by then remarried, Richardson completed the phenomenally successful *PAMELA* (1740), which promotes the triumph of virtue over villainy. A sequel, the less-successful *Pamela in Her Exalted Condition*, appeared in 1742. Richardson's finest novel is the tragic, more complex *CLARISSA* (1747–48), published in seven volumes. An admitted "poor pruner," Richardson has been faulted for the extraordinary length of his novels and their rigid moral tone, complaints that continued to plague him with the publication of *The History of Sir Charles Grandison* (1753–54), another seven-volume tome. Nonetheless, Richardson's works were highly influential during the 18th century, proving a source of inspiration for many later writers, including Choderlos de LACLOS and JANE AUSTEN.

Richler, Mordecai (January 27, 1931–July 2, 2001). Canadian novelist, screenwriter, short-story writer, and children's book author. Richler is best known for his witty, mordantly comic novels that mine his working-class Jewish upbringing. Born, raised, and educated in Montreal, he wrote many of his most admired novels during two decades when he lived in London and Paris: the bestseller *The Apprenticeship of Duddy Kravitz* (1959), *The Incomparable Atuk* (1963), *Cocksure* (1968), and *St. Urbain's Horseman* (1971). Skewering the hypocrisies of contemporary Canadian life, Richler's narratives satirize Montreal gentiles and Jews alike. His many works include screenplays, essays, short-story collections, a series of *Jacob Two-Two* books for children, and a volume of memoirs,

The Street (1975). His tenth novel, *Barney's Version* (1997), won Canada's Giller Prize.

Riley, James Whitcomb (October 7, 1849–July 22, 1916). American poet. Often called the "Hoosier poet," Riley captures in his colloquial and homey verse an image of a cherished and romanticized rural Midwest that was immensely popular not only in his native Indiana, but also throughout the rest of America. He was, as Hamlin GARLAND observed, "the poet of the plain American." Born in Greenfield, Indiana, Riley received little formal education (at school, he recalled, he was "a failure in everything except reading"). He was by turns a traveling sign painter (including a year's stint working for a patent-medicine peddler), an actor, and a newspaperman. Riley began composing poems for recitation during his travels around Indiana because he could not find any printed ones that were "natural enough to speak." The poems that won him both fame and fortune were first published in the Indianapolis *Journal* and later collected as *The Old Swimmin'-hole and 'leven More Poems* (1883). As the popularity of Riley's verse soared, many more volumes followed, including *Afterwhiles* (1887), *Home-Folks* (1900), and *A Hoosier Romance, 1868* (1910). Among his best-known poems are "Little Orphant Annie" and "The Raggedy Man." The ten-volume *Complete Works* was issued in 1916 and *The Complete Poetical Works* in 1937.

Rilke, Rainer Maria, *original name* René Maria Rilke (December 4, 1875–December 29, 1926). German poet. Born in Prague, for much of his life Rilke journeyed restlessly across Europe, stopping for longer periods in Germany, France, and Switzerland. Two trips to Russia (1899–1900) helped inspire his first significant verse, published as *The Book of Hours* (*Das Stundenbuch*, 1905), a cycle celebrating life and man's perception of God. Frequently residing in Paris, he wrote about and befriended the sculptor Auguste Rodin, whose influence is felt in *New Poems* (*Neue Gedichte*, 1907–8). Here, as in *The Book of Images* (*Das Buch der Bilder*, 1902, expanded edition 1906), Rilke experimented with the "Dinggedicht" ("object-poem"), attempting to capture in verse the essence of the physical object. To this period also belong the prose poem *The Lay of the Love and Death of Cornet Christopher Rilke* (*Die Weise von Liebe und Tod des Cornets Christoph Rilke*, 1906), which many a German World War I soldier carried in his knapsack, and Rilke's only novel, *The Notebooks of Malte Laurids Brigge* (*Die Aufzeichnungen des Malte Laurids Brigge*, 1910). Rilke's two greatest achievements appeared after a long silence that concluded in an astonishing burst of creativity: in a single month in 1922, he completed the last six of ten *DUINO ELEGIES* (*Duineser Elegien*, 1923), a cycle begun a decade earlier, together with 55 *SONNETS TO ORPHEUS* (*Die Sonette an Orpheus*, 1923). Influenced by Friedrich HÖLDERLIN, the *Elegies* struggle with man's relation to the divine, while the *Sonnets* celebrate the power of the poet's voice to mediate between life and death. Rilke is among the most highly esteemed and widely read poets in German; he is also widely popular in the English-speaking world, thanks to a steady stream of translations, many by well-known poets such as Randall JARRELL and Robert BLY. In Robert MUSIL's judgment, "This great poet did nothing other than to make the German poem perfect for the first time."

Rimbaud, [Jean-Nicolas-]**Arthur** (October 20, 1854–November 10, 1891). French poet. Prodigy of the Symbolist movement, self-professed visionary, and free-spirited adventurer, Rimbaud exerted a lasting influence on the modern poetic imagination with a literary output of barely five years. Intensely imagined, experimental in method, and purposively "deranged" in syntax and meaning, his lyric poetry pioneered the use of free-verse chant and was a precursor of 20th-century Surrealism. Born in the town of Charleville in northeastern France, he was raised in poverty by a pious, strong-willed mother after his father, an army captain, deserted the family. A quiet boy and brilliant student, he rebelled at age 15 and ran away. After a year of wandering, during which he began writing seriously, he was invited to Paris by Paul VERLAINE, who became his lover and literary champion, although their personal relationship was to be extremely

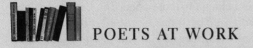

POETS AT WORK

Three things are certain: death, taxes, and the fact that poetry rarely pays the rent.

Poets and freezing garrets seem to go together in the public imagination, perhaps especially since the premiere of Giacomo Puccini's ever-popular opera *La Bohème* in 1906. In the first act of that romantic tragedy, the hero, Rodolfo, a poverty-stricken poet, burns the manuscript of one of his dramas to keep himself warm in his attic apartment. In fact, poets (except those with the good sense to have been born wealthy) have always scrambled to keep themselves in pen and paper, and the wolf—or the landlord—from the door.

The great poet Robert Burns struggled to make ends meet throughout his short life, even though his *Poems, Chiefly in the Scottish Dialect* created a sensation in 1786. Three years later, never having been able to make a go of it as a tenant farmer, Burns finally secured a civil service position as a tax inspector, which brought some financial stability to his life. Other poets who were employed as civil servants include John Milton, during the Puritan Commonwealth; Paul Valéry, who worked for the French War Office from 1897 to 1900; and Constantine Cavafy, who for 30 years earned his primary livelihood working for the Irrigation Service of the Ministry of Public Works in Alexandria, Egypt, retiring with the rank of assistant director in 1923. Many distinguished poets have also served their countries as diplomats or consuls:

Chaucer, Sir Philip Sidney, James Russell Lowell, Rubén Darío, Paul Claudel, Pablo Neruda, Octavio Paz, James Weldon Johnson, George Seferis, Alfonso Reyes, Miguel Angel Asturias, and Saint-John Perse, to name a few.

Some poets, although never truly "successful" in a worldly sense in their own time, managed to eke out a relatively decent living. William Blake, for one, earned a modest income as an engraver, while steadily issuing illuminated editions of his own works (which, however, went virtually unnoticed by his contemporaries). Another was Walt Whitman. After working as a teacher, carpenter, newspaper reporter and editor, and volunteer nurse during the Civil War, Whitman was settling in as a government clerk when, in June 1865, he was fired after his personal copy of *Leaves of Grass* (1855) was discovered in his desk by the Secretary of the Interior, who was scandalized by it. (Through influential friends, Whitman quickly secured another government post.) Never as obscure as Blake was during his own lifetime, Whitman died a famous (or infamous) man, but hardly a rich one.

Poets sometimes find success in both the artistic and the "real" worlds. T. S. Eliot was first a banker, then editor-in-chief of Faber & Faber. The contemporary American poet Dana Gioia spent 14 years with Kraft Foods (where he helped to develop Jell-O Jigglers) before he decided to pursue a full-time career in literature. He had, understandably, grown tired of squeezing his "literary work into the little pockets of time" that his busy life afforded. Two of the 20th century's most influential poets, Wallace Stevens and William Carlos Williams, each carried on two full-time professions. William Carlos Williams, M.D., devoted himself not only to his writing, but also for more than 40 years to his successful obstetric and pediatric practice (nearly 2,000 babies delivered). And Stevens, a vice-president of Hartford Accident and Indemnity Company in Connecticut, was described by a fellow lawyer there as "a kind of sane schizophrenic." There was no mention of business in Stevens's poetry, and no poetry in his business writings.

For some, though, the world of business, even publishing, holds no allure. After graduating from Harvard, E. E. Cummings landed a job in the mail-order division of a New York publishing house, but he could take it for only two months; for the remainder of his life, Cummings managed to support himself—often barely—with his pen. Allen Ginsberg (not yet the king of the Beats) labored in "serious business industry" (including advertising) for a while in the early 1950s, even, at first, with some enthusiasm. But by the time he wrote "My Alba" (1953), Ginsberg was despairing of his "youth of my twenties / fainted in offices / wept on typewriters . . . ." The rest is history.

Arthur Rimbaud was poet-of-many-trades *after* he had reached his literary zenith. Determined "to become a real adventurer instead of a mystic vagabond," Rimbaud abandoned poetry at 21 and set out to wander the world. He traveled throughout Europe, the Middle East, and Africa, working as a laborer, explorer, coffee trader, and arms runner. He even joined the Dutch Foreign Legion, but soon deserted in the East Indies. In the last years of his short life, Rimbaud seems to have been so completely occupied with business considerations that his extensive surviving correspondence contains no mention of poetry.

It is the rare poet whose résumé is as colorful as Rimbaud's. Yet poets' day jobs (like the greatest poems) seem to come in an almost inexhaustible variety. Marianne Moore worked as an assistant at the Hudson Park Branch of The New York Public Library from 1921 to 1925. Frank O'Hara was a curator at New York's Museum of Modern Art, with a self-described talent for "playing the typewriter," who dashed off poems on napkins during business meetings. Maya Angelou was a cocktail waitress, nightclub singer, stage actress, and school administrator, among other things, before becoming a best-selling memoirist and poet. In a wide-ranging and peripatetic career, Jack Kerouac worked as a railroad brakeman, a sports reporter, and even as a fire lookout for the U.S. Agricultural Service in Washington State in the summer of 1956, the latter experience inspiring his novel *Desolation Angels* (1965).

But perhaps the most common "occupation" of poets is un- (or under-) employment. In Hal Sirowitz's poem, "Get a Job," a mother asks her wayward son why he spends all his time reading, why he can't get a summer job like the rest of his class. She concludes, "You're not satisfied / just being a bum, but have to sit / in your room all day studying to be a better one."

tumultuous. Rimbaud's best-known works are "THE DRUNKEN BOAT" ("Le Bâteau Ivre," 1871), a hallucinatory journey of the imagination and spirit; *Illuminations* (*Les Illuminations*, 1886), a cycle of rhythmic, dreamlike prose poems; and *A SEASON IN HELL* (*Une Saison en Enfer*, 1873), a tortured, fragmentary confession of spiritual disillusionment and failed love. Abandoning poetry at age 20, he traveled through Europe and Africa as a trader, gunrunner, and explorer, and died of cancer in Marseille at 37.

Robbe-Grillet, Alain (August 18, 1922–). French novelist, critic, and screenwriter. Robbe-Grillet is a founder and proponent of the *nouveau roman*, the new novel or "anti-novel," part of the French New Wave in literature and film during the 1950s. Born in Brest, he trained as an agronomist and biologist before turning to writing. Because his novels and films lack conventional narrative structure, plot, character development, and analysis, the reader must infer what has happened from precise details, recurring images, and disjunctive events. His best-known novels are *The Erasers* (*Les Gommes*, 1953), *The Voyeur* (*Le Voyeur*, 1955), and *Jealousy* (*La Jalousie*, 1957); later novels include *Topology of a Phantom City* (*Topologie d'une Cité Fantôme*, 1976) and *Djinn* (1981). Robbe-Grillet also wrote and directed the films *The Immortal One* (*L'Immortelle*, 1963) and *The Man Who Lies* (*L'Homme Qui Ment*, 1968), and wrote the screenplay for Alain Resnais's classic film *Last Year at Marienbad* (*L'Année Dernière à Marienbad*, 1961).

Robinson, Edwin Arlington (December 22, 1869–April 6, 1935). American poet. Robinson used traditional forms and a plainspoken style and everyday language in poems about failure and cynicism, as well as courage. Raised in Gardiner, Maine, he attended Harvard University. His first four collections brought him few readers, but revealed his gift for character study. His best and most popular poems are short, spare, and intimate portraits of the residents of a fictional New England village, Tilbury Town, including "Richard Cory" and "Luke Havergal" in *The Children of the Night* (1897) and

"Miniver Cheevy" in *The Town Down the River* (1910). Robinson's verse is often melancholy, as was his own life, marked by family tragedy, alcoholism, and career frustration. His financial struggles eased when admirer President Theodore Roosevelt secured a job for him in the U.S. Customs House in New York. After 1910, Robinson was able to devote himself to writing. His breakthrough collection, *The Man Against the Sky* (1916), was followed by three major, Pulitzer Prize–winning volumes, *Collected Poems* (1921), *The Man Who Died Twice* (1924), and the long narrative poem *Tristram* (1927). The latter completed the Arthurian trilogy in blank verse he had begun with *Merlin* (1917) and *Lancelot* (1920).

Rochester, John Wilmot, [2nd] Earl of (April 10, 1647–July 26, 1680). English poet and satirist. Rochester, considered the most gifted and brilliant poet of the Restoration wits, led a life of notorious debauchery. Born in Oxfordshire and educated at Oxford, he became, while still in his early teens, a member of the court of Charles II, and later served bravely in the war against the Dutch (1665–67). He wrote a wide range of bawdy verse, polished lyrics and songs, and dazzling verse satires, including the powerful *A Satire Against Mankind* (1675), a scathing indictment of man's pretenses to rationality. In his last years, he repudiated his licentious ways; an account of his apparent religious conversion is contained in Gilbert Burnet's *Some Passages of the Life and Death of the Right Honourable John, Earl of Rochester* (1680).

Roethke, Theodore (May 25, 1908–August 1, 1963). American poet. Roethke is known for deeply personal poetry that uses nature as both a source of imagery and as a metaphor for the inner life. Born in Saginaw, Michigan, he spent many hours in his father's greenhouse, an experience reflected in the prominent images of growth and decay in his poetry, from the early collection *The Lost Son* (1948) to the posthumously published *The Far Field* (1964). He attended the University of Michigan and Harvard University, then held a series of university and college teaching posts. In 1935, Roethke experienced the first of the several mental breakdowns that would torment him throughout his life, experiences that informed his work. Praised for his clever wordplay and stylistic experimentation, he was awarded a Pulitzer Prize for his 1953 collection *The Waking,* which contains the frequently anthologized "Elegy for Jane." *Words for the Wind* (1958) garnered a National Book Award, as did *The Far Field.* Roethke's other notable works include the essays and lectures gathered in *On the Poet and His Craft* (1966) and the poetry collections *Praise to the End* (1951) and *Sequence, Sometimes Metaphysical* (1964).

Rølvaag, O[le] E[dvart], *surname also spelled* Rölvaag (April 22, 1876–November 5, 1931). Norwegian-born American novelist, writing in Norwegian. Rølvaag's novels dramatically recount the hardships of immigrant pioneer life in America. Rølvaag left Norway for the United States at age 20, living first on the South Dakota prairie, then settling in Minnesota. His experiences in the New World are related in *Letters from America* (*Amerika-Breve,* 1912). A strong advocate of preserving his fellow immigrants' native culture, he taught Norwegian language and history for more than two decades at St. Olaf College in Northfield, Minnesota, where he had been educated. The best known among his six novels is his starkly realistic epic trilogy consisting of GIANTS IN THE EARTH (*I de Dage,* 1924–25), *Peder Victorious* (*Peder Seier,* 1929), and *Their Fathers' God* (*Den Signede Dag,* 1931).

Rossetti, Christina (December 5, 1830–December 29, 1894). English poet. The sister of William Michael and DANTE GABRIEL ROSSETTI, Christina Rossetti was among the most accomplished Victorian poets. Born into a highly cultured family, she early on showed a lively imagination and a technical facility for verse. In the 1850s she began contributing poetry and prose—often under the pseudonym "Ellen Alleyne"—to various periodicals, including *Macmillan's Magazine* and the short-lived journal of the Pre-Raphaelite Brotherhood, *The Germ,* which was edited by her brother William

Michael. A devout High Anglican, she rejected two Roman Catholic suitors rather than stray from her faith, and religion remained a strong current running through her work. The volumes *Goblin Market and Other Poems* (1862) and *The Prince's Progress and Other Poems* (1866) contain her best-known and finest verse. Shortly before her children's verse collection *Sing-Song* was published in 1872, Rossetti was afflicted with Graves' disease. She became reclusive, thereafter dedicating herself primarily to melancholy devotional prose. The notable *Time Flies,* combining prose and verse, appeared in 1885. In 1904, William Michael Rossetti compiled his sister's *Poetical Works* and, in 1908, her letters.

Rossetti, Dante Gabriel, *original name* Gabriel Charles Dante Rossetti (May 12, 1828–April 9, 1882). English poet. Rossetti, who was also a painter, was the most prominent member of the Pre-Raphaelite Brotherhood, a group of painters and poets who advocated a return to medieval imagery and styles in art and literature. Born in London into a highly cultured family, Rossetti was educated at King's College and the Royal Academy of Arts. In 1850, he helped to establish the Brotherhood, publishing his first poems in *The Germ,* its journal, which was edited by his brother, William Michael Rossetti. That year Rossetti met his future wife and model, Elizabeth Siddal. He immortalized her and a later love—William Morris's wife, Jane—in his lush, dramatic paintings, which were often signed "PRB." After Siddal's death from a laudanum overdose in 1862, the grief-stricken Rossetti buried with her the only complete manuscript of his verse, which he later disinterred and published as *Poems* (1870). His poems about life, love, and death are distinguished by their sensuousness and emotional power. Despite his declining health, Rossetti published his two finest volumes in 1881: *Poems: A New Edition,* containing his masterpiece, the sonnet sequence "The House of Life," and *Ballads and Sonnets,* which includes the superb ballads "The King's Tragedy" and "Sister Helen."

Roth, Henry (February 8, 1906–October 13, 1995). American novelist. Roth's novel CALL IT SLEEP (1934) is a classic of Jewish-American literature. As an infant, Roth was brought to New York City by his parents from their native Galicia in Eastern Europe, and he grew up poor on the Lower East Side and in Harlem. After graduating from the City College of New York in 1928, he began work on *Call It Sleep*, the remarkable narrative of a young Jewish boy facing the terrors of the urban Jewish ghetto. Despite good reviews, the novel quickly went out of print and Roth retired from writing. He worked at various jobs, from machinist to psychiatric aide, until Alfred KAZIN helped to revive interest in *Call It Sleep* in the late 1950s. Roth resumed writing, publishing a collection of essays and short stories, *Shifting Landscape*, in 1987. Of the six projected volumes of his autobiographical novel *Mercy of a Rude Stream*, Roth completed four: *A Star Shines over Mt. Morris Park* (1994), *A Diving Rock on the Hudson* (1994), *From Bondage* (1996), and *Requiem for Harlem* (1998).

Roth, Philip (March 19, 1933–). American novelist and short-story writer. A leading contemporary satirical writer in the tradition of KAFKA, WAUGH, and ORWELL, Roth has scrutinized with comic precision and sometimes

---

"Reading novels is a deep and singular pleasure, a gripping and mysterious human activity that does not require any more moral or political justification than sex."

Philip Roth, in an interview in *The Paris Review* (Fall 1984)

---

shocking frankness Jewish-American life and post–World War II America to reveal the paradoxes, conflicts, and complexities of both. He was born and raised in New Jersey, graduated from Bucknell University, and took a master's degree from the University of Chicago. Scoring a literary coup, Roth won the National Book Award for his first collection of wry short fiction,

Goodbye, Columbus (1959), then turned to writing novels with *Letting Go* (1962). Roth's most famous book, PORTNOY'S COMPLAINT (1969), uproariously brought masturbation into literary fiction. Novels that followed include *Patrimony* (1991), *Operation Shylock* (1993), and *Sabbath's Theater* (1995; National Book Award); the novels featuring his alter ego, Nathan ZUCKERMAN: *My Life as a Man* (1974), THE GHOST WRITER (1979), THE ANATOMY LESSON (1983), *The Counterlife* (1986), *American Pastoral* (1997; Pulitzer Prize), *I Married a Communist* (1998), and *The Human Stain* (2000), the last three of which are sometimes called his "American trilogy"; and several featuring another alter ego, David Kepesh: *The Breast* (1972), *The Professor of Desire* (1977), and *The Dying Animal* (2001). *Reading Myself and Others* (1975) is a collection of essays, articles, and interviews. Media adaptations of Roth's work include the films *Goodbye, Columbus* (1969) and *Portnoy's Complaint* (1972), and a television production of *The Ghost Writer*, shown on the Public Broadcasting System in 1984.

Rousseau, Jean-Jacques (June 28, 1712–July 2, 1778). Swiss-born philosopher, novelist, autobiographer, and essayist, writing in French. Rousseau was perhaps the most influential of all 18th-century European thinkers; his ideas had a crucial impact on the intellectual currents that led to the American and French Revolutions, on Romanticism in the arts, on progressivism in education, and on sociopolitical thought down to the present day. Born in Geneva, Rousseau sought literary fame in the Paris of the 1740s, where he befriended Denis DIDEROT and contributed articles on musical topics to Diderot's *Encyclopédie* (he was also a composer). He established his reputation with a prize-winning essay, the *Discourse on the Sciences and Arts* (*Discours sur les Sciences et les Arts*, 1750), arguing that science and art had corrupted man, rather than improving him, a notion that ran counter to the entire thrust of the Enlightenment. His single most seminal work was *The Social Contract* (*Du Contrat Social*, 1762), with its celebrated opening line, "Man was born free, but he is everywhere in chains," which contained his proposals for restoring man's liberty by improving the structure of society. Other major works include the *Discourse on Inequality* (*Discours sur l'Origine et les Fondements de l'Inégalité parmi les Hommes*, 1755), speculating further on the corruption of "natural" man by civilization's advances; two novels of ideas, the hugely popular *Julie: or, the New Heloise* (*Julie: ou, La Nouvelle Héloïse*, 1761), on the philosophy of love, and *ÉMILE: OR, ON EDUCATION* (*Émile: ou, De l'Éducation*, 1762), a radical treatise on pedagogy that was widely condemned as blasphemous; and two posthumously published works, the lyrical essays *Reveries of the Solitary Walker* (*Les Rêveries du Promeneur Solitaire*, 1782) and the great autobiography *CONFESSIONS* (*Les Confessions*, 1782–89), which anticipated the contemporary vogue for public self-scrutiny. Starting with *Émile*, Rousseau's works were frequently condemned by civil and religious authorities, and he was subject to persecution and banishment. He fled France, and was driven from canton to canton in Switzerland, eventually finding refuge in England with the philosopher David Hume. His sanity wavered, and he grew convinced that his friends were conspiring to destroy his reputation. In 1767, he returned to France, where he continued to write until his death, a decade before the great Revolution he helped to foment.

Roy, [Suzanna] **Arundhati** (November 24, 1961–). Indian novelist and essayist. One of South Asia's rising contemporary authors, she garnered popular and critical acclaim for her bestselling novel *The God of Small Things* (1997; Booker Prize). Born in Bengal, she trained as an architect and worked as a screenwriter before the publication of her first novel brought her international attention. A lyrical tale dense with sensuous language, *The God of Small Things* has been translated into dozens of languages. Roy has become increasingly involved in social activism; two essays addressing controversial policies in India were issued together as *The Cost of Living* (1999).

Rūmī, Jalāl od-Dīn (c. 1207–1273). Persian Ṣūfī poet and mystic. Descending from a tradition of spiritual poets in Islam, Rūmī is distinguished for the economic simplicity and delicacy of his poems, evoking vast spiritual dimensions in just a few words. The volume of his verse is extraordinary: thousands of odes form the *Dīvān-e Shams* (The Complete Poetry of Shams), based on the mysteries imparted to the poet by the wandering dervish, Shams ad-Dīn, while the six books of the *Masnāvī-ye Ma'navī* (Spiritual Couplets) contain more than 25,000 couplets, and the *Robā'īyāt* comprises approximately 1,600 quatrains. Rūmī is best known for exploring mystical states of ecstasy and love. His elliptical verse, like the paradoxical parables of Zen Buddhism and Lao Tzu's *Tao Te Ching*, is intended to guide the reader into closer proximity with spiritual and holy truths. Rūmī's direct disciples, the Whirling Dervishes, are legendary for their ritual dances, which elicit hypnotic states. Intimate and mystically resonant, Rūmī's poetry continues to find wide readership among the Muslim faithful and across the world.

Runyon, Damon, *original name* Alfred Damon Runyan (October 4, 1880?–December 10, 1946). American journalist, sportswriter, and short-story writer. By the age of 15, Runyon, who had only a sixth-grade education, was working full time for a Colorado newspaper. After service in the Spanish-American War, he returned to newspaper work, and in 1911 began a lifelong affiliation with the *New York American*, for which he covered current events and sports. His unorthodox approach to sportswriting, focusing on vivid descriptions and down-to-earth details rather than statistics, would be reflected in his stories of the denizens of New York's Broadway–Times Square area. First published in *Collier's*, *The Saturday Evening Post*, and *Cosmopolitan* magazines, the stories were collected in *GUYS AND DOLLS* (1931), *Blue Plate Special* (1934), *Money from Home* (1935), and other volumes. In them, Runyon created amusing, sometimes sentimental, portraits of gamblers, gangsters, and their girlfriends ("dolls"), who speak in a Runyonesque brand of street slang and live by a code of their own, based on loyalty to friends. The characters and milieu of these tales inspired the Broadway musical *Guys and Dolls* (1950), which has ensured their enduring fame. When Runyon died of throat cancer, his ashes were scattered from a plane over Times Square.

Rushdie, [Ahmed] Salman (June 19, 1947–). Indian-born English novelist and critic. Rushdie was surrounded by controversy in 1989 when Iran's Ayatollah Khomeini issued a *fatwa* ordering his assassination for the ostensible blasphemy of his novel THE SATANIC VERSES (1988); the event resulted in considerable international criticism of Iran and protests on behalf of free speech. Rushdie, born a Muslim in Bombay, was educated in England and graduated from Cambridge University. He worked in advertising until his second novel, MIDNIGHT'S CHILDREN (1981; Booker Prize), found a critical and popular audience. Rushdie's often allegorical and fantastic fiction satirizes contemporary politics and religious and cultural conventions. *Shame* (1983) is a parable about Pakistani politics, and *The Satanic Verses* follows a humanized Muhammad, among others, through morally symbolic adventures. Despite the multimillion-dollar bounty that sent Rushdie into hiding, he continued to write, publishing the collection for children *Haroun and the Sea of Stories* (1990), the short-story collection *East, West* (1994), and the novels *The Moor's Last Sigh* (1995) and *The Ground Beneath Her Feet* (1999). After nearly ten years, the Iranian government lifted Rushdie's death sentence in 1998.

Russell, George William. *See Æ*

Sábato, Ernesto (June 24, 1911–). Argentinean novelist and essayist. A physicist by training, Sábato was educated at the National University of La Plata in Argentina, the Curie Laboratory, and the Massachusetts Institute of Technology. He became a professor in his home country, but his metaphysical questioning led him to writing, and he published a successful book of literary essays, *One and the Universe* (*Uno y el Universo*, 1945). In novels, beginning with *The Outsider* (*El Túnel*, 1948), he expanded his

reflections on personal alienation, the need for enduring meaning, and the limits of rational thinking. Sábato's other major novels include *On Heroes and Tombs* (*Sobre Héroes y Tumbas*, 1961) and *Angel of Darkness* (*Abaddón, el Exterminador*, 1974). He was awarded the prestigious Spanish literature award, the Cervantes Prize, in 1984.

Saʿdāwī, Nawāl al- (October 27, 1931–). Egyptian novelist, short-story writer, and playwright. The author of more than 40 books in Arabic, many of which were banned in Egypt, Saʿdāwī infuses her writing with concern for the women and poor of her country. In psychiatric case studies such as *Women and Sex* (*al-Maʾrah wa-al-Jins*, 1971), she charged that the widespread practice of female circumcision caused needless suffering; she expanded her critique of abuses against Arab women in *The Hidden Face of Eve* (*al-Wajh al-ʿĀrī lil-Marʾah al-ʿArabīyah*, 1977). Much of Saʿdāwī's fiction portrays powerless characters struggling against a hostile society. *Woman at Point Zero* (*Imraʾah ʿinda Nuqṭat al-Ṣifr*, 1975), her best-known novel, follows a prostitute, Firdaus, who kills her pimp rather than submit to his domination; in *God Dies by the Nile* (*Mawt al-Rajul al-Waḥīd ʿalá al-Arḍ* 1976), the heroine, Zakeya, considers murdering a corrupt and lustful politician. Although jailed briefly for her political and sexual frankness, Saʿdāwī continues to write stories, plays, and widely translated novels, including *Searching* (*al-Ghāʾib*, 1968) and *The Circling Song* (*Ughnīyat al-Aṭfāl al-Dāʾirīyah*, 1977); she recounts her own life in *A Daughter of Isis* (1999).

Sade, Donatien-Alphonse-François, Comte de, *known as* the **Marquis de Sade** (June 2, 1740– December 2, 1814). French novelist, short-story writer, and playwright. A cavalry officer in the Seven Years' War, Sade led an infamously contentious life, matched by an equally controversial literary career, after returning home. Imprisoned for more than 30 years for offenses including sexual misconduct, Sade wrote most of his best-known works while incarcerated and died in custody at the insane asylum at Charenton. His works graphically depict rituals of sexual perversion and were not legally permitted to be published in France until the 20th century. Considered by some critics to be a precursor of NIETZSCHE and FREUD, Sade remains important for his iconoclastic treatments of morality, sexuality, and power. The term "sadism" derives from Sade's legendary penchant for sexual cruelty. His novels include *JUSTINE* (1791); *Juliette* (1797), a sequel to *Justine*; and *THE 120 DAYS OF SODOM* (*Les 120 Journées de Sodome*, 1785).

Saikaku, Ihara or **Ibara**, *pen name of* Hirayama Togo (1642–1693). Japanese poet and novelist. A central figure in the literary renaissance of 17th-century Japan, Saikaku is remembered as the first important novelist of the Genroku era and a prolific writer of haikai (*sing.* haiku). Saikaku would have found this designation ironic, since his verses were intended not for posterity, but to amuse the rising merchant class of Osaka with witty descriptions of their secular pursuits, namely, love and money. Challenging the slowness of traditional court poets, he initiated a haiku-writing competition and reportedly created 23,500 verses in a single day and night. His novels, reflecting the growing power of the commercial classes in Japan, present satiric and entertaining tales about the lives of businessmen and merchant-class women, tradesmen, samurai warriors, and prostitutes. Among his best-known works are *The Life of an Amorous Man* (*Kōshoku Ichidai Otoko*, 1682), *The Life of an Amorous Woman* (*Kōshoku Ichidai Onna*, 1686), *Five Women Who Loved Love* (*Kōshoku Gonin Onna*, 1686), *The Mirror of Love Between Men* (*Nanshoku Ōkagami*, 1687), and *Worldly Mental Calculations* (*Seken Munesan'yō*, 1692).

Saint-Exupéry, Antoine de (June 29, 1900–July 31, 1944). French novelist and essayist. An aviator involved in exploratory flights and commercial aviation, Saint-Exupéry wrote about the life of piloting and its spiritual dimensions. His novels, including *Southern Mail* (*Courrier Sud*, 1929) and *Night Flight* (*Vol de Nuit*, 1931), are autobiographical, incorporating his own experiences as a pilot in West Africa and South Amer-

ica. His memoirs *Wind, Sand and Stars* (*Terre des Hommes*, 1939) and *Flight to Arras* (*Pilote de Guerre*, 1942) more explicitly interweave themes of spiritual grace with lyrical depictions of flying. Saint-Exupéry is perhaps best known, however, for *THE LITTLE PRINCE* (*Le Petit Prince*, 1943), a whimsical story of a boy and his discovery of human values. Saint-Exupéry disappeared over France in 1944 while on a reconnaissance mission.

Saki, *pen name of* H[ector] H[ugh] Munro (December 18, 1870–November 14, 1916). Burmese-born Scottish short-story writer. Saki's darkly humorous, often macabre short stories, which frequently invoke supernatural worlds. Cleverly satirizing human foibles, his stories often feature the protagonists Reginald and Clovis, who wreak vengeance on conventional society. The son of a military policeman in Burma, Munro was raised in England by aunts after his mother's death. He returned to Burma for a short time to follow the precedent of his father's military career, but ultimately chose to pursue writing in London. Saki's collections include *Reginald* (1904), *Reginald in Russia* (1910), *The Chronicles of Clovis* (1911), *Beasts and Super-Beasts* (1914), and the posthumous *The Square Egg* (1924). He also wrote the novels *The Unbearable Bassington* (1912) and *When William Came* (1913). When World War I erupted, Saki enlisted, only to be killed at the front. *The Complete Works of Saki* was published in 1976. He took his pen name from the *Rubáiyát of 'Omar Khayyám*, in which Saki is the cupbearer to the gods.

Salinger, J[erome] D[avid] (January 1, 1919–). American novelist and short-story writer. As famous for his reclusiveness as for his writing, Salinger is the subject of both widespread admiration and speculation. His novel *THE CATCHER IN THE RYE* (1951) is the vivid, first-person story of quintessential alienated New York adolescent Holden CAULFIELD, who searches for meaning apart from the "phony" world of adults; Salinger's only novel, the book rapidly became a cult classic. *NINE STORIES* (1953) collects some of Salinger's short stories, seven of which originally appeared in *THE NEW YORKER* and several of which feature members of the GLASS FAMILY, as does *FRANNY AND ZOOEY* (1961), two stories of young siblings who struggle with spiritual belief in their disaffection from middle-class society. The Glass family also appeared in *Raise High the Roof-Beam, Carpenters*; and *Seymour: An Introduction* (1963) and in "Hapworth 16 1924," published in *The New Yorker* in 1965. Salinger has refrained from publication and withdrawn from the public eye since that time.

Sand, George, *pen name of* Amandine-Aurore-Lucile Dupin, later Baronne Dudevant (July 1, 1804–June 8, 1876). French novelist, playwright, and essayist. Immensely popular during her lifetime, Sand is perhaps best known today, outside of France, as an unconventional and flamboyant public figure and friend to such celebrated writers and artists as Gustave FLAUBERT, Franz Liszt, Alfred de Musset, Eugène Delacroix, Frédéric Chopin, Heinrich HEINE, and Ivan TURGENEV, among others. Sand was born in Paris to a father who descended from the Polish aristocracy and a lower-class French mother; on the death of her father when she was four, she was sent to be raised by her strict paternal grandmother and received a convent education. In a misguided bid for liberation, she married the Baron Dudevant at the age of 18, but the marriage was unfulfilling and, after a series of affairs, she left him in 1831 to live in Paris. There she established herself as a prolific writer and acquired a provocative reputation, wearing men's clothes and having open affairs with Musset, Chopin, and others. The appeal of Sand's novels in her time derived from their Balzacian mixture of realism and romance, and from her feminist and socialist ideas (as well as, perhaps, from the public's fascination with her notorious private life). Novels such as *Indiana* (1832), *Valentine* (1832), and *Lélia* (1833) portray women's experiences of sensual love and criticize bourgeois conventions of marriage. Her later, pastoral novels include *Devil's Pool* (*La Mare au Diable*, 1846), *Little Fadette* (*La Petite Fadette*, 1849), and *The Country Waif* (*François le Champi*, 1850). Sand presented a fictionalized account of her affair with Musset

in *She and He* (*Elle et Lui*, 1859), and published her autobiography in the four-volume *Story of My Life* (*Histoire de Ma Vie*, 1854–55). Her correspondence with Flaubert has been published in a translation by Francis STEEGMULLER and Barbara Bray as *Flaubert-Sand: The Correspondence* (1993).

Sandburg, Carl (January 6, 1878–July 22, 1967). American poet, novelist, and biographer. Influenced by WHITMAN, Sandburg's poems in free verse use colloquial vocabulary and everyday imagery to celebrate the lives of ordinary working people and American democracy. The child of Swedish immigrants, Sandburg traveled across America as an itinerant manual laborer before joining the staff of the *Chicago Daily News*. He became associated with a group of Chicago literati, including SHERWOOD ANDERSON and Edgar Lee MASTERS, who attained prominence for their realistic depictions of modern regional life. His now famous poem "CHICAGO" was published in his collection *Chicago Poems* in 1916. His other volumes include *Cornhuskers* (1918), *Slabs of the Sunburnt West* (1922), *Good Morning America* (1928), and *Complete Poems* (1950; Pulitzer Prize). Sandburg also wrote a six-volume biography of Abraham Lincoln, *Abraham Lincoln: The Prairie Years* (2 vols.; 1926) and *Abraham Lincoln: The War Years* (4 vols.; 1939; Pulitzer Prize). His other works include an epic novel of an American family, *Remembrance Rock* (1948), and numerous children's books, the best known of which is *Rootabaga Stories* (1922). Sandburg compiled folk ballads in *The American Songbag* (1927) and *The New American Songbag* (1950).

Sappho (c. 610 B.C.–580 B.C.). Greek poet. One of the earliest and finest Greek lyric poets, Sappho earned the honor of being called "the Tenth Muse" by classical writers. She lived on the island of Lesbos, where she is thought to have guided a coterie of young women in music and poetry; the word "lesbian" is derived from the island's name and its association with Sappho's young devotees. Often dedicated to these women, Sappho's poetry is intimately subjective in tone and frequently treats themes of love and friendship. Little is known of her life, and her poems survive only in fragments. She is believed to have been exiled to Sicily for a time, owing perhaps to a repressive regime in Lesbos. Modern and ancient authors have circulated the apocryphal story of Sappho's throwing herself into the sea after being rebuffed by a handsome boatman, Phaon.

Saramago, José (November 16, 1922–). Portuguese novelist, poet, and playwright. A writer whose first published work appeared in 1947, Saramago's first real success did not come until 1982, when he was 60 years old. Born in a small village some 100 kilometers from Lisbon to working-class parents, Saramago was forced to leave school at the age of 12 because of his family's precarious finances, and trained as a mechanic. But the curriculum, mostly technical, also included literature and he began to visit the public library where, while working at his trade, he began to develop a taste for reading. Subsequently he worked for the social welfare service, and in book and newspaper publishing, first as a production manager, then as an editor, critic, and translator. His first book, *Terra do Pecado: Romance* (Land of Sin), was published in 1947, but although he worked on other books, he did not publish again until 1966, when his *Os Poemas Possíveis* (Possible Poems) appeared. His return to the novel came with *Manual of Painting and Calligraphy* (*Manual de Pintura e Caligrafia*, 1977), concerning the origins of an artistic vocation. This was followed by *Baltasar and Blimunda* (*Memorial do Convento*, 1982), a densely textured, symbolic novel incorporating fantasy, myth, and history; *The Year of the Death of Ricardo Reis* (*O Ano da Morte de Ricardo Reis*, 1984), depicting the tensions between a visionary priest and the Church (reflecting the dictatorship in power in Lisbon in 1936), and incorporating visits by the dead poet Fernando PESSOA to the protagonist, who is himself one of Pessoa's characters; *The Stone Raft* (*A Jangada de Pedra*, 1986), which imagines that the Iberian peninsula has floated away from Europe; and the controversial *The Gospel According to Jesus Christ* (*O Evangelho Segundo Jesus Cristo*, 1991), in which JESUS questions his role and challenges God. The accomplished novels *Blindness* (*Ensaio Sobre a Cegueira*, 1995), a parable of a repressive city beset with an epidemic of blindness, and *All the Names* (*Todos os Nomes*, 1997), about the tragic obsession of a clerk in a population registration office, preceded the awarding to him of the Nobel Prize in Literature in 1998.

Saroyan, William (August 31, 1908–May 18, 1981). American short-story writer, novelist, and playwright. Earning wide popularity during the Depression, Saroyan wrote stories and plays that celebrate the vitality of life in the face of hardship. Self-educated after dropping out of high school, he found instant recognition with the publication of his first short-story collection, *The Daring Young Man on the Flying Trapeze* (1934). Subsequent stories were published in many magazines and gathered in collections, including the autobiographical *My Name Is Aram* (1940). After his first play, *My Heart's in the Highlands* (1939), Saroyan wrote his most successful drama, *The Time of Your Life* (1939), for which he was awarded, but did not accept, the Pulitzer Prize. Saroyan's writings also include the novels *The Human Comedy* (1943), *Rock Wagram* (1951), and *The Laughing Matter* (1953). His memoirs include *Here Comes, There Goes, You Know Who* (1961) and *Places Where I've Done Time* (1975).

Sarraute, Nathalie, *original name* Nathalie Ilyanova Tcherniak (July 18, 1900–October 19, 1999). Russian-born French novelist, playwright, and essayist. Educated in France, England, and Germany, Sarraute worked as a lawyer before devoting herself to writing. Her first book, *Tropisms* (*Tropismes*, 1939), comprises a series of brief sketches of everyday domestic life, focusing on the sensations of existence that travel below conscious awareness. Rejecting traditional plot and structure in favor of open-ended depictions of human relationships, Sarraute labelled her *Portrait of a Man Unknown* (*Portrait d'un Inconnu*, 1948) an "antinovel." Her criticism, centered in *The Age of Suspicion* (*L'Ère du Soupçon*, 1956), elaborates the principles of the *nouveau roman* (new novel), a form of fiction that seeks to represent psychological ambiguities. Sarraute's other novels include *The Planetarium* (*Le Planétarium* 1959), *The Golden Fruits* (*Les Fruits d'Or*, 1963), and the autobiographical *Childhood* (*Enfance*, 1984).

Sartre, Jean-Paul (June 21, 1905–April 15, 1980). French novelist, playwright, philosopher, and critic. An imposing figure in 20th-century French intellectual life, Sartre was the principal developer of Existentialism, a philosophy concerned with the freedom and responsibility of the individual in a world without transcendent values. He was educated at the École Normale Supérieure, studied in Germany under Heidegger and Husserl, and taught in *lycées* in various parts of France for many years. During World War II, he joined the army and escaped Nazi imprisonment to aid the Resistance. In 1943, his play THE FLIES (*Les Mouches*), a symbolic examination of authoritarianism, was banned by the Nazis, and he published his major philosophical work, *Being and Nothingness* (*L'Être et le Néant*). Sartre's novels, including NAUSEA (*La Nausée*, 1938) and THE AGE OF REASON (*L'Âge de Raison*, 1945), and plays, such as NO EXIT (*Huis Clos*, 1945) and *Dirty Hands* (*Les Mains Sales*, 1948), eloquently illustrate Existentialist ideas. At the center of the Left Bank's intelligentsia in Paris for decades, with his long-time companion Simone de BEAUVOIR he founded and edited the important postwar review *Les Temps Modernes*. His other works include *Saint Genet* (1952), a critical study of Jean GENET, and *The Words* (*Les Mots*, 1964), a memoir about his early relationship with literature. Three volumes of a planned four-volume study of Gustave FLAUBERT, *The Family Idiot* (*L'Idiot de la Famille*), appeared in 1971 and 1972. He declined the Nobel Prize in Literature in 1964.

Sassoon, Siegfried (September 8, 1886–September 1, 1967). English poet and autobiographer. After studying at Cambridge, Sassoon privately published his poetry until he enlisted to fight in World War I. At the front he began writing verse, his best known published in *The Old Huntsman and Other Poems* (1917) and *Counter-Attack and Other Poems* (1918), that vigorously opposed the war with satire and open anger. When Sassoon issued a public treatise protesting the war, the War Office deemed him mentally unstable and confined him to a military hospital. There he met fellow antiwar poet Wilfred OWEN, who was later killed in action; Sassoon was instrumental in the publication of Owen's work in 1920. Sassoon wrote an autobiographical trilogy *The Complete Memoirs of George Sherston* (1928–37) and the memoirs *The Old Century and Seven More Years* (1938), *The Weald of Youth* (1942), and *Siegfried's Journey, 1916–1920* (1945). He published spiritual poetry in *Vigils* (1935) and *Sequences* (1956) and converted to Roman Catholicism in 1957. His *Collected Poems* was published in 1961.

Sayers, Dorothy L[eigh] (June 13, 1893–December 17, 1957). English novelist and playwright. Best known for her sophisticated detective novels, Sayers was also a literary scholar and one of the first women to receive a degree from Oxford University. She left a career in advertising to write full time once her mysteries found an audience. Most of her novels feature amateur detective Lord Peter Wimsey and are noted for clever plotting, well-developed characters, and wit. Among her most popular books are *Whose Body?* (1923), *The Unpleasantness at the Bellona Club* (1928), *Strong Poison* (1930), which features the first appearance of Lord Peter's future wife, the mystery writer Harriet Vane, *The Nine Tailors* (1934), *Gaudy Night* (1935), and *Busman's Honeymoon* (1937). Also interested in theology and medieval literature, Sayers focused on writing Christian-themed radio plays after 1937. She published translations of DANTE's *Inferno* and *Purgatorio* in 1949 and 1955, but did not live to complete her translation of the *Paradiso* (completed by Barbara Reynolds, it appeared in 1962).

Schiller, Friedrich [Johann Christoph] **von** (November 10, 1759–May 9, 1805). German playwright and poet. Schiller's early plays, including *The Robbers* (*Die Räuber*, 1781), are in the *Sturm und Drang* style, marked by passionately emotional romanticism. Beginning with the verse drama *Don Carlos* (1787), Schiller underwent a decade-long refinement of his literary purpose and wrote several important scholarly essays, including *On Naïve and Reflective Poetry* (*Über Naive und Sentimentalische Dichtung*, 1795–96). In 1789, he became a professor of history at the University of Jena, a center of progressive thought during the fertile period of German Romanticism; there he became closely associated with GOETHE, with whom he founded the movement known as Weimar Classicism. Schiller's later plays, including *Wallenstein* (1799), *The Maid of Orleans* (*Die Jungfrau von Orleans*, 1801), *The Bride of Messina* (*Die Braut von Messina*, 1803), and *WILLIAM TELL* (*Wilhelm Tell*, 1804), are historical verse dramas, exploring issues of morality, individuality, and social corruption. His many fine lyric poems include "Ode to Joy" ("An die Freude," 1785), which was set to music by Beethoven as the finale of his 9th Symphony.

Schnitzler, Arthur (May 15, 1862–October 21, 1931). Austrian playwright and novelist. The son of a physician, Schnitzler was trained in medicine and psychiatry in FREUD's Vienna and brought an acuity to the psychological depiction of his characters. His stories and plays are darkly ironic and typically concern love relationships in a bourgeois society. His plays include *Anatol* (1891), a group of sketches about the title character; *Light-o'-Love* (*Liebelei*, 1896), about a tragic love triangle; and *Professor Bernhardi* (1918), a criticism of anti-Semitism. His erotically charged collection of interlocking dramatic dialogues, *La Ronde* (*Reigen*, 1897), was not performed for years because of its subject matter but has since been the basis for several notable films and plays, including Max Ophuls's 1950 French film *La Ronde* and David Hare's 1998 free adaptation for theater, *The Blue Room*. Among Schnitzler's novels are *None But the Brave* (*Leutnant Gustl*, 1901), an interior monologue that satirizes the military code of honor, and *The Road to the Open* (*Der Weg ins Freie*, 1908), a story of a turbulent love affair. His novella *Dream Story* (*Traumnovelle*, 1926) was the basis for Stanley Kubrick's 1999 film *Eyes Wide Shut*.

Schulberg, Budd (March 27, 1914–). American novelist and screenwriter. As a novelist, Schulberg is best known for his acerbic portrayal of the unscrupulous moviemaker Sammy GLICK in *What Makes Sammy Run?* (1941). He wrote from his own observations of Hollywood as the son of prominent film producer B. P. Schulberg. Budd Schulberg served in World War II and assisted in the prosecution of war crimes, returning to writing novels with *The Harder They Fall* (1947), an exposé of corruption in professional boxing, and *The Disenchanted* (1950), a fictionalized depiction of F. SCOTT FITZGERALD. Like Fitzgerald, Schulberg also wrote screenplays in Hollywood, including the Academy Award–winning script for *On the Waterfront* (1954). He has also written essays on boxing and short stories, and has established foundations for the arts in Los Angeles and New York. His autobiography is *Moving Pictures: Memories of a Hollywood Prince* (1981).

Schwartz, Delmore (December 8, 1913–July 11, 1966). American poet, critic, and short-story writer. A New Yorker educated at the University of Wisconsin and Harvard, Schwartz is best known for *In Dreams Begin Responsibilities* (1938), in which he combined lyrical, ironic poems with a play and the title short story. His other major works include another prose and poem compilation, *Genesis* (1943), *Summer Knowledge: New and Selected Poems 1938–1958* (1959), the short-story collections *The World Is a Wedding* (1948) and *Successful Love* (1962), and the collection of his most important critical writings, *Selected Essays* (1970). He was poetry editor at *PARTISAN REVIEW* and *THE NEW REPUBLIC* during the 1940s and 1950s, and was awarded the Bollingen Prize in Poetry in 1960. Mental instability and drug and alcohol abuse prevented him from sustaining his early success and resulted in his death at age 52. But his work deeply influenced a number of writers of his generation, including Saul BELLOW (who based the character of Von Humboldt FLEISHER in

HUMBOLDT'S GIFT in part on Schwartz) and Bernard MALAMUD.

Scott, Paul (March 25, 1920–March 1, 1978). English novelist. Scott's experience in the British army in India during World War II figures prominently in his subsequent writing, which concerns the role of Westerners in Asia. Scott worked in publishing and headed a literary agency before committing himself to full-time writing, beginning with the novel *Johnnie Sahib* (1952). Scott's masterpiece is his series of books collectively known as THE RAJ QUARTET, which powerfully chronicles the end of British rule in India from multiple points of view; the series comprises *The Jewel in the Crown* (1966), *The Day of the Scorpion* (1968), *The Towers of Silence* (1971), and *A Division of the Spoils* (1975). In the novel *Staying On* (1977; Booker Prize), Scott focused on two of the work's peripheral characters. *The Raj Quartet* was adapted in 1984 as the television miniseries *The Jewel in the Crown*.

Scott, [Sir] Walter (August 15, 1771–September 21, 1832). Scottish poet and novelist. Although trained as a barrister, Scott made his career writing novels and verse inspired by the folklore of the Border country between Scotland and England. He edited the collection of traditional ballads *Minstrelsy of the Scottish Border* (1802–3) before publishing his own verse, romantic narrative poems set in medieval Scotland, including *The Lay of the Last Minstrel* (1805) and THE LADY OF THE LAKE (1810). From 1811 onward, Scott struggled with financial problems with a publishing partner and was forced to write tirelessly to pay off his debts, producing the enormously popular historical novels for which he is now best known. These colorfully drawn stories (published anonymously until 1827) include *Rob Roy* (1817), *The Bride of Lammermoor* (1819), IVANHOE (1819), *Kenilworth* (1821), and *Castle Dangerous* (1831), which are part of the Scottish series THE WAVERLEY NOVELS. He eventually settled the accounts with his prolific production of novels, criticism, and contributions to the major reference work *Encyclopaedia Britannica*.

Seferis, George, *or* **Geōrgos Sepherēs,** *pen name of* Georgos Seferiadis *or* Geōrgos Sepheriadēs (March 13, 1900–September 20, 1971). Greek poet. Born and raised in the Greek community in Smyrna on the Aegean coast of Turkey, Seferis studied law in France and made a career in the Greek foreign service, holding various posts in the Middle East and serving as his country's ambassador to England. He published his first volume of poetry, *Turning Point* (*Strophē*), in 1931; his greatest work, *Mythistorima* (*Mythistorema*), a sequence of 24 related poems based on HOMER's ODYSSEY, appeared in 1935. Influenced by the French Symbolists and T. S. ELIOT, Seferis brought a modernist sensibility and a spare, precise style to a poetry steeped in the Greek cultural tradition. Much of his writing contrasts the tragic condition of modern Greece with its glorious past. Prominent in his home country, Seferis received international recognition in 1963 when he became the first Greek to receive the Nobel Prize in Literature. His work has been widely translated by, among others, HENRY MILLER; collections in English include the bilingual *Collected Poems* (1981). Other works in English include *Days of 1945–1951: A Poet's Journal* (1974) and *On the Greek Style: Selected Essays in Poetry and Hellenism* (1982).

Seifert, Jaroslav (September 23, 1901–January 10, 1986). Czech poet. A beloved literary figure in Czechoslovakia, and a courageous dissident voice during the Nazi and Communist regimes there, Seifert was little known outside his country until he received the Nobel Prize in Literature in 1984. From 1921 until his death, he published some 30 books of poetry, as well as children's books and essays, despite long periods when he could be published only privately or abroad. His simple, unpretentious, lyrical poems lament his country's political travails and celebrate its culture as well as explore private themes of love and beauty. Only a handful of his works have been translated into English, including the long poem *The Plague Column* (*Morový Sloup*, 1977; also translated as *The Plague Monument*), as well as *The Casting of Bells* (*Odlévání Zvonů*, 1967) and *An Umbrella* from Piccadilly (*Deštník z Piccadilly*, 1979). *The Selected Poetry of Jaroslav Seifert* (1986) and *The Early Poetry of Jaroslav Seifert* (1997) are collections in English.

Selby, Hubert, Jr. (July 23, 1928–). American novelist. The Brooklyn-born Selby is best known for the controversial and powerful bestseller *Last Exit to Brooklyn* (1964), an unrelenting portrait of a nocturnal world teeming with depravity and amorality. Selby wrote from his own encounters with the world of drugs and prostitution after his recovery from tuberculosis (contracted during a stint in the Merchant Marine as a teenager) left him wandering and despondent. His next novel was the stream-of-consciousness narrative of a psychopath, *The Room* (1971), followed by the haunting story of a sexual obsessive, *The Demon* (1976), and a novel about heroin addiction, *Requiem for a Dream* (1979). Other works include the short-story collection *Song of the Silent Snow* (1986) and the novel *The Willow Tree* (1998).

Seneca, Lucius Annaeus, *known as* **Seneca (the younger)** (c. 4 B.C.–A.D. 65). Roman philosopher, poet, and playwright. Tutor to the young Nero, the Spanish-born Seneca found great favor at the court. He taught and wrote extensive treatises on Stoicism, a philosophy of moderation, restraint, and mercy. His plays, mainly revisions of Greek myths, including *Thyestes*, *Medea*, *Phaedra*, and *Oedipus*, also emphasize the moral dangers of excessive passion and are noted for their sensational dramaturgy. When Nero became emperor, Seneca accepted a position as a trusted adviser, but found himself in conflict with imperial policy and ultimately resigned. Soon after, he was accused of sedition and committed suicide under Nero's orders. Although Seneca's plays were only privately performed in his day, they became widely known during the Renaissance and particularly influenced Elizabethan playwrights.

Senghor, Léopold Sédar (October 9, 1906–). Senegalese poet. With Aimé CÉSAIRE, Senghor was a leader of the Négritude movement, which affirmed traditional African culture in the face of imperialist domination. He studied at the Sorbonne in Paris before he was drafted into the French army during World War II, when he was interned by the Nazis for two years. Entering politics after the war, he served in the French parliament as a Socialist and was elected president of the newly independent Senegal in 1960, holding the post until 1980. A champion of African artists, Senghor cofounded the cultural journal *Présence Africaine* in 1947 and edited the seminal collection of African poetry *Anthologie de la Nouvelle Poésie Nègre et Malgache* (1948; Anthology of the New Negro and Malagasy Poetry). His own poetry examines his ambivalent relationship with European culture and explores fundamental human concerns from a markedly African perspective. His collections include *Chants d'Ombre* (1945; Shadow Songs), *Éthiopiques* (1956), *Nocturnes* (1961), and *The Collected Poetry* (*Oeuvre Poétique*, 1990). In 1984, he became the first black writer elected to the Académie Française.

Service, Robert (January 16, 1874–September 11, 1958). English-born Canadian poet and novelist. Raised in Glasgow, Service moved in 1895 to Canada, where life in the Yukon Territory inspired his famous ballads "The Shooting of Dan McGrew" and "The Cremation of Sam McGee," published in *Songs of a Sourdough* (1907). Service's popular verse, also including *Ballads of a Cheechako* (1909), and novels, such as *The Trail of '98* (1910), weave colorful, humorous tales of the Gold Rush and life on the Canadian frontier. Service fought in the Canadian army during World War I and settled in France after the war. He published the memoirs *Ploughman of the Moon* (1945) and *Harper of Heaven* (1948), and his *Collected Verse* appeared in 1960.

Sévigné, Marie de Rabutin-Chantal, Marquise de, *known as* **Madame de Sévigné** (February 5, 1626–April 17, 1696). French writer. One of the world's supreme letter writers, whose epistolary portrait of the age of Louis XIV is rivaled only by that recorded by SAINT-SIMON in his memoirs, Marie de Rabutin-Chantal was born in Paris into a family of ancient Burgundian nobility. Before she was ten, she had lost both her parents; an uncle took her into his household, where she received a remarkably liberal education for a young woman of her class. She knew Latin and was fluent in Italian, and her inimitable letters are enlivened with apt quotations from and allusions to the writers she admired, including TASSO, MOLIÈRE, LA FONTAINE, and CORNEILLE. Her unsatisfactory marriage to the rakish Henri de Sévigné ended when in 1651 he was killed in a duel, leaving his widow with two young children. In early 1671 her daughter joined her husband at his ancestral estates in Provence, and it is primarily because of this that French literature gained one of its greatest treasures, for Madame de Sévigné wrote to her daughter obsessively. A vivacious, shrewd, and witty chronicler of the social, sexual, and political intrigues of the court and of the aristocratic and literary salons she herself adorned (Madame de Lafayette and LA ROCHEFOUCAULD were her intimates), through her letters Madame de Sévigné became, as Leigh HUNT observed, "one of the classics of her language, without effort and without intention."

Sexton, Anne, *original surname* Harvey (November 9, 1928–October 4, 1974). American poet. Her teacher and fellow poet ROBERT LOWELL remembered Sexton "as having the large, transparent, breakable, and increasingly ragged wings of a dragonfly—her poor, shy, driven life, the blind terror behind her bravado, her deadly increasing pace... her bravery while she lasted." After one year of junior college, the Massachusetts-born Anne Harvey eloped in 1948 with Alfred "Kayo" Muller Sexton II. After the birth of their first daughter in 1953, she became depressed; finally she was hospitalized and, in November 1956, attempted suicide. About a month later, after seeing a Harvard professor explaining a sonnet on television, Sexton wrote her first poem, and then another. "Rebirth at 29," she called it; within six months she had written more than 50 poems, pouring into formally elegant lines the raw and precise details of her life, including "the commonplaces of the asylum." Popular and critically acclaimed from her first collection, *To Bedlam and Part Way Back* (1960), she frankly explored her lifelong spiritual conflicts and struggles with mental illness, using vernacular imagery, simple rhythms, and sardonic humor. Her major collections include *All My Pretty Ones* (1962), *Live or Die* (1966; Pulitzer Prize), *Love Poems* (1969), *Transformations* (1971), which poetically retells GRIMM fairy tales, and *The Death Notebooks* (1974); posthumous publications include *The Awful Rowing Toward God* (1975) and *No Evil Star: Selected Essays, Interviews, and Prose* (1985). As Sexton explained it, "in the first book I was giving the experience of madness; and in the second book, the causes of madness; and in the third book, finally I find that I was deciding whether to live or to die." She continued struggling against her "terrible taste" for death until her fourth suicide attempt succeeded, on October 4, 1974. She left behind a letter for her oldest daughter, Linda, suggesting, "Talk to my poems."

Shaffer, [Sir] **Peter** (May 15, 1926–). English playwright. Raised in Liverpool and educated at Cambridge, Shaffer first achieved wide success as a playwright with *Five Finger Exercise* in 1958. The play, about a tutor nearly destroyed by a middle-class family, incorporates Shaffer's characteristic interest in psychological dynamics and the nature of deception. *Black Comedy* (1965) cleverly depicts a blackout on a lit stage, and *Equus* (1973) is a disturbing psychological drama about the relationship between a psychiatrist and a young patient, whose psychosis leads him to torture horses. Shaffer's popular *Amadeus* (1980; also screenplay, 1984; Academy Award) dramatizes the life of Mozart through the eyes of his competitor, Salieri. Shaffer's other plays include a pair of one-acts, *The Private Ear* and *The Public Eye* (1962), *The Royal Hunt of the Sun* (1964), and *Lettice and Lovage* (1988). Shaffer's twin brother, Anthony, is also a playwright, best known as the author of the long-running *Sleuth* (1970). Under the joint pseudonym of Peter Anthony, the brothers have published several mystery novels.

Shakespeare, William (baptized April 26, 1564–April 23, 1616). English playwright and poet. For more than four centuries, Shakespeare, with his overwhelming command of language and his peerless ability to create plays and sonnets that capture the essential qualities of human conflict and frailty and characters that explore mankind's deepest existential dilemmas, has exercised an incalculable influence on world literature. His plays have been translated into scores of languages and are constantly performed around the world, and have inspired countless adaptations in other media, including ballets, operas, films, as well as other works of literature. While the facts of Shakespeare's life are relatively well documented in court records and other such prosaic sources, we know nothing of his inner life: no manuscripts, letters, or recorded conversations survive. We do know that he was born in Stratford-upon-Avon into a family of some social standing; that he must have received a solid classical education, to judge from the work; that at 18 he married Anne Hathaway, who was pregnant and eight years his senior; and that he spent most of his professional career in London, his wife and three children remaining in Stratford. By at least 1592, he was well established in the capital as an actor and playwright, for in that year a pamphlet written by a fellow dramatist included a sarcastic reference to the "upstart crow" who "is in his own conceit the only Shake-scene in a country." He then wrote the narrative poems "Venus and Adonis" (1593) and "The Rape of Lucrece" (1594), as well as a sequence of brilliant sonnets, which were published in 1609 without his consent. By 1594, Shakespeare was a member of the theatrical company the Lord Chamberlain's Men, which used the newly built Globe Theatre as its base from 1599 on. Shakespeare's plays were printed in his lifetime from unreliable sources in editions later known as "bad quartos." A somewhat more accurate collection, the "First Folio," was published in 1623. Critics generally group the plays into early works, mainly comedies and histories, and later works, mainly tragedies, with 1600 as a dividing point. Shakespeare's comedies, with estimated dates of composition, include THE COMEDY OF ERRORS (c. 1592), THE TAMING OF THE SHREW (c. 1593), LOVE'S LABOUR'S LOST (c. 1594–95), TWO GENTLEMEN OF VERONA (c. 1594–95), A MIDSUMMER NIGHT'S DREAM (c. 1595–96), THE MERCHANT OF VENICE (c. 1596–97), THE MERRY WIVES OF WINDSOR (c. 1598), MUCH ADO ABOUT NOTHING (c. 1598–99), AS YOU LIKE IT (c. 1599), and TWELFTH NIGHT (c. 1601–2). The histories comprise HENRY VI (Parts I, II, and III, 1589–92), RICHARD III (c. 1594), RICHARD II (c. 1595), KING JOHN (c. 1595), HENRY IV (Parts I and II, c. 1597–98), HENRY V (1599), and the late, unfinished HENRY VIII (c. 1612–13). Mixed-genre tragicomedies include TROILUS AND CRESSIDA (c. 1601–2), ALL'S WELL THAT ENDS WELL (1602), MEASURE FOR MEASURE (c. 1604–5), PERICLES (c. 1608–9), and CYMBELINE (c. 1610). Shakespeare's early tragedies TITUS

"An honest tale speeds best being plainly told."

William Shakespeare, *Richard III* (c. 1594)

ANDRONICUS (c. 1593–94) and ROMEO AND JULIET (1595) were followed by JULIUS CAESAR (c. 1599), HAMLET (c. 1601), OTHELLO (1604), KING LEAR (c. 1605–6), MACBETH (c. 1605–6), ANTONY AND CLEOPATRA (1607), TIMON OF ATHENS (c. 1607), and CORIOLANUS (c. 1608). Shakespeare's late plays THE WINTER'S TALE (c. 1610–11) and THE TEMPEST (c. 1611) inventively blend tragedy, comedy, and romance. By the early 1610s, Shakespeare seems to have begun gradually withdrawing from London's theatrical life, eventually retiring to Stratford. The last surviving work for the theater in which he had a hand is the tragicomedy *The Two Noble Kinsmen* (1613–14), cowritten with John Fletcher. Shakespeare's admirers in the world of literature make a distinguished company, including GOETHE, STENDHAL, PUSHKIN, and HEINE, to name only a few. There have been detractors, including, notably, VOLTAIRE and TOLSTOY, as well as critics ranging from 19th-century moralizers offended by Shakespeare's ribaldry to 20th-century theorists who question the entire concept of literary "greatness." But the general consensus still remains that Shakespeare, as his arch-defender, Harold BLOOM, has put it, "is the largest writer we will ever know."

Shaw, George Bernard (July 26, 1856–November 2, 1950). British playwright and critic. In his time, Shaw was known as much for his larger-than-life personality, and his social activism, as for his sophisticated plays of uncompromising intellectual and ethical passion. Born in Dublin, Shaw moved to London in 1876, where he published music and drama criticism and spoke publicly on behalf of socialist and progressive causes. His early play MRS. WARREN'S PROFESSION, a defense of prostitution, was banned from public performance for its controversial subject matter, but received wide attention (and a production four years later, in 1902) when Shaw published it in *Plays Pleasant and Unpleasant* (1898). The collection also included *Widower's Houses* (1892), ARMS AND THE MAN (1894), and CANDIDA (1897) as well as Shaw's celebrated critical prefaces. Shaw was influential in advocating realistic dramas about social issues, rather than the idealized romantic plays of his time; indeed, he strongly opposed romanticism of any kind. His own dramas deftly criticize social conventions of class and gender with a light but penetrating tone. Shaw's plays also include CAESAR AND CLEOPATRA (1901), MAN AND SUPERMAN (1905), *The Doctor's Dilemma* (1906), MAJOR BARBARA (1907), PYGMALION (1913), *Androcles and the Lion* (1916), HEARTBREAK HOUSE (1920), and SAINT JOAN (1924). He was awarded the Nobel Prize in Literature in 1925; the presentation speech, which compared him to MOLIÈRE and VOLTAIRE, noted the radical ideas that combined in Shaw "with a ready wit, a complete absence of respect for any kind of convention, and the merriest humor—all gathered together in an extravagance which has scarcely ever before appeared in literature."

Sheed, Wilfrid (December 27, 1930–). English-born American novelist, essayist, and biographer. Sheed immigrated to the United States with his parents, the founders of a Roman Catholic publishing house. Educated at Oxford University, he began his career writing literary and film criticism in New York. His satiric novels frequently draw on his own experience in the publishing world. Sheed's first novel, *The Hack* (1963), is set in the offices of a Catholic parish periodical, while *Max Jamison* (1970) portrays the world of Broadway theater critics. Sheed's other novels include *Office Politics* (1966), *Transatlantic Blues* (1978), and *The Boys of Winter* (1987). He has written biographies of subjects ranging from *Muhammad Ali* (1975) and *Clare Booth Luce* (1982) to his own parents in *Frank and Maisie* (1985). *In Love with Daylight* (1995) is a memoir of his struggles with illness and drug and alcohol addiction.

Shelley, Mary, *original name* Mary Wollstonecraft Godwin (August 30, 1797–February 1, 1851). English novelist. The only child of reformist social philosopher William Godwin and feminist Mary Wollstonecraft, Mary Godwin eloped to Europe with a man destined to become another great literary figure, the poet PERCY BYSSHE SHELLEY, in 1814. While in Geneva with her husband and the poet BYRON, she wrote her classic novel FRANKENSTEIN (1818). Uniquely Gothic, romantic, and philosophical, the novel tells the story of a scientist who brings to life a body assembled from cadavers and then must accept accountability for the creature's unbounded actions. During the 1810s and 1820s, Shelley suffered personal tragedies, including several miscarriages, the death of two of her children, and her husband's death by drowning in 1822. Perhaps with autobiographical resonance, her novel *The Last Man* (1826) portrays the sole survivor of a future world beset by plague. Shelley's other novels include *Valperga* (1823) and *Lodore* (1835). She also edited several editions of her husband's poetry and prose.

Shelley, Percy Bysshe (August 4, 1792–July 8, 1822). English poet. The son of a politician, the rebellious and imaginative Shelley rejected the path set before him at Eton and Oxford and was expelled from college after printing "The

Necessity of Atheism" in 1811. He journeyed to Europe with Mary Godwin, who would achieve fame as a novelist (as MARY SHELLEY), in 1814, and traveled throughout the Continent with the poet BYRON. When Shelley's first wife drowned in 1816, he married Godwin. From his early poems, including "HYMN TO INTELLECTUAL BEAUTY" (1816), Shelley explored the romantic themes of love, imagination, and the moral redemption of humanity, with a powerfully lyrical voice. Under duress from creditors, poor health, and his wife's breakdown upon the death of their two children, he nonetheless produced the major verse drama PROMETHEUS UNBOUND (1820), a philosophical revision of AESCHYLUS's classical tragedy PROMETHEUS BOUND. Shelley's best-known works also include the lyrics "TO A SKYLARK" and "ODE TO THE WEST WIND" (1820), the historical verse drama THE CENCI (1819), the elegy for Keats, "ADONAIS" (1821), and the philosophical "Defence of Poetry" (1821). He drowned in the Gulf of Spezia in Italy at age 29.

Shepard, Sam, *original name* Samuel Shepard Rogers (November 5, 1943–). American playwright and screenwriter. Shepard's lyrical, surrealist-influenced plays examine moral issues in American cultural history, and frequently employ imagery from popular mythology, particularly the western. Born in Illinois and raised mainly in southern California, Shepard dropped out of college to pursue a theatrical career in New York. He found success off-off-Broadway, where dozens of his plays were produced in the ten-year period 1965–74, including the Obie Award–winning trio *Chicago* (1965), *Icarus' Mother* (1965), and *Red Cross* (1966) as well as *The Tooth of Crime* (1972) and *Geography of a Horse Dreamer* (1974). Shepard's mature plays, including BURIED CHILD (1978; Pulitzer Prize), TRUE WEST (1980), and FOOL FOR LOVE (1983), explore his themes in the context of domestic family life. Shepard is also an actor, screenwriter, and film director, whose credits include the screenplay for *Paris, Texas* (1984). Short-story collections include *Cruising Paradise* (1996).

Sheridan, Richard Brinsley (November 4, 1751–July 7, 1816). British playwright. "Whatever Sheridan has done or chosen to do has been, *par excellence*, always the *best* of its kind," noted BYRON in his journal in 1813. Indeed, Sheridan's two comic masterpieces of the 18th-century comedy of manners, THE RIVALS (1775) and THE SCHOOL FOR SCANDAL (1777), are still performed more frequently than the works of any other playwright between SHAKESPEARE and SHAW. Among the many indelible characters he created—Lydia Languish, Sir Anthony Absolute, Sir Peter and Lady Teazle, Sir Benjamin Backbite, Joseph and Charles Surface—one, the language-mangling Mrs. Malaprop, has even given a word, "malapropism," to the English lexicon. Raised in a theatrical family, Sheridan attained renown in 1775 with his first play, *The Rivals*, which was followed the same year by *St. Patrick's Day* and the operetta *The Duenna*. In 1776 he became co-owner and manager of the Drury Lane Theatre when he purchased the actor-manager David Garrick's share; there he produced his best-known play, *The School for Scandal*, which wittily portrays the deceptions and misunderstandings between a husband and wife and a father and his two sons. Sheridan's comedies also include the frequently revived *The Critic* (1779), a satire of the sentimental dramas popular in his day. Turning to politics in 1780, he served in Parliament as a Whig until 1812, distinguishing himself as an orator. Several fires at Drury Lane (and the need to rebuild the theater thereafter) led him into debt (and debtor's prison) and he died a pauper. He is buried in Westminster Abbey. *The Letters of Richard Brinsley Sheridan* appeared in three volumes in 1966.

Shields, Carol (June 2, 1935–). American-born Canadian novelist and short-story writer. Shields is acclaimed as a subtle, powerful chronicler of personal struggles with isolation and identity. Born outside Chicago, she married a Canadian engineer and immigrated to Canada, where she has taught at the University of Manitoba and elsewhere. She wrote poetry and sold stories to television before publishing her first novel, *Small Ceremonies*, in 1976.

Shields gained international recognition with the bestselling novel *The Stone Diaries* (1994), which won both Canada's Governor General's Award and the Pulitzer Prize. A fictional account of the life of an ordinary woman born in 1905, the novel is told from multiple points of view and includes mock photographs and letters. Shields often plays with narrative form and genre in her fiction, alluding to the Victorian novel in *Republic of Love* (1992) and incorporating the essay form in *Larry's Party* (1997).

Sholom Aleichem, *pen name of* Solomon J. Rabinowitz (February 18, 1859–May 13, 1916). Russian-born short-story writer, novelist, and playwright, writing in Yiddish. Sholom Aleichem's tragicomedies about Jewish life in Eastern Europe and America helped to establish the vitality and credibility of Yiddish literature. Born in Kiev, Ukraine, he served as a government rabbi in Russia before escaping the 1905 pogroms and later immigrating to the United States. Sometimes referred to as "the Jewish Mark TWAIN," this widely translated humorist wrote more than 40 volumes of novels, plays, and stories; his stories about TEVYE the dairyman formed the basis for the popular musical *Fiddler on the Roof.* His work in English translation is gathered in a number of collections, including *Adventures of Mottel, the Cantor's Son* (1953), *Collected Stories of Sholom Aleichem* (1965), *The Adventures of Menahem-Mendl* (1979), *The Best of Sholom Aleichem* (1979), and *Tevye the Dairyman and the Railroad Stories* (1987). His pen name (variously transliterated) is a common Yiddish greeting that means "peace be with you."

Sidney, [Sir] Philip (November 30, 1554–October 17, 1586). English poet and critic. Born to an aristocratic family, Sidney was educated at Oxford University and held numerous court posts throughout the 1570s and 1580s. His posthumously published writings were a great influence on Elizabethan literature. Sidney's prose romance ARCADIA (1590) contributed to the revival of the pastoral genre. His sonnet sequence "ASTROPHEL AND STELLA"

(1591), which explores an unfulfilled love relationship, is considered among the finest Elizabethan sonnet cycles, along with those by SHAKESPEARE and SPENSER. Sidney also wrote the critical work *The Defense of Poesie* (1595) and an interpretation of the *Psalms*, which remained unpublished until 1823. Sidney was fatally wounded in a military campaign with his uncle, the Earl of Leicester. It was said that as he lay dying, he gave his water bottle to another soldier, saying, "Thy necessity is greater than mine."

Sillitoe, Alan (March 4, 1928–). English novelist and short-story writer. Sillitoe first gained prominence as one of the Angry Young Men, a group of English writers in the 1950s who vividly indicted the class system. His body of fiction portrays the everyday lives of the English working class and their struggles with moral and social conventions. Raised in a poor family in the north of England, Sillitoe worked in factories and enlisted in the Royal Air Force. After publishing his successful first novel, SATURDAY NIGHT AND SUNDAY MORNING (1958), he produced his best-known work, the short-story collection *The Loneliness of the Long Distance Runner* (1959). Sillitoe's other works include the novels *The Ragman's Daughter* (1963), *The Widower's Son* (1976), and *Her Victory* (1982), the short-story collections *Men, Women and Children* (1973) and *Collected Stories* (1995), and *Sun Before Departure: Poems 1974–1982* (1984).

Silone, Ignazio, *pen name of* Secondo Tranquilli (May 1, 1900–August 22, 1978). Italian novelist and journalist. Orphaned by an earthquake as a child, in adulthood Silone rose to prominence as a socialist activist and a humanist writer. He became a founding member of the Italian Communist Party in 1921 and worked at several of the party's newspapers. His early novels, including *Fontamara* (1930) and BREAD AND WINE (*Pane e Vino*, 1937), realistically portray the lives of peasants and criticize their exploitation by landowners. When Italy was overtaken by the Fascists, Silone escaped into exile in Switzerland. He lost faith in communism and broke with the party. Returning to Italy after the war, Silone wrote novels examining contemporary political and social life, including *A Handful of Blackberries* (*Una Manciata di More*, 1952) and *The Fox and the Camelias* (*La Volpe e le Camelie*, 1960). He published the memoir *Emergency Exit* (*Uscita di Sicurezza*) in 1965.

Simenon, Georges (February 13, 1903–September 4, 1989). Belgian novelist. The prolific Simenon enjoyed both critical esteem and popular affection, sustaining through some 300 books a signature style noted for its economy, vivid characterization, and skillful evocation of daily life in collision with the darkest events. Born in Liège, Belgium, Simenon lived in Paris as well as his home country. Beginning as a crime reporter, he wrote countless pulp detective novels under pseudonyms and published his first substantial novel, *The Case of Peter the Lett* (*Pietr-le-Letton*), under his own name in 1931. The novel introduced the Parisian police inspector Jules MAIGRET, whom Simenon would feature in more than 80 mysteries. He also wrote psychological novels, which he called his "Non Maigrets," including *The Stain on the Snow* (*La Neige Était Sale*, 1948), *The Little Saint* (*Le Petit Saint*, 1961), and *The Innocents* (*Les Innocents*, 1972).

Simic, Charles (May 9, 1938–). Yugoslavian-born American poet and translator. Simic's dreamlike, surreal poetry is often folkloric in tone and explores Eastern European cultural themes as well as family, love, and sexuality. Simic immigrated with his family to America in 1954 and studied at New York University. His first collection of poetry, *What the Grass Says*, was published in 1967 to wide acclaim. His collections include *Somewhere Among Us a Stone Is Taking Notes* (1969), *Dismantling the Silence* (1971), *Unending Blues* (1986), *The World Doesn't End* (1989; Pulitzer Prize), *The Book of Gods and Devils* (1990), *Hotel Insomnia* (1993), and *Jackstraws* (1999). *Dime Store Alchemy* (1992) is a group of prose pieces in homage to artist Joseph Cornell, and *Orphan Factory* (1997) is a collection of Simic's memoirs.

Simon, Claude (October 10, 1913–). French novelist. Frequently compared to FAULKNER, Simon writes densely detailed prose that plays with a fragmented sense of time and subjective perception, and sometimes dispenses with punctuation. Born in Madagascar, Simon lived in France and fought for the Resistance after escaping Nazi imprisonment. His first novel, *The Trickster* (*Le Tricheur*, 1945), concerns the German invasion of France. Since publishing *The Wind* (*Le Vent*, 1957), he has been a leading practitioner of the *nouveau roman* (new novel), an experimental mode of storytelling that emphasizes ambiguity. His major work is the cycle of novels that includes *The Grass* (*L'Herbe*, 1959), *The Flanders Road* (*La Route des Flandres*, 1960), *The Palace* (*Le Palace*, 1962), and *Histoire* (1967). Simon's later novels include *Triptych* (*Triptyque*, 1973) and *The Acacia* (*L'Acacia*, 1989). His work became internationally known when he received the Nobel Prize in Literature in 1985.

Simon, [Marvin] Neil (July 4, 1927–). American playwright and screenwriter. Probably the most commercially successful Broadway playwright of the 20th century, Simon has delivered witty dialogue and sharp observations on middle-class life for 40 years. After studying at New York University and writing for the U.S. Army newspaper, Simon was a radio and television gag writer with his brother Danny for more than a decade. Simon's first play, the autobiographical *Come Blow Your Horn* (1960), was a popular success on Broadway. His subsequent comedies, most of which he also adapted for film, include *Barefoot in the Park* (1963), *The Odd Couple* (1965), *Plaza Suite* (1968), *Last of the Red Hot Lovers* (1969), *The Sunshine Boys* (1972), and *Chapter Two* (1977). Simon also wrote an acclaimed autobiographical trilogy comprising *Brighton Beach Memoirs* (1984), *Biloxi Blues* (1985), and *Broadway Bound* (1986), and received the Pulitzer Prize for *Lost in Yonkers* (1991), a darkly comic play about a troubled Jewish family. More recent works include *The Dinner Party* (2000). Simon also wrote the books for several musicals, including

Sweet Charity (1966), *Promises, Promises* (1968), and *They're Playing Our Song* (1979).

Sinclair, Upton (September 20, 1878–November 25, 1968). American novelist, journalist, and essayist. A prolific author who wrote dime novels to pay for his college education, Sinclair was among the best known of the muckrakers, early 20th-century writers who denounced unethical conduct in business and government. His best-known novel, THE JUNGLE (1906), a fictionalized exposé of the Chicago meat-packing industry, generated a public sensation and led to passage of the federal Pure Food and Drug Act. A socialist activist, Sinclair organized a social movement in California against poverty in the 1930s and ran for governor of California in 1934. Other novels include *King Coal* (1917), *Oil!* (1927), and *Boston* (1928), based on the Sacco-Vanzetti trial. The novel *World's End* (1940) initiated an 11-volume series featuring the idealistic Lanny Budd, wealthy scion of an arms dealer, who sets about righting the world's wrongs. Sinclair's *Autobiography* was published in 1962.

Singer, Isaac Bashevis (c. July 14, 1904–July 24, 1991). Polish-born short-story writer and novelist, writing in Yiddish. Singer's work explores Jewish history and culture in both the Old World and the New, and at the same time illuminates universal human conditions. Singer was raised in Poland and educated to be a Hasidic rabbi, following the path of his father and grandfather. Turning to a writing career, he immigrated in 1935 to New York, where he initially worked as a journalist for the *Jewish Daily Forward*. Singer's fiction, written in Yiddish and then translated into English, often by Singer himself in collaboration with professional translators, has a complex publishing history. His works were sometimes first published serially in Yiddish in the *Forward*. In book form, English translations of his works often appeared before editions in Yiddish, and were sometimes split into two books from a single Yiddish original. His novels include *Satan in Goray* (1955; *Der Sotn in Goray*, 1935), THE FAMILY MOSKAT (1950; *Di Familye Mushkat*, 1950), *The Magi-*

cian of Lublin (1960; *Der Kunstnmakher fun Lublin*, 1971), *The Manor* (1967) and *The Estate* (1969) ("Der Hoyf," 1953–55), and

---

"Children...have no use for psychology. They detest sociology. They still believe in God, the family, angels, devils, witches, goblins, logic, clarity, punctuation, and other such obsolete stuff.... When a book is boring, they yawn openly. They don't expect their writer to redeem humanity, but leave to adults such childish illusions."

Isaac Bashevis Singer, Nobel Lecture (1978)

Shosha (1978; "Neshome-Ekspeditsyes," 1974). Among his acclaimed short-story collections are GIMPEL THE FOOL (1957; *Gimpl Tam*, 1963), THE SPINOZA OF MARKET STREET (1961), *A Crown of Feathers* (1973; National Book Award), and *The Image* (1985). Singer wrote several memoirs, including *In My Father's Court* (1966; *Mayn Tatn's Bes-Din-Shtub*, 1956), and the autobiographical trilogy *Love and Exile* (1984; *A Little Boy in Search of God*, 1976; *A Young Man in Search of Love*, 1978; *Lost in America*, 1981) ("Gloybn un Tsveyfel," 1974–78). His *Shadows on the Hudson*, first published in the *Forward* in 1957, was published in English translation in 1998. He was awarded the Nobel Prize in Literature in 1978 for his "impassioned narrative art."

Sitwell, [Dame] **Edith** (September 7, 1887– December 9, 1964). English poet and critic. The iconoclastic Sitwell first attained prominence as a champion of experimental poetry. She coedited the avant-garde anthology *Wheels* (1916–21) with her brothers Osbert and Sacheverell Sitwell and issued her own books of poetry, including *The Mother and Other Poems* (1915) and *Clown's Houses* (1918). Sitwell's early poetry is eccentrically modernist, marked by a highly stylized, musical prosody. Indeed, in 1922 she caused a sensation by reading her long poem *Façade* to the accompaniment of a jazz composition by William Walton. Sitwell became more widely recognized for the grave, spiritual poems she wrote during World War II, such as "Still Falls the Rain" (1942), which links the London blitz with the Crucifixion. Other volumes of poetry in this vein include *Street Songs* (1942), *The Song of the Cold* (1945), *Gardeners and Astronomers* (1953), and *Music and Ceremonies* (1963). She also published many prose works, including *The English Eccentrics* (1933), the novel *I Live Under a Black Sun* (1937), *A Poet's Notebook* (1943), and *Taken Care Of: An Autobiography* (1965).

Skelton, John (c. 1460–June 21, 1529). English poet. With his wit and energetic verse, Skelton was renowned in academic and court circles. He was named Poet Laureate (an academic honor) at Oxford and Cambridge and served, from 1512 onward, as an adviser to his former pupil, King Henry VIII. Skelton's distinctive verse, labeled "skeltonic," falls between medieval and Renaissance modes of poetry. It is noted for a quick, loose meter, an irregular use of rhyme, and an often disjunctive tone. Skelton's major extant works, published in 1568, include the self-laudatory "A Garlande of Laurell," the scathing satires of court life "The Bowge of Courte" and "Why Come Ye Not to Courte," the morally critical "The Tunnyng of Elynour Rummyng," and the complaint about hypocritical clergymen, "Collyn Cloute." Skelton spent his last years at Westminster Abbey, where he apparently took sanctuary from his longtime adversary, Cardinal Wolsey, the powerful Lord Chancellor.

Škvorecký, Josef (September 27, 1924–). Czech-born novelist, short-story writer, screenwriter, and translator. Škvorecký's first novel, *The Cowards* (*Zbabělci*, 1958), an autobiographical satire about the Soviet takeover of a small Czech town at the end of World War II, was banned on publication by the Czech Communist government. The adventures of its narrator, Danny Smiřický, were continued through several books, including *The Republic of Whores* (*Tankový Prapor*, 1971), *The Bass Saxophone* (*Bassaxofon*, 1967), *The Miracle Game* (*Mirákl*,

1972), and *The Engineer of Human Souls* (*Příběh Inženýra Lidských Duší*, 1977). In 1969, the author and his wife, the writer Zdena Salivarová, immigrated to Canada, where in 1971 they started Sixty-Eight Publishers to publish the writing of Czech exiles and dissidents. Škvorecký's other works include collections of mystery stories, such as *The Mournful Demeanor of Lieutenant Borvka* (*Smutek Poručíka Borůvky*, 1966) and *Sins for Father Knox* (*Hříchy pro Pátera Knoxe*, 1973); and two historical novels, *Dvorak in Love* (*Scherzo Capriccioso*, 1984), based on the Czech composer's two sojourns to America in the 1890s, and *The Bride of Texas* (*Nevěsta z Texasu*, 1992), about Czech soldiers who fought for the Union during the American Civil War.

Smith, Stevie, *original name* Florence Margaret Smith (September 20, 1902–March 7, 1971). English poet and novelist. Smith is best known as a darkly comic poet, although she also published several acclaimed novels, including *Novel on Yellow Paper* (1936). Her mordant, witty, idiosyncratic poetry treats such topics as English culture, women's experience, and human pain. Her collections, often illustrated with her own line drawings, include *A Good Time Was Had by All* (1937), *Not Waving But Drowning* (1957), and *The Frog Prince* (1966). Smith lived most of her life with the maiden aunt who raised her, in the London suburb of Palmers Green. She worked as a secretary at a publishing house for 20 years while pursuing her vocation as a writer. She was awarded the Queen's Gold Medal for Poetry in 1969. Her *Collected Poems* was released in 1975.

Smollett, Tobias (baptized March 19, 1721–September 17, 1771). English novelist, poet, and critic. Known for his novels of adventurous travel, Smollett himself sailed for several years with the British Navy. Trained as a surgeon in his native Scotland, Smollett joined the Navy as a surgeon's mate in 1740 and, after becoming an M.D. in 1750, practiced medicine in London. His first novels, *The Adventures of* RODERICK RANDOM (1748) and *The Adventures of* PEREGRINE PICKLE (1751), are picaresque tales, colorfully depicting their roguish protagonists' journeys and satirizing 18th-century British society. Also the editor of various magazines, Smollett was imprisoned for three months in 1760 after his Tory *Critical Review* published a libelous article. In 1763, he moved to the Continent, writing the acidulous *Travels Through France and Italy* (1766). His last work, the renowned *The Expedition of HUMPHRY CLINKER* (1771), is an epistolary novel about a family's travels and their discovery of an illegitimate relation.

Snow, C[harles] **P**[ercy] [Baron Snow of Leicester] (October 15, 1905–July 1, 1980). English novelist. Raised in a lower-middle-class family, Snow earned a Ph.D. in physics at Cambridge and joined the faculty as a research physicist. From 1945 onward, he held numerous government posts in scientific departments. His best-known novels are those in the 11-volume series *Strangers and Brothers* (1940–70), which draw from his own experiences as they trace the life of Lewis Eliot, a lawyer whose career takes him into academic, political, and scientific circles. Concerned with the ethical and moral problems arising at the intersection of science and society, the series includes the acclaimed *The Masters* (1951), a study of power dynamics at a university, and *Corridors of Power* (1964), observations on life in Parliament. Snow also wrote critical studies and essays, among them the important *The Two Cultures and the Scientific Revolution* (1959), which began as a lecture. In it, he raised an alarm about the lack of communication between humanists and scientists. His argument received wide attention, and is still a reference point in contemporary discussion.

Snyder, Gary (May 8, 1930–). American poet and essayist. A visionary poet and ecological activist/philosopher, Snyder believes passionately that the "world is our consciousness, and it surrounds us." Born in San Francisco, he began his lifelong immersion in Amerindian and East Asian cultures while studying at Reed College in Portland, Oregon, and later studied Oriental languages at Berkeley. In 1956, he moved to

Japan and began an intensive Zen Buddhist practice (he returned permanently to the United States in 1968, and now makes his home in the foothills of the California Sierras). Associated with the San Francisco Beat poets (he took part in the famous reading at the Six Gallery in 1956 when Allen GINSBERG read *Howl*, and appears in Jack KEROUAC's novel *The Dharma Bums* as Japhy Ryder), he published his first collection, *Riprap*, in 1959. Snyder's subsequent volumes of poetry include *The Back Country* (1967), *Regarding Wave* (1970), *Turtle Island* (1974; Pulitzer Prize), *No Nature: New and Selected Poems* (1992), and *Mountains and Rivers Without End* (1996). His essays are collected in *The Practice of the Wild* (1990).

Solzhenitsyn, Aleksandr (December 11, 1918–). Russian novelist. Born in the Caucasus and educated at Rostov University, Solzhenitsyn served in the army during World War II, until he was arrested and sent to prison camp in 1945 for writing a letter denigrating Stalin. Released eight years later, Solzhenitsyn was not allowed

---

"A great writer is, so to speak, a second government in his country. And for that reason no regime has ever loved great writers, only minor ones."

Aleksandr Solzhenitsyn, *The First Circle* (1968), translated by Thomas P. Whitney

---

back into central Russia until 1956. His portrayal of labor camp life in the novella *ONE DAY IN THE LIFE OF IVAN DENISOVICH* (*Odin Den' Ivana Denisovicha*, 1962) caused a sensation upon its publication in the magazine *NOVYĬ MIR*. His novels *THE CANCER WARD* (*Rakovyĭ Korpus*, 1968), *THE FIRST CIRCLE* (*V Kruge Pervom*, 1968), and *August 1914* (*Avgust 1914*, 1971), were first published only in the West, raising Solzhenitsyn's international stature. He was awarded the Nobel Prize in Literature in 1970, but was forced to leave the Soviet Union a year after the Paris publication of the searing

Gulag Archipelago (*Arkhipelag GULag*, 1973), a historical account of prisoners' experiences in Soviet labor camps. While living in the United States, he completed the four-novel cycle *The Red Wheel* (*Krasnoe Koleso*, 1971–91), incorporating an expanded version of *August 1914*, which portrays the origins of the Russian Revolution. Under perestroika, Solzhenitsyn's citizenship was restored in 1990, and he returned to Russia in 1994.

Sophocles, *in Greek,* Sophoklēs (c. 496 B.C.–406 B.C.). Greek playwright. One of the three great classical Greek tragedians (the others being AESCHYLUS and EURIPIDES), Sophocles wrote powerful dramas that were praised by ARISTOTLE as exemplary of the genre. Sophocles' tragic heroes seek moral truths, even if they bring about destruction, as in OEDIPUS THE KING (Greek *Oidipous Tyrannos*, Latin *Oedipus Rex*) and *Oedipus at Colonus* (*Oidipous epi Kōlōnōi*). Of his more than 100 plays, only seven complete works are extant: the Oedipus works, ANTIGONE (*Antigonē*), *The Women of Trachis* (*Trachiniai*), *Philoctetes* (*Philoktētēs*), ELECTRA (*Ēlektra*), and *Ajax* (*Aias*). Renowned for the precise, taut construction of his plays, Sophocles also contributed innovations to Greek dramatic form, adding a third lead actor to the traditional two, and producing self-contained tragedies rather than trilogies. Celebrated throughout Athens as a playwright, Sophocles was also a noted musician, priest, and statesman.

Soyinka, Wole, *in full* Akinwande Oluwole Soyinka (July 13, 1934–). Nigerian playwright, poet, and critic. Educated in England, Soyinka studied drama before returning to Nigeria, where he established the Masks theater company and taught at various universities. A staunch advocate of political freedom, he was jailed twice by the Nigerian military regime in the 1960s. Soyinka's writing examines moral and ethical conflict in modern African society and frequently draws on native folk traditions. His dramas include *Dance of the Forests* (1960), *The Lion and the Jewel* (1962), *Madmen and Specialists* (1970), *Death and the King's Horseman* (1975), and *The Beatification of Area Boy*

(1996). Among his poetry collections are *Idanre* (1967), *Poems from Prison* (1969), and *Mandela's Earth* (1988). Soyinka has also written novels, including *The Season of Anomy* (1974), and numerous works of literary and social criticism on African subjects. He published an autobiography, *Aké: The Years of Childhood*, in 1981. In 1986, he became the first black African to be awarded the Nobel Prize in Literature.

Spark, [Dame] **Muriel,** *original name* Muriel Camberg (February 1, 1918–). British novelist and short-story writer. A brilliant satirist in the tradition of EVELYN WAUGH and Graham GREENE, Spark is best known for THE PRIME OF MISS JEAN BRODIE (1961), which was adapted into a celebrated film. She was raised in Edinburgh by a Jewish father and Protestant mother, converting to Catholicism in her mid-30s. Having something of an outsider's perspective has fed her fiction, as did periods living abroad, in South Africa, Rome, and New York. She began her literary career in London as editor of *The Poetry Review* (1947–49) and as a poet, critic, and biographer, writing the first of many novels, *The Comforters*, in 1957. Her fiction, which often turns on serious ethical or moral dilemmas or on the relation between illusion and reality, has consistently earned critical esteem for crisp plotting, sly irony, and acerbic wit. Among her other works are MEMENTO MORI (1959), *The Ballad of Peckham Rye* (1960), THE GIRLS OF SLENDER MEANS (1963), *The Mandelbaum Gate* (1965), *Loitering with Intent* (1981), *The Stories of Muriel Spark* (1985), *A Far Cry from Kensington* (1988), *Reality and Dreams* (1998), and *Aiding and Abetting* (2000). Her autobiography, *Curriculum Vitae*, appeared in 1992.

Spender, [Sir] **Stephen** (February 28, 1909–July 16, 1995). English poet, short-story writer, and critic. Although his poetry is often personal and lyrical, Spender is also known for his early leftist political poetry. As a student at Oxford University, he counted the socially committed poets W. H. AUDEN, Louis MACNEICE, and C. DAY-LEWIS among his friends; the group gained the nickname "the pylon poets," after Spender's poem about industry and mechanization, "The Pylons" (1933). The writer Christopher ISHERWOOD was also a friend at this time, the two sharing a flat in Berlin during the early 1930s. Among Spender's volumes of poetry are *Poems* (1933), *The Still Centre* (1939), *Ruins and Visions* (1942), *Poems of Dedication* (1947), *The Edge of Being* (1949), and *The Generous Days* (1971); his short stories are collected in *The Burning Cactus* (1936). He was the coeditor of the magazines HORIZON (from 1939 to 1941) and *Encounter* (from 1953 to 1967), and his critical writing is collected in *The Destructive Element* (1935), *The Creative Element* (1953), *The Making of a Poem* (1955), and *The Struggle of the Modern* (1963). His *Collected Poems: 1928–1985* appeared in 1986. His autobiography, *World Within World* (1951), superbly records his intellectual development and artistic milieu.

Spenser, Edmund (c. 1552–January 13, 1599). English poet. Spenser's innovative sonnets and rich epic poetry made him one of the greatest Elizabethan poets. Born in London, Spenser was educated at Cambridge and joined the household of the Earl of Leicester, the uncle of the poet Sir Philip SIDNEY. There he wrote his first major work, *The Shepheardes Calender* (1579), comprising twelve pastoral poems in lively metrical form. Soon after, Spenser moved to Ireland, where he headed an estate in Cork and wrote an elegy for Sidney, "Astrophel" (1591), and his best-known work, the epic THE FAERIE QUEENE (1590–96). A heroic romance telling of the adventures of 12 knights, *The Faerie Queene* incorporates moral allegory into its dynamic narrative. It introduced a new, influential poetic form, the Spenserian stanza, based on the Italian scheme of ottava rima. Spenser's other works include the sonnet sequence *Amoretti* (1595), about courtship, and the marriage hymn "Epithalamion" (1595), both of which reflect his own marriage in 1594. The notable short poems "The Ruines of Time" and "The Teares of the Muses" were published in 1591.

Stead, Christina (July 17, 1902–March 31, 1983). Australian novelist. With cutting political and social truths and a protofeminist perspective, Stead's work provides dark commentary on 20th-century life and obsessions. Raised and educated in Sydney, Stead traveled extensively with her American husband, novelist William Blake, living in New York and Europe. Her first book, the collection *The Salzburg Tales* (1934), was followed the same year by the novel *Seven Poor Men of Sydney*. Her best-known novel, THE MAN WHO LOVED CHILDREN (1940), is an ironic indictment of the American family and is acclaimed for its psychological and social perceptiveness. Stead's other novels include *For Love Alone* (1945), *Letty Fox: Her Luck* (1946), and *Dark Places of the Heart* (1966), all of which feature ambitious women in search of themselves.

Stegner, Wallace (February 18, 1909–April 13, 1993). American novelist. Born in Iowa and transplanted to Utah with his family in 1921, Stegner wrote insightful fiction about life in the American West, exploring both its myths and realities. His first novel, *Remembering Laughter* (1937), was followed by *On a Darkling Plain* (1940) and the popular frontier tale *The Big Rock Candy Mountain* (1943). His best-known novels are *Angle of Repose* (1971; Pulitzer Prize), about an elderly historian who investigates the frontier lives of his grandparents, and *The Spectator Bird* (1976; National Book Award), which portrays a man's journey to his mother's birthplace in Denmark. Among Stegner's many historical studies of the West are *Mormon Country* (1941), *Wolf Willow* (1962), and *The Gathering of Zion* (1964). His collection of autobiographical essays, *Where the Bluebird Sings to the Lemonade Springs*, was published in 1992.

Stein, Gertrude (February 3, 1874–December 20, 1946). American poet, novelist, playwright, and essayist. Stein spent her childhood in Germany, France, and California, then studied psychology with William James at Radcliffe College and anatomy at Johns Hopkins University, before immigrating to Paris in 1902. Living there for the rest of her life with her companion and secretary, Alice B. Toklas, Stein was at the center of the modernist literary and artistic scene and counted Picasso, Matisse, HEMINGWAY, and FORD MADOX FORD among her intimates. An important modern art collector, Stein modeled her experimental compositional style on Cubism, exploring techniques of repetition, concreteness, and immediacy. Her works include *Three Lives* (1909), a portrait of working-class women; the poetry collection *TENDER BUTTONS: OBJECTS, FOOD, ROOMS* (1914); novels, including the thousand-page-long *The Making of Americans* (1925; written 1906–8), and *Lucy Church Amiably: A Novel of Romantic Beauty and Nature and Which Looks Like an Engraving* (1930); and the librettos for two operas composed by Virgil Thomson, *Four Saints in Three Acts* (1934) and *The Mother of Us All* (1947). She published her memoirs as *THE AUTOBIOGRAPHY OF ALICE B. TOKLAS* (1933) and *Everybody's Autobiography* (1937). Widely known for her bons mots and literary quips, Stein originated the line "rose is a rose is a rose" (in her *Geography and Plays*, 1922).

Steinbeck, John (February 27, 1902–December 20, 1968). American novelist and short-story writer. Combining social realism and romantic lyricism, Steinbeck's fiction affirms the lives of simple, hard-working people. His native California is the setting for much of his work, including his first successful novel, *TORTILLA FLAT* (1935). A marine biology major at Stanford University, Steinbeck expressed his deep feelings for the sea in his journal *Sea of Cortez* (1941) and in the novella *The Pearl* (1947). His most widely known novels, however, center on impassioned depictions of the itinerant farm worker and the rural landscape, as in *OF MICE AND MEN* (1937). *THE GRAPES OF WRATH* (1939; Pulitzer Prize) chronicles the migration of a Dust Bowl refugee family from Oklahoma to California. Other notable works include *CANNERY ROW* (1945), the family epic *EAST OF EDEN* (1952), and the short-story collection *THE RED PONY* (1937). He recounted a trip across America with his elderly poodle in

Travels with Charley (1962). Steinbeck won the Nobel Prize in Literature in 1962.

Stendhal, *pen name of* Marie Henri Beyle (January 23, 1783–March 23, 1842). French novelist. One of France's greatest and most cosmopolitan writers, Stendhal was for the most part ignored by his contemporaries (although BALZAC was an admirer); he asserted that he wrote for another century, and the prophecy came true. He has been and is revered by the greatest artists of the 20th century, Wallace STEVENS calling him "the embodiment of the principle of prose," adding, "No doubt Stendhal will survive FLAUBERT, because Stendhal is a point of reference for the mature, while Flaubert is a point of reference for the artist, and perhaps for the immature." A realist in an age of Romantics, he contributed—posthumously—to the evolution of the novel with works noted for their social and psychological penetration, limpid and cool prose, ironic detachment, subtle analysis of the follies of the heart, and realist precision, the latter brilliantly manifest in the Waterloo chapters of *THE CHARTERHOUSE OF PARMA* (*La Chartreuse de Parme*, 1839). The novel, he said famously, should be a "mirror of life," reflecting both the "blue of the skies and the mire of the road below." Born in Grenoble, Beyle passed the examinations for the École Polytechnique in Paris but did not attend, instead securing a position in the Ministry of War, and later joining Napoleon's campaigns in Italy, Germany, Austria, Hungary, and Russia. Following the fall of Napoleon, he lived and worked in both Italy and France, serving desultorily as French Consul at Civatavecchia, the port city near Rome, from 1831 until his death. His thrilling masterpieces, *The Charterhouse of Parma* and *THE RED AND THE BLACK* (*Le Rouge et le Noir*, 1830), chronicle the rise and fall of ambitious heroes "making themselves"—much like their creator—in the Napoleonic and post-Napoleonic eras. "No one," wrote V. S. PRITCHETT, "has so defined and botanized the fervour, uncertainty, conceit, timidity and single-mindedness of young men, their dash, their shames, their calculation for tactics and gesture." Of his superb style, which

strikes contemporary readers as so quintessentially modern, Pritchett said accurately: "Each
sentence of his plain prose is a separate shock."
Stendhal's other works include his first published
book, *Lives of Haydn, Mozart and Metastasio*
(*Vies de Haydn, de Mozart et de Métastase*,
1814); *Love* (*De L'Amour*, 1822), an obsessive
dissection of the secrets of seduction and
romance, and Stendhal's favorite among his
works; *Racine and Shakespeare* (*Racine et
Shakespeare I and II*, 1823 and 1825), a Romantic manifesto that defines Classicism as that
which gives "the greatest possible pleasure to
[one's] great-grandfathers"; and *The Life of
Rossini* (*Vie de Rossini*, 1823), a huge and fascinating biography of one of his heroes, the great
Italian opera composer Giacomo Rossini.
Posthumously published works include the
autobiographical *Memoirs of an Egotist* (*Souvenirs d'Égotisme*, 1892); *The Life of Henry Brulard* (*La Vie de Henri Brulard*, 1890), a thinly
disguised autobiography masquerading as a
novel; and the unfinished *Lucien Leuwen* (first
"complete" edition published 1894), a novel
whose purpose was to be, said Stendhal, "exact
chemistry," describing "with exactitude what
others indicate with a vague and eloquent
phrase." Beyle, who had assumed more than
200 pseudonyms throughout the course of his
life, most probably adopted his most famous
pen name (adding the "h") from the small German city of Stendal, where a general he had
once served as an aide-de-camp had enjoyed a
military victory.

Sterne, Laurence (November 13, 1713–March
18, 1768). Irish-born English novelist and clergyman. Sterne's eccentric nine-volume comic
masterpiece, *The Life and Opinions of TRIS-
TRAM SHANDY, Gentleman* (1759–67), broke
new ground, as its author experimented with
innovative narrative devices and an early form
of stream-of-consciousness writing, based on the
philosopher John Locke's theories of perception
and the free association of ideas; as critic Q. D.
Leavis noted, the book "requires careful and
persevering reading, but the reward is an
extremely subtle kind of pleasure." Born at
Clonmel, Sterne was educated at Cambridge

and began writing while serving as a vicar in
York. His first book, a satire on the ecclesiastical
courts, *A Political Romance*, was burned upon
its publication in 1759. Later that year, the first
two volumes of *Tristram Shandy* appeared,
bringing Sterne instant celebrity, although the
book's critical reception was poor. Despite his
wife's nervous breakdown and his own chronic
weakness owing to tuberculosis, Sterne continued to work on *Tristram Shandy*, publishing
four volumes in 1761, two in 1766, and the
final volume in 1767. His family moved to
France in 1762, inspiring his last book, the
comic novel *A Sentimental Journey Through
France and Italy* (1768).

Stevens, Wallace (October 2, 1879–August 2,
1955). American poet. "Wallace Stevens,"
wrote Marianne MOORE, a great admirer, "is
beyond fathoming, he is so strange, it is as if he
had a morbid secret he would rather perish
than disclose, and just as he tells it out in his
sleep, he changes into an uncontradictable
judiciary with a gown and gavel." One of the
greatest modernist poets, Stevens received relatively scant critical recognition during his lifetime, although in the last year of his life his
Collected Poems (1954) won both the National
Book Award and the Pulitzer Prize. Part of
Stevens's secret strangeness is that, to many, he
seemed so little the poet: he was a portly, prosperous insurance lawyer who went to work
every day for 39 years with the Hartford Accident and Indemnity Company, he never traveled to Europe, and he periodically stopped
writing poetry altogether, once for almost a
decade, with apparently no damage to his psyche—or, when he resumed, to his verse. Born
and raised in Reading, Pennsylvania, the son of
a lawyer and a schoolteacher, he was educated
at Harvard and worked briefly as a journalist (a
tedious profession, he thought) before declaring that he would henceforth pursue the "literary life." However, he soon bowed to his father's
wishes and enrolled in law school in New York
City. Stevens took his law degree, and thereafter his life was remarkably unremarkable–
except that, as Frank KERMODE has observed,
"no poet ever wrote so fixedly from within the

human head as Stevens." With a spectacularly pinwheeling imagination he explored favorite themes, including his longing to show that poetry could fill the modern void created by the absence of God; and, especially, the nature of poetry itself in such great poems as "The Man with the Blue Guitar" (1937), an inquiry into the imagination and its role in the tangible world. Stevens was a methodical and cautious man, and his first volume, *Harmonium* (1923), containing such celebrated poems as "Thirteen Ways of Looing at a Blackbird" and "The Emperor of Ice-Cream," was published when he was 44. Other major collections include *Ideas of Order* (1935; enl. ed. 1936), *The Man with the Blue Guitar & Other Poems* (1937), *Parts of a World* (1942), *Transport to Summer* (1947), and *The Auroras of Autumn* (1950). *The Necessary Angel: Essays on Reality and the Imagination* appeared in 1951. Long condescended to as an aesthete whose work was overly abstract, symbolic, and "philosophical," Stevens was in fact deeply engaged with the real world: "The significance of the poetic act," he stressed in a speech upon being awarded an honorary degree from Bard College, "is that it is evidence. It is instance and illustration.... Above all it is a new engagement with life." The *Collected Poems* and various posthumously published collections of uncollected poetry and prose, fragments, and diaries are now all superseded by the Library of America's *Collected Poetry and Prose* (1997), edited by Kermode and Joan Richardson.

Stevenson, Robert Louis (November 13, 1850–December 3, 1894). Scottish novelist, travel writer, poet, essayist, and short-story writer. Stevenson was born in Edinburgh and studied law, although he never practiced it. Plagued with tubercular illnesses throughout his life, he traveled widely in search of remedies and healthful climates. He began publishing essays and travel writings in the late 1870s. To entertain his stepson, he invented a story about a search for pirate treasure, which grew to become the beloved adventure novel *TREASURE ISLAND* (1883). The book brought him considerable acclaim, as did his subsequent works: *KID-*

NAPPED (1886), a romantic adventure story set in 18th-century Scotland, and *The Strange Case of DR. JEKYLL AND MR. HYDE* (1886), a nightmarish tale of chemically induced dual personality. Among Stevenson's other popular volumes are *A Child's Garden of Verses* (1885) and *THE MASTER OF BALLANTRAE* (1889). In 1889, the peripatetic writer settled on a Samoan island, and died there five years later, leaving behind the unfinished *Weir of Hermiston* (1896).

Stoker, Bram, *in full* Abraham Stoker (November 8, 1847–April 20, 1912). Irish novelist. Stoker made his name by creating one of the 20th century's most popular and fearsome characters, the suave but deadly vampire known as Count Dracula. Born in Dublin and educated at Trinity College, Stoker began his career as a civil servant, writing theater reviews and horror stories on the side. In 1878 he became secretary and manager to the esteemed actor Sir Henry Irving and his London-based Lyceum Theatre, a position he held for 27 years. During this time, he was also hard at work on his first novel, *The Snake's Pass* (1890), and then on *DRACULA* (1897). Stoker's other works include *The Jewel of Seven Stars* (1904), *The Lair of the White Worm* (1911), and *Personal Reminiscences of Henry Irving* (1906).

Stone, Robert (August 21, 1937–). American novelist and short-story writer. Widely praised for novels that combine gripping plots and gritty realism with broad historical, political, and moral themes, Stone vividly captures the drug use, violence, and distrust of authority of the Vietnam War era and beyond. Born in Brooklyn, Stone dropped out of high school shortly before graduation to join the Navy. Later, he attended New York and Stanford universities. Critics praised his first novel, *A Hall of Mirrors* (1967), as an exceptional debut. Stone went to Vietnam as a journalist in 1971, and drew on this experience for his novel *Dog Soldiers* (1974; National Book Award), the story of a Marine veteran double-crossed in a heroin-smuggling scheme. Among Stone's other works are the novels *A Flag for Sunrise* (1981), set in a turbulent Central America; *Children of Light*

(1986), a dark portrait of Hollywood; *Outerbridge Reach* (1992), about a round-the-world sailing race gone awry; *Damascus Gate* (1998), which explores religious conflicts in contemporary Jerusalem; and the story collection *Bear and His Daughter* (1997).

Stoppard, [Sir] Tom, *original name* Tomas Straussler (July 3, 1937–). Czech-born English playwright. One of England's most intellectually dazzling contemporary playwrights, Stoppard explores the fundamental questions of human existence with brilliance and wit. Born in Zlin, Czechoslovakia, Stoppard moved with his family to Bristol, England, as a child, taking the name of his English stepfather. In 1954 he left school to work as a journalist, and in 1960 settled in London. His early, audacious play ROSENCRANTZ AND GUILDENSTERN ARE DEAD (1966) brought him international attention for its focus on minor characters in SHAKESPEARE's *HAMLET.* Further success followed with *Jumpers* (1972), a philosophical farce; *TRAVESTIES* (1974), in which the figures James JOYCE, V. I. Lenin, and Tristan Tzara collaborate on an Oscar WILDE play; and *The Real Thing* (1982), a wry drama of love and adultery. Among his more recent works are *ARCADIA* (1993), a comedy of ideas set in two centuries; *Indian Ink* (1994), about a woman poet's journey to India in the 1930s; and *The Invention of Love* (1997), about scholar/poet A. E. HOUSMAN. Stoppard's numerous radio, television, and film credits include coauthoring the screenplays for Terry Gilliam's *Brazil* (1985) and for *Shakespeare in Love* (1998; Academy Award).

Stout, Rex (December 1, 1886–October 27, 1975). American novelist. Stout is best known as the author of detective novels and stories starring master sleuth Nero WOLFE, who operated from a New York City brownstone, aided by his able, wise-cracking legman (and narrator of the tales), Archie GOODWIN. Over four decades, the gourmandizing, orchid-fancying Wolfe cracked 73 apparently insoluble cases, from *Fer-de-Lance* (1934) to *A Family Affair* (1975)—a long run all the more remarkable considering that Stout began the series in his late 40s, after a career

as a magazine writer and critically respected (but little-known) novelist. Early experiences in the Navy—he served on Theodore Roosevelt's yacht—and years spent traveling around the country working at odd jobs (storing "11,000 impressions a minute") nourished his imagination as he crafted his complex, elegant tales without notes or outlines. P. G. WODEHOUSE praised Stout's mysteries as "rereadable": on repeated readings, "I know exactly what is coming and how it is all going to end, but it doesn't matter. That's *writing.*"

Stowe, Harriet Beecher (June 14, 1811–July 1, 1896). American novelist. Stowe's novel *UNCLE TOM'S CABIN* (1852) brought the cruel realities of American slavery to the attention of an international audience. Born in Litchfield, Connecticut, Stowe was the daughter of a well-known Congregationalist minister. At age 18, she and her family moved to Cincinnati, a city divided over race. There, she worked as a teacher, married an eminent clergyman, and became involved in the Abolitionist movement. A vision of an old black slave, experienced during a church service in Maine, moved her to write *Uncle Tom's Cabin*, a novel whose depiction of "life among the lowly" immediately attracted a devoted readership worldwide. Within ten years, some three million copies of the novel had been sold, and it had been translated into more than 30 languages. President Abraham Lincoln jokingly credited Stowe with having started the Civil War with her book. Stowe was also a frequent contributor to *THE ATLANTIC MONTHLY.* Her other works include *A Key to Uncle Tom's Cabin* (1853), in which she recounts the real-life sources for her famous novel, and *The Minister's Wooing* (1859) and *Oldtown Folks* (1869), novels that capture the flavor of life in rural New England.

Strand, Mark (April 11, 1934–). American poet. One of America's most acclaimed contemporary poets and poetry advocates, Strand, who served as U.S. Poet Laureate for 1990–91, writes haunting, dreamlike poems of masterful brevity that juxtapose the magical with the commonplace. Born on Prince Edward Island in

Canada, Strand was brought to the United States as a child. He was educated at Antioch College, Yale University, the University of Florence, and the University of Iowa, and has held several teaching posts. Strand made his debut with the collection *Sleeping with One Eye Open* (1964), and received widespread critical attention for his second volume, *Reasons for Moving* (1968), which included surreal poems such as "Eating Poetry." Self and family figure prominently in his 1970s collections, *Darker* (1970); *The Story of Our Lives* (1973), which includes the well-known "Elegy for My Father"; and *The Late Hour* (1978). Strand has also published translations, books on art, children's books, and short stories, and has edited a number of distinguished anthologies. Among his later collections are the book-length poem *Dark Harbor* (1993) and the Pulitzer Prize–winning *Blizzard of One* (1998).

Strindberg, [Johan] **August** (January 22, 1849–May 14, 1912). Swedish playwright, novelist, short-story writer, autobiographer, and essayist. Strindberg is the protean central figure of Swedish literature. Despite a tormented personal life (three failed marriages deeply marked his writing) and a contentious public life, he was astoundingly prolific, a virtuoso of wide-ranging themes, moods, styles, and forms. His initial success came with his novel about Stockholm bohemians, *The Red Room* (*Röda Rummet*, 1879), a breakthrough for Swedish realism. His work eventually evolved into the naturalism and psychological determinism of two celebrated tragedies about the battle of the sexes, *THE FATHER* (*Fadren*, 1887) and his most frequently performed play, *MISS JULIE* (*Fröken Julie*, 1889). Other works of this period include the provocative short-story collection *Married* (*Giftas*, 1884–85), which occasioned a trial for blasphemy; the autobiographical *The Son of a Servant* (*Tjänstekvinnans Son*, 1886); and another popular novel, *The People of Hemsö* (*Hemsöborna*, 1887). After a near breakdown in the mid-1890s (the "Inferno crisis," described in *Inferno*, 1897), Strindberg turned to Symbolism and Expressionism, often influenced by a Swedenborgian mysticism, as in the poignant *A*

Dream Play (*Ett Drömspel*, published 1902, performed 1907); the "chamber drama" *GHOST SONATA* (*Spöksonaten*, 1908); and his last play, the symbolically autobiographical *The Great Highway* (*Stora Landsvägen*, 1910). This period also produced *THE DANCE OF DEATH* (*Dödsdansen*, published 1901, performed 1905), about a deadlocked marriage; an important cycle of plays about Swedish rulers; and the exquisite miniature *Tales* (*Sagor*, 1903). The seminal influence on modernist literature of Strindberg's complex late style and his restless formal experimentation has been acknowledged by writers as diverse as Franz KAFKA, Eugene O'NEILL, and Bertolt BRECHT.

Styron, William (June 11, 1925–). American novelist. Oppression, depression, loss of innocence, the nature of evil, and the human consequences of historical upheaval are among the powerful and controversial subjects Styron tackles in his work. Born in Newport News, Virginia, Styron was educated at Duke University and served as a Marine in both World War II and the Korean War. During the 1950s, he spent time in Europe and became one of the founders of *THE PARIS REVIEW*. His first novel, *Lie Down in Darkness* (1951), about a suicidal young Southern woman, invited comparisons with William FAULKNER and THOMAS WOLFE. His novels *The Long March* (1956) and *Set This House on Fire* (1960) draw on his war and postwar experiences. *THE CONFESSIONS OF NAT TURNER* (1967; Pulitzer Prize) is a controversial treatment of a slave revolt in Virginia, while in *SOPHIE'S CHOICE* (1979) Styron focuses on a Polish refugee and her Jewish lover in a story of a Holocaust survivor's guilt. Among his other works are the essay collection *This Quiet Dust* (1982), a memoir of serious depression, *Darkness Visible* (1990), and the story collection *A Tidewater Morning* (1993).

Svevo, Italo, *pen name of* Aron Hector [Ettore] Schmitz (December 19, 1861–September 13, 1928). Italian novelist and short-story writer. Although Svevo's psychological, introspective, experimental, witty fiction was not widely known until after his death, he is now recognized as a groundbreaking figure in Italian literature. Born in Trieste, Svevo left school at age 19 in order to pursue a career in business to support himself and, later, his wife. His first two novels, *A Life* (*Una Vita*, 1892) and *As a Man Grows Older* (*Senilità*, 1898), were commercial failures and made him turn away from writing. After a 25-year hiatus, he produced his masterpiece, THE CONFESSIONS OF ZENO (*La Coscienza di Zeno*, 1923), about a man writing a fictionalized version of his life story for his psychiatrist. His friend and admirer James JOYCE helped the novel to gain attention in Europe. Svevo's posthumously published story collections include *The Nice Old Man and the Pretty Girl* (*La Novella del Buon Vecchio e della Bella Fanciulla*, 1930) and *Short Sentimental Journey and Other Stories* (*Corto Viaggio Sentimentale e Altri Racconti Inediti*, 1949).

Swift, Jonathan (November 30, 1667–October 19, 1745). Irish satirist. A satirical genius who wrote about religion, politics, and society, Swift is best known for GULLIVER'S TRAVELS, his mocking fiction about the follies and abuses of humankind. Born to English parents in Dublin, he attended Trinity College and Oxford, and was ordained a priest in the Church of Ireland in 1694. He worked for a decade, until 1699, as secretary to the diplomat Sir William Temple. Swift's first major works, both published in 1704, were "A Tale of a Tub," a satirical history of the church, and "The Battle of the Books," a mock epic debating the relative merits of the ancients and the moderns. In 1710, Swift moved to London and became active in Tory politics, an experience chronicled in his *Journal to Stella* (1710–13). He returned to Dublin in 1713 as dean of St. Patrick's Cathedral. There, he published *Drapier's Letters* (1724), which influenced Irish politics and made Swift a national hero; poems such as "Cadenus and Vanessa" (1726) and "Stella's Birthday" (1727), tributes to two of the women in his life; and "A Modest Proposal" (1729), which satirically recommends that poor Irish children be fattened up and used as food for the wealthy. Swift remained active throughout most of the 1730s, but by late in the decade his health began to

fail; in 1742 he was declared of "unsound mind and memory" and placed under guardianship. Although he is renowned as the most savage satirist in the English language, Swift was not a misanthrope. He maintained an energetic correspondence with a wide circle of intimates, and his will directed that a large portion of his considerable estate go to the founding of a hospital for the mentally ill. As he once wrote to his friend Alexander POPE, "I have ever hated all Nations professions and Communityes, and all my love is towards individualls."

Swinburne, Algernon Charles (April 5, 1837–April 10, 1909). English poet and critic. A rebellious writer who glorified sensuality and freedom and coined the phrase "art for art's sake," Swinburne led an early life of drunken excess and sexual recklessness that compromised his health and career. Born in London, Swinburne attended Oxford, left without a degree, and joined the circle of Pre-Raphaelites led by William Morris, Edward Burne-Jones, and DANTE GABRIEL ROSSETTI. He gained widespread attention with his poetic dramas *Atalanta in Calydon* (1865) and *Chastelard* (1865). His first poetry collection, *Poems and Ballads, First Series* (1866), was praised for its keen rhythms and intricate imagery, but condemned for its overt sensuality, sadomasochism, and antireligious sentiment. In 1868, he published an elegy on Charles BAUDELAIRE—*Ave Atque Vale*—one of the high points of his career. He went on to publish *Songs Before Sunrise* (1871), a poetic celebration of democracy inspired by the Italian republican revolution, and *Poems and Ballads: Second Series* (1878), but his most creative period was over. Living under a friend's care during the final decades of his life, Swinburne produced some of his best critical works, including studies on William BLAKE, CHARLOTTE BRONTË, William SHAKESPEARE, Victor HUGO, and Ben JONSON.

Synge, John Millington (April 16, 1871–March 24, 1909). Irish playwright. A leading dramatist of the Irish Literary Renaissance, Synge wrote realistic and at times controversial tragedies and comedies about the peasants of the Irish countryside. Synge was born in Rathfarnham, and studied languages at Trinity College in Dublin. He enjoyed a literary life in Paris for several years before following William Butler YEATS's advice to move to the Aran Islands off the coast of Ireland and write about the people there. His time on the islands inspired all his writings: the one-acts *In the Shadow of the Glen* (1903) and *RIDERS TO THE SEA* (1904) as well as the full-length dramas *The Well of the Saints* (1905), *THE PLAYBOY OF THE WESTERN WORLD* (1907)—his most popular work—and *The Tinker's Wedding* (1908). In 1906, Synge become a director of the Abbey Theatre, where most of his plays were produced. At 37, he lost his life to Hodgkin's disease. His final work, produced posthumously, was *Deirdre of the Sorrows* (1910).

Szymborska, Wisława (July 2, 1923–). Polish poet, critic, and translator. Ever astonished by the world and its workings, Szymborska writes restrained, contemplative poems that reflect her belief that "in the language of poetry...nothing is usual or normal. Not a single stone and not a single cloud above it. Not a single day and not a single night after it. And above all, not a single existence, not anyone's existence in this world." Szymborska was born in Bnin (now Kornik) in western Poland, and studied literature and sociology at Jagiellonian University in Krakow. Her first collection was published in 1952. From 1953 to 1981, she served as poetry editor and columnist for the magazine *ŻYCIE LITERACKIE* (Literary Life). In the 1980s, during her country's struggle for democracy, she published under a pseudonym in dissident magazines. Her poems in English translation are collected in *Sounds, Feelings, Thoughts* (1981), *People on a Bridge* (1990), *View with a Grain of Sand* (1996), *Nothing Twice* (*Nic Dwa Razy*; bilingual ed., 1996), *Poems, New and Collected: 1957–1997* (1998), and *Miracle Fair* (2001). Szymborska received the Nobel Prize in Literature in 1996.

Tagore, Rabindranath (May 7, 1861–August 7, 1941). Indian poet, playwright, songwriter, short-story writer, novelist, and essayist. One of modern India's most versatile, prolific, and beloved writers, Tagore is noted for his deeply spiritual, lyrical poetry, written in Bengali. Born in Calcutta to a wealthy Hindu family—his father was a well-known religious leader—Tagore began writing poems as a boy and published his first book at age 17. He was educated at home, although he spent two years at University College, London, studying law. *The Ideal One* (*Mānasī*, 1890), published when he was 29, was his first major poetry collection. In 1912, *GITĀÑJĀLI: SONG OFFERINGS* (*Gitāñjāli*, 1910), now his best-known work, was published in his own English translation, with an introduction by William Butler YEATS; the following year Tagore won the Nobel Prize in Literature. Among other collections of his poems in English translation are *The Gardener* (1913), *Fruit-Gathering* (1916), and *The Fugitive* (1921). Tagore's stories of village life in East Bengal are gathered in the collections *The Hungry Stones* (1916) and *Broken Ties* (1925). Several of Tagore's works, including the novel *The Home and the World* (*Ghare-bāire*, 1916), were brought to the screen by Indian director Satyajit Ray.

Tanizaki, Jun'ichirō (July 24, 1886–July 30, 1965). Japanese novelist. One of Japan's greatest modern writers, Tanizaki used his fiction to explore love, obsession, eroticism, beauty, and the tensions between traditionalism and Westernization in Japanese society. Tanizaki was born in Tokyo and studied literature at the Imperial University there. His early writings, such as "The Tattooer" ("Shisei," 1911), a story about a girl who is transformed through bodily decoration, reflect an interest in contemporary Western ideals and literary styles, while the writings of his middle period, following his 1923 move to the countryside, went in a markedly traditional direction. His masterpiece, *THE MAKIOKA SISTERS* (*Sasameyuki*, 1943–48), is a family saga set in prewar Osaka. Among his other well-known works are *SOME PREFER NETTLES* (*Tade Kuu Mushi*, 1928), a tale of an unhappy marriage; *Quicksand* (*Manji*, 1928–30), a novel of erotic obsession; and *Diary of a Mad Old Man* (*Fūten Rōjin Nikki*, 1961), a grotesque comedy about an elderly man with a foot fetish and a raging libido. Japan's Tanizaki Prize is named in his honor.

Tarkington, [Newton] **Booth** (July 29, 1869–May 19, 1946). American novelist, playwright, and short-story writer. A popular writer and winner of two Pulitzer Prizes, Tarkington made his name by realistically portraying the lives of small-town Midwesterners around the turn of the 20th century. He was born in Indianapolis, Indiana, educated at Purdue University and Princeton, and served a term as a state legislator before turning to writing. His novels *The Gentleman from Indiana* (1899), a tale of political corruption, and *Monsieur Beaucaire* (1900), an 18th-century romance that he adapted for the stage the following year, brought him early fame; THE MAGNIFICENT AMBERSONS (1918), about a prominent family in decline, and *Alice Adams* (1921), in which a young girl seeks to marry well, both won Pulitzer Prizes. His young people's novel *Penrod* (1914) and its sequel, *Penrod and Sam* (1916), recount the adventures of a 12-year-old boy in TOM SAWYER fashion, while *Seventeen* (1916) tells of a one-sided adolescent romance. Tarkington also wrote or collaborated on some two dozen plays, including *The Man from Home* (1907), *Master Antonio* (1916), and *Clarence* (1919).

Tasso, Torquato (March 11, 1544–April 25, 1595). Italian poet. Born in Sorrento, Italy, the son of the prominent poet Bernardo Tasso, Torquato Tasso studied law and philosophy at the University of Padua. In 1565 he entered the service of the Este family at the court of Ferrara. It was there that his fabled doomed romance with Leonora d'Este—immortalized by MILTON, BYRON, GOETHE, and Donizetti but later proven untrue—purportedly unfolded. Although his life's work includes an extensive body of poems, letters, literary criticism, philosophical and moral dialogues, and the pastoral play *Aminta* (1573), Tasso is most remembered for *Jerusalem Delivered* (*Gerusalemme Liberata*, 1575), one of the most distinguished and influential epic poems of the Renaissance. Set during the First Crusade and filled with romance,

heroism, and a mixture of historical and mythological characters, Tasso's great poem tells the story of Godfrey of Boulogne's conquest of Jerusalem. In 1594 Tasso was invited to Rome by Pope Clement VIII to be crowned Poet Laureate; he died before receiving the honor.

Tennyson, Alfred, 1st Baron Tennyson of Aldworth and Freshwater, *known as* **Alfred, Lord Tennyson** (August 6, 1809–October 6, 1892). English poet. Venerated in his day by critics and the public at large, Tennyson wrote of faith and doubt, evoking the values of the Victorian age with his gift for image, lyric, and meter. One of 12 children of a rector, Tennyson was born in a small village in Lincolnshire. He began writing poetry as a child, collaborating with his brothers on a volume of verse while still in grammar school. He studied at Cambridge and published his first important work, *Poems, Chiefly Lyrical* (1830), which includes the well-known "Mariana," while he was a student there. In 1832, his *Poems* introduced such admired verses as "The Lotos-Eaters" and "THE LADY OF SHALOTT." The death in 1833 of Arthur Henry Hallam, a close friend from Cambridge who was engaged to Tennyson's sister, moved him to write the masterful elegy *In Memoriam*, published in 1850. That year, Queen Victoria named Tennyson as William WORDSWORTH's successor as Poet Laureate. His subsequent books include *Maud, and Other Poems* (1855), which contains "THE CHARGE OF THE LIGHT BRIGADE"; IDYLLS OF THE KING (1859–85), a poetic epic based on the King ARTHUR legend; *Enoch Arden* (1864); and *Demeter and Other Poems* (1889), which contains "Crossing the Bar."

Terence, *Latin in full* Publius Terentius Afer (c. 185 B.C.–c. 159 B.C.). Roman playwright. Terence is best known for introducing sophisticated humor and realistic characters to Roman theater. Although the details of his life are uncertain, it is believed that he was born in Carthage, brought to Rome as a slave, and purchased by a senator who was so impressed with the young man's wit, intelligence, and good looks that he set him free. In his short life, Terence wrote six comedies, all of them drawn from earlier Greek plays — typically, he combined scenes and characters from several plays to fashion a new work written in an elegant colloquial Latin. His dramas were popular among artists and critics but were not well known in his time. In 159 B.C., on his way home from a trip to Greece, he was apparently lost at sea. Among his plays are *The Woman of Andros* (*Andria*, 166 B.C.), *The Eunuch* (*Eunuchus*, 161 B.C.), *Phormio* (161 B.C.), and *The Brothers* (*Adelphoe*, 160 B.C.).

Thackeray, William Makepeace (July 18, 1811–December 24, 1863). English novelist and satirist. One of the great Victorian novelists, Thackeray gained his reputation with urbane, moralistic portrayals of 19th-century British society, notably VANITY FAIR (1848). The son of a wealthy merchant, he was born in India and returned to England for his education. He attended Cambridge but did not complete his studies, read law but never practiced, and studied art but turned to writing for his livelihood. He achieved success in the flourishing magazine industry as a contributor of sketches and satirical pieces. *The Book of Snobs* (1848), a collection of satires from the magazine *Punch*, and the panoramic *Vanity Fair*, which first appeared in monthly magazine installments, were popular and critical successes; the latter was the first work published under his own name. These were followed by the fictional autobiography *Pendennis* (1849–50); the Queen Anne–period historical novel *Henry Esmond* (1852) and its sequel, *The Virginians* (1859); BARRY LYNDON (1852; revised 1856); *The Newcomes* (1854–55); several Christmas books; and a number of essays and articles. *The English Humourists of the Eighteenth Century* (1851) and *The Four Georges* (1855–60) are lecture series he delivered in London and the United States.

Theocritus, *in Greek* Theokritos (c. 310 B.C.– c. 250 B.C.). Greek poet. Considered the father of the pastoral tradition, Theocritus left only 30 short poems, called idylls, and about 20 epigrams. He wrote in the Doric dialect and is believed to have been born in Syracuse. The

form and characteristics of his bucolic poems were perpetuated in VIRGIL'S *ECLOGUES* and widely imitated up through the 18th century. Although his reputation derives chiefly from his dozen or so pastoral pieces, with their evocations of arcadian landscapes and innocent shepherd life, the idylls also evidence his interest in other forms: hymns, panegyrics, mythological narratives, and dramatic sketches. Theocritus is believed to have lived for a time on the Aegean island of Kos and in Alexandria.

Theroux, Paul (April 10, 1941–). American novelist and travel writer. An inveterate traveler and bestselling author, the Massachusetts-born Theroux has engaged contemporary readers with his fictional and personal accounts of life in remote places. His experiences as a teacher in Africa and Asia provided material for the early novels *Girls at Play* (1969), *Jungle Lovers* (1971), and *Saint Jack* (1973). Later fiction includes *The Family Arsenal* (1976), about a terrorist group in London; and *The Mosquito Coast* (1982), about an American engineer in the jungles of Honduras. Of his more than two dozen books, the best known are accounts of railroad journeys: from England to Japan in *The Great Railway Bazaar* (1975), through South America in *The Old Patagonian Express* (1979), and through China in *Riding the Iron Rooster* (1988). *The Kingdom by the Sea* (1983) describes a hike through Great Britain; *The Happy Isles of Oceania* (1992) finds him kayaking in the South Pacific; and *The Pillars of Hercules* (1995) is a tour of the Mediterranean. *Sir Vidia's Shadow* (1998) tells of his friendship with V. S. NAIPAUL.

Thomas, Dylan (October 27, 1914–November 9, 1953). Welsh poet and prose writer. Known for his complex, highly charged lyric verse and stormy personal life, Thomas was among the most admired and mythologized literary figures of the mid-20th century. The son of an English instructor at the Swansea Grammar School he attended as a boy, Thomas produced his first collections — *Eighteen Poems* (1934), *Twenty-Five Poems* (1936), and *The Map of Love* (1939) — while in his early 20s. Their energy and originality won him a devoted following and a reputation as an important new voice in modern poetry. Later volumes included *Deaths and Entrances* (1946), *In Country Sleep* (1952), which contains the famous poem "DO NOT GO GENTLE INTO THAT GOOD NIGHT," and *Collected Poems* (1952). Thomas began writing stories and radio scenarios to support his family, and these, too, met with success. Among his prose writings are the short-story collections *Portrait of the Artist as a Young Dog* (1940) and *Adventures in the Skin Trade* (1955), and the popular radio plays *UNDER MILK WOOD* (1954) and *A Child's Christmas in Wales* (1955). Thomas's flamboyant personality, turbulent marriage, and heavy drinking were highly publicized, as was his death from alcoholism in New York City during a poetry-reading tour.

Thompson, Jim (September 27, 1906–April 7, 1977). American novelist and screenwriter. An obscure writer of crime pulp-fiction in the 1950s and early 1960s, Thompson was not recognized as a master of the genre until his work was rediscovered a decade after his death. The son of an Oklahoma sheriff and itinerant oil worker, he had an unsettled childhood and tried his hand at a number of jobs—including newspaper reporting and directing the Federal Writers' Project in Oklahoma during the 1930s—before achieving modest success with *The Killer Inside Me* (1952), his signature work. Thompson's novels, which also include *Savage Night* (1953), *After Dark, My Sweet* (1955), *The Getaway* (1959), *The Grifters* (1963), and more than 20 others, are known for their violently explicit portrayals of small-town losers, petty criminals, con artists, corrupt police officers, and psychopathic killers. Thompson collaborated with Stanley Kubrick on the screenplays for *The Killing* (1956) and *Paths of Glory* (1957).

Thoreau, Henry David (July 12, 1817–May 6, 1862). American essayist and natural history writer. Thoreau published only two books during his lifetime and earned little money from literature, but his writings on nature, society, and the spirit of individualism stand as classics of American letters. He was born in Concord, Massachusetts, home of the Transcendentalist movement, with which he was associated, and, with the exception of nature excursions and lecture outings, spent much of his adult life there doing odd jobs. After graduating from Harvard in 1837, he taught school, wrote poems and articles for *THE DIAL* and other magazines, and began the journal he would keep to the end of his life. His first book, *A Week on the Concord and Merrimack* (1849), based on a boating trip with his brother, sold barely two hundred

---

"How many a man has dated a new era in his life from the reading of a book. The book exists for us perchance which will explain our miracles and reveal new ones."

Henry David Thoreau, *Walden* (1854)

---

copies. The work on which his reputation chiefly rests, *WALDEN, or Life in the Woods* (1854), an account of his two-year experiment in "simple living" in a Walden Pond cabin, also attracted little immediate attention. It was during those years that Thoreau spent a night in jail for refusing to pay his poll tax and defended his action in the influential essay "Civil Disobedience" (1849). His *Journals*, the source of many posthumously published works, appeared in 14 volumes in 1906.

Thurber, James (December 8, 1894–November 2, 1961). American humorist. Remembered for his sardonic, deadpan depictions of human folly and the absurdities of modern life, Thurber—who brought to his stories, sketches, and essays a simplicity and tenderness of style, often complemented by his own line drawings—set the standard for sophisticated American humor at mid-century. He was born and raised in Columbus, Ohio, a milieu he would frequently satirize, and began his career in journalism before entering into a long association with *THE NEW YORKER* magazine in 1927. His contributions, many of which were collected in books, helped to establish the style and reputation of that publication. "The Secret Life of Walter Mitty," recounting the heroic fantasies of a meek "everyman," is his best-known short story; *The Male Animal* (1940) was a play cowritten with Elliott Nugent. His 22 books include *Is Sex Necessary?* (1929), a collaboration with E. B. WHITE; *The Middle-Aged Man on the Flying Trapeze* (1935); *My World—And Welcome to It* (1942); *The Thurber Carnival* (1945); *Thurber Country* (1953); and *The Years with Ross* (1959), a reminiscence about *New Yorker* founder Harold ROSS.

Tolkien, J[ohn] **R**[onald] **R**[euel] (January 3, 1892–September 2, 1973). English novelist. An Oxford professor of Anglo-Saxon and English language and literature, Tolkien won unexpected fame for his original mythological fantasies THE HOBBIT (1937) and THE LORD OF THE RINGS trilogy (*The Fellowship of the Ring*, 1954; *The Two Towers*, 1954; and *The Return of the King*, 1955). Born in South Africa, he moved to England as a young boy after the death of his father. He attended Oxford on a scholarship, fought in France during World War I, and taught at the University of Leeds before returning to his alma mater in 1925. Tolkien earned his reputation as a medieval scholar with an edition of SIR GAWAIN AND THE GREEN KNIGHT (1925) and the critical study *Beowulf: The Monsters and the Critics* (1936). At the urging of fellow medievalist C. S. LEWIS, he wrote *The Hobbit*, based on bedtime stories he told his children. The publisher asked for a sequel, and Tolkien spent the next 12 years developing *The Lord of the Rings*. His own favorite "Middle Earth" romance, *The Silmarillion*, begun in 1917, was edited by his son and published posthumously in 1977.

Tolstoy, [Count] **Leo** [*or* **Lev**] (September 9, 1828–November 20, 1910). Russian novelist and moral philosopher. Tolstoy's two masterpieces of fictional realism, WAR AND PEACE (*Voĭna i Mir*, 1868–69) and ANNA KARENINA (1878), have led many to agree with VIRGINIA WOOLF that he was "the greatest of all novelists." His writings on nonviolence, material renunciation, and social reform earned him a reputation

as "the conscience of humanity." Tolstoy was born on the Yasnaya Polyana family estate outside Moscow, where he spent much of his life. Orphaned at age nine, he was raised by aunts and educated by tutors; his early experiences are recounted in *Childhood* (*Detstvo*, 1852), *Boyhood* (*Otrochestvo*, 1854), and *Youth* (*Yunost'*, 1857). An uninspired student, Tolstoy left the university and served in the Russian army in the Caucasus and Crimea; his *Sevastopol Sketches* (*Sevastopol'skie Rasskazy*, 1855–56), based on the defense of that city, were well received in literary circles. After traveling in Europe, he returned to his estate in 1859, married, and devoted himself to the education of serf children; it was during this period also that he wrote his great psychological novels. Tolstoy suffered a deepening spiritual crisis that culminated in a religious and moral conversion based on Christianity, experiences described in *A Confession* (*Ispoved'*, 1882). In the decades that followed, he created an extensive body of philosophical writings and moralizing tales for "the people." Literary achievements of his late period include the novellas THE DEATH OF IVAN ILYICH (*Smert' Ivana Il'icha*, 1886), *The Kreutzer Sonata* (*Kreĭtserova Sonata*, 1890), and *Master and Man* (*Khozyain i Rabotnik*, 1895), and a last long novel, *The Resurrection* (*Voskresenie*, 1899).

Toomer, Jean (December 26, 1894–March 30, 1967). American fiction writer and poet. A central figure in the Harlem Renaissance of the 1920s, Toomer is known primarily for his mixed-genre fictional work CANE (1923). The importance of *Cane*, a study of African-American identity in short prose pieces, poetry, and drama, was not fully recognized until it was republished in 1967, the year of its author's death. Toomer all but abandoned serious writing after the book's publication, devoting himself instead to the spiritual teachings of G. I. Gurdjieff and the ideal of racial unity. The latter theme figured prominently in his last noteworthy published piece, the long philosophical poem "Blue Meridian" (1936). A native of Washington, D.C., he lived for years in New York City, spent time in rural Georgia, led meditation groups in Chicago and Wisconsin, and settled in Doylestown, Pennsylvania, where he lived for 30 years in relative obscurity. *Collected Poems* appeared in 1988.

Trevor, William, *pen name of* William Trevor Cox (May 28, 1928–). Irish short-story writer and novelist. A wry, sometimes ironic observer of the marginalized and eccentric, usually in an Irish setting, Trevor was born in County Cork, attended Trinity College, and worked as a teacher and sculptor before turning to writing full time. His second novel, *The Old Boys* (1964), about eight old men at a class reunion, gained critical notice and was followed by, among others, *Mrs. Eckdorf in O'Neill's Hotel* (1969); three Whitbread Award–winners, *The Children of Dynmouth* (1976), *Fools of Fortune* (1983), and *Felicia's Journey* (1994); and *Death in Summer* (1998). Trevor's reputation, however, rests chiefly on short fiction. His stories of personal defeat and isolation, in the realist tradition of MAUPASSANT, have been published in a number of volumes, from *The Day We Got Drunk on Cake* (1967) to *The Hill Bachelors* (2000). Trevor's *Collected Stories* appeared in 1992 and his personal essays, *Excursions in the Real World*, two years later. He has also written for the stage and screen, and many of his stories have been adapted for television.

Trollope, Anthony (April 24, 1815–December 6, 1882). English novelist. A writer whose books were "as English as a beef-steak" (according to Nathaniel HAWTHORNE), exhibiting "a complete appreciation of the usual" (in the opinion of HENRY JAMES), Trollope was among the most popular writers of his day, appreciated for his depictions of clerical, political, and everyday life in Victorian England and his portrayals of memorable characters in richly imagined settings. The son of a failed gentleman farmer and the writer Frances Trollope, he grew up in relative poverty and took a job as a postal clerk while in his 20s. He worked as a civil servant through much of his adult life and rose to a position of prominence in the postal service, all the while writing with remarkable energy and discipline. His output included 47 novels as well as travel books, biographies, and prose collections. He is best known for two novel sequences, a form he introduced to English literature: the BARSETSHIRE NOVELS, the chronicle of clerical life in the fictional cathedral town of Barchester (including *The Warden*, 1855; *Barchester Towers*, 1857; *Doctor Thorne*, 1858; and *The Last Chronicle of Barset*, 1867); and, after running unsuccessfully for Parliament, the politically steeped PALLISER NOVELS (including *Can You Forgive Her?*, 1864; *Phineas Finn*, 1869; *The Eustace Diamonds*, 1873; and *The Prime Minister*, 1876). His two-volume *Autobiography* appeared posthumously, in 1883.

Tsvetayeva, Marina (October 8, 1892–August 31, 1941). Russian poet. Little known outside Russia during her lifetime, Tsvetayeva is now ranked as one of the greatest Russian poets of the 20th century, along with Anna AKHMATOVA, Osip MANDELSHTAM, and her friend and admirer Boris PASTERNAK. Born and raised in Moscow, she published her first book, *Verchernii Al'bom* (1910; Evening Album), at her own expense, to unexpected critical praise. She married Sergei Efron, a White Russian army officer, in 1911 or 1912, in 1922 joining him in Berlin; by 1925 they had settled in Paris. In 1939, Tsvetayeva followed her daughter and Efron (now a Soviet agent) to Moscow with her 14-year-old son, only to see her daughter imprisoned and her husband shot during the Stalinist terror. In 1941, as part of the evacuation of Moscow, she and her son were sent to the Tatar Republic, where, deprived of both financial and emotional sustenance, she hanged herself. Despite abundant personal hardships, Tsvetayeva wrote prolifically and her work was published in numerous volumes of poetry and prose during her lifetime. Among her works translated into English are the poetry volumes *After Russia* (*Posle Rossii*, 1928); *The Demesne of the Swans* (*Lebediny Stan'*, 1957), a bilingual edition that includes the definitive Russian text; and *The Ratcatcher: A Lyrical Satire* (2000; "Krysolov," first published in a Russian journal). Selected poems in English include *In the Inmost Hour of the Soul* (1989), *Black Earth* (1992), *Selected Poems* (1993), and *Poem of the End = Poema*

Kontsa: Selected Narrative Lyrical Poetry (1998). Prose collections include *A Captive Spirit: Selected Prose* (1980) and *Art in the Light of Conscience: Eight Essays on Poetry* (1992). The correspondence of Tsvetayeva, Pasternak, and Rainer Maria RILKE appears in *Letters, Summer 1926* (1985).

Turgenev, Ivan (November 9, 1818–September 3, 1883). Russian novelist, short-story writer, and playwright. Although his reputation was later eclipsed by that of TOLSTOY and DOSTOYEVSKY, Turgenev was Russia's most widely celebrated writer of the late 19th century. After attending universities in Moscow and St. Petersburg, he continued his studies in Berlin, where he encountered prominent liberal intellectuals and became, as he later said, a "Westerner for life." His critical portrayals of Russian serfdom and national culture—beginning with the stories that made up *A Sportsman's Sketches* (*Zapiski Okhotnika*, 1852) and continuing in such novels as *Rudin* (1856), *A Nest of Gentlefolk* (*Dvoryanskoe Gnezdo*, 1859), *On the Eve* (*Nakanune*, 1860), and the classic *FATHERS AND SONS* (*Ottsy i Deti*, 1862)—alienated both the older tsarist generation and the younger radicals. He left Russia in 1863, returning only for brief visits, and lived thereafter in Germany and France. Later works include *Smoke* (*Dym*, 1867), a fictional response to critics; *Torrents of Spring* (*Veshnie Vody*, 1872), a lyrical novella; and *Virgin Soil* (*Nov'*, 1877), a last, controversial novel about his native land. His most important play is *A MONTH IN THE COUNTRY* (*Mesyats v Derevne*, 1855).

Tutuola, Amos (June 20, 1920–June 8, 1997). Nigerian novelist and short-story writer. Raised on his father's farm and educated for only a few years in missionary schools, Tutuola worked at a variety of odd jobs even after the international success of his first novel, *THE PALM-WINE DRINKARD AND HIS DEAD PALM-WINE TAPSTER IN THE DEAD'S TOWN* (1952), which recounts, in Yoruba-inflected English dialect, the adventures of a young alcoholic who journeys to the land of the dead to find the deceased bartender who used to serve him. The book sold especially well outside of Africa, thanks in part to favorable reviews by such respected critics as V. S. PRITCHETT, who praised Tutuola's imaginative storytelling and highly original use of language, and Dylan THOMAS, who described the novel as a "brief, thronged, grisly and bewildering story... a nightmare of indescribable adventures, all simply and carefully described in the spirit-bristling bush." But in Nigeria he was controversial, some critics suggesting that his work was too heavily influenced by the writings of D. O. Fagunwa, another Nigerian author who wrote in the same vein, but in Yoruba. In recent years, Tutuola's unique talent as well as his preservation of Yoruba mythology and folk culture have gained wider appreciation in Africa. Other works include *My Life in the Bush of Ghosts* (1954), *The Feather Woman of the Jungle* (1962), *Ajaiyi and His Inherited Poverty* (1967), *Witch-Herbalist of the Remote Town* (1981), *Pauper, Brawler and Slanderer* (1987), and *The Village Witch Doctor and Other Stories* (1990).

Twain, Mark, *pen name of* Samuel Langhorne Clemens (November 30, 1835–April 21, 1910). American humorist, novelist, and travel writer. A child of the frontier and master of the Gilded Age, Twain brought to American letters an irreverent humor, ear for the vernacular, and stubborn egalitarian spirit that have had a major influence on the nation's literature and popular consciousness. Youthful experiences on the Mississippi River provided the source for his most beloved works—*The Adventures of TOM SAWYER* (1876) and *The Adventures of HUCKLEBERRY FINN* (1884), episodic novels marked by unforgettable characters, free-flowing idioms, and undercurrents of social commentary; and *Life on the Mississippi* (1883), a reminiscence of his days as a steamboat pilot. (His pseudonym is river slang for "two fathoms.") Born and raised in Hannibal, Missouri, Twain began his career as a journeyman printer and journalist, first achieving celebrity with the publication of his comic folk tale "The Celebrated Jumping Frog of Calaveras County" in 1865. With the impious humor that became his hallmark, he entertained a growing readership and lecture-circuit audience with rollicking accounts of his travels, notably THE INNOCENTS ABROAD (1869), about a tour of the Mediterranean and Holy Land. Attacking pretense, privilege, and greed wherever he saw them, he took aim at English history and folklore in the children's novel *The Prince and the Pauper* (1882) and in the satirical A CONNECTICUT YANKEE IN KING ARTHUR'S COURT (1889), and at religion, politics, and social injustice in countless other writings. Personal misfortunes in his later years, including bankruptcy and the deaths of his wife and two daughters, are reflected in the pessimism and misanthropy of his late writings. His autobiography was published posthumously, in 1924.

Tyler, Anne (October 25, 1941–). American novelist. Raised in Quaker communities in the Midwest and South, Tyler was a precocious child who entered Duke University at 16 and finished in three years. Her fiction portrays idiosyncratic characters who turn to varied occupations—cooking, mothering, hitchhiking, falling in love, doing odd jobs, and committing bank robbery (the last in *Earthly Possessions*, 1977)—as devices to make sense of their lives. Tyler's popular and critically acclaimed novels, which include *Celestial Navigation* (1974), *Dinner at the Homesick Restaurant* (1982), *The Accidental Tourist* (1985), *Breathing Lessons* (1988; Pulitzer Prize), *Saint Maybe* (1991), *Ladder of Years* (1995), and *A Patchwork Planet* (1998), explore rhythms of repetition and change in families that both support and constrain. She has also published more than 50 short stories and a children's book, *Tumble Tower* (1993), with pictures by her daughter, Mitra Modaressi. Considering herself a Southern writer, Tyler sets her fiction primarily in North Carolina or Baltimore, where she has lived since 1967.

Unamuno [y Jugo], **Miguel de** (September 29, 1864–December 31, 1936). Spanish essayist, novelist, poet, and playwright. Iconoclastic philosophical writings and innovative literary works established Unamuno as his nation's most influential 20th-century thinker and writer. A central figure in the "Generation of 1898," he was deeply concerned with the state of Spanish society and culture. His essays argued passionately against dogmatism and conformity, and examined the existential conflicts between faith and reason. Born in Bilbao and raised in the Basque Catholic tradition, he became a professor of ancient Greek at the University of Salamanca in 1891. With the exception of a self-imposed political exile (1924–30), he remained there until his death. Notable among his essays and treatises are *Life of Don Quixote and Sancho* (*Vida de Don Quijote y Sancho*, 1905), *The Tragic Sense of Life* (*Del Sentimiento Trágico de la Vida*, 1912), and *The Agony of Christianity* (*La Agonía del Cristianismo*, 1924). Literary works include the novels *Mist* (*Niebla*, 1914), *Abel Sanchez* (1917), *Three Exemplary Novels* (*Tres Novelas Ejemplares*, 1920), and *St. Manuel Bueno, Martyr* (*San Manuel Bueno, Mártir*, 1933); several plays; and the modernist verse work, *The Christ of Velázquez* (*El Cristo de Velázquez*, 1920).

Undset, Sigrid (May 20, 1882–June 10, 1949). Norwegian novelist. The daughter of an archaeologist who introduced her to the Nordic past, which became a prominent element in her work, Undset worked as a secretary in Kristiania (Oslo) while beginning her writing career. Her early novels, including *Jenny* (1911) and *Images in a Mirror* (*Splinten av Troldspeilet*, 1917), examined the lives of contemporary young Norwegian women. In the 1920s, she produced KRISTIN LAVRANSDATTER (1920–22), the meticulously detailed historical novel about a woman's spiritual evolution for which she became world-famous; and *The Master of Hestviken* (*Olav Audunssøn*, 1925–27), another historical saga. After her conversion to Catholicism in 1924, religious themes deepened in her work. She fled her country when the Nazis invaded in 1940, and spent the war years in the United States as a sort of Norwegian cultural ambassador. Her journey into exile is described in *Return to the Future* (*Tilbake til Fremtiden*, 1942). Undset was awarded the Nobel Prize in Literature in 1928.

Unsworth, Barry (August 10, 1930–). English novelist. Born in Durham, England, Unsworth graduated from the University of Manchester and served in the Royal Corps of Signals before taking up a career as a teacher and writer. Known for his meticulously researched explorations of the darker side of history and for his moral and philosophical themes, he is the author of more than a dozen novels, including *Pascali's Island* (1980), about a spy on an Aegean island; *Sacred Hunger* (1992; Booker Prize), about the 18th-century slave trade; *Morality Play* (1995), a detective story set in 14th-century England concerning a priest who joins a troupe of actors; and *Losing Nelson* (1999), about a scholar obsessed with the British naval hero Horatio Nelson.

Updike, John (March 18, 1932–). American novelist, short-story writer, poet, and critic. Born in the small town of Shillington, Pennsylvania, Updike began his extraordinarily successful and prolific career right out of Harvard University, when he was hired by THE NEW YORKER in 1955 to write occasional pieces. His first book, *The Carpentered Hen*, a collection of poems, appeared in 1958, followed the next year by his first novel, *The Poorhouse Fair*. RABBIT, RUN (1960), about a former high school athlete who abandons his wife and child, was a bestseller and, in the minds of many, is one of Updike's best novels. The character of Harry "Rabbit" ANGSTROM later appeared in four sequels: *Rabbit Redux* (1971), *Rabbit Is Rich* (1981; Pulitzer Prize), *Rabbit at Rest* (1990; Pulitzer Prize), and *Rabbit Remembered*, a novella included in the collection *Licks of Love* (2000). Updike's fiction is primarily concerned with the lives of middle- and upper-class Protestants, and is bolstered by strong moral and religious themes. A great many of his novels and stories are set in New England, where Updike lived after 1960, and the author frequently makes reference to that region's Calvinist heritage. He is also a prose stylist of great accomplishment. Of his more than 20 novels, some of the more important are *The Centaur* (1963), *Couples* (1968), *Marry Me* (1976), *The Witches of Eastwick* (1985), *Brazil* (1994), *In the Beauty of the Lilies* (1996), and *Gertrude and Claudius* (2000). Story collections include *Museums and Women* (1972), *Trust Me* (1987), and *The Afterlife and Other Stories* (1994). He is also the author of numerous collections of poetry, several volumes of criticism, and a memoir, *Self-Consciousness* (1989).

Valenzuela, Luisa (November 26, 1938–). Argentinean novelist and short-story writer. One of Latin America's preeminent women writers, Valenzuela has won an international following for her highly expressive, structurally innovative novels, many with strong sexual themes. Intellectually challenging, her work is informed by her feminism and by the writings of such postmodern thinkers as Michel FOUCAULT and Jacques Lacan. The daughter of writer Luisa Mercedes Levinson, Valenzuela was raised in Buenos Aires, where she began working as a journalist at age 17. Her first novel, *Clara* (*Hay Que Sonreir*, 1966), about a maimed prostitute, is told in a naturalistic manner. However, with her second novel, *The Efficient Cat* (*El Gato Eficaz*, 1972), she abandoned conventional narration for a highly baroque style, employing elaborate wordplay and altered spelling to create a unique narrative texture. Other works of note, most with strong sociopolitical themes, include *He Who Searches* (*Como en la Guerra*, 1977), *Other Weapons* (*Cambio de Armas*, 1982), *The Lizard's Tail* (*Cola de Lagartija*, 1983), *Black Novel with Argentines* (*Novela Negra con Argentinos*, 1990), and *Bedside Manners* (*Realidad Nacional desde la Cama*, 1990). A voluntary exile from her native country after 1979, Valenzuela has taught at a number of American colleges, including New York University, Columbia University, and the University of Iowa.

Valéry, Paul (October 30, 1871–July 20, 1945). French poet and critic. Although he is now recognized as one of the leading French poets of the modern period, fame came slowly to Valéry, who abandoned his writing career in his early 20s after a series of personal setbacks, notably an unsuccessful love affair. He continued to write daily in private notebooks but published no verse until 1917, when, encouraged by André GIDE, a longtime friend from Valéry's schooldays at Montpellier, he returned to poetry. *The Young Fate* (*La Jeune Parque*, 1917), a lengthy monologue in the voice of a young maiden, and *Album de Vers Anciens* (1920), a collection of new and revised work, swiftly propelled him to prominence. The collection *Charmes* appeared in 1922, and contains many of his most famous poems, including "The Graveyard by the Sea" ("Le Cimetière Marin"). Although Valéry introduced no important technical innovations to verse writing, his highly crafted poems display a formidable intelligence and are bound by the author's lifelong concern over the contest between reason and passion in human affairs. Valéry was elected to the Académie Française in 1925, and occupied a number of distinguished academic positions. His 29 volumes of notebooks, posthumously published as *Cahiers* (1957–61), provide insight into his creative process and aesthetic philosophy.

van der Post, Laurens (December 13, 1906–December 15, 1996). South African travel writer, essayist, and novelist. Van der Post's adventurous early life provided him with much material: he sailed on a whaler for three seasons (from which came *The Hunter and the Whale*, 1967); founded an antiracist magazine, *Voorslag* (The Lash of the Whip); traveled to Japan where, nearly 20 years later, he was a prisoner of war; and became a friend and adherent of C. G. JUNG. Van der Post's primary subject was sub-Saharan Africa, and the role of white South Africans in the struggle against racism informs a great deal of his work. *The Lost World of the Kalahari* (1958), perhaps his best-known book, describes lyrically the South African desert and the universal meanings he saw in the tribal lives of its inhabitants. His many other works include the autobiographical *Yet Being Someone Other* (1982), *The Heart of the Hunter* (1961), *A Portrait of Japan* (1968), and *First Catch Your Eland: A Taste of Africa* (1982).

Van Dine, S. S. *See* **Wright, Willard Huntington** [in Other Influential Figures]

Vargas Llosa, [Jorge] **Mario** (March 28, 1936–). Peruvian novelist and literary critic. A leading figure in the renaissance of modern Latin American literature, Vargas Llosa has probed the tragic social history of his native Peru in complex, multilayered works of fiction. Among these are THE TIME OF THE HERO (*La Ciudad y los Perros*, 1963); *The Green House* (*La Casa Verde*, 1966); *Conversation in the Cathedral* (*Conversación en la Catedral*, 1969); *The War of the End of the World* (*La Guerra del Fin del Mundo*, 1981), set in Brazil; and *The Storyteller* (*El Hablador*, 1987). In a lighter vein are the satiric *Captain Pantoja and the Special Service* (*Pantaleón y las Visitadores*, 1973), the autobiographical comedy *Aunt Julia and the Scriptwriter* (*La Tía Julia y el Escribidor*, 1977), and the romantic fantasy *The Notebooks of Don Rigoberto* (*Los Cuadernos de Don Rigoberto*, 1997). Vargas Llosa has also written critical studies on Gabriel GARCÍA MÁRQUEZ, Gustave FLAUBERT, and on Jean-Paul SARTRE and Albert CAMUS as well as essays and memoirs on literature and politics. An outspoken advocate of social change, he ran unsuccessfully for the Peruvian presidency against Alberto Fujimori in 1990.

Vega [Carpio], **Lope** [Félix] **de** (November 25, 1562–August 27, 1635). Spanish playwright and poet. The great dramatist of Spain's Golden Age, Lope de Vega founded the national theater, or *comedia nueva*, with highly popular three-act plays written for the broad public rather than the aristocracy. He defined the tenets of the new dramaturgy in a verse treatise, *The New Art of Writing Plays* (*El Arte Nueva de Hacer Comedias*, 1609). Dubbed by CERVANTES a *monstruo de la naturaleza* (prodigy of nature), Lope wrote some 1,500 plays—of which nearly 500 survive—as well as sketches, interludes, lyric poems, and narratives. The dramatic works fall into several categories: works based on Spanish history and legend, such as *The Sheep Well* (*Fuente Ovejuna*, c. 1611–14), *Peribáñez and the Comendador of Ocaña* (*Peribáñez y el Comendador de Ocaña*, c. 1614), and *The King, the Greatest Alcalde* (*El Major Alcalde, el Rey*, c. 1620–23); "cloak and sword" comedies (romantic adventures of the Spanish nobility), including *Steel of Madrid* (*El Acero de Madrid*, c. 1608–12) and *The Dog in the Manger* (*El*

Perro del Hortelano, c. 1613); religious and biblical dramas; and *autos sacramentales,* one-act canonical allegories. His poetry, most of which was written early in his career, includes some of the finest sonnets in Spanish literature. His best-known nondramatic work, *Dorothy* (*La Dorotea,* 1632), is an autobiographical romance in verse form. Lope himself had a dramatic, often turbulent life, rising from humble origins in Madrid, marrying twice and carrying on numerous love affairs (the most scandalous of which led to an eight-year exile), sailing with the Spanish Armada in 1588, and entering the priesthood.

Verlaine, Paul (March 30, 1844–January 8, 1896). French poet. A master of lyrical verse, Verlaine helped to launch the Symbolist movement with images of fleeting beauty and emotion. Born in Metz, he attended school in Paris and soon joined the antitraditionalist "Parnassian" poets in the city's literary salons and journals. In his first books, *Les Poèmes Saturniens* (1866; Saturnine Poems) and *Fêtes Galantes* (1869), Verlaine refined his distinctly musical, informal style. Scandal followed when he left his wife and infant son for the 17-year-old poet Arthur RIMBAUD, whom he later shot in the wrists. Nevertheless, Verlaine composed some of his best poems during this period, including "Il pleure dans mons coeur..." ("There is weeping in my heart..."), published in *Romances sans Paroles* (1874; Songs Without Words). Later works reflecting Verlaine's turn to Catholicism include *Sagesse* (1880; Wisdom), *Amour* (1888; Love), and *Bonheur* (1891; Happiness); *Parallèlement* (1889; In Parallel) contains both pious verses and erotica. His prose study of six tragically misunderstood poets, *Les Poètes Maudits* (1884; Accursed Poets), drew attention to the Symbolists he inspired, including Stéphane MALLARMÉ and Rimbaud, with their common rejection of Romantic impressionism and stilted themes. His poem "Ars Poétique," published in *Jadis et Naguère* (1884; Yesteryear and Yesterday), is a manifesto for a poetry of music and nuance rather than of description and wit. English-language editions of his works include *One Hundred and One Poems by Paul Verlaine* (1999; translator, Norman R. Shapiro), *Selected Poems* (1948; translator, C. F. Macintyre), and *Selected Poems* (1999; editor, Martin Sorrell).

Verne, Jules (February 8, 1828–March 24, 1905). French novelist. A visionary writer and pioneer of modern science fiction who anticipated the birth of the submarine, television, and space travel, Verne achieved a popularity that is universal and apparently timeless. He was born in Nantes and studied law in Paris, then worked as a secretary for a theater company and as a stockbroker. After some early success writing opera libretti, dramas, and stories, he turned to the novel with a short romantic adventure tale called *Five Weeks in a Balloon* (*Cinq Semaines en Ballon,* 1863). His next book, A JOURNEY TO THE CENTER OF THE EARTH (*Voyage au Centre de la Terre,* 1964), about a geologic expedition into an Icelandic crater, was a great popular success. His renown increased with each subsequent work: the great submarine novel TWENTY THOUSAND LEAGUES UNDER THE SEA (*Vingt Mille Lieues sous les Mers,* 1870); the masterpiece of adventure writing AROUND THE WORLD IN EIGHTY DAYS (*Le Tour du Monde en Quatre-vingt Jours,* 1873); and *The Mysterious Island* (*L'Île Mystérieuse,* 1874), about a group of castaways on an undiscovered island. Verne published more than 50 novels in his lifetime, all part of a series he called *Les Voyages Extraordinaires* (Extraordinary Voyages).

Vidal, [Eugene Luther] **Gore** (October 3, 1925–). American novelist, essayist, playwright, screenwriter, and pundit. Vidal's long career has been built in large part on his satirical skill—on his ability, as one critic said, to show that the emperor has no clothes and then to remove his skin as well. In addition, Vidal has an erudite and vivid command of history. The grandson of Senator Thomas P. Gore of Oklahoma, he made two unsuccessful bids (in 1960 and 1982) for Congress and wrote a Broadway play, *The Best Man* (1960), set at a presidential nominating convention. Vidal's first novel, *Williwaw* (1946), drew on his World War II Army experience. Two years later, *The City and the Pillar* broke ground with its sympathetic portrayal of the homosexual demimonde, a first for a mainstream American novel; 20 years later, MYRA BRECKINRIDGE (1968), perhaps his best-known novel, and its sequel, *Myron* (1974), satirized American attitudes toward sexuality through the adventures of the transsexual Myron/Myra. A number of Vidal's novels are set in the distant past (*Julian*, 1964; *Creation*, 1981; *Live from Golgotha: The Gospel According to Gore Vidal*, 1992), but his primary theme has been the United States—"I do nothing but think about my country," he once wrote, although he has lived in Italy for many years. Among his American-historical novels are *Washington, D.C.* (1967), *Burr* (1973), *1876* (1976), *Lincoln* (1984), and *Hollywood* (1990). His essay collections, including *United States: Essays, 1952–1992* (1993; National Book Award) and *The Last Empire: Essays, 1992–2000* (2001), have received consistent critical acclaim. Under the name Edgar Box, he published three mystery novels—*Death in the Fifth Position* (1952), *Death Before Bedtime...* (1953), and *Death Likes It Hot* (1954)—collected in *Three by Box* (1978). A memoir, *Palimpsest*, appeared in 1995.

Villon, François, *pen name of* François de Montcorbier *or* François des Loges (1431–c. 1463). French poet. The preeminent lyric poet of the late Middle Ages who in his *Testament* posed the question, "But where are the snows of yesteryear?" ("Mais où sont les neiges d'antan?"), Villon is as renowned for his criminal past and mysterious personal history as he is for his formally disciplined and emotionally moving poetry. Little is known about his early life except that he was raised by a chaplain and educated at the University of Paris. Despite some academic success, the rowdy company he cultivated during his student days led to frequent run-ins with the law. Over the course of his short life, he was imprisoned several times and in 1455 was banished from Paris after fatally wounding a priest. Villon composed two major works. His *Little Testament* (*Le Petit Testament*, written 1456; published 1489) features bequests to his friends and enemies that are alternately wry and sincere, while his *Testament*

or *Great Testament* (*Le Testament* or *Le Grand Testament*, written 1461; published 1489) is a candid portrait of the author and his times. In 1463, after narrowly escaping a death sentence, Villon left Paris and was never heard from again.

Virgil *or* **Vergil,** *Latin in full* Publius Vergilius Maro (70 B.C.–19 B.C.). Roman poet. The author of the great epic poem the AENEID, and a man who "sang of flocks and farms and heroes," as his own inscription for his tombstone proclaims, Virgil had a profound influence on literature that resounds in the work of DANTE, SPENSER, MILTON, and SHAKESPEARE. Virgil was born in the village of Andes near Mantua in northern Italy and was educated in a wide range of subjects. When his family's farmland was confiscated in 41 B.C. during the civil war, he left his village and became part of the prestigious circle supported by Emperor Augustus's imperial arts patron Maecenas. Virgil aimed to create works that would equal those of the Greeks; ultimately, he transcended his goal with writing that was uniquely Italian and uniquely his. His first published work was the *Eclogues* (*Bucolica*, 37 B.C.), a collection of idyllic pastoral poems written in the manner of THEOCRITUS. He then began work on the *Georgics* (*Georgica*, 30 B.C.), a realistic tribute to farm life based on HESIOD's *Works and Days*. He devoted the final decade of his life to composing his patriotic Homeric epic, the *Aeneid* (*Aeneis*, c. 29–19 B.C.). During a trip to Greece in 19 B.C., Virgil became ill and died upon his return, leaving his great masterwork unfinished.

Vittorini, Elio (July 23, 1908–February 13, 1966). Italian novelist, translator, and critic. One of Italy's foremost novelists and men of letters, in his neorealist fiction Vittorini explored life under fascism. Born in Sicily, Vittorini began his literary career as a short-story writer and translator of American and English authors, including D. H. LAWRENCE, T. S. ELIOT, Edgar Allan POE, William FAULKNER, and Ernest HEMINGWAY. Hemingway, in turn, wrote the introduction to the American edition of Vittorini's best-known work, *In Sicily* (*Conversazione in*

Sicilia, 1941). The antifascist sentiments expressed in this allegorical tale about a young man's search for truth led to Vittorini's imprisonment. Nevertheless, his literary career continued undeterred with such novels as *The Twilight of the Elephant* (*Il Sempione Strizza l'Occhio al Frejus*, 1947) and *The Red Carnation* (*Il Garofano Rosso*, 1948). The short 1956 novels *Erica* and *La Garibaldina* were published together in English as *The Dark and the Light* (1961).

Voltaire, *pen name of* François-Marie Arouet (November 21, 1694–May 30, 1778). French philosopher, poet, playwright, and novelist. Foremost among the 18th-century *philosophes* and a passionate crusader for humanism, justice, and free thought, Voltaire embodied the genius and values of the Age of Enlightenment. Early literary creations, including the tragic dramas *Oedipe* (1718) and *Zaïre* (1732) and the epic poem *La Henriade* (1728), earned him a reputation among contemporaries as the premier poet and playwright of his century. His place in history, however, rests chiefly on his essays and letters in defense of reason and tolerance, and on such "philosophical tales" as *Zadig* (1747) and CANDIDE (1759). Born of a middle-class Parisian family, he was educated at a Jesuit school and gave up his legal studies for writing. Both admired and condemned for his liberal views and attacks on the church, nobility, and the *ancien régime,* he was imprisoned and exiled on several occasions. Banished to England from 1726 to 1729, he was drawn to the political ideas of John Locke, Isaac Newton, and others, about which he wrote in *Letters Concerning the English Nation* (*Lettres Philosophiques,* 1734). The book was banned in France, and Voltaire took refuge at the estates of wealthy admirers. In 1758 he moved to a French-Swiss border town, where he remained until returning to Paris just before his death. Other major works include *Essay on the Manners and Spirit of Nations* (*Essai sur les Moeurs et l'Esprit des Nations,* 1756–69), a seven-volume world history, and *Philosophical Dictionary* (*Dictionnaire Philosophique,* 1764), a compendium of ideas.

Vonnegut, Kurt, [Jr.] November 11, 1922–). American novelist and short-story writer. Vonnegut's darkly humorous vision of the modern world, conveyed through a unique blend of science fiction, realism, and satire, made him one of America's most popular and original writers of the 1960s and 1970s. Vonnegut was born in Indianapolis, Indiana, and studied biochemistry at Cornell and anthropology at the University of Chicago, an education that was interrupted by service in World War II. His time as a prisoner-of-war in Dresden would later provide the basis for his famed antiwar novel SLAUGHTERHOUSE-FIVE (1969). Vonnegut first came onto the scene with *Player Piano* (1951), a novel about the dehumanizing effects of the corporate workplace. CAT'S CRADLE (1963), an apocalyptic fantasy that uses science fiction to address serious social concerns, earned him a wide readership. Since then, he has produced a steady stream of popular fiction, notably the story collections *Welcome to the Monkey House* (1968) and *Bagombo Snuff Box* (1999), and the novels *Breakfast of Champions* (1973) and *Timequake* (1994).

Walcott, Derek (January 23, 1930–). West Indian poet and playwright. Winner of the 1992 Nobel Prize in Literature, Walcott is celebrated for his poetic and dramatic meditations on Caribbean cultural identity. Born of mixed descent in Castries, St. Lucia, he completed his studies at the University of the West Indies in Jamaica before moving to Trinidad. In 1959 he launched the Trinidad Theatre Workshop, where many of his plays have been produced. His first poetry collection, *In a Green Night* (1962), was praised for its lush blending of island imagery and rhythms. Subsequent collections — including the autobiographical *Another Life* (1973), *Sea Grapes* (1976), and *The Star-Apple Kingdom* (1979) — preserved these stylistic qualities while exploring the folk heritage of the Caribbean. *The Fortunate Traveller* (1981) and *Midsummer* (1984) deal with experiences in the United States, where he has spent much time teaching, and with the theme of cultural estrangement. The sea epic OMEROS (1990), a reworking of the Homeric legends, and other works examine the conflicts and connections among European and Caribbean traditions. Walcott's plays, drawn heavily from island lore, include *Ti-Jean and His Brothers* (1957), *Dream on Monkey Mountain* (1967), and *Pantomime* (1978). He also wrote the book for the 1998 Broadway musical *The Capeman*.

Walker, Alice (February 9, 1944–). American novelist, short-story writer, poet, and essayist. Walker's background as a Georgia sharecropper's daughter, a scholarship student at Sarah Lawrence College, and a civil rights activist has given her a wider view of American culture than that of many of her contemporaries. After publishing two novels, two volumes of poetry, and one collection of short stories, she achieved seemingly overnight critical and commercial success with THE COLOR PURPLE (1982), which won the Pulitzer Prize and became a popular film (1985). In its message of hope and celebration and in its concern with the obstacles faced by black women, the novel is typical of Walker's work. Often writing from the perspective of women who refuse to give up, Walker refers to her approach as "womanist" (rather than feminist). Other significant Walker novels are *Meridian* (1976) and *The Temple of My Familiar* (1989). Her other books include *Revolutionary Petunias and Other Poems* (1973), *In Love and Trouble: Stories of Black Women* (1973), and *In Search of Our Mothers' Gardens* (1983), a collection of essays. *The Way Forward Is with a Broken Heart* (2000) is a collection of fiction and autobiographical stories.

Walton, Izaak (August 9, 1593–December 15, 1683). English prose writer, biographer, and poet. A tradesman with wide-ranging scholarly interests, Walton is remembered as the author of one of the most regularly reprinted works in the English language, THE COMPLEAT ANGLER (1653), an idyllic treatise on the joys of fishing and pastoral life. The son of an alehouse-keeper in Staffordshire, Walton had a modest education and moved to London as an apprentice to an ironmonger. He prospered there as a small shop owner, read extensively, and befriended prominent Anglican clergymen and men of let-

ters. Among them was the vicar John DONNE, a frequent fishing companion. Walton's other notable works include biographies of the poets Donne (1640), Sir Henry Wotton (1651), and GEORGE HERBERT (1670) and of the theologians Richard Hooker (1665) and Robert Sanderson (1678)—referred to collectively as the *Lives*. Walton also wrote elegiac and pastoral verse that appeared in prefaces to books by friends. He spent his later years at Winchester, immersed in writing and editing, church history, and outdoor leisure.

Warner, Sylvia Townsend (December 6, 1893–May 1, 1978). English short-story writer, novelist, and poet. Warner claimed that she began writing poetry "accidentally," on receipt of paper with a "particularly tempting surface." Both the whimsy and the poetic impulse implied in that statement are evident in her work. Her first publication was a poetry collection, *The Espalier* (1925). Her novels include *Lolly Willowes* (1926), a bestseller about a single woman who becomes a witch in order to gain independence; the equally successful *Mr. Fortune's Maggot* (1927), about a South Seas missionary whose soul is saved by the people he sets out to convert; and the acclaimed *The Corner That Held Them* (1948), a historical novel portraying everyday life in a 14th-century convent. Although she thought of herself as a poet first, she is probably best known for her numerous short stories, 144 of which were first published in THE NEW YORKER. Story collections include *Kingdoms of Elfin* (1977), in which her fantasy fairy-world offers the reader an ironic view of human society. Warner also made contributions to *Grove's Dictionary of Music and Musicians* and wrote the travel guide *Somerset* (1949), as well as a critical study, *Jane Austen* (1951, rev. 1957), and a well-received biography, *T. H. White* (1967).

Warren, Robert Penn (April 24, 1905–September 15, 1989). American poet, novelist, and critic. Born in Guthrie, Kentucky, Warren attended Vanderbilt University, where he joined the Fugitive group of poets, which embraced the Southern agrarian tradition. From 1934 to

1973, he taught at Louisiana State University (where he cofounded *The Southern Review*), the University of Minnesota, and Yale. Distinguished alike for his fiction, poetry, and criticism, he is best known for his novel ALL THE KING'S MEN (1946; Pulitzer Prize), which traces the career of a Southern political demagogue. Other fiction includes the novel *World Enough and Time* (1950) and the short-story collection *The Circus in the Attic* (1947). His 14 books of verse — among them *Promises* (1957; Pulitzer Prize), *Now and Then* (1978; Pulitzer Prize), *Being Here* (1980), and *New and Selected Poems* (1985) — established him as a major voice in postwar American poetry; he was named U.S. Poet Laureate in 1985. As a literary critic, he promoted the New Criticism in influential textbooks cowritten with CLEANTH BROOKS — *Understanding Poetry* (1938) and *Understanding Fiction* (1943) — and numerous essays.

Wasserstein, Wendy (October 18, 1950–). American playwright. A native New Yorker, Wasserstein studied at Mount Holyoke, the City College of New York, and the Yale School of Drama. Her first play, *Any Woman Can't* (1973), was also her master's thesis and announced the central concerns of much of her work: the negotiations and compromises made by intelligent middle-class women in a world where family and career are still often felt to be at odds. This fundamentally serious outlook is enlivened by an acute ear and extraordinary sense of humor; Wasserstein's plays escape pigeonholing as drama or comedy. Her sweet-and-sour style has been successful with both critics and audiences, and she was the first woman to receive a Tony Award for playwriting, for *The Heidi Chronicles* (1989), which also won the Pulitzer Prize. Other plays include *Uncommon Women and Others* (1977), *The Sisters Rosensweig* (1993), and *An American Daughter* (1997). In 1999 Wasserstein ventured into opera with her libretto *Festival of Regrets*, one-third of the trilogy *Central Park* (other libretti by Terrence MCNALLY and A. R. Gurney), reinforcing her position as a quintessentially New York playwright.

Waugh, Evelyn (October 28, 1903–April 10, 1966). English novelist. Sophisticated, witty, and staunchly moralistic, Waugh's early novels — including DECLINE AND FALL (1928), VILE BODIES (1930), *Black Mischief* (1932), A HANDFUL OF DUST (1934), and SCOOP (1938) — are highly regarded works of modern satiric fiction. His caustic attacks on English high society and modern culture gave way to more serious and pessimistic novels after World War II, including BRIDESHEAD REVISITED (1945), *Helena* (1950), and the wartime trilogy *Men at Arms* (1952), *Officers and Gentlemen* (1955), and *Unconditional Surrender* (1961). Born in London and

---

"I think to be oversensitive about clichés is like being oversensitive about table manners."

Evelyn Waugh, "Fan-Fare" (1946), in *A Little Order: A Selection from His Journalism* (1981)

---

educated at Lancing College, Sussex, and Hertford College, Oxford, Waugh converted to Roman Catholicism in 1930 and traveled extensively as a journalist. His books include several travelogues of Africa and South America, including the collection *When the Going Was Good* (1946). Waugh saw extensive action in the Royal Marines and Royal Horse Guard during World War II, settling thereafter at his home in Somerset. *The Ordeal of Gilbert Pinfold* (1957) is a fictional self-caricature about a middle-aged Catholic writer who suffers from hallucinations. *A Little Learning* (1964) recounts his childhood and education. His highly revealing *Diaries* appeared posthumously in 1976.

Webster, John (c. 1580–c. 1634). English playwright. Beginning in 1602, Webster's plays (mostly collaborations with such dramatists as John Ford, Thomas Middleton, and William Rowley) were performed by some of the most prestigious companies in London. Several of his works are now lost; extant plays include two written with Thomas Dekker: *Westward Ho* (1604) and *Northward Ho* (1605). Webster's modern reputation, however, is based on his sole authorship of the blank verse tragedies THE WHITE DEVIL (1612) and THE DUCHESS OF MALFI (c. 1613), and to a lesser degree on his tragicomedy *The Devil's Law-Case* (1610?). The preoccupation with death and corruption in his two best-known plays, which are more frequently revived than any Jacobean tragedies except SHAKESPEARE's, is captured in T. S. ELIOT's "Whispers of Immortality" (1920): "Webster was much possessed by death / And saw the skull beneath the skin."

Wedekind, [Benjamin] **Frank**[lin] (July 24, 1864–March 9, 1918). German playwright, journalist, and poet. Considered a forerunner of the Expressionists for his provocative, antibourgeois, and sexually candid dramas, which occasioned public controversy and difficulties with the censors, Wedekind was also a contributor to the Munich satirical weekly *Simplicissimus*, and an actor and cabaret performer who sometimes appeared in his own plays with his wife, Tilly. He is best remembered for *Spring Awakening* (*Frühlingserwachen*, published 1891; produced 1905), a harsh, sometimes lyrical drama of adolescent sexuality, and two plays, *Earth Spirit* (*Erdgeist*, 1898) and PANDORA'S BOX (*Die Büchse der Pandora*, 1904), that together constitute a "monster drama" about the *femme fatale* LULU, who destroys numerous lovers before dying at the hands of Jack the Ripper. Wedekind's diaries were published posthumously as *The Diary of an Erotic Life* (*Die Tagebücher: Ein Erotisches Leben*, 1986).

Weiss, Peter (November 8, 1916–May 10, 1982). German playwright and novelist. In exile from Nazi Germany from 1934 onward, Weiss settled permanently in Sweden in 1939, where his first career was as an artist and filmmaker. He began writing in Swedish, but soon switched to German, publishing several short novels and memoirs. His breakthrough came in 1964 with the play *The Persecution and Assassination of Jean-Paul Marat as Performed by the Inmates of the Asylum of Charenton under the Direction of the Marquis de Sade*, commonly known as MARAT/SADE. An international sensation, it was followed by other political dramas, such as *The Investigation* (*Die Ermittlung*, 1965), based on documents of the Frankfurt Auschwitz trial, and *Viet Nam Discourse* (*Viet Nam Diskurs*, 1968). An engaged leftist, Weiss returned to the novel in the 1970s with *The Aesthetics of Resistance* (*Die Ästhetik des Widerstands*, 1975–81) to record his interpretation of the political turmoil of the 20th century.

Weldon, Fay, *original name* Franklin Birkinshaw (September 22, 1931?–). English novelist, short-story writer, playwright, and scriptwriter. Noted for her witty, idiosyncratic portrayals of contemporary women and their tragicomic family relationships, Weldon has entertained a vast audience with bestselling works of fiction as well as adaptations and original plays for television, radio, and the stage. Born in London and raised in New Zealand, she attended St. Andrew's University in Scotland and worked as an advertising copywriter during the 1960s. Her first novel, *The Fat Woman's Joke* (1967), began as a television play, and was followed by a string of successes in the 1970s, including *Down Among the Women* (1971), *Female Friends* (1974), *Praxis* (1978), and *Puffball* (1979). Her skillful use of dialogue led to a thriving career as a playwright and scriptwriter, even as her production of fiction remained steady. Later novels include *The Life and Loves of a She-Devil* (1983), *The Cloning of Joanna May* (1989), *Darcy's Utopia* (1990), *Worst Fears* (1996), and *Rhode Island Blues* (2000). Among her story collections are *Polaris* (1985), *Wicked Women* (1995), and *A Hard Time to Be a Father* (1999).

Wells, H[erbert] **G**[eorge] (September 21, 1866–August 13, 1946). English novelist, journalist, and historian. The son of lower-middle-class parents, Wells attended the Normal School of Science on scholarship, where he was greatly influenced by the biologist T. H. Huxley. His scientific training is reflected in the novels for which he is best known today— THE TIME MACHINE (1895), *The Island of Dr. Moreau* (1886), THE INVISIBLE MAN (1897), and

THE WAR OF THE WORLDS (1898) — in which he developed the modern concept of science fiction. In his own day, however, his novels in the realist tradition were also admired. *TONO-BUNGAY* (1909), providing a critical view of society, was well received, as was the comic *History of Mr. Polly* (1910). But in *Boon* (1915) Wells antagonized many of the literati with a parody of his former friend HENRY JAMES. Sympathetic to socialism and hoping that technology would save civilization, Wells published political discussions throughout his lifetime. Although he never despaired, he nonetheless saw an urgent need to awaken society to dangers at large, declaring in *The Outline of History* (1920) that "History is more and more a race between education and catastrophe."

Welty, Eudora (April 13, 1909–July 23, 2001). American novelist, short-story writer, critic, and essayist. A connoisseur of ordinary lives, with a fierce wit and a brilliant ear for the Southern vernacular, Welty was the kind of artist, as Carol SHIELDS put it, who made great literature "out of the humble clay of home." Born in Jackson, Mississippi, into a bookish family, Welty attended Mississippi State College for Women, but took her B.A. at the University of Wisconsin in 1929. She was studying advertising in New York when her father's unexpected death forced her back to Jackson, where she lived for the rest of her life. During the Depression, she traveled throughout Mississippi for the WPA, interviewing and photographing people from all walks of life, an experience that she would later mine in her fiction. Welty began to place her work in magazines in the late 1930s, publishing her first collection, *A Curtain of Green* (with an admiring introduction by Katherine Anne PORTER) in 1941. This volume, which helped to establish her reputation, includes three of her most popular stories, "The Petrified Man," "The Worn Path," and "WHY I LIVE AT THE P.O." Later collections include *The Wide Net* (1943), *The Golden Apples* (1949), and *The Bride of Innisfallen* (1955). Among her novels are *THE PONDER HEART* (1954), a masterpiece of absurdist

humor; *Delta Wedding* (1946) and *Losing Battles* (1970), which work on a larger canvas to portray extended Southern families; and *THE OPTIMIST'S DAUGHTER* (1972; Pulitzer Prize), which describes the aftermath of a beloved father's death. *A Writer's Eye* (1994) collects her book reviews; her photographs have been published in *Eudora Welty: Photographs* (1989) and *Eudora Welty: Country Churchyards* (2000). Among her many honors and awards were the French Legion of Honor and the American Medal of Freedom. At the end of her memoir, *One Writer's Beginnings* (1984), she wrote, "As you have seen, I am a writer who came of a sheltered life. A sheltered life can be a daring life as well. For all serious daring starts from within."

West, Nathanael, *original name* Nathan Weinstein (October 17, 1903–December 22, 1940). American novelist and screenwriter. The New York–born son of Lithuanian-German-Jewish immigrants, West legally changed his name in 1926. Bitterly resenting American society for snubbing him because of the Jewish heritage he himself had disavowed, he concentrated on its grotesques and marginals in the four slender, mordantly satirical novels for which he is remembered: the bizarre, scatological, and misogynistic *The Dream Life of Balso Snell* (1931); *MISS LONELYHEARTS* (1933), considered his most accomplished work, about an advice columnist more desperate than his wretched supplicants; *A Cool Million* (1934), an anti–Horatio Alger, rags-to-ashes saga; and the acid-edged *THE DAY OF THE LOCUST* (1939), about misfits on the fringes of Hollywood's dream factory. The last was the fruit of his sojourn in late-1930s Hollywood as a moderately successful screenwriter. In 1940, West married Eileen McKenney, the "Eileen" of Ruth McKenney's bestseller, *My Sister Eileen*; his own sister, Laura, was the wife of his lifelong friend S. J. PERELMAN. West and his wife were killed in a car accident later that year. He had made a little over a thousand dollars from his novels; he is now widely ranked among the century's major American novelists.

THE NEW YORK PUBLIC LIBRARY IN FICTION

The New York Public Library has frequently been depicted in fiction, no doubt because it is located in the literary and publishing center of the United States, and because it serves the many writers who live in New York or who visit either for pleasure or work. The following passages all refer to the Library's Beaux-Arts building at Fifth Avenue and 42nd Street, which is guarded by two famous stone lions.

A few days after his arrival he happened to emerge upon Fifth Avenue just opposite the Public Library. Awed by its rhetorical façade, so unlike a haunt of studious peace, he stood wondering if it were one of the swell hotels he'd heard about—the Ritz or the St. Regis—till looking more closely he read its designation. Instantly he dashed up the vast steps, entered the doors unabashed, and asked the first official he met if he could go in and read....He could, it appeared, and without paying a cent, and for many hours of the day. At first he was perplexed as to his next step; but where books were concerned some instinct seemed to guide him, and presently he had been made free of a series of card-catalogues, and was lost in them as in the murmurs of a forest....It was wonderful...to sit in a recess of a quiet room, with a pile of volumes in front of him, his elbows on the table, his hands plunged in his hair, his soul immersed in a new world...his hours at the Library were so engrossing, and his ignorance had revealed itself on a scale so unsuspected and overwhelming, that each day drew him back to the lion-guarded gates of knowledge.

Edith Wharton, *Hudson River Bracketed* (1929)

Bernard Clare looked around vaguely in the large reading room of the New York Public Library....He fingered his pencils. He gazed upward at the high ceiling. He listened to vague sounds from the remote world of New York beyond the walls of this building.... A seedy old woman took a book from a clerk by the board, clutched it, scurried to the first

---

West, [Dame] Rebecca, *original name* Cicily Isabel Fairfield (December 25, 1892–March 15, 1983). English journalist, novelist, and critic. An ardent feminist and advocate for women's suffrage, West took her name from the heroine of Henrik IBSEN's play *Rosmersholm*. Born in London and educated at George Watson's Ladies' College in Edinburgh, she briefly pursued a career in acting before turning to political journalism in 1912. She is best known for her two-volume sociopolitical history and travelogue of the Balkans, *Black Lamb and Grey Falcon* (1941), and for her reports for THE NEW YORKER on the treason trial of World War II propagandist "Lord Haw-Haw," collected in *The Meaning of Treason* (1947), and on the Nuremberg war-crimes trials, collected in *A Train of Powder* (1955). Her writings also include seven

table, and bent over the book. In front of him, he noticed a bald-headed man whom he had seen here before working out chess problems, reading and poring over volumes on chess. The library! The world of the inner life of man.

James T. Farrell, *Bernard Clare* (1946)

How many wonderful days and nights I spent at the 42nd Street Library, seated at a long table, one among thousands, it seemed, in that main reading room. The tables themselves excited me. It was always my desire to own a table of extraordinary dimensions, a table so large that I could not only sleep on it but dance on it, even skate on it....Yes, it gave one a good feeling to be working amidst so many other industrious students in a room the size of a cathedral, under a lofty ceiling which was an imitation of heaven itself....Sometimes I sat and meditated, wondering what question I could put to the genius which presided over the spirit of this vast institution that it could not answer.

Henry Miller, *Plexus* (1953)

He left Fifth Avenue and walked west towards the movie houses. Here on 42nd Street it was less elegant but no less strange. He loved this street, not for the people or the shops but for the stone lions that guarded the great main building of the Public Library, a building filled with books and unimaginably vast, and which he had never yet dared to enter. He might, he knew, for he was a member of the branch in Harlem and was entitled to take books from any library in the city. But he had never gone in because the building was so big that it must be full of corridors and marble steps, in the maze of which he would be lost and never find the book he wanted. And then everyone, all the white people inside, would know that he was not used to great buildings, or to many books, and they would look at him with pity. He would enter on another day, when he had read all the books uptown, an achievement that would, he felt, lend him the poise to enter any building in the world.

James Baldwin, *Go Tell It on the Mountain* (1953)

novels—among them *The Judge* (1922), *The Thinking Reed* (1936), *The Fountain Overflows* (1956), and *The Birds Fall Down* (1966)—and critical studies of HENRY JAMES, D. H. LAWRENCE, and St. Augustine. A ten-year liaison with H. G. WELLS beginning in 1912 produced her only child, the writer Anthony West. She was later married to the banker Henry Maxwell Andrews.

"Just how difficult it is to write biography can be reckoned by anybody who sits down and considers just how many people know the real truth about his or her love affairs."

Rebecca West, "The Art of Skepticism," *Vogue* (November 1952)

Westmacott, Mary. *See* **Christie, Agatha**

Wharton, Edith, *original name* Edith Newbold Jones (January 24, 1862–August 11, 1937). American novelist, short-story and nonfiction writer, and poet. Wharton, raised in the United States and Europe, is renowned as the preeminent chronicler of the Old New York society into which she was born. Her first literary experiments were published anonymously in THE ATLANTIC MONTHLY in 1880, but she wrote little over the next ten years. In 1885, she entered into an unsatisfying and passionless marriage to Edward "Teddy" Wharton, a banker; the couple divided their time between the United States and France. Within a few years, Wharton was writing short stories of particular psychological acuity, culminating in *The Greater Inclination* (1899), and by 1902 had published a novel, *The Valley of Decision.* Her first major work, THE HOUSE OF MIRTH (1905), depicting the tragic struggle of the individual to rise above rigid social conventions, was a critical and popular success. After moving to France in 1907, Wharton produced ETHAN FROME (1911), a novel about a painful love triangle, set against the backdrop of a dreary New England winter. By 1913, Teddy had suffered numerous nervous illnesses and been discovered embezzling her funds, and Wharton divorced him. The same year, her scathing satire, *The Custom of the Country,* which chronicles the devastating career of a heartless American social-climber, was published. THE AGE OF INNOCENCE (1920; Pulitzer Prize) followed a thwarted love affair over the course of a lifetime and is considered Wharton's most distinguished work. Her nonfiction includes *The Writing of Fiction* (1924), which shows her debt to her lifelong friend, HENRY JAMES; and *A Backward Glance* (1934), her autobiography. She left unfinished at her death a novel, *The Buccaneers* (1938).

Wheatley, Phillis (c. 1753–December 5, 1784). American poet. The first African-American woman poet of note, she was captured in her native West Africa in 1761 and brought to America in a slave ship. As a servant to the family of John Wheatley, a Boston tailor, she was allowed to learn to read and write, quickly mastering English and moving on to Latin, Greek, ancient history, and mythology. She wrote her first mature verse as a teenager, and her collection *Poems on Various Subjects, Religious and Moral* (1773) was published during a family visit to London. Her lively personality and classically inspired poems won admirers in London social circles, where she was known as the "sable muse." Several more poems found their way into print after her return to America, but no second volume was published in her lifetime. Granted her freedom after the death of the Wheatleys, she married in 1778, took work as a maid, and died in obscurity. *Memoir and Poems of Phillis Wheatley* (1834) and *Letters of Phillis Wheatley* (1864) were published posthumously.

White, Patrick (May 28, 1912–September 30, 1990). Australian novelist and playwright. Awarded the Nobel Prize in Literature in 1973, White was cited "for an epic and psychological narrative art which has introduced a new continent into literature." Born in London to Australian parents, he spent his early years in Sydney and the Outback; the latter would provide the imaginative landscape for many of his works. He earned a university degree in 1932 at King's College, Cambridge, and served in the RAF as an intelligence officer during World War II, finally settling on a farm outside Sydney. His novels, steeped in myth and allegory, center on the search for reason and spiritual truth among the isolated and dispossessed. *Happy Valley* (1939), his first published fiction, is the story of a small town in New South Wales. *The Tree of Man* (1955) began a series of award-winning novels set largely in the Australian interior, among them *VOSS* (1957), *Riders in the Chariot* (1961), and *The Eye of the Storm* (1973). Dramatic works include *Four Plays* (1965) and *Signal Driver* (1962). *Flaws in the Glass* (1981) and *Memoirs of Many in One* (1986) are autobiographical.

Whitman, Walt[er] (May 31, 1819–March 26, 1892). American poet and journalist. Seeking a poetry that would reflect a vitally American experience—vast in scope, democratic in spirit, vigorous, free-flowing, celebrating the self and nature—Whitman achieved a uniquely important place in the national literature with his life's work, *LEAVES OF GRASS*. Born on a small farm on Long Island, New York, he was raised from the age of five in Brooklyn, where he attended public schools and learned the printing trade. He began work as a teacher, typesetter, and newspaperman, becoming editor of the *Brooklyn Eagle,* the city's leading daily, from 1846 to 1848. Except for a brief stay in New Orleans, he lived and worked at odd jobs in Brooklyn through the 1850s. The first edition of *Leaves of Grass,* hand-printed and consisting of 12 untitled poems, appeared in 1855. Although hardly a popular success, the work did not go unnoticed: "I greet you at the beginning of a great career," wrote EMERSON. Whitman went on to produce eight expanded editions, the last in 1892. Meanwhile, in 1862, he traveled to Virginia to nurse his brother George, who had been wounded in the Civil War. Staying on in Washington as a hospital volunteer and government clerk, he produced two collections of war poems, *Drum Taps* (1865) and *Sequel to Drum Taps* (1865–66), the latter containing his famous elegies for Lincoln, "When Lilacs Last in the Dooryard Bloom'd" and "O Captain! My Captain!" After a paralytic stroke in 1873, he moved to Camden, New Jersey, where he lived out his life attended by celebrity.

Whittier, John Greenleaf (December 17, 1807–September 7, 1892). American poet and journalist. A Quaker raised on his father's farm in Massachusetts, Whittier was the most popular poet of 19th-century rural New England and a highly influential polemicist of the Abolitionist movement. His early poems and essays gained the notice of William Lloyd Garrison, who became a lifelong friend, and led to work on various antislavery publications. His pamphlet *Justice and Expediency* (1833) and subsequent writings established him as a leading spokesman for Abolitionism. Meanwhile, his first volumes of original poems and sketches, beginning with *Legends of New England* (1831), were having little success, and it was not until the publication of the poem "SNOW BOUND" in 1866 that he won widespread recognition as a writer of literary merit. Other poems on which his reputation now rests include "Maud Miller" (1854), "The Barefoot Boy" (1855), and "Barbara Fritchie" (1863). Departing from the bucolic and reformist themes of his pre–Civil War writings, Whittier's later work is marked by a devotional piety, grounded in Quakerism, that has led some to call him "America's finest religious poet."

Wiesel, Elie[zer] (September 30, 1928–). Romanian-born novelist and essayist. A passionate spokesman for and activist on behalf of victims and survivors of the Nazi Holocaust—efforts for which he was awarded the Nobel Peace Prize in 1986—Wiesel has written more than 30 books of testimony, consecration, and reconciliation of faith. Raised in a traditional Jewish household in the village of Sighet, Romania, he was deported with his family to the Auschwitz concentration camp in 1944. He settled in Paris after the war and moved to the United States in 1956, taking teaching positions at City College of New York and later Boston University. His first account of Holocaust experiences was the powerful novella *Night* (*La Nuit,* 1958). Subsequent novels—many written in French and translated by his wife, Marion—include *Dawn* (*L'Aube,* 1961), *The Accident* (*Le Jour,* 1961), *A Beggar in Jerusalem* (*Le Mendiant de Jérusalem,* 1968), and *Twilight* (*Le Crépuscule au Loin,* 1987). He has also written on Jewish lore and biblical characters in *Souls on Fire* (*Célébration Hassidique,* 1972) and other volumes. *All Rivers Run to the Sea* (*Tous les Fleuves Vont à la Mer,* 1994) and *And the Sea Is Never Full* (*Et la Mer N'est Pas Remplie,* 1996) are memoirs.

Wilbur, Richard (March 1, 1921–). American poet, translator, critic, and editor. One of the most distinguished post–World War II American poets writing in traditional meters and forms, Wilbur was born in New York City and grew up on a farm in rural New Jersey, an experience that sparked his lifelong fascination with "how things work" in nature. He studied at Amherst College and, after serving in the U.S. Army in Italy and Germany during World War II, took his M.A. from Harvard University in 1947, in the same year publishing his first collection, *The Beautiful Changes and Other Poems*. Like MARIANNE MOORE, one of his models, Wilbur has been acclaimed for the felicitous precision with which he evokes the things and creatures of the world. Other collections of Wilbur's poetry include *Ceremony and Other Poems* (1950), *Things of This World: Poems* (1956; Pulitzer Prize, National Book Award), *Advice to a Prophet and Other Poems* (1961), *The Mind-Reader: New Poems* (1976), *New and Collected Poems* (1988; Pulitzer Prize), and *Mayflies: New Poems and Translations* (2000). Named Poet Laureate of the United States for 1987–88, Wilbur is also a prolific translator, especially renowned for his brilliant versions of the plays of RACINE and MOLIÈRE. Other works include *Responses: Prose Pieces, 1953–1976* (1976; expanded edition 2000) and *The Catbird's Song: Prose Pieces, 1963–1995* (1997).

Wilde, Oscar, *original name* Fingal O'Flahertie Wills Wilde (October 16, 1854–November 30, 1900). Irish playwright, novelist, short-story writer, poet, and critic. Born in Dublin, Wilde was educated at Trinity College, Dublin, and Magdalen College, Oxford, then moved to London, making a name for himself as a wit, dandy, and leader of the Aesthetic movement. Had he written nothing other than THE IMPORTANCE OF BEING EARNEST (1895), his admission to the pantheon of English letters would be secure. That play is the quintessential comedy of manners, linking the Restoration wit of CONGREVE and the 18th-century brilliance of SHERIDAN with the 20th-century drawing-room polish of COWARD and the absurdism of PINTER and STOPPARD. But Wilde also wrote the novel THE PICTURE OF DORIAN GRAY (1891), a moral allegory that is at the same time the epitome of the *fin-de-siècle* decadence it decries. Among his other works are three assured comedies, LADY WINDERMERE'S FAN (1892), *A Woman of No Importance* (1893), and AN IDEAL HUSBAND (1895);

several collections of children's stories, including *The Happy Prince* (1888) and *A House of Pomegranates* (1891); and a drama in French, *Salomé* (1896). An ill-advised lawsuit for libel against the Marquess of Queensberry, the father of his lover, Lord Alfred Douglas ("Bosie"), resulted in Wilde's trial and conviction for "gross indecency." He was sentenced to two years' hard labor, during which time he wrote a long letter to Bosie, published posthumously as *De Profundis* (1905). On his release from prison, he moved to France, where he wrote his most famous poem, THE BALLAD OF READING GAOL (1897), and died in exile.

Wilder, Thornton (April 17, 1897–December 7, 1975). American playwright, novelist, and screenwriter. Born in Wisconsin, Wilder grew up in China and California. After graduating from Yale, he studied history and the classics in Rome—subjects that would inform his first novel, *The Cabala* (1926), and others, including *The Ides of March* (1948). While in Rome, he was influenced by the experimental playwright PIRANDELLO. On his return to the United States, he began writing professionally while earning a master's degree from Princeton. His second novel, THE BRIDGE OF SAN LUIS REY (1927), won the Pulitzer Prize. After writing several successful one-act plays employing ancient Greek stagecraft, such as direct address and minimal scenery, he further developed this approach in the full-length OUR TOWN (1938; Pulitzer Prize; also screenplay, 1940), which has become the most-produced play in America, and THE SKIN OF OUR TEETH (1942; Pulitzer Prize), a more experimental work that uses anachronism to make the point that human nature is unchanging. Direct address is also used in *The Matchmaker* (1954), which became the basis for the musical *Hello, Dolly!* Other novels include *The Eighth Day* (1967; National Book Award) and THEOPHILUS NORTH (1973). Wilder also coscripted *Shadow of a Doubt* (1942), the favorite film of its director, Alfred Hitchcock.

Williams, Tennessee, *original name* Thomas Lanier Williams II (March 26, 1911–February

25, 1983). American playwright. Williams is generally acknowledged, with Eugene O'NEILL and ARTHUR MILLER, as one of the three great playwrights of the American stage. Renowned for treating the earthiest of subjects with lyrical delicacy, most of his work reveals an attachment to a romanticized although not uncritical vision of America's Deep South. His first major achievement was THE GLASS MENAGERIE (1945), a poetic, loosely autobiographical "memory play." This was followed by the overwhelming success of A STREETCAR NAMED DESIRE (1947; Pulitzer Prize), which features one of the most memorable lines in American drama, Blanche DuBois's "I have always depended on the kindness of strangers." Other plays of the next decade-and-a-half include Summer and Smoke (1948), The Rose Tattoo (1950), CAT ON A HOT TIN ROOF (1955; Pulitzer Prize), Orpheus Descending (1957), SUDDENLY LAST SUMMER (1958), SWEET BIRD OF YOUTH (1959), and his last unqualified success, THE NIGHT OF THE IGUANA (1961). Williams continued to write for the rest of his life, but his later plays—including The Milk Train Doesn't Stop Here Anymore (1962), Out Cry (1971), and Clothes for a Summer Hotel (1981)—were generally dismissed by critics. In 1998, an early, previously unproduced play, Not About Nightingales, written in 1939, was staged to acclaim in England and subsequently on Broadway. Williams's other works include the novel The Roman Spring of Mrs. Stone (1950) and the short-story collection Hard Candy (1954). He also adapted a number of his works for the screen; his screenplay for Baby Doll (1954), based on two of his one-act plays, was directed by his frequent collaborator Elia Kazan.

Williams, William Carlos (September 17, 1883–March 4, 1963). American poet, novelist, and short-story writer. A practicing physician for more than 50 years in his birthplace of Rutherford, New Jersey, Williams produced a body of poetry considered among the most innovative, influential, and distinctively American of the 20th century. Epitomized by his five-volume epic, PATERSON (1946–58), based on the manu-

facturing city near his home, his fresh poetic vision sprang from the experiences and idioms of everyday life. His 45 books of verse and prose, predominantly American in subject matter, reflect his "objectivist" approach in their emphasis on the concrete rather than the abstract. Williams's unique poetic style and philosophy took shape in several early volumes: The Tempers (1913), Al Que Quiere! (1917), Kora in Hell (1920), and Sour Grapes (1921). Subsequent verse was gathered in Collected Poems (1934), Collected Later Poems (1950), Collected Earlier Poems (1951), and PICTURES FROM BRUEGHEL (1962; Pulitzer Prize), a three-volume compilation. Among his works of fiction are the Steche trilogy of novels, the saga of an American immigrant family, and more than 50 short stories. Other essential prose includes In the American Grain (1925), a look at early American history and culture, his Autobiography (1951), and Selected Essays (1954).

Wilson, A[ndrew] **N**[orman] (October 27, 1950–). English novelist, biographer, critic, and journalist. Educated at Rugby and Oxford, Wilson is a prolific writer of social comedy in the tradition of EVELYN WAUGH and Barbara PYM. His literary bent combines satire, aimed particularly at the upper and middle classes, with a serious concern with religion, especially the Church of England. Wilson's novels, the best received of which have been Wise Virgin (1982), Daughters of Albion (1991), and The Vicar of Sorrows (1994), are populated by clergymen, capitalists, artists, physicians, actors, and teachers, whose difficulties with sexuality, family, greed, and belief in God he portrays with acerbic accuracy. His interests in England and religion have extended to his nonfiction work: he has written biographies—often popular, sometimes controversial—of JESUS, Saint Paul, MILTON, SIR WALTER SCOTT, and C. S. LEWIS, among others, and edited both The Faber Book of Church and Clergy (1992) and The Faber Book of London (1993).

Wilson, [Sir] Angus (August 11, 1913–May 31, 1991). English novelist, short-story writer, and literary biographer. The author of some 50 books—even though he did not begin writing until his mid-30s—Wilson satirized British middle-class society with a distinctive mixture of wit and compassion in such novels as *Hemlock and After* (1952), *Anglo-Saxon Attitudes* (1956), *The Middle Age of Mrs. Eliot* (1958), and *Old Men at the Zoo* (1961), and the short-story collections *The Wrong Set* (1949), *Such Darling Dodos* (1950), and *A Bit off the Map* (1957). Raised in an unsettled middle-class family in London, he attended Merton College, Oxford, and worked in the Foreign Service during World War II. He later served as deputy supervisor at the British Library Reading Room and, from 1966 to 1978, professor of English at the University of East Anglia. His work as a scholar includes distinguished critical biographies of Émile ZOLA, Charles DICKENS, and Rudyard KIPLING. *The Wild Garden* (1963) tells of his own life and creative processes. *Diversity and Depth in Fiction* (1984) is a selection of critical essays.

Wilson, August, *original name* Frederick August Kittel (April 27, 1945–). American playwright. Wilson's best-known works are part of a projected ten-play cycle set mostly in The Hill, a black neighborhood in Pittsburgh, where he was raised. Each play takes place in a different decade of the 20th century and examines a different aspect of African-American history. Completed works in the cycle are *Jitney* (1982), MA RAINEY'S BLACK BOTTOM (1984), FENCES (1985; Pulitzer Prize), *Joe Turner's Come and Gone* (1986), THE PIANO LESSON (1987; Pulitzer Prize), *Two Trains Running* (1990), *Seven Guitars* (1995), and *King Hedley II* (1999). Developed in regional theaters, all but the first have also been produced on Broadway; a revised *Jitney* received an acclaimed Off-Broadway production in 2000. Wilson's work is notable for its creative incorporation of African-American culture and folk tradition; he credits as his chief influences "the four B's": Romare Bearden, Amiri BARAKA, Jorge Luis BORGES, and the Blues. Cofounder/director of the Pittsburgh theater company Black Horizons on The Hill (1968–78), he is an outspoken supporter of the development of an African aesthetic in American theater.

Wilson, Lanford (April 13, 1937–). American playwright. Wilson's career was launched in the 1960s heyday of the Off-Off-Broadway movement. Of his early works, perhaps the best known is *Balm in Gilead* (1965), which explores the aspirations of a loose community of New York street types who frequent the same coffee shop. It exemplifies his style, which employs virtuosic monologues, direct address, and unusual approaches to time and place, yet remains fundamentally realistic, and makes use of naturalistic devices such as overlapping dialogue. In 1969, Wilson became cofounder and resident playwright of Off-Broadway's Circle Repertory Company, where many of his subsequent works were developed. *The Hot l Baltimore* (1973), about the residents of a hotel slated for demolition, won critical acclaim and several awards, enjoyed an extended run, and was adapted as a television series. *Fifth of July* (1978) and *Talley's Folly* (1979; Pulitzer Prize), the first two plays of the Talley family trilogy set in his hometown of Lebanon, Missouri, achieved Broadway runs and garnered important awards. Later plays include *Angels Fall* (1982), *Burn This* (1987), *Redwood Curtain* (1991), and *Sympathetic Magic* (1998).

Winterson, Jeanette (August 27, 1959–). English novelist and essayist. Winterson was adopted into an evangelical Christian family in the north of England and was a child preacher before her coming-out as a lesbian caused an irreparable break with her family. She was educated at Oxford and burst onto the literary scene with *Oranges Are Not the Only Fruit* (1985), an extraordinarily well-received volume that won the Whitbread Prize for a first novel. Combining autobiographical elements with inset parables and fairy tales, *Oranges* reads like a British answer to magic realism. Winterson's concerns with love, sex, language, and ethics are carried further in her novels *The Passion* (1987), *Sexing the Cherry* (1989), *Written on the Body* (1992), and *Gut Symmetries* (1997), written in an inventive, approachably experimental style with settings ranging from Renaissance Venice to Russia during the Napoleonic Wars to late 20th-century England. Winterson's essays are collected in *Art Objects: Essays on Ecstasy and Effrontery* (1995).

Wodehouse, [Sir] **P**[elham] **G**[renville] (October 15, 1881–February 14, 1975). English-born novelist, short-story writer, playwright, and lyricist. One of the world's great humorists, Wodehouse wrote 73 novels and 291 stories, all based (whatever their ostensible setting) in an idealization of the Edwardian world in which he reached maturity. His many much-loved characters, including Psmith, Mulliner, Sally, Ukridge, The Oldest Member, and the inhabitants of Blandings Castle, are featured in various popular series; the best known are the engagingly dim Bertie WOOSTER and his imperturbable gentleman's gentleman, JEEVES. Wodehouse's narrative style, juxtaposing classical allusions with breezy slang, and unexpected imagery ("He floated noiselessly through the doorway like a healing zephyr") with unconventional modifiers ("I balanced a thoughtful lump of sugar on the teaspoon"), secured his reputation as a grand master of English prose. He was also the author or coauthor of 16 plays, and librettist (and often lyricist) of 22 musicals; musical collaborators included George Gershwin, Victor Herbert, and Cole Porter. His whimsical, politically naive 1941 radio broadcasts about his experiences as a German prisoner-of-war were misunderstood in England and denounced as treasonous; in 1947 he moved permanently to the United States. His works include *My Man Jeeves* (1919); *Leave It to Psmith* (1923); *Carry On, Jeeves* (1925); *Doctor Sally* (1932); *Mulliner Nights* (1933); *Blandings Castle* (1935); *The Code of the Woosters* (1938); *Pigs Have Wings* (1952); *Service with a Smile* (1961); and *Aunts Aren't Gentlemen* (1974; U.S. title, *The Cat Nappers*). Autobiographical works include *Performing Flea: A Self-Portrait in Letters* (1953; U.S. title, *Author! Author!*) and *America, I Like You* (1956; revised 1957 as *Over Seventy: An Autobiography with Digressions*).

Wolf, Christa (March 18, 1929–). German novelist and essayist. Although Wolf is closely identified with the former East Germany, she is a sophisticated and demanding writer who received honors and provoked controversy in both the former German states as well as in reunited Germany. Committed to Marxist social ideals, she explores in her novels the personal crises of individuals, especially women, caught up in difficult historical currents. *Divided Heaven* (*Der Geteilte Himmel*, 1963), praised in East Germany, is about a woman who refuses to follow her lover to West Germany, while *The Quest for Christa T.* (*Nachdenken über Christa T.*, 1968), admired in West Germany, describes the heroine's failure to flourish under socialism. Wolf examined her Nazi-era childhood in the autobiographical novel *A Model Childhood* (*Kindheitsmuster*, 1976). After reunification, she confessed to a brief and distant period of cooperation with East German state surveillance authorities, and published a novel, *Medea* (1996), in which the mythic title character metaphorically voiced Wolf's sense of uprootedness in the new Germany.

Wolfe, Thomas (October 3, 1900–September 15, 1938). American novelist. Four epic novels, the lyrical energy of his prose, and an output of manuscript that allegedly bordered on the unmanageable have contributed to Wolfe's reputation as one of the leading—and legendary—figures of modern American fiction. Early ambitions as a playwright led him to the University of North Carolina, Harvard, and New York City, where he lived from 1923 to the end of his short life. Turning to fiction in 1926, he began work on what would become his first, most acclaimed novel, LOOK HOMEWARD, ANGEL (1929). Set in the North Carolina town of Altamount, modeled after his native Asheville, and recounting the youth of Eugene GANT, his autobiographical protagonist, the final version was born of a close working relationship with Scribner's editor Maxwell PERKINS. OF TIME AND THE RIVER (1935), also edited by Perkins, continues Gant's story after leaving home. Wolfe died unexpectedly in 1938, leaving a voluminous manuscript from which another editor, Edward Aswell at Harper's, produced the novels *THE WEB AND THE ROCK* (1939) and *YOU CAN'T GO HOME AGAIN* (1940)—featuring a new autobiographical hero, George Webber—and a collection of shorter pieces, *The Hills Beyond* (1942).

Wolfe, Tom, *in full* Thomas Kennerly Wolfe, Jr. (March 2, 1931–). American journalist and novelist. A leading practitioner of New Journalism—mixing objective reportage with personal observation and techniques borrowed from fiction—Wolfe has portrayed contemporary American society in a succession of highly animated, amusing, often controversial narratives and essays. He received a doctorate in American Studies from Yale University in 1957 and wrote for several newspapers and magazines before publishing *The Kandy-Kolored Tangerine-Flake Streamline Baby* (1965), a collection of satiric essays on popular culture. Later works include several major bestsellers: *The Electric Kool-Aid Acid Test* (1968), recounting the psychedelic adventures of writer Ken KESEY and friends during the 1960s; *The Right Stuff* (1979), about the original American astronauts; and his first novel, *THE BONFIRE OF THE VANITIES* (1987), a story of greed and corruption in New York City during the "go-go" 1980s. *The Painted Word* (1975) and *From Bauhaus to Our House* (1981) are critical commentaries on modern art and architecture, respectively. Other works include *The Pump House Gang* (1968), *Radical Chic & Mau-Mauing the Flak Catchers* (1970), and the novel *A Man in Full* (1998).

Woolf, Virginia, *original name* Adeline Virginia Stephen (January 25, 1882–March 28, 1941). English novelist, short-story writer, essayist, critic, and diarist. One of the most innovative and influential writers of the 20th century, Woolf was born into a family that was part of the intellectual elite of Great Britain. Unlike her brothers, she was educated at home under the guidance of her father, Sir Leslie STEPHEN, the distinguished man of letters and editor of the *Dictionary of National Biography*, who gave her free run of his library. In 1904, Woolf became a

professional author when *THE TIMES LITERARY SUPPLEMENT* published her first essay (a subtle meditation on a pilgrimage she had made to the BRONTË homestead at Haworth), the beginning of a singularly productive career that would establish her as one of the most important essayists and critics of her generation. After her father's death, Woolf, her two brothers, and her sister (the painter Vanessa Bell) moved to London's Bloomsbury district, where their Gordon Square home became the center of the now-legendary Bloomsbury Group, a circle of writers, artists, and intellectuals (including her future husband, the economist and writer

---

"I have sometimes dreamt, at least, that when the Day of Judgment dawns and the great conquerors and lawyers and statesmen come to receive their rewards...the Almighty will turn to Peter and will say, not without a certain envy when He sees us coming with our books under our arms, 'Look, these need no reward. We have nothing to give them. They have loved reading.'"

Virginia Woolf, "How Should One Read a Book?," in *The Second Common Reader* (1932)

LEONARD WOOLF) that was avant-garde in art and modernist in literature. Woolf published two fairly conventional novels (*The Voyage Out*, 1915; and *Night and Day*, 1919) before making a decisive break with the realist tradition with *JACOB'S ROOM* (1922), the first of her works to employ the "stream-of-consciousness" technique, creating a rounded portrait of the absent title character through a series of interior monologues by various other characters. She continued experimenting, with ever-increasing mastery of her craft, in the novels *MRS. DALLOWAY* (1925), *TO THE LIGHTHOUSE* (1927), and *THE WAVES* (1931). Woolf also wrote biographies, including the pseudo-historical romp *ORLANDO* (1928) and *Flush* (1933), the latter written from the point of view of ELIZABETH BARRETT BROWNING's dog. Although prodigiously well read, Woolf felt the lack of a formal education keenly, a key factor in the development of her influential feminist essays "A ROOM OF ONE'S OWN" (1929) and "Three Guineas" (1938). In addition to writing prolifically in many forms, in 1917 Woolf founded with her husband the distinguished Hogarth Press, which would publish the work of many significant literary modernists, including the first English edition of T. S. ELIOT's *THE WASTE LAND*. Her other novels are *The Years* (1937) and *Between the Acts* (1941); her major essays were collected in *The Common Reader* (1925), *The Second Common Reader* (1932), *The Death of the Moth* (1942), and *Granite and Rainbow* (1958). Woolf was also a supreme practitioner of writing on a more intimate scale, as was demonstrated with the posthumous publication of her *Letters* (6 vols.; 1975–80) and her extraordinary *Diary* (5 vols.; 1977–84). For most of her life, Woolf suffered from emotional instability, and recurring bouts of severe depression tormented her; in 1941, she drowned herself in the River Ouse near her Sussex home.

Wordsworth, William (April 7, 1770–April 23, 1850). English poet. One of his country's greatest poets, whose early work helped spark the Romantic movement in English literature, Wordsworth began his career as a revolutionary who brought a new voice to English poetry and ended it as a widely revered, orthodox-minded Poet Laureate (1843–50). Born in the Lake District, whose natural beauty would profoundly stamp his life and work, he studied at Cambridge, where he was an indifferent student. In 1790, during his summer break, he took a long walking tour of France, returning to England fired with enthusiasm for the French Revolution (his ardor cooled as the full scale of the Terror became known). After several restless years, in 1795 Wordsworth began his close association with the poet Samuel Taylor COLERIDGE. Three years later, the two friends published (anonymously) their epochal *LYRICAL BALLADS*, a slim collection of poems that, in daringly rejecting then-prevailing neo-classical models, was savaged by the critics (it opens with Coleridge's "THE RIME OF THE ANCIENT

MARINER" and closes with Wordsworth's "TINTERN ABBEY," now two of the most famous poems in the English language). In the celebrated Preface to the second edition (1800), Wordsworth stated that their objective was to write of daily life and ordinary people "in a selection of the language really used by men"—a radical notion at the time. In 1802, Wordsworth married a childhood friend, who joined him and his devoted sister Dorothy at their home at Grasmere in the Lake District. Five years later he published his *Poems, in Two Volumes*, which includes his masterful "ODE: INTIMATIONS OF IMMORTALITY FROM RECOLLECTIONS OF EARLY CHILDHOOD." He continued to write prolifically for the next four decades, but with few exceptions (including such superior works as *The Excursion*, 1814, and the sonnet sequence *The River Duddon*, 1820), his later poetry displays a falling off in quality and inspiration. Politically and religiously he grew more conservative as he aged, evoking the scorn of younger Romantics like SHELLEY and BYRON. Wordsworth's uncontested masterpiece, the vastly ambitious autobiographical epic *THE PRELUDE*, tracing the "Growth of a Poet's Mind" (first version, 1798–1805; continuously revised by the poet until his death) was published posthumously in 1850.

Wouk, Herman (May 27, 1915–). American novelist. One of the bestselling authors of the late 20th century, Wouk achieved his greatest success with three dramatic, plot-intensive novels set during World War II: *THE CAINE MUTINY* (1951; Pulitzer Prize), about cruelty and rebellion aboard a Navy minesweeper, and the two-volume saga *The Winds of War* (1971) and *War and Remembrance* (1978), about a naval officer and his family from 1939 to the war's aftermath. An observant Jew, Wouk was born and raised in New York City and educated at Columbia University. He entered the Navy as a line officer in 1942 and served for four years before embarking on his writing career. Other works include *The Caine Mutiny Court-Martial*, a 1954 stage adaptation of his novel; the bestselling novel *MARJORIE MORNINGSTAR* (1955), the story of a working-class Jewish girl who pursues a life in the theater; the novel *Youngblood Hawke* (1962), about an artist turned businessman; and several late writings on his religious roots.

Wright, Richard (September 4, 1908–November 28, 1960). American novelist and short-story writer. With the publication of his bestselling novel NATIVE SON (1940) — hailed by James BALDWIN as "the most powerful and celebrated statement we have yet of what it means to be a Negro in America" — Wright made his name as one of the most influential African-American writers of the century. Born on a sharecroppers' farm near Natchez, Mississippi, Wright, the grandson of slaves, was raised in Memphis, and drifted to Chicago at age 19. The self-educated author entered the literary world by joining the Federal Writers' Project. His first book, UNCLE TOM'S CHILDREN (1938), a collection of four novellas about racial discrimination, was critically acclaimed. During the Depression, Wright joined the Communist Party. He worked for a time in New York City, lived in Mexico, and settled permanently in Paris after World War II. In addition to *Native Son*, Wright's major works include the autobiography BLACK BOY (1945); the novel *The Outsider* (1953), about a man trying to live outside the law; and the posthumously published story collection *Eight Men* (1961).

Wycherley, William (c. 1640–January 1, 1716). English playwright. One of the great comic playwrights of the English Restoration, Wycherley and his biting satires were praised for their penetrating critiques of social and sexual mores. Wycherley was born in Clive, near Shropshire, and educated in France and at Oxford, although he never obtained a degree. His first play, *Love in a Wood, or, St. James Park* (1671), was a great success, winning the admiration of the Duchess of Cleveland — mistress of King Charles II — along with a place in her circle at court. But after his marriage to the countess of Drogheda, he fell out of favor, and was plagued by financial troubles for most of his days. His finest works include THE COUNTRY WIFE (1675), a bawdy tale about a jealous husband and his naive, vulnerable wife, and *The Plain Dealer* (1676), in which an honest man relentlessly attacks the hypocrisy around him.

Wylie, Elinor, *original name* Elinor Morton Hoyt (September 7, 1885–December 16, 1928). American poet and novelist. Known for her formal, musical verse and fiction, Wylie dramatizes the tension between individual ideals and life's disappointments. Born in Somerville, New Jersey, to a prominent family, Wylie married in 1905 but left her husband and child to run away to England with a married man. Her vivacious looks and notorious personal life — including three marriages, the last to poet WILLIAM ROSE BENÉT — sometimes overshadowed her literary works. Wylie established her reputation as a poet with the collections *Nets to Catch the Wind* (1921) and *Black Armour* (1923). Her novels include *Jennifer Lorn* (1923), the story of a woman bored with her husband and his practical world; *The Venetian Glass Nephew* (1925), a fantasy in which a boy made of glass falls in love; and *The Orphan Angel* (1926), an imaginative story featuring the poet PERCY BYSSHE SHELLEY.

Yeats, William Butler (June 13, 1865–January 28, 1939). Irish poet and playwright. In a lecture delivered to the Friends of the Irish Academy at the Abbey Theatre one year after the poet's death, T. S. ELIOT placed Yeats in the company of those few poets "whose history is the history of their own time, who are a part of the consciousness of an age which cannot be understood without them." Born in Dublin and raised in London, Yeats initially followed in the footsteps of his painter father by attending Dublin's Metropolitan School of Art, but at 21 he turned to writing. His early works reflect his lifelong interests in Irish folklore, nationalism, spiritualism, mysticism, and the conflicts between art and life. In 1889 he met and fell in love with actress and political firebrand Maud Gonne, a great inspiration and influence in the years to come, although she did not return his affections. Near the end of the century, Yeats worked with Isabella Augusta, Lady GREGORY, to found the Irish Literary Theatre, which became the influential Abbey Theatre in 1904, and the center of the Irish literary renaissance. *The Countess Cathleen* (1892), *The Land of Heart's Desire* (1894), *Cathleen ni Houlihan* (1902), and many other of Yeats's plays were originally staged there. The accomplished poems of Yeats's later years veer toward the modern, utilizing a spare, realistic, often colloquial style and a system of symbolic images. Among the most celebrated of these are "EASTER, 1916" (1916), "THE WILD SWANS AT COOLE" (1917), "THE SECOND COMING" (1921), "The Tower" (1926), and "SAILING TO BYZANTIUM" (1927). He was awarded the Nobel Prize in Literature in 1923.

Yehoshua, A[vraham] B. (December 9, 1936–). Israeli novelist, short-story writer, and playwright. One of his country's leading writers, Yehoshua examines the moral and social dilemmas of contemporary Israel. Yehoshua was born in Jerusalem, moved to Haifa in his 20s, and has taught at several universities. His first novel, *The Lover* (*Ha-me'ahev*, 1977), the story of a husband's search for his wife's lover during the Yom Kippur War, was an instant success. *A Late Divorce* (*Gerushim Me'uharim*, 1982) tells of a troubled Israeli family whose conflicts reflect those of Israel itself. *Mr. Mani* (*Mar Mani*, 1990) is a multigenerational saga that traces recent Jewish history from the mid-19th century to the present. *A Journey to the End of the Millennium* (*Masot 'al Tom ha-Elef*, 1999) is a novel set in 1999, on the eve of the second millennium. Yehoshua's short fiction in English translation is collected in *The Continuing Silence of a Poet* (1991).

Yevtushenko, Yevgeny (July 18, 1933–). Russian poet. A gifted orator as well as a popular poet, Yevtushenko is known for his lively public readings and political activism. Born in Zima, Siberia, Yevtushenko first came to attention as a spokesperson for Russia's post-Stalin generation. By the early 1960s, he was at times controversial for writings that alternately praised and criticized Soviet policy. Among his notable works are the narrative poem *Winter Station* (*Stantsiya Zima*, 1956), set in his childhood hometown; the poem "Babi Yar" ("Babiĭ Yar," 1962), detailing the Nazi massacre of Jews near the city of Kiev; and the poem cycle *The Bratsk Station* (*Bratskaya GES*, 1965), in which he compares the slaves who built the Egyptian pyramids to self-sacrificing Russian laborers. Yevtushenko is also the author of the memoir *A Precocious Autobiography* (1963; *Primechaniya k Avtobiografii*, 1964), the novel *Wild Berries* (*Yagodnye Mesta*, 1981), and the collection of poetry and prose in English translation, *Almost at the End* (1987).

Young, Marguerite (August 28, 1908–November 17, 1995). American novelist. Young's single, massive novel, *MISS MACINTOSH, MY DARLING* (1965), earned her a reputation for literary inventiveness. Born in Indianapolis, Indiana, she graduated from the University of Chicago and pursued a career in academia. Although Young also published poetry, stories, essays, and a nonfiction book about utopian communities, she is best known for her 1,200-page novel, which has been praised as a work of great, if underappreciated, distinction. A lush tale told in musical language and with rollicking humor, the novel revolves around a band of eccentric characters and their epic quest in a small Iowa town, while questioning the relationship between reality and illusion.

Yourcenar, Marguerite, *pen name and anagram of* Marguerite de Crayencour (June 8, 1903–December 17, 1987). Belgian-born French novelist, short-story writer, and essayist. The first woman elected (in 1981) to the Académie Française, Yourcenar brought to her historical novels a combination of erudition, classicism, and worldly philosophical reflection on such subjects as destiny, heroism, and human solitude. Born in Brussels, she displayed a gift for writing and scholarship as a teenager. After her mother died, she traveled extensively with her father until 1939, when she moved to the United States and settled permanently with her companion and translator, Grace Frick, on Mount Desert Island, Maine. Her masterpiece, *MEMOIRS OF HADRIAN* (*Mémoires d'Hadrien*, 1951), takes the form of a letter from the dying Roman emperor as he looks back over his tumultuous life. Other historical novels include *Alexis* (*Alexis; ou, Le Traité du Vain Combat*, 1929; rev. 1965), *A Coin in Nine Hands* (*Denier du Rêve*, 1934; rev. 1959), *Coup de Grâce* (*Le Coup de Grâce*, 1939), and *The Abyss* (*L'Oeuvre au Noir*, 1968). Collections of her essays include *The Dark Brain of Piranesi and Other Essays* (*Sous Bénéfice d'Inventaire*, 1962) and *That Mighty Sculptor, Time* (*Le Temps, Ce Grand Sculpteur*, 1983). Her autobiography, collectively entitled *The Labyrinth of the World* (*Le Labyrinthe du Monde*), consists of *Dear Departed* (*Souvenirs Pieux*, 1974), *How Many Years* (*Archives du Nord*, 1977), and *Quoi? L'Éternité* (1988, English translation under this title). Yourcenar also published stories, translations, prose poems, and plays.

Zamyatin, Yevgeny (February 1, 1884–March 10, 1937). Russian novelist, short-story writer, and playwright. With its powerful evocation of the totalitarian "One State," Zamyatin's dystopian novel *We* (*My*, 1924) influenced such later works as George ORWELL's *NINETEEN EIGHTY-FOUR*. Born in Lebedyan in central Russia, Zamyatin became involved in Bolshevik activities as a student in St. Petersburg. But his disenchantment following the Russian Revolution led him to write *We*, an indictment of the dictatorial iron hand of Russia's new society. Published abroad in a Russian-language edition, the novel was banned at home, as, eventually, were all his writings. With the help of

---

"True literature can exist only where it is created not by diligent and trustworthy officials, but by madmen, heretics, dreamers, rebels and sceptics. But when a writer must be sensible...there can be no bronze literature, there can only be a newspaper literature, which is read today, and used for wrapping soap tomorrow."

Yevgeny Zamyatin, "I Am Afraid" (1921), in *A Soviet Heretic* (1991), translated by Mirra Ginsberg

---

Maxim GORKY, Zamyatin was permitted to emigrate, going to Paris in 1931. *The Dragon* (1966) is a collection of many of his best stories in English translation. His plays include *The Fires of St. Dominic* (*Ogni Svyatogo Dominika*, 1922) and *The Flea* (*Blokha*, 1925). *A Soviet Heretic* (*Litsa*, 1955) is a collection of essays.

Zola, Émile (April 2, 1840–September 28, 1902). French novelist. Believing that the writer should observe reality with the dispassion of a scientist, Zola wrote shocking, minutely detailed novels in which social forces and heredity were shown to shape the lives of his characters. Born in Paris, Zola was raised in Aix-en-Provence, where a childhood friend was artist Paul Cézanne. Following a spotty education, he worked for a time at a publishing house before becoming a freelance journalist. His early novel *THÉRÈSE RAQUIN* (1867) is written in the naturalist style he pioneered. His monumental 20-novel cycle, *Les Rougon-Macquart* (1871–93), chronicles the fortunes of a 19th-century French family over several generations. Among the well-known works in this series are *L'Assommoir* (1877), in which a working-class couple is destroyed by liquor; *NANA* (1880), the story of a prostitute; *GERMINAL* (1885), Zola's masterpiece about a coal-miners' strike; and *The Debacle* (*La Débâcle*, 1892), set during the Franco-Prussian War. Zola explained his theories of writing in *The Experimental Novel* (*Le Roman Expérimental*, 1880).

Zweig, Stefan (November 28, 1881–February 22, 1942). Austrian poet, playwright, novelist, short-story writer, biographer, and critic. One of the most-translated German-language authors in the 1920s and 1930s, Zweig is now best known to English-reading audiences as the author of *The World of Yesterday: An Autobiography* (1943; *Die Welt von Gestern: Erinnerungen eines Europäers*, 1944), which one reviewer described as "an unwaveringly civilized account of a civilization's collapse." Born in Vienna to a wealthy Austrian-Jewish family, Zweig began publishing poetry while still in his teens, and studied literature at the University of Vienna. Early encounters with the Belgian poet Émile

Verhaeren and the French writer Romain Rolland helped form his convictions, and Zweig became a lifelong humanist and pacifist. His antiwar play *Jeremiah: A Drama in Nine Scenes* (*Jeremias: Eine Dramatische Dichtung in Neun Bildern*, 1917) and a number of inspired translations contributed to his developing career as a multifaceted man of letters. In the realm of fiction, he wrote several novellas, usually psychological explorations, ranging from the early work *Amok* (1922), the story of a doctor's suicide, to *The Royal Game* (*Schachnovelle*, 1942), about a mentally unstable chess player, which appeared together in English translation in *The Royal Game; Amok; Letter from an Unknown Woman* (1944); his only novel is *Beware of Pity* (*Ungeduld des Herzensa: Roman*, 1939). Zweig was also a prolific literary and historical biographer, whose frank, psychologically probing works include *Paul Verlaine* (*Verlaine*, 1905), *Émile Verhaeren* (1910), *Romain Rolland: The Man and His Work* (*Romain Rolland: Der Mann und das Werk*, 1921), *The Struggle with the Daimon: Hölderlin. Kleist. Nietzsche* (*Der Kampf mit dem Dämon*, 1925), *Adepts in Self-Portraiture: Casanova. Stendhal. Tolstoy* (*Drei Dichter ihres Lebens*, 1928), *Marie Antoinette: The Portrait of an Average Woman* (*Marie Antoinette: Bildnis eines Mittleren Charakters*, 1932), and *Balzac* (*Balzac: Der Roman seines Lebens*, 1946). In 1934, after the Nazis' rise to power, he fled to London and then in 1940 to Brazil where, in despair, he and his second wife committed joint suicide. Other notable collections of Zweig's work in English translation include *Kaleidoscope: Thirteen Stories and Novelettes* (1934) and *The Old-Book Peddler and Other Tales for Bibliophiles* (1937), which includes "Books Are the Gateway to the World," "The Invisible Collection: An Episode from the Post-war Inflation Period," and "Thanks to Books."

Other Influential Figures

BIOGRAPHERS, CRITICS, EDITORS, PUBLISHERS, THINKERS, TRANSLATORS

Addison, Joseph (May 1, 1672–June 17, 1719). English essayist, poet, and playwright. Educated at Oxford, where he met his future collaborator, Richard STEELE, Addison enjoyed many successes during his career as a highly versatile man of letters whose shrewd political instincts (and fluid pen) brought him increasingly important government appointments when the Whigs were in power. But today he is best known for the brilliant essays he contributed to the distinguished London periodicals *The Tatler* (1709–11), which was launched by his friend Steele, and its successor, *The Spectator* (1711–12; 1714), which the friends cofounded. Aiming to divert as well as to instruct, both periodicals covered a wide range of topics, while always endeavoring "to enliven morality with wit, and to temper wit with morality." Writing in a lively, conversational style that would profoundly influence the development of the English essay, Addison strove to rescue philosophy from the confines of the library that it might find a home, as he said, "in clubs and assemblies, at tea-tables and coffee-houses." Other important works include *The Campaign* (1705), a long poem addressed to the Duke of Marlborough celebrating his victory at Blenheim; *Cato* (1713), a verse tragedy; and two influential series of papers, both published in *The Spectator*, on "The Pleasures of the Imagination or Fancy" and on MILTON's *PARADISE LOST*.

Anderson, Margaret (November 24, 1886–October 18, 1973). American editor. As founder and editor of the literary magazine *THE LITTLE REVIEW* (1914–29), Anderson provided a pioneering forum for modernist writing, publishing such writers as James JOYCE, Ezra POUND, Gertrude STEIN, and WILLIAM CARLOS WILLIAMS as well as essays on art, feminism, and psychoanalysis. The Indiana-born Anderson's affinity for avant-garde ideas took her to Chicago, where she founded *The Little Review*, and in 1917 to New York City's Greenwich Village, where she published the magazine with her companion, associate editor Jane Heap. Struggling against censors and financial difficulties, the two women were convicted of obscenity in 1921 after serializing Joyce's *ULYSSES*. Anderson's autobiographical writings include *My Thirty Years' War* (1930), *The Fiery Fountains* (1951), and *The Strange Necessity* (1970).

Aristotle, *in Greek* Aristotelēs (384–322 B.C.). Greek philosopher. Born in Stagira in Macedonia to a court physician, Aristotle went to Athens at 17 to study at Plato's Academy and remained there for 20 years, until the death of his teacher. He then left Athens for more than a decade, lecturing and writing, and serving as tutor to the future Alexander the Great. He returned to Athens in 335 B.C., where he directed and lectured at the Lyceum. Aristotle's thought has come down largely through lecture notes that were originally edited and published in the first century B.C. by Andronicus of Rhodes, the Lyceum's last director. His works cover such subjects as logic, ethics, metaphysics, physics, politics, rhetoric, and poetics, but his seminal influence on literary theory and criticism has derived chiefly from his *Poetics* (*Peri Poiētikēs*). In this work, he focuses on Greek tragedy and elaborates on the influential concepts of *mimesis*, *katharsis*, and the unities (of time, place, and action). He wrote, "Tragedy is an imitation [mimesis] of an action that is serious, complete and of a certain magnitude... through pity and fear effecting the proper purgation [catharsis] of these emotions." One of the foundational thinkers of Western civilization, Aristotle forged his ideas about literature in opposition to those of his master, Plato, who embraced literature for its moral worth, rather than for the knowledge that it brings.

Artaud, Antonin (September 4, 1896–March 4, 1948). French playwright, poet, and theorist. An avant-garde visionary, Artaud is best known for his influential theoretical writings on drama. Born in Marseilles, he moved in 1920 to Paris, where he worked as a stage and film actor. He was a member of the Surrealist group from 1924 to 1927, parting ways over the movement's allegiance to communism. Throughout the 1920s and 1930s, Artaud directed experimental plays and wrote strikingly original poetry, screenplays, and criticism. His theoretical work *The Theater and Its Double* (*Le Théâtre et Son Double*, 1938), which contains his famous essay "The Theater of Cruelty" ("Le Théâtre de la Cruauté"), promoted a mode of theater that would break down the barriers between performers and audience, while challenging rational logic and habits of thought. Artaud, who suffered from lifelong psychological instability as well as opium addiction, was diagnosed as schizophrenic in 1937 and spent the next nine years in mental hospitals; he died of cancer in a convalescent home outside of Paris in 1948. *Selected Writings* (1976, edited by Susan SONTAG) is an anthology in English translation.

Auerbach, Erich (November 9, 1892–October 13, 1957). German-American critic and philologist. A specialist in Romance philology, Auerbach is counted among the 20th century's seminal literary critics for his comprehensive survey, *Mimesis: The Representation of Reality in Western Literature* (*Mimesis: Dargestellte Wirklichkeit in der Abendländischen Literatur*, 1946). Covering 3,000 years of European narrative, from HOMER to VIRGINIA WOOLF, he traces an evolving definition of reality in Western culture and examines the social and historical implications of its literary expression. Born and educated in Germany, Auerbach fled the Nazi regime in 1936 and settled in Turkey, where he taught at the state university while writing *Mimesis*. Immigrating to the United States in 1948, he took teaching positions at Pennsylvania State and later Yale, where he was Sterling Professor of Romance Philology from 1956 until his death. His other works are devoted chiefly to the languages and literatures of medieval Europe.

Azorín, *pen name of* José Martínez Ruiz (June 8, 1873–March 2, 1967). Spanish critic, novelist, and playwright. Azorín was the leading critic of the Generation of '98, an important circle of early 20th-century Spanish writers who sought to revive interest in Spanish cultural traditions and promote a revitalized national literature. After first studying law, Azorín turned to literature in 1893, producing a body of work marked by a personal, impressionistic style, a commitment to the Spanish cultural heritage, and an appreciation for vernacular pueblo life. In works such as *The Castilian Soul* (*El Alma Castellana*, 1900), *Classical and Modern Authors* (*Clásicos y Modernos*, 1913), and *Marginal Notes to the Classics* (*Al Margen de los Clásicos*, 1915), Azorín explores Spanish social history and medieval and Renaissance literature, insightfully examining their relevance for contemporary life. Azorín's novels include *Don Juan* (1922).

Babbitt, Irving (August 2, 1865–July 15, 1933). American critic. Prominent in the second and third decades of the 20th century, Babbitt was the major figure of the New Humanists, a conservative group who espoused a critic's code of morality, rationality, and responsibility to uphold social standards of behavior. Babbitt remains best known for his outspoken critiques of Romanticism, realism, and modernist literature, in such works as *The New Laokoön: An Essay on the Confusion of the Arts* (1910) and *Rousseau and Romanticism* (1919). Babbitt also wrote widely on religion, education, and politics, as in the essay collection *Literature and the American College* (1908) and *Democracy and Leadership* (1924), a work of political philosophy. Raised in the Midwest and educated at Harvard, Babbitt was a professor at Harvard from 1894 until his death.

Baker, Carlos (May 5, 1909–April 18, 1987). American critic and biographer. Baker is best known for his major studies of Ernest HEMINGWAY. His *Hemingway: The Writer as Artist* (1952) is a significant analysis of the novelist's life and work, while *Ernest Hemingway: A Life Story* (1969) is considered the definitive biography of the writer and was both a critical and popular success. Baker was noted for his subtle, insightful approach and his ability to draw out his subjects' own truths, rather than impose his views on his material. In addition to his work on Hemingway, Baker also wrote the important *Shelley's Major Poetry* (1948), which examines the poet's personal and philosophical vision. He received his Ph.D. in 1940 from Princeton, where he taught from 1938 until 1977.

Bakhtin, Mikhail (November 17, 1895–March 7, 1975). Russian literary theorist. Long suppressed in Russia, Bakhtin's writings have been influential since the 1960s for their philosophical explorations of the interaction of language and its social context. In the 1920s, Bakhtin published under others' names but was nonetheless exiled to Kazakhstan by Stalinist authorities. He continued to write and teach in Saransk, interrupted only by World War II. His major works include *Problems of Dostoevsky's Poetics* (*Problemy Tvorchestva Dostoevskogo*, 1929), *Rabelais and His World* (*Tvorchestvo Fransua Rable i Narodnaya Kul'tura Srednevekov'ya i Renessansa*, 1965), and *The Dialogic Imagination* (*Voprosy Literatury i Estetiki*, 1975). Bakhtin's work critiques both narrowly formalist and sociological approaches to literature. He created the concept of "dialogism" to explore the dynamic, creative interrelationship

among author, text, and sociocultural realities. Studying RABELAIS, he also examined the "carnivalesque," parodic folk humor that he suggests opens up hierarchical ideologies to new points of view.

Barthes, Roland (November 12, 1915–March 26, 1980). French critic and cultural theorist. A leading intellectual of the 1960s and 1970s, Barthes remains influential for his probing investigations of cultural forms. Drawing upon Marxism and semiotics (the study of signs), his writings are concerned with how meaning is produced through linguistic and cultural operations. Two of his best-known works, *Writing Degree Zero* (*Le Degré Zéro de l'Écriture*, 1953) and *The Pleasure of the Text* (*Le Plaisir du Texte*, 1973), elucidate literary texts. Barthes is also noted for extending semiotics to nonlinguistic fields, such as popular culture in *Mythologies* (1957) and Japanese customs in *The Empire of Signs* (*L'Empire des Signes*, 1970). His searching, increasingly lyrical and allusive writings are collected in *Image-Music-Text* (1977) and *A Barthes Reader* (1982). In 1977, Barthes was appointed the first chair of literary semiology at the Collège de France.

Barzun, Jacques (November 30, 1907–). French-born American cultural historian and educator. A product and champion of the humanist tradition, Barzun has written with authority and erudition on diverse aspects of cultural history and intellectual life in the West —literature, education, music, art, philosophy, politics, science, and the revolutions that have encompassed all of them. The son of a French literary scholar, he came to the United States in 1920 and attended Columbia University, where he joined the history faculty and eventually became a full professor, dean, and provost. His advocacy of liberal arts education and indictments of education in America are forcefully articulated in such works as *The House of Intellect* (1959), *The American University* (1968), and *Begin Here: The Forgotten Conditions of Teaching and Learning* (1991). His wide-ranging intellect is reflected in some 30 books, also including *Romanticism and the Modern Ego*

(1943); *Berlioz and the Romantic Century* (2 vols., 1950); *A Catalogue of Crime* (with Wendell Hertig Taylor; 1971, revised and enlarged, 1989), an annotated bibliography of some 5,000 books of crime fiction and the literature of true crime; *The Use and Abuse of Art* (1974); *On Writing, Editing, and Publishing: Essays Explicative and Hortatory* (1971); and *The Culture We Deserve* (1989). The self-acknowledged culmination of his studies is *From Dawn to Decadence: 500 Years of Western Cultural Life, 1500 to the Present* (2000).

Bataille, Georges (September 10, 1897–July 9, 1962). French cultural theorist and novelist. An important intellectual figure in mid-20th-century France, Bataille has gained increasing renown for his critical investigations of sexuality and irrationality. After abandoning his initial intention to become a Catholic monk, Bataille worked as a librarian throughout his life, mainly in Paris at the Bibliothèque Nationale. In the 1920s he became interested in psychoanalysis and Surrealism, which inform his unsettling, experimental erotic novels, including the well-known *The Story of the Eye* (*Histoire de l'Oeil*, 1928). In 1936 he formed the Collège de Sociologie, which offered lectures by leading intellectuals such as Jean-Paul SARTRE and Claude Lévi-Strauss, and in 1946 founded the journal *Critique*, publishing the early writings of Jacques DERRIDA and Roland BARTHES. Bataille's critical works concern the transgression of rational thinking; they include *The Accursed Share* (*La Part Maudite*, 1949), on sacrificial rituals, and *Death and Sensuality* (*L'Érotisme*, 1957), on sexuality and mortality.

Bayley, John (March 27, 1925–). English critic, memoirist, and novelist. The son of a military officer, Bayley was born in what is now Pakistan and educated at Eton and Oxford, where he became a fellow at New College and later Warton Professor of English Literature at St. Catherine's College. Early critical writings, such as *The Romantic Survival* (1957), *The Characters of Love: A Study in the Literature of Personality* (1960), and *Tolstoy and the Novel* (1966), established Bayley's reputation as a learned, nonideological literary critic. These were followed by works on PUSHKIN, HARDY, KEATS, A. E. HOUSMAN, the tragedies of SHAKESPEARE, and the art of the short story, among other subjects. His critical essays appear regularly in *THE NEW YORK REVIEW OF BOOKS* and elsewhere. His first novel, *In Another Country* (1955), was well received, but he did not write fiction again until the 1990s, when he produced *Alice* (1994), *The Queer Captain* (1995), *George's Lair* (1996), and *The Red Hat* (1998). *Elegy for Iris* (1999) and *Iris and Her Friends* (2000) are personal memoirs of his life with his wife, novelist Iris MURDOCH, focusing particularly on her struggle with Alzheimer's disease.

Beach, Sylvia (March 14, 1887–October 5, 1962). American bookshop proprietor and publisher. As owner of Shakespeare and Company, a Paris shop and lending library carrying English-language books, Beach provided an invaluable gathering place for French, English, and American writers in the fertile modernist period. Raised in Princeton, she moved to Paris in 1916; there she ran her shop from 1919 until the Nazi occupation in 1941. She provided writers such as F. SCOTT FITZGERALD, Gertrude STEIN, Ezra POUND, and André GIDE with the opportunity to read, meet, and exchange ideas, and offered them practical aid. Beach also courageously published the first edition of James JOYCE's ULYSSES in 1922 after it was banned for obscenity in the United States. Her memoir, *Shakespeare and Company* (1959), presents a vivid account of the expatriate scene in Paris.

Belinsky, Vissarion (June 11, 1811–June 7, 1848). Russian critic, journalist, editor, and philosopher. Although his career was relatively short, and his life plagued by poverty and poor health, Belinsky exerted a profound influence on his contemporaries and on the entire course of 19th-century Russian literature. The preeminent literary and cultural critic of his generation, he was an early and insightful supporter of many writers, including LERMONTOV, GOGOL, TURGENEV, and DOSTOYEVSKY, who would come to be seen as giants of the Golden Age of Russian literature. Stressing that Russian writers should explore and cultivate *narodnost'* (national character or national distinctiveness) in their work, and not simply imitate European models, he also emphasized the importance of representing "real life" and contemporary issues —such as the quest for social justice—in literature, above all urging Russian writers to grapple with the conditions of the poor and others on the margins of society. In this, his impact can be traced even well into the next century, when Socialist Realism became the officially sanctioned doctrine of Soviet letters. English translations of some of his most significant works are available in *Belinsky, Chernyshevsky, and Dobrolyubov* (1976) and *Selected Philosophical Works* (1981).

Benchley, Robert (September 15, 1889– November 1, 1945). American humorist, theater critic, and screenwriter. One of the celebrated wits of modern American letters, Benchley was raised in Worcester, Massachusetts, and educated at Harvard, where he contributed to the *Harvard Lampoon*. In New York, he was managing editor (1919–20) of *Vanity Fair*, drama editor (1920–29) of *Life* magazine, and a contributor to and columnist for THE NEW YORKER (1929–40). As a member of the Algonquin Round Table, the gathering of wits that included Dorothy PARKER, George S. KAUFMAN, and Alexander WOOLLCOTT, he more than held his own, famously quipping, "I've got to get out of these wet clothes and into a dry martini." Benchley also wrote and acted in 46 short films, including *The Treasurer's Report* (1928), based on a monologue he had performed on Broadway, *The Sex Life of the Polyps* (1928), *How to Read* (1936), *How to Figure Income Tax* (1938), and the Academy Award–winning *How to Sleep* (1935). The many features in which he appeared include *The Major and the Minor* (1942) and *Week-end at the Waldorf* (1945); he also cowrote the screenplay for *Foreign Correspondent* (1940), directed by Alfred Hitchcock. Benchley's comic essays, reprinted in such volumes as *My Ten Years in a Quandary and How They Grew* (1936), *Benchley Beside Himself* (1943), and *The Benchley*

Roundup (edited by his son, Nathaniel Benchley; 1954), offer farcical commentaries on middle-class, modern American life in an often deliberately incongruous style. *Benchley at the Theatre* (1986) collects his criticism.

Benét, William Rose (February 2, 1886– May 4, 1950). American poet, essayist, critic, and editor. A prolific and accomplished poet (and the older brother of poet and novelist STEPHEN VINCENT BENÉT), Benét nonetheless made his greatest mark on the literary world as an editor and anthologist. Born in Brooklyn and educated at Yale, he achieved fame first as a contributor and editor for the New York *Evening Post Literary Review*, then as founding editor of THE SATURDAY REVIEW of *Literature*, a post he held from 1924 until his death. He also wrote a regular literary column, "The Phoenix Nest," for *The Saturday Review*. His verse — playful, highly crafted, alternately humorous and melancholy—was much admired and sometimes described as "Browningesque" for its similarity to the work of English poet ROBERT BROWNING. Collections include *Merchants from Cathay* (1913), *Moons of Grandeur* (1920), *With Wings as Eagles* (1940), and the autobiographical *The Dust Which Is God* (1941), which received the 1942 Pulitzer Prize for poetry. *Rip Tide* (1932) is a novel in verse. Benét was also the first editor of *The Reader's Encyclopedia* (1948). He was married to the American poet Elinor WYLIE from 1923 until her death in 1928.

Benjamin, Walter (July 15, 1892–September 26, 1940). German critic. A provocative cultural analyst, Benjamin produced searching, philosophical reflections on literature, visual art, and the mass media, and their relationship to modern, capitalist society. Born into an upper-middle-class Jewish family, he wrote critical essays in Berlin throughout the 1920s and continued writing in exile, mainly in Paris, after leaving Germany following the Nazis' rise to power in 1933. While fleeing occupied France in 1940, he committed suicide at the Spanish-French border when he was threatened with capture by the Gestapo. His penetrating, nuanced, often elliptical writing includes the highly influential 1936 essay "The Work of Art in the Age of Mechanical Reproduction," published in the collection *Illuminations* (*Illuminationen*, 1961). *Reflections* (1978) represents a further collection of significant writings in English translation. *The Arcades Project* (*Das Passagen-Werk*, 1983), unfinished at his death, is a montage of quotations and reflections about the shopping arcades of Paris, which embodied for Benjamin the process of commodification characteristic of the modern age.

Bentley, Eric (September 14, 1916–). English-born American theater critic, translator, editor, and playwright. The foremost theater critic of his generation, whose prose is admired for its intellectuality, freedom from cant, and gusto, Bentley was born in Bolton, Lancashire, England, and educated at Oxford, where he studied with C. S. LEWIS. His first book, *A Century of Hero-Worship: A Study of the Idea of Heroism in Carlyle and Nietzsche* (1944; also published as *The Cult of the Superman*), is an expansion of his Yale doctoral dissertation. He has served as an indefatigable champion of playwrights he admires, most notably Bertolt BRECHT, and has helped to shape critical consensus as to which works are the classics of modern drama with his critical writings and with such influential anthologies as *The Modern Theatre* (6 vols., 1955–60) and *The Classic Theatre* (4 vols., 1958–61). Scornful of commercial theater because of the compromises it forces on writers (a "playwright is either a rebel and an artist or a yes man and a hack"), he has translated plays by PIRANDELLO, GOGOL, CHEKHOV, SCHILLER, BÜCHNER, WEDEKIND, and others, in addition to his many translations of Brecht. Among his most important works are the now-classic *The Playwright as Thinker* (1946), *Bernard Shaw: A Reconsideration* (1947), and *The Life of the Drama* (1964). *Bentley on Brecht* (1998) gathers his writings on the playwright, including the book-length "Brecht Memoir." Bentley's theater criticism is collected in *What Is Theatre? Incorporating the Dramatic Event, and Other Reviews, 1944–1967* (1968), while *Thinking About the Playwright: Comments from Four*

Decades (1987) assembles his occasional writings and lectures. Among his plays are *The Kleist Variations* (1978–81), adaptations of three plays by Heinrich von KLEIST.

Bergson, Henri (October 18, 1859–January 4, 1941). French philosopher. An important influence on modernist writers, including Marcel PROUST, Bergson offered a critique of rationalist, scientific thinking and explored intuition, creativity, and lived, qualitative experience. He is best known for distinguishing mechanically measured time from the inner, fluid experience of time and memory. Raised in Paris, Bergson began teaching in 1897 at the Collège de France, where his lectures were remarkably popular with both academic and general audiences; as a Jew, he renounced his chair at the Collège during World War II. His major writings include *Matter and Memory* (*Matière et Mémoire*, 1896), *Creative Evolution* (*L'Évolution Créatrice*, 1907), and *The Two Sources of Morality and Religion* (*Les Deux Sources de la Morale et de la Religion*, 1932). He was awarded the Nobel Prize in Literature in 1927.

Blackmur, R[ichard] **P**[almer] (January 21, 1904–February 2, 1965). American critic and poet. A leading theorist and practitioner of the New Criticism, Blackmur is known for his meticulous and penetrating analyses of modern American and British poetry. With no formal education beyond high school, he began his literary career as a contributor to, and then editor of, the periodical *Hound & Horn*. He was awarded a Guggenheim Fellowship to write a study of Henry ADAMS, a work he never completed, before joining the faculty at Princeton University in 1940; he taught there for 25 years. In *The Double Agent* (1935), Blackmur argued the importance of both form and content in establishing the meaning of a poetic text. In *Language as Gesture* (1952), another influential essay collection, he focused on the importance of linguistic technique. Other critical works include *The Expense of Greatness* (1940), *The Lion and the Honeycomb* (1955), *Form and Value in Modern Poetry* (1957), and the posthumous *A Primer of Ignorance* (1967). Blackmur also published three volumes of poetry, *From Jordan's Delight* (1937), *The Second World* (1942), and *The Good European* (1947).

Bloom, Harold (July 11, 1930–). American critic and literary scholar. Raised in New York City in a Yiddish-speaking household, Bloom took his Ph.D. from Yale in 1955, the same year that he joined the faculty; he later held simultaneous professorships at Yale and New York University. Trained as a scholar of Romantic poetry, he published three volumes of criticism before writing the book that made his reputation, *The Anxiety of Influence* (1973). In that work, he proposed a theory, based in part on the principles of Freudian psychoanalysis, that literature is the result of a struggle between the poet and his "precursor," whose work he must deliberately misread. Enormously influential, his ideas found further expression in such works as *A Map of Misreading* (1975), *Poetry and Repression: Revisionism from Blake to Stevens* (1976), and *Agon: Towards a Theory of Revisionism* (1982). The prolific Bloom also included the Bible in his researches, resulting most controversially in *The Book of J* (1990), in which he proposed that the author of the J-text, one of the oldest narrative threads in the Old Testament, was a woman. In *The Western Canon* (1994), Bloom offered a list of the writers and books he considers the most important in all literature; *Shakespeare: The Invention of the Human* (1998) credits the playwright with inventing the modern conception of human personality; *How to Read and Why* (2000) is Bloom's gathering of observations about authors he admires, from the Romantics to Oscar WILDE.

Booth, Wayne C[layson] (February 22, 1921–). American critic and educator. Booth's best-known work, *The Rhetoric of Fiction* (1961; rev. ed. 1983), offers a method of literary criticism based on principles of Aristotelian rhetoric. A Mormon, Booth was born and raised in Utah, took his B.A. at Brigham Young University in Salt Lake City, and received his Ph.D. from the University of Chicago, where he became much enamored of the Neo-Aristotelian Chicago school of criticism led by R. S. CRANE. Booth occupied teaching posts at Haverford College in Haverford, Pennsylvania, and Earlham College in Richmond, Indiana, before returning to the University of Chicago, where he became the Pullman Professor of English in 1962. He expanded his discussion of rhetorical interpretation in several subsequent volumes, including *A Rhetoric of Irony* (1974), *Critical Understanding: The Powers and Limits of Pluralism* (1979), and *The Company We Keep: An Ethics of Fiction* (1988), considered a seminal work in the revival of ethical criticism. *The Vocation of a Teacher: Rhetorical Occasions, 1967–1988* (1988) contains Booth's reflections on a lifetime in the English classroom.

Bradbury, Malcolm (September 7, 1932– November 27, 2000). English critic and novelist. Bradbury's studies of American and English literary history are noted for their sensitive assessments and graceful, accessible prose. Among his acclaimed surveys are *The Modern American Novel* (1983, revised 1992), *From Puritanism to Postmodernism: A History of American Literature* (1991, written with Richard Ruland), and *The Modern British Novel* (1993). *Dangerous Pilgrimages* (1995) examines the cross-pollination between American and English literatures in the 19th and 20th centuries. A dedicated teacher, Bradbury was a longtime professor of American studies at the University of East Anglia in Norwich. There he also established in 1970 Britain's first master's level creative writing program; his students included Ian MCEWAN and Kazuo ISHIGURO. Bradbury's novels, often satirizing academia, include *Eating People Is Wrong* (1959), *The History Man* (1975), *Rates of Exchange* (1983), *Doctor Criminale* (1992), and *To the Hermitage* (2000). Among his many other works is a guide to important literary meccas, *The Atlas of Literature* (1996).

Brandes, Georg (February 4, 1842–February 19, 1927). Danish critic, philosopher, and biographer. Influenced by such thinkers as John Stuart Mill and the young Émile ZOLA, Brandes became the catalyst of what he termed the "modern breakthrough" in Scandinavian literature and a guiding figure for modernist and naturalist movements elsewhere, particularly Germany, where he lived and lectured for several years. His 1870s Copenhagen lectures on *Main Currents in 19th-century Literature* (*Hovedstrømninger i det 19de Århundredes Litteratur*, published 1872–90) were instrumental in persuading Scandinavian writers to break with Romanticism's ideals and engage themselves in the movement for realism and social reform. Among those he championed and corresponded with were the Norwegians Bjørnstjerne Bjørnson and Henrik IBSEN, and the Swede August STRINDBERG; beyond Scandinavia, he extolled FLAUBERT, the GONCOURT brothers, TURGENEV, and DOSTOYEVSKY. Later, after studying the then little-known Friedrich NIETZSCHE, Brandes elaborated a philosophy of "aristocratic radicalism" (*Aristokratisk Radikalisme*, 1889), and published studies of such "great men" as SHAKESPEARE, GOETHE, VOLTAIRE, Julius Caesar, and Michelangelo. Nietzsche called Brandes a "good European"; he constantly strove, as Ibsen had urged him, to further the "revolution of the human spirit."

Brod, Max (May 17, 1884–December 20, 1968). Prague-born Israeli editor, biographer, and novelist, writing in German. Brod is remembered primarily for preserving the manuscripts of unpublished works by Franz KAFKA, which Kafka had asked him to burn upon his death. Making an incalculable contribution to 20th-century literature, Brod ignored his friend's wishes and as Kafka's literary executor edited and published THE TRIAL (*Der Prozess*, 1925), THE CASTLE (*Das Schloss*, 1926), and *Amerika* (1927), as well as Kafka's diaries and correspondence. Unfortunately, his editions are unreliable, for he freely altered Kafka's spelling, punctuation, word order, and chapter divisions; a new critical edition of Kafka's complete works, based more closely on the author's manuscripts, began to appear in German in 1982. However, the decades-long intimacy between the two Prague-born writers made Brod's 1937 biography, *Franz Kafka*, authoritative. Other Prague writers also benefited from his advocacy, including Franz Werfel and Jaroslav HAŠEK. In his own right, Brod was a prolific author; among his works translated into English are the novels *The Redemption of Tycho Brahe* (*Tycho Brahes Weg zu Gott*, 1915) and *Three Loves* (*Die Frau, nach der Man Sich Sehnt*, 1927; a film version starred Marlene Dietrich), and a 1934 biography of Heinrich HEINE, translated as *Heinrich Heine: The Artist in Revolt*.

Brooks, Cleanth (October 16, 1906–May 10, 1994). American critic. Brooks was a major practitioner of the New Criticism, an influential approach in the 1930s through the 1950s that emphasized the close reading and structural analysis of literature, rather than the exploration of its historical or cultural properties. Educated at Vanderbilt, the launching site of the New Critics, and at Tulane, Brooks subsequently taught at Louisiana State University at Baton Rouge and at Yale. At LSU, he coedited the New Critics' journal, *The Southern Review*, from 1935 to 1942. He also cowrote landmark college textbooks, including *Understanding Poetry* (1938) and *Understanding Fiction* (1943), which spread New Critical ideas. Brooks's *Modern Poetry and the Tradition* (1939) and *The Well Wrought Urn* (1947) provide close readings of classic poems, while his *Literary Criticism* (1957, cowritten with William K. Wimsatt) is acclaimed as an important examination of the history of literary criticism.

Brooks, Van Wyck (February 16, 1886–May 2, 1963). American critic and literary historian. Educated at Harvard, Brooks struggled financially as a young critic, working at various teaching, editing, and writing jobs. His books *The Wine of the Puritans* (1908) and *America's Coming-of-Age* (1915) criticized the American culture of Puritanism and pragmatic materialism, which he felt were destructive to literary achievement. Brooks also controversially attacked contemporary modernists as being too aesthetically divorced from American life. Searching for high-quality literature rooted in American life, Brooks wrote *The Flowering of New England: 1815–1865* (1936), which won the Pulitzer Prize. It was the first of the five volumes in his important series, *Makers and Finders* (1936–52), which examines the American literary tradition.

Burke, Kenneth (May 5, 1897–November 19, 1993). American critic and philosopher. Believing that criticism should "use all that there is to use," Burke combined insights from psychology, philosophy, linguistics, and sociology to develop an innovative, complex, and highly influential theory of literature as "symbolic action": the use of rhetoric as a symbolic acting out of psychological motives and conflicts. Burke attended Ohio State and Columbia universities but did not earn a degree. Early in his career he wrote music criticism and book reviews for THE DIAL and THE NATION, turning to literary criticism in the late 1930s. He lectured at the University of Chicago and then moved to Bennington College, where he taught from 1943 to 1962. *The Philosophy of Literary Form* (1941) lays the foundation of his theory, elaborated in *A Grammar of Motives* (1945), *A Rhetoric of Motives* (1950), and *Language as Symbolic Action* (1966). Other works include *Permanence and Change* (1935), *Attitudes Toward History* (2 vols., 1937), *Dramatism and Development* (1972), and *On Symbols and Society* (1989), as well as collections of poetry and short stories and translations of Thomas MANN, Oswald Spengler, and other modern German authors.

Carlyle, Thomas (December 4, 1795–February 5, 1881). Scottish-born English essayist and historian. A prominent Victorian writer and thinker, Carlyle was shaped philosophically by the German Romantics, especially GOETHE, whose work he devoted many years to translating. Raised in a deeply religious Presbyterian household, he received his education at the University of Edinburgh and planned to enter the ministry, but put this aside for writing, and a life of poverty from which he never fully escaped. *Sartor Resartus* (1836), his first major work, is a loosely affiliated gathering of philosophy, memoir, and personal reflection written in an exuberant, difficult style that would come to be known in his lifetime as "Carlylese." This was followed by his remarkable three-volume *The French Revolution* (1837), a historical work that secured his reputation and won him the sobriquet "The Sage of Chelsea," after the London neighborhood where he lived. A writer of prodigious energy (he rewrote one volume of the history entirely after the manuscript was mistakenly used to light a fire), Carlyle continued to produce a major work of cultural criticism every few years. Major works include *Chartism* (1840), *On Heroes, Hero-Worship and the Heroic in History* (1841), *Oliver Cromwell's Letters and Speeches, with Elucidations* (1845), and *The History of Friedrich II of Prussia, Called Frederick the Great* (1858–65). After his death his literary legacy suffered as critics came to see his beliefs as innately fascistic; nevertheless, he remains an important subject of study as both an example of, and a spokesman for, the complexities of Victorian social thought.

Carruth, Hayden (August 3, 1921–). American critic, poet, and essayist. An influential critic, Carruth served as editor of the journal POETRY (1949–50) and as poetry editor of HARPER'S (1977–82). He was also a National Book Award–winner in poetry for his collection *Scrambled Eggs & Whiskey* (1996). Educated at the University of North Carolina and the University of Chicago, he lived many years in Vermont and upstate New York (where he taught at Syracuse University), a landscape that figures prominently in his work. He began his career writing poems notable for their use of formal structures, as in his collection *The Crow and the Heart: 1946–1959* (1959). His hospitalization for alcoholism in 1953, an experience recorded in the long poem *The Bloomingdale Papers* (1975), led him to a more confessional approach and an association with the "deep image" school led by James Wright and Robert BLY. *Brothers, I Loved You All* (1978), among his most praised collections, also bears evidence of Carruth's interest in jazz and the blues. *Selected Essays and Reviews* (1996) contains writings on such poets as Robert FROST, Richard Hugo, and Allen GINSBERG, as well as Carruth's writings on jazz.

Caxton, William (c. 1422–1491). English printer and publisher. Caxton earned lasting renown for producing the first printed book in English in 1475, *The Recuyell of the Historyes of Troye*, his own translation from the French of a work by Raoul Le Fèvre. A prominent Bruges textile merchant, Caxton turned to printing around 1471, studying the trade in Germany before founding a press in Bruges, where he published *The Recuyell*. In 1476, he established a press in his native England, producing the first book printed in England, *Dictes and Sayenges of the Phylosophers*, the next year. Caxton ultimately printed nearly one hundred works, mostly in English, including CHAUCER's *THE CANTERBURY TALES*, MALORY's *LE MORTE D'ARTHUR*, and AESOP's *FABLES*.

Cerf, Bennett (May 25, 1898–August 27, 1971). American editor and publisher. The cofounder and longtime president of the trade publisher Random House, Cerf was born in New York City and educated at Columbia University. After working briefly on Wall Street, he joined the publishing house Boni and Liveright in 1923. Two years later, he and his friend Donald Klopfer bought Liveright's Modern Library, a series of inexpensive editions of literary classics, and then, in 1927, established Random House, to publish "at random" (Cerf's words) other books that interested them. At the new firm, Cerf demonstrated exceptional dedication to literary quality, along with commercial acumen, and the house attained international prominence when it successfully defended in court its 1934 publication of JOYCE's *ULYSSES* (1922), which had been banned in the United States. Under Cerf's leadership, the company also published such major authors as FAULKNER, O'NEILL, PROUST, STEIN, and ELLISON. He was also a prolific editor of anthologies of wit and humor, short stories, and plays; *Try and Stop Me: A Collection of Anecdotes and Stories, Mostly Humorous* (1944) led to his syndicated column of the same name for the King Features newspaper syndicate. Cerf's public celebrity was enhanced by his weekly appearances as a panelist on television's "What's My Line?" from 1951 to 1967. *At Random: The Reminiscences of Bennett Cerf*, edited by his widow, Phyllis Cerf Wagner, and Albert Erskine, was published posthumously, in 1977.

Chapman, George (c. 1559–May 12, 1634). English translator, poet, and playwright. Chapman is best known for his major early English translations of HOMER's *ILIAD*, from 1598 to 1611, and *ODYSSEY*, in 1615. Although they do not employ rigorous scholarship, his translations are credited with capturing the spirit of the texts; among those who praised them is John KEATS, who wrote a sonnet called "ON FIRST LOOKING INTO CHAPMAN'S HOMER." Chapman also wrote philosophical poems, including *Ovid's Banquet of Sense* (1595) and *Euthymiae Raptus* (1609), which adopted a formal, controlled style similar to that of his close friend Ben JONSON. His plays include *Bussy D'Ambois* (c. 1607), a tragedy of a man in love with the wife of his aristocratic patron, and the comedies *The Widowes Teares* (c. 1612) and *All Fools* (1605).

Chesterton, G[ilbert] K[eith] (May 29, 1874–June 14, 1936). English journalist, essayist, poet, critic, novelist, biographer, and editor. Although he claimed to be nothing more than a "jolly journalist," Chesterton in fact wrote prolifically in a wide variety of genres, producing works brimming with wit, paradox, and gusto. Born in London, he was educated at the Slade School of Art, and worked for a few years as a publisher's reader before embarking on a career as a freelance journalist, quickly establishing his reputation. Politically and philosophically an arch-conservative, Chesterton was also a passionate defender of the Catholic faith, which he embraced in 1922. Among his major literary works are the phantasmagoric allegorical novels *The Napoleon of Notting Hill* (1904) and *The Man Who Was Thursday: A Nightmare* (1908); the long poem *The Ballad of the White Horse* (1911); and critical studies of CHAUCER, the Victorian age in literature, ROBERT BROWNING, and Charles DICKENS, especially *Appreciations and Criticisms of the Works of Charles Dickens* (1911). An essayist and biographer of distinction, Chesterton wrote lives of, among others,

William Cobbett, Robert Louis STEVENSON, and St. Thomas Aquinas. He also created the popular series of short stories featuring the priest-sleuth Father Brown, which were first collected in *The Innocence of Father Brown* (1911). His *Autobiography* was published posthumously in 1936.

Child, Francis (February 1, 1825–September 11, 1896). American scholar and editor. Child is renowned as the compiler of the multivolume *The English and Scottish Popular Ballads* (1857–58, rev. 1882–98), which remains the definitive collection of these verses. Born in Boston, Child was educated at Harvard and taught there from 1851 on. In 1849, he studied philology in Germany, inspired by the GRIMM brothers' famous studies of linguistics and folklore. His classic collection of ballads is distinguished by its scrupulous scholarship, comprehensiveness, and sensitive critical notes, which place the verses in historical context. Child gathered the ballads from manuscripts rather than printed sources, providing an invaluable document of the important folk ballad tradition.

Connolly, Cyril (September 10, 1903–November 26, 1974). English critic, essayist, and editor. The son of an English army officer, Connolly was born in Coventry, raised in Ireland and South Africa, and educated at Eton and Balliol College, Oxford. He cofounded and edited *HORIZON* magazine, a premier English literary review, from 1939 to its closure in 1950, publishing the most influential writers of his time, including W. H. AUDEN, Elizabeth BOWEN, T. S. ELIOT, Arthur KOESTLER, EVELYN WAUGH, George ORWELL, Jean-Paul SARTRE, and Dylan THOMAS. As a critic, his interests ranged widely, focusing especially on English and French modernism and 18th-century literature. His work is noted for its flexible, often personal approach, as well as its liberality of thought and the insight it offers into issues of aesthetic form. After serving at *Horizon*, he wrote columns for the *NEW STATESMAN*, was literary editor of the *Observer*, and was on the literary staff of the *Sunday Times* of London from 1951 to 1972. Connolly's books include *Ene-*

mies of Promise (1938), about the toll taken on talented writers by politics, conversation, drink, domesticity, advertising, and journalism; the essay collections *The Condemned Playground* (1945), *Ideas and Places* (1953), *Previous Convictions* (1963), and *The Evening Colonnade* (1973); the bibliographic essay *The Modern Movement: One Hundred Key Books from England, France, and America, 1880–1950* (1965); and the novel *The Rock Pool* (1936). *The Unquiet Grave* (1944; rev. ed 1945), a book difficult to categorize and published under the pseudonym "Palinurus," is an introspective collection of epigrams, reflections, and quotations, in which Connolly draws upon his knowledge of classical culture, travel, and art; it has been called a minor classic.

Cowley, Malcolm (August 24, 1898–March 27, 1989). American critic, literary historian, and editor. Cowley is best known for his attention to American writers of the 1920s. Having himself composed poetry and studied literature in Paris in the 1920s, Cowley wrote a major, partly autobiographical account of the expatriate culture of the period, *Exile's Return* (1934). His acclaimed *A Second Flowering* (1973) further examines the American writers of the period. Settling in New York, Cowley served as literary editor of *THE NEW REPUBLIC* from 1929 to 1944 and edited in 1946 the classic *The Portable Faulkner*, which revived FAULKNER's visibility at a time when he was largely ignored. Cowley's writings also include *The Literary Situation* (1954), a study of the writer's position in American society; *And I Worked at the Writer's Trade: Chapters of Literary History, 1918–1978* (1978); and *The Dream of the Golden Mountains: Remembering the 1930s* (1980).

Crane, R[onald] S[almon] (January 5, 1886–July 12, 1967). American critic. Distinguished for his rigorous scholarship and complexity of vision, Crane was an esteemed professor of English at the University of Chicago from 1924 on and a leading figure among the "Chicago critics," also known as the Neo-Aristotelians, who included Elder Olson and, later, Wayne C. BOOTH. The group is noted for stressing a formalist, rather than a historical or cultural, approach to studying texts, and promoting a flexible use of multiple methods of investigation. Crane's major book, *The Languages of Criticism and the Structure of Poetry* (1935), is considered seminal to the Chicago school, as is his body of essays, collected in *The Idea of the Humanities* (1967) and *Critical and Historical Principles of Literary History* (1971). He also edited the influential *Critics and Criticism: Ancient and Modern* (1952).

de Man, Paul (December 6, 1919–December 21, 1983). Belgian-born American critic and theorist. One of the leading advocates of deconstruction—a critical method, first articulated by French philosopher Jacques DERRIDA, that asserts that language refers to no reality beyond its own ambiguities and social contexts—de Man was one of a cadre of intellectuals who made Yale University the hub of deconstructionist criticism in the United States in the 1970s. He emigrated from Brussels to the United States in 1947, attended Harvard, and taught at Johns Hopkins and Cornell before joining the Yale faculty in 1970. *Blindness & Insight: Essays in the Rhetoric of Contemporary Criticism* (1971) propelled him to the forefront of the movement; this was followed by, among other volumes, *Allegories of Reading: Figural Language in Rousseau, Nietzsche, Rilke, and Proust* (1979), *The Rhetoric of Romanticism* (1984), and *The Resistance to Theory* (1986). *Aesthetic Ideology* (1996) collects essays he was working on at his death. De Man's reputation suffered when, not long after his death, it was learned that he had worked for a pro-Nazi, anti-Semitic newspaper in Belgium during World War II.

Derrida, Jacques (July 15, 1930–). French philosopher and critic. The founder of the deconstructionist movement in contemporary philosophy and criticism, Derrida has been a central and controversial figure in poststructuralist intellectual life. His critical method, initially directed at Western metaphysics and later applied to literature, psychoanalysis, and the social sciences, is based on the theory that language is inherently ambiguous and that a written text defies absolute, definitive interpretation. Deconstructionist criticism therefore consists in revealing the metaphysical, linguistic, and political assumptions hidden in a text. Eschewing any specific philosophical doctrine, Derrida has used the approach to reveal the uncertainty of traditional metaphysical concepts and modern social ideology. Born to Jewish parents in Algeria, Derrida moved to France at age 19 to enter military service. He attended the École Normale Supérieure in Paris, where he taught from 1965 to 1980; he has also held teaching positions at the Sorbonne and Yale, and lectured widely in Europe and the United States. Notable writings include *Speech and Phenomena* (*La Voix et la Phénomène*, 1967), *Writing and Difference* (*L'Écriture et la Différence*, 1967), *Of Grammatology* (*De la Grammatologie*, 1967), *Dissemination* (*La Dissémination*, 1972), *Margins of Philosophy* (*Marges de la Philosophie*, 1972), *Positions* (1972), *The Truth in Painting* (*La Vérité en Peinture*, 1978), and *Specters of Marx* (*Spectres de Marx*, 1993).

Deutsch, Babette (September 22, 1895–November 13, 1982). American poet, critic, novelist, and translator. The author of a number of books used in schools throughout the United States, including *Poetry in Our Time* (1952) and *Poetry Handbook: A Dictionary of Terms* (1957), Deutsch was born and raised in New York City. She published her first poems while a student at Barnard College and issued her first collection, *Banners*, in 1919. Two years later, she married scholar Avrahm Yarmolinsky, with whom she translated many works from Russian or German into English. *Honey Out of the Rock* (1925), *Fire for the Night* (1930), *One Part Love* (1939), *Take Them, Stranger* (1944), *Animal, Vegetable, Mineral* (1954), and *The Collected Poems* (1969) contain most of her poetry. *A Brittle Heaven* (1926) and *Mask of Silenus* (1933) are novels, and *Potable Gold* (1929), *This Modern Poetry* (1935), and *The Reader's Shakespeare* (1946) are critical works.

Doubleday, Frank Nelson (January 8, 1862–January 30, 1934). American publisher. The cofounder and longtime president of the publishing house that bears his name, Doubleday was born in Brooklyn and began working at age 15 at the publisher Charles Scribner's Sons; in 1887 he became manager of the new *Scribner's Magazine*. He left Scribners after 20 years to cofound his own firm, Doubleday & McClure, in 1897, with Samuel Sidney McClure. Throughout a century of subsequent incarnations (as Doubleday, Page & Company; Doubleday, Doran, and Company; and Doubleday & Co.) the firm has prospered in both literary and commercial terms, expanding into bookselling through its own chain of bookstores and through the Literary Guild, the bookclub founded by Doubleday's son, Frank, in 1927, five years after he joined the firm. In addition, the Doubleday house initiated one of the industry's most distinguished lines of paperbacks, Anchor Books, in 1953. During the 30 years of the senior Doubleday's tenure, the company published such major American and British authors as Joseph CONRAD, Jack LONDON, SINCLAIR LEWIS, O. HENRY, Frank NORRIS, Arthur Conan DOYLE, and Edna FERBER. It was Rudyard KIPLING, who became a lifelong friend, who gave Doubleday the nickname by which he was known throughout his life: "effendi," Turkish for "chief," from his initials (F.N.D.). It was also Kipling who introduced the publisher to T. E. LAWRENCE, whose *The Seven Pillars of Wisdom* the firm published in 1935. Doubleday was also the first publisher of DREISER's controversial *SISTER CARRIE* (1900), albeit in expurgated form.

Du Bois, W[illiam] E[dward] B[urghardt] (February 23, 1868–August 27, 1963). American scholar and editor. Primarily known as a political thinker and black nationalist, and one of the founders of the National Association for the Advancement of Colored People (NAACP), Du Bois exercised his influence partly through writing and editing, especially of the NAACP journal THE CRISIS: *A Record of the Darker Races*, which he launched and edited from 1910 to 1934. Du Bois earned a B.A. from Fisk University in Nashville and a doctorate at Har-

vard before studying economy and sociology at the University of Berlin. He was a professor of economics and history at Atlanta University from 1897 to 1910. During the Harlem Renaissance, he published the works of many black writers in *The Crisis* and contributed to publications such as the *Pittsburgh Courier, Chicago Defender, Current History*, and *Foreign Affairs*. JAMES WELDON JOHNSON praised his collection *The Souls of Black Folk* (1903) as having had "a greater effect upon and within the Negro race in America than any single book published in this country since UNCLE TOM'S CABIN." Among Du Bois's other works are *The Philadelphia Negro* (1899), *Black Reconstruction in America* (1935), and *Dusk of Dawn* (1940). His autobiography was published posthumously in 1968.

Eagleton, Terry, *in full* Terence Eagleton (February 22, 1943–). English critic. A preeminent Marxist literary theorist, Eagleton has directed critical attention to the social ideologies at work in literature. Examining works of literature, criticism, and cultural analysis, Eagleton links texts to their sociohistorical contexts and explores their political implications. His incisive, often provocative political vision and his grasp of contemporary intellectual currents, including psychoanalysis, poststructuralism, and postmodernism, have given his writings wide renown. Among his best-known books are *Literary Theory: An Introduction* (1983), *The Ideology of the Aesthetic* (1990), and *The Illusions of Postmodernism* (1996). A frequent contributor to such distinguished journals as *The London Review of Books* and THE TIMES LITERARY SUPPLEMENT, Eagleton has also written several works on Irish literature and culture, including *Heathcliff and the Great Hunger: Studies in Irish Culture* (1995). The anthology *The Eagleton Reader* was published in 1998. Eagleton was educated at Cambridge and is a professor of English at Oxford University.

Eastman, Max (January 12, 1883–March 25, 1969). American editor and political writer. A significant figure in New York's radical,

VICE VERSA: WRITERS TRANSLATING WRITERS

Why was Boris Pasternak, unlike so many of his literary friends in the USSR, spared the purges of the 1930s? Some speculate that Stalin (who was from Georgia) admired his translations of the dictator's favorite Georgian poets. Translation was indeed Pasternak's livelihood during those dangerous years, and his renderings into Russian of Shakespeare, Goethe, the English Romantics, Paul Verlaine, and Rainer Maria Rilke have been hailed as masterpieces. "A translation," he wrote in 1944, "must issue from an author who has experienced the effect of the original long before he embarks on his labors." According to Vladimir Nabokov, a notable translator of both Pushkin and his own works, there are three types of translators: the scholar, who works to "make the world appreciate an obscure genius as much as he does himself"; the well-intentioned hack; and the professional writer, who enjoys "relaxing in the company of a foreign confrère."

When distinguished writers tackle translations, they bring their own genius to what William Gass has called the "obdurate, complex and compacted" lines of a foreign author, unraveling sense from the myriad possibilities of words and images. Cicero translated the Greek philosophers into Latin. John Dryden began translating Virgil's *Aeneid* and the satires of Juvenal and Ovid in the 1680s, making the heroes of the classical world speak, as he put it, as if they were Englishmen. A young Alexander Pope began translating Homer's *Iliad* in 1713. The fruit of his seven-year labor won praise from Samuel Johnson.

Dante Alighieri's poetry is visionary, musical, profound—and exceptionally difficult to translate, a fact that seems to have challenged several writer/translators. In 1843, Ralph Waldo Emerson made perhaps the earliest translation into English of Dante's "La Vita Nuova" (but it was not published until more than a hundred years later, in 1957). The poet Henry Wadsworth Longfellow translated the *Divine Comedy* during 1865–67. Dorothy L. Sayers, an accomplished scholar and creator of the popular detective Lord Peter Wimsey, published translations of the *Inferno* and the *Purgatorio* in 1949 and 1955, respectively, but did not live to complete her translation of the *Paradiso*. And more recently, two American poets have published acclaimed translations: Robert Pinsky of

---

bohemian Greenwich Village in the years surrounding World War I, Eastman edited two prominent socialist literary periodicals, *The Masses* from 1912 to 1917 and *The Liberator* from 1918 to 1922. Raised on a farm in New York state, after completing his education Eastman taught at Columbia University and became involved in socialist and feminist causes. As editor of *The Masses*, he published radical social commentary and works of literary realism by such writers as SHERWOOD ANDERSON and Carl SANDBURG. The magazine was suppressed in 1917, and in 1918 Eastman was tried twice for sedition for publishing commentary opposing World War I; both trials ended in hung juries. In 1918, Eastman founded and edited *The Libera-*

the *Inferno* in 1994, and W. S. Merwin of the *Purgatorio* in 2000.

Sometimes the translator's voice overpowers or even appropriates his or her material. An anonymous Chinese translator, working from oral versions of Charles Dickens, once created neo-Confucian parables, *The Old Curiosity Shop* becoming, for example, "The Story of the Filial Daughter Nell." Edward FitzGerald, a frustrated poet and dedicated sporting gentleman, translated *The Rubáiyát of 'Omar Khayyám* from Persian to English in 1859 and published it anonymously. Decades and countless editions later, critics knowledgeable in Persian began to point out that, while retaining the meaning of the poems, FitzGerald's translation was so loose as to be unrecognizable. Robert Lowell called his own renderings of the poems of Pasternak, Arthur Rimbaud, and Charles Baudelaire "imitations." Ezra Pound translated Japanese Nō plays and Chinese poetry while admitting that he did not know the original languages; he "adapted" the English translations of the American Orientalist Ernest Fenollosa.

Czech novelist Milan Kundera was so enraged by the English version of his 1968 novel *The Joke* (important passages had been excised and others senselessly reordered) that he suspected the translator could not read Czech at all. In *The Art of the Novel*, he created a guide for future translators, a 30-page personal dictionary of key words, problem words, and words he loves. Now, when a translator tells him, "That's not the way we say it in German (or Spanish)," Kundera replies, "That's not the way we say it in Czech either."

It is the rare translator, though, who, like Vladimir Nabokov, will admit that he has come up short. Nabokov spent almost a decade on a literal translation of his beloved Pushkin's long novel-in-verse, *Eugene Onegin*. Published in 1964, the translation provoked a furious debate with his friend the American critic Edmund Wilson, whose harsh attack effectively ended his longtime friendship with Nabokov. In a 1964 interview, Nabokov admitted that his translation was, "of course, a literal one, a crib, a pony. And to the fidelity of transposal I have sacrificed everything: elegance, euphony, clarity, good taste, modern usage, and even grammar." Realizing that his version of *Eugene Onegin* was "not close enough and not ugly enough," Nabokov began a revision to "eliminate the last vestiges of bourgeois poesy" that was finally published in 1975, two years before the great novelist's death.

tor, but resigned in 1922 owing to his anti-Stalinist views following a visit to the USSR. He worked as editor-at-large of *Reader's Digest* from 1941 to 1969. His memoirs were published as *Enjoyment of Living* (1948) and *Love and Revolution: My Journey Through an Epoch* (1964).

Edel, Leon (September 9, 1907–September 5, 1997). American literary biographer and critic. Edel is renowned for his multivolume study of HENRY JAMES. Born in Pittsburgh to Russian-Jewish immigrants and raised mainly in Canada, Edel wrote on James both for his master's thesis at McGill University and for his doctoral dissertation at the University of Paris. In 1953 he published *Henry James: The Untried Years, 1843–1870*, the first book of his major five-volume biography (1953–72). Edel's work is distinguished by its scholarship and artful composition as well as by its sometimes controversial psychoanalytic interpretations. Among Edel's other works are *Bloomsbury: A House of Lions* (1979), a group portrait of the Bloomsbury literary circle; *Writing Lives: Principia Biographica* (1984), about writing biography; and the abridged, single-volume *Henry James: A Life* (1985).

Ellmann, Richard (March 15, 1918–May 13, 1987). American literary biographer and critic. Ellmann's meticulous, suggestive studies of modern Irish writers brought him acclaim as one of the 20th century's most distinguished literary biographers. Educated at Yale University and Trinity College, Dublin, he later taught at Harvard, Northwestern, and Yale, as well as at Oxford, where he was the first American to teach English literature. His works include three masterly biographical and critical studies, *Yeats: The Man and the Masks* (1948), *James Joyce* (1959; National Book Award), and the posthumously published *Oscar Wilde* (1987). Other notable works include *The Identity of Yeats* (1954), *Edwardians and Late Victorians* (1960), *Eminent Domain: Yeats Among Wilde, Joyce, Pound, Eliot, and Auden* (1967), *Ulysses on the Liffey* (1972), *The Consciousness of Joyce* (1977), and *Four Dubliners: Wilde, Yeats, Joyce, and Beckett* (1987).

Empson, [Sir] William (September 27, 1906–April 15, 1984). English critic and poet. Considered one of the most influential critics of his time, Empson is renowned for highly original, often irreverent works that explore the properties of poetic language, including the way that it reveals complex cultural attitudes. Studying mathematics and literature at Cambridge in the 1920s, he worked under the professor and critic I. A. RICHARDS, who promoted the close analysis of textual forms rather than historical or biographical approaches to literature. Empson subsequently taught at universities in Japan and China and worked at the BBC, before taking a position at Sheffield University, where he held the Chair of English Literature from 1953 until his retirement in 1971. His major works include *Seven Types of Ambiguity* (1930), *Some Versions of Pastoral* (1935), *The Structure of Complex Words* (1951), and *Using Biography* (1984). Empson is equally distinguished for his intelligent, argumentative, and witty poetry — F. R. LEAVIS called him the first true successor to John DONNE — which is gathered in *The Complete Poems* (2000).

Epstein, Barbara, *original surname* Zimmerman (August 30, 1929–). American editor. With Robert SILVERS, JASON EPSTEIN, and others, Barbara Epstein founded the respected literary-intellectual magazine THE NEW YORK REVIEW OF BOOKS during the New York City newspaper strike of 1963. Epstein and Silvers have served as editors of the publication from the first issue. Featuring articles and reviews by leading writers and scholars, *The New York Review* quickly gained a following and continues to publish on a biweekly basis; national circulation now exceeds 100,000. Born in Boston, Epstein graduated from Radcliffe in 1949 and began her publishing career as a junior editor at Doubleday & Company. She worked at PARTISAN REVIEW before cofounding *The New York Review.*

Epstein, Jason (August 25, 1928–). American editor, publishing executive, and author. A leading innovator and entrepreneur in postwar American publishing, Epstein served from 1958 to 1997 as editorial director and literary steward at Random House, Inc., which grew into the world's largest English-language trade-book publisher. A native of Cambridge, Massachusetts, Epstein earned B.A. and M.A. degrees at Columbia University. As a young editor at Doubleday in the early 1950s, he introduced the concept of the quality paperback with a new imprint of literary and intellectual titles, Anchor Books. In 1963 he was one of the founders of the prominent NEW YORK REVIEW OF BOOKS, to which he has been a frequent contributor of articles and reviews, and in the early 1980s he was the moving force in the creation of The Library of America, a nonprofit imprint dedicated to preserving American literary classics in standard hardcover editions. His own books include *The Great Conspiracy Trial: An Essay on Law, Liberty, and the Constitution* (1970), *East Hampton: A History and Guide* (1975), and a postretirement assessment, *Book Business: Publishing—Past, Present, and Future* (2001). He received a National Book Award for Lifetime Achievement in 1988.

Fauset, Jessie Redmon (April 27, 1882–April 30, 1961). American editor, novelist, and poet. Dubbed the "midwife" of Harlem Renaissance literature by LANGSTON HUGHES, Fauset served from 1919 to 1926 as literary editor of the major African-American journal of the period, THE CRISIS. Providing a significant public forum for black poets and novelists, Fauset published writers such as Hughes, Countee CULLEN, and Jean TOOMER. Her own novels, which include *THERE IS CONFUSION* (1924), *Plum Bun* (1928), *The Chinaberry Tree* (1931), and *Comedy, American Style* (1933), insightfully portray the lives of middle-class African-Americans, particularly women. Born in New Jersey, Fauset taught French in a black high school in Washington, D.C., while pursuing a master's degree from the University of Pennsylvania; she returned to teaching after her tenure at *The Crisis*.

Fiedler, Leslie A[aron] (March 8, 1917–). American critic, short-story writer, and novelist. Best known for his critique of the American novel, Fiedler was born in Newark, New Jersey, earned his Ph.D. at age 22, served in World War II as a Japanese interpreter, and taught at the University of Montana and the State University of New York at Buffalo. In the 1948 *PARTISAN REVIEW* essay "Come Back to the Raft Ag'in, Huck honey," he argued that central to *HUCKLEBERRY FINN, MOBY-DICK,* and the national consciousness is the "chaste" homoerotic bond between men of different races— Huck and Jim, Ishmael and Queequeg—each pair fleeing both women and civilization. He traced this controversial theme throughout American fiction in *Love and Death in the American Novel* (1960), which introduced Freudian psychoanalysis to American literary criticism, and two sequels, *Waiting for the End* (1964) and *The Return of the Vanishing American* (1968). With his respect for 1960s youth culture ("The New Mutants," 1965), defense of popular fiction (*What Was Literature?*, 1982), and interest in the role of the outsider (*The Stranger in Shakespeare*, 1972; *Fiedler on the Roof: Essays on Literature and Jewish Identity*, 1991), Fiedler became an antiestablishment hero.

Fish, Stanley (April 19, 1938–). American critic. A prominent academic figure since the 1980s, Fish earned renown for establishing "reader-response" criticism, an approach that emphasizes the reader's role in creating the meaning of the text. Fish pioneered this approach in *Surprised by Sin: The Reader in "Paradise Lost"* (1967), which suggests that the reader plays the central role in MILTON's classic, as the poem orchestrates the reader's own self-examination. Fish's best-known work, *Is There a Text in This Class?* (1980), and his essay collection *Doing What Comes Naturally* (1989) further develop the theory. Provocative as well as erudite, Fish has examined legal and political issues in later volumes, including *There's No Such Thing as Free Speech, and It's a Good Thing, Too* (1994). Fish has held professorships at Johns Hopkins and Duke universities and was appointed dean of Liberal Arts and Sciences at the University of Illinois in 1999. His *How Milton Works* appeared to critical acclaim in 2001.

Flanner, Janet (March 13, 1892–November 7, 1978). American journalist. As Paris correspondent for THE NEW YORKER, Flanner wrote the renowned "Letters from Paris" column under the pseudonym "Genêt" for a half century, from 1925 to 1975, except for the war years 1939 to 1944, when she lived in New York City. Her astute observations on French art, politics, and society strongly influenced opinion on life in France in the English-reading world. Born in Indianapolis, Flanner moved to Paris in 1922, where her friends included expatriate writers DJUNA BARNES and Gertrude STEIN. Most of her essays are collected in her two-volume *Paris*

Journal (1965–71), *Paris Was Yesterday, 1925–1939* (1972), and *Janet Flanner's World: Uncollected Writings 1932–1975* (1979). She also published a novel, *The Cubical City* (1926).

Foucault, Michel (October 15, 1926–June 25, 1984). French philosopher and historian. Born in Poitiers, the son of a surgeon, Foucault studied philosophy, psychology, and psychopathology at the École Normale Supérieure and the Sorbonne. He received a doctorate in 1960, publishing his thesis the next year as *Folie et Déraison: Histoire de la Folie à l'Âge Classique* (abridged in English as *Madness and Civilization: A History of Insanity in the Age of Reason*, 1965), a work that exemplifies Foucault's lifelong fascination with figures who live on the margins of society and with what he called the "principles of exclusion." Professor of the History of Systems of Thought at the Collège de France in Paris from 1970 until his death, Foucault exerted a profound influence upon postmodern literary criticism, especially in the United States. His writings scrutinized not literature *per se*, but rather the laws and codes that govern intellectual discourse and power structures in Western society. His skeptical analyses sought to demonstrate that systems once thought to be "universal necessities" are in fact the result of precise historical changes and the power strategies employed by society to maintain order and consensus. Other major works include *The Birth of the Clinic: An Archaeology of Medical Perception* (*Naissance de la Clinique: Une Archéologie du Regard Médical*, 1963), *The Order of Things: An Archeology of the Human Sciences* (*Les Mots et les Choses: Une Archéologie des Sciences Humaines*, 1966), *The Archeology of Knowledge* (*L'Archéologie du Savoir*, 1969), *Discipline and Punish: The Birth of the Prison* (*Surveiller et Punir: Naissance de la Prison*, 1975), and *The History of Sexuality* (*Histoire de la Sexualité*, 1976–84), of which Foucault lived to complete only three of the six planned volumes.

Frazer, [Sir] James George (January 1, 1854–May 7, 1941). Scottish anthropologist and folklorist. One of the pioneers of modern anthropology, Frazer is best known as the author of the classic compendium of folklore, myth, and pagan ritual, *The Golden Bough* (2 vols., 1890; enlarged to 12 vols., 1911–15). Publication of the work generated enormous interest in the field and had a profound influence on the literary imagination in the first decades of the 20th century. His material, based entirely on secondary sources, led him to an evolutionary theory of societal development—from magical to religious to scientific thought—that is now generally disregarded. His comparative approach to culture and the distinction he made between magic and religion, however, are still widely followed in anthropology. Frazer was born in Glasgow and attended the university there before completing his studies at Trinity College, Cambridge, where he remained for most of the rest of his life. His other works include *Totemism and Exogamy* (1910) and *Folk-lore in the Old Testament* (1918) as well as translations of Pausanius, OVID, and other classical writers.

Freud, Sigmund (May 6, 1856–September 23, 1939). Austrian psychiatrist. Controversial from the beginning, Freud's pioneering theories of the subconscious mind have done more to shape the modern understanding of human experience than the work of any other individual of the age. Freud received his medical degree at the University of Vienna in 1881, where he developed a specialty in neuropathology; in 1885 he moved to Paris where, working with neurologist Jean-Martin Charcot, he began to formulate his theories of the mind and his groundbreaking use of free association in the treatment of various mental disorders, recorded in *Studies in Hysteria* (*Studien über Hysterie*, 1895). This was followed, four years later, by the landmark volume *The Interpretation of Dreams* (*Die Traumdeutung*, 1899), Freud's treatise on the symbolic framework of the unconscious. Freud's division of the human psyche into its three fundamental components —id, ego, and superego—and his insistence on the primacy of sexuality as the engine of the unconscious have become touchstones in the modern conversation about human nature, creativity, and culture. His work has been a source of contention especially among some feminists, who take exception to Freud's presentation of female sexuality. Other major writings by Freud include *Three Essays on the Theory of Sexuality* (*Drei Abhandlungen zur Sexualtheorie*, 1905), *Totem and Taboo* (*Totem und Tabu*, 1913), and *Civilization and Its Discontents* (*Das Unbehagen in der Kultur*, 1930). A Jew, in 1938 Freud fled with his family to England, where he lived the last year of his life.

Frye, [Herman] **Northrop** (July 14, 1912–January 23, 1991). Canadian literary and social critic and educator. One of the most influential postwar literary theorists writing in English, Frye began what would become a more than 50-year teaching and administrative career at Victoria College, University of Toronto, his alma mater, in 1939, eventually rising to University Professor of the University of Toronto (1967–91) and, finally, Chancellor, Victoria University, Toronto (1978–91). His first book, *Fearful Symmetry* (1947), is a landmark exploration of the Romantic poet William BLAKE's symbols and ideas in which Frye argued that all symbolism "in all art and religion is mutually intelligible among all men." Frye continued to develop this idea in his most famous and influential work, *Anatomy of Criticism* (1957), which, through four essays analyzing historical, ethical, archetypal, and rhetorical criticism, attempts to give a comprehensive view of the scope, theory, and techniques of literary criticism. In addition to his theoretical work and his writings on education and Canadian culture, Frye wrote much distinguished practical criticism, including books on T. S. ELIOT (1963), MILTON (1965), and the English Romantics (1968), as well as studies of SHAKESPEARE's comedies (1965) and tragedies (1967). Two of Frye's most ambitious works, *The Great Code: The Bible and Literature* (1982) and its sequel, *Words with Power* (1990), survey the cross-fertilization of symbols and myths in biblical, classical, and secular literatures and traditions.

Fujiwara, Sadaie, *also called* Teika (1162–September 26, 1241). Japanese critic and poet. The son of the important poet TOSHINARI FUJI-WARA, Sadaie Fujiwara was a critic and theorist whose writings shaped the practice of poetry in Japan for centuries. His critical writings include *Eiga Taigai* (1216; Essentials of Poetic Composition) and *Superior Poems of Our Time* (*Kindai Shūka*, 1209), considered the first history of poetry in Japan. He also assembled a number of influential anthologies, including *The Little Treasury of One Hundred People, One Poem Each* (*Ogura Hyakunin Isshū*, c. 1235), and was a co-compiler of the eighth Imperial anthology, *Shin Kokinshū* (1205; New Collection of Ancient and Modern Times), as well as the sole compiler of the ninth, *Shin Chokusenshū* (1235; New Imperial Collection)—the only person ever to be chosen by the Emperor to work on more than one royal collection. In his remarkable poetry, he initially emphasized the concept of *yūen*, or "ethereal beauty," building upon the centuries-old traditions of Japanese versemaking but introducing technical innovations. Later, he began to write in a new, less formal style, favoring *ushin*, or "conviction of feeling."

Fuller, [Sarah] **Margaret,** Marchesa Ossoli (May 23, 1810–July 19, 1850). American critic, journalist, and editor. One of the most prominent intellectuals of her generation, Fuller's major American feminist work *Woman in the Nineteenth Century* (1845) powerfully argued for women's equality and right to self-fulfillment. Born in Massachusetts, she received an exceptionally rigorous education at home from her father. Closely associated with the major Transcendentalist writers, she edited the movement's influential quarterly, THE DIAL, from 1840 to 1842. In the early 1840s she also supported herself by holding a series of educational "conversations" for groups of women that proved a great success, for the witty and brilliant Fuller provided, as her admirer EMERSON said, "the most entertaining conversation in America." In 1844, the progressive newspaper editor Horace Greeley hired Fuller as literary critic for his *New York Tribune*, for which she also produced much serious critical reporting. *Papers on Literature and Art*, collecting some of her work for the *Tribune*, appeared in 1846; in the same year she sailed to Europe as the paper's European correspondent. Fuller settled in Italy in 1847, where she became deeply involved in the movement for Italian independence, and secretly married an Italian nobleman and ardent Republican, Giovanni Angelo, Marchese Ossoli. Forced to leave Italy, they sailed for America in May 1850, Fuller bringing with her the manuscript history of the revolution she had witnessed. On July 9, Fuller, her husband, and their infant son were all drowned when their ship foundered on a sandbar and broke apart, within sight of land, just off New York's Fire Island.

Gallimard, Gaston (January 18, 1881–December 25, 1975). French publisher and editor. As the founder and longtime president of Librairie Gallimard (later Éditions Gallimard), Gallimard established the most respected French book-publishing company of the 20th century. Under his direction, the firm published many of the nation's foremost modern writers, from André GIDE, Marcel PROUST, Paul Claudel, and Paul VALÉRY to André MALRAUX, Jean-Paul SARTRE, and Albert CAMUS. The company also became known for such series as La Pléiade, a line of distinguished editions of French literary classics. The son of a prominent art collector, Gallimard was born in Paris and studied law and literature at the University of Paris before embarking on a career in journalism. In 1911 he was invited by Gide and Jean Schlumberger, founders of the literary review *LA NOUVELLE REVUE FRANÇAISE,* to join in launching a book-publishing operation. Gallimard became sole proprietor of the firm, called Éditions de la Nouvelle Revue Française, in 1913 and reestablished the business under his own name in 1919. He managed the company until the early 1970s, when he turned over control to his son.

Garnett, Constance, *original surname* Black (December 19, 1861–December 17, 1946). English translator. Garnett was the first to translate the works of DOSTOYEVSKY and CHEKHOV into English; although many of her translations have been superseded, she remains an important early figure in the spread of Russian lit-

erature to the English-speaking world. She attended Newnham College, Cambridge, and worked as a librarian in London. Through her husband, the critic Edward Garnett, she met a group of exiled Russian revolutionaries who helped her to learn Russian. She later traveled to Russia, where she carried messages from the exiles in London and met TOLSTOY, some of whose works she would later translate. She also translated works by GONCHAROV and the complete works of TURGENEV and GOGOL.

Gates, Henry Louis, Jr. (September 16, 1950–). American critic and educator. A leading scholar and high-profile advocate of African-American studies and culture, Gates has advanced the black perspective in literary criticism and argued powerfully for greater cultural diversity in the Western canon. Born in a small town in West Virginia, he earned a B.A. from Yale in 1973 and won a fellowship to Cambridge, where he studied under the Nigerian writer Wole SOYINKA. In 1979, he became the first African American to be awarded a Ph.D. at Cambridge. His historical perspective on African-American literature derives in part from his discovery and collection of previously unknown works, including *Our Nig* by Harriet E. Adams, which had been attributed to a white man but which he proved to be the earliest known novel by a black American (1859). An able administrator and prolific author, he taught at Yale, Cornell, and Duke before being appointed, in 1991, W. E. B. DuBois Professor of the Humanities and head of African-American Studies at Harvard. Major works of literary criticism are *Figures in Black* (1987), *The Signifying Monkey* (1988), and *Loose Canons* (1992). Other books include *Colored People* (1994), a childhood memoir; *The Future of the Race* (1996), with Cornel West; and *Thirteen Ways of Looking at a Black Man* (1997), essays on racial identity. He has also edited the 30-volume *Schomburg Library of Nineteenth-century Black Women Writers* (1988–91) and coedited *The Norton Anthology of African American Literature* (1996).

Girodias, Maurice, *original surname* Kahane (April 12, 1919–July 3, 1990). French publisher. Born in Paris, Girodias was the publisher of Olympia Press, which specialized in erotic literature, including important avant-garde works as well as strictly pornographic novels. Girodias's father, Jack Kahane, founded and operated the Obelisk Press, which published such controversial novelists as HENRY MILLER and Radclyffe Hall. After Kahane's death, Girodias (who had begun using his mother's non-Jewish maiden name during World War II) carried on in his father's tradition, founding Olympia Press in 1953. Publishing controversial writers who had difficulty finding outlets elsewhere, Olympia issued works by such major authors as Samuel BECKETT, Jean GENET, WILLIAM S. BURROUGHS, and Georges BATAILLE, and was the first to publish Vladimir NABOKOV's *LOLITA* (1955). Repeatedly tried by French authorities for obscenity, the press gradually folded in the 1960s. Girodias's anthology *The Olympia Reader* (1965) gathers selections from the press's eminent works of literature.

Goncourt, Edmond (May 26, 1822–July 16, 1896) and **Jules** (December 17, 1830–June 20, 1870). French novelists and belle-lettrists. The founders of the Académie Goncourt and its literary award, the Prix Goncourt, the Goncourt brothers were also early practitioners of the naturalistic novel, a 19th-century form of objective realism. Thanks to an inheritance from their parents, the brothers were able to devote themselves to cultural pursuits, collaboratively writing art criticism, social histories, and fiction. Novels such as *Charles Demailly* (1860; originally titled *Les Hommes des Lettres*), about newspaper journalism, and *Germinie Lacerteux* (1864), about the hidden sex life of a punctilious servant, are distinguished by their realistic observations of social milieus. The Goncourts' private *Journal*, published between 1887 and 1896 in nine volumes, gives a vivid account of contemporary Parisian life. The Prix Goncourt, awarded annually to a work of literary prose, was established in 1903 according to the brothers' wishes and remains a highly respected French literary prize.

Greenblatt, Stephen (November 7, 1943–). American critic and literary scholar. A Renaissance specialist and a founder of the critical practice called New Historicism, Greenblatt has been a prominent figure in literary studies since the 1980s. Born in Cambridge, Massachusetts, he received his B.A. and Ph.D. from Yale (1964, 1969), and an M.Phil. from Cambridge University (1966). He was professor of English at the University of California at Berkeley from 1969 to 1997, when he moved to the English Department at Harvard. New Historicism—simply defined as a method of interpretation that situates works of art and literature in their historical and political contexts—developed out of a cross-disciplinary study group at Berkeley that drew upon the ideas of Michel FOUCAULT and included, in addition to Greenblatt, the scholars Denis Hollier, Lynn Hunt, Walter Benn Michaels, Svetlana Alpers, and Thomas Laqueur. Greenblatt founded the journal *Representations* as a forum for the group in 1983. His 1986 essay on the new approach, "Towards a Poetics of Culture," was widely reprinted and contributed to the growth of the even broader critical tendency known as cultural studies. Among his major works are *Three Modern Satirists: Waugh, Orwell, and Huxley* (1965), *Renaissance Self-fashioning: More to Shakespeare* (1980), *Shakespearean Negotiations: The Circulation of Social Energy in Renaissance England* (1988), *Learning to Curse: Essays in Early Modern Culture* (1990), *Marvelous Possessions: The Wonder of the New World* (1991), and *Hamlet in Purgatory* (2001); as coeditor, with Giles Gunn, *Redrawing the Boundaries: The Transformation of English and American Literary Studies* (1992); as associate general editor, *The Norton Shakespeare* (1997) and *The Norton Anthology of English Literature: The Major Authors* (2000); and, as coauthor with Catherine Gallagher, *Practicing New Historicism* (2000). His writing also appears in THE NEW YORKER, *The New York Times,* THE NEW REPUBLIC, and THE TIMES LITERARY SUPPLEMENT, as well as other general-interest publications.

Grimm, Jacob (January 4, 1785–September 20, 1863) and **Wilhelm** (February 24, 1786–

December 16, 1859). German philologists and folklorists. They are known and beloved worldwide as the Brothers Grimm for the collection usually called *Grimms' Fairy Tales* (*Kinder- und Hausmärchen*, 1812–15; six enlarged editions, 1819–57; first translated as *German Popular Stories*, 1823–26). On his own, Jacob was a pioneering linguist; in his treatise on the comparative and historical grammar of the Germanic languages, *Deutsche Grammatik* (1819–37), he formulated what is still known as "Grimm's Law" of consonant correspondences. Wilhelm is generally considered the stylist who shaped the final form of the *Fairy Tales*. The Grimms began work on their second enduring monument, their great historical and etymological German dictionary (*Deutsches Wörterbuch*, 1854–1960), in 1838; it was finally finished a century after their deaths. Academicians and librarians by profession, honored throughout the learned world, the brothers believed in their responsibility to assert their principles in an increasingly reactionary era. In 1837, both were dismissed from professorships in Göttingen for protesting the rescindment of a liberal constitution. In 1841, they found refuge in then liberal Berlin, as members of the Prussian Academy of Sciences.

Hale, Sarah Josepha (October 24, 1788–April 30, 1879). American editor and writer. Hale was widely influential in 19th-century America as the editor of *The Ladies' Magazine* from 1828 to 1837 and of its subsequent incarnation, *Godey's Lady's Book*, from 1837 to 1877. Under her guidance, both were popular periodicals for women, publishing articles on middle-class women's issues as well as fashion reports and sentimental poems and stories. Hale's editorials encouraged women's domestic and moral role and advocated their exclusion from the public realms of work and politics. She also, however, supported the progressive causes of women's education and property rights. Self-educated, Hale began her career in letters as a young widow in order to support her five children. Her own writings include *Woman's Record* (1853), an encyclopedia of illustrious women

in history, and the classic children's poem "Mary Had a Little Lamb" (1830).

Hardwick, Elizabeth (July 27, 1916–). American critic, novelist, and editor. A celebrated essayist, Hardwick is best known for her perceptive, eloquent contributions to PARTISAN REVIEW and *THE NEW YORK REVIEW OF BOOKS*, which she cofounded in 1963. Born and raised in Kentucky, she has lived in New York City for most of her life, and was married to poet ROBERT LOWELL from 1949 to 1972. Hardwick has written several acclaimed novels, including *The Ghostly Lover* (1945) and *Sleepless Nights* (1979), which are noted for the same original observation and elegant style that characterize her critical writing. Collections of Hardwick's essays include *A View of My Own: Essays in Literature and Society* (1962), *Seduction and Betrayal: Women and Literature* (1974), *Bartleby in Manhattan and Other Essays* (1983), and *Sight-Readings: American Fictions* (1998). *Herman Melville* (2000) is a critical study.

Hartman, Geoffrey (August 11, 1929–). German-born American critic and educator. A central figure in the "Yale School" of deconstructionists, who dominated literary criticism in the 1970s and early 1980s, Hartman urged critics to look "within literature, not outside of it" for the meaning of a text and viewed criticism itself as a creative endeavor. Born and raised in Germany, he immigrated to the United States in 1946 and studied at Queens College in New York, the University of Dijon in France, and Yale. He joined the faculty at Yale in 1955 and has spent most of his teaching career there. Hartman gained notice with his early writings on critical theory and Romantic poetry in *The Unmediated Vision* (1954) and *Wordsworth's Poetry, 1787–1814* (1964). Other works on literature and culture include *Beyond Formalism* (1970), *The Fate of Reading* (1975), *Criticism in the Wilderness* (1980), *Saving the Text* (1981), *Easy Pieces* (1985), *Minor Prophecies* (1991), *The Fateful Question of Culture* (1997), and *A Critic's Journey: Literary Reflections, 1958–1998* (1999). In 1982 he became director of Yale's Video Archive of Holocaust

Testimonies; his lectures on the subject appear in *The Longest Shadow: In the Aftermath of the Holocaust* (1996).

Hazlitt, William (April 10, 1778–September 18, 1830). English essayist and critic. Hazlitt was a Romantic critic and brilliant prose stylist who argued for the superiority of passion, experience, and creative imagination over strict literary rules. He befriended many of the leading literary figures of his time, including WORDSWORTH and COLERIDGE, and quarreled with them all; only Charles LAMB remained a lifelong friend. Hazlitt studied religion, then painting, but financial difficulties drove him to work as a reporter for the *Morning Chronicle*. Working his way out of poverty, he became a well-known lecturer, and a respected theater critic and journalist writing for THE EXAMINER, *Champion*, EDINBURGH REVIEW, and THE LONDON MAGAZINE. His essays and lectures can be found in such collections as *Characters of Shakespear's Plays* (1817), *Lectures on the English Poets* (1818), *Lectures on the English Comic Writers* (1819), *Lectures Chiefly on the Dramatic Literature of the Age of Elizabeth* (1820), *Table-Talk* (1821), *The Spirit of the Age* (1825), and *The Plain Speaker* (1826) as well as in various modern editions of his selected essays and collected works.

Hearn, [Patricio] **Lafcadio** (June 27, 1850–September 26, 1904). Irish-Greek-American-Japanese travel writer, novelist, and journalist. An eccentric and colorful figure of multicultural background and experience, Hearn introduced Japanese and other exotic traditions to Western readers through his essays, novels, folklore collections, travel accounts, and translations. Of Irish-Greek heritage, he was born in the Ionian Islands and educated in Dublin, England, and France. He settled in the United States in 1869, writing for newspapers in Cincinnati and New Orleans before moving to Martinique. Writings from this period include a collection of oriental legends and stories, *Stray Leaves from Strange Literature* (1884); the novels *Chita: A Memory of Last Island* (1889) and *Youma: The Story of a West-Indian Slave*

(1890); and the travelogue *Two Years in the French West Indies* (1890). Hearn traveled to Japan in 1890, where he married, naturalized (taking his wife's surname, Koizumi, and the given name Yakumo), and lived out his life. He introduced English-language literature to Japanese university students while writing voluminously for Western readers on the culture, customs, and character of his adopted country. *Glimpses of Unfamiliar Japan* (1894), "Out of the East" (1895), *Kokoro* (1896), *A Japanese Miscellany* (1901), and *Japan: An Attempt at Interpretation* (1904) are representative works.

Heilbrun, Carolyn (January 13, 1926–). American critic and novelist. Heilbrun is widely known for her investigations of gender roles and her work to promote greater recognition of women's voices in literature. Raised in a Russian-Jewish family in New Jersey and Manhattan, she studied at Wellesley College and Columbia University, and taught literature at Columbia from 1960 to 1993. A committed feminist, Heilbrun has been prominently outspoken about the difficulties women face in academia. Her best-known critical works include *Toward a Recognition of Androgyny* (1973), on conceptions of gender in literature, and *Reinventing Womanhood* (1979) and *Writing a Woman's Life* (1988), which explore women's identity and autobiographical writing. Additional works include *Hamlet's Mother and Other Women* (1990) and *The Last Gift of Time: Life Beyond Sixty* (1997). Under the name Amanda Cross, Heilbrun has also written numerous popular mystery novels that incorporate feminist and literary elements.

Herder, Johann Gottfried (August 25, 1744–December 18, 1803). German philosopher, critic, and theologian. In the 1770s, influenced by ROUSSEAU and G. E. LESSING, Herder sparked the proto-Romantic German literary movement *Sturm und Drang* (Storm and Stress). In particular, the young GOETHE owed much to him, and repaid the debt in 1776 by securing him a Weimar court position. Although their relations eventually grew strained, some have speculated that Herder was one of the models for Goethe's

FAUST. Herder applied his views of the organic nature of historical phenomena in several fields, as in the "fragments" *On Recent German Literature* (*Über die Neuere Deutsche Litteratur: Fragmente*, 1767) and the *Essay on the Origin of Language* (*Abhandlung über den Ursprung der Sprache*, 1772). Championing the individuality of national cultures and the art of the "natural," he invented the term "folk song" ("Volkslied"); his international collection of *Volkslieder* (1778) influenced generations of German poets. Herder's magnum opus, *Outlines of a Philosophy of the History of Man* (*Ideen zur Philosophie der Geschichte der Menschheit*, 1784–91), is a comprehensive synthesis emphasizing humanity's evolution toward an elevated state. His protean influence was felt in a wide range of intellectual movements in Europe and the young United States. DE QUINCEY, writing in 1823, called him "the German COLERIDGE."

Hicks, Granville (September 9, 1901–June 18, 1982). American critic, editor, and novelist. A significant literary critic in the 1930s, Hicks employed a Marxist perspective to evaluate authors' portrayals of economic and social conditions. After graduating from Harvard in 1929, Hicks served as literary editor of the Communist Party periodical *New Masses* from 1933 to 1939 and wrote books of Marxist criticism, including *The Great Tradition* (1933), a study of American literary history, and *Figures of Transition* (1939), an examination of late Victorian literature. An outspoken critic of the USSR's nonaggression pact with Nazi Germany, he resigned from the Communist Party in 1939. Hicks subsequently wrote literary reviews and novels, including *There Was a Man in Our Town* (1952), and collected his early essays in *Granville Hicks in the "New Masses"* (1974).

Hirsch, E[ric] D[onald] (March 22, 1928–). American scholar, educator, and critic. Trained at Cornell University, Hirsch taught at Yale for a decade before joining the faculty of the University of Virginia in 1966. Although his scholarship in the field of Romantic poetry is distinguished, he is more widely known as the author, coauthor, and editor of a number of popular books on cultural literacy: *Cultural Literacy: What Every American Needs to Know* (1987), *The Dictionary of Cultural Literacy* (coauthored with Joseph Kett and James Trefil, 1988), and *A First Dictionary of Cultural Literacy: What Our Children Need to Know* (1989). Although disputed in some circles as narrow and polemical, Hirsch's work in the field won praise among many educators and parents for rehabilitating the value of a common body of cultural information. *The Schools We Need and Why We Don't Have Them* (1996) is Hirsch's treatise on the American education system's overemphasis on critical thinking skills at the expense of "core knowledge" in history, literature, civics, science, and the arts. He also served as the editor of the Core Knowledge Series of books for elementary schools. Hirsch's works of literary interpretation and writing instruction include *Validity in Interpretation* (1967), *The Aims of Interpretation* (1976), and *The Philosophy of Composition* (1977).

Holroyd, Michael (August 27, 1935–). English biographer. Esteemed for his critical biographies of major cultural figures, Holroyd, in his two-volume *Lytton Strachey: A Critical Biography* (1967–68), brought renewed attention to Strachey's own venerable biographical writing, and to the Bloomsbury circle of intellectuals with whom STRACHEY associated. A revised, single-volume *Lytton Strachey* appeared in 1994. Holroyd also wrote *Augustus John* (1974–75), the definitive biography of the painter, and the comprehensive, five-volume *Bernard Shaw* (1988–92). Born in London, Holroyd has famously asserted that he obtained his literary education in the public library. He has worked commitedly on behalf of writers with such organizations as the National Book League and PEN. His *Basil Street Blues: A Memoir* (1999) explores his childhood history and reflects on the roots of the biographer's vocation.

Howe, Irving (June 11, 1920–May 5, 1993). American critic. Coining the term "New York Intellectuals" in his essay of that title (1968),

Howe was prominent among the midcentury circle of New York Jewish literary critics that included Lionel TRILLING and Alfred KAZIN. A lifelong democratic socialist, Howe founded the political magazine *Dissent* in 1954 and was its coeditor. He also insightfully examined literature's relationship to history and politics, in works including *William Faulkner* (1952), *Politics and the Novel* (1957), and *Decline of the New* (1970). The son of Russian-Jewish immigrants, he promoted Jewish writers such as Saul BELLOW and Isaac Bashevis SINGER throughout his career, and edited several anthologies of Yiddish literature. His bestselling *World of Our Fathers* (1976) presents a sociocultural history of Eastern European Jews in America. His *A Margin of Hope: An Intellectual Autobiography* appeared in 1982.

Howells, William Dean (March 1, 1837–May 11, 1920). American critic, editor, and novelist. Influential in late 19th-century American letters, as a critic and editor Howells promoted realistic fiction and examined questions of morality and ethics in an industrializing, materialistic society. Raised in Ohio, Howells worked from childhood, first for his father, a printer, and then as a journalist. In Boston he served as subeditor (1866–71) and editor-in-chief (1871–81) of *THE ATLANTIC MONTHLY*, and in New York he wrote a column (1886–92) for *HARPER'S MAGAZINE*. In his articles and critical works, including *Criticism and Fiction* (1891), he promoted the work of such writers as Mark TWAIN, HENRY JAMES, and STEPHEN CRANE. Also a prolific novelist, in *A Modern Instance* (1882) and *THE RISE OF SILAS LAPHAM* (1885) he scathingly depicted moral corruption in the business world, while in *A Hazard of New Fortunes* (1890) he portrayed labor issues in magazine publishing.

Hulme, T[homas] **E**[rnest] (September 16, 1883–September 28, 1917). English critic and poet. Publishing little in his short lifetime, Hulme nonetheless strongly influenced modernist poetry, particularly the Imagists, a group that included Ezra POUND, H. D., and Amy Lowell. After completing his diffident studies in

1906, Hulme published poems, including the well-known "Autumn" (1908), held an intellectual salon in London, and translated the writings of French philosopher Henri BERGSON. His critical writings were published from his notebooks, after his death in action in World War I, in the volumes *Speculations* (1924) and *Notes on Language and Style* (1929). Hulme advocated the "hard, dry image," valuing precise, concrete imagery over discursive or effluent poetry. His writing criticizes Romantic optimism about human nature, contending that human capacity is limited and that concrete, concentrated images may poetically convey the challenging, modern complexity of experience.

Hunt, [James Henry] **Leigh** (October 19, 1784–August 28, 1859). English poet, critic, and journalist. An accomplished essayist and champion of Romanticism, Hunt defended poets such as SHELLEY and KEATS from their detractors at *BLACKWOOD'S EDINBURGH MAGAZINE*. He began publishing essays and dramatic criticism in various journals in 1801 and with his brother John started a political journal, *THE EXAMINER* (1806–21). Politically radical, Hunt even edited from jail after he was arrested in 1813 for issuing an article critical of the future George IV. While in Italy in 1822, he began the journal *The Liberal*, a brief venture with BYRON and Shelley. Known for his one-man periodicals, Hunt also edited *The Reflector* (1810–11), *The Indicator* (1819–21), *Literary Pocket-Book* (1819–23), *The Tatler* (1830–32), *The Companion* (1828), and *Leigh Hunt's London Journal* (1834–35), among others. Some of his best-known works include *The Story of Rimini* (1816), *Lord Byron and Some of His Contemporaries* (1828), *Imagination and Fancy* (1844), and his *Autobiography* (1850).

Irigaray, Luce (1930–). Belgian-born French psychoanalyst and critic. Irigaray is an influential feminist thinker whose ideas have had some currency in academic literary studies since the 1960s. In examining the relationship between discourse and cultural power, she concluded that language was "phallocentric" and constructed to reinforce the authority of men. Focusing on linguistics, philosophy, and psychoanalysis, she studied with Jacques Lacan and became a member of his École Freudienne in Paris. But she was expelled from the school after the publication of her doctoral dissertation, *Speculum of the Other Woman* (*Speculum de l'Autre Femme*, 1974), which questioned many psychoanalytic ideas about women, including FREUD's concept of the Oedipus complex and his treatment of women as existing only in relation to men (as daughters, wives, and mothers). Irigaray has also written about gender representation in philosophical and canonical texts. She holds doctorates in linguistics and philosophy, and in 1986 became a director of research at the Centre Nationale de la Recherche Scientifique in Paris. Her works include *The Language of the Demented* (*Le Langage des Deménts*, 1973), *This Sex Which Is Not One* (*Ce Sexe Qui n'en Est pas Un*, 1977), and *An Ethics of Sexual Difference* (*Éthique de la Différence Sexuelle*, 1984).

Ivanov, V[yacheslav] **I**[vanovich] (February 28, 1866–July 16, 1949). Russian poet, philosopher, scholar, and critic. Ivanov's first book of poetry, *Kormchiya Zvezdy* (1903; Lodestars), made him a seminal figure in the Russian Symbolist movement. After studying classics under historian Theodor Mommsen at the University of Berlin, in 1905 he established an important literary salon in his St. Petersburg apartment. Ivanov rejected the concepts of individualism and "art for art's sake," arguing that the creation of art is the realization of the struggle for the divine, and that dramatic and literary characters should be symbols, not psychological probes of individuals (like many of DOSTOYEVSKY's protagonists). Among his many volumes of poetry are *Prozrachnost'* (1904; Translucency), *Eros* (1907), *Cor Ardens* (1911), and *Zimnie Sonety* (1921; Winter Sonnets). His critical works on aesthetics include *Po Zvezdam* (1909; Following the Stars) and *Borozdy i Mezhi* (1916; Furrow and Landmarks). *Freedom and the Tragic Life: A Study in Dostoevsky* (1952) is a critical work published in English.

Jakobson, Roman (October 11, 1896–July 18, 1982). Russian linguist and critic. As a founding member of the Prague Linguistics Circle, Jakobson in the late 1920s and 1930s studied the relation between language and literature; his work proved central to the theory and practice of structuralist criticism. On the basis of such innovative concepts as the "dominant"—the prevailing structural element of a text—and groundbreaking work in grammar, phonology, speech analysis, and language acquisition, he advanced general theories of linguistics and applied them to readings of Slavic epic literature and verse. A professor at Masarykova University in Brno, Czechoslovakia, beginning in 1933, he was forced to flee with the rise of Nazism and was a visiting professor at several other European universities before immigrating to the United States. He taught at Columbia from 1943 to 1949 and was professor of Slavic languages and general linguistics at Harvard from 1949 to 1967. Important works include *Fundamentals of Language* (1956), *Main Trends in the Science of Language* (1973), *The Framework of Language* (1980), and *Selected Writings* (8 vols., 1962–88).

Jolas, Eugene (October 26, 1894–May 26, 1952). American editor and poet. Jolas was a cofounder and editor of the influential magazine *TRANSITION* (1927–38), dedicated to innovative modern literature exploring the unconscious and the imagination, "the language of the night" as Jolas titled a volume of his poems (1932). Based in Paris, *transition* provided a forum for modernist authors, including Samuel BECKETT, H. D., E. E. CUMMINGS, and HART CRANE, publishing, for example, 17 segments of James JOYCE's experimental *FINNEGANS WAKE*. Born in New Jersey, Jolas was raised in Lorraine, France, and New York and worked as a journalist in both the United States and Paris before editing *transition*. He later worked in American government service during and after World War II. His volumes of poems, including *Cinema* (1926) and *I Have Seen Monsters and Angels* (1938), explore in a Surrealist-influenced style the need for a vital inner life.

Jowett, Benjamin (April 15, 1817–October 1, 1893). English educator, scholar, and translator. Jowett is best known for his translations, especially of Plato's *Dialogues* (4 vols., 1871), Thucydides' *History of the Peloponnesian War* (2 vols., 1881), ARISTOTLE's *Politics* (2 vols., 1885), and Plato's *Republic* (1894). He was educated at Balliol College, Oxford, where he went on to serve as a fellow, tutor, lecturer, and eventually master, becoming one of the most influential educators of his day. He was also an Anglican priest, and his *The Epistles of St. Paul to the Thessalonians* (1855) and other unorthodox (some said heretical) writings earned him enemies and made him a controversial figure.

Jung, C[arl] **G**[ustav] (July 26, 1875–June 6, 1961). Swiss psychiatrist. The founder of analytical psychology, Jung worked closely with Sigmund FREUD from 1907 to 1912, but broke with him over Freud's insistence on the sexual basis of neuroses and the purely sexual nature of libido. In such books as *The Psychology of the Unconscious* (*Wandlungen und Symbole der Libido*, 1912) and *Psychological Types* (*Psychologische Typen*, 1921), Jung introduced and elaborated on his pioneering ideas about the existence of archetypes, or universal patterns and figures, in myths, dreams, and literature; a collective unconscious; and masculine and feminine components of the psyche (the *animus* and *anima*). Jungian thought soon went beyond psychology and psychiatry to affect religious studies and literary criticism. Jung taught at the universities of Zurich (1933–41) and Basel (1944–61).

Kakutani, Michiko (January 9, 1955–). American critic. Senior Book Critic at *The New York Times*, Kakutani joined the newspaper's staff as a cultural news reporter in 1979 and began reviewing books there in 1983. Born in New Haven, Connecticut, she attended Yale University, where she edited the *Yale Daily News*. She then worked as a reporter for the *Washington Post* and a staff writer for *Time* magazine before moving to the *Times*. In 1988, she published *The Poet at the Piano: Portraits of Writers, Filmmakers, Playwrights, and Other Artists at Work.*

In awarding her the 1998 Pulitzer Prize for criticism, the Pulitzer jury praised her "passionate, intelligent writing on books and contemporary literature."

Kaplan, Justin (September 5, 1925–). American biographer and editor. Kaplan is chiefly known for his contributions to American literary biography, including *Mr. Clemens and Mark Twain* (1966; Pulitzer Prize and National Book Award), *Lincoln Steffens: A Biography* (1974), and *Walt Whitman: A Life* (1980). Born in New York City, he attended Harvard University and later lectured there and elsewhere. His other books include *Mark Twain and His World* (1974) and *The Language of Names* (with Anne Bernays, 1997). In addition, he edited *With Malice Toward Women: A Handbook for Women-Haters Drawn from the Best Minds of All Time* (1952) and the 16th edition of *Bartlett's Familiar Quotations* (1992).

Kazin, Alfred (June 5, 1915–June 5, 1998). American editor, critic, and cultural historian. One of America's preeminent men of letters, Kazin influenced a generation of thinkers through his perceptive, erudite, eloquent, yet highly accessible writings. Born in Brooklyn to Russian immigrant parents, he was educated at the City College of New York and Columbia University. In his early 20s he joined the staff of THE NEW REPUBLIC, where he soon became literary editor. At 27, Kazin won instant recognition with his first book of criticism, *On Native Grounds* (1942), a sweeping survey of American literature and society from the late 19th century to the beginning of World War II. His other works include *Bright Book of Life: American Novelists and Storytellers from Hemingway to Mailer* (1973), *An American Procession* (1984), and *God and the American Writer* (1997) as well as several evocative memoirs—*A Walker in the City* (1951), *Starting Out in the Thirties* (1965), *New York Jew* (1978), *Writing Was Everything* (1995), and *A Lifetime Burning in Every Moment: From the Journals of Alfred Kazin* (1996).

Kenner, [William] Hugh (January 7, 1923–). Canadian critic. Kenner is best known for his interpretations of modernists and for helping to make writers such as James JOYCE, T. S. ELIOT, WYNDHAM LEWIS, and especially Ezra POUND more accessible to a wide audience. Kenner earned his B.A. and M.A. at the University of Toronto before receiving a Ph.D. from Yale in 1950. He taught at the University of California, Santa Barbara, for 14 years, then joined the faculty of Johns Hopkins University. Being introduced to Ezra Pound as a young man profoundly affected his interests and his commitment to meeting his subjects and even visiting sites described in their works. His principal works of criticism include *The Poetry of Ezra Pound* (1951), *Wyndham Lewis* (1954), *Dublin's Joyce* (1955), *Gnomon: Essays on Contemporary Literature* (1958), *The Invisible Poet: T. S. Eliot* (1959), *Samuel Beckett* (1961), *The Pound Era* (1971), *A Colder Eye: The Modern Irish Writers* (1983), *The Sinking Island: The Modern English Writers* (1988), and *Historical Fictions* (1990).

Kermode, [Sir] [John] **Frank** (November 29, 1919–). English critic and literary historian. Born on the Isle of Man, Kermode graduated from Liverpool University in 1940. He spent six years in the Royal Navy before beginning his teaching career, which included professorships at several universities in England and the United States; from 1974 to 1982, he was Edward VII Professor of English Literature at King's College, Cambridge. A specialist in the English Renaissance, he is the author of several works on DONNE and SHAKESPEARE, including *John Donne* (1957), *William Shakespeare: The Final Plays* (1963), *The Patience of Shakespeare* (1964), *On Shakespeare's Learning* (1965), and *Shakespeare's Language* (2000). His critical writings on a variety of other periods and subjects include *Romantic Image* (1957), *The Sense of an Ending* (1967), *The Classic: Literary Images of Permanence and Change* (1975), *The Genesis of Secrecy: On the Interpretation of Narrative* (1979), *The Art of Telling: Essays on Fiction* (1983), *Forms of Attention* (1985), *An Appetite for Poetry* (1989), and *The Uses of Error* (1991). In 1979, he helped to found the *London Review of Books*. His autobiography, *Not Entitled*, appeared in 1995. A voice of moderation and tolerance, Kermode does not fit into any

distinct school of criticism, but has increasingly opposed some of the more extreme forms of postmodern theory. He is also appreciated for his ability to speak intelligently on scholarly subjects to a general audience.

Kerr, Walter (July 8, 1913–October 9, 1996). American theater critic and playwright. Kerr, who wrote theater criticism for *The New York Times* from 1966 to 1983, won the Pulitzer Prize for criticism in 1978. Born in Evanston, Illinois, he received his B.A. and M.A. from Northwestern University, and taught speech and drama at Catholic University before becoming drama critic for *Commonweal* magazine in 1950. In 1951, he began writing for the *New York Herald Tribune*, where he remained until 1966 before moving to the *Times*. His critical writings include *How Not to Write a Play* (1955), *Pieces at Eight* (1957), *The Decline of Pleasure* (1962), *The Theater in Spite of Itself* (1963), *Thirty Plays Hath November* (1969), *God on the Gymnasium Floor and Other Theatrical Adventures* (1971), *Silent Clowns* (1975), and *Journey to the Center of the Theater* (1979). Kerr also wrote several plays, including the musical *Goldilocks* (1958), cowritten with his wife, humorist and playwright Jean Kerr. When restoration was completed on the Ritz Theater in Manhattan, it was renamed the Walter Kerr Theater in 1990.

Kierkegaard, Søren (May 5, 1813–November 11, 1855). Danish philosopher and religious thinker. Kierkegaard's writings occupy a middle ground between imaginative literature and discursive philosophy. Critical of systematic, rational philosophic schemes (especially Hegelianism) because of their remoteness from life, he published his best-known works under pseudonyms, employing fictitious personae to further his aim "to deceive people into the truth." They include *Either/Or* (*Enten-Eller*, 1843), about the necessity of individual choice between "aesthetic" (or merely sensory) and "ethical" ways of life; *Fear and Trembling* (*Frygt og Bæven*, 1843), concerned with the purpose of sacrifice; *The Concept of Anxiety* (*Begrebet Angest*, 1844), which proposes anxiety as a necessary condition for freedom; *Stages on Life's Way* (*Stadier paa Livets Vej*, 1845), which further distinguishes the stage of faith from the aesthetic and ethical "stages"; and *The Sickness unto Death* (*Sygdommen til Døden*, 1849), which scrutinizes despair, proposing a radical Christian faith as its only antidote. Little known outside Denmark and Germany until the 20th century, Kierkegaard is sometimes called "the father of existentialism" because of the profound influence his work exerted on modern existentialist thinking.

Kirkus, Virginia (December 7, 1893–September 10, 1980). American editor and book reviewer. After working as a children's book editor at Harper & Brothers from 1926 to 1932, Kirkus in 1933 founded the Kirkus Review Service, a prepublication book review service dedicated to providing informative, unpretentious, unbiased reviews of books; it is now published under the title *Kirkus Reviews*, and is widely respected. She studied at Vassar College and Teachers College at Columbia University, and taught English and history in Wilmington, Delaware, before beginning a career in magazine and book publishing. She worked for *The Pictorial Review* and *McCall's*, and as a freelance writer and editor, before joining Harper's.

Knopf, Alfred A[braham] (September 12, 1892–August 11, 1984). American publisher. Founder of the New York firm that bears his name, Knopf was born into a well-to-do family in New York City and received his B.A. from Columbia University in 1912. He then traveled to Europe, spending much time in bookshops, and returned to New York with a heightened interest in the aesthetics of book design and determined to become a publisher, not a lawyer as his family had intended. Knopf worked at Doubleday, Page & Company (where he helped to promote Joseph CONRAD, one of his favorite writers) and at Mitchell Kennerley (a house noted for its quality book design) before founding, in the summer of 1915, the firm of Alfred A. Knopf, Inc., with the financial backing of his father and the support of his future wife, Blanche Wolf. Knopf was resolved to pub-

lish the very best in American literature and he championed the work of such writers as Willa CATHER (his personal favorite). But his firm also gained renown for its translations of writers from around the world, introducing American readers to such masters as Knut HAMSUN, Thomas MANN, André GIDE, Sigrid UNDSET, Simone de BEAUVOIR, Jorge AMADO, Yukio MISHIMA, and many others. Knopf was keenly interested in the physical look and quality of the books he published, and over the years hired many important designers, including the legendary W. A. Dwiggins, who began working with the firm in the 1920s. Its colophon—"the coursing Borzoi"—became synonymous with the standards set by the firm's founder, whose description of the ideal publisher could be a self-portrait: "[H]e will have great curiosity, broad interests, and that very old-fashioned quality, taste." Random House, Inc., purchased Alfred A. Knopf in 1960.

Korda, Michael (October 8, 1933–). American editor, publisher, novelist, and memoirist. In more than 30 years at Simon & Schuster, where he rose to become editor-in-chief, Korda concentrated on commercial fiction, publishing such popular authors as Mary Higgins Clark, Jackie Collins, Harold Robbins, and Jacqueline Susann, as well as on works by such literary figures as Graham GREENE, Larry MCMURTRY, and TENNESSEE WILLIAMS, and by historians and public figures such as Henry Kissinger, David McCullough, and Richard Nixon. The son of a Hungarian-Jewish father and an English actress, and the nephew of film producer Alexander Korda, Michael Korda was educated in Switzerland and at Magdalene College, Cambridge. He went to Budapest in 1956 to support the Hungarian Revolution, and spent two years in the Royal Air Force. Among his works are *Charmed Lives: A Family Romance* (1979), about the lives of his father and uncles in the film industry; *Queenie* (1985), a novel based on the life of actress Merle Oberon, who was married to his uncle; *Man to Man: Surviving Prostate Cancer* (1996); *Another Life: A Memoir of Other People* (1999); and *Country Matters: The Pleasures and Tribulations of Moving from a*

Big City to an Old Country Farmhouse (2001). He has been a frequent contributor to THE NEW YORKER.

Kramer, Hilton (March 25, 1928–). American art critic, essayist, and editor. Kramer began his career in art criticism as a reviewer for *Art Digest* in 1954; from 1955 to 1961, he served as managing editor, then chief editor of *Arts Magazine*. He became the art news editor for *The New York Times* in 1965, and from 1973 to 1982 served as chief art critic there, solidifying his reputation as an influential commentator and learned art historian. Disillusioned by what he considered the decline of intellectual life in America, in 1982 Kramer founded *The New Criterion*, a conservative critical journal of art and culture. His first and most important book, *The Age of Avant-Garde* (1973), was followed by *The Revenge of the Philistines: Art and Culture, 1972–1984* (1985) and *The Twilight of the Intellectuals: Culture and Politics in the Era of the Cold War* (1999).

Kristeva, Julia (June 24, 1941–). Bulgarian-born French critic and psychoanalyst. Upon leaving her native Bulgaria, Kristeva became a major actor in the intellectual and political ferment in Paris in the late 1960s. She was a primary editor of the journal TEL QUEL, which covered and instigated debates in Marxism, psychoanalysis, and literary studies. Always interested in the linguistic aspects of femininity, Kristeva has had an ambivalent relationship with feminism as a political movement. Her commitment to social engagement is unquestionable, however, as in the early work *Revolution in Poetic Language* (*La Révolution du Langage Poétique*, 1974). A practicing psychoanalyst since 1979, Kristeva has incorporated her clinical as well as literary interests into such later books as *Powers of Horror: An Essay on Abjection* (*Pouvoirs de l'Horreur: Essai sur l'Abjection*, 1980), *Tales of Love* (*Histoires d'Amour*, 1983), *Black Sun: Depression and Melancholia* (*Soleil Noir: Dépression et Mélancolie*, 1987), and *New Maladies of the Soul* (*Les Nouvelles Maladies de l'Âme*, 1993). Her autobiographical novel, *The Samurai* (*Les Samouraïs*, 1990), portrays characters based on real figures in the Parisian intellectual milieu of the 1960s. *The Portable Kristeva*, an anthology, appeared in 1997.

Krutch, Joseph Wood (November 25, 1893–May 22, 1970). American critic and essayist. Krutch earned his M.A. and Ph.D. from Columbia University and, after a brief period of teaching, became a book and theater critic for THE SATURDAY REVIEW *of Literature* and THE NATION. He joined *The Nation* full time in 1924, writing theater reviews and commentary on American culture. From 1937 on, he took a less active role at *The Nation* and instead accepted a teaching post at Columbia University, where he remained until 1952. He then moved to Arizona to concentrate on environmental interests. *The Modern Temper* (1929), *The Measure of Man* (1954), *Human Nature and the Human Condition* (1959), and *If You Don't Mind My Saying So . . .* (1964) are collections of his essays. His criticism includes *Edgar Allan Poe* (1926), *Five Masters* (1930), *Experience and Art* (1932), *Samuel Johnson* (1944), *Henry David Thoreau* (1948), and "Modernism" in *Modern Drama* (1953).

Lamb, Charles (February 10, 1775–December 27, 1834). English essayist and critic. A friend of COLERIDGE, HAZLITT, Southey, WORDSWORTH, and other figures in the English Romantic movement, Lamb is best known for the series of essays he wrote for THE LONDON MAGAZINE under the pseudonym Elia between 1820 and 1825. Mostly autobiographical, these exemplars of the personal essay were collected in two volumes titled *Elia* (1823 and 1828), and in a third volume, *The Last Essays of Elia* (1833). Lamb suffered from a speech impediment that kept him from pursuing his education beyond the age of 15, when he took a job as a clerk for the East India Company, a post he held until retirement. With his sister Mary, he collaborated on the two-volume *Tales from Shakespear* (1807), a retelling of SHAKESPEARE's plays for young readers. An avid and talented letter writer, Lamb corresponded with many of his contemporaries, especially Coleridge; his letters are reprinted in the multivolume *The Letters of Charles and Mary Anne Lamb* (1975–).

Lapham, Lewis H[enry] (January 8, 1935–). American journalist, social critic, and editor. After studying at Yale and Cambridge universities, Lapham embarked on a career in journalism. He began as a reporter for the *San Francisco Examiner* and spent two years with the *New York Herald Tribune* before switching to magazines, including *The Saturday Evening Post* and *Life*. Lapham had served as the managing editor of HARPER'S MAGAZINE for four years when in 1975 he was made editor of the magazine, helping it to survive and prosper after its parent company threatened to close it. Lapham's skill at identifying and examining social ills in America and his disdain for greed, abuses of power, and pretension can be seen in *Money and Class in America* (1988), *Imperial Masquerade* (1990), *The Wish for Kings* (1993), *Hotel America: Scenes in the Lobby of the Fin-de-siècle* (1995), and *Waiting for the Barbarians* (1997). *Fortune's Child: A Portrait of the United States as Spendthrift Heir* (1980) is a collection of previously published essays on modern America.

Lattimore, Richmond (March 6, 1906–February 26, 1984). American poet and translator. Lattimore is best known for his brilliant translations of ancient Greek classics. After completing his graduate studies at Oxford and the University of Illinois in 1934, Lattimore joined the faculty in Greek at Bryn Mawr College, where he remained for 36 years. During that time, he produced his best-known translations, many of which remain standard versions, including *The Odes of PINDAR* (1947), *The ILIAD of HOMER* (1951), *The ORESTEIA of AESCHYLUS* (1953), ARISTOPHANES' *THE FROGS* (1962), *The ODYSSEY of Homer* (1967), and EURIPIDES' *Iphigeneia in Tauris* (1973). Lattimore also wrote poetry diverse in form and subject, characterized by controlled, simple eloquence. His poems are collected in *Poems from Three Decades* (1972).

Laughlin, James (October 30, 1914–November 12, 1997). American publisher and poet. As the founder and longtime head of New Directions press, Laughlin created one of the most important American literary publishing houses. The son of a wealthy Pittsburgh steel manufacturer, Laughlin attended Choate and Harvard, and traveled to Europe to pursue his interest in experimental literature, meeting such writers as Gertrude STEIN and Ezra POUND. At Pound's suggestion he founded New Directions in 1936. Noted for its integrity and dedication to literary values, the house has published such writers as TENNESSEE WILLIAMS, Dylan THOMAS, HENRY MILLER, Vladimir NABOKOV, and many of the Beat poets as well as translations of important non-English-language writers and reprints of neglected works by early modern authors. Laughlin was also a well-regarded poet; his fluent, expressive compositions were gathered in *Collected Poems* (1994).

Leavis, F[rank] **R**[aymond] (July 14, 1895–April 14, 1978). English critic. Leavis was educated at Emmanuel College, Cambridge University, and spent his entire academic career teaching at Cambridge. A controversial and opinionated figure, he left a strong and contentious mark on the literary criticism of his day. While many of his contemporaries emphasized literary biography and history, Leavis insisted that criticism focus on the text. He also thought the critic should be an advocate for high moral and cultural standards and steer literature, tradition, and therefore life away from cultural decline. Leavis wrote *Mass Civilisation and Minority Culture* (1930), *New Bearings in English Poetry* (1932), *Revaluation, Tradition and Development in English Poetry* (1936), *The Great Tradition: George Eliot, Henry James, Joseph Conrad* (1948), and *The Common Pursuit* (1952), in addition to several books on D. H. LAWRENCE, whom he considered the greatest novelist of the 20th century. With his wife, critic Q. D. ("Queenie") Leavis, he founded the highly influential journal *SCRUTINY* in 1932.

Lee, Hermione (February 29, 1948–). English literary biographer. Following the success of her critically acclaimed and bestselling *Virginia Woolf: A Biography* (1996), Lee was named Goldsmiths' Professor of English Literature at

New College, Oxford, in 1998. A specialist in women's writing, 19th- and 20th-century fiction, and the art of autobiography, she has also published books on Willa CATHER, Elizabeth BOWEN, and PHILIP ROTH, and edited the letters of William Hogarth and a selection of writings by Stevie SMITH. Lee earned her academic degrees at Oxford and held teaching positions at the College of William and Mary in Virginia, the University of Liverpool, and the University of York before returning to Oxford. She is a frequent commentator on literature and the arts in the British media.

Lehmann, [Rudolph] **John** (June 2, 1907–April 7, 1987). English editor, poet, and publisher. Lehmann began his literary career as general manager of LEONARD and VIRGINIA WOOLF's Hogarth Press in 1931–32. After several years as a journalist in Vienna and the Soviet Union, he returned to the Press as a partner in 1938; he later wrote about the Woolfs in *Virginia Woolf and Her World* (1975) and *Thrown to the Woolfs: Leonard and Virginia Woolf and the Hogarth Press* (1978). In 1938 Lehmann also became editor of the left-leaning periodical *New Writing* (called *Penguin New Writing* from 1946 on), continuing in that position until 1950. Four years later, he founded the literary journal *The London Magazine*. Lehmann's autobiography, *In My Own Time* (1969), shed light on the literary scene of his time and on the writers he published over the years. His poetry can be found in *A Garden Revisited and Other Poems* (1931), *The Noise of History* (1934), *The Sphere of Glass* (1944), *The Reader at Night* (1974), and *New and Selected Poems* (1985).

Leslie, Frank, *original name* Henry Carter (March 29, 1821–January 10, 1880). American engraver and publisher. Leslie's highly successful *Frank Leslie's Illustrated Newspaper*, which featured graphic images of murders, fires, fights, and, later, the Civil War, with little accompanying text, exemplified his motto: "Never shoot over the heads of the people." Leslie also established a book-publishing company that flourished by selling cheap editions to railway passengers. Born Henry Carter in Ipswich, England, he changed his name because his father disapproved of his nascent career as a wood engraver for magazines and newspapers. He eventually began working for *The Illustrated London News*, and in 1848 immigrated to the United States. After working for several publications in Boston and New York, Leslie began publishing his own periodicals in 1853; the first issue of his *Illustrated Newspaper* appeared in 1855. In 1874, Leslie created a scandal when the wife of his magazine's chief editor divorced her husband to marry Leslie. Together, the new husband-and-wife team headed an empire that churned out magazines, joke books, scandal sheets, and books for every market. Owing to their extravagant lifestyle and the financial panic of 1877, Leslie filed for bankruptcy and was still trying to pay off his debts when he died three years later. His resourceful wife, Miriam, had her name legally changed to Frank Leslie, took over the business, and successfully repaid the debts, leaving $2 million to the cause of women's suffrage at her death in 1914.

Liveright, Horace (December 10, 1886–September 24, 1933). American publisher. A pioneer of the American book-publishing industry, Liveright was cofounder and president of the firm of Boni and Liveright (renamed Horace Liveright, Inc. in 1928), known for originating The Modern Library—inexpensive reprints of literary classics and popular fiction—and discovering some of the most important writers in 20th-century American letters. Raised in Philadelphia, he dropped out of high school to work at a brokerage house and, after several other ventures, joined with Albert Boni in 1917 to start a book business. With a keen instinct for literary talent, he published the first books of Ernest HEMINGWAY (*In Our Time*, 1925), E. E. CUMMINGS (*THE ENORMOUS ROOM*, 1922), and other notables as well as such modern classics as T. S. ELIOT's *THE WASTE LAND* (1922), Theodore DREISER's *AN AMERICAN TRAGEDY* (1925), and the major plays of Eugene O'NEILL. Among the many publishing careers he launched were those of Bennett CERF and Richard SIMON. Nicknamed "the Firebrand," he indulged his attraction to bright lights and high society as a Broadway producer; a 1927 *Dracula* starring Bela Lugosi was his only major success. Losses sustained on Broadway and Wall Street forced him out of business in 1930.

Lowell, James Russell (February 22, 1819–August 12, 1891). American poet, critic, and editor. Born to a wealthy and distinguished family in Cambridge, Massachusetts, Lowell edited the Harvard college magazine and was elected class poet, but was suspended from school for violating rules. He later received a law degree from Harvard, but decided instead to pursue his literary ambitions, publishing his poetry in such leading reviews as THE DIAL, and in 1843 founding *The Pioneer*, which failed quickly despite contributions from POE, HAWTHORNE, and Elizabeth Barrett (later to become ELIZABETH BARRETT BROWNING). In 1848, he published *The Biglow Papers: First Series*, a collection of satirical political essays featuring the Yankee farmer Hosea Biglow and demonstrating Lowell's mastery of New England dialect; the work was a tour de force that enhanced its author's growing literary reputation. From 1857 to 1861, he was the first editor of THE ATLANTIC MONTHLY, and from 1863 to 1872 edited the distinguished literary journal THE NORTH AMERICAN REVIEW. He taught at Harvard for many years, and served as United States minister to Spain (1877–80) and ambassador to Great Britain (1880–85). Other important writings by Lowell include the satirical A FABLE FOR CRITICS (1848) and the poem "Commemoration Ode" (1865), honoring Harvard students who died in the Civil War.

Lukács, Georg *or* **György** (April 13, 1885–June 4, 1971). Hungarian philosopher and literary theorist, writing in German and Hungarian. Lukács was born in Budapest and studied there as well as in Berlin, Heidelberg, and Moscow. Although he was a member of the Hungarian Communist Party from 1918 on, Lukács had a tumultuous relationship with the Communist International and was forced to relocate several times during a 25-year exile from Hungary. After returning to Budapest in 1945, he served

in the parliament and taught at the university, but was arrested and deported briefly after his role in the Hungarian uprising in 1956. In literature, he brought his own brand of Marxism to a more general interest in form, championing the great 19th- and 20th-century realists against more modernist writers. His critical works include *Soul and Form* (*Die Seele und die Formen*, 1911), *The Theory of the Novel* (*Die Theorie des Romans*, 1920), *The Historical Novel* (*Der Historische Roman*, 1955), and *Realism in Our Time* (*Wider den Missverständenen Realismus*, 1958).

Macdonald, Dwight (March 24, 1906–December 19, 1982). American political and cultural writer and editor. A sometimes severe critic of capitalism and American popular culture, Macdonald graduated from Yale University and worked as an editor and writer for *Fortune* and PARTISAN REVIEW before founding the journal *Politics* in 1944 as a vehicle for anarchist and pacifist opinion. His radical politics of the 1930s and 1940s evolved into a wry disenchantment with dogmatism in any form, traced in the essays contained in *Memoirs of a Revolutionist: Essays in Political Criticism* (1957). Turning to sociocultural criticism, he became a staff writer for THE NEW YORKER and a movie critic for *Esquire*. Notable essays and reviews are collected in *Against the American Grain* (1962), concerning mass culture and its effects on the arts; *Dwight Macdonald on Movies* (1969); and *Discriminations: Essays & Afterthoughts, 1938–1974* (1974). Other books include *Henry Wallace: The Man and the Myth* (1948) and *The Ford Foundation: The Men and the Millions* (1956).

Matthiessen, F[rancis] O[tto] (February 19, 1902–March 31, 1950). American critic and scholar. Matthiessen devoted his life to the study of American writers and, as a member of the faculty at Harvard (1929–50), did much to cement the notion of a cohesive American literary tradition connecting authors as disparate as Walt WHITMAN and Theodore DREISER. He is known particularly for his studies of T. S. ELIOT and HENRY JAMES as well as for *The Oxford Book* *of American Verse* (1950), which he edited. His suicide is the basis of a novel, *Faithful Are the Wounds* (1955), by May Sarton.

Menand, Louis (January 21, 1952–). American critic, journalist, and scholar. Menand received his Ph.D. from Columbia and has taught since 1988 at the Graduate Center of the City University of New York. His early criticism included an influential re-reading of T. S. ELIOT (*Discovering Modernism: T. S. Eliot and His Context*, 1987); he has also written on EDMUND WILSON, Rudyard KIPLING, and Oscar WILDE, among others. In 2000, the seventh volume of the *Cambridge History of Literary Criticism*, covering (and subtitled) *Modernism and the New Criticism*, edited by Menand with A. Walton Litz and Lawrence Rainey, appeared to great acclaim. In addition to literary criticism, Menand writes cultural journalism for a wider audience and has been a contributing editor of *THE NEW YORK REVIEW OF BOOKS, HARPER'S*, and *THE NEW REPUBLIC*, and a staff writer for *THE NEW YORKER*. Although he is an acknowledged liberal, Menand's work is free of dogmatism and is not easily categorized; much of his later work is on the history of pragmatism, including *The Metaphysical Club: A Story of Ideas in America* (2001) and, as editor, *Pragmatism: A Reader* (1997).

Mencken, H[enry] **L**[ouis] (September 12, 1880–January 29, 1956). American journalist and critic. Widely renowned in the 1920s for his caustically witty attacks on American provincialism, Mencken brought candor and vitality to the journalism of his day. He began his career in 1899 as a newspaper reporter at the Baltimore *Herald*, rising to become editor in chief in 1906 and then working as a columnist and editor for several other newspapers. He then led the literary magazine *The Smart Set* to prominence during his coeditorship with George Jean NATHAN from 1914 to 1923, and with Nathan in 1924 cofounded the influential *AMERICAN MERCURY*, which Mencken edited until 1933. His iconoclastic essays in both magazines—published under his own name as well as many pseudonyms—aggressively critiqued

hypocrisy, puritanical attitudes, and bourgeois culture (the "booboisie"). He also promoted and published controversial contemporary writers such as Theodore DREISER, SINCLAIR LEWIS, Sherwood ANDERSON, and Eugene O'NEILL. Mencken largely retired from public life after the death of his wife in 1935, returning to his native Baltimore and writing a series of autobiographical essays, published in *THE NEW YORKER* and collected in *Happy Days, 1880–1892* (1940), *Newspaper Days, 1899–1906* (1941), and *Heathen Days, 1890–1936* (1943) and reprinted as *The Days of H. L. Mencken* (1947). Other essays are collected in the multivolume series *Prejudices* (1919–27). He is also remembered for *The American Language* (1919), a classic chronicle of the development of American English. Since his death in 1956, many anthologies of his work, as well as of his letters and diaries, have appeared; *My Life as Author and Editor* (1993), edited by Jonathan Yardley, is one of several volumes culled from the 2,000-page manuscript memoir Mencken left uncompleted.

Millett, Kate (September 14, 1934–). American critic and memoirist. Millett is best known for her groundbreaking *Sexual Politics* (1970), which analyzes the political dimensions of power in sexual relationships through a close reading of the representations of sexuality in such important modern male authors as D. H. LAWRENCE, HENRY MILLER, and Jean GENET. Based on her Ph.D. dissertation for Columbia University, *Sexual Politics* had an enormous impact on the development of radical feminism and women's studies. Born in Minnesota, Millett worked as a sculptor in Japan and New York in the early 1960s. She was a prominent early member of the National Organization for Women and founded the Women's Art Colony Farm in Poughkeepsie, New York, where she continues to write and sculpt. Her autobiographical writings include *Going to Iran* (1982), on her work in Iran for women's rights; *Flying* (1974); *Sita* (1977); *The Loony Bin Trip* (1990), on her experiences with mental illness; and *A.D.* (1995).

Monroe, Harriet (December 23, 1860–September 26, 1936). American editor and poet. As the founder and editor of the little magazine *POETRY* from 1912 to 1936, Monroe published innovative new American poets. A native and lifelong resident of Chicago, Monroe was associated with the writers of the second Chicago literary renaissance, who portrayed the modern, urban, industrialized region. *Poetry* published work by leading Chicago writers Carl SANDBURG, Edgar Lee MASTERS, and Sherwood ANDERSON as well as early work by such significant modernists as T. S. ELIOT, H. D., Wallace STEVENS, MARIANNE MOORE, and Ezra POUND, who served as the magazine's foreign editor. Monroe also coedited the anthology *The New Poetry* (1917, rev. 1923, 1932). Monroe's own poems are gathered in *Chosen Poems* (1935), while her autobiography, *A Poet's Life*, was published in 1938.

Mount, [William Robert] Ferdinand (July 2, 1939–). English editor, journalist, and novelist. A Conservative political writer, former adviser to Parliamentary committees (1962–65) and Prime Minister Margaret Thatcher (1982–83), and prolific novelist, Mount became editor of the prestigious *TIMES LITERARY SUPPLEMENT* in 1991. The son of a peer, he was born in London and educated at Eton and Christ Church College, Oxford. He has been a political correspondent, editor, and contributor for such publications as the *Daily Sketch, Daily Mail, Spectator, Standard,* and *Daily Telegraph,* among others. His books on politics and society include *The Theatre of Politics* (1972), *The Subversive Family: An Alternative History of Love and Marriage* (1982), and *The British Constitution Now: Recovery or Decline?* (1992). His novels, typically historical in setting, are *Very Like a Whale* (1967), *The Man Who Rode Ampersand* (1975), *The Clique* (1978), *The Selkirk Strip* (1987), *Of Love and Asthma* (1991), *Umbrella* (1994), *The Liquidator* (1995), *Jem (and Sam)* (1998), and *Fairness* (2001).

Murry, John Middleton (August 6, 1889–March 13, 1957). English writer and editor. Murry wrote prolifically on a wide variety of subjects and in many genres, but today he is remembered chiefly as the husband of the more gifted writer Katherine MANSFIELD, as an intimate friend of D. H. LAWRENCE from 1913 until Lawrence's death in 1930, and as the object of merciless satire in Aldous HUXLEY's novel *POINT COUNTER POINT* (1928), where he appears as Burlap, a pompous, self-intoxicated, woolly-headed literary editor. Of humble origins, Murry won a scholarship to Oxford, where he excelled academically and cofounded *Rhythm* (later *Blue Review*), a short-lived but distinguished modernist journal. He began his career as a literary journalist in London in 1913, becoming editor of *THE ATHENAEUM* six years later. During his brief tenure there (he resigned in 1921 when it merged with the *Nation*), the journal published such important younger writers as T. S. ELIOT, Robert GRAVES, and Huxley. In 1923 he founded a new journal, the *Adelphi* (later *New Adelphi*), with which he was associated until 1948. After Mansfield's death in 1923, Murry became increasingly preoccupied with religious, political, economic, and social issues, such as pacifism, although he continued to write about literature. Among his voluminous works are critical studies of DOSTOYEVSKY, KEATS, BLAKE, Lawrence, Mansfield, and SWIFT. He was also instrumental in securing Mansfield's posthumous reputation, editing and introducing numerous volumes of her work, including her journals and letters. Gudrun Brangwen and Gerald Crich, the doomed couple in Lawrence's *WOMEN IN LOVE* (1920), were at least partially inspired by Mansfield and Murry, whose marriage was tumultuous.

Nathan, George Jean (February 14, 1882–April 8, 1958). American theater critic and editor. In the first half of the 20th century, Nathan's pungent, astute newspaper and magazine criticism was enormously influential. Born in Fort Wayne, Indiana, Nathan was a child of privilege who traveled widely, studying in Germany, France, and Italy as a teenager. After graduating from Cornell University in 1904, he became a cub reporter and then theater critic for the *New York Herald* before moving to the magazines

Outing and *Bohemia*. In 1909, he became head of the drama department at the literary magazine *The Smart Set*, where he met H. L. MENCKEN, who became a friend and close collaborator when the two coedited the magazine (1914–23). With Mencken he cofounded THE AMERICAN MERCURY in 1924, but soon resigned his editorship in a disagreement about the new magazine's direction. Thereafter, he concentrated on freelance criticism except for a three-year interval (1932–35) when he edited *The American Spectator*, which he cofounded with Eugene O'NEILL, Theodore DREISER, and others. Although his critical stance was exacting, he passionately championed writers whose work he admired, including O'Neill, Henrik IBSEN, and George Bernard SHAW, who described him as "intelligent playgoer number one." A bon vivant and ladies' man, Nathan served as the model for the critic Addison De Witt in the classic film about Broadway, *All About Eve* (1950). His reviews and essays have been collected in such volumes as *The Critic and the Drama* (1922), *The World of George Jean Nathan* (1952), and *A George Jean Nathan Reader* (1990). In his will he established the George Jean Nathan Award for drama criticism, which has been presented annually since 1958 to a drama critic who uses his position to "stimulate intelligent playgoing"; the award is administered by his alma mater, Cornell University.

Nietzsche, Friedrich (October 15, 1844–August 25, 1900). German-born philosopher, cultural critic, and poet. An impassioned opponent of what he saw as the weaknesses of Western philosophy in the Judeo-Christian tradition, Nietzsche strove to prepare the way for "the age which will carry heroism into knowledge, and wage war for the sake of ideas and their consequences." His provocative, visionary works were little heeded in his lifetime but have exerted an extraordinary, often controversial, influence since his death. They include *The Birth of Tragedy* (*Die Geburt der Tragödie aus dem Geiste der Musik*, 1872), about the dynamic opposition of "Apollonian" and "Dionysian" forces in life and art; *Thus Spake Zarathustra*

(*Also Sprach Zarathustra*, 1883–85), an ecstatic, ironic prose poem presenting Nietzsche's views on humanity's future after the "death of God"; *Beyond Good and Evil* (*Jenseits von Gut und Böse*, 1886), his "critique of modernity" and morality; and *Ecce Homo* (written 1888; published 1908), a stylized intellectual self-portrait that Walter Kaufmann called "one of the treasures of world literature." An amateur composer for whom music was centrally important, Nietzsche first championed Richard Wagner as a thinker and a composer, then vehemently denounced him. In 1889, he suffered a mental breakdown from which he never recovered.

Norton, Charles Eliot (November 16, 1827–October 21, 1908). American scholar and editor. A professor of fine arts at Harvard, Norton was also a passionate advocate of reform who devoted considerable energies to a variety of social causes. The most lasting of these was cofounding and editing THE NATION, the reformist political journal, in 1865. With his friend JAMES RUSSELL LOWELL he also edited THE NORTH AMERICAN REVIEW, which remains an important literary journal. In addition to Lowell, Norton kept company with many important writers and thinkers of his day, such as John RUSKIN, Henry Wadsworth LONGFELLOW, and Ralph Waldo EMERSON. His correspondence with these associates later became important material for biographers and critics, and Norton himself edited the works of a number of major figures, including John DONNE, Anne Bradstreet, and Thomas CARLYLE.

Ocampo, Victoria (April 7, 1890–January 27, 1979). Argentinean essayist, editor, and publisher. Known as Argentina's "queen of letters," Ocampo wrote extensively on literature, the arts, and contemporary society and, through her contacts with intellectuals and artists from other countries, served for decades as her nation's unofficial cultural ambassador. In 1931 she founded the literary review SUR, which would become the most respected publication of its kind in Latin America; it was the first to publish many important writers, including Jorge Luis BORGES. Born into an upper-class family,

Ocampo spent much of her childhood in Europe and studied at the Sorbonne in Paris. She gained notice with her first book, *From Francesca to Beatrice* (*De Francesca a Beatrice*, 1924), an essay on DANTE's *DIVINE COMEDY*. She produced 26 volumes of essays, including the multivolume *Testimonies* (*Testimonios*, 1935–80). Her six-volume *Autobiography* (*Autobiografía*, 1979–84) was published posthumously. Ocampo also translated numerous works into Spanish, recorded poetry, and in 1939 recited André GIDE's *Perséphone* to music by Igor Stravinsky. She was the sister of poet and short-story writer Silviana Ocampo.

Ortega y Gasset, José (May 9, 1883–October 18, 1955). Spanish philosopher and essayist. Promoting a national cultural awakening, the cause of republicanism, and his own humanist philosophy, Ortega y Gasset was a leading figure in the intellectual life of 20th-century Spain. Born and educated in Madrid, he studied for five years in Germany before becoming professor of metaphysics at Madrid University in 1910. To cultivate interest in contemporary European thought, he launched the journal *Review of the West* (*Revista de Occidente*) in 1923. An active republican, he went into exile with the outbreak of civil war in 1936, not returning until 1945; three years later he founded the Institute of Humanities in Madrid. In his best-known book, *The Revolt of the Masses* (*La Rebelión de las Masas*, 1929), he argues for leadership of the masses by a benevolent intellectual elite. His philosophy of "vital reason" (*razón vital*), in which life is the fundamental reality and reason a function of individual perspective, is articulated in *The Modern Theme* (*El Tema de Nuestro Tiempo*, 1923). Other principal writings are *Invertebrate Spain* (*España Invertebrada*, 1921), *The Dehumanization of Art* (*La Deshumanización del Arte*, 1925), and *The Idea of Principle in Leibnitz* (*La Idea de Principio en Leibniz*, 1958).

Palgrave, Francis (September 28, 1824–October 24, 1897). English anthologist, poet, and critic. Palgrave is best known as the editor of *The Golden Treasury of the Best Songs and Lyrical Poems in the English Language* (1861), an anthology that has never been out of print since its publication. Compiled with the aid of Palgrave's longtime friend, the poet Alfred, Lord TENNYSON, the anthology is considered a classic representation of the Victorian perspective on poetry. Palgrave's own volumes of poetry include *The Visions of England* (1881), a popular cycle portraying events in English history, and the collections *Idyls and Songs* (1854) and *Hymns* (1867). Educated at Oxford, Palgrave worked as a civil servant from 1849 to 1884 and taught at Oxford from 1885 to 1895. *Landscape in Poetry from Homer to Tennyson* (1897) includes several lectures on art and poetry.

Pater, Walter (August 4, 1839–July 30, 1894). English critic, essayist, and novelist. Pater's studies of Renaissance painters and sculptors, and his writings on the nature of art, became cornerstones of the Aesthetic Movement in Victorian England. Born in London, Pater was educated at Queens College, Oxford, and later became a fellow of Brasenose College, where he began to publish his highly personal studies of such Renaissance figures as Michelangelo, Botticelli, and da Vinci. These he collected in his first major book, *Studies in the History of the Renaissance* (1873), in which he articulated his belief that art serves no purpose beyond itself (famously urging his followers to thus embrace experience and "burn with a hard gemlike flame"). The book garnered much attention (Oscar WILDE described it as "the holy writ of beauty") and won Pater the companionship of members of the Pre-Raphaelite circle, including DANTE GABRIEL ROSSETTI and SWINBURNE, with whom he maintained close ties. Other notable works include the ambitious philosophical novel *Marius the Epicurean* (1885), an examination of the aesthetic life set in ancient Rome; *Imaginary Portraits* (1887); *Plato and Platonism* (1893); and an unfinished novel, *Gaston de Latour* (1896).

Perkins, Maxwell (September 20, 1884–June 17, 1947). American editor. Educated at Harvard University, Perkins began his publishing career at Charles Scribner's Sons in 1910, working in the advertising department; by the time he retired, he was editorial director and vice-president of the company, and the much-celebrated discoverer of some of the century's literary luminaries. His greatest gift was seeing talent where others did not, a reputation he acquired in 1918 when he championed the twice-rejected manuscript of a young F. SCOTT FITZGERALD. Perkins helped the writer to pare down the text's exuberant language, and the novel, retitled THIS SIDE OF PARADISE, became a breakout success in 1920. Over the next three decades, Perkins mentored and edited, among others, Ernest HEMINGWAY, Erskine CALDWELL, James JONES, Ring LARDNER, Alan PATON, and THOMAS WOLFE, whose unwieldy 1,114-page manuscript Perkins substantially reshaped to make the novel LOOK HOMEWARD, ANGEL (1929).

Pivot, Bernard (May 5, 1935–). French print and broadcast journalist. Born and educated in Lyon, Pivot took a diploma in journalism before beginning his career at *Figaro Littéraire*, where he worked from 1958 to 1974. He is best known for the series of book discussion programs he produced for French television, starting with "Ouvrez les Guillemets" (1973–74; Quote Unquote), "Apostrophes" (1975–90; Apostrophes or Rude Remarks), and "Bouillon de Culture" (1991–2001; Culture Medium); he retired from weekly television in June 2001. At the center of French literary life for more than 25 years, Pivot served as the genial host of programs featuring almost every great literary and intellectual figure of his generation, but in a distinctly unstuffy atmosphere which, he said, should be "like that of a dinner party, not of a reception at the Académie Française." His guests ranged from distinguished writers, intellectuals, and scholars, such as Marguerite DURAS, Vladimir NABOKOV, Umberto ECO, and George STEINER, to politicians, including French President Valéry Giscard d'Estaing, who talked about the Pléiade edition of the complete works of MAUPASSANT, whom he loved (sales of Maupassant's works soared). By the 1980s, publishers understood that an author's appearance on Pivot's program would deter-

mine the fate of a book. From 1975 to 1993, he was also editorial director of the monthly magazine *Lire* (To Read), and at different times wrote a column for the newspapers *Point* and *Journal du Dimanche*. Although he is also the author of a novel, *L'Amour en Vogue* (1959; Love in Style), he claimed in an interview in the June 2001 issue of *Le Nouvel Observateur* that he had little urge to write, saying, "My happiness, my vice, my passion, is reading."

Plimpton, George (March 18, 1927–). American journalist, editor, and sportswriter. Plimpton is most widely known as a participatory journalist, whose exploits have included brief tours as a quarterback for the Detroit Lions, a *Playboy* magazine centerfold photographer, a benchwarmer for the Boston Celtics, a New York Yankee pitcher, a percussionist for the New York Philharmonic, and a trapeze artist with a professional circus. From these escapades and others came a number of best-selling books, including *Out of My League* (1961), *Paper Lion* (1966), *The Bogey Man* (1968), *Fireworks* (1984), *Open Net* (1985), and *The Best of Plimpton* (1990). In literary circles, however, Plimpton is most highly regarded as the editor of THE PARIS REVIEW, which he established with author PETER MATTHIESSEN in Paris in 1953. A showcase for literary fiction and poetry, *The Paris Review* also pioneered the literary interview, publishing conversations with noted authors in every issue. The magazine moved in 1965 to Plimpton's native New York City, where for four decades it operated out of his apartment on the Upper East Side of Manhattan. A prolific writer, Plimpton has contributed journalistic pieces on sports and culture to many major magazines, and adapted *The Paris Review*'s interview format for a number of literary "oral biographies," including *Truman Capote: In Which Various Friends, Enemies, Acquaintances, and Detractors Recall His Turbulent Career* (1997).

Praz, Mario (September 6, 1896–March 23, 1982). Italian critic, editor, and translator. Educated in Bologna, Rome, and Florence, Praz lectured in Italian and Italian culture at universities in England for ten years before becoming professor of English literature in 1934 at the University of Rome, where he taught for more than 30 years. An authority on English Baroque and Romantic literature, he established his reputation with his landmark study *The Romantic Agony* (*La Carne, la Morte e il Diavolo nella Letteratura Romantica*, 1930; literally, "Flesh, Death, and the Devil in Romantic Literature"), an analysis of the macabre, sadistic, and erotic strains in Romantic literature and art. Praz is also renowned for his explorations of the interconnections between English and Italian literature, and between the written and the visual arts. Among his many other works are *Unromantic Spain* (*Penisola Pentagonale*, 1928) and *Studies in Seventeenth-century Imagery* (*Studi sul Concettismo*, 1934), both of which Praz himself translated into English; *On Neoclassicism* (*Gusto Neoclassico*, 1940); *The Hero in Eclipse in Victorian Fiction* (*La Crisi dell'Eroe nel Romanzo Vittoriano*, 1952); *The Flaming Heart: Essays on Crashaw, Machiavelli, and Other Studies in the Relations Between Italian and English Literature from Chaucer to T. S. Eliot* (1958); and *Mnemosyne: The Parallel Between Literature and the Visual Arts* (1970). His autobiography, *The House of Life* (*La Casa della Vita*, 1958), is considered by many critics to be his masterpiece. He also edited a number of literary anthologies and translated into Italian works by SHAKESPEARE, Ben JONSON, John WEBSTER, Walter PATER, Jane AUSTEN, and T. S. ELIOT, among others.

Putnam, Samuel (October 10, 1892–January 15, 1950). American critic, editor, and translator. Putnam's legacy rests largely on the attention he brought in the United States to European writers whose work he published and translated. His greatest achievement was his translation of Miguel de CERVANTES's *DON QUIXOTE*, published in 1949 after nearly two decades of labor. Educated at the University of Chicago, which he left without a degree, Putnam worked for a time as a journalist and art critic in Chicago before moving to Europe, where he founded *The New Review* (1931–32).

He also translated the works of many Italian and French writers and wrote a literary history of Brazil, *Marvelous Journey* (1948).

Rahv, Philip, *original name* Ivan Greenberg (March 10, 1908–December 22, 1973). Ukrainian-born American critic and editor. Greenberg fled with his family to Palestine after the Russian Revolution of 1917, and at age 14 joined an older brother who had immigrated to Rhode Island. An enormously erudite autodidact who dropped out of high school at 16, he arrived in New York City during the Depression, supporting himself as a freelance writer for a number of leftist or radical publications, including *New Masses*, THE NEW REPUBLIC, *New Leader*, and *The Daily Worker*, and joining the Communist Party in 1932, when he adopted the name Philip Rahv (*Rav* means rabbi, or teacher, in Hebrew). In 1934, Rahv and William Phillips cofounded PARTISAN REVIEW, a literary and political journal, to critique literature and culture from the point of view of "the revolutionary working class," while also promoting opposition to imperialism and fascism. When the horrors of the Stalinist show trials became clear to the world in the mid-1930s, *Partisan Review* severed its ties with the Communist Party, although the staff's political orientation remained, as Rahv put it, "a kind of independent and critical Marxism." The first issue of the newly reconstituted—and now staunchly anti-Stalinist—*Partisan Review* featured work by an array of American writers and intellectuals, including EDMUND WILSON, James T. FARRELL, Dwight MACDONALD, Mary McCARTHY, Sidney Hook, and Rahv himself, and the *Review* has continued to provide a forum for many academic and artistic luminaries. A trenchant and admiring critic of literary modernism who was deeply concerned with how historical, social, and political forces intersect with or impinge on works of the creative imagination, Rahv collected his essays in *Image and Idea* (1949; rev. and enl. edition, 1957), *The Myth and the Powerhouse* (1965), and *Literature and the Sixth Sense* (1969), the last published the year he was forced out of *Partisan Review* in a power struggle with Phillips. One of his most famous essays, "Paleface and Redskin" (1939), analyzed the split in the American literary tradition between gentile patricians (like HENRY JAMES) and uncouth rebels (like Walt WHITMAN), a distinction that retains its currency. The posthumous *Essays on Literature and Politics, 1932–1972* (1978) includes previously unpublished or uncollected work. Rahv was professor of English at Brandeis University from 1957 until his death.

Ransom, John Crowe (April 30, 1888–July 4, 1974). American critic and poet. The originator of the term New Criticism, Ransom was a major figure in that movement, influential in the mid-20th century for emphasizing the internal coherence of works of literature, rather than their historical, biographical, or cultural properties. While teaching at Vanderbilt University, Ransom was among the writers there who published THE FUGITIVE (1922–25), a literary magazine that promoted an adherence to traditional Southern values. Ransom's essays, collected in books including *The World's Body* (1938) and *Beating the Bushes* (1972), explore the distinct linguistic structures of poetry, while his *The New Criticism* (1941) examines contemporary criticism from a formalist stance. Ransom also edited the critical journal THE KENYON REVIEW from 1939 to 1958, while teaching at Kenyon College in Ohio.

Rhys, Ernest (July 17, 1859–May 25, 1946). English editor and writer. As originating editor of the popular Everyman's Library — a series of world literary classics in inexpensive, pocket-sized, hardcover format — Rhys oversaw the publication of nearly one thousand volumes from 1906 to 1940, thereby influencing 20th-century reading habits. Born in London and raised in Wales, he abandoned his career as a mining engineer to pursue his literary ambitions. Having befriended prominent figures in London's literary circles, he was invited to edit the 30-volume Camelot Series (1886–1900) and the ten-volume Lyric Poets series (1895–1905), the latter published by J. M. Dent. It was Dent who conceived the "democracy of books" that Rhys dubbed Everyman's Library; Rhys

also chose the series epigraph — "Everyman, I will go with thee, and be thy guide." — from the late 15th-century morality play EVERYMAN. A founder of the famous Rhymers' Club in 1891, he produced several original poetry collections, plays, novels, and essays as well as a number of literary anthologies. His writings include the autobiographical *Everyman Remembers* (1931) and *Wales England Wed* (1940).

Rich, Frank (June 2, 1949–). American theater and cultural critic. Born and raised in Washington, D.C., and educated at Harvard University, Rich developed an early love for theater, particularly Broadway musicals; this enthusiasm is at the center of his memoir of his youth, *Ghost Light* (2000). After college, he wrote film and theater criticism for a number of publications, including the *New York Post* and *Time* magazine, before joining *The New York Times*. As that newspaper's chief drama critic from 1980 to 1993, he exerted enormous influence on the commercial viability of individual productions through his perceptive, often passionate reviews. This power led some detractors to dub him "the Butcher of Broadway" and in one instance resulted in a headline-grabbing feud with playwright David Hare ("Hare Airs Rich Bitch," noted the show-business weekly *Variety*), who denounced Rich after the latter's 1989 review of Hare's play *The Secret Rapture*. Resigning his post as theater critic at the end of 1993, Rich has since 1994 written on culture and politics for the paper's Op-Ed page; in 1999, he was given the additional title of senior writer for *The New York Times Magazine*. His theater criticism is collected in *Hot Seat: Theater Criticism for The New York Times, 1980–1993* (1998). With Lisa Aronson, he is coauthor of *The Theatre Art of Boris Aronson* (1987), an illustrated biography of the famed scenic designer.

Richards, I[vor] A[rmstrong] (February 26, 1893–September 7, 1979). English critic, poet, and educator. Establishing the foundation of what would be called the New Criticism, Richards developed a method of close textual analysis that looked to semantics as the essence of meaning and emotional effect. He earned a B.A. at Magdalene College, Cambridge, where he taught from 1922 to 1929 and devised his essential critical theories. Collaborating with the linguist C. K. Ogden, he pioneered the study of semantics in *Foundations of Aesthetics* (1922) and *The Meaning of Meaning* (1923), elaborating his critical method in *Principles of Literary Criticism* (1924) and *Practical Criticism* (1929). Richards also worked with Ogden in developing Basic English, a system of 850 words designed to simplify the language and promote universal understanding. He taught Basic as a visiting professor in China during the 1930s, translated Plato's *Republic* (1942), and wrote the primer *Basic English and Its Uses* (1943). The imagination was another area of interest, reflected in *Mencius on the Mind* (1932) and *Coleridge on Imagination* (1934). Richards's own poetry appears in *Goodbye Earth* (1958), *Internal Colloquies* (1971), and *New and Selected Poems* (1978). He was a professor of English at Harvard from 1944 to 1963.

Riffaterre, Michael (November 20, 1924–). French-American critic and theorist. Highly respected as a theorist and practitioner of structuralist criticism, Riffaterre advanced a novel approach to semiotic text analysis that addresses the subjective responses of the reader. His critical theories, tested in close readings of French and English literature, remain at the forefront of academic debate. His first book, *Le Style des Pléiades de Gobineau: Essai d'Application d'une Méthode Stylistique* (1957; The Style of Gobineau's *Pléiades*: Essay on a Stylistic Method), introduced his method of stylistic criticism, extended in *Essais de Stylistique Structurale* (1971; Essays on Structural Stylistics) with the concept of the *archilecteur*, or "average reader." Subsequent works—*Semiotics of Poetry* (1978), *Text Production* (*La Production du Texte*, 1979), and *Fictional Truth* (1990)—present defenses of principal and new perspectives on semiotic interpretation and narratology. Riffaterre attended the University of Lyons and the Sorbonne, earning his Ph.D. from Columbia in 1955. He began teaching at Columbia later that year, becoming a full professor in 1964. He has been affiliated with the Dartmouth College School of Criticism and Theory and has been a visiting professor or guest lecturer at several other universities.

Ripley, George (October 3, 1802–July 4, 1880). American journalist and social reformer. Ripley's importance in 19th-century American letters derives from his association with the Transcendentalists and, in particular, his work as founder and director of Brook Farm, a utopian community in Massachusetts guided by the principles of cooperative labor and the support of creative pursuits. Educated at Harvard Divinity School, Ripley was a Unitarian minister from 1826 to 1841 in Boston, where he contributed to the Transcendentalist journal THE DIAL. In 1841, he founded Brook Farm, where he also edited the commune's paper, *The Harbinger*, which was influential for its radically idealistic commentary on politics and the arts. Among the community's original shareholders was Nathaniel HAWTHORNE, who based his novel *The Blithedale Romance* (1852) on his experiences there; others who lived at or visited the community included Ralph Waldo EMERSON and Bronson Alcott. Ripley closed the financially struggling Brook Farm in 1847, and thereafter served as book reviewer for the *New York Tribune* from 1849 to 1880, remaining prominent for his principled intellect.

Rivière, Jacques (July 15, 1886–February 14, 1925). French critic and editor. Rivière attained prominence in French letters for cofounding and editing from 1919 to 1925 LA NOUVELLE REVUE FRANÇAISE (1909–43), a leading review of literature and the other arts. Rivière's own essays are gathered in *Études* (1911; Essays) and *Nouvelles Études* (1947; New Essays), while his book-length studies include *Marcel Proust* (1924). Rivière's writing frequently reflects his experience as a German prisoner of war in World War I and his profound struggles with spiritual belief. His acclaimed, personal *À la Trace de Dieu* (1925; On the Track of God) combines an epistolary form with diary selections and theological contemplations. He is also known for his revealing correspondence with contemporary intellectuals, including his brother-in-law, novelist Alain-Fournier, poet Paul Claudel, and avant-garde figure Antonin ARTAUD.

Roget, Peter Mark (January 18, 1779–September 12, 1869). English philologist and physician. Roget is primarily remembered for his famous *Thesaurus of English Words and Phrases* (1852), which has remained a standard work in many editions. Born in London, Roget studied medicine at the University of Edinburgh and served as a physician in London until his retirement in 1840. At age 61 he began compiling his idiosyncratic thesaurus, based on a conceptual system of classifying words that he had formulated some 30 years earlier. Published when he was 73, the *Thesaurus* went through 28 editions in his lifetime and continues to be frequently revised and updated.

Ross, Harold (November 6, 1892–December 6, 1951). American editor and publisher. Although he lacked a college degree, grew up in the far west, and did not set foot on the island of Manhattan until he was 21, Ross became the guiding spirit behind a magazine that defined eastern, urban sophistication: THE NEW YORKER. His career prior to founding the magazine was spent in newspaper journalism. Born in Aspen, Colorado, and raised in Salt Lake City, Ross began to work as a reporter at age 13 for the *Salt Lake City Tribune*; by the time he first traveled to New York in 1917, he had worked for newspapers in California, Panama, New Orleans, and Atlanta. During World War I, Ross enlisted in the Army and became the editor of *Stars and Stripes*, a weekly newspaper of the American Expeditionary Forces, based in Paris. After the armistice he returned to New York, and in 1925 he launched *The New Yorker* with financial backing from Raoul Fleischmann, a private investor with whom Ross played poker, and contributions from members of the Algonquin Round Table circle of wits, including Dorothy PARKER, Alexander WOOLLCOTT (a former *New York Times* theater critic and a colleague of Ross's at *Stars and Stripes*), and Robert BENCHLEY. The magazine quickly became a beacon for New York's smart set, and over the next 25 years Ross, who reportedly never lost his coarse, western ways (he allegedly mailed his underclothes to columnist Walter Winchell, who had accused him of not wearing any), piloted it to editorial prominence and financial success. Among the many writers whom Ross brought aboard were E. B. WHITE, James THURBER, and JOSEPH MITCHELL, and by the time of his death in 1951, *The New Yorker* was generally recognized as one of the country's premiere outlets for sophisticated humor, fiction, criticism, and commentary.

Rosset, Barney (May 28, 1922–). American publisher. The guiding force of the publishing house Grove Press, the Chicago-born Rosset settled in New York City in 1951 when he purchased the firm, then a small reprint publisher located in Greenwich Village. By the late 1950s, he had built the press into a leading publisher of avant-garde literature and a touchstone for the intellectual counterculture. Championing freedom of expression, Rosset waged successful, highly publicized legal battles to publish in 1959 the first unexpurgated edition of D. H. LAWRENCE'S *LADY CHATTERLEY'S LOVER* (1928) and in 1961 the first American edition of HENRY MILLER'S *TROPIC OF CANCER* (1934). Rosset's prestigious roster of authors also included BECKETT, BURROUGHS, DURAS, GENET, IONESCO, KEROUAC, and ROBBE-GRILLET, many of whom he also featured in *EVERGREEN REVIEW*, a house literary journal published from 1957 to 1973. After struggling financially in the 1970s, Rosset sold Grove Press in 1985; the firm and Rosset's backlist remain distinguished. Rosset established an online incarnation of *Evergreen Review* in 1999.

Ruskin, John (February 8, 1819–January 20, 1900). English art and social critic. A master prose stylist who revolutionized the field of art criticism, Ruskin articulated aesthetic and social principles that had a far-reaching influence on European culture. His artistic ideal of "truth to nature"—exemplified in the paintings of J. M. W. Turner, Gothic architecture, and the poetic imaginations of DANTE and SPENSER—was a guiding principle in the work of Marcel PROUST and other contemporaries. His abhorrence of industrialism and belief that the morals of society are reflected in its art gained a following among the likes of Charles DICKENS and George Bernard SHAW. In the field of literary criticism, his aesthetic theory found expression in the term *pathetic fallacy*, which he coined to describe an anthropomorphic formulation that is false to nature. The son of a wealthy wine merchant, Ruskin developed his interest in art and architecture on extended trips through Europe as a boy. He began a serious study of art at Oxford and, in 1843, a year after graduating, produced the first volume in his series *Modern Painters* (5 vols., 1843–60). *The Seven Lamps of Architecture* (1849) and *The Stones of Venice* (3 vols., 1851–53) established him as a leading critic and theorist. Notable later writings on social and economic justice include *"Unto This Last"* (1862), *Essays on Political Economy* (1862–63), and *Fors Clavigera: Letters to the Workmen and Labourers of Great Britain* (1871–84). *Praeterita* (1885–87), written during a period when Ruskin suffered from severe bouts of depression, is an autobiographical fragment. Ruskin was Slade Professor of Fine Art at Oxford from 1870 to 1885.

Said, Edward W[illiam] (November 1, 1935–). Palestinian-American critic and social theorist. A versatile, distinguished, and at times controversial intellect, Said is best known in literary circles for *Orientalism* (1978), a critical work that examines Western misunderstandings of Arabic literature and Islamic culture. Born in Jerusalem, Said was educated in Egypt and at Princeton and Harvard universities and began teaching at Columbia University in 1963. As in *Orientalism*, many of his writings deal with issues of imperialism, both in terms of its literary representations and its social and political mechanisms. In *Culture and Imperialism* (1993) he extended this discourse to non-Arab writers, such as Jane AUSTEN and Joseph CONRAD, about whom he had also written in *Joseph Conrad and the Fiction of Autobiography* (1966). Other influential works of literary criticism include *Beginnings: Intention and Method* (1975), *The World, the Text, and the Critic* (1983), and *Reflections on Exile and Other Essays* (2000). His books about Palestine and the Middle East include *After the Last Sky: Palestinian Lives* (1986) and *The Politics of Dispossession: The Struggle for Palestinian Self-Determination* (1994). Also a classical music critic, Said published *Musical Elaborations* in 1991. *Out of Place* (1999) is a memoir.

Sainte-Beuve, Charles (December 23, 1804–October 13, 1869). French critic. The foremost literary commentator of 19th-century France, Sainte-Beuve has been called the father of modern professional criticism. Writing for the *Revue de Paris*, REVUE DES DEUX MONDES, *Constitutionnel, Moniteur, Temps*, and other journals and newspapers, he produced a voluminous body of criticism on virtually all of French literature. Expounding on the historical and social background of a work as well as the experiences and temperament of the author, his reviews placed a premium on natural and behavioral authenticity that remained standards of criticism for decades. Sainte-Beuve gave up his medical education in 1827 to pursue wholeheartedly a career in literary journalism that was already well under way. His early period was marked by a fascination with French Romanticism, later renounced, and publication of his own work—several poetry collections and the novel *Volupté: The Sensual Man* (*Volupté*, 1834). His most celebrated essays were written after 1850 and collected in 28 volumes as *Monday-Chats* (*Causeries du Lundi*, 15 vols., 1851–62; *Nouveaux Lundis*, 13 vols., 1863–70). Earlier collections include *Portraits Littéraires* (1832–39), *Portraits of Women* (*Portraits de Femmes: Mmes de Sévigné, de La Fayette, de Staël et Mme Roland*, 1844), and *Portraits Contemporains* (1846). A lecture series on Jansenism, published as *Port-Royal* (6 vols., 1840–59), is also highly regarded.

Saintsbury, George (October 23, 1845–January 28, 1933). English critic, literary historian, and biographer. The preeminent English literary scholar of his generation, Saintsbury is known for his engaging and insightful studies of European literary tradition. His emphasis on style over substance has given way to more formal analytic methods, but the scope and enthusiasm of his writings remain unsurpassed. He earned a master's degree at Merton College, Oxford, in 1868, but was denied a fellowship and spent the next several years as a schoolteacher and headmaster. Turning to writing full time in 1876, he made his name with magazine essays and reviews and with his first book, *A Primer of French Literature* (1880). Extensive writings on French and English literary history led to his appointment in 1895 as professor of rhetoric and literature at Edinburgh University, where he taught for 20 years and produced numerous major works, including *A History of Nineteenth Century Literature (1780–1895)* (1896), *A Short History of English Literature* (1898), *The History of Criticism and Literary Taste in Europe* (1900–4), *A History of English Prosody* (1906–10), *Sir Walter Scott* (1897), and *Matthew Arnold* (1899).

Saint-Simon, Louis de Rouvroy, duc de (January 15, 1675–March 2, 1755). French courtier and memoirist. The aristocrat Saint-Simon is celebrated for his *Mémoires* (43 vols., 1879–1928), an eloquent portrayal of court life during the last years of Louis XIV and the early years of Louis XV. A dedicated documentarian, Saint-Simon kept copious records of his experience at court and based his *Mémoires* on these and on the testimony of fellow courtiers. Personally opposed to the extravagant, autocratic Louis XIV, Saint-Simon examined the intrigues of power and ambition among the French aristocracy, offering a stimulating, vivid depiction of personalities and rivalries in the 18th-century court before the French Revolution. Composed between 1740 and 1750, the *Mémoires* were confiscated by the state at Saint-Simon's death and were not published until 1879. Many abridged editions of the *Mémoires* have appeared in French and in translation, including the excellent three-volume English translation by Lucy Norton.

Santayana, George, *original name* Jorge Augustín Nicolás Ruiz de Santayana (December 16, 1863–September 26, 1952). Spanish-American philosopher, critic, poet, and novelist. One of the great speculative philosophers of the 20th century, Santayana developed systematic theories of ontology, aesthetics, and ethics that reconciled the imagination and reality in literature, art, religion, science, and everyday life. His theory of poetics and defense of the classical ideal of beauty, as presented in *The Sense of Beauty* (1896) and *Interpretations of Poetry and Religion* (1900), had a direct influence on the work of T. S. ELIOT, Wallace STEVENS, Conrad AIKEN (all of whom were his students at Harvard), and others. Among his contributions to the study of literary history is the notion of "the genteel tradition." Born in Avila, Spain, Santayana moved to the United States at age eight and attended the Boston Latin School and Harvard. After completing his doctorate in 1889, he joined the Harvard faculty and remained there until 1912. Works of this period include *The Life of Reason, or, The Phases of Human Progress* (5 vols., 1905–6); *Three Philosophical Poets: Lucretius, Dante, and Goethe* (1910); and several volumes of original poetry. He spent his last 40 years in Europe — first at Oxford, later in Rome — where he produced his most extensive and serious philosophical works, notably *Scepticism and Animal Faith* (1923), a "critical introduction"; and *The Realms of Being* (4 vols., 1927–40), a rigorous statement of naturalist theories. *The Last Puritan* (1935) is an autobiographical novel, and *Persons and Places* (1944–53) is a three-volume memoir.

Schlegel, August Wilhelm von (September 8, 1767–May 12, 1845). German critic and translator. Schlegel was a key figure of early German and international Romanticism. Around 1800, he was at the center of the "Jena circle" of Romantic writers and thinkers that included his wife, Caroline (afterwards Frederick Schelling's wife); his brother, FRIEDRICH VON SCHLEGEL; Friedrich's future wife, Dorothea Mendelssohn Veit; NOVALIS; Ludwig Tieck; and Schelling; with his brother he founded and edited *Athenaeum* (Berlin, 1798–1800), the organ of Romanticism. After the circle's breakup,

Schlegel traveled and lectured widely, chiefly as the associate of Germaine de STAËL from 1804 until her death in 1817. A Vienna lecture series grew into his most important theoretical work, *A Course of Lectures on Dramatic Art and Literature* (*Über Dramatische Kunst und Litteratur: Vorlesungen*, 1809–11), in which he exalted playwrights he considered in accord with Romanticism, such as SHAKESPEARE and CALDERÓN, over the French and other Neoclassicists; COLERIDGE and PUSHKIN were among those influenced by it. Schlegel's most enduring accomplishments are probably his translations, especially of Shakespeare (17 plays, 1797–1810, which began the "Schlegel-Tieck" translation, the form in which Shakespeare became central to German culture) and Calderón (*Spanisches Theater*, 1803–9).

Schlegel, [Karl Wilhelm] Friedrich von (March 10, 1772–January 12, 1829). German essayist, critic, and novelist. Schlegel's contributions (*Fragmente*, or "Fragments") to the journal *Athenaeum* (Berlin, 1798–1800), which he edited with his brother AUGUST WILHELM VON SCHLEGEL, made him the principal theoretician of early Romanticism; indeed, he gave the movement its name. In the seminal "116th fragment," he defined "Romantic poetry" as a "progressive universal poetry" encompassing all forms and genres. While part of the "Jena circle" of early Romantics (including his brother; his future wife, Dorothea Mendelssohn Veit; his brother's wife, Caroline; NOVALIS; Ludwig Tieck; and Friedrich Schelling), he published his only novel, the experimental, autobiographical *Lucinde* (1799). With its scandalously explicit descriptions of his extramarital affair with Dorothea, it became probably the most widely read novel of German Romanticism. When the Jena circle broke up, Schlegel lectured on his theories in Paris and Cologne; his championing of medievalism in art and literature influenced the Gothic revival style in architecture. He also became a pioneering Sanskrit scholar with *On the Language and Wisdom of India* (*Über die Sprache und die Weisheit der Indier*, 1808). After converting to Catholicism, he moved to Vienna, where he entered the service of Metternich's government, while continuing to lecture and publish as an increasingly conservative spokesman for the Viennese-Catholic school of Romanticism.

Schuster, Max (March 2, 1897–December 20, 1970). American publisher and editor. Schuster, the cofounder of the publishing house Simon & Schuster, was born to American parents in Austria, raised in New York City, and educated at Columbia University. He began his career writing for and editing numerous periodicals and the United Press news syndicate. After Richard SIMON, then a piano salesman, contacted him in 1921 about a potential sale, the men discovered a mutual love of books and literature and began what would prove to be a lifelong friendship. In 1924, they became business partners, establishing Simon & Schuster. With its initial publication, a crossword puzzle book, the new firm had its first success, which would be followed by such publishing landmarks as Will Durant's *The Story of Philosophy* (1926), written at Schuster's suggestion, and Dale Carnegie's *How to Win Friends and Influence People* (1938). The partners' enthusiasm for literature and their astute assessment of the general audience, as well as Simon & Schuster's groundbreaking use of modern marketing methods, made the firm a leading force in the publishing industry. In 1939, he and Simon cofounded Pocket Books, one of the first major sellers of paperback books. Schuster guided Simon & Schuster for more than 40 years, acting variously as president, editor-in-chief, and chairman of the board. His own publications included the bestselling anthology *A Treasury of the World's Great Letters, from Ancient Days to Our Own Time* (1940) and its 1941 sequel.

Scribner Family. American publishers. A firm of perhaps unequalled achievement in the publishing of major American writers, Charles Scribner's Sons was founded in 1846 by **Charles Scribner** (February 21, 1821–August 26, 1871) and Isaac D. Baker (April 1, 1819–November 23, 1850), as Baker & Scribner. (The firm's name underwent various permutations until in 1878 it was given the name under

THE EDITOR REGRETS...:
SHORTSIGHTED REJECTION LETTERS

Many books that ultimately became bestsellers or are now widely considered classics were initially turned down by publishing houses. Often rejection letters simply state that a manuscript is "not quite suitable for our list," as Agatha Christie was told upon the submission of *The Mysterious Affair at Styles*. Other rejections have cited the supposedly limited market for the author's submission, as in the case of a letter to Pearl S. Buck about *The Good Earth*, which declared that "the American public is not interested in anything on China," or a reply to Colette about *Claudine in School*, which read, "I wouldn't be able to sell ten copies." When offered the right to serialize Margaret Mitchell's *Gone with the Wind* before its publication, the editor of the *Pictorial Review* replied, "A period novel! About the Civil War! Who needs the Civil War now—who cares?"

Other editors delivered much harsher criticism. Editor Marc Humbolt rejected Marcel Proust's *Remembrance of Things Past* in 1912, commenting, "My dear fellow, I may perhaps be dead from the neck up, but wrack my brains as I may, I can't see why a chap should need thirty pages to describe how he turns over in bed before going to sleep." An editor commenting on E. L. Doctorow's *Welcome to Hard Times* wrote, "Things improve a bit with the rebuilding of the village but then go to hell in a hack at the end. Perhaps there is a public that can take all this with a straight face but I am not one of them."

William Faulkner's *Sanctuary* elicited a memorable response: "Good God, I can't publish this," declared a prospective publisher. "We'd both be in jail." Faulkner also received a pointed letter regarding *Sartoris*, which read, "If the book had a plot and structure, we might suggest shortening and revisions but it is so diffuse that I don't think this would be any use. My chief objection is that you don't have any story to tell." Similarly, Gustave Flaubert had his talents criticized in a letter rejecting *Madame Bovary*, which stated, "You have buried your novel underneath a heap of details which are well done but utterly superfluous."

which it is best known.) Its first book, a collection of lectures by Edwin Hall, *The Puritans and Their Principles* (1846), is characteristic of the firm's early lists, on which philosophical and theological works predominated. In 1870, Charles Scribner formed a new firm, Scribner & Company, to publish magazines, launching the very successful *Scribner's Monthly* (later the *Century Magazine*), an "illustrated magazine for the people"; three years later, Scribner & Company published the first issue of the famous children's magazine *St. Nicholas*, which featured such distinguished contemporary writers as Mark TWAIN, Bret HARTE, Louisa May ALCOTT, and Rudyard KIPLING. After Charles Scribner's death, the firm was headed in succession by his three sons, **John Blair Scribner** (June 4, 1850–January 20, 1879),

James Joyce is among the writers who prove that persistence pays off. His *Dubliners* was rejected by 22 publishers, one of whom advised Joyce to "Rewrite it with another sense." The perennial childhood favorite, Dr. Seuss, had his *And to Think I Saw It in Mulberry Street* rejected 23 times, receiving comments such as "Fantasy doesn't sell," "Verse doesn't sell," and "It has no pattern and is not practical for a child."

Frank Herbert received a batch of contradictory reactions to his fantasy masterpiece *Dune*, including "Too long," "Too short," "Too clearcut and old fashioned," and "Confusing and irritating." After being turned down by 13 publishers, *Dune* was finally published in 1965 and has now sold more than 12 million copies.

After a thoughtful review of the manuscript of George Orwell's *Animal Farm*, an editor at the British publishing house Jonathan Cape responded, "I think the choice of pigs as the ruling caste will no doubt give offense to many people, and particularly to anyone who is a bit touchy, as undoubtedly the Russians are." As an editor at Faber & Faber, T. S. Eliot con-

curred, stating, "We doubt...whether this is the right point of view from which to criticize the political situation at the present time."

John Irving had fun with a rejection letter he once received. The main character of Irving's *The World According to Garp* gets his literary start with a short story, "The Pension Grillparzer." Irving decided to publish the story on its own before it was released as part of the novel, but received rejections from *American Review*, *The New Yorker*, *Esquire*, and *The Paris Review*, the last commenting, "The story is only mildly interesting, and it does nothing new with language or form." Irving then decided to include this rejection letter in the novel. His editor argued that the letter was too harsh and agreed to keep it in the manuscript only when Irving proved that it was not fictitious. "The Pension Grillparzer" is now routinely cited as one of the strongest parts of the novel.

Even *The Diary of Anne Frank* was not above the scrupulous (or clouded) eyes of wary editors. One responded to the submission, "This girl doesn't, it seems to me, have a special perception or feeling which would lift that book above the 'curiosity' level."

Charles Scribner II (October 18, 1854–April 19, 1930), and **Arthur Hawley Scribner** (March 15, 1859–July 3, 1932). During the second Charles Scribner's long tenure as president, Scribner's published works by an astonishing panoply of great writers, such as Henry ADAMS, Edith WHARTON, HENRY JAMES (including the 26-volume *New York Edition* of his works), Robert Louis STEVENSON, George SANTAYANA,

F. SCOTT FITZGERALD, and Ernest HEMINGWAY. Charles Scribner II also helped to underwrite the 1905 founding of the Princeton University Press as an outlet for scholarly books not feasible for commercial firms, and subsequently proved to be a generous donor to the Press (the Scribner men were all Princetonians). In 1932, his only son, **Charles Scribner III** (January 26, 1890–February 11, 1952) took over the firm;

20 years later, his son, also named Charles and known as **Charles Scribner, Jr.** (July 13, 1921–November 11, 1995), became president. Charles Scribner, Jr. established the well-known Scribner Library of quality paperbacks, and also served as Hemingway's personal editor during the last part of the novelist's career. The Scribner firm's highly respected reference book division (which produced, for example, the original *Dictionary of American Biography*) is now part of the Gale Group. Scribner's trade division is now owned by Simon & Schuster, Inc.

Shawn, William, *original name* Wallace Chon (August 31, 1907–December 8, 1992). American editor. The editor of THE NEW YORKER for 35 years (1952–87), Shawn is remembered as a man whose personal shyness was exceeded only by his editorial exactitude. The son of a Chicago cutlery salesman, Shawn studied briefly at the University of Michigan and worked as a journalist and musician before joining *The New Yorker* in 1933 as a contributor to the "Talk of the Town" section. He was named managing editor six years later and assumed the editor's position in 1952, after the death of the magazine's founder, Harold ROSS. Under Shawn's leadership, *The New Yorker* grew from a publication known primarily for humor to a venue for serious journalism on political and cultural affairs. Among the most significant pieces Shawn published, wholly or in serial form, were Rachel Carson's *Silent Spring*, a groundbreaking examination of the effects of pesticides (1962); Truman CAPOTE's IN COLD BLOOD, a nonfiction novel about a murder in Kansas (1965); Hannah Arendt's *Eichmann in Jerusalem: A Report on the Banality of Evil*, about the trial of the former Gestapo officer (1963); and James BALDWIN's essay "Letter from a Region of My Mind" (1962), which would form the basis of his book about racism, *The Fire Next Time*. Other important writers Shawn published included John McPhee, Garrison Keillor, John UPDIKE, John CHEEVER, Ann BEATTIE, Roger Angell, and Pauline Kael. After *The New Yorker* was acquired by S. I. Newhouse in 1987 and Shawn was asked to step down,

longtime staffers staged a protest, presenting a petition asking the new editor, Robert Gottlieb, not to take the job. Shawn was the father of Wallace Shawn, author of the screenplay for *My Dinner with André* (1981), in which he also costarred, and of plays including *Marie and Bruce* (1980).

Showalter, Elaine (January 21, 1941–). American critic. A formative influence on feminist literary study since the 1970s, Showalter has written several accessible scholarly works on women's writing and cultural experience. Born in Massachusetts, she received her Ph.D. from the University of California at Davis and taught at Douglass College, Rutgers University, from 1969 to 1984; in 1985, she became a professor of English at Princeton, eventually becoming chair of the department. Her first book, the groundbreaking *A Literature of Their Own: British Women Novelists from Brontë to Lessing* (1977), brought to light a host of marginalized women writers. Her later works include *The Female Malady: Women, Madness, and English Culture, 1830–1980* (1985), a historical study of women's relationship with psychiatric medicine; *Sexual Anarchy: Gender and Culture at the Fin de Siècle* (1990), on late 19th-century literature; and *Histories* (1997), a cultural study of epidemics of hysteria.

Silvers, Robert B. (December 31, 1929–). American editor. A cofounder of the literary and intellectual journal THE NEW YORK REVIEW OF BOOKS, Silvers has served, with BARBARA EPSTEIN, as coeditor of the biweekly publication since its inception in 1963. His broad editorial direction and emphasis on political and economic issues have helped to establish the *Review*'s reputation for seriousness, breadth, and currency of ideas. Born in Mineola, New York, he graduated from the University of Chicago in 1947 and served as press secretary to Connecticut Governor Chester Bowles in 1950. He worked on THE PARIS REVIEW from 1954 to 1956, and as associate editor of *HARPER'S MAGAZINE* from 1959 to 1963. He has edited or coedited *Writing in America* (1960), with John Fischer; *The First Anthology: Thirty*

Years of the New York Review of Books (1993), with Epstein and Rea S. Hederman; *Hidden Histories of Science* (1995); and *Doing It: 5 Performing Arts* (2001), with Tom STOPPARD and Garry Wills, among others.

Simon, Richard L[eo] (March 6, 1899–July 29, 1960). American publisher. The cofounder and longtime guiding force of the major book publishing house Simon & Schuster, Simon was born in New York City to a family with a passionate love of music. After graduating from Columbia University and serving in World War I, he worked as a piano salesman. In 1921, he met Max SCHUSTER, who would become a lifelong friend, and with him established Simon & Schuster three years later. Simon pioneered the use of modern promotion and merchandising techniques in bookselling, and his acumen at marketing contributed to Simon & Schuster's growth from a one-room operation to a dominant force in publishing. During his tenure, the company published bestsellers ranging from how-to books to works of philosophy and literature. Simon is particularly noted for steering the firm's commercially successful focus on music and photography books, and for introducing to the American public the work of Arthur SCHNITZLER, translating the latter's *Leutnant Gustl* as *None But the Brave* (1926). In 1939, he and Schuster established Pocket Books, one of the first major sellers of paperback books. The Simon family's love of music is reflected in his own children, who include singer-songwriter Carly Simon, opera singer Joanna Simon, and singer-songwriter Lucy Simon.

Sontag, Susan (January 16, 1933–). American critic, essayist, novelist, and screenwriter. Born in New York City, Sontag grew up in Arizona and California, and studied philosophy and literature at the University of Chicago, Harvard University, St. Anne's College, Oxford, and the University of Paris. She applied her work in philosophy to the study of the avant-garde and to modern culture, publishing essays and stories in such magazines as THE NEW YORK REVIEW OF BOOKS, HARPER'S, *Commentary*, and THE NATION, first gaining wide notoriety for her essay "Notes on 'Camp'" in PARTISAN REVIEW in 1964. Her best-known collection, *Against Interpretation, and Other Essays* (1966), elaborated her belief that art should be experienced rather than analyzed. Other works include the novels *The Benefactor* (1963), *Death Kit* (1967), *The Volcano Lover* (1992), and *In America* (2000; National Book Award), and the critical works *Styles of Radical Will* (1969), *On Photography* (1977), *Illness As Metaphor* (1978), *Under the Sign of Saturn* (1980), and *AIDS and Its Metaphors* (1988).

Staël, Germaine de, *original name* Anne-Louise-Germaine Necker, Baronne de Staël-Holstein, *known as* **Madame de Staël** (April 22, 1766–July 14, 1817). French-Swiss novelist and woman of letters. Madame de Staël's celebrated salon attracted writers, intellectuals, and political figures, and her essays exerted a profound influence on European letters by introducing German Romantic thought to France. Her father, Jacques Necker, was the chief minister to Louis XVI. Her mother, the Swiss-born Suzanne Curchod, maintained a salon in Paris, which introduced her daughter to the witty intellectual conversation that would become her forte. She married the Swedish ambassador in Paris, Baron Erik de Staël-Holstein, in 1786, separating from him permanently in 1797. Her support of the French Revolution and her personal enmity against Napoleon resulted in her periodic exile from France, so her salon was sometimes conducted from Coppet, near Geneva. Her most important works include the essays *A Treatise on the Influence of the Passions upon the Happiness of Individuals and Nations* (*De l'Influence des Passions sur le Bonheur des Individus et des Nations*, 1796), *The Influence of Literature upon Society* (*De la Littérature Considérée dans Ses Rapports avec les Institutions Sociales*, 1800), and *Germany* (*De l'Allemagne*, 1810). Her novels *Delphine* (1802) and *Corinne* (1807), early feminist works, reflect her passion for individualism and the theme of the intense loneliness of intellectual women.

Steegmuller, Francis (July 3, 1906–October 20, 1994). American literary biographer, translator, critic, and novelist. Best known for his distinguished biographies of modern French masters —among them *Flaubert and Madame Bovary* (1939), *Maupassant, A Lion in the Path* (1949), *Apollinaire, Poet Among the Painters* (1963), and *Cocteau* (1970; National Book Award)—and his translations, including MADAME BOVARY (1957) and *The Letters of Gustave Flaubert* (1980 and 1982), which he also edited and annotated, Steegmuller also wrote several works of comic fiction, critical biographies under the pseudonym Byron Steel, and crime novels under the pseudonym David Keith. He earned a bachelor's degree from Dartmouth and a master's from Columbia, where he began contributing sketches to THE NEW YORKER. His novels include *States of Grace* (1946), *The Christening Party* (1960), and *Silence at Salerno: A Comedy of Intrigue* (1978). The first of three David Keith crime novels, *A Matter of Iodine* (1940), was critically acclaimed. Byron Steel titles included *O Rare Ben Jonson* (1927) and *Sir Francis Bacon: The First Modern Mind* (1930). Steegmuller was married to the novelist Shirley HAZZARD.

Steele, Richard (1672–September 1, 1729). English essayist, editor, and playwright. Steele is best known as the founder of *The Tatler* (1709–11) and cofounder of *The Spectator* (1711–12), both pioneering journals of literary essays. Born in Dublin, Steele was educated in England, where he met his lifelong associate Joseph ADDISON, a prominent contributor to *The Tatler*. The two cofounded *The Spectator*, which they cleverly presented as a series of essays written by members of a fictional "Spectator Club." Their influential essays in both journals commented on manners, mores, and contemporary social life for a genteel, middle-class audience. Affiliated with the Whig party, Steele also founded several short-lived political journals, and served as the government-appointed director of the Drury Lane Theatre from 1714 on. Steele's own plays, including *The Conscious Lovers* (1723), are important examples of sentimental comedy, an 18th-century form marked by moralistic ideals.

Steiner, George (April 23, 1929–). French-born American critic and novelist. Steiner's distinguished critical writing focuses on the relationships between cultural history and literature. Born in Paris and educated at the Sorbonne, he fled with his Jewish family to America in 1940 and became a United States citizen in 1944. After studying at the University of Chicago, Harvard, and Oxford, he taught at Cambridge and the University of Geneva. His works include *Language and Silence* (1967), which examines the effects of the Holocaust on literature; *Extraterritorial* (1971), on the literature of exile; *After Babel* (1975), which explores questions of similarity and difference among languages and cultures; and *Real Presences* (1989), on the nature of meaning. His best-known novel, *The Portage to San Cristóbal of A. H.* (1981), imagines Hitler's life as a fugitive in South America. Other works include *Tolstoy or Dostoevsky* (1959), *The Death of Tragedy* (1961), *In Bluebeard's Castle: Some Notes Towards the Redefinition of Culture* (1971), and *Antigones* (1984). *Errata: An Examined Life*, his intellectual memoir, appeared in 1998.

Stephen, [Sir] Leslie (November 28, 1832–February 22, 1904). English critic, scholar, and editor. A formidable Victorian intellectual figure, Stephen was educated at Cambridge, where he took orders for the clergy. He had become an agnostic by 1864, when he embarked on a literary career in London, but theological concerns recur throughout his work. He edited THE CORNHILL MAGAZINE, a prominent literary periodical, from 1871 to 1882, attracting essays and fiction from the most distinguished writers of the day, and was the first editor of and major contributor to the monumental *Dictionary of National Biography* from 1882 to 1891. His major works are *History of English Thought in the Eighteenth Century* (1876) and *English Literature and Society in the Eighteenth Century* (1904). Stephen was the father of the writer VIRGINIA WOOLF and the basis for the character Mr. RAMSAY in her novel TO THE LIGHTHOUSE (1927).

Strachey, [Giles] **Lytton** (March 1, 1880–January 21, 1932). English biographer and critic. A celebrated member of the Bloomsbury Group in London, Strachey transformed the art of biography with his witty, irreverent, often satiric portrayals of illustrious figures. The eleventh child of India civil administrator Sir Richard Strachey, he was a sickly child and spent a year at Liverpool University before attending Trinity College, Cambridge, from 1899 to 1903. He began his literary career writing journal articles and a book of criticism, *Landmarks in French Literature* (1912). This was followed by an iconoclastic collection of biographical sketches, *Eminent Victorians* (1918), which brought him enduring fame but engendered controversy. He fixed his reputation for highly personal—some called it exaggerated or eccentric—literary portraiture with *Queen Victoria* (1921), *Elizabeth and Essex* (1928), and *Portraits in Miniature* (1931). His writings also include two essay collections, *Books and Characters, French & English* (1922) and *Characters and Commentaries* (1933).

Straus, Roger W[illiams], **Jr.** (January 3, 1917–). American publisher. The cofounder and guiding force of the book-publishing house Farrar, Straus & Giroux, Inc. (originally Farrar and Straus), Straus has set standards for literary quality and editorial independence through more than five decades of industry commercialization and conglomeration. The son of prominent industrialist Roger Williams Straus and Gladys Guggenheim Straus, he grew up in New York and studied journalism at the University of Missouri. After a brief career in newspapers and a four-year stint in the Navy during World War II, he joined with publisher John Farrar in establishing the New York firm in 1945. Dedicated to high editorial standards and the support of literary talent, Farrar, Straus gained a reputation for award-winning books and authors, especially in the areas of fiction and poetry. Championing the work of commercially inauspicious or politically suppressed foreign writers—such as Elias CANETTI, Aleksandr SOLZHENITSYN, and Pablo NERUDA—it has retained some 20 Nobel Prize winners and earned uncommon loyalty among the ranks of its many notable authors. In 1994 Straus sold a majority share of the firm to the German company Verlagsgruppe Georg von Holtzbrinck, but stayed on as its flamboyant and independent-minded president.

Symons, Arthur (February 28, 1865–January 22, 1945). English poet, translator, and critic. Born in Wales, the son of an itinerant Methodist minister, Symons became an influential figure in London literary circles. He gained recognition with his early poetry, characterized by disillusionment and aestheticism and collected in *Silhouettes* (1892) and *London Nights* (1895). A member of the Rhymers' Club (whose membership also included YEATS), Symons contributed to the influential YELLOW BOOK and was an editor of *The Savoy*, a magazine focusing on new writers and artists. In his translations of MALLARMÉ and VERLAINE and in *The Symbolist Movement in Literature* (dated 1899 but published 1900), he introduced the French Symbolists to the English reader. In 1908 Symons suffered a mental breakdown and was institutionalized until 1910. Afterward, he wrote little of significance except for his account of the breakdown, *Confessions: A Study in Pathology* (1930).

Tate, Allen (November 19, 1899–February 9, 1979). American critic, poet, and novelist. An important figure in the renaissance of Southern literature in the first half of the 20th century, Tate was associated with the formalist New Critics. As a student at Vanderbilt University, he was one of the group of Southern writers who published THE FUGITIVE (1922–25), an influential literary magazine that promoted a conservative vision of the agrarian South. In all his work as a critic and poet, he explored, with intellectual complexity, issues of tradition, the decline of coherent values, and the distinct qualities of Southern literature. Collections of his critical writings include *Essays of Four Decades* (1968) and *Memoirs and Opinions, 1926–1974* (1975). His poetry, including the well-known "Ode to the Confederate Dead" (1926), is gathered in *Collected Poems, 1919–1976* (1977).

Thurman, Wallace (August 16, 1902–December 22, 1934). American editor, critic, novelist, and playwright. Versatile and eclectic, Thurman is best known for his involvement in the 1920s with the Harlem Renaissance, a fertile period of African-American literature and art. Born in Utah and educated at the University of Southern California, Thurman moved to Harlem in 1925 to be a part of the literary scene there. He edited and contributed to the short-lived but important magazines *Fire!!* (1926) and *Harlem* (1928), publishing new black writers such as LANGSTON HUGHES and Zora Neale HURSTON. Thurman's essays explore the need for African-American authenticity and criticize writers such as W. E. B. DU BOIS for being overly concerned with white values. His novel *The Blacker the Berry* (1929) examines racism among blacks, while his best-known novel, *Infants of the Spring* (1932), satirizes the Harlem Renaissance, presenting a contentious but stimulating portrait of its milieu.

Trilling, Lionel (July 4, 1905–November 5, 1975). American critic. A leading figure among the New York Intellectuals, Trilling became one of the 20th century's most influential literary critics. The son of Jewish immigrants to New York, Trilling taught English literature at Columbia University from 1931 until his death and counted among his students Allen GINSBERG, John Hollander, and Norman Podhoretz. He won academic celebrity with *The Liberal Imagination* (1950), a book of essays on the interplay between literature, culture, and politics. By arguing that literature played an important role in politics and life, Trilling opposed the New Critics of the 1930s and 1940s, who considered art apart from its context. He took the 19th-century English poet and critic Matthew ARNOLD as his hero, devoting his first book to him (*Matthew Arnold*, 1939, rev. 1949) and emulating his genteel prose style and belief in the moral potential of art. Despite one early novel (*The Middle of the Journey*, 1947), Trilling is best known for essays on Jane AUSTEN, HENRY JAMES, William WORDSWORTH, and even Alfred Kinsey's *Sexual Behavior in the Human Male* (1948); many are reprinted in *The Moral Obligation to Be Intelligent: Selected Essays* (2000).

Tynan, Kenneth (April 2, 1927–July 26, 1980). English theater critic. With a B.A. in English from Magdalen College, Oxford, Tynan embarked on a short career as a director and actor before starting to write influential theater reviews in London for the *Spectator*, the *Evening Standard*, the *Daily Sketch*, and especially the *Observer*, establishing a reputation in the 1950s and 1960s as Britain's foremost drama critic. During this time he championed the "new realism" of the group of writers known as the Angry Young Men and served as the literary manager of the National Theatre of Great Britain. He collaborated on the erotic revue *Oh! Calcutta!* (1969) and, in the late 1970s, contributed acclaimed profiles and essays to THE NEW YORKER. Collections of his criticism, essays, and profiles include *He That Plays the King* (1950), *Curtains* (1961), *Tynan Right and Left* (1968), *A View of the English Stage 1944–1965* (1975), and *Show People: Profiles in Entertainment* (1979). After his death, his widow, Kathleen Tynan, edited *Profiles* (1990; rev. ed. 1995) and *Kenneth Tynan, Letters* (1995).

Underwood, Francis (January 12, 1825–August 7, 1894). American editor. The son of a Massachusetts farmer, Underwood spent a year at Amherst College before moving to Kentucky to teach. There, he became a lawyer and an increasingly fervent abolitionist. Returning to Massachusetts in the 1850s to advance the antislavery cause, he became a literary editor at the Boston publishing house of Phillips, Sampson & Company. His long-cherished idea of founding an antislavery literary magazine was realized in 1857 when THE ATLANTIC MONTHLY was launched with the help of such impressive figures as Harriet Beecher STOWE, JAMES RUSSELL LOWELL, Ralph Waldo EMERSON, Oliver Wendell Holmes, and Henry Wadsworth LONGFELLOW; Lowell served as editor and Underwood as assistant editor. *Quabbin, the Story of a Small Town with Outlooks Upon Puritan Life* (1893) is based on his memories of Enfield, Massachusetts, where he grew up. He also wrote biographies of Longfellow, Lowell, and WHITTIER, and served as United States consul to Glasgow, Scotland, during Grover Cleveland's two terms as President.

Untermeyer, Louis (October 1, 1885–December 19, 1977). American poet, anthologist, and editor. Untermeyer's literary influence has resulted primarily from the more than 50 anthologies he edited, especially *Modern American Poetry* (1919) and *Modern British Poetry* (1920), published in many editions. His extensive knowledge of poetry helped him to bring an eclectic mix of poets to the general public and earned him a chair on the Pulitzer Prize jury for many years. Untermeyer began his literary career as a prolific contributor to scholarly, academic, and humorous journals. In his six years as an editor of the socialist journal *The Masses*, he became friendly with Robert FROST, and their correspondence was published in 1963. While working as the poetry editor for *THE AMERICAN MERCURY*, he compiled *Play in Poetry* (1938), from his lectures on light verse. *Treasury of Great Poems, English and American* (1955), *Lives of the Poets* (1959), and *Treasury of Great Humor* (1972) are other Untermeyer anthologies. In addition to his autobiographies *From Another World* (1939) and *Bygones* (1965), Untermeyer published collections of his own poetry, including *Burning Bush* (1935), *Selected Poems and Parodies* (1935), and *Long Feud* (1962).

Van Doren, Carl (September 10, 1885–July 18, 1950). American editor, critic, and biographer. The brother of poet MARK VAN DOREN, Carl Van Doren taught at Columbia University from 1911 to 1930, and helped to elevate the status of American writers in university programs at a time when most scholars and critics still focused on European literature. Van Doren was also the managing editor of *The Cambridge History of American Literature* (4 vols., 1917–21) and the literary editor of both *THE NATION* (1919–22) and *The Century* (1922–25), and a founder and editor (1926–34) of The Literary Guild book club. His biography of Benjamin Franklin received the Pulitzer Prize in 1938, and he also wrote biographies of Thomas Love PEACOCK, Jonathan SWIFT, and SINCLAIR LEWIS, and the autobiography *Three Worlds* (1936). Van Doren's many critical works include *The American Novel* (1921) and *Contemporary American Novelists, 1900–1920* (1922).

Van Doren, Mark (June 13, 1894–December 10, 1972). American poet, critic, and editor. The brother of CARL VAN DOREN and an influential professor at Columbia, Mark Van Doren inspired students such as Allen GINSBERG, John BERRYMAN, and Thomas Merton. During his career, Van Doren served as the literary editor (1924–28) and film critic (1935–38) for *THE NATION*, wrote critical studies including *The Poetry of John Dryden* (1920), *Shakespeare* (1939), and *Nathaniel Hawthorne* (1949), and edited *An Anthology of English and American Poetry* (1928), *American Poets, 1630–1930* (1932), *Walt Whitman* (1945), and *The Portable Emerson* (1946). His poetry, influenced by Romanticism and the English pastoral tradition, often featured the people and rural settings of New England. His *Collected Poems, 1922–1938* (1939) won the Pulitzer Prize. He published his *Autobiography* in 1958.

Vendler, Helen, *original surname* Hennessy (April 30, 1933–). American critic. The foremost American poetry critic of her generation, Vendler was born in Boston, the daughter of schoolteachers, and studied chemistry as an undergraduate because she did not approve of the way literature was taught at the religious college that her parents insisted she attend. From her study of science and mathematics, however, she learned "the beauty of clear thought, the satisfaction of providing a chain of demonstrable evidence, and the virtue of rational and logical exposition," all admired strengths of her critical writing. After receiving her B.A. in 1954, Vendler went to Belgium as a Fulbright Fellow for a year and later studied at Boston College, receiving her Ph.D. from Harvard University in 1960. She taught at a number of American colleges and universities before becoming a visiting professor at Harvard in 1981, where she has since risen to University Professor. Vendler practices what she calls "aesthetic criticism," whose first task is to describe the elements—formal, aesthetic, psychological, metaphorical—that generate the "unique configuration" of a particular poem or group of poems. Her work has appeared regularly in such publications as *The New York Times Book Review*, THE NEW YORKER, THE NEW YORK REVIEW OF BOOKS, THE NEW REPUBLIC, and *The London Review of Books*, among others. Her essays and reviews have been collected in *Part of Nature, Part of Us: Modern American Poets* (1980; National Book Critics Circle Award for criticism), *The Music of What Happens: Poems, Poets, Critics* (1988), and *Soul Says: On Recent Poetry* (1995). Vendler has also written widely praised studies of individual poets, including YEATS, Wallace STEVENS, GEORGE HERBERT, KEATS, SHAKESPEARE, and Seamus HEANEY.

Ward, Artemus, *pen name of* Charles Farrar Browne (April 26, 1834–March 6, 1867). American humorist. In 1858, while working for the *Cleveland Plain Dealer*, Charles Farrar Browne created the character of Artemus Ward, supposedly a carnival manager who wrote letters to the editor commenting on everything from slavery and Mormonism to politicians and temperance. His letters were rife with comical misspellings, gross exaggerations, tall tales, and ridiculous caricatures that poked fun at anything he found hypocritical in American society. Browne began lecturing as Ward in 1861, perfecting his deadpan delivery and pioneering a type of comic lecture that influenced Mark TWAIN. He moved to New York in 1859 and had continued success writing for *Vanity Fair*. He also contributed to the British magazine *Punch* and achieved popularity in England as well as the United States. His books include *Artemus Ward, His Book* (1862), *Artemus Ward, His Travels* (1865), and *Artemus Ward in London* (1867).

Waugh, Auberon (November 17, 1939–January 16, 2001). English journalist and novelist. The son of EVELYN WAUGH, Auberon Waugh is known for his biting wit and conservative political commentary. He began writing after sustaining a serious injury during a training exercise in the British military. He spent a year at Christ Church, Oxford, then began his journalism career with the *Daily Telegraph*. Waugh was a columnist for the *Catholic Herald*, the *Spectator*, and the *Daily Mail*, and contributed political and satirical columns to *Private Eye* and the *Sunday Telegraph*. In 1968, he founded *The Literary Review*, which he edited until his death. His novels include *The Foxglove Saga* (1960), *Path of Dalliance* (1963), and *Consider the Lilies* (1968). His autobiographical works are *Four Crowded Years* (1976), *Auberon Waugh's Yearbook* (1981), *The Diaries of Auberon Waugh* (1985), and *Will This Do? The First Fifty Years of Auberon Waugh* (1991).

Weaver, William (July 24, 1923–). American translator, critic, and biographer. An eminent translator of modern and contemporary Italian authors including Giorgio Bassani, Italo CALVINO, Umberto ECO, Primo LEVI, and Luigi PIRANDELLO, Weaver received the National Book Award for *Cosmicomics*, his 1968 translation of Calvino's *Le Cosmicomiche* (1965), and the PEN Translation Prize for THE NAME OF THE ROSE, his 1983 rendition of Eco's *Il Nome della Rosa* (1980). His translations are highly regarded for making accessible in English the challenging linguistic play of modern Italian writers, while remaining faithful to the original texts. Also an opera critic, Weaver has published numerous books on Italian opera, including *Verdi, A Documentary Study* (1977). Among his other publications are *Duse* (1984), an acclaimed biography of Italian actress Eleonora Duse, and the anthology *Open City: Seven Writers in Postwar Rome* (1999). Weaver has taught at universities in Europe and the United States and is a professor of literature at Bard College.

Webster, Noah (October 16, 1758–May 28, 1843). American lexicographer. Webster's *An American Dictionary of the English Language* (1828) had an unsurpassed effect on American pronunciation and word usage. The son of a Connecticut farmer, Webster graduated from

Yale University and, while working as a teacher in New York, wrote his first textbook, *Grammatical Institute of the English Language,* a three-volume compendium that helped to standardize American spelling. Recognizing the need for a copyright law, he worked diligently until one was passed in 1790. Webster's first dictionary, *A Compendious Dictionary of the English Language* (1806), proved financially disappointing and he spent more than 20 years compiling his larger and more scholarly dictionary, which included nonliterary words as well as both American and British terms, setting a new standard. Webster also helped to found Amherst College in Massachusetts.

White, E[lwyn] **B**[rooks] (July 11, 1899–October 1, 1985). American essayist, stylist, and children's writer. The graceful clarity and unaffected elegance of White's prose style raised the quality of American magazine commentary and influenced the craft of writing for generations. His contributions to THE NEW YORKER helped to establish the tone and reputation of that publication, and *The Elements of Style* (1959), his update and revision of notes by William Strunk, Jr., has remained a standard manual for students and professional writers. White was born in Mount Vernon, New York, and graduated from Cornell University in 1921. He joined *The New Yorker's* staff in 1927, writing the "Notes and Comment" column, essays, poems, and other pieces. In 1937 he moved with his wife, *New Yorker* editor Katherine Angell, to a farm in Maine, where he continued to write for the magazine. His books include *Is Sex Necessary?* (1929), a satire cowritten with James THURBER; *One Man's Meat* (1942), a selection of columns for HARPER'S; and several other collections and anthologies, including *Essays of E. B. White* (1977) and *Poems and Sketches of E. B. White* (1981). *Stuart Little* (1945), *Charlotte's Web* (1952), and *The Trumpet of the Swan* (1970) are modern children's classics. He was awarded the Presidential Medal of Freedom in 1963 and a special Pulitzer Prize in 1978.

Wieseltier, Leon (June 14, 1952–). American journalist and editor. In 1983 Wieseltier became literary editor of THE NEW REPUBLIC, where he has published highly distinguished and influential reviews and criticism. The son of Holocaust survivors, he grew up in Brooklyn, studied at Columbia, Oxford, and Harvard universities, then pursued a career in journalism. In addition to his articles and essays in various magazines and the monthly column he contributed during one period to *Vanity Fair* under the pen name Tristan Vox, his 1983 book *Nuclear War, Nuclear Peace* brought him recognition as a prominent strategic thinker and journalist. The death of his father in 1996 inspired *Kaddish* (1998), meditations on his year of mourning and the history of the Jewish prayer for the dead. He is the editor of *The Moral Obligation to Be Intelligent: Selected Essays* by Lionel TRILLING (2000).

Wilson, Edmund (May 8, 1895–June 12, 1972). American critic and novelist. Skeptical of literary theory, Wilson addressed his criticism to the general reader, and published books on an eclectic array of topics as well as novels, plays, notebooks, and diaries. After graduating from Princeton, he took a job reporting for the *New York Evening Sun,* but left to serve in World War I. After the war, he worked for *Vanity Fair* (1920–21), THE NEW REPUBLIC (1926–31), and THE NEW YORKER (1944–48). *To the Finland Station* (1940) is his history of socialism in Europe. His works of literary criticism include *Axel's Castle: A Study in the Imaginative Literature of 1870–1930* (1931), *The Triple Thinkers: Ten Essays on Literature* (1938), *The Wound and the Bow: Seven Studies in Literature* (1941), *Classics and Commercials: A Literary Chronicle of the Forties* (1950), *The Shores of Light: A Literary Chronicle of the Twenties and Thirties* (1952), *Patriotic Gore: Studies in the Literature of the American Civil War* (1962), *The Bit Between My Teeth: A Literary Chronicle of 1950–1965* (1965), and, as editor, *The Shock of Recognition: The Development of Literature in the United States Recorded by the Men Who Made It* (1943). He also wrote the novels *I Thought of Daisy* (1929, rev. 1967) and *Memoirs of Hecate County* (1946); the plays *This Room and This Gin and These Sandwiches*

(1937) and *The Blue Light* (1950), among others; and the autobiographical *A Prelude* (1967) and *Upstate* (1971). Other biographical sources include his correspondence with Vladimir NABOKOV, published in 1979, and his journals, published from 1975 to 1993 as *The Twenties*, *The Thirties*, *The Forties*, *The Fifties*, and *The Sixties*.

Winfrey, Oprah (January 29, 1954–). American television talk-show host and magazine editor. Long a highly influential figure on daytime television, Winfrey became a phenomenon in the publishing world as well when in 1996 her popular talk show added a new feature, Oprah's Book Club, "to get the country excited about reading." Winfrey was born into humble circumstances on a farm in Kosciusko, Mississippi, and was raised there by her maternal grandmother until she was six years old, when she went to live with her mother in Milwaukee. She later lived with her father, who encouraged her to excel academically, demanding weekly book reports from his daughter. While studying at Tennessee State University, Winfrey began a series of jobs in television, including one as the first African-American woman to coanchor the evening news in Nashville. In 1984, she took a job hosting a local morning television talk show in Chicago; two years later the program went national as the still-running "Oprah Winfrey Show," one of the most successful shows in television history. It was Winfrey's lifelong love of reading that inspired her to found Oprah's Book Club, an on-air (and online) reading club featuring some 8–10 titles (almost exclusively contemporary fiction) each year. To date, each selection of the Book Club has become an instant bestseller; the Club's impact on book sales has been called the "Oprah Effect." Writers selected by Winfrey for the Club include such novelists as Joyce Carol OATES, André Dubus III, Barbara KINGSOLVER, Toni MORRISON, Isabelle ALLENDE, Jane Hamilton, Bernhard Schlink, Edwidge Danticat, and Alice Hoffman. Also a producer of movies for television and an actress, Winfrey has starred in the film adaptations of Alice WALKER's *THE COLOR PURPLE* (1985) and Toni Morrison's *BELOVED* (1998). In April 2000, Winfrey launched O, *The Oprah Magazine*, of which she serves as editor-in-chief.

Winters, Yvor (October 17, 1900–January 25, 1968). American poet and critic. Winters's criticism aroused controversy for its insistence that critics should pass moral judgment on literary works; Winters himself objected, sometimes vehemently, to the work of POE, T. S. ELIOT, and HENRY JAMES. He received his Ph.D. from Stanford University, where he taught English from 1928 until his death. His major works of criticism include *In Defense of Reason* (1947; collecting the earlier works *Primitivism and Decadence*, *Maule's Curse*, and *The Anatomy of Nonsense*), *The Function of Criticism* (1957), and *Forms of Discovery* (1967). Winters's poetry is collected in *The Immobile Wind* (1921), *The Magpie's Shadow* (1922), *The Proof* (1930), *Collected Poems* (1952), and *Selected Poems* (1999).

Wolff, Kurt (March 3, 1887–October 21, 1963), and **Wolff, Helen**, *original surname* Mosel (July 27, 1906–March 28, 1994). American publishers. Kurt Wolff was born in Bonn, where his father was a professor of music history, and studied at the universities of Bonn, Munich, Marburg, and Leipzig. He entered the world of publishing at age 21 when he joined the Leipzig firm of Ernst Rowohlt Verlag. He eventually became a partner and then proprietor, in 1913 renaming the firm Kurt Wolff Verlag, the earliest publications of which included the first published work (a book of short stories) by Franz KAFKA. Following World War I, he steered his company through financial and other difficulties, but overwork, the stress of divorcing his first wife, and the increasingly difficult political situation in Germany took their toll, and he closed the firm in the early 1930s and moved to France when the Nazis came to power. In 1933, he married Helen Mosel, who had been a translator for the Pantheon imprint of Kurt Wolff Verlag. The couple lived in Italy and France until 1941, when, after brief periods of incarceration by the French as enemy aliens, they were allowed to immigrate to New York. There, in February 1942, they founded a new company, Pantheon Books, which grew from a one-room enterprise to a firm with a formidable reputation, noted for publishing in English translation the works of such European writers as Günter GRASS, Hermann BROCH, Paul VALÉRY, Franz Werfel, Émile ZOLA, and Boris PASTERNAK (the first American edition of *DOCTOR ZHIVAGO*); Pantheon also had great commercial success with such popular titles as Anne Morrow Lindbergh's *Gift from the Sea* (1955). In 1959, they returned to Italy and subsequently resigned from Pantheon, with plans to leave publishing permanently. But then, in 1960, they accepted publisher William Jovanovich's offer to head a new imprint, Helen and Kurt Wolff Books, at Harcourt, Brace and World. They worked from Italy until Kurt Wolff's death in 1963; thereafter, Helen Wolff returned to New York to oversee the imprint. Writers whose works were published under her leadership include Grass, Italo CALVINO, Umberto ECO, Max FRISCH, Stanislaw LEM, Amos OZ, and Georges SIMENON, who called the Wolffs "the most astonishing couple in the world of publishing." Helen Wolff, who inspired great loyalty in her roster of European writers because of the attention she paid to the nuances of translation, retired in 1986.

Wood, James (November 1, 1965–). English critic. As senior editor and "house critic" of *THE NEW REPUBLIC*, Wood has established himself as one of the leading literary commentators of his generation. His collection of previously published journal essays, *The Broken Estate: Essays on Literature and Belief* (1999), was widely praised for its perceptive critical judgment and incisive polemical style. In its 21 essays, the work explores connections between literature and religious belief in writers as diverse as VIRGINIA WOOLF, Philip ROTH, Thomas MANN, Toni MORRISON, and Thomas More. A child of evangelical Anglicans, Wood was born in Durham, England, and studied at Cambridge during the 1980s. He has contributed reviews and essays to a variety of other British and American publications, including *The London Review of Books*, *The Guardian*, and *THE NEW YORKER*. He also edited the *Selected Stories of D. H. Lawrence* (1999).

Woolf, Leonard (November 25, 1880–August 14, 1969). English essayist, journalist, novelist, and publisher. A founding member of the Bloomsbury Group and a versatile man of letters, Woolf devoted his literary and journalistic efforts to the pursuit of social and political causes. At Cambridge he befriended E. M. FORSTER, John Maynard Keynes, and Lytton STRACHEY, who formed the core of the Bloomsbury circle. His first novel, *The Village in the Jungle* (1913), and the short fiction collected in *Stories of the East* (1916) expressed his anti-imperialist sentiments after eight years as a civil servant in Ceylon. *The Wise Virgins* (1914) tells of a young Jew who yearns to marry a beautiful upper-class woman, paralleling his own courtship of VIRGINIA (Stephen) WOOLF. In 1917 the couple founded the Hogarth Press, which published such writers as Forster, T. S. ELIOT, and Gertrude STEIN. Woolf promoted his socialist and internationalist convictions as a contributing editor for several prominent journals and in such books as *International Government* (1916), *Imperialism and Civilization* (1928), *After the Deluge* (2 vols., 1931–39), and *Principia Politica* (1953). His major work, by many accounts, is a five-volume autobiography: *Sowing* (1960), *Growing* (1961), *Beginning Again* (1964), *Downhill All the Way* (1967), and *The Journey Not the Arrival Matters* (1969).

Woollcott, Alexander (January 19, 1887–January 23, 1943). American theater and literary critic and radio personality. A colorful and respected figure on the New York cultural scene for nearly three decades—and doyen of the fabled Algonquin Round Table—Woollcott influenced the success or failure of Broadway shows and the tastes of the reading public with his witty, often biting, critical commentaries. A graduate of Hamilton College, he began his career as a drama critic with *The New York Times* in 1914. After reporting for the *Stars and Stripes* during World War I, he returned to the *Times* and later wrote for the *New York Herald* —where he became known as one of the

"Three Fat Fates of Broadway"—and the *New York World*. As host of the CBS radio show "The Town Crier" from 1929 to 1942, he gained a national following with his anecdotes, gossip, and waggish conversation. His curmudgeonly personality inspired the character of Sheridan Whiteside in George S. KAUFMAN and Moss HART's play *The Man Who Came to Dinner* (1939), a role Woollcott himself once played. His reviews, essays, and reminiscences are collected in *Shouts and Murmurs: Echoes of a Thousand and One First Nights* (1922), *Enchanted Aisles* (1924), *Going to Pieces* (1928), *While Rome Burns* (1934), *Long, Long Ago* (1943), and other works.

Wright, Willard Huntington, *pen name* S. S. Van Dine (October 15, 1888–April 11, 1939). American literary and art critic, editor, and detective novelist. Born in Virginia, Wright briefly attended a number of colleges, including Harvard, before studying art and music in Munich and Paris. In 1907, he became literary editor of the *Los Angeles Times* and in 1912, on the recommendation of his friend H. L. MENCKEN, became the editor of *Smart Set* in New York. A great supporter of modern literature, he published such writers as Floyd Dell, Ezra POUND, and Joseph CONRAD. Wright was also an art critic, championing modernist art and helping to organize the Forum Exhibition of Modern American Painters at New York's Anderson Gallery in 1916. Among his books are a collection of travel essays (cowritten with Mencken and George Jean NATHAN), *Europe After 8:15* (1914); *Modern Painting* (1915); *What Nietzsche Taught* (1915); and *The Man of Promise* (1916), a novel. While recovering from a breakdown, Wright spent two years systematically studying detective stories; from this study came his "Twenty Rules for Writing Detective Stories," published in *American Magazine* in 1928. Thereafter, he turned to writing a series of best-selling detective novels under the pen name S. S. Van Dine. These novels, featuring the wealthy and erudite sleuth Philo Vance, include *The Benson Murder Case* (1926), *The Scarab Murder Case* (1930), *The Kidnap Murder Case* (1936), and *The Winter Murder Case* (1939).

Authors' Awards

NOBEL PRIZE IN LITERATURE

Awarded annually by the Swedish Academy in Stockholm to the person of any nationality who "shall have produced in the field of literature the most outstanding work in an ideal direction."

2000	Gao Xingjian, Chinese
1999	Günter Grass, German
1998	José Saramago, Portuguese
1997	Dario Fo, Italian
1996	Wisława Szymborska, Polish
1995	Seamus Heaney, Irish
1994	Kenzaburo Oe, Japanese
1993	Toni Morrison, American
1992	Derek Walcott, West Indian
1991	Nadine Gordimer, South African
1990	Octavio Paz, Mexican
1989	Camilo José Cela, Spanish
1988	Naguib Mahfouz, Egyptian
1987	Joseph Brodsky, Russian-American
1986	Wole Soyinka, Nigerian
1985	Claude Simon, French
1984	Jaroslav Seifert, Czech
1983	William Golding, British
1982	Gabriel García Márquez, Colombian
1981	Elias Canetti, Bulgarian
1980	Czesław Miłosz, Polish-American
1979	Odysseus Elytis, Greek
1978	Isaac Bashevis Singer, American
1977	Vicente Aleixandre, Spanish
1976	Saul Bellow, American
1975	Eugenio Montale, Italian
1974	Eyvind Johnson, Swedish, and Harry Edmund Martinson, Swedish
1973	Patrick White, Australian
1972	Heinrich Böll, German
1971	Pablo Neruda, Chilean
1970	Aleksandr Solzhenitsyn, Russian
1969	Samuel Beckett, Irish-French
1968	Yasunari Kawabata, Japanese
1967	Miguel Angel Asturias, Guatemalan
1966	Samuel Joseph Agnon, Israeli, and Nelly Sachs, Swedish
1965	Mikhail Sholokhov, Russian
1964	Jean-Paul Sartre, French (declined the prize)
1963	George Seferis, Greek
1962	John Steinbeck, American
1961	Ivo Andric, Yugoslav
1960	Saint-John Perse, French
1959	Salvatore Quasimodo, Italian
1958	Boris Pasternak, Russian (declined the prize)
1957	Albert Camus, French
1956	Juan Ramón Jiménez, Spanish
1955	Halldór Laxness, Icelandic
1954	Ernest Hemingway, American
1953	Sir Winston Churchill, British
1952	François Mauriac, French
1951	Pär Lagerkvist, Swedish
1950	Bertrand Russell, British
1949	William Faulkner, American
1948	T. S. Eliot, British
1947	André Gide, French

NOBEL PRIZE IN LITERATURE, BY COUNTRY

■ **AUSTRALIA**

1973   Patrick White

■ **BELGIUM**

1911   Maurice Maeterlinck

■ **CHILE**

1945   Gabriela Mistral
1971   Pablo Neruda

■ **CHINA**

2000   Gao Xingjian

■ **COLOMBIA**

1982   Gabriel García Márquez

■ **CZECHOSLOVAKIA**

1984   Jaroslav Seifert

■ **DENMARK**

1917   Karl A. Gjellerup and Henrik Pontoppidan
1944   Johannes V. Jensen

■ **EGYPT**

1988   Naguib Mahfouz

■ **FINLAND**

1939   Frans Eemil Sillanpää

■ **FRANCE**

1901   René F. A. Sully-Prudhomme
1904   Frédéric Mistral
        (with José Echegaray, Spain)
1915   Romain Rolland
1921   Anatole France
1927   Henri Bergson
1937   Robert Martin du Gard
1947   André Gide
1952   François Mauriac
1957   Albert Camus
1960   Saint-John Perse

1964   Jean-Paul Sartre (declined the prize)
1985   Claude Simon

■ **GERMANY**

1902   Theodor Mommsen
1908   Rudolf Eucken
1910   Paul J. L. Heyse
1912   Gerhart Hauptmann
1929   Thomas Mann
1972   Heinrich Böll
1999   Günter Grass

■ **GREAT BRITAIN**

1907   Rudyard Kipling
1925   George Bernard Shaw
1932   John Galsworthy
1948   T. S. Eliot (b. United States)
1950   Bertrand Russell
1953   Sir Winston Churchill
1981   Elias Canetti (b. Bulgaria,
        writing in German)
1983   William Golding

■ **GREECE**

1963   George Seferis
1979   Odysseus Elytis

■ **GUATEMALA**

1967   Miguel Angel Asturias

■ **ICELAND**

1955   Halldór Laxness

■ **INDIA**

1913   Rabindranath Tagore

■ **IRELAND**

1923   William Butler Yeats
1969   Samuel Beckett
1995   Seamus Heaney

■ ISRAEL

1966   Samuel Joseph Agnon
        (with Nelly Sachs, Sweden)

■ ITALY

1906   Giosuè Carducci
1926   Grazia Deledda
1934   Luigi Pirandello
1959   Salvatore Quasimodo
1975   Eugenio Montale
1997   Dario Fo

■ JAPAN

1968   Yasunari Kawabata
1994   Kenzaburo Oe

■ MEXICO

1990   Octavio Paz

■ NIGERIA

1986   Wole Soyinka

■ NORWAY

1903   Björnstjerne Björnson
1920   Knut Hamsun
1928   Sigrid Undset

■ POLAND

1905   Henryk Sienkiewicz
1924   Władysław S. Reymont
1980   Czesław Miłosz
1996   Wisława Szymborska

■ PORTUGAL

1998   José Saramago

■ RUSSIA

1933   Ivan A. Bunin
1958   Boris Pasternak (declined the prize)
1965   Mikhail Sholokhov
1970   Aleksandr Solzhenitsyn

■ SOUTH AFRICA

1991   Nadine Gordimer

■ SPAIN

1904   José Echegaray
        (with Frédéric Mistral, France)
1922   Jacinto Benavente
1956   Juan Ramón Jiménez
1977   Vicente Aleixandre
1989   Camilo José Cela

■ SWEDEN

1909   Selma Lagerlöf
1916   Verner von Heidenstam
1931   Erik A. Karlfeldt
1951   Pär Lagerkvist
1966   Nelly Sachs (b. Germany, writing in German)
        (with Samuel Joseph Agnon, Israel)
1974   Eyvind Johnson
        and Harry Edmund Martinson

■ SWITZERLAND

1919   Carl F. G. Spitteler
1946   Hermann Hesse

■ UNITED STATES

1930   Sinclair Lewis
1936   Eugene O'Neill
1938   Pearl S. Buck
1949   William Faulkner
1954   Ernest Hemingway
1962   John Steinbeck
1976   Saul Bellow
1978   Isaac Bashevis Singer (b. Poland, writing
        in Yiddish)
1987   Joseph Brodsky (b. Russia, writing in
        Russian and English)
1993   Toni Morrison

■ WEST INDIES

1992   Derek Walcott

■ YUGOSLAVIA

1961   Ivo Andric

(Nobel Prize in Literature, continued)

1946	Hermann Hesse, Swiss-German
1945	Gabriela Mistral, Chilean
1944	Johannes V. Jensen, Danish
1940–43	No award
1939	Frans Eemil Sillanpää, Finnish
1938	Pearl S. Buck, American
1937	Robert Martin du Gard, French
1936	Eugene O'Neill, American
1935	No award
1934	Luigi Pirandello, Italian
1933	Ivan A. Bunin, Russian
1932	John Galsworthy, British
1931	Erik A. Karlfeldt, Swedish
1930	Sinclair Lewis, American
1929	Thomas Mann, German
1928	Sigrid Undset, Norwegian
1927	Henri Bergson, French
1926	Grazia Deledda, Italian
1925	George Bernard Shaw, British
1924	Władysław S. Reymont, Polish
1923	William Butler Yeats, Irish
1922	Jacinto Benavente, Spanish
1921	Anatole France, French
1920	Knut Hamsun, Norwegian
1919	Carl F. G. Spitteler, Swiss
1918	No award
1917	Karl A. Gjellerup, Danish, and Henrik Pontoppidan, Danish
1916	Verner von Heidenstam, Swedish
1915	Romain Rolland, French
1914	No award
1913	Rabindranath Tagore, Indian
1912	Gerhart Hauptmann, German
1911	Maurice Maeterlinck, Belgian
1910	Paul J. L. Heyse, German
1909	Selma Lagerlöf, Swedish
1908	Rudolf Eucken, German
1907	Rudyard Kipling, British
1906	Giosuè Carducci, Italian
1905	Henryk Sienkiewicz, Polish
1904	Frédéric Mistral, French, and José Echegaray, Spanish
1903	Björnstjerne Björnson, Norwegian
1902	Theodor Mommsen, German
1901	René F. A. Sully-Prudhomme, French

THE BOLLINGEN PRIZE IN POETRY

Currently awarded biannually, under the administration of the Yale University Library, to a writer or writers for achievement in American poetry.

2001	Louise Glück
1999	Robert Creeley
1997	Gary Snyder
1995	Kenneth Koch
1993	Mark Strand
1991	Laura Riding Jackson and Donald Justice
1989	Edgar Bowers
1987	Stanley Kunitz
1985	John Ashbery and Fred Chappel
1983	Anthony Hecht and John Hollander
1981	Howard Nemerov and May Swenson
1979	W. S. Merwin
1977	David Ignatow
1975	A. R. Ammons
1973	James Merrill
1971	Richard Wilbur and Mona Van Duyn
1969	John Berryman and Karl Shapiro
1967	Robert Penn Warren
1965	Horace Gregory
1963	Robert Frost
1962	John Hall Wheelock and Richard Eberhart
1961	Yvor Winters
1960	Delmore Schwartz
1959	Theodore Roethke
1958	E. E. Cummings
1957	Allen Tate
1956	Conrad Aiken
1955	Léonie Adams and Louise Bogan
1954	W. H. Auden
1953	Archibald MacLeish and William Carlos Williams
1952	Marianne Moore
1951	John Crowe Ransom
1950	Wallace Stevens
1949	Ezra Pound

POETS LAUREATE

English Poets Laureate

Appointed for life by the English monarch, the Poet Laureate was formerly
expected to compose commemorative verse for special occasions of state.
The first appointment, in 1668, was made by King James II.

LAUREATESHIP	POET	LAUREATESHIP	POET
1999–	Andrew Motion	1790–1813	Henry James Pye
1984–98	Ted Hughes	1785–90	Thomas Warton
1972–84	Sir John Betjeman	1757–85**	William Whitehead
1968–72	C. Day-Lewis	1730–57	Colley Cibber
1930–67	John Masefield	1718–30	Laurence Eusden
1913–30	Robert Bridges	1715–18	Nicholas Rowe
1896–1913	Alfred Austin	1692–1715	Nahum Tate
1850–92*	Alfred, Lord Tennyson	1689–92	Thomas Shadwell
1843–50	William Wordsworth	1668–88	John Dryden
1813–43	Robert Southey		

* The 1850 appointment was declined by Samuel Rogers.

** The 1757 appointment was declined by Thomas Gray.

American Poets Laureate

This position, appointed by the U.S. Library of Congress, has existed
under two separate titles: from 1937 to 1986 as "Consultant in Poetry to
the Library of Congress" and from 1986 forward as "Poet Laureate Consultant in Poetry." Appointments are for October through May.

LAUREATESHIP	POET	LAUREATESHIP	POET
2001–	Billy Collins	1984	Reed Whittemore (Interim Consultant in Poetry)
2000–2001	Stanley Kunitz		
1997–2000	Robert Pinsky (first to serve three consecutive terms) Special Consultants: Rita Dove, Louise Glück, and W. S. Merwin	1984	Robert Fitzgerald (appointed and served in a health-limited capacity, but did not come to the Library of Congress)
1995–97	Robert Hass	1982–84	Anthony Hecht
1993–95	Rita Dove	1981	Maxine Kumin
1992	Mona Van Duyn	1978–80	William Meredith
1991	Joseph Brodsky	1976–78	Robert Hayden
1990	Mark Strand	1974–76	Stanley Kunitz
1988–90	Howard Nemerov	1973	Daniel Hoffman
1987	Richard Wilbur	1971–73	Josephine Jacobsen
1986	Robert Penn Warren	1970	William Stafford
1985	Gwendolyn Brooks	1968–70	Jay Smith

(American Poets Laureate, continued)

LAUREATESHIP	POET
1966–68	James Dickey
1965	Stephen Spender
1964	Reed Whittemore
1963	Howard Nemerov
1961–63	Louis Untermeyer
1959–61	Richard Eberhart
1958	Robert Frost
1956–58	Randall Jarrell
1952	William Carlos Williams (appointed in 1952 but did not serve)

LAUREATESHIP	POET
1950–52	Conrad Aiken (first to serve two terms)
1949	Elizabeth Bishop
1948	Léonie Adams
1947	Robert Lowell
1946	Karl Shapiro
1945	Louise Bogan
1944	Robert Penn Warren
1943	Allen Tate
1937–41	Joseph Auslander (Auslander's appointment had no fixed term)

Sources in Literary Biography

1 REFERENCE BOOKS

Biographical Indexes

Author Biographies Master Index: A Consolidated Index to More Than 1,140,000 Biographical Sketches. 5th ed. Geri Speace, ed. 2 vols. Detroit: Gale, 1997.

Authors: Critical & Biographical References. 2nd ed. Richard E. Combs and Nancy R. Owen. Metuchen N.J.: Scarecrow Press, 1993.

Index to Black American Writers in Collective Biographies. Dorothy W. Campbell. Littleton, Colo.: Libraries Unlimited, 1983.

Index to the Wilson Author Series. Rev. ed. New York: H. W. Wilson, 1997.

Interviews and Conversations with 20th-Century Authors Writing in English: An Index. Stan A. Vrana. 3 vols. Metuchen, N.J.: Scarecrow Press, 1982–90.

Twentieth-Century Author Biographies Master Index: A Consolidated Index to More Than 170,000 Biographical Sketches Concerning Modern Day Authors as They Appear in a Selection of the Principal Biographical Dictionaries Devoted to Authors, Poets, Journalists, and Other Literary Figures. Barbara McNeil, ed. Detroit: Gale, 1984.

Current Writers Directories

A Directory of American Poets and Fiction Writers. New York: Poets & Writers, 1980/81– . Biennial.

International Authors and Writers Who's Who. 7th ed. Cambridge: International Biographical Centre, 1976– .

The Writers Directory. New York: St. Martin's Press, 1971/73– .

General Biographical Sources
(with important coverage of literary figures)

American National Biography. John A. Garraty and Mark C. Carnes, eds. 24 vols. New York: Oxford University Press, 1999.

The Cambridge Biographical Encyclopedia. David Crystal, ed. Cambridge: Cambridge University Press, 1998.

Current Biography Yearbook. New York: H. W. Wilson, 1940– .

Dictionary of National Biography. Leslie Stephen and Sidney Lee, eds. 66 vols., with supplementary volumes through 1986–90 published by Oxford University Press. London: Smith, Elder, 1885–1901.

Literary Biographical Sources: General

Cyclopedia of World Authors. 3rd rev. ed. Frank N. Magill, ed. 5 vols. Pasadena, Calif.: Salem Press, 1997.

Dictionary of Literary Biography. Detroit: Gale, 1978– . This major series publishes bio-bibliographical, critical, and documentary essays on a wide range of writers and literary movements. Each volume in the series treats a distinct author, subject, or period, from the first volume, *The American Renaissance in New England* (1978), through such recent titles as *Twentieth-Century Eastern European Writers. Second Series* (2000). Complementary Gale series include the *Dictionary of Literary Biography Documentary Series* (1982–) and the *Dictionary of Literary Biography Yearbook* (1981–), which covers the year's literary highlights and also includes revised and updated entries from earlier volumes of the *Dictionary of Literary Biography*.

Everyman's Dictionary of Literary Biography, English & American. Rev. ed., with supplement. John W. Cousin and D. C. Browning, comps. New York: Dutton, 1970.

Nobel Laureates in Literature: A Biographical Dictionary. Rado Pribic, ed. New York: Garland, 1990.

CONTEMPORARY

Contemporary Authors. Detroit: Gale, 1962– . A bio-bibliographical guide to current writers in fiction, non-fiction, poetry, journalism, drama, motion pictures, television, and other fields. Revised and updated author entries from the earlier volumes in this series can be found in Gale's *Contemporary Authors. New Revision Series* (1981–). A complementary series is Gale's *Contemporary Authors. Autobiographical Series* (1984–), which reprints autobiographical writings by authors of note.

Contemporary Popular Writers. Dave Mote, ed. Detroit: St. James Press, 1996.

Contemporary World Writers. 2nd ed. Tracy Chevalier, ed. Detroit: St. James Press, 1993.

Literary Exile in the Twentieth Century: An Analysis and Biographical Dictionary. Martin Tucker, ed. New York: Greenwood Press, 1991.

Literary Journalism: A Biographical Dictionary of Writers and Editors. Edd Applegate. Westport, Conn.: Greenwood Press, 1996.

200 Contemporary Authors: Bio-bibliographies of Selected Leading Writers of Today with Critical and Personal Sidelights. Barbara Harte and Carolyn Riley, eds. Detroit: Gale, 1969.

World Authors, 1900–1950. Martin Seymour-Smith and Andrew Kimmens, eds. 4 vols. New York: H. W. Wilson, 1996. An expanded and revised version of the classic but now out-of-date *Twentieth Century Authors: A Biographical Dictionary of Modern Literature*, Stanley J. Kunitz and Howard Haycraft, eds. (1942). Wilson followed *Twentieth Century Authors* with a number of supplementary volumes providing biographical sketches of additional authors, including: *World Authors, 1950–1970* (1975), *World Authors, 1970–1975* (1980), *World Authors, 1975–1980* (1985), *World Authors, 1980–1985* (1991), and *World Authors, 1985–1990* (1995).

HISTORICAL

Ancient Greek Authors. Ward W. Briggs, ed. Detroit: Gale, 1997. (Vol. 176 of the *Dictionary of Literary Biography*.)

Ancient Roman Authors. Ward W. Briggs, ed. Detroit: Gale, 1999. (Vol. 211 of the *Dictionary of Literary Biography*.)

Greek and Latin Authors, 800 B.C.–A.D. 1000: A Biographical Dictionary. Michael Grant. New York: H. W. Wilson, 1980.

Literary Biographical Sources: By Nationality or Ethnicity

AMERICAN

American Authors, 1600–1900: A Biographical Dictionary of American Literature. Stanley J. Kunitz and Howard Haycraft. New York: H. W. Wilson, 1966. Reprint of the 1938 edition.

American Diversity, American Identity: The Lives and Works of 145 Writers Who Define the American Experience. John K. Roth, ed. New York: Henry Holt, 1995.

American Dramatists. Matthew C. Roudané, ed. Detroit: Gale, 1989. (*Contemporary Authors Bibliographical Series*, vol. 3.)

American Nature Writers. John Elder, ed. 2 vols. New York: Charles Scribner's Sons, 1996.

American Novelists. James J. Martine, ed. Detroit: Gale, 1986. (*Contemporary Authors Bibliographical Series*, vol. 1.)

American Poets. Ronald Baughman, ed. Detroit: Gale, 1986. (*Contemporary Authors Bibliographical Series*, vol. 2.)

American Writers: A Collection of Literary Biographies. Leonard Unger, ed. 4 vols., with supplements. New York: Charles Scribner's Sons, 1974–79.

American Writers Before 1800: A Biographical and Critical Dictionary. James A. Levernier and Douglas R. Wilmes, eds. 3 vols. Westport, Conn.: Greenwood Press, 1983.

Biographical Dictionary of Contemporary Catholic American Writing. Daniel J. Tynan, ed. New York: Greenwood Press, 1989.

Concise Dictionary of American Literary Biography. 7 vols. Detroit: Gale, 1987–99.

Who's Who of Pulitzer Prize Winners. Elizabeth A. Brennan and Elizabeth C. Clarage. Phoenix, Ariz.: Oryx, 1999.

[See also relevant volumes of the *Dictionary of Literary Biography*, including, for example, vol. 11, *American Humorists, 1800–1950*; vol. 7, *Twentieth-Century American Dramatists*; and vol. 16, *The Beats: Literary Bohemians in Postwar America*.]

African-American Writers

African American Women Playwrights: A Research Guide. Christy Gavin, ed. New York: Garland, 1999.

African American Writers. Valerie Smith, ed. New York: Charles Scribner's Sons, 2000.

African-American Writers: A Dictionary. Shari Dorantes Hatch and Michael R. Strickland, eds. Santa Barbara, Calif.: ABC-CLIO, 2000.

Contemporary Black American Playwrights and Their Plays: A Biographical Directory and Dramatic Index. Bernard L. Peterson. New York: Greenwood Press, 1988.

Early Black American Playwrights and Dramatic Writers: A Biographical Directory and Catalog of Plays, Films, and Broadcasting Scripts. Bernard L. Peterson. New York: Greenwood Press, 1990.

The Harlem Renaissance and Beyond: Literary Biographies of 100 Black Women Writers, 1900–1945. Lorraine Elena Roses and Ruth Elizabeth Randolph. Boston: G. K. Hall, 1990.

Asian-American Writers

Asian American Novelists: A Bio-bibliographical Critical Sourcebook. Emmanuel S. Nelson, ed. Westport, Conn.: Greenwood Press, 2000.

Jewish-American Writers

Contemporary Jewish-American Dramatists and Poets: A Bio-critical Sourcebook. Joel Shatzky and Michael Taub, eds. Westport, Conn.: Greenwood Press, 1999.

Contemporary Jewish-American Novelists: A Bio-critical Sourcebook. Joel Shatzky and Michael Taub, eds. Westport, Conn.: Greenwood Press, 1997.

Native-American Writers

Contemporary Native American Authors: A Biographical Dictionary. Kay Juricek and Kelly J. Morgan. Golden, Colo.: Fulcrum, 1997.

Native North American Literature: Biographical and Critical Information on Native Writers and Orators from the United States and Canada from Historical Times to the Present. Janet Witalec, ed. New York: Gale, 1994.

American Regional Writers

Biographical Dictionary of Transcendentalism. Wesley T. Mott, ed. Westport, Conn.: Greenwood Press, 1996.

Contemporary Fiction Writers of the South: A Bio-bibliographical Sourcebook. Joseph M. Flora and Robert Bain, eds. Westport, Conn.: Greenwood Press, 1993.

Contemporary Poets, Dramatists, Essayists, and Novelists of the South: A Bio-bibliographical Sourcebook. Robert Bain and Joseph M. Flora, eds. Westport, Conn.: Greenwood Press, 1994.

Contemporary Southern Writers. Robert Matuz, ed. Detroit: St. James Press, 1999.

American Women Writers

American Women Writers: A Critical Reference Guide: From Colonial Times to the Present. 2nd ed. Taryn Benbow-Pfalzgraf, ed. Detroit: St. James Press, 2000.

Modern American Women Writers. Lea Baechler and A. Walton Litz, eds. New York: Charles Scribner's Sons, 1991.

SPANISH AMERICAN, LATIN AMERICAN, AND CARIBBEAN

Biographical Dictionary of Hispanic Literature in the United States: The Literature of Puerto Ricans, Cuban Americans, and Other Hispanic Writers. Nicolás Kanellos. New York: Greenwood Press, 1989.

A Dictionary of Contemporary Latin American Authors. David William Foster, comp. Tempe: Center for Latin American Authors, Arizona State University, 1975.

Fifty Caribbean Writers: A Bio-bibliographical Critical Sourcebook. Daryl Cumber Dance. Westport, Conn.: Greenwood Press, 1986.

Hispanic Writers: A Selection of Sketches from Contemporary Authors. Bryan Ryan, ed. Detroit: Gale, 1991.

Jewish Writers of Latin America: A Dictionary. New York: Garland, 1997.

Latin American Literature in the 20th Century: A Guide. New York: Frederick Ungar, 1986.

Latin American Writers. Carlos A. Solé, ed. 2 vols. New York: Charles Scribner's Sons, 1989.

Spanish American Authors: The Twentieth Century. Angel Flores. New York: H. W. Wilson, 1992.

[See also relevant volumes of the *Dictionary of Literary Biography,* including, for example, vols. 113 and 145, *Modern Latin-American Fiction Writers, First Series* and *Second Series.*]

BRITISH AND IRISH

A Biographical Dictionary of English Women Writers, 1580–1720. Maureen Bell, George Parfitt, and Simon Shepherd. Boston: G. K. Hall, 1990.

Biographical Dictionary of Irish Writers. Anne M. Brady and Brian Cleeve, eds. Westmeath, Ireland: Lilliput Press, 1985.

A Biographical Dictionary of Renaissance Poets and Dramatists, 1520–1650. J. W. Saunders. Totowa, N.J.: Barnes & Noble, 1983.

British Authors Before 1800: A Biographical Dictionary. Stanley J. Kunitz and Howard Haycraft, eds. New York: H. W. Wilson, 1952.

British Authors of the Nineteenth Century. Stanley J. Kunitz, ed. New York: H. W. Wilson, 1964. Reprint of the 1936 edition.

British Women Writers: A Critical Reference Guide. Janet Todd, ed. New York: Continuum, 1989.

British Writers. Ian Scott-Kilvert, ed. 7 vols. New York: Charles Scribner's Sons, 1979–84. With *Supplements* in 6 vols., vol. 5 of which includes a cumulative index for *British Writers,* 1–7, and *Supplements,* 1–5.

Concise Dictionary of British Literary Biography. 8 vols. Detroit: Gale, 1991–92.

An Encyclopedia of British Women Writers. Paul and June Schlueter, eds. New Brunswick, N.J.: Rutgers University Press, 1998.

Modern Irish Writers: A Bio-critical Sourcebook. Alexander G. Gonzalez, ed. Westport, Conn.: Greenwood Press, 1997.

[See also relevant volumes of the *Dictionary of Literary Biography,* including, for example, vol. 21, *Victorian Novelists Before 1885;* vol. 19, *British Poets, 1880–1914;* and vol. 10, *Modern British Dramatists, 1900–1945.*]

CANADIAN

Canada's Playwrights: A Biographical Guide. Don Rubin and Allison Cranmer-Byng. Downsview, Ontario: Canadian Theatre Review Publications, 1980.

ECW's Biographical Guide to Canadian Novelists. Toronto: ECW Press, 1993.

ECW's Biographical Guide to Canadian Poets. Toronto: ECW Press, 1993.

EUROPEAN

A Companion to Twentieth-Century German Literature. Raymond Furness and Malcolm Humble. New York: Routledge, 1997.

European Authors, 1000–1900: A Biographical Dictionary of European Literature. Stanley J. Kunitz and Vineta Colby, eds. New York: H. W. Wilson, 1967.

European Writers. William T. H. Jackson and George Stade, eds. 14 vols. New York: Charles Scribner's Sons, 1983–91.

Spanish Women Writers: A Bio-bibliographical Source Book. Linda Gould Levine, Ellen Engelson Marson, and Gloria Feiman Walman, eds. Westport, Conn.: Greenwood Press, 1993.

[See also relevant volumes of the *Dictionary of Literary Biography*, including, for example, vol. 90, *German Writers in the Age of Goethe, 1789–1832*; vol. 56, *German Fiction Writers, 1914–1945*; vol. 192, *French Dramatists, 1789–1914*; vol. 217, *Nineteenth-century French Poets*; vols. 215 and 220, *Twentieth-century Eastern European Writers, First Series* and *Second Series*.]

AFRICAN

African Authors: A Companion to Black African Writing, 1300–1973. Donald E. Herdeck. Washington, D.C.: Black Orpheus Press, 1973.

African Writers. C. Brian Cox, ed. 2 vols. New York: Charles Scribner's Sons, 1997.

Postcolonial African Writers: A Bio-bibliographical Critical Sourcebook. Pushpa Naidu Parekh and Siga Fatima Jagne, eds. Westport, Conn.: Greenwood Press, 1998.

Who's Who in African Literature: Biographies, Works, Commentaries. Janheinz Jahn, Ulla Schild, and Almut Nordmann. Tübingen, Germany: H. Erdmann, 1972.

[See also relevant volumes of the *Dictionary of Literary Biography*, including, for example, vol. 225, *South African Writers*; and vols. 117, 125, and 157, *Twentieth-Century Caribbean and Black African Writers, First Series, Second Series*, and *Third Series*.]

JAPANESE

Biographical Dictionary of Japanese Literature. Sen'ichi Hisamatsu. Tokyo: Kodansha International, 1977.

Japanese Women Novelists of the 20th Century: 104 Biographies, 1900–1993. Sachiko Schierbeck. Copenhagen, Denmark: Museum Tusculanum Press; University of Copenhagen, 1994.

Japanese Women Writers: A Bio-critical Sourcebook. Chieko I. Mulhern, ed. Westport, Conn.: Greenwood Press, 1994.

Modern Japanese Novelists: A Biographical Dictionary. John Lewell. Tokyo: Kodansha International, 1993.

BLACK WRITERS — INTERNATIONAL

Black Writers: A Selection of Sketches from Contemporary Authors. 3rd ed. Detroit: Gale, 1999.

The Schomburg Center Guide to Black Literature from the Eighteenth Century to the Present. Roger M. Valade III, ed. Detroit: Gale, 1995.

Selected Black American, African, and Caribbean Authors: A Bio-Bibliography. James A. Page and Jae Min Roh. Littleton, Colo.: Libraries Unlimited, 1985.

Twentieth-Century Caribbean and Black African Writers. First Series, Second Series, Third Series. Bernth Lindfors and Reinhard Sander, eds. Detroit: Gale, 1992–96. [Vols. 117, 125, and 157 of the *Dictionary of Literary Biography*.]

WOMEN WRITERS — INTERNATIONAL

A Dictionary of British and American Women Writers, 1660–1800. Janet Todd, ed. Totowa, N.J.: Rowman & Allanheld, 1985.

Great Women Writers: The Lives and Works of 135 of the World's Most Important Women Writers, from Antiquity to the Present. Frank N. Magill, ed. New York: Henry Holt, 1994.

Women Writers of Great Britain and Europe: An Encyclopedia. Katharina M. Wilson, Paul Schlueter, and June Schlueter, eds. New York: Garland, 1997.

2 NOTABLE BIOGRAPHICAL WORKS

Autobiographies, Memoirs, Diaries, Letters

Aciman, André, *Out of Egypt: A Memoir*

Ackerley, J. R., *My Father and Myself*

Adams, Henry, *The Education of Henry Adams*

Amis, Martin, *Experience: A Memoir*

Angelou, Maya, *I Know Why the Caged Bird Sings*

Arenas, Reinaldo, *Before Night Falls*

Baker, Russell, *Growing Up*

Baldwin, James, *Notes of a Native Son* and *The Price of the Ticket*

Baraka, Amiri, *The Autobiography of LeRoi Jones*

Beauvoir, Simone de, *Memoirs of a Dutiful Daughter, The Prime of Life, Force of Circumstance,* and *All Said and Done*

Behan, Brendan, *Borstal Boy*

Bennett, Alan, *Writing Home*

Berberova, Nina, *The Italics Are Mine*

Brodkey, Harold, *This Wild Darkness: The Story of My Death*

Burgess, Anthony, *Little Wilson and Big God*

Byron, George Gordon, Lord, *The Letters of Lord Byron*

Canetti, Elias, *The Tongue Set Free, The Torch in My Ear,* and *The Play of the Eyes*

Christie, Agatha, *An Autobiography*

Coetzee, J. M., *Boyhood: Scenes from Provincial Life*

Connolly, Cyril, *Enemies of Promise*

Cowley, Malcolm, *Exile's Return* and *The Dream of the Golden Mountains: Remembering the 1930s*

Dillard, Annie, *Pilgrim at Tinker Creek*

Dinesen, Isak, *Out of Africa*

Flaubert, Gustave, *Letters* (2 volumes), ed. by Francis Steegmuller

Frame, Janet, *To the Is-Land, An Angel at My Table,* and *The Envoy from Mirror City*

Gide, André, *If It Die*

Ginzburg, Natalia, *Family Sayings* (also published as *The Things We Used to Say*)

Gorky, Maxim, *My Childhood, My Apprenticeship,* and *My Universities*

Gosse, Edmund, *Father and Son*

Graves, Robert, *Goodbye to All That*

Green, Henry, *Pack My Bag: A Self-Portrait*

Hardy, Thomas, *The Life and Work of Thomas Hardy,* ed. by Michael Millgate

Hazzard, Shirley, *Greene on Capri: A Memoir*

Hellman, Lillian, *Pentimento, An Unfinished Woman,* and *Scoundrel Time*

Holmes, Richard, *Footsteps: Adventures of a Romantic Biographer* and *Sidetracks: Explorations of a Romantic Biographer*

Howard, Maureen, *Facts of Life*

Hurston, Zora Neale, *Dust Tracks on a Road*

Isherwood, Christopher, *Christopher and His Kind, 1929–1939*

James, Henry, *A Small Boy and Others, Notes of a Son and Brother, The Middle Years,* and *Henry James: A Life in Letters*

Kazin, Alfred, *A Walker in the City, New York Jew, Starting Out in the Thirties,* and *Writing Was Everything*

Kingston, Maxine Hong, *The Woman Warrior: Memoirs of a Girlhood Among Ghosts*

Lawrence, Frieda, *"Not I, but the Wind…"*

Lawrence, T. E., *The Seven Pillars of Wisdom*

Lee, Laurie, *Cider with Rosie* and *As I Walked Out One Midsummer Morning*

Levi, Carlo, *Christ Stopped at Eboli: The Story of a Year*

Levi, Primo, *If This Is a Man, The Periodic Table,* and *The Drowned and the Saved*

McCarthy, Mary, *How I Grew, Memories of a Catholic Girlhood,* and *Intellectual Memoirs: New York 1936–1938*

McCourt, Frank, *Angela's Ashes*

Mehta, Ved, *Daddyji and Mammaji*, *Vedi*, *The Stolen Light*, and *Up at Oxford*

Mencken, H. L., *My Life as Author and Editor*

Merrill, James, *A Different Person*

Miller, Arthur, *Timebends*

Moore, George, *Hail and Farewell...*

Moravia, Alberto, *Life of Moravia*

Mortimer, John, *Clinging to the Wreckage*

Nabokov, Vladimir, *Speak, Memory*

Orwell, George, *Such, Such Were the Joys*

Osborne, John, *A Better Class of Person: An Autobiography 1929–1959*

Pepys, Samuel, *The Diary of Samuel Pepys* or *The Shorter Pepys*

Pritchett, V. S., *A Cab at the Door: An Autobiography: Early Years* and *Midnight Oil*

Pym, Barbara, *A Very Private Eye*

Roth, Philip, *Patrimony* and *The Facts: A Novelist's Autobiography*

Rousseau, Jean-Jacques, *Confessions*

Saint-Simon, Duc de, *Memoirs*

Sartre, Jean-Paul, *The Words*

Simenon, Georges, *Intimate Memoirs*

Spark, Muriel, *Curriculum Vitae: Autobiography*

Spender, Stephen, *World Within World: Autobiography*

Stein, Gertrude, *The Autobiography of Alice B. Toklas* and *Everybody's Autobiography*

Steinbeck, John, *Travels with Charley*

Styron, William, *Darkness Visible: A Memoir of Madness*

Theroux, Paul, *Sir Vidia's Shadow: A Friendship Across Five Continents*

Thurber, James, *The Years with Ross*

Tolstoy, Leo, *Childhood, Boyhood, and Youth*

Trilling, Diana, *The Beginning of the Journey: The Marriage of Diana and Lionel Trilling*

Twain, Mark, *Autobiography*

Updike, John, *Self-Consciousness*

Vidal, Gore, *Palimpsest*

Waugh, Evelyn, *The Letters*, *The Diaries*, and *A Little Learning*

Welty, Eudora, *One Writer's Beginnings*

Wilson, Edmund, *The Twenties*, *The Thirties*, *The Forties*, *The Fifties*, and *The Sixties*

Wodehouse, P. G., *Wodehouse on Wodehouse* (comprising *Performing Flea*, *Bring on the Girls*, and *Over Seventy*)

Wolff, Kurt, *Kurt Wolff: A Portrait in Essays and Letters*

Wolff, Tobias, *This Boy's Life*

Woolf, Virginia, *Diaries* and *Letters*

Wordsworth, Dorothy, *Journals* and *Letters*

Wright, Richard, *Black Boy*

Yeats, William Butler, *Autobiographies*

Zweig, Stefan, *The World of Yesterday: An Autobiography*

Biographies

Ackroyd, Peter, *Blake*

Ackroyd, Peter, *Dickens*

Ackroyd, Peter, *T. S. Eliot*

Alpers, Antony, *The Life of Katherine Mansfield*

Annan, Noel, *Leslie Stephen: The Godless Victorian*

Atlas, James, *Bellow: A Biography*

Backscheider, Paula, *Daniel Defoe: His Life*

Bair, Deirdre, *Simone de Beauvoir*

Baker, Carlos, *Ernest Hemingway: A Life Story*

Barker, Juliet, *The Brontës*

Barnes, Christopher, *Boris Pasternak: A Literary Biography*

Bate, Walter Jackson, *John Keats*

Bate, Walter Jackson, *Samuel Johnson*

Bayley, John, *Elegy for Iris*

Bell, Quentin, *Virginia Woolf 1882–1941*

Berg, A. Scott, *Max Perkins: Editor of Genius*

Boswell, James, *Life of Johnson*

Boyd, Brian, *Vladimir Nabokov: The American Years* and *Vladimir Nabokov: The Russian Years*

Boyle, Nicholas, *Goethe: The Poet and the Age*

Bruccoli, Matthew J., *Some Sort of Epic Grandeur: The Life of F. Scott Fitzgerald*

Bulgakov, Mikhail, *Molière: Life of Monsieur de Molière*

Burke, Carolyn, *Becoming Modern: The Life of Mina Loy*

The Cambridge Biography of D. H. Lawrence: Worthen, John, *D. H. Lawrence, the Early Years, 1885–1912*; Kinkead-Weekes, Mark, *D. H. Lawrence, Triumph to Exile, 1912–1922*; Ellis, David, *D. H. Lawrence, Dying Game, 1922–1930*

Carpenter, Humphrey, *A Serious Character: The Life of Ezra Pound*

Carpenter, Humphrey, *W. H. Auden: A Biography*

Cohen, Morton, *Lewis Carroll: A Biography*

Crick, Bernard, *George Orwell: A Life*

Davenport-Hines, Richard, *Auden*

Davis, Linda H., *Badge of Courage: The Life of Stephen Crane*

Dearborn, Mary V., *The Happiest Man Alive: A Biography of Henry Miller*

Donald, David Herbert, *Look Homeward: A Life of Thomas Wolfe*

Duddon, F. Homes, *Fielding: His Life, Works and Times*

Edel, Leon, *The Life of Henry James*

Ehrenpreis, Irwin, *Swift: The Man, His Works and the Age*

Ellmann, Richard, *James Joyce*

Ellmann, Richard, *Oscar Wilde*

Ellmann, Richard, *Yeats: The Man and His Masks*

Feinstein, Elaine, *A Captive Lion: The Life of Marina Tsvetayeva*

Foster, R. F., *W. B. Yeats: A Life*

Frank, Elizabeth, *Louise Bogan: A Portrait*

Frank, Joseph, *Dostoevsky* (3 volumes: *The Seeds of Revolt 1821–1849*, *The Years of Ordeal 1850–1859*, *The Stir of Liberation 1860–1865*)

Furbank, P. N., *E. M. Forster: A Life*

Gaskell, Elizabeth, *The Life of Charlotte Brontë*

Gibson, Ian, *Federico García Lorca: A Life*

Gill, Stephen, *William Wordsworth: A Life*

Glendinning, Victoria, *Edith Sitwell: A Unicorn Among the Lions*

Glendinning, Victoria, *Trollope*

Gooch, Brad, *City Poet: The Life and Times of Frank O'Hara*

Gordon, Lyndall, *Charlotte Brontë: A Passionate Life*

Gordon, Lyndall, *Eliot's Early Years*

Gorky, Maxim, *Reminiscences of Leo Nikolayevitch Tolstoy*

Haight, Gordon, *George Eliot*

Hamilton, Nigel, *The Brothers Mann*

Harding, Walter, *The Days of Henry David Thoreau*

Hardwick, Elizabeth, *Herman Melville*

Hastings, Selina, *Evelyn Waugh: A Biography*

Hedrick, Joan D., *Harriet Beecher Stowe*

Hemenway, Robert E., *Zora Neale Hurston: A Literary Biography*

Holden, Anthony, *William Shakespeare*

Holmes, Richard, *Coleridge: Early Visions, 1772–1804* and *Coleridge: Darker Reflections, 1804–1834*

Holmes, Richard, *Dr. Johnson & Mr. Savage*

Holmes, Richard, *Shelley: The Pursuit*

Holroyd, Michael, *Bernard Shaw* (Vol. 1: *The Search for Love*, Vol. 2: *The Pursuit of Power*)

Holroyd, Michael, *Lytton Strachey: A Biography*

Honan, Park, *Jane Austen: Her Life*

Honan, Park, *Shakespeare: A Life*

Hughes, Kathryn, *George Eliot: The Last Victorian*

Johnson, Edgar, *Charles Dickens, His Tragedy and Triumph*

Johnson, Samuel, *Lives of the English Poets*

Kaplan, Fred, *Dickens: A Biography*

Kaplan, Justin, *Mr. Clemens and Mark Twain*

Karl, Frederick R., *Joseph Conrad: The Three Lives*

Karl, Frederick R., *William Faulkner: American Writer*

Keats, John, *You Might As Well Live: The Life and Times of Dorothy Parker*

Kennedy, Richard S., *Dreams in the Mirror: A Biography of E. E. Cummings*

Kent, George E., *A Life of Gwendolyn Brooks*

Kunkel, Thomas, *Genius in Disguise: Harold Ross of The New Yorker*

Lahr, John, *Prick Up Your Ears: The Biography of Joe Orton*

Lee, Hermione, *Virginia Woolf*

Lee, Hermione, *Willa Cather: Double Lives*

Leeming, David, *James Baldwin: A Biography*

Lewis, Jeremy, *Cyril Connolly: A Life*

Lewis, R.W.B., *Edith Wharton: A Biography*

Mack, Maynard, *Alexander Pope: A Life*

Malcolm, Janet, *The Silent Woman: Sylvia Plath and Ted Hughes*

Mandelshtam, Nadezhda, *Hope Abandoned* and *Hope Against Hope*

Marchand, Leslie Alexis, *Byron: A Biography*

Mariani, Paul, *Lost Puritan: A Life of Robert Lowell*

Marnham, Patrick, *The Man Who Wasn't Maigret: A Portrait of Georges Simenon*

Maurois, André, *Byron*

Maurois, André, *Prometheus: The Life of Balzac*

Mellen, Joan, *Hellman and Hammett: The Legendary Passion of Lillian Hellman and Dashiell Hammett*

Middlebrook, Diane Wood, *Anne Sexton: A Biography*

Miller, Edwin Haviland, *Salem Is My Dwelling Place: A Life of Nathaniel Hawthorne*

Mitford, Nancy, *Voltaire in Love*

Molesworth, Charles, *Marianne Moore: A Literary Life*

Monsarrat, Ann, *An Uneasy Victorian: Thackeray the Man*

Motion, Andrew, *Phillip Larkin: A Writer's Life*

Nicholl, Charles, *Somebody Else: Arthur Rimbaud in Africa 1880–91*

O'Brien, Edna, *James Joyce*

Origo, Iris, *Leopardi*

Painter, George D., *Marcel Proust*

Parker, Hershel, *Herman Melville: A Biography*

Pawel, Ernst, *The Nightmare of Reason: A Life of Franz Kafka*

Pearson, Hesketh, *Conan Doyle*

Pichois, Claude, *Baudelaire*

Polito, Robert, *Savage Art: A Biography of Jim Thompson*

Polizzoti, Mark, *Revolution of the Mind: The Life of André Breton*

Pritchard, William H., *Randall Jarrell: A Literary Life*

Pritchett, V. S., *Chekhov: A Spirit Set Free*

Pritchett, V. S., *The Gentle Barbarian: The Life and Work of Turgenev*

Rampersad, Arnold, *Life of Langston Hughes*

Rayfield, Donald, *Anton Chekhov: A Life*

Reeder, Roberta, *Anna Akhmatova: Poet and Prophet*

Reynolds, David S., *Walt Whitman's America: A Cultural Biography*

Robb, Graham, *Balzac: A Biography*

Robb, Graham, *Victor Hugo*

Rusk, Ralph L., *The Life of Ralph Waldo Emerson*

Samuels, Ernest, *Henry Adams*

Scammel, Michael, *Solzhenitsyn*

Schiff, Stacy, *Saint Exupéry: A Biography*

Schoenbaum, S., *William Shakespeare: A Compact Documentary Life*

Scott, Geoffrey, *The Portrait of Zélide*

Scott-Stokes, Henry, *The Life and Death of Yukio Mishima*

Scribner, Charles, Jr., *In the Company of Writers: A Life in Publishing*

Sewall, Richard B., *The Life of Emily Dickinson*

Shakespeare, Nicholas, *Chatwin*

Sheaffer, Louis, *O'Neill, Son and Artist*

Sherry, Norman, *The Life of Graham Greene*

Silverman, Kenneth, *Edgar A. Poe: Mournful and Never-Ending Remembrance*

Spark, Muriel, *Mary Shelley*

Spoto, Donald, *The Kindness of Strangers: The Life of Tennessee Williams*

Steegmuller, Francis, *Apollinaire: Poet Among the Painters*

Steegmuller, Francis, *Cocteau: A Biography*

Stern, Madeleine, *Louisa May Alcott*

Stevenson, Anne, *Bitter Fame: A Life of Sylvia Plath*

Symons, A.J.A., *The Quest for Corvo*

Thompson, Lawrence, *Robert Frost*

Thurman, Judith, *Isak Dinesen: The Life of a Storyteller*

Thurman, Judith, *Secrets of the Flesh: A Life of Colette*

Tomalin, Claire, *Jane Austen: A Life*

Tomalin, Claire, *Katherine Mansfield: A Secret Life*

Treglown, Jeremy, *Romancing: The Life and Work of Henry Green*

Trelawny, Edward, *Records of Shelley, Byron, and the Author*

Troyat, Henri, *Tolstoy*

Turkov, Andrei, ed., *Anton Chekhov and His Times*

Tynan, Kathleen, *The Life of Kenneth Tynan*

Vitale, Serena, *Pushkin's Button*

Ward, Aileen, *John Keats: The Making of a Poet*

Warner, Sylvia Townsend, *T. H. White: A Biography*

West, James L. W., III, *William Styron*

White, Edmund, *Genet*

Wilson, A. N., *The Life of John Milton*

Wilson, A. N., *Tolstoy*

Wilson, Angus, *The Strange Ride of Rudyard Kipling*

Wineapple, Brenda, *Genêt, a Biography of Janet Flanner*

Woodress, James, *Willa Cather: A Literary Life*

Wreszin, Michael, *A Rebel in Defense of Tradition: The Life And Politics of Dwight Macdonald*

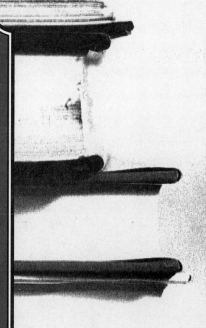

WORKS

OF

LITERATURE

Works of Literature

Novels, Plays, Poems, Stories, Essays

Aaron's Rod (1922). An autobiographical novel by D. H. LAWRENCE, the title of which alludes to the biblical story of Aaron, the brother of MOSES, and refers to the flute played by the protagonist, Aaron Sisson.

Absalom, Absalom! (1936). A novel by William FAULKNER, marked by stream-of-consciousness dialogue and Faulkner's vision of a doomed South, that follows the misfortunes of the SUTPEN family from the Civil War to the early 20th century.

Adam Bede (1859). The first novel by GEORGE ELIOT. Although Adam BEDE courts the self-centered Hetty Sorrel, she chooses Arthur Donnithorne, who leaves her pregnant and alone. The unfortunate Hetty is convicted of killing her baby, while Adam marries Dinah Morris, a preacher.

"Adonais" (1821). A poem by PERCY BYSSHE SHELLEY, a lament on the death of Shelley's fellow poet John KEATS. The title is a reference to Adonis, the hero of Greek mythology.

Adventures of Augie March, The (1953). A National Book Award–winning novel by Saul BELLOW. A "larky and boisterous" Jewish-American youngster growing up in Depression-era Chicago, Augie MARCH lives through a series of alternately funny and tragic experiences while encountering a variety of extraordinary characters, as he quests after a "worthwhile fate." His adventures continue in Canada, Mexico, the African Sea, and Europe.

Adventures of Sherlock Holmes, The (1892). A collection of detective stories by Sir Arthur Conan DOYLE, including "The Red-Headed League," "A Scandal in Bohemia," and "The Adventure of the Speckled Band." The stories featuring the methodical pipesmoking Sherlock HOLMES and his partner Dr. WATSON first appeared in *The Strand* magazine in 1891–92, following the success of the first two novels starring Holmes (*A Study in Scarlet*, 1887; *The Sign of Four*, 1890). Two more novels and three more story collections followed, concluding with *The Case Book of Sherlock Holmes* (1927). Among the many stage, screen, and television adaptations of the Holmes stories and novels are the 1899 play by American actor William Gillette, which was revived successfully by the Royal Shakespeare Company in London and New York in the 1970s; a series of 14 films starring Basil Rathbone and Nigel Bruce, beginning with *The Hound of the Baskervilles* (1939) and ending with *Dressed to Kill* (1946); several British television series starring Jeremy Brett in the 1980s and 1990s; and even a Broadway musical, *Baker Street* (1965).

Aeneid, The (*Aeneis*, c. 29–19 B.C.). An epic poem in 12 books by the Roman poet VIRGIL about the founding of Rome, a landmark of Western literature. Major characters are AENEAS, prince of defeated Troy; his son, Ascanius; DIDO, queen of Carthage; Latinus, king of Latium; and his daughter, Lavinia.

Aesop's Fables (*Aisopou Mythoi*, c. 6th century B.C.; also known as *Fables of Aesop*). The conventional name for a group of around 200 brief allegories that point a moral, often representing animals in human situations, traditionally ascribed to AESOP. Whether or not a Greek fabulist by this name actually existed, these works effectively established the fable genre in the Western tradition. Pioneer English printer William CAXTON's translation (1484) was the first of countless English-language versions and adaptations. Perennial favorites include "The Wolf in Sheep's Clothing" and "The Tortoise and the Hare."

After the Fall (1964). A play by ARTHUR MILLER, with autobiographical overtones, that explores the idealism of 1930s leftists and the disillusionment that followed in its wake. The character of Maggie is based on Miller's ex-wife, actress Marilyn Monroe.

Against the Grain (À *Rebours*, 1884). A novel by Joris-Karl HUYSMANS about a wealthy but neurasthenic French nobleman, Des Esseintes, who goes "against the grain" of conventional morality by indulging in refined sensualism. Admired by Oscar WILDE, it was a key text of the *fin-de-siècle* Decadent movement.

Agamemnon. *See* Oresteia

Age of Anxiety, The (1947). A long narrative poem by W. H. AUDEN that follows four strangers who meet in a bar in New York during World War II. A meditation on the spiritual emptiness of modern life, it won the Pulitzer Prize for poetry.

Age of Innocence, The (1920). A Pulitzer Prize–winning novel by Edith WHARTON, an acerbic exploration of the manners and mores of wealthy turn-of-the-century New Yorkers. The conflict centers on Newland Archer, who marries May Welland but struggles with an unconsummated passion for his wife's more worldly, unconventional cousin, Ellen OLENSKA.

Age of Reason, The (*L'Âge de Raison*, 1945). A novel by Jean-Paul SARTRE, whose main character is Mathieu, a man obsessed with discovering the nature of ethical freedom. Meant as the first of a four-book project called *Roads to Freedom* (*Les Chemins de la Liberté*), it was followed by only two subsequent volumes, *The Reprieve* (*Le Sursis*, 1945) and *Troubled Sleep* (*La Mort dans l'Âme*, 1949).

Ah, Wilderness! (1933). A play by Eugene O'NEILL, the author's only comedy, set in a small New England town. Called by the author "a comedy of recollection," it takes its title from the *RUBÁIYÁT* of 'OMAR KHAYYÁM. (For adaptations, see Variations.)

Alexandria Quartet, The (1957–60). Four novels—*Justine* (1957), *Balthazar* (1958), *Mountolive* (1958), and *Clea* (1960)—that form a single, intertwined work by Lawrence DURRELL. The four works tell the same story from four different points of view. The book is named for Alexandria, Egypt, a city whose decayed cosmopolitanism attracted Durrell.

Alice's Adventures in Wonderland (1865). A novel by Lewis CARROLL relating the story of Alice and her descent down a rabbit hole into a world of nonsense and fantasy. Originally written as a gift for a young girl, Alice Liddell, this work has become a classic of English literature. Alice's adventures continue in *THROUGH THE LOOKING-GLASS*.

All My Sons (1947). A play by ARTHUR MILLER about the unraveling of the Keller family after Chris Keller discovers that his father, Joe, knowingly sold defective airplane parts to the military and that these same parts may have played a role in the wartime death of his brother.

All Quiet on the Western Front (*Im Westen Nichts Neues*, 1929). A novel by Erich Maria REMARQUE, perhaps the most vivid and certainly the best-known book about the horrors of trench warfare in World War I. (For adaptations, see Variations.)

All's Well That Ends Well (1602). A comedy by William SHAKESPEARE, an exploration into the war of desire and wits between the sexes, focusing on HELENA and Bertram.

All the King's Men (1946). A Pulitzer Prize–winning novel by Robert Penn WARREN about the rise and fall of a demagogic Southern politician named Willie STARK, modeled on Huey Long of Louisiana. (For adaptations, see Variations.)

All the Pretty Horses. *See* Border Trilogy, The

Ambassadors, The (1903). A late-period novel by HENRY JAMES about the clash of social propriety and the individual urge for self-fulfillment. The setting is Paris and the major characters are Lambert STRETHER, Mrs. Newsome, Chad, and Mme de Vionnet.

American, The (1877). An early novel by HENRY JAMES, set in France, about the encounter between a wealthy American, Christopher Newman, and the French aristocrats he meets: American directness and simplicity meet European sophistication and subtlety, to the mutual incomprehension of all, a favorite Jamesian theme.

American Buffalo (1975). A play by David MAMET that centers on two small-time hustlers, Donny and Teach, as they plan a burglary they never carry out. Mamet's first play to reach Broadway (in 1977), it established him as a major American dramatist.

American Dream, An (1965). A novel by Norman MAILER whose central character, Stephen Rojack, a psychology professor, murders his wife.

American Dream, The (1961). A one-act play by Edward ALBEE featuring five characters—Mommy, Daddy, Grandma, Mrs. Barker, and the Young Man—who engage in occasionally absurd, often acid conversation the purpose of which is to strip bare the hypocrisy of family lies.

American Tragedy, An (1925). A novel by Theodore DREISER inspired in part by the real-life New York murder trial of Chester Gillette. The protagonist, Clyde GRIFFITHS, desperate to escape the poverty in which he was raised, is torn between two women: Roberta Alden, a factory worker, and the wealthy socialite Sondra Finchley. When Roberta becomes pregnant, he plans to drown her, with ambiguous, but tragic consequences. (For adaptations, see Variations.)

Anatomy Lesson, The (1983). A novel by PHILIP ROTH, the third in a trilogy that includes *THE GHOST WRITER* (1979) and *ZUCKERMAN UNBOUND* (1981), about novelist Nathan ZUCKERMAN, who suffers from writer's block. The title refers to a painting by Rembrandt.

Anatomy of Melancholy, The (1621). A book-length essay by Robert BURTON on what he calls the "inbred malady" of melancholy, defined as the anguish of love and religious faith.

Andersonville (1955). A Pulitzer Prize–winning novel by MacKinlay KANTOR set in the notorious American Civil War prison camp.

Angels in America: A Gay Fantasia on National Themes (1991–93). A pair of plays by Tony KUSHNER, comprising *Millennium Approaches* and *Perestroika*, that depicts the dilemmas faced by gay men in the United States at the end of the 20th century. The character of Roy Cohn is based on the right-wing lawyer and behind-the-scenes dealmaker who died of AIDS in 1986. *Millennium Approaches* won the Pulitzer Prize for drama in 1993.

Animal Farm (1945). A novel by George ORWELL satirizing Stalinist communism in the Soviet Union. Set in a barnyard, the novel describes a revolt of the animals against the farmer: the idealistic chickens and donkeys establish a stateless socialist commune, which is rapidly taken over by the cunning and ruthless pigs who set up a police state to keep the power for themselves. (For adaptations, see Variations.)

"Annabel Lee" (1849). A poem by Edgar Allan POE. In this late meditation on love and death, ANNABEL LEE, who died following an idyllic romance "many and many a year ago, / In a kingdom by the sea," still comes to the narrator's memory at night when the moon and stars evoke her "bright eyes."

Anna Christie (1921). A Pulitzer Prize–winning play by Eugene O'NEILL about Anna, a prostitute, and the melodramatic series of events that lead her to a path toward a more respectable life. (For adaptations, see Variations.)

Anna Karenina (1878). A novel by Leo TOLSTOY, one of the masterpieces of Russian literature, which begins with the famous line, "Happy families are all alike; every unhappy family is unhappy in its own way." Anna KARENINA leaves her husband and young son to live with VRONSKY, a dashing young army officer.

Shunned by society, longing for her child, and increasingly unstable, she commits suicide. (For adaptations, see Variations.)

Anna of the Five Towns (1902). A novel by Arnold BENNETT, the first of several works that deal with the people and customs of the Potteries, the area in Staffordshire where Bennett was born.

Antic Hay (1923). A novel by Aldous HUXLEY that explores the nihilistic existence of Theodore Gumbril and his bohemian friends as they stumble aimlessly through their lives in post–World War I London.

Antigone (*Antigonē*, c. 442–441 B.C.). A tragedy by SOPHOCLES in which the heroine, ANTIGONE, defies the state and buries her brother Polyneices, a traitor. She is sentenced to death and commits suicide.

Antony and Cleopatra (1607). A tragedy by William SHAKESPEARE in which the hero, Mark ANTONY, a ruler of the Roman Empire, is doomed by a tragic flaw, his passion for CLEOPATRA, queen of Egypt.

Appointment in Samarra (1934). The first, and perhaps best, novel by JOHN O'HARA, chronicling the final days of Julian English. It takes place in the fictional town of Gibbsville, Pennsylvania, a frequent setting for O'Hara's works.

Arcadia (1993). A play by Tom STOPPARD that explores the changing nature of time and truth by contrasting two different eras (the early 19th and late 20th centuries) and sets of characters.

Areopagitica (1644). A pamphlet by John MILTON. Written during the wrangling between Parliament and Charles I that preceded the Puritan revolution, this is a protest against censorship in general and censorship laws that had been passed by the Puritan Parliament in particular.

Ariel (1965). A posthumous collection of poems by Sylvia PLATH that includes many of her best-known works, such as "Daddy," "Lady Lazarus," and the title poem.

Arms and the Man (1894). A comedy by George Bernard SHAW, which takes its name from the first line of the AENEID. In Bulgaria,

then at war with Serbia, a fugitive Swiss mercenary fighting on the Serbian side becomes entangled with the fiancée of a Bulgarian officer. It served as the basis for the operetta *The Chocolate Soldier* (1909), by Oscar Straus.

Around the World in Eighty Days (*Le Tour du Monde en Quatre-vingts Jours*, 1873). An adventure novel by Jules VERNE, recounting the adventures of Phileas FOGG and his French valet Passepartout (literally, "go everywhere") as they speed around the world to win a bet. (For adaptations, see Variations.)

Arrowsmith (1925). A Pulitzer Prize–winning novel by SINCLAIR LEWIS about the career of Dr. Martin Arrowsmith, a medical researcher torn between the rigor of science and the need to help patients during an epidemic.

"Ash Wednesday" (1930). A poem by T. S. ELIOT, an exploration of religious themes, written after the poet's conversion to Anglicanism in 1927.

As I Lay Dying (1930). A novel by William FAULKNER describing the numerous trials undergone by the relatives of Addie Bundren as they try to return her rotting corpse to the fictional town of Jefferson, Mississippi, for burial.

Aspern Papers, The (1888). A novella by HENRY JAMES, inspired by the rumor that one of Lord BYRON's mistresses possessed some of the poet's letters. A researcher attempts unsuccessfully to obtain the papers of a deceased Romantic poet, Jeffrey Aspern, by scheming to manipulate the poet's now elderly former mistress, who lives in Venice. (For adaptations, see Variations.)

Assistant, The (1957). A novel by Bernard MALAMUD, set in Brooklyn and portraying the relationship between a struggling, elderly Jewish grocer and the young Italian-American petty criminal whom he hires as his assistant.

"Astrophel and Stella" (1591). A sonnet sequence, one of the greatest of the Elizabethan period, by Sir Philip SIDNEY.

As You Like It (c. 1599). A comedy by William SHAKESPEARE set in the pastoral Forest of Arden, the theme of which is summarized in its famous lines, "All the world's a stage, / And all the men and women merely players." The major characters are ORLANDO and ROSALIND.

Atala (*Atala, ou Amours de Deux Sauvages dans le Désert*, 1801). A novel by François-Auguste-René de CHATEAUBRIAND, considered a germinal work of early Romanticism. Set in North America, the story traces the life of Atala, a Christian, half-Spanish, half-American-Indian girl who falls in love with René, a Natchez man, despite her religious vow of chastity. It was revised as *Atala and René* in 1805.

Atlas Shrugged (1957). A novel by Ayn RAND elaborating in fiction her political philosophy of radical individualism, self-determination, and free enterprise (known as objectivism). The central character is Dagny Taggart.

Aurora Leigh (1857). A long poem by ELIZABETH BARRETT BROWNING, often described as a novel in verse, that narrates the life and career of its title character, who defies Victorian convention to become a successful woman poet. Widely read in its day, the poem later fell out of favor until its rediscovery in the 1970s.

Autobiography of Alice B. Toklas, The (1933). A celebrated memoir by Gertrude STEIN in which Stein slyly chronicles her own life as though from the viewpoint of her companion, Alice B. Toklas. Toklas's own account is *What Is Remembered* (1963).

Autobiography of an Ex-Colored Man, The (1912). A novel by JAMES WELDON JOHNSON, in which the mixed-race protagonist, a gifted concert pianist from Connecticut, confronts issues of racial identity. First published anonymously as if it were a genuine autobiography, the novel attracted wide attention when Johnson republished it under his own name in 1927 as an acknowledged work of fiction.

Auto-da-Fé (*Die Blendung*, 1935; also translated under the title *Tower of Babel*). A novel by Elias CANETTI, his first, that relates the descent into madness of a hermetic scholar, Peter Kien, after his wife drives him from his house and beloved library.

Awake and Sing (1935). A play by Clifford ODETS, in which Bessie Berger's relentless pursuit of bourgeois respectability for her lower-class Jewish family leads to tragedy.

Awakening, The (1899). A novel by Kate CHOPIN describing the awakening of a woman (Edna PONTELLIER) to her own desires and potential, set against the backdrop of stifling social conventions.

Babbitt (1922). A satirical novel by SINCLAIR LEWIS that follows the protagonist George Follansbee BABBITT, a dull realtor, and his pedestrian, middle-class existence in Zenith, "the Zip City"; threats of ostracism discourage his desultory attempts to change or seek wider horizons. The character's name came to represent a particular mix of the provincial and the philistine.

"Babette's Feast" (1952; published in the author's native Danish as "Babettes Gæstebud," 1958). A short story by Isak DINESEN. Babette, formerly a celebrated Parisian chef, works as a cook for two pious Norwegian sisters who know nothing of her illustrious past. Upon winning the lottery, she uses her winnings to prepare a sumptuous feast for the sisters and the devout followers of their late father, an ascetic pastor. Gabriel Axel's 1987 film version starred Stéphane Audran as Babette.

Bacchae, The (*Bakchai*, 408–406 B.C.; also translated under the title *The Bacchants*). A tragedy by EURIPIDES, written while in exile. Pentheus, king of Thebes, defies and even imprisons the disguised god Dionysus (also known as Bacchus, hence the title). As punishment, Pentheus is torn to pieces by his own mother, Agave, and the women of Thebes. The play recalls tragedy's roots in Dionysian fertility rites.

Balcony, The (*Le Balcon*, 1956). An avant-garde play by Jean GENET, influenced by the Theater of Cruelty. While a revolution rages outside the Grand Balcony, a brothel run by Madame Irma, her customers, including the chief of police and the rebel leader, enact their fantasies, and Irma takes on the role of the absent queen.

Bald Soprano, The (*La Cantatrice Chauve*, 1950). A one-act play by Eugène IONESCO, a highly influential masterpiece of the Theater of the Absurd in which two couples exchange increasingly banal non sequiturs. At the "end" of the play, the couples switch roles and the play starts over. Ionesco forces the audience to confront the absurdity of existence and the meaninglessness of bourgeois social interaction.

Balkan Trilogy, The. A trilogy of novels by Olivia MANNING comprising *The Great Fortune* (1960), *The Spoilt City* (1962), and *Friends and Heroes* (1965), and continued in *The Levant Trilogy*, published posthumously in 1981; the whole sequence of six books is collectively known as *The Fortunes of War*. The series, set in Romania and Greece during World War II, vividly portrays the effects of war upon daily life.

Ballad of Reading Gaol, The (1898). A tragic ballad by Oscar WILDE, his last published work, written while the author was jailed for sodomy (officially, "indecent acts"). The poem recounts the story of a prisoner condemned to death for murdering his lover. Wilde subordinates his characteristic wit in order to make a generous and impassioned call for prison reform and to demand that society question the power it has over those deemed "criminal."

Ballad of the Sad Café, The (1951). A Southern Gothic novella by Carson MCCULLERS about a strange love triangle consisting of the hulking Amelia Evans; her former husband, Marvin Macy, newly released from jail; and the hunchbacked dwarf Lyman, who claims to be her cousin. The work was adapted for the stage by Edward ALBEE in 1963.

Balthazar. *See* **Alexandria Quartet, The**

Barabbas (1950). A bestselling novel by Pär LAGERKVIST, portraying the New Testament criminal set free in place of JESUS.

Barber of Seville, The (*Le Barbier de Séville; ou, La Précaution Inutile*, 1775). A comedy by Pierre-Augustin Caron de BEAUMARCHAIS. Dr. Bartholo is hiding away his lovely ward, Rosine, whom he plans to wed against her will. Count Almaviva enlists the aid of the barber FIGARO, a delightful trickster, to gain access to her. The play was the basis of Rossini's opera *Il Barbiere di Siviglia* (1816). (For this and other adaptations, see Variations.)

Barchester Towers. *See* **Barsetshire Novels**

Barry Lyndon (1856). A satirical novel by William Makepeace THACKERAY, which was originally serialized in *Fraser's Magazine* (1844) as *The Luck of Barry Lyndon: A Romance of the Last Century*, published in 1852 and then revised in 1856 as *The Memoirs of Barry Lyndon, Esquire, by Himself*. Redmond Barry, an Irish gambler and adventurer, recounts his immoral exploits, always depicting himself as ill-used by others. He eventually marries a widow named Lyndon, and takes her aristocratic name. It was filmed in 1975 by Stanley Kubrick.

Barsetshire Novels (1855–67). Also known as the *Cathedral Stories*, this series of novels by Anthony TROLLOPE consists of *The Warden* (1855), *Barchester Towers* (1857), *Doctor Thorne* (1858), *Framley Parsonage* (1861), *The Small House at Allington* (1864), and *The Last Chronicle of Barset* (1867). These pleasantly ironic novels detail life, centered among the clergy, in the county of Barset, one of the great fictional locales in literature.

"Bartleby the Scrivener: A Story of Wall Street" (1853). A long story by Herman MELVILLE, about BARTLEBY, a copier of legal documents, who declines all requests from his employer with the enigmatic but insistent phrase, "I would prefer not to." His eventual refusal to participate in life leads to his death in prison, his final gesture of utter negation.

"Batter My Heart" (1633). A religious sonnet by John DONNE, which argues that knowledge of sinfulness opens the sinner to the grace of God. It was originally published in *Songs and Sonnets* as part of a series of 19 spiritual poems known as the "Divine Meditations" or the "Holy Sonnets."

Bear, The (1935). A novella by William FAULKNER, originally published as "Lion" in

Harper's Magazine and later as part of *GO DOWN, MOSES* (1942). As a boy, Ike McCaslin was apprenticed to Sam Fathers, a Native American, for a rite of passage: hunting a bear known as Old Ben. Five years later, Ike gives an account of the hunt in order to explain his refusal of the family inheritance, simultaneously an act of penitence and cowardice.

Beautiful and Damned, The (1922). A novel by F. SCOTT FITZGERALD. Anthony and Gloria Patch waste their lives waiting for an inheritance from Anthony's grandfather, only to be disinherited because of their profligate lifestyle.

"Because I Could Not Stop for Death" (written c. 1863; published posthumously in 1890). A poem by Emily DICKINSON, in which death is envisioned as a silent and restrained escort to the grave.

"Belle Dame sans Merci, La" (1820). A ballad by John KEATS. An allegory of the pains of love, the poem takes its title from a medieval poem about a man whose love for a supernatural woman ruins him.

Bell Jar, The (1963). An autobiographical novel by Sylvia PLATH about a Smith College student named Esther Greenwood who, during a summer internship with a Manhattan-based magazine, examines her psychological frailty and compulsion to suicide. First published under the pseudonym Victoria Lucas, it gained particular poignancy with Plath's suicide in the same year. It is her only novel.

Beloved (1987). A Pulitzer Prize–winning novel by Toni MORRISON, relating the haunting story of SETHE, an African-American woman who escapes slavery just before the Civil War, and kills one of her children (called only "Beloved" on her tombstone) to prevent the child's capture and enslavement by a brutal slaveholder. When a young woman appears years later calling herself "Beloved," Sethe believes that her lost daughter has returned.

Bend in the River, A (1979). A novel by V. S. NAIPAUL that explores the legacy of colonialism in Africa through the character Salim.

Ben-Hur (1880). A bestselling novel by the American author Lew Wallace (1827–1905), set in biblical times and telling the story of Judah Ben-Hur, a young Jew wrongly accused of assassination by his false friend Messala. Notable adaptations include the 1907 silent film with Ramon Novarro as Ben-Hur and Francis X. Bushman as Messala, and the 1959 film directed by William Wyler, which won 11 Academy Awards, including Best Picture, Best Director, and Best Actor (Charlton Heston as Ben-Hur).

Beowulf (sole surviving manuscript c. 1000, date of composition controversial, but c. 700–50 is often suggested; first published 1815). An Old English epic poem relating the deeds of the hero BEOWULF in Denmark, where he slays the monster GRENDEL, and in southern Sweden, where he reigns as king of the Geats. It is the oldest surviving Germanic epic and the longest and most important Old English poem. Seamus HEANEY's award-winning translation was published in 1999.

Berlin Stories, The (1946). A pair of two previously published novels (*The Last of Mr. Norris*, 1935, and *Goodbye to Berlin*, 1939) by Christopher ISHERWOOD. With the phrase, "I am a camera with its shutter open," the character Isherwood follows the lives of down-and-out expatriates living in the decadent pre-Nazi Berlin of the early 1930s. (For adaptations, see Variations.)

Betrothed, The (*I Promessi Sposi*, 1827). A historical novel by Alessandro MANZONI, set in the kingdom of Lombardy during the early 17th century, a time of the plague and the bloody Thirty Years' War. A high point of Italian Romanticism, it concerns two young peasant lovers whose marriage is blocked by a despotic local lord and a craven priest.

Bhagavadgītā (c. 2nd to 1st century B.C.). A section of the Hindu epic poem known as the *Mahābhārata*, written down from traditional oral sources and consisting of 700 Sanskrit verses. This work within a work chronicles a dialogue between Arjuna, a hero of the warlike Pāndava family, and his chariot driver, Krishna.

The title means "Song of the Lord" in Sanskrit and the work is one of the essential statements of Hindu faith.

Bible (c. 8th century B.C. to 1st century A.D.). A collection of sacred books, written from oral traditions. The Hebrew Bible consists of books on Jewish law, mythical and actual history, and prophecies. The Christian Bible is divided into two parts, the Old and New Testaments. The Old Testament slightly rearranges the order of the Hebrew Bible, and the New Testament contains books that tell the story of Jesus and the establishment of the Christian church. The various books of the Old and New Testaments were written originally in Hebrew, Aramaic, and Greek, and were translated into Latin and gathered together in their present form in the Vulgate by St. Jerome in A.D. 382. The Reformation of the 16th century prompted Protestant versions of the Bible in many European languages. In English, the best-known edition is the King James Bible, first printed in 1611.

"Big Blonde" (1929). An autobiographical story by Dorothy PARKER, winner of an O. Henry Memorial Prize, telling of Hazel Morse's tragic slide into alcoholism and depression.

Big Money, The. *See* **U.S.A.**

Billiards at Half-Past Nine (*Billard um Halbzehn*, 1959). A novel by Heinrich BÖLL probing the moral terrain of postwar Germany through three generations of architects in the Fähmel family as they try to come to terms with their role in the events of the Nazi period.

Billy Budd, Foretopman (published posthumously in 1924). A novella by Herman MELVILLE. Completed but not published at Melville's death in 1891, the story follows the torment of the good-hearted, innocent protagonist, Billy BUDD, a common sailor, on his last sea voyage as he becomes the victim of irrational persecution by the twisted master-at-arms, Claggart. (For adaptations, see Variations.)

Birds, The (*Ornithes*, 414 B.C.). A comedy by ARISTOPHANES written to spoof human pretensions generally and the 415 B.C. Athenian military campaign against Sicily in particular. Pisthetaerus, an elderly Athenian, has grown tired of living in his crowded, contentious native city and joins the birds in building Nephelo-Kokkygia ("Cloud-Cuckoo-land"), a utopia that must be protected from humans.

Birthday Party, The (1958). A play by Harold PINTER, the author's first so-called comedy of menace. At a depressing party thrown for Stanley, a layabout, by the landlady of his seedy rooming house, two strangers appear, alarming Stanley with their announcement that they must "punish" him for unknown offenses.

Black Boy: A Record of Childhood and Youth (1945). An autobiography, considered a seminal work of African-American literature, by Richard WRIGHT, the title of which is meant to mock the use of the word *boy* by segregationists in the rural South to describe black men. It is continued by *American Hunger* (1977).

Bleak House (1853). A novel by Charles DICKENS that indicts the English court system through the endless case of *Jarndyce vs. Jarndyce*. The novel also relates the search for her true identity by Esther Summerson, an illegitimate child who has been raised by her guardian, the lawyer Mr. JARNDYCE.

"Bliss" (1920). A short story by Katherine MANSFIELD in which Bertha Young's particularly radiant day is ruined when she discovers that her husband is having an affair.

Blithe Spirit (1941). A comedy by Noël COWARD that expertly captures the fantasy life of English urban sophisticates in the pre–World War II era. Charles Condomine's home life is upset by the jealous ghost of his first wife (Elvira); Madame Arcati is the medium he uses to rid himself of Elvira and then of his second wife, Ruth.

Blood Wedding (*Bodas de Sangre*, 1933). Part of a trilogy of plays by Federico GARCÍA LORCA that includes *YERMA* and *THE HOUSE OF BERNARDA ALBA*. This play tells the story of a bride who runs away with a married man on her wedding day. Death, in the form of a beggar, leads the jilted groom to the lovers, and the men kill each other. (For adaptations, see Variations.)

Blue Flower, The (1995). A novel by PENELOPE FITZGERALD, a fictionalized account of the early life of 18th-century German poet Friedrich von Hardenberg, best known under the pseudonym NOVALIS.

Bonfire of the Vanities, The (1987). A bestselling satirical novel by TOM WOLFE about Sherman MCCOY, a wealthy New York stockbroker who becomes entangled in urban politics and the corrupt judicial system following a hit-and-run accident in which he badly injures a young boy in the South Bronx.

Bonjour Tristesse (1954). A novel by the French author Françoise Sagan (1935–), written when she was 18, in which the teenaged narrator describes the boredom, hedonism, and ultimate tragedy of a summer spent with her father and his mistress in a Mediterranean villa.

Book of Disquiet, The (*Livro do Desassossego*, 1982). A fragmentary prose masterpiece by Portuguese poet Fernando PESSOA, written as if by Bernardo Soares, exploring the difficulties of communication. It was first published long after the poet's 1935 death.

Book of Laughter and Forgetting, The (*Kniha Smíchu a Zapomnění*, 1979). A novel by Milan KUNDERA, originally published in French translation, that explores the fragile and changing nature of personal and national history and memory. A powerful protest against the Communist regime in Czechoslovakia, the book caused Kundera to be stripped of his Czech citizenship.

Border Trilogy, The (1992–98). A trilogy of novels by CORMAC MCCARTHY consisting of *All the Pretty Horses* (1992), *The Crossing* (1994), and *Cities of the Plain* (1998), and telling in lyrical language the story of the young John Grady Cole and his companions struggling against great odds on the violent Texas-Mexico border in the 1940s. *All the Pretty Horses* won a National Book Award and a National Book Critics Circle Award.

Boris Godunov (written 1824–25; published 1831). A historical drama by Aleksandr PUSHKIN that recounts the tragic life of the Russian tsar who ruled from 1598 to 1605. The author's first

play, it is considered one of the masterpieces of European theater in the 19th century and, along with his poetry, established Pushkin as the greatest master in the Russian language. (For adaptations, see Variations.)

Borstal Boy (1958). An autobiographical novel by Brendan BEHAN that tells the story of a troubled Irish teenager, Paddy, who briefly joins the Irish Republican Army and ends up in a borstal (an English reformatory) on political charges.

Bostonians, The (1886). A novel by HENRY JAMES satirizing American progressive liberalism, whose home he locates in Boston. Verena Tarrant, a young protégée of the feminist Olive Chancellor, falls in love with Basil Ransom, a Mississippi lawyer, and deserts the women's movement for a life of marriage and domesticity. The novel is notable for its subtle exploration of Olive's passionate attraction to Verena.

"Boule de Suif" (1880). A short story by Guy de MAUPASSANT centered on a prostitute known as Boule de Suif ("Ball of Fat"), who refuses to accommodate a German officer while traveling by train through German-occupied France. The author contrasts her noble behavior with the hypocrisy of the respectable bourgeois travelers on the train.

Bourgeois Gentleman, The (*Le Bourgeois Gentilhomme*, 1670; also translated under the title *The Would-Be Gentleman*). A comedy by MOLIÈRE that exposes, with the author's characteristic understanding of human nature, the pretensions of a socially ambitious tradesman, Monsieur JOURDAIN, and his efforts to master fencing and philosophy, fashionable dress and dancing. (For adaptations, see Variations.)

Box Man, The (*Hakootoko*, 1973). An absurdist novel by Kōbō ABE about a man who cuts a peephole in an empty cardboard box and places it over his body, thus escaping the world and its anxieties. Yet he still has one fear: that he will meet another "box man."

Brave New World (1932). A futuristic fable by Aldous HUXLEY, celebrated for its darkly imagined vision of a society in which all human beings are hatched from incubators and are graded, sorted, and brainwashed from birth to

OPENING BIDS: FIRST LINES

Presented in chronological order, the following are some memorable, famous, and striking first lines in literature.

Rage—Goddess, sing the rage of Peleus' son
    Achilles,
murderous, doomed, that cost the Achaeans
    countless losses,
hurling down to the House of Death so many
    sturdy souls,
great fighters' souls, but made their bodies
    carrion,
feast for the dogs and birds,
and the will of Zeus was moving toward its
    end.
Begin, Muse, when the two first broke and
    clashed,
Agamemnon lord of men and brilliant
    Achilles.

Homer, *Iliad* (8th century B.C.), translated by Robert Fagles (1990)

Arms, and the man I sing, who, forc'd by fate,
And haughty Juno's unrelenting hate,
Expell'd and exil'd, left the Trojan shore.

Virgil, *The Aeneid* (c. 29–19 B.C.), translated by John Dryden (1697)

In the beginning was the word, and the Word was with God, and the Word was God.

The Gospel According to St. John 1:1, New Testament, Bible, King James Version (1611)

In the middle of the journey of our life
I came to myself within a dark wood
where the straight way was lost.

Dante Alighieri, *Inferno* (1320), translated by John D. Sinclair (1939)

Now is the winter of our discontent
Made glorious summer by this son of York,
And all the clouds that loured upon our house
In the deep bosom of the ocean buried.

William Shakespeare, *Richard III* (c. 1594)

Of Man's first disobedience, and the fruit
Of that forbidden tree whose mortal taste
Brought death into the World, and all our woe,
With loss of Eden, till one greater Man
Restore us, and regain the blissful Seat,
Sing, Heavenly Muse...

John Milton, *Paradise Lost* (1667)

As I walked through the wilderness of this world, I lighted on a certain place where was a Den, and I laid me down in that place to sleep: and, as I slept, I dreamed a dream.

John Bunyan, *The Pilgrim's Progress* (Part I, 1678)

Know then thy self, presume not God to scan;
The proper study of mankind is Man.

Alexander Pope, *An Essay on Man*, Epistle II (1733–34)

I was ever of opinion, that the honest man who married and brought up a large family, did more service than he who continued single, and only talked of population.

Oliver Goldsmith, *The Vicar of Wakefield* (1766)

It is a truth universally acknowledged, that a single man in possession of a good fortune, must be in need of a wife.

Jane Austen, *Pride and Prejudice* (1813)

Marley was dead: to begin with.

Charles Dickens, *A Christmas Carol* (1843)

Whether I shall turn out to be the hero of my own life, or whether that station will be held by anybody else, these pages must show.

Charles Dickens, *David Copperfield* (1850)

Call me Ishmael.

Herman Melville, *Moby-Dick* (1851)

It was the best of times, it was the worst of times, it was the age of wisdom, it was the age of foolishness, it was the epoch of belief, it was the epoch of incredulity, it was the season of Light, it was the season of Darkness, it was the spring of hope, it was the winter of despair, we had everything before us, we had nothing before us, we were all going direct to Heaven, we were all going direct the other way—in short, the period was so far like the present period, that some of its noisiest authorities insisted on its being received, for good or for evil, in the superlative degree of comparison only.

Charles Dickens, *A Tale of Two Cities* (1859)

All happy families are alike; each unhappy family is unhappy in its own way.

Leo Tolstoy, *Anna Karenina* (1878), translated by Richard Pevear and Larissa Volokhonsky (2000)

For reasons which many persons thought ridiculous, Mrs. Lightfoot Lee decided to pass the winter in Washington.

Henry Adams, *Democracy* (1880)

You don't know about me without you have read a book by the name of *The Adventures of Tom Sawyer*; but that ain't no matter. That book was made by Mr. Mark Twain, and he told the truth, mainly.

Mark Twain, *The Adventures of Huckleberry Finn* (1884)

The Superintendent said to me: "I only keep you out of regard for your worthy father; but for that you would have been sent flying long ago." I replied to him: "You flatter me too much, your Excellency, in assuming that I am capable of flying." And then I heard him say: "Take that gentleman away; he gets upon my nerves."

Anton Chekhov, "My Life: The Story of a Provincial" (1896), translated by Constance Garnett (1920)

For a long time I used to go to bed early.

Marcel Proust, *Remembrance of Things Past* (1913–27), translated by C. K. Scott Moncrieff and Terence Kilmartin (1981)

This is the saddest story I have ever heard.

Ford Madox Ford, *The Good Soldier* (1915)

People from the big cities have no idea of standards and proportions in the small towns.

Knut Hamsun, *The Women at the Pump* (1920), translated by Arthur G. Chater (1928)

Stately plump Buck Mulligan came from the stairhead, bearing a bowl of lather on which a mirror and a razor lay crossed.

James Joyce, *Ulysses* (1922)

(Opening Bids: First Lines, continued)

During these last decades the interest in professional fasting has markedly diminished.

Franz Kafka, "The Hunger Artist" (1922), translated by Willa and Edwin Muir (1952)

In the fall the war was always there, but we didn't go to it any more.

Ernest Hemingway, "In Another Country," in *Men Without Women* (1927)

Ours is essentially a tragic age, so we refuse to take it tragically.

D. H. Lawrence, *Lady Chatterley's Lover* (1928)

I had a farm in Africa, at the foot of the Ngong Hills.

Isak Dinesen, *Out of Africa* (1937)

Ships at a distance have every man's wish on board. For some they come in with the tide. For others they sail forever on the horizon, never out of sight, never landing until the Watcher turns his eyes away in resignation, his dreams mocked to death by Time. That is the life of men.

Zora Neale Hurston, *Their Eyes Were Watching God* (1937)

Last night I dreamt I went to Manderley again.

Daphne Du Maurier, *Rebecca* (1938)

If you really want to hear about it, the first thing you'll probably want to know is where I was born, and what my lousy childhood was like, and how my parents were occupied and all before they had me, and all that David Copperfield kind of crap, but I don't feel like going into it, if you want to know the truth.

J. D. Salinger, *The Catcher in the Rye* (1951)

I am an American, Chicago born—Chicago, that somber city—and go at things as I have taught myself, free-style, and will make the record in my own way: first to knock, first admitted, sometimes an innocent knock, sometimes not so innocent.

Saul Bellow, *The Adventures of Augie March* (1953)

The past is a foreign country: they do things differently there.

L. P. Hartley, *The Go-Between* (1953)

---

accept their place in the social order. The title is taken from MIRANDA's words in SHAKESPEARE's *THE TEMPEST*: "O brave new world, that has such people in it!"

Bread and Wine (*Pane e Vino*, 1937). A novel by Ignazio SILONE, written during Benito Mussolini's fascist reign in Italy, about the return to Italy after 15 years' absence of Pietro Spina, an underground opponent of the regime.

Breakfast at Tiffany's (1958). A novella by Truman CAPOTE about a country girl from Texas who moves to Manhattan and reinvents herself as Holly GOLIGHTLY, a free and easy sophisticate. It takes up some of Capote's favorite themes: hidden identities, the glamour of wealth, the city as a place to create oneself anew. (For adaptations, see Variations.)

Brideshead Revisited (1945). A novel by EVELYN WAUGH about an eccentric English Roman

Lolita, light of my life, fire of my loins.

Vladimir Nabokov, *Lolita* (1955)

Granted: I am an inmate of a mental hospital; my keeper is watching me, he never lets me out of his sight; there's a peephole in the door, and my keeper's eye is the shade of brown that can never see through a blue-eyed type like me.

Günter Grass, *The Tin Drum* (1959), translated by Ralph Manheim (1963)

The cradle rocks above an abyss, and common sense tells us that our existence is but a brief crack of light between two eternities of darkness.

Vladimir Nabokov, *Speak, Memory* (rev. ed. 1966)

She was so deeply imbedded in my consciousness that for the first year of school I seem to have believed that each of my teachers was my mother in disguise.

Philip Roth, *Portnoy's Complaint* (1969)

Over the weekend the vultures got into the presidential palace by pecking through the screens on the balcony windows and the flapping of their wings stirred up the stagnant time inside, and at dawn on Monday the city awoke out of its lethargy of centuries with the warm, soft breeze of a great man dead and rotting grandeur.

Gabriel García Márquez, *The Autumn of the Patriarch* (1975), translated by Gregory Rabassa (1976)

You are about to begin reading Italo Calvino's new novel, *If on a Winter's Night a Traveler*. **Relax. Concentrate.**

Italo Calvino, *If on a Winter's Night a Traveler* (1979), translated by William Weaver (1981)

This is a true story but I can't believe it's really happening.

It's a murder story, too. I can't believe my luck.

And a love story (I think), of all strange things, so late in the century, so late in the goddamned day.

Martin Amis, *London Fields* (1989)

In the beginning there was a river. The river became a road and the road branched out to the whole world. And because the road was once a river it was always hungry.

Ben Okri, *The Famished Road* (1991)

Catholic family, the Flytes (Lord and Lady MARCHMAIN and their children, including the central character Lord Sebastian FLYTE), and their friend, Charles RYDER, and an ironic reflection on a style of English country life that would disappear after the war. A 1982 British television miniseries, adapted by John MORTIMER and starring Anthony Andrews and Jeremy Irons, was hugely successful on both sides of the Atlantic.

Bridge, The (1930). A poem by HART CRANE, one of his best-known works, which uses the bridge as a metaphor for crossing from old to new, past to present.

Bridge of San Luis Rey, The (1927). A Pulitzer Prize–winning novel by Thornton WILDER, the story of the collapse of a bridge in 18th-century Peru in which five travelers perish, and of Brother Juniper's search for evidence of divine intervention to explain their deaths.

Brighton Rock (1938). A novel by Graham GREENE about Pinkie Brown, a teenaged gang leader and murderer who marries Rose, a nice but dim local girl, to keep her silent about his crimes. After Pinkie dies while trying to kill Rose, a priest assures Rose that Pinkie was not all bad and that God's mercy may have saved him from his actions.

Bronze Horseman, The (*Mednyĭ Vsadnik*, 1837). A narrative poem by Aleksandr PUSHKIN about a poor clerk, Evgeni, who curses the famous statue of Peter the Great, whose imperious decision to place St. Petersburg in a swamp Evgeni blames for the death of his fiancée during a flood. In his delirium, Evgeni imagines that Peter and his horse come down from their pedestal to chase him through the city.

Brothers Karamazov, The (*Bratya Karamazovy*, 1880). A philosophical novel by Fyodor DOSTOYEVSKY, one of the great novels in world literature. Focusing on Fyodor KARAMAZOV and his three sons, Dmitri, Ivan, and Alyosha, the book combines the story of a patricide with the exploration of religious and ethical ideas. The search for God at the heart of the book is dramatized in the famous "Legend of the GRAND INQUISITOR." (For adaptations, see Variations.)

Buddenbrooks: The Decline of a Family (*Buddenbrooks: Verfall einer Familie*, 1901). In this first novel by Thomas MANN, a multigenerational tale of the degeneration and ruin of the wealthy and respectable Buddenbrook family in l9th-century Lübeck, the major themes that would dominate Mann's work are already present: the decadence of the bourgeoisie and the isolation of the artist in bourgeois society.

Burger's Daughter (1979). A novel by Nadine GORDIMER in which Rosa BURGER, the daughter of a white communist leader who has been murdered in prison, seeks to lead a nonpolitical life but is confronted by the ugly realities of apartheid in the aftermath of the Soweto uprising.

Buried Child (1978). A Pulitzer Prize–winning play by Sam SHEPARD that portrays the lies and delusions of a Gothically dysfunctional late-20th-century American family.

Burnt Norton (1936). A poem by T. S. ELIOT, one of his *FOUR QUARTETS*, pondering the meaning of time and of paths taken and not taken. The famous opening lines are, "Time present and time past / Are both perhaps present in time future, / And time future contained in time past. /…What might have been and what has been / Point to one end, which is always present."

Burnt-Out Case, A (1961). A novel by Graham GREENE that explores the possibility of spiritual redemption in the modern materialist world.

Caesar and Cleopatra (1906). A play by George Bernard SHAW, portraying the conflict between Julius CAESAR, the aged Roman conquerer, and Egypt's inexperienced queen CLEOPATRA, based on the Greek biographer PLUTARCH's account of Caesar's life. (For adaptations, see Variations.)

Caine Mutiny, The (1951). A bestselling novel by Herman WOUK about a World War II mutiny against the mentally incompetent Captain QUEEG. Wouk's stage adaptation of the novel, *The Caine Mutiny Court-Martial*, premiered on Broadway in 1954; the same year, a film adaptation of the novel starred Humphrey Bogart as Captain Queeg.

Cairo Trilogy, The (*al-Thulāthīyah*, 1956–57). A trilogy of novels by Naguib MAHFOUZ consisting of *Palace Walk* (*Bayna al-Qaṣrayn*, 1956), *Palace of Desire* (*Qaṣr al-Shawq*, 1957), and *Sugar Street* (*al-Sukkarīyah*, 1957), chronicling several generations in the Egyptian al-Jawad family and offering a masterful portrait of post–World War I Egyptian society.

Cakes and Ale (1930). A novel by W. Somerset MAUGHAM, a thinly disguised treatment of London literary life in the 1920s. Willie Ashenden, a character much like Maugham, tells the story of Alroy Kear's attempt to write a biography of Edward Driffield, a successful novelist based on Thomas HARDY.

Call It Sleep (1934). An autobiographical novel by HENRY ROTH, describing, through the story of seven-year-old David Schearl, the difficulties of assimilation and family strife in a

Yiddish-speaking Jewish household in early 20th-century New York.

Call of the Wild, The (1903). A novel by Jack LONDON, in which the unusual protagonist, a dog named BUCK, is transformed after a series of travails into a mythical creature, the "Ghost Dog" of the Klondike. The story is a parable about endurance and justice in the face of adversity.

Cancer Ward, The (*Rakovyĭ Korpus*, 1968). A novel by Aleksandr SOLZHENITSYN, about the protagonist Oleg Kostoglotov's treatment for cancer shortly after his release from a Soviet concentration camp (a plot mirroring events in the life of Solzhenitsyn, who served eight years in Soviet prison camps at the end of World War II). Suppressed by Soviet authorities, the manuscript was smuggled out to the West, where it was first published simultaneously in English and Russian.

Candida (1897). A play by George Bernard SHAW, exploring the power dynamics within a marriage. Candida Morell, the wife of the Reverend James Morell, must choose between her staid husband and the much younger Eugene Marchbanks, an irrepressible poet.

Candide; or, Optimism (*Candide; ou, L'Optimisme*, 1759). A satirical novel by VOLTAIRE. The innocent title character, instructed in Leibnizian optimism by Dr. PANGLOSS, embarks on a series of adventures that sorely test the motto "All is for the best in this best of all possible worlds." (For adaptations, see Variations.)

Cane (1923). An experimental work by Jean TOOMER, one of the most important works of the Harlem Renaissance, combining a variety of genres, including fiction and poetry, to explore the experience of African Americans. The title may refer to sugar cane and to the biblical Cain.

Cannery Row (1945). A novel by John STEINBECK interweaving the stories of a cast of characters living in Monterey, California's run-down cannery district ("a poem, a stink, a grating noise, a quality of light, a tone, a habit, a nostalgia, a dream"). The plot centers on a marine biologist, Doc, and the genial bums of the Palace Flophouse.

Canterbury Tales, The (c. 1387–1400). A Middle English verse masterpiece by Geoffrey CHAUCER, consisting of 24 tales told by a group of pilgrims to pass the time as they make their way to the shrine of THOMAS À BECKET at Canterbury. (For adaptations, see Variations.)

Canto General (1950; revised editions appeared through 1963). An epic poem in 15 cantos by Chilean poet Pablo NERUDA. Setting out to tell the story of South America from a Marxist viewpoint, Neruda creates a panoramic view of a culture, honoring the spirit of the land and its many peoples.

Cantos, The (1925–68). A series of connected poems by Ezra POUND, considered among the most important and influential American poetic works of the 20th century. An attempt to create a modernist epic, *The Cantos* interweaves various fragments, combining references to Greek and Roman mythology, Eastern poetry, Renaissance literature, and American politics. *The Pisan Cantos* (1948), written during Pound's incarceration for treason after World War II, won the Bollingen Prize.

Can You Forgive Her? *See* **Pallisers, The**

Captains Courageous (1897). An adventure novel by Rudyard KIPLING. Harvey Cheyne, the spoiled, cocky son of a millionaire, learns responsibility from fishing-boat captain Disko Troop. Hard work and responsibility for others transform the pampered boy into a man of integrity and honor, a favorite theme of the author.

Captive, The. *See* **Remembrance of Things Past**

Caretaker, The (1960). An enigmatic play by Harold PINTER that explores the precarious nature of human interaction. When slow-witted Aston invites a vagrant named Davies to the one-room flat he shares with his volatile brother, Mick, a power struggle erupts.

Carmen (1846). A novella by the French writer Prosper Mérimée (1803–1870). For love of a Gypsy named CARMEN, Don José abandons his military post and sets out on a life of crime and debauchery. Uncontrollably jealous, he murders her when she falls in love with another man, and is sentenced to death. The author wrote the tragic romance out of financial necessity, according to legend in order to pay for a pair of pants. The story is best known today as the source of the opera by Georges Bizet. (For adaptations, see Variations.)

Carrie (1974). The first novel by Stephen KING, about Carrie White, an unpopular girl with powerful telekinetic powers. She is tormented by her fanatically religious mother and her fellow high school students until she takes revenge. (For adaptations, see Variations.)

"Cask of Amontillado, The" (1846). A short story by Edgar Allan POE, a chilling tale of revenge in which Montresor, a European aristocrat, recounts how he buried alive a foe, Fortunato, who had insulted him.

Castle, The (*Das Schloss*, 1926). An unfinished allegorical novel by Franz KAFKA, published posthumously. Summoned to a castle in his capacity as land surveyor, the hero, known simply as K., is continually denied admittance by the authorities for unspecified reasons. Max BROD, who prepared the novel for publication, notes that Kafka intended his hero to die of exhaustion at the end.

Castle of Otranto, The (1765). A Gothic novel, the first in English, by the English writrer Horace Walpole (1717–1797), whose themes and style were widely imitated. The story centers around Manfred, the evil prince who has murdered the castle of Otranto's rightful inhabitant, Alfonso. Ultimately, Alfonso's ghost rises up and destroys the castle.

Catcher in the Rye, The (1951). A novel by J. D. SALINGER. Expelled from his prep school, alienated teenager Holden CAULFIELD complains about the "phoniness" of the adult world in this brilliant and affecting first-person narrative. The title refers to his mistaken recollection of a poem by Robert BURNS; Holden imagines protecting children at play in a rye field from falling off a nearby cliff. Its frank language has made the book a frequent target of book banners.

Catch-22 (1961). A satirical World War II novel by Joseph HELLER, characterized by black humor. Attempting to avoid flying further missions, Captain John YOSSARIAN is foiled by catch-22: a soldier who is insane is exempt from combat, but he must file a formal request to be relieved of duty; however, filing such a request indicates that he is sane, and so he will have to continue on active duty. "Catch-22" has become a catch phrase for bureaucratic perversity. In 1994, Heller published a sequel, *Closing Time*.

Cathedral Stories. *See* **Barsetshire Novels**

Cat on a Hot Tin Roof (1955). A Pulitzer Prize–winning play by TENNESSEE WILLIAMS about conflict among members of the Pollitt family over control of the estate of the dying patriarch, BIG DADDY. Guilty over the death of his friend Skipper, the alcoholic son Brick scorns his wife, MAGGIE. Yearning for him, she explains that, like a cat on a hot tin roof, she is just trying to hold on.

Cat's Cradle (1963). A science-fiction novel by Kurt VONNEGUT. As he awaits the end of the world, the journalist-narrator, Jonah, records the events that led to the apocalypse. A former atomic scientist named Dr. Felix Hoenikker invented ice-nine, a crystal that freezes any liquid it touches. On the island nation of San Lorenzo, Jonah is converted to Bokonism, a religion based on lies, and witnesses the strange circumstances that release ice-nine into the ocean.

Caucasian Chalk Circle, The (*Der Kaukasische Kreidekreis*, written 1944–45). A play by Bertolt BRECHT, first performed in English in 1948. Based on a 13th-century Chinese play, and harkening back to the biblical King Solomon, the story illuminates a property dispute between two Soviet communes. During a rebellion, Grusha, a servant, rescues the governor's infant son. When the governor's wife sues to regain her child, a judge places the boy in a chalk circle, saying that whoever pulls him out will gain custody. The wise judge recognizes by Grusha's unwillingness to hurt the child that she is the true mother.

Cenci, The (1819). A verse drama by PERCY BYSSHE SHELLEY, published in 1819 but not performed until 1886. Based on the story of the 16th-century Cenci family, it is a sensational tale of incest, murder, and revenge. The work greatly influenced the 20th-century French dramatist Antonin ARTAUD's conception of the Theater of Cruelty.

"Charge of the Light Brigade, The" (1855). An occasional poem by Alfred, Lord TENNYSON, published to commemorate the doomed Crimean War attack at Balaclava on October 25, 1854, when a British brigade of 600 men charged the Russian position and were slaughtered.

Charterhouse of Parma, The (*La Chartreuse de Parme*, 1839). A historical novel by STENDHAL in which Fabrice del Dongo, after seeking military glory in the Napoleonic wars and living an adventurous life, retires to a charterhouse, or monastery. The antiheroic battle scene inspired TOLSTOY's *WAR AND PEACE* (1868–69).

Chéri (1920). A novel by COLETTE about an affair between an older woman and a rich young man. The title refers to the woman's nickname for her lover, *chéri*, which means "darling." The novel helped to establish Colette's reputation and was followed by *La Fin de Chéri* (*The Last of Chéri*) in 1926.

Cherry Orchard, The (*Vishnevyĭ Sad*, 1904). A play by Anton CHEKHOV depicting the declining fortunes of the RANEVSKY family. When LOPAKHIN, a crass businessman, suggests that the family save its estate by cutting down the cherry orchard to lease the land for summer homes, the family does nothing and loses the entire estate, while Lopakhin buys the property to carry out his plan. The play depicts the inertia that gripped the Russian aristocracy when faced with historic change.

"Chicago" (1916). A poem by Carl SANDBURG written in boisterous free verse and celebrating the working people and industrious fervor of Chicago.

Childe Harold's Pilgrimage (1812–18). A narrative poem in four cantos by Lord BYRON. Weary of a pointless life devoted to pleasure, Childe Harold, whose title is the medieval term for a nobleman yet to be knighted, undertakes a journey to exotic lands. Encountering representative and historical figures, he records his reflections on each foreign land. In canto IV, the poet abandons his hero, and speaks to the audience directly.

Children's Hour, The (1934). The first play by Lillian HELLMAN, banned in several American cities for its controversial theme. The play concerns the destructive result when a spiteful student accuses two boarding-school teachers of having a lesbian affair. (For adaptations, see Variations.)

Christmas Carol, A (1843). A classic Christmas fable by Charles DICKENS. The miserly Ebenezer SCROOGE is visited on Christmas Eve by ghosts who show him the damaging effects of his avarice, especially on his ill-used employee, Bob CRATCHIT, father of TINY TIM, one of Dickens's most famous characters. (For adaptations, see Variations.)

Cid, Le (1637). A verse tragedy by Pierre CORNEILLE, generally regarded as the first French classical drama, based upon Guillén de Castro y Bellvis's treatment of the Spanish medieval epic. During the campaign to win back territory conquered by the Moors, the title character and military hero, Don Rodrigue, is torn between honor and love when forced into a duel with the father of his intended, Chimène.

Cities of the Plain. *See* **Border Trilogy, The**

Cities of the Plain. *See* **Remembrance of Things Past**

Clarissa; or, The History of a Young Lady (1747–48). An epistolary novel by SAMUEL RICHARDSON. The upright country girl Clarissa HARLOWE runs off with Robert Lovelace, an alluring rogue, who places her in a brothel. Refusing his subsequent marriage proposal, which would make her an honorable woman, the heroine withdraws from society and dies of shame. At more than a million words, it is the longest novel in the English language.

Clea. *See* **Alexandria Quartet, The**

"Clean, Well-lighted Place, A" (1933). A short story by Ernest HEMINGWAY. As an old man lingers in a café past closing time, two waiters must postpone their departure. Despite the impatience of the younger waiter, the older man, himself already defeated by life, understands the customer's need for the simple human contact offered by the café.

Clockwork Orange, A (1962). An anti-utopian novel by Anthony BURGESS, written in an argot partly derived from Russian. The narrator, Alex, is a teenaged member of a gang that indulges in orgies of violence and sex. Imprisoned after one attack, he is subjected to behavioral conditioning to rehabilitate him. The novel was filmed memorably by Stanley Kubrick in 1971.

Cloister and the Hearth, The (1861). A historical romance by the English writer Charles Reade (1814–1844), set in 15th-century Holland. Gerard Eliasson and Margaret Brandt are prevented from marrying by the machinations of his father. They separate, with Gerard unaware that Margaret has borne him a son, and their eventual reunion is complicated by Gerard's having taken monastic vows. The novel's surprise twist is that their son grows up to be the esteemed scholar Erasmus.

Clouds, The (*Nephelai*, 423 B.C.). A satire on education by ARISTOPHANES that links SOPHOCLES to the Sophists, known for rhetoric so convincing as to be capable of proving false arguments. Wishing to evade his debtors, Strepsiades enrolls his son in Sophocles' academy, the Phrontisterion or Thinking Shop. Initially pleased with his son's new-found abilities, he regrets his decision when those skills come back to haunt him.

Cocktail Party, The (1949). A play in verse by T. S. ELIOT, a combination of drawing-room comedy and morality play in which the marital dissatisfaction of Edward and Lavinia Chamberlayne suggests the spiritual anomie of their fashionable milieu. Their marriage is saved by the self-sacrifice of Edward's mistress, who becomes a Christian martyr. The play is Eliot's exploration of the possibilities for redemption.

Cold Comfort Farm (1932). A novel by the English author Stella Gibbons (1902–1989) that parodies the British rural novel popularized by Thomas HARDY and others. Flora Poste visits her relatives, the Starkadders of Sussex, confronting their gloom with the zeal of a reformer.

Color Purple, The (1982). A Pulitzer Prize–winning epistolary novel by Alice WALKER, consisting of a series of letters written to God and to her sister Nettie by a young Southern African-American woman named CELIE. Abused by her stepfather and married at 14 to the brutal Mr—, Celie finds support through a community of women, including her sister; the defiant Sofia; and the sensual Shug Avery, who becomes her lover. Despite the final redemption of Mr—, the novel raised controversy over its negative portrayals of African-American men. The 1985 film version, directed by Steven Spielberg, starred Whoopi Goldberg and Oprah Winfrey.

Come Back, Little Sheba (1950). A drama by William INGE about a frustrated marriage. A middle-aged husband and wife, Doc and Lola, each suffer alone the disillusionment of their empty existence. Both seek ways of denying their pain: Doc through alcohol and sexual fantasies, Lola through memories of her lost youth, symbolized by her dog, Little Sheba, who has run away. Doc's violent outbreak forces her to face the truth of her life and the knowledge that Little Sheba will never return.

Comedy of Errors, The (c. 1592). A play by William SHAKESPEARE, his first comedy, about the farcical events attending the separation and eventual reunion of a family with twin sons both named Antipholus and a pair of slaves, both named Dromio. (For adaptations, see Variations.)

Compleat Angler, The, or The Contemplative Man's Recreation (1653). A treatise by Izaak WALTON, both practical how-to and meditative discourse, celebrating the sport of fishing in prose, poetry, and song. It is the third most-reprinted book in the English language, after the BIBLE and SHAKESPEARE's collected works.

Comus (1634). A masque by John MILTON, written to commemorate the appointment of John Egerton, earl of Bridgewater, to the position of Lord President of Wales, in which Comus, the son of Dionysus and Circe, whisks a girl away from her two brothers and tries to convince her to become his consort.

"Concord Hymn" (1836). A poem by the Transcendentalist poet and philosopher Ralph Waldo EMERSON, commemorating the skirmish between British soldiers and Paul Revere and some 500 American minutemen in Concord, Massachusetts, on April 19, 1775.

Confessions (1782–89). A 4-volume autobiography by Jean-Jacques ROUSSEAU. Rousseau's obsessive interest in his own feelings, ideas, and beliefs heralded a new form of autobiography appropriate to the Romantic era.

Confessions of a Mask (*Kamen no Kokuhaku*, 1949). An autobiographical novel by Yukio MISHIMA, in which the narrator describes his experiences growing up homosexual in Japan.

Confessions of an English Opium-Eater (1822). A book-length autobiographical essay by English writer Thomas DE QUINCEY, providing a poetic and often terrifying glimpse into opium addiction, common in England during the early 19th century.

Confessions of Felix Krull, Confidence Man (*Bekenntnisse des Hochstaplers Felix Krull*, 1954). An unfinished, picaresque novel by Thomas MANN, exploring the theme of the incompatibility of art and morality through the life of an unprincipled con artist.

Confessions of Nat Turner, The (1967). A Pulitzer Prize–winning historical novel by William STYRON. Narrated by the leader of an 1831 Virginia slave revolt, the book explores the mysteries of one man's life as well as the idea that violence may be justified as a response to racism. Although he based the work on a historical incident, Styron took some liberties with the facts, for which he came under criticism.

Confessions of St. Augustine, The (*Confessiones*, 397–401). An account of his own spiritual development by Saint Augustine (354–430), who recalls a youth bent on sexual self-indulgence and rebellion and his conversion to Christianity. Augustine was the first writer to focus exclusively upon his own inner life, thereby establishing many of the features of the genre of autobiography.

Confessions of Zeno (*La Coscienza di Zeno*, 1923). A novel by Italo SVEVO, using modernist techniques new to Italian literature, in which the title character's attempts to understand his smoking habit through his talks with his psychiatrist reveal the intricacies of his life.

Connecticut Yankee in King Arthur's Court, A (1889). A satirical novel by Mark TWAIN, describing the journey, occasioned by a blow to the head, of Hank Morgan, a superintendent in the Colt firearms factory, back to Camelot in the 6th century. The novel served as the basis for the 1927 Broadway musical *A Connecticut Yankee*, by Richard Rodgers, Lorenz Hart, and Herbert Fields.

Cool Million, A (1934). A satirical novel by NATHANAEL WEST, examining the collision of Lemuel Pitkin's naive hope in the American dream of financial success with the nightmarish reality of life in the Great Depression.

Coriolanus (c. 1608). A play by William SHAKESPEARE, the last of his political tragedies, dramatizing the rise and fall of Roman general Caius Marcius (given the cognomen Coriolanus after his victory at Corioli).

Counterfeiters, The (*Les Faux-Monnayeurs*, 1926). A novel by André GIDE, narrated through a series of unconnected events, about a group of schoolboys who pass counterfeit money. This book is a meditation on youth's hypocritical conformity to the social values that it consciously rejects.

Count of Monte Cristo, The (*Le Comte de Monte Cristo*, 1844). A novel of adventure and intrigue by Alexandre DUMAS PÈRE, narrating the story of the unjustly accused Edmond Dantès and the painstaking revenge he exacts for the 14 years he was imprisoned. Stage adaptations of the novel were popular in the 19th century and into the 20th; James O'Neill, the actor father of playwright Eugene O'NEILL, toured in the play for decades.

Country Girls Trilogy, The. A series of novels by EDNA O'BRIEN, consisting of *The Country Girls* (1960), *The Lonely Girl* (1962), and *Girls in Their Married Bliss* (1964), which relate the story of Caithleen Brady and Bridget Brennan, two young women who leave the harshness of the countryside for Dublin, and then London, without achieving the happiness they seek. For their frank depiction of sexuality, all three works were banned in Ireland.

Country of the Pointed Firs, The (1896). A collection of short pieces by Sarah Orne JEWETT, conveying the local color of Dunnet Landing, a fictional seaside town in Maine.

Country Wife, The (1675). A play by William WYCHERLEY. Through the characters of Pinchwife, his young, unsophisticated wife Margery, and the libertine Horner, this comedy of manners mocks the hypocritical sexual mores of the Restoration era.

Cousin Bette. *See* **Human Comedy, The**

Crack-Up, The (1936). An essay by F. SCOTT FITZGERALD, describing the difficult time Fitzgerald endured beginning in 1930 with the first breakdown of his wife, Zelda, and the author's own subsequent decline.

Crime and Punishment (*Prestuplenie i Nakazanie*, 1867). A novel by Fyodor DOSTOYEVSKY. A great realist novel, this work narrates the story of RASKOLNIKOV, a student who suffers a mental breakdown, murders a miserly pawnbroker, and is thereafter tortured by guilt. (For adaptations, see Variations.)

Crome Yellow (1921). The first novel by Aldous HUXLEY, about a party given for a cast of eccentric characters at the country house of Mrs. Wimbush. Denis Stone, a young writer, commits a number of gaffes that prevent a desired love affair.

Crossing, The. *See* **Border Trilogy, The**

"Crossing Brooklyn Ferry." *See* **Leaves of Grass**

Crucible, The (1953). A play by ARTHUR MILLER, dramatizing an incident imagined during the time of the Salem witchcraft trials in the late 1600s. This work served as a not-so-veiled protest against the purges of suspected Communists being conducted by Senator Joseph McCarthy and the U.S. House Committee on Un-American Activities during the early 1950s.

Crying of Lot 49, The (1966). A complexly plotted novel by Thomas PYNCHON in which Southern California housewife Oedipa Maas, while serving as executor to her former lover Pierce Inverarity's will, uncovers the mysterious Tristero organization, an alternative postal system hinted at in his will.

Cry, the Beloved Country (1948). A novel by Alan PATON about two South African fathers, a black minister and a white landowner, trying to come to terms with the murder of the landowner's son by the son of the minister. In highly poetic language, the book explores the consequences of South Africa's racial policies. (For adaptations, see Variations.)

Custom of the Country, The (1913). A satirical novel by Edith WHARTON, critiquing the "custom of the country" in upper-class New York society at the turn of the 20th century whereby women were left ignorant of their husbands' business affairs, and had nothing to turn to but a callow materialism. The ambitious heroine is Undine Spragg. This was the novelist's own favorite among her works.

Cymbeline (c. 1610). A play by William SHAKESPEARE. Nominally based on the story of an early king of Britain, the comedy centers on the popular medieval story of a wager about a woman's virtue. Major characters are Posthumus, the husband; Imogen, his wife and King Cymbeline's daughter; and Iachimo, the aspiring seducer.

Cyrano de Bergerac (1897). A tragicomic verse drama by the French playwright Edmond Rostand (1868–1918), fancifully based on the life of the 17th-century French author of the title. Renowned for his ornate diction and unusually large nose, CYRANO DE BERGERAC helps his shy and soft-spoken friend, Christian, woo the beautiful ROXANE, with whom Cyrano himself is secretly in love. (For adaptations, see Variations.)

Daisy Miller: A Study (1878). A novel by HENRY JAMES, exploring the differences between American and European manners. The work contrasts the naive openness of the title character with the nuanced, worldly approach of her European acquaintances.

Dance of Death (*Dödsdansen*, 1901, performed 1905). A play by August STRINDBERG that explores with keen psychological insight the complex struggle for power between a dying, tyrannical husband and his wife. The play takes its name from the medieval *danse macabre*, the allegorical representation of death as alone equalizing worldly rank.

Dance to the Music of Time, A (1951–75). A *roman-fleuve* of 12 novels by ANTHONY POWELL. Grouped in three series of four novels, each representing a season and beginning with winter, the novels are narrated by Nicholas Jenkins, who describes life as it has been experienced over a period of 50 years by himself and his upper-class circle from public school into adulthood. The title comes from Nicolas Poussin's painting of the same name. The series includes *A Question of Upbringing* (1951), *A Buyer's Market* (1952), *The Acceptance World* (1955), *At Lady Molly's* (1957); *Casanova's Chinese Restaurant* (1960), *The Kindly Ones* (1962), *The Valley of Bones* (1964), *The Soldier's Art* (1966); and *The Military Philosophers* (1968), *Books Do Furnish a Room* (1971), *Temporary Kings* (1973), *Hearing Secret Harmonies* (1975).

Daniel Deronda (1876). The final novel by GEORGE ELIOT, exploring Victorian anti-Semitism through the title character and the two women with whom he is involved, Gwendolyn Harleth and Mirah Cohen.

Danton's Death (*Dantons Tod*, published 1835, performed 1902). A play by Georg BÜCHNER, dramatizing the last days in the life of Georges Jacques Danton, a disillusioned hero of the French Revolution sentenced to death in 1794 by his former political allies.

Daphnis and Chloe (*Daphnis kai Chloē*, c. 300–500). A pastoral poem attributed to the Greek sophist Longus about two innocents, Daphnis and Chloe, who are separated by kidnappers but eventually reunite. It greatly influenced later English and French pastorals, including *Rosalynde* (1590) by Thomas Lodge (c. 1557–1625), the principal source for William SHAKESPEARE's *AS YOU LIKE IT*.

Darkness at Noon (1940). A political novel by Arthur KOESTLER. The story follows the moral and physical destruction of Nicholas RUBASHOV, an old Bolshevik, who has spoken out against the tyranny of his former comrades.

David Copperfield (in full: *The Personal History of David Copperfield*, 1850). Autobiographical novel by Charles DICKENS, narrated by its title character, David COPPERFIELD. Among his most beloved works for its humor, humanity, and large cast of unforgettable characters, such as the optimistic spendthrift Mr. MICAWBER and the hypocritical, "umble" Uriah HEEP, it also has room for Dickens's characteristically trenchant observations on social injustice. Dickens said of the work, "Like many fond parents, I have in my heart of hearts a favourite child. And his name is David Copperfield."

Day of the Locust, The (1939). A novel by Nathanael WEST, depicting the bleak lives of people at the margins of the Hollywood film industry through the eyes of a young painter working as a film set designer.

Day of the Scorpion, The. *See* **Raj Quartet, The**

"Dead, The" (1914). A short story by James JOYCE, centering on Gabriel CONROY, who spends an evening with his wife at his aunts' Christmas party, and later reflects movingly on mortality. Considered among the author's finest stories, it is included in the collection *DUBLINERS*. (For adaptations, see Variations.)

Dead Souls (*Mertvye Dushi*, 1842). A satirical novel by Nikolai GOGOL about wily Pavel Ivanovich CHICHIKOV, who schemes to make his fortune by buying from landowners at a reduced price serfs (or "souls") who have died

PARTING WORDS: LAST LINES

Presented in chronological order, the following are some memorable, famous, and striking last lines in literature.

My work is complete: a work which neither Jove's anger, nor fire nor sword shall destroy, nor yet the gnawing tooth of time.... If there be any truth in poets' prophecies, I shall live to all eternity, immortalized by fame.

Ovid, *Metamorphoses* (c. A.D. 8), translated by Mary M. Innes (1955)

For never was a story more full of woe
Than this of Juliet and her Romeo.

William Shakespeare, *Romeo and Juliet* (1595)

L – – d! said my mother, what is all this story about?———

A COCK and a BULL, said Yorick———And one of the best of its kind, I ever heard.

Laurence Sterne, *Tristram Shandy* (1759–67)

Melmoth and Monçada exchanged looks of silent and unutterable horror, and returned slowly home.

Charles Robert Maturin, *Melmoth the Wanderer* (1820)

When they attempted to detach this skeleton from the one it was embracing, it fell to dust.

Victor Hugo, *The Hunchback of Notre Dame* (1831), translated by Jessie Haynes (1903)

And so, as Tiny Tim observed, God bless Us, Every One!

Charles Dickens, *A Christmas Carol* (1843)

I lingered round them [the head-stones], under that benign sky; watched the moths fluttering among the heath and harebells, listened to the soft wind breathing through the grass, and

---

since the last census, and then mortgaging these "dead souls" to raise money to buy his own estate.

"Death Be Not Proud" (1633). A poem in sonnet form by John DONNE. One of his series of devotional lyrics known as the *Holy Sonnets*, this work begins, "Death be not proud, though some have called thee / Mighty and dreadful, for thou art not so."

Death Comes for the Archbishop (1927). A novel by Willa CATHER depicting the struggles of Jean LATOUR, a French Catholic priest, as he strives to establish a diocese in 19th-century New Mexico.

Death in the Family, A (1957). A Pulitzer Prize–winning, unfinished autobiographical novel by James AGEE, describing an accident that destroys a family's way of life. Told through the eyes of six-year-old Rufus, the story explores the reactions of the family members to the death of one of their own. The novel was adapted for the stage by Tad Mosel as *All the Way Home* (1960; Pulitzer Prize) and was filmed in 1963.

wondered how any one could ever imagine unquiet slumber for the sleepers in that quiet earth.

Emily Brontë, *Wuthering Heights* (1847)

Now small fowls flew screaming over the yet yawning gulf; a sullen white surf beat against its steep sides; then all collapsed, and the great shroud of the sea rolled on as it rolled five thousand years ago.

Herman Melville, *Moby-Dick* (1851)

"It is a far, far better thing that I do, than I have ever done; it is a far, far better rest that I go to than I have ever known."

Sydney Carton, just before he is guillotined, in Charles Dickens's *A Tale of Two Cities* (1859)

Like a fallen spirit shut out from eternal life, Tempest looked at him a moment, then, as the old fire blazed up within him for the last time, he drove a hidden dagger into his breast, and, dropping on his knees, gathered the dead woman in his arms, saying with mingled love and defiance in his despairing voice, "Mine first—mine last—mine even in the grave."

Louisa May Alcott, *A Long Fatal Love Chase* (written 1866; first published 1995)

But I reckon I got to light out for the Territory ahead of the rest, because Aunt Sally she's going to adopt me and sivilize me and I can't stand it. I been there before.

Mark Twain, *The Adventures of Huckleberry Finn* (1884)

He steered his course out towards the new Christmas star, out over the sea, the mother of all, in whose womb the first spark of life was lit, the inexhaustible well of fertility and love, life's source, and life's enemy.

August Strindberg, *By the Open Sea* (1890), translated by Mary Sandbach (1984)

The offing was barred by a black bank of clouds, and the tranquil waterway leading to the uttermost ends of the earth flowed sombre under an overcast sky—seemed to lead into the heart of an immense darkness.

Joseph Conrad, *Heart of Darkness* (1902)

Death in Venice (*Der Tod in Venedig*, 1912). A novella by Thomas MANN. On holiday in Venice, the respected author Gustav von ASCHENBACH, whose life has been one of discipline and sober self-restraint, yields to an unbridled passion for the "perfect beauty" of a 14-year-old boy, Tadzio. It was filmed by Luchino Visconti (1971) and adapted as an opera by Benjamin Britten (1973).

Death of Artemio Cruz, The (*La Muerte de Artemio Cruz*, 1962). A novel by Carlos FUENTES. Structured as a dispute among the different parts of the soul of a dying man, Artemio CRUZ, this novel weighs the meaning of his life through an examination of the former revolutionary's compromised idealism and his place in 20th-century Mexican history.

Death of a Salesman (1949). A Pulitzer Prize–winning play by ARTHUR MILLER. A savage indictment of the spiritual costs of American consumerism, this drama looks at the life of Willy LOMAN, a failed, 63-year-old salesman who realizes that he has not achieved success on any terms.

"Death of Ivan Ilyich, The" ("Smert' Ivana Il'icha," 1886). A short story by Leo TOLSTOY,

(Parting Words: Last Lines, continued)

…and I thought well as well him as another and then I asked him with my eyes to ask again yes and then he asked me would I yes to say yes my mountain flower and first I put my arms around his and drew him down to me so that he could feel my breasts all perfume yes and his heart was going like mad and yes I said yes I will Yes.

Molly Bloom, in James Joyce's *Ulysses* (1922)

Moments there were, when out of death, and the rebellion of the flesh, there came to thee, as thou tookest stock of thyself, a dream of love. Out of this universal feast of death, out of this extremity of fever, kindling the rain-washed evening sky to a fiery glow, may it be that Love one day shall mount?

Thomas Mann, *The Magic Mountain* (1924), translated by H. T. Lowe-Porter (1927)

And the widow bird, startled, flew away, describing wider and wider circles until it became (what she called her soul) remote as a crow which has been startled up into the air by a stone thrown at it.

Virginia Woolf, *Mrs. Dalloway* (1925)

So we beat on, boats against the current, borne back ceaselessly into the past.

F. Scott Fitzgerald, *The Great Gatsby* (1925)

The broken flower drooped over Ben's fist and his eyes were empty and blue and serene again as cornice and façade flowed smoothly once more from left to right, post to tree, window and doorway and signboard each in its ordered place.

William Faulkner, *The Sound and the Fury* (1929)

He disliked bars and bodegas. A clean, well-lighted café was a very different thing. Now,

---

whose title character, a judge absorbed in bureaucratic routine and conventional values, undergoes a crisis of meaning when he discovers he has terminal cancer.

Death of the Heart, The (1938). A novel by Elizabeth BOWEN. A coming-of-age story that follows the disillusionment of Portia Quayne, a 16-year-old orphan who goes to live in London with her superficial and callous half-brother and his wife.

"Death of the Hired Man, The" (1914). A narrative poem by Robert FROST. Published in the volume *North of Boston*, the poem is a meditation on the nature of home as seen through the

return of Silas, an old farm hand, to the farm where he used to work.

Death of Virgil, The (*Der Tod des Vergil*, 1945). A novel by Hermann BROCH, a meditation on the role of literature in times of historical tumult as portrayed through the last 18 hours in the life of the poet VIRGIL.

Death on the Installment Plan (*Mort à Credit*, 1936). An autobiographical novel by Louis-Ferdinand CÉLINE that traces Ferdinand Bardamu's troubled coming of age amid squalor and poverty.

Decameron, The (*Decamerone*, 1351–53). A collection of 100 stories by Giovanni BOCCAC-

without thinking further, he would go home to his room. He would lie in the bed and finally, with daylight, he would go to sleep. After all, he said to himself, it is probably only insomnia. Many must have it.

Ernest Hemingway, "A Clean, Well-lighted Place" (1933)

When the flames reached him at last, he laughed out loud, louder than he had ever laughed in all his life.

Elias Canetti, *Auto-da-Fé* (1935), translated by C. V. Wedgwood (1946)

"Tomorrow, I'll think of some way to get him back. After all, tomorrow is another day."

Scarlett O'Hara, in Margaret Mitchell's *Gone with the Wind* (1936)

He heard the ring of steel against steel as a far door clanged shut.

Richard Wright, *Native Son* (1940)

The creatures outside looked from pig to man, and from man to pig, and from pig to man again; but already it was impossible to say which was which.

George Orwell, *Animal Farm* (1945)

"And now," he said, "I am going to tell you the story of Pnin, rising to address the Cremona Women's Club and discovering that he had brought the wrong lecture."

Vladimir Nabokov, *Pnin* (1957)

This ecstasy at its peak may glow on a body stripped by penury, bared to its own aridity, but on a will that the challenge of joy has made free.

Naguib Mahfouz, *Wedding Song* (1980), translated by Olive E. Kenny (1984)

To the both of them and to you I say: put an egg in your shoe, and beat it. Make like a tree, and leave. Tell your story walking.

Jonathan Lethem, *Motherless Brooklyn* (1999)

CIO. A masterpiece of the Renaissance, this work recounts tales told to one another over the course of ten days by ten young people who have fled to a rural retreat to avoid an outbreak of the Black Plague in Florence in 1348. The title literally means "Ten Days." (For adaptations, see Variations.)

Decline and Fall (1928). A satiric novel by EVELYN WAUGH, recounting the travails of Paul Pennyfeather, whose troubles begin when he is expelled from Oxford and is forced to take a job as a teacher at a British public school.

Deerslayer, The. *See* **Leatherstocking Tales, The**

"Dejection: An Ode" (1802). An autobiographical poem by Samuel Taylor COLERIDGE, written as a letter in verse to his beloved and describing the poet's fear of aging, which he feels has led to a loss of his artistic ability and the keenness of his appreciation for nature.

De Profundis (published posthumously in 1905). A letter written in prison by Oscar WILDE to his lover, Lord Alfred Douglas, in which Wilde recalls their relationship with both resentment and hope for the possibility of a renewed friendship. The title, the first two words of Psalm 130, means "out of the depths." The complete, unexpurgated text of this very long letter was first published in Rupert

Hart-Davis's 1962 edition of Wilde's collected correspondence.

Design for Living (1933). A play by Noël COW-ARD. This comedy, shocking in its day, explores the complicated but clever ménage à trois formed by three worldly, witty characters—a painter, a playwright, and the woman they both love—who devise a satisfying way of life beyond convention.

Desire Under the Elms (1924). A play by Eugene O'NEILL. This drama tells the story of a father and son, Ephraim and Eben, both of whom lust for the father's calculating young bride, Abbie, and of the tragic consequences that follow Abbie's pregnancy with Eben's child.

Dharma Bums, The (1958). An autobiographical novel by Jack KEROUAC that deals with the search for alternatives to the stultifying values of conventional American society. The character of Japhy Ryder is based on Kerouac's poet friend Gary SNYDER.

"Diamond as Big as the Ritz, The" (1922). An early short story by F. SCOTT FITZGERALD, published in *Tales of the Jazz Age*, about a man's obsession with preserving his own wealth, even at the cost of his death and the deaths of his wife and son.

Diary of a Country Priest, The (*Journal d'un Curé de Campagne*, 1936). A novel by Georges BERNANOS, about a priest's struggle to live his faith in the face of the indifference and hostility of his parishioners. The 1950 French film adaptation was directed by Robert Bresson.

"Diary of a Madman" ("Zapiski Sumasshed-skogo," 1835). A story by Nikolai GOGOL, included in the collection *Arabesques* (*Ara-beski*, 1835). Gogol's only experiment with first-person narrative, "Diary of a Madman" is a comical and disturbing series of diary entries written by Poprishchin, an inept civil servant in St. Petersburg who is gradually going insane.

"Diary of a Superfluous Man" ("Dnevnik Lishnego Cheloveka," 1850). A short story by Ivan TURGENEV that vividly depicts the triviality and emptiness of upper-class life in 19th-

century Russia. The story introduced the term "superfluous man" to describe the alienated, disillusioned men of the gentry. In the form of diary entries, the work recounts the last two weeks of Chulkaturin's life and his unrequited love for Liza.

Divine Comedy, The (*La Divina Commedia*, c. 1314–21). A long, allegorical poem by DANTE Alighieri, one of the masterworks of Western literature. Written in terza rima, the poem describes Dante's imaginary tour through the afterworlds of Inferno, Purgatorio, and Paradiso, accompanied in the first two by the Roman poet VIRGIL and in Paradise by his beloved BEATRICE.

Division of the Spoils, A. *See* **Raj Quartet, The**

Doctor Faustus (*Doktor Faustus*, 1947). A novel by Thomas MANN. This modern adaptation of the FAUST legend is meant to symbolize the tragic consequences of Germany's embrace of Nazism. The protagonist, Adrian LEVER-KÜHN, a talented musician, sells his soul to the Devil in exchange for 24 years of fame as the world's greatest living composer.

Doctor Faustus, The Tragicall History of (c. 1588). A tragedy by Christopher MARLOWE based on the medieval FAUST legend of a man who sells his soul to the devil in exchange for a lifetime of power and knowledge.

Doctor Thorne. *See* **Barsetshire Novels**

Doctor Zhivago (*Doktor Zhivago*, 1957). A novel by Boris PASTERNAK, set in Russia during and after the Revolution. The young doctor/poet Yury ZHIVAGO, who struggles to survive the brutality of the Bolshevik regime, is in love with LARA, the wife of a revolutionary. The book's anti-Marxism made it unpublishable in the Soviet Union until 1987; it appeared in print first in Italy in 1957.

Doll's House, A (*Et Dukkehjem*, 1879; also translated under the title *A Doll House*). A play by Henrik IBSEN, examining how Nora HELMER comes to be disillusioned by her husband and to question her role as a cosseted wife, after her husband repudiates her when he discovers that she once committed a forgery to obtain a loan of money needed to save his life. At play's end, Nora leaves her husband, an action that has become a symbol of women's liberation.

Dombey and Son (in full: *Dealings with the Firm of Dombey and Son, Wholesale, Retail, and for Exportation*, 1848). A novel by Charles DICKENS with a central character, Paul DOMBEY, who pushes away his daughter, Florence, in favor of his son Paul, whom Dombey wants to inherit the family shipping business.

Don Juan (1819–24). A comic epic by Lord BYRON, consisting of 16 cantos in ottava rima as well as a fragment of a 17th canto, left unfinished at his death. Byron's Don JUAN is not the roguish philanderer of Spanish legend, but rather a man struggling against the petty dictates of conventional society. Exiled from Spain at 16 after a scandalous affair, Byron's hero embarks on colorful adventures that take him around the world, giving Byron ample opportunity to satirize the political, philosophical, and social hypocrisies of his age. *Don Juan* is considered Byron's supreme accomplishment.

"Do Not Go Gentle into That Good Night" (1952). A villanelle by Dylan THOMAS, included in the collection *In Country Sleep*. Addressed to his dying father, the poem reflects on the multiple, yet ultimately unsatisfactory, ways of greeting death, while exhorting humanity to cling to life, despite inevitable failure.

Don Quixote (*El Ingenioso Hidalgo Don Quijote de la Mancha*, 1605–15). A picaresque novel by Miguel de CERVANTES y Saavedra. Generally considered the first Western novel, this is a tale of the adventures of an idealistic old man, Don QUIXOTE de la Mancha, who, inspired by reading too many gallant knight-errant romances, sets out to right the world's wrongs, only to mistake windmills for giants and sheep for soldiers. He is accompanied by his squire, the pragmatic Sancho PANZA, and falls in love with the lady DULCINEA DEL TOBOSO, in reality an ordinary peasant girl named Aldonza. (For adaptations, see Variations.)

"Dover Beach" (1867). A poem by Matthew ARNOLD, published in *New Poems* (1867), about

the loss of faith that plagues the modern era, with the famous lines, "And we are here as on a darkling plain / Swept with confused alarms of struggle and flight, / Where ignorant armies clash by night."

Down and Out in Paris and London (1933). The first published work by George ORWELL, chronicling in fictional form the period the author spent living among the impoverished of the two cities.

Dracula (1897). A Gothic novel by Bram STOKER. Based on vampire folklore and the historical prince Vlad the Impaler, this classic work relates the story of Count Dracula; Jonathan Harker; Harker's fiancée, Mina; and Mina's friend Lucy, whom Dracula turns into a vampire. (For adaptations, see Variations.)

Dream of the Red Chamber (*Honglou Meng*, c. 1763). A novel by CAO ZHAN, probably with additions by Gao E. This autobiographical work, considered one of the greatest Chinese novels, tells the story of Bao-yu, the much indulged youngest son of a large clan, who prefers the company of women to the serious pursuits his father demands of him.

"Dreary Story, A" ("Skuchnaya Istoriya," 1889). A short story by Anton CHEKHOV, exploring the fears and sorrows of Professor Nikolai Stepanovich as he approaches death, and the lack of communication between him and his ward Katya.

Dr. Jekyll and Mr. Hyde, The Strange Case of (1886). A novella by Robert Louis STEVENSON about the duality of good and evil. The honorable Dr. Henry JEKYLL develops a formula that will isolate his sinister aspects, giving rise to the evil Mr. Edward Hyde. Unable to control this metamorphosis, Jekyll commits suicide, destroying both personas. (For adaptations, see Variations.)

"Drunken Boat, The" ("Le Bateau Ivre," 1871). A poem by Arthur RIMBAUD. Written when the author was 16 years old, this description of a boat tossed at sea by the violent and overwhelming forces of a storm parallels the poet's internal experience of the creative process.

"Dry Salvages, The" (1941). A poem by T. S. ELIOT, the third of the *FOUR QUARTETS*, which takes its title from a rock formation near Cape Ann, Massachusetts. The strong internal unity of this poem contrasts sharply with Eliot's earlier work. "Salvages" rhymes with "assuages."

Dubliners (1914). A collection of short stories by James JOYCE. Written in what Joyce called a spirit of "scrupulous meanness," these stories lay bare the hypocrisy, provincialism, and occasional humor of the city he eventually fled. The final story, "THE DEAD," is considered to be among the world's greatest short stories.

Duchess of Malfi, The (c. 1613). A revenge tragedy by JOHN WEBSTER. The last of the great Elizabethan dramas, it concerns the widowed duchess's marriage to her steward, Antonio, which is kept secret for fear of angering her status-conscious and greedy brothers.

Duino Elegies (*Duineser Elegien*, 1923). A cycle of ten poems by Rainer Maria RILKE, begun at Duino Castle near Trieste. The poems took ten years to write, although the last five were composed in a three-week burst of creativity that also produced the *SONNETS TO ORPHEUS*. Elegies in mood, if not in form, these influential and haunting poems respond to the problems of the modern era by invoking the great mysteries of the universe and affirming the essential and creative unity of life and death.

Duke's Children, The. *See* **Pallisers, The**

Dunciad, The (1728, revised 1729, 1742, 1743). A mock epic by Alexander POPE. Written to belittle Pope's critics, these caustic heroic couplets describe the career of the goddess Dulness and her favorite, the King of the Dunces, with their minions of foolish scholars and critics. Pope's first King of the Dunces was Lewis Theobald (1688–1744), a scholar who had criticized Pope's edition of SHAKESPEARE. The object of derision was changed to second-rate playwright and Poet Laureate Colley Cibber (1671–1757) in the 1742 version.

Dune (1965). A Hugo and Nebula Award–winning science fiction epic by FRANK HERBERT. Marrying fantasy with ecological concerns, the story is set on the desert planet of Arrakis (Dune), where a young man's exposure to a unique herb gives him the power to resist a violent regime. Herbert followed his bestselling novel with a series of sequels: *Dune Messiah* (1969), *Children of Dune* (1976), *God Emperor of Dune* (1981), *Heretics of Dune* (1981), and *Chapterhouse: Dune* (1985). Brian Herbert and Kevin Anderson have written a "prequel," *Dune: House Harkonnen* (2000).

Dust Tracks on a Road (1942). A memoir by Zora Neale HURSTON that engagingly describes the author's spirited childhood in the all-black town of Eatonville, Florida; her development as a young writer; and her pioneering work to collect Southern black folklore. The work has been controversial since its publication for its factual unreliability and its marked reticence to confront the issue of racism.

Dutchman (1964). A play by Amiri BARAKA. This one-act drama exploring racism is set in a New York City subway car, where a provocatively dressed white woman flirts with a bourgeois black man, then stabs him when he is goaded into revealing his anger at white society. The title alludes to the legendary cursed ship, *The Flying Dutchman* (the stage directions describe the subway as "the flying underbelly of the city").

Dybbuk, The (*Der Dibek*, 1920). An Expressionist drama by the Russian ethnologist S. Ansky (1863–1920), based on the Hasidic legend of the *dybbuk*, a disembodied spirit in search of a human body to inhabit.

"East Coker" (1940). A poem by T. S. ELIOT, the second of the *FOUR QUARTETS*. Named for the Somersetshire village of his ancestors and the place he chose to be buried, the poem continues Eliot's search, begun in the first quartet, for spiritual and artistic fulfillment.

"Easter, 1916" (1921). A poem by William Butler YEATS, paying tribute to the martyrs of the April 24, 1916, Easter Rising, when Irish nationalists demanded that England honor its promise of Irish home rule. British forces quashed the insurrection, and 16 rebel leaders, including acquaintances of the poet, were later executed.

East of Eden (1952). A novel by John STEIN-BECK. Through a reworking of the Cain and Abel story, the novel examines the nature of evil and the question of free will. Set mainly in California's Salinas Valley, the story covers two generations of the TRASK family, with the emphasis on the second generation—the troubled Caleb and his twin, the righteous Aron, who is psychologically destroyed when Caleb reveals that their mother is a notorious prostitute. (For adaptations, see Variations.)

Education of Henry Adams, The (privately published, 1907; posthumously published, 1918). A Pulitzer Prize–winning autobiography by Henry ADAMS, grandson of President John Quincy Adams, in which the author uses his life story as a framework for a meditation on the nature and effects of education.

Edward II (c. 1592). A play by Christopher MARLOWE, generally considered his masterpiece, condensing the 34-year reign of England's King Edward II into a single year.

Effi Briest (1895). A novel by Theodor FONTANE, portraying the short, unhappy life of the title character, married by arrangement to an older husband, Baron von Instetten, who is "as noble as one can be who is without real love," but who cannot forgive her fleeting affair with an army major when he learns about it several years after the fact. The 1974 Rainer Werner Fassbinder film starred Hanna Schygulla.

Egoist, The: A Comedy in Narrative (1879). A comic novel by George MEREDITH about a self-absorbed, domineering man, Sir Willoughby PATTERNE, engaged in a difficult search for a wife.

Electra (*Ēlektra*, c. 413 B.C.). A tragedy by EURIPIDES about ELECTRA's desire to kill her mother, Clytemnestra, to avenge the murder of her father, AGAMEMNON. In contrast to the treatments by AESCHYLUS (in the *ORESTEIA*) and SOPHOCLES, Euripides makes Clytemnestra a sympathetic character, and makes clear his belief that blood vengeance is evil.

Electra (*Ēlektra*, 4th century B.C.). A tragedy by SOPHOCLES. Believing her brother ORESTES dead and herself powerless to avenge their father's death, Sophocles' ELECTRA achieves heroic status through her fierce desire for justice. Clytemnestra is portrayed as an unfeeling monster, in contrast to the more generous portrayal of her by Euripides.

Elegy Written in a Country Churchyard, An (1751). A poem by Thomas GRAY. The melancholy speaker in this poem mourns the lost potential of those who lie buried in a rural graveyard and meditates on the transitory nature of existence.

Elmer Gantry (1927). A novel by SINCLAIR LEWIS. A savage satire of fundamentalist religion, this is the story of a charismatic evangelist, Elmer GANTRY, whose personal charm conceals his ambition and self-interest.

Émile, or, On Education (*Émile, ou, De l'Éducation*, 1762). A novel of ideas by Jean-Jacques ROUSSEAU, describing the title character's education. Based on the author's belief that individuals are oppressed by a constricting society, it proposes a "negative education," in which the young "savage" is isolated from the larger world so that he may develop naturally. The work enormously influenced 19th-century pedagogy.

Emma (1816). A novel by Jane AUSTEN, following the intrusive and deluded Emma WOODHOUSE, who interferes in her friends' romances with nearly catastrophic and amusing results, finally to be set right when she marries George Knightley. (For adaptations, see Variations.)

Emperor Jones, The (1920). An Expressionist play by Eugene O'NEILL, dramatizing the adventures of Brutus JONES, an African-American ex-Pullman porter and escaped convict, who establishes himself as dictator of a West Indian island. (For adaptations, see Variations.)

Endgame (*Fin de Partie*, 1957). A play by Samuel BECKETT. A leading example of Theater of the Absurd, this play, generally considered one of Beckett's finest works, offers a bleak and spare account of four characters—a demanding blind man (Hamm), his attendant (Clov), and

Hamm's elderly parents (Nagg and Nell)—who live in a world seemingly at its end. Punctuated with crucifixion and chess imagery, *Endgame* poses existential questions about life, death, human relationships, and the nature of God.

End of the Affair, The (1951). A novel by Graham GREENE, exploring themes of personal guilt and religious faith through the adulterous affair between Sarah Miles and Maurice Bendrix during the blitz of London in World War II and the years that follow. Bendrix narrates the story, but the diaries of Sarah contribute a counter point of view.

Endymion: A Poetic Romance (1818). A book-length narrative poem by John KEATS, about the shepherd Endymion's quest for a beautiful woman he saw in a dream, eventually revealed as the moon goddess Cynthia. The opening lines are among Keats's most famous: "A thing of beauty is a joy for ever: / Its loveliness increases; it will never / Pass into nothingness . . ." The reviews were savage, but Keats had already grown beyond the work with which he said he "leaped headlong into the sea" of poetry.

Enemy of the People, An (*En Folkefiende*, 1882). A play by Henrik IBSEN. When Dr. Stockman, commissioned to investigate the condition of the local baths, the town's sole tourist attraction, reports that its water is dangerously contaminated, the town persecutes him for his integrity.

Enfants Terribles, Les (1929). A novel by Jean COCTEAU. Translated as *The Holy Terrors* and as *The Children of the Game*, but often published in translation under its original title, the work examines the close relationship between a brother and sister who live in their own elaborate fantasy world. Cocteau adapted the novel for the screen in 1950.

Enormous Room, The (1922). An autobiographical novel by E. E. CUMMINGS about a man who is wrongly suspected of treason and imprisoned in a French military concentration camp during World War I.

Entertainer, The (1959). A play by John OSBORNE. Filled with harsh realism and anti-establishment sentiments, the play presents a portrait of a third-rate music hall comedian whose struggles to hide his failure simultaneously evoke admiration and pity. His deterioration and the decrepit Empire Music Hall where he performs also serve as metaphors for Great Britain's faltering world power.

Erewhon (1872). A satirical novel by Samuel BUTLER. In this anti-utopian novel, a traveler-narrator visits the utopia of Erewhon (an anagram for "nowhere") and gradually loses faith in the creeds of eternal human progress and a perfectible world. *Erewhon Revisited*, a sequel, was published in 1901.

Essay on Criticism, An (1711). A didactic poem by Alexander POPE that lays out rules of literary taste and style based on a classical understanding of art. It includes the famous couplet, "A little learning is a dangerous thing; / Drink deep, or taste not the Pierian spring."

Essay on Man, An (1733–34). A philosophical poem by Alexander POPE that attempts to "vindicate the ways of God to man." Inspired by and addressed to Lord Bolingbroke, Pope's patron, the poem advocates a religion based on reason rather than revelation.

Essays (First Series, 1841; Second Series, 1844). Collections of essays by Ralph Waldo EMERSON, presenting his Transcendentalist views on the immanence of God and the absolute importance of the individual.

Essays (*Essais*, 1580–88). A collection of essays by Michel de MONTAIGNE, in which the author examines human nature through an examination of his own life. The work introduced to Western literature, and gave a name to, the modern form of short, secular, personal exploration.

Ethan Frome (1911). A novel by Edith WHARTON, a grim tale of futility and psychological alienation set on an isolated farm in turn-of-the-century New England, where Ethan FROME seeks solace from a confining marriage in the company of his sickly wife's cousin, Mattie. The author compared her characters to the "granite outcroppings" of their native soil.

Eugene Onegin (*Evgeniĭ Onegin*, 1833). A novel in verse by Aleksandr PUSHKIN, generally considered the finest work of Russia's greatest poet. The world-weary Onegin spurns the naive, provincial Tatyana, and kills his best friend in a petty duel. Years later it is Tatyana, now married and a dazzling sophisticate, who rejects Onegin. Besides its brilliant poetry, the work contains sharply incisive portraits of contemporary Russian society. (For adaptations, see Variations.)

Eugénie Grandet. *See* **Human Comedy, The**

Eumenides. *See* **Oresteia**

Eustace Diamonds, The. *See* **Pallisers, The**

Evangeline, A Tale of Acadie (1847). A narrative poem by Henry Wadsworth LONGFELLOW, relating the tale of lovers separated when the British cast out the Acadians (French colonists) from Nova Scotia.

"Eve of St. Agnes, The" (1820). A narrative poem by John KEATS, based on a legend that on St. Agnes's feast day (January 20) a maiden will receive a vision of her future husband while she sleeps.

Everyman (late 15th century). An English morality play by an unknown author, based on the Flemish play *Elckerlyc*, which was first printed in 1495. Summoned by Death to give a reckoning of his life before God, Everyman learns that he must meet his fate unaccompanied by any of his gifts except those he has bestowed on others: his Good Deeds.

"Everything That Rises Must Converge" (1961). A short story by FLANNERY O'CONNOR, reprinted in the collection of the same name (1965). An embittered young Southern white man with delusions of moral superiority is confronted with his own inadequacies when his mother suffers a fatal stroke after a confrontation with a black woman, who takes her condescending gesture of friendliness amiss. The title is taken from the Jesuit Pierre Teilhard de Chardin's (1881–1955) theory that human evolution continues beyond the biological to the spiritual.

Executioner's Song, The (1979). A Pulitzer Prize–winning so-called "true-life" novel by Norman MAILER about the life and execution of murderer Gary Gilmore. Based on research and Mailer's interviews with Gilmore, the novel presents the story of an articulate, violent convict who chooses to die for his crimes rather than appeal his death sentence.

Eye in the Door, The. *See* **Regeneration Trilogy, The**

Eyeless in Gaza (1936). An autobiographical novel by Aldous HUXLEY, which charts the spiritual awakening of Anthony Beavis, who, critical of his society and his own aimless life, accompanies a friend to join the Mexican Revolution. The title is taken from MILTON's *SAMSON AGONISTES* (1671).

Fable for Critics, A (1848). A verse satire containing JAMES RUSSELL LOWELL's shrewd and wittily rhymed assessments of William Cullen BRYANT, James Fenimore COOPER, Ralph Waldo EMERSON, Margaret FULLER, Nathaniel HAWTHORNE, WASHINGTON IRVING, Henry Wadsworth LONGFELLOW, Edgar Allan POE, Henry David THOREAU, John Greenleaf WHITTIER, and other contemporary American writers, including Lowell himself. The full original title is a hundred-word jingle, beginning, "Reader! walk up at once (it will soon be too late) and buy at a perfectly ruinous rate A *Fable for Critics*..."

Fables (*Fables Choisies Mises en Vers*, 1668–94). A collection by Jean de LA FONTAINE, comprising some 240 rhymed miniatures drawn chiefly from AESOP and other ancient sources, including "The Grasshopper and the Ant," "The Hare and the Tortoise," and "Philemon and Baucis." La Fontaine retells the familiar stories of animals, gods, and ordinary country folk in poised and elegant verse, often leaving it to the reader to supply the moral. The *Fables* has been widely imitated and frequently translated; one English version is by MARIANNE MOORE.

Faerie Queene, The (1590–96). An allegorical poem in six books by Edmund SPENSER in praise of Christian virtue. GLORIANA, ruler of the land of Faerie, represents Queen

Elizabeth, while knights of the mythic realm personify Holiness, Temperance, Chastity, Friendship, Justice, and Courtesy. The poet created a nine-line stanza, now called Spenserian in his honor, for this work, which was originally intended to comprise 12 books. Fragments of a seventh book were published as *Two Cantos of Mutabilitie* in the folio edition of 1609.

Fahrenheit 451 (1953). An anti-utopian novel by Ray BRADBURY, a classic of speculative fiction. In a future time when the written word is forbidden, firemen whose helmets bear the number "451" (the flashpoint of paper) are sent out to burn all surviving books. One of them, Montag, begins hoarding books, and joins a group of people who memorize books to preserve them. The novel was filmed by François Truffaut in 1966.

Fall, The (*La Chute*, 1956). A short novel by Albert CAMUS about a personal confession to a stranger in an Amsterdam bar that turns into a meditation on the absurdity and alienation of the human condition and the impossibility of innocence.

"Fall of the House of Usher, The" (1839). A Gothic short story by Edgar Allan POE, first published in 1839 and collected in *Tales of the Grotesque and Arabesque* (1840). The unnamed first-person narrator visits the gloomy mansion of his childhood friend Roderick USHER. During his stay, Usher's sister, Madeleine, apparently dies and is entombed in a vault in the house. When she escapes and appears before them, the narrator runs from the house, which collapses upon the Ushers, apparently under the weight of terrible family secrets. (For adaptations, see Variations.)

Family Moskat, The (*Di Familye Mushkat*, 1950). A novel by Isaac Bashevis SINGER about several generations of a Jewish family living in Warsaw. The saga paints a vivid portrait of Jewish life in Poland from the turn of the 20th century until the outbreak of World War II.

Farewell to Arms, A (1929). Ernest HEMINGWAY's novel, based on his war experiences in the Italian ambulance corps, is both a tragic love story and a prime expression of the Lost Generation's disillusionment with the ideals that led to the Great War. "I was always embarrassed by the words *sacred, glorious,* and *sacrifice* and the expression *in vain*," remarks American lieutenant Frederic HENRY, shortly before deserting to be with British nurse Catherine BARKLEY, who is carrying his child. (For adaptations, see Variations.)

Far from the Madding Crowd (1874). A novel by Thomas HARDY. Bathsheba Everdene inherits, and learns how to run, a Wessex farm. She marries the feckless Sergeant Troy, enraging her prosperous neighbor, William Boldwood, whom she has irresponsibly encouraged, with disastrous results. Eventually she finds peace in marriage with Gabriel Oak, a farmer who remains loyal to her throughout changes in his fortune and hers. The title derives from Thomas GRAY's *ELEGY WRITTEN IN A COUNTRY CHURCHYARD* (1751).

Father, The (*Fadren*, 1887). A tragedy by August STRINDBERG. Like *MISS JULIE* (1889), this play employs a raw, naturalistic style to illustrate Strindberg's idea of the battle of the sexes, this time within a tortuous marriage where the wife has the upper hand. She drives her husband to madness by causing him to doubt that he is the father of their child.

Father and Son (1907). An autobiography by the English author Edmund Gosse (1849–1928) detailing his struggle against his father, zoologist Philip Henry Gosse, and his ultimate rejection of his father's strict religious views. The father/son clash, in which the son chooses science, intellect, and rational thought over religious faith, reflects a key confict of its era. Gosse published the work anonymously.

Fathers and Sons (*Ottsy i Deti*, 1862). A novel by Ivan TURGENEV about generational conflict, in which the young, arrogant, nihilist intellectual Bazarov visits his friend Arkady and clashes with Arkady's uncle Pavel Kirsanov, who belongs to the older, more conservative generation. The novel was severely criticized by both radicals and conservatives and its reception contributed to Turgenev's decision to leave Russia.

Faust: A Tragedy, Parts I and II (*Faust, eine Tragödie*, published 1808, performed 1829; *Faust, der Tragödie Zweiter Teil*, published 1832, performed 1854). A dramatic poem by Johann Wolfgang von GOETHE, his greatest poetic achievement and a pinnacle of world literature. Written over a span of 60 years, it contains a dazzling variety of styles, subjects, and verse forms, woven around the familiar theme of a magician's pact with the Devil, to which Goethe adds a wager: FAUST bets MEPHISTOPHELES that he will never cease to strive; until he does, Mephisto must be his servant. Adaptations in many media include Gounod's opera (1859) and Murnau's film (1926).

Fences (1986). A Pulitzer Prize–winning play by AUGUST WILSON. Set in 1950s Pittsburgh, it tells the story of a former Negro League ballplayer whose fruitless struggles against racism blind him to the fences he sets around his own family.

Fictions (*Ficciones*, 1944). A collection of short narratives by Jorge Luis BORGES, comprising the eight stories of his first collection, *The Garden of Forking Paths* (*El Jardín de Senderos que se Bifurcan*, 1942), and nine new pieces grouped under the title "Artifices." These multilayered "fictions," often without both characters and plots, are playful and profound ruminations on the nature of language, time, and reality. This collection contains perhaps Borges's most famous story, "The Library of Babel."

Finnegans Wake (1939). James JOYCE's last novel. Written primarily in English, it contains multilingual wordplay (including words of Joyce's own devising), literary, psychological, historical, cultural, classical, and personal references, and myriad approaches to time, space, and narration. Cyclical and expansive rather than linear in its structure, it was designed to defy conventional reading, interpretation, and summary, and is generally acknowledged to be indecipherable without a key (or keys) to its meanings.

First Circle, The (*V Kruge Pervom*, 1968). A novel by Aleksandr SOLZHENITSYN about a group of intellectuals forced to conduct scientific research in a Stalinist prison camp. Unlike the laborers in Siberia, the prisoner-scientists live in relative comfort, but must confront the knowledge that their work will further Stalin's repressive efforts. The title refers to the first circle of hell, in which, according to DANTE's *DIVINE COMEDY*, poets, philosophers, and pagan scholars are condemned to spend eternity.

First Love (*Pervaya Lyubov'*, 1860). An autobiographical novella by Ivan TURGENEV. A poignant and nostalgic love story recounted in the first person, the novella tells of 16-year-old Vladimir's love for his neighbor's daughter, Zinaida, and explores the full range of adolescent love.

Fixer, The (1966). A Pulitzer Prize– and National Book Award–winning novel by Bernard MALAMUD. Based on the true story of Mendel Beilis, who was arrested in Kiev in 1911, *The Fixer* recounts the travails of Yakov Bok, a Russian Jew and handyman (or "fixer") who is accused of "ritual murder" after a 12-year-old boy is found dead near the brick factory Yakov manages. The novel focuses on the two years Yakov spends in jail, ending when he is taken to trial.

Flies, The (*Les Mouches*, 1943). A play by Jean-Paul SARTRE, a rewriting of the last two parts of AESCHYLUS's trilogy, the *ORESTEIA*. Here, ORESTES, in killing his mother and her lover, Aegisthus, is driven not by fate but by conscious choice. The crowd of flies, counterpart of the Furies in Aeschylus's drama, here represent conscious responsibility for one's actions.

"Flowering Judas" (1930). A short story by Katherine Anne PORTER, reprinted in the collection of the same name. The author's experiences and acquaintances in 1920s Mexico are transformed into the story of an American schoolteacher (a lapsed Catholic) who secretly aids Mexican revolutionaries. Disillusionment with a local socialist leader who tries to seduce her, and with other would-be lovers, disturbs her increasingly fragile faith in the cause and her own actions.

Flowers of Evil, The (*Les Fleurs du Mal*, 1857; expanded editions, 1861 and 1868). The only collection of poems in book form by Charles BAUDELAIRE. Publicly condemned as obscene when it appeared, it is now considered among the most masterly works of its era, combining sensuous and macabre imagery with great formal control. Baudelaire's apostrophe to the reader ("Hypocrite reader, my double, my brother") was quoted in French in T. S. ELIOT's *THE WASTE LAND* (1922).

Fool for Love (1983). A play by Sam SHEPARD, set in the claustrophobic confines of a motel room at the edge of the Mojave Desert, which dissects the insular, consuming relationship of half-brother and -sister Eddie and May. The play was filmed in 1985 with the playwright starring as Eddie.

Forsyte Saga, The (1922). The first sequence in a larger novel-and-short-story series (*The Forsyte Chronicles*) by John GALSWORTHY, comprising *The Man of Property* (1906), "Indian Summer of a Forsyte" (in *Five Tales*, 1918), *In Chancery* (1920), "Awakening" (1920), and *To Let* (1921). The changing fortunes of several generations of the English upper-middle-class family of Soames FORSYTE, the spiritually empty title character of the first novel, are set against the changing society of the late Victorian through Edwardian eras. In 1967, the *Saga's* popularity was revived by the worldwide success of a British television serial adaptation.

Fortunata and Jacinta (*Fortunata y Jacinta*, 1886–87). A four-volume novel by Benito PÉREZ GALDÓS, part of a longer series of novels offering a panorama of Spanish society and an important work of Spanish fiction. In this psychological exploration of two unhappy marriages, Fortunata is the mistress of Jacinta's husband and bears his children.

42nd Parallel, The. *See* **U.S.A.**

For Whom the Bell Tolls (1940). A novel by Ernest HEMINGWAY, inspired by his journalistic coverage of the Spanish Civil War, and arguably his masterpiece. The title comes from a 1623 sermon by John DONNE: "... and therefore never send to know for whom the bell tolls; it tolls for thee."

Fountainhead, The (1943). Ayn RAND's first bestselling novel and the first fully formed fictional treatment of her "objectivist" philosophy. Architect Howard ROARK (who bears some resemblance to Frank Lloyd Wright) is an individualist genius struggling against collectivist mediocrity; he destroys a housing complex rather than permit his creative vision to be altered. Dominique Francon is the woman who loves him but successively marries two of his enemies. Rand wrote the screenplay for the 1949 King Vidor film, starring Gary Cooper and Patricia Neal.

Four Million, The (1906). A collection of stories by O. HENRY inspired by his experiences in New York City. Among the 25 stories are the well-known "THE GIFT OF THE MAGI" and "The Furnished Room." The title refers to the population of New York City at the time.

Four Quartets (1943). A collection of four poems by T. S. ELIOT: "BURNT NORTON," "EAST COKER," "THE DRY SALVAGES," and "LITTLE GIDDING." In this work, each poem of which follows the structure of a five-movement sonata, Eliot examines the role of memory, the cyclical nature of time, and the close relationship between past and present. Pervaded with Christian faith and stressing a universal harmony, these poems contrast with Eliot's earlier masterpiece, *THE WASTE LAND* (1922), with its vision of fragmentation and despair.

"Fra Lippo Lippi" (1855). A blank-verse dramatic monologue by ROBERT BROWNING, from his collection *Men and Women*. Fra Lippo LIPPI, the Florentine painter/monk, stopped by the night watch as he leaves a brothel, defends himself in a colorful verbal self-portrait. In art as in life, Lippi favors the flesh over the spirit: "If you get simple beauty and naught else, / You get about the best thing God invents: /...you'll find the soul you have missed, / Within yourself, when you return him thanks."

Framley Parsonage. *See* **Barsetshire Novels**

Frankenstein: or, The Modern Prometheus (1818). A Gothic novel by MARY SHELLEY. Scientist Victor FRANKENSTEIN usurps the roles of God and Woman by generating artificial life.

His creature, hideously cobbled together from assorted corpses, is unable to find affection anywhere, and in despair turns on the creator who rejected him at the moment of his animation. (For adaptations, see Variations.)

Franny and Zooey (1961; stories published separately in 1955 and 1957). Two connected stories by J. D. SALINGER about the youngest members of his fictional clan of gifted Irish-Jewish eccentrics, the GLASS family, and one of Salinger's most popular and critically acclaimed works. Twenty-year-old Franny seeks escape from Eisenhower-era "ego, ego, ego" by obsessively reciting "the Jesus prayer," and suffers a breakdown. Her older brother Zooey draws on mystic wisdom and family lore to help her through the crisis, urging her to seek spiritual transcendence in her worldly vocation as an actor.

French Lieutenant's Woman, The (1969). A novel by John FOWLES. Set in London in 1867, the novel tells of a Victorian love affair, with frequent contemporary comments from the narrator, who is writing 100 years later. Charles Smithson is engaged to Ernestina, but falls in love with Sarah Woodruff, the jilted lover of a French officer, who is treated by the townspeople like a whore and an outcast. Fowles toys with the conventions of the Victorian novel and provides the reader with three different endings.

Friends and Heroes. *See* **Balkan Trilogy, The**

Frogs, The (*Batrachoi*, 405 B.C.). A comedy by ARISTOPHANES satirizing both governmental misrule and contemporary drama. Set in Hades and produced the year before the defeat of Athens in the Peloponnesian War, the play uses confusion and bickering in the Underworld to reflect conditions in Athens. The plot concerns the efforts of Dionysus to determine which playwright—AESCHYLUS or EURIPIDES—can best serve a troubled society in need of inspiration. He concludes that Aeschylus, with his traditional values and lofty verse, is the more inspirational.

From Here to Eternity (1951). A National Book Award–winning novel by James JONES, the first book in a trilogy about World War II that also includes *The Thin Red Line* (1962) and *Whistle* (1978). Set in Hawaii just before the Japanese attack on Pearl Harbor, the book recounts the stories of peacetime soldiers asserting their individualism, focusing on the honorable and defiant Private Robert E. Lee PREWITT, whose refusal to join the company's boxing team brings down the wrath of his commanding officer and eventually destroys Prewitt. The book's sexual situations and frank language shocked the public when the novel was published in 1951. Two years later, the film adaptation, directed by Fred Zinnemann and starring Montgomery Clift as Prewitt, received eight Academy Awards, including Best Picture.

"Garden Party, The" (1922). A short story by Katherine MANSFIELD, published in a collection of the same name. The shallow, romantic preconceptions of a sheltered young woman in middle-class New Zealand society are challenged when news of the accidental death of a working-class family man from the neighborhood interrupts preparations for her own family's lavish garden party. Mansfield's attempt to show "The diversity of life and how we try to fit in everything, Death included" is widely regarded as an exemplar of the short-story form.

Gargantua and Pantagruel (*Cinq Livres de la Vie, Faicts et Dicts Héroiques de Gargantua, et de Son Fils Pantagruel*, 1565, originally published separately, 1532–64; attribution of the Fifth Book is disputed). A series of comic novels by François RABELAIS about the learned giants GARGANTUA and PANTAGRUEL, father and son, and their fantastic companions and adventures, in the form of mock-heroic, often exuberantly scatological parodies of chivalrous romances; variously condemned by the Sorbonne and the Paris Parlement as obscene or heretical. The immense, voracious, and coarsely witty title characters inspired the English adjectives "gargantuan" and "pantagruelian."

Germinal (1885). A novel by Émile ZOLA, part of his 20-novel *Rougon-Macquart* series, which follows Étienne Lantier as he participates in an ill-fated miners' strike.

Ghost Road, The. *See* **Regeneration Trilogy, The**

Ghosts (*Gengangere*, 1882). A "family drama" by Henrik IBSEN. As the late Captain Alving's hidden vices haunt his survivors—his widow, who concealed the truth about him; his son, dying of syphilis inherited from him; and a young woman revealed as his illegitimate daughter—so society is haunted by "dead ideas and lifeless old beliefs." Considered too scandalous for the contemporary European stage, the play had its premiere in Chicago.

Ghost Sonata, The (*Spöksonaten*, 1908; also translated under the title *The Spook Sonata*). Like other works of August STRINDBERG's Expressionist period, this most famous of his "chamber plays" anticipated Surrealism with its dreamlike apparent haphazardness and nightmarish grotesqueries. The action unfolds in an analogy to three-part sonata structure, and involves a quest to expose the shameful secrets behind the attractive facade of a mysterious house.

Ghost Writer, The (1979). A partly autobiographical novel by Philip ROTH, in which the young writer Nathan ZUCKERMAN, searching for a father-figure and confused about his Jewish identity, visits the home of established Jewish novelist E. I. Lonoff (said to be based on Bernard MALAMUD). The story of Zuckerman is continued in *ZUCKERMAN UNBOUND* (1981) and *THE ANATOMY LESSON* (1983). The three works were collected in one volume, along with "The Prague Orgy," as *Zuckerman Bound: A Trilogy and Epilogue* (1985). Zuckerman also appears as a character in several other Roth novels.

Giant (1952). A bestselling novel by Edna FERBER about 25 years on a two-million-acre Texas cattle ranch, as observed by Leslie Lynnton Benedict, the free-thinking Virginian wife of Texas chauvinist Jordan "Bick" Benedict, patriarch of Reata Ranch, in an era of conflict between cattle and oil interests and entrenched Anglo prejudice against Mexican Americans. George Stevens's 1956 blockbuster film starred Elizabeth Taylor, Rock Hudson, and James Dean (in his final role) as disgraced ranch hand Jett Rink, who becomes an oil-rich parvenu.

Giants in the Earth (*I De Dage,* literally "In Those Days," 1924–25). A novel by the Norwegian-American O. E. RØLVAAG. Subtitled "A Saga of the Prairie," this story of a Norwegian pioneer family in the harsh and alien land that was 19th-century Dakota Territory takes its English-language title from Genesis: "In those days there were giants in the earth."

"Gift of the Magi, The" (1906). A short story by O. HENRY collected in *THE FOUR MILLION* (1906), telling the gently ironic story of an impoverished couple, each of whom sells a prized possession in order to give the other a thoughtful gift for Christmas. Della sells her hair to purchase a new watch chain for her husband, while Jim pawns his watch to buy hair combs for Della.

Giles Goat-Boy, or The Revised New Syllabus (1966). A satiric novel by John BARTH, in which the world of the Cold War era is represented by a university. The hero, a man raised by a herd of goats, begins a mythic journey of discovery and rediscovery to become the leader of the Western world. The book includes a lengthy and detailed sham introduction purporting to be by the main text's four (fictional) editors.

Gilgamesh (c. 2000 B.C.). A Babylonian epic that recounts the adventures of GILGAMESH, the legendary ruler of Erech, and his heroic journey over the earth in search of immortality. Along the way, he encounters monsters, gods, and the wise man, Utnapishtim, who relates to him the story of a great flood and an ark. Discovered on clay tablets (which date to 668–626 B.C.), the epic of *Gilgamesh* has taken its place alongside the *ILIAD* and the *ODYSSEY* as an important heroic epic.

"Gimpel the Fool" ("Gimpel Tam," 1945). A short story by Isaac Bashevis SINGER, set in a small Jewish *shtetl* around the turn of the 20th century. First published in the periodical *Yidisher Kemfe*, the story was collected in *Gimpel the Fool and Other Stories* (1957). The narrator, the gullible Gimpel, is treated like a fool by his fellow villagers, who tease and trick him. Throughout, Gimpel maintains a strong faith, responding with childlike simplicity and inherent goodness to the cruelty of others.

Ginger Man, The (1955). A novel by J. P. DONLEAVY that recounts the antics and comic adventures of Sebastian Dangerfield, a lazy and irresponsible American in Ireland who prefers drinking and womanizing to work or his studies at Trinity College. First published in Paris in 1955, the novel appeared in 1958 in an expurgated version in the United States, where it was not printed in its entirety until 1965.

Giovanni's Room (1956). A novel by James BALDWIN about social expectations and the conflicted sexual identity of an American expatriate in Paris in the 1950s. After asking a woman, Hella, to marry him, David has an affair with an Italian bartender named Giovanni. Unable to reconcile his homosexual impulses with his desire to live a socially acceptable life, the narrator is alone at the end. Coming after Baldwin's earlier, race-conscious works, the novel surprised readers and reviewers with its all-white cast of characters.

Girls in Their Married Bliss. *See* **Country Girls Trilogy, The**

Girls of Slender Means, The (1963). A novel by Muriel SPARK, set during World War II and focusing on a group of young women living in the May of Teck Club, a hostel in London. Forced to earn their living in the city, they cope, with youthful energy and resourcefulness, with day-to-day concerns brought on by their own modest circumstances and the privations of wartime. Spark's own experience living at the Helena Club in London provided the background of the novel.

Gītāñjali: Song Offering (*Gītāñjali*, 1910). A collection of poems by Rabindranath TAGORE, translated from Bengali into English by the poet himself and published with an introduction by W. B. YEATS in 1912. Primarily concerned with love and brimming with natural imagery, some of the poems also meditate on the tension between spiritual and worldly desires. Although the poetry and its author are still extremely influential in India, their popularity has gradually waned in the West.

Glass Menagerie, The (1945). An autobiographical play by TENNESSEE WILLIAMS about the WINGFIELD family. In this memory play, Tom Wingfield recalls the night that he invited a "gentleman caller" back to his home in St. Louis to meet his mother, Amanda, a faded Southern belle, and his painfully shy sister, Laura, whose only friends are found in her collection of glass animals (the menagerie of the title).

Glengarry Glen Ross (1983). A Pulitzer Prize–winning play by David MAMET about a group of unscrupulous real-estate agents attempting to sell lots in two dubious Florida land developments.

"Go and Catch a Falling Star" (1633). A poem by John DONNE, written in the 1590s and published in the collection *Songs and Sonnets*, describing the many challenges less difficult than discovering a woman "true and faire."

Go Down, Moses (1942). A collection of short stories by William FAULKNER. Forming a novel of interconnecting generations and races, these stories feature the McCaslin family, who bear the guilt of their legacy as slave owners. The collection includes the masterpiece "The Bear."

God's Little Acre (1933). A novel by Erskine CALDWELL. A tragicomedy that was the object of an obscenity trial, this story follows the wavering religious commitment of Ty Ty Walden, an amoral Georgia mountaineer who, as he digs for gold, continually shifts the location of the acre of his farm that he is going to consecrate to God.

God's Trombones: Seven Negro Sermons in Verse (1927). A volume of poetry by JAMES WELDON JOHNSON. Consisting of an introductory prayer and seven sermons written in verse, this collection conveys the power of African-American religious oratory.

"Gold Bug, The" (1843). A mystery story by Edgar Allan POE, included in *Tales of the Grotesque and Arabesque*, about William Legrand, whose strange discovery of a golden beetle ultimately leads him to buried pirate treasure.

Golden Ass, The (*Metamorphoses*, 2nd century A.D.). A satirical romance by Lucius APULEIUS, probably based on Lucius of Patraes's *Metamorphoses*, a Greek work no longer extant. BOCCACCIO, CERVANTES, and RABELAIS were among the writers influenced by it.

Golden Bowl, The (1904). The last great novel by HENRY JAMES. Examining the social niceties that mask betrayal, the novel concerns the wealthy American expatriate Adam Verver and his daughter, Maggie, who discover that their respective spouses are involved in an adulterous affair.

Golden Notebook, The (1962). A novel by DORIS LESSING, a classic of feminist literature, concerning the struggle of a writer, Anna WULF, to come to terms with her identity through her writing.

Gone with the Wind (1936). A Pulitzer Prize–winning historical novel by MARGARET MITCHELL (her only novel), set against the backdrop of the Civil War and Reconstruction, which follows the life of Scarlett O'HARA, a determined Southern belle who, after the hardships of the war, famously vows, "As God is my witness, I'll never go hungry again." The title is taken from Ernest DOWSON's poem "Non Sum Qualis Eram Bonae sub Regno Cynarae." The 1939 film adaptation, starring Vivien Leigh and Clark Gable, is one of the most popular movies of all time. In 1991, an authorized sequel, *Scarlett*, by Alexandra Ripley, was published; an unauthorized parody, Alice Randall's *The Wind Done Gone* (2001) appeared only after a court battle with the Mitchell Trusts, which control the copyright of Mitchell's novel.

Good-bye, Mr. Chips (1934). A novel by the English novelist James Hilton (1900–1954), narrating the life of Arthur Chipping [Mr. CHIPS], a schoolmaster at an English public school who, after his young wife's death, returns to bachelordom and the education of generations of young boys at Brookfield School. (For adaptations, see Variations.)

Good Earth, The (1931). A Pulitzer Prize–winning novel by Pearl BUCK, offering a sympathetic representation of Chinese peasant life in the 1920s through the story of Wang Lung and his wife, O-Lan.

Good Man Is Hard to Find, A (1955). A collection of short stories by FLANNERY O'CONNOR, including such masterpieces as "The Artificial Nigger," "Good Country People," and the title story.

Good Soldier, The: A Tale of Passion (1915). A novel by FORD MADOX FORD. Generally considered the author's finest work, this tragic story is a study of the complex emotional connections, as well as the deceptions, in two marriages. The author begins with the line, "This is the saddest story I have ever heard."

Good Soldier Schweik and His Fortunes in the War, The (*Osudy Dobrého Vojáka Švejka za Světové Války*, 1921–23). A satirical novel in four volumes by Jaroslav HAŠEK. Drawn from the author's experiences in the Austro-Hungarian army during World War I, this is the story of an honest but bumbling soldier whose basic decency stands at odds with the rigid military bureaucracy enforced by his commanding officers. Hašek died before he could write the final two intended volumes.

Good Woman of Setzuan, The (*Der Gute Mensch von Sezuan*, 1943). A play by Bertolt BRECHT. In this parable about capitalism, the good-hearted Shen Te, a former prostitute, is forced to assume the role of Shui Ta, a tough-minded businessman, to fend off the connivers who try to take advantage of her naturally generous nature.

Go Tell It on the Mountain (1953). An autobiographical novel by James BALDWIN, set in Harlem, about the struggle between 14-year-old John Grimes and his preacher stepfather, Gabriel. The novel ends with John's religious conversion at a Pentecostal church service.

Grapes of Wrath, The (1939). A Pulitzer Prize–winning novel by John STEINBECK about the JOAD family, migrant farmworkers who trek from Oklahoma to California during the Great

Depression of the 1930s. John Ford's 1940 film adaptation starred Henry Fonda as Tom Joad.

Gravity's Rainbow (1973). A National Book Award–winning novel by Thomas PYNCHON, in which Tyrone SLOTHROP, an American intelligence agent, searches for the connection between his erections and the flights of a rocket developed by the Nazis at the end of World War II.

Great Expectations (1861). A novel by Charles DICKENS, set in Victorian England, which chronicles the coming of age of PIP, an orphan, whose illusions about the world are lost when he moves to London to improve his social status. (For adaptations, see Variations.)

Great Fortune, The. *See* **Balkan Trilogy, The**

Great Gatsby, The (1925). A novel by F. SCOTT FITZGERALD that explores the decadent and morally bankrupt society of the Jazz Age through the story of self-made millionaire Jay GATSBY and his love for Daisy BUCHANAN. (For adaptations, see Variations.)

Green Mansions (1904). A novel by the English author W. H. Hudson (1841–1922) that tells the story of Mr. Abel, a wealthy man who moves to Guyana to live among the Indians, and Rima, a mystical Indian girl with whom Abel falls in love.

Group, The (1963). A novel by MARY MCCARTHY that traces the lives of eight Vassar graduates.

Group Portrait with Lady (*Gruppenbild mit Dame*, 1971). A novel by Heinrich BÖLL expressing his protest against the dehumanizing forces of capitalism. The story follows the life of subversive heroine Leni Pfeiffer from the pre-Nazi period to the 1970s.

Guermantes Way, The. *See* **Remembrance of Things Past**

Gulliver's Travels (original title: *Travels into Several Remote Nations of the World*; 1726). A novel by Jonathan SWIFT, one of the most popular novels of the 18th century, a satire on political cant and hypocrisy. The story follows the fantastic voyages of Lemuel GULLIVER to the lands of Lilliput, Brobdingnag, Laputa, and Houyhnhmland.

Guys and Dolls (1931). The first collection of short stories by Damon RUNYON, featuring his trademark colorful Broadway gamblers, chorus girls, and moochers. The title *Guys and Dolls* is identified today with Runyon's collected stories, not merely those in this volume, in part as a result of its use as the title of the hit 1950 Broadway musical, which is based primarily on only one story, "The Idyll of Miss Sarah Brown" (first published in *Collier's* in 1933 and collected in *Runyon à la Carte*, 1944). (For adaptations, see Variations.)

Gypsy Ballads, The (*Romancero Gitano*, 1928). A series of ballads by Federico GARCÍA LORCA. This highly popular collection of 18 lyrical poems, all composed in eight-syllable lines, revitalized Spanish balladry.

Hairy Ape, The (1922). An Expressionistic play by Eugene O'NEILL about the dehumanizing effects of industrialization. The bullying Yank Smith, a ship's stoker, is taunted by the upper-class Mildred Douglas, who calls him a "hairy ape." Later, on shore leave, Yank tries to fit in to conventional society but is rejected, even by a gorilla at the zoo, whom he releases from his cage and who then tramples him to death. (For adaptations, see Variations.)

Hamlet, The (1940). The first novel of the SNOPES trilogy by William FAULKNER, exploring the rise of capitalism, and its consequences, in the South. Set in the fictional Yoknapatawpha county in Mississippi, the story focuses on the early years of the heartless and unscrupulous Flem Snopes and his family. The other novels in the trilogy are *THE TOWN* (1957) and *THE MANSION* (1959).

Hamlet, Prince of Denmark (c. 1601). A play of great psychological complexity by William SHAKESPEARE. It is the story of HAMLET, who learns from his father's ghost that his uncle and now stepfather, CLAUDIUS, king of Denmark, has murdered his father, the former king. Feigning madness to cover his plans for revenge, Hamlet is inexorably drawn into a tragedy that ends in the death of most of the major characters, including himself. One of the most analyzed dramatic texts in history, *Hamlet* is also among

Shakespeare's most popular and frequently staged works. (For adaptations, see Variations.)

Handful of Dust, A (1937). A darkly comic novel by EVELYN WAUGH that portrays the spiritual barrenness and amorality of London society in the 1920s and 1930s.

Hard Times (1854). A novel by Charles DICK-ENS, a critique of industrialization, centering around Thomas GRADGRIND, a man who believes in practicality at the expense of imagination, and his children Tom and Louisa. When Tom robs a bank and Louisa abandons the loveless marriage she has made to a much older man, their father acknowledges the shortcomings of his method of child-rearing.

Harlot High and Low, A. *See* **Human Comedy, The**

Heartbreak House (1919). An allegorical play by George Bernard SHAW, focusing on a group of eccentric characters gathered in the bohemian household of Captain Shotover. Shaw uses these characters to demonstrate the irresponsibility of the cultured class.

Heart Is a Lonely Hunter, The (1940). A novel by Carson McCULLERS, an outstanding example of Southern Gothic fiction. This sensitive and compelling treatment of loneliness and isolation centers on John Singer, a deaf-mute in a small Southern town in the 1930s.

Heart of Darkness (1902). A novella by Joseph CONRAD about the brutalities of European colonialism and man's capacity for evil. The narrator, MARLOW, journeys into the jungle in search of the ivory trader KURTZ. The depraved Kurtz's dying words, "The horror, the horror!" reflect humanity's capacity for evil, the heart of darkness. (For adaptations, see Variations.)

Heart of Midlothian, The. *See* **Waverley Novels, The**

Heart of the Matter, The (1948). A novel by Graham GREENE, set in West Africa during World War II. The protagonist, Scobie, a married man, struggles with his sense of personal morality while conducting an affair with a young widow.

Heat and Dust (1975). A novel by Puth Prawer JHABVALA that tells two interrelated tales: the story of Olivia, the wife of a British officer, who leaves her husband in 1923 for an Indian prince, and the story of her granddaughter, who comes to India to reconstruct her grandmother's life.

Hedda Gabler (1890). A play by Henrik IBSEN, featuring one of the most richly drawn women characters in dramatic literature. Out of jealousy and boredom, the selfish and neurotic Hedda GABLER destroys a former lover, with tragic consequences for herself.

Heights of Macchu Picchu, The (*A Huras de Macchu Picchu*, 1947). A long poem by Pablo NERUDA, inspired by his 1943 visit to the Incan ruins. The poem, in 12 sections that describe a literal and metaphorical journey, is widely viewed as one of Neruda's greatest works.

Henderson the Rain King (1959). A comic novel by Saul BELLOW, examining the hard-drinking millionaire Eugene Henderson's quest for meaning during a journey to Africa.

Henry IV, Parts I and II (c. 1597–98). History plays by William SHAKESPEARE, set in the early 15th century. HENRY IV, having usurped the crown from RICHARD II, must deal with various rebellions, notably one led by HOTSPUR and Northumberland. With much comic support from FALSTAFF, the central character is Henry's son, the apparently dissolute Prince Hal (later HENRY V). After the final suppression of the rebels, Hal repudiates his riotous friends and prepares to become king.

Henry V (1599). A history play, a continuation of *HENRY IV*, by William SHAKESPEARE. HENRY V, formerly Prince Hal, leads an army into France and defeats the French at Agincourt. On his marriage to Catherine, he becomes heir to the French throne.

Henry VI, Parts I and III (c. 1589–92). History plays by William SHAKESPEARE. Part I dramatizes the struggles between the English and French during the Hundred Years' War, starting with the inheritance of HENRY V's throne by the child king Henry VI. Parts II and III cover the Wars of the Roses, the battles within England that pitted

Henry VI's House of Lancaster against Richard Plantagenet and the House of York.

Henry VIII (c. 1612–13). A history play by William SHAKESPEARE, probably cowritten with John Fletcher (1579–1625). Before Buckingham is executed for treason, he offers a prophecy to beware of false friends, a warning heeded by the tempestuous Henry VIII as, with the help of the archbishop of Canterbury, he divorces Catherine of Aragon to marry Anne Boleyn.

Hero of Our Time, A (*Geroĭ Nashego Vremeni*, 1840). A novel by Mikhail LERMONTOV about the "hero" Grigory Pechorin, a cynical and apathetic aristocrat.

Herzog (1964). A National Book Award–winning novel by Saul BELLOW. Bellow's most autobiographical work, it is the story of Moses Herzog, a professor tormented by betrayal and his failed relationships and troubles with women.

Hiawatha, The Song of (1855). A narrative poem by Henry Wadsworth LONGFELLOW, following the quest of the Ojibway Indian Hiawatha to right the wrongs done by his father to his mother and to promote peace among the Ojibway and their neighbors.

"Hills Like White Elephants" (1927). A short story by Ernest HEMINGWAY, marked by the author's characteristic ironic distance and told almost entirely through the conversation of an American man and young woman as they wait for a train in Spain. It becomes clear that the woman is pregnant and the man wants her to have an abortion.

Hobbit, The (1937). A novel by J. R. R. TOLKIEN about Bilbo Baggins and his fellow hobbits, small creatures with furry feet who live in Middle Earth. Bilbo comes into possession of a magic ring, which he uses to help his companions. The story was continued in the trilogy THE LORD OF THE RINGS (1954–56).

"Hollow Men, The" (1925). A poem by T. S. ELIOT. Called by Eliot "the last work of an old world," this fragmented poem expresses the spiritual emptiness of England after World War I.

Holy Sonnets, The (1633). A sonnet sequence by John DONNE, including the works beginning "I am a little world made cunningly," "DEATH BE NOT PROUD," and "BATTER MY HEART," revealing the rapture, pain, awe, and fear that made up the poet's conception of God. The 19 sonnets were first published posthumously in Donne's *Songs and Sonnets.*

Homecoming, The (1965). A play by Harold PINTER. This work, with its menacing, erotically charged atmosphere, dramatizes the return to his home and family in North London of Teddy, an academic, with his beautiful wife, Ruth, and stories of his success in America. In the course of the play, Teddy's brothers, Lenny and Joey, become sexually entangled with Ruth; at play's end, Ruth stays behind in the odd household as her strangely aloof husband leaves to return to their home and three children in America.

Home to Harlem (1928). A novel by Claude MCKAY. One of the classic depictions of the culture of the Harlem Renaissance in the 1920s, this work contrasts Jake, who is determined to enjoy life despite the racial oppression of American society, and Ray, a Haitian immigrant who perceives fully the alienation and damage of racism.

Hopscotch (*Rayuela*, 1963). A novel by Julio CORTAZAR, tracing the fantastic adventures and checkered career of Horacio Oliveira. Following the disappearance in Paris of his lover, "La Maga," and his dissatisfaction with the logical approach to life, Oliveira returns to Buenos Aires and undertakes a series of unusual jobs, becoming the trainer of a talking cat and an attendant in an insane asylum. This inventive, playfully postmodern narrative asks readers to proceed chronologically through the first 56 chapters, and then to reread the text, "hopscotching" from one chapter to another and back again, and only then to read the later chapters.

Horla, The (*Le Horla*, 1887). A novella by Guy de MAUPASSANT, tracing the descent into madness of a narrator who views his illness as an external being, a demonic figure who has recently arrived in France aboard a Brazilian ship. The title means "the thing out there."

Horse's Mouth, The (1944). The last novel of a comic trilogy by Joyce CARY, including *Herself Surprised* (1941) and *To Be a Pilgrim* (1942). Gulley JIMSON, an irreverent, alcoholic, ex-convict artist engaged in painting his masterpiece, accidentally kills his lover, Sara Monday. Alec Guinness wrote and starred in a 1958 film adaptation, directed by Ronald Neame.

Hostage, The (1958). A play by Brendan BEHAN. Illuminating the futility of sectarian violence and political partisanship, this tragicomedy employs music-hall songs and Irish ballads to tell the story of a captured British soldier being held hostage by the IRA in a combined whorehouse and pub.

Hotel Du Lac (1984). A Booker Prize–winning novel by Anita BROOKNER about a repressed, middle-aged woman, a writer of romance novels, who unexpectedly breaks loose.

House for Mr. Biswas, A (1961). A novel by V. S. NAIPAUL, set in Naipaul's native Trinidad, which follows the life of Mr. BISWAS: his mishaps as a journalist, his conflicts with in-laws (with whom he is forced to live out of economic necessity), and his efforts to win independence through a house of his own. The novel is one of the earliest and most insightful depictions of the postcolonial situation, particularly in its investigation of the conflict between traditional cultural values and the ways of the modern world.

House in Paris, The (1935). A novel by Elizabeth BOWEN that focuses on two children visiting the Fisher home in Paris: 11-year-old Henrietta Mountjoy, en route from England to Menton, and nine-year-old Leopold, who is waiting there to meet his mother for the first time. The first and third sections of the novel, set in the present, serve as a frame for the center section, set in the past, which concerns Leopold's mother and tells the story of the affair that resulted in his conception.

House of Bernarda Alba, The (*La Casa de Bernarda Alba: Drama de Mujeres en los Pueblos de España*, written 1936, performed 1945).

A play by Federico GARCÍA LORCA. The last work in the trilogy that includes *YERMA* and *BLOOD WEDDING*, this tragedy explores outmoded Spanish moral customs through Bernarda, who exerts rigid control over her spinster daughters, with inexorably tragic consequences. The play is notable for the fact that only female characters appear on stage.

House of Mirth, The (1905). A novel by Edith WHARTON, chronicling the downfall of Lily BART, a beautiful young woman who is torn between her desire to be free of the constraints placed on women in turn-of-the-century New York high society and a need to join that same society permanently through a "good" marriage.

House of the Seven Gables, The (1851). A novel by Nathaniel HAWTHORNE. Drawing on Hawthorne's own family history, it finds the once wealthy and proud PYNCHEON family at its lowest ebb. Because of a curse placed on the family by Mathew Maule, a victim of the Salem witch trials, all that remains of the family's former glory is a dilapidated seven-gabled mansion, inhabited by the spinster Hepzibah; her brother Clifford, just released from prison for a murder he did not commit; and their young cousin, Phoebe, whose marriage to a descendant of Maule's eventually lifts the hex. The author's preface provides a key clarification of his conception of the romance genre.

Howards End (1910). A novel by E. M. FORSTER, examining the modernizing England of the early 20th century through the relationship between the bohemian SCHLEGEL sisters and the bourgeois Wilcox family, and the fate of the Wilcoxes' country home, Howards End. Forster's famous dictum, "Only connect," serves as the novel's epigraph. The 1992 film version was directed by James Ivory from a screenplay by Ruth Prawer JHABVALA.

Howl (1956). A major poem by Allen GINSBERG, included in a volume of the same name and generally regarded as the anthem of the Beat Generation. Beginning with the lines, "I saw the best minds of my generation destroyed by madness, / starving hysterical naked," the poem is an embittered rant against the conservative orthodoxy of the Eisenhower years and represented a radical departure from traditional formality in verse.

Huckleberry Finn, The Adventures of (1884). A classic novel by Mark TWAIN, following the misadventures and scrapes of Huckleberry FINN, one of the most memorable characters in American literature, as he makes his way down the Mississippi River on a raft with a runaway slave named JIM, whom Huck helps to evade the authorities. Ernest Hemingway said of it, "All modern American literature comes from one book by Mark Twain called *Huckleberry Finn.*"

Hugh Selwyn Mauberley (1920). A poetic sequence by Ezra POUND, in 13 fragmented, elliptical poems, that forms an epitaph for an imaginary poet and for the values and idealism of the generation that came of age during World War I. The work includes homages to Max Beerbohm ("Brennbaum") and FORD MADOX FORD ("Mr. Nixon"), and concludes with an "Envoi" attesting to the permanence of beauty preserved in artistic works.

Human Comedy, The (*La Comédie Humaine*, 1829–47). A series of 90 interconnected realistic novels and novellas by Honoré de BALZAC, including the well-known volumes *Père Goriot* (*Le Père Goriot*, 1835), *Eugénie Grandet* (1833), *Cousin Bette* (*La Cousine Bette*, 1846), *Cousin Pons* (*Le Cousin Pons*, 1847), *Lost Illusions* (*Illusions Perdues*, 1837–43), and *A Harlot High and Low* (*Splendeurs et Misères des Courtisanes*, 1839–47). The monumental work was intended as a comprehensive study of French society from the revolution of 1789 to the July monarchy in 1830, a society the author saw as increasingly dominated by social ambition and greed.

Humboldt's Gift (1975). A Pulitzer Prize–winning novel by Saul BELLOW, following the split allegiance of the narrator, Charlie Citrine, toward his dual gods, poetry and money. The book is notable for the portrait of Bellow's mentor, Delmore SCHWARTZ, through the title character, Von Humboldt FLEISHER, a writer who is constantly broke but unwilling to sacrifice his artistic integrity.

Humphry Clinker, The Expedition of (1771). An epistolary novel by Tobias SMOLLETT, depicting a journey through England and Scotland of Welsh squire Matthew Bramble and Bramble's encounter with the title character, whom he eventually recognizes as his lost son. The novel cleverly presents individual episodes through the eyes of different characters, who have widely varying interpretations of the same events.

Hunchback of Notre Dame, The (*Notre-Dame de Paris*, 1831). A novel by Victor HUGO about life in and around the great Parisian cathedral in the late 15th century. The principal characters are the bell ringer QUASIMODO, grotesquely deformed and deaf; his adored, the beautiful Gypsy dancer Esmeralda; and the wicked archdeacon Claude Frollo, who lustfully pursues Esmeralda. (For adaptations, see Variations.)

Hunger (*Sult*, 1890). An impressionist novel by Knut HAMSUN. The unnamed narrator, an unsuccessful writer losing his grasp on reality as hunger breaks down his body and mind, describes a series of loosely connected episodes.

"Hymn to Intellectual Beauty" (1816). A lyric poem by PERCY BYSSHE SHELLEY, one of the author's important early works, describing an elusive sense of spiritual illumination that appears only in glimpses, but "gives grace and truth to life's unquiet dream."

Iceman Cometh, The (written 1939, performed 1946). A play by Eugene O'NEILL. One of O'Neill's last and most acclaimed plays, the drama examines the lives of rundown regulars at Harry HOPE's saloon, a seedy waterfront bar in Manhattan, who find solace in fantasies about attaining better lives until HICKEY, a traveling salesman, arrives to puncture their "pipe dreams."

I, Claudius (1934). A historical novel by Robert GRAVES, combining historical detail with psychological insight to tell the story of court intrigues and imperial workings of power in 1st-century Rome during the reigns of Augustus, Tiberius, and Caligula, as narrated by the future emperor CLAUDIUS. It was followed by a sequel, *Claudius the God* (1934), which carries the story into Claudius's own reign. The two novels were adapted into a critically acclaimed 13-part television miniseries in 1976; the title character was portrayed by Derek Jacobi.

Ideal Husband, An (1895). A play by Oscar WILDE that shrewdly depicts the hypocrisy of the titled Victorian upper class. An English parliamentarian must extricate himself from a blackmailer and justify his past misdeeds to his wife, who has thought him "the ideal husband."

Idiot, The (*Idiot*, 1874). A novel by Fyodor DOSTOYEVSKY about the encounter between the guileless Prince MYSHKIN, a "positively good man" of profound religious faith, and the wealthy, sophisticated circle he enters after coming into an inheritance. (For adaptations, see Variations.)

Idylls of the King (1859–85). A series of poems by Alfred, Lord TENNYSON. Written and published over the course of many years, these 12 poems retell the story of King ARTHUR and the rise and fall of the idealistic court of Camelot. The work is particularly noted for its dramatic portrayal of Queen GUINEVERE's adultery with LANCELOT.

If on a Winter's Night a Traveler (*Se una Notte d'Inverno un Viaggiatore*, 1979). An experimental novel by Italo CALVINO that probes the nature of literature itself by directly addressing the reader as a central character. The reader begins the novel only to find that part of another novel has been interposed in its pages. In a labyrinthine pursuit of the incomplete storyline, the reader finds ten different beginnings of novels within the novel, as Calvino playfully reflects on the operations of narrative.

Iliad (*Ilias*, 8th century B.C.). An epic poem, one of the great works of European literature, attributed to HOMER, that focuses on a brief period in the tenth year of the Greek assault on Troy. Major characters include the warrior ACHILLES, whose wrath sets the story in motion; AGAMEMNON, commander of the Greek forces; and HECTOR, prince of Troy. The *Iliad* and its companion piece, the *ODYSSEY*, in their powerful and moving explorations of the heroic ideal, have served as models for all epics in the classical tradition. (For adaptations, see Variations.)

Illuminations (*Les Illuminations*, 1886). A collection of experimental verse and prose poems by Arthur RIMBAUD, in which, through "the hallucination of words," the ordinary rules of time, space, and logic are suspended in favor of a deeper consciousness. The cycle was most likely written when the author was between 17 and 19 years old, shortly before he abandoned literature. It was published without his knowledge by Paul VERLAINE.

Imaginary Invalid, The (*Le Malade Imaginaire*, 1673). A satirical play by MOLIÈRE. Argan, a hypochondriac, opposes the marriage of his daughter Angelique to Cléante because he wants her to marry a doctor. His brother, Beralde, and Toinette, a clever servant, contrive to show him that he is being conned by his doctors and by his second wife, Beline, who is interested only in his money. While playing the title role in the play's fourth performance, Molière collapsed of a lung hemorrhage and died the following day.

Immoralist, The (*L'Immoraliste*, 1902). A short novel by André GIDE, written in the first person, examining the consequences of egoism. The protagonist, Michel, believes himself to be a Nietzschean superman beyond the grip of conventional morality. He intends his narrative to be a justification of his life, but the brutishness of his behavior is not lost on the reader.

I'm Not Stiller (*Stiller*, 1954). A novel by Max FRISCH, exploring the subject of identity, about an American named J. C. White who is detained after he is identified as a missing Swiss sculptor named Anatol Stiller. The novel, presented as his journal, insists that he is not Stiller, despite the conviction of Stiller's wife, Julika, and ultimately of a Swiss court.

Importance of Being Earnest, The (1895). A play by Oscar WILDE, one of the wittiest in the English language, in which Jack WORTHING adopts an alter ego, his fictional brother Ernest, so that from time to time he may escape his settled life in the country and go down to London, a practice his friend, Algernon MONCRIEFF, dubs "Bunburying," after his own fictional friend Bunbury, who suffers from a series of illnesses that make possible Algy's escape from the city to the country. Confusion ensues when both men realize that they wish to marry young women determined to wed only men named Ernest. Lady BRACKNELL, the mother of Jack/Ernest's fiancée Gwendolen FAIRFAX, is one of the great gorgons in literature.

In Chancery. *See* **Forsyte Saga, The**

In Cold Blood: A True Account of a Multiple Murder and Its Consequences (1965). An acclaimed "nonfiction novel" by Truman CAPOTE examining the murder of the Clutter family in Holcomb, Kansas, and the trial of their killers, Dick Hickock and Perry Smith.

Independence Day (1995). A Pulitzer Prize–winning novel by RICHARD FORD, narrated by its protagonist, Frank BASCOMBE, a sportswriter turned real-estate salesman, who is trying to come to terms with his divorce and his troubled son, Paul, over a Fourth of July weekend. It is a sequel to *The Sportswriter* (1986).

Independent People: An Epic (*Sjálfstætt Fólk*, 1934–35). A novel by Halldór LAXNESS. Guðbjartur Jónsson, called Bjartur of Summerhouses after the miserable croft he has purchased, is a sheep farmer in Iceland's remote wastes, struggling to maintain the one thing he treasures, his independence, in the face of overwhelming difficulties presented by nature, society, and incipient societal change—and perhaps by spirits from the mythic Icelandic past. His grudging, long unacknowledged love for his rebellious stepdaughter, Ásta Sóllilja, is his life's sole bright spot.

Infernal Machine, The (*La Machine Infernale*, 1934). A play by Jean COCTEAU, a modern version of the OEDIPUS myth in which Oedipus functions as a plaything of the gods.

Inferno. *See* **Divine Comedy, The**

Innocents Abroad, The; or, The New Pilgrim's Progress (1869). A travel narrative by Mark TWAIN, based on letters he wrote as newspaper columns during his 1867 visit to Europe and the Holy Land, which gently ridicules tourist guidebooks and people whose experiences of foreign lands never exceed those prescribed by such manuals.

Inspector General, The (*Revizor*, 1836). A satirical play by Nikolai GOGOL, describing the fawning reception by small-town notables of Ivan Khlestakov, a minor official who is mistaken for the powerful inspector general when he arrives in a provincial Russian town.

"In the Ravine" ("V Ovrage," 1900). A realistic short story by Anton CHEKHOV, depicting the unsavory ambition of Aksina, daughter-in-law of peasant shopkeeper Tsybukin, who causes the death of her nephew while taking over the family's business.

Intruder in the Dust (1948). A novel by William FAULKNER. A meditation on American racism, this is the story, set in Faulkner's fictional Yoknapatawpha County, Mississippi, of Lucas Beauchamp, an elderly African-American man who is wrongly accused of murder, and Chick Mallison, a 16-year-old white boy who helps to prove him innocent.

Invisible Man (1952). A National Book Award–winning novel by RALPH ELLISON, concerning an unnamed African-American man who recognizes that blackness renders him effectively invisible in the United States.

Invisible Man, The (1897). A science-fiction novel by H. G. WELLS, portraying Griffin, a mad scientist who learns the secret of invisibility and uses this knowledge for evil ends.

Ironweed (1983). A National Book Award– and Pulitzer Prize–winning novel by William KENNEDY, the third in a six-novel "Albany cycle." Through the protagonist, down-and-out Francis PHELAN, Kennedy sought to express the "central eloquence of every human being." Kennedy wrote the screenplay for the 1987 film, starring Jack Nicholson and Meryl Streep. The other novels in the cycle are *Legs* (1975), *Billy Phelan's Latest Game* (1978), *Quinn's Book* (1988), *Very Old Bones* (1992), and *The Flaming Corsage* (1996).

"I Sing the Body Electric." *See* **Leaves of Grass**

Ivanhoe (1819). A historical novel by SIR WALTER SCOTT. In England at the end of the 12th century, during the reign of Richard the Lion-Hearted, the fictional knight Wilfred of IVANHOE falls in love with Rowena and defends Rebecca, a Jew, from charges of witchcraft. (See also *THE WAVERLEY NOVELS.*)

Jacob's Room (1922). An experimental novel by VIRGINIA WOOLF, tracing the life of Jacob Flanders from childhood to his years at Cambridge University, and finally to his death in World War I. Through her description of Jacob's empty room, the author powerfully evokes his loss. The protagonist was based on Woolf's younger brother, Thoby Stephen, who died as a young man of typhoid fever contracted during a trip to Greece.

Jane Eyre (1847). A novel by CHARLOTTE BRONTË, about Jane EYRE, a strong-willed and intelligent governess, and Edward ROCHESTER, her Byronic, brooding employer, whose long-concealed secret threatens to thwart the love that develops between them. The complex characterizations and powerful delineation of a woman's self-assertion are inimitable. (For adaptations, see Variations.)

Jean-Christophe (1904–12). A series of ten novels by the French writer Romain Rolland (1866–1944), depicting the life of Jean-Christophe Krafft, a German musical genius partly modeled on Ludwig von Beethoven, who pursues moral truth through his art with no regard for material gain.

Jerusalem: The Emanation of the Giant Albion (1804–20). A prophetic poem by William BLAKE, illustrated with 100 etchings by the poet, in which England is personified as Albion and called to reunion with Jerusalem.

Jewel in the Crown, The. *See* **Raj Quartet, The**

Jew of Malta, The (in full: *The Famous Tragedy of the Rich Jew of Malta*, c. 1590). A play in blank verse by Christopher MARLOWE, portraying the unintended consequences of the revenge taken by Barabas, a wealthy merchant, when his entire property is taken from him by the Christian governor of Malta.

John Brown's Body (1928). A Pulitzer Prize–winning epic poem about the Civil War by STEPHEN VINCENT BENÉT, beginning with the famous attack led by abolitionist John Brown on the U.S. Arsenal at Harper's Ferry, Virginia, in 1859; Brown was hanged for his part in the raid. "John Brown's Body" was the title of a popular Civil War song.

Joseph and His Brothers (*Joseph und Seine Brüder*, 1933–43). A tetralogy of novels by Thomas MANN, comprising *The Tales of Jacob* (*Die Geschichten Jaakobs*), *Young Joseph* (*Der Junge Joseph*), *Joseph in Egypt* (*Joseph in Ägypten*), and *Joseph the Provider* (*Joseph der Ernährer*). With scholarly seriousness of purpose leavened by a certain playfulness, Mann retells the events of the second half of Genesis on a vast canvas of 2,000 pages.

Joseph Andrews (in full: *The History of the Adventures of Joseph Andrews and of His Friend, Mr. Abraham Adams, Written in Imitation of the Manner of Cervantes*, 1742). A novel by Henry FIELDING about the picaresque adventures of Joseph ANDREWS, a footman in the employ of the wealthy Lady Booby. Begun as a parody of SAMUEL RICHARDSON's *PAMELA* (1740) (Joseph is Pamela's brother), the novel transcended its origins to become a significant work in its own right.

Joseph in Egypt. *See* **Joseph and His Brothers**

Joseph the Provider. *See* **Joseph and His Brothers**

Journal of the Plague Year, A (1722). A fictional chronicle of the 1664–65 Great Plague of London by Daniel DEFOE, notable for its vivid description of a city living in close quarters with death.

Journey to the Center of the Earth, A (*Voyage au Centre de la Terre*, 1864). A novel by Jules VERNE. In this early work of science fiction, German geologist Otto Lidenbrock journeys through an extinct volcano to the Earth's core.

Journey to the End of Night, A (*Voyage au Bout de la Nuit*, 1932). A novel by Louis-Ferdinand CÉLINE, following the wanderings of its antihero, Ferdinand Bardanu, through war-ravaged Europe. This bleak and misanthropic novel angered Céline's contemporaries, but proved inspiring to post-Holocaust writers.

Jude the Obscure (1895). A tragic novel by Thomas HARDY, examining the idea of incomprehensible Fate through the luckless Jude FAWLEY, his wife Arabella, and his cousin, Sue Bridehead, whom he loves. The negative reception of the novel by critics led Hardy to abandon fiction-writing; he wrote only poetry thereafter.

Julius Caesar (c. 1599). A tragedy by William SHAKESPEARE about the fall of the Roman Emperor Julius CAESAR, and the ensuing civil conflict. The central figure is BRUTUS; other major characters are Caesar himself, Cassius, and Mark ANTONY.

Jungle, The (1906). A muckraking novel by Upton SINCLAIR, exposing the harsh, unsanitary conditions of the Chicago stockyards. Public outcry following its publication led to the passage of the Pure Food and Drug Act.

Juno and the Paycock (1924). A tragicomedy by Sean O'CASEY, following the misfortunes of the Boyle family during the Irish civil disturbances of 1922–23. The "paycock" (peacock) is the charming but shiftless Captain Jack Boyle; Juno is his wife. (For adaptations, see Variations.)

Justine. *See* **Alexandria Quartet, The**

Justine; or, The Misfortunes of Virtue (*Justine, ou Les Malheurs de la Vertu*, 1791). A sexually explicit novel by Donatien-Alphonse-François, Marquis de SADE, in which the title character suffers one form of sexual abuse after another.

Kaddish (1961). A poem by Allen GINSBERG based on the traditional Jewish prayer for the dead. It is a memorial to his mother, who suffered from mental illness.

Kenilworth. *See* **Waverley Novels, The**

Kidnapped (1886). A novel by Robert Louis STEVENSON, in which David Balfour is kidnapped and shipped away by his greedy uncle Ebenezer Shaw.

Kim (1901). A novel by Rudyard KIPLING, about a resourceful Lahore beggar boy. The orphaned son of an Irish sergeant, he is taken for an Indian, and becomes the disciple and helper of a Tibetan lama in search of the holy "River of the Arrow." After he is discovered by members of his father's regiment and educated, he distinguishes himself as a British secret agent in the "great game" of international espionage.

King John (c. 1595). A history play by William SHAKESPEARE, telling of the English king's futile efforts to save his endangered throne.

King Lear (c. 1605–6). A tragedy by William SHAKESPEARE, often considered his greatest. King LEAR, the aged title character, creates personal and political chaos when he lets himself be deceived by the effusive flattery of his two elder daughters, REGAN and GONERIL, rather than accept the sincere love of his youngest daughter, CORDELIA. (For adaptations, see Variations.)

Kiss of the Spider Woman (*El Beso de la Mujer Araña*, 1976). A novel by Manuel PUIG, in which a political revolutionary and a homosexual are brought together in prison. (For adaptations, see Variations.)

Krapp's Last Tape (1958). A one-act, one-character play by Samuel BECKETT, in which an alienated old man listens to tapes of himself as a youth.

Kristin Lavransdatter (1920–22). A trilogy by Sigrid UNDSET, consisting of *The Bridal Wreath* (*Kransen*, 1920), *The Mistress of Husaby* (*Husfrue*, 1921), and *The Cross* (*Korset*, 1922), and following the life of Kristin Lavransdatter, a devout Christian woman of the Middle Ages.

"Kubla Khan; or, A Vision in a Dream" (written 1797, published 1816). A poem by Samuel Taylor COLERIDGE, inspired by an opium dream. The poem begins with the celebrated lines, "In Xanadu did KUBLA KHAN / A stately pleasure dome decree…"

Labyrinths (1962, enlarged 1964). A collection of short prose pieces by Jorge Luis BORGES, compiled for English-language readers. Included are such significant works as "The Lottery in Babylon," "The Garden of Forking Paths," and "Pierre Menard, Author of the Quixote."

Lady Chatterley's Lover (1928). A novel by D. H. LAWRENCE about a passionate affair between an upper-class woman, Lady Constance CHATTERLEY, and her gamekeeper, Oliver MELLORS. Because of its explicit descriptions of sex and its use of taboo terms, the novel appeared legally only in expurgated form until 1959 in the United States and 1960 in England, where it was the subject of a landmark obscenity trial.

"Lady of Shalott, The" (1832, revised 1842). A narrative poem by Alfred, Lord TENNYSON, a version of the Arthurian legend of Elaine.

Lady of the Lake, The (1810). A narrative poem by SIR WALTER SCOTT, retelling the legend of the romance between Ellen Douglas, the daughter of the outlaw James Douglas, and Malcolm Graeme.

Lady Windermere's Fan (1892). A comedy of manners by Oscar WILDE, his first stage success. The major characters include Lady Margaret WINDERMERE and Mrs. ERLYNNE, who, unbeknownst to Lady Margaret, is actually her mother.

"Lady with a Lap Dog, The" ("Dama s Sobachkoï," 1899). A short story by Anton CHEKHOV, one of his best known, about an adulterous affair.

Lafcadio's Adventures (*Les Caves du Vatican*, 1914). A satiric novel (or "sortie") by André GIDE, in which a group of con men take advantage of a rumor that the Pope has been kidnapped. Lafcadio is characterized by his gratuitous murder of a friend.

"Lament for the Death of a Bullfighter" ("Llanto por Ignacio Sanchez Mejías," 1935; also translated under the title "Lament for Ignacio Sanchez Mejías"). An elegy by Federico GARCÍA LORCA, written for a bullfighter and friend.

Last Chronicle of Barset, The. *See* **Barsetshire Novels**

Last of the Mohicans, The. *See* **Leatherstocking Tales, The**

Last Post, The. *See* **Parade's End**

Last Tycoon, The (1941). An unfinished novel by F. SCOTT FITZGERALD, published posthumously as edited by EDMUND WILSON. It was reedited by Matthew Bruccoli (1993). In the novel the principled hero, Monroe STAHR, is pitted against corrupt Hollywood moguls.

Leatherstocking Tales, The (1823–41). A series of five novels by James Fenimore COOPER. A stirring epic of the American frontier, these books—in narrative order, *The Deerslayer* (1841), *The Last of the Mohicans* (1826), *The Pathfinder* (1840), *The Pioneers* (1823), and *The Prairie* (1827)—follow the westward migration of skilled woodsman Natty BUMPPO.

Leaves of Grass (1855). A collection of poems by Walt WHITMAN, which was expanded and revised throughout his lifetime. Included are such significant poems as "Song of Myself," "I Sing the Body Electric," and "There Was a Child Went Forth." Owing to its frank expressions of sexuality, charges of indecency haunted the radical work.

"Leda and the Swan" (1924). A sonnet by William Butler YEATS, describing Leda's rape by the Greek god ZEUS in the form of a swan.

Left Hand of Darkness, The (1969). A science-fiction novel by Ursula K. LE GUIN, in which an interplanetary organization sends an envoy, Genly Ai, to the planet of the androgynous Gethians. The novel won both the Hugo and Nebula awards.

Leopard, The (*Il Gattopardo*, 1959). A historical novel by Giuseppe di LAMPEDUSA, set against Garibaldi's invasion of Sicily and the unification of Italy, and covering 50 years in the life of an aristocratic Sicilian family.

Liaisons Dangereuses, Les (1782; also translated under the titles *Dangerous Connections* and *Dangerous Acquaintances*). An epistolary novel by Pierre Choderlos de LACLOS. The unscrupulous, scheming Viscount de Valmont and Madame de Merteuil manipulate and seduce everyone around them, ostensibly to redress old grievances, but largely for the perverse pleasure of dominating others. A sordid tale told with refinement, it was called a "byword for literary infamy" by Edmund Gosse. (For adaptations, see Variations.)

Libation Bearers, The. *See* **Oresteia**

Libra (1988). A novel by Don DELILLO, taking as its subject the assassination of President John F. Kennedy. The major characters are Lee Harvey Oswald, Win Everett, and Nicholas Branch.

Life of Samuel Johnson, LL.D., The (1791). A biography by James BOSWELL, perhaps the greatest of all literary biographies in English. The work offers a vivid account of the life of English writer SAMUEL JOHNSON and of 18th-century London.

Life Studies (1959). A National Book Award–winning collection by ROBERT LOWELL, consisting of a prose memoir and three sections of poetry. The volume, which offered some of the earliest examples of "confessional" poetry, includes the memorable poems "Skunk Hour," "Waking in Blue," and "Home After Three Months Away."

Light in August (1932). A novel by William FAULKNER, telling the connected stories of Lena Grove and Joe CHRISTMAS. The placid and pregnant Lena is a contrast to the tormented, racially ambiguous Christmas.

Lincoln (1984). A novel by Gore VIDAL (part of his American Chronicle series), depicting Abraham Lincoln from 1861 to 1865. The President is seen as a great man but one who places more value on ends than on means.

Little Disturbances of Man, The (1959). The first collection of short stories by Grace PALEY. Combining the syntax of the New York streets with a vocabulary derived from a broad knowledge of literature, the stories explore the New York Jewish experience.

Little Dorrit (1857). A novel by Charles DICKENS, protesting the hypocrisy of the English justice system. The title refers to Amy DORRIT, who faithfully cares for her father as he languishes in the Marshalsea debtors' prison, where Dickens's own father was imprisoned when he was a young boy.

Little Foxes, The (1939). A play by Lillian HELLMAN. Set in the South in 1900, this drama about the Hubbard family, owners of a cotton mill, scathingly depicts greed for money and power. Regina, the relentlessly manipulative sister, is one of the most arresting female villains in modern drama. The title is taken from the biblical Song of Solomon. Hellman's 1946 play *Another Part of the Forest* was a prequel. (For adaptations, see Variations.)

"Little Gidding" (1942). A poem by T. S. ELIOT, the last of his *Four Quartets*, continuing and resolving the cycle's themes in the lengthening shadow of World War II; fire, the fourth element, is the dominant image. The title alludes to a utopian community once visited by a "broken king" (Charles I); its chapel, now ruined, still abounds with spiritual meaning. Eliot's Westminster Abbey memorial quotes this poem: "The communication / Of the dead is tongued with fire beyond the language of the living."

Little Prince, The (*Le Petit Prince*, 1943). An interplanetary fable written and illustrated by Antoine de SAINT-EXUPÉRY about a child prince who leaves his tiny planet to travel to Earth, meeting a wise fox and a pilot stranded in the Sahara Desert. Written for children, it has become equally popular with adults around the world.

Lolita (1955). A highly controversial novel by Vladimir NABOKOV about a sexual affair between the middle-aged Humbert HUMBERT and his 12-year-old stepdaughter, LOLITA, a "nymphet." Published first in France, the work created a furor upon its 1958 publication in the United States. (For adaptations, see Variations.)

London Fields (1989). A novel by MARTIN AMIS, chronicling the decline of morality at the end of the millennium, as narrated by American novelist Sampson Young. *Femme fatale* Nicola Six has a premonition that a man she meets in a pub will murder her. At the pub, she spots two likely suspects—working-class knave Keith

Talent and wealthy, well-mannered Guy Clinch—and initiates her plan to exact revenge.

Lonely Girl, The. *See* **Country Girls Trilogy, The**

Lonely Passion of Judith Hearne, The (1955). A novel by BRIAN MOORE. An unmarried, middle-aged, alcoholic Belfast Catholic with genteel pretensions has a crisis of faith when her dream of a "home, [and] children to raise up to honour and reverence [God]," disintegrates irrevocably. Banned in the Republic of Ireland on publication, it was in other respects a great critical and popular success.

Lonesome Dove (1985). An epic western novel by Larry MCMURTRY that won the Pulitzer Prize. *Lonesome Dove* recounts the dangerous, exciting, sometimes comedic, sometimes deadly events that take place during a cattle drive from Texas to Montana led by two former Texas Rangers, Augustus (Gus) McCrae and Woodrow CALL.

Long Day's Journey into Night (written 1940–41, performed 1956). An autobiographical, posthumously produced play by Eugene O'NEILL, exploring the love, resentment, and interdependence among the members of the TYRONE family: James and Mary, and their sons, Jamie and Edmund. The searing work, considered by many to be the greatest American play, won a 1957 Pulitzer Prize.

Look Back in Anger (1957). A play by John OSBORNE. A defining drama that introduced the Angry Young Man to 1950s Britain, it depicts the tensions of the English class struggle through the protagonist, Jimmy Porter, a restless, working-class young man with a university education, and his gentle, middle-class wife.

Look Homeward, Angel (1929). A novel by THOMAS WOLFE. Based on the author's experiences growing up in Asheville, North Carolina, this classic coming-of-age novel concerns Eugene GANT, a young man who strives to escape his tumultuous family and the limitations of small-town life. Editor Maxwell PERKINS worked with Wolfe to shape and cut the original manuscript for publication. Eugene's story was continued in a sequel, *OF TIME AND THE RIVER* (1935). (For adaptations, see Variations.)

Lord Jim (1900). A novel by Joseph CONRAD about a man's efforts to expiate an act of cowardice. The novel is narrated by MARLOW, who appears in other major novels of Conrad.

Lord of the Flies (1954). An allegorical novel by William GOLDING. A group of English schoolboys marooned on a tropical island degenerate into an irrationally destructive tribe of savages, despite the efforts of their elected leader, Ralph, and his friend PIGGY to maintain order. Golding defined his theme as "an attempt to trace the defects of society back to the defects of human nature." Hugely popular with college-age readers since the late 1950s, the work was filmed twice, notably by Peter Brook (1963).

Lord of the Rings, The (1954–56). An epic trilogy of fantasy novels by J. R. R. TOLKIEN that includes *The Fellowship of the Ring* (1954), *The Two Towers* (1955), and *The Return of the King* (1956). The trilogy continues the saga of Middle Earth begun in *THE HOBBIT* (1937) and tells the story of Frodo Baggins, a humble and peaceful hobbit, whose adoptive father, Bilbo Baggins, has bequeathed to him a magic ring of unimaginable power. In this classic tale of good versus evil, the reluctant Frodo must destroy the ring to keep it from the variety of evil creatures who seek its power. Based on an intricate mythology created by the author, this popular series features characters such as wizards, elves, trolls, dwarfs, and ringwraiths.

Lorna Doone: A Romance of Exmoor (1869). A historical romance by the English novelist Richard Blackmore (1825–1900) set in late 17th-century England. Yeoman John Ridd falls in love with a young maiden named Lorna, who as a little girl was captured and adopted by a murderous band of outlaws, the Doones. John's love for Lorna is complicated by the fact that the Doones killed his father and he has vowed revenge on them.

Lost Honor of Katharina Blum, The (*Die Verlorene Ehre der Katharina Blum*, 1974). A novel by Heinrich BÖLL, in which the author attacks a German newspaper for irresponsibility and sensationalism in its reporting of the trial of the Baader-Meinhof gang. Falsely accusing a young woman of terrorist activity, the newspaper destroys her life.

Lost Horizon (1933). A novel by the English novelist James Hilton (1900–1954) in which Hugh Conway, a British diplomat, finds an earthly paradise nestled in the Tibetan Himalayas. "Shangri-La," the name of the paradise, is now used to signify a utopia. (For adaptations, see Variations.)

Lost Illusions. *See* **Human Comedy, The**

Lost Lady, A (1923). A novel by Willa CATHER. The central character is Marian Forrester, a charming woman whose eventual corruption reflects that of the American West.

"Lottery, The" (1948). A frequently anthologized short story by SHIRLEY JACKSON, first published in *The New Yorker* and then in the collection *The Lottery; or The Adventures of James Harris* in 1949. The chilling allegory describes the events of an annual lottery held in a small New England town. The reader discovers at the end of the story that the lottery is used to determine which of the villagers will be stoned to death by the others.

Loved One, The: An Anglo-American Tragedy (1948). A novel by EVELYN WAUGH. A satire on American manners, this book relates the cross-cultural experiences of a young Englishman in Los Angeles who takes a job at a pet cemetery to be closer to his lover, an embalmer at a funeral home for Hollywood celebrities.

Love in the Time of Cholera (*El Amor en los Tiempos del Cólera*, 1985). A novel by Gabriel GARCÍA MÁRQUEZ about a love that triumphs despite the lovers' having spent almost 52 years apart, and despite the pervading atmosphere of disease. The main characters are Fermina Daza and Florentino Ariza.

Love's Labours Lost (c. 1594–95). A comedy by William SHAKESPEARE, in which the King of Navarre and three noblemen foolishly swear to abstain from the company of women for three years and then break the vow as soon as four comely women appear on the scene. The play concludes with the much-admired companion songs "Winter" and "Spring."

"Love Song of J. Alfred Prufrock, The" (1915). A poem by T. S. ELIOT, in which the middle-aged speaker reviews his decorous, wasted life: "I have measured out my life with coffee spoons." Said to have been written while the author was a student at Harvard, the poem is the first major work of modernist poetry in English.

Lower Depths, The (*Na Dne*, 1902). A play by Maxim GORKY. Set in a flophouse, *The Lower Depths* was first performed at Stanislavsky's Moscow Art Theater and was recognized for its insightful portrayal of the lives of its bitter, downtrodden characters, including laborers, thieves, drunks, prostitutes, and card sharks.

"Luck of Roaring Camp, The" (1869). A short story by Bret HARTE, featuring a hardened group of gold miners who adopt a child when his prostitute mother dies in childbirth. Nicknamed "Luck," the boy inspires uncharacteristic tenderness in the miners and changes their lives. The story was collected in *The Luck of Roaring Camp and Other Sketches* (1870).

Lucky Jim (1954). A comic novel by KINGSLEY AMIS about Jim DIXON, a young historian from a working-class background who has difficulty fitting into the academic establishment.

Lusiads, The (*Os Lusíadas*, 1572). An epic poem in ten cantos by Luís de CAMÕES. The national epic of Portugal, it is a mythicized retelling of Vasco da Gama's 1497–99 expedition to discover a sea route to India via the Cape of Good Hope, aided by Venus, but opposed by Bacchus. A long digression recapitulates the history of the Portuguese (or Lusitanians) and their struggles against Spain and the Moors. It ends with a vision of Portugal's future glory.

Lyre of Orpheus, The (1988). The final work in Robertson DAVIES' satirical Cornish trilogy, which examines the intertwined worlds of academia, philanthropy, and grand opera. It follows *THE REBEL ANGELS* (1981) and *WHAT'S BRED IN THE BONE* (1985).

Lyrical Ballads, with a Few Other Poems (1798, expanded edition 1800). The landmark collection with which William WORDSWORTH and Samuel Taylor COLERIDGE inaugurated England's Romantic movement, employing "the language of conversation" to write poems about ordinary "human passions, human characters, and human incidents." The first edition included "THE RIME OF THE ANCIENT MARINER" and three other poems by Coleridge, and "TINTERN ABBEY" and 18 others by Wordsworth. The 1800 edition added a second volume with 37 poems by Wordsworth, including his "Lucy" poems; its preface contained his famous dictum that poetry originates in "emotion recollected in tranquillity."

Lysistrata (*Lysistratē*, 411 B.C.). A comedy by ARISTOPHANES, known for its satire and ribald humor. The title character, a plucky Athenian woman outraged by the ravages of the 20-year Peloponnesian War, convinces the women of Athens and the rest of Greece to seize the Athenian treasury, occupy the Acropolis, and deny their husbands sexual satisfaction until the bloodshed ends. (For adaptations, see Variations.)

Macbeth (c. 1605–6). A tragedy by William SHAKESPEARE, the shortest of his plays. Encouraged by the prophecy of three witches he meets on the heath, and urged on by his wife, MACBETH, a Scottish general, rises to the throne of Scotland by murdering the king, DUNCAN. He is overthrown by the sons of Duncan and of BANQUO, a fellow general for whose murder Macbeth is also responsible. The play was a tribute to King James I (1566–1625), who had recently ascended to the English throne and who traced his ancestry back to the sons of Banquo. (For adaptations, see Variations.)

Madame Bovary (1857). A novel by Gustave FLAUBERT, a landmark of literary realism. The novel's heroine, Emma BOVARY, is a middle-class woman bored with both her provincial life and her dull yet devoted husband. Impelled by her reading of romantic novels, she pursues reckless love affairs, amasses a large debt, and eventually commits suicide. Several passages were removed from the work when it first appeared serially in the *Revue de France* from October to December 1856. The author, printer, and publisher were acquitted of obscenity charges in early 1857 and the novel was published in two volumes later that year. (For adaptations, see Variations.)

Magic Mountain, The (*Der Zauberberg*, 1924). A novel by Thomas MANN. Both an ironic Bildungsroman and an allegory of European intellectual life on the eve of World War I, it is set in a Swiss tuberculosis sanitarium, where young Hans CASTORP spends seven years recovering from a "moist spot" on his lung, as he learns about clashing world views from fellow patients Naphta and Settembrini, and about the more carnal passions from Mme Clavdia Chauchat.

Magister Ludi (*Das Glasperlenspiel*, 1943; also translated under the title *The Glass Bead Game*). A Bildungsroman by Hermann HESSE about the character Joseph Knecht, set in a 23rd-century utopia where the highest intellectual achievement is mastering the Glass Bead Game, the goal of which is the synthesis of art and science. In the end, Knecht becomes a Magister Ludi, or Master of the Game.

Magnificent Ambersons, The (1918). A Pulitzer Prize–winning novel by Booth TARKINGTON, later published as part of the trilogy *Growth* (1927), also comprising *The Turmoil* (1915) and *The Midlander* (1924, also titled *National Avenue*). As the modern era—symbolized by the advent of the motor car—shifts the foundation of American aristocracy from social connection to commercial success, the Amberson dynasty's fortunes are eclipsed by the rise of a new manufacturing class. Orson Welles's 1942 film version was drastically reedited by RKO Studios, including the addition of a conventional happy ending, without Welles's knowledge or consent.

Magus, The (1965). A novel by John FOWLES about an English schoolmaster living on a Greek island and his relations with an enigmatic local millionaire.

Mahābhārata, The (final form c. 400; Great Epic of the Bharata Dynasty). One of the two great Sanskrit epics of Ancient India (the other being the RĀMAYĀṆA). The narrative framework (the struggle for succession of the Kauravas and the Pandavas) is a means to convey philosophical and political ideas, especially prescribed codes of conduct, or *dharma*. It includes the BHAGAVADGĪTA, the key Hindu religious text.

Main Street (1920). A satirical novel by SINCLAIR LEWIS that denounces small-town provincialism. The protagonist, Carol KENNICOTT, attempts in vain to combat the narrowness and tedium of Gopher Prairie (modeled after Lewis's hometown, Sauk Center, Minnesota), before finally accepting its limitations.

Major Barbara (1905). A play by George Bernard SHAW that sees poverty as the result of systemic inequities rather than individual weakness or vice. The major characters are the practical-minded Sir Andrew Undershaft, a munitions manufacturer, and his naively idealistic daughter, Barbara, a major in the Salvation Army.

Making of Americans, The (completed 1911, published 1925). An autobiographical novel by Gertrude STEIN in which she casts three generations of her own family as representative of the American people as a whole. The 925-page modernist chronicle dispenses with such traditional literary devices as plot, dialogue, and conventional syntax.

Makioka Sisters, The (*Sasameyuki*, 1948). A novel by Jun'ichirō TANIZAKI, the title of which means literally "a light snowfall." In describing the four Makioka sisters' relationships and marriages, Tanizaki explores the passing of an era in Japanese culture and history.

Malone Dies (*Malone Meurt*, 1951). A novel by Samuel BECKETT, part of a trilogy that also includes *MOLLOY* (1951) and *THE UNNAMABLE* (1953). The title character, a dying man, recalls and reconstructs his past through stories about a character based on himself. The novel, like other Beckett works, poses existential questions about personal identity.

Maltese Falcon, The (1930). A detective novel by ex-Pinkerton man Dashiell HAMMETT, introducing the quintessential hard-boiled detective,

Sam SPADE. Looking for his partner's killer, Spade is caught up in the hunt for a mysterious statuette along with *femme fatale* Brigid O'Shaughnessy and an assortment of shady characters, all motivated by greed, lust, and a passion for treachery. Of several film versions, John Huston's 1941 film, starring Humphrey Bogart, is the best known.

Mambo Kings Play Songs of Love, The (1989). A Pulitzer Prize–winning novel by Oscar HIJUELOS, acclaimed for its tragicomic exuberance and its vivid recreation of post–World War II New York. With dreams of becoming musical stars like fellow Cubans Desi Arnaz and Xavier Cugat, brothers Nestor and Cesar Castillo immigrate to America in the late 1940s and form their own group, the Mambo Kings. They enjoy notable success for a period, and even appear on an episode of "I Love Lucy" with Arnaz and Lucille Ball.

Man and Superman: A Comedy and a Philosophy (first performed 1905, first complete performance 1915). A satirical play by George Bernard SHAW that revises the Don JUAN legend. The play exemplifies Shaw's philosophical concept of the Life Force. A mere man (the intellectual John TANNER) becomes a superman by yielding to this Force (marrying the instinctive Ann Whitefield). The dream scene, "Don Juan in Hell," is often omitted from performances, and is frequently performed on its own.

Manchild in the Promised Land (1965). An autobiographical novel by the American writer Claude Brown (1937–) that traces the coming of age of a young black delinquent in Harlem.

Man Could Stand Up, A. *See* **Parade's End**

Mandarins, The (*Les Mandarins*, 1954). An autobiographical novel by Simone de BEAUVOIR, awarded the Prix Goncourt. Against the backdrop of the Holocaust, Hiroshima, and Stalinist atrocities, it explores the role of intellectuals in a changing society. The central characters, Anne and Robert Dubreuilh, are based on the author and Jean-Paul SARTRE. Lewis Brogan is based on the American writer Nelson ALGREN.

Man of Property, The. *See* Forsyte Saga, The

Manon Lescaut (*Histoire du Chevalier des Grieux et de Manon Lescaut*, 1731). The last novel of *Mémoires et Aventures d'un Homme de Qualité* (1728–31; Memories and Adventures of a Man of Quality) by the French writer Abbé Prévost (Antoine-François Prévost d'Exiles, 1697–1763), telling of the aristocrat des Grieux's destructive passion for the courtesan Manon Lescaut. Operatic versions appeared in 1884 (by Massenet) and 1893 (by Puccini).

Mansfield Park (1814). A novel by Jane AUSTEN, set on the English country estate of the title. An elaborate variation on the Cinderella story, the novel follows Fanny Price, who is taken in by her wealthy aunt and uncle, the Bertrams, as a favor to Lady Bertram's sister, who had foolishly married for love.

Mansion, The (1959). A novel by William FAULKNER, the third in the SNOPES trilogy, which also includes *THE HAMLET* (1940) and *THE TOWN* (1957).

Man Who Loved Children, The (1940). A novel by Christina STEAD, presenting the story of the Pollitts, an American family torn apart by jealousy and hostility. Self-effacing Sam Pollitt smothers and dominates his children with "love"; his wife, Henrietta, rages against his passivity and lack of ambition and repeatedly abuses the talented Louisa, Sam's daughter by a previous marriage. Neglected and unappreciated at the time of its publication, the novel was reissued in 1965 and is now acknowledged as the Australian writer's masterpiece.

Man Who Was Thursday, The (1908). A novel by G. K. CHESTERTON, set in London at the turn of the 20th century. The hero, Gabriel Syme, is a policeman and poet who must go undercover and infiltrate an anarchist organization.

"Man Who Would Be King, The" (1899). A short story by Rudyard KIPLING, originally collected in *The Phantom Rickshaw*. A social parable about imperialism, "The Man Who Would Be King" recounts the tale of two white men, Daniel Dravot and Peachey Carnahan, who convince the people of Kafristan that they are gods and establish themselves as the heads of the country. Sean Connery and Michael Caine starred in John Huston's 1975 film version.

Man Without Qualities, The (*Der Mann ohne Eigenschaften*, 1930–43; most comprehensive edition, 1978). An unfinished 2,000-page novel by Robert MUSIL about life in the twilight of the Austro-Hungarian Empire ("Kakania"); roughly one-third is unorganized material, published posthumously. In 1913, Ulrich, the protagonist, is made honorary secretary of a "Parallel Campaign" planning the emperor's 1918 jubilee, a campaign that will be made pointless by the intervening war. In the later chapters, Ulrich retreats into a quasi-mystical union with his sister Agathe. The multifaceted, ironic narrative is considered a landmark of modernist fiction.

Man with the Golden Arm, The (1949). A novel by Nelson ALGREN that won the first National Book Award for fiction. It concerns the tormented efforts of Francis Majcinek (known as Frankie Machine), a poker dealer with a "golden arm," to cope with morphine addiction and his manipulative wife, whom he injured during a binge. Otto Preminger directed the 1955 film version, starring Frank Sinatra as Frankie, Eleanor Parker as his wheelchair-bound wife, and Kim Novak as the other woman in his life.

Ma Rainey's Black Bottom (1984). A play by AUGUST WILSON. A Chicago recording studio in 1927 becomes the setting for a blistering examination of racial injustice and the complex evolution of black identity and aspiration in America. It is told through the stories of four African-American session musicians and the "mother of the blues," whose singing they have been hired by white executives to support.

Marat/Sade (in full: *The Persecution and Assassination of Jean-Paul Marat as Performed by the Inmates of the Asylum of Charenton under the Direction of the Marquis de Sade; Die Verfolgung und Ermordung Jean Paul Marats, Dargestellt durch die Schauspielgruppe des Hospizes zu Charenton unter Anleitung des Herrn de Sade*, 1964). A drama by Peter WEISS, presenting a confrontation between the revolutionary Marat and the voluptuary Sade as a play performed by madmen. The play was inspired by amateur theatricals actually staged at Charenton by the historical Marquis de SADE. The Royal Shakespeare Company's stage production was filmed by Peter Brook in 1966.

Marjorie Morningstar (1955). A coming-of-age novel by Herman WOUK. Marjorie, a middle-class Jewish girl in 1930s New York City, rebels against her parents' conservative values. She struggles to become an actress and has a love affair with a charismatic and bohemian director. Eventually she settles down, marries, and comes to accept the traditional values she once found so stifling.

"Marquise of O..., The" ("Die Marquise von O...," 1810). A short story by Heinrich von KLEIST. The aristocratic heroine becomes unaccountably pregnant; secure in her sense of her own virtue, she offers in a newspaper advertisement to marry the unknown father. French director Eric Rohmer filmed the story in 1976.

Marriage of Figaro, The (*La Folle Journée, ou, Le Mariage de Figaro*, 1784). A comedy by Pierre-Augustin Caron de BEAUMARCHAIS. The clever FIGARO, who was "the barber of Seville" in Beaumarchais's previous play, plans to marry Suzanne, but his master, Count Almaviva, has his own designs on the Countess's pretty maid. With its frequent jibes at the aristocracy, the work points toward the impending French Revolution. It served as the basis for Mozart's opera *Le Nozze di Figaro* (1786). (For this and other adaptations, see Variations, under *The Barber of Seville*.)

Marriage of Heaven and Hell, The (c. 1790). A satirical work in prose and poetry by William BLAKE. A complex work, shot through with Blake's humor and socially subversive sensibility, this book uses parables, proverbs, and poetry to examine the idea of religion.

Martin Chuzzlewit (1844). A novel by Charles DICKENS. The protagonist, Martin Chuzzlewit, renounces the greedy, selfish ways of his family after a failed attempt to seek his fortune in America. The part of the novel that takes place in the United States greatly offended American readers.

Master and Margarita, The (*Master i Margarita*, 1973). A satirical and ribald novel by the Russian writer Mikhail Bulgakov (1891–1940). The main plot line, about SATAN's visit to Moscow in the 1930s, is interwoven with a version of the story of Pontius Pilate set in ancient Jerusalem, but the philosophical subtext is about the struggle between good and evil. Bulgakov wrote the novel in the 1930s but was not able to publish it until 1966–67 (in an expurgated version). The work was finally published in its entirety in the Soviet Union in 1973.

Master Builder, The (*Bygmester Solness*, 1893). The first drama of Henrik IBSEN's late period, when symbolism began to dominate in his works; here, buildings symbolize artistic accomplishments, and the play has autobiographical overtones. The title character, Solness, is an aging architect who has abandoned church-building to construct "homes for people" (as Ibsen gave up poetic dramas for realistic ones about social problems).

Master of Ballantrae, The: A Winter's Tale (1889). A novel by Robert Louis STEVENSON, set in 18th-century Scotland and America, about the decades-long, deadly rivalry between two brothers of opposing temperaments: James Durrisdeer, the charismatic, demonic Master of Ballantrae, and Henry Durrisdeer, his noble, stolid younger brother.

Maxims (*Réflections, ou Sentences et Maximes Morales*, 1665–78). A collection of more than 600 witty, often caustic aphorisms by François VI, duc de LA ROCHEFOUCAULD. An example of the author's pithy and cynical observations is, "We all have enough strength to bear the misfortunes of others."

Mayor of Casterbridge, The (1886). A tragic novel by Thomas HARDY. In a state of drunkenness, the novel's protagonist, Michael Henchard, sells his wife Susan and baby daughter to a sailor. When he realizes what he has done, he gives up drink and searches for them, to no avail. The reformed Henchard becomes mayor of the town of Casterbridge, and although Susan returns many years later, Henchard is eventually ruined both publicly and emotionally.

McTeague: A Story of San Francisco (1899). Frank NORRIS's first novel, indebted to Émile ZOLA, but a landmark of naturalism in its own right. McTeague, a dull-witted former miner working as a dentist, marries Trina, who had been his friend Schouler's girl, then declines into alcoholism and brutishness, murdering Trina to get at the lottery winnings she greedily hoards. (For adaptations, see Variations.)

Measure for Measure (c. 1604–5). A comedy by William SHAKESPEARE, ranked among his "problem plays" for its disturbing themes and forced resolution. For the crime of fornication—with his betrothed—Claudio is condemned to death by Angelo, deputy Duke of Vienna; Claudio's sister Isabella, a novice nun, pleads with Angelo for his life, and is told that the price will be her chastity.

Medea (*Mēdeia*, 431 B.C.). A tragedy by EURIPIDES. MEDEA, deserted by her husband, Jason, for the daughter of King Creon of Corinth, takes agonizing revenge by murdering the Corinthian princess and then her own children, in order to leave her husband with nothing. This treatment of the ancient Greek legend has inspired countless adaptations in all media, including plays by SENECA and Jean ANOUILH, and a ballet by Martha Graham with a Samuel Barber score. (For additional adaptations, see Variations.)

Melmoth the Wanderer (1820). A Gothic novel by the Irish clergyman and author Charles Robert Maturin (1782–1824) about John Melmoth, who has sold his soul to the Devil and is forced to spend 150 years searching for someone to take his place, so that he may die a natural death.

Member of the Wedding, The (1946). A novel by Carson MCCULLERS. The author's preoccupation with the loneliness of freaks and outcasts is developed in the story of 12-year-old Frankie, a white Southern girl who does not fit the roles prescribed for her age, sex, and race. She has more in common with Berenice, the "colored" cook-housekeeper, and her seven-year-old cousin John Henry, than with her father or the older brother of whose wedding she yearns to be a "member." McCullers's own hit stage adaptation (1950) was filmed in 1952.

Memento Mori (1959). A novel by Muriel SPARK, a black comedy in which a group of aging Londoners individually receive an anonymous call with the message, "Remember you must die." In accordance with his or her established pattern, each reacts differently.

Memoirs of Hadrian (*Mémoires d'Hadrien*, 1951). A historical novel by Marguerite YOURCENAR, her greatest work. It consists of a series of letters, meditating on such topics as politics, war, art, love, and fate, from the brilliant 2nd-century Roman Emperor Hadrian, nearing death, mostly to his 17-year-old heir and adoptive grandson, Marcus Aurelius. Yourcenar's interest in Hadrian arose when she read Gustave FLAUBERT's description of his era: "Just when the gods had ceased to be and the Christ had not yet come, there was a unique moment in history, between Cicero and Marcus Aurelius, when man stood alone."

"Mending Wall" (1914). A poem in blank verse by Robert FROST, in which trenchant images—the neighbor hoisting a rock is "like an old-stone savage armed"—drive home Frost's point that the boundaries separating human beings from each other are of their own making: "Good fences make good neighbors."

Merchant of Venice, The (c. 1596–97). A comedy by William SHAKESPEARE. Antonio borrows money from the Jewish moneylender SHYLOCK and agrees to forfeit "a pound of flesh" if he cannot repay the loan. When his ships are reported wrecked and Shylock demands the flesh, the clever PORTIA disguises herself as a male lawyer and appeals to Shylock's compassion: "The quality of mercy is not strain'd . . ." The portrayal of Shylock as greedy and callous has caused much controversy over whether Shakespeare was anti-Semitic.

Merry Wives of Windsor, The (c. 1598). A comedy by William SHAKESPEARE that follows the misadventures of FALSTAFF (introduced in Shakespeare's *HENRY IV*) as he plots to seduce two wealthy married women. According to unsubstantiated legend, the play was written at the behest of Elizabeth I, who asked to see Falstaff in love. (For adaptations, see Variations.)

Messiah of Stockholm, The (1987). A novel by Cynthia OZICK, in which a book reviewer undertakes a quest for *The Messiah*, the lost masterpiece of the Polish writer Bruno Schulz, who was killed by the Nazis and whom the reviewer believes to be his father.

Metamorphoses (c. A.D. 8). A long poem in 15 books by the Roman poet OVID. It includes approximately 250 tales, each based on myth or legend and involving a supernatural transformation.

Metamorphosis, The (*Die Verwandlung*, 1915). A novella by Franz KAFKA, his most famous work, about Gregor SAMSA, who awakens to find himself transformed inexplicably into a gigantic insect.

Middlemarch: A Study of Provincial Life (1872). A novel by GEORGE ELIOT, generally considered her masterpiece, that explores provincial Victorian society and expectations. The main characters include the intelligent and idealistic Dorothea BROOKE, her incompatible, scholarly husband Edward CASAUBON, Casaubon's attractive cousin Will LADISLAW, the young doctor Tertius Lydgate, his frivolous wife, Rosamond Vincy, her unlucky brother Fred, and his longtime love, Mary Garth.

Midnight's Children (1981). A Booker Prize–winning novel by Salman RUSHDIE, in which two infants, one the product of an adulterous union of a low-caste Hindu woman and an Englishman, and one from an affluent Muslim family, are switched at birth. The two, Saleem and Shiva, grow up to play significant roles in the first 30 years of India's independence from Britain.

Midsummer Night's Dream, A (c. 1595–96). A romantic comedy by William SHAKESPEARE, in which the playwright looks whimsically at the capriciousness of love. The most memorable characters are the fairy king OBERON, his wife TITANIA, the playful sprite PUCK, and the weaver BOTTOM. (For adaptations, see Variations.)

Mill on the Floss, The (1860). A novel by GEORGE ELIOT about Maggie TULLIVER and her brother Tom, in which Tom's sense of family honor and duty leads him to renounce Maggie, whose passion and imagination often put her in conflict with her provincial community. The siblings are finally reunited during a disastrous and deadly flood.

Misanthrope, The (*Le Misanthrope*, 1666). A satirical comedy by MOLIÈRE, showing that a virtue in excess can lose its value. ALCESTE, a sympathetic character at first, renders himself ridiculous by his obsessive railing against the hypocrisy of society.

Miser, The (*L'Avare*, 1668). A satiric play by MOLIÈRE, the first of his domestic comedies. The title character is Harpagon, who connives to marry off his daughter, Elise, to an older man who demands no dowry, even though she loves someone else. He also plots to marry himself to a young woman, Mariane, with whom his son is in love.

Misérables, Les (1862). A novel by Victor HUGO, set against the social and political conditions of France in the first half of the 19th century. Although there is a panorama of characters and events, the focus is on the unrelenting search by Police Inspector JAVERT for the escaped convict Jean VALJEAN, who had been imprisoned for stealing a loaf of bread. (For adaptations, see Variations.)

Miss Julie (*Fröken Julie*, 1889). A naturalistic tragedy by August STRINDBERG, probably his most frequently performed play. On Midsummer Night, in a manor-house kitchen, the manservant Jean and the count's daughter Julie engage in a skirmish of sexual and class warfare that will end in humiliation and suicide for one of the mismatched pair.

Miss Lonelyhearts (1933). A novel by NATHANAEL WEST. "Miss Lonelyhearts" (he has no other name) is a male advice-to-the-lovelorn columnist in Depression-era New York who agonizes over his correspondents' insoluble problems and his powerlessness to help them.

GREAT LINES FROM GREAT POEMS: A MATCHING QUIZ

Match the quotation to the poet:

1 "Hope" is the thing with feathers—
That perches in the soul—
And sings the tune without the words—
And never stops—at all—

2 And was Jerusalem builded here
Among these dark Satanic mills?

3 Do I contradict myself?
Very well then. . . . I contradict myself;
I am large. . . . I contain multitudes.

4 Glory be to God for dappled things—
For skies of couple-colour as a brinded
cow;
For rose-moles all in stipple upon trout
that swim;
Fresh-firecoal chestnut-falls; finches'
wings . . .

5 I saw the best minds of my generation
destroyed by madness,
starving hysterical naked . . .

6 Hail to thee, blithe spirit!
Bird thou never wert . . .

7 And we are here as on a darkling plain
Swept with confused alarms of struggle
and flight,
Where ignorant armies clash by night.

8 A Book of Verses underneath the Bough
A Jug of Wine, a Loaf of Bread—and
Thou
Beside me singing in the wilderness—

9 Take us the foxes, the little foxes, that
spoil the vines:
for our vines have tender grapes.

10 You may shoot me with your words,
You may cut me with your eyes,
You may kill me with your hatefulness,
But still, like air, I'll rise.

11 When you are old and grey and full of
sleep,
And nodding by the fire, take down this
book . . .

12 It is not a carol of joy or glee,
But a prayer that he sends from his
heart's deep core . . .
I know why the caged bird sings!

13 All nature is but art, unknown to thee;
All chance, direction which thou canst
not see . . .

14 Teach me to hear mermaids singing,
Or to keep off envy's stinging,
And find
What wind
Serves to advance an honest mind.

15 unless statistics lie he was
more brave than me:more blond than
you.

16 I love thee with the breath,
Smiles, tears, of all my life!—and, if God
choose,
I shall but love thee better after death.

17 Where are the songs of Spring? Ay, where
are they?
Think not of them, thou hast thy music
too,—

18 Looking up at the stars, I know quite well
That, for all they care, I can go to hell,
But on earth indifference is the least
We have to dread from man or beast.

19 Guns aren't lawful;
Nooses give;
Gas smells awful;
You might as well live.

20 Shall I part my hair behind? Do I dare to
        eat a peach?
I shall wear white flannel trousers, and
        walk upon the beach.
I have heard the mermaids singing, each
        to each.

21 Let us roll all our strength and all
Our sweetness up into a ball,
And tear our pleasures with rough strife
Through the iron gates of life.

22 I've stayed in the front yard all my life.
I want to peek at the back
Where it's rough and untended and
        hungry weed grows.
A girl gets sick of a rose.

(A) Maya Angelou
(B) Matthew Arnold
(C) W. H. Auden
(D) William Blake
(E) Gwendolyn Brooks
(F) Elizabeth Barrett Browning
(G) E. E. Cummings
(H) Emily Dickinson
(I) John Donne
(J) Paul Laurence Dunbar
(K) T. S. Eliot
(L) Edward FitzGerald
(M) Allen Ginsberg
(N) The Holy Bible (King James Version)
(O) Gerard Manley Hopkins
(P) John Keats
(Q) Andrew Marvell
(R) Dorothy Parker
(S) Alexander Pope
(T) Percy Bysshe Shelley
(U) Walt Whitman
(V) William Butler Yeats

ANSWERS:

1-H, Emily Dickinson, "No. 254"; 2-D, William Blake, "The New Jerusalem" (*Milton*, prefatory poem); 3-U, Walt Whitman, "Song of Myself"; 4-O, Gerard Manley Hopkins, "Pied Beauty"; 5-M, Allen Ginsberg, Howl; 6-T, Percy Bysshe Shelley, "To a Skylark"; 7-B, Matthew Arnold, "Dover Beach"; 8-L, Edward FitzGerald, *The Rubáiyát of Omar Khayyám*; 9-N, The Holy Bible (King James Version), *Song of Solomon*; 10-A, Maya Angelou, "Still I Rise"; 11-V, William Butler Yeats, "When You Are Old"; 12-J, Paul Laurence Dunbar, "Sympathy"; 13-S, Alexander Pope, *An Essay on Man*; 14-I, John Donne, "Song"; 15-G, E. E. Cummings, "i sing of Olaf glad and big"; 16-F, Elizabeth Barrett Browning, *Sonnets from the Portuguese*, 43; 17-P, John Keats, "To Autumn"; 18-C, W. H. Auden, "The More Loving One"; 19-R, Dorothy Parker, "Résumé (Enough Rope)"; 20-K, T. S. Eliot, "The Love Song of J. Alfred Prufrock"; 21-Q, Andrew Marvell, "To His Coy Mistress"; 22-E, Gwendolyn Brooks, "A Song in the Front Yard"

Eventually, he intervenes in the case of one unhappy couple, with disastrous results. The novel was adapted for the screen as *Lonelyhearts* (1959), starring Montgomery Clift.

Miss MacIntosh, My Darling (1965). A novel by Marguerite YOUNG. A multilayered poetic epic in 82 chapters, this discursive meditation on illusion versus reality focuses on Vera Cartwheel, who takes a bus to Indiana in a quixotic search for her long-missing nursemaid, Miss MacIntosh, who supposedly drowned herself when Vera was 14. Although little known by the general public, it is considered an underrated masterpiece by a cult of devoted admirers, including several well-known writers and critics.

Moby-Dick, or, The Whale (1851). A novel by Herman MELVILLE. This vast, epic masterpiece about men and whales, little heeded on publication, is now considered one of the greatest novels in English, from its famous opening line—"Call me ISHMAEL."—through the details of Captain AHAB's obsessive pursuit of the white whale that maimed him, to the final, cataclysmic confrontation, which brings death to the *Pequod*'s entire crew; only the narrator escapes to tell the story. (For adaptations, see Variations.)

Moll Flanders (in full: *The Fortunes and Misfortunes of the Famous Moll Flanders*, 1722). A picaresque novel by Daniel DEFOE; one of the first English novels, still enjoyed for its resourceful heroine. Defoe's subtitle summarized the story of Moll FLANDERS: "Born in Newgate, and during a Life of continu'd Variety…was Twelve Year a Whore, five times a Wife (whereof once to her own Brother), Twelve Year a Thief, Eight Year a Transported Felon in Virginia, at last grew Rich, liv'd Honest, and died a Penitent."

Molloy (1951). A novel in French by Samuel BECKETT, his first major work in the language he said allowed him to write "without style," although the characters' predicaments and preoccupations are quintessentially Beckettian. It consists of two blackly humorous monologues; in the first, Molloy tells of his vain quest to find his mother; in the second, Moran narrates his equally vain pursuit of Molloy. The first part of a trilogy, it was followed by *MALONE DIES* (1951) and *THE UNNAMABLE* (1953).

Month in the Country, A (*Mesyats v Derevne*, 1855). A play by Ivan TURGENEV, an important early landmark in the use of realistic psychological characterization in European theater. Natalya, a landowner's restless wife, discovers that both she and her young ward, Vera, are attracted to her son's tutor, Belyayev. The women's rivalry and the dynamics of love and marriage in provincial Russia are played out in the month that Belyayev spends with the family.

Mont-Saint-Michel and Chartres (1904, revised 1913). A travel narrative by Henry ADAMS, subtitled *A Study of Thirteenth-century Unity*. In evoking the spirit of the great cathedrals, Adams implicitly contrasts the unified medieval view of God and Humanity with the uncertainty and spiritual confusion of the modern world.

Moon and Sixpence, The (1919). A novel by W. Somerset MAUGHAM, loosely based on the life of artist Paul Gauguin. Charles Strickland renounces his comfortable life as a wealthy London stockbroker, leaves his wife and children, and moves to Paris to become a painter. He cruelly ignores the pain he causes others and, obsessed with painting, settles in Tahiti, where he marries a native woman, and dies of leprosy. The title alludes to a saying about a man who is so engrossed in staring at the moon that he does not see the sixpence at his feet.

Moon for the Misbegotten, A (written 1943; performed 1957). The last play by Eugene O'NEILL. In this epilogue to *LONG DAY'S JOURNEY INTO NIGHT*, embittered alcoholic Jamie TYRONE and his contentious tenant's "giantess" daughter, Josie Hogan, find a brief interlude of peace and understanding over the course of a moonlit night and the following dawn. Initially a failure, the play has since achieved critical stature, enhanced by a celebrated 1973 Broadway revival, and is now one of the playwright's most frequently produced works.

"Moons of Jupiter, The" (1977). A short story by Alice MUNRO, reprinted in the collection of the same name (1982). An unnamed narrator struggles to remain detached while visiting her critically ill father at a hospital. She is driven to examine her roles as the child of a difficult parent, and the loving parent of two now-adult children—daughters who are, in their own ways, as ill at ease with her as she is with her demanding father.

Moonstone, The (1868). A detective novel by Wilkie COLLINS, one of the earliest English examples of the genre. The tale, about a stolen diamond that was once part of an ancient Hindu talisman, is narrated by several characters, but the case is pursued officially by Sergeant Cuff.

Morte d'Arthur, Le (c. 1469–70; first printed by William Caxton, 1485). A retelling and translation from French verse, probably by Sir Thomas MALORY, of eight chivalric romances. Among these are the quest by Sir GALAHAD and Sir LANCELOT for the Holy Grail, the story of TRISTAN and ISEULT, and the adventures of King ARTHUR and his Knights of the Round Table.

Mother Courage and Her Children (*Mutter Courage und Ihre Kinder*, 1941). A play by Bertolt BRECHT, set against the destruction of the Thirty Years' War. The title character is a vendor who supports herself and her family by following regiments. Even the loss of her three children to the violence does not dampen her resolve to profit from it, as she becomes the embodiment of the heartlessness and greed associated with war.

Mountolive. *See* **Alexandria Quartet, The**

Mourning Becomes Electra (1931). A dramatic trilogy by Eugene O'NEILL, based on AESCHYLUS's *ORESTEIA* and consisting of "Homecoming," "The Hunted," and "The Haunted," performed in one sitting. Replacing the Greek concept of fate with psychological determinism and setting his work in post–Civil War New England, O'Neill examines the lusts and hatreds of the MANNON family, whose members are torn between passion and puritanism. (For a film adaptation, see Variations, under *Oresteia*.)

Moviegoer, The (1961). Walker PERCY's first, and National Book Award–winning, novel, depicting Binx BOLLING's existential quest for purpose and redemption. Bolling, a successful professional in the "New South," espouses a wry philosophy as he finds meaning in the movies.

Mr. Sammler's Planet (1970). A National Book Award–winning novel by Saul BELLOW. Artur Sammler, an old-world Jewish intellectual now in his 70s, has survived the Holocaust in Poland, but finds himself something of a displaced person in late 1960s New York City. Dispassionately observing the chaotic world around him, he attempts to make sense of people and events to which he is necessarily connected yet from which he feels removed.

Mrs. Dalloway (1925). A novel by VIRGINIA WOOLF, presenting a day in the life of Clarissa DALLOWAY, whose preoccupation with a planned dinner party is contrasted with her reflections on her past, and also with the struggle for inner peace of Great War veteran Septimus Smith. Woolf's masterly use of time and internal monologue to link the stories and concerns of two characters who never meet make this one of her finest works.

Mrs. Warren's Profession (1902). One of three "Plays Unpleasant" in George Bernard SHAW's first collection (1898), it was denied a public performance license until the 1920s (the 1902 production was private) because the "profession" in question is prostitution, which Shaw said was caused "by underpaying, undervaluing and overworking women." The main characters are Kitty Warren, now a prosperous brothel owner, and her daughter Vivie, a brilliant "new woman" who has been raised apart from her, and only now learns her story.

Much Ado About Nothing (c. 1598–99). A comedy by William SHAKESPEARE, in which the villainous Don John causes Claudio to doubt the chastity of his fiancée, Hero. The play is best remembered for the malapropisms of the comic, incompetent Constable Dogberry and for the sparkling, combative repartee of BEATRICE and BENEDICK.

Mule Bone (written 1931, published 1990, performed 1992). A drama written jointly by Zora Neale HURSTON and LANGSTON HUGHES. Hoping to create a drama that countered the conventions of minstrelsy, the two African Americans based their work on the Southern black tradition, using the folktale "The Bone of Contention" as a suggestion for a comic play of romantic rivals. Differences over the play kept Hurston and Hughes from further association with one another.

Mumbo Jumbo (1972). A novel by Ishmael REED. In this satirical hybrid of styles and genres, a detective story is interwoven with African-American and Egyptian myths, historical citations, newspaper articles, and photographs. The plot follows Neo-Hoodoo detective PaPa LaBas in his quest for a lost Hoodoo text so that its followers, the Jes Grew, can practice their beliefs openly. In this endeavor he is opposed by the Atonists, the authorities and preservers of Western civilization.

Murder in the Cathedral (1935). A play in verse by T. S. ELIOT about the martyrdom of St. THOMAS À BECKET, Archbishop of Canterbury, in 1170. The work turns on the conflict between allegiance to the state and to one's own conscience.

"Murders in the Rue Morgue, The" (1841). A short story by Edgar Allan POE, considered the first detective story. Poe's master of ratiocination, C. Auguste DUPIN, is the archetype of the cerebral sleuth, and his account of how Dupin solves the riddle of the bestial murders in a quiet Parisian street is the archetypal "locked room" mystery. With this and two other stories featuring Dupin, "THE PURLOINED LETTER" and "The Mystery of Marie Rogêt" (1842–43), Poe established many of the genre's still-prevailing conventions.

Murphy (1938). A novel by Samuel BECKETT. "The sun shone, having no alternative, on the nothing new," begins Beckett's first published novel, sounding one of his most persistent themes: there being "no alternative" to what exists, how may one occupy a lifetime of "the nothing new"? Murphy, an Irishman in Lon-

don, would prefer no occupation at all, to his lover Celia's dismay, but he finally takes a job in an asylum, Magdalen Mental Mercyseat, where he encounters kindred spirits.

Mutiny on the Bounty (1932). The first novel in the *Bounty Trilogy* (followed by *Men Against the Sea*, 1934, and *Pitcairn's Island*, 1935), by the American writers Charles B. Nordhoff (1887–1947) and James Norman Hall (1887–1951). This carefully researched work offers a fictional account of the events surrounding the real-life 1787 mutiny in the South Seas, led by Fletcher CHRISTIAN against Captain William BLIGH. A bestseller, it became the basis for at least five films, notably a 1935 version starring Charles Laughton and Clark Gable, as well as various stage and television adaptations. It has also inspired continued research leading to countless nonfiction print and film histories of the mutiny.

My Ántonia (1918). A novel by Willa CATHER that vividly conveys both the romance and the harshness of frontier life. The narrator, Jim Burden, presents a series of reminiscences of his childhood friend Ántonia SHIMERDA, the daughter of Bohemian settlers in Nebraska. Ántonia's hard work, steadfastness, generosity, and enthusiasm make her the embodiment of the pioneer woman.

My Brilliant Career (1901). A novel by the Australian author Miles Franklin (1879–1954). Sybylla Melvyn is the feminist heroine of a satiric romance set in turn-of-the-20th-century Australia. Written when the author was 16, it excited comparisons to *JANE EYRE* and caused a sensation on the mistaken assumption that it was autobiographical. Franklin restricted its reprinting until ten years after her death, but sought publication of a "corrective" sequel, *My Career Goes Bung* (written 1902, published 1946). The 1979 film version brought international attention to this hitherto neglected Australian classic.

"My Last Duchess" (1842). A poem by ROBERT BROWNING, one of his best-known dramatic monologues. The Duke of Ferrara describes how his late wife had displeased him with her indiscriminate smiles and insufficient deference to himself, as he shows her portrait to an emissary of his prospective next wife: "I gave commands, then all smiles stopped together."

My Man Jeeves (1919). The first collection of stories by P. G. WODEHOUSE, featuring his popular characters Bertie WOOSTER (the inept aristocrat) and JEEVES (the capable valet). Subsequent collections include *The Inimitable Jeeves* (1923), *Carry On, Jeeves* (1925, including some stories from *My Man Jeeves* substantially revised), and *Very Good, Jeeves* (1930). Some of the novels featuring Wooster and Jeeves are *Right Ho, Jeeves* (1922), *Jeeves and the Feudal Spirit* (1954), *Stiff Upper Lip, Jeeves* (1963), and *Jeeves and the Tie That Binds* (1971).

My Mortal Enemy (1926). A short novel by Willa CATHER, written in the austere style that she called the "novel *démeublé*," or "unfurnished novel." It offers a portrait of the willful, extravagant, and strangely captivating Myra Birdseye, who as a young woman was disinherited by her wealthy great-uncle when she married for love. At the end, Myra and her husband have been reduced to living in a shabby hotel on the California coast.

Myra Breckinridge (1968). A fantasy by Gore VIDAL that satirizes gender roles and media obsession in American culture. His protagonist is transsexual Myron/Myra. *Myron: A Novel* (1974) is a sequel.

Mysteries of Udolpho, The (1794). A Gothic novel by Ann RADCLIFFE, one of the best-known and most popular works of the genre, following the adventures of Emily de St. Aubert, an orphan who is sent to live with her vain aunt and the aunt's outlaw husband.

Mystery of Edwin Drood, The (1870). The last, uncompleted novel of Charles DICKENS. The principal characters are John Jasper and his nephew, the title character, who is murdered. Because the story was only half-finished when Dickens died, much controversy has arisen about the mystery's intended resolution. Rupert Holmes's musical adaptation (1985) allows audiences to vote for the ending they prefer.

Naked and the Dead, The (1948). The first novel by Norman MAILER, relating the fates of American infantrymen struggling to take the fictional Japanese-held Pacific island of Anopopei during World War II. Widely hailed on publication as the first major novel about the recent war, it today ranks high among American war novels for its unstinting depictions of the minutiae of war, as seen by the men of Sergeant Sam Croft's Intelligence and Reconnaissance Platoon.

Naked Lunch (1959). A Beat Generation novel by WILLIAM S. BURROUGHS, based on his own experiences with drugs. The surreal, disturbing, and often comic text recreates the world as experienced by a drug addict.

Name of the Rose, The (*Il Nome della Rosa*, 1980). An erudite but extremely popular murder mystery by Umberto ECO, set in a medieval Benedictine monastery and reflecting the author's interest in semiotics. On one level about the investigation, conducted by the monk William of Baskerville, into a series of murders, it also explores the nature of truth and knowledge.

Nana (1880). A novel by Émile ZOLA, the ninth in his *Rougon-Macquart* series about a family of the French Second Empire. The beautiful Nana rises from the slums, has a brief theatrical career, and becomes a courtesan who wreaks destruction among her lovers. The novel reflects the "survival of the fittest" theme inherent in literary naturalism, of which Zola was a founder.

Native Son (1940). A novel by Richard WRIGHT, a bestseller and one of the masterpieces of African-American literature. This story of Bigger THOMAS, who kills two women (one accidentally, one deliberately), deals unflinchingly with the consequences of American racism. (For adaptations, see Variations.)

Natural, The (1952). The first novel by Bernard MALAMUD, in which a modern baseball fable is structured upon the quest for the Holy Grail. Roy Hobbs, a gifted player with a powerful, perhaps supernatural bat ("Wonderboy"), leads his team to amazing success, but then creates his own downfall.

"Nature" (1836). A long philosophical essay by Ralph Waldo EMERSON, derived from a series of lectures and published anonymously. The work established the main tenets of Transcendentalism. Emerson believed that nature is the physical manifestation of the Divine, to which humans can turn to realize their own divinity, their souls being contained in the all-pervading spirit of God.

Nausea (*La Nausée*, 1938). The first novel by Jean-Paul SARTRE, a major work of Existentialism. Through the diaries of the protagonist, Antoine Roquentin, the novel portrays the individual's struggle to find meaning in a world in which former systems are no longer relevant. The alienated Roquentin becomes physically sick as he confronts inanimate objects and finds himself unable to connect with other people.

"Negro Speaks of Rivers, The" (1921). A poem by LANGSTON HUGHES, dedicated to W. E. B. DU BOIS, affirming the survival of African Americans despite the legacy of slavery. ("My soul has grown deep like the rivers.") Stylistically, it combines the cadences of the American spiritual with the free verse form of Walt WHITMAN.

Nibelungenlied (c. 1200; also translated under the titles *The Lay of the Nibelungs*; *The Song of the Nibelungs*). An epic poem in Middle High German, retelling episodes from Germanic history and myth in terms of 13th-century courtly life. It culminates in a massacre of the Nibelungs (here meaning the Burgundians, whose kingdom was annihilated by the Huns in 437), which is the fulfillment of Kriemhild's revenge for the treacherous slaying of her husband, Siegfried. Wagner adapted portions for his four-opera cycle, *The Ring of the Nibelung* (1876); it was also the source of a two-part film by Fritz Lang (1924).

Nicholas Nickleby (in full: *The Life and Adventures of Nicholas Nickleby*, 1839). A novel by Charles DICKENS, whose description of Dotheboys Hall, run by the tyrannical schoolmaster Squeers, exposed the horrors of many contemporary English schools, where children were beaten, half-starved, and taught little. The book led to reforms throughout England. Other memorable characters are young Nicholas NICKLEBY's wicked uncle, moneylender Ralph Nickleby; lame, simpleminded Smike; and the good-hearted brothers Cheeryble. Adaptations include David Edgar's eight-hour stage version for the Royal Shakespeare Company (1980), which was later telecast.

Nigger of the "Narcissus," The (1897). A novel by Joseph CONRAD, based on the author's experiences while serving in the British merchant navy. James Wait, a black sailor dying of tuberculosis, is at the center of a story that explores the behavior of and relationships among a crew of sailors in the face of unpredictable conditions, rising stress, violent storms, and the possibility of mutiny.

Night of the Iguana, The (1961). A play by TENNESSEE WILLIAMS, set at a rundown Mexican hotel. The guilt-ridden Shannon, a defrocked priest, brings a busload of women teachers to the hotel run by his old friend, Maxine Faulk. The other principal character is Hannah Jelkes, an ascetic artist attending her dying poet-grandfather. The title refers to an iguana (symbolic of the leading characters) caught and tormented by local boys.

Nightwood (1936). An experimental, poetic novel by DJUNA BARNES, set in Paris, Berlin, and rural New York. The author explores the nature of relationships (including lesbian relationships) and the search for identity. The most famous of Barnes's works, the novel became a cult classic. The introduction was written by T. S. ELIOT, who was also the book's editor.

Nine Stories (1953). A collection of short stories by J. D. SALINGER. Included are "A Perfect Day for Banana Fish" (which introduces the enigmatic Seymour GLASS, whose family will appear in many of Salinger's later works), "For Esmé—With Love and Squalor" (in which a young girl enables a shell-shocked soldier to regain his ability to love, and usually considered Salinger's best story), and "Pretty Mouth and Green My Eyes" (concerning casual adultery).

Nineteen Eighty-four (1949). An anti-utopian novel by George ORWELL, portraying the tyranny of a fictional totalitarian regime based on Stalinist Russia, symbolized by the icon BIG BROTHER. Capturing totalitarianism's disturbing logic, the work introduced to the language such formulations as "thought police," "newspeak," "thoughtcrime," and "doublethink," along with the chilling notion that "Big Brother is watching you."

1919. *See* **U.S.A.**

Njal's Saga (*Njáls Saga*; also known as *Njála* and *Brennu-Njáls Saga*, late 13th century; also translated under the title *The Story of Burnt Njal*). A Norse saga, classed among the "sagas of Icelanders" or "family sagas," about heroes from earlier Icelandic history. The chief heroes here are the impetuous warrior Gunnar and his friend and counselor Njal (Njáll), whose stoic acceptance of his fate—to be burned in his dwelling with his family—is the story's climax. It is often considered the greatest of all the sagas for its broad panorama of medieval Icelandic life, vivid action scenes, and complex, vibrantly drawn characters.

No Exit (*Huis Clos*, 1944). A play by Jean-Paul SARTRE, illustrating the Existentialist dictum that "Hell is other people." The setting is a Second Empire drawing room in which three people are condemned to coexist eternally in mutual recrimination and unrequited lust. The three are Garcin (a political coward who abused his wife), Inez (a lesbian killed by her lover), and Estelle (who murdered her illegitimate child).

No More Parades. *See* **Parade's End**

Northanger Abbey (1817). A novel by Jane AUSTEN, a parody of the Gothic novels then popular in England, which follows the life of young Catherine Morland, who, after a series of adventures, learns that life does not much resemble a Gothic novel.

Nostromo: A Tale of the Seaboard (1904). A novel by Joseph CONRAD. The author's seagoing experiences provided him with raw material for this tale of idealism and corruption centered around a South American silver mine. The complicated narrative structure, intertwining four major character studies and varied points of view, troubled early critics, but it elevates the story from what could have been a straight-forward romantic adventure to a more profound examination of human nature. It is considered by many modern critics to be Conrad's greatest work.

Notes from the Underground (*Zapiski iz Podpol'ya*, 1864). A long short story by Fyodor DOSTOYEVSKY, in which the unnamed "underground" man both elucidates and embodies the author's antipositivist philosophy that people are inherently irrational and often petty and spiteful. It explores many of the themes found in Dostoyevsky's strongest novels and is a key philosophical work for Existentialists.

Oblomov (1859). A satirical novel by Ivan GONCHAROV about OBLOMOV, a lazy Russian landowner who idles away his days in St. Petersburg, daydreaming and rarely even getting up from his couch. In Russian, the title character's name came to stand for the inertia and back-wardness of 19th-century Russia and the social situation of the nobility prior to the emancipation of the serfs.

"O Captain! My Captain!" *See* **Leaves of Grass**

Octopus, The: A Story of California (1901). A novel by Frank NORRIS. In this story of greed, dishonesty, and courage, California wheat farmers confront the Pacific and Southwestern Railroad monopoly, the "octopus" whose tentacles surround them and threaten to crush them. Conceived as part of a projected trilogy about the wheat industry, it is an early example of American naturalism. *The Octopus* was followed by *The Pit* (1903); Norris died in 1902 without having written the final book of the trilogy, which was to have been called *The Wolf*.

"Ode: Intimations of Immortality from Recollections of Early Childhood" (1807). A poem by William WORDSWORTH, in which the poet finds solace in the memory of childhood experiences, but is still left with "thoughts that do often lie too deep for tears."

"Ode on a Grecian Urn" (1820). An ode by John KEATS; its moving last lines—"Beauty is truth, truth beauty—that is all / Ye know on earth, and all ye need to know"—have made it one of the best-known in British poetry.

"Ode to a Nightingale" (1820). A poem by John KEATS, who was ill with tuberculosis when he wrote it. The poem conveys an intense awareness of the pleasures of living, the imminence of death, and the incapacity of art to make up for the pains of living on earth.

"Ode to the West Wind" (1820). An ode by PERCY BYSSHE SHELLEY, addressed to the autumnal wind, nature's "destroyer and preserver." Shelley wishes fervently for the wind's power and eloquence ("Make me thy lyre, even as the forest is") to spread his message to mankind. The final line hints at optimism: "If Winter comes, can Spring be far behind?"

Odyssey (*Odysseia*, 8th century B.C.). An epic poem traditionally ascribed to HOMER. With its companion work, the *Iliad*, it is among the oldest and most significant works of Western literature. The *Odyssey* relates the post–Trojan War adventures of ODYSSEUS (called Ulysses by the Romans) on his ten-year voyage home to Ithaca, where he reclaims his kingdom and his faithful wife, PENELOPE, with the help of his son Telemachus and the goddess Athena. Translated by poets (George CHAPMAN, Alexander POPE, William Cullen BRYANT) and scholars, it has inspired innumerable works of art, including James JOYCE'S *ULYSSES*. (For this and other adaptations, see Variations, under the *Iliad*.)

Oedipus the King (*Oidipous Tyrannos*; Latin, *Oedipus Rex*, c. 430 B.C.). A tragedy by SOPHOCLES about the mythical king who unknowingly kills his father and marries his mother. The action takes place on the day that OEDIPUS discovers that, in trying to avoid his prophesied fate, he has, ironically, carried it out. In atonement, he blinds himself with needles, even though his appalling acts were committed in ignorance. In his *Poetics*, ARISTOTLE found Sophocles' *Oedipus* an exemplary work of dramatic art; centuries later, Sigmund FREUD argued that the play's grip on audiences stemmed from its portrayal of the basic truth of the human psyche, the Oedipus Complex.

Of Human Bondage (1915). An autobiographical novel by W. Somerset MAUGHAM, exploring the forces that limit one mentally and spiritually. After breaking free of the forms of bondage imposed by his background and his club foot, Philip Carey, a medical student, becomes infatuated with Mildred Rogers, a Cockney waitress who cruelly manipulates and exploits him.

Of Mice and Men (1937). A novella by John STEINBECK about the fate of innocence in a corrupt world. Lennie Small, a mentally retarded giant, and George Milton, Lennie's friend and protector, are itinerant farm workers who fantasize about owning their own farm. When Lennie inadvertently breaks the neck of a flirtatious woman, George must kill his friend to save him from a lynch mob. (For adaptations, see Variations.)

Of Time and the River: A Legend of Man's Hunger in His Youth (1935). A novel by THOMAS WOLFE, the sequel to *LOOK HOMEWARD, ANGEL* (1929), depicting further events in the life of Eugene GANT as he attends Harvard, suffers the death of his father, and becomes involved in literary circles in New York and Europe.

Old Man and the Sea, The (1953). A Pulitzer Prize–winning short novel by Ernest HEMINGWAY, exemplifying human grace and dignity in the face of defeat. It raises to mythic grandeur the Cuban fisherman SANTIAGO (who has gone 84 days without a catch) and his quest for a large marlin (whom he calls his "brother"). The work was first published in *Life* magazine in September 1952.

Oliver Twist (1838). A novel by Charles DICKENS, which recounts the colorful adventures of the orphan Oliver TWIST. By depicting the cruelty of workhouses and the reality of poverty and crime in Victorian England, Dickens used his novel to criticize social abuses of the poor and attack the Poor Law of 1834. (For adaptations, see Variations.)

Omeros (1990). A long narrative poem by Derek WALCOTT, a postcolonial epic that reworks the Homeric legends, casting them in the Caribbean. The poem identifies a beautiful black Helen ("oblique but magnetic") with the island of St. Lucia, eagerly sought by imperialists. Other significant characters are the fisherman Achille, the taxi-driver Hector, the expatriate Plunkett family, the Obeah Ma Kilman, and Walcott himself. It was for this work especially that Walcott was awarded the 1992 Nobel Prize in Literature.

Once and Future King, The (1938–58). A tetralogy by the English author T. H. White (1906–1964). Based on Sir Thomas MALORY's LE MORTE D'ARTHUR, White's epic retelling of Arthurian legend includes *The Sword and the Stone* (1938), *The Queen of Air and Darkness* (originally titled *The Witch in the Wood*, 1939), *The Ill-Made Knight* (1940), and *The Candle in the Wind* (1958). The four books were published in a single volume in 1958. A fifth, related tale was found among White's papers after his death and published as *The Book of Merlyn* in 1977.

One Day in the Life of Ivan Denisovich (*Odin Den' Ivana Denisovicha*, 1962). The first novel by Aleksandr SOLZHENITSYN, based on the eight years the author spent in a Soviet labor camp, and recounting a single grueling day in the life of a peasant serving a ten-year sentence in a Stalinist prison camp in Siberia. The most important novel of the post-Stalin "thaw" period in the Soviet Union, *One Day* was authorized for publication by Premier Nikita Khrushchev and established Solzhenitsyn as a major writer.

One Flew Over the Cuckoo's Nest (1962). A novel by Ken KESEY, examining the nature of tyranny and the fate of those who too rashly oppose it. Chief Bromden, a Native American inmate in a psychiatric ward, narrates the arrival in the ward of R. P. McMurphy, who brings life and energy to the docile, cowed patients. However, McMurphy's exuberant defiance of the authoritarian Nurse Ratched brings her wrath down upon him; she has him lobotomized. Milos Forman's 1975 film adaptation won five Academy Awards, including Best Picture, Best Director, Best Actor (Jack Nicholson as McMurphy), and Best Actress (Louise Fletcher as Nurse Ratched).

120 Days of Sodom, The (*Les 120 Journées du Sodome, ou L'École du Libertinage*, written 1784–85, published 1904). A philosophical and erotic novel by Donatien-Alphonse-François, Marquis de SADE, written during his imprisonment and originally believed to have been destroyed during the storming of the Bastille. In the work, called by its author "the most impure tale which has ever been told since our world began," four notorious libertines kidnap unwilling participants and sequester themselves in a castle for a four-month orgy of sex, torture, and murder.

One Hundred Years of Solitude (*Cien Años de Soledad*, 1967). A novel by Gabriel GARCÍA MÁRQUEZ, his masterpiece, in which the fictional town of Macondo and its citizens serve as a microcosm not only of Latin America, but also of all humanity, the town's history representing the history of civilization. The work focuses on six generations of the remarkable BUENDÍA family.

"On First Looking into Chapman's Homer" (1816). A sonnet by John KEATS, written on first encountering the translations of the *Odyssey* and the *Iliad* by the Elizabethan poet George CHAPMAN. After reading all night with his friend Charles Cowden Clarke, Keats went home and wrote his poem of exhilarated discovery: "Then felt I like some watcher of the skies / When a new planet swims into his ken…" He finished the poem and delivered it to Clarke by ten the next morning.

On the Road (1957). A novel by Jack KEROUAC, a *roman à clef* tracing a cross-country search for "kicks" in prose heavily influenced by poetry, jazz, and artificial stimulants. Gilbert Millstein's *New York Times* review accurately predicted that, "Just as, more than any other novel of the Twenties, THE SUN ALSO RISES came to be regarded as the testament of the 'Lost Generation,' so it seems certain that *On the Road* will come to be known as that of the 'Beat Generation.'"

"Open Boat, The" (1898). A frequently anthologized short story by STEPHEN CRANE about four men who escape from a sinking ship and attempt to row to safety in a tiny dinghy. Collected in *The Open Boat and Other Tales of Adventure* (1898), the story is based on Crane's own survival of a shipwreck on the way to Cuba in 1897.

O Pioneers! (1913). A novel by Willa CATHER, the title of which comes from Walt WHITMAN. Alexandra BERGSON, the daughter of immigrants, gains control of her family's farm on the Nebraska prairies and, introducing unconventional farming methods, turns it into a success.

Optimist's Daughter, The (1972). An autobiographical Pulitzer Prize–winning novel by Eudora WELTY, focusing on the intricacies of the tie between parent and child, and manifesting the author's characteristic ironic sensibility.

Oresteia (458 B.C.). A trilogy of plays by AESCHYLUS, the only trilogy extant from the Greek Classical period. The topic is the curse on the House of Atreus (i.e., the descendants of the Mycenaen king Atreus), here including AGAMEMNON, son of Atreus; Agamemnon's wife, Clytemnestra; and their children ORESTES, IPHIGENIA, ELECTRA, and Chrysothemis. In *Agamemnon* (*Agamemnōn*), the title character returns home as the triumphant hero of the Trojan War only to be murdered by his wife because he had sacrificed their eldest daughter, Iphigenia, in exchange for favorable winds for the Greek fleet. In *The Libation Bearers* (*Choēphoroi*), Orestes returns from exile to avenge his father's murder and—with encouragement from his sister Electra—kills Clytemnestra and her lover, Aegisthus. He then flees, pursued by the Furies. In the *Eumenides*, the curse on the House of Atreus is lifted as Athena organizes a trial by a jury of Athenian citizens who exonerate the tormented Orestes of the crime of matricide. Thus the Athenian model of rational justice prevails over the primitive code of blood retribution. (For adaptations, see Variations.)

Orlando: A Biography (1928). A novel by VIRGINIA WOOLF that comments whimsically on four centuries of English society and literature through the character ORLANDO, who confounds gender roles by changing from male to female, and confutes chronology by aging scarcely at all through generations. Inspired by the character and family history of Woolf's intimate friend, Vita Sackville-West, *Orlando* was an instant success. It has endured and outlived fashionable critical readings ever since, much as Orlando transcends sex, time, and death.

Orlando Furioso (1532). An epic poem in 46 cantos by Ludovico ARIOSTO, about the wondrous adventures and exotic ordeals of knights, princesses, and a woman warrior in search of true love. Ariosto's serene command of his medium transforms material from Carolingian and Arthurian romances (Orlando is "ROLAND" from *THE SONG OF ROLAND*) and the classical tradition into one of the supreme literary achievements of the Italian Renaissance, by turns ironic, uplifting, and purely enchanting.

Othello, the Moor of Venice (1604). One of the major tragedies of William SHAKESPEARE, dramatizing the passion of OTHELLO, a North African general serving Venice, for his wife, DESDEMONA, and the treachery of IAGO, one of Othello's soldiers, who turns Othello against Desdemona. (For adaptations, see Variations.)

Our Lady of the Flowers (*Notre-Dame des Fleurs*, 1944, limited edition 1943). A novel by Jean GENET, written while he was in prison for burglary. Within an elaborate and fantastic urban underworld of outcasts, traditional values are inverted; evil becomes sacred. The major characters are Divine (a male prostitute and thief), Darling (his pimp), and Our Lady of the Flowers (a brutal murderer). The work, with its abandonment of conventional morality and its lyrical prose style, was acclaimed by many French intellectuals, notably Jean-Paul SARTRE, leading to a pardon for Genet.

Our Man in Havana (1958). A comic novel by Graham GREENE about a British Secret Service agent in Cuba. Alec Guinness starred in the 1960 film version.

Our Mutual Friend (1865). The last completed novel by Charles DICKENS. Beyond the usual Dickensian trademarks—a convoluted plot, colorful characters—the work is dominated by motifs and imagery of waste, dust, and death. Mistakenly declared dead, the title character assumes a false identity to test the young woman who was to have been his bride, while another of the principals, a jaded lawyer, must almost literally die to be deemed worthy of the working-class woman who loves him.

Our Town (1938). A Pulitzer Prize–winning play by Thornton WILDER. "Do any human beings ever realize life while they live it?—every, every minute?" Set in New England, using minimal props and scenery, and a "stage manager" as Chorus, on the surface the play presents a snapshot album of small-town Americana. On a deeper level, in the playwright's words, "It is an attempt to find a value above all price for the smallest events in our daily life." (For adaptations, see Variations.)

"Outcasts of Poker Flat, The" (1870). A short story by Bret HARTE, collected in *The Luck of Roaring Camp and Other Sketches*. Professional gambler John Oakhurst, two prostitutes named "the Duchess" and "Mother Shipton," and the drunkard "Uncle Billy" are expelled from Poker Flat. On their way to the next town, the "outcasts" meet a young couple and selflessly try to save them from a blizzard.

Out of Africa (1937). A memoir by Isak DINESEN, written in English and translated the same year by the author into Danish (*Den Afrikanske Farm*). In this work, which may be partly fictitious, the author relates her experiences running a coffee plantation in Kenya from 1914 until it failed in 1931.

"Out of the Cradle Endlessly Rocking." *See* **Leaves of Grass**

Out of the Silent Planet. *See* **Space Trilogy, The**

"Overcoat, The" ("Shinel'," 1842). A short story by Nikolai GOGOL. Low-level clerk Akaky Bashmachkin scrimps and saves to buy a new overcoat before the bitter-cold St. Petersburg winter begins, only to have the coat stolen the first time he wears it. He seeks in vain for assistance from an important bureaucrat, then falls ill and dies a few days later. Soon after, a ghost begins haunting the city, snatching overcoats. The ghost disappears only after stealing the coat of the heartless bureaucrat. This important social satire influenced the work of many Russian writers and the development of Russian realism.

Ox-Bow Incident, The (1940). A novel by the American author Walter van Tilburg Clark (1909–1971), examining frontier justice in 1880s Nevada. Three innocent men are lynched, and the men who perform the deed must confront its consequences. William Wellman's celebrated film version (1943) starred Henry Fonda.

"Ozymandias" (1818). An irregularly rhymed sonnet by PERCY BYSSHE SHELLEY; among his best-known poems, it is a meditation on vainglory and transitoriness. The ruined statue of the pharaoh Ramses II, called Ozymandias by the Greeks, bears an inscription—"Look on my works, ye mighty, and despair!"—that its current state has rendered profoundly ironic.

Painted Bird, The (1965). A putatively autobiographical novel by Jerzy KOSINSKI about a Polish child separated from his parents during World War II, surviving amid violence, ignorance, and depravity. As the boy roams the countryside, he is victimized repeatedly by brutal peasants who believe that he is either a Jew or a Gypsy. The novel, Kosinski's first, appeared only eight years after he had immigrated to the United States and taught himself English. While its autobiographical claims have since been questioned, it remains an impressive work of literature.

Palace of Desire. *See* **Cairo Trilogy, The**

Palace Walk. *See* **Cairo Trilogy, The**

Pale Fire (1962). A novel by Vladimir NABOKOV consisting of two parts: a 999-line poem by a fictional American, John Shade, and the commentary (the bulk of the book) of a psychotic professor, Charles KINBOTE. In Nabokov's satire of literary criticism, the delusional Kinbote turns every line of the poem into a reference to himself and his fantasy realm of Zembla, of which he is the exiled king.

Pale Horse, Pale Rider (1939). A collection of three novellas by Katherine Anne PORTER. In "Old Mortality," two young sisters confront the truth, which has been obscured by family mythologizing. "Noon Wine" concerns a farmer overwhelmed by shame and guilt after killing a man, perhaps accidentally. The title story, set during the influenza epidemic of 1918, depicts a woman's journey into truth after nearly dying.

Pallisers, The (1864–80). The informal collective title for six novels by Anthony TROLLOPE, including *Can You Forgive Her?* (1864), *Phineas Finn* (1869), *The Eustace Diamonds* (1873), *Phineas Redux* (1874), *The Prime Minister* (1876), and *The Duke's Children* (1880). Political aspirant Plantagenet PALLISER (of the ducal house of Omnium), and his wife, Lady Glencora, were introduced as minor characters in Trollope's *The Small House at Allington* (1864). With Phineas Finn, an Irish member of Parliament, they serve as the thread connecting this series, in which the author trains his eye on Victorian England, its policies, manners, and mores. Trollope considered *The Pallisers* "the best work of my life." It was the basis of a popular BBC television miniseries (1974).

Palm-Wine Drinkard, The (in full: *The Palm-Wine Drinkard and His Dead Palm-Wine Tapster in the Dead's Town*, 1952). A novel by the Nigerian writer Amos TUTUOLA, written in Yoruban English. The fantastic episodes (including a visit to the afterlife) were inspired by Yoruban oral tradition.

Pamela: or, Virtue Rewarded (1740). A novel by SAMUEL RICHARDSON. A young servant-girl preserves her innocence against the depredations of her lovesick master. Her virtue is rewarded by marriage and eventual triumph over all who object to the elevation in her status. Although *Pamela's* reputation as either the first novel or the first in epistolary form is erroneous, its success did much to establish and expand the possibilities of the medium in English. It was satirized by Henry FIELDING in *Shamela* (1741) and *JOSEPH ANDREWS* (1742).

Pandora's Box (*Die Büchse der Pandora*, 1904). The second part of Frank WEDEKIND's "monster tragedy" about the *femme fatale* LULU, following *Earth Spirit* (*Erdgeist*, 1898). Lulu is here represented in her decline. She is finally reduced to prostituting herself in a London garret, where her last customer is Jack the Ripper. (For adaptations, see Variations.)

Parade's End (1950). A tetralogy of novels by FORD MADOX FORD, consisting of *Some Do Not...* (1924), *No More Parades* (1925), *A Man Could Stand Up* (1926), and *The Last Post* (1928), in which Ford examines the radical disruptions of society before, during, and after World War I. His protagonist is Christopher Tietjens, out of step with his times and miserably married to a malicious woman.

Paradise Lost (1667). A Christian epic in blank verse by John MILTON. A vastly ambitious work in 12 books, modeled on the epics of HOMER, DANTE, and VIRGIL, this is Milton's retelling of Genesis, in which ADAM and EVE, deceived by the wily snake, fall from obedience to God and are expelled from Eden.

Paradiso. *See* **Divine Comedy, The**

Part of Speech, A: Poems (*Chast' Rechi*, 1977; English translation with added poems, 1980). A collection of poems by Joseph BRODSKY, dealing largely with emotional and physical exile. Several date to the time of the poet's persecution in the Soviet Union; others are set in the United States or in locations that he visited while en route there. Among the pieces are "Odysseus to Telemachus," "Lullaby of Cape Cod," and the title poem.

Parzival (c. 1210). An epic poem in Middle High German by the German poet Wolfram von Eschenbach (1170–c. 1220), freely adapted from CHRÉTIEN DE TROYES, about the mystical adventures of the future Grail King and his spiritual metamorphosis from a "guileless fool" to a worthy guardian of the miraculous Grail. It served as the source for Wagner's last opera, *Parsifal* (1882).

Passage to India, A (1924). A novel by E. M. FORSTER. A visit by two Englishwomen, Mrs.

Moore and Adela QUESTED, to India's Marabar Caves with the young Muslim doctor AZIZ has unforeseen consequences, as Anglo-Indian relations are strained to the breaking point during the twilight of the British Raj. Arguably the author's masterpiece, the novel continues his exploration (begun in *HOWARDS END*) of the need for social and spiritual connection. It was adapted for film in 1984 by David Lean.

Paterson (1946–58, 1963). A long poem by WILLIAM CARLOS WILLIAMS, published in five separate volumes; an additional fragment appeared posthumously (1963). The title refers not only to the New Jersey city but also to a character inextricably bound to his community ("a man is himself a city"). The poem is a collage of prose, poetry, letters, notes, and historical details.

Pathfinder, The. *See* **Leatherstocking Tales, The**

"Paul Revere's Ride" (1861). A ballad by Henry Wadsworth LONGFELLOW, first published in *The Atlantic Monthly* and included as the "Landlord's Tale" in Longfellow's *Tales of a Wayside Inn* (1863); it tells of the Revolutionary War hero's legendary ride to warn "every Middlesex village and farm" that a British raid was impending. Familiar to generations of American schoolchildren, it begins with a famous couplet in its characteristic "galloping" meter: "Listen, my children, and you shall hear / Of the midnight ride of Paul Revere...."

Peer Gynt (1867). A fantastic verse drama by Henrik IBSEN that recounts the adventures of the charming, irresponsible, and boastful Peer Gynt. Among his many experiences in his epic search to find his true self, Peer woos the daughter of the troll king, survives a shipwreck, becomes a rich slave trader, and is confined to a madhouse. At the end of his life, Peer is finally redeemed by Solveig, who has always loved him.

Pelleas and Melisande (*Pelléas et Mélisande*, 1893). A play by Maurice MAETERLINCK, a dark Symbolist fable in spare, evocative prose, set in a mythical medieval kingdom. "If I were God, I would have pity on the hearts of men," remarks old King Arkel about the tragic love triangle that develops among his grandsons, Golaud and Pelléas, and Golaud's ethereal, waiflike wife, Mélisande. It was adapted as an opera by Debussy (1902).

Père Goriot, Le. *See* **Human Comedy, The**

Peregrine Pickle (in full: *The Adventures of Peregrine Pickle, In Which Are Included Memoirs of a Lady of Quality,* 1751). A picaresque novel by Tobias SMOLLETT, relating the rapscallion title character's escapades in England and on the continent (where the parodistic "grand tour" includes an "ancient" banquet inspired by PETRONIUS). Finally, a stint in Fleet Prison induces him to reform, preparing the way for a happy ending. The work is notable for Smollett's satirical attacks on contemporaries, and for its colorfully drawn secondary characters, like the landlocked mariner Commodore Trunnion. The scandalous "Memoirs" Smollett included are by Lady Frances Anne Vane.

Perelandra. *See* **Space Trilogy, The**

Pericles, Prince of Tyre (c. 1608–9). A play attributed to William SHAKESPEARE, although parts of it may have been written by another author or pieced together from actors' recollections. As with other Shakespearean romances of this period (*CYMBELINE, THE WINTER'S TALE, THE TEMPEST*), the plot concerns the violent separation and the eventual reconciliation of family members. In this case, Pericles is reunited with his wife and daughter after a period of many years.

Periodic Table, The (*Il Sistema Periodico,* 1975). A collection of 21 interconnected autobiographical stories by Primo LEVI. The title of each is a chemical element, and each is related to an episode in the author's life. Among the topics are his approach to his profession as chemist, his identity as an Italian Jew, and his experiences as a concentration-camp survivor.

Persians, The (*Persai,* 472 B.C.). A play by AESCHYLUS, unique among extant Greek tragedies in that its subject matter is from contemporary events rather than from myth. The topic is the expelling of the Persian army from Greece in 480 B.C., marking the end of the Persian Wars. The tragic hero is the Persian King Xerxes, a sympathetic victim of the arrogance that leads to his downfall. Even though Aeschylus himself fought against the Persians, he portrays them with compassion and respect.

Personae: The Collected Poems of Ezra Pound (1926). A collection of short poems by Ezra POUND, most of which had earlier appeared in *Personae* (1909) and *Exultations* (1909). Included are such Pound classics as "The Tree," "Sestina: Altaforte," and "In a Station of the Metro."

Persuasion (1817). The last finished novel by Jane AUSTEN, which portrays the gradual reunion of Anne Elliot and Captain Frederick Wentworth and the social life of Bath, the fashionable British spa town.

Phaedra (*Phèdre*, 1677). A tragedy by Jean RACINE, reworking EURIPIDES' *Hippolytus*, shifting the emphasis to the stepmother. Believing incorrectly that her husband, King Theseus, is dead, PHAEDRA reveals her passion for his son Hippolytus to the young man himself; he contemptuously scorns her. The consequences are tragic as the humiliated Phaedra allows her husband to believe that his son was the aggressor.

Phineas Finn. *See* **Pallisers, The**

Phineas Redux. *See* **Pallisers, The**

Physicists, The (*Die Physiker*, 1962). A comedy by Friedrich DÜRRENMATT. Three apparently delusional physicists are confined to an asylum, where each commits a murder. The asylum's megalomaniac director appears poised to take over the world with secrets she steals from one of them. But things may not be what they seem, as this sinister absurdist farce constructed of paradoxes reveals itself to be a kind of modern morality play about the responsibility of science and the nature of sanity.

Piano Lesson, The (1987). A Pulitzer Prize–winning play by AUGUST WILSON, the fourth in his series exploring African-American culture. In 1936 Pittsburgh, the conflict between a brother and sister over the fate of a piano (carved by their great-grandfather with

depictions of the family's history) is related to the legacy of slavery and the need to reclaim the African-American cultural tradition.

Pickwick Papers, The (in full: *The Posthumous Papers of the Pickwick Club*, 1837). A picaresque comic novel by Charles DICKENS, first published in installments and originally commissioned to accompany a series of engravings by a well-known artist. The hilarious misadventures of the genial, ingenuous Samuel PICKWICK and the members of his Pickwick Club proved to be enormously popular, making Dickens famous almost overnight.

Picnic (1953). A Pulitzer Prize–winning play by William INGE, in which a handsome misfit, Hal, drifts into a small Kansas town and serves as the catalyst for the revealing of hidden tensions and frustrations among the town's women. Especially affected is the town beauty, Madge. The play grew from an earlier work by Inge, *Front Porch* (1952), and was later revised by him as *Summer Brave* (1962).

Picture of Dorian Gray, The (1891). Oscar WILDE's only novel. Under the Mephistophelean influence of Lord Henry Wotton, an aesthete in the Wildean mode, Dorian GRAY wishes he might forever retain his youthful beauty. His wish is granted; he remains untouched by passing time, but his newly painted portrait grows ever more hideous with the marks of his sins and vices. The novel was adapted repeatedly for the screen, notably by Albert Lewin (1945), with George Sanders as Lord Henry and Hurd Hatfield in the title role. The portrait for the film was painted by American artist Ivan Albright.

Pictures from Brueghel, and Other Poems (1962). A Pulitzer Prize–winning collection of poems by WILLIAM CARLOS WILLIAMS. The title piece is a reflection on ten paintings by the 16th-century Flemish artist Pieter Brueghel the elder.

Pierre; or, The Ambiguities (1852). A novel by Herman MELVILLE, stressing the conflict between obsession and balance and between conscience and convention. Upon his discovery of an illegitimate half-sister, Pierre Glendinning defies his family in an attempt to expiate the sin of his father, going so far as to pretend to marry the young woman (so that she can claim the family name).

Piers Plowman (in full: *The Vision of Piers Plowman*, mid–late 14th century). A Middle English epic poem usually attributed to William Langland (c. 1330–1400). A Christian allegory in alliterative verse, it exists in three main versions. The poet-narrator, Will, describes a series of visions that show him the need for societal reform and individual spiritual awakening. Piers the Plowman, who appears in an early vision as a simple farmer and fellow seeker of Truth, is in Will's last dream (in the later versions) identified with God.

Pilgrimage (1938, enlarged 1967). A *roman-fleuve* of 13 "chapter-volumes" by DOROTHY M. RICHARDSON. Eleven were first published individually: *Pointed Roofs* (1915), *Backwater* (1916), *Honeycomb* (1917), *The Tunnel* (1919), *Interim* (1919), *Deadlock* (1921), *Revolving Lights* (1923), *The Trap* (1925), *Oberland* (1927), *Dawn's Left Hand* (1931), and *Clear Horizon* (1935). "Dimple Hill" was added to the first collection, "March Moonlight" to the 1967 edition. The autobiographical work is noted for its use of stream-of-consciousness technique.

Pilgrim's Progress, The (Part I, 1678; Part II, 1684). The popular shortened title of a prose allegory by Puritan preacher John BUNYAN. In a dream, the narrator, Christian, journeys from the City of Destruction to the Celestial City in search of salvation, which he finds in steadfast faith alone. Its realism and humor made the work an early bestseller; it has never been out of print, influencing writers as diverse as William Makepeace THACKERAY, who found his title for *VANITY FAIR* therein, and Louisa May ALCOTT, whose "little women" deemed it a reliable source of comfort and inspiration.

Pillow Book of Sei Shonagon, The (*Makura no Sōshi*, c. 1000). Written by the Japanese diarist and poet Sei Shōnagon (966/67–c. 1013), the work provides details of court life in 10th-century Japan, during the Heian period. In this miscellany, the author describes the events, annoyances, and joys of her daily life, enumerates the faults of men, observes nature, and comments on life at court.

Pioneers, The. *See* **Leatherstocking Tales, The**

"Pit and the Pendulum, The" (1842). A short story by Edgar Allan POE. The first-person narrator of this terrifying story is being tortured during the Spanish Inquisition. Strapped to a board, he is forced to watch a razor-sharp swinging pendulum slowly descend on him. He escapes from the pendulum only to be forced ever closer to an equally deadly pit in his cell, before being saved by the invading French army.

Plague, The (*La Peste*, 1947). A novel by Albert CAMUS, illustrating the Existentialist challenge of confronting evil in an absurd world. An epidemic of bubonic plague forces the inhabitants of an Algerian city to face a terrifying and indiscriminate force. The main character is Dr. Rieux, who cannot agree with the Jesuit Father Paneloux, who sees the epidemic as God's justice. Rieux's failure in the struggle to save lives is inevitable, but he derives dignity from the struggle itself.

Playboy of the Western World, The (1907). A comedy by J. M. SYNGE, one of the most significant works of the Irish Literary Renaissance. Christy MAHON, a stranger in County Mayo, quickly becomes the focus of hero worship— especially among the local women—when he claims to have killed his bullying father, who eventually turns up, very much alive. The play provoked riots at its Abbey Theatre premiere, both because of its satire of small-town Ireland and because one of its characters utters the word "shift," in scandalously improper reference to a woman's undergarment.

Play It As It Lays (1970). A novel by Joan DIDION, on the surface depicting the glittering and superficial world of Hollywood, but on a deeper level the emptiness of modern life. Didion and her husband, novelist and screenwriter John Gregory Dunne, adapted the novel for the screen in 1972.

Plough and the Stars, The (1926). A tragicomedy by Sean O'CASEY, set during the Easter Rising of 1916 and showing the human toll taken by the political violence. The play's premiere at the Abbey Theatre led to riots by Nationalists, who felt that it demeaned Irish patriotism.

Pnin (1957). A comic and affectionate novel by Vladimir NABOKOV, in which a hapless émigré Russian professor, Timofey Pnin, struggles to adapt to American culture. Pnin returns as a minor character in Nabokov's *PALE FIRE* (1962).

Poem of the Cid, The (*Poema de Mio Cid*; also known as *Cantar de Mio Cid*, c. 1200; published 1779). The only medieval Spanish epic poem to have survived in near-complete form, it relates the adventures of Spain's national hero, Rodrigo (Ruy) Díaz de Vivar (c. 1043–1099), called the Cid ("Lord") and Campeador ("Champion"), as he battles the Moors to regain the favor of King Alfonso, who had unjustly exiled him. The Cid's career inspired countless other works; Pierre CORNEILLE's 1637 *Le Cid* and Anthony Mann's 1961 film starring Charlton Heston are largely based on other sources.

Point Counter Point (1928). A novel by Aldous HUXLEY that explores, from a variety of perspectives, contemporary British society, art, literature, music, and politics as well as several love affairs. A number of its characters were based on real literary figures, including D. H. LAWRENCE and his wife Frieda, Charles BAUDELAIRE, Katherine MANSFIELD, and John Middleton MURRY.

Ponder Heart, The (1954). A novel by Eudora WELTY. In this first-person narrative, Miss Edna Earle Ponder, a lonely hotelkeeper in Clay, Mississippi, tells the story of the townspeople and her Uncle Daniel (a slow-witted and generous man with a penchant for giving away his fortune and his belongings) to a traveling salesman stranded at her inn. With colloquial rhythms, colorful imagery, and vivid digressions, the gently humorous story paints a rich portrait of small-town Southern life.

Porgy (1925). A novel by the American writer DuBose Heyward (1885–1940), a romance by a white author about African-American life in Charleston's "Catfish Row." The story of Porgy's doomed love for Bess is now better known in its incarnation as the opera *Porgy and Bess* (1935) by Heyward and George and Ira Gershwin, which is based on the 1927 stage version of *Porgy* by Heyward and his wife, Dorothy.

Portnoy's Complaint (1969). A comic novel by PHILIP ROTH that explores the neuroses of the modern Jewish male. Alexander PORTNOY relates his life story to his analyst, Dr. Spielvogel. He blames his parents—a domineering mother and a passive father—for causing his adolescent compulsive masturbation and his later preference for Gentile women. Although some readers have condemned the work as dealing in stereotypes, many critics consider it a minor masterpiece of Jewish-American literature.

Portrait of a Lady, The (1881). A novel by HENRY JAMES, depicting the encounter between European sophistication and decadence (represented by the fortune hunter Gilbert Osmond) and American innocence and forthrightness (represented by the heiress Isabel ARCHER).

Portrait of the Artist as a Young Man, A (1916). An autobiographical, stream-of-consciousness novel by James JOYCE, following the development of Stephen DEDALUS from an unformed boy into an artist sure of his calling. Rejecting the bonds of family, church, and country, Stephen has determined by the novel's end to travel to Paris and, as he says, "to encounter for the millionth time the reality of experience and to forge in the smithy of my soul the uncreated conscience of my race." Stephen is also a character in *ULYSSES* (1922).

Possessed, The (*Besy*, 1872; also translated under the titles *The Devils* and *The Demons*). A novel by Fyodor DOSTOYEVSKY. Suggested by actual events, it concerns the activities of a revolutionary group led by the brilliant, diabolical Nikolai Stavrogin. The work reflects Dostoyevsky's belief that intellect divorced from emotion can lead only to destruction, his hatred of Western philosophy, and his conviction that the salvation of Russia lies in a return to Eastern Orthodoxy.

Postman Always Rings Twice, The (1934). A crime novel by James M. CAIN. A drifter and the wife of a roadside café owner plot to murder her husband, in hard-boiled prose as remarkable for its attention to the minutiae of down-and-out life in Depression-era California as for sex scenes so steamy that the book was banned in Boston. It was filmed in 1942 by Luchino Visconti (*Ossessione*) and twice in the United States (1946, with Lana Turner and John Garfield, and 1981, with Jessica Lange and Jack Nicholson).

Power and the Glory, The (1940). A novel by Graham GREENE about the martyrdom of a sinful Mexican Catholic priest. In the novel, set in Mexico when anticlerical revolutionary sentiment was at its height, the "whiskey priest" is pursued by an unnamed police lieutenant.

Prairie, The. *See* **Leatherstocking Tales, The**

Praisesong for the Widow (1983). A novel by the American novelist Paule Marshall (1929–) in which the 64-year-old, recently widowed Avey Johnson travels to the West Indies, where she achieves spiritual renewal by immersing herself in African-Caribbean history and ritual.

Prelude, The, or, Growth of a Poet's Mind (1850; first versions written 1798–1805). An autobiographical book-length epic poem by William WORDSWORTH, who worked on it from 1798 until his death. It describes Wordsworth's Lake District childhood, his young manhood during the French Revolution ("Bliss was it in that dawn to be alive, / But to be young was very heaven!") and its tumultuous aftermath, and the maturing of his imaginative powers; of these untraditional epic subjects, he wrote, "What [souls] do within themselves while yet / The yoke of earth is new to them … / This is, in truth, heroic argument."

Pride and Prejudice (1813). A novel by Jane AUSTEN, with the famous opening line, "It is a truth universally acknowledged, that a single man in possession of a good fortune must be in want of a wife." Elizabeth BENNET and Fitzwilliam DARCY are, in fact, in want of each other, but pride and prejudice long delay their mutual acknowledgment of that truth. (For adaptations, see Variations.)

Prime Minister, The. *See* **Pallisers, The**

Prime of Miss Jean Brodie, The (1961). A novel by Muriel SPARK, set in 1930s Edinburgh. Loosely based on Spark's own school experiences, the novel tells of Jean BRODIE, an eccentric and fanatical schoolteacher who wields an unhealthy influence over a group of girls whom she calls her "crème de la crème." The story is narrated by a nun looking back on her time as a chosen member of the set, and on the events that led her to betray Miss Brodie. The novel was successfully adapted to the stage by Jay Presson Allen in 1966 and to the screen in 1969 with Maggie Smith in the title role.

Princess of Cleves, The (*La Princesse de Clèves*, 1678). A novel by the French writer Madame de La Fayette (1634–1693), first published anonymously. The work deals with the numerous and successful efforts of a virtuous married woman to overcome her passion for a nobleman not her husband. Because of its psychological exploration of a woman's internal conflict, it is considered by some to be the first modern novel.

Private Lives (1930). A comedy by Noël COWARD, depicting a couple (Elyot and Amanda) who are recently divorced from one another and newly married to other persons but who find that they cannot stay apart. Their very bickering is a sign of the passion that fuels the relationship. Coward himself played Elyot in the first production, in a cast that also included Gertrude Lawrence and Laurence Olivier.

Professor's House, The (1925). A novel by Willa CATHER. A middle-aged scholar, estranged from his family and disillusioned by society's materialism, faces loneliness and depression. Inserted into the story is the tragedy of the professor's gifted student, Tom Outland.

Prometheus Bound (*Promētheus Desmōtēs*, date uncertain). A tragedy by AESCHYLUS, depicting the punishment of the Titan who incurred the wrath of ZEUS by bringing fire to mankind. Prometheus is first bound to a remote rock and then cast into the underworld. The play stands as an extraordinary illustration of the refusal to yield to tyranny. It is the only surviving work of a trilogy that also included *Prometheus Unbound* and *Prometheus, the Fire Bearer.*

Prometheus Unbound (1820). A lyrical drama by PERCY BYSSHE SHELLEY, countering AESCHYLUS's *PROMETHEUS BOUND.* For the Romantic Shelley, Prometheus represents the heroic potential of humanity when faced with tyranny. When Prometheus is freed from his bonds by the primal power of Demogorgon, the dictatorial rule of Jupiter (ZEUS) ends. A golden age of love, liberty, and joy commences.

Prophet, The (1923). A collection of 26 poetic sermons by Kahlil GIBRAN, in which the mystic Almustafa offers "wisdom" on such basic matters as love, marriage, beauty, and death. Although critics have been less than enthusiastic about the book's literary value, it has enjoyed great popular acclaim. The work was followed by the posthumously published *The Garden of the Prophet* (1933) and *The Death of the Prophet* (1998).

Purgatorio. *See* **Divine Comedy, The**

"Purloined Letter, The" (1845). A mystery story by Edgar Allan POE, in which C. Auguste DUPIN uses psychological reasoning to determine the whereabouts of a stolen letter that is being used to blackmail a woman. It is the third story featuring Dupin; the others are "THE MURDERS IN THE RUE MORGUE" (1841) and "The Mystery of Marie Rogêt" (1842–43).

Pygmalion (1913). A romantic comedy by George Bernard SHAW, in which a Greek myth is adapted for purposes of satirizing human pretensions and the British class system. Eliza DOOLITTLE, a cockney flower girl, is transformed into a "lady" under the tutelage of the smug linguist Henry HIGGINS. A particularly notable adaptation of the play is Lerner and Loewe's 1956 Broadway musical version, *My Fair Lady.* (For this and other adaptations, see Variations.)

"Queen of Spades, The" ("Pikovaya Dama," 1834). A short story by Aleksandr PUSHKIN, a psychological thriller. A Russian officer's obsession with getting the secret for winning at faro causes him to commit manslaughter and then to go mad. The story was the basis for an 1890 opera by Tchaikovsky.

Quentin Durward. *See* **Waverley Novels, The**

Qur'ān (or Koran, canonical text established 651–52). The sacred text of Islam, the infallible word of Allah (God) as revealed to the prophet Muhammad (c. 570–632) over a period of 20 years. Comprised of 114 sūras (chapters), it teaches of the one God, who created the universe and who demands from humans total submission to his will. In addition, it provides a moral and legal code for Muslims. Much of its material derives from Hebrew sources as well as Arabic and Christian legend. The language of the Qur'ān determined classic Arabic.

Rabbit, Run (1960). A novel by John UPDIKE, the first work in which Harry ANGSTROM ("Rabbit") figures as the protagonist. Against the background of the cultural forces of late 1960s America, Rabbit tries unsuccessfully to cope with his personal frustrations, failing to find satisfaction in his job, his wife, or his mistress. Updike continued Rabbit's story in *Rabbit Redux* (1971), *Rabbit Is Rich* (1981), *Rabbit at Rest* (1990), and "Rabbit Remembered" (2000).

Rainbow, The (1915). A novel by D. H. LAWRENCE, exploring relationships between men and women. Although it follows three generations of the BRANGWEN family, the main focus is on the unconventional, sensitive Ursula Brangwen, who refuses to yield to marriage with the rigid Anton Skrebensky. The novel was officially declared obscene and subsequently banned. Ursula and her sister Gudrun are the central figures of the sequel, *WOMEN IN LOVE* (1921).

Raisin in the Sun, A (1959). A play by Lorraine HANSBERRY, the title of which is taken from LANGSTON HUGHES's poem "Harlem" ("What happens to a dream deferred? Does it dry up / like a raisin in the sun?..."). The dreams of each member of the African-American Younger family are revealed as they consider how to spend the insurance money gained from the father's death.

Raj Quartet, The (1966–75). The collective title for a series of novels by PAUL SCOTT, comprising *The Jewel in the Crown* (1966), *The Day of the Scorpion* (1968), *The Towers of Silence* (1971), and *A Division of the Spoils* (1975). A young Englishwoman, Daphne Manners, is raped during an anti-British riot in Mayapore; her lover, Hari KUMAR, born in India but raised in England, is charged with the crime. The final years of British colonial rule in India are explored through the reactions of Hindu, Muslim, and English characters as the case progresses. Inspired by the author's Indian experiences, the *Quartet* was the basis of a popular 1984 television miniseries, *The Jewel in the Crown*. The author's 1977 novel *Staying On* continues the story.

Rāmāyaṇa, The (3rd century B.C.?). An epic poem of India, traditionally attributed to Vālmīki, consisting of 24,000 Sanskrit couplets. It narrates the heroic life of Prince Rāma.

"Ransom of Red Chief, The" (1910). A humorous short story by O. HENRY, in which two kidnappers realize that the mischievous ten-year-old redhead they are holding for ransom is more trouble than he is worth and agree to pay the boy's father a sum to take him back. First published in *Whirligigs* (1910), it is one of O. Henry's most anthologized stories.

Rape of the Lock, The (1714). A mock-epic poem by Alexander POPE. Written originally to reconcile the parties in an actual incident in which a young nobleman surreptitiously snipped a lock of a young gentlewoman's hair, Pope's "heroi-comical poem" amusingly describes a trivial affair among the foppish beaux and pampered belles of Augustan London in terms traditionally employed to sing the grandiose deeds and battles of gods and heroes.

"Rappaccini's Daughter" (1844). A short story by Nathaniel HAWTHORNE. Dr. Rappaccini, an Italian scientist, in an attempt to immunize his daughter, BEATRICE, against unhappiness, has rendered her literally poisonous by raising her on toxic plants from his garden. The unfortunate young woman contaminates any male with whom she comes into contact.

"Rashōmon" (1917). A short story by the Japanese writer Ryūnosuke Akutagawa (1892–1927), which gave Akira Kurosawa's celebrated 1950 film its title and its setting by the ruined Rashomon gate in Kyoto. Another Akutagawa story, "In a Grove" ("Yabu no Naka," 1921), supplied the film's plot and its unusual narrative method (several characters relate mutually contradictory versions of a rape and murder), which has entered the language as "Rashomon-like." Both stories derive from the 12th-century collection *Tales of a Time Now Past* (*Konjaku Monogatari*). (For additional adaptations, see Variations.)

Rasselas (in full: *The History of Rasselas, Prince of Abissinia*; first published as *The Prince of Abissinia: A Tale*, 1759). A novel by SAMUEL JOHNSON in the form of a fable examining the nature of happiness. Although the title character mistakenly believes that bliss can be attained through a deliberate search, the book's theme is that, on earth, happiness is elusive.

"Raven, The" (1845). A poem by Edgar Allan POE. This ballad of 18 six-line stanzas, collected in *The Raven and Other Poems* (1845), was an immediate critical and popular success and demonstrates Poe's mastery of rhythmic effects. Overcome with grief over the death of his beloved Lenore, the first-person narrator questions a mysterious raven that has tapped on his door. To each of his anguished questions, the raven responds "Nevermore," which drives the narrator into a frenzy of despair.

Razor's Edge, The (1944). A novel by W. Somerset MAUGHAM, detailing the spiritual journey of Larry Darrell, who returns from World War I yearning for more than material success as a Chicago businessman. His search takes him from America to Europe and Asia. The five years Darrell spends in study and meditation in India are loosely based on Maugham's own experiences in India. The title is taken from the *Kaṭha-Upaniṣad*, a book of Hindu wisdom that advises, "The sharp edge of a razor is difficult to pass over: thus the wise say the path to Salvation is hard."

Real Life of Sebastian Knight, The (1941). Vladimir NABOKOV's first novel written in English. A man known only as "V." sets out to write a biography of his half-brother, the writer Sebastian Knight. The "real" events in the elusive writer's life prove difficult to uncover; thus the tale becomes a literary detective story with V. searching in Knight's fiction for clues to his life and learning about himself in the process.

Rebecca (1938). A Gothic romance novel by Daphne DU MAURIER. "Last night I dreamt I went to Manderley again." A nameless young woman struggles to free her marriage from the specter of her aristocratic husband's late wife, Rebecca. She meets obstacles set by Rebecca's friends, family, and loyal housekeeper, Mrs. Danvers, who is determined never to let the second Mrs. de Winter become the lady of the house. A bestselling psychological thriller, it was strikingly filmed by Alfred Hitchcock in 1940 with Joan Fontaine, Laurence Olivier, and Dame Judith Anderson.

Rebel Angels, The (1981). A novel by Robertson DAVIES. This mysterious novel, set at a Canadian university, is the first in his Cornish trilogy, which also includes *WHAT'S BRED IN THE BONE* (1985) and *THE LYRE OF ORPHEUS* (1988).

Recognitions, The (1955). The first novel by William GADDIS. Experimental in form and encyclopedic in scope, it focuses on the corruption and eventual redemption of the artistic, spiritual Wyatt Gwyon, who has been caught up in a superficial, dishonest society.

Red and the Black, The (*Le Rouge et le Noir*, 1830). A novel by STENDHAL about the low-born, fiercely ambitious Julien SOREL and the two women who love him, Madame de Rênal, a mayor's wife, and Mathilde, a marquis's daughter. One of the great love stories of French literature, it is also a profound psychological character study and a mordant critique of French society under the Bourbon restoration.

Red Badge of Courage, The (1895). A novel by STEPHEN CRANE, set during the Civil War, often considered the first modern war novel. The story focuses on the internal struggles of the young recruit Henry FLEMING, who has dreamed of the excitement and glory of being a soldier but instead is overcome with fear. Although Crane had never fought in a war, *The Red Badge of Courage* was praised for its realism and earned Crane international recognition.

Red Pony, The (1937, enlarged 1945). A sequence of four stories by John STEINBECK, each focusing on the young Jody Tiflin. Growing up on his family's California ranch, Jody encounters love and pain as he learns elemental truths about hope, compromise, the inevitability of change, and the cycle of life and death. The stories are "The Gift," "The Great Mountains," "The Promise," and "The Leader of the People."

"Red Wheelbarrow, The" (1923). A short poem by WILLIAM CARLOS WILLIAMS exemplifying his credo, "No ideas but in things." In four stanzas of two short lines each, the poet—with painterly detail—evokes a barnyard scene.

Reflections in a Golden Eye (1941). A Southern Gothic novel by Carson MCCULLERS noted for its controlled depiction of disturbed characters. Set in an army camp in the 1930s, the novel portrays the lives of six lonely, self-centered people, each of whom is tormented by darkly irrational impulses.

Regeneration. *See* **Regeneration Trilogy, The**

Regeneration Trilogy, The (1991–95). A series of critically admired novels by Pat BARKER about World War I, comprising *Regeneration* (1991), *The Eye in the Door* (1993), and *The Ghost Road* (1995; Booker Prize). *Regeneration* is about the treatment of British soldiers traumatized by trench warfare; some of the characters are based on real people, including army psychologist Dr. William H. R. Rivers and the poets Siegfried SASSOON and Wilfrid OWEN. The next two titles continue the story of Rivers and his patients, especially the working-class bisexual lieutenant, Billy Prior.

Remains of the Day, The (1989). A Booker Prize–winning novel by Kazuo ISHIGURO, narrated by Stevens, who was for 30 years the loyal butler of an Englishman who became a Nazi sympathizer. In 1956 Stevens must come to terms with his own ethical blindness. In a moving narrative, he discloses the truth of his moral cowardice to the reader at the same time that he discloses it to himself. A 1993 film version, directed by James Ivory, starred Anthony Hopkins and Emma Thompson.

Remembrance of Things Past (*À la Recherche du Temps Perdu*, 1913–27; also translated under the title *In Search of Lost Time*). A 7-volume autobiographical novel by Marcel PROUST, one of the greatest works of the 20th century. Proust's inspiration came from eating a French teacake called a *madeleine*, an act that evoked a vivid, long-forgotten childhood memory. Throughout, he explores the nature of a reality that is always in flux, that can be captured only through the re-creation of a pattern of sensations that transcend time itself. The *roman-fleuve* consists of *Swann's Way* (*Du Côté de Chez Swann*, 1913), *Within a Budding Grove* (*À l'Ombre des Jeunes Filles en Fleurs*, 1919; Prix Goncourt), *The Guermantes Way* (*Le Côté de Guermantes*, 1920), *Cities of the Plain* (*Sodome et Gomorrhe*, 1922), *The Captive* (*La Prisonnière*, 1923), *The Sweet Cheat Gone* (or *The Fugitive*; *Albertine Disparue*, 1925), and *Time Regained* (or *The Past Recaptured*; *Le Temps Retrouvé*, 1927).

"Renascence" (1912, reprint 1917). A poem by Edna St. Vincent MILLAY that brought her immediate attention when it first appeared in an anthology of young poets. The poem is complex in language and subject, the poet an isolated soul reaching for ultimate understanding. At the conclusion, Millay feels that one can sense the infinite: "The soul can split the sky in two, / And let the face of God shine through."

Requiem (*Rekviem*, completed 1940, published 1963). A poetic cycle by Anna AKHMATOVA, written at the height of the Stalinist Terror. A record of her personal suffering following the death of her husband and the imprisonment of her son,

it also honors all the victims: "For them I have woven a wide shroud."

Residence on Earth (*Residencia en la Tierra*, 1933–47). Three collections of poems by Pablo NERUDA, presenting a unified philosophical exploration of the idea of decay.

Return of the Native, The (1878). A tragic novel by Thomas HARDY about the inhabitants of Egdon Heath, a gloomy stretch of land in southern England. The title refers to the character Clym YEOBRIGHT, who returns to Egdon Heath and marries the fiery Eustacia VYE, with disastrous consequences.

Rhinoceros (*Le Rhinocéros*, 1959). An absurdist drama by Eugène IONESCO, expressing outrage at the spread of mindless conformity. Bérenger is initially startled and then appalled as, one by one, his associates metamorphose into rhinoceroses. By the play's end, he is the only human being left.

Richard II (c. 1595). A history play by William SHAKESPEARE, the first of a tetralogy that also includes *HENRY IV, PARTS I AND II*, and *HENRY V*. The egotistical and erratic RICHARD II incurs the wrath of Henry Bolingbroke, who later deposes him. After Bolingbroke has assumed the throne as HENRY IV, the imprisoned Richard achieves self-knowledge and dignity, revealed in a moving soliloquy. This is the only Shakespearean play written entirely in verse.

Richard III (c. 1594). A history play by William SHAKESPEARE about a man who brutally eliminates anyone who stands between him and the throne of England. To attain his goal, the deformed and conniving—but also gifted—Richard, Duke of Gloucester, plots the deaths not only of King Henry VI and his son, but of his own two nephews. He himself is eventually deposed, and Henry VII ascends the throne. RICHARD III's fierce intelligence and malignant imagination place him among the most intriguing villains of English literature.

Riders to the Sea (1904). A one-act tragedy by John Millington SYNGE, first performed at the Abbey Theatre in Dublin. Based on a story heard by Synge and set in the Aran Islands, the play tells the story of Maurya, a woman who has lost her husband and five sons to the sea and who loses her last son before the play ends.

Right You Are—If You Think You Are (*Così È (Se Vi Pare)*, 1917; also translated under the title *Right You Are (If You Think So)*). A play by Luigi PIRANDELLO, his first major dramatic success and his greatest contribution to the "theater of the grotesque." Signora Frola and Signor Ponza are newcomers in town. She is his mother-in-law—or is she his *former* mother-in-law? Each claims the other is mad. Whose story is true? The townspeople are perplexed, and the only person who can enlighten them is Ponza's wife—who insists that the truth is whatever they choose to believe.

"Rime of the Ancient Mariner, The" (1798; originally spelled "The Rime of the Ancyent Marinere"). A poem by Samuel Taylor COLERIDGE, perhaps the most famous English literary ballad. In simple but hallucinatorily vivid language, the title character recounts a disastrous voyage on which he slew an albatross, a bird of good omen, and suffered a terrible retribution from natural and supernatural forces. The ship's entire crew perished, and the mariner alone survived to expiate his crime by compulsively retelling it. It was included in the *LYRICAL BALLADS* of Coleridge and William WORDSWORTH.

Ring and the Book, The (1868–69). A book-length poem by ROBERT BROWNING, based on a 17th-century murder case, concerning an elderly Italian nobleman tried for killing his young wife. Each of the poem's 12 sections presents the story from a different character's point of view, offering a series of partial, subjectively told tales from which the events of the story can be pieced together by the reader.

"Rip Van Winkle" (1819). A short story by WASHINGTON IRVING, based on a German folktale and published in Irving's *The Sketch Book of Geoffrey Crayon, Gent.* Rip VAN WINKLE, a Colonial idler, falls asleep in New York's Catskill Mountains, awakening 20 years later to find that America has gone from being an English colony to a free nation.

Rise of Silas Lapham, The (1885). A novel by William Dean HOWELLS that provides a portrait of Gilded Age America, and illustrates the conflict between old money and new riches through the story of Silas Lapham. A self-made businessman, Lapham clumsily tries to enter wealthy Boston society and regains his humanity only when he loses his fortune.

Rivals, The (1775). A comedy by Richard Brinsley SHERIDAN. Well-bred Captain Jack Absolute loves incurable romantic Lydia Languish. To win her heart, he woos her in the guise of his own rival, the penniless Ensign Beverly. To gain her hand, he must secure the approval of her dragonlike aunt, the immortal Mrs. MALAPROP, whose opinion of her own erudition as "a progeny of learning" is woefully misplaced, and whose name has contributed the word "malapropism" to the English language.

"Road Not Taken, The" (1915). A poem by Robert FROST, written in iambic tetrameter, first published in *The Atlantic Monthly* in August 1915, then collected in Frost's *Mountain Interval* (1916). While walking in the woods, the narrator is confronted by a fork in the path. Years later, he views the choice he made that day as symbolic of the "less traveled" road he has followed in life.

Robinson Crusoe (in full: *The Life and Strange Surprizing Adventures of Robinson Crusoe, of York, Mariner*, 1719). An adventure novel by Daniel DEFOE. Englishman Robinson CRUSOE is shipwrecked for 28 years on an island near present-day Venezuela. He finds and rescues from cannibals an island native and names him FRIDAY. Screen adaptations for adults include Luis Buñuel's 1954 film and *Crusoe* (1988), starring Aidan Quinn.

Rob Roy. *See* **Waverley Novels, The**

Roderick Random, The Adventures of (1748). Tobias SMOLLETT's first novel, which combined the traditions of the picaresque novel and the verse satire with elements of fictionalized autobiography. Like his title character, Smollett served as a surgeon's mate on a man-of-war and witnessed the siege of Cartagena (1741), experiences reflected in the excruciating but true-to-life naval scenes, which may have inspired reforms. Random's many other adventures are related with a view to arousing the reader "against the sordid and vicious disposition of the world."

Romance of 'Antar (*Sīrat 'Antar*, 8th–12th centuries). A series of 32 poetic tales involving the black, pre-Islamic Arab poet and hero 'Antarah ibn Shaddād (6th century). Apparent in the stories are the successive influences of Islam, Persian culture, and Christianity. This romance predates the European chivalric romances.

Romance of the Rose (*Roman de la Rose*, 13th century). A 21,000-line medieval French poem begun by Guillaume de Lorris (c. 1230; 4,058 lines) and completed by Jean de Meun (c. 1280). The first part—a dream allegory of a love affair—is the more moving. Jean de Meun's lengthy addition is filled with digressions on such topics as human nature, economics, and astronomy. In the early 1360s, Geoffrey CHAUCER translated Guillaume de Lorris's section and 3,000 lines of the remainder into Middle English.

Romeo and Juliet (1595). A play by William SHAKESPEARE, set in Verona. Born into families that are bitter enemies, Romeo MONTAGUE and Juliet CAPULET fall in love at a masked ball and are secretly married. Romeo's exile from Verona after a duel sets in motion a series of events that ends in the suicide of both lovers. (For adaptations, see Variations.)

Room at the Top (1957). A novel by the English novelist John Braine (1922–1987). In a Yorkshire factory town, working-class John Lampton is led by social ambition into a loveless marriage with the daughter of a rich industrialist. A typical product of the British Angry Young Man era, it is perhaps better known in its 1959 film adaptation, which starred Laurence Harvey and Simone Signoret.

"Room of One's Own, A" (1929). An essay by VIRGINIA WOOLF, addressing the problems of women writers. Her central point is that in order to write, a woman must have privacy and financial independence.

Room with a View, A (1908). A novel by E. M. FORSTER. While staying at an Italian *pensione*, proper young Englishwoman Lucy Honeychurch and her cousin complain that their room does not have a view. The modest, elderly Mr. Emerson and his son, George, offer to trade rooms with the women. Lucy eventually falls in love with George, but becomes engaged to Cecil Vyse, a snobbish and drab member of her own class. Forced to choose between passion and propriety, Lucy finally breaks free of social convention. The 1986 film version was directed by James Ivory from an Academy Award–winning screenplay by Ruth Prawer JHABVALA.

Roots: A Saga of an American Family (1976). A novel by Alex HALEY that provides a fictionalized account of seven generations of Haley's family through slavery, emancipation, and Jim Crow, concluding with the death of the author's father in 1967. Based on many years of research, the work begins with the birth of Kunta Kinte in a village in Gambia, Africa, in 1750, then describes his abduction by slave traders and his harrowing passage to America. A runaway bestseller, *Roots* was the basis for a phenomenally successful television miniseries (1977). Although the book aroused controversy over some historical inaccuracies, it remains a groundbreaking work in African-American literature and heritage. It was awarded a special Pulitzer Prize.

Rosencrantz and Guildenstern Are Dead (1966). A play by Tom STOPPARD. On the premise that every exit is "an entrance somewhere else," Stoppard examines the off-stage life of HAMLET's schoolfellows, ROSENCRANTZ AND GUILDENSTERN, who ponder (among other things) the laws of chance and the meaning or meaninglessness of life and death in a universe beyond their comprehension. (For a film adaptation, see Variations, under *Hamlet*.)

Rubáiyát of 'Omar Khayyám, the Astronomer-Poet of Persia, The (1859; revised editions, 1868–89). Edward FitzGerald's metrical paraphrase of some 600 epigrammatic qua-trains (each is a "rubái") currently or formerly ascribed to the 12th-century Persian ʻOMAR KHAYYÁM. FitzGerald condensed, conflated, and arranged the poems as a hundred-stanza elegy, lamenting life's brevity and praising its tangible joys. It contains many familiar lines, such as "A jug of wine, a loaf of bread—and thou / Beside me singing in the wilderness," and "The moving finger writes…"

"Sailing to Byzantium" (1927). One of William Butler YEATS's best-known poems, first collected in *October Blast* (1927), and then in *The Tower* (1928). The spiritual journey to the titular "holy city" symbolizes the 62-year-old poet's acceptance of his exile from the country of the young and merely sensual ("That is no country for old men") and his desire to escape from transience and mortality through the per-manence of art, the "artifice of eternity." A Byzantine mosaic in Ravenna reportedly sug-gested the image of "sages standing in God's holy fire."

Saint Joan (1923). A play by George Bernard SHAW about the life and martyrdom of JOAN OF ARC. Shaw was motivated by the Roman Catholic canonization of Joan. Shaw's heroine is frank, unfeminine, intuitive, and persistent— qualities that frighten people enough for them to wish her dead. Facing death, Joan cries, "O God that madest this beautiful earth, when will it be ready to receive Thy Saints?"

Samson Agonistes (1671). A blank-verse tragedy by John MILTON, the story of the final triumph and death of the biblical Samson. Per-sonally, the blind poet must have felt a kinship with his blinded, imprisoned hero. Milton con-sciously modeled his work on Greek tragedy "as it was anciently composed."

Sanctuary (1931). A novel by William FAULKNER. This sensational story of rape, mur-der, and injustice focuses on Temple Drake, a debutante, and Popeye, a brutal bootlegger. In his preface to the novel, Faulkner described it as "a cheap idea…deliberately conceived to make money." He continued Temple Drake's

story in *Requiem for a Nun* (1951). (For adapta-tions, see Variations.)

Satanic Verses, The (1988). A novel by Salman RUSHDIE. Set mainly in London, the work comi-cally depicts the battle between good and evil (represented by Gibreel FARISHTA and Saladin CHAMCHA). It received undesired publicity when the Ayatollah Khomeini, condemning it as blasphemous to Islam, declared a fatwah (sentence of death) against the author, who lived in hiding until the Iranians lifted the decree in 1998.

Satires (*Saturae*, c. 100–c. 128). Sixteen poems by the Roman writer JUVENAL, published sepa-rately in five books. These have long served as models for bitter, angry satire (in contrast to the lighter satire of HORACE). Juvenal aims at a broad range of targets, including crime, homo-sexuals, the behavior of women, Roman intel-lectuals, and hereditary nobility.

Saturday Night and Sunday Morning (1958). The first novel by Alan SILLITOE, one of En-gland's original Angry Young Men. Arthur Seaton, a Nottingham factory worker, has noth-ing to look forward to from week to week except Saturday nights spent at the pub or in bed with other men's wives. The widely praised 1960 film adaptation was directed by Karel Reisz from a screenplay by Sillitoe.

Satyricon (c. A.D. 60s). A comic novel ascribed to Gaius PETRONIUS ARBITER, Nero's "arbiter of taste," relating the wanderings of a dissolute trio in the posh Bay of Naples area. Only frag-ments survive; the longest and best known describes in mordant detail the banquet of the *nouveau riche* freedman Trimalchio. It is prized by modern scholars and readers for its intimate, often ribald, glimpses of daily life in an ancient society usually recalled for more monumental achievements. It was the basis of a 1969 film by Federico Fellini.

Scarlet Letter, The (1850). A novel by Nathaniel HAWTHORNE, set in Puritan New England. The novel tells the story of Hester PRYNNE, who must wear a scarlet letter "A" on her clothing as punishment for adultery. Her estranged husband returns to the community disguised as Roger CHILLINGWORTH and uncovers the truth that the town minister Arthur DIMMESDALE is the father of Prynne's illegitimate daughter. This tale of sin, pride, guilt, hypocrisy, and revenge is a classic of American literature. (For adaptations, see Variations.)

Scarlet Pimpernel, The (1905). A novel by Hungarian-born English novelist Baroness Orczy (1865–1947). Orczy and her husband, Montagu Barstow, adapted her unpublished novel for the stage in 1903 to great acclaim; this led to the publication of the original novel, which proved an enormous success, and to a series of equally popular sequels featuring "that damned elusive" SCARLET PIMPERNEL—an incognito English nobleman whose forte is rescuing French aristocrats from the Reign of Terror. Film, television, and musical theater adaptations all followed.

Schindler's List (U.S. title; U.K. *Schindler's Ark*, 1982). A historical novel by Thomas KENEALLY, based on the real-life activities of Oskar Schindler, who saved more than 1,200 Jews from concentration camps. Keneally focuses on the paradox of the flawed antihero unexpectedly becoming a savior. Steven Spielberg's 1993 film adaptation won seven Academy Awards, including Best Picture.

School for Scandal, The (1777). A comedy of manners by Richard Brinsley SHERIDAN, satirizing the gossipmongering of Restoration England. In the course of the play, the true nature of each of the Surface brothers is revealed. The obsequious Joseph is unmasked as a hypocrite, while the hedonistic Charles is found to be honest and charitable.

School for Wives, The (*L'École des Femmes*, 1662). A comedy by MOLIÈRE. Arnolphe, believing that women cannot be trusted, hopes to marry his unsophisticated ward, Agnès, and to keep her naive so that she will not cuckold him. His plan is thwarted when she falls in love with his friend Horace. The most commercially successful of Molière's plays in his lifetime, it nevertheless occasioned considerable literary and moral debate.

Scoop (1938). A novel by EVELYN WAUGH, satirizing journalistic rivalry and greed. The novel is set in the fictional African country of Ishmaelia and concerns two competing newspapers, *The Beast* and *The Brute*. It is based on Waugh's 1930s stint as a reporter for the *Daily Mail* in Abyssinia.

Screwtape Letters, The (1942). An epistolary novel by C. S. LEWIS, in which the author undertakes a defense of Christianity by satirical means. The book is cast as a series of 31 letters from Screwtape, a senior, successful devil, to Wormwood, a mere novice, thus far less skilled in the business of corrupting souls.

Seagull, The (*Chaĭka*, 1896). A play by Anton CHEKHOV, exploring the role of the creative artist in a petty society and characterized by his typically subtle rendering of human interaction. The major characters, all guests at a country estate, are Irina Nikolaevna ARKADINA, an actress; her lover, the writer Boris Alexeyevich TRIGORIN; her son Konstantin Gavrilovich TREPLEV; and a young actress, Nina ZARECHNAYA, whom Treplev loves. Against a backdrop of jealousy and emotional cruelty, a seagull is shot—symbolizing the broken hopes of the characters.

Sea of Fertility, The (*Hojo no Umi*, 1969–71). A tetralogy by Yukio MISHIMA, which includes *Spring Snow* (*Haru no Yuki*, 1969), *Runaway Horses* (*Honba*, 1969), *The Temple of Dawn* (*Akatsuki no Tera*, 1971), and *The Decay of the Angel* (*Tennin Gosui*, 1971). The four books range in time from 1912 to the post–World War II period and depict what Mishima considered the decline of Japanese culture and tradition.

Season in Hell, A (*Une Saison en Enfer*, 1873). A collection of nine prose-poems by Arthur RIMBAUD, the title of which likely refers to the period of his relationship with the poet Paul VERLAINE. The dreamlike pieces demonstrate Rimbaud's efforts to forge a new poetic reality. Although the early Symbolist was only 19 when the work was published, he gave up writing soon thereafter.

Sea, the Sea, The (1978). A Booker Prize–winning novel by Iris MURDOCH, a psychological study of a man's slowly growing awareness that his existence has been a matter of delusions and misconceptions. The sea is a symbol of the unexplored depths of his soul.

Sea-Wolf, The (1904). An adventure novel by Jack LONDON, a Darwinian tale of survival. The narrator, intellectual dilettante Humphrey Van Weyden, is shipwrecked in foggy San Francisco Bay. Rescued by a mysterious sealing schooner, he becomes engaged in a struggle with the ship's captain, Wolf Larsen, who forces the "miserable weakling" to serve as cabin boy to "make or break him."

"Second Coming, The" (1920). One of the best-known poems by William Butler YEATS, with lines and phrases that have entered the language, such as "Things fall apart; the centre cannot hold" and "Slouching towards Bethlehem." In it, Yeats presents his cyclical theory of history as a vivid vision of disorder and apocalyptic transformations to come.

Secret Agent, The: A Simple Tale (1907). A novel by Joseph CONRAD, considered one of the first international spy stories. The foreign spy Verloc, who is also an informer to Scotland Yard, poses as the owner of a shop where anarchists gather. (For adaptations, see Variations.)

Seize the Day (1956). A novella by Saul BELLOW that tells of the middle-aged Tommy Wilhelm, unemployed, separated from his wife, and burdened with feelings of failure, as he strives to attain a sense of dignity and inner peace.

Sense and Sensibility (1811). Jane AUSTEN's first novel, originally drafted around 1795, about two sisters with diametrically opposed attitudes to life and love: the stable, rational Elinor DASHWOOD and the impulsive, romantic Marianne Dashwood. Ang Lee's 1995 film version had an Oscar-winning screenplay by Emma Thompson, who played Elinor.

Sentimental Education, A (*L'Éducation Sentimentale: Histoire d'un Jeune Homme*, 1869). A novel by Gustave FLAUBERT about coming of age in Paris in the 1840s. Frédéric Moreau's passion for Madame Arnoux (an older, married woman) and his political disillusionment are projected against the background of the failed revolution of 1848.

"September 1, 1939" (1940). A poem by W. H. AUDEN, composed "As the clever hopes expire / Of a low dishonest decade," on the day the Germans invaded Poland, triggering World War II. Although it is perhaps Auden's most frequently quoted poem, he eventually repudiated it as "dishonest," denouncing the famous line, "We must love one another or die" as "a damned lie! We must die anyway."

Seven Against Thebes (*Hepta epi Thēbas*, 467 B.C.). A tragedy by AESCHYLUS, the third and only surviving play of a trilogy about the curse on the House of Laius. The first play was *Laius*, the second *Oedipus*. This play concerns a fight to the death between the sons of OEDIPUS: Eteocles, who is defending Thebes, and Polyneices, who (along with six chieftains) is attacking it. Scholars believe that an unknown author tacked on an additional conclusion, probably so that the play's plot would agree with that of SOPHOCLES' ANTIGONE and EURIPIDES' *Phoenician Women*.

Seven Gothic Tales (1934; translated into her native Danish by the author as *Syv Fantastike Fortællinger*, 1935). A collection of stories by Isak DINESEN, set in an ornate, decadent past, in which the ironic, the supernatural, and the psychological intensify one another.

Shadows on the Rock (1931). A novel by Willa CATHER that explores the world of 17th-century Quebec, especially the pioneering spirit and Catholic traditions of the colonists.

Shakespeare's Sonnets (1609). A series of 154 sonnets, the most famous sonnet sequence in British literature, by William SHAKESPEARE, sometimes addressed to a young man, other times to a woman. These poems are meditations on love and the power of time over human affairs.

She (1886). A fantasy-adventure novel by H. Rider HAGGARD, set in a mysterious African city, Kôr, ruled by the beautiful white-skinned AYESHA, or "She-Who-Must-Be-Obeyed." The queen finds in an explorer the reincarnation of the lover whom she killed 2,000 years before. Her story is continued in *Ayesha: The Return of She* (1905), *She and Allen* (1921), and *Wisdom's Daughter* (1923).

Sheltering Sky, The (1948). The first novel by Paul BOWLES, about an American couple, Port and Kit Moresby, who travel in North Africa in the hope of reviving their failing marriage, but meet with tragic ends. Sometimes compared to Joseph CONRAD's *HEART OF DARKNESS* (1902), the novel illustrates the couple's increasing estrangement, both from each other and from societal conventions, as they move deeper into the Sahara and farther from civilization.

She Stoops to Conquer; or The Mistakes of a Night (1773). A comedy of mistaken identity by Oliver GOLDSMITH. The "She" of the title is Kate HARDCASTLE, a young lady who stoops, by impersonating a barmaid, to conquer the heart of Richard Marlow, a suitor so bashful he cannot even look at a woman he thinks is his social equal. The supporting role of Tony Lumpkin has proved a comic tour de force for many actors.

Shield of Achilles, The (1955). A collection of poetry by W. H. AUDEN, exemplifying his mature style. The title poem, embellishing an episode from the *Iliad* in order to comment on the devastation of war, is one of his most famous. Also included are the "Horae Canonicae" and "Bucolics" series.

Ship of Fools (1962). A novel by Katherine Anne PORTER, suggested by an ocean voyage that she took in 1931. The ship is a microcosm of the Western world in the years leading up to World War II. Although the Jew-baiting German passengers are the most contemptible, no character is without serious flaws. Those who are not fools are irresponsible or brutal. Porter borrowed her title from Sebastian Brant's *Das Narren Schyff* (1494).

Shipping News, The (1993). A Pulitzer Prize–winning novel by Annie PROULX. After the death of his wife and her lover, R. G. Quoyle and his daughters move to his forbidding ancestral home, a fishing town in New-foundland, to start over. Quoyle begins writing the shipping news column for the local paper and undergoes a memorable transformation, finding love and a stable home among the eccentric locals.

Shirley (1849). A novel by CHARLOTTE BRONTË set in Yorkshire against the background of the anti-industrial Luddite movement. In this story of tangled romantic relationships, the strong-minded, gifted title character may have been modeled on Brontë's novelist sister EMILY BRONTË. The novel's concerns with class differences, the conflicts of the Industrial Revolution, and the social plight of women make it Brontë's most political work.

"Short Happy Life of Francis Macomber, The" (1936). One of Ernest HEMINGWAY's most famous short stories, about an American couple and their English guide on an African safari. Along with "THE SNOWS OF KILIMANJARO," it appeared in the collection *The Fifth Column and the First Forty-nine Stories* (1938).

Shropshire Lad, A (1896). A collection of poems by A. E. HOUSMAN. The "Shropshire" of the title refers to a fictional "land of lost content" more than it does to the English county of the same name. The patriotism of these poems, along with the themes of failed love, nostalgia, and war, made the book very popular during World War I.

Siddhartha (1922). A novel by Hermann HESSE, following a Brahmin's lifelong search for enlightenment. The pleasures of the mind and body cannot satisfy Siddhartha; not even Buddha can give him the answer. Only when he learns to search within himself does he find Nirvana.

Silas Marner: The Weaver of Raveloe (1861). A novel by GEORGE ELIOT. Among the author's most popular works, it relates how the fate of the weaver Silas MARNER, an embittered miser, becomes intertwined with that of the two sons of the village squire in Raveloe, where Marner has taken refuge after being falsely accused of a theft. Eliot took her epigraph from William WORDSWORTH, whose pioneering efforts to treat country people realistically in his poetry parallels hers in her fiction.

Silent Cry, The (*Man 'en Gannen no Futtoboru*, 1967). A novel by Kenzaburo OE, the poetic and often surreal story of two extremely different brothers who clash violently. This technically innovative novel won the Tanizaki Prize.

Sir Gawain and the Green Knight (c. 1375–1400). An Arthurian romance of 2,500 alliterative lines by an unknown author about GAWAIN, a knight who engages in a quest for another knight who possesses magical powers.

Sister Carrie (1900). Theodore DREISER's influential naturalistic first novel, long available only in an edition bowdlerized by the publisher; a reconstructed, unexpurgated edition appeared in 1981. Country girl Carrie MEEBER works in a Chicago shoe factory, but falls on hard times and is forced into a compromising relationship with a traveling salesman. A new, wealthier lover, George Hurstwood, steals money to travel with her to New York. There, as he sinks into degradation, she rises to Broadway stardom. That Carrie's unconventional behavior goes unpunished made the book scandalous to contemporary readers.

Six Characters in Search of an Author (*Sei Personaggi in Cerca d'Autore*, 1921). A play by Luigi PIRANDELLO that significantly influenced the Theater of the Absurd. The author obscures the boundaries between reality and illusion when a rehearsal of one of his own plays is interrupted by six characters, who were created and then abandoned by their own author. Chaos ensues as the recent arrivals play havoc with the traditional concepts of theater.

Skin of Our Teeth, The (1942). A comic, experimental play by Thornton WILDER, the topic of which is humanity's determined survival in the face of catastrophe. The audience follows the family of Mr. and Mrs. ANTROBUS (from *anthropos*, "human"), who seem to confront every major natural and manmade disaster from the Flood through World War II. The play won a Pulitzer Prize.

Slaughterhouse-Five; or, The Children's Crusade: A Duty-Dance with Death (1969). An allegorical novel by Kurt VONNEGUT, a landmark of antiwar literature inspired by Vonnegut's experiences as a soldier during World War II, blending historical fact, absurdist humor, and time-traveling fantasy. Kidnapped by aliens to their planet Tralfamadore, Billy PILGRIM becomes "unstuck in time," reliving various parts of his life, centrally his experiences as an American prisoner of war during World War II. "Slaughterhouse-Five" refers to the building where Billy and the other P.O.W.'s are held prisoner.

Sleepwalkers, The (*Die Schlafwandler*, 1931–32). A trilogy of novels by Hermann BROCH about the collapse of German bourgeois values in the era concluding with World War I, comprising *The Romantic* (*Pasenow oder die Romantik* 1888), *The Anarchist* (*Esch oder die Anarchie* 1903), and *The Realist* (*Huguenau oder die Sachlichkeit* 1918). Each has as its theme one stage of the disintegration, with its title character representing the type Broch saw as defining his era. Finally, with the war's end, the character Huguenau's amoral, materialistic realism triumphs.

Small House at Allington, The. *See* **Barsetshire Novels**

"Snow-Bound: A Winter Idyll" (1866). A poem by John Greenleaf WHITTIER, which he saw as a "Yankee pastoral." It is memorable for its vivid descriptions of nature and for its portrayal of a snug, warm family sheltered from the winter elements raging outside the door.

Snow Country (*Yukiguni*, 1948). A short lyrical novel by Yasunari KAWABATA that recounts the tragic love affair between Komako, a beautiful country geisha, and Shimamura, a wealthy Tokyo dilettante.

"Snows of Kilimanjaro, The" (1936). A short story by Ernest HEMINGWAY about Harry, a writer who develops gangrene while on an African safari. As he slowly dies, Harry meditates on his life and unfulfilled dreams. The story was included in *The Fifth Column and the First Forty-nine Stories* (1938).

"Soldier, The" (1915). A sonnet by Rupert BROOKE, in which a British soldier speaks of participating in World War I. A contrast to the many bitter poems inspired by that war, this one is remembered for its beginning lines: "If I should die, think only this of me: / That there's some corner of a foreign field / That is for ever England."

Soldier's Play, A (1981). A Pulitzer Prize–winning play by the American playwright Charles Fuller (1939–). Inspired by Herman Melville's *Billy Budd*, this play also won a special Edgar Award and was filmed as *A Soldier's Story* (1984). When a black soldier is murdered at a Louisiana Army base during World War II, the investigating officer, also black, finds his efforts hampered by racism from both within and without the segregated unit.

Some Do Not. . . . *See* **Parade's End**

Some Prefer Nettles (*Tade Kuu Mushi*, 1928–29). A novel by Jun'ichirō TANIZAKI, in which the author explores one of his favorite themes: the conflict between traditional Japanese and modern, Westernized culture.

"Song of Myself." *See* **Leaves of Grass**

Song of Roland, The (*La Chanson de Roland*, c. 1100). The great medieval French epic poem (perhaps by Turold), it is a *chanson de geste* ("song of great deeds"). The work recounts (with scant historical accuracy) the Battle of Roncesvalles (778) and the heroism and foolhardiness of ROLAND, nephew of Charlemagne. Betrayed by his malicious stepfather, Ganelon, and too proud to blow his horn to summon Charlemagne, Roland leads his men to slaughter.

Song of the Lark, The (1915). A novel by Willa CATHER, in which the protagonist, Thea Kronberg, overcomes the narrow-mindedness of her small Nebraska town and works with constant determination to become a successful opera singer.

"Song of the Open Road." *See* **Leaves of Grass**

Songs of Innocence and of Experience: Shewing the Two Contrary States of the Human Soul (1794). A volume of lyric poems written and illustrated by William BLAKE, setting poems on the power of love against others on the power of evil and disillusionment.

Sonnets from the Portuguese (1850). A sequence of 44 sonnets by ELIZABETH BARRETT BROWNING, written for her husband, ROBERT BROWNING, and given to him in 1849. The poems depict the stages of their ardent romance and marriage. The most famous is the 43rd, beginning "How do I love thee? Let me count the ways." The title of the collection refers to Browning's pet name for his wife.

Sonnets to Orpheus (*Die Sonette an Orpheus*, 1923). Two linked sonnet cycles by Rainer Maria RILKE. The 55 poems, ranging from the traditional to experimental in form, invoke ORPHEUS, the mythical Greek musician who represents the artist's transcendence of the boundary between life and death.

Sons and Lovers (1913). An autobiographical first novel by D. H. LAWRENCE, exploring a mother's strong hold on her son. Paul MOREL, an aspiring artist, abandons two relationships with women because he cannot free himself from the passive dominance of his mother. He is freed only by her death. The novel is noteworthy for its psychological insight, its frank portrayal of sexuality, and its depiction of working-class life.

Sophie's Choice (1979). A novel by William STYRON, in which an aspiring novelist, Stingo, gradually learns the harrowing history of Sophie Zawistowska, a beautiful concentration-camp survivor. The novel raises complex questions of guilt and the meaning of survival. Meryl Streep won an Oscar for her performance in the 1982 film.

Sorrows of Young Werther, The (*Die Leiden des Jungen Werthers*, 1774). An epistolary novel by Johann Wolfgang von GOETHE, one of the most significant works of Germany's *Sturm und Drang* ("storm and stress") movement. From the unconsummated love of sensitive young WERTHER for the married Lotte spring memorable expressions of passion. Werther's suicide gave rise to a rash of suicides across Europe.

Sot-Weed Factor, The (1960, revised 1967). A picaresque historical novel by John BARTH that is also a burlesque of the genre. The title comes from a 1708 poem by Ebenezer Cooke, who becomes the protagonist of Barth's novel. Despite its status as fantasy, the book has been praised for Barth's realistic rendering of the language, style, and cultural details of 17th-century Maryland.

Sound and the Fury, The (1929). A novel by William FAULKNER, his first stream-of-consciousness work. It traces the decline of the aristocratic COMPSON family in the fictional Yoknapatawpha County, Mississippi, from four different perspectives, those of the three Compson sons (Benjy, an "idiot"; Quentin; and Jason) and of Dilsey, one of the family's black servants. Among its themes are the curse laid upon the South by slavery, and the values (represented by Dilsey) of love and endurance. The title is from SHAKESPEARE's *MACBETH*: "Life's but a walking shadow, a poor player, / That struts and frets his hour upon the stage / And then is heard no more; it is a tale / Told by an idiot, full of sound and fury, / Signifying nothing."

Space Trilogy, The (1938–45). A science-fiction sequence by C. S. LEWIS, consisting of *Out of the Silent Planet* (1938), *Perelandra* (1943), and *That Hideous Strength* (1945). As his protagonist, Dr. Elwin Ransom, travels from planet to planet, Lewis explores a theme always dear to his heart: the battle between good and evil.

Spinoza of Market Street, The (1961). A short-story collection by Isaac Bashevis SINGER. The title story (published in Yiddish as "Der Spinozist," 1944) is a charming tale of the unlikely love between a scholar devoted to Spinoza and his illiterate neighbor.

Spoilt City, The. *See* **Balkan Trilogy, The**

Spoon River Anthology (1915). A volume of verse by Edgar Lee MASTERS that includes 245 free-verse monologues. Inspired by J. W. Mackail's *Select Epigrams from the Greek Anthology*, Masters wrote the monologues in the form of epitaphs from the points of view of the dead residing in the cemetery of the fictional Spoon River, a compound of two small Illinois towns.

Sportsman's Sketches, A (*Zapiski Okhotnika*, 1852). A collection of short stories by Ivan TURGENEV. The work has been compared to Harriet Beecher STOWE's *UNCLE TOM'S CABIN* (1852) for its direct criticism of Russia's system of serfdom and for its sympathetic and realistic look at the life of the Russian peasant.

Stand, The (1978). A popular novel by Stephen KING that incorporates elements of fantasy, science fiction, and horror. Set in the near future after a rapidly mutating virus has killed 99.4 percent of the world's population, the story details the battle between good and evil fought by the survivors.

Steppenwolf (*Der Steppenwolf*, 1927). A novel by Hermann HESSE. The main character, Harry Haller, a lonely, isolated intellectual, thinks of himself as a "Steppenwolf," or a wolf from the steppes. He strives to come to terms with bourgeois society, which he hates yet needs.

"Stopping by Woods on a Snowy Evening" (1923). A lyric poem by Robert FROST, which describes a brief pause in a long day's (or life's) work: "The woods are lovely, dark and deep. / But I have promises to keep, / And miles to go before I sleep, / And miles to go before I sleep."

Strange Interlude (1928). A Pulitzer Prize–winning play in nine acts by Eugene O'NEILL, notable for its innovative use of Freudian soliloquies and its extraordinary length (it was performed in two parts with a break for dinner). Nina Leeds compensates for her fiancé's death with a succession of ill-advised marriages and affairs, and gives birth to an illegitimate son. One by one the men in her life abandon her, except for long-suffering friend Charles Marsden, with whom she at last settles into passionless matrimony.

Stranger, The (*L'Étranger*, 1942). The first novel by Albert CAMUS, in which a dispassionate young French Algerian (MEURSAULT) faces murder charges for killing an Arab. His trial focuses on his antisocial character, as the prosecutor introduces such evidence as his failure to cry at his mother's funeral. Convicted and facing execution, Meursault experiences a moral awakening and attains a reverence for human existence.

Stranger in a Strange Land (1961). A Hugo Award–winning novel by Robert A. HEINLEIN about the first human born on Mars, who returns to Earth after being raised by aliens. The book earned a cult following and became the first science-fiction bestseller.

Streetcar Named Desire, A (1947). A Pulitzer Prize–winning drama by TENNESSEE WILLIAMS. Williams places in opposition Blanche DuBOIS, a faded Southern belle clinging to illusions of a past gentility, and her brother-in-law, the carnal, savage Stanley KOWALSKI. In such an encounter, Blanche is doomed to lose; at the play's end she is removed to a mental institution, noting that she has "always depended on the kindness of strangers." (For adaptations, see Variations.)

Studs Lonigan (1935). A trilogy of novels by James T. FARRELL, consisting of *Young Lonigan: A Boyhood in Chicago Streets* (1932), *The Young Manhood of Studs Lonigan* (1934), and *Judgment Day* (1935). The novels, set in the early 20th-century Chicago slums, trace the unsuccessful, generally halfhearted efforts of William "Studs" LONIGAN to move beyond the lower-middle-class Irish Catholic milieu into which he was born.

Suddenly Last Summer (1958). A play by TENNESSEE WILLIAMS, originally performed on a double bill called *Garden District* with *Something Unspoken*. The play concerns the efforts of a wealthy woman, Violet Venable, to have a young woman, Catherine Holly, lobotomized, in order to prevent Catherine from revealing that Mrs. Venable's son was homosexual and that his death was marked by violence and cannibalism. Even for Williams, the play is unusually bleak. The 1959 film version, directed by Joseph L. Mankiewicz from a screenplay by Gore VIDAL, starred Elizabeth Taylor as Catherine and Katharine Hepburn as Mrs. Venable.

Sugar Street. *See* **Cairo Trilogy, The**

Sun Also Rises, The (or *Fiesta*, 1926). A novel by Ernest HEMINGWAY about the "lost generation" of American and British expatriates after

World War I. Set in France and Spain, it depicts the despair of a group of friends, most of whom have had their lives shattered by the war. Most memorable are the narrator, Jake BARNES, the promiscuous Lady Brett ASHLEY, and the bullfighter Pedro Romero.

"Sunday Morning" (1915). A poem by Wallace STEVENS, tracing the musings of a 20th-century woman, frightened by the certainty of death and seeking an "imperishable bliss." The answer given in the poem is that belief in the supernatural is impossible. One can only accept the inevitability of death and embrace "the heavenly fellowship of men that perish."

Suttree (1979). An autobiographical novel by CORMAC McCARTHY, which shows the influence of William FAULKNER and other Southern Gothic writers. Cornelius Suttree travels through corruption, depravity, and violence before achieving spiritual redemption.

Swann's Way. *See* **Remembrance of Things Past**

Sweeney Agonistes: Fragments of an Aristophanic Melodrama (serialized 1926–27, performed 1933). A poetic drama by T. S. ELIOT that intersperses dialogue with musical numbers, reminiscent of the style and rhythms of music halls. The work suggests that contemporary life is characterized by spiritual and cultural impoverishment. Sweeney is the subject of two other poems by Eliot, "Sweeney Erect" and "Sweeney Among the Nightingales."

Sweet Bird of Youth (1959). A play by TENNESSEE WILLIAMS. The gigolo Chance Wayne returns to his hometown with the Princess Kosmonopolis, a fading movie star. By play's end she has left, and Wayne, rather than fleeing, is awaiting castration, the price he must pay for having in the past infected Heavenly Finley (the daughter of the local political boss) with a venereal disease. Chance possesses the rootlessness and the alienation typical of many of Williams's protagonists.

Sweet Cheat Gone, The. *See* **Remembrance of Things Past**

READING IN THE TRENCHES

War often consists of days of tedium broken by the sudden violence of battle, so soldiers typically fill the hours with games, letter writing, and reading. At such times, reading is not simply a diversion but a comfort, sometimes even an inspiration. For soldiers facing the possibility of death, the Bible has been a frequent companion. In World War II, a steel-jacketed New Testament was carried by servicemen in their breast pocket, where it could provide spiritual comfort and also stop a shell fragment.

During the American Civil War, many soldiers eagerly sought out daily and weekly newspapers, twenty-five-cent yellow-backed novels, and dime novels. These exotic love and adventure stories were the rage among the troops: "Miserable worthless novels were sold by the thousand," recalled one soldier in disgust. To counteract their influence, alarmed religious groups such as the Christian Commission distributed pious works in the camps, but some soldiers avoided both sermons and trash. One recruit, fresh from Harvard, sent home for *Hamlet* and *Macbeth*: "I want something to read," he wrote, "and know nothing as condensed as Shakespeare."

With World War I, an unprecedented number of educated men joined the ranks. English soldiers of all classes were familiar with their country's literary giants—Shakespeare, Donne, Milton, Tennyson—and many of them carried *The Oxford Book of English Verse* in their rucksacks. Jane Austen's novels, set among the tearooms, card games, and gardens of England at the turn of the 19th century, were also popular and calming, evoking a typically British serenity. Other soldiers, seeking to understand the events around them, immersed themselves in the darker depictions of human nature in the novels of Conrad and Hardy. "I didn't want to die—not before I'd finished *Return of the Native* anyhow," wrote the English soldier and celebrated war poet Siegfried Sassoon.

"Swimmer, The" (1964). A short story by John CHEEVER that combines realism and fantasy. Neddy Merrill decides to return home from a suburban pool party by swimming through all the pools along the way. The bizarre, increasingly grotesque journey provides him with an opportunity to examine his life and finally to recognize his own failure and his emptiness.

Tale of Genji, The (*Genji Monogatari*, early 11th century). A prose narrative by Lady MURASAKI, a classic of Japanese literature. A second author may have written the last 14 chapters. Focusing on the romantic affairs of the cultivated Prince Genji, the work is an elegant tapestry of highly refined court life.

Tale of Two Cities, A (1859). A historical novel by Charles DICKENS set in London and Paris during the French Revolution. The novel illustrates the injustices leading to the Revolution and the chaotic violence that characterized it. The focus is on Sydney CARTON's sacrifice of his life to save that of Charles Darnay. It begins memorably: "It was the best of times, it was the worst of times...."

When the United States entered World War II, book publishers saw an unparalleled opportunity to expose 12 million servicemen to reading. The Council on Books in Wartime, whose motto was, "Books Are Weapons in the War of Ideas," offered Armed Services Editions—paperback works designed (at 4 × 5½ inches) to fit in the left-hand pocket of a soldier's shirt. Among the 1,322 titles were works by Whitman, Melville, Twain, Faulkner, Homer, Keats, Wordsworth, and Dickens, but not the bleak war poetry of Wilfred Owen or novels tinged with the disillusion of World War I, such as *All Quiet on the Western Front* and *A Farewell to Arms*. Other book publishers came out with their own cheap editions. In 1945, the serviceperson's periodical *Stars and Stripes* surveyed American troops, asking them to name their favorite titles among Pocket Books editions: among the top choices were *The Pocket Book Dictionary*; *The Pocket Book of Cartoons*; *The Pocket Book of Boners*; *See Here, Private Hargrove*; *The Case of the Curious Bride*; Zola's *Nana*; and *The Pocket Book of Verse*.

For English readers on the homefront, W. Somerset Maugham reviewed the merits of detective stories in a radio broadcast, "Reading Under Bombing." The Penguin publishing house produced paperback books that fit perfectly into the left pants-pocket, designed for a shovel but now dubbed the "Penguin pocket."

But the most popular reading for American soldiers during World War II, and later the Vietnam War, was comic books. One comic-book hero, Major Mighty, bravely led his troops into battle; his devotees could join a club complete with membership cards and a secret code. In its heyday during World War II the club had hundreds of thousands of members, about half of them servicepeople, according to the comic's editor, Stanley Kauffmann (who would go on to become a distinguished film critic). As Kauffmann recalled in his memoir *Albums of Early Life*, "I saw many a letter from a serviceman overseas confiding his troubles to the Major because there was no one around he could really talk to."

Tamburlaine the Great (c. 1587). A tragedy in two parts by Christopher MARLOWE, based on the triumphs and death of the 14th-century Mongol conqueror (also called Tamerlane or Timur). The work is credited with establishing blank verse as the poetic form for Elizabethan drama.

Taming of the Shrew, The (c. 1593). A comedy by William SHAKESPEARE, in which PETRUCHIO, a man seeking a fortune, wins the hand and thus the dowry of the irritable, manhating KATE, whom he must first "tame." The drama, containing some of Shakespeare's most ribald language, is a play within a play: a drunken tinker is made to watch it. (For adaptations, see Variations.)

"Taras Bulba" ("Taras Bul'ba," 1835). A story by Nikolai GOGOL, first published in the collection *Mirgorod* (1835) and later expanded. Set in Gogol's native Ukraine, the story recounts the epic adventures and tragic deaths of the aging Cossack Taras Bulba and his two sons during the 17th-century wars against Poland. It is sometimes referred to as the "Cossack *ILIAD*."

Tartuffe (*Le Tartuffe, ou L'Imposteur*, 1664). A satirical comedy by MOLIÈRE. The fraudulent Tartuffe presents himself to the wealthy and gullible Orgon as a pious and good man so convincingly that Orgon signs over the deed to his property and offers his daughter in marriage to the imposter. Tartuffe's true nature is exposed only when he is caught making advances to Orgon's beautiful wife, Elmire. The play was banned when first produced in 1664 and again in a revised version in 1667. In 1669, *Tartuffe* was finally licensed for full performance. (For adaptations, see Variations.)

"Tell-Tale Heart, The" (1843). A short story by Edgar Allan POE. In this Gothic tale, the narrator kills the old man in his care because he is tormented by the man's diseased eye. He dismembers his victim and hides him beneath the floorboards. While talking to the police, he places his chair over the body, but is convinced that he can hear the man's heart beating. Terrified that the police will hear it too, he is overcome with madness and confesses to the murder.

Tempest, The (c. 1611). A comedy by William SHAKESPEARE, set on an enchanted island and known for its atmosphere of magic. PROSPERO, the deposed and exiled Duke of Milan, contrives a shipwreck to bring his political enemies to his shores and under his power. The play's characters exemplify the "chain of being"— from the spirit ARIEL to the subhuman CALIBAN. As *The Tempest* was probably Shakespeare's final play, audiences enjoy seeing parallels between Prospero's renunciation of magic and Shakespeare's ending his writing career. (For adaptations, see Variations.)

Temple of the Golden Pavilion, The (*Kinkakuji*, 1956). A novel by Yukio MISHIMA about a disturbed and alienated Buddhist monk who sets fire to a beloved temple. The book is based on the actual destruction of a temple in Kyoto in 1950.

Tenant of Wildfell Hall, The (1848). A novel by the English writer Anne Brontë (1820–1849). The heroine, Helen Graham, defies Victorian society, escapes from an abusive husband, supports her son by painting landscapes, and eventually marries Gilbert Markham, a man who loves her deeply. Much of the story is told through letters written by Gilbert and Helen and through Helen's journal entries, which she allows Gilbert to read so that he may understand her past and her mysterious seclusion.

Tender Buttons: Objects, Food, Rooms (1914). A collection of prose poems by Gertrude STEIN. In these pieces focusing on everyday objects, Stein brought the characteristics of Cubism to bear upon language, creating "verbal collages" designed to evoke (rather than explain) meaning.

Tender Is the Night (1934). A novel by F. SCOTT FITZGERALD, focusing on a psychiatrist whose youthful promise and vitality are sapped by his wife (formerly his patient) and the emptiness of the expatriate group with whom he associates. The major characters are Dick and Nicole DIVER, based partly on Fitzgerald and his wife, Zelda. The book was reissued posthumously with a revised plot structure (1948). The title is from KEATS's "ODE TO A NIGHTINGALE."

Tess of the d'Urbervilles: A Pure Woman Faithfully Presented (1891). A tragic novel by Thomas HARDY, considered scandalous at the time of its publication because of its empathetic treatment of a socially disgraced woman. Struggling against poverty, Tess DURBEYFIELD, a virtuous girl hired out to work for a wealthy family, is used cruelly by men, first seduced by the licentious Alec D'Urberville, and later abandoned by Angel Clare, the man she loves, when he learns of her history.

Testament, The (*Le Grande Testament*, written c. 1461, published 1489; also translated under the title *The Great Testament*). A long poem by François VILLON, consisting of eight-line stanzas interspersed with other poetic forms. In tones of regret and grief, the poet mourns bygone days and lost opportunity. Incorporated into the work is "Ballade of the Ladies of Time Past," with the melancholy line, "Where are the snows of yesteryear?"

"Thanatopsis" (1817; expanded version 1821). A poem in blank verse by William Cullen

BRYANT. The first version, written before Bryant turned 19, was quickly recognized as one of the strongest American poems to that date. An editor of the *North American Review* supplied the title, to mean "reflections on Death." The poet exhorts those troubled by thoughts of mortality to "Go forth, under the open sky, and list / To Nature's teachings," seeking courage in the fact that death claims all who live.

That Hideous Strength. *See* **Space Trilogy, The**

Their Eyes Were Watching God (1937). A lyrical novel by Zora Neale HURSTON. Set in the all-black town of Eatonville, Florida, the story traces the life and growing maturity of Janie CRAWFORD as she struggles for identity and independence. Writing in a fluid vernacular style, Hurston draws upon African-American folk rituals and oral storytelling traditions.

them (1969). A novel by Joyce Carol OATES, portraying the turbulent lives of Maureen Wendall, her mother Loretta, and her brother Jules, all of whom strive to overcome their environment, which includes alcoholism, prostitution, and domestic violence. The story is based on the actual family history of a young woman Oates taught at the University of Detroit.

Theophilus North (1973). A novel by Thornton WILDER, presenting a portrait of the wealthy residents of Newport, Rhode Island, in the 1920s. The loosely linked episodes are the reminiscences of the aging narrator, the gentle and helpful Theophilus North. It was the author's last work of fiction.

There Is Confusion (1924). The first novel by Jessie Redmon FAUSET, which interweaves the stories of three black Philadelphians, each struggling with the legacy of racial definitions in America. Peter works to comprehend his mixed-race heritage, Maggie yearns for middle-class respectability, and Joanna strives to be a successful dancer.

Thérèse Desqueyroux (1927). A novel by François MAURIAC. Set in Mauriac's native Bordeaux, the story concerns Thérèse DESQUEY-ROUX, an unhappily married woman who attempts to poison her husband but is acquitted at trial. The novel probes her troubled inner life before and after her crime, painting a portrait of her profound spiritual isolation within a constraining society of complacent, middle-class landowners.

Thérèse Raquin (1867). An early novel by Émile ZOLA, the first in which he applied a scientific, analytical technique (the naturalist method) to fiction, portraying, with careful detachment, the title character and her lover, who murder her husband and then are driven to suicide by their mutual guilt.

Things Fall Apart (1958). The first novel by Nigerian writer Chinua ACHEBE. An insightful portrayal of traditional social relations in Eastern Nigeria and the tragic destruction wrought by colonial invasion, the novel, set in the 19th century, concerns OKONKWO, a spirited, combative young man who struggles with both his own community's ethics and the Western assault on his culture.

Thin Man, The (1934). Dashiell HAMMETT's last novel. With humor, logic, and tough talk, ex-detective Nick CHARLES, aided by wealthy, witty wife Nora Charles (based on Hammett's companion, Lillian HELLMAN), solves the double mystery of a woman's murder and the title character's disappearance. (For adaptations, see Variations.)

This Side of Paradise (1920). The first novel by F. SCOTT FITZGERALD, which gained him a reputation for capturing the mood of "flaming youth." Following the career of Amory Blaine (based on the author) from his college days to an advertising job, the novel implies that the costs of involvement in a frivolous, superficial society are high.

Thousand and One Nights, The (*Alf Laylah wa Laylah*, present form 14th or 15th century; also translated under the title *The Arabian Nights*). A collection of stories of Persian, Indian, and Arabian origin, of varied and uncertain authorship. According to the frame story, Shahrazad (SCHEHERAZADE) contrives to keep her husband, the king, in suspense by telling him each night a gripping tale that is left incomplete until the next night. She thus saves herself from execution. The collection includes such legends as SINBAD THE SAILOR, Ali Baba, and ALADDIN.

Thousand Cranes (*Senbazuru*, 1952). A novel by Yasunari KAWABATA, in which the traditional tea ceremony becomes a vehicle for a critique of the nihilism of modern culture. This loosely structured work is classically Japanese yet anticipates the postmodern novel.

Three Musketeers, The (*Les Trois Mousquetaires*, 1844). A novel by Alexandre DUMAS *PÈRE* about D'ARTAGNAN and the "three musketeers" —ATHOS, PORTHOS, and ARAMIS—swashbuckling guardsmen for Louis XIII who defend their queen and king against the intrigues of Cardinal Richelieu.

Three Sisters, The (*Tri Sestry*, 1901). A play by Anton CHEKHOV, in which sisters Olga, Masha, and Irina PROZOROV endure a stultifying life in the country by dreaming of a new beginning in Moscow.

Three Tall Women (1994). A Pulitzer Prize– winning play by Edward ALBEE, in which three characters—identified only as A, B, and C— represent, in Act I, an old woman, her middle- aged caregiver, and her attorney, and, in Act II, three stages in the life of the same woman. A fourth character, a silent young man who appears in Act II, is A's son. The play is considered to be Albee's somewhat conciliatory portrait of his adoptive mother, with whom he had a troubled relationship.

Through the Looking-Glass (and What Alice Found There) (1872). Lewis CARROLL's sequel to *ALICE'S ADVENTURES IN WONDERLAND*, continuing Alice's fantasy adventures after she climbs through the looking-glass and finds a world in reverse. The work includes the well- known poems "Jabberwocky" and "The Walrus and the Carpenter," and the characters of Humpty Dumpty and the Red and White Queens.

Time Machine, The (1895). A novel by H. G. WELLS, his first book of science fiction, which reflects the author's fears of class strife. After building a machine that projects him into the future, the Time Traveller discovers a world starkly divided between the shallow and beautiful Eloi and the Morlocks, a worker group who support and prey on their social superiors.

Time of the Hero, The (*La Ciudad y los Perros*, 1963). A nonlinear novel by the Peruvian writer Mario VARGAS LLOSA, depicting the brutality of a military academy he had attended. The novel condemns the violence and deceit of military institutions and, by extension, of the author's native Peru.

Time Regained. *See* **Remembrance of Things Past**

Timon of Athens (c. 1607). A tragedy by William SHAKESPEARE about a man who becomes a traitor to his state out of fury at his friends' ingratitude. Because this portrait of a misanthrope lacks the character development of Shakespeare's great tragedies, some scholars speculate that it is an unrevised draft or that it was written only partially by Shakespeare.

Tin Drum, The (*Die Blechtrommel*, 1959). A novel by Günter GRASS narrated from an asylum for the criminally insane by the dwarfish Oskar MATZERATH. Oskar's claim that at the age of three he decided to stop growing suggests that he symbolizes the morally stunted Germany under the Nazis and in the immediate postwar period. The novel was filmed by Volker Schlöndorff in 1979.

"Tintern Abbey" (in full: "Lines Composed a Few Miles Above Tintern Abbey, on Revisiting the Banks of the Wye During a Tour, July 13, 1798," 1798). A poem by William WORDS- WORTH, inspired by a walk he took with his sister Dorothy, in which natural beauty is personified as a moral force. It was published in *LYRICAL BALLADS* (1798), the collection of poems by Wordsworth and Samuel Taylor COLERIDGE that helped to ignite English Romanticism.

'Tis Pity She's a Whore (1633). A play by En- glish dramatist John Ford (1586–1639?) about a tragic love triangle between Annabella and Giovanni, the incestuous daughter and son of an Italian nobleman, and Soranzo, the man Annabella tricks into marrying her when she becomes pregnant by her brother.

Titus Andronicus (c. 1593–94). A tragedy by William SHAKESPEARE. After defeating the Goths, Roman general Titus Andronicus has Alarbus, son of the vanquished Queen Tamora, put to death, setting in motion a series of gruesome acts of revenge, including the rape and mutilation of Titus's daughter Lavinia, and the unwitting cannibalism by Tamora of her other sons, Demetrius and Chiron, the perpetrators of Lavinia's torture. This foray into Senecan tragedy is the only one of Shakespeare's Roman plays not based in historical fact.

"To an Athlete Dying Young" (1896). A poem by A. E. HOUSMAN about a young man who is brought home for burial. The poem appears in the collection *A SHROPSHIRE LAD.*

"To a Skylark" (1820). One of PERCY BYSSHE SHELLEY's best-known and most frequently anthologized poems, inspired by birdsong heard on a summer evening's stroll near Livorno; first published with *PROMETHEUS UNBOUND.* In a series of similes, the poet addresses the "blithe spirit, / Bird thou never wert," in whose song he hears "profuse strains of unpremeditated art," concluding that the unconscious, natural songster's music surpasses that of human poets, constrained by sorrow, yearning, and "Hate, and pride, and fear."

Tobacco Road (1932). A novel by Erskine CALDWELL about the fortunes and (mostly) misfortunes of Jeeter Lester and his wretchedly poor clan, once sharecroppers, now squatters on the rural Georgian land their ancestors had owned, back when the "tobacco road" was built to roll hogsheads of tobacco to the river. Caldwell's novel became a bestseller only after the runaway success of Jack Kirkland's 1933 dramatization (3,182 performances on Broadway), which treated the material in a comic vein. John Ford directed the 1941 film.

To Have and Have Not (1937). A novel by Ernest HEMINGWAY about Harry Morgan, a boat owner in Key West during the Depression, who resorts to smuggling and aiding criminals to support himself and his family. The protagonist's dying words, "One man alone ain't got… no chance," reflect Hemingway's growing social awareness. Howard Hawks's memorable 1944 film starring Humphrey Bogart as Harry Morgan was only loosely based on the book; it represented the first screen pairing of Bogart with Lauren Bacall, making her screen debut as his love interest.

"To His Coy Mistress" (1681). A love poem by Andrew MARVELL, in which the amorous speaker urges his beloved to cease resisting his advances, saying "But at my back I always hear / Time's wingèd chariot hurrying near." The work is one of the most celebrated poems on the theme of "carpe diem" ("seize the day").

To Kill a Mockingbird (1960). A Pulitzer Prize–winning novel by HARPER LEE. Scout, the six-year-old daughter of lawyer Atticus FINCH, learns of racism, hypocrisy, and injustice when her father defends a black man accused of raping a white woman. Lee's only novel was adapted by screenwriter Horton Foote and director Robert Mulligan into a critically acclaimed 1962 film.

To Let. *See* **Forsyte Saga, The**

Tom Jones (in full: *The History of Tom Jones, a Foundling*, 1749). A comic novel by Henry FIELDING, in which lusty, good-hearted Tom JONES learns the secret of his birth and wins the hand of Sophia Western, despite numerous obstacles. Among the other memorable characters in this panorama of 18th-century Britain are Tom's hateful enemy Blifil, Tom's adoptive father Squire ALLWORTHY, and the irritable Squire Western. One of the first English novels, *Tom Jones* has greatly influenced the genre. Albert Finney played Tom in a 1963 film adaptation.

Tom Sawyer, The Adventures of (1876). A novel by Mark TWAIN, offering a humorous view of small-town life in 1830s America. Tom, seeking adventure and avoiding propriety, is said by some to be an archetype of American youth. Twain wrote three sequels, including *HUCKLEBERRY FINN* (1884).

"Tonio Kröger" (1903). A short story by Thomas MANN, describing the struggles of a writer whose artistic temperament conflicts with his yearning for bourgeois ordinariness.

Tono-Bungay (1908). A novel by H. G. WELLS. The narrator, George Ponderevo, helps his uncle Edward, a druggist, market a bogus medical elixir known as Tono-Bungay, and together they make a fortune until their company collapses. Throughout this social satire, George comments on the corruption of British society and the foolishness of a public that is so easily duped.

Tortilla Flat (1935). A novel by John STEINBECK. This humorous and realistic story of a group of Mexican-Americans in Monterey, California, helped to establish Steinbeck's reputation.

To the Lighthouse (1927). A novel by VIRGINIA WOOLF. The Great War's effect on Mr. and Mrs. RAMSAY and their friends is revealed through multiple perspectives rendered in stream-of-consciousness writing; the story is organized in three sections: before, during, and after the war. Mrs. Ramsay's nurturing optimism is contrasted with Mr. Ramsay's stolid pragmatism, and with their painter friend Lily BRISCOE's dedication to her art. Loosely autobiographical, it is one of the most successful examples of Woolf's modernist approach to the novel.

Towers of Silence, The. *See* **Raj Quartet, The**

Town, The (1957). A novel by William FAULKNER, part of his SNOPES trilogy. Dismayed by postbellum social changes, Faulkner created the sometimes comic, usually contemptible Snopes family as a symbol of the "new" South's degradation. In this novel the scurrilous Flem Snopes rises to power and wealth in Yoknapatawpha County. The trilogy also includes *THE HAMLET* (1940) and *THE MANSION* (1959).

Travesties (1974). A play by Tom STOPPARD. The coincidental residence of James JOYCE, Tristan Tzara, and V. I. Lenin in Zurich during World War I provides the springboard for this comedy. Ostensibly the memoirs of Henry Carr, a British consular official whom Joyce cast in a production of Oscar WILDE's *THE IMPORTANCE OF BEING EARNEST* (1895), it is an intellectual vaudeville composed of equal parts philosophical, artistic, and political debate, replete with puns, parody, and music-hall pastiche.

Treasure Island (1883). A pirate adventure novel by Robert Louis STEVENSON. After finding a map to a pirate captain's hidden treasure, the intrepid young narrator, Jim Hawkins, joins the crew of a schooner seeking the prize, only to learn that the ship's cook, one-legged Long John Silver, heads a pirate faction plotting a mutiny to seize the loot for themselves. Courageous and quick-witted, he helps defeat the villains and claims his share of the treasure.

Tree Grows in Brooklyn, A (1943). A novel by the American writer Betty Smith (1896–1972), the poignant story of Francie Nolan, an imaginative young girl coming of age in turn-of-the-century Brooklyn. The title refers to a tree that, like Francie, grows in the slums yet flourishes despite many hardships. Elia Kazan directed the 1945 film adaptation, starring Peggy Ann Garner as Francie.

Trial, The (*Der Prozess*, 1925). A posthumously published novel by Franz KAFKA, addressing the drift toward totalitarianism, the absurdist nature of bureaucracy, and the irrationality of guilt. JOSEPH K., a thoroughly unremarkable bank employee, is arrested, put on trial, and executed—all on charges that are never clarified. Kafka ordered his literary executor, Max BROD, to destroy the manuscript. Instead, Brod edited it for publication.

Trilby (1894). A novel by English caricaturist George du Maurier (1834–1896). *Fin-de-siècle* Left Bank artist's model Trilby O'Ferrall is transformed into a singing sensation by the mesmerizing SVENGALI, whose name has entered the English language as a synonym for an evil, controlling mentor. A triumph of marketing and merchandising, *Trilby* gave rise to a hit play, songs, several films (notably *Svengali*, 1931, starring John Barrymore), and a slew of products from shoes, sausages, soaps, toys, writing paper, and ice cream to the still-worn eponymous hat.

Tristram Shandy (in full: *The Life and Opinions of Tristram Shandy, Gentleman*, 1759–67). A novel by Laurence STERNE. Perhaps the first experimental novel in English, and a forerunner of the stream-of-consciousness novel, the book includes such devices as one-sentence chapters, missing chapters, blacked-out pages, and pages of marbled paper. The primary characters are Tristram's father, his Uncle Toby, Corporal Trim, Parson Yorick, and Widow Wadman. Tristram SHANDY himself is a relatively minor character; although the work begins with his conception, he is not born until the fourth of the work's nine volumes.

Troilus and Cressida (c. 1601–2). A play by William SHAKESPEARE, one of his "problem plays"—neither a comedy nor a traditional tragedy. Defecting to the Greeks, Cressida (or CRISEYDE) betrays her pledge of love to the Trojan prince TROILUS. In this generally pessimistic view of a corrupt world, the Trojan War is characterized by petty squabbling and cowardly behavior. Only HECTOR meets the test of a hero.

Troilus and Criseyde (c. 1385). A narrative poem by Geoffrey CHAUCER, based on the legendary love of the Trojan prince TROILUS and the faithless CRISEYDE.

Trojan Women, The (*Trōades*, 415 B.C.). A tragedy by EURIPIDES that depicts the cruelty of the Greek victors toward the women of Troy. Even the royal women—Hecuba (the Queen), Andromache (HECTOR's wife), and CASSANDRA (his sister)—are enslaved. Andromache's little son is hurled to his death. Presented shortly after the Athenian massacre of the citizens of Melos, the play can be seen as Euripides' veiled protest.

Tropic of Cancer (1934). An autobiographical novel by HENRY MILLER, published in Paris but, because of charges of obscenity, not legally available in the United States until 1961. In recounting his escapades as an expatriate in 1930s Paris, Miller illustrates his creed that sex is life-affirming, is indeed the life force itself. His fictionalized reminiscences continue in *Black Spring* (1936) and *Tropic of Capricorn* (1939).

True West (1980). A play by Sam SHEPARD about the rivalry between two brothers who find themselves exchanging roles. At the beginning, Austin is a relatively successful screenwriter, while Lee has lived from hand to mouth, stealing when it is convenient. The play's themes are those associated with Shepard: the breakdown of the American family, the sham inherent in the mythology of the American West, and the violence barely beneath the surface of civility.

Turn of the Screw, The (1898). A novella by HENRY JAMES, one of the most celebrated modern ghost stories. A young governess believes the two beautiful children in her charge, Miles and Flora, are haunted by two evil revenants, who may or may not be projections of her imagination. (For adaptations, see Variations.)

Twelfth Night; or, What You Will (c. 1601–2). A comedy by William SHAKESPEARE, the title of which refers to the Feast of the Epiphany, a time of celebration, 12 nights after Christmas. After her twin, Sebastian, is lost at sea, VIOLA disguises herself as a man. Merry confusion ensues. All is sorted out by the play's end, as the pairs of lovers (Viola and Orsino, Olivia and Sebastian) are happily united. An especially memorable character is the self-righteous MALVOLIO, a satire on Puritans. (For adaptations, see Variations.)

Twenty Love Poems and a Song of Despair (*Veinte Poemas de Amor y una Canción Desesperada*, 1924). An early verse collection by Pablo NERUDA, in which the poet expresses love in frankly erotic language. Although some readers were scandalized, the collection brought the young Neruda immediate recognition.

Twenty Thousand Leagues Under the Sea (*Vingt Mille Lieues sous les Mers*, 1869–70). A novel by Jules VERNE, considered a precursor of modern science fiction. It describes the fantastic but scientifically plausible undersea adventures of three men held captive by the mysterious Captain NEMO in his giant submarine, the Nautilus; unabridged editions contain many digressions on scientific topics. The earliest film version was by Georges Méliès (1905); the 1954 Disney Studios adaptation starred James Mason.

Twice-Told Tales (1837, enlarged 1842). A collection of short stories by Nathaniel HAW-THORNE. "The May-Pole of Merry Mount" and "The Minister's Black Veil" examine New England's sin-obsessed Puritan legacy; a psychological rendering of human mystery is seen in "Wakefield"; and "Dr. Heidegger's Experiment" is another of Hawthorne's treatments of fallible scientific research.

Two Gentlemen of Verona, The (c. 1594–95). A comedy by William SHAKESPEARE. "Heaven! were man / But constant, he were perfect" (V, iv). Valentine of Verona travels to Milan to elope with Silvia. He is soon followed by his aptly named friend Proteus, who abandons his betrothed Julia to court his friend's inamorata. Julia disguises herself as a boy and follows her love to Milan. Complications and double-crosses ensue until the end, when the original pairings are reinstated.

2001: A Space Odyssey (1968). A science-fiction novel by Arthur C. CLARKE. In collaboration with film director Stanley Kubrick, Clarke adapted his short story "The Sentinel" (1951) for the screenplay of the film *2001: A Space Odyssey* in 1968. In the same year, Clarke released the work in the form of a novel. *2001* is about astronauts who must investigate a mysterious monolith on Mars and contend with HAL 9000, a computer capable of human thought and emotions. The work was followed by *2010: Odyssey Two* (1982), *2061: Odyssey Three* (1987), and *3001: The Final Odyssey* (1997).

Two Women (*La Ciociara*, 1957). A novel by Alberto MORAVIA, in which an Italian widow, Cesira, and her 18-year-old daughter, Rosetta, suffer numerous forms of humiliation and privation, including rape, as they flee to Rome during World War II. A highly regarded 1961 film adaptation, directed by Vittorio de Sica, starred Sophia Loren in an Academy Award–winning performance.

Two Years Before the Mast (1840). A realistic novel by Richard Henry DANA about the harsh lives of sailors. The work is based on Dana's own experiences sailing from Boston to California.

Ubu Roi (1896). A play by Alfred JARRY, his best-known work and an important influence on avant-garde theater. Marked by raucous, satirical humor, punning (often scatological) wordplay, and hallucinatory imagery, the play was highly controversial when it premiered in Paris, but was particularly esteemed by Dadaists and Surrealists. The central figure, Père Ubu (later Ubu Roi, the King of Poland) is a grotesquely bloated buffoon who parodically represents the ruling classes. Jarry wrote several lesser-known sequels.

"Ulalume" (1847). A poem by Edgar Allan POE, which first appeared in the *American Review* in 1847 and was later collected in *The Works of Edgar Allan Poe* (1849). In this haunting ballad, the grief-stricken narrator, conflicted over whether to relinquish his devotion to his dead love, Ulalume, wanders in a dreamlike state, ending up at her tomb and coming to the realization that he cannot escape his melancholy preoccupation with her.

Ulysses (serialized 1918–20, book 1922). A stream-of-consciousness novel by James JOYCE, fusing multiple styles to re-create the rich and abundant experiences of a single day (June 16, 1904) in Dublin. Using HOMER's *ODYSSEY* as a mythological frame, Joyce focuses on the alienated Jew Leopold BLOOM (ULYSSES); his wife, Molly Bloom (PENELOPE); and the artist Stephen DEDALUS (Telemachus), from the author's *A PORTRAIT OF THE ARTIST AS A YOUNG MAN* (1916). An especially remarkable chapter is the final one, consisting of Molly's rambling but life-affirming interior monologue. Viewed as indecent and banned in the United States until 1933, the work is now generally considered the most significant English-language novel of the 20th century. Today, June 16 is celebrated worldwide as Bloomsday (after Leopold Bloom) with marathon readings of *Ulysses* and, in Dublin, with pilgrimages to places mentioned in the novel. (For adaptations, see Variations.)

Unbearable Lightness of Being, The (1984). A novel by Milan KUNDERA, written in Czech (*Nesnesitelná Lehkost Bytí*) but first published in English and then in French translation. It was banned in Czechoslovakia until 1989. Tomas's philandering, and its implied freedom, is set against the constraints of the post-1968 totalitarian regime in Prague.

Uncle Tom's Cabin; or, Life Among the Lowly (1852). A novel by Harriet Beecher STOWE, illustrating the evils of slavery. Although banned in the South, it was an amazing commercial success and its influence reached far beyond its literary value. Abraham Lincoln referred to Stowe as "the little lady who wrote the book that made this big war." The names of two of its characters—Uncle TOM and Simon LEGREE—have entered the English language as derogatory labels. Stage adaptations, notably one by George Aiken, were immensely popular in the 19th century.

Uncle Tom's Children (1938, enlarged 1940). A collection of four novellas by Richard WRIGHT about black people and their struggle against racism in the Deep South. For this book, his first, Wright won *Story* magazine's award for the best work by anyone employed by the WPA Federal Writers Project. The original edition consisted of "Big Boy Leaves Home," "Down by the Riverside," "Long Black Song," and "Fire and Cloud." For the enlarged edition Wright added "The Ethics of Living Jim Crow" (a preface) and the story "Bright and Morning Star."

Uncle Vanya (*Dyadya Vanya*, 1897). A play by Anton CHEKHOV, typical of the author's work in its moving and sympathetic glimpse into lives characterized by delusion and inertia. For years VANYA has managed the estate of his brother-in-law, Serebryakov, so that the latter could dedicate himself to scholarship. Too late, Vanya must admit that his self-sacrifice has been futile. In varying ways, all the characters share Vanya's psychological immobility. (For adaptations, see Variations.)

Under Milk Wood (1953). A play by Dylan THOMAS, evoking the texture of life in the Welsh village of Llareggub ("buggerall" spelled backwards). The script consists of a collage of comic monologues, conversations, and choral pieces through which the characters are revealed. Written as a radio play, it was first performed as a staged reading at Harvard during Thomas's American tour, and has since received many theatrical productions.

Under the Net (1954). The first novel by Iris MURDOCH, following the efforts of Jake Donaghue to discover a philosophy on which to pattern his life. Eventually, he realizes that this is impossible—made so by the presence of chance and other people. Like other early works by Murdoch, this novel was influenced by the French Existentialists.

Under the Volcano (1947). A novel by Malcolm LOWRY. Set in 1930s Mexico, the novel details the final, increasingly irrational 12 hours in the life of Geoffrey Firmin, an alcoholic former British consul in Quauhnahuac, Mexico.

Unnamable, The (*L'Innommable*, 1953). A novel by Samuel BECKETT, the last and most formally experimental novel in the trilogy that also includes *MOLLOY* (1951) and *MALONE DIES* (1951). It is presented as a poetic monologue, in which an "unnamable" narrator reflects on the difficulties of representation and the elusiveness of reality.

U.S.A. A trilogy by John DOS PASSOS, comprising *The 42nd Parallel* (1930), *1919* (1932), and *The Big Money* (1936), which creates a portrait of America from the turn of the 20th century to the start of the Depression. It is notable for Dos Passos's use of fictional devices, such as the "newsreel" technique (the use of quotations from newspapers, popular songs, and contemporary speeches), the "camera eye" (including brief autobiographical sketches in the narrative), and the use of short biographies of prominent contemporary figures.

V. (1963). A novel by Thomas PYNCHON. In this intricate, modernist work, "schlemiel" Benny Profane is a complacent slacker, working at dead-end jobs and frittering away time with his friends, The Whole Sick Crew. Profane becomes an active participant in life, however, when he meets Herbert Stencil, an industrious

TO BE CONTINUED: THE SERIAL

Serialized novels came into their own with young Charles Dickens's first novel, *The Pickwick Papers*, which appeared monthly during 1836–37 and became a publishing phenomenon; by the summer of 1837, 40,000 copies of each installment were being sold. The 24-year-old author received £2,000 for his efforts and his publishers made £10,000. Dickens capitalized on his success by beginning another serial, *Oliver Twist*, before *Pickwick* was even finished. He continued to publish his novels serially for much of his career, creating a pantheon of exceedingly popular characters. So beloved was Little Nell in *The Old Curiosity Shop*, for example, that when the sweet, self-effacing girl took sick at the end of one episode, her illness prompted hysterical speculation on both sides of the Atlantic. In New York, mail boats from London were met by crowds of frustrated readers, yelling, "Is Little Nell dead?" (She was.)

Victorian readers loved serialized poetry as well. Tennyson's *Idylls of the King* retold the romance of King Arthur at intervals over several decades, and Coventry Patmore's epic portrayal of a marriage, *Angel in the House*, was published over a period of nine years. Because serialized works can take years to be completed, the relationship between author and work, work and audience, is singular. Current events had an uncanny way of making their way into the narrative, and critical reviews and readers' suggestions also exerted an influence.

The golden age of serial literature was undoubtedly the 19th century, but in a bid to revitalize flagging readerships at the end of the 20th century, newspapers and magazines were once again serializing stories and novels. A harbinger of this revival was the serialization of Norman Mailer's novel *An American Dream* in *Esquire*, January–August 1964. Another was the *San Francisco Chronicle*'s publication, in the 1970s, of Armistead Maupin's "Tales of the City," stories of colorful oddballs that evolved into bestselling novels and several television

---

18-year-old obsessed with discovering the identity of a woman named V., who was mentioned in his dead father's notebooks and has mysteriously disappeared.

"Valediction Forbidding Mourning, A" (1633). A poem by John DONNE, published posthumously in his *Songs and Sonnets*. The poet, departing on a journey, assures his beloved that distance cannot divide them, urging the eternal, circular nature of their love in metaphysical analogies: "And so I end, where I begun."

Vanity Fair, a Novel Without a Hero (1848; published serially as *Vanity Fair, Pen and Pencil Sketches of English Society*, 1847–48). A novel by William Makepeace THACKERAY. Set in England around the time of the Battle of Waterloo, it follows Becky SHARP, a scheming and ambitious young woman, as she attempts to climb the social ladder. The title is a reference to the

miniseries. Stephen King published *The Green Mile* in six parts in 1996, and John Grisham's *A Painted House* appeared in his hometown (Oxford, Mississippi) newspaper throughout 1999–2000. *Time* magazine premiered *Killing Time*, a five-part science-fiction novel by Caleb Carr, in 2000.

An interesting aspect of the serialized novel is that the writer is often only one step ahead of the reader, writing a new chapter just as the previous chapter is going into print. Colin McEnroe, author of "The Resurrection of Caleb Quine," which appeared in the *Hartford Courant* over a period of six months, told a reporter in 1994 that each installment prompted a rash of suggestions and critiques from readers. His response: "gnawing fear." Deadline dread aside, McEnroe said he could not imagine writing a novel in the traditional way. "You go in a room and write and write and write and nobody sees it until you're done? What's that like?"

The rapid dissemination and response made possible by electronic publishing and the Internet encourages ever-higher levels of public interaction. In July 2000, Stephen King launched the Internet-first serial publication of *The Plant*, a novel written years earlier but rejected by publishers. The novel was to appear online in monthly installments, with readers paying under a highly unusual honor system. The catch was that King would write new installments only if 75 percent or more of the readers who downloaded installments actually paid for them. As King put it, "If you pay, the story rolls. If you don't, the story folds." The first installment of *The Plant* was downloaded by 120,000 readers, but by November, sales had fallen off drastically and King decided to suspend publication so that he could concentrate on other, more conventional books. While still bullish on the potential of online publication, King observed that his experience with *The Plant* led him to draw three conclusions: Internet users have the attention span of "grasshoppers"; Internet users have come to expect that everything on the Internet is (or should be) free; and for most readers, e-books are not "real" books. As King explained, such readers are like people who say, "I love corn on the cob but creamed corn makes me gag."

town in John BUNYAN's *PILGRIM'S PROGRESS* (1678–84), which represents human venality. (For adaptations, see Variations.)

Vicar of Wakefield, The (1766). A novel by Oliver GOLDSMITH about the continuing trials of Dr. Charles PRIMROSE, a vicar in rural England, and his family. Sale of this novel saved Goldsmith from debtor's prison.

View from the Bridge, A (1955). A play by ARTHUR MILLER about a Brooklyn dockworker whose incestuous attachment to his niece brings about his undoing. (For adaptations, see Variations.)

Vile Bodies (1930). A satirical novel by EVELYN WAUGH, about a vapid young Londoner, Adam Fenwick-Symes, who persistently attempts to raise enough money to wed his fiancée.

Violent Bear It Away, The (1960). The last novel by FLANNERY O'CONNOR, acclaimed for its vivid rendering of fervent Christian faith, dark emotions, and gritty, rural Southern settings. It concerns a poor orphan, Francis Marion Tarwater, whose great-uncle, a fierce fundamentalist, is convinced that the boy is destined to be a religious prophet. The novel conveys the intensity of spiritual quests, as Francis agonizes about his ostensible religious calling and ultimately learns to recognize its power.

Visit, The (*Der Besuch der Alten Dame*, 1956). A play by Friedrich DÜRRENMATT, in which a wealthy old woman returns to her hometown to offer the citizens a fortune to murder the man who had seduced and ruined her years before.

Volpone, or The Fox (1606). A play by Ben JONSON. A comedy set in Venice, *Volpone* is the story of a wealthy man who pretends to be near death in order to swindle eager gold diggers. The names of all the major characters are derived from the Italian words for various animals: Mosca ("Fly"), Volpone's henchman; and Corvino ("Raven"), Voltore ("Vulture"), and Corbaccio ("Crow"), Volpone's dupes. (For adaptations, see Variations.)

Voss (1957). A novel by PATRICK WHITE, set in mid-19th-century Australia, contrasting the rough life of an Australian frontiersman with the civilized society of his fiancée in Sydney.

Waiting for Godot (*En Attendant Godot*, 1953). A tragicomedy by Samuel BECKETT, a landmark work of the Theater of the Absurd. In the course of two days, two tramps (VLADIMIR and ESTRAGON) discuss their hardships, contemplate suicide, and continue their vigil for Godot, who daily sends them a message that he will arrive the following day. The play ends with the pair still waiting.

Waiting for Lefty (1935). A one-act proletarian drama by Clifford ODETS, in which members of a taxi drivers' union are aroused to fight for their rights upon hearing that their leader, Lefty Costello, has been murdered. Odets breaks down the "fourth wall" (the barrier between audience and stage) by having the actors address the audience directly and by having other actors play audience members.

Walden; or, Life in the Woods (1854). A unified collection of 18 essays by Henry David THOREAU, and a masterpiece of American Transcendentalism. Emphasizing self-reliance, simplicity, and the rewards of a close relationship with nature, Thoreau writes of his withdrawal from materialist, urban society to the shore of Walden Pond. (For literary purposes, he condenses two years into one.) Throughout, he stresses that the sojourn at Walden was a "deliberate" experiment, an attempt to examine himself and to avoid the plight of "the mass of men [who] lead lives of quiet desperation."

Walk on the Wild Side, A (1956). The last novel by Nelson ALGREN, a reworking of an earlier work, *Someone in Boots* (1935). With savage humor, Algren presents drifter and sometime con-man Dove Linkhorn and his Depression-era wanderings among the outcasts of society.

Wapshot Chronicle, The (1957). A National Book Award–winning novel by John CHEEVER, which has parallels to his own life. In this episodically structured work, Cheever, with grim humor, traces the decline of the Wapshot family and their town. The title refers to the journals kept by the father, Leander. The family's story was continued in *The Wapshot Scandal* (1964).

War and Peace (*Voĭna i Mir*, 1868–69). An epic novel by Leo TOLSTOY. Set against the backdrop of the Napoleonic Wars, this massive work, written in the realist tradition, illustrates Tolstoy's belief in historical determinism. At the emotional center are the lovely, vibrant Natasha ROSTOVA and the two men who love her: Andrei BOLKONSKY, a man of brilliant but uncreative intellect, and Pierre BEZUKHOV, an awkward and ineffectual idealist. Offering a panorama of 19th-century Russian society, the work is a masterpiece of world literature. (For adaptations, see Variations.)

Warden, The. *See* **Barsetshire Novels**

"Ward Number Six" ("Palata No. 6," 1892; also translated under the title "Ward No. 6"). A short story by Anton CHEKHOV, in which a mismanaged mental ward represents Russia. Dr. Andrei Ragin, who passively accepts the status quo, is shaken by the patient Ivan Gromov, who rails against the brutality and stupidity rampant in the institution. Ragin, symbolizing the aristocracy who prefer to ignore injustice, ends up a patient in his own hospital.

War of the Worlds, The (1898). A science-fiction novel by H. G. WELLS, in which Martians invade England. (For adaptations, see Variations.)

Washington Square (1881). A novel by HENRY JAMES, typical of the author in its psychological subtlety and moral concerns. Catherine SLOPER, a plain, awkward spinster, is unloved and ridiculed by her father, which makes her easy prey for the fortune-hunting Morris Townsend. In finally rejecting Townsend, Catherine shows an acquired self-respect. She is one of several Jamesian heroines who learn to accept their lot with dignity. (For adaptations, see Variations.)

Wasps (*Sphēkes*, 422 B.C.). A comedy by ARISTOPHANES that lampoons the Athenian court system. Attacked by the playwright but not actually appearing on stage as a character is Cleon (earlier ridiculed by Aristophanes in *The Knights*), who regularly pays jurors. The plot consists of the efforts of Bdelycleon ("Cleon-hater") to restrain his father, Philocleon ("Cleon-lover"), who is obsessed with serving on juries. The most absurd part of the play is the trial of a dog for stealing cheese. Wasps—jurymen who delight in "stinging" defendants for pay—make up the Chorus.

Waste Land, The (1922). A poem in five parts by T. S. ELIOT, arguably the most famous and most influential English-language poem of the 20th century. The poem depicts the search for meaning and rejuvenation in the modern desert of spiritual waste. Former promises of renewal are no longer relevant: "April is the cruellest month." Mingling disparate literary, historical, and mythical allusions (many in the original languages), along with colloquial dialogue and rich symbolism, Eliot gives poetic form to the fragmentation of a land in ruins. He cut the poem nearly in half at the suggestion of Ezra POUND, to whom it is dedicated.

Watt (written 1942–45, published 1953). A comic novel by Samuel BECKETT. From within a mental institution, Watt, a former servant of Mr. Knott (both names are puns), tries to make sense of his ultimately senseless experiences. The convoluted structure of the novel and the premise that Watt is dictating to another mental patient reinforce the absence of rational explanation.

Waverley Novels, The (1814–32). A series of 32 novels, including *Rob Roy* (1818) and *Ivanhoe* (1820), by SIR WALTER SCOTT, published anonymously until 1827. In these works covering several centuries of Scottish and English history, Scott created and defined the historical novel as a genre.

Waves, The (1931). A novel by VIRGINIA WOOLF, generally considered her masterpiece. Three men and three women move through seven stages of their lives. The novel is a series of interior monologues interspersed with references to the changing tides and the movement of the sun, signifying the passing of time. The six characters seem to flow in and out of one another like waves. Even for Woolf, this work is experimental in its rejection of conventional notions of plot and character.

Way of All Flesh, The (1903). A posthumously published semiautobiographical novel by Samuel BUTLER chronicling four generations of the PONTIFEX family in 19th-century England, focusing on the youngest, the unhappy clergyman and future writer Ernest Pontifex.

Way of the World, The (1700). A comedy by William CONGREVE, in which the characters Millamant and Mirabell attempt to obtain the consent of Mirabell's aunt for their marriage. Although now considered Congreve's masterpiece, it was poorly received when first produced and prompted the author to give up writing plays.

Way We Live Now, The (1875). A satirical novel by Anthony TROLLOPE, concerning the financier Augustus Melmotte and his circle of unscrupulous friends as they try to maintain their social status in Victorian England.

Weary Blues, The (1926). The first collection of poems by LANGSTON HUGHES, renowned for introducing the technique, featured in the title poem, of adapting the traditional African-American musical form of the blues to literary verse. The poems also include "Dream Variations" and "THE NEGRO SPEAKS OF RIVERS."

Web and the Rock, The (1939). An autobiographical novel by THOMAS WOLFE, compiled from manuscripts by Wolfe's editor after the author's death. George Webber flees his provincial childhood home in North Carolina and moves to New York City, where he becomes involved with an older, married woman, Esther Jack. Webber's story is continued in YOU CAN'T GO HOME AGAIN (1940).

What Maisie Knew (1897). A novel by HENRY JAMES, noted for its skillful presentation of events from the perspective of a child. Maisie witnesses, with limited understanding, her divorced parents' self-absorption, their spiteful behavior to each other, and their adulterous betrayals of their new spouses. The novel masterfully charts the developing consciousness of a young girl in a corrupt, bewilderingly unstable world of adults.

What's Bred in the Bone (1985). The second book in Robertson DAVIES's Cornish trilogy, which also includes THE REBEL ANGELS (1981) and THE LYRE OF ORPHEUS (1988). In the novel, the adventures of eccentric art collector Francis Cornish are narrated by two "biographer" angels.

What We Talk About When We Talk About Love (1981). The third collection of short stories by Raymond CARVER, acclaimed for its highly spare prose; repetitive, conversational rhythms; and deadpan tone. Focusing on the ambiguous, complex dynamics of relationships, the stories convey the mundanely painful lives of ordinary people. The volume's best-known stories include the title work and "Why Don't You Dance?" about a jilted man who mysteriously places all of the furniture from his house on his front lawn.

"When Lilacs Last in the Dooryard Bloom'd." *See* **Leaves of Grass**

White Devil, The, or, Vittoria Corombona (1612). A Jacobean revenge tragedy by JOHN WEBSTER, based on a 16th-century Italian murder case, in which Vittoria's lover, Bracciano, and her brother, Flamineo, murder Bracciano's wife and Vittoria's husband. The murders are eventually avenged by Francisco, the murdered woman's brother.

White Fang (1905). A novel by Jack LONDON. A companion to London's THE CALL OF THE WILD (1903), this popular work tells of the domestication of White Fang, part dog and part wolf. White Fang learns to survive among humans, enduring mistreatment until he is befriended by a young prospector, whose life he eventually saves. London equates the struggle for existence among animals—"hunting and being hunted, eating and being eaten, all in blindness and confusion, with violence and disorder, a chaos of gluttony and slaughter, ruled over by chance"—with human society.

White Noise (1985). Don DELILLO's novel about Jack Gladney, Chair of Hitler Studies at College-on-the-Hill in a small Midwestern town. Jack is morbidly afraid of death (a colleague tells him, "Hitler is larger than death. You thought he would protect you."). He hopes for respite from his fear in a drug said to repress it, but is unable to bring himself to kill a man to obtain it.

Who's Afraid of Virginia Woolf? (1962). A play by Edward ALBEE, his first full-length drama and often considered his best work. After a campus party, a middle-aged couple, George and Martha, invite a younger couple, Nick and Honey, for a nightcap. No holds are barred as these four ruthless, unhappy people wound, humiliate, and betray one another in an evening of "fun and games." In the process they lay bare the illusions to which they have clung over the years.

"Why I Live at the P.O." (1941). A short story in the Southern Gothic vein by Eudora WELTY, first published in *The Atlantic Monthly*, then collected in *A Curtain of Green* (1941). The story is cast in the form of an often hilarious monologue by Sister, a young woman who has gone to live in the post office of her Mississippi town to escape her family. A classic of American literature, it captures with pitch-perfect realism a story of Southern eccentricity.

Wide Sargasso Sea (1966). A novel by Jean RHYS, the protagonist of which is *JANE EYRE*'s "madwoman," Bertha Mason. Here called Antoinette, the first Mrs. Rochester is an exotic, vulnerable young woman from the West Indies. Her fortune-hunting husband—with his xenophobia and inhibitions—cannot understand her. As he comes to display only contempt for her sexuality and her un-English spontaneity, his cruelty and the isolation of her life in England drive her mad. (For a film adaptation, see Variations, under *Jane Eyre*.)

Wild Ass's Skin. *See* **Human Comedy, The**

Wild Duck, The (*Vildanden*, 1884). A drama by Henrik IBSEN. Gregers Werle, in rebellion against his father's bourgeois values, determines to reveal to his old friend, Hjalmar EKDAL, the long-held secrets that bind their families together. The results shatter the lives of the Ekdals, dramatically calling into question the value of unmasking false beliefs.

"Wild Swans at Coole, The" (1917). A poem by William Butler YEATS, in which he reflects wistfully on lost youth and the uncertainties of the future. Coole Park was the County Galway estate of Yeats's patron, Lady Augusta GREGORY, the distinguished Irish playwright and poet.

Wilhelm Meister's Apprenticeship (*Wilhelm Meisters Lehrjahre*, 1795–96). A novel by Johann Wolfgang von GOETHE. The prototypical Bildungsroman, it relates Wilhelm's disillusioning experiences in pursuit of a theatrical career and his spiritual maturing. The beautiful songs given to two tragic characters, Mignon and the Harper, have been set by many composers, including Schubert, Schumann, and Hugo Wolf.

William Tell (*Wilhelm Tell*, 1804). A drama in blank verse by Friedrich SCHILLER, inspired by 13th-century Swiss history and the spirit of the American Revolution. Tell, the Swiss national hero, slays the tyrant Gessler and frees his countrymen from Austrian oppression. It is the basis of Rossini's opera, with its well-known overture.

Winesburg, Ohio (1919). A collection of 23 related short stories by SHERWOOD ANDERSON, all set in a typical Midwestern town. The central figure, George WILLARD, is a young reporter who longs to transcend the town's narrowly provincial horizons.

Wings of the Dove, The (1902). A novel by HENRY JAMES, in which a conniving woman, Kate CROY, engineers a marriage between her own sweetheart, Merton DENSHER, and a dying heiress, Milly Theale, only to have the plan go awry. The novel is an instance of James's treatment of the contrast between European corruption and American innocence. The title comes from Psalm 55: "Oh that I had wings like a dove!"

Winter's Tale, The (c. 1610–11). A comedy by William SHAKESPEARE, with traces of tragedy, also called one of his romances. Its themes include the wages of jealousy and the healing power of nature. Sorrow ensues when King Leontes imprisons his innocent wife for adultery and orders that their infant daughter be abandoned. Years later—and in Springtime—joy is restored, as the king and queen are reunited, and their daughter is restored to them. The play has one of the theater's most amusing stage directions: "Exit pursued by a bear."

Winter's Tales (*Vinter-eventyr*, 1942). A collection of 11 short stories by Isak DINESEN, supposedly suggested by SHAKESPEARE's *THE WINTER'S TALE*. These strange and symbolic tales are set largely in the author's native Denmark, and attention is given to realistic detail; yet they have a touch of the unworldly. Included are "Sorrow Acre" (based on a tragic Danish folk legend), "The Invincible Slave-Owners," "The Heroine," and "The Sailor-Boy's Tale."

Wise Blood (1952). FLANNERY O'CONNOR's first novel, representative of her fiction in its use of dialect, humor, and irony. In this Southern Gothic work stressing the grotesque, Hazel MOTES's very denial of Christianity becomes a religious obsession as he proselytizes for the Church Without Christ.

Within a Budding Grove. *See* **Remembrance of Things Past**

Woman in the Dunes, The (*Suna no Onna*, 1962). A novel by Kōbō ABE, an allegory of the human condition. Niki Jumpei, an amateur entomologist seeking a rare beetle, discovers a remote seaside town surrounded by sand dunes. The inhabitants hold him captive in a sand pit with an outcast woman, and force them to shovel away the ever advancing sand that threatens to bury the town. Are they "shoveling to survive, or surviving to shovel"? Abe adapted his own work for a highly regarded 1964 film.

Woman in White, The (1860). A popular mystery novel by Wilkie COLLINS. The memorable villains Percival Glyde and Count FOSCO plan to steal the inheritance of young heiress Laura Fairlie. Their plan is complicated by a mysterious woman in white named Anne Catherick, who is confined to a mental institution and greatly resembles Laura.

Women in Love (privately printed 1920, published 1921). A novel by D. H. LAWRENCE, a sequel to *THE RAINBOW* (1915), in which the writer continues his examination of marriage and the relationships between men and women. Ursula BRANGWEN and Rupert Birkin, a couple modeled on Lawrence and his wife, Frieda, work through their conflicts and toward harmony, with each respecting the individuality of the other, while Ursula's sister, Gudrun Brangwen, and the cold industrialist Gerald Crich are doomed by their unyielding natures.

Women of Brewster Place, The (1982). A loosely unified novel by Gloria NAYLOR, focusing on the intertwining lives of seven African-American women in a walled-off, dead-end street of an unnamed Northeastern city. Each woman's tale of the struggle leading her to Brewster Place brings her into contact with the others. The novel won the American Book Award for a first novel. Oprah Winfrey coproduced and starred in a television miniseries adaptation in 1989, which was followed by a less-successful weekly television series in 1990.

World According to Garp, The (1978). JOHN IRVING'S comic novel featuring T. S. Garp. Named for the rank (Technical Sergeant) of the near-comatose soldier his mother chose to conceive him with, Garp grows up to be a successful novelist, strongly influenced by his mother, Jenny Fields, who becomes a famous feminist writer.

"World Is Too Much with Us, The" (1807). A sonnet by William WORDSWORTH, in which he laments that humankind is out of harmony with the natural world.

Woyzeck (written 1835–37, performed 1913). A dramatic fragment by Georg BÜCHNER, pathbreaking for its treatment of a man from society's dregs as a tragic subject; the title character is a destitute soldier harassed by poverty and jealousy into madness and murder. It was adapted as an opera (*Wozzeck*, 1921) by Alban Berg.

"Wreck of the Deutschland, The" (written c. 1876, published 1918). A long, spiritual poem by Gerard Manley HOPKINS. Occasioned by the wreck of a ship whose passengers included five nuns expelled from Germany for their faith, the poem is in the poet's celebrated "sprung rhythm." Hopkins, a Jesuit priest, relates his own religious crises as well as the Crucifixion of Christ to the sufferings of one of the drowned, whom he calls the "tall nun."

Wuthering Heights (1847). A novel by EMILY BRONTË, published under the pseudonym Ellis Bell. This masterpiece of British Romanticism, with its adept use of a narrative within a narrative, is the story of the passionate bond between the tempestuous Catherine EARNSHAW and her soulmate, the diabolical HEATHCLIFF. When Catherine betrays this bond by marrying the good but insipid Edgar Linton, Heathcliff's rage and misery threaten to destroy two generations of Earnshaws and Lintons. (For adaptations, see Variations.)

"Yellow Wallpaper, The" (1892). A short story by Charlotte Perkins GILMAN, a classic of feminist literature that hauntingly portrays a woman's mental breakdown when she undergoes the "rest cure" for depression.

Yerma (1934). A tragedy by Federico GARCÍA LORCA, written in the author's characteristically spare and haunting language and depicting the grim consequences of a woman's thwarted desires. Yerma ("barren land"), trapped with an indifferent husband and attracted to a young shepherd, yearns for a child. But rather than commit adultery, she escapes into madness and strangles her husband. The work is the middle play of a trilogy that also includes *BLOOD WEDDING* and *THE HOUSE OF BERNARDA ALBA*.

You Can't Go Home Again (1940). The last novel by THOMAS WOLFE, a sequel to *THE WEB AND THE ROCK* (1939), which continues the story of George Webber as he returns from Europe to visit his North Carolina hometown.

You Can't Take It with You (1936). A Pulitzer Prize–winning comedy by George S. KAUFMAN and Moss HART about the farcically eccentric Vanderhof family.

Young Joseph. *See* **Joseph and His Brothers**

Zoo Story, The (1959). A one-act play by Edward ALBEE, which focuses on an ultimately violent confrontation between two strangers who meet on a park bench.

Zorba the Greek (*Vios kai Politeia tou Alexē Zormpa*, 1946). A novel by Nikos KAZANTZAKIS, set on the Greek island of Crete, tracing the friendship between an ascetic scholar and the life-embracing Zorba. The story was filmed in 1964 (starring Anthony Quinn) and adapted as a Broadway musical by Kander and Ebb in 1968.

Zuckerman Unbound (1981). A novel by PHILIP ROTH, the second in a trilogy that includes *THE GHOST WRITER* (1979) and *THE ANATOMY LESSON* (1983). *Zuckerman Unbound* tells of the controversy aroused by novelist Nathan ZUCKERMAN's latest book. The three novels were collected as *Zuckerman Bound: A Trilogy and Epilogue* (1985).

Book Awards

PULITZER PRIZE FOR FICTION

Awarded annually by Columbia University in New York for distinguished fiction by an American author, preferably dealing with American life.

2001   *The Amazing Adventures of Kavalier & Clay*, Michael Chabon

2000   *Interpreter of Maladies*, Jhumpa Lahiri

1999   *The Hours*, Michael Cunningham

1998   *American Pastoral*, Philip Roth

1997   *Martin Dressler: The Tale of an American Dreamer*, Stephen Millhauser

1996   *Independence Day*, Richard Ford

1995   *The Stone Diaries*, Carol Shields

1994   *The Shipping News*, E. Annie Proulx

1993   *A Good Scent from a Strange Mountain*, Robert Olen Butler

1992   *A Thousand Acres*, Jane Smiley

1991   *Rabbit at Rest*, John Updike

1990   *The Mambo Kings Play Songs of Love*, Oscar Hijuelos

1989   *Breathing Lessons*, Anne Tyler

1988   *Beloved*, Toni Morrison

1987   *A Summons to Memphis*, Peter Taylor

1986   *Lonesome Dove*, Larry McMurtry

1985   *Foreign Affairs*, Alison Lurie

1984   *Ironweed*, William Kennedy

1983   *The Color Purple*, Alice Walker

1982   *Rabbit Is Rich*, John Updike

1981   *A Confederacy of Dunces*, John Kennedy Toole

1980   *The Executioner's Song*, Norman Mailer

1979   *The Stories of John Cheever*, John Cheever

1978   *Elbow Room*, James Alan McPherson

1977   No award

1976   *Humboldt's Gift*, Saul Bellow

1975   *The Killer Angels*, Michael Shaara

1974   No award

1973   *The Optimist's Daughter*, Eudora Welty

1972   *Angle of Repose*, Wallace Stegner

1971   No award

1970   *Collected Stories*, Jean Stafford

1969   *House Made of Dawn*, N. Scott Momaday

1968   *The Confessions of Nat Turner*, William Styron

1967   *The Fixer*, Bernard Malamud

1966   *The Collected Stories of Katherine Anne Porter*, Katherine Anne Porter

1965   *The Keepers of the House*, Shirley Ann Grau

1964   No award

1963   *The Reivers*, William Faulkner

1962   *The Edge of Sadness*, Edwin O'Connor

1961   *To Kill a Mockingbird*, Harper Lee

1960   *Advise and Consent*, Allen Drury

1959   *The Travels of Jaimie McPheeters*, Robert Lewis Taylor

(Pulitzer Prize for Fiction, continued)

1958	*A Death in the Family*, James Agee
1957	No award
1956	*Andersonville*, MacKinlay Kantor
1955	*A Fable*, William Faulkner
1954	No award
1953	*The Old Man and the Sea*, Ernest Hemingway
1952	*The Caine Mutiny*, Herman Wouk
1951	*The Town*, Conrad Richter
1950	*The Way West*, A. B. Guthrie, Jr.
1949	*Guard of Honor*, James Gould Cozzens
1948	*Tales of the South Pacific*, James A. Michener
1947	*All the King's Men*, Robert Penn Warren
1946	No award
1945	*A Bell for Adano*, John Hersey
1944	*Journey in the Dark*, Martin Flavin
1943	*Dragon's Teeth*, Upton Sinclair
1942	*In This Our Life*, Ellen Glasgow
1941	No award
1940	*The Grapes of Wrath*, John Steinbeck
1939	*The Yearling*, Marjorie Kinnan Rawlings
1938	*The Late George Apley*, John P. Marquand
1937	*Gone with the Wind*, Margaret Mitchell
1936	*Honey in the Horn*, Harold L. Davis
1935	*Now in November*, Josephine Winslow Johnson
1934	*Lamb in His Bosom*, Caroline Miller
1933	*The Store*, T. S. Stribling
1932	*The Good Earth*, Pearl S. Buck
1931	*Years of Grace*, Margaret Ayer Barnes
1930	*Laughing Boy*, Oliver LaFarge
1929	*Scarlet Sister Mary*, Julia M. Peterkin
1928	*The Bridge of San Luis Rey*, Thornton Wilder
1927	*Early Autumn*, Louis Bromfield
1926	*Arrowsmith*, Sinclair Lewis
1925	*So Big*, Edna Ferber
1924	*The Able McLaughlins*, Margaret Wilson
1923	*One of Ours*, Willa Cather
1922	*Alice Adams*, Booth Tarkington
1921	*The Age of Innocence*, Edith Wharton
1920	No award
1919	*The Magnificent Ambersons*, Booth Tarkington
1918	*His Family*, Ernest Poole

PULITZER PRIZE FOR POETRY

Awarded annually by Columbia University in New York for a distinguished volume of original verse by an American author.

2001	*Different Hours*, Stephen Dunn
2000	*Repair*, C. K. Williams
1999	*Blizzard of One*, Mark Strand
1998	*Black Zodiac*, Charles Wright
1997	*Alive Together: New and Selected Poems*, Lisel Mueller
1996	*The Dream of the Unified Field*, Jorie Graham
1995	*Simple Truth*, Philip Levine
1994	*Neon Vernacular*, Yusef Komunyakaa
1993	*The Wild Iris*, Louise Glück
1992	*Selected Poems*, James Tate
1991	*Near Changes*, Mona Van Duyn
1990	*The World Doesn't End*, Charles Simic
1989	*New and Collected Poems*, Richard Wilbur
1988	*Partial Accounts: New and Selected Poems*, William Meredith
1987	*Thomas and Beulah*, Rita Dove
1986	*The Flying Change*, Henry Taylor
1985	*Yin*, Carolyn Kizer
1984	*American Primitive*, Mary Oliver
1983	*Selected Poems*, Galway Kinnell
1982	*The Collected Poems*, Sylvia Plath
1981	*The Morning of the Poem*, James Schuyler
1980	*Selected Poems*, Donald Justice

1979	*Now and Then: Poems 1976–1978,* Robert Penn Warren	1946	No award
1978	*Collected Poems,* Howard Nemerov	1945	*V-Letter and Other Poems,* Karl Shapiro
1977	*Divine Comedies,* James Merrill	1944	*Western Star,* Stephen Vincent Benét
1976	*Self-Portrait in a Convex Mirror,* John Ashbery	1943	*A Witness Tree,* Robert Frost
1975	*Turtle Island,* Gary Snyder	1942	*The Dust Which Is God,* William Rose Benét
1974	*The Dolphin,* Robert Lowell	1941	*Sunderland Capture,* Leonard Bacon
1973	*Up Country,* Maxine Kumin	1940	*Collected Poems,* Mark Van Doren
1972	*Collected Poems,* James Wright	1939	*Selected Poems,* John Gould Fletcher
1971	*The Carrier of Ladders,* William S. Merwin	1938	*Cold Morning Sky,* Marya Zaturenska
1970	*Untitled Subjects,* Richard Howard	1937	*A Further Range,* Robert Frost
1969	*Of Being Numerous,* George Oppen	1936	*Strange Holiness,* Robert P. T. Coffin
1968	*The Hard Hours,* Anthony Hecht	1935	*Bright Ambush,* Audrey Wurdemann
1967	*Live or Die,* Anne Sexton	1934	*Collected Verse,* Robert Hillyer
1966	*Selected Poems,* Richard Eberhart	1933	*Conquistador,* Archibald MacLeish
1965	*77 Dream Songs,* John Berryman	1932	*The Flowering Stone,* George Dillon
1964	*At the End of the Open Road,* Louis Simpson	1931	*Collected Poems,* Robert Frost
1963	*Pictures from Breughel,* William Carlos Williams	1930	*Selected Poems,* Conrad Aiken
1962	*Poems,* Alan Dugan	1929	*John Brown's Body,* Stephen Vincent Benét
1961	*Times Three: Selected Verse from Three Decades,* Phyllis McGinley	1928	*Tristram,* Edwin Arlington Robinson
1960	*Heart's Needle,* W. D. Snodgrass	1927	*Fiddler's Farewell,* Leonora Speyer
1959	*Selected Poems 1928–1958,* Stanley Kunitz	1926	*What's O'Clock,* Amy Lowell
1958	*Promises: Poems 1954–1956,* Robert Penn Warren	1925	*The Man Who Died Twice,* Edwin Arlington Robinson
1957	*Things of This World,* Richard Wilbur	1924	*New Hampshire: A Poem with Notes and Grace Notes,* Robert Frost
1956	*Poems, North & South,* Elizabeth Bishop	1923	*The Ballad of the Harp-Weaver and Other Poems,* Edna St. Vincent Millay
1955	*Collected Poems,* Wallace Stevens	1922	*Collected Poems,* Edwin Arlington Robinson
1954	*The Waking,* Theodore Roethke	1921	No award
1953	*Collected Poems 1917–1952,* Archibald MacLeish	1920	No award
1952	*Collected Poems,* Marianne Moore	1919	*Old Road to Paradise,* Margaret Widdemer
1951	*Complete Poems,* Carl Sandburg		*Corn Huskers,* Carl Sandburg
1950	*Annie Allen,* Gwendolyn Brooks	1918	*Love Songs,* Sara Teasdale
1949	*Terror and Decorum,* Peter Viereck		
1948	*The Age of Anxiety,* W. H. Auden		
1947	*Lord Weary's Castle,* Robert Lowell		

PULITZER PRIZE FOR DRAMA

Awarded annually by Columbia University in New York for a distinguished dramatic work by an American playwright.

2001   *Proof*, David Auburn

2000   *Dinner with Friends*, Donald Margulies

1999   *Wit*, Margaret Edson

1998   *How I Learned to Drive*, Paula Vogel

1997   No award

1996   *Rent*, book, music, and lyrics by Jonathan Larson

1995   *The Young Man from Atlanta*, Horton Foote

1994   *Three Tall Women*, Edward Albee

1993   *Angels in America: Millennium Approaches*, Tony Kushner

1992   *The Kentucky Cycle*, Robert Schenkkan

1991   *Lost in Yonkers*, Neil Simon

1990   *The Piano Lesson*, August Wilson

1989   *The Heidi Chronicles*, Wendy Wasserstein

1988   *Driving Miss Daisy*, Alfred Uhry

1987   *Fences*, August Wilson

1986   No award

1985   *Sunday in the Park with George*, music and lyrics by Stephen Sondheim; book by James Lapine

1984   *Glengarry Glen Ross*, David Mamet

1983   *'night, Mother*, Marsha Norman

1982   *A Soldier's Play*, Charles Fuller

1981   *Crimes of the Heart*, Beth Henley

1980   *Talley's Folly*, Lanford Wilson

1979   *Buried Child*, Sam Shepard

1978   *The Gin Game*, Donald L. Coburn

1977   *The Shadow Box*, Michael Cristofer

1976   *A Chorus Line*, conceived, choreographed, and directed by Michael Bennett; book by James Kirkwood and Nicholas Dante; music by Marvin Hamlisch and lyrics by Edward Kleban

1975   *Seascape*, Edward Albee

1974   No award

1973   *That Championship Season*, Jason Miller

1972   No award

1971   *The Effect of Gamma Rays on Man-in-the-Moon Marigolds*, Paul Zindel

1970   *No Place to Be Somebody*, Charles Gordone

1969   *The Great White Hope*, Howard Sackler

1968   No award

1967   *A Delicate Balance*, Edward Albee

1966   No award

1965   *The Subject Was Roses*, Frank D. Gilroy

1964   No award

1963   No award

1962   *How to Succeed in Business Without Really Trying*, music and lyrics by Frank Loesser; book by Abe Burrows

1961   *All the Way Home*, Tad Mosel

1960   *Fiorello!*, book by Jerome Weidman and George Abbott; music by Jerry Bock; lyrics by Sheldon Harnick

1959   *J.B.*, Archibald MacLeish

1958   *Look Homeward, Angel*, Ketti Frings

1957   *Long Day's Journey into Night*, Eugene O'Neill

1956   *The Diary of Anne Frank*, Albert Hackett and Frances Goodrich

1955   *Cat on a Hot Tin Roof*, Tennessee Williams

1954   *The Teahouse of the August Moon*, John Patrick

1953   *Picnic*, William Inge

1952   *The Shrike*, Joseph Kramm

1951   No award

1950   *South Pacific*, music by Richard Rodgers; book by Oscar Hammerstein II and Joshua Logan; lyrics by Hammerstein

1949   *Death of a Salesman*, Arthur Miller

1948	*A Streetcar Named Desire*, Tennessee Williams
1947	No award
1946	*State of the Union*, Russel Crouse and Howard Lindsay
1945	*Harvey*, Mary Chase
1944	No award
1943	*The Skin of Our Teeth*, Thornton Wilder
1942	No award
1941	*There Shall Be No Night*, Robert E. Sherwood
1940	*The Time of Your Life*, William Saroyan
1939	*Abe Lincoln in Illinois*, Robert E. Sherwood
1938	*Our Town*, Thornton Wilder
1937	*You Can't Take It with You*, Moss Hart and George S. Kaufman
1936	*Idiot's Delight*, Robert E. Sherwood
1935	*The Old Maid*, Zoë Akins
1934	*Men in White*, Sidney Kingsley
1933	*Both Your Houses*, Maxwell Anderson
1932	*Of Thee I Sing*, book by George S. Kaufman and Morrie Ryskind; lyrics by Ira Gershwin
1931	*Alison's House*, Susan Glaspell
1930	*The Green Pastures*, Marc Connelly
1929	*Street Scene*, Elmer L. Rice
1928	*Strange Interlude*, Eugene O'Neill
1927	*In Abraham's Bosom*, Paul Green
1926	*Craig's Wife*, George Kelly
1925	*They Knew What They Wanted*, Sidney Howard
1924	*Hell-Bent Fer Heaven*, Hatcher Hughes
1923	*Icebound*, Owen Davis
1922	*Anna Christie*, Eugene O'Neill
1921	*Miss Lulu Bett*, Zona Gale
1920	*Beyond the Horizon*, Eugene O'Neill
1919	No award
1918	*Why Marry?*, Jesse Lynch Williams

NATIONAL BOOK AWARD FOR FICTION

Awarded annually, under the auspices of the National Book Foundation, to a work of fiction of the highest quality written by an American and published by an American publisher.

2000	*In America*, Susan Sontag
1999	*Waiting*, Ha Jin
1998	*Charming Billy*, Alice McDermott
1997	*Cold Mountain*, Charles Frazier
1996	*Ship Fever and Other Stories*, Andrea Barrett
1995	*Sabbath's Theater*, Philip Roth
1994	*A Frolic of His Own*, William Gaddis
1993	*The Shipping News*, E. Annie Proulx
1992	*All the Pretty Horses*, Cormac McCarthy
1991	*Mating*, Norman Rush
1990	*The Middle Passage*, Charles Johnson
1989	*Spartina*, John Casey
1988	*Paris Trout*, Pete Dexter
1987	*Paco's Story*, Larry Heinemann
1986	*World's Fair*, E. L. Doctorow
1985	*White Noise*, Don DeLillo
1984	*Victory over Japan*, Ellen Gilchrist
1983	*The Color Purple*, Alice Walker
1982	*Rabbit Is Rich*, John Updike
1981	*Plains Song*, Wright Morris
1980	*Sophie's Choice*, William Styron
1979	*Going After Cacciato*, Tim O'Brien
1978	*Blood Ties*, Mary Lee Settle
1977	*The Spectator Bird*, Wallace Stegner
1976	*J.R.*, William Gaddis
1975	*Dog Soldiers*, Robert Stone
	The Hair of Harold Roux, Thomas Williams
1974	*Gravity's Rainbow*, Thomas Pynchon
	A Crown of Feathers and Other Stories, Isaac Bashevis Singer
1973	*Chimera*, John Barth
1972	*The Complete Stories of Flannery O'Connor*, Flannery O'Connor

(*National Book Award for Fiction, continued*)

1971	*Mr. Sammler's Planet*, Saul Bellow
1970	*them*, Joyce Carol Oates
1969	*Steps*, Jerzy Kosinski
1968	*The Eighth Day*, Thornton Wilder
1967	*The Fixer*, Bernard Malamud
1966	*The Collected Stories of Katherine Anne Porter*, Katherine Anne Porter
1965	*Herzog*, Saul Bellow
1964	*The Centaur*, John Updike
1963	*Morte D'Urban*, J. F. Powers
1962	*The Moviegoer*, Walker Percy
1961	*The Waters of Kronos*, Conrad Richter
1960	*Goodbye, Columbus*, Philip Roth
1959	*The Magic Barrel*, Bernard Malamud
1958	*The Wapshot Chronicle*, John Cheever
1957	*Field of Vision*, Wright Morris
1956	*Ten North Frederick*, John O'Hara
1955	*A Fable*, William Faulkner
1954	*The Adventures of Augie March*, Saul Bellow
1953	*Invisible Man*, Ralph Ellison
1952	*From Here to Eternity*, James Jones
1951	*The Collected Stories of William Faulkner*, William Faulkner
1950	*The Man with the Golden Arm*, Nelson Algren

NATIONAL BOOK AWARD FOR POETRY

Awarded annually, under the auspices of the National Book Foundation, to a volume of poetry of the highest quality written by an American and published by an American publisher.

2000	*Blessing the Boats: New and Selected Poems 1998–2000*, Lucille Clifton
1999	*Vice: New & Selected Poems*, Ai
1998	*This Time: New and Selected Poems*, Gerald Stern
1997	*Effort at Speech: New & Selected Poems*, William Meredith
1996	*Scrambled Eggs & Whiskey*, Hayden Carruth
1995	*Passing Through: The Later Poems*, Stanley Kunitz
1994	*A Worshipful Company of Fletchers*, James Tate
1993	*Garbage*, A. R. Ammons
1992	*New & Selected Poems*, Mary Oliver
1991	*What Work Is*, Philip Levine
1984–90	No award
1983	*Selected Poems*, Galway Kinnell
1982	*Life Supports: New and Collected Poems*, William Bronk
1981	*The Need to Hold Still*, Lisel Mueller
1980	*Ashes*, Philip Levine
1979	*Mirabell: Book of Numbers*, James Merrill
1978	*The Collected Poems of Howard Nemerov*, Howard Nemerov
1977	*Collected Poems, 1930–1976*, Richard Eberhart
1976	*Self-Portrait in a Convex Mirror*, John Ashbery
1975	*Presentation Piece*, Marilyn Hacker
1974	*The Fall of America: Poems of These States*, Allen Ginsberg
	Driving into the Wreck: Poems 1971–1972, Adrienne Rich
1973	*Collected Poems, 1951–1971*, A. R. Ammons
1972	*Selected Poems*, Howard Moss
	The Collected Poems of Frank O'Hara, Frank O'Hara
1971	*To See, To Take*, Mona Van Duyn
1970	*The Complete Poems*, Elizabeth Bishop
1969	*His Toy, His Dream, His Rest*, John Berryman
1968	*The Light Around the Body*, Robert Bly
1967	*Nights and Days*, James Merrill
1966	*Buckdancer's Choice: Poems*, James Dickey
1965	*The Far Field*, Theodore Roethke

1964	*Selected Poems*, John Crowe Ransom
1963	*Traveling Through the Dark*, William Stafford
1962	*Poems*, Alan Dugan
1961	*The Woman at the Washington Zoo*, Randall Jarrell
1960	*Life Studies*, Robert Lowell
1959	*Words for the Wind*, Theodore Roethke
1958	*Promises: Poems, 1954–1956*, Robert Penn Warren
1957	*Things of the World*, Richard Wilbur
1956	*The Shield of Achilles*, W. H. Auden
1955	*The Collected Poems of Wallace Stevens*, Wallace Stevens
1954	*Collected Poems*, Conrad Aiken
1953	*Collected Poems*, Archibald MacLeish
1952	*Collected Poems, 1917–1952*, Marianne Moore
1951	*The Auroras of Autumn*, Wallace Stevens
1950	*Paterson*, Book III and *Selected Poems*, William Carlos Williams

THE NATIONAL BOOK CRITICS CIRCLE FICTION AWARD

Awarded by the National Book Critics Circle (consisting of more than 700 book reviewers) for the year's best work of fiction.

2000	*Being Dead*, Jim Crace
1999	*Motherless Brooklyn*, Jonathan Lethem
1998	*The Love of a Good Woman*, Alice Munro
1997	*The Blue Flower*, Penelope Fitzgerald
1996	*Women in Their Beds*, Gina Berriault
1995	*Mrs. Ted Bliss*, Stanley Elkin
1994	*The Stone Diaries*, Carol Shields
1993	*A Lesson Before Dying*, Ernest J. Gaines
1992	*All the Pretty Horses*, Cormac McCarthy

1991	*A Thousand Acres*, Jane Smiley
1990	*Rabbit at Rest*, John Updike
1989	*Billy Bathgate*, E. L. Doctorow
1988	*The Middleman and Other Stories*, Bharati Mukherjee
1987	*The Counterlife*, Philip Roth
1986	*Kate Vaiden*, Reynolds Price
1985	*The Accidental Tourist*, Anne Tyler
1984	*Love Medicine*, Louise Erdrich
1983	*Ironweed*, William Kennedy
1982	*George Mills*, Stanley Elkin
1981	*Rabbit Is Rich*, John Updike
1980	*The Transit of Venus*, Shirley Hazzard
1979	*The Year of the French*, Thomas Flanagan
1978	*The Stories of John Cheever*, John Cheever
1977	*Song of Solomon*, Toni Morrison
1976	*October Light*, John Gardner
1975	*Ragtime*, E. L. Doctorow

THE NATIONAL BOOK CRITICS CIRCLE POETRY AWARD

Awarded by the National Book Critics Circle (consisting of more than 700 book reviewers) for the year's best volume of poetry.

2000	*Carolina Ghost Woods*, Judy Jordan
1999	*Ordinary Words*, Ruth Stone
1998	*The Bird Catcher*, Marie Ponsot
1997	*Black Zodiac*, Charles Wright
1996	*Sun Under Wood*, Robert Hass
1995	*Time and Money*, William Matthews
1994	*Rider*, Mark Rudman
1993	*My Alexandria*, Mark Doty
1992	*Collected Shorter Poems 1946–1991*, Hayden Carruth
1991	*Heaven and Earth: A Cosmology*, Albert Goldbarth
1990	*Bitter Angel*, Amy Gerstler
1989	*Transparent Gestures*, Rodney Jones
1988	*The One Day*, Donald Hall

(*National Book Critics Circle Poetry Award, continued*)

1987 *Flesh and Blood*, C. K. Williams

1986 *Wild Gratitude*, Edward Hirsch

1985 *The Triumph of Achilles*, Louise Glück

1984 *The Dead and the Living*, Sharon Olds

1983 *The Changing Light at Sandover*, James Merrill

1982 *Antarctic Traveler*, Katha Pollitt

1981 *A Coast of Trees*, A. R. Ammons

1980 *Sunrise*, Frederick Seidel

1979 *Ashes: Poems New and Old*, Philip Levine

1978 *Hello Darkness: The Collected Poems of L. E. Sissman*, L. E. Sissman

1977 *Day by Day*, Robert Lowell

1976 *Geography III*, Elizabeth Bishop

1975 *Self-Portrait in a Convex Mirror*, John Ashbery

THE BOOKER PRIZE FOR FICTION

Awarded annually by the Booker McConnell company for a full-length novel by an English-language writer from the United Kingdom, the Commonwealth countries, the Republic of Ireland, or South Africa.

2000 *The Blind Assassin*, Margaret Atwood

1999 *Disgrace*, J. M. Coetzee

1998 *Amsterdam*, Ian McEwan

1997 *The God of Small Things*, Arundhati Roy

1996 *Last Orders*, Graham Swift

1995 *The Ghost Road*, Pat Barker

1994 *How Late It Was, How Late*, James Kelman

1993 *Paddy Clark Ha Ha Ha*, Roddy Doyle

1992 *The English Patient*, Michael Ondaatje

Sacred Hunger, Barry Unsworth

1991 *The Famished Road*, Ben Okri

1990 *Possession*, A. S. Byatt

1989 *The Remains of the Day*, Kazuo Ishiguro

1988 *Oscar and Lucinda*, Peter Carey

1987 *Moon Tiger*, Penelope Lively

1986 *The Old Devils*, Kingsley Amis

1985 *The Bone People*, Keri Hulme

1984 *Hotel du Lac*, Anita Brookner

1983 *Life and Times of Michael K*, J. M. Coetzee

1982 *Schindler's Ark*, Thomas Keneally

1981 *Midnight's Children*, Salman Rushdie

1980 *Rites of Passage*, William Golding

1979 *Offshore*, Penelope Fitzgerald

1978 *The Sea, the Sea*, Iris Murdoch

1977 *Staying On*, Paul Scott

1976 *Saville*, David Storey

1975 *Heat and Dust*, Ruth Prawer Jhabvala

1974 *The Conservationist*, Nadine Gordimer

Holiday, Stanley Middleton

1973 *The Siege of Krishnapur*, J. G. Farrell

1972 *G*, John Berger

1971 *In a Free State*, V. S. Naipaul

1970 *The Elected Member*, Bernice Rubens

1969 *Something to Answer For*, P. H. Newby

THE WHITBREAD AWARD FOR THE BEST BRITISH NOVEL

Sponsored by Whitbread PLC, the annual Whitbread Book Awards honor the best of contemporary British writing. The winner of the Whitbread Book of the Year Award—first presented in 1980 and given annually since 1985—is chosen from among the winners of the Poetry, Biography, First Novel, and Novel Awards. (A Whitbread Book of the Year is indicated by an asterisk.)

2000 *English Passengers*, Matthew Kneale*

1999 *Music and Silence*, Rose Tremain

1998 *Leading the Cheers*, Justin Cartwright

1997	*Quarantine*, Jim Crace
1996	*Every Man for Himself*, Beryl Bainbridge
1995	*The Moor's Last Sigh*, Salman Rushdie
1994	*Felicia's Journey*, William Trevor*
1993	*Theory of War*, Joan Brady*
1992	*Poor Things*, Alasdair Gray
1991	*The Queen of the Tambourine*, Jane Gardam
1990	*Hopeful Monsters*, Nicholas Mosley*
1989	*The Chymical Wedding*, Lindsay Clarke
1988	*The Satanic Verses*, Salman Rushdie
1987	*The Child in Time*, Ian McEwan
1986	*An Artist of the Floating World*, Kazuo Ishiguro*
1985	*Hawksmoor*, Peter Ackroyd
1984	*Kruger's Alp*, Christopher Hope
1983	*Fools of Fortune*, William Trevor
1982	*Young Shoulders*, John Wain
1981	*Silver's City*, Maurice Leitch
1980	*How Far Can You Go?*, David Lodge*
1979	*The Old Jest*, Jennifer Johnston
1978	*Picture Palace*, Paul Theroux
1977	*Injury Time*, Beryl Bainbridge
1976	*The Children of Dynmouth*, William Trevor
1975	*Docherty*, William McIlvanney
1974	*The Sacred & Profane Love Machine*, Iris Murdoch
1973	*The Chip-Chip Gatherers*, Shiva Naipaul
1972	*The Bird of Night*, Susan Hill
1971	*The Destiny Waltz*, Gerda Charles

THE WHITBREAD AWARD FOR FIRST NOVEL

Sponsored by Whitbread PLC, the annual Whitbread Book Awards honor the best of contemporary British writing. The winner of the Whitbread Book of the Year Award—first presented in 1980 and given annually since 1985—is chosen from among the winners of the Poetry, Biography, First Novel, and Novel Awards. (A Whitbread Book of the Year is indicated by an asterisk.)

2000	*White Teeth*, Zadie Smith
1999	*White City Blue*, Tim Lott
1998	*The Last King of Scotland*, Giles Foden
1997	*The Ventriloquist's Tale*, Pauline Melville
1996	*The Debt to Pleasure*, John Lanchester
1995	*Behind the Scenes at the Museum*, Kate Atkinson*
1994	*The Longest Memory*, Fred D'Aguiar
1993	*Saving Agnes*, Rachel Cusk
1992	*Swing Hammer Swing!*, Jeff Torrington*
1991	*Alma Cogan*, Gordon Burn
1990	*The Buddha of Suburbia*, Hanif Kureishi
1989	*Gerontius*, James Hamilton-Paterson
1988	*The Comforts of Madness*, Paul Sayer*
1987	*The Other Garden*, Francis Wyndham
1986	*Continent*, Jim Crace
1985	*Oranges Are Not the Only Fruit*, Jeanette Winterson
1984	*A Parish of Rich Women*, James Buchan
1983	*Flying to Nowhere*, John Fuller
1982	*On the Black Hill*, Bruce Chatwin
1981	*A Good Man in Africa*, William Boyd

THE WHITBREAD AWARD FOR POETRY

Sponsored by Whitbread PLC, the annual Whitbread Book Awards honor the best of contemporary British writing. The Whitbread Award for Poetry was presented for the first time in 1971 and has been awarded annually since 1985. The winner of the Whitbread Book of the Year Award—first presented in 1980 and given annually since 1985—is chosen from among the winners of the Poetry, Biography, First Novel, and Novel Awards. (A Whitbread Book of the Year is indicated by an asterisk.)

2000	*The Asylum Dance*, John Burnside
1999	*Beowulf*, Seamus Heaney*
1998	*Birthday Letters*, Ted Hughes*
1997	*Tales from Ovid*, Ted Hughes*
1996	*The Spirit Level*, Seamus Heaney*
1995	*Gunpowder*, Bernard O'Donoghue
1994	*Out of Danger*, James Fenton
1993	*Mean Time*, Carol Ann Duffy
1992	*The Gaze of the Gorgon*, Tony Harrison
1991	*Gorse Fires*, Michael Longley
1990	*Daddy, Daddy*, Paul Durcan
1989	*Shibboleth*, Michael Donaghy
1988	*The Automatic Oracle*, Peter Porter
1987	*The Haw Lantern*, Seamus Heaney
1986	*Stet*, Peter Reading
1985	*Elegies*, Douglas Dunn*
1972–84	No award
1971	*Mercian Hymns*, Geoffrey Hill

PRIX GONCOURT

The major French literary award, bestowed by the ten-member Académie Goncourt, for an outstanding work of imaginative prose published during the year.

2000	*Ingrid Caven*, Jean-Jacques Schuhl
1999	*Je m'en Vais*, Jean Echenoz
1998	*Confidence pour Confidence*, Paule Constant
1997	*La Bataille*, Patrick Rambaud
1996	*Le Chasseur Zéro*, Pascale Roze
1995	*Le Testament Français*, Andrei Makine
1994	*Un Aller Simple*, Didier Van Cauwelaert
1993	*Le Rocher de Tanios*, Amin Maalouf
1992	*Texaco*, Patrick Chamoiseau
1991	*Les Filles du Calvaire*, Pierre Combescot
1990	*Les Champs d'Honneur*, Jean Rouaud
1989	*Un Grand Pas vers le Bon Dieu*, Jean Vautrin
1988	*L'Exposition Coloniale*, Erik Orsenna
1987	*La Nuit Sacrée*, Tahar Ben Jelloun
1986	*Valet de Nuit*, Michel Host
1985	*Les Noces Barbares*, Yann Queffélec
1984	*L'Amant*, Marguerite Duras
1983	*Les Égarés*, Frédérick Tristan
1982	*Dans la Main de l'Ange*, Dominique Fernandez
1981	*Anne Marie*, Lucien Bodard
1980	*Le Jardin d'Acclimatation*, Yves Navarre
1979	*Pélagie-la-Charrette*, Antonine Maillet
1978	*Rue des Boutiques Obscures*, Patrick Modiano
1977	*John l'Enfer*, Didier Decoin
1976	*Les Flamboyants*, Patrick Grainville
1975	*La Vie Devant Soi*, Emile Ajar, pseudonym of Romain Gary
1974	*La Dentellière*, Pascal Lainé
1973	*L'Ogre*, Jacques Chessex
1972	*L'Épervier de Maheux*, Jean Carrière
1971	*Les Bêtises*, Jacques Laurent
1970	*Le Roi des Aulnes*, Michel Tournier
1969	*Creezy*, Félicien Marceau
1968	*Les Fruits de l'Hiver*, Bernard Clavel
1967	*La Marge*, André Pieyre de Mandiargues
1966	*Oublier Palerme*, Edmonde Charles-Roux
1965	*L'Adoration*, Jacques Borel
1964	*L'État Sauvage*, Georges Conchon

1963	*Quand la Mer se Retire*, Armand Lanoux
1962	*Les Bagages de Sable*, Anna Langfus
1961	*La Pitié de Dieu*, Jean Cau
1960	*Dieu Est Né en Exil*, Vintila Horia
1959	*Le Dernier des Justes*, André Schwarz-Bart
1958	*Saint-Germain ou La Négociation*, Francis Walder
1957	*La Loi*, Roger Vailland
1956	*Les Racines du Ciel*, Romain Gary
1955	*Les Eaux Mêlées*, Roger Ikor
1954	*Les Mandarins*, Simone de Beauvoir
1953	*Les Bêtes*, Pierre Gascar
1952	*Léon Morin, Prêtre*, Béatrice Beck
1951	*Le Rivage des Syrtes*, Julien Gracq
1950	*Les Jeux Sauvages*, Paul Colin
1949	*Week-End à Zuydcoote*, Robert Merle
1948	*Les Grandes Familles*, Maurice Druon
1947	*Les Forêts de la Nuit*, Jean-Louis Curtis
1946	*Histoire d'un Fait Divers*, Jean-Jacques Gautier
1945	*Mon Village à l'Heure Allemande*, Jean-Louis Bory
1944	*Le Premier Accroc Coûte Deux Cents Francs*, Elsa Triolet
1943	*Passage de l'Homme*, Marius Grout
1942	*Pareils à des Enfants*, Marc Bernard
1941	*Le Vent de Mars*, Henri Pourrat
1940	*Les Grandes Vacances*, Francis Ambrière
1939	*Les Enfants Gâtés*, Philippe Hériat
1938	*L'Araigne*, Henri Troyat
1937	*Faux Passeports*, Charles Plisnier
1936	*L'Empreinte du Dieu*, Maxence Van Der Meersch
1935	*Sang et Lumières*, Joseph Peyré
1934	*Capitaine Conan*, Roger Vercel
1933	*La Condition Humaine*, André Malraux
1932	*Les Loups*, Guy Mazeline
1931	*Mal d'Amour*, Jean Fayard

1930	*Malaisie*, Henri Fauconnier
1929	*L'Ordre*, Marcel Arland
1928	*Un Homme se Penche sur Son Passé*, Maurice Constantin-Weyer
1927	*Jérôme, 60° Latitude Nord*, Maurice Bedel
1926	*Le Supplice de Phèdre*, Henri Deberly
1925	*Raboliot*, Maurice Genevoix
1924	*Le Chèvrefeuille*, Thierry Sandre
1923	*Rabevel ou Le Mal des Ardents*, Lucien Fabre
1922	*Le Vitriol de Lune*, Henri Béraud
1921	*Batouala*, René Maran
1920	*Nène*, Ernest Pérochon
1919	*À l'Ombre des Jeunes Filles en Fleurs*, Marcel Proust
1918	*Civilisation*, Georges Duhamel
1917	*La Flamme au Poing*, Henri Malherbe
1916	*Le Feu*, Henri Barbusse
1915	*Gaspard*, René Benjamin
1914	*L'Appel du Sol*, Adrien Bertrand
1913	*Le Peuple de la Mer*, Marc Elder
1912	*Les Filles de la Pluie*, André Savignon
1911	*Monsieur des Lourdines*, Alphonse de Châteaubriant
1910	*De Goupil à Margot*, Louis Pergaud
1909	*En France*, Marius-Ary Leblond
1908	*Écrit sur l'Eau*, Francis de Miomandre and François Durand
1907	*Terres Lorraines*, Émile Moselly
1906	*Dingley l'Illustre Écrivain*, Jérôme and Jean Tharaud
1905	*Les Civilisés*, Claude Farrère
1904	*La Maternelle*, Léon Frapié
1903	*La Force Ennemie*, John-Antoine Nau

PEN / BOOK-OF-THE-MONTH CLUB TRANSLATION PRIZE

Awarded annually for a distinguished book-length translation of a work of literary
character, from any language into English, published in the current calendar
year in the United States by a translator of any nationality.

YEAR	TRANSLATOR	BOOK	AUTHOR
2000	Richard Sieburth	*Selected Writings*	Gérard de Nerval
1999	Michael Hofmann	*The Tale of the 1002nd Night*	Joseph Roth
1998	Peter Constantine	*Six Early Stories*	Thomas Mann
1997	Arnold Pomerans	*The Letters of Vincent Van Gogh*	Vincent Van Gogh
1996	Stanisław Baránczak and Clare Cavanagh	*View with a Grain of Sand*	Wisława Szymborska
1995	Burton Watson	*Selected Poems of Su Tung-p'o*	Su Tung-p'o
1994	Bill Zavatsky and Zack Rogow	*Earthlight*	André Breton
1993	Thomas Hoisington	*The Adventures of Mr. Nicholas Wisdom*	Ignacy Krasicki
1992	David Rosenberg	*The Poet's Bible*	
1991	Richard Pevear and Larissa Volokhonsky	*The Brothers Karamazov*	Fyodor Dostoyevsky
1990	William Weaver	*Foucault's Pendulum*	Umberto Eco
1989	Matthew Ward	*The Stranger*	Albert Camus
1988	Madeline Levine and Francine Prose	*A Scrap of Time*	Ida Fink
1987	John E. Woods	*Perfume: The Story of a Murderer*	Patrick Süskind
1986	Prose: Barbara Bray	*The Lover*	Marguerite Duras
	Poetry: Dennis Tedlock	*Popul Vuh: The Mayan Book of the Dawn of Life*	
1985	Prose: Helen R. Lane	*The War at the End of the World*	Mario Vargas Llosa
	Poetry: Seamus Heaney	*Sweeney Astray: A Version from the Irish*	Seamus Heaney
1984	William Weaver	*The Name of the Rose*	Umberto Eco
1983	Richard Wilbur	*Four Comedies: The Misanthrope, Tartuffe, The Learned Ladies, The School for Wives*	Molière
1982	Hiroaki Sato and Burton Watson	*From the Country of Eight Islands: An Anthology of Japanese Poetry*	
1981	John E. Woods	*Evening Edged in Gold*	Arno Schmidt
1980	Charles Simic	*Homage to the Lame Wolf*	Vasco Popa
1979	Charles Wright	*The Storm and Other Poems*	Eugenio Montale
1978	Adrienne Foulke	*One Way or Another*	Leonardo Sciascia
1977	Gregory Rabassa	*Autumn of the Patriarch*	Gabriel García Márquez
1976	Richard Howard	*A Short History of Decay*	E. M. Cioran

YEAR	TRANSLATOR	BOOK	AUTHOR
1975	Helen R. Lane	*Count Julian*	Juan Goytisolo
1974	Hardie St. Martin and Leonard Mades	*The Obscene Bird of Night*	José Donoso
1973	J. P. McCullough	*The Poems of Sextus Propertius*	Sextus Propertius
1972	Richard and Clara Winston	*Letters of Thomas Mann*	Thomas Mann
1971	Max Hayward	*Hope Against Hope*	Nadezhda Mandelshtam
1970	Sidney Alexander	*The History of Italy*	Francesco Guicciardini
1969	W. S. Merwin	*Selected Translations 1948–1968*	
1968	Vladimir Markov and Merrill Sparks, editors	*Modern Russian Poetry*	
1967	Harriet de Onis	*Sagarana*	João Guimarães Rosa
1966	Geoffrey Skelton and Adrian Mitchell	*Marat/Sade*	Peter Weiss
1965	Joseph Barnes	*The Story of a Life*	Konstantin Paustovsky
1964	Ralph Manheim	*The Tin Drum*	Günter Grass
1963	Archibald Colquhoun	*The Viceroys*	Federico de Roberto

EDGAR ALLAN POE AWARD ("THE EDGAR") FOR BEST MYSTERY NOVEL

Awarded annually by The Mystery Writers of America to honor the best in mystery fiction.

2001 *The Amazing Adventures of Kavalier & Clay*, Michael Chabon

2000 *Bones*, Jan Burke

1999 *Mr. White's Confession*, Robert Clark

1998 *Cimarron Rose*, James Lee Burke

1997 *The Chatham School Affair*, Thomas A. Cook

1996 *Come to Grief*, Dick Francis

1995 *The Red Scream*, Mary Willis Walker

1994 *The Sculptress*, Minette Walters

1993 *Bootlegger's Daughter*, Margaret Maron

1992 *A Dance at the Slaughterhouse*, Lawrence Block

1991 *New Orleans Mourning*, Julie Smith

1990 *Black Cherry Blues*, James Lee Burke

1989 *A Cold Red Sunrise*, Stuart M. Kaminsky

1988 *Old Bones*, Aaron Elkins

1987 *A Dark-adapted Eye*, Barbara Vine

1986 *The Suspect*, L. R. Wright

1985 *Briarpatch*, Ross Thomas

1984 *La Brava*, Elmore Leonard

1983 *Billingsgate Shoal*, Rick Boyer

1982 *Peregrine*, William Bayer

1981 *Whip Hand*, Dick Francis

1980 *The Rheingold Route*, Arthur Mailing

1979 *The Eye of the Needle*, Ken Follett

1978 *Catch Me: Kill Me*, William H. Hallahan

1977 *Promised Land*, Robert B. Parker

1976 *Hopscotch*, Brian Garfield

1975 *Peter's Pence*, Jon Cleary

1974 *Dance Hall of the Dead*, Tony Hillerman

1973 *The Lingala Code*, Warren Kiefer

1972 *The Day of the Jackal*, Frederick Forsyth

1971 *The Laughing Policeman*, Maj Sjöwall and Per Wahlöö

1970 *Forfeit*, Dick Francis

(Edgar Allan Poe Award, continued)

1969 *A Case of Need*, Jeffrey Hudson

1968 *God Save the Mark*, Donald E. Westlake

1967 *The King of the Rainy Country*, Nicolas Freeling

1966 *The Quiller Memorandum*, Adam Hall

1965 *The Spy Who Came In from the Cold*, John le Carré

1964 *The Light of Day*, Eric Ambler

1963 *Death and the Joyful Woman*, Ellis Peters

1962 *Gideon's Fire*, J. J. Marric

1961 *The Progress of a Crime*, Julian Symons

1960 *The Hours Before Dawn*, Celia Fremlin

1959 *The Eighth Circle*, Stanley Ellin

1958 *Room to Swing*, Ed Lacy

1957 *A Dram of Poison*, Charlotte Armstrong

1956 *Beast in View*, Margaret Millar

1955 *The Long Goodbye*, Raymond Chandler

1954 *Beat Not the Bones*, Charlotte Jay

GOLD DAGGER AWARD FOR BEST CRIME NOVEL

Awarded annually by the British Crime Writers' Association.

2000 *Motherless Brooklyn*, Jonathan Lethem

1999 *A Small Death in Lisbon*, Robert Wilson

1998 *Sunset Limited*, James Lee Burke

1997 *Black and Blue*, Ian Rankin

1996 *Popcorn*, Ben Elton

1995 *The Mermaids Singing*, Val McDermid

1994 *The Scold's Bridle*, Minette Walters

1993 *Cruel and Unusual*, Patricia Cornwell

1992 *The Way Through the Woods*, Colin Dexter

1991 *King Solomon's Carpet*, Barbara Vine

1990 *Bones and Silence*, Reginald Hill

1989 *The Wench Is Dead*, Colin Dexter

1988 *Ratking*, Michael Dibdin

1987 *A Fatal Inversion*, Barbara Vine

1986 *Live Flesh*, Ruth Rendell

1985 *Monkey Puzzle*, Paula Gosling

1984 *The Twelfth Juror*, B. M. Gill

1983 *Accidental Crimes*, John Hutton

1982 *The False Inspector Dew*, Peter Lovesey

1981 *Gorky Park*, Martin Cruz Smith

1980 *The Murder of the Maharajah*, H. R. F. Keating

1979 *Whip Hand*, Dick Francis

1978 *The Chelsea Murders*, Lionel Davidson

1977 *The Honourable Schoolboy*, John le Carré

1976 *A Demon in My View*, Ruth Rendell

1975 *The Seven Per Cent Solution*, Nicholas Meyer

1974 *Other Paths to Glory*, Anthony Price

1973 *The Defection of A. J. Lewinter*, Robert Littell

1972 *The Levanter*, Eric Ambler

1971 *The Steam Pig*, James McClure

1970 *Young Man I Think You're Dying*, Joan Fleming

1969 *A Pride of Heroes*, Peter Dickinson

1968 *Skin Deep*, Peter Dickinson

1967 *Murder Against the Grain*, Emma Lathen

1966 *A Long Way to Shiloh*, Lionel Davidson

1965 *The Far Side of the Dollar*, Ross Macdonald

1964 *The Perfect Murder*, H. R. F. Keating

1963 *The Spy Who Came In from the Cold*, John le Carré

1962 *When I Grow Rich*, Joan Fleming

1961 *The Spoilt Kill*, Mary Kelly

1960 *The Night of Wenceslas*, Lionel Davidson

1959 *Passage of Arms*, Eric Ambler

1958 *Someone from the Past*, Margot Bennett

1957 *The Colour of Murder*, Julian Symons

1956 *The Second Man*, Edward Grierson

1955 *The Little Walls*, Winston Graham

NEBULA AWARD FOR BEST SCIENCE FICTION / FANTASY NOVEL

Awarded by the Science Fiction and Fantasy Writers of America, Inc., for the best science fiction or fantasy novel of the year.

2000	*Darwin's Radio*, Greg Bear
1999	*Parable of the Talents*, Octavia E. Butler
1998	*Forever Peace*, Joe Haldeman
1997	*The Moon and the Sun*, Vonda N. McIntyre
1996	*Slow River*, Nicola Griffith
1995	*The Terminal Experiment*, Robert J. Sawyer
1994	*Moving Mars*, Greg Bear
1993	*Red Mars*, Kim Stanley Robinson
1992	*Doomsday Book*, Connie Willis
1991	*Stations of the Tide*, Michael Swanwick
1990	*Tehanu: The Last Book of Earthsea*, Ursula K. Le Guin
1989	*The Healer's War*, Elizabeth Ann Scarborough
1988	*Falling Free*, Lois McMaster Bujold
1987	*The Falling Woman*, Pat Murphy
1986	*Speaker for the Dead*, Orson Scott Card
1985	*Ender's Game*, Orson Scott Card
1984	*Neuromancer*, William Gibson
1983	*Startide Rising*, David Brin
1982	*No Enemy But Time*, Michael Bishop
1981	*The Claw of the Conciliator*, Gene Wolfe
1980	*Timescape*, Gregory Benford
1979	*The Fountains of Paradise*, Arthur C. Clarke
1978	*Dreamsnake*, Vonda N. McIntyre
1977	*Gateway*, Frederik Pohl
1976	*Man Plus*, Frederik Pohl
1975	*The Forever War*, Joe Haldeman
1974	*The Dispossessed*, Ursula K. Le Guin
1973	*Rendezvous with Rama*, Arthur C. Clarke
1972	*The Gods Themselves*, Isaac Asimov
1971	*A Time of Changes*, Robert Silverberg
1970	*Ringworld*, Larry Niven
1969	*The Left Hand of Darkness*, Ursula K. Le Guin
1968	*Rite of Passage*, Alexei Panshin
1967	*The Einstein Intersection*, Samuel R. Delany
1966	*Babel-17*, Samuel R. Delany
	Flowers for Algernon, Daniel Keyes
1965	*Dune*, Frank Herbert

THE HUGO AWARD FOR BEST SCIENCE FICTION NOVEL (A.K.A. THE SCIENCE FICTION ACHIEVEMENT AWARD)

Awarded annually by the World Science Fiction Society.

2000	*A Deepness in the Sky*, Vernor Vinge
1999	*To Say Nothing of the Dog*, Connie Willis
1998	*Forever Peace*, Joe Haldeman
1997	*Blue Mars*, Kim Stanley Robinson
1996	*The Diamond Age*, Neal Stephenson
1995	*Mirror Dance*, Lois McMaster Bujold
1994	*Green Mars*, Kim Stanley Robinson
1993	*A Fire Upon the Deep*, Vernor Vinge
	Doomsday Book, Connie Willis
1992	*Barrayar*, Lois McMaster Bujold
1991	*The Vor Game*, Lois McMaster Bujold
1990	*Hyperion*, Dan Simmons
1989	*Cyteen*, C. J. Cherryh
1988	*The Uplift War*, David Brin
1987	*Speaker for the Dead*, Orson Scott Card
1986	*Ender's Game*, Orson Scott Card
1985	*Neuromancer*, William Gibson
1984	*Startide Rising*, David Brin
1983	*Foundation's Edge*, Isaac Asimov

(Hugo Award, continued)

1982   *Downbelow Station*, C. J. Cherryh

1981   *The Snow Queen*, Joan D. Vinge

1980   *The Fountains of Paradise*, Arthur C. Clarke

1979   *Dreamsnake*, Vonda McIntyre

1978   *Gateway*, Frederik Pohl

1977   *Where Late the Sweet Birds Sang*, Kate Wilhelm

1976   *The Forever War*, Joe Haldeman

1975   *The Dispossessed*, Ursula K. Le Guin

1974   *Rendezvous with Rama*, Arthur C. Clarke

1973   *The Gods Themselves*, Isaac Asimov

1972   *To Your Scattered Bodies Go*, Philip José Farmer

1971   *Ringworld*, Larry Niven

1970   *The Left Hand of Darkness*, Ursula K. Le Guin

1969   *Stand on Zanzibar*, John Brunner

1968   *Lord of Light*, Roger Zelazny

1967   *The Moon Is a Harsh Mistress*, Robert A. Heinlein

1966   *...And Call Me Conrad*, Roger Zelazny

      Dune, Frank Herbert

1965   *The Wanderer*, Fritz Leiber

1964   *Way Station*, Clifford D. Simak

1963   *The Man in the High Castle*, Philip K. Dick

1962   *Stranger in a Strange Land*, Robert A. Heinlein

1961   *A Canticle for Leibowitz*, Walter M. Miller, Jr.

1960   *Starship Troopers*, Robert A. Heinlein

1959   *A Case of Conscience*, James Blish

1958   *The Big Time*, Fritz Leiber

1957   No award

1956   *Double Star*, Robert A. Heinlein

1955   *They'd Rather Be Right*, Mark Clifton

1954   No award

1953   *The Demolished Man*, Alfred Bester

Influential
Literary Periodicals

The following list identifies periodicals from around the world (but primarily from America and Great Britain) that have had, since the 17th century, an important influence on literary life. Longevity characterizes many of them, but some with the longest runs achieved distinction or influence during specific periods, and then declined in importance or were suppressed. A few journals on the list existed only briefly, but are included because they were groundbreaking, or interesting enough to have become legendary. Entries include dates, places, and frequency of publication; notes on first and subsequent notable editors, contributors, and editorial character; and, whenever possible, sources for further reading.

AMERICAN MERCURY, THE (1924–80, New York). Monthly founded by H. L. Mencken and George Jean Nathan, "to attempt a realistic presentation of the whole gaudy, gorgeous American scene." Edited by Mencken 1924–33, with Nathan 1924–25, it published fiction, skeptical critical commentary, and satirical essays by an array of celebrated contributors, including Dreiser, O'Neill, Sherwood Anderson, Sandburg, Sinclair Lewis, and Edgar Lee Masters. In 1952, after several changes in ownership, it became a right-wing journal published in California with no connection to the original. See *The American Mercury Reader* (1944), *H. L. Mencken and the American Mercury Adventure* by Marvin Singleton (1962), and *My Life as an Author and Editor* by H. L. Mencken (1993).

ATHENAEUM, THE (1828–1921, London). Subtitled "A Journal of Literature, Science, the Fine Arts, Music, and the Drama." Weekly literary and critical journal, founded by James S. Buckingham. Among the 19th-century contributors were Robert Browning, Thomas Carlyle, Thomas Hood, Charles Lamb, and Walter Pater; in the 20th century, Max Beerbohm, T. S. Eliot, Robert Graves, Thomas Hardy, Katherine Mansfield, John Middleton Murry, Edith Sitwell, and Virginia Woolf. After 1921, *The Athenaeum* merged with *The Nation*, as *The Nation and Athenaeum*; in 1931, that journal was absorbed by *The New Statesman*.

ATLANTIC MONTHLY, THE (1857–present, Boston). Monthly journal of literature and opinion, publishing literature (including serialized novels) and literary criticism as well as political commentary, with a regional emphasis at first. Founded by Moses Dresser Phillips and Francis H. Underwood. Subsequent notable editors included James Russell Lowell (1857–61) and William Dean Howells (1871–81). Among contributors were Ralph Waldo Emerson, Henry Wadsworth Longfellow, and Oliver Wendell Holmes, and later Henry James, Francis Parkman, and Sarah Orne Jewett, to name a few. *The Atlantic* endures as a respected journal of literature and contemporary affairs. See *Jubilee* (1957), an anthology of its first century, and *The Atlantic Monthly, 1857–1909: Yankee Humanism at High Tide and Ebb* by Ellery Sedgwick (1994).

BELL, THE (1940–54, Dublin). Monthly that aimed to present "the best work of Irish writers," and that became an important intellectual journal. Founded by Sean O'Faolain, its editor until 1946, it carried new fiction, poetry, plays, reminiscences, and reviews, especially those with some reflection on being Irish. Some of the celebrated writers who appeared in its pages were Frank O'Connor, Elizabeth Bowen, Jack Butler Yeats, Flann O'Brien, Brendan Behan, Louis MacNeice, G. B. Shaw, Sean O'Casey, and O'Faolain. See *The Best from "The Bell": Great Irish Writing*, ed. by Sean MacMahon (1978).

BLACK MOUNTAIN REVIEW, THE (1954–57, Black Mountain, N.C.). Quarterly founded by Robert Creeley and Charles Olson. A widely influential forum for avant-garde American poetry, especially as practiced by the poets Robert Creeley, Robert Duncan, and Charles Olson while they were teaching at Black Mountain College in North Carolina. In addition to the above, it featured the work of such writers as William Carlos Williams, Paul Blackburn, Denise Levertov, Allen Ginsberg, Gary Snyder, Jack Kerouac, and Louis Zukofsky. See *Black Mountain: An Exploration in Community* by Martin Duberman (1972).

BLACKWOOD'S EDINBURGH MAGAZINE (1817–1980, Edinburgh). Monthly, referred to familiarly as "the Maga." It started as *Edinburgh Monthly Magazine* in 1817, but was soon retitled *Blackwood's Edinburgh Magazine* and, in 1906, *Blackwood's Magazine.* Founded by William Blackwood, a book publisher, to compete with the Whig *Edinburgh Review*, it became notorious for attacks on what it called the "Cockney School of Poetry," which included Leigh Hunt, Keats, and Hazlitt. Contributors Thomas De Quincey, George Eliot, Joseph Conrad, Alfred Noyes, and others made it an important literary force in the 19th century. See *Annals of a Publishing House: William Blackwood, His Sons, Their Magazine, and Friends* by Mrs. Oliphant (1897–98).

BLAST: THE REVIEW OF THE GREAT ENGLISH VORTEX (two issues only: July 1914 [date on cover 20 June] and July 1915, London). Edited by Wyndham Lewis, with the collaboration of Ezra Pound. Despite its fleeting existence, it is considered significant because of its daring modernism in art, prose, and poetry, and its publication of manifestoes and challenges to the reigning world of English art. The first issue included Lewis's "Enemy of the Stars" and the second, Eliot's "Preludes." World War I broke out only a few weeks after issue No. 1, sealing its fate. See *Blasting and Bombardiering* by Wyndham Lewis (1967).

BUNGAKU-KAI (The Literary Circle) (1933–?, Tokyo). A leading Japanese journal for a decade, before becoming a major commercial monthly after World War II. Founding members included Hideo Kobayashi (who became editor in 1935), Yasunari Kawabata, Koji Uno, Hirotsu Kazuo, Fusao Hayashi, Rintaro Takeda, and Kyuya Fukada. It published such important contemporary novelists as Kenzaburo Oe.

BUNGEI (The Literary Arts) (1944–57, 1962–present, Tokyo). A leading Japanese monthly, publishing original contemporary literature and criticism, with contributions from such major writers as Yasunari Kawabata and Yukio Mishima.

CONTACT (1920–32, New York, then Paris). Published irregularly, *Contact* was an avant-garde journal founded by the American author Robert McAlmon, aided by the poet William Carlos Williams. Contributors included Kay Boyle, H. D., Marianne Moore, Ezra Pound, Wallace Stevens, Glenway Wescott, E. E. Cummings, and S. J. Perelman. See *Being Geniuses Together, 1920–1930* by Robert McAlmon and Kay Boyle (1984).

CORNHILL MAGAZINE, THE (1860–1975, suspended pub. 1940–43; London). William Makepeace Thackeray was its first editor, attracting brilliant contributors and achieving an unprecedented circulation of 80,000 during his two-year tenure. From 1871 to 1882, under the editorship of Leslie Stephen, who published major fiction and more literary essays, it reached even greater heights of literary interest and quality while declining in circulation. Among those whose work appeared in the *Cornhill* were George Eliot, Thomas Hardy, Alfred, Lord Tennyson, Robert Browning, Algernon Charles Swinburne, John Ruskin, Henry James, Edmund Gosse, Robert Louis Stevenson, and Stephen himself. See *Leslie Stephen: The Godless Victorian* by Noel Annan (1990).

CRISIS, THE: A RECORD OF THE DARKER RACES (1910–40, 1964–69, New York). Monthly published by the NAACP, launched by W. E. B. Du Bois and edited by him for its first 24 years. An important vehicle for writers of the Harlem Renaissance, especially from 1919 to 1926, when literary editor Jessie Redmon Fauset published Arna Bontemps, Langston Hughes, Countee Cullen, and Jean Toomer, among others.

CRITERION, THE (1922–39, London). Quarterly edited by T. S. Eliot. Eliot's *The Waste Land* appeared for the first time in its first issue, along with criticism by Ezra Pound and stories by D. H. Lawrence. Over its life, contributors included William Empson, W. H. Auden, and Stephen Spender, as well as numerous modern European writers, including Paul Valéry, Marcel Proust, and Jean Cocteau, many of whom were introduced to English-language readers for the first time in its pages.

DIAL, THE (1840–44, Boston). Quarterly magazine of literature, philosophy, and religion, edited first by Margaret Fuller and later by Ralph Waldo Emerson, as a vehicle for the work of the New England Transcendentalists, including poems and essays by Emerson, Fuller, Thoreau, and Bronson Alcott. See *The New England Transcendentalists and the Dial: A History of the Magazine and Its Contributors* by Joel Myerson (1980).

DIAL, THE (1880–1929, Chicago; New York from 1918). Monthly founded by Francis F.

Browne and edited at various times by Conrad Aiken, Van Wyck Brooks, Scofield Thayer, and Marianne Moore, among others, reaching its pinnacle of literary distinction after 1920 under Thayer and Moore. A champion of modern currents in art and literature, it introduced some of the best 20th-century writers and artists, including Thomas Mann, T. S. Eliot, Sherwood Anderson, Djuna Barnes, D. H. Lawrence, and E. E. Cummings, and published excellent reproductions of modern graphic art. See *Scofield Thayer and The Dial: An Illustrated History* by Nicholas Joost (1964).

DOUBLE DEALER, THE (1921–26, New Orleans). The first magazine to publish the fiction of Ernest Hemingway, and a champion of the early work of Hart Crane, Thornton Wilder, Jean Toomer, and Kenneth Fearing. Other contributors included Robert Penn Warren, Edmund Wilson, Amy Lowell, and John Crowe Ransom.

EDINBURGH REVIEW, OR THE CRITICAL JOURNAL (1802–1929, Edinburgh). Quarterly founded by Francis Jeffrey, Sydney Smith, and Henry Brougham, with Jeffrey as its first and longtime editor. The literary section was highly influential. Contributors included Sir Walter Scott, William Hazlitt, and Thomas Babington Macaulay as well as most of the major writers and critics of the day. But the prestigious journal was also notoriously critical of Wordsworth, Coleridge, and Southey, whom it called the "Lake School." See *Scotch Reviewers: The Edinburgh Review, 1802–1815* by John Clive (1957); *Politics and Reviewers: The 'Edinburgh' and the 'Quarterly' in the Early Victorian Age* by Joanne Shattock (1989); and *Heirs of the Enlightenment: Edinburgh Reviewers and Writers, 1800–1830* by George Pottinger (1992).

EGOIST, THE (1914–19, London; originally named *The New Freewoman: An Individualist Review*). An avant-garde periodical founded by Harriet Shaw Weaver and Dora Marsden as a feminist paper; under the editorial influence of

Ezra Pound, it became *The Egoist* and a vehicle for the Imagist poets. Appearing at first semimonthly, then monthly, it published the work of such writers as H. D., Richard Aldington, Rebecca West, T. S. Eliot, and Ezra Pound. James Joyce's *A Portrait of the Artist as a Young Man* was serialized in its pages. See *Dear Miss Weaver: Harriet Shaw Weaver, 1876–1961* by Jane Lidderdale and Mary Nicholson (1970).

ENGLISH REVIEW, THE (1908–37, London). Monthly literary review notable for several brilliant editors, especially its founding editor, Ford Madox Ford (then Hueffer), 1908–9, who described its purpose as "giving imaginative literature a chance in England." The first issue included the serialization of H. G. Wells's *Tono-Bungay* and Thomas Hardy's poem "A Sunday Morning Tragedy"; other early volumes featured D. H. Lawrence, Wyndham Lewis, Ezra Pound, E. M. Forster, W. B. Yeats, Arnold Bennett, John Galsworthy, G. K. Chesterton, Joseph Conrad, and Henry James. As editor from 1910 to 1923, Austin Harrison opened the roster to writers from around the world, including Sherwood Anderson, Anton Chekhov, Maxim Gorky, Hermann Hesse, Vladimir Nabokov, Aldous Huxley, Bertrand Russell, and Ivan Turgenev, among others. Douglas Jerrold, editor from 1931 to 1935, was the last of the journal's editors of literary distinction. See *South Lodge: Reminiscences of Violet Hunt, Ford Madox Ford and the English Review* by Douglas Goldring (1943).

EVERGREEN REVIEW (1957–73, New York). Quarterly, then bimonthly progressive magazine of ideas and literature edited by Barney Rossett of Grove Press. With a penchant for the avant-garde, the erotic, and foreign authors, the magazine published the work of, among others, Vladimir Nabokov, Jack Kerouac, Allen Ginsberg, Samuel Beckett, Henry Miller, and E. E. Cummings.

EXAMINER, THE (1808–81, London). Radical weekly founded by John and Leigh Hunt, and edited by Leigh Hunt for the first 20 years, during which time it published the work of Shelley, Keats, and Hazlitt.

FORTNIGHTLY REVIEW (1865–1934, London). Biweekly first edited by G. H. Lewes. A general periodical best known for the quality of its literary contributions and notable in the history of literary journals for insisting on signed articles, a break with the tradition of anonymous reviewing. Contributors included William Makepeace Thackeray, George Eliot, Matthew Arnold, George Meredith, Leslie Stephen, Thomas Hardy, Henry James, Rudyard Kipling, and James Joyce.

FUGITIVE, THE (1922–25, Nashville, Tenn.). Bimonthly little magazine produced by a conservative group of Southern poets and critics who embraced the Southern agrarian ideal. Most were associated with Vanderbilt University. Major participants were John Crowe Ransom, Allen Tate, Robert Penn Warren, Merrill Moore, and Laura Riding. See *Fugitive Anthology* (1928) and *The Fugitive Group: A Literary History* by Louise Cowan (1959).

GRANTA (1979–present, Cambridge, England). Avant-garde literary and cultural review, first edited by Bill Buford, appearing irregularly. It publishes fiction and journalism by an international but predominantly English roster of writers, including Martin Amis, Ian McEwan, George Steiner, Salman Rushdie, Emma Tennant, Angela Carter, and A. N. Wilson. Each issue has a distinctive theme and title.

HARPER'S MAGAZINE (1850–present, New York). Monthly journal of literature and opinion, founded as *Harper's New Monthly Magazine* by the book publisher Harper & Brothers. The first editor was Henry J. Raymond, who served until 1856. Originally, it published mostly retreaded material already published in England, including works by Dickens, Thackeray, Trollope, and Hardy. Under the editorship of Henry M. Alden (1869–1919), it began to feature American writers, including Melville, Twain, Dreiser, Tarkington, James, William Dean Howells, Sarah Orne Jewett, and Jack London. Since then, ownership has changed hands several times. The current magazine, with its "Harper's Index," "Readings," and other new elements, and now operated by a foundation, was formed under the editorship of Lewis Lapham, who continues to publish outstanding journalism and fiction in its pages. See *New York Days* by Willie Morris (1993).

HORIZON (1940–50, London). Monthly founded in 1939 by Cyril Connolly, Stephen Spender, and Peter Watson, it was first issued in 1940 as a medium for literature in wartime England. Connolly was editor for its life; among the contributors were some of the foremost writers of the 20th century, including Evelyn Waugh, W. H. Auden, George Orwell, Angus Wilson, Laurie Lee, and more. See *Friends of Promise: Cyril Connolly and the World of Horizon* by Michael Shelden (1989) and *World Within World* by Stephen Spender (1951).

JOURNAL DES SÇAVANS, LE (later, *Journal des Savants*) (Learned Journal) (1665–1753, irregular, Paris). Founded by Denis de Sallo under the authorization of Louis XIV, who wanted a periodical to monitor currents in the sciences and arts, it reviewed French and other European books. One of the important pioneering organs of literary journalism. See *Histoire du Journal des Sçavans depuis 1665 jusqu'en 1701* by Betty T. Morgan (1929).

KENYON REVIEW, THE (1939–70, 1979–present, Gambier, Ohio). Quarterly of literary criticism, founded by faculty members of Kenyon College. John Crowe Ransom was the first editor. From 1939 to 1958, it was influential as a mouthpiece of the New Criticism, publishing commentary by Ransom, William Empson, Yvor Winters, I. A. Richards, Cleanth Brooks, Allen Tate, Robert Penn Warren, and Mark Van Doren, and poetry by Marianne Moore,

Stephen Spender, Wallace Stevens, John Berryman, and Dylan Thomas. See *The Kenyon Review, 1939–1970: A Critical History* by Marian Janssen (1989).

KNICKERBOCKER MAGAZINE, THE (1833–65, New York). Monthly edited by Lewis G. and Willis G. Clark, which published work of the so-called Knickerbocker School (the name deriving from Washington Irving's *A History of New York* "by Diedrich Knickerbocker"), including that of Irving, the novelist J. K. Paulding, Henry Wadsworth Longfellow, Nathaniel Hawthorne, James Fenimore Cooper, and William Cullen Bryant. See the anthology *The Knickerbocker Gallery* (1855).

LITTLE REVIEW, THE (1914–29, Chicago, then Paris). One of the most influential avant-garde literary magazines of its time, founded as a monthly in Chicago by Margaret Anderson. It became a quarterly in 1921, changed editors in 1922 when Jane Heap took over, and moved to Paris in 1927. Its serialization of James Joyce's *Ulysses*, beginning in March 1918, set in motion a landmark obscenity trial in the U.S. courts. Other contributors included T. S. Eliot, Wyndham Lewis, W. B. Yeats, Malcolm Cowley, Ford Madox Ford, Sherwood Anderson, Ernest Hemingway, Gertrude Stein, William Carlos Williams, Ezra Pound, and Wallace Stevens. See *My Thirty Years' War: An Autobiography* by Margaret Anderson (1930); *Pound/The Little Review: The Letters of Ezra Pound to Margaret Anderson: The Little Review Correspondence* (1988); and *Girls Lean Back Everywhere: The Law of Obscenity and the Assault on Genius* by Edward De Grazia (1992).

LONDON MAGAZINE, THE (1820–29, London). Monthly especially devoted to exploring writers and books. John Scott, the first editor, was killed in a duel that ensued from a dispute with its rival, *Blackwood's Edinburgh Magazine*. Scott was assisted by William Hazlitt, Thomas Hood, and Mary Russell Mitford. Thomas De Quincey's *Confessions of an English Opium*

Eater and the series of essays by Charles Lamb that were eventually collected as *Essays of Elia* were published here, along with the work of other young English writers, including Thomas Carlyle, Leigh Hunt, John Keats, and William Wordsworth.

MERCURE DE FRANCE, LE (1672 [as *Le Mercure Galant*]–1965, with interruptions: suppressed in 1811, resumed in 1815, then ceased in 1820s, revived in 1889; name changed in 1924; Paris). Long-lived French journal founded by Jean Donneau de Visé as *Le Mercure Galant*, publishing literature and criticism and political commentary. During the 18th century, Voltaire and Jean-François de La Harpe were involved in it and used it to promote the *Encyclopédie*. The revival in 1889 was virtually a new periodical, but one that became one of the most important literary periodicals of the 20th century. With a particular focus on Symbolism, it published the work of Alfred Jarry and Stéphane Mallarmé, among others. See *Le Mercure Galant de Dufresny (1710–1714), ou, Le Journalisme à la Mode* by François Moureau (1982) and *Le Mercure de France: Cent Un Ans d'Édition* (Bibliothèque Nationale de France, 1995).

MONTHLY REVIEW (1749–1845, London). Founded by a bookseller, Ralph Griffiths, as a journal of extracts, by around 1780 it had become what many critics now consider to be the first great English literary review. Among those published in its pages were Richard Brinsley Sheridan, Charles Burney, and Oliver Goldsmith.

NATION, THE (1865–present, New York). Established by a group of abolitionists, *The Nation* is America's oldest weekly magazine. The first editor was E. L. Godkin. Primarily a journal of opinion, it has also had a distinguished history of literary publishing; literary editors have included Carl and Mark Van Doren, John Macy, Ludwig Lewisohn, and Joseph Wood Krutch. Such writers as W. H. Auden, James Baldwin, Langston Hughes, Sylvia Plath, Henry James, Thomas Mann, Alice Walker, Carlos Fuentes, E. L. Doctorow, Gore Vidal, Toni Morrison, and William Styron have appeared in its pages.

NEA GRAMMATA, TA (The New Letters) (1935–40, 1944–45, Athens). Avant-garde literary magazine, the most important to emerge between the wars in Greece. Founded anonymously as a monthly in 1935 by George Katsimbalis working with fellow critic Andreas Karandonis, it later appeared on a quarterly, then bimonthly, basis. It served as the prime vehicle for the poetry of the "Generation of the '30s," including that of George Seferis and Odysseus Elytis, who in 1979 won the Nobel Prize in Literature. It also published Constantine Cavafy and others.

NEW REPUBLIC, THE (1914–present, New York, then Washington, D.C.). A weekly journal of opinion founded by Willard D. Straight and first edited by Herbert Croly, who famously said that its purpose was "less to inform or entertain its readers than to start little insurrections in the realm of their convictions." It has long had an influential "back of the book" and a distinguished line of literary and associate editors, including Malcolm Cowley, Edmund Wilson, Alfred Kazin, and Leon Wieseltier. See *The New Republic: A Voice of Modern Liberalism* by David Seideman (1986) and *Coming of Age with The New Republic, 1938–1950* by Merrill D. Peterson (1999).

NEW STATESMAN, THE (1913–present, London). A weekly founded by Sidney and Beatrice Webb as an organ of the Fabian Society. The first editor was Clifford Sharp and the first literary editor J. C. Squire; early regular contributors included the Webbs and G. B. Shaw. In 1931, its impressive circulation enabled it to take over *The Nation and Athenaeum* (see *Athenaeum*), changing its title to *The New Statesman & Nation (incorporating Athenaeum)*; other name changes occurred over the years, and it is now again simply *The New Statesman*. However, the original policy of "dissent, of skepticism, of inquiry, of nonconformity" is still in force. Contributors have included Leonard Woolf, J. B. Priestley, and V. S. Pritchett.

NEW YORKER, THE (1925–present, New York). Weekly, founded and initially edited by Harold Ross; edited subsequently by William Shawn, Robert Gottlieb, Tina Brown, and David Remnick. Intended as an urbane, sophisticated, witty magazine "not for the old lady in Dubuque," it has been a regular vehicle for such writers and cartoonists as E. B. White, James Thurber, Wolcott Gibbs, Ogden Nash, Charles Addams, Saul Steinberg, John O'Hara, S. J. Perelman, John Updike, and many others. While still featuring longtime departments like "Talk of the Town," the character of the magazine has in fact varied with its editors, some of whom have also featured serious reportage. See *The Years with Ross* by James Thurber (1959), *Here at The New Yorker* by Brendan Gill (1975), *Remembering Mr. Shawn's New Yorker* by Ved Mehta (1998), *About Town: The New Yorker and the World It Made* by Ben Yagoda (2000), and *Gone* by Renata Adler (2000).

NEW YORK REVIEW OF BOOKS, THE (1963–present, New York). Biweekly (monthly in July, Aug., Sept., Dec., Jan.). It was founded during the New York newspaper strike of 1963 by its present editors, Robert Silvers and Barbara Epstein, and a group of friends that included Jason Epstein and Elizabeth Hardwick. Early issues contained articles by such writers as W. H. Auden, Edmund Wilson, Susan Sontag, Robert Penn Warren, Lillian Hellman, Norman Mailer, Gore Vidal, Saul Bellow, Robert Lowell, Truman Capote, William Styron, Mary McCarthy, and Hardwick. Today one of the premier intellectual and literary magazines in the English-speaking world, the *NYRB* continues to publish a distinguished roster of writers and scholars. It is illustrated with caricatures and other witty drawings by David Levine. See *Intellectual Skywriting: Literary Politics and The New York Review of Books* by Philip Nobile (1974) and *Book Business: Publishing: Past, Present, and Future* by Jason Epstein (2001).

NORTH AMERICAN REVIEW, THE (1815–1939, Boston, later New York; revived 1963–present, Cedar Falls, Iowa). Quarterly, later monthly, that became one of the country's leading literary journals of the 19th and 20th centuries. A distinguished line of editors included C. E. Norton, Jared Sparks, Edward Everett, James Russell Lowell, Henry Adams, and Henry Cabot Lodge, but it especially flourished under the editorships of Lowell (1863–72) and Adams (1872–76). In 1877, Allen Thorndike Rice (editor until 1889) moved it to New York, and changed it from a local to a national organ. Early contributors included William Cullen Bryant (who first published his "Thanatopsis" here in 1817), Daniel Webster, John Adams, Henry Wadsworth Longfellow, and Francis Parkman, as well as such European authors as Goethe and Schiller, and later Walt Whitman, Henry James, William Gladstone, Oliver Wendell Holmes, Mark Twain, and H. G. Wells.

NOUVELLE REVUE FRANÇAISE, LA (The New French Review) (1909–43, 1953–present, Paris). Monthly review of literature and the other arts, founded by André Gide, Jacques Copeau, and Jean Schlumberger. Under the editors Jacques Rivière (1919–25) and Jean Paulhan (1925–40), it became France's leading literary journal, publishing Paul Valéry, Jean Giraudoux, Paul Claudel, Charles Montherlant, and François Mauriac. It ceased for a time during the war, but in 1953 reappeared as *La Nouvelle Nouvelle Revue Française*, reverting to its original name in 1959.

NOVYI MIR (New World) (1925–present, Moscow). A once highly influential Soviet monthly. The work of such liberal Soviet writers and poets as Aleksey Tolstoy, Boris Pasternak, and Osip Mandelshtam appeared in it from its inception. In 1932, it became an official organ of the writers' union of the USSR, making it the vehicle for more traditional Marxist writers. After World War II and until

Stalin's death in 1953, it was often the instrument of the dictator's attacks on writers out of favor with the Communist Party. In 1956, the journal rejected Pasternak's *Doctor Zhivago* because of its anti-Soviet bias, but, during one period of liberalization, it published such works as Aleksandr Solzhenitsyn's *One Day in the Life of Ivan Denisovich* (1962). Censorship of the magazine in the 1970s and 1980s contributed to the development of a large underground press in the Soviet Union. *Novyi Mir* has now greatly declined in influence, but continues to publish new fiction and essays.

ORPHEU (1915 [2 issues], Lisbon). Subtitled *Revista Trimestral de Literatura* (Trimesterly Review of Literature). Edited by Antonio Ferro, this avant-garde review, shortlived as it was, is considered a landmark in Portuguese literary history for serving as the vehicle for the introduction of Modernismo in Portugal, an event considered controversial, even scandalous, at the time. Among the writers whose work was published here were Fernando Pessoa, Mário de Sá-Carneiro, Alvaro de Campos, Luis de Montalvor, and Eduardo Guimarães. Unable to survive financially, the magazine ceased publication after only two issues.

OVERLAND MONTHLY, THE (1868–75 and 1883–1935, San Francisco). Edited for the first two-and-a-half years by Bret Harte, this monthly sought to gain recognition and legitimacy for the literature of the American West. Harte's "The Luck of Roaring Camp" and "The Outcasts of Poker Flat" first appeared in its pages. Other contributors were Ina Coolbrith, Jack London, and Frank Norris.

PARIS REVIEW, THE (1953–present, Paris, New York). English-language quarterly founded by Peter Matthiessen, Harold L. Humes, George Plimpton, William Pène Du Bois, Thomas H. Guinzburg, and John Train, and edited by George Plimpton and others up to the present. Recent poetry editors have included Jonathan Galassi (1978–88) and Patricia Storace (1988–92). Known for its interviews with writers, it has published fiction and poetry by such writers as Malcolm Cowley, Philip Roth, Jack Kerouac, Joyce Carol Oates, Raymond Carver, and others.

PARTISAN REVIEW (1934–present, New York, Boston). Quarterly, published irregularly 1934–62, and quarterly thereafter, founded by William Phillips and Philip Rahv in 1933. Originally associated with the John Reed Club and Marxism, it became more politically independent after 1937. Notable editors have included Rahv (1934–69) and Delmore Schwartz (1943–55), while among the contributors have been Auden, Beckett, Bellow, Jarrell, Kazin, Lowell, Dwight Macdonald, Mary McCarthy, Levertov, Mailer, Sontag, Trilling, and Edmund Wilson. See *A Partisan View: Five Decades of the Literary Life* by William Phillips (1983) and *Partisans: Marriage, Politics, and Betrayal Among the New York Intellectuals* by David Laskin (2000).

POETRY: A MAGAZINE OF VERSE (1912–present, Chicago). Monthly founded by poet and critic Harriet Monroe, who edited it until her death in 1936. At first it published such figures as Carl Sandburg, Edgar Lee Masters, Vachel Lindsay, and Sherwood Anderson, but it also championed more experimental work, including that of T. S. Eliot, Wallace Stevens, Marianne Moore, D. H. Lawrence, and William Carlos Williams. Becoming over time the most influential American poetry magazine, it has by now published most of the major American poets of the century.

PRAIRIE SCHOONER, THE (1927–present, Lincoln, Nebraska). Quarterly founded by Lowry Charles Wimberly (editor, 1927–56) and associated with the University of Nebraska. Karl Shapiro succeeded Wimberly from 1956 to 1963. It began with a focus on literature and criticism relevant to the Midwest but became more inclusive.

QUARTERLY REVIEW, THE (1809–1967, London). Conservative literary and political journal founded by publisher John Murray, and one of the most influential journals of its day (the other being the *Edinburgh Review*, its Whig rival). Its first editor, until 1825, was William Gifford, who scorned most of the young writers of the age (including Keats, Shelley, Tennyson, Dickens, and Brontë), but supported the so-called Lake School poets (Wordsworth, Coleridge, Robert Southey) and Byron, thus playing a major role in the development of Romanticism in England. Sir Walter Scott and Southey were its best-known early contributors. Writers published under subsequent editors included Thackeray, Arnold, and Swinburne. For a scathing assessment of Gifford's editorship, see *The Spirit of the Age, or, Contemporary Portraits* by William Hazlitt (1859); see also *Politics and Reviewers: The 'Edinburgh' and the 'Quarterly' in the Early Victorian Age* by Joanne Shattock (1989).

REVUE BLANCHE, LA (The White Review) (1891–1903, Paris). An important Symbolist journal that published (monthly, then semimonthly) the work of such writers as Stéphane Mallarmé and Henri de Régnier. Debussy was its music critic and Léon Blum reviewed theater and literature.

REVUE DES DEUX MONDES, LA (Review of Two Worlds) (1829, 1831–1944, 1948–present, sometimes called *La Nouvelle Revue des Deux Mondes*, Paris). Fortnightly journal of literature, culture, politics, and economics. François Buloz, editor 1831–77, attracted contributions from such figures as Guy-Augustin Sainte-Beuve, Honoré de Balzac, Victor Hugo, Guy de Maupassant, Hippolyte Taine, Alfred de Vigny, George Sand, and Ernest Renan. It was the most widely read and influential journal of its day up until the 1890s, and continues today.

SATURDAY REVIEW, THE (1924–72, New York). Called until 1952 *The Saturday Review of Literature*. It was founded by Henry Seidel Canby and edited by him from 1924 to 1936, then by Bernard De Voto from 1936 to 1938. Both of these editors published the work of new writers, including many foreign writers in translation;

early contributors included Edgar Lee Masters and G. K. Chesterton. Norman Cousins, who was editor from 1940 to 1972, enlarged its scope, and for a time the magazine was published as four separate reviews of the arts, society, education, and the sciences.

SCRUTINY (1932–53, Cambridge, England). Quarterly literary review edited by the renowned critic F. R. Leavis along with L. C. Knights, Donald Culver, and Denys Thompson. It was notable as an influential vehicle for the critical views of Leavis and the Cambridge school of criticism (including I. A. Richards and William Empson), who favored close scrutiny of the text over historical, biographical, and other external factors. Pitting itself against what it considered the literary establishment, it ignored or attacked most of the work of such modern figures as Virginia Woolf, Dylan Thomas, George Orwell, W. H. Auden, and Stephen Spender. See *F. R. Leavis: A Literary Biography* by G. Singh (1995), which includes Q. D. Leavis's "Memoir" of her husband.

SEWANEE REVIEW, THE (1892–present, Sewanee, Tenn.). Quarterly cultural review emphasizing literature, founded at the University of the South in Sewanee, Tennessee, by William Peterfield Trent when he was a professor there. Allen Tate was editor from 1944 to 1946. Its emphasis is on Southern writers and the place of the South in American literature, but contributors have included national and international as well as local figures, including Cleanth Brooks, Robert Lowell, Wallace Stevens, Robert Penn Warren, Malcolm Cowley, W. H. Auden, Dylan Thomas, Louise Bogan, and others.

SINN UND FORM. BEITRÄGE ZUR LITERATUR (Meaning and Form) (1949–present, with many interruptions; Berlin). Bimonthly founded by J. R. Becher and P. Wiegler; its first editor was P. Huchel. The major literary organ of the German Democratic Republic and Marxist in orientation, it was also a vehicle of the international avant-garde. As such, it had to weather attacks and suspensions for publishing such authors as Sartre, Kafka, and Hemingway, whose works had been banned in East Germany. Other contributors were Paul Celan, Pablo Neruda, Louis Aragon, Thomas Mann, Hans Magnus Enzensburger, and Nathalie Sarraute. It resumed publication after the reunification of Germany in 1990.

SOLARIA: REVISTA MENSILE DI LETTERATURA (Solaria: Monthly Review of Literature) (1926–33, Florence). Edited by Alberto Carocci, it published poems by such major Italian writers as Giuseppe Ungaretti, Eugenio Montale, Carlo Emilio Gadda, and Elio Vittorini. At the same time it aimed to promote the Europeanization of Italian culture by seeking to establish as models the work of such writers as Kafka, Proust, and Joyce.

SOVREMENNIK (The Contemporary) (1836–66, St. Petersburg). Quarterly until 1846, then monthly. Founded by Aleksandr Pushkin the year before he died, this journal gained major influence only under the editorship of N. A. Nekrasov (1847–66). In the 1840s and 1850s, contributors included Tolstoy, Turgenev, A. A. Fet, F. I. Tiutchev, and Apollon Maikov. From 1856 to 1866, it became more provocative, espousing a so-called "nihilist" ideology (positivist, socialist, feminist, antireligion, antitradition). See Nikolai Smirnov-Sokolsky, "How Pushkin's Magazine 'The Contemporary' Was Born (1836–1837)," *Soviet Literature* 1 (1987), 161–67, and *Literary Journals in Imperial Russia*, ed. by Deborah A. Martinsen (1997).

SUR (1931–70, Buenos Aires). Leading Latin American literary journal, founded and edited by the Argentinean writer and publisher Victoria Ocampo. Frequency varied. See *Victoria Ocampo: Against the Wind and the Tide, with a selection of essays by Victoria Ocampo* by Doris Meyer (1979) and *Victoria Ocampo: Writer, Feminist, Woman of the World*, selections from her work, edited by Patricia Owen Steiner (1999).

TAIYO (The Sun) (1895–1928, Tokyo). A leading Japanese monthly general-interest periodical with distinguished literary contributions in criticism, contemporary fiction, and translations of such Western authors as Poe, Flaubert, Maupassant, Twain, and Tolstoy.

TEL QUEL (1960–82, Paris). Avant-garde literary review founded by Philippe Sollers and others. Such New Wave authors as Alain Robbe-Grillet and Nathalie Sarraute published in its pages, as did James Joyce, Francis Ponge, Antonin Artaud, Georges Bataille, Ezra Pound, and later the Structuralists Michel Foucault, Jacques Derrida, Julia Kristeva, Roland Barthes, and Jacques Lacan.

TIMES LITERARY SUPPLEMENT, THE (1902–present, London). Weekly journal, founded as a supplement to *The Sunday Times* of London, long famous for its sophisticated, authoritative coverage of literature, scholarship, and the arts. It became separate from the *Times* in 1914. Publishing topical essays and some 50 comprehensive book reviews in each issue, it covers both fiction and nonfiction, and major works in every language. The first editor was Bruce Richmond, the current one (as of spring 2001) is Ferdinand Mount; among its notable fiction editors have been Anthony Powell and Martin Amis. Literary essayists and reviewers have included Henry James, T. S. Eliot, Seamus Heaney, George Steiner, E. M. Forster, Virginia Woolf, Italo Calvino, Elizabeth Hardwick, Philip Larkin, Anita Brookner, Milan Kundera, Mario Vargas Llosa, Joseph Brodsky, Anthony Burgess, and Gore Vidal, to name a few. Reviewers were anonymous until 1974.

TRANSATLANTIC REVIEW, THE (Jan. 1924–Jan. 1925, Paris). Legendary but short-lived literary monthly founded and edited by Ford Madox Ford in Paris, with the involvement of Ernest Hemingway, Robert McAlmon, and Ezra Pound. Among the writers it published were James Joyce, E. E. Cummings, and Gertrude Stein. See *Ford Madox Ford and the Transatlantic Review* by Bernard J. Poli (1967).

TRANSITION (1927–38, suspended 1930–32, Paris). Monthly (quarterly from 1928) founded and edited by Eugene and Maria Jolas (initially with Elliot Paul). Subtitled first "an international workshop for orphic creation," then "an international quarterly for creative experiment." It published serially a *Work in Progress* by James Joyce, which became *Finnegans Wake*. Among other avant-garde contributors were Gertrude Stein, Hart Crane, Archibald MacLeish, H. D., Henry Miller, William Carlos Williams, Robert Desnos, Philippe Soupault, Georg Trakl, Beckett, Breton, Kafka, Michel Leiris, and Anaïs Nin. See *transition: The History of a Literary Era 1927–1938* by Dougald McMillan (1975) and *Man from Babel* by Eugene Jolas (1998).

YELLOW BOOK, THE: AN ILLUSTRATED QUARTERLY (1894–97, London). Edited by Henry Harland. For the first four issues, the art editor was Aubrey Beardsley; he was fired in 1895 because of his association with Oscar Wilde. Lavishly produced, each volume ran to approximately 300 pages; its bright yellow cover accounted for its title. *The Yellow Book* was associated with *fin-de-siècle* decadence, Aestheticism, and art nouveau, and with the denizens of such gathering places as the Rhymers Club, the New English Art Club, and the Café Royale. Among the contributors were Arthur Symons, Max Beerbohm, Ernest Dowson, Henry James, and a fair number of lesser-known women writers and artists.

ŻYCIE LITERACKIE (Literary Life) (1951–90, suspended during martial law in the 1980s, Cracow, Poland). A biweekly then weekly journal that from 1953 to its demise was the voice of Cracow's literary community. The first editor was Henryk Markiewicz, a literary historian and critic. Nobel Prize–winner Wisława Szymborska was its poetry editor 1952–81. Although it followed the Stalinist party line through 1954 (concentrating on Socialist Realism), it subsequently introduced Western literature in Polish translation, and also published the work of such Polish émigré writers as Czesław Miłosz and Witold Gombrowicz, as well as Polish literature from the interwar period (1919–39).

Variations

ADAPTATIONS
INTO OTHER MEDIA

Great works of literature often serve as grist for the creative mills of artists working in other genres. The entries on these pages can only begin to suggest some of the ways that filmmakers, playwrights, novelists, opera composers, musical theater artists, choreographers, and others have been inspired by earlier works. The emphasis here is on notable, interesting, and sometimes even downright peculiar adaptations. The selection is of necessity subjective, with an emphasis on U.S. adaptations and others in English, and makes no claim to comprehensiveness. Titles of adaptations are the same as those of the original work (or exact translations of the original title) except where a different title is indicated. Names in boldface type highlight for the reader some of the significant or surprising figures who have contributed to adaptations.

AH, WILDERNESS!
(play by Eugene O'Neill; 1933)

The first of the two film versions of O'Neill's only comedy (directed by Clarence Brown; 1935) starred **Lionel Barrymore** and **Spring Byington** as Nat and Essie Miller, Eric Linden as teenaged Richard, and **Mickey Rooney** and Bonita Granville as the younger Miller children. Thirteen years later, in the musical *Summer Holiday* (directed by Rouben Mamoulian; 1948), with songs by Harry Warren and Ralph Blane, Rooney (by then 28) had graduated to playing the teenaged son, with **Walter Huston** and Selena Royle as his parents.

Another musical, this time for Broadway, was *Take Me Along* (1959), with a score by Bob Merrill and a book by Joseph Stein and Robert Russell. The production starred **Jackie Gleason** and **Walter Pidgeon**, with Robert Morse (also 28 at the time) as teenaged Richard.

ALL QUIET ON THE WESTERN FRONT
(novel by Erich Maria Remarque; 1929)

The 1930 adaptation of Remarque's novel by screenwriters **George Abbott, Maxwell Anderson**, and Del Andrews still stands as one of the greatest antiwar films of all time. Academy Awards went to director Lewis Milestone and to the film as Best Picture. The cast included **Lew Ayres** as Paul Baumer and Louis Wolheim as Katczinsky.

A 1979 CBS television adaptation featured **Richard Thomas** (Paul), **Ernest Borgnine** (Katczinsky), and **Patricia Neal** (Paul's mother).

In 1982, a song by **Elton John** and Bernie Taupin based on the theme of the novel was included on John's album *Jump Up*.

ALL THE KING'S MEN
(novel by Robert Penn Warren; 1946)

The Pulitzer Prize–winning political tale became an Academy Award–winning film in 1949, garnering Oscars for Best Picture, Best Actor (**Broderick Crawford** as Willie Stark), and Best Supporting Actress (**Mercedes McCambridge** as Sadie Burke); director Robert Rossen and actor John Ireland (for Best

Supporting Actor, as Jack Burden) were also nominated.

The opera *Willie Stark*, by composer Carlisle Floyd, premiered at the Houston Grand Opera in 1981.

AMERICAN TRAGEDY, AN
(novel by Theodore Dreiser; 1925)

Dreiser's novel has been adapted for Broadway twice: by Patrick Kearney in 1926, with a cast including Morgan Farley, **Miriam Hopkins**, and Katherine Wilson; and then as *The Case of Clyde Griffiths* (1936), a Group Theater production adapted by Erwin Piscator and Lena Goldschmidt and directed by **Lee Strasberg**; the cast included Morris Carnofsky, Luther Adler, and Sanford Meisner.

On film, **Josef von Sternberg**'s 1931 adaptation starred Phillips Holmes as Clyde Griffiths, **Sylvia Sidney** as Roberta Alden, and Frances Dee as Sondra Finchley. The better-known 1951 film changed not only the title—to *A Place in the Sun*—but also the characters' names: Clyde became George Eastman (played by **Montgomery Clift**); Sondra, Angela Vickers (**Elizabeth Taylor**); and Roberta, Alice Tripp (**Shelley Winters**). The Academy Award for Best Director went to **George Stevens**.

ANIMAL FARM
(novel by George Orwell; 1945)

Orwell's satire of Stalinist politics has been filmed twice: first for the big screen, as a British animated film in 1955, with Gordon Heath as the narrator and Maurice Denham supplying the voices for all the characters; and then for television (TNT, 1999), in a version combining animatronics and live action. For the latter, animal voices were supplied by **Kelsey Grammer** (Snowball, the Trotsky figure), **Patrick Stewart** (Napoleon/Stalin), **Peter Ustinov** (Old Major/Lenin), and, in other roles, Julia Louis-Dreyfus, Julia Ormond, Pete Postlethwaite, and Paul Scofield.

ANNA CHRISTIE
(play by Eugene O'Neill; 1921)

The two 1923 film versions of O'Neill's drama suggest the play's universal appeal. In the United States, John Griffith Wray directed **Blanche Sweet** as Anna, William Russell as Matt Burke, George F. Marion as Chris Christopherson, and Eugenie Besserer as Marthy Owens. Meanwhile, across the world, in Japan, Kenji Mizoguchi directed *Foggy Harbor* (*Kiri no Minato*).

This universality was reflected also in the best-known film adaptation, heralded in 1930 by the advertising slogan "Garbo talks!" And that **Greta Garbo** did, both in English and German, in her first sound film—shot in two versions, with separate supporting casts and directors, but using the same sets. The English-language film, directed by Clarence Brown, featured Charles Bickford as Matt, George F. Marion (again) as Chris, and **Marie Dressler** as Marthy. The German version was directed by French director Jacques Feyder, with Theo Shall as Matt, Hans Junkermann as Chris, and Salka Viertel as Marthy.

New Girl in Town (1957) brought O'Neill's heroine to the Broadway musical stage, with words and music by Bob Merrill, a book by **George Abbott** (who also directed), choreography by **Bob Fosse**, and starring performances by **Gwen Verdon** as Anna and **Thelma Ritter** as Marthy.

ANNA KARENINA
(novel by Leo Tolstoy; 1878)

Tolstoy's tragic love story was adapted to the silent screen in Russia (1914), Hungary (1918), and the United States (1915, starring Danish stage actress Betty Nansen). At the very end of the silent era, in 1927, **Greta Garbo** portrayed Anna in *Love*, directed by Edmund Goulding and costarring **John Gilbert** as Vronsky.

Eight years later, Garbo played the role again, under Clarence Brown's direction. This time, **Fredric March** was Vronsky, with **Basil Rathbone** as Alexei Karenin, Maureen O'Sullivan as Kitty, and **Freddie Bartholomew** as Sergius

[Sergei]. In 1948, **Vivien Leigh** was Anna, under Julien Duvivier's direction; **Ralph Richardson** was Karenin and Kieron Moore was Vronsky.

The Russians reclaimed the material in 1967, when Aleksandr Zarkhy directed Tatyana Samoilova as Anna. The supporting cast included famed ballerina **Maya Plisetskaya**, in a small dramatic role; she would dance the role of Anna in 1972 in a ballet she choreographed for the Bolshoi Ballet, filmed in 1974 with Alexander Godunov as Vronsky. The music for all of these was by Rodion Shchedrin.

More recently, in 1997, Bernard Rose directed **Sophie Marceau** as Anna, Sean Bean as Vronsky, **James Fox** as Karenin, **Alfred Molina** as Levin, and Mia Kirshner as Kitty.

On television, PBS's "Masterpiece Theatre" has aired two adaptations of the novel: a ten-part, ten-hour miniseries (1978) starring Nicola Pagett as Anna, Eric Porter as Karenin, and Stuart Wilson as Vronsky; and a two-part, four-hour version (2001) with Helen McCrory as Anna, Stephen Dillane as Karenin, and Kevin McKidd as Vronsky. A 1985 CBS version featured Jacqueline Bisset as Anna, Christopher Reeve as Vronsky, and Paul Scofield as Karenin.

Anna Karenina has also been transformed into an opera by Iain Hamilton (London, 1981) and a 1992 Broadway musical, with book and lyrics by Peter Kellogg and music by Daniel Levine. Starring Ann Crumb as Anna, Scott Wentworth as Vronsky, Gregg Edelman as Levin, Melissa Errico as Kitty, and John Cunningham as Karenin, the Broadway version was a critical disaster.

In **Thomas Tryon**'s novella *Fedora* (included in *Crowned Heads*, 1976), filmed by **Billy Wilder** in 1978, a director tries to convince a reclusive, Garbo-like actress to make a screen comeback as Anna Karenina. The actress, who harbors a secret, instead commits suicide, like Anna in the novel, by throwing herself in the path of an oncoming train. The film starred **William Holden** as the director, **Marthe Keller** as Fedora, and **Michael York** as himself (as the intended Vronsky of the film-within-the-film).

AROUND THE WORLD IN EIGHTY DAYS
(novel by Jules Verne; 1873)

Verne's novel became a Mercury Theatre extravaganza produced and directed by **Orson Welles** on Broadway in 1946. Despite a lavish production and songs by **Cole Porter**, the show was a failure. Nearly 20 years later, in 1973, another stage musical, with book by Sig Herzig, music by Victor Young and Sammy Fain, and lyrics by Harold Adamson, was a summer offering at the outdoor Jones Beach Theatre on Long Island, New York; Fritz Weaver and Robert Clary starred as Fogg and Passepartout.

To raise money to finance his stage production, Orson Welles had been forced to sell off the movie rights to the book; **Mike Todd**, who snapped them up, scored a spectacular success in 1956 with his film version. Under Michael Anderson's direction, an all-star international cast, headed by **David Niven** as Fogg, **Cantinflas** as Passepartout, **Shirley MacLaine** as Princess Aouda, and Robert Newton as Mr. Fix (and including, in cameo roles, John Gielgud, Noël Coward, Trevor Howard, Fernandel, Charles Boyer, José Ferrer, Frank Sinatra, Gilbert Roland, Cesar Romero, Ronald Colman, Peter Lorre, George Raft, Red Skelton, Marlene Dietrich, Buster Keaton, John Carradine, Joe E. Brown, Victor McLaglen, Beatrice Lillie, John Mills, Glynis Johns, Hermione Gingold, and many others) romped about in the 1956 Academy Award–winning Best Picture.

A 1989 NBC miniseries starred **Pierce Brosnan** as Fogg, Eric Idle as Passepartout, Julia Nickson-Soul as Princess Aouda, and **Peter Ustinov** as Detective Fix. In the SCI FI Channel television series "The Secret Adventures of Jules Verne," the author-inventor travels the world with Phileas Fogg, Fogg's cousin Rebecca, and Passepartout, engaging in a series of historically based escapades. The series, featuring Chris Demetral as Verne and Michael Praed as Fogg, premiered in fall 2000.

ASPERN PAPERS, THE
(novella by Henry James; 1888)

Loosely inspired by the love affair between the poet Lord Byron and Claire Clairmont, the step-sister of *Frankenstein* author Mary Shelley, James's novella was filmed in 1947 as *The Lost Moment*. Under Martin Gabel's direction, **Robert Cummings** was Lewis Venable, an American publisher searching for the love letters exchanged by the aged Juliana Bordereau (played by **Agnes Moorehead**) and the long-dead poet Jeffrey Aspern. **Susan Hayward** appeared as the disturbed niece, Tina Bordereau.

In his off-Broadway play *The Golden Age* (1981), A. R. Gurney moved the action to the contemporary United States, where a young writer pursues a lost chapter of *The Great Gatsby*, allegedly in the possession of a woman who had known F. Scott Fitzgerald in the 1920s.

For his opera based on the novella, American composer Dominick Argento transformed Jeffrey Aspern into a composer, and the quest to a search for the manuscript of a lost opera based on *Medea*. Argento's opera premiered at Dallas Opera in 1988.

BARBER OF SEVILLE, THE; MARRIAGE OF FIGARO, THE; GUILTY MOTHER, THE
(plays by Beaumarchais; 1775, 1784, 1792)

Beaumarchais's trilogy about the barber Figaro is best known today through the operas based on the plays and the character: **Gioacchino Rossini's** *The Barber of Seville* (Rome, 1816); **Wolfgang Amadeus Mozart's** *Le Nozze di Figaro* (Vienna, 1786); and **John Corigliano's** *The Ghosts of Versailles* (Metropolitan Opera, New York, 1991). An earlier opera based on the first play, by Giovanni Paisiello (St. Petersburg, 1782), was enormously popular until Rossini's version eclipsed it.

Most of the films based on the plays are adaptations of the operas, even the 22-minute silent *Barber of Seville* (1904), directed by film pioneer **Georges Méliès** and accompanied by a soundtrack featuring excerpts from Rossini's score. Rossini's opera was filmed in 1946, with **Tito Gobbi** as Figaro, Ferruccio Tagliavini as Almaviva, and Nelly Corradi as Rosina; in 1949, with Roger Bussonet as Figaro and Raymond Amade as Almaviva; in 1955, with Tito Gobbi (again) as Figaro, Armando Francioli as Almaviva, and Irene Genna as Rosina (singing voice supplied by Giulietta Simionato); and in 1973, with Hermann Prey as Figaro, Luigi Alva as Almaviva, and **Teresa Berganza** as Rosina.

Mozart's opera was filmed in 1945, with Willy Domgraf-Fassbaender as Figaro; in 1973, with **Kiri Te Kanawa** as the Countess and **Frederika von Stade** as Cherubino; in 1991, with Ruggero Raimondi as the Count, Marie McLaughlin as Susanna, and Cheryl Studer as the Countess; and, despite its title, as *Le Barbier de Séville* in 1933, with André Baugé as Figaro, Josette Day as Suzanne, Monique Rolland as Chérubin, and Jean Galland as Almaviva.

Nonmusical adaptations of *The Marriage of Figaro* include the French film *Figaro* (1929), with Ernst Van Duren as Figaro, Marie Bell as Suzanne, and Tony D'Algy as Almaviva. In 1959, a filmed production by the French theatrical company La Comédie-Française featured Jean Piat as Figaro, Georges Descrières as Almaviva, Micheline Boudet as Suzanne, and Michèle Grellier as Chérubin.

Rabbit of Seville (1950) is a **Bugs Bunny** cartoon featuring Rossini's music. Earlier, in 1944, **Woody Woodpecker** had appeared in his own *Barber of Seville*.

BERLIN STORIES, THE
(two novels by Christopher Isherwood; 1946)

Isherwood's stories of pre–World War II Berlin were first adapted for Broadway in 1951, as *I Am a Camera*, written by John Van Druten. **Julie Harris** was the doomed Sally Bowles, and William Prince played Christopher Isherwood, the play's narrator. The film version (1955) again starred Harris, with **Laurence Harvey** as Chris. The principal subplot concerned a young couple, Natalia (**Shelley Winters**) and Fritz (Anton Diffring), whose romance is threatened by anti-Semitism.

But Isherwood's work is better known today as the source of *Cabaret*, the 1966 Broadway musical based on both Van Druten's play and the original stories. With music by **John Kander**, lyrics by **Fred Ebb**, and a book by Joe Masteroff, the stage production, directed by **Harold Prince**, alternated traditionally plotted scenes with production numbers set in the Kit Kat Klub, where Sally performs and where she meets the writer-narrator (now called Cliff Bradshaw). The principal subplot concerns the romance of gentile landlady Fraulein Schneider and Jewish grocer Herr Schmitt. A new character, the club's Emcee, sets the sleazy, disquieting tone. The original cast included Jill Haworth as Sally, Bert Convy as Cliff, Jack Gilford as Herr Schultz, and **Joel Grey** as the Emcee; adding period authenticity, Fraulein Schneider was played by **Lotte Lenya**, whose husband, Kurt Weill, composed *The Threepenny Opera* (1928), in which she created the role of Jenny.

Cabaret was filmed by **Bob Fosse** in 1972; **Liza Minnelli** was Sally, **Michael York** was Brian Roberts (the character previously known as Chris/Cliff, and here for the first time depicted as a bisexual), Marisa Berenson was Natalia, and Fritz Wepper was Franz (the Natalia-Franz subplot had been restored, and the Fraulein Schneider–Herr Schultz characters omitted). Joel Grey repeated his Broadway role as the Emcee. Academy Awards went to Fosse as Best Director, Minnelli as Best Actress, and Grey as Best Supporting Actor.

BILLY BUDD, FORETOPMAN
(novella by Herman Melville; posthumously published, 1924)

Melville's story of good and evil aboard ship was dramatized in 1951 by Louis O. Coxe and Robert Chapman in the Broadway play *Billy Budd*; the cast included Dennis King, Charles Nolte, Torin Thatcher, and, in his Broadway debut, **Lee Marvin**.

A 1962 film, based on both the play and the novella, and directed by **Peter Ustinov**, starred Terrence Stamp as Billy, **Robert Ryan** as Claggart, and Ustinov as Vere. The French film *Beau Travail* (1999) was a loose adaptation of the story, told through flashbacks, against a French Foreign Legion background.

The novella has also inspired a one-act opera by Giorgio Ghedini (Venice, 1949) and, far better known, the full-length opera by **Benjamin Britten** (London, 1951; revised 1960). In addition, the characters sang and danced in a Broadway musical, *Billy* (1969), with music and lyrics by Ron Dante and Gene Allan, and a book by Stephen Glassman. *Billy* (originally *Billy Be Damned*) closed on opening night.

BLOOD WEDDING
(play by Federico García Lorca; 1933)

García Lorca's drama has been interpreted on film through dance: **Carlos Saura**'s *Bodas de Sangre* (1961) is a ballet-flamenco version, featuring both a full-length performance of the work as choreographed by **Antonio Gades** to music by Emilio de Diego as well as some rehearsal and backstage footage. The principal roles are danced by Gades, **Cristina Hoyos**, and Juan Antonio.

BORIS GODUNOV
(play by Aleksandr Pushkin; 1824–25)

Soviet director Sergei Bondarchuk filmed Pushkin's play in 1986, playing the title role himself. But the more significant adaptation of the work is the opera by **Modest Mussorgsky**. The composer's original version, although generally preferred today, did not receive its premiere until 1928, in Leningrad; the work's St. Petersburg premiere, in 1873, was in a revised version by Mussorgsky. A subsequent revision by **Rimsky-Korsakov**, made after Mussorgsky's death, was performed in St. Petersburg, 1896, and became the standard version for most of the 20th century. Another revision, edited by **Shostakovich**, premiered in Leningrad in 1959. A 1955 film by Vera Stroyeva captures the opera on film, with Aleksandr Pirogov in the title role.

BOURGEOIS GENTLEMAN, THE
(play by Molière; 1670)

Described by its author as a "comédie-ballet," Molière's satire originally featured music by **Jean-Baptiste Lully** (who danced one of the roles in the premiere). A 1958 film preserved a performance by the French theater company La Comédie-Française; the cast included Jacques Charon as the dancing master, Louis Seigner as Monsieur Jourdain, and the director, Jean Meyer, as Covielle. Another French film, in 1982, featured Frank David as Cléonte, Michel Galabru as Monsieur Jourdain, and director Roger Coggio as Covielle.

In addition to Lully, the work has attracted the interest of other composers, notably **Richard Strauss**, whose opera *Ariadne auf Naxos* includes a prologue inspired by Molière's play in which the composer comments on art and music. The opera exists in two versions: the first, without the prologue, premiered in Stuttgart in 1912; the second was first performed in Vienna in 1916 with the prologue.

The ballet *Le Bourgeois Gentilhomme*, choreographed by **George Balanchine** to a concert suite by Richard Strauss, premiered at the Ballets-Russes de Monte-Carlo in 1932; principal roles were danced by David Lichine and Tamara Toumanova. Balanchine rechoreographed the work as a companion piece to Purcell's *Dido and Aeneas* at New York City Opera in 1979, where it was performed by Rudolf Nureyev and Patricia McBride, and again for his New York City Ballet in 1980 for **Suzanne Farrell** and Peter Martins.

Charles Ludlam's 1983 play *Le Bourgeois Avant-Garde* updated Molière's satire to the downtown New York art scene of the early 1980s; the characters included a graffiti artist. Produced by Ludlam's Ridiculous Theatrical Company, with Ludlam as Mr. Foufas (the Monsieur Jourdain character), the play had a long run off-Broadway.

BREAKFAST AT TIFFANY'S
(novella by Truman Capote; 1958)

Capote's charmingly amoral Holly Golightly came to the screen in 1961, in a somewhat sanitized adaptation that also satisfied the audience's demand for a conventional happy ending. Under **Blake Edwards**'s direction, **Audrey Hepburn** was Holly and **George Peppard** was the writer Paul Varjak. The film introduced the Oscar-winning song "Moon River," by **Henry Mancini** and **Johnny Mercer**.

Some of the changes made in the transition from page to screen are suggested in an episode of NBC's "Seinfeld," in which George Constanza (**Jason Alexander**) joins a reading club. Too lazy to read the (very short) novella, George instead watches the movie on video. Later, when he comments in the book discussion on the romantic happy ending, another member of the group points out that the story's unnamed narrator is a homosexual!

In 1966, Broadway producer David Merrick produced a musical version, which was initially called *Holly Golightly* but reverted to the original title before it began preview performances in New York. The show had music and lyrics by Bob Merrill, a book by **Edward Albee**, and **Mary Tyler Moore** and **Richard Chamberlain** in the leading roles. After only four preview performances, Merrick took the nearly unprecedented step of closing the show *before* its opening night, rather than subject critics and paying audiences to what he saw as "an excruciatingly boring evening."

BROTHERS KARAMAZOV, THE
(novel by Fyodor Dostoyevsky; 1880)

Silent film versions of Dostoyevsky's novel were produced in Russia, Germany, Italy, and the United States; the German version (1920) starred **Emil Jannings** (as Dmitri Karamazov) and Werner Krauss. The next version, again from Germany, was *The Murderer Dmitri Karamazov* (1931), with Fritz Kortner as Dmitri and Anna Sten as Grushenka. An Italian version appeared in 1948.

The Hollywood treatment came in 1958, courtesy of director Richard Brooks. **Yul Brynner** was Dmitri; the cast also included **Maria Schell** (Grushenka), **Claire Bloom** (Katya), **Richard Basehart** (Ivan Karamazov), Albert Salmi (Smerdyakov), and **Lee J. Cobb** as the family patriarch. A 1968 Russian adaptation starred Mikhail Ulyanov.

Operas based on the novel include those by Otakar Jeremiás (Prague, 1928), Boris Blacher (*Der Grossinquisitor*; Berlin, 1948), and Renzo Rossellini (*La Leggenda del Ritorno*; Milan, 1966).

Concentrating on the psychological and emotional entanglements of the novel, Boris Eifman choreographed *The Karamazovs* (St. Petersburg, 1995), set to Rachmaninov, Mussorgsky, and Wagner, for his then five-year-old ballet company.

CAESAR AND CLEOPATRA
(play by George Bernard Shaw; 1906)

Shaw himself was responsible for the screenplay when *Caesar and Cleopatra* was filmed in 1946; the director was Gabriel Pascal, who had produced the screen adaptation of *Pygmalion* several years earlier. The young Cleopatra was played by **Vivien Leigh**, opposite the Caesar of **Claude Rains**. **Stewart Granger** was Apollodorus, and Flora Robson was Ftatateeta.

After the success of *My Fair Lady*, it may have seemed logical to musicalize another Shaw play. *Her First Roman* (1968) opened on Broadway with Richard Kiley as Caesar, **Leslie Uggams** as Cleopatra, and Claudia McNeil as Ftatateeta. The show, with book, music, and lyrics by Ervin Drake, proved to be a disaster all down the Nile; Drake even changed the ending, sending Cleopatra off to Rome to live happily ever after with Caesar (leaving Antony, her second Roman, out in the cold).

CANDIDE
(philosophical novel by Voltaire; 1759)

Candide's satire on optimism was updated to the 20th century in the 1961 French film *Candide, or the Optimist in the Twentieth Century* (*Candide, ou L'Optimiste au XXe Siècle*), in which Candide's experience of the world includes inspecting a World War II concentration camp. Directed by Norbert Carbonnaux, the film starred Jean-Pierre Cassel as Candide, Daliah Lavi as his much-raped beloved, Cunegonde, and Pierre Brasseur as Dr. Pangloss.

O Lucky Man! (1973), **Lindsay Anderson**'s picaresque film about the adventures of young Mick Travis (played by **Malcolm McDowell**), is generally considered a loose take on *Candide*, although the relationship is not acknowledged in the film's credits. On the other hand, *Candy*, **Terry Southern**'s 1964 novel and its 1968 film adaptation, is clearly inspired by Voltaire, but Southern's satire is directed at pornographic literature, not optimism. Directed by Christian Marquand, the film featured Ewa Aulin as the naive Candy, who proceeds from one sexual exploit to another, and, in cameo roles, such major stars as **Richard Burton, Marlon Brando, Walter Matthau, James Coburn**, and even ex-Beatle **Ringo Starr**.

By far the best-known adaptation of Voltaire's work is the musical composed by **Leonard Bernstein**; like its hero, it has gone through changes over time. With lyrics by **Richard Wilbur**, John Latouche, **Dorothy Parker**, and Bernstein himself, and a book by **Lillian Hellman**, *Candide* premiered on Broadway in 1956. Bernstein's glorious music could not compensate for the production's uneasy mixture of operetta and satire, and the show ran fewer than ten weeks. In 1973, for a revival at Brooklyn's Chelsea Theater Center, director **Harold Prince** commissioned a new book from Hugh Wheeler and additional lyrics from **Stephen Sondheim**. Prince's environmental staging of the revised work was a great success, moving to Broadway for a run of almost two years. The work was then revised again, incorporating music cut from earlier versions (some of it never previously performed), for the "Opera House Version," which premiered, again under Prince's direction, at the New York City Opera in 1982 and has since been produced by opera companies around the world.

CANTERBURY TALES, THE
(poem by Geoffrey Chaucer; c. 1387–1400)

Chaucer's earthy Middle English poem has inspired two notable films. The first, *A Canterbury Tale* (1944), written and directed by **Michael Powell** and **Emeric Pressburger**, is a modern variation on the pilgrimage theme, set in World War II–era England, as two soldiers (one American, one English), a magistrate, and a London shopgirl journey to Canterbury. Eric Portman starred as the magistrate, Dennis Price was the English sargeant, Sheila Sim was the shopgirl, and Bob Johnson, an amateur actor and actual U.S. serviceman, played the American soldier.

The second film (1971) was a more literal adaptation of Chaucer's tales, including all the bawdry and licentiousness the censors would allow. It was the work of Italian director **Pier Paolo Pasolini**, who played Chaucer; the cast also included Hugh Griffith as Sir January and Laura Betti as the Wife of Bath.

Musical adaptations range from *The Canterbury Pilgrims*, an opera by Reginald De Koven (Metropolitan Opera, New York, 1917), to a 1968 London musical comedy hit, *Canterbury Tales*, with book by Martin Starkie and Nevill Coghill, music by Richard Hill and John Hawkins, and lyrics by Coghill. The show's pilgrimage to Broadway the following year turned out badly, however; the show had only a brief run. A month before that show's opening, another musical, *Get Thee to Canterbury*, with a book by Jan Steen and David Secter, music by Paul Hoffert, and lyrics by Secter, opened off-Broadway, but it was gone by the time the Broadway pilgrims reached New York.

CARMEN
(novella by Prosper Merimée; 1846)

Probably best remembered for the 1875 French opera by **Georges Bizet**, Merimée's story has also been retold, with and without Bizet's music, in dozens of films and theatrical adaptations.

Among the films are **Charlie Chaplin**'s silent burlesque (1915), with Chaplin as "Darn Hosiery" (Don José) and Edna Purviance as Carmen; *The Loves of Carmen* (directed by Charles Vidor; 1948), with **Rita Hayworth** and **Glenn Ford**; the sexploitation film *Carmen, Baby* (directed by Radley Metzger; 1967); *Carmen* (directed and choreographed by **Carlos Saura** and **Antonio Gades**; Spain, 1983), which combined excerpts from Bizet's opera with flamenco dance; *First Name, Carmen* (*Prénom Carmen*) (directed by **Jean-Luc Godard**; France, 1984), loosely inspired by the Merimée story, with Maruschka Detmers as a Gypsy gang member involved in an affair with a policeman; and *Carmen* (directed by Francesco Rosi; France/Italy, 1984), a film of the opera, featuring **Julia Migenes** and **Placido Domingo**.

In 1943, the all-black Broadway musical *Carmen Jones* moved the story to the American South and paired Bizet's music with new lyrics by **Oscar Hammerstein II**; the film version (directed by **Otto Preminger**; 1954) starred **Dorothy Dandridge**, **Harry Belafonte**, and **Pearl Bailey** (the singing voices of Dandridge and Belafonte were provided by opera singers **Marilyn Horne** and LeVern Hutcherson, respectively). For her performance, Dandridge became the first African American to be nominated for an Academy Award as Best Actress.

Roland Petit's hot three-character (Carmen, Don José, and the Toreador) ballet, an early work for his Ballets de Paris (London, 1949), rocketed his ballerina-wife, Renée "Zizi" Jeanmaire, to stardom.

CARRIE
(novel by Stephen King; 1974)

Brian De Palma's 1976 screen version of King's novel is a classic, both as a horror story and as a popular-teens-vs.-the-geeks tale. The film made a star of **Sissy Spacek** in the title role; the cast also included **Piper Laurie** as Carrie's Bible-thumping mother; **Amy Irving** as Sue Snell, the only major character to survive the bloodbath that ended the film; and **Betty Buckley** as gym teacher Miss Collins.

Irving was the link between the original film and *The Rage: Carrie II* (1999), directed by Katt Shea, in which another Bates High School outsider finds that she has telekinetic powers. Irving's Snell, now a guidance counselor at the school, tries (unsuccessfully) to help Emily Bergl's Rachel deal with her unusual gift.

Carrie's other manifestation, as a 1988 Broadway musical, has earned a place in history as one of the great Broadway catastrophes; the show has even been enshrined in a book title (*Not Since Carrie: 40 Years of Broadway Musical Flops*, Ken Mandelbaum's 1991 history). The Broadway *Carrie*, linked to the original film by the casting of Betty Buckley as Carrie's mother, was coproduced with the Royal Shakespeare Company. Directed by Terry Hands, the show had music by Michael Gore (of *Fame* fame), lyrics by Dean Pitchford, and a book by Lawrence D. Cohen.

CHILDREN'S HOUR, THE
(play by Lillian Hellman; 1934)

Hellman's stage play turned on an accusation of lesbianism brought against two schoolteachers by a mean-spirited child. To comply with Hollywood's Production Code, which prohibited the original subject matter, Hellman, in her own screenplay, altered the accusation to a charge that one of the teachers is in love with her friend's fiancé. Retitled *These Three* (1936), the film was directed by **William Wyler** and starred **Miriam Hopkins** and **Merle Oberon** as the two teachers, with Bonita Granville as their young accuser.

Nearly three decades later, in 1961, Wyler took another crack at the material; with the Production Code a thing of the past, he restored both the original title and the lesbian aspect. This time, **Shirley MacLaine** and **Audrey Hepburn** were the teachers, with Karen Balkin as young Mary, **James Garner** as the fiancé, and Fay Bainter as Mary's grandmother. Although the later version, with its screenplay by John Michael Hayes, may be more faithful to the original play, *These Three* is generally considered the better film.

CHRISTMAS CAROL, A
(short novel by Charles Dickens; 1843)

This holiday perennial is perhaps Dickens's most-adapted work, for both stage and screen. Dickens himself often gave public readings of an abridged text; this public reading version has been published by The New York Public Library and is still used today by actors giving holiday readings.

Silent film versions include *Scrooge* (1901, 1922, 1923), *The Virtue of Rags* (1912), and *The Right to Be Happy* (1916); with sound came *Scrooge* (1935); *A Christmas Carol* (1938), with Reginald Owen and Gene Lockhart; *A Christmas Carol* (1951), with **Alastair Sim** and Mervyn Johns (the version most often televised at holiday time); the musical *Scrooge* (1970), with songs by Leslie Bricusse and starring **Albert Finney**; and *Scrooged* (1988), a contemporary adaptation with **Bill Murray** as a television executive.

Animated versions have starred some of the world's most popular cartoon characters: the made-for-video short *Mickey's Christmas Carol* (1983), featuring **Mickey Mouse** as Bob Cratchit, Scrooge McDuck as Ebenezer Scrooge, Goofy as Marley's Ghost, Jiminy Cricket as the Ghost of Christmas Past, and **Donald Duck** as Scrooge's nephew Fred; and, on television, *Mr. Magoo's Christmas Carol* (NBC, 1962), with Jim Backus's **Mr. Magoo** and songs by Jule Styne and Bob Merrill. The not-quite-human Muppets also took a turn with the material in *The Muppet Christmas Carol* (1992), in which **Michael Caine**'s human Scrooge interacts with **Kermit the Frog**'s Bob Cratchit and **Miss Piggy**'s Mrs. Cratchit.

Television adaptations have starred **Fredric March** and **Basil Rathbone** (CBS, 1954), **Walter Matthau** (*The Stingiest Man in Town*; NBC, 1978), **George C. Scott** (CBS, 1984), and **Patrick Stewart** (TNT, 1999). Several other television adaptations featured twists or unusual settings. *A Carol for Another Christmas* (ABC, 1964), directed by **Joseph L. Mankiewicz** from a teleplay by **Rod Serling** (creator of "The Twilight Zone"), set the story in cold war America, where an isolationist named Grudge (played by Sterling Hayden) was given an apocalyptic glimpse of the aftermath of World War III; the program was a propaganda effort on behalf of the United Nations. *An American Christmas Carol* (ABC, 1979), set in Depression-era New England, featured **Henry Winkler** as Scrooge-like businessman Benedict Slade. And female Scrooges were depicted in *Ebbie* (Lifetime, 1995), with **Susan Lucci** as Elizabeth "Ebbie" Scrooge, a ruthless department-store owner, and in *Ms. Scrooge* (USA, 1997), with **Cicely Tyson** as Ebenita Scrooge, a miserly banker. Finally, England's "Blackadder" television series did a complete comic reversal: in *Blackadder's Christmas Carol* (1988), **Rowan Atkinson**'s Ebenezer Blackadder was perhaps the first and only decent, thoroughly selfless Scrooge.

In 1979, Scrooge went uptown, to Harlem, in the Broadway musical *Comin' Uptown*. Starring **Gregory Hines** as Scrooge, the show had music by Gary Sherman, lyrics by Peter Udell, and a book by Udell and Philip Rose. That show's run was short, but in the 1990s, *A Christmas Carol* became a perennial on the New York stage. On Broadway, actor Patrick Stewart performed his own one-man adaptation of Dickens's story for limited runs at Christmastime in 1991 and 1992. And, since 1994, Madison Square Garden has offered each year a musical adaptation composed by Alan Menken, with lyrics by Lynn Ahrens and a book by Ahrens and Mike Okrent. The cast is different each year; among the actors who have portrayed Scrooge are **Tony Randall**, **Roddy McDowall**, Walter Charles, Hal Linden, Frank Langella, and The Who's **Roger Daltrey**.

Several composers have based operas on the story: in 1954, **Bernard Herrmann**; in 1974, Thea Musgrave; and in 1963, as *Mr. Scrooge*, Ján Cikker.

COMEDY OF ERRORS, THE
(play by William Shakespeare; c. 1592)

Shakespeare's farcical treatment of mistaken identity involving two sets of identical twins has never received a straightforward film treatment.

The closest it has come is the screen version (1940) of the hit Broadway musical *The Boys from Syracuse* (1938), with music by **Richard Rodgers**, lyrics by **Lorenz Hart**, and a book by **George Abbott**. Although in stage productions of the musical (as of Shakespeare's original play) the two Dromios and the two Antipholuses are played by individual actors, the film medium made it possible for each pair of twins to be played by a single actor: Allan Jones as the Antipholuses and Joe Penney as the Dromios. **Martha Raye** and Rosemary Lane played the women in their lives.

A 1985 PBS telecast preserved a Lincoln Center Theater production of Shakespeare's play, directed by Gregory Mosher and Robert Woodward. Starring the juggling troupe **The Flying Karamazov Brothers** as well as comic Avner the Eccentric (Avner Eisenberg) and drag performer Ethyl Eichelberger, the production turned the play into a New Vaudeville circus, showing at times a gleeful disregard for Shakespeare's text.

Jim Abrahams's film *Big Business* (1988) is a contemporary variation: two sets of twins (played by **Bette Midler** and **Lily Tomlin**) are separated at birth, with one set raised in rural West Virginia and the other in the Northeast; the four women are reunited as adults when the corporation run by the New York pair threatens to take over the town where their sisters live.

Undaunted by the success of *The Boys from Syracuse*, composer Michael Valenti and lyricist-librettist Donald Driver created *Oh, Brother!*, set in the Persian Gulf. Two sets of twins are separated as infants when the plane on which one set is traveling is hijacked to Iraq. The musical ran for only two days after it opened on Broadway in 1981.

CRIME AND PUNISHMENT
(novel by Fyodor Dostoyevsky; 1867)

Of the Russian, German, and American silent films of Dostoyevsky's novel, the most significant is the German *Raskolnikov* (1923), directed by Robert Wiene and using Expressionist sets designed by **Andrei Andreyev**; the cast was recruited from the Moscow Art Theater. An American version from 1917 begins in Russia, but then moves to the United States, where the murders and the subsequent action occur; at the end, Raskolnikov is imprisoned in the Tombs, the famous New York City prison.

Among the sound film adaptations are those from Sweden (1945), Mexico (1951), the Soviet Union (1969), and Peru (two versions, 1994 and 1996). There were two adaptations in 1935, one French, one American. The French film, directed by Pierre Chenal, starred Pierre Blanchar as Raskolnikov, with Harry Baur as the magistrate and Madeline Ozeray as Sonya. In the American film, directed by **Josef von Sternberg**, **Peter Lorre** was Raskolnikov, **Edward Arnold** was the inspector, Marian Marsh was Sonya, and, in a rare film role, the British stage actress **Mrs. Patrick Campbell** was the pawnbroker. Later adaptations changed the setting and the time of the story. *Crime et Châtiment* (directed by Georges Lampin; 1956) was set in contemporary France, where police commissioner **Jean Gabin** pursued Robert Hossein (as René Brunel/Raskolnikov); Marina Vlady played Lili Marcelin/Sonya. *Crime and Punishment, USA* (directed by Denis Sanders; 1959) set the story in Santa Monica, California, where **George Hamilton**'s Robert was pursued by Frank Silvera's police inspector. And *Rikos ja Rangaistus* (directed by Aki Kaurismäki; 1983) moved the story to Helsinki, Finland, and altered the plot: the Raskolnikov figure (played by Makku Toika) shoots the man responsible for the death of his fiancée several years earlier in a hit-and-run accident.

In 1980, a four-part PBS "Masterpiece Theatre" miniseries featured **John Hurt** as Raskolnikov, Timothy West as the inspector, and Yolanda Palfrey as Sonya. A 1998 CBS adaptation starred Patrick Dempsey, **Ben Kingsley**, and Julie Delpy.

Operas based on the novel include *Raskolnikoff* (Stockholm, 1948), by Heinrich Sutermeister, and *Crime and Punishment* (Helsinki, 1970), by Emil Petrovics.

CRY, THE BELOVED COUNTRY
(novel by Alan Paton; 1948)

Paton's novel of racial injustice in South Africa was filmed in 1951 by Zoltan Korda, with a cast headed by Canada Lee, **Sidney Poitier** (in only his second film role), and Charles Carson. Shot on location in South Africa and London, the film benefited from Paton's involvement as cowriter and coproducer.

But this was not the first adaptation of the novel: two years earlier it had been adapted for Broadway as the musical *Lost in the Stars* (1949), with book and lyrics by **Maxwell Anderson** and music by **Kurt Weill**. The production, directed by Rouben Mamoulian and starring Todd Duncan and Leslie Banks, received mixed reviews and had only a short initial run, but its score—Weill's last work for the musical theater—has endured. The musical was brought to the screen in 1974 by Delbert Mann, as part of the American Film Theatre project, which provided films to audiences on a subscription basis. Brock Peters, Melba Moore, Raymond St. Jacques, and Clifton Davis starred.

CYRANO DE BERGERAC
(play by Edmond Rostand; 1897)

On stage and screen, two actors have been closely identified with Rostand's poet with a heart and soul as large as his nose: **José Ferrer** and **Christopher Plummer**.

After playing the title role to critical acclaim in a Broadway production, Ferrer won an Academy Award for his performance in the 1950 film (directed by Michael Gordon, and with Mala Powers as Roxane). He had already appeared in the role on television, on NBC in 1949, and would do so again on NBC in 1955, with Plummer as his Christian. Ferrer also starred in the musical *A Song for Cyrano* (1972), for which he wrote the book (under a pseudonym); the music and lyrics were by Robert Wright and George Forrest. The show closed during its pre-Broadway tryout. He also played Cyrano in **Abel Gance**'s 1963 *Cyrano et d'Artagnan*, but that film was based not on Rostand but on the life of the actual Cyrano.

After playing Christian in the 1955 NBC production, Plummer graduated to the title role of the 1962 NBC adaptation and of the Broadway musical *Cyrano* (1973), with book and lyrics by **Anthony Burgess** and music by Michael J. Lewis. The show failed, but Plummer won a Tony Award as Best Actor in a Musical.

The first film version of *Cyrano* was a French-Italian coproduction in 1923, and in 1990, **Gérard Depardieu** took on the role in a French film that used the Anthony Burgess translation in its English subtitles. In a rare instance of a performer being considered for an Oscar for a role in a foreign-language film, Depardieu received a Best Actor nomination.

In a lighter vein, **Steve Martin** wrote and starred in *Roxanne* (1987), in which a modern-day Cyrano named C. D. Bales vies with the dimwitted Chris (Rick Rossovich) for the love of an astronomer (**Daryl Hannah**). (Incidentally, the real Cyrano de Bergerac wrote early fantasies about travel to the moon and the sun.) And *The Truth About Cats and Dogs* (1996) turns the sexual tables, as a sharp-witted but physically unassuming radio call-in host (Abby, played by **Janeane Garofalo**) asks her beautiful but none-too-bright friend Noelle (**Uma Thurman**) to impersonate her when one of her callers (Ben Chaplin) asks to meet her.

Another television presentation (PBS, 1985) preserved the Royal Shakespeare Company's stage production with **Derek Jacobi**.

Other attempts to set Rostand's play to music range from Walter Damrosch's opera *Cyrano* (Metropolitan Opera, New York, 1913) to the 1993 *Cyrano*, which reached Broadway via Holland, where the show originated. Its authors were Ad van Dijk (music) and Koen van Dijk (book and lyrics); English lyrics were credited to Peter Reeves and Sheldon Harnick.

"DEAD, THE"
(short story by James Joyce; collected in *Dubliners*, 1914)

The 1987 film adaptation of Joyce's story was a family affair, directed by **John Huston** from a screenplay by his son, Tony Huston, and starring the director's daughter, **Anjelica Huston**, as Gretta Conroy. Other members of the Anglo-Irish cast included Donal McCann as Gabriel Conroy, Dan O'Herlihy as Mr. Browne, Donal Donnelly as Freddy Malins, and Helena Carroll and Cathleen Delany as aunts Kate and Julia.

In 1999, a musical adaptation (*James Joyce's The Dead*) composed by Shaun Davey, with lyrics by Richard Nelson and Davey, opened off-Broadway at the nonprofit Playwrights Horizons; the lyrics were inspired not only by Joyce's text but also by a number of 18th- and 19th-century Irish poems. With a cast including **Blair Brown** as Gretta, **Christopher Walken** as Gabriel, Brian Davies as Mr. Browne, Stephen Spinella as Freddy, and Marni Nixon and Sally Ann Howes as aunts Kate and Julia, the production moved to Broadway in January 2000.

DECAMERON, THE
(collection of tales by Boccaccio; 1351–53)

Boccaccio's tales have been adapted to film a number of times, even inspiring a series of soft-core pornographic Italian films in 1972. Among the more significant films based on the tales as a whole are *Decameron Nights* (1924), from a British stage adaptation by Robert McLaughlin and Boyle Laurence. The international cast of this English-German coproduction was headed by **Lionel Barrymore** and Randle Ayrton. The 1953 film of the same title featured three tales and a framing story; the cast included **Joan Collins, Joan Fontaine**, and **Louis Jourdan**. The Italian *Il Decameron* (1970), directed by **Pier Paolo Pasolini**, offered a dozen tales; the director appeared as the painter Giotto, who served as narrator, and the cast also included Franco Citti. *Boccaccio '70* (1962) had four segments, each the work of a different noted Italian director: **Vittorio De Sica, Federico Fellini**, Mario Monicelli, and **Luchino Visconti**. The cast included **Anita Ekberg**, Sylvia Koscina, **Sophia Loren**, and **Romy Schneider**. The Hungarian film *A Tyrant's Heart, or Boccaccio* *in Hungary* (1981), set in 15th-century Hungary, was directed by Miklós Jancsó.

A Broadway musical, *Boccaccio* (1975), with book and lyrics by Kenneth Cavender and music by Richard Peaslee, ran only seven performances, several days short of the ten days in Boccaccio's original work.

DON QUIXOTE
(novel by Miguel de Cervantes; 1605–15)

After silent adaptations from Spain, the United States, Denmark, and England, the first important film adaptation was directed by **G. W. Pabst** in 1933, in three versions (in German, French, and English), and starred the great Russian opera singer **Fyodor Chaliapin**, who had played the title role in the Monte Carlo premiere of **Jules Massenet**'s opera in 1910. Pabst's film is not a film of the opera, however, but a dramatic retelling (although a few songs were interpolated, to take advantage of Chaliapin's vocal talent).

Other adaptations include *Dulcinea* (Spain, 1947), *Don Quijote de la Mancha* (Spain, 1948), *Dan Quihote v'Sa'adia Pansa* (Israel, 1956), and *Don Kikhot* (Soviet Union, 1957), directed by Grigory Kosintsev. *Dulcinea* (1962), an Italian-Spanish-West German coproduction with two American stars (Millie Perkins as Dulcinea and Cameron Mitchell as a priest), was the story of a barmaid (Perkins) whose encounter with Don Quixote leads her to take the name Dulcinea and devote herself to helping the poor; she is eventually burned at the stake when she will not renounce her mission.

Orson Welles began filming a *Don Quixote* in the mid-1950s; not completed until the early 1970s, Welles's film remained unreleased until 1992, when it appeared with additional footage by director Jesús Franco.

A 1973 film preserves a performance of the ballet composed by Ludwig Minkus, with choreography by **Rudolf Nureyev** after Marius Petipa. The principal roles in the ballet, which does not closely follow Cervantes's story, were danced by Robert Helpmann (Don Quixote),

Nureyev (Basilo), and Ray Powell (Sancho Panza). **George Balanchine** fashioned his own ballet on the subject (New York City Ballet, 1965), to a commissioned score by Nicolas Nabokov, for his then muse, Suzanne Farrell. In its first season, Balanchine himself occasionally stepped in unannounced as the Don.

In addition to Massenet, whose opera is mentioned above, scores of composers have been inspired by Cervantes's work, among them **Felix Mendelssohn** (*Die Hochzeit des Camacho*; Berlin, 1827); **Manuel de Falla** (*Master Peter's Puppet Show* [*El Retablo de Maese Pedro*], a marionette opera in which Don Quixote mistakes the puppets for real people in need of his help; Seville, 1923); and Vito Frazzi (Florence, 1952).

The Tony Award–winning musical *Man of La Mancha* (1965), with music by Mitch Leigh, lyrics by Joe Darion, and a book by Dale Wasserman, was based on Cervantes by way of Wasserman's own 1959 CBS teleplay *I, Don Quixote*, which starred **Lee J. Cobb** as the Don, **Colleen Dewhurst** as Aldonza/Dulcinea, and **Eli Wallach** as Sancho Panza. The Broadway musical starred Richard Kiley as Don Quixote, Joan Diener as Aldonza, and Irving Jacobson as Sancho Panza; introduced the song "The Impossible Dream"; and ran five-and-a-half years. Arthur Hiller's 1972 film version starred **Peter O'Toole** as Don Quixote, **Sophia Loren** as Aldonza, and **James Coco** as Sancho Panza.

DRACULA
(novel by Bram Stoker; 1897)

Dracula's early screen appearances were courtesy of some distinguished directors: **F. W. Murnau**'s *Nosferatu* (Germany, 1922), starring Max Schreck; **Tod Browning**'s *Dracula* (1931), with **Bela Lugosi** in the role that made him famous (he first played Dracula on Broadway, in a 1927 stage adaptation by Hamilton Deane and John L. Balderston); and **Carl Theodor Dreyer**'s *Vampyr* (Germany, 1932), although this film was based on stories by Sheridan Le Fanu, not on Stoker's novel. Years later, **Werner Herzog**'s 1979 *Nosferatu: Phantom of the Night*, with

Klaus Kinski in the title role, ushered in a new series of "prestige" Dracula films, including John Badham's 1979 version, starring **Frank Langella** (reprising his role from the successful 1977 Broadway revival of the Deane-Balderston play) and **Laurence Olivier**; and **Francis Ford Coppola**'s *Bram Stoker's Dracula* (1992), with **Gary Oldman** as the Count, and featuring **Winona Ryder, Anthony Hopkins**, and **Keanu Reeves**.

In the nearly 50 years that separated Dreyer's and Herzog's efforts, Dracula was a frequent presence on screen, if not always bearing much resemblance to Stoker's creation. The Hammer Studios initiated its series in 1958, with Terence Fisher's *Dracula*, starring **Christopher Lee** as the Count and **Peter Cushing** as Van Helsing; other Hammer entries include *Dracula Has Risen from the Grave* (1968), *Scars of Dracula* (1970), and *Dracula A.D. 1972* (1972). *House of Dracula* (1945) was a sequel to *House of Frankenstein* (1944; see under *Frankenstein*, below) with the same stars, except for Boris Karloff, who did not appear in the second film. *Count Dracula* (Italy, 1970), although not a Hammer film, starred Christopher Lee as Dracula, with Klaus Kinski as Renfield (Kinski returned to the role of the vampire in the 1986 Italian film *Nosferatu in Venice*). And in 1974, Andy Warhol associate Paul Morrissey directed *Blood for Dracula*, with Udo Kier as the Count and **Joe Dallesandro** as the Count's servant (the three collaborated the same year on a *Frankenstein*; see below).

Dracula's relations appear in *Dracula's Daughter* (1936), *House of Dracula's Daughter* (1973), *Son of Dracula* (1943), and *Dracula's Widow* (1989), and Dracula's encounters with other screen favorites have included *Billy the Kid vs. Dracula* (1966) and *Allen and Rossi Meet Dracula and Frankenstein* (1974) as well as an appearance in *Abbott and Costello Meet Frankenstein* (1948). Other variations, many of them comic, include *I Was a Teenage Vampire* (1967); *The Fearless Vampire Killers* (1972), directed by **Roman Polanski**; *Blacula* (1972), with William Marshall; *Old Dracula* (1974;

also known as *Vampira*), with **David Niven** as the aging Count in contemporary England; *Love at First Bite* (1979), with George Hamilton as a contemporary Count adrift in New York; *Vampire in Brooklyn* (1995), with **Eddie Murphy**; and *Dracula: Dead and Loving It* (1995), directed by **Mel Brooks** and starring **Leslie Nielsen** as an accident-prone Count and Brooks himself as Van Helsing, with Peter MacNicol as Renfield.

Shadow of the Vampire (directed by E. Elias Merhige; 2000) is a fanciful account of the making of *Nosferatu*, in which director Murnau (John Malkovich) employs an actual vampire (**Willem Dafoe**) to play the leading role, with predictably unfortunate (but wickedly amusing) results.

A 1974 CBS adaptation starred **Jack Palance** as the Count, and the syndicated 1990 "Dracula: The Series," shot in Luxemburg, concerned A[lexander] Lucard ("dracula" spelled backwards), the head of a multinational corporation. Unlike previous vampires, he was able to tolerate sunlight, but his powers were activated only after sundown. Geordie Johnson starred in the 26-episode series.

DR. JEKYLL AND MR. HYDE, THE STRANGE CASE OF
(novel by Robert Louis Stevenson; 1886)

A half-dozen silent versions (in Denmark, England, and the United States) culminated in the two that appeared in 1920: the U.S. version starred John Barrymore, while the freer Geman adaptation, *The Head of Janus* (*Der Januskopf*), directed by **F. W. Murnau**, starred Conrad Veidt as a scientist transformed under the influence of a two-headed statue. **Bela Lugosi**, in an early screen role, played the doctor's butler.

Two important Hollywood versions followed, in 1931 and 1941. In the first, Rouben Mamoulian directed **Fredric March** (who shared the Academy Award for Best Actor that year with Wallace Beery in *The Champ*) as the title characters, with Miriam Hopkins and Rose Hobart as the women in their lives. In the later film,

Victor Fleming directed **Spencer Tracy, Ingrid Bergman**, and **Lana Turner**.

The Two Faces of Dr. Jekyll (1960) was England's Hammer Studios entry; it is distinguished for being the first film in which Hyde is actually better-looking than Jekyll. In *I, Monster* (1971), Christopher Lee took his turn in the dual role, but the characters are here called Charles Marlowe and Edward Blake. *Edge of Sanity* (1989), although set in the 19th century, provided a late 20th-century spin: Jekyll (**Anthony Perkins**) accidentally turns into Hyde after sniffing crack cocaine.

Two films offer a Jekyll who is transformed into a woman: *Dr. Jekyll and Sister Hyde* (1971) with Ralph Bates and Martine Beswick; and *Dr. Jekyll and Ms. Hyde* (1995) with Timothy Daly and **Sean Young**. The latter is played for laughs. Other comic versions include *Abbott and Costello Meet Dr. Jekyll and Mr. Hyde* (1953), with Boris Karloff as Jekyll/Hyde; and *Jekyll & Hyde... Together Again* (1982), a contemporary updating in which Mark Blankfield's shy, humanitarian scientist turns into a sex-crazed party animal. In **Jerry Lewis**'s zany *The Nutty Professor* (1963), a shy chemistry professor is transformed into "cool cat" Buddy Love; **Eddie Murphy** appeared in a 1996 remake of the Lewis film and in a 2000 sequel, *Nutty Professor II: The Klumps*. In addition, several of America's best-known cartoon characters have appeared in short films influenced by the story: *Mighty Mouse Meets Jekyll and Hyde Cat* (1944); *Dr. Jekyll and Mr. Mouse* (1947), featuring **Tom and Jerry**; and *Dr. Jekyll's Hyde* (1958), with **Sylvester the Cat**.

The Son of Dr. Jekyll (1951) and *Daughter of Dr. Jekyll* (1957) present flip sides of the same story: in the next generation, suspicion is cast on Jekyll's adult children (played by Louis Hayward and Gloria Talbot, respectively) when a series of murders occurs in the community; in both cases, they are vindicated when the real murderer is discovered.

Mary Reilly (directed by Stephen Frears; 1996), based on Valerie Martin's 1990 novel, looked at the story from the point of view of Jekyll's young housemaid, played by **Julia Roberts**. **John Malkovich** was Jekyll/Hyde. In **Paddy Chayefsky**'s novel *Altered States* (1978), a scientist exploring varying states of consciousness through the use of hallucinogenic drugs and a sensory-deprivation chamber finds himself regressing physically to an earlier state of evolution. **Ken Russell**'s 1980 film version featured William Hurt, Blair Brown, and, as their daughter, five-year-old **Drew Barrymore** in her big screen debut.

Television adaptations have starred Jack Palance (ABC, 1968); **Kirk Douglas** (NBC, 1973), in a musical with songs by Lionel Bart, Mel Mandel, and Norman Sachs; Anthony Andrews (Showtime, 1989); and **Michael Caine** (ABC, 1990).

The Broadway musical *Jekyll & Hyde* (1997), with music by Frank Wildhorn and book and lyrics by Leslie Bricusse, achieved the transformation of Jekyll to Hyde with a flip of the leading actor's mane of hair.

EAST OF EDEN
(novel by John Steinbeck; 1952)

The 1955 film version of Steinbeck's novel was the first of **James Dean**'s three films; here he appeared as the troubled Cal Trask. **Elia Kazan** directed a cast including **Julie Harris** as Abra, Raymond Massey as the patriarch Adam Trask, Richard Davalos as Aron Trask, and, as Kate, **Jo Van Fleet**, who won an Academy Award as Best Supporting Actress.

Although Kazan's film began midway in Steinbeck's story, with the high school graduation of Cal and Aron, the eight-hour ABC miniseries (*John Steinbeck's East of Eden*, 1981) began at the beginning, with the story of Cal and Aron's parents. The cast was led by **Jane Seymour** (Kate), Timothy Bottoms (Adam), Sam Bottoms (Cal), Hart Bochner (Aron), and **Karen Black** (Abra).

In 1968, an attempt to turn the novel into a Broadway musical resulted in *Here's Where I Belong*, which closed on its opening night. The music was by Robert Waldman, the lyrics by

Alfred Uhry, and the book by Terrence McNally (credited under a pseudonym because he was unhappy with changes made without his permission). The cast included Walter McGinn, Ken Kercheval, and Heather MacRae as the younger generation, and Paul Rogers and Nancy Wickwire as Adam and Kate.

EMMA
(novel by Jane Austen; 1816)

Austen's charmingly meddlesome heroine made her screen debut in 1996 in the person of **Gwyneth Paltrow**. Directed by Douglas McGrath, the film also featured Jeremy Northam as Mr. Knightley, **Toni Collette** as Harriet Smith, and **Alan Cumming** as the Rev. Elton.

At almost the same time, Emma's 20th-century incarnation, Cher Horowitz, made her own screen debut, in *Clueless* (1995), in which writer-director Amy Heckerling stayed true to the general outlines of Austen's novel even as she updated it to contemporary California. **Alicia Silverstone** was the clueless heroine, Brittany Murphy was Tai Fraiser (the Harriet Smith character), Paul Rudd was Josh (Mr. Knightley), and Jeremy Sisto was Elton.

Because too much of a good thing apparently *isn't* too much, a 1997 A&E miniseries presented Kate Beckinsale as Emma, Mark Strong as Mr. Knightley, Samantha Morton as Harriet, and Dominic Rowan as Elton.

EMPEROR JONES, THE
(play by Eugene O'Neill; 1920)

O'Neill's drama was filmed in 1933 by director Dudley Murphy, with a screenplay by **DuBose Heyward** (the author of *Porgy*). **Paul Robeson**, who had appeared in a 1925 revival of the stage play, starred as Brutus Jones; Dudley Digges was Smithers. The cast also included Fredi Washington and the comedienne **Jackie "Moms" Mabley**. That same year, composer Louis Gruenberg's opera was premiered by the Metropolitan Opera, New York.

The play was dramatically realized by the modern dance choreographer-dancer **José Limón**

as a series of superstition-generated hallucinations, set to a commissioned score by Heitor Villa-Lobos and first performed by Limón as the Emperor, Lucas Hoving as the White Man, and a small ensemble of men at the Empire State Music Festival (Ellenville, New York, 1956).

EUGENE ONEGIN
(novel in verse by Aleksandr Pushkin; 1833)

Pushkin's influential work eluded a significant dramatic screen adaptation until 1999, when, under the direction of Martha Fiennes, it finally came to the screen as *Onegin*, starring her brother **Ralph Fiennes** in the title role. Tatyana, Onegin's great love, was played by **Liv Tyler**, and Toby Stephens was Vladimir Lensky.

Of course, Pushkin's work had already served as the basis for the opera by **Tchaikovsky**, which premiered in Moscow in 1879. A Russian film of the opera was made in 1959 by Roman Tikhomirov.

The ballet by John Cranko (Stuttgart, 1965), called *Onegin*, set to music by Tchaikovsky (none from the opera itself, for copyright reasons), is a signature work in the repertory of the Stuttgart Ballet.

"FALL OF THE HOUSE OF USHER, THE"
(story by Edgar Allan Poe; 1839)

Poe's tale was first filmed in 1928, in France, with Jean Debucourt and Marguerite Abel-Gance as the Usher siblings. A British version followed in 1950, with Kay Tendeter and Gwen Watford as the Ushers. The next adaptation, in 1960, is by far the best known: *House of Usher*, directed by **Roger Corman**, with **Vincent Price** and Myrna Fahey as Roderick and Madeline Usher, and Mark Damon as Philip Winthrop (the narrator of the story). The film took some liberties, making the narrator Roderick's enemy, rather than his friend, and a suitor for Madeline.

Some later films appropriated the Usher name and some of the characters, but are not true adaptations or even sequels; these include *Revenge in the House of Usher* (1982), with

Howard Vernon as Eric Usher, the last descendant of the family; and *The House of Usher* (1988), with **Oliver Reed** as Roderick Usher and **Donald Pleasence** as Walter Usher.

Czech animator Jan Svankmajer's variation on the theme is one of eight short films included in *Jan Svankmajer: Alchemist of the Surreal* (1989).

On NBC in 1982, **Martin Landau** was Roderick Usher, opposite Dimitra Arliss (as Madeline), Charlene Tilton, Ray Walston, and Robert Hays.

Philip Glass composed an opera on the subject that premiered in Cambridge, Massachusetts, in 1988. Roger Sessions began an opera based on the story around 1925; it was incomplete at Sessions's death in 1985.

FAREWELL TO ARMS, A
(novel by Ernest Hemingway; 1929)

Hemingway's story of the love of a World War I ambulance driver for a battlefield nurse has been adapted to the screen twice: in 1932, directed by Frank Borzage, with **Helen Hayes** and **Gary Cooper** as Catherine and Frederic, and **Adolphe Menjou** as Major Rinaldi; and in 1957, directed by Charles Vidor, with, respectively, **Jennifer Jones, Rock Hudson**, and **Vittorio De Sica**.

The events that inspired Hemingway's novel were dramatized in **Richard Attenborough**'s 1997 film *In Love and War*, based on the diaries of Agnes von Kurowsky, the nurse on whom Hemingway based the character of Catherine. The film starred **Sandra Bullock** as Agnes and Chris O'Donnell as Hemingway, who had in fact been an ambulance driver during the war.

FRANKENSTEIN
(novel by Mary Shelley; 1818)

Since 1910, when the first silent film version of the novel appeared, Frankenstein has conquered the screen, although many of the movies bearing his name have little or nothing to do with Mary Shelley's original vision.

It was **James Whale**'s 1931 film, and its 1935 sequel, *Bride of Frankenstein*, that put Dr. Frankenstein, his monster, and actor **Boris Karloff** on the cinematic map. The sequel began with a prologue depicting Mary Shelley, her husband, Percy Bysshe Shelley, and Lord Byron discussing the novel; **Elsa Lanchester** played Mary as well as the Bride. Many years later, the circumstances of the novel's germination in the summer of 1816 would be explored in Anne Edwards's novel *Haunted Summer* (1972), filmed in 1988 by Ivan Passer, with Alice Krige as Mary Godwin (later Shelley), **Eric Stoltz** as Shelley, Philip Anglim as Byron, and **Laura Dern** as Claire Clairmont (Mary's stepsister and Byron's lover, on whom Henry James based *The Aspern Papers*). And the later life and mysterious death of director James Whale were the subject of Christopher Bram's novel *Father of Frankenstein* (1995), filmed by Bill Condon as *Gods and Monsters* (1998), with **Ian McKellen** as Whale.

The success of Whale's two films led to a flood of Frankenstein films (none directed by Whale), some of which teamed the monster with Hollywood's other screen creatures; these included *Son of Frankenstein* (1939), with Karloff and **Bela Lugosi** as Ygor; *The Ghost of Frankenstein* (1942), with **Lon Chaney, Jr.** and Lugosi again as Ygor; *Frankenstein Meets the Wolf Man* (1942), with Lugosi and Chaney as the Wolf Man; *House of Frankenstein* (1944), with Glenn Strange, Chaney as the Wolf Man, John Carradine as Dracula, and Karloff as the mad scientist Dr. Gustav Niemann; and *Abbott and Costello Meet Frankenstein* (1948), with Strange, Chaney as the Wolf Man, and Lugosi as Dracula.

England's Hammer Studios began its series with *The Curse of Frankenstein* (1957), a reasonably faithful adaptation of Shelley's story, starring Peter Cushing as Frankenstein and Christopher Lee as the monster. Sequels, all with Cushing, include *The Revenge of Frankenstein* (1958), *The Evil of Frankenstein* (1964), *Frankenstein Created Woman* (1967), *Frankenstein Must Be Destroyed* (1969), and *Frankenstein and the Monster from Hell* (1993).

LITERARY REFERENCES IN POP CULTURE

When politicians or television pundits accuse someone of "tilting at windmills" or of living in a "never, never land," one can fairly wonder if they have any idea that they are alluding to, respectively, Cervantes's Don Quixote *and James M. Barrie's* Peter Pan. *Literary allusions are in fact everywhere in popular culture, and are regularly employed by people one would never suspect of ever having read a book. Following is a selection of generally well-known proper names, all of whose origins can be traced to great writers and their works.*

AJAX (Colgate-Palmolive brand of household cleansers). "The foaming cleanser" and the laundry detergent (both "stronger than dirt") were presumably named for the prototypical big lug (frequently compared to a wall) in Homer's epic the *Iliad* (8th century B.C.).

BALTIMORE RAVENS (National Football League team, 1996–). Founded in 1946 as the Cleveland Browns, the franchise moved to Baltimore in 1996 and cast about for a new name. After a *Baltimore Sun* telephone poll received a record number of calls supporting it, the choice fell on "a ghostly bird immortalized by a writer of haunting stories and poems" (as the *Sun* reported): the eponymous bird from Edgar Allan Poe's poem "The Raven" (1845). Poe died in Baltimore in 1849.

"BIG BROTHER" (reality television show, 1999–). Originating in the Netherlands, the show spawned local variants in many countries, including the United States. The name (in English even in the Netherlands) is from the all-seeing icon of the State in George Orwell's anti-utopian novel *Nineteen Eighty-four* (1949).

CABARET VOLTAIRE (birthplace of Dada, 1916; Sheffield-based techno rock group, 1974–). The original Cabaret Voltaire was started in Zurich by Dada guru Hugo Ball—it is the legendary site of the founding of the "anti-art" Dada movement—and took its name from the great genius of the French Enlightenment, Voltaire. The rock group revived the name as a tribute to Dada, acknowledging the movement as an influence on the "confrontational energy of punk."

THE DOORS (rock group, 1967–72). The name is borrowed from a work on the effects of mescaline and LSD on the human psyche: Aldous Huxley's *The Doors of Perception* (1954). Huxley took his title from another of group leader Jim Morrison's favorite writers, William Blake: "If the doors of perception were cleansed, every thing would appear to man as it is, infinite" (*The Marriage of Heaven and Hell*, c. 1790).

THE FLYING KARAMAZOV BROTHERS (juggling and performance art troupe, 1974–). Named after Fyodor Dostoyevsky's novel *The Brothers Karamazov* (1880); the troupe's various individual members over the years have sported Dostoyevskian monikers: Alyosha, Dmitri, Ivan, Fyodor, Alexi, Smerdyakov, and Rakitin.

HEAVEN 17 (British synth-pop-funk band, 1980–88). Their name was taken from a Top 10 list in the record store scene in Anthony Burgess's anti-utopian novel A *Clockwork Orange* (1962).

LE FIGARO (Paris daily newspaper, 1826–). Named after the effervescent, slyly subversive title character in Pierre-Augustin Caron de Beaumarchais's comedies *The Barber of Seville* (1775) and *The Marriage of Figaro* (1784).

LONG JOHN SILVER'S FISH 'N' CHIPS (fast-food restaurant chain, 1969–). Inspired by the one-legged buccaneer in Robert Louis Stevenson's classic adventure story *Treasure Island* (1883). Among his many other talents, Long John served as ship's cook on the treasure hunt.

LORNA DOONE (Nabisco brand of shortbread cookies, 1912–). Named for the heroine of *Lorna Doone: A Romance of Exmoor* (1869), a bestseller by R. D. Blackmore. Held captive since her youth by a 17th-century Devonshire outlaw band, Lorna is ultimately revealed to be the child of Scottish nobility. A Nabisco executive once commented on the product name, "Shortbread biscuits were considered a product of Scottish heritage, and the Lorna Doone character was symbolic of Scotland."

MOBY (techno vocalist; real name Richard Melville Hall, 1965–). From Herman Melville's whaling epic *Moby-Dick; or, The Whale* (1851). As a direct descendant of Melville, Moby comes by his artist's name legitimately.

PERE UBU (Cleveland-based avant-garde rock group, 1975–). Named for "Father Ubu," the central character in *Ubu Roi* (1896) and other absurdist dramas by Alfred Jarry, because, according to the group's founder, David Thomas, "It seemed like a good idea at the time; the name looked good, sounded good, had 3 syllables, and wasn't likely to mean much of anything to anyone."

PETER PAN PEANUT BUTTER (1920–). The brand is currently owned by ConAgra Foods, and comes in creamy, crunchy, and five other varieties; named after the flying boy from James M. Barrie's play *Peter Pan; or, The Boy Who Would Not Grow Up* (1904), although in some periods the label showed a clearly female adult Peter in high-heeled shoes.

ROB ROY (cocktail, early 20th century). This Caledonian variation (Scotch, vermouth, a dash of bitters) on the classic Manhattan cocktail was named ultimately for Robert MacGregor, the hero of Sir Walter Scott's novel *Rob Roy* (1818), apparently with reference to a Broadway show of the era, possibly Reginald De Koven's operetta *Rob Roy* (1894).

THE SHANGRI-LAS (girl group, 1964–68). Composed of two sets of Queens (N.Y.) high-school-aged sisters, the group performed under a pluralized form of the name of the mythical hidden lamasery in James Hilton's utopian novel, *Lost Horizon* (1933). (See Imaginary Worlds.)

STARBUCKS (upscale coffee purveyors, 1970–). The environmentally conscious corporation was named for Ahab's life-respecting First Mate, Starbuck, in Herman Melville's *Moby-Dick; or, The Whale* (1851).

(Literary References in Pop Culture, continued)

STEELY DAN (rock band, 1972–81; revived in the 1990s). The name was "unceremoniously lifted" from a term applied to a dildo in William S. Burroughs's novel *Naked Lunch* (1959).

STEPPENWOLF (rock band, 1967–). The band's German-born founder, John Kay, took the name for his band from the sobriquet of Hermann Hesse's outsider hero Harry Haller, who likened himself to a "wolf of the steppes" in Hesse's novel *Steppenwolf* (1927). Also, the Chicago-based Steppenwolf Theatre Company, founded in Highland Park, Illinois, in 1974 by actors Gary Sinise, Terry Kinney, and Jeff Perry, an acclaimed ensemble whose members include John Malkovich, Laurie Metcalf, Joan Allen, and John Mahoney.

THIS MORTAL COIL (series of rock albums, 1984–90). The pet project of rock producer Ivo Watts-Russell was named for one of the title character's celebrated soliloquies in Shakespeare's tragedy *Hamlet, Prince of Denmark* (c. 1601): "For in that sleep of death what dreams may come / When we have shuffled off this mortal coil, / Must give us pause."

3 MUSKETEERS (candy bar, 1933–). Originally a three-flavor bar (chocolate, vanilla, and strawberry nougat), it was changed to all chocolate nougat in 1945, but the name was retained, evoking the swashbuckling Athos, Porthos, and Aramis of the Alexandre Dumas *père* classic, *The Three Musketeers* (1844).

TINY TIM (pop singer; real name Herbert Khaury, 1932–1996). The lanky fellow with the little-girl falsetto took his name from the heart-wrenching tot in Charles Dickens's fable *A Christmas Carol* (1843).

URIAH HEEP (rock band, 1969–). The group took its present name just before the 1970 cen-

---

Andy Warhol's Frankenstein (1974; also known as *Flesh for Frankenstein*), directed, despite the title, by Paul Morrissey, is a sexy, blood-soaked version, featuring Udo Kier as the Baron, Joe Dallesandro as a stableboy, Monique van Vooren as the Baroness, and both male and female monsters. **Mel Brooks**'s *Young Frankenstein* (1974) is a loving send-up of the Whale films, starring **Gene Wilder** as Dr. Friedrich von Frankenstein (grandson of the Baron) and **Peter Boyle** as the monster. *The Bride* (directed by Franc Roddam; 1985) combines elements from the two Whale movies, with **Sting** as Dr. Frankenstein, Jennifer Beals as the Bride, and Clancy Brown as the monster. *Roger Corman's Frankenstein Unbound* (1990) begins when a 21st-century scientist (John Hurt) is transported back to 1816, where Mary Godwin (**Bridget Fonda**) is writing the story of a neighbor, Dr. Victor Frankenstein (**Raul Julia**), whose creature is played by Nick Brimble. Jason Patric is Byron and Michael Hutchence is Shelley. **Kenneth Branagh**'s *Mary Shelley's Frankenstein* (1994) starred Branagh as Dr. Frankenstein and **Robert De Niro** as the monster.

Other appropriations of the Frankenstein name include *I Was a Teenage Frankenstein* (1957), with Gary Conway as the adolescent monster; Japan's *Frankenstein Conquers the World* (1965); *Blackenstein* (1973); France's *Frankenstein 90* (1984), presenting the first computer-literate monster (Frankenstein, a cybernetics engineer, fits the creature with a microprocessor for a brain); and *Frankenhooker* (1990), set in

tenary of the death of Charles Dickens, choosing a moniker from among Dickens's panoply of colorful characters. Uriah Heep is the obsequious law clerk in *David Copperfield* (1850).

U.S.S. *NAUTILUS* (nuclear submarine, SSN-571, launched 1954, decommissioned 1980). The nautilus is a cephalopod with a chambered shell allowing it to float or sink to the sea bottom. The name had long been popular for ships, but it was Jules Verne's use of it for Captain Nemo's fantastic craft in his adventure novel *Twenty Thousand Leagues Under the Sea* (1869–70) that inspired the naming of the first nuclear-powered submarine, which was also the first "true" submarine capable of prolonged submersion—the first vessel capable of realizing Verne's vision, as her skipper, Commander William R. Anderson, acknowledged in his account of the ship's 1958 voyage beneath the North Pole's ice cap, *Nautilus 90 North* (1959).

VANITY FAIR (magazines). The title of a number of periodicals, most recently a New York–based monthly (1983–) published by Condé Nast, was taken from John Bunyan's allegory *The Pilgrim's Progress* (1678–84). In his new magazine, Nast promised to cover everyone who, "through some striking merit of one kind or another, makes what Bunyan called a 'great stir at the Fair.'" Bunyan's work also inspired the title of W. M. Thackeray's *Vanity Fair, a Novel Without a Hero* (1848). (See Imaginary Worlds.)

WALDENBOOKS (bookstore chain, 1933–). Originated as a rental library chain in the Great Depression; in 1962, the first "Walden Book Store" was so named in tribute to Henry David Thoreau's classic, *Walden; or, Life in the Woods* (1854); the name "Waldenbooks" was adopted nationwide in 1972.

suburban New Jersey, where a young scientist tries to reassemble his dead girlfriend with body parts from streetwalkers. Two actors associated with the role of the monster returned later in life in variations: Karloff in *Frankenstein—1970* (1958), playing a descendant of the original Baron Frankenstein; and Lugosi in **Ed Wood, Jr.**'s *Bride of the Monster* (1956), a Grade Z variation on the mad scientist theme.

One of the best-known variations on the subject is the midnight-movie audience-participation classic *The Rocky Horror Picture Show* (1975), starring **Tim Curry** as Dr. Frank-N-Furter and **Susan Sarandon** and Barry Bostwick as the apple-cheeked innocents Janet and Brad. The film was an adaptation of composer-lyricist Richard O'Brien's rock musical, *The Rocky Horror Show*. A smash hit in London in 1973, the stage show failed the first time around on Broadway, in 1975, but a revival in 2000, starring rocker **Joan Jett**, comedian/talk show host **Dick Cavett**, and actor Tom Hewitt, fared better.

Television adaptations starred Robert Foxworth as Frankenstein and Bo Svenson as the monster (ABC, 1973) and Patrick Bergin as Frankenstein and Randy Quaid as the monster (TNT, 1993).

Victor Gialanella's play *Frankenstein*, starring David Dukes as Dr. Frankenstein, opened and closed on Broadway on the same night in 1981, becoming one of the costliest failures in theater history up to that time.

GOOD-BYE, MR. CHIPS
(novel by James Hilton; 1934)

Hilton's gentle novel about a schoolteacher reviewing his life first reached the screen in 1939 under Sam Wood's direction. **Robert Donat** starred as Mr. Chipping (affectionately known as Mr. Chips), with **Greer Garson** as his wife, Katherine; John Mills as one of his students; and Paul Henreid as Staefel. Donat received the Academy Award as Best Actor.

The other film incarnation of the story was a musical, directed by Herbert Ross and with a score by Leslie Bricusse. **Peter O'Toole** was Mr. Chips, **Petula Clark** was his wife (the role was expanded to take advantage of Clark's singing ability), and **Michael Redgrave** was the Headmaster.

In 1987, a three-hour PBS "Masterpiece Theatre" miniseries starred Ray Marsden as Mr. Chips and Jill Meagher as Katherine.

GREAT EXPECTATIONS
(novel by Charles Dickens; 1861)

Dickens's story of a young man's coming-of-age came to the silent screen twice: in America in 1917 and in Denmark in 1923. Sound versions followed, beginning in the United States in 1934, when Phillips Holmes was Pip, **Jane Wyatt** was Estella, Florence Reed was Miss Havisham, and Henry Hull was Magwitch. The 1946 British version is better known: directed by **David Lean**, it starred **John Mills** as Pip, **Jean Simmons** and Valerie Hobson as, respectively, the younger and older Estella, Martita Hunt as Miss Havisham, and Finlay Currie as the convict Magwitch.

When *Great Expectations* next reached the screen, in 1998, it had experienced a sea change: although the title and the general outlines of the story remained, the setting, time, and most of the characters' names were different. Alfonso Cuarón's film begins in Florida, where Finn (**Ethan Hawke**), an artist, becomes involved with the wealthy eccentric Nora Diggers Dinsmoor (**Anne Bancroft**) and her young niece Estella (**Gwyneth Paltrow**). Finn's "great expectations" find expression in the opportunity to have a show of his paintings in a New York art gallery, courtesy of the escaped convict Lustig (**Robert De Niro**).

On television, a 1974 NBC production featured **Michael York** as Pip, **Sarah Miles** as Estella, **Margaret Leighton** as Miss Havisham, and **James Mason** as Magwitch. A 1989 Disney Channel adaptation featured Anthony Calf as Pip, Kim Thomson as Estella, Jean Simmons (the young Estella of the 1946 film) as Miss Havisham, and **Anthony Hopkins** as Magwitch.

The American composer Dominick Argento has written two one-act operas based on episodes from the novel: *Miss Havisham's Fire* (New York City Opera, 1979) and *Miss Havisham's Wedding Night* (Minnesota Opera, 1981).

GREAT GATSBY, THE
(novel by F. Scott Fitzgerald; 1925)

The first film version of Fitzgerald's Jazz Age classic, in 1928, starred Warner Baxter (Gatsby), Lois Wilson (Daisy Buchanan), Neil Hamilton (Nick Carraway), Hale Hamilton (Tom Buchanan), and Georgie Hale and **William Powell** (Myrtle and George Wilson).

The next film, in 1949, was based not only on the novel but also on a theatrical adaptation by Owen Davis that had a three-month run on Broadway in 1926 under **George Cukor**'s direction; on stage, James Rennie was Gatsby and Florence Eldridge was Daisy. For the 1949 film, directed by Elliott Nugent, the cast included **Alan Ladd** (Gatsby), Betty Field (Daisy), Macdonald Carey (Nick), Barry Sullivan (Tom), **Shelley Winters** (Myrtle), and Howard Da Silva (George). Jordan Baker was played by Ruth Roman; the character was more prominent than in other versions because here she served as Nick's love interest.

The next incarnation, directed by Jack Clayton, was the star-studded 1974 films with **Robert Redford** (Gatsby), **Mia Farrow** (Daisy), **Sam Waterston** (Nick), Bruce Dern (Tom), Karen Black (Myrtle), and Scott Wilson (George); the

1949 George, Howard Da Silva, made an appearance as gangster Meyer Wolfsheim.

In 1999, an opera by John Harbison had its world premiere at the Metropolitan Opera in New York City, with soprano **Dawn Upshaw** as Daisy and tenor Jerry Hadley as Gatsby.

For A. R. Gurney's 1981 play *The Golden Age*, see above, under *The Aspern Papers*.

GUYS AND DOLLS
(stories by Damon Runyon)

Runyon's stories of Broadway's gamblers, moochers, and hangers-on have found their way into other media many times. The following stories (published in various collections of the author's works) have been adapted to stage and screen.

"The Idyll of Miss Sarah Brown." This is the story that served as the kernel for the Broadway musical *Guys and Dolls* (1950), which its authors (Abe Burrows and Jo Swerling) described as based on "a story and characters by Damon Runyon." It concerns a bet that gambler Sky Masterson makes with Salvation Army "doll" Miss Sarah Brown; for the musical, that incident was augmented with other characters from Runyon's stories (Nathan Detroit, Nicely Nicely Johnson, Harry the Horse, and others) and newly invented plotlines and characters. With music and lyrics by **Frank Loesser**, the show ran three years the first time around, had a highly successful revival in the 1990s, and is arguably the great American musical comedy. It came to the screen in 1955, under **Joseph L. Mankiewicz**'s direction, with a cast including **Frank Sinatra** as Nathan, **Vivian Blaine** as Miss Adelaide (reprising her Broadway role), **Marlon Brando** as Sky Masterson, and **Jean Simmons** as Sarah Brown.

"Madame La Gimp." This story inspired two memorable films, both directed by **Frank Capra**: *Lady for a Day* (1933) and *Pocketful of Miracles* (1961). Both hew closely to the original Runyon story, which has an unabashedly happy ending. The story's Madame La Gimp becomes Apple Annie (played, respectively, by May Robson and **Bette Davis**), a gin-soaked, down-at-the-heels Broadway beggar who becomes lady for a day when Dave the Dude (Warren William and **Glenn Ford**) engineers an elaborate masquerade to impress Annie's young daughter, raised since infancy in a Spanish convent and believing her mother to be the wife of a prominent man. **Ann-Margret** made her film debut in 1961 as the daughter.

"Little Miss Marker." Of the four screen versions, the first is the most faithful, although it takes liberties that are repeated in later versions. *Little Miss Marker* (1934), with moppet **Shirley Temple** in her first starring role, featured **Adolphe Menjou** as Sorrowful Jones, the bookie who accepts a little girl as a marker for a $2 bet. In the film, the child's father is killed before he can "redeem" his child (in the story, the father has amnesia, but turns up at the end to reclaim little Marky); the film also added a love interest for Sorrowful, played by Dorothy Dell. These changes were retained in the next adaptation, *Sorrowful Jones* (1949), starring **Bob Hope** and **Lucille Ball**; Mary Jane Saunders played Marky. *Forty Pounds of Trouble* (1963) did not acknowledge the story as its source, but this tale of a Lake Tahoe casino manager (**Tony Curtis**) follows the general outlines of the earlier films; **Suzanne Pleshette** was the love interest, Claire Wilcox was the abandoned child, and **Stubby Kaye** (who had played Nicely Nicely Johnson in *Guys and Dolls* on both stage and screen) provided an additional touch of Runyon flavor. Finally, 1980's *Little Miss Marker* offered **Walter Matthau** as Sorrowful, **Julie Andrews** as his love interest, and Sara Stimson as The Kid.

"The Lemon Drop Kid." The 1934 film stays close to the original plot, although the Kid's baby is no longer born dead (his wife still dies in childbirth), making possible a bittersweet Hollywood ending when the Kid is reunited with the child. Lee Tracy played the title character (called Wally Brooks, but unnamed except for the moniker in the Runyon story), opposite Helen Mack as his wife, Alice. The 1951 film took the Runyon story as a starting point only, inventing most of the plot incidents and tailoring the role of the Kid to suit the talents of star **Bob Hope**.

"Hold 'em Yale." This story was filmed in 1935 with the basic concept—a group of typically Runyonesque ticket scalpers attend the Harvard-Yale football game—intact, but some changes in plot. The film's cast included William Frawley and Andy Devine as two of the scalpers, Cesar Romero as Gigolo Georgie, and **Buster Crabbe** as a college student romancing Patricia Ellis as heiress Clarice Van Cleve.

"Little Pinks." This tale of the enduring love of a busboy named Pinkerton (known as Little Pinks) for a nightclub performer was adapted for the screen as *The Big Street* in 1942. **Henry Fonda** played the timid hero, opposite Lucille Ball as the golddigging Gloria. After she is paralyzed in a fall (pushed down a flight of stairs by a rejected lover), which does nothing to improve her demanding personality, Pinks stands by her as her better-heeled companions disappear. Impoverished and sick, Gloria yearns to go to Florida, for her health and, she hopes, to reunite with the wealthy man she has set her sights on. Pinks gets her there, by hitching rides and sometimes even pushing her south in her wheelchair—down a very big street, from Broadway to the Sunshine State. As in Runyon's story, Gloria dies in Florida, but (in the film) not without recognizing the single-minded devotion and love Pinks has for her. The supporting cast includes Sam Levene, who eight years later would star as Nathan Detroit in Broadway's *Guys and Dolls*, and, as himself, bandleader and later TV dad **Ozzie Nelson**.

"Butch Minds the Baby." The 1942 film, starring **Broderick Crawford**, appears to have taken little from the story other than the character of a tough safecracker entrusted with the care of a child; in the film Butch goes straight, through the influence of his neighbor's child, but Runyon's story concerns a safecracking conducted with the little boy (Butch's own son) in tow.

"Johnny One-Eye." As with other Runyon adaptations, this 1950 film starring Pat O'Brien and Wayne Morris altered the story's plot somewhat and changed the characters' names—and even, in one case, a character's species: Johnny, a one-eyed cat in Runyon's story, here becomes a dog!

"The Bloodhounds of Broadway." The 1989 **Madonna** film (without the "The" and based on several stories by Runyon) has little in common with the title story, except for a few characters: Regret, played by **Matt Dillon**; Lovey Lou, played by Jennifer Grey; and Anita Morris as Miss Missouri Martin. Beat writer **William S. Burroughs** has a cameo role as a butler.

Television adaptations. "Damon Runyon Theatre" was a half-hour weekly series on CBS from April 1955 to June 1956; most of the episodes were based on Runyon's writings.

HAIRY APE, THE
(play by Eugene O'Neill; 1922)

O'Neill's Expressionistic drama was brought to the screen in 1944 under Alfred Santell's direction. The film takes some liberties with the original material, deleting much of the play's guttural dialect and changing the ending: in the play, ship's stoker Yank (called Hank in the film) frees an ape in the zoo and is crushed to death; in the film, Hank (William Bendix) makes peace with the world, does not free the ape, and returns to the ship. The film featured **Susan Hayward** as the society woman who entices Hank.

HAMLET
(play by William Shakespeare; c. 1601)

This tragedy has been adapted to the screen literally dozens of times, in England, the United States, Russia, Finland, India, France, and elsewhere. Among the actors who have embodied the title character on screen are **Sarah Bernhardt** (directed by Clement Maurice; France, 1900), **Laurence Olivier** (directed by Olivier; 1948; Academy Awards: Best Picture, Best Actor), **Richard Burton** (directed by **John Giel-**

gud; 1964), **Mel Gibson** (directed by **Franco Zeffirelli**; 1990), and (in a four-hour version) **Kenneth Branagh** (directed by Branagh; 1996). In 2000, under Michael Almereyda's direction, **Ethan Hawke**'s up-to-the-minute Hamlet took on corporate politics at the rotten Denmark Corporation, where his murdered father (**Sam Shepard**) had been the CEO; Julia Stiles's Ophelia drowned herself in the pool of New York City's Solomon R. Guggenheim Museum. A 1964 Russian film (directed by Grigory Kosintsev) had a screenplay by **Boris Pasternak** and a score by **Shostakovich**. Television Hamlets include Maurice Evans (NBC, 1953), Richard Chamberlain (NBC, 1970), and Kevin Kline (PBS, 1990).

More off-beat film approaches include *Johnny Hamlet* (1972), an Italian-American spaghetti-western in which a soldier returns home to find his father dead and his mother married to his uncle. Although the plot follows Shakespeare fairly closely, the ending is different: like any good western hero, Johnny rides off into the sunset. *A Midwinter's Tale* (1995; U.K. title: *In the Bleak Midwinter*), written and directed by Kenneth Branagh, is a comedy about a provincial English theater company attempting to stage *Hamlet*; the cast includes **Joan Collins** and Richard Briers. And *Strange Brew* (1983), written and directed by its stars, **Rick Moranis** and **Dave Thomas**, offers a curious homage to Shakespeare: Bob and Doug McKenzie, characters created by Moranis and Thomas on the television comedy series "SCTV," here become involved in a plot to gain control of the Elsinore Brewery, run by Claude Elsinore.

Of the operas based on *Hamlet*, the one by Ambroise Thomas (Paris, 1868) is notable, not least for its happy ending—Hamlet lives to ascend the throne of Denmark. *Hamlet* has also inspired composers of popular music: Frank Loesser's song "Hamlet," introduced by Betty Hutton in the 1949 film *Red, Hot and Blue*, gives the tale of Hamlet a jive/swing slant, and the rock musical *Hair* (1968) includes a musical setting by Galt MacDermot of one of the play's best-known soliloquies, "What a piece

of work is man." A rock musical, *Rockabye Hamlet*, with book, music, and lyrics by Cliff Jones, began its life in Canada in 1973 on the Canadian Broadcasting Corporation; two years later, it came to Broadway where, under the direction of Gower Champion, it lasted just a week.

The ravages of war-torn England may have prompted the radical style in which Robert Helpmann choreographed his one-act ballet, to Tchaikovsky's Fantasy Overture, for the Sadler's Wells Ballet (London, 1942); it was classical ballet put to dramatic-mimetic use within swift, cinematic scenes, each ending with a blackout. Boris Eifman used the play as an analogue for his ballet *Russian Hamlet* (St. Petersburg, 1999), to explore through surreal spectacle the psychological underpinnings of the sad, dramatic story of Catherine the Great's son, eventually Tsar Paul II, all the revealed emotions heightened by the music of Beethoven and Mahler. *Hamlet Connotations* (American Ballet Theatre, New York, 1976) is a dance piece choreographed by John Neumeier to music by **Aaron Copland**; in its world premiere performance, **Mikhail Baryshnikov** danced the role of Hamlet.

Tom Stoppard's *The Fifteen-minute Hamlet* (produced on Broadway in 1992 and adapted as a short film in 1995 by Todd Luiso) reduces Shakespeare's play to its most famous lines, spoken by actors who rush madly on and off stage. Earlier, in *Rosencrantz and Guildenstern Are Dead* (1966), Stoppard presented *Hamlet* from the point of view of two of its seemingly insignificant characters; in 1990, his film version of his play starred **Gary Oldman, Tim Roth**, and **Richard Dreyfuss**. Also adopting a shift in point of view, John Updike's novel *Gertrude and Claudius* (2000) relates the life of Hamlet's mother, from her point of view.

HAMLET, THE
(novel by William Faulkner; 1940)

Characters and elements from this novel, along with others from two Faulkner stories, "Barn

Burning" and "Spotted Horses," were loosely combined by screenwriters Irving Ravetch and Harriet Frank, Jr. to become *The Long Hot Summer* (directed by Martin Ritt; 1958). The film's cast included **Paul Newman** as Ben Quick, **Joanne Woodward** as Clara Varner (a character not in any of the Faulkner sources), Anthony Franciosa as Jody Varner, **Lee Remick** as Eula Varner (Jody's wife in the film, but his sister in the novel), Orson Welles as Will Varner, and **Angela Lansbury** as Minnie Littlejohn.

The movie inspired an hourlong weekly television series on ABC that ran for one season, in 1965–66. The cast was headed by Edmond O'Brien (replaced halfway through the season by Dan O'Herlihy) as Will Varner, Roy Thinnes as Ben Quick, Nancy Malone as Clara Varner, Paul Geary as Jody Varner, Ruth Roman as Minnie Littlejohn, and Lana Wood as Eula Harker (in this version, neither Will's daughter nor Jody's wife).

In 1985, an NBC miniseries starred Don Johnson as Ben, **Jason Robards** as Will, Judith Ivey as Clara, Cybill Shepherd as Eula (once again a Varner), **Ava Gardner** as Minnie, and William Russ as Jody.

HEART OF DARKNESS
(novella by Joseph Conrad; 1902)

For his Vietnamese war epic *Apocalypse Now* (1979), director **Francis Ford Coppola** borrowed elements from Conrad's novel for the journey down the river by Captain Willard (played by **Martin Sheen**) to find the madman Kurtz (**Marlon Brando**). Although the film is not officially an adaptation of *Heart of Darkness*, it was the closest the novella came to the big screen in the 20th century.

An acknowledged, official adaptation did appear on cable television, on TNT, in 1994. Directed by **Nicolas Roeg**, the cast included Tim Roth as Marlow and **John Malkovich** as Kurtz.

HUNCHBACK OF NOTRE DAME, THE
(novel by Victor Hugo; 1831)

Hugo's tale of the tortured hunchback Quasimodo and his love for the Gypsy girl Esmeralda has been filmed many times. Two notable silent screen adaptations were *The Darling of Paris* (1917), starring vamp **Theda Bara** as Esmeralda and focusing on her trial; and a 1923 version with the master of horror makeup, **Lon Chaney**, as Quasimodo and Patsy Ruth Miller as Esmeralda.

The best-known film, at least until the Disney version, was William Dieterle's 1939 adaptation, starring **Charles Laughton** as Quasimodo, **Maureen O'Hara** as Esmeralda, and Cedric Hardwicke as Frollo. Next came a French-Italian coproduction, *Notre Dame de Paris* (1956), with a mostly French cast but starring Italian actress **Gina Lollobrigida** as Esmeralda and American actor **Anthony Quinn** as Quasimodo. Then, confounding all expectations, came the 1996 animated Disney musical. Despite Quasimodo's cute gargoyle companions, this was essentially a serious film, not a watered-down children's version. The songs were by Alan Menken and Stephen Schwartz, and the voice cast included Tom Hulce as Quasimodo, **Demi Moore** as Esmeralda, Kevin Kline as Captain Phoebus, and Jason Alexander and Charles Kimbrough as the gargoyles Hugo and Victor.

A 1982 CBS "Hallmark Hall of Fame" adaptation starred **Anthony Hopkins** as Quasimodo, **Derek Jacobi** as Frollo, and **Lesley-Anne Down** as Esmeralda; and *The Hunchback* (TNT, 1997) featured **Mandy Patinkin** as Quasimodo, Richard Harris as Frollo, and Selma Hayek as Esmeralda.

Among the operas on the subject are those by Alexander Dargomizhsky (*Esmeralda*; Moscow, 1847) and Franz Schmidt (*Notre Dame*; Vienna, 1914).

A famous Romantic ballet, *La Esmeralda* (1844), was choreographed and danced by Jules Perrot as Gringoire and his partner, Carlotta Grisi, in the title role.

Idiot, The
(novel by Fyodor Dostoyevsky; 1874)

Dostoyevsky's novel of the saintly Prince Myshkin has attracted the interest of filmmakers in several countries and cultures, including versions from France in 1946 (with **Gérard Philipe** as Myshkin and Edwige Feuillère as Nastasia) and 1985 (*L'Amour Braque*, a free adaptation set in 1980s Paris); the Soviet Union (1958); and India (1991, set in contemporary Bombay). **Akira Kurosawa**'s *Hakuchi* (1951) takes place in Japan; Rogoshin, played by **Toshiro Mifune**, joins Myshkin in madness.

Robert Montgomery's off-Broadway play with music, *Subject to Fits: A Response to Dostoyevsky's The Idiot* (1971), is a comment on the novel, rather than a straightforward adaptation.

Operas based on the novel include *L'Idiota* by Luciano Chailly (Rome, 1970) and *Myshkin* (commissioned by PBS, 1970) by John Charles Eaton.

The Idiot was one of Russian choreographer Boris Eifman's earliest uses of literary text as scenario in his ballet set to Tchaikovsky's Sixth Symphony (St. Petersburg, 1980).

Iliad *and* Odyssey
(epic poems by Homer; 8th century B.C.)

The Trojan War and its chief players—Helen of Troy, Achilles, Odysseus—have appeared in many works over the millennia; listed here are a few that acknowledge a specific debt to Homer.

The Hollywood extravaganza *Helen of Troy* (1956), directed by Robert Wise, had an international cast, with Italian actress **Rossana Podestà** as Helen, the Frenchman Jacques Sernas as Paris, British actors Cedric Hardwicke, Stanley Baker, and Torin Thatcher as, respectively, Priamus, Achilles, and Odysseus, and French bombshell **Brigitte Bardot** as Andraste. More recently, *O Brother, Where Art Thou?* (2000), directed by **Joel Coen** from a screenplay cowritten with his brother Ethan, follows the Depression-era odyssey of Ulysses Everett McGill (**George Clooney**) and his fellow fugitives-from-a-chain-gang (John Turturro and Tim Blake Nelson), as McGill tries to get home in time to prevent his ex-wife, Penny (**Holly Hunter**), from remarrying. Along the way, they encounter a blind prophet (Lee Weaver), the one-eyed Big Dan Teague (**John Goodman**), mayoral candidate Homer Stokes (Wayne Duvall), and a group of sirens, not to mention gangster George "Babyface" Nelson (Michael Badaluco) and the Ku Klux Klan. The film's title is an allusion to the Preston Sturges film classic *Sullivan's Travels* (1942), in which film director John L. Sullivan (Joel McCrea) undertakes his own Depression-era odyssey in search of the meaning of life—and material for a film he hopes to make, called...*O Brother, Where Art Thou?*

The Odyssey, a 1997 NBC "Hallmark Hall of Fame" miniseries, directed by Andrei Konchalovsky, boasted an all-star cast: Armand Assante as Odysseus, Greta Scacchi as Penelope, Isabella Rossellini as Athene, and, in other roles, Bernadette Peters, Eric Roberts, Irene Papas (an authentic touch of Greece), Jeroen Krabbé, Geraldine Chaplin, Christopher Lee, and Vanessa L. Williams.

Musical adaptations include two operas—**Claudio Monteverdi**'s *Il Ritorno d'Ulisse in Patria* (*The Return of Ulysses to His Country*) (Venice, 1641), and **Gabriel Fauré**'s *Pénélope* (Paris, 1913)—and three Broadway musicals. *The Golden Apple* (1954), with book and lyrics by John Latouche and music by Jerome Moross, was set in Washington State (chosen as the locale because there is a Mount Olympus there), and Ulysses became a veteran of the Spanish-American War. The show was so critically acclaimed that it became the first off-Broadway musical to transfer to Broadway, where, unfortunately, it never found an audience. The second musical, *Home Sweet Homer* (1976), reached Broadway after its own odyssey of more than a year on the road, undergoing an alteration in title (from *Odyssey*) and other changes in the directing and writing areas (**Erich Segal**, a classics scholar best known as the author of *Love Story*, was among those who jumped ship). It starred **Yul Brynner**, had music by Mitch Leigh, lyrics by Charles Burr and Forman Brown, and a book by Roland Kibbee and Albert Marre. The show's New York sojourn ended as soon as it began; *Home Sweet Homer* closed on opening night. The third, *The Human Comedy* (1983), with music by Galt MacDermot and a libretto by William Dumaresq, was an adaptation of William Saroyan's 1943 novel, set during World War II in the town of Ithaca, California. The novel, its 1943 film version (directed by Clarence Brown and starring **Mickey Rooney** and Van Johnson), and the musical all follow the fortunes of the Macauley family: eldest son, Marcus, away at war; his brother Homer, who works in a telegraph office to help support the family; and youngest brother Ulysses, who watches the trains pass by. The musical was acclaimed in its original production at the New York Shakespeare Festival's Public Theater, but a transfer to Broadway in 1984 was unsuccessful.

More seriously, the *Odyssey* has inspired several major works of literature, including one of the greatest books of the 20th century, **James Joyce**'s *Ulysses* (1922; see below for adaptations). In 1938, **Nikos Kazantzakis** composed *The Odyssey: A Modern Sequel*, a philosophical epic poem that continues the story of Odysseus's journeys. And the epic poem *Omeros* (1990) is **Derek Walcott**'s homage to the *Odyssey*; the title is Greek for "Homer."

JANE EYRE
(novel by Charlotte Brontë; 1847)

This classic tale has been filmed many times, including silent versions in 1915 (as *The Castle of Thornfield*), 1918 (as *Woman and Wife*, with Alice Brady as Jane), 1921, and 1926 (in Germany, as *Die Waise von Lowood*).

The first sound version, in 1934, featured Virginia Bruce as Jane, Colin Clive as Rochester, and Beryl Mercer as Mrs. Fairfax. Notably, in 1944 Robert Stevenson directed **Joan Fontaine** as Jane, **Orson Welles** as Rochester, child stars Margaret O'Brien as Adele and Peggy Ann Garner as the young Jane, and Edith Barrett as Mrs.

Fairfax. And in 1996, **Franco Zeffirelli** directed French actress **Charlotte Gainsbourg** as Jane, **William Hurt** as Rochester, **Anna Paquin** as young Jane, and **Elle Macpherson** as Blanche Ingram.

Television adaptations include a 1971 NBC presentation (first shown in theaters in England) starring **Susannah York** and **George C. Scott**, and a 1997 A&E miniseries with Samantha Morton and Ciarán Hinds.

Courtney Burr's 1958 Broadway dramatic adaptation starred Eric Porter and Jan Brooks. A musical adaptation, with book and direction by John Caird, and music and lyrics by Paul Gordon, opened on Broadway in fall 2000, with Marla Schaffel as Jane and James Barbour as Rochester.

A prequel to *Jane Eyre*, **Jean Rhys**'s novel *Wide Sargasso Sea* (1966) tells the story of Antoinette Cosway, a Jamaican who marries an Englishman and moves with him to England, where she goes mad and is confined in the attic of her husband's home. Antoinette is, of course, the Bertha of *Jane Eyre*, and her husband, the reader eventually discovers, is Rochester. Rhys's novel was filmed in 1993 by John Duigan, with Karina Lombard as Antoinette and Nathaniel Parker as Rochester.

A looser variation is *I Walked with a Zombie* (1943), a classic Jacques Tourneur horror film, about a young Canadian nurse (Frances Dee) who journeys to the West Indies to care for the wife (presumed insane) of a tortured English plantation owner. Like Jane Eyre, she falls in love with her employer and is united with him when his wife, who is not mad but is in a zombie state as the result of a voodoo curse, is drowned by her lover, the plantation owner's half brother.

JUNO AND THE PAYCOCK
(play by Sean O'Casey; 1924)

The film version of O'Casey's play represents a curiosity in the career of master of suspense **Alfred Hitchcock**, who directed it in 1930 from a screenplay by Alma Reville (Hitchcock's wife). The cast included Sara Allgood as Juno, Edward Chapman as Cap'n Boyle, and Sydney Morgan as Joxer Daly.

Juno (1959), with music and lyrics by **Marc Blitzstein** and a book by Joseph Stein, was a Broadway musical adaptation starring **Shirley Booth** as Juno, Melvyn Douglas as Boyle, and Jack MacGowran as Joxer, under **José Ferrer**'s direction. Although the show had only a short run (16 performances), Blitzstein's score is memorable.

KING LEAR
(play by William Shakespeare; c. 1605–6)

Shakespeare's king was depicted in a number of undistinguished silent films in the United States (1909, 1916) and Italy (1910), but in the sound era the play attracted the interest of four of the world's most prominent directors: the Soviet Union's Grigory Kosintsev, England's **Peter Brook**, Japan's **Akira Kurosawa**, and France's **Jean-Luc Godard**.

Both Kosintsev (1969) and Brook (1971) chose to use black and white, rather than color, to emphasize the starkness of the story. Kosintsev's casting is also of interest: Lear was played by a frail, diminutive actor, and the Fool was presented as a shaven-headed starveling, resembling a concentration camp inmate. Brook's Lear was **Paul Scofield**, who had triumphed in the role on the London stage; **Irene Worth** was Goneril.

Kurosawa's *Ran* (1985) was inspired not only by Shakespeare's play, but also by the story of a 16th-century Japanese warrior. The plot closely resembles that of *King Lear*, although here the warlord Hidetora/Lear wishes to divide his land among three sons (rather than daughters). Lady Kaede, one of the warlord's daughters-in-law, is a ruthless combination of Shakespeare's Regan and Goneril.

Godard's 1987 film is the freest, and strangest, of the adaptations. The main character, called William Shakespeare Jr. the Fifth (played by avant-garde theater director **Peter Sellars**), tries to recapture the works of his ancestor, which

have somehow been destroyed in the post-Chernobyl world. Burgess Meredith is Don Learo, a Mafia capo, and **Molly Ringwald** is his daugher Cordelia. Godard himself appears as the Professor, **Woody Allen** appears briefly as a film editor seen splicing film with a safety pin and a needle and thread, and writer **Norman Mailer** and his actress daughter Kate Mailer appear briefly in a prologue.

Another interesting variation is *Der Yidisher Kenig Lir* (*The Yiddish King Lear*), Harry Thomashefsky's 1934 film adaptation of Jacob Gordin's play, set in turn-of-the-century Vilna, Lithuania. In this American film, in Yiddish with English subtitles, a Jewish patriarch announces at a Passover seder his intention to divide his fortune among his daughters and then leave for Jerusalem.

A CBS television adaptation in 1953 starred Orson Welles as Lear, under Peter Brook's direction; Beatrice Straight was Goneril, and Natasha Perry was Cordelia. A 1997 PBS "Masterpiece Theatre" adaptation preserved Ian Holm's acclaimed London stage performance of the role, in which he notoriously appeared nude during the storm on the heath.

Operas based on Shakespeare's play include Stafano Gobatti's *Cordelia* (Bologna, 1881), Vito Frazzi's *Re Lear* (Florence, 1939), and Aribert Reimann's *Lear* (Munich, 1978).

Jane Smiley's Pulitzer Prize–winning novel *A Thousand Acres* (1991) updated the story of *King Lear* to an Iowa farm; a screen version in 1997, directed by Jocelyn Moorhouse, starred **Michelle Pfeiffer, Jessica Lange**, and Jennifer Jason Leigh as the Cook sisters, with **Jason Robards** as Larry Cook, the family patriarch.

KISS OF THE SPIDER WOMAN
(novel by Manuel Puig; 1976)

Puig's highly cinematic novel of cellmates in a Bolivian prison came to the screen in 1985 in a Brazilian-U.S. coproduction directed by Hector Babenco. **William Hurt**, in his Oscar-winning role, was the windowdresser Molina, who shared his movie memories with **Raul**

Julia's Valentin; **Sonia Braga** played the woman in his cinematic fantasies.

The movie-fantasy sequences made the material a natural for the Broadway musical stage (even if the political-prison setting did not). With music by John Kander, lyrics by Fred Ebb, a book by **Terrence McNally**, and direction by **Harold Prince**, the show reached Broadway in 1993, quickly winning the Tony Award as Best Musical as well as Tonys for its stars, Brent Carver as Molina and Chita Rivera as the Spider Woman.

LIAISONS DANGEREUSES, LES
(novel by Pierre Choderlos de Laclos; 1782)

Laclos's epistolary novel has seduced its way onto the screen four times. **Roger Vadim**'s *Les Liaisons Dangereuses* (France, 1959) set the story in contemporary France, where **Jeanne Moreau** and **Gérard Philipe** (as Merteuil and Valmont) plot against Annette Vadim and Jeanne Valérie (as Madame de Tourvel and Cécile); a tape recording substitutes for a letter as the instrument of Cécile's destruction. In 1988, Christopher Hampton's stage adaptation *Les Liaisons Dangereuses* (presented by the Royal Shakespeare Company in London in 1986 and on Broadway in 1987) was filmed by Stephen Frears as *Dangerous Liaisons*, starring **Glenn Close, John Malkovich, Michelle Pfeiffer**, and **Uma Thurman**. The next year, Milos Forman's *Valmont* featured **Colin Firth** as Valmont, **Annette Bening** as Merteuil, **Meg Tilly** as Madame de Tourvel, and Fairuza Balk as Cécile. Finally, in 1999, Roger Kumble's *Cruel Intentions* moved the story to present-day Manhattan, where overprivileged teenaged step-siblings Kathryn Merteuil (**Sarah Michelle Gellar**) and Sebastian Valmont (Ryan Phillippe) set out to destroy Annette (**Reese Witherspoon**) and Cecile (Selma Blair), their classmates at exclusive Manchester Prep. Despite the late-1990s setting, letters, not e-mail correspondence, still figure in the proceedings. A television series based on *Cruel Intentions*, called "Manchester Prep," was scheduled by

FOX for the 1999–2000 television season, but was withdrawn before the first episode aired.

The ballet *Coup d'Estoc*, choreographed by Christian Holder to music by Mozart, was performed by the New Amsterdam Ballet at the Jacob's Pillow Dance Festival in 1991. As *Les Liaisons Dangereuses*, the work is in the repertory of American Ballet Theatre, where it premiered in 1993.

LITTLE FOXES, THE
(play by Lillian Hellman; 1939)

Hellman's drama came to the screen in 1941, directed by **William Wyler**, with **Bette Davis** as Regina Giddins, Herbert Marshall as Horace Giddins, Teresa Wright as Alexandra Giddins, Dan Duryea as Leo Hubbard, Charles Dingle as Ben Hubbard, and Patricia Collinge as Birdie Hubbard.

Five years later, Hellman's Broadway play *Another Part of the Forest* was a prequel to *The Little Foxes*, set 20 years earlier and exploring the events that established the balance of power among the Hubbard siblings. When this play reached the screen in 1948, the cast was headed by Ann Blyth as Regina, Dan Duryea as Oscar (the father of the character he had played in *The Little Foxes*), Edmond O'Brien as Ben, and **Fredric March** and **Florence Eldridge** as the parents of this brood.

Marc Blitzstein's *Regina* (1949) straddled the worlds of theater and opera. First produced on Broadway, where it had a short (56-performance) run, it was presented in 1953 by the New York City Opera (in whose repertory it remains), and subsequently by the Santa Fe Opera and Houston Grand Opera, among other opera companies.

LOLITA
(novel by Vladimir Nabokov; 1955)

This novel has reached the screen twice: in 1962, directed by **Stanley Kubrick**, with **James Mason** (Humbert Humbert), **Peter Sellers** (Clare Quilty), **Shelley Winters** (Charlotte Haze), and **Sue Lyon** (Lolita); and in 1997, directed by Adrian Lyne, with **Jeremy Irons** (Humbert), Frank Langella (Quilty), Melanie Griffith (Charlotte), and Dominique Swain (Lolita).

Two attempts were made to bring *Lolita* to Broadway. The musical *Lolita, My Love* (1971), composed by John Barry with book and lyrics by Alan Jay Lerner, starred John Neville as Humbert and Dorothy Loudon as Charlotte; the show closed during its pre-Broadway tryout. In 1981, **Edward Albee**'s dramatic adaptation included a new character, A Certain Gentleman, played by Ian Richardson, who served as an on-stage narrator. **Donald Sutherland** played Humbert, Clive Revill was Quilty, Shirley Stoler was Charlotte, and Blanche Baker was Lolita. Albee's *Lolita* lasted only 12 performances on Broadway.

Pia Pera's *Lo's Diary*, a novel first published in Italy that retold the story from Lolita's point of view, was published in English translation in the United States in 1999.

LOOK HOMEWARD, ANGEL
(novel by Thomas Wolfe; 1929)

Although it has never made its way to the big screen, Wolfe's story of the coming of age of Eugene Gant became a Pulitzer Prize–winning Broadway play in 1957. Adapted by Ketti Frings, better known as a screenwriter than a playwight, the play ran more than a year and starred **Anthony Perkins** as Eugene. A 1972 CBS television adaptation of the play starred **Geraldine Page**, E. G. Marshall, Timothy Bottoms, and Pamela Payton-Wright.

The play's success was not repeated when *Angel* (1978), a musical adaptation by Gary Geld (music), Peter Udell (lyrics), and Frings and Udell (book), opened on Broadway. For its five performances, the cast was headed by Frances Sternhagen and Fred Gwynne as the elder Gants, and Don Scardino as Eugene.

LOST HORIZON
(novel by James Hilton; 1933)

Director **Frank Capra**'s 1937 film version of Hilton's tale of Shangri-La was an instant classic, with a cast that included **Ronald Colman** as Robert Conway, Jane Wyatt as Sandra, his love interest, Margo as Maria, Sam Jaffe as the High Lama, and H. B. Warner as Chang.

The 1973 musical film, with a score by **Burt Bacharach** and **Hal David**, was less successful. Directed by Charles Jarrott, the cast included Peter Finch as Robert Conway, **Liv Ullmann** as Catherine, his love interest, Olivia Hussey as Maria, **Charles Boyer** as the High Lama, and **John Gielgud** as Chang. Less successful still was an earlier Broadway musical, *Shangri-La* (1956), with music by Harry Warren, lyrics by Jerome Lawrence and Robert E. Lee, additional lyrics by Sheldon Harnick, and a book by Hilton (who had died in 1954), Lawrence, and Lee. For its two-and-a-half-week run, it starred Dennis King and Shirley Yamaguchi.

LYSISTRATA
(play by Aristophanes; 411 B.C.)

Updated from Peloponnesian War–era Athens and Sparta to Kansas in the 1880s, *The Second Greatest Sex* (1955) is a film musical, directed by George Marshall with songs by Pony Sherell and Phil Moody. As the men of rival towns fight over the location of the county seat, Liza/Lysistrata (**Jeanne Crain**) organizes a marital strike to bring the men (chief among them Liza's brand-new husband, Matt, played by George Nader) to their senses.

A 1968 Swedish film, *The Girls* (*Flickorna*), directed by **Mai Zetterling**, is set in the present and concerns a group of actresses (**Bibi Andersson, Harriet Andersson**, and Gunnel Lindblom) on tour with a production of *Lysistrata*. Off stage, the women are involved in feminist and peace issues that mirror the themes of Aristophanes' play. The cast also included **Erland Josephson**.

Emil Petrovics's opera premiered in Budapest in 1962, and on Broadway *The Happiest Girl in the World* (1961) combined music by **Jacques**

Offenbach with new lyrics by **E. Y. Harburg**. In this moderately successful production, Pluto (played by Cyril Ritchard) descended to earth, where he met up with the goddess Diana (Janice Rule), who was trying to bring peace to all those warlike humans. Dran Seitz played Lysistrata.

MACBETH
(play by William Shakespeare; c. 1605–6)

Shakespeare's tale of bloody ambition has attracted filmmakers from the beginning: silent versions were produced in the United States (1908, 1916), Italy (1909), France (1910, 1915), England (1911), and Germany (1913).

Several noted directors have adapted the story, beginning with **Orson Welles** in 1948; Welles also played the title role, with Jeannette Nolan as Lady Macbeth, Dan O'Herlihy as Macduff, and **Roddy MacDowall** as Malcolm. **Akira Kurosawa** transposed the story to Japan in *Throne of Blood* (1957); **Toshiro Mifune** played the samurai Washizu, and Isuzu Yamada was his wife. **Roman Polanski**'s 1971 adaptation starred Jon Finch as Macbeth and **Francesca Annis** as Lady Macbeth.

Macbeth has also inspired looser adaptations. The French film *The Red Curtain* (*Le Rideau Rouge*), from a screenplay by **Jean Anouilh**, uses a performance of the play as the backdrop for a murder mystery. Michel Simon is the director of the play, who is killed just before the opening-night performance, Pierre Brasseur is the murderous actor reliving his crime as he portrays Macbeth on stage, and Monelle Valentin is the woman who came between them. And two English-language films have used Shakespeare's work as the outline for stories of ambition within the world of organized crime: *Joe Macbeth* (1955), featuring Paul Douglas as Joe Macbeth, Ruth Roman as his wife, Grégoire Aslan as Duca, Sid James as Banky, and Nicholas Stuart as Duffy; and *Men of Respect* (1991), with **John Turturro** as Mike Battaglia, Katherine Borowitz as his wife, Dennis Farina as Bankie Como, and Peter Boyle as Duffy.

Television adaptations have starred Maurice Evans and Judith Anderson on the "Hallmark Hall of Fame" (NBC, 1954), and, all on PBS, Eric Porter and Janet Suzman (1970), Ian McKellen and Judi Dench (1979), Jeremy Brett and Piper Laurie (1981), Philip Anglim and Maureen Anderman (1982), and Nicol Williamson and Jane Lapotaire (1983).

Operatic treatments of *Macbeth* have been composed by, most prominently, **Giuseppe Verdi** (Florence, 1847) as well as Lauro Rossi (*Biorn*; London, 1877), Ernest Bloch (Paris, 1910), and Lawrance Collingwood (London, 1934). A 1987 film of the Verdi opera, directed by Claude d'Anna, features Leo Nucci as Macbeth and **Shirley Verrett** as Lady Macbeth.

Russian writer Nikolai Leskov's 1865 story *Lady Macbeth of the Mtsensk District* concerns a young woman, Katerina, who murders first her father-in-law and then her husband, until, betrayed by her lover, she commits suicide, taking her lover's new mistress with her. Leskov's story was adapted by **Dmitri Shostakovich** as an opera that premiered in Leningrad in 1934. The opera was filmed in 1992 by Petr Weigl, and several Eastern European films have been based on the Leskov novel, notably the Polish/Yugoslav *The Siberian Lady Macbeth* (1961), directed by **Andrzej Wajda**.

Off-Broadway in 1967, *MacBird!* by Barbara Garson borrowed Shakespeare's plot for a political satire focusing on the conflict between President Lyndon B. Johnson and Senator Robert F. Kennedy. His performance as MacBird made **Stacy Keach** a star.

Richard Nelson's play *Two Shakespearean Actors* (1990) focuses on the background of the historical Astor Place Riots of 1849, prompted by rival productions of *Macbeth* in New York City that year starring, respectively, the American actor Edwin Forrest and the English actor William Charles Macready. The play premiered in London at the Royal Shakespeare Company; its subsequent Broadway production starred Victor Garber as Forrest and Brian Bedford as Macready.

MADAME BOVARY
(novel by Gustave Flaubert; 1857)

The first (alleged) adaptation of Flaubert's novel of romantic yearning, *Unholy Love* (1932), was set in Rye, New York, in the 1930s, but its principal characters, played by H. B. Warner, Lila Lee, and Lyle Talbot, seem to have little to do with Flaubert. Two years later, however, French director **Jean Renoir** was responsible for a faithful version, with exteriors shot on location in Normandy; Valentine Tessier was Emma Bovary, Pierre Renoir (the director's brother) was Charles Bovary, and Fernand Fabre was Rodolphe. A German version followed in 1937, with **Pola Negri** as Emma, Aribert Wascher as Charles, and Ferdinand Marian as Rodolphe. An Argentinean version appeared in 1947.

In 1949, director **Vincente Minnelli** gave the story the full Hollywood treatment; **Jennifer Jones** was Emma, **Van Heflin** was Charles, and **Louis Jourdan** was Rodolphe; **James Mason** played Flaubert himself, in scenes depicting a trial at which the author defends his novel and its title character.

In the ensuing decades there were adaptations from Germany (1969), Poland (1976), the Soviet Union (1989), and India (*Maya Memsaab*, 1992) as well as another from France; directed by **Claude Chabrol**, this 1991 film features **Isabelle Huppert** as Emma, Jean-François Balmer as Charles, and Christophe Malavay as Rodolphe.

A four-part miniseries aired in 1976 on PBS's "Masterpiece Theatre"; it starred **Francesca Annis** as Emma, **Tom Conti** as Charles, and Dennis Lill as Rodolphe. A two-part adaptation, also on "Masterpiece Theatre," starred Frances O'Connor in 2000.

McTEAGUE
(novel by Frank Norris; 1899)

Norris's story of murderous greed was brought to the silent screen several times. The first version, *Desert Gold* (1914), starred Clara Williams, Charles Ray, and Frank Borzage (who would soon become far better known as a director). Two years later, *Life's Whirlpool* (1916) featured Holbook Blinn and Fania Marinoff as McTeague and his wife.

But it was with *Greed* (1925), directed by **Erich Von Stroheim**, that Norris's work achieved screen immortality. Working with a cast headed by Gibson Gowland as McTeague, **Zasu Pitts** as Trina, and Jean Hersholt as Marcus Schouler, Von Stroheim insisted on verisimilitude, shooting as much as possible on location, rather than on the studio backlot; the final scenes were even filmed in Death Valley itself, where Norris had set them (inflicting great hardship on the cast and crew, who had to work in blistering heat). The original version of the film ran more than nine hours; Von Stroheim himself cut it to four-and-a-half hours, before it was reedited by the studio to just over two hours. Notorious for years as one of the most-butchered films in history, *Greed* was restored in 1999 to 280 minutes by film historian Rick Schmidlin, who used archival still photographs to represent much of the missing footage; the restored *Greed* was shown on cable's TCM in December 1999.

An opera by William Bolcom premiered at the Lyric Opera of Chicago in 1992.

MEDEA
(play by Euripides; 431 B.C.)

One of the best examples of the vengeance of a woman scorned, *Medea* was brought to the screen in 1970, directed by **Pier Paolo Pasolini** and starring opera diva **Maria Callas** in a nonsinging role. Callas had, however, previously sung the role in a production of Luigi Cherubini's opera *Médée*, which premiered in Paris in 1797. Other operas based on the story include those by Marc-Antoine Charpentier (*Médée*; Paris, 1693), **Darius Milhaud** (*Médée*; Angers, 1939), and Johann Mayr (*Medea in Corinto*; Naples, 1813). For Dominick Argento's 1988 opera *The Aspern Papers*, see above, under *The Aspern Papers*.

For the theater, Euripides' tragedy has been adapted by other playwrights and poets, notably

Pierre Corneille in *Médée* (1635) and **Robinson Jeffers** in *Medea* (1946). The Jeffers version is the best-known English-language adaptation; it was first performed on Broadway by **Judith Anderson** (who also appeared in a syndicated 1959 "Play of the Week" television adaptation) and, in more recent revivals, by **Zoe Caldwell** and **Diana Rigg**.

The interior life of the protagonist was famously taken on by **Martha Graham** in one of her great, stark, psychological ballets, *Cave of the Heart* (New York, 1946), with commissioned music by **Samuel Barber** and sets by **Isamu Noguchi**. The Royal Spanish National Ballet has a sizzling flamenco version (1984) in its repertory. And historically, a rendition by Jean-Georges Noverre, *Médée et Jason* (1763), set the stage for ballet with dramatic narrative thrust, rather than simply entrances and exits.

In 1999, *Marie Christine*, a Broadway musical adaptation by Michael John LaChiusa, moved the action to 1890s America, where Marie Christine L'Adrese, a New Orleans Creole versed in the art of *vodun*, meets Dante Keyes, a politically ambitious young man. The plot mirrors that of Euripides' play, although after exacting her revenge, Marie Christine is sent to prison, turn-of-the-century America offering no possibility of a *deus ex machina*.

MERRY WIVES OF WINDSOR, THE
(play by William Shakespeare; c. 1598)

Allegedly written because Queen Elizabeth I wanted to see the character of Falstaff in love, this play has been frequently adapted by composers, but has not had a notable film adaptation (although films both sound and silent have been produced in the United States, England, France, and Germany). The most memorable attempt to bring Falstaff to the screen is *Chimes at Midnight* (1965), directed by and starring **Orson Welles**, which weaves together elements from several of Shakespeare's history plays (*Richard II*, *Henry IV, Parts I and II*, *Henry V*) as well as from Holinshed's *Chronicle* (one of Shakespeare's own sources), and from *The Merry Wives of Windsor*.

Of the operas, Otto Nicolaï's *Die Lustigen Weiber von Windsor* (Berlin, 1849) has been preserved in a 1950 East German film featuring Paul Esser as Falstaff, and in a 1965 Austrian film with the American bass Norman Foster as Falstaff. Operas titled *Falstaff* include those by Antonio Salieri (Vienna, 1799), Adolphe Adam (Paris, 1856), and, notably, **Giuseppe Verdi** (Milan, 1893). *Sir John in Love*, by **Ralph Vaughan Williams**, premiered in London in 1929.

MIDSUMMER NIGHT'S DREAM, A
(play by William Shakespeare; c. 1595–96)

Silent film versions of Shakespeare's fantasy were produced in the United States (1909), France (1909), Italy (1913), and Germany (1924; with an original, jazz-inflected music score). But the first significant film adaptation was the first sound version, codirected in 1935 by **William Dieterle** and **Max Reinhardt**, with a cast including some of Hollywood's biggest stars—**James Cagney** as Bottom, **Dick Powell** as Lysander, **Mickey Rooney** as Puck, **Victor Jory** as Oberon, **Olivia de Havilland** as Hermia, and **Joe E. Brown** as Flute—and featuring Felix Mendelssohn's music on the soundtrack.

Perhaps because this was a hard act to follow, there was no important adaptation for more than 30 years, until the Peter Hall–Royal Shakespeare Company version of 1968, featuring **Diana Rigg** as Helena, **Helen Mirren** as Hermia, Ian Richardson as Oberon, **Judi Dench** as Titania, and David Warner as Lysander. Another Royal Shakespeare Company production was filmed in 1996 by Trevor Nunn; the cast was headed by Lindsay Duncan as Titania, Alex Jennings as Oberon, and Desmond Barrit as Bottom.

And at century's end, Michael Hoffman's 1999 film offered another all-star cast: **Kevin Kline** as Bottom, **Michelle Pfeiffer** as Titania, **Rupert Everett** as Oberon, Stanley Tucci as Puck, **Calista Flockhart** as Helena, Christian Bale as Demetrius, **Sophie Marceau** as Hippolyta, and **Roger Rees** as Peter Quince.

Swingin' the Dream (1939), for Broadway, was set in New Orleans in 1890. The show, with music by James Van Heusen, lyrics by Eddie de Lange, and a book by Gilbert Seldes and Erik Charell, had only a brief run, despite the contributions of a remarkable cast, including **Louis Armstrong** as Bottom, **Butterfly McQueen** as Puck, jazz singer Maxine Sullivan as Titania, **Dorothy Dandridge** (as part of the singing group The Dandridge Sisters) as a pixie, and comedienne Jackie "Moms" Mabley as Quince. Musical accompaniment was provided by the **Benny Goodman** Sextet. The score included the song "Darn That Dream."

The New York City Ballet's production of the ballet choreographed by **George Balanchine** in 1962 to **Mendelssohn**'s music was filmed in 1966; the film cast **Suzanne Farrell** as Titania, **Edward Villella** as Oberon, **Arthur Mitchell** as Puck, and **Patricia McBride** as Hermia.

Operas based on the play include those by **Henry Purcell** (*The Fairy Queen*; London, 1692) and, most famously, **Benjamin Britten** (Aldeburgh, 1960).

MISÉRABLES, LES
(novel by Victor Hugo; 1862)

Les Misérables may have inspired more film versions than almost any other work of nondramatic literature: there have been more than 20, in France and the United States as well as Italy, the Soviet Union, Mexico, Egypt, and Japan. And some of these adaptations rank among the longest films ever made, running three or more hours in their original versions. What follows is a list of select French- and English-language adaptations.

In French. In 1911, the great French music-hall star **Mistinguett** appeared as Eponine. In 1934, Harry Baur played Jean Valjean. In 1958, it was **Jean Gabin**'s turn, with Bernard Blier (later an important director) as Javert, and Bourvil as Thenardier. In 1982, Lino Ventura played Valjean and Michel Bouquet was Javert, under Robert Hossein's direction. **Claude Lelouch**'s 1995 film was a variation, in which a simple Frenchman (**Jean-Paul Belmondo**) finds purpose in life when he meets a Jewish family fleeing the Nazis and is introduced by them to Hugo's novel.

In English. The first critically important adaptation, in 1935, was directed by Richard Boleslawski, with **Fredric March** as Jean Valjean, **Charles Laughton** as Javert, Florence Eldridge as Fantine, and Cedric Hardwicke as Bishop Bienvenu. In 1952, Lewis Milestone's film starred Michael Rennie as Valjean, Robert Newton as Javert, Debra Paget as Cosette, and **Sylvia Sidney** as Fantine. In 1998, **Bille August**'s film (a German production, but shot in English) starred **Liam Neeson** as Valjean, **Geoffrey Rush** as Javert, **Uma Thurman** as Fantine, and **Claire Danes** as Cosette.

A 1978 CBS television adaptation starred Richard Jordan as Valjean and **Anthony Perkins** as Javert, with Cyril Cusack, Claude Dauphin, John Gielgud, and Ian Holm in other roles.

The novel is also known to many through its musical theater incarnation. Originally produced in Paris in 1980, with music by Claude-Michel Schönberg and lyrics by Alain Boublil and Jean-Marc Natel, *Les Misérables* premiered in English, with lyrics by Herbert Kretzmer, Trevor Nunn, and John Caird, at the Royal Shakespeare Company in London in 1985 and then on Broadway in 1987. The English-language productions were codirected by Trevor Nunn and John Caird, and Colm Wilkinson played the role of Jean Valjean on both sides of the ocean. A video concert version, *Les Misérables in Concert*, features a British and American "dream cast": Wilkinson as Valjean, Ruthie Henshall as Fantine, **Lea Salonga** as Eponine, Michael Ball as Marius, and Judy Kuhn as Cosette.

MOBY-DICK
(novel by Herman Melville; 1851)

When the great white whale came to the screen in 1926 as *The Sea Beast*, the title was not all that had changed; Ahab (played by **John Barrymore**) had a fiancée (Dolores Costello) back home in New Bedford, whose horror at his missing leg was what motivated his revenge against the whale. And Ishmael, who narrates Melville's novel, was nowhere in sight. Four years later, *Moby Dick* was virtually a remake of *The Sea Beast*, but with sound; Barrymore again played Ahab, with Joan Bennett as his lady-love. The next year, *Dämon des Meeres* was a German version of the latter film, with William Dieterle as Ahab.

With *Moby Dick* (directed by **John Huston**; 1956), the novel received a more faithful screen treatment: there were no women, and Ishmael, played by **Richard Basehart**, finally made it onto the screen. **Orson Welles** played Father Mapple, and Ahab was **Gregory Peck**, who returned to *Moby Dick*, but not as Ahab, in a 1998 USA television adaptation that featured **Patrick Stewart** as Ahab, Henry Thomas as Ishmael, and Peck as Father Mapple.

An earlier television adaptation, on NBC's "Hallmark Hall of Fame" series in 1954, was one of the first live dramatic broadcasts from Hollywood. It featured Victor Jory as Ahab and Lamont Johnson as Ishmael.

If *Moby Dick* on a television sound stage sounds difficult to pull off, imagine *Moby Dick* on a Broadway stage. Orson Welles did, and his adaptation, using a play-within-a-play structure and directed by Douglas Campbell, had a brief run on Broadway in 1962. **Rod Steiger** starred as Ahab.

Native Son
(novel by Richard Wright; 1940)

Wright's classic novel of racial conflict was adapted to the stage by Wright and playwright Paul Green in 1940; the Broadway production, directed by Orson Welles, starred Canada Lee as Bigger Thomas. But the novel's controversial subject matter kept it off the screen until 1950, when Wright and director Pierre Chenal obtained financing from the Argentinean film industry. Shot in Buenos Aires, the film starred the 42-year-old Wright as the 20-year-old Bigger Thomas.

In 1986, Jerrold Freedman directed a new film version for PBS's "American Playhouse" series, with the film shown first in theaters and then, some months later, on television. This time, Victor Love was Bigger and **Oprah Winfrey** was Mrs. Thomas. Playwright Richard Wesley, who wrote the screenplay, had a small role as a bartender.

Oedipus the King
(play by Sophocles; c. 430 B.C.)

Film versions of Sophocles' play have been an international affair. The 1957 *Oedipus Rex*, based on a stage production by the Stratford Festival of Canada, used **William Butler Yeats**'s adaptation of Sophocles and starred Douglas Campbell as Oedipus, Donald Davis as Tiresias, and Eleanor Stuart as Jocasta, under **Tyrone Guthrie**'s direction. Italian director **Pier Paolo Pasolini**'s 1967 *Edipo Re* was shot in the Moroccan desert and starred Silvano Mangano as Jocasta, Franco Citti as Oedipus, Alida Valli as Merope, and Julian Beck as Tiresias. In his adaptation, Pasolini moved through time, beginning with a prologue set in the 20th century and then moving back to the ancient Greece of Sophocles (whose play is unacknowledged in the film's credits).

The next year, the British *Oedipus the King*, filmed in Greece with a partly Greek cast, offered **Christopher Plummer** as Oedipus, Orson Welles as Tiresias, Lilli Palmer as Jocasta, Cyril Cusack as the Messenger, and **Donald Sutherland** as the Chorus Leader. And in 1996, *Edipo Alcalde*, a Colombian-Mexican-Spanish coproduction with a screenplay cowritten by **Gabriel García Márquez**, featured Angela Molina as Jocasta and Jorge Perugorría as Oedipus.

Pierre Corneille's 1659 tragedy *Oedipe* was based on Sophocles' version of the myth, but includes a new character, Dirce, the sister of Oedipus. Similarly, **Voltaire**'s play *Oedipe* (1718) introduces the character of Philoctetes, Jocasta's former lover.

Sophocles' play has inspired a number of musical works: **Igor Stravinsky**'s cantata *Oedipus*

Rex (Paris, 1927), sung in Latin from a libretto translated from the French of **Jean Cocteau**; Carl Orff's opera *Oedipus der Tyrann* (Stuttgart, 1959), a setting of Friedrich Hölderlin's German translation of Sophocles; **Ruggiero Leoncavallo**'s opera *Edipo Rè* (Chicago, 1920), the composer's last work; and *Oedipe* (Paris, 1936), the only opera by Romanian composer **George Enescu**.

OF MICE AND MEN
(novel by John Steinbeck; 1937)

When the stage version of his novel opened on Broadway in November 1937 (the year the book was published), it was Steinbeck himself who was responsible for the adaptation. Under George S. Kaufman's direction, the cast included **Broderick Crawford** as the childlike Lennie and Wallace Ford as his protector, George. Claire Luce was the flirtatious Mae, whom Lennie accidentally strangles.

The 1939 film version, directed by Lewis Milestone, starred Burgess Meredith as George, Lon Chaney, Jr. as Lennie, and Betty Field as Mae. A 1992 film, made for PBS's "American Playhouse" but released first to theaters, was directed by **Gary Sinise**, who also played George; **John Malkovich** was Lennie, and Sherilynn Fenn was Mae.

A 1968 ABC television production starred **George Segal** as George, Nicol Williamson as Lennie, and **Joey Heatherton** as Mae. In 1981, on NBC, **Robert Blake** was George, Randy Quaid was Lennie, and Cassie Yates was Mae.

The novel has been set to music twice: as an opera by Carlisle Floyd (Seattle, 1970) and as an off-Broadway musical (1958). With book by Ira J. Bilowit, lyrics by Bilowit and Wilson Lehr, and music by Alfred Brooks, the latter, with a cast headed by Art Lund and Jo Sullivan, ran only a few weeks.

OLIVER TWIST
(novel by Charles Dickens; 1838)

Film adaptations of Dickens's story abounded from as early as 1897, when *The Death of*

Nancy Sykes featured Mabel Fenton in the title role. Other silent versions appeared in 1909, 1912, 1916, 1921, and 1922. In the 1916 adaptation, Oliver was played by a young woman, Marie Doro, with Hobart Bosworth as Bill Sykes, Tully Marshall as Fagin, and W. S. Van Dyke as Dickens himself. The 1921 *Oliver Twist, Jr.* updated the story to the contemporary United States; Harold Goodwin was Oliver. And for the 1922 version, Hollywood brought out the star power: child star **Jackie Coogan** as Oliver and **Lon Chaney** as Fagin.

In 1933, Oliver spoke on screen for the first time, in the person of Dickie Moore; Irving Pichel was Fagin, William Boyd was Bill, and Doris Lloyd was Nancy. But the most successful dramatic adaptation is probably that of 1948, directed by **David Lean**. John Howard Davies was Oliver, **Alec Guinness** was Fagin, Robert Newton was Bill Sykes, Kay Walsh was Nancy, and **Anthony Newley** was the Artful Dodger.

After that, Dickens profited from an infusion of song and dance: in 1960, Lionel Bart wrote book, music, and lyrics for *Oliver!*, which followed a successful London stage production with a Broadway triumph in January 1963; the cast included Clive Revill as Fagin and Georgia Brown as Nancy. And when the musical was adapted to the screen, it became the Best Picture of 1968. Directed by **Carol Reed** (who won the Academy Award as Best Director), it featured Ron Moody as Fagin, Shani Wallis as Nancy, **Oliver Reed** as Bill Sykes, Mark Lester as Oliver, and Jack Wild as the Artful Dodger.

And the music didn't stop there: in 1988, Walt Disney's animated *Oliver & Company* moved the action to New York City, as the kitten Oliver joined a gang of dogs engaged in petty larceny. The voice cast included Joey Lawrence as Oliver, **Billy Joel** as the Dodger, Robert Loggia as Sykes, Dom DeLuise as Fagan [sic], **Cheech Marin**, and **Bette Midler**. The songs were by **Billy Joel**, **Barry Manilow**, and J. A. C. Redford.

More offbeat was *Twisted* (1997), a contemporary adaptation set within the gay subculture of New York City.

Television adaptations include a 1959 CBS production, with Eric Portman as Fagin, Tom Clancy and Nancy Wickwire as Bill and Nancy, William Hickey as the Artful Dodger, and, in a small role as a consumptive orphan, **Richard Thomas**; a 1985 version on CBS with **George C. Scott** as Fagin, **Tim Curry** as Bill, and Cherie Lunghi as Nancy; and a 1997 ABC "Wonderful World of Disney" adaptation, with **Richard Dreyfuss** and **Elijah Wood**.

ORESTEIA
(trilogy of plays by Aeschylus; 458 B.C.)

Aeschylus's tragedy was adapted for Broadway in 1931 by **Eugene O'Neill** as *Mourning Becomes Electra*. Originally intended as a trilogy (running 14 hours), to be performed over three nights, the play was cut to five hours so that it could be performed in one evening, with a dinner break. O'Neill changed the setting to post–Civil War New England, but followed the basic plot of the Greek original, as Christine Mannon (played by **Alla Nazimova**) and her daughter Lavinia (Alice Brady) await the return of their husband and father, Ezra Mannon (Earle Lattimore), who will be murdered by Christine and her young lover. A 1947 film version, cut still more to run just under three hours, was directed by Dudley Nichols and starred **Rosalind Russell** as Lavinia, Katina Paxinou as Christine, Raymond Massey as Ezra, **Michael Redgrave** as Lavinia's brother, Orin, and, in one of his earliest film roles, **Kirk Douglas** as Lavinia's suitor. A five-part PBS "Great Performances" production in 1979 starred Joan Hackett, Roberta Maxwell, and Bruce Davison.

Poet-playwright **T. S. Eliot** borrowed elements from the *Oresteia* for *The Family Reunion* (1939), a verse drama in which Harry, who may have murdered his wife, is pursued by the Eumenides, who figure in the third play of Aeschylus's trilogy. Jean-Paul Sartre's play *The Flies* (*Les Mouches*, 1943), a version of the story of Clytemnestra's murder written during World War II in occupied France, emphasizes the triumph of human freedom over the power of the gods.

An opera based on Aeschylus's work, composed by Sergei Tanayev, premiered in St. Petersburg in 1895. Like O'Neill's play, it calls itself a trilogy but resembles more a three-act opera.

OTHELLO
(play by William Shakespeare; 1604)

The Moor of Venice has been popular on film from the beginning. Silent versions were produced in Germany (1907, 1918, 1922), Italy (1907, 1909, 1914, 1920), and the United States (1908); the 1922 German version featured **Emil Jannings** as Othello and Werner Krauss as Iago. Of the sound versions, those starring **Orson Welles** (1952), Sergei Bondarchuk (Soviet Union, 1955), **Laurence Olivier** (1965), and **Laurence Fishburne** (1995) are notable.

The Welles version took three years to film because of financial problems; filming stopped when the money ran out and resumed when Welles could afford it. As a result, Welles was often unable to assemble his entire cast in one place at one time; to compensate, the film relies heavily on close-ups, with actors often playing scenes to their costars' doubles. Nevertheless, this *Othello*, which was restored and rereleased to theaters in 1992, is considered one of the most important film versions of the play. Micheál MacLiammóir was Iago, and Suzanne Cloutier was Desdemona.

The Olivier version, based on a production at England's National Theatre, featured Frank Finlay as Iago and **Maggie Smith** as Desdemona. The Fishburne version was the first major adaptation to star a black actor (although Yaphet Kotto had played the role in a 1980 film that was never commercially released). Fishburne's Iago was **Kenneth Branagh**, with **Irène Jacob** as Desdemona.

A few contemporary versions are worth noting. *All Night Long* (directed by Basil Dearden; 1961) set the story in London among a group of jazz musicians. Jealous of bandleader Aurelius Rex/Othello (Paul Harris), Johnnie (the Iago figure, played by Patrick McGoohan), a drummer, casts suspicion on the fidelity of Aurelius's

THE ELUSIVE MR. SALINGER

The 1949 film *My Foolish Heart*, directed by Mark Robson, has the distinction of being the first and only film adapted from any work by J. D. Salinger with the author's permission. The film, which starred Susan Hayward, Dana Andrews, and Kent Smith, took liberties with the source material, the short story "Uncle Wigily in Connecticut," first published in *The New Yorker* magazine in 1948 and collected in *Nine Stories* (1953). Salinger's unhappiness with the film led to his subsequent unwillingness to subject other works to the adaptation process.

The Iranian film *Pari* (1995), directed by Dariush Mehrjui, is, according to its director, loosely based on Salinger's *Franny and Zooey*. But when the Film Society of Lincoln Center scheduled a screening of the film as part of an Iranian film festival in New York City in 1998, Salinger threatened legal action and the screening was canceled. The director told the press that he had written to Salinger to request permission to adapt the novella, but received no reply. Taking that as tacit consent, he had proceeded to make his film.

W. P. Kinsella's book *Shoeless Joe* (1982) features Salinger as a principal character; for the film version, *Field of Dreams* (1989), the character was transformed into a civil rights activist, played by James Earl Jones, after Salinger refused to allow himself to be depicted in the film.

---

wife, Delia (Betsy Blair). Among the musicians who play themselves and provide the soundtrack music are **Dave Brubeck, Charles Mingus,** Tubby Hayes, and John Dankworth. Thirteen years later, McGoohan moved to the other side of the camera to direct *Catch My Soul* (1974), a rock version with **Richie Havens** as Othello, Lance LeGault as Iago, and Season Hubley as Desdemona. Conceived and written by Jack Good, *Catch My Soul* began as a stage musical in Los Angeles in 1968, then went on to a two-year run on the London stage before making it to the screen. The setting is a desert commune in the American West; Othello is a preacher who marries a young convert. In another contemporary version, from 1982, Othello is a U.S. mercenary in Africa who falls in love with the daughter of a senator from Boston. Max H. Boulois, who also directed, played Othello, opposite **Tony Curtis** as Iago and Joanna Pettet as Desdemona.

In *A Double Life* (directed by **George Cukor**; 1947), **Ronald Colman** plays Anthony John, a stage actor with a tendency to overidentify with the characters he plays. His former wife, Brita (Signe Hasso), becomes concerned when he takes on the role of Othello. Off stage, John eventually kills a young woman (**Shelley Winters**) in a reenactment of Othello's murder of Desdemona. Colman received the Academy Award as Best Actor.

Paula Vogel's off-Broadway play *Desdemona* (1993) offered a sexual turnabout: focusing on only the three women characters (Desdemona, Emilia, and Bianca), Vogel suggested that Desdemona might, in fact, have been guilty of everything Othello suspected her of—and more!

Operas on the subject have been composed by **Gioacchino Rossini** (Naples, 1816) and **Giuseppe Verdi** (Milan, 1887).

Dance versions of *Othello* include **José Limón's** *The Moor's Pavane*, to music by **Henry Purcell** (New London, Connecticut, 1949), in whose premiere Limón and Lucas Hoving danced; and a ballet by Lar Lubovitch, to music by Elliot Goldenthal, for American Ballet Theatre (New York, 1997).

OUR TOWN
(play by Thornton Wilder; 1938)

The 1940 film (directed by Sam Wood) retains much of the play's highly theatrical structure, but appends a happy ending: although in the play Emily dies in childbirth, the film's Emily lives to see her newborn child (many of the film's events turn out to have been a dream). Martha Scott as Emily and Frank Craven as Mr. Morgan (the Stage Manager of the play) re-created their Broadway roles; **William Holden** played George.

In 1955, NBC presented a musical adaptation with a score by **Jimmy Van Heusen** and **Sammy Cahn**; among the songs was the now-standard "Love and Marriage." **Frank Sinatra** was the Stage Manager, **Eva Marie Saint** was Emily, and **Paul Newman** was George. In the mid-1980s, the composer-lyricist team of Harvey Schmidt and Tom Jones adapted Wilder's play as *Grover's Corners*; intended for Broadway, the show has not been produced in New York.

PANDORA'S BOX
(play by Frank Wedekind; 1904)

Wedekind's two Lulu plays, *Erdgeist* (1898) and *Der Büchse der Pandora* (1904), were twice memorably transformed into other media: first, by film director **G. W. Pabst** in 1929 in his *Pandora's Box*, a German silent film that made a star of American actress **Louise Brooks**, and then in the three-act opera *Lulu*, composed by **Alban Berg** (Acts I and II, Zurich, 1937, two years after the composer's death; complete, Paris, 1979).

The plays were adapted to the screen three more times, in each case under the title *Lulu*: an Austrian version in 1962; an American version in 1978, directed by Ronald Chase, that is almost entirely silent but features Berg's music on the soundtrack; and a French-West German-Italian version in 1980, in which Lulu was played by Anne Bennent. None of the films approached Pabst's achievement.

PRIDE AND PREJUDICE
(novel by Jane Austen; 1813)

The only 20th-century big-screen adaptation of Austen's best-known novel starred **Greer Garson** and **Laurence Olivier** as Elizabeth Bennet and Fitzwilliam Darcy. The 1940 film, directed by Robert Z. Leonard from a screenplay by **Aldous Huxley**, featured **Maureen O'Sullivan**, Ann Rutherford, Marsha Hunt, and Heather Angel as the other Bennet sisters, Mary Boland and Edmund Gwenn as the Bennet parents, and Edward Ashley as Mr. Wickham.

A six-part PBS "Masterpiece Theatre" mini-series, shown in 1980, starred Elizabeth Garvie as Elizabeth and David Rintoul as Mr. Darcy; the adaptation was by feminist writer **Fay Weldon**. A 1995 A&E miniseries starred **Jennifer Ehle** as Elizabeth and **Colin Firth** as Mr. Darcy. Firth would play Mr. Darcy again (sort of) in the 2001 film adaptation of Helen Fielding's 1996 novel *Bridget Jones's Diary*, in which the very contemporary Mark Darcy proves, at last, to be Mr. Right to the endearing Bridget (Renée Zellweger), a much less self-assured variation on Austen's Elizabeth Bennet.

Pride and Prejudice has also twice made its way to Broadway. In 1935, a dramatic adaptation by Helen Jerome featured Adrianne Allen, Colin-Keith Johnston, and Lucile Watson. Presumably for reasons of economy, of which Mr. and Mrs. Bennet might have approved, the number of Bennet daughters was reduced from five to three. Then, in 1959, Jerome's play was adapted by Abe Burrows as the musical *First Impressions*, with songs by Robert Goldman, Glen Paxton, and George Weiss. The cast included **Polly Bergen** as Elizabeth, Farley Granger as Mr. Darcy, and **Hermione Gingold** as Mrs. Bennet. Although the dramatic adaptation had had a healthy run of six months, the musical lasted only ten weeks.

PYGMALION
(play by George Bernard Shaw; 1913)

For the 1938 film version of his play, starring **Wendy Hiller** as Eliza Doolittle and **Leslie Howard** as Henry Higgins, Shaw himself received an Academy Award for Best Screenplay, with a separate Oscar for Best Adaptation going to Ian Dalrymple, Cecil Lewis, and W. P. Liscomb. Anthony Asquith and Leslie Howard shared the directing credit.

My Fair Lady (1956) is probably the most successful musical comedy, both from a critical and popular standpoint, to have been inspired by a classic work of literature. Some of its popularity may stem from a critical change from the source material: although Shaw makes it clear that Higgins and Eliza do not wind up together (Eliza will presumably marry the adoring, if a bit dim, Freddie Eynsford-Hill), *My Fair Lady* ends with Eliza returning to Higgins as he sings "I've Grown Accustomed to Her Face." With music by **Frederick Loewe**, and book and lyrics by **Alan Jay Lerner**, the show ran more than six years on Broadway and became an Academy Award–winning film in 1964, receiving Oscars for Best Picture, Director (**George Cukor**), and Actor (**Rex Harrison** as Henry Higgins, re-creating his Broadway role). **Audrey Hepburn** played Eliza (replacing **Julie Andrews**, who created the role on stage), Stanley Holloway repeated his stage role as Alfred Doolittle, and Gladys Cooper was Mrs. Higgins.

In the 1999 teen film *She's All That*, Zach Silver (Freddie Prinze, Jr.), jilted by his teen-queen girlfriend, Taylor (Jodi Lyn O'Keefe), bets a friend that he can turn any girl into the prom queen, and proceeds to do just that with Laney Boggs (Rachael Leigh Cook)—although in the end, he learns more from her than she from him.

RASHŌMON
(story by Ryūnosuke Akutagawa; 1917)

Akutagawa's story was filmed by Japanese director **Akira Kurosawa** in 1950, in combination with another story by Akutagawa, "In a Grove" (1921). Kurosawa's masterpiece, set in the Heian period (794–1184), presents four accounts of a rape and murder; the story is told by each of the participants—a samurai, his bride, and a bandit; the dead samurai gives his version with the help of a spirit medium—and by a woodcutter who witnessed the events. No attempt is made to determine which version is "true," since "truth" is by its very nature relative.

A stage adaptation by husband-and-wife Fay and Michael Kanin premiered on Broadway in 1959, with a cast headed by **Rod Steiger, Claire Bloom**, Akim Tamiroff, and Oscar Homolka. The following year, the play was televised as part of the syndicated "Play of the Week" series. Under **Sidney Lumet**'s direction, James Mitchell, Carol Lawrence, Ricardo Montalban, and Oscar Homolka (repeating his Broadway role) headed the cast.

Playwright Michael Kanin was responsible for the screenplay for Martin Ritt's 1964 film of the play, retitled *The Outrage* and now set in the American Southwest in the 1870s. The samurai became a southern gentleman (**Laurence Harvey**); the bandit, a Mexican outlaw (**Paul Newman**); and the woodcutter, a prospector (Howard Da Silva). The wife was played by Claire Bloom, reprising her Broadway role, and **Edward G. Robinson** appeared as a con-man to whom the prospector tells his version of the story.

Iron Maze (1991) loosely updated the story to a fictional small town in Pennsylvania. An unemployed steelworker, Barry (Jeff Fahey), a Japanese businessman, Sugita (Hiroaki Murakami), and the businessman's wife, Chris (**Bridget Fonda**), offer conflicting stories about the beating of Sugita and the possible rape of Chris by Barry. J. T. Walsh is the police sergeant who must try to make sense of the confessions.

ROMEO AND JULIET
(play by William Shakespeare; 1595)

The Bard's star-crossed lovers have lived unhappily ever after on screen since the beginning of the silent era, with versions from England (1908, 1923), France (1900), Italy (1908, 1911), and the United States, where **Francis X.**

Bushman was Romeo in 1916, Wallace Reid was Oniatore in the *Indian Romeo and Juliet* (1912), and, notably, screen vamp **Theda Bara** was Juliet in 1916, with Harry Hilliard as her Romeo.

Of the sound films, four are of particular interest. In 1936, **George Cukor** directed **Norma Shearer** as Juliet, **Leslie Howard** as Romeo, **John Barrymore** as Mercutio, Basil Rathbone as Tybalt, Edna May Oliver as the Nurse, and Andy Devine (best known later as Roy Rogers's sidekick) as the Nurse's servant. A 1954 British-Italian coproduction, directed by Renato Castellani, starred **Laurence Harvey** as Romeo and newcomer Susan Shentall as Juliet, with Flora Robson as the Nurse. Then, in 1968, **Franco Zeffirelli** directed newcomers Leonard Whiting and Olivia Hussey in an adaptation noted more for its prettiness than its dramatic power. Finally, Baz Luhrmann's *Romeo + Juliet* (1996) was a *very* contemporary, hip version, set in Verona Beach, with the Capulets and Montagues as two warring Mafia families. **Leonardo di Caprio** was Romeo to **Claire Danes**'s Juliet.

Ethnic versions, in addition to the Native-American variation mentioned above, include the Indian *Anjuman* (1948) and the Egyptian *Shuhaddaa el Gharam* (1942). *Love Is All There Is* (1996) is a comedic Italian-American version, featuring families that run rival restaurants in Queens, New York; the parents become even more embattled when their respective children (**Angelina Jolie** and Nathaniel Marston) fall in love while rehearsing a high school production of—what else?—*Romeo and Juliet*. Other comic variations starred Mack Sennett comedian Ben Turpin (1924) and the Mexican comedian Cantinflas (1943). **Peter Ustinov**'s play *Romanoff and Juliet* (1956) is a cold-war variation, in which the young lovers are the son and daughter, respectively, of rival Russian and American ambassadors. In the 1961 screen version, **Sandra Dee** was Juliet Moulsworth and John Gavin was Igor Romanoff. Finally, even further afield, there are *Tromeo and Juliet* (1996), a punk adaptation from the Troma studio, and *The Secret Sex Lives of Romeo and Juliet* (1968).

Three films have captured performances of the ballet scored by **Serge Prokofiev**: a 1955 film of a Bolshoi Ballet performance, choreographed by Leonid Lavrovsky, with Galina Ulanova as Juliet; a 1966 performance by London's Royal Ballet, featuring Kenneth MacMillan's choreography; and a 1982 performance at La Scala, in Milan; in the latter two films, **Margot Fonteyn** and **Rudolf Nureyev** dance the leads.

Among those who have composed operas on the subject are Niccolò Zingarelli (Naples, 1796), Vincenzo Bellini (*I Capuleti e i Montecchi*; Venice, 1830), **Charles Gounod** (Paris, 1867), and Heinrich Sutermeister (Dresden, 1940).

For Broadway, *Romeo and Juliet* inspired one of the most acclaimed musicals ever: *West Side Story* (1957), with a book by Arthur Laurents, music by **Leonard Bernstein**, lyrics by **Stephen Sondheim**, and choreography and direction by **Jerome Robbins**. In this version, the starcrossed lovers, Tony and Maria (played by Larry Kert and Carol Lawrence), are divided by gang rivalries in New York City. After the show's nearly two-year run on Broadway, it became one of the great screen musicals in 1961 as filmed by codirectors Robert Wise and Jerome Robbins. Starring **Natalie Wood** and Richard Beymer, the film received ten Oscars, including Best Picture, Best Director, Best Supporting Actor (George Chakiris as Bernardo), and Best Supporting Actress (**Rita Moreno** as Anita).

Last but not least, in 1998's *Shakespeare in Love*, Academy Award–winning screenwriters Marc Norman and **Tom Stoppard** offered a fanciful notion about the origin of *Romeo and Juliet*, as the film's William Shakespeare (Joseph Fiennes) alters his original concept for *Romeo and Ethel, the Pirate's Daughter* when he falls in star-crossed love with his own Juliet, Viola de Lesseps (**Gwyneth Paltrow**). The film garnered Oscars also as Best Picture and for Paltrow as Best Actress.

SANCTUARY
(novel by William Faulkner; 1931)

Filmed as *The Story of Temple Drake* (1933), Faulkner's sensational novel necessarily underwent some changes, even in character names (Popeye became Trigger, and Horace Benbow became Stephen Benbow). The title role was played by Miriam Hopkins, with Jack LaRue as Trigger and William Gargan as Stephen Benbow. In true Hollywood fashion, even before the Production Code went into effect, the title character sacrificed herself to the cause of justice in a very un-Faulknerian ending.

In 1951, Faulkner published *Requiem for a Nun*, a sequel that continued Temple's story in three prose sections followed by a three-act courtroom drama. The novel was adapted for the stage by Faulkner and actress Ruth Ford, and premiered on Broadway in 1959 with a cast including Ford, Zachary Scott, Scott McKay, and Bertice Reading.

Material from both *Requiem for a Nun* and *Sanctuary* was combined and loosely adapted by James Poe into a second film, *Sanctuary* (1961), directed by **Tony Richardson**. The cast included **Lee Remick** as Temple, **Yves Montand** as Candy (a composite of three characters from Faulkner's original works), and the folksinger **Odetta** as Nancy Mannigoe (another composite character). Bradford Dillman played Gowan Stevens, a character from *Requiem for a Nun* who appears also in other works by Faulkner.

SCARLET LETTER, THE
(novel by Nathaniel Hawthorne; 1850)

Hawthorne's novel was first filmed in 1917, with Stuart Holmes as the Reverend Arthur Dimmesdale, Dan Mason as Roger Chillingworth, and Mary Martin as Hester Prynne. Far more memorable was the 1926 film directed in America by the Swedish director Victor Sjöström [Seastrom]. **Lillian Gish**, perhaps the greatest actress of the silent era, was Hester, Swedish actor Lars Hanson was Dimmesdale, and Chillingworth was Henry B. Walthall, who would play the character again, in 1934,

opposite Colleen Moore's Hester and Hardie Albright's Dimmesdale.

When the story next came to the screen, Hawthorne's characters spoke German, in **Wim Wenders**'s *Der Scharlachrote Buchstabe* (1972), shot in Spain but still set in New England. Senta Berger was Hester, Hans Christian Blech was Chillingworth, and Lou Castel was Dimmesdale. For the critically lambasted 1995 version, directed by Roland Joffé, **Demi Moore** was Hester, **Gary Oldman** was Dimmesdale, and **Robert Duvall** was Chillingworth.

A four-part PBS 1979 miniseries starred Meg Foster as Hester, John Heard as Dimmesdale, and Kevin Conway as Chillingworth.

An opera by Walter Damrosch premiered, appropriately, in Boston in 1896.

Hawthorne's tale has also been reimagined by later writers. **John Updike**'s trilogy of novels— *A Month of Sundays* (1975), *Roger's Version* (1986), and *S.* (1988)—presents contemporary variations on the characters of, respectively, Dimmesdale, Chillingworth, and Hester. *In the Blood* (1999), an off-Broadway play by Suzan-Lori Parks, reinvents Hawthorne's heroine as Hester, La Negrita, a woman on welfare who lives with her five children under a bridge in New York City; illiterate, she is trying to learn the alphabet, but has not progressed beyond "A."

SECRET AGENT, THE
(novella by Joseph Conrad; 1907)

The first film version of Conrad's story was called *Sabotage* (1936), and was directed by **Alfred Hitchcock**, whose previous film, also released in 1936, was called *Secret Agent* but was based on stories by W. Somerset Maugham. *Sabotage* starred Oskar Homolka as Verloc, **Sylvia Sidney** as Mrs. Verloc, and Desmond Tester as Stevie, with John Loder as the police sergeant.

Under its own title, the novella was filmed in 1996 by Christopher Hampton, with a cast headed by **Bob Hoskins** as Verloc, **Patricia Arquette** as his wife, Christian Bale as Stevie,

Jim Broadbent as the Chief Inspector, and, unbilled, **Robin Williams** as the Professor.

STREETCAR NAMED DESIRE, A
(play by Tennessee Williams; 1947)

Williams's Pulitzer Prize–winning drama was filmed in 1951 by **Elia Kazan**, with **Vivien Leigh, Marlon Brando, Karl Malden**, and **Kim Hunter** in the leads (except for Leigh, who replaced Jessica Tandy, all were repeating their roles from the original Broadway production). Leigh received the Oscar as Best Actress.

Television adaptations were presented in 1984 (ABC) and 1995 (CBS). The earlier version featured **Ann-Margret**, Treat Williams, Randy Quaid, and Beverly D'Angelo. The later presentation, starring **Jessica Lange**, Alec Baldwin, John Goodman, and Diane Lane, had its origin in a 1992 Broadway revival in which Lange and Baldwin costarred.

In 1998, **André Previn**'s opera premiered at the San Francisco Opera; with acclaimed American soprano **Renée Fleming** as Blanche, the production aired later that year on PBS's "Great Performances."

The torrid confrontation between Blanche DuBois and Stanley Kowalski was choreographed as a one-act ballet duo for Mia Slavenska and Frederic Franklin by Valerie Bettis (Montreal, 1952), who was better known for modern dance choreography. The music was adapted from Alex North's film score.

TAMING OF THE SHREW, THE
(play by William Shakespeare; c. 1593)

Shakespeare's version of the battle of the sexes was translated to the silent screen in Italy (1908), France (1911), and England (1911, 1913, 1923); sound versions appeared in Mexico (1948), Spain (1955), and the Soviet Union (1961). In the United States, the earliest version (1908) was directed by film pioneer **D. W. Griffith**, with Florence Lawrence as Katharina. The next American film that claimed a connection to Shakespeare's play was *Daring Youth* (1924), but the relationship was tenuous: a wife (Bebe

Daniels) has an "open marriage" agreement with her new husband (Norman Kerry), but he eventually "tames" her by bringing her to admit that she wants a closer commitment. The last silent version (and one of the very last of all silents), in 1929, featured husband-and-wife stars **Mary Pickford** and **Douglas Fairbanks**, under Sam Taylor's direction; the film was restored and reissued to theaters in 1966, accompanied by a half-hour documentary about Pickford and Fairbanks.

Less than six months after that reissue, another famous couple took on the roles of Katharina and Petruchio; **Elizabeth Taylor** and **Richard Burton**, under **Franco Zeffirelli**'s direction, used their real-life reputation for marital discord to advantage in this lusty, beautifully filmed version.

Ten Things I Hate About You (1999) set the story among contemporary teenagers: Bianca Stratford (Larisa Oleynik) cannot date until her ill-tempered, boy-hating sister, Kat (**Julia Stiles**), has her own boyfriend. Salvation arrives in the figure of Patrick Verona (Heath Ledger), who accepts a bet that he can woo and win Kat.

Television adaptations include a 1956 NBC "Hallmark Hall of Fame" production with Maurice Evans and Lilli Palmer. In November 1986, the ABC series "Moonlighting" presented an episode in which, in a dream sequence, Maddie (Cybill Shepherd) and David (**Bruce Willis**) took on the roles of Katharina and Petruchio, in an adaptation that mirrored the private eyes' own relationship.

Operas based on the play include Hermann Götz's *Der Widerspenstigen Zähmung* (Mannheim, 1874), Ruperto Chapí y Lorente's *Las Bravías* (Madrid, 1896), Ermanno Wolf-Ferrari's *Sly* (Milan, 1927), Rudolf Karel's *The Taming of the Shrew* (unproduced, 1939), and Vittorio Giannini's *The Taming of the Shrew* (Cincinnati, 1953).

John Cranko's ballet (Stuttgart, 1969) made instant stars of its leading dancers, **Marcia Haydée** and Richard Cragun, when the Stuttgart

Ballet burst on the scene during its first U.S. tour.

Of course, many people know *The Taming of the Shrew* from its Broadway incarnation as *Kiss Me, Kate* (1948), with a book by Bella and Samuel Spewack, and music and lyrics by **Cole Porter**. *Kiss Me, Kate* is a play-within-a-play (as, in fact, is *The Taming of the Shrew*); musical numbers based on Shakespeare's play alternate with backstage scenes and songs in which the embattled relationship between actors Lilli Vanessi and Fred Graham mirrors that of Katharina and Petruchio. When *Kiss Me, Kate* came to the screen in 1953, it was the first major musical to be photographed in 3-D, the better to show off **Ann Miller's** high-kicking tap dancing in the role of Lois Lane/Bianca. Directed by George Sidney, the film starred **Kathryn Grayson** and **Howard Keel**. On television in 1958, NBC's "Hallmark Hall of Fame" featured Alfred Drake as Fred/Petruchio and Patricia Morison as Lilli/Katharina in the roles they had created on Broadway. In 1964, ABC's "Armstrong Circle Theatre" presented Robert Goulet and Carol Lawrence in the leads.

TARTUFFE
(play by Molière; 1664)

Molière's satire of religious hypocrisy was first filmed in 1926 by German director **F. W. Murnau**, who used a modern-day framing device, in which a young man uses a film version of *Tartuffe* to alert his uncle to the duplicity of a lecherous rogue. Within the play-within-the-film, Tartuffe was portrayed by **Emil Jannings**, Orgon by Werner Krauss, and Elmire by Lil Dagover. Nearly 60 years later, **Gérard Depardieu** made his directorial debut with *Le Tartuffe* (1984), in which he also played the title role, with François Périer as Orgon and Elisabeth Depardieu as Elmire.

An opera by Arthur Benjamin premiered in London in 1964.

The Broadway play *Tartuffe: Born Again* (1996) attempted to update Molière's satire, making Tartuffe a born-again Christian televangelist and Orgon a Louisiana television station owner.

Written in verse by Freyda Thomas, the play had only a brief run; the leading roles were played by John Glover and David Schramm.

TEMPEST, THE
(play by William Shakespeare; c. 1611)

Shakespeare's great last play is one of his least-filmed works, but each of the adaptations has borne the stamp of its creators.

Derek Jarman's 1979 film has a distinctive visual style, and a great deal of male nudity. It features Heathcote Williams as Prospero, Toyah Wilcox as Miranda, Karl Johnson as Ariel, and Jack Birkett as Caliban. The film concludes with a wedding feast at which blues singer Elisabeth Welch performs "Stormy Weather."

Paul Mazursky's 1982 *Tempest* is a free, contemporary updating: Philip (**John Cassavetes**), an architect in midlife crisis, goes with his teenaged daughter, Miranda (**Molly Ringwald**, in her screen debut), to Greece, where he meets Aretha (**Susan Sarandon**), a free-spirited singer. The three go off to an island inhabited only by the hermit-goatherd Kalibanos (**Raul Julia**), who at one point summons a rendition of "New York, New York" by Liza Minnelli. Philip's wife, Antonia (**Gena Rowlands**), and her lover (Vittorio Gassman) and his son (Sam Robards) are shipwrecked on the island during a storm Philip/Prospero has conjured. Philip and Antonia eventually reconcile and return together to Manhattan.

Peter Greenaway's 1991 *Prospero's Books* is a highly stylized, visual reimagining of Shakespeare's play, in which **John Gielgud's** Prospero doubles as Shakespeare, speaking the lines of all the characters as the playwright conjures them. The film demonstrates a fascination with the books that Prospero has taken with him to the island, and with the entire Renaissance world of learning that they contain.

In the science-fiction classic *Forbidden Planet* (1956), scientist Edward Morbius (**Walter Pidgeon**) and his daughter Altaira (Anne Francis) are the only human inhabitants of the planet Altair-4; the other inhabitant is **Robby the**

Robot, making his screen debut as a sort of Ariel. When a group of astronauts, led by Leslie Nielsen's Commander John J. Adams, arrive, Morbius/Prospero conjures a menace to drive them away; in the end, Morbius must die in order to destroy the menace.

On television, *The Tempest* was presented on NBC's "Hallmark Hall of Fame" in 1960; Maurice Evans was Prospero, **Richard Burton** was Caliban, Roddy McDowall was Ariel, and Lee Remick was Miranda. Another NBC adaptation, in 1998, set the story during the Civil War; **Peter Fonda** was Gideon Prosper, a Mississippi plantation owner fascinated by magic; Harold Perrineau, Jr. was the slave Ariel; and Katherine Heigl was Miranda Prosper.

Among the operas based on the play are those by Fromental Halévy (*La Tempesta*; London, 1850), Nicholas Comyn Gatty (London, 1920), Felice Lattuada (*La Tempesta*; Milan, 1929), Heinrich Sutermeister (*Die Zauberinsel* [*The Magic Island*]; Dresden, 1942), Kurt Atterberg (*Stormen*; Stockholm, 1948), Frank Martin (*Der Sturm*; Vienna, 1956), and John Charles Eaton (San Francisco Opera, 1985).

THIN MAN, THE
(novel by Dashiell Hammett; 1934)

Hammett's debonair husband-and-wife sleuths Nick and Nora Charles came to the screen in 1934 under W. S. Van Dyke's direction. **William Powell** and **Myrna Loy** were Nick and Nora; Edward Ellis played the title character. The film's success led to five sequels: *After the Thin Man* (1936), *Another Thin Man* (1939), *Shadow of the Thin Man* (1941), *The Thin Man Goes Home* (1944), and *Song of the Thin Man* (1947), all with Powell and Loy, but without a thin man in sight.

The Thin Man came to television in September 1957 in a weekly NBC series that ran until June 1959; **Peter Lawford** and Phyllis Kirk played Nick and Nora. And then came Broadway, in 1991: *Nick and Nora*, with music by Charles Strouse, lyrics by Richard Maltby, Jr., and a book by Arthur Laurents, who also directed, had a great pedigree (like Asta, the Charleses' dog),

and a stellar cast headed by **Barry Bostwick** and **Joanna Gleason**, but the show itself was a quick and fabled failure.

TURN OF THE SCREW, THE
(novella by Henry James; 1898)

James's classic ghost story was faithfully adapted for Broadway by playwright William Archibald in 1950; retitled *The Innocents*, the play starred Beatrice Straight and Isabel Elsom. Director Jack Clayton brought the play to the screen in 1961, with **Deborah Kerr** as Miss Giddens (James's unnamed governess), Peter Wyngarde as Peter Quint, Clytie Jessop as Miss Jessel, and Martin Stephens and Pamela Franklin as young Miles and Flora. The screenplay was coauthored by **Truman Capote**.

In the Spanish film *Otra Vuelta de Tuerca* (1985), the setting is the Basque area, and James's governess has become a male tutor (played by Pedro Maria Sánchez). Otherwise, the film follows James's story fairly closely, except for a hint of homosexual attraction between the tutor and his young male charge. A 1992 British film starred Patsy Kensit, Stéphane Audran, Julian Sands, and **Marianne Faithfull** (as the Narrator).

Ingrid Bergman made her television acting debut in a 1959 NBC adaptation of the novel. Later television versions starred **Lynn Redgrave** (ABC, 1974), Amy Irving (Showtime, 1990), and, as a present-day American governess abroad, **Valerie Bertinelli** in *The Haunting of Helen Walker* (CBS, 1995).

Benjamin Britten's English-language opera, one of the most significant operas of the second half of the 20th century, premiered in Venice in 1954.

TWELFTH NIGHT
(play by William Shakespeare; c. 1601–2)

Shakespeare's story of shipwreck and lovesickness is one of the least-filmed of all the Bard's plays. A silent version appeared in 1910 in the United States; the next version was from the Soviet Union, in 1956. *Viola and Sebastian*

(1973) was a West German version, essentially faithful to the play but with a contemporary German setting. Not until 1996 did the film receive a lavish production in English. Directed by **Trevor Nunn**, that film starred **Helena Bonham Carter** as Olivia, Imogen Stubbs as Viola/Cesario, Toby Stephens as Orsino, **Nigel Hawthorne** as Malvolio, and **Ben Kingsley** as Feste.

On television, Rosemary Harris and Frances Hyland starred as Viola and Olivia, with Lloyd Bochner as Orsino, in a 1957 NBC "Hallmark Hall of Fame" production. In 1998, PBS's "Live from Lincoln Center" presented the Lincoln Center Theater production, with **Helen Hunt** as Viola, Kyra Sedgwick as Olivia, and Paul Rudd as Orsino.

Perhaps because of the play's first line—"If music be the food of love, play on"—*Twelfth Night* has attracted composers of all sorts. The Czech composer Bedřich Smetana left *Viola* (c. 1875) unfinished at his death, but his countryman Ivan Jirko completed his opera in 1964. In a more popular vein, *Your Own Thing* (1968) was a rock musical, with music and lyrics by Hal Hester and Danny Apolinar, book by Donald Driver; it had a two-year run off-Broadway. On the other hand, *Music Is* (1976), with music by Richard Adler, lyrics by Will Holt, and a book and direction by George Abbott, ran only a week on Broadway. *Play On!* (1997) was a loose adaptation, set in the Harlem of the 1940s and focusing on a would-be songwriter. Conceived and directed by Sheldon Epps, the show had a book by Cheryl West; 20 songs associated with the late **Duke Ellington**, including "Take the 'A' Train," "Mood Indigo," "Don't Get Around Much Anymore," and "Prelude to a Kiss"; and choreography by Ellington's granddaughter, Mercedes Ellington. Despite the talent involved, *Play On!* had only a short Broadway run.

ULYSSES
(novel by James Joyce; 1922)

Joyce's great experimental novel, itself inspired by Homer's *Odyssey* (see above, under the *Iliad*), presents significant challenges to anyone attempting an adaptation. Nevertheless, the novel was filmed in 1967 by Joseph Strick, who directed and cowrote the screenplay. Shot in Ireland and retaining much of the complexity of Joyce's language, the film concentrates on the novel's chief characters, Leopold Bloom (played by **Milo O'Shea**), Molly Bloom (Barbara Jefford), and Stephen Dedalus (Maurice Roëves); the final section of the film is devoted to Molly Bloom's famous soliloquy. A far looser adaptation, with a nod also to Homer, was the West German film *Uliisses* (1983), directed by Werner Nekes.

In 1958, Marjorie Barkentin's *Ulysses in Nighttown*, an adaptation of the book's "Nighttown" sequence, ran for six months off-Broadway. Under Burgess Meredith's direction, the cast included **Zero Mostel** as Leopold Bloom as well as **Carroll O'Connor, Beatrice Arthur, Anne Meara**, and John Astin. A Broadway revival in 1974, again starring Mostel and directed by Meredith, was less successful.

Fans of Mel Brooks and of Joyce may have wondered if it was mere coincidence that the mousy accountant in the film *The Producers* (1968) is named Leo Bloom. Brooks's 2001 Broadway musical adaptation of his film makes the reference explicit: according to the show's program, the second scene (in which Leo first meets Max Bialystock) is set on June 16, the day on which the action of Joyce's novel takes place, known as Bloomsday (Leo even asks, "When is it gonna be Bloomsday?").

UNCLE VANYA
(play by Anton Chekhov; 1897)

The first film version of Chekhov's play, in 1958, was a transfer to film of an off-Broadway production from two years earlier, with the same cast: Franchot Tone (who codirected with John Goetz) as Dr. Astrov, George Voskovec as Vanya, Dolores Dorn-Heft as Yelena, Clarence Derwent as Professor Serebryakov, and Peggy McCay as Sonya. A Russian version in 1971, directed by Andrei Konchalovsky, starred Sergei Bondarchuk.

In the 1990s, several films altered the setting or took a novel approach. *Vanya on 42nd Street* (1994), directed by **Louis Malle**, features a play-within-the-film structure, as a theatrical company assembles to perform the play on a bare stage in a crumbling New York City theater. Theatrical director **André Gregory** appears as himself, and his *My Dinner with André* costar, **Wallace Shawn**, appears as Vanya. The cast also includes Larry Pine as Astrov, **Julianne Moore** as Yelena, George Gaynes as the Professor, and Brooke Smith as Sonya. In *Country Life* (directed by Michael Blakemore; 1994), the action is transplanted to rural Australia in the 1920s. **Sam Neill** is Dr. Max Askey, Blakemore is Professor Alexander Voysey, **Greta Scacchi** is his wife, Deborah, John Hargreaves is Jack Dickens (the Vanya character), and Kerry Fox is Sally Voysey. *August* (1996) moves the story to turn-of-the-19th-century South Wales. **Anthony Hopkins** (who also directed) is Ieuan Davies (Vanya), Leslie Phillips is Professor Max Brathwaite, **Kate Burton** is his American wife, Helen, Gawn Grainger is Dr. Michael Lloyd, and Rhian Morgan is Sian Brathwaite.

Television productions include a British stage production shown on public television in 1967 on "NET Playhouse," which starred Laurence Olivier as Astrov, Michael Redgrave as Vanya, Rosemary Harris as Yelena, Max Adrian as the Professor, and Joan Plowright as Sonya.

VANITY FAIR
(novel by William Makepeace Thackeray; 1848)

Silent film adaptations of Thackeray's satirical novel include a 1911 version with Helen Gardener as Becky Sharp; a 1915 version starring the great American stage actress **Minnie Maddern Fiske**, then 50 years old (the director, Eugene Nowland, avoided shooting his star in close-up); a 1922 British version, with Cosmo Kyrle Bellew as Becky and Clive Brook as Rawdon Crawley; and a 1923 version, directed by Hugo Ballin, with Hobart Bosworth as the Marquis of Steyne and starring the director's wife, Mabel Ballin (in this case, the director was generous with the close-ups).

In 1932, a modern-dress version starred **Myrna Loy** as Becky, with Montagu Love as the Marquis of Steyne and Conway Tearle as Rawdon Crawley. But by far the most important film adaptation was *Becky Sharp* (1935), directed by Rouben Mamoulian, with **Miriam Hopkins** in the title role and with a supporting cast headed by Frances Dee as Amelia Sedley, Cedric Hardwicke as the Marquis of Steyne, Billie Burke as Lady Beauacres, Nigel Bruce as Joseph Sedley, and Alan Mowbray as Rawdon Crawley. What gives this film its place in history is that it was the first feature film to be shot using the three-strip color process invented by Technicolor.

Television adaptations include a five-hour 1972 PBS "Masterpiece Theatre" miniseries, with Susan Hampshire as Becky; and a six-hour A&E 1998 miniseries, with Natasha Little as Becky, Nathaniel Parker as Rawdon Crawley, and Miriam Margolyes as Miss Crawley.

VIEW FROM THE BRIDGE, A
(play by Arthur Miller; 1955)

The 1961 film version of Miller's play about Italian Americans and illegal Italian immigrants on the Brooklyn waterfront was a French production, in English, with an international cast headed by an Italian star. Under **Sidney Lumet**'s direction, Raf Vallone was Eddie Carbone, whose jealousy of his young niece's attraction to a young Italian immigrant leads to betrayal. Carol Lawrence was the niece, and Jean Sorel was her young suitor. **Maureen Stapleton** played Eddie's wife, Beatrice, and Morris Carnovsky was the lawyer Alfieri.

Operas based on the play have been composed by Renzo Rossellini (Rome, 1961) and William Bolcom (Lyric Opera of Chicago, 1999).

VOLPONE
(play by Ben Jonson; 1606)

Jonson's bawdy satire has been filmed several times, notably in 1940 in France by director Maurice Tourneur, with two of France's best-known actors in the leading roles: Harry Baur as Volpone (the Fox) and **Louis Jouvet** as Mosca (the Fly). In 1967, director **Joseph L. Mankiewicz** loosely adapted and updated the play as *The Honey Pot*, in which Cecil Fox (played by **Rex Harrison**), with the help of his assistant William McFly (**Cliff Robertson**), tries to dupe former mistresses played by **Susan Hayward**, Capucine, and **Edie Adams**. Other film versions include the Mexican *Tiburón* (1933) and the Italian *Il Volpone* (1988).

On Broadway, the short-lived *Foxy* (1964), set in the Yukon, had music by Robert Emmett Dolan, lyrics by **Johnny Mercer**, and a book by Ian McLellan Hunter and Ring Lardner, Jr. Its greatest asset was **Bert Lahr** in the leading role. Twelve years later, Larry Gelbart's Broadway comedy *Sly Fox* (1976), starring **George C. Scott** as Foxwell S. Sly, updated the action to the turn-of-the-century Barbary Coast.

WAR AND PEACE
(novel by Leo Tolstoy; 1868–69)

Tolstoy's monumental, 600,000-word-long masterpiece was turned by Hollywood into a film nearly three-and-a-half hours long in 1956. Directed by **King Vidor**, the production's all-star, international cast was headed by **Henry Fonda** as Pierre, **Audrey Hepburn** as Natasha, and **Mel Ferrer** as Andrei, with Vittorio Gassman, Anita Ekberg, Oskar Homolka, Herbert Lom, and John Mills in supporting roles.

But the Soviets did Hollywood one better in the 1960s with a seven-hour-long, four-part adaptation, which was released in the United States in 1968 in two parts, abridged to just over six hours (the Battle of Borodino sequence alone ran an hour). Directed by **Sergei Bondarchuk**, who also played Pierre, the film was dubbed into English, rather than subtitled, for the English-speaking audience, which was the only misstep in a film noted for its visual style.

A 1973 PBS miniseries starred **Anthony Hopkins** as Pierre, Morag Hood as Natasha, and Alan Dobie as Andrei.

Sergei Prokofiev's opera (Leningrad, 1946), probably his greatest work, no doubt had special significance for the audience at its premiere, with the events of World War II fresh in their minds.

WAR OF THE WORLDS, THE
(novel by H. G. Wells; 1898)

Wells's novel inspired perhaps the most "successful" literary adaptation ever. When **Orson Welles** chose *The War of the Worlds* as the subject for the October 30, 1938, installment of his "Mercury Theater on the Air" CBS radio series, he could not have foreseen the widespread panic the show would induce in its listeners, many of whom believed the Halloween-eve broadcast to be a breaking-news account of a Martian landing in New Jersey. Overnight, Welles (who had narrated the broadcast and coadapted the novel with Howard Koch) became famous.

For the 1953 film version, the action was transplanted to Southern California. Byron Haskin directed the film, whose true stars were its spectacular special effects. The humans included **Gene Barry**, Les Tremayne, and Ann Robinson.

A 1988–90 syndicated television series was a contemporary sequel to both the radio broadcast and the film: in the plotline, which involved a threatened invasion of Earth by a group of aliens from the planet Mortax, references were made to an alien reconnaissance mission in 1938 and to a first war in 1953. By the end of the run, the evil Malzor was destroyed and the remaining aliens sought a peaceful coexistence with humankind.

WASHINGTON SQUARE
(novel by Henry James; 1881)

James's novel concerns the transformation of shy heiress Catherine Sloper after she is abandoned by a gold-digging suitor; the novel was itself transformed and dramatized as *The Heiress* in 1947. Written by Ruth and Augustus Goetz, the Broadway success starred **Wendy Hiller** as Catherine, Basil Rathbone as Dr. Sloper, and Peter Cookson as Morris Townsend.

Two years later, the play was brought to the screen, directed by **William Wyler** and starring **Olivia de Havilland** (Academy Award for Best Actress), **Ralph Richardson**, and **Montgomery Clift**; Miriam Hopkins was Aunt Lavinia Penniman.

In 1997, the novel came to the screen again with the original title; directed by **Agnieszka Holland**, this version did not draw from the Goetzes' play. **Jennifer Jason Leigh** was Catherine, **Albert Finney** was Dr. Sloper, Ben Chaplin was Morris, and **Maggie Smith** was Aunt Lavinia.

Washington Square (Michigan Opera Theatre, Detroit, 1976) is an opera by Thomas Pasatieri.

WUTHERING HEIGHTS
(novel by Emily Brontë; 1847)

Brontë's tale of passion has been filmed several times, in several languages, beginning with a 1920 British silent version. The best-known English-language version is the 1939 Hollywood classic featuring **Laurence Olivier** as Heathcliff, **Merle Oberon** as Cathy, and **David Niven**, Flora Robson, and **Geraldine Fitzgerald** (as Isabella Linton) in supporting roles, under William Wyler's direction. A 1970 version starred Timothy Dalton and Anna Calder-Marshall, and in 1992, **Ralph Fiennes** and **Juliette Binoche** took on the leading roles; singer **Sinéad O'Connor** appeared (uncredited) as Emily Brontë. The latter version is significant in that it takes into account the entire story of the novel, including Heathcliff's return

after Cathy's death, his control of her daughter and of Wuthering Heights, and his death.

Overseas, Spanish director **Luis Buñuel** adapted the second part of the novel as *Abismos de Pasión* (1953). Although the plot is truncated, the passion remains. The cast included Jorge Mistral as Alejandro/Heathcliff, Irasema Dilián as Catalina/Cathy, and Lilia Prado as Isabel. In France, **Jacques Rivette**'s *Hurlevent* (1985) moved the story to the French countryside in the 1930s. Fabienne Babe was Cathy and Lucas Belvaux was Roch/Heathcliff.

A stage adaptation had a brief run on Broadway in 1939; written by Randolph Carter, it starred Don Terry and Edith Barrett, under Stewart Chaney's direction.

On television, Richard Burton and Rosemary Harris starred in CBS's 1958 adaptation.

Operas based on the novel have been composed by **Bernard Herrmann** (unproduced; 1950) and Carlisle Floyd (Santa Fe, New Mexico, 1958).

The influence of the novel on its young women readers was suggested in Mike Leigh's 1997 film *Career Girls*, whose title characters, Hannah and Annie, use a well-worn copy of the Penguin edition of the novel to resolve life crises: faced with a problem, they chant "Miz Brontë, Miz Brontë, [insert problem]" and point randomly to a passage in the book. No matter the question or the passage, Emily Brontë always seems to give them useful advice.

Recommended Reading

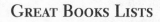

GREAT BOOKS LISTS

BOOKS OF THE CENTURY

To commemorate the New York Public Library's Centennial in May 1995, librarians identified books that played defining roles in history and culture from 1895 to 1995—the Library's first one hundred years. The resulting list, which first appeared in an exhibition and later in a book, includes great books and landmarks; books that influenced the course of events; books that interpreted new worlds; and books that simply delighted millions of readers. The list is international; the only restriction was "one book per author." Below are the works of literary interest featured on the list, a full account of which can be found in *The New York Public Library's Books of the Century*, edited by Elizabeth Diefendorf (New York: Oxford University Press, 1996).

1895	H. G. Wells, *The Time Machine*
1896	Sarah Orne Jewett, *The Country of the Pointed Firs*
1897	Bram Stoker, *Dracula*
1898	Henry James, *The Turn of the Screw*
1900	L. Frank Baum, *The Wonderful Wizard of Oz*
	Joseph Conrad, *Lord Jim*
1901	Anton Chekhov, *The Three Sisters*
	Rudyard Kipling, *Kim*
	Beatrix Potter, *The Tale of Peter Rabbit*
1902	Arthur Conan Doyle, *The Hound of the Baskervilles*
1903	Helen Keller, *The Story of My Life*

1906	J. M. Barrie, *Peter Pan in Kensington Gardens*
	Upton Sinclair, *The Jungle*
1907	Henry Adams, *The Education of Henry Adams*
1911	G. K. Chesterton, *The Innocence of Father Brown*
1912	Edgar Rice Burroughs, *Tarzan of the Apes*
	Zane Grey, *Riders of the Purple Sage*
1913–27	Marcel Proust, *Remembrance of Things Past*
1914	Juan Ramón Jiménez, *Platero and I: An Andalusian Elegy*
	George Bernard Shaw, *Pygmalion*
	Gertrude Stein, *Tender Buttons: Objects Food Rooms*
1915	Charlotte Perkins Gilman, *Herland*
	Franz Kafka, *The Metamorphosis*
1917	Edna St. Vincent Millay, *Renascence and Other Poems*
	William Butler Yeats, *The Wild Swans at Coole*
1919	Siegfried Sassoon, *The War Poems*
1920	Agatha Christie, *The Mysterious Affair at Styles*
	Edith Wharton, *The Age of Innocence*
1920–23	Jaroslav Hašek, *The Good Soldier Schweik*
1921	Luigi Pirandello, *Six Characters in Search of an Author*
1922	T. S. Eliot, *The Waste Land*
	James Joyce, *Ulysses*
1923	Kahlil Gibran, *The Prophet*

(Books of the Century, continued)

P. G. Wodehouse, *The Inimitable Jeeves*

1924 E. M. Forster, *A Passage to India*

Thomas Mann, *The Magic Mountain*

1925 F. Scott Fitzgerald, *The Great Gatsby*

1926 A. A. Milne, *Winnie-the-Pooh*

1927 Virginia Woolf, *To the Lighthouse*

1928 Federico García Lorca, *Gypsy Ballads*

Erich Maria Remarque, *All Quiet on the Western Front*

1931 Willa Cather, *Shadows on the Rock*

1932 Aldous Huxley, *Brave New World*

1933 James Hilton, *Lost Horizon*

1935–40 Anna Akhmatova, *Requiem*

1936 Margaret Mitchell, *Gone with the Wind*

1937 John Dos Passos, *U.S.A.*

J. R. R. Tolkien, *The Hobbit*

1939 Raymond Chandler, *The Big Sleep*

John Steinbeck, *The Grapes of Wrath*

Nathanael West, *The Day of the Locust*

1940 Ernest Hemingway, *For Whom the Bell Tolls*

Richard Wright, *Native Son*

1941 Arthur Koestler, *Darkness at Noon*

1942 Albert Camus, *The Stranger*

Zora Neale Hurston, *Dust Tracks on a Road*

1943 Betty Smith, *A Tree Grows in Brooklyn*

1944 Jorge Luis Borges, *Fictions*

Lillian Smith, *Strange Fruit*

1946 William Faulkner, *The Portable Faulkner*

1947 W. H. Auden, *The Age of Anxiety: A Baroque Eclogue*

Margaret Wise Brown, *Goodnight Moon*

1948 Alan Paton, *Cry, the Beloved Country*

B. F. Skinner, *Walden Two*

1949 George Orwell, *Nineteen Eighty-four*

1950 C. S. Lewis, *The Lion, the Witch and the Wardrobe*

1951 J. D. Salinger, *The Catcher in the Rye*

1952 Samuel Beckett, *Waiting for Godot*

Ralph Ellison, *Invisible Man*

The Holy Bible. Revised Standard Version

E. B. White, *Charlotte's Web*

1953 Ray Bradbury, *Fahrenheit 451*

1955 Vladimir Nabokov, *Lolita*

1956 Grace Metalious, *Peyton Place*

1957 Jack Kerouac, *On the Road*

Ayn Rand, *Atlas Shrugged*

Dr. Seuss, *The Cat in the Hat*

1958 Chinua Achebe, *Things Fall Apart*

Elie Wiesel, *Night*

1960 Harper Lee, *To Kill a Mockingbird*

1961 Robert A. Heinlein, *Stranger in a Strange Land*

Joseph Heller, *Catch-22*

Langston Hughes, *The Best of Simple*

1962 Anthony Burgess, *A Clockwork Orange*

Ezra Jack Keats, *The Snowy Day*

Ken Kesey, *One Flew over the Cuckoo's Nest*

Doris Lessing, *The Golden Notebook*

1963 Maurice Sendak, *Where the Wild Things Are*

1965 Truman Capote, *In Cold Blood: A True Account of a Multiple Murder and Its Consequences*

1966 Jean Rhys, *Wide Sargasso Sea*

1967 Gabriel García Márquez, *One Hundred Years of Solitude*

1969 Maya Angelou, *I Know Why the Caged Bird Sings*

Philip Roth, *Portnoy's Complaint*

Tayeb el-Salih, *Season of Migration to the North*

1973–75 Aleksandr I. Solzhenitsyn, *The Gulag Archipelago, 1918–1956: An Experiment in Literary Investigation*

1974 Stephen King, *Carrie*

1975 V. S. Naipaul, *Guerrillas*

1976 Bruno Bettelheim, *The Uses of Enchantment*

Buchi Emecheta, *The Bride Price*

1977 Toni Morrison, *Song of Solomon*

1982 Alice Walker, *The Color Purple*

1983 Elizabeth Bishop, *The Complete Poems, 1927–1979*

1984 Marguerite Duras, *The Lover*

1985 Patricia MacLachlan, *Sarah, Plain and Tall*

1986 Margaret Atwood, *The Handmaid's Tale*

1986–91 Art Spiegelman, *Maus: A Survivor's Tale* (2 vols.)

1987 Tom Wolfe, *The Bonfire of the Vanities*

BOOKS TO REMEMBER, 1990–2000

Books to Remember is an annual list of 25 fiction and nonfiction titles chosen by the librarians of The New York Public Library for their distinct and lasting contributions to literature. The following selection includes works of fiction, poetry, and literary biography chosen from 1990 to 2000.

2000

Laure Adler, *Marguerite Duras: A Life*

Michael Chabon, *The Amazing Adventures of Kavalier & Clay: A Novel*

Tracy Chevalier, *Girl with a Pearl Earring*

Myla Goldberg, *Bee Season*

Thom Gunn, *Boss Cupid*

Seamus Heaney, *Beowulf: A New Verse Translation*

Sheri Holman, *The Dress Lodger*

David Leavitt, *Martin Bauman; or, A Sure Thing*

Ernesto Quiñonez, *Bodega Dreams*

Anne Roiphe, *For Rabbit, with Love and Squalor: An American Read*

Akhil Sharma, *An Obedient Father*

1999

Toni Cade Bambara, *Those Bones Are Not My Child*

Raymond Briggs, *Ethel and Ernest*

Amit Chaudhuri, *Freedom Song: Three Novels*

Rita Dove, *On the Bus with Rosa Parks: Poems*

Nathan Englander, *For the Relief of Unbearable Urges*

Lyndall Gordon, *T. S. Eliot: An Imperfect Life*

Barbara Hamby, *The Alphabet of Desire*

Kent Haruf, *Plainsong*

Ha Jin, *Waiting*

Wayne Johnston, *The Colony of Unrequited Dreams: A Novel*

Thom Jones, *Sonny Liston Was a Friend of Mine: Stories*

Phillip Kimball, *Liar's Moon: A Long Story*

Jhumpa Lahiri, *The Interpreter of Maladies: Stories*

Pauline Melville, *The Migration of Ghosts*

Stewart O'Nan, *A Prayer for the Dying*

Annie Proulx, *Close Range: Wyoming Stories*

Judith Thurman, *Secrets of the Flesh: A Life of Colette*

1998

Thomas Bernhard, *The Voice Imitator*

Edwidge Danticat, *The Farming of Bones*

Mark Doty, *Sweet Machine: Poems*

Nick Hornby, *About a Boy*

Ted Hughes, *Birthday Letters*

Barbara Kingsolver, *The Poisonwood Bible*

David Lehman, *The Last Avant-Garde: The Making of the New York School of Poets*

Simon Mawer, *Mendel's Dwarf*

Jill McCorkle, *Final Vinyl Days*

Steven Millhauser, *The Knife Thrower and Other Stories*

Iain Pears, *An Instance of the Fingerpost*

(Books to Remember, continued)

1997

Peter Cameron, *Andorra*

Patrick Chamoiseau, *Texaco*

Don DeLillo, *Underworld*

Stephen Dobyns, *The Church of Dead Girls*

Arthur Golden, *Memoirs of a Geisha*

Audre Lorde, *The Collected Poems of Audre Lorde*

Thomas Lux, *New and Selected Poems: 1975–1995*

Haruki Murakami, *The Wind-up Bird Chronicle*

Peter Nadas, *A Book of Memories*

Charles T. Powers, *In the Memory of the Forest*

Arundhati Roy, *The God of Small Things*

Charles Wright, *Black Zodiac*

1996

Peter Ackroyd, *Blake*

Carlos Baker, *Emerson Among the Eccentrics: A Group Portrait*

Andrea Barrett, *Ship Fever and Other Stories*

Hayden Carruth, *Scrambled Eggs and Whiskey: Poems 1991–1995*

Stephen Dobyns, *Common Carnage*

Deborah Iida, *Middle Son*

Jamaica Kincaid, *The Autobiography of My Mother*

Javier Marias, *A Heart So White*

Frank McCourt, *Angela's Ashes: A Memoir*

Harry Mulisch, *The Discovery of Heaven*

Joyce Carol Oates, *We Were the Mulvaneys*

Salman Rushdie, *The Moor's Last Sigh*

Mary Doria Russell, *The Sparrow*

Jackie Wullschläger, *Inventing Wonderland: The Lives and Fantasies of Lewis Carroll, Edward Lear, J. M. Barrie, Kenneth Grahame, and A. A. Milne*

Rafael Yglesias, *Dr. Neruda's Cure for Evil*

Akira Yoshimura, *Shipwrecks*

1995

Isabel Allende, *Paula*

Nicholas A. Basbanes, *A Gentle Madness: Bibliophiles, Bibliomanes, and the Eternal Passion for Books*

Fred D'Aguiar, *The Longest Memory*

Robertson Davies, *The Cunning Man*

Richard Ford, *Independence Day*

Mark Helprin, *Memoir from the Antproof Case*

Mary Karr, *The Liars' Club: A Memoir*

Dionisio D. Martinez, *Bad Alchemy: Poems*

Alvaro Mutis, *The Adventures of Maqroll: Four Novellas*

Tim Pears, *In the Place of Fallen Leaves*

Hilda Schiff, compiler, *Holocaust Poetry*

A. J. Verdelle, *The Good Negress*

Marina Warner, *From the Beast to the Blonde: On Fairy Tales and Their Tellers*

1994

Miguel Algarin and Bob Holman, eds., *Aloud: Voices from the Nuyorican Poets Cafe*

Beryl Bainbridge, *The Birthday Boys*

Pat Barker, *The Eye in the Door*

Jane Hamilton, *A Map of the World*

David Leeming, *James Baldwin: A Biography*

Doris Lessing, *Under My Skin: Volume One of My Autobiography, to 1949*

Heather McHugh, *Hinge & Sign: Poems 1968–1993*

Alice Munro, *Open Secrets: Stories*

Howard Norman, *The Bird Artist*

Grace Paley, *The Collected Stories*

Caryl Phillips, *Crossing the River*

Reynolds Price, *A Whole New Life*

David Sedaris, *Barrel Fever: Stories and Essays*

John Updike, *The Afterlife and Other Stories*

1993

Reinaldo Arenas, *Before Night Falls*

Margaret Atwood, *The Robber Bride*

Michael Collins, *The Man Who Dreamt of Lobsters*

Marita Golden, ed., *Wild Women Don't Wear No Blues: Black Women Writers on Love, Men and Sex*

Peter Hoeg, *Smilla's Sense of Snow*

Audre Lorde, *The Marvelous Arithmetics of Distance: Poems 1987–1992*

Patrick Marnham, *The Man Who Wasn't Maigret: A Portrait of Georges Simenon*

Patrick McCabe, *The Butcher Boy*

Brian Moore, *No Other Life*

Fae Myenne Ng, *Bone*

Chet Raymo, *The Dork of Cork*

Colm Tóibín, *The Heather Blazing*

1992

Bebe Moore Campbell, *Your Blues Ain't Like Mine*

Maryse Conde, *I, Tituba, Black Witch of Salem*

Annie Dillard, *The Living*

Cristina Garcia, *Dreaming in Cuban*

Robert Harris, *Fatherland*

Alice McDermott, *At Weddings and Wakes*

Sharon Olds, *The Father*

Abraham Rodriguez, Jr., *The Boy Without a Flag: Tales of the South Bronx*

1991

Louis Begley, *Wartime Lies*

Larry Brown, *Joe*

Countee Cullen, *My Soul's High Song: The Collected Writings of Countee Cullen, Voice of the Harlem Renaissance*

Mark Helprin, *A Soldier of the Great War*

Glyn Hughes, *The Antique Collector*

Paule Marshall, *Daughters*

Mary McGarry Morris, *A Dangerous Woman*

Jane Smiley, *A Thousand Acres*

Anne Tyler, *Saint Maybe*

1990

Christine Bell, *The Perez Family*

Brian Boyd, *Vladimir Nabokov: The Russian Years*

A. S. Byatt, *Possession: A Romance*

Bob Cook, *Paper Chase*

Nadine Gordimer, *My Son's Story*

Alice Hoffman, *Seventh Heaven*

Valerie Martin, *Mary Reilly*

Brian Moore, *Lies of Silence*

Joyce Carol Oates, *Because It Is Bitter, and Because It Is My Heart*

Jay Parini, *The Last Station*

Rosamond Smith [Joyce Carol Oates], *Nemesis*

Derek Walcott, *Omeros*

THE MODERN LIBRARY 100

In 1998, The Modern Library, an imprint of Random House, sponsored the compilation, by a panel of ten writers and historians, of this list of "the 100 best novels written in the English language and published since 1900." The publication of The Modern Library 100 sparked lively debate, and numerous lists were created in response. The list appears in order of ranking by the panel of judges.

1 James Joyce, *Ulysses*

2 F. Scott Fitzgerald, *The Great Gatsby*

3 James Joyce, *A Portrait of the Artist as a Young Man*

4 Vladimir Nabokov, *Lolita*

5 Aldous Huxley, *Brave New World*

6 William Faulkner, *The Sound and the Fury*

7 Joseph Heller, *Catch-22*

8 Arthur Koestler, *Darkness at Noon*

9 D. H. Lawrence, *Sons and Lovers*

10 John Steinbeck, *The Grapes of Wrath*

11 Malcolm Lowry, *Under the Volcano*

12 Samuel Butler, *The Way of All Flesh*

13 George Orwell, *Nineteen Eighty-four*

14 Robert Graves, *I, Claudius*

15 Virginia Woolf, *To the Lighthouse*

16 Theodore Dreiser, *An American Tragedy*

17 Carson McCullers, *The Heart Is a Lonely Hunter*

18 Kurt Vonnegut, *Slaughterhouse-Five*

19 Ralph Ellison, *Invisible Man*

20 Richard Wright, *Native Son*

21 Saul Bellow, *Henderson the Rain King*

22 John O'Hara, *Appointment in Samarra*

23 John Dos Passos, *U.S.A.*

(The Modern Library 100, continued)

24 Sherwood Anderson, *Winesburg, Ohio*

25 E. M. Forster, *A Passage to India*

26 Henry James, *The Wings of the Dove*

27 Henry James, *The Ambassadors*

28 F. Scott Fitzgerald, *Tender Is the Night*

29 James T. Farrell, *The Studs Lonigan Trilogy*

30 Ford Madox Ford, *The Good Soldier*

31 George Orwell, *Animal Farm*

32 Henry James, *The Golden Bowl*

33 Theodore Dreiser, *Sister Carrie*

34 Evelyn Waugh, *A Handful of Dust*

35 William Faulkner, *As I Lay Dying*

36 Robert Penn Warren, *All the King's Men*

37 Thornton Wilder, *The Bridge of San Luis Rey*

38 E. M. Forster, *Howards End*

39 James Baldwin, *Go Tell It on the Mountain*

40 Graham Greene, *The Heart of the Matter*

41 William Golding, *Lord of the Flies*

42 James Dickey, *Deliverance*

43 Anthony Powell, *A Dance to the Music of Time*

44 Aldous Huxley, *Point Counter Point*

45 Ernest Hemingway, *The Sun Also Rises*

46 Joseph Conrad, *The Secret Agent*

47 Joseph Conrad, *Nostromo*

48 D. H. Lawrence, *The Rainbow*

49 D. H. Lawrence, *Women in Love*

50 Henry Miller, *Tropic of Cancer*

51 Norman Mailer, *The Naked and the Dead*

52 Philip Roth, *Portnoy's Complaint*

53 Vladimir Nabokov, *Pale Fire*

54 William Faulkner, *Light in August*

55 Jack Kerouac, *On the Road*

56 Dashiell Hammett, *The Maltese Falcon*

57 Ford Madox Ford, *Parade's End*

58 Edith Wharton, *The Age of Innocence*

59 Max Beerbohm, *Zuleika Dobson*

60 Walker Percy, *The Moviegoer*

61 Willa Cather, *Death Comes for the Archbishop*

62 James Jones, *From Here to Eternity*

63 John Cheever, *The Wapshot Chronicles*

64 J. D. Salinger, *The Catcher in the Rye*

65 Anthony Burgess, *A Clockwork Orange*

66 W. Somerset Maugham, *Of Human Bondage*

67 Joseph Conrad, *Heart of Darkness*

68 Sinclair Lewis, *Main Street*

69 Edith Wharton, *The House of Mirth*

70 Lawrence Durell, *The Alexandria Quartet*

71 Richard Hughes, *A High Wind in Jamaica*

72 V. S. Naipaul, *A House for Mr. Biswas*

73 Nathanael West, *The Day of the Locust*

74 Ernest Hemingway, *A Farewell to Arms*

75 Evelyn Waugh, *Scoop*

76 Muriel Spark, *The Prime of Miss Jean Brodie*

77 James Joyce, *Finnegans Wake*

78 Rudyard Kipling, *Kim*

79 E. M. Forster, *A Room with a View*

80 Evelyn Waugh, *Brideshead Revisited*

81 Saul Bellow, *The Adventures of Augie March*

82 Wallace Stegner, *Angle of Repose*

83 V. S. Naipaul, *A Bend in the River*

84 Elizabeth Bowen, *The Death of the Heart*

85 Joseph Conrad, *Lord Jim*

86 E. L. Doctorow, *Ragtime*

87 Arnold Bennett, *The Old Wives' Tale*

88 Jack London, *The Call of the Wild*

89 Henry Green, *Loving*

90 Salman Rushdie, *Midnight's Children*

91 Erskine Caldwell, *Tobacco Road*

92 William Kennedy, *Ironweed*

93 John Fowles, *The Magus*

94 Jean Rhys, *Wide Sargasso Sea*

95 Iris Murdoch, *Under the Net*

96 William Styron, *Sophie's Choice*

97 Paul Bowles, *The Sheltering Sky*

98 James M. Cain, *The Postman Always Rings Twice*

99 J. P. Donleavy, *The Ginger Man*

100 Booth Tarkington, *The Magnificent Ambersons*

The Best Fiction on the Black Experience

The titles on this list are drawn from *No Crystal Stair: A Booklist on the Black Experience* (2001), compiled by the branch librarians of The New York Public Library, and include fiction published through 1999.

Raymond Andrews, *Appalachee Red*

Tina McElroy Ansa, *Baby of the Family*

Sterling Anthony, *Cookie Cutter*

Calvin Baker, *Naming the New World*

James Baldwin, *Go Tell It on the Mountain*

Toni Cade Bambara, *The Salt Eaters*

Marci Blackman, *Po Man's Child*

Eleanor Taylor Bland, *See No Evil*

Arna Bontemps, *Black Thunder*

David Bradley, *The Chaneysville Incident*

Connie Briscoe, *Sisters & Lovers*

William Wells Brown, *Clotel, or, The President's Daughter*

Octavia E. Butler, *Kindred*

Bebe Moore Campbell, *Your Blues Ain't Like Mine*

Lorene Cary, *The Price of a Child*

Colin Channer, *Waiting in Vain*

Barbara Chase-Riboud, *Sally Hemmings*

Charles Waddell Chesnutt, *The Marrow of Tradition*

Maxine Clair, *Rattlebone*

Breena Clarke, *River, Cross My Heart*

Pearl Cleage, *What Looks Like Crazy on an Ordinary Day*

Michelle Cliff, *The Store of a Million Items*

Cyrus Colter, *City of Light*

Clarence L. Cooper, *The Scene*

J. California Cooper, *In Search of Satisfaction*

Steven Corbin, *Fragments That Remain*

Fred D'Aguiar, *Feeding the Ghosts*

Edwidge Danticat, *Breath, Eyes, Memory*

Thulani Davis, *Maker of Saints*

Virginia DeBerry and Donna Grant, *Tryin' to Sleep in the Bed You Made*

Samuel R. Delany, *Tales of Nevèrÿon*

Melvin Dixon, *Trouble the Water*

Tananarive Due, *My Soul to Keep*

Larry Duplechan, *Tangled Up in Blue*

Grace F. Edwards, *No Time to Die*

Trey Ellis, *Home Repairs*

Ralph Ellison, *Invisible Man*

Jessie Redmon Fauset, *Plum Bun*

Carolyn Ferrell, *Don't Erase Me*

Lolita Files, *Scenes from a Sistah*

Albert French, *Billy*

Ernest J. Gaines, *A Lesson Before Dying*

Donald Goines, *Daddy Cool*

Jewelle Gomez, *The Gilda Stories*

Sam Greenlee, *The Spook Who Sat by the Door*

Bonnie Greer, *Hanging by Her Teeth*

James Earl Hardy, *B-Boy Blues*

Frances Ellen Watkins Harper, *Iola Leroy; or Shadows Uplifted*

E. Lynn Harris, *Invisible Life: A Novel*

David Haynes, *Somebody Else's Mama*

Gar Anthony Haywood, *When Last Seen Alive*

Chester B. Himes, *Cotton Comes to Harlem*

John Holman, *Luminous Mysteries*

Nalo Hopkinson, *Brown Girl in the Ring*

Langston Hughes, *The Ways of White Folks*

Zora Neale Hurston, *Their Eyes Were Watching God*

Brian Keith Jackson, *The View from Here*

Sheneska Jackson, *Li'l Mama's Rules*

Roland S. Jefferson, *The School on 103rd Street*

Yolanda Joe, *He Say, She Say*

Charles R. Johnson, *Middle Passage*

James Weldon Johnson, *The Autobiography of an Ex-Colored Man*

Gayl Jones, *Corregidora*

Kwadwo Agymah Kamau, *Flickering Shadows*

John C. Keene, *Annotations*

William Melvin Kelly, *dem*

Randall Kenan, *Let the Dead Bury Their Dead: And Other Stories*

John Oliver Killens, *Youngblood*

(Best Fiction on the Black Experience, continued)

Jamaica Kincaid, *Annie John*

Florence Ladd, *Sarah's Psalm*

Nella Larsen, *Passing*

Victor D. LaValle, *Slapboxing with Jesus*

Helen Elaine Lee, *The Serpent's Gift*

Benilde Little, *Good Hair: A Novel*

Audre Lorde, *Zami: A New Spelling of My Name*

Clarence Major, *All-Night Visitors*

devorah major, *Open Weave*

Claude McKay, *Home to Harlem*

Diane McKinney-Whetstone, *Tumbling*

Kim McLarin, *Taming It Down*

Terry McMillan, *Mama*

James Alan McPherson, *Elbow Room: Stories*

Louise Meriwether, *Daddy Was a Number Runner*

Penny Mickelbury, *Where to Choose: A Carol Ann Gibson Mystery*

Toni Morrison, *Paradise*

Walter Mosley, *Blue Light*

Albert Murray, *Train Whistle Guitar*

Gloria Naylor, *The Women of Brewster Place*

Gordon Parks, *The Learning Tree*

Alexs Pate, *Finding Makeba*

Charles Perry, *Portrait of a Young Man Drowning*

Phyllis Alesia Perry, *Stigmata*

Richard Perry, *The Broken Land*

Ann Petry, *The Street*

Robert Deane Pharr, *S. R. O.*

Caryl Phillips, *Crossing the River*

John Calvin Rainey, *The Thang That Ate My Grandaddy's Dog*

Ishmael Reed, *Mumbo, Jumbo*

Jewell Parker Rhodes, *Voodoo Dreams*

Dori Sanders, *Clover*

Sapphire, *Push*

Danzy Senna, *Caucasia*

Ntozake Shange, *Sassafrass, Cypress, & Indigo*

Herbert Simmons, *Corner Boy*

April Sinclair, *Coffee Will Make You Black*

Faye McDonald Smith, *Flight of the Blackbird*

Mary Burnett Smith, *Miss Ophelia*

Vern E. Smith, *The Jones Men*

Sister Souljah, *The Coldest Winter Ever*

Wallace Thurman, *The Blacker the Berry*

Jean Toomer, *Cane*

Dawn Turner Trice, *Only Twice I've Wished for Heaven*

Henry Van Dyke, *The Dead Piano*

J. Verdelle, *The Good Negress*

Alice Walker, *The Color Purple*

Margaret Walker, *Jubilee*

Dorothy West, *The Richer, the Poorer*

John Edgar Wideman, *Philadelphia Fire*

John Alfred Williams, *Clifford's Blues*

Sherley Anne Williams, *Dessa Rose*

Harriet E. Wilson, *Our Nig, or Sketches from the Life of a Free Black*

Richard Wright, *Native Son*

THE 100 BEST LESBIAN AND GAY NOVELS

The Publishing Triangle, an association of gay men and women in publishing, created this list, selected by a panel of lesbian and gay writers. It was announced March 30, 2000, in New York City. The list appears in order of ranking by the panel of judges.

1 Thomas Mann, *Death in Venice*

2 James Baldwin, *Giovanni's Room*

3 Jean Genet, *Our Lady of the Flowers*

4 Marcel Proust, *Remembrance of Things Past*

5 André Gide, *The Immoralist*

6 Virginia Woolf, *Orlando*

7 Radclyffe Hall, *The Well of Loneliness*

8 Manuel Puig, *Kiss of the Spider Woman*

9 Marguerite Yourcenar, *The Memoirs of Hadrian*

10 Audre Lorde, *Zami: A New Spelling of My Name*

11 Oscar Wilde, *The Picture of Dorian Gray*

12 Djuna Barnes, *Nightwood*

13 Herman Melville, *Billy Budd*

14 Edmund White, *A Boy's Own Story*

15 Andrew Holleran, *Dancer from the Dance*

16 E. M. Forster, *Maurice*

17 Gore Vidal, *The City and the Pillar*

18 Rita Mae Brown, *Rubyfruit Jungle*

19 Evelyn Waugh, *Brideshead Revisited*

20 Yukio Mishima, *Confessions of a Mask*

21 Carson McCullers, *The Member of the Wedding*

22 John Rechy, *City of Night*

23 Gore Vidal, *Myra Breckinridge*

24 Isabel Miller, *Patience and Sarah*

25 Gertrude Stein, *The Autobiography of Alice B. Toklas*

26 Truman Capote, *Other Voices, Other Rooms*

27 Henry James, *The Bostonians*

28 Jane Bowles, *Two Serious Ladies*

29 Dorothy Allison, *Bastard Out of Carolina*

30 Carson McCullers, *The Heart Is a Lonely Hunter*

31 Virginia Woolf, *Mrs. Dalloway*

32 Mary Renault, *The Persian Boy*

33 Christopher Isherwood, *A Single Man*

34 Alan Hollinghurst, *The Swimming Pool Library*

35 Dorothy Bussy, *Olivia*

36 Patricia Highsmith, *The Price of Salt*

37 Carol Anshaw, *Aquamarine*

38 James Baldwin, *Another Country*

39 Colette, *Cheri*

40 Henry James, *The Turn of the Screw*

41 Alice Walker, *The Color Purple*

42 D. H. Lawrence, *Women in Love*

43 Louisa May Alcott, *Little Women*

44 Mary Renault, *The Friendly Young Ladies*

45 Robert Musil, *Young Torless*

46 James Purdy, *Eustace Chisholm and the Works*

47 Terry Andrews, *The Story of Harold*

48 John Horne Burns, *The Gallery*

49 June Arnold, *Sister Gin*

50 Neil Bartlett, *Ready to Catch Him Should He Fall*

51 Christopher Bram, *Father of Frankenstein*

52 William S. Burroughs, *Naked Lunch*

53 Christopher Isherwood, *The Berlin Stories*

54 Charles Henri Ford and Parker Tyler, *The Young and Evil*

55 Jeanette Winterson, *Oranges Are Not the Only Fruit*

56 Randall Kenan, *A Visitation of Spirits*

57 Gertrude Stein, *Three Lives*

58 Ronald Firbank, *Concerning the Eccentricities of Cardinal Pirelli*

59 Sarah Schulman, *Rat Bohemia*

60 Vladimir Nabokov, *Pale Fire*

61 André Gide, *The Counterfeiters*

62 Jeanette Winterson, *The Passion*

63 Bertha Harris, *Lover*

64 Herman Melville, *Moby Dick*

65 Violette Leduc, *La Bâtarde*

66 Willa Cather, *Death Comes for the Archbishop*

67 Harper Lee, *To Kill a Mockingbird*

68 Petronius, *Satyricon*

69 Lawrence Durrell, *The Alexandria Quartet*

70 Roger Peyrefitte, *Special Friendships*

71 Jo Sinclair, *The Changelings*

72 José Lezama Lima, *Paradiso*

73 Irving Rosenthal, *Sheeper*

74 Monique Wittig, *Les Guérillères*

75 Christa Winsloe, *The Child Manuela (Mädchen in Uniform)*

76 Mark Merlis, *An Arrow's Flight*

77 William Talsman, *The Gaudy Image*

78 Alfred Chester, *The Exquisite Corpse*

79 Geoff Ryman, *Was*

80 Violette Leduc, *Thérèse and Isabelle*

81 Michel Tournier, *Gemini*

82 Edmund White, *The Beautiful Room Is Empty*

83 Rebecca Brown, *The Children's Crusade*

FAVORITES

"...it is not possible, when you are reading Charlotte Brontë, to lift your eyes from the page."

Virginia Woolf, "Charlotte Brontë," *Times Literary Supplement* (April 13, 1916)

"I liked Yeats! That wild Irishman. I really loved his love of language, his flow. His chaotic ideas seemed to me just the right thing for a poet. Passion! He was always on the right side. He may be wrongheaded, but his heart was always on the right side."

Chinua Achebe, in an interview with Jerome Brooks in *The Paris Review* (Winter 1994)

"There exists one [book] which, to my taste, provides the most felicitous treatise on natural education....What, then, is this marvelous book? Is it Aristotle? Is it Pliny, is it Buffon? No. It is *Robinson Crusoe*."

Jean-Jacques Rousseau, *Émile; or, On Education* (1762), translated by Alan Bloom (1979)

"'What do I think of *Middlemarch*?' What do I think of glory—except that in a few instances this 'mortal has already put on immortality.'"

Emily Dickinson, letter to Louise and Frances Norcross, April 1873, in *The Letters of Emily Dickinson* (1958)

"That book [Robert Louis Stevenson's *Treasure Island*] and I loved each other, and I don't mean just its text: that book, which then was new, its cover slick and shiny, its paper agleam with the tossing sea and armed, as Long John Silver was, for a fight, its binding tight as the elastic of new underwear, not slack as it is now, after so many openings and closings, so many dry years; that book would be borne off to my room, where it lived through my high school miseries in a dime-store bookcase, and it would accompany me to college too, and be packed in the duffel bag I carried as a sailor."

William H. Gass, "In Defense of the Book," *Harper's Magazine* (November 1999)

"The first play that amazed me (I thought it was the most powerful thing of all—not only in theater but in painting, film, everything!) was Beckett's *Waiting for Godot*. I saw the play in Paris and I didn't understand a word of the French, but I left the theater as if I'd been hit over the head. I understood every moment of it. That play had a profound influence on me. When I returned from Europe, I started writing."

Maria Irene Fornes, in an interview in Kathleen Betsko and Rachel Koenig, *Interviews with Contemporary Women Playwrights* (1987)

"Tolstoy is the greatest Russian writer of prose fiction. Leaving aside his precursors Pushkin and Lermontov, we might list the greatest artists in Russian prose thus: first, Tolstoy; second, Gogol; third, Chekhov; fourth, Turgenev. This is rather like grading students' papers and no doubt Dostoevski and Saltykov are waiting at the door of my office to discuss their low marks."

Vladimir Nabokov, "Leo Tolstoy," in *Lectures on Russian Literature* (1981)

"If I knew that by grinding Mr. Eliot into a fine dry powder and sprinkling that powder over Mr. Conrad's grave, Mr. Conrad would shortly reappear, looking very annoyed at the forced return, and commence writing, I would leave for London early tomorrow morning with a sausage-grinder."

Ernest Hemingway, quoted in Carlos Baker, *Hemingway: The Writer as Artist* (1952)

"When I read something saying I've not done anything as good as *Catch-22* I'm tempted to reply, 'Who has?'"

Joseph Heller, in *The Times* (London) (June 9, 1993)

"Kafka arouses pity and terror, Joyce admiration, Proust and Gide respect, but no modern writer that I can think of, except Camus, has aroused love."

Susan Sontag, *Against Interpretation* (1966)

"I always like comedies where there's suddenly a chill, like *Much Ado About Nothing*, when you get the line 'Kill Claudio!' And you think, 'Aha!'"

Julian Barnes, quoted in "Julian Barnes on Love, etc." by Brendan Bernhard, *LA Weekly* (March 30–April 5, 2001)

"I suspect that the detective novels of Eduardo Gutiérrez and a volume of Greek mythology and *The Student of Salamanca* and the rea-sonable and not at all fanciful fantasies of Jules Verne and Stevenson's grandiose romances and the first serial novel ever written, *The Thousand and One Nights*, are the greatest literary joys I have experienced. The list is diverse and cannot claim any unity other than the early age at which I read them. I was a hospitable reader in those days, a polite explorer of the lives of others, and I accepted everything with providential and enthusiastic resignation. I believed everything, even errata and poor illustrations."

Jorge Luis Borges, "Literary Pleasure" (1927), translated by Suzanne Jill Levine, in *Selected Non-Fictions* (1999)

"In the beginning—and perhaps still—the most important short story writers to me were Isaac Babel, Anton Chekhov, Frank O'Connor and V. S. Pritchett. I forget who first passed along a copy of Babel's *Collected Stories* to me, but I do remember coming across a line from one of his greatest stories. I copied it into the little notebook I carried around with me everywhere in those days. The narrator, speaking about Maupassant and the writing of fiction, says: 'No iron can stab the heart with such force as a period put just at the right place.'"

Raymond Carver, "A Special Message for the First Edition," in *Where I'm Calling From* (1988)

"If a writer has to rob his mother, he will not hesitate; the *Ode on a Grecian Urn* is worth any number of old ladies."

William Faulkner, in an interview in *The Paris Review* (Spring 1956)

(The 100 Best Lesbian and Gay Novels, continued)

84 Colm Tóibín, *The Story of the Night*

85 Jean Cocteau, *Holy Terrors (Les Enfants Terribles)*

86 José Donoso, *Hell Has No Limits*

87 Elana Nachman (Dykewomon), *Riverfinger Women*

88 Tom Spanbauer, *The Man Who Fell in Love with the Moon*

89 Dennis Cooper, *Closer*

90 Honoré de Balzac, *Lost Illusions*

91 Elizabeth Jolley, *Miss Peabody's Inheritance*

92 Virgilio Pinera, *René's Flesh*

93 Shyam Selvadurai, *Funny Boy*

94 Jo Sinclair, *Wasteland*

95 May Sarton, *Mrs. Stevens Hears the Mermaids Singing*

96 Paul Russell, *Sea of Tranquility*

97 Jacqueline Woodson, *Autobiography of a Family Photo*

98 Jane DeLynn, *In Thrall*

99 Joanna Russ, *On Strike Against God*

100 Kate Millett, *Sita*

THE NEW YORK TIMES FICTION BESTSELLERS, 1917–99

The following list of American bestsellers is drawn from *The New York Times Almanac,* 2001.

1917 H. G. Wells, *Mr. Britling Sees It Through*

1918 Zane Grey, *The U.P. Trail*

1919 V. Blasco Ibañez, *The Four Horsemen of the Apocalypse*

1920 Zane Grey, *The Man of the Forest*

1921 Sinclair Lewis, *Main Street*

1922 A. S. M. Hutchinson, *If Winter Comes*

1923 Gertrude Atherton, *Black Oxen*

1924 Edna Ferber, *So Big*

1925 A. Hamilton Gibbs, *Soundings*

1926 John Erskine, *The Private Life of Helen of Troy*

1927 Sinclair Lewis, *Elmer Gantry*

1928 Thornton Wilder, *The Bridge of San Luis Rey*

1929 Erich Maria Remarque, *All Quiet on the Western Front*

1930 Edna Ferber, *Cimarron*

1931 Pearl S. Buck, *The Good Earth*

1932 Pearl S. Buck, *The Good Earth*

1933 Hervey Allen, *Anthony Adverse*

1934 Hervey Allen, *Anthony Adverse*

1935 Lloyd C. Douglas, *Green Light*

1936 Margaret Mitchell, *Gone with the Wind*

1937 Margaret Mitchell, *Gone with the Wind*

1938 Marjorie Kinnan Rawlings, *The Yearling*

1939 John Steinbeck, *The Grapes of Wrath*

1940 Richard Llewellyn, *How Green Was My Valley*

1941 A. J. Cronin, *The Keys of the Kingdom*

1942 Franz Werfel, *The Song of Bernadette*

1943 Lloyd C. Douglas, *The Robe*

1944 Lillian Smith, *Strange Fruit*

1945 Kathleen Winsor, *Forever Amber*

1946 Daphne du Maurier, *The King's General*

1947 Russell Janney, *The Miracle of the Bells*

1948 Lloyd C. Douglas, *The Big Fisherman*

1949 Mika Waltari, *The Egyptian*

1950 Henry Morton Robinson, *The Cardinal*

1951 James Jones, *From Here to Eternity*

1952 Thomas B. Costain, *The Silver Chalice*

1953 Lloyd C. Douglas, *The Robe*

1954 Morton Thompson, *Not as a Stranger*

1955 Herman Wouk, *Marjorie Morningstar*

1956 William Brinkley, *Don't Go Near the Water*

1957 James Gould Cozzens, *By Love Possessed*

1958 Boris Pasternak, *Doctor Zhivago*

1959 Leon Uris, *Exodus*

1960 Allen Drury, *Advise and Consent*

1961 Irving Stone, *The Agony and the Ecstasy*

1962 Katherine Anne Porter, *Ship of Fools*

1963 Morris L. West, *The Shoes of the Fisherman*

1964 John Le Carré, *The Spy Who Came in from the Cold*

1965 James A. Michener, *The Source*

1966 Jacqueline Susann, *Valley of the Dolls*

1967 Elia Kazan, *The Arrangement*

1968 Arthur Hailey, *Airport*

1969 Philip Roth, *Portnoy's Complaint*

1970 Erich Segal, *Love Story*

1971 Arthur Hailey, *Wheels*

1972 Richard Bach, *Jonathan Livingston Seagull*

1973 Richard Bach, *Jonathan Livingston Seagull*

1974 James A. Michener, *Centennial*

1975 E. L. Doctorow, *Ragtime*

1976 Leon Uris, *Trinity*

1977 J. R. R. Tolkien, *The Silmarillion*

1978 James A. Michener, *Chesapeake*

1979 Robert Ludlum, *The Matarese Circle*

1980 James A. Michener, *The Covenant*

1981 James Clavell, *Noble House*

1982 William Kotzwinkle, *E. T., The Extra-Terrestrial Storybook*

1983 Joan D. Vinge, *Return of the Jedi Storybook*

1984 Stephen King, Peter Straub, *The Talisman*

1985 Jean M. Auel, *The Mammoth Hunters*

1986 Stephen King, *It*

1987 Stephen King, *The Tommyknockers*

1988 Tom Clancy, *The Cardinal of the Kremlin*

1989 Tom Clancy, *Clear and Present Danger*

1990 Jean M. Auel, *The Plains of Passage*

1991 Alexandra Ripley, *Scarlett*

1992 Stephen King, *Dolores Claiborne*

1993 Robert James Waller, *The Bridges of Madison County*

1994 John Grisham, *The Chamber*

1995 John Grisham, *The Rainmaker*

1996 John Grisham, *The Runaway Jury*

1997 John Grisham, *The Partner*

1998 John Grisham, *The Street Lawyer*

1999 John Grisham, *The Testament*

GOOD BOOKS ABOUT GOOD BOOKS: A BRIEF BIBLIOGRAPHY

Bauermeister, Erica, Jesse Larsen, and Holly Smith. *500 Great Books by Women: A Reader's Guide.* New York: Penguin Books, 1994.

Best Books: Experts Choose Their Favourites. Edited by Chris Murray. Oxford: Helicon, 1996.

La Bibliothèque Idéale. Edited by Pierre Boncenne. Paris: Albin Michel, 1997.

Bloom, Harold. *The Western Canon: The Books and School of the Ages.* New York: Harcourt Brace, 1994.

Burgess, Anthony. *Ninety-nine Novels: The Best in English Since 1939: A Personal Choice.* London: Allison & Busby, 1984.

Callil, Carmen, and Colm Tóibín. *The Modern Library: The Two Hundred Best Novels in English Since 1950.* London: Picador, 1999.

Calvino, Italo. *Why Read the Classics?* London: Jonathan Cape, 1999.

Carey, John. *Pure Pleasure: A Guide to the 20th Century's Most Enjoyable Books.* London: Faber and Faber Ltd., 2000.

The Crown Crime Companion: The Top 100 Mystery Novels of All Time. Selected by the Mystery Writers of America, annotated by Otto Penzler, compiled by Mickey Friedman. New York: Crown Trade Paperbacks, 1995.

Denby, David. *Great Books: My Adventures with Homer, Rousseau, Woolf, and Other Indestructible Writers of the Western World.* New York: Simon & Schuster, 1996.

Fadiman, Clifton, and John S. Major. *The New Lifetime Reading Plan.* 4th ed. New York: HarperCollins Publishers, 1997.

For the Love of Books: 115 Celebrated Writers on the Books They Love Most. Edited by Ronald B. Shwartz. New York: Grosset/Putnam, 1999.

(Good Books About Good Books, continued)

Gilbar, Steven. *Good Books: A Book Lover's Companion*. New Haven: Ticknor & Fields, 1982.

Good Fiction Guide. Edited by Jane Rogers, Mike Harris, Douglas Houston, and Hermione Lee. Oxford: Oxford University Press, 2001.

Good Reading: A Guide for Serious Readers. Edited by Arthur Waldhorn, Olga S. Weber, and Arthur Zeiger. New York: R. R. Bowker, 1990.

The Harvard Guide to Influential Books: 113 Distinguished Harvard Professors Discuss the Books That Have Helped to Shape Their Thinking. Edited by C. Maury Devine, Claudia M. Dissel, and Kim D. Parrish. New York: Harper & Row, 1986.

Kanigel, Robert. *Vintage Reading: From Plato to Bradbury: A Personal Tour of Some of the World's Best Books*. Baltimore, Md.: Bancroft Press, 1998.

Katz, Linda Sternberg, and Bill Katz. *Writer's Choice: A Library of Rediscoveries*. Reston, Va.: Reston Publishing Company, 1983.

Keating, H. R. F. *Crime & Mystery: The 100 Best Books*. London: Xanadu, 1987.

McLeish, Kenneth. *Bloomsbury Good Reading Guide*. London: Bloomsbury, 1990.

101 Great Books of Our Time. Selected by the Sunday Times (London, England). Manchester, England: Withy Grove, 1961.

Pearlman, Mickey. *What to Read: The Essential Guide for Reading Group Members and Other Book Lovers*. New York: HarperPerennial, 1994.

Pringle, David. *Science Fiction: The 100 Best Novels: An English-language Selection, 1949–1984*. New York: Carroll & Graf, 1985.

The Reader's Catalog: An Annotated Selection of More than 40,000 of the Best Books in Print in Over 300 Categories. Edited by Geoffrey O'Brien. New York: Reader's Catalog, 1997.

Saal, Rollene. *The New York Public Library Guide to Reading Groups*. New York: Crown Publishers, 1995.

Van Doren, Charles. *The Joy of Reading: 210 Favorite Books, Plays, Poems, Essays, etc.: What's in Them, Why Read Them*. New York: Harmony Books, 1985.

What Do I Read Next? Detroit: Gale, 1990– . Annual. "A reader's guide to current genre fiction."

Landmarks in Literary Censorship

1497

In Florence, Italy, fiery reformer-priest Girolamo Savonarola leads a movement for the regeneration of religion and morality to combat the flowering of humanism. The movement's efforts to suppress "vice and frivolity" find expression in a "bonfire of the vanities," into which the faithful toss onto the flames books (including works by Ovid, Dante, and Propertius), lewd pictures, personal ornaments, and gaming paraphernalia.

1559

The first *Index Auctorum et Librorum Prohibitorum* (Index of Forbidden Authors and Books) is published in Rome, Italy, under Pope Paul IV. The list, new editions of which appear until 1966 when the Vatican ends it, consists of books considered dangerous to the faith or morals of Roman Catholics. Among the many literary works listed on the Index during its existence are Montaigne's *Essays*, Casanova's *Memoirs*, de Sade's *Justine*, and Stendhal's *The Red and the Black*.

1791

The First Amendment to the U.S. Constitution, written by James Madison, states that "Congress shall make no law...abridging the freedom of speech, or of the press...."

1818

Thomas Bowdler publishes an edition of Shakespeare's works (the *Family Shakespeare*) that omits "those words and expressions which cannot with propriety be read aloud in the family." His name becomes a byword for censorship: "to bowdlerize" now means "to expurgate."

1857

Accused of attacking morality and religion in *Madame Bovary*, Gustave Flaubert and the novel's publisher and printer are taken to court. Flaubert's clever lawyers obtain an acquittal by arguing that the author was portraying scenes of vice in order to encourage the practice of virtue.

1873

The U.S. Congress passes the Comstock Law, banning the mailing of materials found to be "lewd," "indecent," "filthy," or "obscene," after a campaign by Anthony Comstock's Society for the Suppression of Vice, which took as its slogans "Morals not Art and Literature!" and "Books are feeders for brothels!" Among the literary classics banned under the law's authority are Aristophanes' *Lysistrata*, Chaucer's *Canterbury Tales*, Boccaccio's *Decameron*, and Defoe's *Moll Flanders*. The law remains on the books, but is no longer enforced.

1884

The Adventures of Huckleberry Finn by Mark Twain is banned by the Concord (Massachusetts) Public Library, one trustee saying that it

■ 541

"deals with a series of adventures of a very low grade of morality; it is couched in the language of a rough dialect, and all through its pages there is a systematic use of bad grammar.... The book is flippant and irreverent.... It is trash of the veriest sort." When Twain hears about the ban, he remarks, "That will sell 25,000 copies for us, sure."

1918–30

Issues of the literary magazine the *Little Review* that contain excerpts from James Joyce's *Ulysses* are burned by the U.S. Post Office. The complete text of the novel is published by Shakespeare and Co. in Paris in 1922; copies imported from France to the United States, Canada, Ireland, and Great Britain are seized and burned. But copies of the book smuggled into the United States in a myriad of ingenious ways force libraries to address the issue of adding Joyce's novel to their collections. In 1930, George F. Bowerman of the Washington, D.C., public library system opines that *Ulysses* is appropriate material for "a medical library or a library of abnormal psychology." (See 1933.)

1920s–80s

In the Soviet Union, clandestinely produced literary and other works known as *samizdat* (Russian *sam* [self] and *izdatelstvo* [publishing]) pass secretly from reader to reader in handwritten or typed carbon copies, allowing the writings of banned authors to circulate in spite of government suppression. The work of such major poets and novelists as Osip Mandelshtam, Anna Akhmatova, Marina Tsvetayeva, Boris Pasternak, Mikhail Bulgakov, and many others are usually available to Soviet readers only through *samizdat* channels.

1928

Radclyffe Hall's *The Well of Loneliness*, the frank portrayal of a lesbian relationship, is condemned by a British court as a work that "glorified unnatural tendencies" and it is ordered that the book be "burnt as an obscene libel which tended to corrupt those into whose hands it

fell." (The ban was lifted in Britain in 1949, and the novel was read on BBC Radio in 1974.) The book is also found obscene in New York, the prosecution citing the Hicklin Rule—that if some passages are obscene, the entire work is obscene—to prove its case. (The Hicklin Rule was overturned in 1934 in the case *United States v. One Book Entitled "Ulysses."*)

When British publishers decline to publish *Lady Chatterley's Lover*, D. H. Lawrence's novel about adultery, the author has it published in Florence, Italy. Almost immediately it is banned in Britain and the United States, the censors being concerned about the explicit sexual content of the novel and its provocative themes. It will not be published in the United States until 1959.

1933

In the early 1930s, according to historian David Clay Large, the Nazis begin organizing book-burnings of so-called "un-German" and "Jewish-Bolshevik" literature in university towns around the country. The largest takes place in Berlin on May 10, 1933, when 20,000 books pillaged from libraries and stores around the capital are burned. Among the authors whose works are chosen for destruction are Karl Marx, Bertolt Brecht, Thomas Mann, Arnold and Stefan Zweig, Erich Maria Remarque, H. G. Wells, Sigmund Freud, Émile Zola, Upton Sinclair, André Gide, Marcel Proust, Ernest Hemingway, and Helen Keller. In that year, Sigmund Freud writes to his colleague Ernest Jones, "What progress we are making. In the Middle Ages they would have burned me. Now they are content with burning my books."

Random House decides to publish James Joyce's *Ulysses* in New York, forcing the landmark 1934 obscenity case *United States v. One Book Entitled "Ulysses."* In his decision, Judge John Woolsey writes, "The question in each case is whether the publication taken as a whole has a libidinous effect," radically changing the definition of obscenity and thereby permitting the American publication of *Ulysses* in that year.

God's Little Acre by Erskine Caldwell comes under fire for its graphic descriptions of casual sexual practices. In 1933, the New York Society for the Suppression of Vice files a complaint of obscenity against the publisher. Magistrate Benjamin Greenspan of New York City dismisses the complaint, noting that the book must be judged not on isolated passages but in its entirety; he further rules that the novel does not "incite lustful desires in normal minds," and that "the court may not require the author to put refined language in the mouths of primitive people." Despite this strong statement, *God's Little Acre* remains a subject of controversy in other parts of the country, and citizens' groups continue to seek to ban it from schools and public libraries. A prominent example is a 1961 crusade by Mothers United for Decency, an Oklahoma City organization that utilizes a trailer known as a "smutmobile," which displays *God's Little Acre* and other works deemed objectionable and dangerous to public morals.

1955

After failing to acquire an American publisher for his novel *Lolita*, Vladimir Nabokov has it published in Paris in 1955. It is quickly denounced as a pornographic work endorsing pedophilia, and France bans the sale of the book a year after publication. After several court cases and the publication of a French-language version in 1959, the courts relent, and the English version legally reappears in France in 1959. In 1957, U.S. Customs determines that the book is not obscene and, thus, can be brought into the country; the following year the first American edition appears.

1956

Upon Josef Stalin's death and the mild liberalization permitted by Nikita Khrushchev in the Soviet Union, Boris Pasternak undertakes the writing of what will become his most famous work. In 1956, he submits copies of *Doctor Zhivago* to the State Publishing House in Moscow as well as to an Italian publisher in Milan. The Soviet authorities ultimately reject the work as defaming the achievements of the Russian Revolution of 1917. It is published in Italy in 1957, and the following year in an English translation. It is only in 1988 that *Doctor Zhivago* is finally published in Russia.

1957

In a test case, Grove Press in New York City publishes an unexpurgated version of D. H. Lawrence's *Lady Chatterley's Lover*, prompting the Postmaster General to ban it from the U.S. mails. In the same year, the courts decide in favor of the publisher; Judge Frederick van Pelt Bryan of the federal district court, acknowledging changing community standards and the mores of a more liberal society, rejects attempts to censor the work, and in his decision cites *Roth v. United States* (1957), which accepted the standard of "redeeming social importance" in determining whether literary works ought to be judged obscene. His decision is upheld by the circuit court of appeals in 1960.

1968–93

After serving eight years at hard labor and spending three years in internal exile for criticizing Josef Stalin, author Aleksandr Solzhenitsyn is prohibited from publishing in the Soviet Union. His novels *The First Circle* (1968), *The Cancer Ward* (1968), and *August 1914* (1971), and his influential work on the history of the Soviet prison camp system, *The Gulag Archipelago, 1918–1956*, are all first published abroad.

1989

On February 14, Iranian revolutionary leader Ayatollah Ruhollah Khomeini calls on all Muslims to kill Salman Rushdie, author of the novel *The Satanic Verses*, for blasphemy against Islam and the Koran—an edict called a *fatwa*. The book is banned in Israel, India, South Africa, Sudan, Bangladesh, Sri Lanka, Pakistan, Iran, Tanzania, Singapore, and Indonesia. Rushdie is forced into hiding until 1998, when the *fatwa* is lifted.

THE 100 MOST FREQUENTLY CHALLENGED BOOKS OF THE 1990s

The Office for Intellectual Freedom of the American Library Association compiled this list of the 100 most frequently challenged books of the decade from a total of 5,718 challenges to library materials reported to or recorded by the Association's Office for Intellectual Freedom from 1990 to 1999.

1 Scary Stories (series) by Alvin Schwartz

2 *Daddy's Roommate* by Michael Willhoite

3 *I Know Why the Caged Bird Sings* by Maya Angelou

4 *The Chocolate War* by Robert Cormier

5 *The Adventures of Huckleberry Finn* by Mark Twain

6 *Of Mice and Men* by John Steinbeck

7 *Forever* by Judy Blume

8 *Bridge to Terabithia* by Katherine Paterson

9 *Heather Has Two Mommies* by Leslea Newman

10 *The Catcher in the Rye* by J. D. Salinger

11 *The Giver* by Lois Lowry

12 *My Brother Sam Is Dead* by James Lincoln Collier and Christopher Collier

13 *It's Perfectly Normal* by Robie Harris

14 Alice (series) by Phyllis Reynolds Naylor

15 Goosebumps (series) by R. L. Stine

16 *A Day No Pigs Would Die* by Robert Newton Peck

17 *The Color Purple* by Alice Walker

18 *Sex* by Madonna

19 Earth's Children (series) by Jean M. Auel

20 *The Great Gilly Hopkins* by Katherine Paterson

21 *In the Night Kitchen* by Maurice Sendak

22 *The Witches* by Roald Dahl

23 *A Wrinkle in Time* by Madeleine L'Engle

24 *The New Joy of Gay Sex* by Charles Silverstein

25 *Go Ask Alice* by Anonymous

26 *The Goats* by Brock Cole

27 The Stupids (series) by Harry Allard

28 Anastasia Krupnik (series) by Lois Lowry

29 *Final Exit* by Derek Humphry

30 *Blubber* by Judy Blume

31 *Halloween ABC* by Eve Merriam

32 *Julie of the Wolves* by Jean Craighead George

33 *Kaffir Boy* by Mark Mathabane

34 *The Bluest Eye* by Toni Morrison

35 *What's Happening to My Body? Book for Girls: A Growing-Up Guide for Parents & Daughters* by Lynda Madaras

36 *Fallen Angels* by Walter Dean Myers

37 *The Handmaid's Tale* by Margaret Atwood

38 *The Outsiders* by S. E. Hinton

39 *The Pigman* by Paul Zindel

40 *To Kill a Mockingbird* by Harper Lee

41 *We All Fall Down* by Robert Cormier

42 *Deenie* by Judy Blume

43 *Flowers for Algernon* by Daniel Keyes

44 *Annie on My Mind* by Nancy Garden

45 *Beloved* by Toni Morrison

46 *The Boy Who Lost His Face* by Louis Sachar

47 *Cross Your Fingers, Spit in Your Hat* by Alvin Schwartz

48 Harry Potter (series) by J. K. Rowling

49 *Cujo* by Stephen King

50 *James and the Giant Peach* by Roald Dahl

51 *A Light in the Attic* by Shel Silverstein

52 *Ordinary People* by Judith Guest

53 *American Psycho* by Bret Easton Ellis

54 *Brave New World* by Aldous Huxley

55 Sleeping Beauty Trilogy by A. N. Roquelaure (Anne Rice)

56 *Bumps in the Night* by Harry Allard

57 *Asking About Sex and Growing Up* by Joanna Cole

58 *What's Happening to My Body? Book for Boys: A Growing-Up Guide for Parents & Sons* by Lynda Madaras

59 *The Anarchist Cookbook* by William Powell

60 *Are You There, God? It's Me, Margaret* by Judy Blume

61 *Boys and Sex* by Wardell Pomeroy

62 *Crazy Lady* by Jane Conly

63 *Athletic Shorts* by Chris Crutcher

64 *Killing Mr. Griffin* by Lois Duncan

65 *Fade* by Robert Cormier

66 *Guess What?* by Mem Fox

67 *Slaughterhouse-Five* by Kurt Vonnegut

68 *Lord of the Flies* by William Golding

69 *Native Son* by Richard Wright

70 *Women on Top: How Real Life Has Changed Women's Fantasies* by Nancy Friday

71 *Curses, Hexes and Spells* by Daniel Cohen

72 *On My Honor* by Marion Dane Bauer

73 *The House of the Spirits* by Isabel Allende

74 *Jack* by A. M. Homes

75 *Arizona Kid* by Ron Koertge

76 *Family Secrets* by Norma Klein

77 *Mommy Laid an Egg* by Babette Cole

78 *Bless Me, Ultima* by Rudolfo A. Anaya

79 *Where Did I Come From?* by Peter Mayle

80 *The Face on the Milk Carton* by Caroline Cooney

81 *Carrie* by Stephen King

82 *The Dead Zone* by Stephen King

83 *The Adventures of Tom Sawyer* by Mark Twain

84 *Song of Solomon* by Toni Morrison

85 *Always Running* by Luis Rodriguez

86 *Private Parts* by Howard Stern

87 *Where's Waldo?* by Martin Hanford

88 *Summer of My German Soldier* by Bette Greene

89 *Tiger Eyes* by Judy Blume

90 *Little Black Sambo* by Helen Bannerman

91 *Pillars of the Earth* by Ken Follett

92 *Running Loose* by Chris Crutcher

93 *Sex Education* by Jenny Davis

94 *Jumper* by Steven Gould

95 *Christine* by Stephen King

96 *The Drowning of Stephen Jones* by Bette Greene

97 *That Was Then, This Is Now* by S. E. Hinton

98 *Girls and Sex* by Wardell Pomeroy

99 *The Wish Giver* by Bill Brittain

100 *Jump Ship to Freedom* by James Lincoln Collier and Christopher Collier

Reprinted by permission of the American Library Association

1998

In May, New York City's nonprofit Manhattan Theatre Club cancels a production of Terrence McNally's new play, *Corpus Christi*, in the face of protests from the Catholic League for Religious and Civil Rights and anonymous telephoned bomb threats against the theater company, the playwright, and the theater building. The play depicts a young gay man, Joshua, and his 12 disciples, and is (sight unseen) deemed by the religious group to be a sacrilegious depiction of Jesus. The theater's decision to cancel is met with an outcry from the artistic community. The theater relents, and McNally's play is reinstated; but *Corpus Christi*'s fall premiere is picketed by members of the League and of the Society for the Defense of Tradition, Family and Property. As a security precaution, throughout the play's run audiences are required to pass through metal detectors before entering the theater.

General

Literary Sources

1 GUIDES TO LITERARY REFERENCE BOOKS

Guide to Reference Works for the Study of the Spanish Language and Literature and Spanish American Literature. 2nd ed. Hensley Charles Woodbridge. New York: Modern Language Association of America, 1997.

The Humanities: A Selective Guide to Information Sources. 5th ed. Ron Blazek and Elizabeth Aversa. Englewood, Colo.: Libraries Unlimited, 2000.

Key Sources in Comparative and World Literature: An Annotated Guide to Reference Materials. George A. Thompson. New York: Frederick Ungar, 1982.

Literary Research Guide: An Annotated Listing of Reference Sources in English Literary Studies. 3rd ed. James L. Harner. New York: Modern Language Association of America, 1998.

A Reference Guide for English Studies. Michael J. Marcuse. Berkeley: University of California Press, 1990.

Reference Works in British and American Literature. James K. Bracken. Englewood, Colo.: Libraries Unlimited, 1998.

2 GUIDES TO DOING LITERARY RESEARCH

The Art of Literary Research. 4th ed. Richard Daniel Altick and John J. Fenstermaker. New York: Norton, 1993.

A Handbook to Literary Research. Simon Eliot and W. R. Owens, eds. New York: Routledge, in association with the Open University, 1998.

The Oxford Guide to Library Research. Rev. ed. Thomas Mann. New York: Oxford University Press, 1998.

A Research Guide for Undergraduate Students: English and American Literature. 5th ed. Nancy L. Baker and Nancy Huling. New York: Modern Language Association of America, 2000.

3 ENCYCLOPEDIAS AND DICTIONARIES

General (with excellent coverage of literature)

The Columbia Encyclopedia. 6th ed. Paul Legassé, ed. New York: Columbia University Press, 2000.

The New Encyclopaedia Britannica. 15th ed. 32 vols. Chicago: Encyclopaedia Britannica, 1990.

Literary

Benét's Reader's Encyclopedia. 4th ed. Bruce Murphy, ed. New York: HarperCollins, 1996.

Cassell's Encyclopaedia of World Literature. S. H. Steinberg, ed. Rev. and enl. by J. Buchanan-Brown. 3 vols. New York: Morrow, 1973.

Columbia Dictionary of Modern European Literature. 2nd ed., fully rev. and enl. Jean-Albert Bédé and William B. Edgerton, eds. New York: Columbia University Press, 1980.

Encyclopedia of Folklore and Literature. Mary Ellen Brown and Bruce A. Rosenberg, eds. Santa Barbara, Calif.: ABC-CLIO, 1998.

Encyclopedia of Literature and Criticism. Martin Coyle, et al., eds. London: Routledge, 1990.

A Handbook to Literature. 7th ed. William Harmon and Hugh Holman. Upper Saddle River, N.J.: Prentice Hall, 1996.

The Harper Handbook to Literature. 2nd rev. ed. Northrop Frye, et al. New York: Longman, 1997.

Literature and Its Times: Profiles of 300 Notable Literary Works and the Historical Events That Influenced Them. Joyce Moss and George Wilson, eds. 5 vols. Detroit: Gale, 1997.

Macmillan Guide to Modern World Literature. 3rd ed., completely rev. Martin Seymour-Smith. London: Macmillan, 1985.

Magill's Survey of World Literature. Frank N. Magill, ed. 8 vols. New York: Marshall Cavendish, 1993–95.

Merriam-Webster's Encyclopedia of Literature. Springfield, Mass.: Merriam-Webster, 1995.

The Reader's Adviser: A Layman's Guide to Literature. 14th ed. Fred Kaplan, ed. 6 vols. New Providence, N.J.: R. R. Bowker, 1994.

4 LITERATURE BY PERIOD, GENRE, PLACE, ETHNICITY AND GENDER

By Period

CLASSICAL LITERATURE

Ancient Writers: Greece and Rome. T. James Luce, ed. 2 vols. New York: Charles Scribner's Sons, 1982.

Cambridge Companion to Greek Tragedy. P. E. Easterling, ed. New York: Cambridge University Press, 1997.

Classical and Medieval Literature Criticism. Detroit: Gale, 1988–.

Classical Literary Criticism. Penelope Murray and T. S. Dorsch, trans. New York: Penguin Books, 2000.

Classical Studies: A Guide to the Reference Literature. Fred W. Jenkins. Englewood, Colo.: Libraries Unlimited, 1996.

A Companion to Greek Tragedy. John Ferguson. Austin: University of Texas Press, 1972.

Dictionary of Latin Literature. James H. Mantinband. New York: Philosophical Library, 1956.

The Handbook of Classical Literature. Lillian Feder. 1986. Reprint, New York: Da Capo Press, 1998.

An Intelligent Person's Guide to Classics. P. V. Jones. London: Duckworth, 1999.

The Oxford Book of Classical Verse in Translation. Adrian Poole and Jeremy Maule, eds. New York: Oxford University Press, 1995.

The Oxford Classical Dictionary. 3rd ed. Simon Hornblower and Antony Spawforth, eds. New York: Oxford University Press, 1996.

The Oxford Companion to Classical Literature. 2nd ed. M. C. Howatson, ed. New York: Oxford University Press, 1989.

Who's Who in Classical Mythology. Rev ed. Adrian Room. Lincolnwood, Ill.: NTC Pub. Group, 1997.

MEDIEVAL AND RENAISSANCE

Classical Myths and Legends in the Middle Ages and Renaissance: A Dictionary of Allegorical Meanings. H. David Brumble. Westport, Conn.: Greenwood Press, 1998.

A Dictionary of Medieval Heroes: Character in Medieval Narrative Traditions and Their Afterlife in Literature, Theatre, and the Visual Arts. Willem P. Gerritsen and Anthony G. van Melle. Rochester, N.Y.: Boydell Press, 1998.

Encyclopedia of Medieval Literature. Robert Thomas Lambdin and Laura Conner Lambdin, eds. Westport, Conn.: Greenwood Press, 2000.

Encyclopedia of the Renaissance. Paul F. Grendler, ed. 6 vols. New York: Charles Scribner's Sons, 1999.

English Renaissance Literary Criticism. Brian Vickers, ed. New York: Oxford University Press, 1999.

The New Arthurian Encyclopedia. Norris J. Lacy, ed. New York: Garland, 1996.

NINETEENTH CENTURY

The Cambridge Companion to American Realism and Naturalism. Donald Pizer, ed. New York: Cambridge University Press, 1995.

Literature of the Romantic Period: A Bibliographical Guide. Michael O'Neill, ed. New York: Oxford University Press, 1998.

Nineteenth-Century Literature Criticism. Detroit: Gale, 1981–.

An Oxford Companion to the Romantic Age: British Culture, 1776–1832. Iain McCalman, ed. New York: Oxford University Press, 1999.

TWENTIETH CENTURY

An Annotated Critical Bibliography of Modernism. Alastair Davies. Totowa, N.J.: Barnes & Noble, 1982.

The Bloomsbury Group: A Reference Guide. Lawrence W. Markert. Boston: G. K. Hall, 1990.

The Bohemian Register: An Annotated Bibliography of the Beat Literary Movement. Moren Hickey. Metuchen, N.J.: Scarecrow Press, 1990.

The Cambridge Companion to Modernism. Michael Levenson, ed. New York: Cambridge University Press, 1999.

Encyclopedia of World Literature in the 20th Century. 3rd ed., completely rev. and enl. Steven R. Serafin, ed. Detroit: St. James Press, 1999.

The Harlem Renaissance: An Annotated Reference Guide for Student Research. Marie E. Rodgers. Englewood, Colo.: Libraries Unlimited, 1998.

Modernisms: A Literary Guide. Peter Nicholls. Berkeley: University of California Press, 1995.

A Reader's Guide to Edwardian Literature. Anthea Trodd. New York: Harvester Wheatsheaf, 1991.

20th-Century Culture: A Dictionary of the Arts and Literature in Our Time. David M. Brownstone. New York: Prentice Hall, 1991.

Twentieth-Century Literary Criticism. Detroit: Gale, 1978–.

Twentieth-Century Literary Movements Dictionary: A Compendium to More Than 500 Literary, Critical, and Theatrical Movements, Schools, and Groups from More Than 80 Nations, Covering the Novelists, Poets, Short-Story Writers, Dramatists, Essayists, Theorists, and Works, Genres, Techniques, and Terms Associated with Each Movement. Helene Henderson and Jay P. Pederson, eds. Detroit: Omnigraphics, 2000.

By Genre

BIOGRAPHY AND DIARY

And So to Bed: A Bibliography of Diaries Published in English. Patricia Pate Havlice. Metuchen, N.J.: Scarecrow Press, 1987.

Biography: An Annotated Bibliography. Carl Rollyson. Pasadena, Calif.: Salem Press, 1992.

St. James Guide to Biography. Paul E. Schellinger, ed. Chicago: St. James Press, 1991.

CRIME, MYSTERY, AND ESPIONAGE

Bloomsbury Good Reading Guide to Murder, Crime Fiction and Thrillers. Kenneth and Valerie McLeish. London: Bloomsbury, 1990.

A Catalogue of Crime. Rev. and enl. ed. Jacques Barzun and Wendell Hertig Taylor. New York: Harper & Row, 1989.

The Crime and Mystery Book: A Reader's Companion. Ian Ousby. London: Thames and Hudson, 1997.

Critical Survey of Mystery and Detective Fiction: Authors. Frank N. Magill, ed. 4 vols. Pasadena, Calif.: Salem Press, 1988.

Detective and Mystery Fiction: An International Bibliography of Secondary Sources. 2nd ed., rev. and expanded. Walter Albert. San Bernardino, Calif.: Brownstone Books, 1997.

Good Old Index: The Sherlock Holmes Handbook: A Guide to the Sherlock Holmes Stories by Sir Arthur Conan Doyle, Persons, Places, Themes, Summaries of all the Tales, with Commentary on the Style of the Author. Thomas Wynne Ross. Columbia, S.C.: Camden House, 1997.

Modern Mystery, Fantasy, and Science Fiction Writers. Bruce Cassiday, ed. New York: Continuum, 1993.

Mystery and Suspense Writers: The Literature of Crime, Detection, and Espionage. Robin W. Winks, ed. 2 vols. New York: Charles Scribner's Sons, 1998.

Mystery Reader's Walking Guide, New York. Alzina Stone Dale. Lincolnwood, Ill.: Passport Books, 1993.

The Oxford Companion to Crime and Mystery Writing. Rosemary Herbert, ed. New York: Oxford University Press, 1999.

Reader's Guide to the Private Eye Novel. Gary Warren Niebuhr. New York: G. K. Hall, 1993.

Reader's Guide to the Spy and Thriller Novel. Nancy-Stephanie Stone. New York: G. K. Hall, 1997.

A Reader's Guide to the Suspense Novel. Mary J. Jarvis. New York: G. K. Hall, 1997.

Reference Guide to Mystery and Detective Fiction. Richard J. Bleiler. Englewood, Colo.: Libraries Unlimited, 1999.

Spy Fiction: A Connoisseur's Guide. Donald McCormick and Katy Fletcher. New York: Facts on File, 1990.

St. James Guide to Crime and Mystery Writers. 4th ed. Jay P. Pederson, ed. Detroit: St. James Press, 1996.

The Subject Is Murder: A Selective Subject Guide to Mystery Fiction. 2 vols. Albert J. Menendez. New York: Garland, 1986–90.

DRAMA

The Back Stage Theater Guide: A Theatergoer's Companion to the World's Best Plays and Playwrights. Trevor R. Griffiths and Carole Woddis, eds. New York: Back Stage Books, 1991.

Brewer's Theatre: A Phrase and Fable Dictionary. London: Cassell, 1994.

The Cambridge Guide to Theatre. Rev. ed. Martin Banham, ed. New York: Cambridge University Press, 1995.

Cassell Companion to Theatre. London: Cassell, 1997.

Concise Oxford Companion to the Theatre. Phyllis Hartnoll and Peter Found, eds. New York: Oxford University Press, 1992.

Contemporary Dramatists. 6th ed. Thomas Riggs, ed. New York: St. James Press, 1996.

The Crown Guide to the World's Great Plays: From Ancient Greece to Modern Times. Rev., updated ed. Joseph Twadell Shipley. New York: Crown Publishers, 1984.

Drama Criticism. Detroit: Gale, 1991–.

McGraw-Hill Encyclopedia of World Drama. 2nd ed. Stanley Hochman, ed. 5 vols. New York: McGraw-Hill, 1984.

Modern World Drama: An Encyclopedia. New York: Dutton, 1972.

Oxford Companion to American Theatre. 2nd ed. Gerald Bordman. New York: Oxford University Press, 1992.

Play Index. New York: H. W. Wilson Co., 1949–.

A Reader's Guide to Modern Irish Drama. Sanford V. Sternlicht. Syracuse, N.Y.: Syracuse University Press, 1998.

Research Guide to Biography and Criticism: World Drama. Walton Beacham, ed. Washington, D.C.: Research Pub., 1986.

The World Encyclopedia of Contemporary Theatre. Don Rubin, ed. 5 vols. New York: Routledge, 1994–99.

ESSAY

Encyclopedia of the Essay. Tracy Chevalier, ed. Chicago: Fitzroy Dearborn, 1997.

Essay and General Literature Index. New York: H. W. Wilson, 1900–.

FICTION

American Best Sellers: A Reader's Guide to Popular Fiction. Karen Hinckley and Barbara Hinckley. Bloomington: Indiana University Press, 1989.

Cambridge Guide to Fiction in English. Ian Ousby. New York: Cambridge University Press, 1998.

Classic Cult Fiction: A Companion to Popular Cult Literature. Thomas Reed Whissen. New York: Greenwood Press, 1992.

Critical Survey of Long Fiction. Carl Rollyson, ed. Pasadena, Calif.: Salem Press, 2000.

Dickinson's American Historical Fiction. A. T. Dickinson. 5th ed., by Virginia Brokaw Gerhardstein. Metuchen, N.J.: Scarecrow Press, 1986.

Fiction Catalog. 13th ed. Juliette Yaakov and John Greenfieldt, eds. New York: H. W. Wilson, 1996.

The Fiction Dictionary. Laurie Henry. Cincinnati: Story Press, 1995.

Genreflecting: A Guide to Reading Interests in Genre Fiction. 5th ed. Diana Tixier Herald. Englewood, Colo.: Libraries Unlimited, 2000.

A Guide to Historical Fiction. 1914. Reprint, New York: Burt Franklin, 1969.

Now Read On: A Guide to Contemporary Popular Fiction. 2nd ed. Mandy Hicken and Ray Prytherch. Brookfield, Vt.: Ashgate Publishing, 1994.

The #1 New York Times Bestseller: Intriguing Facts About the 484 Books That Have Been #1 New York Times Bestsellers Since the First List in 1942. John Bear. Berkeley: Ten Speed Press, 1992.

Popular World Fiction, 1900–Present. Walton Beacham and Suzanne Niemeyer, eds. 4 vols. Washington, D.C.: Beacham Publishing, 1987.

Sequels. 12th ed. Mandy Hicken, comp. Vol. 1: Adult Books. London: Career Development Group, 1998–.

HORROR AND GOTHIC

Dracula: The Connoisseur's Guide. Leonard Wolf. New York: Broadway Books, 1997.

Gothic Horror: A Reader's Guide from Poe to King and Beyond. Clive Bloom, ed. New York: St. Martin's Press, 1998.

The Handbook to Gothic Literature. Marie Mulvey-Roberts, ed. New York: New York University Press, 1998.

Hooked on Horror: A Guide to Reading Interests in Horror Fiction. Anthony J. Fonseca and June Michele Pulliam. Englewood, Colo.: Libraries Unlimited, 1999.

Horror Literature: A Reader's Guide. Neil Barron, ed. New York: Garland, 1990.

The Penguin Encyclopedia of Horror and the Supernatural. Jack Sullivan, ed. New York: Viking, 1986.

St. James Guide to Horror, Ghost & Gothic Writers. David Pringle, ed. Detroit: St. James Press, 1998.

HUMOR AND SATIRE

American Literature in Parody: A Collection of Parody, Satire, and Literary Burlesque of American Writers Past and Present. Robert P. Falk. New York: Twayne, 1955.

Encyclopedia of Satirical Literature. Mary Ellen Snodgrass. Santa Barbara, Calif.: ABC-CLIO, 1996.

Humor in American Literature: A Selected Annotated Bibliography. Don Lee Fred Nilsen. New York: Garland, 1992.

Humor in Eighteenth- and Nineteenth-Century British Literature: A Reference Guide. Don Lee Fred Nilsen. Westport, Conn.: Greenwood Press, 1998.

Humor in Twentieth-Century British Literature: A Reference Guide. Don Lee Fred Nilsen. Westport, Conn.: Greenwood Press, 2000.

Parodies: An Anthology from Chaucer to Beerbohm—and After. Dwight Macdonald, ed. 1960. Reprint, New York: Da Capo Press, 1985.

LITERARY CRITICISM

The Columbia Dictionary of Modern Literary and Cultural Criticism. Joseph Childers and Gary Hentzi, eds. New York: Columbia University Press, 1995.

Contemporary Literary Critics. 2nd ed. Elmer Borklund. Detroit: Gale, 1982.

A *Dictionary of Critical Theory*. Leonard Orr. New York: Greenwood Press, 1991.

Encyclopedia of Contemporary Literary Theory: Approaches, Scholars, Terms. Irene R. Makaryk, ed. Toronto: University of Toronto Press, 1993.

Encyclopedia of Literary Critics and Criticism. Chris Murray, ed. 2 vols. Chicago: Fitzroy Dearborn, 1999.

A *Handbook of Critical Approaches to Literature*. 4th ed. Wilfred L. Guerin, et al. New York: Oxford University Press, 1999.

Literary Theories: A Reader and Guide. Julian Wolfreys, ed. Edinburgh: Edinburgh University Press, 1999.

Literary Theory from Plato to Barthes: An Introductory History. Richard Harland. New York: St. Martin's Press, 1999.

NOVEL

The Cambridge Companion to the Classic Russian Novel. Malcolm V. Jones and Robin F. Miller, eds. New York: Cambridge University Press, 1998.

The Cambridge Companion to the French Novel. Timothy Unwin, ed. New York: Cambridge University Press, 1997.

The Catholic Novel: An Annotated Bibliography. Albert J. Menendez. New York: Garland, 1988.

Civil War Novels: An Annotated Bibliography. Albert J. Menendez. New York: Garland, 1986.

Contemporary Novelists. 6th ed. Susan Windisch Brown, ed. New York: St. James Press, 1996.

The Encyclopedia of Novels into Film. John C. Tibbetts and James M. Welsh. New York: Facts on File, 1998.

Encyclopedia of the Novel. Paul Schellinger, ed. 2 vols. Chicago: Fitzroy Dearborn, 1998.

The English Novel. Richard Kroll, ed. Vols. 1, 2–. New York: Longman, 1998–.

The Reader's Companion to the Twentieth Century Novel. Peter Parker, ed. London: Fourth Estate; Oxford: Helicon, 1994.

Sequels: An Annotated Guide to Novels in Series. 3rd ed. Janet Husband and Jonathan F. Husband. Chicago: American Library Association, 1997.

POETRY

The Columbia Granger's Index to African-American Poetry. Nicholas Frankovich and David Larzelere. New York: Columbia University Press, 1999.

The Columbia Granger's Index to Poetry in Anthologies. 11th ed., completely rev. Nicholas Frankovich, ed. New York: Columbia University Press, 1997. Also available in CD-ROM format.

Contemporary Poets. 6th ed. Thomas Riggs, ed. New York: St. James Press, 1996.

Critical Survey of Poetry: English Language Series. Rev. ed. Frank N. Magill, ed. 8 vols. Englewood Cliffs, N.J.: Salem Press, 1982.

English Poetry: The English Poetry Full-text Database. Alexandria, Va.: Chadwyck-Healey, 1992. CD-ROM edition.

Guide to American Poetry Explication. Boston: G. K. Hall, 1989.

Last Lines: An Index to the Last Lines of Poetry. New York: Facts on File, 1991.

The New Princeton Encyclopedia of Poetry and Poetics. Rev. ed. Alex Preminger and T.V.F. Brogan, eds. Princeton: Princeton University Press, 1993.

The Oxford Companion to Twentieth-Century Poetry in English. Ian Hamilton, ed. New York: Oxford University Press, 1994.

Poetry Criticism. Detroit: Gale, 1991–.

The Poetry Dictionary. John Drury. Cincinnati: Story Press, 1995.

ROMANCE

Classic Love & Romance Literature: An Encyclopedia of Works, Characters, Authors & Themes. Virginia Brackett. Santa Barbara, Calif.: ABC-CLIO, 1999.

Romance Fiction: A Guide to the Genre. Kristin Ramsdell. Englewood, Colo.: Libraries Unlimited, 1999.

Twentieth-Century Romance and Historical Writers. 3rd ed. Aruna Vasudevan, ed. Detroit: St. James Press, 1994.

SCIENCE FICTION AND FANTASY

Anatomy of Wonder: A Critical Guide to Science Fiction. 4th ed. Neil Barron, ed. New Providence, N.J.: R. R. Bowker, 1995.

Critical Terms for Science Fiction and Fantasy: A Glossary and Guide to Scholarship. New York: Greenwood Press, 1986.

The Encyclopedia of Fantasy. John Clute and John Grant, eds. London: Orbit, 1997.

The Encyclopedia of Science Fiction. John Clute and Peter Nicholls, eds. New York: St. Martin's Press, 1993.

Fantasy Literature: A Reader's Guide. Neil Barron, ed. New York: Garland, 1990.

Fluent in Fantasy: A Guide to Reading Interests. Diana Tixier Herald. Englewood, Colo.: Libraries Unlimited, 1999.

Reference Guide to Science Fiction, Fantasy, and Horror. Michael Burgess. Englewood, Colo.: Libraries Unlimited, 1992.

Science Fiction and Fantasy Reference Index, 1878–1985: An International Author and Subject Index to History and Criticism. H. W. Hall, ed. 2 vols. Detroit: Gale, 1987. With supplements, *Science Fiction and Fantasy Reference Index, 1985–1991*, and *Science Fiction and Fantasy Reference Index, 1992–1995*, published by Libraries Unlimited in 1993 and 1997, respectively.

Science Fiction, Fantasy, and Weird Fiction Magazines. Marshall B. Tymn and Mike Ashley, eds. Westport, Conn.: Greenwood Press, 1985.

The Science Fiction Source Book. David Wingrove, ed. New York: Van Nostrand Reinhold, 1984.

Science-Fiction, The Early Years: A Full Description of More Than 3,000 Science-Fiction Stories from Earliest Times to the Appearance of the Genre Magazines in 1930: With Author, Title, and Motif Indexes. Everett Franklin Bleiler and Richard J. Bleiler. Kent, Ohio: Kent State University Press, 1990.

St. James Guide to Science Fiction Writers. 4th ed. Jay P. Pederson, ed. Detroit: St. James Press, 1996.

Supernatural Fiction Writers: Fantasy and Horror. Everett Franklin Bleiler, ed. 2 vols. New York: Scribner, 1985.

Survey of Modern Fantasy Literature. Frank N. Magill, ed. 5 vols. Englewood Cliffs, N.J.: Salem Press, 1983.

The Ultimate Encyclopedia of Fantasy: The Definitive Illustrated Guide. David Pringle, ed. Woodstock, N.Y.: Overlook Press, 1999.

SHORT STORY

Critical Survey of Short Fiction. Frank N. Magill, ed. Rev. ed. 7 vols. Pasadena, Calif.: Salem Press, 1993.

Reference Guide to Short Fiction. 2nd ed. Thomas Riggs, ed. Detroit: St. James Press, 1999.

Short Story Criticism. Detroit: Gale, 1988–. Annual.

Short Story Index: An Index to Stories in Collections and Periodicals. New York: H. W. Wilson, 1950/54–. Annual, with cumulation every five years.

Twentieth-Century Short Story Explication: Interpretations, 1900–1975. 3rd ed. Hamden, Conn.: Shoe String Press, 1977. With *Supplement* in 5 vols. (1980–91); and *New Series* in 4 vols. (1993–99).

WESTERN

The American West from Fiction (1823–1976) into Film (1909–1986). Jim Hitt. Jefferson, N.C.: McFarland, 1990.

Cowboy Poets & Cowboy Poetry. David Stanley and Elaine Thatcher, eds. Urbana: University of Illinois Press, 2000.

Encyclopedia of Frontier and Western Fiction. Jon Tuska and Vicki Piekarski, eds. New York: McGraw-Hill, 1983.

Encyclopedia of Frontier Literature. Mary Ellen Snodgrass. Santa Barbara, Calif.: ABC-CLIO, 1997.

Fifty Western Writers: A Bio-bibliographical Sourcebook. Fred Erisman and Richard W. Etulain, eds. Westport, Conn.: Greenwood Press, 1982.

Twentieth-Century Western Writers. 2nd ed. Geoff Sadler, ed. Chicago: St. James Press, 1991.

By Place: English-speaking World

The Cambridge Guide to Literature in English. New ed. Ian Ousby, ed. New York: Cambridge University Press, 1993.

Encyclopedia of Post-colonial Literatures in English. Eugene Benson and L. W. Conolly, eds. New York: Routledge, 1994.

Guide to English and American Literature. F. W. Bateson and Harrison T. Meserole, assisted by Marilyn R. Mumford. 3rd ed. New York: Longman, 1976.

Literally Entitled: A Dictionary of the Origins of the Titles of Over 1300 Major Works of the Nineteenth and Twentieth Centuries. Adrian Room. Jefferson, N.C.: McFarland, 1996.

The Oxford Companion to Twentieth-Century Literature in English. Jenny Stringer, ed. New York: Oxford University Press, 1996.

Penguin Companion to English Literature. David Daiches, ed. New York: McGraw-Hill, 1971.

Reader's Guide to Literature in English. Mark Hawkins-Dady, ed. London; Chicago: Fitzroy Dearborn, 1996.

Reference Guide to English Literature. 2nd ed. D. L. Kirkpatrick, ed. 3 vols. Chicago: St. James Press, 1991.

Writers of the Indian Diaspora: A Bio-Bibliographical Critical Sourcebook. Emmanuel S. Nelson, ed. Westport, Conn.: Greenwood Press, 1993.

THE UNITED STATES

Benét's Reader's Encyclopedia of American Literature. George Perkins, Barbara Perkins, and Philip Leininger, eds. New York: HarperCollins, 1991.

Encyclopedia of American Literature. Steven R. Serafin, ed. New York: Continuum, 1999.

Encyclopedia of Southern Literature. Mary Ellen Snodgrass. Santa Barbara, Calif.: ABC-CLIO, 1997.

Handbook of American Popular Literature. M. Thomas Inge, ed. New York: Greenwood Press, 1988.

Harvard Guide to Contemporary American Writing. Daniel Hoffman, ed. Cambridge: Harvard University Press, 1979.

Literary History of the United States. 4th ed., rev. Robert E. Spiller, et al., eds. 2 vols. New York: Macmillan, 1974.

Magill's Survey of American Literature. Frank N. Magill, ed. 8 vols. New York: Marshall Cavendish, 1991–94.

Modern American Literature. 5th ed. 3 vols. Detroit: St. James Press, 1999.

The Oxford Book of American Literary Anecdotes. Donald Hall, ed. New York: Oxford University Press, 1981.

The Oxford Companion to American Literature. James David Hart. 6th ed., with revisions and additions by Phillip W. Leininger. New York: Oxford University Press, 1995.

The Penguin Companion to American Literature. Malcolm Bradbury, Eric Mottram and Jean Franco, eds. New York: McGraw-Hill, 1971.

Reference Guide to American Literature. 4th ed. Thomas Riggs, ed. Detroit: St. James Press, 2000.

African-American Writers

Afro-American Fiction, 1853–1976: A Guide to Information Sources. Edward Margolies and David Bakish. Detroit: Gale, 1979.

Afro-American Women Writers, 1746–1933: An Anthology and Critical Guide. Ann Allen Shockley, ed. Boston: G. K. Hall, 1988.

Contemporary African American Novelists: A Bio-bibliographical Critical Sourcebook. Emmanuel S. Nelson, ed. Westport, Conn.: Greenwood Press, 1999.

Masterpieces of African-American Literature. Frank N. Magill, ed. New York: HarperCollins, 1992.

The Oxford Companion to African American Literature. William L. Andrews, Frances Smith Foster, and Trudier Harris, eds. New York: Oxford University Press, 1997.

Asian-American Writers

An Interethnic Companion to Asian American Literature. King-Kok Cheung. New York: Cambridge University Press, 1997.

Hispanic-American Writers

Handbook of Hispanic Cultures in the United States: Literature and Art. Francisco Lornelí, ed. Houston: Arte Público Press, 1993.

The Hispanic Literary Companion. Nicolás Kanellos. Detroit: Visible Ink Press, 1996.

A Sourcebook for Hispanic Literature and Language: A Selected, Annotated Guide to Spanish, Spanish-American, and United States Hispanic Bibliography, Literature, Linguistics, Journals and Other Source Materials. 3rd ed. Donald W. Bleznick. Lanham, Md.: Scarecrow Press, 1995.

Spanish American Women Writers: A Bio-bibliographical Source Book. Diane E. Marting, ed. New York: Greenwood Press, 1990.

U.S. Latino Literature: An Essay and Annotated Bibliography. Marc Zimmerman. Chicago: MARCH/Abrazo Press, 1992.

Native-American Writers

American Indian Literatures: An Introduction, Bibliographic Review, and Selected Bibliography. A. LaVonne Brown Ruoff. New York: Modern Language Association of America, 1990.

Dictionary of Native American Literature. Andrew Wiget, ed. New York: Garland, 1994.

Native American Literatures: An Encyclopedia of Works, Characters, Authors, and Themes. Kathy J. Whitson. Santa Barbara, Calif.: ABC-CLIO, 1999.

GREAT BRITAIN AND IRELAND

The Bloomsbury Dictionary of English Literature. Marion Wynne-Davies, general ed. London: Bloomsbury, 1997.

The Cambridge Companion to English Literature, 1650–1740. New York: Cambridge University Press, 1998.

Dictionary of Irish Literature. Rev. and expanded ed. Robert Hogan, ed. 2 vols. Westport, Conn.: Greenwood Press, 1996.

Modern British Literature. 2nd ed. Laurie Di Mauro, ed. 3 vols. Detroit: St. James Press, 2000.

The New Cambridge Bibliography of English Literature. George Watson, ed. Cambridge: Cambridge University Press, 1969–77.

The New Companion to the Literature of Wales. Meic Stephens, ed. Cardiff: University of Wales Press, 1998.

The Oxford Companion to English Literature. 6th ed. Margaret Drabble, ed. New York: Oxford University Press, 2000.

The Oxford Companion to Irish Literature. Robert Welch, ed. Oxford: Clarendon Press, 1996.

CANADA

Major Canadian Authors: A Critical Introduction to Canadian Literature in English. Lincoln: University of Nebraska Press, 1988.

The Oxford Companion to Canadian Literature. 2nd ed. Eugene Benson and William Toye, eds. New York: Oxford University Press, 1997.

By Place: The Caribbean

Caribbean Literature: A Bibliography. Marian Goslina. Lanham, Md.: Scarecrow Press, 1998.

Caribbean Writers: A Bio-bibliographical-critical Encyclopedia. Donald E. Herdeck, ed. Washington, D.C.: Three Continents Press, 1979.

Fifty Caribbean Writers: Bio-bibliographical Critical Sourcebook. Daryl Cumber Dance, ed. Westport, Conn.: Greenwood Press, 1986. Covers the West Indies, i.e., the English-speaking Caribbean.

Twentieth-Century Caribbean and Black African Writers. Bernth Lindfors and Reinhard Sander, eds. Detroit: Gale, 1992–96.

Writers of the Caribbean and Central America: A Bibliography. M. J. Fenwick. New York: Garland, 1992.

By Place: Latin America

The Cambridge History of Latin American Literature. Roberto González Echevarría and Enrique Pupo-Walker, eds. 3 vols. New York: Cambridge University Press, 1996.

Encyclopedia of Latin American Literature. Verity Smith, ed. Chicago: Fitzroy Dearborn, 1997.

Handbook of Latin American Literature. 2nd ed. David William Foster, ed. New York: Garland, 1992.

Latin American Writers. Carlos A. Sole, ed. 3 vols. New York: Scribner, 1989.

BRAZIL

Brazilian Literature: A Research Bibliography. David William Foster. New York: Garland, 1990.

Dictionary of Brazilian Literature. Irwin Stern, ed. New York: Greenwood Press, 1988.

Portuguese Language and Luso-Brazilian Literature: An Annotated Guide to Selected Reference Works. Bobby J. Chamberlain. New York: Modern Language Association of America, 1989.

By Place: Europe

The Penguin Companion to European Literature. Anthony Thorlby, ed. New York: McGraw-Hill, 1971.

FRANCE

Cassell Guide to Literature in French. Valerie Worth-Stylianou, ed. New York: Cassell, 1996.

A Critical Bibliography of French Literature. D. C. Cabeen, ed. Syracuse, N.Y.: Syracuse University Press, 1947–94. 6 vols. in 9, with supplements.

Dictionary of Modern French Literature: From the Age of Reason through Realism. Sandra W. Dolbow. New York: Greenwood Press, 1986.

Guide to French Literature. Anthony Levi. 2 vols. Chicago: St. James Press, 1992–94.

A Guide to French Literature: Early Modern to Postmodern. Jennifer Birkett and James Kearns. New York: St. Martin's Press, 1997.

Introduction to Library Research in French Literature. Robert K. Baker. Boulder, Colo.: Westview Press, 1978.

Modern French Literature: A Library of Literary Criticism. Debra Popkin and Michael Popkin, eds. 2 vols. New York: Frederick Ungar, 1977.

The New Oxford Companion to Literature in French. Peter France, ed. New York: Oxford University Press, 1995.

GERMANY

A Companion to German Literature: From 1500 to the Present. Eda Sagarra and Peter Skrine. Malden, Mass.: Blackwell, 1997.

A Companion to Twentieth-Century German Literature. 2nd ed. Raymond Furness and Malcolm Humble. New York: Routledge, 1997.

Modern German Literature. 2 vols. New York: Frederick Ungar, 1972.

The Oxford Companion to German Literature. 3rd ed. Henry and Mary Garland. New York: Oxford University Press, 1997.

ITALY

Dictionary of Italian Literature. Rev., expanded ed. Peter Bondanella and Julia Conaway Bondanella, eds. Westport, Conn.: Greenwood Press, 1996.

PORTUGAL

Portuguese Language and Luso-Brazilian Literature: An Annotated Guide to Selected Reference Works. Bobby J. Chamberlain. New York: Modern Language Association of America, 1989.

Portuguese Literature from Its Origins to 1990: A Bibliography Based on the Collections of Indiana University. Hugo Kunoff, ed. Metuchen, N.J.: Scarecrow Press, 1994.

SCANDINAVIA

Dictionary of Scandinavian Literature. Virpi Zuck, ed. New York: Greenwood Press, 1990.

SPAIN

Dictionary of the Literature of the Iberian Peninsula. Germán Bleiberg, Maureen Ihrie, and Janet Peréz, eds. Westport, Conn.: Greenwood Press, 1993.

The Oxford Companion to Spanish Literature. Philip Ward, ed. Oxford: Clarendon Press, 1978.

EASTERN EUROPE AND RUSSIA

Handbook of Russian Literature. Victor Terras, ed. New Haven: Yale University Press, 1985.

The Modern Encyclopedia of Russian and Soviet Literatures. 10 vols. [Vol. 10 has title: *The Modern Encyclopedia of East Slavic, Baltic, and Eurasian Literatures.*] Harry B. Weber, et al., eds. Gulf Breeze, Fla.: Academic International Press, 1977–96.

Reader's Encyclopedia of Eastern European Literature. Robert B. Pynsent, ed. New York: HarperCollins, 1993.

Reference Guide to Russian Literature. Neil Cornwell, ed. Chicago: Fitzroy Dearborn, 1998.

The Slavic Literatures. Richard C. Lewanski, ed. New York: The New York Public Library, Frederick Ungar, 1967.

Soviet Dissident Literature: A Critical Guide. Josephine Woll; with the collaboration of Vladimir G. Treml. Boston: G. K. Hall, 1983.

By Place: Africa

African Literature and Its Times. Joyce Moss and Lorraine Valestuk. Detroit: Gale, 2000.

African Literatures in the 20th Century: A Guide. New York: Frederick Ungar, 1986.

The Companion to African Literatures. Douglas Killam and Ruth Rose, eds. Bloomington: Indiana University Press, 2000.

A New Reader's Guide to African Literature. 2nd, completely rev. and expanded ed. Hans M. Zell, Carol Bundy, and Virginia Coulon, eds. New York: Africana, 1983.

By Place: Middle East

Encyclopedia of Arabic Literature. Julie Scott Meisami and Paul Starkey. New York: Routledge, 1998.

Modern Arabic Literature. Roger Allen, ed. New York: Frederick Ungar, 1987.

Modern Arabic Literature. M. M. Badawi, ed. New York: Cambridge University Press, 1992. Part of the in-progress *Cambridge History of Arabic Literature.*

By Place: Asia

Approaches to the Asian Classics. Wm. Theodore de Bary and Irene Bloom, eds. New York: Columbia University Press, 1990.

Asian Literature in English: A Guide to Information Sources. G. L. Anderson. Detroit: Gale, 1981.

Dictionary of Oriental Literatures. Jaroslav Prusek, ed. 3 vols. New York: Basic Books, 1974.

Far Eastern Literatures in the 20th Century: A Guide. New York: Frederick Ungar, 1986.

A Guide to Eastern Literatures. David Marshall Lang, ed. London: Weidenfeld and Nicolson, 1971.

A Guide to Oriental Classics. 3rd ed. Wm. Theodore de Bary and Ainslee Embree, eds. New York: Columbia University Press, 1989.

The Penguin Companion to Classical, Oriental and African Literature. D. M. Lang and D. R. Dudley, eds. New York: McGraw-Hill, 1971.

CHINA

Classical Chinese Fiction: A Guide to Its Study and Appreciation: Essays and Bibliographies. Winston L. Y. Yang, Peter Li, and Nathan K. Mao. Boston: G. K. Hall, 1978.

A Guide to Chinese Literature. Wilt Idema and Lloyd Haft. Ann Arbor: Center for Chinese Studies, University of Michigan, 1997.

Guide to Chinese Prose. Jordan D. Paper. Boston: G. K. Hall, 1984.

The Indiana Companion to Traditional Chinese Literature. William H. Nienhauser, Jr., ed. Bloomington: Indiana University Press, 1986.

INDIA

A Dictionary of Indian Literature. Sujit Mukherjee. Hyderabad: Orient Longman, 1999.

Encyclopaedia of Indian Literature. Amaresh Datta, ed. 6 vols. New Delhi: Sahitya Akademi, 1987–94.

An Encyclopedia of Indian Literature. Ganga Ram Garg. Delhi: Mittal, 1982.

Indian Literature in English, 1827–1979: A Guide to Information Sources. Amritjit Singh, Rajiva Verma, and Irene M. Joshi. Detroit: Gale, 1981.

Indian Writing in English. K. R. Srinivasa Iyengar. 3rd ed., with a postscript chapter on the seventies and after, in collaboration with Prema Nandakumar. New Delhi: Sterling Publishers, 1983.

A Layman's Guide to Sanskrit Literature. Sures Chandra Banerji. Delhi: AMBER Books, 1997.

JAPAN

Dawn to the West: Japanese Literature of the Modern Era—Fiction and *Dawn to the West: Japanese Literature of the Modern Era—Poetry, Drama, Criticism.* Donald Keene. New York: Columbia University Press, 1998–99. Originally published in 1984.

Guide to Japanese Prose. 2nd ed. Alfred H. Marks and Barry D. Bort. Boston: G. K. Hall, 1984.

The Princeton Companion to Classical Japanese Literature. Earl Roy Miner, Hiroko Odagiri, and Robert E. Morrell. Princeton: Princeton University Press, 1985.

A Reader's Guide to Japanese Literature. J. Thomas Rimer. New York: Kodansha International, 1988.

VIETNAM

Writing about Vietnam: A Bibliography of the Literature of the Vietnam Conflict. Sandra M. Wittman. Boston: G. K. Hall, 1989.

By Place: Australia

The Oxford Companion to Australian Literature. 2nd ed. William H. Wilde, Joy Hooton, and Barry Andrews. New York: Oxford University Press, 1994.

The Oxford Literary History of Australia. Bruce Bennett and Jennifer Strauss, eds. New York: Oxford University Press, 1998.

By Ethnicity and Gender

BLACK WRITERS *(see also literature by place)*

Black Authors: A Selected Annotated Bibliography. James Edward Newby. New York: Garland, 1991.

Black Literature Criticism: Excerpts from Criticism of the Most Significant Works of Black Authors over the Past 200 Years. James P. Draper, ed. 3 vols. Detroit: Gale, 1992.

Modern Black Writers. 2nd ed. Manitou Wordworks, ed. Detroit: St. James Press, 2000.

WOMEN WRITERS

American Women Writers: A Critical Reference Guide: From Colonial Times to the Present.

Taryn Benbow-Pfalzgraf, ed. 4 vols. Detroit: St. James Press, 2000.

The Cambridge Companion to American Women Playwrights. Brenda Murphy, ed. New York: Cambridge University Press, 1999.

The Cambridge Guide to Women's Writing in English. Lorna Sage, ed. New York: Cambridge University Press, 1999.

Caribbean Women Novelists: An Annotated Critical Bibliography. Lizabeth Paravisini-Gebert and Olga Torres-Seda. Westport, Conn.: Greenwood Press, 1993.

The Feminist Companion to Literature in English: Women Writers from the Middle Ages to the Present. Virginia Blain, Patricia Clements, and Isobel Grundy, eds. New Haven: Yale University Press, 1990.

A Guide to Twentieth-Century Women Novelists. Kathleen Wheeler. Cambridge, Mass.: Blackwell, 1997.

The Oxford Companion to Women's Writing in the United States. Cathy N. Davidson and Linda Wagner-Martin, eds. New York: Oxford University Press, 1995.

Third World Women's Literatures: A Dictionary and Guide to Materials in English. Barbara Fister. Westport, Conn.: Greenwood Press, 1995.

Women Playwrights of Diversity: A Bio-bibliographical Sourcebook. Jane T. Peterson and Suzanne Bennett. Westport, Conn.: Greenwood Press, 1997.

Gay & Lesbian Studies

Gay and Lesbian American Plays: An Annotated Bibliography. Ken Furtado and Nancy Hellner. Metuchen, N.J.: Scarecrow Press, 1993.

Gay and Lesbian Characters and Themes in Mystery Novels: A Critical Guide to over 500 Works in English. Anthony Sale. Jefferson, N.C.: McFarland, 1993.

The Gay and Lesbian Literary Heritage: A Reader's Companion to the Writers and Their Works, from Antiquity to the Present. Claude J. Summers, ed. New York: Henry Holt, 1995.

Latin American Writers on Gay and Lesbian Themes: A Bio-Critical Sourcebook. David William Foster, ed. Westport, Conn.: Greenwood Press, 1994.

Lesbians in Print: A Bibliography of 1,500 Books with Synopses. Irvine, Calif.: Bluestocking Books, 1995.

Spanish Writers on Gay and Lesbian Themes: A Bio-critical Sourcebook. David William Foster, ed. Westport, Conn.: Greenwood Press, 1999.

5 Criticism: Collections and Indexes

Contemporary Literary Criticism. Detroit: Gale, 1973– [including the annual *Contemporary Literary Criticism Yearbook,* 1985–].

The Critical Perspective. Harold Bloom, ed. 11 vols. New York: Chelsea House, 1985–89.

The Library of Literary Criticism of English and American Authors. Charles Wells Moulton, ed. 8 vols. Gloucester, Mass.: P. Smith, 1959. Reprint of the 1901–5 edition.

Literature Criticism from 1400 to 1800: Excerpts from Criticism of the Works of Fifteenth, Sixteenth, Seventeenth, and Eighteenth-Century Novelists, Poets, Playwrights, Philosophers, and Other Creative Writers, from the First Published Critical Appraisals to Current Evaluations. Dennis Poupard, ed. Detroit: Gale, 1984–.

MLA International Bibliography of Books and Articles on the Modern Languages and Literatures. New York: Modern Language Association of America, 1921–. Annual.

The New Moulton's Library of Literary Criticism. Harold Bloom, ed. 11 vols. New York: Chelsea House, 1985–90.

Yearbook of Comparative and General Literature. Bloomington: Indiana University [etc.], 1952–.

LITERARY

FACTS

AND

RESOURCES

Characters

Abd al-Jawad, al-Sayyid Ahmad. Central character in Naguib MAHFOUZ's THE CAIRO TRILOGY (1956–57). The patriarch of a middle-class Cairo family experiencing the changes in Egyptian society in the aftermath of World War I, he is the main character of the first novel, *Palace Walk* (*Bayna al-Qasrayn*, 1956), and also appears in the second and third novels.

Absolute, Sir Anthony. Choleric father of protagonist Jack Absolute in Richard Brinsley SHERIDAN's play THE RIVALS (1775), as comically irascible as he is obstinate.

Achilles. Legendary Greek hero in the Trojan War, son of the sea goddess Thetis and the mortal Peleus, said to be vulnerable only in one heel. In HOMER's epic poem the ILIAD (8th century B.C.) he is the greatest Greek warrior, who slays the Trojan champion HECTOR. He appears in many other literary works, including William SHAKESPEARE's play TROILUS AND CRESSIDA (c. 1601–2) and Heinrich von KLEIST's tragedy *Penthesilea* (published 1808, performed 1876).

Adam. The first human being, according to the BIBLE (Genesis). Created to dwell with EVE in the Garden of Eden, he falls with her from divine grace when they are tempted by SATAN. In John MILTON's epic poem PARADISE LOST (1667), he is described as "the goodliest man of men since borne / His sons."

Adams, Nick. Partly autobiographical, prototypical Ernest HEMINGWAY character and protagonist of 16 short stories published in Hemingway's first three collections, *In Our Time* (1925), *Men Without Women* (1927), and *Winner Take Nothing* (1933), including several of his best-known stories, such as "The Big Two-Hearted River" (1925). After Hemingway's death, the series was collected with previously unpublished material, as *The Nick Adams Stories* (1972).

Aeneas. Legendary Trojan founder of Rome, son of the goddess Aphrodite (Venus) and the mortal Anchises, and protagonist of VIRGIL's epic poem the AENEID (c. 29–19 B.C.). A minor character in HOMER's epic poem the ILIAD (8th century B.C.), he becomes a symbol of Roman virtue in the *Aeneid*, fated to love and abandon the Carthaginian queen DIDO and lead the Trojan exiles to Rome.

Agamemnon. Legendary king of Mycenae, scion of the accursed house of Atreus, husband of Clytemnestra, father of IPHIGENIA, ELECTRA, and ORESTES. As leader of the Greek forces in the Trojan War, he is a principal character in HOMER's epic poem the ILIAD (8th century B.C.). His family's misfortunes were popular subjects for later tragedians; he is a leading character in AESCHYLUS's play *Agamemnon* (part of the ORESTEIA, 458 B.C.) and EURIPIDES' play *Iphigenia in Aulis* (*Iphigeneiaē en Aulidi*, c. 405 B.C.).

Ahab, Captain. Monomaniacal captain of the *Pequod* in Herman MELVILLE's whaling epic MBOBY-DICK (1851), who obsessively hunts the white whale that maimed him. Named for the biblical king Ahab (BIBLE, 1 Kings 16–22): "Ahab the son of Omri did evil in the sight of the Lord, above all that were before him."

Aladdin. Plucky protagonist of "Aladdin or the Wonderful Lamp," from the story collection *THE THOUSAND AND ONE NIGHTS* (14th or 15th century), a poor youth who seeks his fortune with the help of two genies.

Alceste. Title character in MOLIÈRE's play *THE MISANTHROPE* (1666), who detests society's hypocrisy, but paradoxically loves the flirtatious Célimène.

Allworthy, Squire. Naive but benevolent guardian of the title character Tom JONES of Henry FIELDING's picaresque novel *TOM JONES* (1749); he raises Tom from infancy after finding him in his bed.

Andrews, Joseph. Adventurous footman and title character of Henry FIELDING's comic novel *JOSEPH ANDREWS* (1742). He is introduced as the virtuous brother of PAMELA ANDREWS, heroine of SAMUEL RICHARDSON'S *PAMELA* (1740); Fielding's picaresque tale originated as a parody of Richardson.

Andrews, Pamela. Virtuous maidservant and title character of SAMUEL RICHARDSON's epistolary novel *PAMELA; OR, VIRTUE REWARDED* (1740). The reward for the beautiful and accomplished young woman's virtue is marriage to her deceased mistress's son, Mr. B., who had striven assiduously to seduce her.

Angstrom, Harry "Rabbit." Former high school basketball star and uneasy middle-class protagonist of John UPDIKE's novels *RABBIT, RUN* (1960), *Rabbit Redux* (1971), *Rabbit Is Rich* (1981), and *Rabbit at Rest* (1990). His story is concluded in the novella *Rabbit Remembered* (2000).

Annabel Lee. Young maiden loved and mourned by the narrator in Edgar Allan POE's poem "ANNABEL LEE" (1849).

Anna Livia Plurabelle. In James JOYCE's experimental novel *FINNEGANS WAKE* (1939), a name for the wife of protagonist H. C. EARWICKER, representing woman as the stream of the life force, a personification of Dublin's River Liffey. She is also called An, Ann, Anna, Anne, Lif, Life, Liffey, Liv, Livia, Livy, Nancy, Nann, and ALP.

Antigone. In Greek mythology, faithful elder daughter of OEDIPUS. She appears in several Greek tragedies, prominently in SOPHOCLES' *ANTIGONE* (c. 442–441 B.C.), where she defies King Creon's order against burying her rebel brother Polyneices. Jean ANOUILH's play *Antigone* (published 1942, performed 1944) recapitulates that story as an allegory of French resistance to the Vichy regime.

Antipova, Lara. *See* **Lara**

Antony, Mark [Marcus Antonius]. Roman general and statesman (c. 82 B.C.–30 B.C.), protégé of JULIUS CAESAR. His deeds are dramatized in William SHAKESPEARE's plays *JULIUS CAESAR* (c. 1599) and *ANTONY AND CLEOPATRA* (1607). In the former, his eloquence ("Friends, Romans, countrymen…") turns the Roman people against Caesar's assassins. In the latter, and in John DRYDEN's tragedy *All for Love; or, The World Well Lost* (1677), he is CLEOPATRA's ally and lover.

Antrobus, Mr. and **Mrs. (George** and **Maggie).** Main characters (with Sabina, their maid) of Thornton WILDER's experimental comedy *THE SKIN OF OUR TEETH* (1942). A "typical American" couple, they are also the archetypal father and mother of the human race in this antic history of the world.

Aramis. One of the title characters in *THE THREE MUSKETEERS* (1844), the novel by ALEXANDRE DUMAS *PÈRE*; his real name is the Chevalier d'Herblay. This member of the trio always wore black and declared he would enter the Church once the adventures ceased.

Archer, Isabel. Heroine of HENRY JAMES's novel *THE PORTRAIT OF A LADY* (1881), an heiress who encounters Europe as the archetypal American innocent; James called her his "conception of a young lady confronting her destiny."

Ariel. 1. "Airy spirit" and supporting character in William SHAKESPEARE's last play, *THE TEMPEST* (c. 1611). Under the control of PROSPERO, he lives on an island with Prospero and MIRANDA, using his magic to aid in Prospero's work of reconciliation. 2. In Alexander POPE's mock-epic poem THE RAPE OF THE LOCK (1714), the guardian sylph of the heroine, BELINDA.

Arkadina, Irina Nikolaevna. Celebrated actress in Anton CHEKHOV's play THE SEAGULL (1896). She neglects and resents her son, the sensitive aspiring author Konstantin TREPLEV, and temporarily loses her lover, TRIGORIN, to the young actress Nina ZARECHNAYA.

Artful Dodger, The. Adept petty thief and would-be corruptor of youths in Charles DICKENS's novel OLIVER TWIST (1838). Born Jack Dawkins, he is a student of FAGIN and in turn introduces Oliver TWIST to the world of crime.

Arthur, King. Legendary king of Britain. He reigns at Camelot over the Knights of the Round Table. Among the basic elements of his story are his removal of a sword from a stone, the act that qualifies him for kingship, and his love triangle with Queen GUINEVERE and Sir LANCELOT. He appears in many works, including Thomas MALORY's romance LE MORTE D'ARTHUR (c. 1469–70), Alfred, Lord TENNYSON's poetic cycle IDYLLS OF THE KING (1859–85), Mark TWAIN's fantasy A CONNECTICUT YANKEE IN KING ARTHUR'S COURT (1889), and T. H. White's tetralogy of novels, THE ONCE AND FUTURE KING (1938–58).

Aschenbach, Gustav von. Protagonist of Thomas MANN's novella DEATH IN VENICE (1912). A respected author on holiday in Venice, he becomes enraptured by a beautiful Polish boy, Tadzio.

Ashley, Lady Brett. Central character in Ernest HEMINGWAY's novel THE SUN ALSO RISES (1926). The most magnetic member of a group of postwar wanderers in Paris and Spain, she loves the impotent Jake BARNES, yet engages in other relationships.

Athos. One of the title characters in THE THREE MUSKETEERS (1844), the novel by ALEXANDRE DUMAS PÈRE; his real name is the Count de la Fère. Of the group, he is the courteous but melancholy aristocrat.

Ayesha. Powerful queen and title character of H. Rider HAGGARD's novel SHE: A HISTORY OF ADVENTURE (1887). Known as She-Who-Must-Be-Obeyed, the mysterious, millenniums-old She is also featured in three sequels, Ayesha: The Return of She (1905), She and Allan (1921), and Wisdom's Daughter (1923).

Aziz, Dr. Main character in E. M. FORSTER's novel A PASSAGE TO INDIA (1924). A Muslim Indian physician, he is accused of sexual assault by English visitor Adela QUESTED during an excursion to the Marabar Caves.

Babbitt, George Follansbee. Self-satisfied middle-class businessman in SINCLAIR LEWIS's satirical novel BABBITT (1922), a staunch booster of the Midwestern town of Zenith. His name and the noun "Babbittry" have become bywords for a mixture of the provincial and the philistine.

Banquo. Fellow general with MACBETH in William SHAKESPEARE's tragedy MACBETH (c. 1605–6). Slain because of a prophecy that his sons would be kings, he returns as a ghost to haunt Macbeth, who ordered the killing.

Barkley, Catherine. Central character in Ernest HEMINGWAY's World War I novel A FAREWELL TO ARMS (1929). A volunteer English nurse in Italy, she loves and becomes pregnant by an American soldier, Frederic HENRY, who deserts from the front to be with her.

Barnes, Jake [Jacob]. Protagonist and narrator of Ernest HEMINGWAY's novel THE SUN ALSO RISES (1926). An American journalist wounded and made impotent in World War I, Barnes travels aimlessly from France to Spain with friends, including Lady Brett ASHLEY, who loves him, but has affairs with others.

Barry Lyndon, Redmond. Title character and narrator of William Makepeace THACKERAY's novel BARRY LYNDON (1856). Irish adventurer Redmond Barry fights on both sides in the Seven Years War (1756–63), travels around Europe as a professional gambler, and marries, then fleeces the countess of Lyndon, before landing in Fleet Prison.

Bart, Lily. Main character of Edith WHARTON's novel of the New York upper class in the Gilded Age, THE HOUSE OF MIRTH (1905). Of a good family but orphaned and without means,

29-year-old Lily strives for a secure life through marriage, but also seeks a husband whom she can respect and love.

Bartleby. Ultimate alienated office worker in Herman MELVILLE's story "BARTLEBY THE SCRIVENER: A STORY OF WALL STREET" (1853). A law firm hireling, Bartleby gradually withdraws from participation in, first, office life, and then life itself, with the reiterated assertion, "I would prefer not to."

Bascombe, Frank. Uneasy protagonist and narrator of RICHARD FORD's novels *The Sportswriter* (1986) and *INDEPENDENCE DAY* (1995). Having left a promising literary career, he works as a sportswriter in suburban New Jersey in the first novel; in the second, he is a real-estate salesman, trying to come to terms with his divorce and his troubled son.

Bathgate, Billy. Resourceful title character and narrator of E. L. DOCTOROW's novel *Billy Bathgate* (1989). A fatherless Bronx teenager who takes his surname from a neighborhood market street, he becomes part of gangster Dutch Schultz's (1902–1935) circle, and observes its deeds until Schultz's death.

Beatrice. 1. Beloved of DANTE ALIGHIERI; often identified as Beatrice (Bice) Portinari (1266–1290). In his prose-and-poetry collection *La Vita Nuova* (c. 1293; The New Life), Dante recounts how he loved her from afar and how she became a spiritual beacon for him after her early death. In the third part, *Paradiso*, of his epic poem *THE DIVINE COMEDY* (c. 1314–21), Beatrice becomes a symbol of divine revelation and his guide through Paradise. 2. Merry heroine of William SHAKESPEARE's comedy *MUCH ADO ABOUT NOTHING* (c. 1598–99). Reluctant to wed, she is surprised to find herself in love with BENEDICK, a soldier with whom she has often engaged in a battle of wits. 3. Title character of Nathaniel HAWTHORNE's short story "RAPPACINI'S DAUGHTER" (1844), who is raised on poison as part of her father's experiments and grows up to be as "poisonous as she is beautiful."

Bede, Adam. Morally upright title character of GEORGE ELIOT's novel *ADAM BEDE* (1859). Infat-

uated with comely Hetty Sorrel, he discovers when they are to be married that she has had a liaison with rake Arthur Donnithorne.

Beelzebub. *See* **Satan**

Belinda. Shorn maiden of Alexander POPE's mock-epic poem *THE RAPE OF THE LOCK* (1714), the "gentle Belle" whom a "well-bred Lord" relieves of a lock of hair. Based on an actual incident in Pope's social circle; the real-life Belinda was Arabella Fermor.

Benedick. Jesting hero of William SHAKESPEARE's comedy *MUCH ADO ABOUT NOTHING* (c. 1598–99). A brave soldier and committed bachelor, he is surprised to find he has met his match in witty BEATRICE, with whom he has often engaged in a war of words. "Benedick" (or "benedict") has become a byword for a confirmed bachelor who yields to matrimony.

Benjy. *See* **Compson family**

Bennet, Elizabeth. Spirited and outspoken heroine of Jane AUSTEN's novel of manners *PRIDE AND PREJUDICE* (1813). One of five unmarried daughters of a family of modest means, she is attracted to handsome, wealthy Fitzwilliam DARCY, and he to her, but pride and prejudice long keep them both from acknowledging this state of affairs.

Beowulf. Prince of the Geats (a southern Swedish people) and hero of the Old English epic poem *BEOWULF* (c. 700–50?). Renowned as a monster-killer, he slays the undersea-dwelling GRENDEL and Grendel's mother in Denmark, then returns home, where he becomes king of his people and reigns for 50 years, before facing a dragon in a final battle. He also appears in JOHN GARDNER's novel *Grendel* (1972).

Bergson, Alexandra. Forbearing farmer and protagonist of Willa CATHER's novel *O PIONEERS!* (1913). When her father dies, she takes over the Nebraska family farm, making it prosper through her ability and love of the land.

Bezukhov, Pierre [Pyotr Kirilovich]. Awkward but good-hearted central character in Leo TOLSTOY's epic novel *WAR AND PEACE* (1868–69);

his complicated relationships with the other characters are at the heart of the work. After many false starts, Pierre's search for meaning is resolved when circumstances permit him to confess his love for Natasha ROSTOVA, with whom he will live in happy acceptance of life.

Bierce, Ambrose. Title character of Carlos FUENTES's novel *The Old Gringo* (*El Gringo Viejo*, 1985), based on the real-life American journalist and poet Ambrose BIERCE, who disappeared mysteriously in Mexico in 1913 while seeking to join Pancho Villa's revolution. The end of his life is imaginatively reconstructed through the voices of several characters involved in the events.

Big Brother. Symbolic head of the Party controlling all aspects of society in Oceania (a state representing the United States and Britain) in George ORWELL's anti-utopian novel *NINETEEN EIGHTY-FOUR* (1949). Big Brother is never seen in person, but his image is everywhere, announcing the Party's omnipotence with the phrase, "Big Brother is watching you."

Big Daddy (Pollitt). Controlling Mississippi patriarch of TENNESSEE WILLIAMS's play *CAT ON A HOT TIN ROOF* (1955), around whose 65th birthday celebration the action is centered.

Biswas, Mr. Title character of V. S. NAIPAUL's novel *A HOUSE FOR MR. BISWAS* (1961). An East Indian living in postcolonial Trinidad, he seeks his true personal and cultural identity, striving to win independence via a house of his own.

Blakeney, Sir Percy. *See* **Scarlet Pimpernel**

Bligh, Capt. William. British captain and severe disciplinarian whose actions prompt a mutiny in Charles Nordhoff and James Norman Hall's novel *MUTINY ON THE BOUNTY* (1932), based on an actual mutiny in 1789. The real-life Bligh (1754–1817) sailed 3,600 miles in a 23-foot longboat after the mutiny, as described in the second book of Nordhoff and Hall's *Bounty Trilogy*, *Men Against the Sea* (1933).

Bloom, Leopold and **Molly.** Main characters in James JOYCE's novel *ULYSSES* (1922). Leopold Bloom is a Jewish advertising canvasser who spends the day of June 16, 1904, wandering around Dublin as if on an epic quest. His wife, Molly, the embodiment of the feminine principle, meditates that night on her personal and erotic life in a lengthy interior monologue. The novel takes its mythological frame from HOMER's epic the *ODYSSEY* (8th century B.C.); Leopold corresponds to Homer's ODYSSEUS (called Ulysses by the Romans) and Molly to his wife PENELOPE.

Bolingbroke, Henry. *See* **Henry IV**

Bolkonsky, Prince Andrey. Central character in Leo TOLSTOY's epic novel *WAR AND PEACE* (1868–69). The searching, intellectual Andrey, a dashing officer who grows increasingly disillusioned as events proceed, is one of two men who love lively Natasha ROSTOVA; the other is his friend, Pierre BEZUKHOV.

Bolling, Binx [John Bickerson Bolling]. Detached protagonist and narrator of Walker PERCY's novel *THE MOVIEGOER* (1961). A New Orleans stockbroker, he lives in the alternate world of movies, where he finds a meaning that he fails to discover in life, until the Mardi Gras week of the novel's events.

Bond, James [Agent 007]. Suave British secret agent and protagonist of Ian FLEMING's novels *Casino Royale* (1953), *From Russia with Love* (1957), *Dr. No* (1958), *Goldfinger* (1959), and others. He is formally granted a license to kill (signified by the "double 0" in his alias), which is indispensable for facing world-threatening villains. Other Bondian trademarks are flashy cars, exotic locales, and beautiful women.

Bottom, Nick. Weaver and amateur thespian in William SHAKESPEARE's comedy *A MIDSUMMER NIGHT'S DREAM* (c. 1595–96). The most enthusiastic of the "rude mechanicals" whose theatricals are to enliven Theseus's wedding feast, he is "translated" by PUCK into a creature with an ass's head as part of a practical joke OBERON plays on TITANIA.

Bountiful, Lady. Supporting character in a play by George Farquhar (1678–1707), *The Beaux' Stratagem* (1707). A benevolent old lady who "has cured more people...within ten years than the doctors have killed in twenty," she is deceived into nursing the perfectly healthy Thomas Aimwell, one of the title's impoverished beaux in search of a wealthy wife. Her name is a byword for a patronizingly generous benefactress.

Bovary, Emma. Yearning title character of Gustave FLAUBERT's novel *MADAME BOVARY* (1857). Dissatisfied with her provincial life and her marriage to a kind but dull doctor, she futilely seeks in adulterous affairs and extravagant spending the romantic fulfillment she knows only from novels.

Bracknell, Lady [Aunt Augusta]. Formidable character in Oscar WILDE's comedy of manners *THE IMPORTANCE OF BEING EARNEST* (1895). As Algernon MONCRIEFF's aunt and Jack WORTHING's prospective mother-in-law, she delivers many of the play's funniest lines. Jack calls her "a Gorgon ... a monster without being a myth, which is rather unfair."

Brangwen sisters (Ursula, Gudrun). Main characters of D. H. LAWRENCE's novels *THE RAINBOW* (1915) and *WOMEN IN LOVE* (privately printed 1920, published 1921). In the former, independent Ursula comes of age, rebelling against her provincial surroundings and vainly seeking sexual and personal fulfillment in a university town. In the latter, Ursula is a teacher who lives in a relationship of equals with Rupert Birkin, while sculptor Gudrun endures a calamitous affair with Birkin's industrialist friend, Gerald Crich.

Briscoe, Lily. Character in VIRGINIA WOOLF's novel *TO THE LIGHTHOUSE* (1927). A painter and friend of the Ramsay family, her intuitive outlook meshes with that of the nurturing MRS. RAMSAY, to whom she is deeply attached. Through her art, she tries to "make of the moment something permanent," as she feels her friend was able to do in her life.

Brodie, Miss Jean. Eccentric title character of Muriel SPARK's novel *THE PRIME OF MISS JEAN BRODIE* (1961). Proud schoolmistress at the Marcia Blaine School for Girls in Edinburgh, she creates the "Brodie set" of five favored

teenaged students, who are drawn into her philosophy and personal life.

Brooke, Dorothea. Intelligent, idealistic central character of GEORGE ELIOT's novel *MIDDLEMARCH* (1872). She marries older scholar Edward CASAUBON, but is frustrated in her hope for a satisfying union; she later comes to love his younger cousin, Will LADISLAW.

Brutus, Marcus Junius. Roman general (c. 85 B.C.–42 B.C.) and assassin of Julius CAESAR, as dramatized in William SHAKESPEARE's *JULIUS CAESAR* (c. 1599). He joins Cassius's conspiracy "for the good of Rome," despite his love for Caesar, whose dying words — "Et tu, Brute?" — are a proverbial expression of betrayal. After his suicide, Mark ANTONY calls him "the noblest Roman of them all." In the *Inferno* section of DANTE's *DIVINE COMEDY* (c. 1314–21), Brutus, Cassius, and Judas are in the lowest circle of Hell, the abode of traitors.

Buchanan, Daisy (Fay). Object of Jay GATSBY's obsessive desire in F. SCOTT FITZGERALD's novel *THE GREAT GATSBY* (1925). A rich, married Southern beauty in fashionable East Egg, Long Island, she was briefly engaged to Gatsby when he was a poor soldier years before. Now mysteriously wealthy, he has moved to West Egg, across the bay, to be near her.

Buck. Canine protagonist of Jack LONDON's adventure novel *THE CALL OF THE WILD* (1903). From fine surroundings in California, Buck is kidnapped into brutal sledge-dog servitude in the Klondike gold rush, then finds a loving master in John Thornton, whom he serves heroically. Eventually, he escapes into legend as the "Ghost Dog" of the Klondike.

Budd, Billy. Doomed title character of Herman MELVILLE's novella *BILLY BUDD, FORETOPMAN* (1924). The "handsome sailor," who stutters badly under stress, is provoked at length by master-at-arms Claggart; falsely accused of planning a mutiny, he accidentally strikes and kills his tormentor.

Buendía family. Central characters in Gabriel GARCÍA MÁRQUEZ's novel *ONE HUNDRED YEARS OF SOLITUDE* (1967). Headed by José Arcadio

Buendía, seven generations of the family live in Macondo, the South American small town the family founded.

Bumppo, Natty [Nathaniel]. Intrepid frontiersman and protagonist of James Fenimore COOPER's novels comprising *THE LEATHERSTOCKING TALES*, in narrative order, *The Deerslayer* (1841), *The Last of the Mohicans* (1826), *The Pathfinder* (1840), *The Pioneers* (1823), and *The Prairie* (1827). The embodiment of uncorrupted natural nobility, he keeps a distance from civilization as it advances through the New York wilderness and westward. Known by many names, including Hawkeye, Leatherstocking, Deerslayer, and Pathfinder.

Burger, Rosa [Rosemarie]. Protagonist of Nadine GORDIMER's novel of South African politics, *BURGER'S DAUGHTER* (1979). Burdened by the political legacy of her white Marxist parents, who both died in prison, Rosa seeks to escape from their shadow. Eventually she is able to develop an independent ethical stance against apartheid.

Butler, Rhett. Dashing main character of MARGARET MITCHELL's novel *GONE WITH THE WIND* (1936). An outcast from fashionable Southern society who makes a fortune as a blockade runner during the Civil War, he loves and is repeatedly spurned by Scarlett O'HARA, who finally marries him, but realizes too late — as he is leaving her — that she has always loved him. His celebrated reply to her despair is, "My dear, I don't give a damn."

Caesar, Julius [Gaius Julius Caesar]. Roman general and dictator (c. 102 B.C.–44 B.C.), whose last days are dramatized in William SHAKESPEARE's *JULIUS CAESAR* (c. 1599). He appears relatively briefly before his murder by BRUTUS and Cassius on the Ides of March (March 15); his ghost appears to Brutus late in the play. George Bernard SHAW's *CAESAR AND CLEOPATRA* (1906), set in 48 B.C., features Caesar's romance with the teenaged CLEOPATRA; it depicts him as wise and practical.

Caliban. "Deformed monster" and supporting character in William SHAKESPEARE's last play, *THE TEMPEST* (c. 1611). Son of the witch Sycorax, he is the rightful heir of the island where PROSPERO landed with his baby daughter, but when he makes advances to the grown MIRANDA, he finds himself reduced by her father to slavery in his own domain. His name is a variant of "Cannibal."

Call, Woodrow. Former Texas Ranger and main character of Larry MCMURTRY's popular novel *LONESOME DOVE* (1985). In the 1870s, he leads a cattle drive from Texas to Montana.

Candide. Naive title character in VOLTAIRE's satirical novel *CANDIDE* (1759). After a series of disastrous adventures have sorely tried his belief in the optimistic doctrines of his master Dr. PANGLOSS, he settles down with Pangloss, his beloved CUNÉGONDE, and other companions of his wanderings, certain of one material truth: "We must cultivate our garden."

Capulet, Juliet. Title character and one of the "star-cross'd lovers" in William SHAKESPEARE's tragedy *ROMEO AND JULIET* (1595). The 14-year-old daughter of a prominent Verona family, Juliet falls in love with Romeo MONTAGUE, scion of her family's bitter enemies, the Montagues, and marries him in secret.

Carbone, Eddie. Self-deceived main character of ARTHUR MILLER's play *A VIEW FROM THE BRIDGE* (1955). The Italian-American longshoreman is consumed by his obsession with his niece Catherine, but his inability to admit the truth about his feelings leads to his ruin.

Cardew, Cecily. Unspoiled English rose and ward of Jack WORTHING in Oscar WILDE's comedy *THE IMPORTANCE OF BEING EARNEST* (1895). She becomes engaged to Algernon MONCRIEFF when he impersonates Jack's reprobate (and nonexistent) brother Ernest, for "it had always been a girlish dream of mine to love someone whose name was Ernest."

Carmen. Gypsy heroine of Prosper Mérimée's novella *CARMEN* (1845). Temperamental and fiercely independent, she beguiles and manipulates Don José and many other lovers, then breaks with them to remain free of the servitude of love.

FROM ACHILLES' HEEL TO YAHOO: LITERARY EPONYMS AND ALLUSIONS

Literary eponyms are words that have become detached from their literary origins or associations to function independently as part of the language. In common usage, capitalization is sometimes retained, sometimes abandoned.

ACHILLES' HEEL The single vulnerable feature or trait in a person, plan, and so forth. From Homer's *Iliad*: the heel is the only spot where the hero Achilles is vulnerable (as a child his mother had dipped him in the river Styx, making him invincible to arrows except at the heel by which she held him).

ALBATROSS A burdensome source of distress, guilt, or impairment. From Samuel Taylor Coleridge's poem "The Rime of the Ancient Mariner" (1798), after the seabird that is slain. As the guilt-ridden Mariner observes, "Instead of the cross, the albatross / About my neck was hung."

BABBITT (BABBITTRY) A smugly complacent upholder of middle-class values and mores who is interested solely in material success and maintaining appearances; a philistine. From Sinclair Lewis's 1922 novel *Babbitt*, after the title character, the small-town businessman George Babbitt.

CASANOVA A man who pursues many love affairs, often simultaneously; a man who is unscrupulous in his search for sexual pleasure; a charming seducer. From *Casanova's Memoirs* (1826–38) by Giacomo Casanova, the Italian author whose adventures established him as the very paragon— and byword—for the amorous rake.

CASSANDRA A person whose prophecies of danger or doom are ignored, often with disastrous consequences; a prophet of misfortune. From Homer's *Iliad*, after Cassandra, the Trojan princess who (although no one believes her) correctly predicts the downfall of Troy to the invading Greeks.

CATCH-22 A problematic situation arising from contradictions inherent in the bureaucratic, legal, or other systems that govern the matter, leading to paralysis and frustration. From Joseph Heller's classic 1961 antiwar novel *Catch-22*, in which "Catch-22" is the paradoxical regulation that prevents Captain John Yossarian from getting out of the Army.

DON JUAN A highly accomplished womanizer; a libertine. From the legendary Spanish nobleman and notoriously unrepentant seducer of women who has been immortalized by many great writers, including Tirso de Molino, Molière, Lord Byron, and George Bernard Shaw, and perhaps most famously by Mozart in his opera *Don Giovanni* (1787).

FAUSTIAN Used to refer to a bargain or pact, especially one in which moral or spiritual principles are sacrificed in the pursuit of worldly, intellectual, or material success. From the legend of the aged German magician and philosopher Johann Faust, who sells his soul to the Devil in exchange for youth, greater knowledge, and worldly success (immortalized notably by Christopher Marlowe and Goethe).

GARGANTUAN Immensely large in size or amount. From François Rabelais's *Gargantua and Pantagruel* (1532–64), after the prodigiously ravenous giant Gargantua.

KNICKERBOCKERS Loose, knee-length men's pants supposedly worn by New York's early Dutch settlers; and KNICKERS, a woman's or girl's bloomerlike undergarment. From Washington Irving's satirical *A History of New York* (1809), after Diedrich Knickerbocker, the pseudonymous author of the book. The use of the word probably had its origin in the old-fashioned pants depicted in George Cruikshank's illustrations for an edition of Irving's book.

LILLIPUTIAN Diminutive; insignificant, petty, or not worth noticing. From Jonathan Swift's *Gulliver's Travels* (1726), after the Lilliputians, a race of tiny people.

LOTHARIO A charmingly suave—and unrepentant—seducer of women. From Nicholas Rowe's tragedy *The Fair Penitent* (1703), after Lothario, a vile womanizer.

MALAPROPISM A misuse of words (especially those sounding alike), often unintentionally comic. From Richard Brinsley Sheridan's 1775 comedy *The Rivals*, after the inimitable Mrs. Malaprop. ("Illiterate him, I say, quite from your memory.") The character's name was itself derived from the French phrase, *mal à propos*, meaning inappropriate.

MAN (OR GIRL) FRIDAY A devoted, right-hand assistant or servant, often with a wide range of responsibilities; a factotum. From Daniel Defoe's *Robinson Crusoe* (1719), after Crusoe's servant, Friday. (Crusoe referred to him as "my man, Friday.")

MUNCHAUSEN SYNDROME A psychological illness in which a patient convincingly pretends to be sick or even makes him or herself ill in order to gain attention. From *The Adventures of Baron Munchausen* (many editions), retellings of the "tall tales" of Karl Friedrich Hieronymus, Baron von Münchausen (1720–1797), a German soldier and adventurer who was celebrated for his colorful exploits.

PANDER To cater to someone's baser passions, ambitions, machinations, and so forth; to act as a go-between in a love-affair or sexual intrigue; a procurer or pimp. From the character Pandarus who helps to unite the lovers in the medieval legend of Troilus and Cressida, later versions of which include Boccaccio's poem *Il Filostrato* (c. 1338), Geoffrey Chaucer's long poem *Troilus and Criseyde* (c. 1385), and William Shakespeare's play *Troilus and Cressida* (c. 1601–2).

PECKSNIFF (PECKSNIFFIAN, PECKSNIFFERY) A thoroughly selfish and despicable person who hypocritically espouses the highest standards of morality and benevolence. From Charles Dickens's novel *Martin Chuzzlewit* (1844), after the oily, ingratiating, "holier-than-thou" Seth Pecksniff.

PETER PAN An adult who retains the naturalness, sense of wonder, and *joie de vivre* associated with children, often used critically in reference to men who irresponsibly "refuse to grow up." From Sir James M. Barrie's play *Peter Pan; or, The Boy Who Wouldn't Grow Up* (1904); see also Dan Kiley's *The Peter Pan Syndrome: Men Who Have Never Grown Up* (1983). Also: PETER PAN COLLAR A small, close-fitting collar with rounded ends, used on women's and children's clothing, from Peter Pan's traditional costume.

POLLYANNA An individual with an extremely sunny and hopeful personality, who is often blindly or irritatingly optimistic. From the heroine of a popular series of books created by the American novelist Eleanor H. Porter (1868–1920).

PUCKISH (PUCKISHNESS) Mischievous; capricious. From the impish fairy, spirit, or demon of folk superstition known as Puck (as well as Robin-Goodfellow and Hobgoblin), brought to life most famously in William Shakespeare's play *A Midsummer Night's Dream* (c. 1595–96).

QUIXOTIC Impractically idealistic or romantic; visionary; exceedingly chivalrous. From Miguel de Cervantes y Saavedra's epic *Don Quixote* (1605–15), after its hero.

ROMEO A man who loves ardently, and usually successfully; a philandering seducer of women. From William Shakespeare's tragedy *Romeo and Juliet* (1595).

SCROOGE An avaricious, penny-pinching curmudgeon; a killjoy. From Charles Dickens's *A Christmas Carol* (1843), after the miserly and misanthropic Ebenezer Scrooge.

SHANGRI-LA A distant, imaginary place of great natural beauty where life is entirely delightful. From James Hilton's novel *Lost Horizon* (1933), in which Shangri-La is imagined as paradise on earth.

SHERLOCK A private detective; a sleuth; a person who is an extraordinarily astute solver of mysteries or puzzles. From Sir Arthur Conan Doyle's *The Adventures of Sherlock Holmes* (1892) and other books and stories, after his detective nonpareil.

SHYLOCK An extortionate moneylender; a merciless creditor. Now considered offensive. It can

---

Carraway, Nick. Narrator of F. SCOTT FITZGERALD's novel *THE GREAT GATSBY* (1925). Cousin of married beauty Daisy BUCHANAN, he reintroduces her to next-door neighbor Jay GATSBY, whose confidant he becomes during Gatsby's doomed pursuit of her.

Carter, Nick. Tough, intrepid detective hero of thousands of pulp magazine stories, dime novels, and paperbacks, created originally by John R. Coryell (1851–1924), continued by Frederic Van Rensselaer Dey (1865–1922) and many others. Beginning with *The Old Detective's Pupil; or, The Mysterious Crime of Madison Square* (serialized in Street & Smith's *New York Weekly*, 1886), the character appeared for decades in various print guises as well as in radio, stage, and screen adaptations. "Nick Carter" was also a pseudonym for authors of such tales.

Carton, Sydney. Central character of Charles DICKENS's novel *A TALE OF TWO CITIES* (1859). A dissipated lawyer, he redeems himself ("It is a far, far better thing I do than I have ever done") by trading identities with French nobleman Charles Darnay, husband of his beloved Lucie,

also be used as a verb. From William Shakespeare's *The Merchant of Venice* (c. 1596–97), after the Jewish usurer Shylock.

SIMON LEGREE A cruel, merciless taskmaster. From Harriet Beecher Stowe's antislavery classic *Uncle Tom's Cabin* (1852), after the vicious slave overseer, Simon Legree.

SIMON-PURE Authentic; unadulterated. From Susanna Centlivre's play *A Bold Stroke for a Wife* (1718), after the character who must prove that he is the "real Simon Pure" after an imposter assumes his identity.

STEPFORD WIFE A "perfect wife," whose complete submissiveness and maniacal attention to detail are robotlike; anyone who behaves like an emotionless and/or mindless domestic automaton. From Ira Levin's horror novel *The Stepford Wives* (1972), in which suburban husbands discover the enormous advantages of replacing their flesh-and-blood wives with robots that are virtually identical to the women they have disposed of. Probably even better known from the 1975 film adaptation ("Something strange is happening in the town of Stepford").

SVENGALI One who exercises a mesmerizing control over another, usually with sinister intentions. From George Du Maurier's best-selling novel *Trilby* (1894), after Svengali, the evil hypnotist who holds the beautiful young Trilby completely under his dominion.

UNCLE TOM A contemptuous characterization of a black man who is thought to be excessively fawning and submissive toward whites. From Harriet Beecher Stowe's antislavery novel *Uncle Tom's Cabin* (1852), after the slave Uncle Tom.

YAHOO A vulgar, brutish, and stupid person; a proudly ignorant or uneducated person; an anti-intellectual. From Jonathan Swift's *Gulliver's Travels* (1726), after the Yahoos, a race of loutish, degraded, humanlike creatures.

to save Darnay from the guillotine in the French Revolution.

Casamassima, Princess [Christina Light]. Central character in HENRY JAMES's novels *Roderick Hudson* (1876) and *The Princess Casamassima* (1886). As a young woman, the beautiful Christina Light is betrothed to Prince Casamassima, but loved obsessively by the dissolute sculptor Hudson. In the later novel, the princess is separated from her husband and turns to radical politics in London under the tutelage of a revolutionary, Hyacinth Robinson.

Casaubon, Rev. Edward. Pompous husband of Dorothea BROOKE in GEORGE ELIOT's novel *MIDDLEMARCH* (1872). A scholar planning an explanatory tome to be called *A Key to All Mythologies* — which never gets past the planning stage — he marries the much younger Dorothea, with ruinous results. His cousin Will LADISLAW calls him a "white-blooded pedantic coxcomb."

Cassandra. Prophetess and daughter of Troy's King Priam in Greek mythology. The god Apollo gave her the power of prophecy, then cursed her so that no one would believe her predictions. Her name has become proverbial for a prophet of doom who is not believed. AGAMEMNON brought her home from Troy as war booty, and Clytemnestra killed them both. She appears in AESCHYLUS's play *Agamemnon* (from his ORESTEIA, 458 B.C.), EURIPIDES' play *THE TROJAN WOMEN* (415 B.C.), and William SHAKESPEARE's play *TROILUS AND CRESSIDA* (c. 1601–2).

Castorp, Hans. Protagonist of Thomas MANN's novel *THE MAGIC MOUNTAIN* (1924). A young engineer who comes to a Swiss tuberculosis sanatorium to visit a cousin, he is diagnosed with a "moist spot" on his lung and remains for seven years, observing his fellow patients and pondering the mysteries of life and death.

Caulfield, Holden. Alienated 16-year-old narrator of J. D. SALINGER's novel *THE CATCHER IN THE RYE* (1951). After flunking out of his prep school, he embarks on a journey of self-discovery in New York. Rebelling against adult "phoniness," he imagines himself the protector of children, their "catcher in the rye."

Celie. African-American protagonist of Alice WALKER's novel of emancipation, *THE COLOR PURPLE* (1982). In letters to God and her sister Nettie, Celie reveals a life of rape and mistreatment by her stepfather and husband. Through relationships with other women, especially her husband's mistress Shug Avery, she comes to realize her worth.

Chamcha, Saladin. Indian expatriate in England and main character of Salman RUSHDIE's novel *THE SATANIC VERSES* (1989). After a plane crash of which Chamcha and Indian movie star Gibreel FARISHTA are the sole survivors, Chamcha finds himself transformed into a devil figure with horns and a tail.

Chance. *See* **Gardiner, Chauncey**

Charles, Nick and **Nora.** Urbane sleuthing couple in Dashiell HAMMETT's detective novel *THE THIN MAN* (1934). Nick is a hard-drinking retired private eye who is drawn into a murder investigation. His Watson, witty, spunky socialite Nora, is based on Hammett's companion, Lillian HELLMAN.

Charlus, Baron Palamède de. A main character in Marcel PROUST's series of novels *REMEMBRANCE OF THINGS PAST* (1913–27); a member of the GUERMANTES family. Appearing for the first time in the first novel, *Swann's Way* (*Du Côté de Chez Swann*, 1913), he is a central character in the fourth, *Cities of the Plain* (*Sodome et Gomorrhe*, 1922). For the narrator, the homosexual Charlus represents the decadence of the aristocracy; he nevertheless admires him for his intelligence and erudition. Charlus's real-life model was the *fin-de-siècle* poet Comte Robert de Montesquiou (1855–1921).

Chatterley, Lady Constance [Connie]. Central character of D. H. LAWRENCE's novel *LADY CHATTERLEY'S LOVER* (1928). Her aristocratic husband was paralyzed by a war wound, and she has a pair of graphically depicted affairs, becoming pregnant by her second lover, the gamekeeper Oliver MELLORS.

Chichikov, Pavel Ivanovich. Main character of Nikolai GOGOL's novel *DEAD SOULS* (1842). A charming schemer in a Russia where serfdom still prevails, he travels across country in a troika buying up large numbers of serfs (or "souls") who have died since the last census, planning to use them as collateral to acquire some actual property.

Chillingworth, Roger. Alias used by the husband of Hester PRYNNE in Nathaniel HAWTHORNE's novel *THE SCARLET LETTER* (1850). Arriving in Boston as his wife is being punished for her crime of adultery, he remains incognito and aims to avenge himself by discovering her partner. His suspicions soon fall on Reverend Arthur DIMMESDALE.

Chingachgook. Laconic central character in James Fenimore COOPER's novel *The Last of the Mohicans* (1826, from his LEATHERSTOCKING TALES, 1823–41). He joins his son Uncas and his friend Hawkeye (Natty BUMPPO) to aid two young female settlers through dangerous territory, becoming "the last of the Mohicans" when Uncas is slain. Chingachgook also appears in another novel in the series, *The Deerslayer*

(1841), which takes place in his and Natty's youth.

Chips, Mr. [Arthur Chipping]. Title character of James Hilton's sentimental novel *GOOD-BYE, MR. CHIPS* (1934). A beloved teacher of Latin and Greek at an English public school, Mr. Chipping, nicknamed Mr. Chips by generations of students, finds solace in his profession when his young wife dies.

Christian, Fletcher. Ship's mate and leader of the rebellion against despotic Captain BLIGH in Charles Nordhoff and James Norman Hall's novel *MUTINY ON THE BOUNTY* (1932), based on an actual mutiny in 1789. The historical Christian (1764–1793) led the mutineers to a remote Pacific refuge where their descendants still live, as related in the third book in the authors' *Bounty Trilogy, Pitcairn's Island* (1934).

Christmas, Joe. Main character of William FAULKNER's novel *LIGHT IN AUGUST* (1932). An orphan of ambiguous race who believes himself to be part black, Christmas kills a white female lover who pushes him to accept his blackness, and becomes the victim of a lynching.

Claudine. Spirited, sensual title character of four novels by COLETTE: *Claudine at School* (*Claudine à l'École*, 1900), *Claudine in Paris* (*Claudine à Paris*, 1901; also translated as *Young Lady of Paris*), *Claudine Married* (*Claudine en Ménage*, 1902; also translated as *The Indulgent Husband*), and *Claudine and Annie* (*Claudine S'en Va*, 1903; also translated as *The Innocent Wife*). Based in part on the author's school years in Burgundy, the books were published under the name of Willy, the pen name of her then-husband Henri Gauthier-Villars. The character's popularity in turn-of-the-20th-century Paris extended to "Claudine" collars, haircuts, and perfume.

Claudius. 1. Fourth Roman emperor (Tiberius Claudius Drusus Nero Germanicus, 10 B.C.–A.D. 54; reigned A.D. 41–54). Title character and narrator of Robert GRAVES's historical novels *I, CLAUDIUS* (1934) and *Claudius the God* (1934); a stammering, deformed, but trenchantly observant amateur historian and minor

member of the imperial family who unexpectedly becomes emperor. 2. HAMLET's uncle and stepfather in William SHAKESPEARE's tragedy *HAMLET, PRINCE OF DENMARK* (c. 1601). Murderer of and successor to his brother, the king of Denmark, he marries Hamlet's mother, Gertrude.

Cleopatra [Cleopatra VII Thea Philopator]. Beautiful, imperious queen of Egypt (61 B.C.–30 B.C.; reigned 51 B.C.–30 B.C.) and main character in William SHAKESPEARE's tragedy *ANTONY AND CLEOPATRA* (1607), in which she kills herself with an asp to unite with her ally and lover, Mark ANTONY, after his suicide; John DRYDEN's tragedy *All for Love, or the World Well Lost* (1678), about the lovers' last day; and George Bernard SHAW's play *CAESAR AND CLEOPATRA* (1906), in which she is a teachable teenager to an older Caesar.

Columbine [in Italian, Columbina, "Little Dove"]. Stock character in the Italian commedia dell'arte, in French and English pantomime, and in 18th-century French comedies. Usually a saucy servant girl or lady's maid, or the daughter or ward of an elderly character, she is the sweetheart of HARLEQUIN.

Compson family (Quentin, Jason, Benjy, Caddy, etc.). Declining dynasty in William FAULKNER's fictional Yoknapatawpha County, Mississippi, the setting for most of his novels. The four Compson siblings who are central characters in *THE SOUND AND THE FURY* (1929)—the "idiot" Benjy, who begins telling this tale "full of sound and fury"; the mean-spirited middle son, Jason; the eldest son, Quentin, who committed suicide while at Harvard; and the only daughter, Constance (Caddy)—are the end of the family line, except for Quentin, Caddy's illegitimate daughter. Several Compsons appear in other Faulkner novels, notably the elder Quentin and his father, Jason, in *ABSALOM, ABSALOM!* (1936).

Conroy, Gabriel. College teacher and central character of James JOYCE's short story "THE DEAD" (from *DUBLINERS*, 1914). His aunts' Christmas party and his wife Gretta's revelations afterward lead Conroy to contemplate the death around him and within himself.

Conselheiro, Antônio [Antonio, the Counselor]. Central character in Mario VARGAS LLOSA's novel *The War of the End of the World* (*La Guerra del Fin del Mundo*, 1981), based on the historical figure of Antônio Vicente Mendes Maciel (1828–1897), who called himself the Counselor as the founder of a millenarian religious movement in late 19th-century rural Brazil; their community, Canudos, was destroyed by the military government, killing tens of thousands, a story first told in the Brazilian classic *Rebellion in the Backlands* (*Os Sertões*, 1902) by Euclides da Cunha.

Copperfield, David. Title character and narrator of Charles DICKENS's autobiographical novel *DAVID COPPERFIELD* (1850). He relates his life from the beginning ("I am born"), through the painful but instructive events of his childhood — after his mother's death, ten-year-old David is taken from a harsh boarding school and forced to work at a menial job, but he escapes and goes to live with his eccentric Aunt Betsey Trotwood — to the struggles of his young adulthood and his eventual success as a writer.

Cordelia. Youngest daughter of the title character in William SHAKESPEARE's tragedy *KING LEAR* (c. 1605–6). She is the only one of the king's three daughters who truly loves him, but unlike her fawning sisters GONERIL and REGAN, she will not make an elaborate show of her affection, and is disinherited. She proves her devotion when her sisters show their true colors.

Cowperwood, Frank Algernon. Unethical businessman and protagonist of Theodore DREISER's "trilogy of desire," comprising *The Financier* (1912), *The Titan* (1914), and *The Stoic* (1947). Closely based on financier and streetcar mogul Charles T. Yerkes (1837–1905), Cowperwood rises to great wealth and prominence in Philadelphia and Chicago in the first two novels, also enjoying an array of sexual adventures. In the last novel, an aging Cowperwood attempts to seize control of the London Underground.

Crane, Ichabod. Lanky, credulous schoolteacher in WASHINGTON IRVING's story "The Legend of Sleepy Hollow" (from his *The Sketch Book of Geoffrey Crayon, Gent.*, 1820). He courts the blooming (and wealthy) Katerina Van Tassel, but vanishes from the town after mistaking his rival Brom Van Brunt for a legendary headless horseman.

Cratchit, Bob. In Charles DICKENS's short novel *A CHRISTMAS CAROL* (1843), clerk to the miserly Ebenezer SCROOGE, and father of a loving and contented family of eight, including the lame son TINY TIM. Scrooge's vision of their happiness is one of the keys to his redemption.

Crawford, Janie [Janie Killicks, Janie Starks, Janie Woods]. Thrice-married protagonist of Zora Neale HURSTON's novel *THEIR EYES WERE WATCHING GOD* (1937). Escaping her first, loveless marriage, she weds a budding politician, who becomes mayor of an African-American town in Florida but leaves her no room to fulfill herself. Her third marriage, to a much younger man, teaches her the value of her own life.

Crécy, Odette de. *See* Odette

Criseyde [Cressida]. Daughter of Trojan prophet Calchas and faithless object of TROILUS's affection in Geoffrey CHAUCER's poem *TROILUS AND CRISEYDE* (c. 1385) and William SHAKESPEARE's play *TROILUS AND CRESSIDA* (c. 1601–2). In both, the couple's bond is broken when Greek warrior Diomedes seduces Criseyde/Cressida.

Croy, Kate. Central character in HENRY JAMES's novel *THE WINGS OF THE DOVE* (1902). A clever but impecunious Englishwoman, Kate loves a journalist, Merton DENSHER, but they cannot marry on his income. When she finds out that a wealthy American friend, Milly Theale, is fatally ill, she devises a scheme for Densher to inherit her fortune.

Crusoe, Robinson. Title character and narrator of Daniel DEFOE's novel *ROBINSON CRUSOE* (1719). Shipwrecked on an island, Crusoe uses ingenuity and salvaged parts to survive for 28 years, confronting nature and cannibals with faith and reason, which sharpen his courage.

The character is based on 18th-century seafarer Alexander Selkirk (1676–1721).

Cruz, Artemio. Central character in Carlos FUENTES's novel *THE DEATH OF ARTEMIO CRUZ* (1962). On his deathbed, corrupt Mexican political leader and former revolutionary Cruz experiences an internal moral debate about his life, which reveals his survival to be the result of his loss of ideals and his wanton use and betrayal of others.

Cunégonde. Baron's daughter and pragmatic beloved of CANDIDE in VOLTAIRE's satirical novel *CANDIDE* (1759). When she and Candide are found together, Candide is expelled from her father's castle, and spends much of the novel searching for her. Meanwhile, she undergoes severe trials of her own.

Cyrano de Bergerac. Title character of Edmond Rostand's play *CYRANO DE BERGERAC* (1897), inspired by French satirist and dramatist Savinien Cyrano de Bergerac (1619–1655). The gallant and poetic Cyrano, a brilliant swordsman in the corps of Gascon cadets, secretly worships the lovely, witty ROXANE, but fears his overlong nose is an insuperable hindrance to romance. He lends his eloquence to a handsome but inarticulate young fellow soldier, who courts her successfully.

Dalloway, Clarissa. Title character of VIRGINIA WOOLF's novel *MRS. DALLOWAY* (1925). A sophisticated society matron in post–World War I London, Mrs. Dalloway reflects on her life and the choices she has made as she prepares for a dinner party.

Darcy, Fitzwilliam. Main character in Jane AUSTEN's novel of manners *PRIDE AND PREJUDICE* (1813). Handsome, well-born, and wealthy, he seems an ideal match for spirited Elizabeth BENNET, but pride and prejudice long keep them both from acknowledging their mutual attraction.

D'Artagnan. Central character in the novel by ALEXANDRE DUMAS *PÈRE*, *THE THREE MUSKETEERS* (1844), modeled on the historical figure of Charles de Batz-Castelmore, comte d'Artagnan (1613?–1673). A poor but intrepid Gascon

who wants to become a guardsman for King Louis XIII, he begins his road to royal service by adventuring with the Three Musketeers: ATHOS, PORTHOS, and ARAMIS.

Dashwood sisters (Elinor and **Marianne).** Main characters of Jane AUSTEN's novel *SENSE AND SENSIBILITY* (1811). Their contrasting characters give the novel its title: Elinor's speech and actions reflect her sound common sense, and Marianne's her romantic impulsiveness and "sensibility" (a contemporary term for poetic sensitivity).

Dead, Milkman [Macon Dead III]. Main character in Toni MORRISON's novel *Song of Solomon* (1977), nicknamed "Milkman" because his mother nursed him until he was eight or nine. The son of wealthy, prominent Michigan blacks, Milkman travels to Shalimar, Virginia, where he tracks his family history back to his great-grandfather, the slave Solomon, who had magical powers and was said to have flown back to Africa.

Dedalus, Stephen. Main character in two novels by James JOYCE. In *A PORTRAIT OF THE ARTIST AS A YOUNG MAN* (1916), the Irish Catholic youth rebels against family and church. Abandoning plans to enter the priesthood, he vows to become an artist, a "priest of the eternal imagination." His name links him to Daedalus, master craftsman of Greek mythology. In *ULYSSES* (1922), he walks around Dublin on June 16, 1904, as a modern version of the mythical Telemachus, the son of Ulysses (Odysseus), who goes in search of his father. See also BLOOM, LEOPOLD and MOLLY; ODYSSEUS.

Defarge, Madame Therese. Supporting character in Charles DICKENS's novel *A TALE OF TWO CITIES* (1859). Wife of a wine-shop owner, she is a fanatical supporter of the French Revolution, stitching the names of enemies marked for the guillotine into her knitting.

Denisovich, Ivan. *See* **Shukhov, Ivan Denisovich**

Densher, Merton. English journalist and central character in HENRY JAMES's novel *THE WINGS OF THE DOVE* (1902). Lacking enough income to marry his lover, Kate CROY, he agrees to her scheme to feign love for a terminally ill American friend, Milly Theale, in order to inherit her fortune.

Desdemona. Devoted wife of the title character in William SHAKESPEARE's tragedy *OTHELLO, THE MOOR OF VENICE* (1604). She defies her father to marry the great general OTHELLO, but becomes the victim of the evil schemes of her husband's ensign, IAGO, who tricks Othello into believing her unfaithful.

Desqueyroux, Thérèse. Title character of François MAURIAC's novel *THÉRÈSE DESQUEY-ROUX* (1927). Confined by an oppressive marriage, she attempts to poison her husband. Her story is continued in Mauriac's novel *The End of the Night* (*La Fin de la Nuit*, 1935); she also appears in two short stories, "Thérèse Chez le Docteur" (Thérèse at the Doctor's) and "Thérèse à l'Hôtel" (Thérèse at the Hotel) (both 1938).

Diamond, Jack "Legs." Real-life Roaring Twenties and Depression-era gangster (1895 or 1896–1931) and title character of the first novel in William KENNEDY's "Albany cycle," *Legs* (1975). As reported by lawyer Marcus Gorman, Diamond and his showgirl paramour Kiki Roberts live a high, dangerous life across the United States. It ends in a rooming house in Albany, New York.

Dido. Founder and queen of Carthage in VIRGIL's *AENEID* (c. 29 B.C.–19 B.C.). Through the instigation of Venus, she falls in love with the goddess's son, the wandering Trojan leader AENEAS, but he is fated to leave her to found Rome. She kills herself in despair. Her story is also told in OVID's poetry collection *Epistles of the Heroines* (*Heroides*, c. 16 B.C.–A.D. 8).

Dimmesdale, Arthur. Guilt-ridden minister in Nathaniel HAWTHORNE's novel *THE SCARLET LETTER* (1850). He hides his liaison with Hester PRYNNE, who has given birth to their child, but is tortured inwardly and by Prynne's vengeful husband, Roger CHILLINGWORTH.

Diver, Dick and **Nicole.** Main characters of F. SCOTT FITZGERALD's novel *TENDER IS THE NIGHT* (1934), set in Paris and on the Riviera. Promising psychiatrist Dick Diver marries his beautiful former patient, Nicole Warren, but her mental instability and his alcoholism strain their marriage and wreck his career. The couple is loosely based on Fitzgerald and his wife, Zelda.

Dixon, Jim [James]. Antiestablishment title character of KINGSLEY AMIS's comic novel *LUCKY JIM* (1954). Lower-middle-class Dixon is an assistant lecturer at a provincial university who loathes the pretentiousness of his surroundings. When he loses his job after making his true feelings known, his luck helps him to a better one in London.

Dobson, Zuleika. Title character of the sole novel by Max Beerbohm (1872–1956), *Zuleika Dobson; or, An Oxford Love Story* (1911), who is so beautiful that all men fall in love with her. While visiting Oxford, she enthralls the Duke of Dorset and the entire undergraduate class. Except for one man, Noaks, they all drown themselves for her sake. After Noaks kills himself too, Zuleika moves on to Cambridge.

Dombey, Paul. Proud businessman and title character of Charles DICKENS's novel *DOMBEY AND SON* (1848). Desiring only a son who will join his business, Mr. Dombey neglects his daughter, Florence, even after his son Paul's early death. Finally, in his decline, he embraces Florence.

Doolittle, Eliza. Unschooled Cockney flower peddler transformed by phonetics professor Henry HIGGINS into a lady in George Bernard SHAW's comedy *PYGMALION* (1913). She also appears in Alan Jay Lerner and Frederick Loewe's Broadway musical version, *My Fair Lady* (1956).

Dorrit, Little (Amy). Title character and selfless daughter of William Dorrit in Charles DICKENS's novel *LITTLE DORRIT* (1857). Born and raised in London's Marshalsea debtor's prison, where her father is incarcerated, she remains humble and submissive even when her father unexpectedly inherits a fortune.

DuBois, Blanche. Fragile, fading Southern belle, the tragic heroine of TENNESSEE WILLIAMS's play *A STREETCAR NAMED DESIRE* (1947). Driven by a series of failures and disappointments to seek refuge with her sister and brother-in-law, Stella and Stanley KOWALSKI, in New Orleans, she tries desperately to find "magic" and salvation amid squalid surroundings. Her intrusion into her relatives' lives precipitates the final crisis that tips her into madness.

Dulcinea del Toboso. Idealized object of QUIXOTE's affection in Miguel de CERVANTES's novel *DON QUIXOTE* (1605–15). In reality, she is a strapping peasant woman named Aldonza Lorenzo, who has never paid any attention to him, but in his vision, she is endowed with flowing hair, rosy cheeks, and alabaster skin.

Duncan. King of Scotland in William SHAKE-SPEARE's tragedy *MACBETH* (c. 1605). Urged on by LADY MACBETH, MACBETH slays him and usurps his throne.

Dupin, C. Auguste. Amateur detective who solves the case of "THE MURDERS IN THE RUE MORGUE" in Edgar Allan POE's short story (1841), and clears up two other Poe puzzlers in "The Mystery of Marie Rogêt" (1842–43) and "THE PURLOINED LETTER" (1845). Dupin's method of deductive reasoning has become standard procedure for generations of literary sleuths.

Durbeyfield, Tess. Title character of Thomas HARDY's novel *TESS OF THE D'URBERVILLES* (1891). A poor but "pure" girl from a rural family, Tess becomes pregnant by the son of a wealthy neighbor, and is later rejected by the man she loves because of her past. Victimized and frustrated by men and contemporary mores, she is eventually driven to commit murder.

Earnshaw, Catherine [Cathy; Catherine Linton]. Tempestuous central character of EMILY BRONTË's novel *WUTHERING HEIGHTS* (1847). Having loved the family's ward HEATHCLIFF since they were children roaming the moors together, she says of him, "He's more myself than I am…I am Heathcliff! He's always, always in my mind." Yet she betrays her own heart, and breaks Heathcliff's, by marrying Edgar Linton, a man of refinement and social standing—a choice she will come to regret bitterly.

Earwicker, Humphrey Chimpden. Irish pubkeeper and protagonist of James JOYCE's experimental novel *FINNEGANS WAKE* (1939); husband of ANNA LIVIA PLURABELLE. He is frequently represented by his initials, HCE, which appear throughout the book as a myriad of expanded acronyms, such as Here Comes Everybody and Haveth Childer Everywhere.

Ekdal family (Hjalmar, Gina, Hedvig). Main characters in Henrik IBSEN's play *THE WILD DUCK* (1884). Photographer Hjalmar and former housemaid Gina are a devoted couple, despite Hjalmar's delusions about his own genius, until the chronically truth-telling Gregers Werle reveals circumstances that cause Hjalmar to doubt his paternity of his and Gina's beloved daughter, Hedvig.

Electra. In Greek legend, daughter of AGAMEMNON, sister of IPHIGENIA and ORESTES. She urges her brother Orestes to avenge their father's death by killing his murderers, their mother Clytemnestra and her lover Aegisthus. Electra's story is told in AESCHYLUS's play *The Libation Bearers* (part of the ORESTEIA, 458 B.C.), SOPHOCLES' play *ELECTRA* (4th century B.C.), and EURIPIDES' play *ELECTRA* (413 B.C.). It is retold in a post–Civil War American setting in Eugene O'NEILL's dramatic trilogy *MOURNING BECOMES ELECTRA* (1931), where the character is named Lavinia Mannon.

Eliza (Harris). Young slave woman in Harriet Beecher STOWE's antislavery novel *UNCLE TOM'S CABIN* (1852). Her escape with her son Harry across the ice floes of the Ohio River and her reunion with her husband George are central to the story.

Erlynne, Mrs. (Margaret). Scandal-tainted mother of Lady WINDERMERE in Oscar WILDE's comedy of manners *LADY WINDERMERE'S FAN* (1892). Without divulging her true identity to her "Puritan" daughter, who thinks her mother is dead, she protects her from disgrace and teaches her a lesson in tolerance.

Estragon [Gogo]. Central character in Samuel BECKETT's absurdist play *WAITING FOR GODOT* (1953). For two days, he and fellow tramp VLADIMIR (Didi) vainly await the arrival of the mysterious Mr. Godot, while discoursing on a variety of topics. Estragon is the more timid, emotional, and easily confused of the pair.

Eva [Little Eva; Evangeline St. Clare]. Frail, angelic child heroine of Harriet Beecher STOWE's antislavery novel *UNCLE TOM'S CABIN* (1852). She is rescued from drowning by the slave Uncle TOM, who is then purchased by her grateful father, a "benevolent" slave owner. Eva idolizes her rescuer, and they become friends.

Eve. The first woman, fashioned from one of ADAM's ribs to be his companion, according to the BIBLE (Genesis) and John MILTON's epic poem *PARADISE LOST* (1667). Tempted by SATAN in the form of a serpent, she eats the forbidden fruit, then shares it with Adam. For this sin, they are driven from the Garden of Eden. She is, says Genesis 3:20, the "mother of all living."

Eyre, Jane. Intelligent, persevering governess and narrator of CHARLOTTE BRONTË's novel *JANE EYRE* (1847). Orphaned, Jane is educated at the draconian Lowood Institution until she leaves to take a position at Thornfield Hall, where she falls in love with her brooding employer, Edward ROCHESTER.

Fagin. In Charles DICKENS's novel *OLIVER TWIST* (1838), the aged and repulsive head of a band of juvenile thieves encountered in London by young Oliver TWIST. Fagin and his gang, including the ARTFUL DODGER, try to train Oliver for the criminal life. Apparently repenting late in life the casual anti-Semitism that caused him frequently to refer to Fagin simply as "the Jew," Dickens revised the later chapters of an 1867 edition to nearly eliminate this epithet.

Fairfax, Gwendolen. Urbane daughter of Lady BRACKNELL in Oscar WILDE's comedy *THE IMPORTANCE OF BEING EARNEST* (1895). She becomes engaged to Jack WORTHING after meeting him under his "town" alias of "Ernest Worthing," for "my ideal has always been to love someone of the name of Ernest."

Falstaff, Sir John. One of the great comic characters of all time, Falstaff appears in three plays by William SHAKESPEARE: as a boon companion to the roistering Prince Hal in *HENRY IV*, Parts I and II (c. 1597–98), and as the would-be seducer of *THE MERRY WIVES OF WINDSOR* (c. 1598). In all, he is larger than life, "a marvelous congregation of charms and vices" (H. W. Hudson). He says of himself, "I am not only witty in myself, but the cause that wit is in other men." In *HENRY V* (1599), Falstaff dies offstage, as movingly described by Mistress Quickly.

Farishta, Gibreel. Top Indian movie star and main character of Salman RUSHDIE's novel *THE SATANIC VERSES* (1989). After a plane crash of which Farishta and Bombay expatriate Saladin CHAMCHA are the sole survivors, Farishta finds himself transformed into a figure resembling the archangel Gabriel, complete with a halo.

Faust. German scholar and magician who sells his soul to the Devil (or MEPHISTOPHELES, an emissary of SATAN) in return for knowledge and power, in popular legends and in many works of literature. In Christopher MARLOWE's tragedy *DOCTOR FAUSTUS* (c. 1588), he is Dr. John Faustus, whose pursuit of forbidden knowledge is punished with eternal damnation. In the two parts of J. W. von GOETHE's dramatic poem *FAUST* (published 1808 and 1832; performed 1829 and 1854), he is Heinrich Faust, whose constant striving is rewarded with an angelic rescue. In Thomas MANN's novel *DOCTOR FAUSTUS* (1947), his 20th-century counterpart is the musician Adrian Leverkühn, whose extraordinary career ends in madness.

Fawley, Jude. Stonemason and title character of Thomas HARDY's last novel, *JUDE THE OBSCURE* (1895). His life is a series of failures and catastrophes. His "obscure" birth prevents him from studying as he wishes; his marriage fails, and an extramarital relationship with a beloved cousin, Sue Bridehead, ends disastrously with the death of his three children and his abandonment by Sue.

Figaro. Clever and subversive archetype of the servant who is superior to his master in wit and intelligence, in Pierre-Augustin de BEAUMARCHAIS's plays *THE BARBER OF SEVILLE* (1775), *THE MARRIAGE OF FIGARO* (1784), and *A Mother's Guilt* (*La Mère Coupable*, 1792). In the first play, he is the town barber and factotum who helps dashing Count Almaviva to win a wife; in the second, he is in the Count's service, trying to keep his own intended wife from the Count's clutches; in the third, he still serves the Count as a subordinate figure in a bourgeois melodrama.

Filippovna, Nastasya. Central character in Fyodor DOSTOYEVSKY's novel *THE IDIOT* (1874). Sexually abused by an older man in her youth and the mistress first of Ganya and then of ROGOZHIN, the beautiful but fragile "fallen woman" arouses pity from kind Prince MYSHKIN, whom she eventually agrees to marry. Tormented, she leaves him at the altar to return to Rogozhin.

Finch, Atticus. Depression-era small-town Alabama lawyer representing the values of tolerance, honesty, and moral courage in HARPER LEE's novel *TO KILL A MOCKINGBIRD* (1960). When he defends Tom Robinson, a black man wrongly accused of raping a white woman, he impresses upon his children, Jem and Scout, the necessity of pursuing equal justice for all.

Finn, Huckleberry. Fourteen-year-old protagonist and narrator of Mark TWAIN's novel *HUCKLEBERRY FINN* (1884). To escape from his brutal father, Huck flees on a raft down the Mississippi River with runaway slave JIM. After many adventures, including "stealing back" a captured Jim — Huck decides he would rather "go to hell" than do the "right" thing and return Jim to his owner — he comes home to be "sivilized," but vows that he will soon "light out for the Territory." Huck was introduced as Tom SAWYER's pal in Twain's earlier novel *TOM SAWYER* (1876).

Flanders, Moll. Resourceful title character of Daniel DEFOE's novel *MOLL FLANDERS* (1722). Child of a thief, she was, as Defoe's subtitle put it, "Twelve Year a Whore, five times a Wife (whereof once to her own Brother), Twelve Year a Thief, Eight Year a Transported Felon in Virginia, at last grew Rich, liv'd Honest, and died a Penitent."

Fleisher, Von Humboldt. Deceased author whose life and work consume fellow writer Charles Citrine in Saul BELLOW's novel *HUMBOLDT'S GIFT* (1975). He is generally understood as a portrait of Bellow's mentor, American poet Delmore SCHWARTZ.

Fleming, Henry. Union soldier and protagonist of STEPHEN CRANE's Civil War novel *THE RED BADGE OF COURAGE* (1895). When the images of glory that led him to enlist are dispersed by the horrifying reality of combat, he flees and is wounded accidentally by a retreating Union soldier. Eventually, he fights bravely, having come to know the true meaning of courage.

Flor, Dona [Florípedes Paiva, Florípedes Guimarães, Florípedes Madureira]. Title character and protagonist of Jorge AMADO's novel *Dona Flor and Her Two Husbands* (*Dona Flor e Seus Dois Maridos*, 1966). After the rakish husband of cooking teacher Flor dies, she marries again, to a noble, steady pharmacist. When she longs for her first husband's lovemaking, his ghost returns to her marriage bed.

Flyte, Lord Sebastian. Profligate main character in EVELYN WAUGH's novel *BRIDESHEAD REVISITED* (1945). The apostate second son of a wealthy Catholic aristocratic family — his parents are Lord and Lady MARCHMAIN — he befriends narrator Charles RYDER at Oxford, where he is known for his good looks and eccentricity, and from which he is sent down for heavy drinking. Alcoholism and a liaison with a young German, Kurt, dominate the following years; in later life, he returns to the Church.

Fogg, Phileas. Main character in Jules VERNE's novel *AROUND THE WORLD IN EIGHTY DAYS* (1873). After he accepts a bet at his gentlemen's club in London, he and his valet Passepartout take steamer, rail, elephant, and other conveyances to cover the globe in 80 days, overcoming obstacles by following Fogg's dictum, "The unforeseen does not exist."

Forsyte family (Soames, Irene, Jolyon, Old Jolyon, etc.). Title characters of John GALSWORTHY's novel-and-short-story cycle published collectively as THE FORSYTE SAGA (1922). It chronicles the lives and fortunes of the upper-middle-class clan typified by solicitor Soames Forsyte, the spiritually empty title character of the first novel in the series, *The Man of Property* (first published 1906), from the 1880s to the early 1920s. After *The Forsyte Saga* appeared, their story was continued in several more novels and stories.

Fosco, Count [Isidore Ottavio Baldassore]. Obese but sinisterly attractive villain and husband of heroine Laura Fairlie's aunt Eleanor in Wilkie COLLINS's mystery novel THE WOMAN IN WHITE (1860). He plots to steal Laura's inheritance.

Frankenstein, Victor. Title character of MARY SHELLEY's Gothic novel FRANKENSTEIN: OR THE MODERN PROMETHEUS (1818). Natural science student Frankenstein assembles and animates a "creature" (often erroneously called Frankenstein) from cadaver parts, but quickly regrets his action and abandons his creation. Ultimately, he pursues the creature to the Arctic, determined to kill it.

Friday. Servant and sole human companion of the title character in Daniel DEFOE's novel ROBINSON CRUSOE (1719). After 25 years of island solitude, CRUSOE rescues the young "savage" from cannibals and dubs him his "Man Friday" (for the day they met). Part African and part Indian, he becomes Europeanized under Crusoe's tutelage.

Frome, Ethan. Tragic title character of Edith WHARTON's novel ETHAN FROME (1911). The beleaguered New England farmer and unhappy spouse finds brief solace in the company of Mattie, the visiting cousin of his sickly wife ZENOBIA (Zeena), before an unforeseen turn of events confines the hapless lovers to a lifetime in Zeena's care.

Gabler, Hedda. Willful, self-destructive protagonist of Henrik IBSEN's play HEDDA GABLER (1890). Having buried herself in a loveless marriage to George Tesman, she goads her former lover Eilert Løvborg to revert to his dissipated ways, then incites him to commit suicide. But he dies sordidly, not "beautifully" as she envisioned; afraid of having her own role in the affair exposed, she shoots herself, causing family friend Judge Brack to exclaim, "People don't *do* such things!"

Galahad, Sir. Legendary knight of the Round Table, the illegitimate son of Sir LANCELOT and Princess Elaine. In Sir Thomas MALORY's romance LE MORTE D'ARTHUR (c. 1469–70), he is the purest knight, who achieves the quest of the Holy Grail. He appears in many other Arthurian works, including Alfred, Lord TENNYSON's poetic cycle IDYLLS OF THE KING (1859–85) and T. H. White's tetralogy of novels, THE ONCE AND FUTURE KING (1938–58).

Galt, John. Research engineer and central character of Ayn RAND's novel ATLAS SHRUGGED (1957). An embodiment of rational self-interest, he organizes a strike against a society aimed at fostering collective well-being through altruism.

Gant, Eugene. Sensitive protagonist of THOMAS WOLFE's autobiographical novels LOOK HOMEWARD, ANGEL (1929) and OF TIME AND THE RIVER (1935). In the first book, he is an observant romantic growing up in a small Southern town ("Altamont," a fictionalized Asheville, North Carolina); in the second, he is an aspiring writer whose spiritual development is traced during his sojourns in New York, at Harvard, and in Europe.

Gantry, Elmer. Handsome, fast-talking Midwestern minister in SINCLAIR LEWIS's novel ELMER GANTRY (1927), whose road to fame and fortune as a religious huckster is repeatedly sidetracked by scandals involving women. Gantry begins his career as a Baptist, later joining forces with a leading female evangelist; when last seen, he is the pastor of a large Methodist flock in New York. His name has become shorthand for a religious hypocrite.

Gardiner, Chauncey [Chance]. Guileless protagonist of Jerzy KOSINSKI's satirical novel BEING

THERE (1971). A taciturn, perhaps mentally damaged gardener, he obtains his only education from television. When he is thrust into upper-class society and the Washington power elite through a series of misunderstandings— his introduction of himself as "Chance, the gardener," is heard as "Chauncey Gardiner"—his comments on gardening are taken as sage metaphors, and his habit of relating all human activity to television ("I like to watch you") is misread as a sexual proclivity.

Gargantua. Giant and father of PANTAGRUEL; title character of François RABELAIS's satirical work *GARGANTUA AND PANTAGRUEL* (1565). Son of the King of Utopia, he is born from his mother's ear shouting "Drink, drink, drink!" and educated in Paris. After his victories in wars with Utopia's neighbors, he founds the unorthodox abbey at Thélème, where the motto is "Do what you will" and poverty, celibacy, and obedience are unwanted. His name lives on in the word "gargantuan."

Gatsby, Jay [James Gatz]. Title character of F. SCOTT FITZGERALD's Jazz Age novel *THE GREAT GATSBY* (1925). Born James Gatz, he has reinvented himself as a mysterious millionaire and taken a mansion in less-than-fashionable West Egg, Long Island, where he gives lavish parties, hoping to lure back his lost beloved, married beauty Daisy BUCHANAN, who lives across the bay in fashionable East Egg.

Gauthier, Marguerite. Title character of *Camille*, a popular novel (*La Dame aux Camélias*, 1848) and play (1852) by ALEXANDRE DUMAS *FILS*. A dazzling courtesan, she is said to be based on the real-life Marie Duplessis (1824–1847). She abandons her glamorous life to live simply with Armand Duval, whom she loves, but Armand's father convinces her to end the liaison for the sake of the young man's sister. The lovers are reunited only at her deathbed. Dumas's work is the source of Verdi's opera *La Traviata* (1853).

Gawain, Sir [Gawayne, Gawaine]. Nephew of King ARTHUR and valorous knight in Arthurian legend; his strength was said by some to wax and wane with the sun. 1. Title character of the Middle English verse romance *SIR GAWAIN AND THE GREEN KNIGHT* (c. 1375–1400), who answers the challenge of the Green Knight. 2. Character in other Arthurian works. In Sir Thomas MALORY's romance *LE MORTE D'ARTHUR* (c. 1469–70), his desire for revenge against Sir LANCELOT, who has killed his brothers, leads to the final battle.

Gilgamesh. King of Erech (Uruk) in Sumerian and Babylonian legend, son of a goddess and a mortal. In the Babylonian epic *GILGAMESH* (c. 2000 B.C.), he has many adventures with his friend Enkidu, a "wild man" created to be his companion. After Enkidu dies, he embarks on a quest to discover the secret of immortality.

Glass family (Seymour, Buddy, Zooey, Franny). Precocious, eccentric protagonists of a series of stories by J. D. SALINGER. Various Glass family members appear in "A Perfect Day for Bananafish" (1948), in other stories included in Salinger's collection *NINE STORIES* (1953), in *FRANNY AND ZOOEY* (two related stories published as a novel in 1961), in "Raise High the Roof Beam, Carpenters" (1955), in "Seymour: An Introduction" (1959), and in "Hapworth 16 1924" (1965).

Glick, Sammy [Sammele Glickstein]. Driven movie mogul and title character of Budd SCHULBERG's satirical novel *What Makes Sammy Run?* (1941). As he climbs the ladder in Hollywood, the transplanted New Yorker, "a man with a positive genius for being a heel," finds that the coarse ways of his childhood suit the glittery movie business.

Gloriana. Title character and virgin queen in Edmund SPENSER's allegorical poem *THE FAERIE QUEENE* (1590). The "greatest Glorious Queene of Faerie lond," she stands for England's Queen Elizabeth I. She sends the RED CROSS KNIGHT on the quest—to free a lady's parents from a dragon—with which the work begins.

Gloucester, Duke of. *See* **Richard III**

Golightly, Holly [Holiday Golightly, Lulamae Barnes Golightly]. Waif-about-town in 1940s New York and central character of Truman

CAPOTE's novella *BREAKFAST AT TIFFANY'S* (1958). Her glamorous, hand-to-mouth lifestyle enchants the narrator, who eventually discovers that she fled a marriage to an elderly horse doctor in Tulip, Texas.

Goneril. Eldest daughter of the title character in William SHAKESPEARE's tragedy *KING LEAR* (c. 1605). She wins half of LEAR's kingdom by falsely professing her love, but her treachery soon leads Lear to utter a curse that she might one day feel "How sharper than a serpent's tooth it is / To have a thankless child." She will also prove to be vicious, adulterous, and murderous.

Goodwin, Archie. Former police detective and legman for private detective Nero WOLFE in around 80 novels, novellas, and short stories by Rex STOUT, from *Fer-de-Lance* (1934) to *A Family Affair* (1975); he also serves as the series' narrator. He extracts information through a mix of familiarity and cheekiness.

Goriot, Père. Title character of Honoré de BALZAC's novel *Père Goriot* (*Le Père Goriot*, 1835), perhaps the most celebrated novel in his cycle *THE HUMAN COMEDY* (1829–47). Having dispensed much of the fortune he made in the noodle business on dowries for his two daughters, who have married noblemen, Goriot lives in a boardinghouse and is forbidden to visit them in their homes. He continues to lavish affection and his remaining money on them, even though they repay him with neglect.

Gradgrind, Thomas. Founder of an experimental school in the industrial city of Coketown and father of Tom and Louisa in Charles DICKENS's novel *HARD TIMES* (1845). His motto is, "Facts alone are wanted in life." He raises his children to be severely practical, but they lack the intuitive values they need to find happiness.

Grand Inquisitor. Aged cardinal and Spanish Inquisition leader in the parable related by Ivan KARAMAZOV in Fyodor DOSTOYEVSKY's novel *THE BROTHERS KARAMAZOV* (1880). The Grand Inquisitor visits JESUS, who has returned to earth and been taken prisoner by the Inquisition, and explains to him why he must die for the good of the Church.

Gray, Dorian. Protagonist of Oscar WILDE's novel *THE PICTURE OF DORIAN GRAY* (1890). In a bargain resembling FAUST's, young Dorian's wish to retain eternal youth and beauty is granted, but as he pursues a libertine's life, his portrait changes, aging and growing ever more hideous to reflect his depravity.

Grendel. Man-eating monster in the Old English epic poem *BEOWULF* (c. 700–50?), reported to be a descendant of Cain, the first murderer. With his equally monstrous mother, he lives in an undersea den and ravages the men of the Danish King Hrothgar; BEOWULF defeats him without weapons, since Grendel uses none. JOHN GARDNER retold the story from the monster's point of view in his novel *Grendel* (1972).

Griffiths, Clyde. Ambitious protagonist of Theodore DREISER's novel *AN AMERICAN TRAGEDY* (1925). The impoverished son of traveling evangelists, he is working at a factory in upstate New York when he plots to drown fellow worker Roberta Alden, who is pregnant by him, to be free to court wealthy socialite Sondra Finchley.

Grundy, Mrs. Exemplary but unseen character in a comedy by Thomas Morton (1764–1838), *Speed the Plough* (1798); a neighbor constantly worries about what Mrs. Grundy will think. Her name is a byword for the censorship imposed by conventional opinion.

Guermantes family. Aristocratic central characters in Marcel PROUST's multipart novel *REMEMBRANCE OF THINGS PAST* (1913–27). Figuring prominently in the book *The Guermantes Way* (*Le Côté de Guermantes*, 1920) and others, the large family includes siblings Baron Palamède de CHARLUS, Mme de Marsantes, and Duc Basin, husband of Oriane, Duchesse de Guermantes.

Guildenstern. *See* **Rosencrantz** and **Guildenstern**

Guinevere. Legendary queen of Britain and wife of King ARTHUR. Her illicit affair with Sir LANCELOT in Sir Thomas MALORY's romance

LE MORTE D'ARTHUR (c. 1469–70) contributes to the demise of Camelot. She appears in many other works, including CHRÉTIEN DE TROYES's romance *Lancelot* (*Le Chevalier de la Charrette; ou, Lancelot,* c. 1180); Alfred, Lord TENNYSON's poetic cycle *IDYLLS OF THE KING* (1859–85); and T. H. White's tetralogy of novels, *THE ONCE AND FUTURE KING* (1938–58).

Guishar, Lara. *See* **Lara**

Gulliver, Lemuel. Narrator and protagonist of Jonathan SWIFT's satirical novel *GULLIVER'S TRAVELS* (1726). Over four books, he takes many illuminating voyages: to Lilliput, an island of six-inch inhabitants (Book I); to Brobdingnag, an island of inhabitants 12 times his size (Book II); to the flying island of Laputa (Book III); and to the country inhabited by the horselike Houyhnhnms, wise and reasonable creatures whom Gulliver comes to appreciate, and the humanlike Yahoos, beasts lacking reason and conscience (Book IV).

Hal, Prince. *See* **Henry V**

Hamlet. 1. Protagonist of William SHAKESPEARE's tragedy *HAMLET, PRINCE OF DENMARK* (c. 1601). Son and namesake of the late king of Denmark, he is spurred by his father's ghost to avenge his "murder most foul." Feigning madness, he fails to take his revenge upon CLAUDIUS, his father's brother and successor. His inaction leads to calamity. The audience is granted insight into his thoughts in soliloquies such as the famous "To be, or not to be." 2. In Tom STOPPARD's comedy *ROSENCRANTZ AND GUILDENSTERN ARE DEAD* (1966), Hamlet is a secondary character.

Hammer, Mike. Ultra-hard-boiled private eye and narrator of more than a dozen popular detective novels by Mickey Spillane (Frank Morrison Spillaine, 1918–), beginning with *I, the Jury* (1947) and including *Kiss Me Deadly* (1952) and *Black Alley* (1996). Hammer's hallmark fondness for graphically portrayed "gratuitous" violence and sex aroused critical indignation and tested the limits of the hard-boiled genre.

Hardcastle, Kate. The "she" of the title in Oliver GOLDSMITH's comedy *SHE STOOPS TO CONQUER; OR, THE MISTAKES OF A NIGHT* (1773). Because her suitor Marlow is too bashful to woo a woman of his own social class, Kate "stoops" to play the role of a servant in her own home, which Marlow has mistaken for an inn.

Harlequin [in Italian, **Arlecchino**]. Stage clown and stock character in the Italian commedia dell'arte, in French and English pantomime, and in 18th-century French comedies. Masked, clad in a color-block costume and tights, and carrying a "batte," or "slapstick," he is a fool for the love of COLUMBINE.

Harlowe, Clarissa. Title character and tragic heroine of SAMUEL RICHARDSON's epistolary novel *CLARISSA; OR, THE HISTORY OF A YOUNG LADY* (1747–48). Clarissa's letters recount her imprisonment by her family and her supposed rescue by the handsome rake Robert Lovelace. After he drugs and rapes her, her letters tell of her decline and death.

Harris, Eliza. *See* **Eliza**

Havisham, Miss. Wealthy, eccentric old lady in Charles DICKENS's novel *GREAT EXPECTATIONS* (1861). Jilted on her wedding day long ago, she preserves her house as it was then and always wears her bridal attire. Wanting to "wreak revenge on all the male sex," she raises her ward, Estella, to break all men's hearts, including that of PIP (Philip Pirrip), the book's narrator. Pip long believes her to be the source of his "expectations."

Haze, Dolores. *See* **Lolita**

Heathcliff. Passionate central character of EMILY BRONTË's novel *WUTHERING HEIGHTS* (1847), a "fierce, pitiless, wolfish man." A ward of the Earnshaws, he has loved his foster sister Catherine EARNSHAW since they were children roaming the moors together, but she betrays their bond and marries another. Years later, when she dies, he cries out to her ghost to haunt him: "I cannot live without my life! I cannot live without my soul!"

PROTOTYPES: WRITERS AND OTHERS PORTRAYED IN FICTION

Real people often serve as models for characters in fiction. The well-known figures in the left-hand column—writers, actors, politicians, and others— have been identified (and, in some cases, acknowledged) as the primary inspiration for the character or characters listed in the center column. Individuals in the left-hand column are writers and critics unless otherwise indicated.

ORIGINAL	CHARACTER	SOURCE
Nelson Algren (1909–1981)	Lewis Brogan	*The Mandarins* (1954) by Simone de Beauvoir
Kingsley Amis (1922–1995)	Lester Ince	*The Affair* (1960) by C. P. Snow
Sherwood Anderson (1876–1941)	Dawson Fairchild	*Mosquitoes* (1927) by William Faulkner
W. H. Auden (1907–1973)	Nigel Strangeways	A *Question of Proof* (1938) and subsequent novels in the detective series by Nicholas Blake (pen name of C. Day-Lewis)
	Hugh Weston	*Lions and Shadows* (1938) by Christopher Isherwood
Charles Baudelaire (1821–1867)	Maurice Spandrell	*Point Counter Point* (1928) by Aldous Huxley
Allan Bloom, University of Chicago professor (1930–1992)	Ravelstein	*Ravelstein* (2000) by Saul Bellow
Claire Bloom, English actress (1931–)	Eve Frame	*I Married a Communist* (1999) by Philip Roth
George Gordon, Lord Byron (1788–1824)	Jeffrey Aspern	*The Aspern Papers* (1888) by Henry James
	Lord Cadurcis	*Venetia* (1837) by Benjamin Disraeli
	Mr. Cypress	*Nightmare Abbey* (1818) by Thomas Love Peacock
	Euphorion	*Faust*, part 2 (1832) by Johann Wolfgang von Goethe
Albert Camus (1913–1960)	Henri Perron	*The Mandarins* (1954) by Simone de Beauvoir

ORIGINAL	CHARACTER	SOURCE
G. K. Chesterton (1874–1936)	Dr. Gideon Fell	*Hag's Nook* (1933) and subsequent novels in the detective series by John Dickson Carr
Bill and Hillary Clinton, U.S. president and first lady (Bill, 1946–; Hillary, 1947–)	Jack and Susan Stanton	*Primary Colors: A Novel of Politics* (1996) by Anonymous [Joe Klein]
Eleanora Duse, Italian actress (1858–1924)	La Foscarina	*The Flame of Life* (1900) by Gabriele D'Annunzio
F. Scott Fitzgerald (1896–1940)	Manley Halliday	*The Disenchanted* (1950) by Budd Schulberg
E. M. Forster (1879–1970)	Benjamin Dexter	*The Third Man* (1950) by Graham Greene
William Gaddis (1922–1998)	Harold Sand	*The Subterraneans* (1958) by Jack Kerouac
Allen Ginsberg (1926–1997)	Irwin Garden	*Visions of Cody* (1960), *Book of Dreams* (1961), *Big Sur* (1962), *Desolation Angels* (1966), *Vanity of Duluoz* (1968) by Jack Kerouac
Oliver St. John Gogarty (1878–1957)	Buck Mulligan	*Ulysses* (1922) by James Joyce
Thomas Hardy (1840–1928)	Edward Driffield	*Cakes and Ale* (1930) by W. Somerset Maugham
Lillian Hellman (1905–1984)	Nora Charles	*The Thin Man* (1934) by Dashiell Hammett
Leigh Hunt (1784–1859)	Harold Skimpole	*Bleak House* (1853) by Charles Dickens
Henry James (1843–1916)	George Boon	*Boon* (1915) by H. G. Wells
James Joyce (1882–1941)	James-Julius Ratner	*The Apes of God* (1930) by Wyndham Lewis
Arthur Koestler (1905–1983)	Victor Scriassine	*The Mandarins* (1954) by Simone de Beauvoir
François, duc de La Rochefoucauld (1613–1680)	Duc de Nemours	*The Princess of Cleves* (1678) by Madame de Lafayette
D. H. and Frieda Lawrence (D. H., 1885–1930; Frieda, 1879–1956)	Mark and Mary Rampion	*Point Counter Point* (1928) by Aldous Huxley

(Prototypes: Writers and Others Portrayed in Fiction, continued)

ORIGINAL	CHARACTER	SOURCE
Sinclair Lewis (1885–1951)	Lloyd McHarg	*You Can't Go Home Again* (1940) by Thomas Wolfe
Huey Long, Louisiana governor and senator in the 1920s and 1930s (1893–1935)	Willie Stark	*All the King's Men* (1946) by Robert Penn Warren
György Lukács (1885–1971)	Naptha	*The Magic Mountain* (1924) by Thomas Mann
Dwight Macdonald (1906–1981)	Macdougal Macdermott	*The Oasis* (1949) by Mary McCarthy
Norman Mailer (1923–)	Harvey Marker	*Desolation Angels* (1965) by Jack Kerouac
Bernard Malamud (1914–1986)	E. I. Lonoff	*The Ghost Writer* (1979) by Philip Roth
Katherine Mansfield (1888–1923)	Susan Paley	*Point Counter Point* (1928) by Aldous Huxley
W. Somerset Maugham (1874–1965)	Kenneth Marchal Toomey	*Earthly Powers* (1980) by Anthony Burgess
Aimee Semple McPherson, American evangelist (1890–1944)	Mrs. Melrose Ape	*Vile Bodies* (1930) by Evelyn Waugh
	Sharon Falconer	*Elmer Gantry* (1927) by Sinclair Lewis
A. A. Milne (1882–1956)	Rodney Spelvin	"Rodney Has a Relapse," in *Nothing Serious* (1950) by P. G. Wodehouse
Helena Modjeska, Polish actress (1840–1909)	Maryna Zalezowska	*In America* (2000) by Susan Sontag
Molière (1622–1673)	Élomire	*Zélinde* (1663) by Jean Donneau de Visé
Marilyn Monroe, American actress (1926–1962)	Maggie	*After the Fall* (1964) by Arthur Miller
Ottoline Morrell, English hostess and member of the Bloomsbury Group (1873–1938)	Hermione Roddice	*Women in Love* (1920) by D. H. Lawrence
	Lady Septuagesima Goodley	*Triple Fugue* (1924) by Osbert Sitwell
Nadar (Gaspard Félix Tournachon), French photographer and balloonist (1820–1910)	Michel Ardan	*From the Earth to the Moon* (1864) and *Around the Moon* (1870) by Jules Verne

ORIGINAL	CHARACTER	SOURCE
V. S. Naipaul (1932–)	Victor Mehta	*A Map of the World* (1983) by David Hare
George Jean Nathan (1882–1958)	Maury Noble	*The Beautiful and Damned* (1922) by F. Scott Fitzgerald
Anaïs Nin (1903–1977)	Carla Blankton	*In a Yellow Wood* (1947) by Gore Vidal
	Maria Verlaine	*The City and the Pillar* (1948) by Gore Vidal
George Orwell (1903–1950)	Alf, Viscount Erridge, Earl of Warminster	*A Dance to the Music of Time* (1951–75) by Anthony Powell
Maxwell Perkins (1884–1947)	Foxhall Morton Edwards	*You Can't Go Home Again* (1940) by Thomas Wolfe
Aleksandr Pushkin (1799–1837)	Khlestakov	*The Government Inspector* (1836) by Nikolai Gogol
Franklin Delano Roosevelt, U.S. president (1882–1945)	Winston Niles Rumfoord	*The Sirens of Titan* (1959) by Kurt Vonnegut
Delmore Schwartz (1913–1966)	Von Humboldt Fleisher	*Humboldt's Gift* (1975) by Saul Bellow
Al Sharpton, New York minister and civil rights activist (1954–)	Reverend Bacon	*The Bonfire of the Vanities* (1987) by Tom Wolfe
Percy Bysshe Shelley (1792–1822)	Scythrop Glowry	*Nightmare Abbey* (1818) by Thomas Love Peacock
Stephen Spender (1909–1995)	Brian Botsford	*While England Sleeps* (1995) by David Leavitt
Sir Leslie Stephen (1832–1904)	Mr. Ramsay	*To the Lighthouse* (1927) by Virginia Woolf
	Vernon Whitford	*The Egoist* (1879) by George Meredith
Irving Thalberg, movie producer (1899–1936)	Monroe Stahr	*The Last Tycoon* (1941) by F. Scott Fitzgerald
Alexander Woollcott (1887–1943)	Sheridan Whiteside	*The Man Who Came to Dinner* (1939) by George S. Kaufman and Moss Hart
Frank Lloyd Wright, American architect (1867–1959)	Howard Roark	*The Fountainhead* (1943) by Ayn Rand

Hector. Eldest son of King Priam of Troy in HOMER's epic the *ILIAD* (8th century B.C.). He is the noblest and greatest Trojan warrior in the Trojan War, but his fate is sealed when he kills ACHILLES' friend Patroclus. Achilles kills him in retaliation. Hector also appears in William SHAKESPEARE's play *TROILUS AND CRESSIDA* (c. 1601–2).

Heep, Uriah. "'Umble" law clerk in Charles DICKENS's novel *DAVID COPPERFIELD* (1850). Employed by Mr. Wickfield, lawyer for David COPPERFIELD's Aunt Betsey Trotwood, he eventually becomes Wickfield's partner, constantly scheming to destroy those he ostensibly serves. His name has become shorthand for an obsequious hypocrite.

Helena. 1. Heroine of William SHAKESPEARE's comedy *ALL'S WELL THAT ENDS WELL* (1602). A physician's daughter, she cures the ailing King of France and is rewarded with the hand of the reluctant Bertram, Count of Rossillon, who considers her his inferior. When he flees after marrying her, she devises a stratagem to force him to recognize her as his wife. 2. In Shakespeare's comedy *A MIDSUMMER NIGHT'S DREAM* (c. 1595–96), one of the mortal lovers whom the events of the night first mismatch, then unite.

Helen of Troy. In Greek legend, the world's most beautiful woman, daughter of ZEUS and Leda, wife of MENELAUS, king of Sparta. Her husband's determination to get her back from the Trojan prince PARIS caused the Trojan War. She appears in HOMER's epic the *ILIAD* (8th century B.C.); in EURIPIDES' tragedy *THE TROJAN WOMEN* (415 B.C.); in Euripides' *Helen* (*Helenē*, 412 B.C.), where we learn that the Helen who went to Troy was only a phantom, and the real Helen is sought by Menelaus in Egypt; and in versions of the FAUST legend, including Christopher MAR-LOWE's tragedy *DOCTOR FAUSTUS* (c. 1588) and J. W. von GOETHE's dramatic poem *FAUST*, Part II (1832), where Faust's magic conjures her as the greatest beauty of the past. Marlowe's Faustus addresses her: "Was this the face that launched a thousand ships?"

Helmer, Nora. Heroine of Henrik IBSEN's play *A DOLL'S HOUSE* (1879). Nora passed from her father's house to her husband's as a "doll-child," denied a sense of her own worth. As a newly-wed, she forged a signature to save her husband's life, and has struggled ever since to repay a secret loan. When this is discovered, her husband's selfish reaction causes her to realize she has been "living with a stranger" for eight years, and she slams the door on the doll-house marriage.

Henry IV. King of England (1367–1413; reigned 1399–1413) and first monarch of the House of Lancaster. In William SHAKESPEARE's history play *RICHARD II* (c. 1595), as Henry Bolingbroke, he overthrows Richard II and gains the throne. His reign is depicted in two other Shakespeare plays, *HENRY IV*, Parts I and II (c. 1597–98), in which he suppresses HOTSPUR's rebellion and passes on the throne to his son, HENRY V.

Henry V. King of England (1387–1422; reigned 1413–22). In William SHAKESPEARE's history plays *HENRY IV*, Parts I and II (c. 1597–98), he is Prince Hal, chiefly devoted to making merry with his friend FALSTAFF, but he breaks with Falstaff upon assuming the throne at the end of the latter play. As the title character of Shakespeare's *HENRY V* (c. 1598–99), he is a model soldier and statesman, defeating a larger French army at Agincourt and successfully wooing French princess Katharine.

Henry, Frederic. Narrator and protagonist of Ernest HEMINGWAY's novel *A FAREWELL TO ARMS* (1929). An American serving in the Italian army in World War I, he falls in love with British volunteer nurse Catherine BARKLEY, eventually deserting from the front to be with her when she is to give birth to their child.

Hickey [Theodore Hickman]. Traveling salesman and central character of Eugene O'NEILL's play *THE ICEMAN COMETH* (written 1939, performed 1946). Appearing sober for his annual visit to Harry HOPE's saloon, he harangues the regulars, compelling them to acknowledge the emptiness of their "pipe dreams."

Higgins, Henry. Professor of phonetics and protagonist of George Bernard SHAW's play *PYGMALION* (1913). To win a bet, he trains Cockney flower-seller Eliza DOOLITTLE in upper-class English and the social niceties, enabling her to pass as a duchess in society.

Holmes, Sherlock. Peerless detective of 221B Baker Street, London, in Sir Arthur Conan DOYLE's novels *A Study in Scarlet* (1887; book edition, 1888), *The Sign of Four* (1890), *The Hound of the Baskervilles* (1902), and *The Valley of Fear* (1915), and in 56 short stories, published in *THE ADVENTURES OF SHERLOCK HOLMES* (1892) and several other collections. The most celebrated of all literary amateur sleuths, he solves complex crimes with pure deductive reasoning, following his dictum, "When you have eliminated the impossible, whatever remains, however improbable, must be the truth." His friend and associate is Dr. John WATSON.

Hope, Harry. Owner of the New York watering hole (called the "No Chance Saloon" by a regular) in Eugene O'NEILL's play *THE ICEMAN COMETH* (written 1939, performed 1946). His 60th birthday celebration is the occasion for the visit by traveling salesman HICKEY that the play is centered around.

Horatio. HAMLET's loyal friend in William SHAKESPEARE's tragedy *HAMLET, PRINCE OF DENMARK* (c. 1601). It is he who informs Hamlet of the sightings of Hamlet's father's ghost, and, present at Hamlet's death, takes leave of him with the words "Good-night, sweet prince."

Hornblower, Horatio. British Napoleonic War–era naval hero in a series of ten popular novels by C. S. FORESTER: *The Happy Return* (published in the United States as *Beat to Quarters*, 1937), *A Ship of the Line* (1938), *Flying Colours* (1939), and seven others, concluding with *Hornblower and the Hotspur* (1962). The books trace Hornblower's career from midshipman to naval commander.

Hotspur [Sir Henry Percy]. Hot-tempered nobleman (1364–1403) and character in two of William SHAKESPEARE's history plays. In *RICHARD II* (c. 1595), he and his father, the earl of Northumberland, aid Henry Bolingbroke (HENRY IV) in winning the throne. In *HENRY IV*, Part I (c. 1597), he and Northumberland rebel against Henry IV. Hotspur is killed in the Battle of Shrewsbury by the king's son, Prince Hal (HENRY V).

Humbert, Humbert. Narrator of Vladimir NABOKOV's novel *LOLITA* (1955). A middle-aged European author, he marries the mother of 12-year-old "nymphet" Dolores Haze (LOLITA) to be near the girl. When her mother dies, he becomes Lolita's lover and traveling companion on two memorable motel-to-motel trips across mid-century America.

Hunter, Richard. *See* **Ragged Dick**

Hyde, Edward. *See* **Jekyll, Dr. Henry**

Iago. OTHELLO's ensign and antagonist in William SHAKESPEARE's tragedy *OTHELLO, THE MOOR OF VENICE* (1604). Angry that Othello has promoted Cassio instead of him, Iago schemes to destroy them both by making Othello believe that his faithful wife DESDEMONA has betrayed him with Cassio. The unsuspecting Moor styles him "Honest Iago."

Iphigenia. In Greek legend, eldest child of AGAMEMNON and Clytemnestra. Her father sacrifices her to gain favorable winds for the Greek armies to sail to the Trojan War; this motivates his murder by Clytemnestra when he returns from the war (as described in AESCHYLUS's tragedy *Agamemnon*, part of the *ORESTEIA*, 458 B.C.). In EURIPIDES' play *Iphigenia in Aulis* (*Iphigeneiaē en Aulidi*, c. 405 B.C.), she agrees to be sacrificed. In plays titled *Iphigenia in Tauris* by Euripides (*Iphigeneiaē en Taurois*, c. 414 B.C.) and J. W. von GOETHE (*Iphigenie auf Tauris*, published 1787, performed 1800), she is found alive in the savage land of Tauris, where Artemis transported her from her funeral pyre. There she intervenes to rescue her brother ORESTES.

Irina. *See* **Prozorov sisters**

Iseult [Iseult the Fair, Isolde, Isolt, Ysolt]. Legendary Irish princess and lover of TRISTAN [Tristram]. She and Tristan fall helplessly in love when they drink a magic potion on the way to the court of Tristan's uncle, King Mark [Marke] of Cornwall, whom she is to marry. The tragic story has often been told, notably in Gottfried von Strassburg's unfinished Middle High German epic poem *Tristan and Isolde* (*Tristan und Isolde*, c. 1210; one of the principal sources for Wagner's 1859 opera), and in Sir Thomas MALORY's romance *LE MORTE D'ARTHUR* (c. 1469–70).

Ishmael. Narrator of Herman MELVILLE's whaling epic *MOBY-DICK* (1851). "Call me Ishmael," he introduces himself, and relates the expedition of the *Pequod* in search of the white whale that has maimed Captain AHAB — an expedition that he alone survives. His assumed name, "God hears" in Hebrew, is that of the outcast son of Abraham and Hagar (handmaiden of Sarah) in the BIBLE (Genesis).

Ivanhoe, Sir Wilfred of. Chivalrous Saxon knight and title character of SIR WALTER SCOTT's novel *IVANHOE* (1819). Banished by his father for loving his father's ward, Rowena, Ivanhoe returns from the Holy Land, where he fought beside Richard Lionheart, to England, where further knightly challenges await him.

Jarndyce, John. Benevolent main character and party in the interminable court case *Jarndyce v. Jarndyce* in Charles DICKENS's novel *BLEAK HOUSE* (1853). A "humane but singular man," he serves as guardian to three other major characters, who live at his Hertfordshire estate, Bleak House: Esther Summerson and the "wards in Jarndyce," Richard Carstone and Ada Clare.

Jason. *See* **Compson family**

Javert, Police Inspector. Implacable detective in Victor HUGO's novel *LES MISÉRABLES* (1862). He discovers the true identity of former convict Jean VALJEAN after he has established a new life, and pursues him relentlessly.

Jeeves. Incomparably unflappable gentleman's gentleman to Bertie WOOSTER in P. G. WODE-HOUSE's story collection *MY MAN JEEVES* (1919), and many others in a long series of comic stories and novels. He first appeared as a minor character in a short story, "Extricating Young Gussie" (1917), and swiftly became as indispensable to readers as he is to his master, whom he frequently rescues from the most extraordinary jams.

Jekyll, Dr. Henry/Hyde, Edward. Title character(s) of Robert Louis STEVENSON's popular novella *DR. JEKYLL AND MR. HYDE* (1886). Investigating the duality of human nature, Dr. Jekyll tests a serum to separate out the evil aspects of the human personality. Afterward, he struggles to control his transformations into his own evil side, an ever-more-dominant separate personality he calls "Mr. Hyde."

Jesus. Founder of Christianity, regarded by Christians as the incarnate Son of God. 1. In the BIBLE's New Testament, the Gospels of Matthew, Mark, Luke, and John tell of his life (c. 4 B.C.–c. A.D. 29), crucifixion, and resurrection; the Book of Revelation prophesies his second coming at the end of time. 2. John MILTON's epic poem *Paradise Regained* (1671) recounts SATAN's temptation of Jesus in the wilderness; the latter's resistance regains the paradise lost by the fall of ADAM and EVE. 3. Nikos KAZANTZAKIS's novel *The Last Temptation of Christ* (1951) retells Jesus' life in the context of the author's idea of the conflict between flesh and spirit. 4. In Fyodor DOSTOYEVSKY's novel *THE BROTHERS KARAMAZOV* (1880), Ivan KARAMAZOV relates a parable in which Christ returns to earth during the Spanish Inquisition and is accused of heresy by the GRAND INQUISITOR.

Jim. Runaway slave and central character in Mark TWAIN's novel *HUCKLEBERRY FINN* (1884). With Huckleberry FINN, who is escaping from his brutal father, he flees on a raft down the Mississippi River. After many adventures, in the course of which he teaches Huck valuable lessons about the meaning of friendship and loyalty, Jim learns that his owner, Miss Watson, has died, and freed him in her will.

Jim, Lord [Tuan]. Title character of Joseph CONRAD's novel *LORD JIM* (1900). When he was chief mate on the *Patna*, he had fled in a lifeboat when he erroneously believed the damaged ship was sinking, and was formally condemned for cowardice. As observer MARLOW reports, he finds redemption as Tuan (Lord) Jim, leader of the Malay community of Patusan.

Jimson, Gulley. Self-involved artist and narrator of Joyce CARY's comic novel THE HORSE'S MOUTH (1944). In his struggles to continue to paint what he hopes will be his masterpieces, he stops at nothing, including theft, and accidentally kills a former model and lover, Sara Monday. He is a secondary character in the other novels of Cary's "First Trilogy": *Herself Surprised* (1941) and *To Be a Pilgrim* (1942).

Joad family (Granma, Grampa, Ma, Pa, Tom, Rose of Sharon, etc.). Oklahoma farm family in John STEINBECK's novel THE GRAPES OF WRATH (1939). Displaced by Depression-era dust storms, they head for California, where they are disparaged as "Okies" and exploited as migrant farm workers. As the family group is gradually dispersed, they develop solidarity with others in their plight.

Joan of Arc [Jeanne d'Arc, La Pucelle d'Orléans, The Maid of Orleans]. French national heroine (1412?–1431) and saint (canonized 1920). During the Hundred Years War, she led the troops of the French dauphin (King Charles VII) into battle; captured by the English, she was tried and burned as a heretic. She appears in many works, including William SHAKESPEARE's history play HENRY VI, Part I (c. 1591–92), where she is portrayed as a witch; Friedrich von SCHILLER's "romantic tragedy" *The Maid of Orleans* (*Die Jungfrau von Orleans*, 1801), where she dies in battle; and George Bernard SHAW's play SAINT JOAN (1923), where she is a prophet of an age yet to come.

Jocasta. In Greek mythology, queen of Thebes and mother and wife of OEDIPUS, who was fated to kill his father and marry his mother; abandoned in infancy, he was raised without knowledge of his true parentage. Jocasta marries him after he has slain her first husband, his father King Laius, and becomes the mother of his children and siblings, ANTIGONE, Ismene, Eteocles, and Polyneices. Her story is told by SOPHOCLES in the play OEDIPUS THE KING (c. 430 B.C.).

John, Annie. Protagonist of Jamaica KINCAID's novel *Annie John* (1985), about a girl growing up on Antigua. Annie lives her day-to-day life under the strong influence of her mother, until she is 17 and leaves by herself for England.

John, the Savage. Central character in Aldous HUXLEY's anti-utopian novel BRAVE NEW WORLD (1932). A savage in a scientifically controlled world, he is brought from the "Savage Reservation" to caste-bound London, where his knowledge of forbidden matters such as the works of William SHAKESPEARE aids him in a debate with the resident World Controller about the state of society.

Jones, Brutus. Black prison escapee who has become the "emperor" of a West Indian island in Eugene O'NEILL's play THE EMPEROR JONES (1920). Learning of a rebellion, he flees into the forest, and relives episodes from his past in a series of nightmarish vignettes enacted by "ghosts," which he believes the rebels have sent after him.

Jones, Tom. Title character and protagonist of Henry FIELDING's comic novel TOM JONES (1749). Found as an infant in Squire ALLWORTHY's bed, he is raised as his ward, and falls in love with comely neighbor Sophia Western, promised to Allworthy's odious nephew Blifil. Youthful exuberance and Blifil's machinations cause young Tom to be banished from Allworthy's home, propelling him into a series of adventures in quest of his fortune and the hand of Sophia.

Jordan, Robert. Protagonist of Ernest HEMINGWAY's Spanish Civil War novel FOR WHOM THE BELL TOLLS (1940). An American Loyalist volunteer, he is part of a group planning the demolition of a bridge; with one of them, war victim Maria, he shares an intense, doomed passion. Although he comes to question the validity of his cause, indeed of all causes, he acts with courage in extreme straits for his friends' sake: "You can do nothing for yourself, but perhaps you can do something for another."

Joseph K. Central character in Franz KAFKA's novel *THE TRIAL* (1925). A bank employee, he is arrested "one fine morning...without having done anything wrong" and prosecuted by a faceless authority for a nameless crime.

Jourdain, Monsieur. Wealthy tradesman and title character of MOLIÈRE's *THE BOURGEOIS GENTLEMAN* (1670). Wanting to become a gentleman, Jourdain is tutored in fashionable matters such as music, dancing, and fencing; a philosophy master informs him that without knowing it, he has been speaking "prose" all his life.

Juan, Don. Legendary womanizer of Seville, introduced to literature as Don Juan Tenorio in a tragedy by Tirso de Molina (1571?–1648), *Don Juan, the Libertine of Seville and the Stone Guest* (*El Burlador de Sevilla y el Convadado de Piedra*, 1630); Mozart's opera *Don Giovanni* (1787) is partly based on this source. He appears in many other works, including MOLIÈRE's comedy *Don Juan* (*Dom Juan; ou, Le Festin de Pierre*, 1665); Lord BYRON's satire *DON JUAN* (1819–24), in which he is a lover and adventurer; *Don Juan Tenorio* (1844), a popular Spanish play by José Zorrilla (1817–93); and George Bernard SHAW's satirical play MAN AND SUPERMAN (1915), in which his modern counterpart, Jack Tanner, flees from a woman bent on matrimony, and in the third act, "Don Juan in Hell," dreams of his illustrious "ancestor."

Juliet. *See* **Capulet, Juliet**

Julius Caesar. *See* **Caesar, Julius**

Jupiter. *See* **Zeus**

Karamazov family (Fyodor; Dmitri, *sometimes called* **Mitya; Ivan; Alexei,** *usually called* **Alyosha).** Provincial businessman and his three sons, main characters of Fyodor DOSTOYEVSKY's novel *THE BROTHERS KARAMAZOV* (1880). The father, Fyodor, and his sons by two wives embody contrasting emotional and moral types: Fyodor, the reprobate; Dmitri, the sensualist; Ivan, the intellectual; Alyosha, the spiritual and compassionate. There is also Smerdyakov,

Fyodor's illegitimate son, who represents all the brothers' worst qualities.

Karenina, Anna. Passionate heroine of Leo TOLSTOY's tragic novel *ANNA KARENINA* (1878). Unhappily married to an unfeeling bureaucrat, she falls in love with a young officer, Count Alexei VRONSKY, and leaves her husband and young son for his sake. She gives birth to her lover's child and travels abroad with him, but finding on her return that society can come to terms with Vronsky's behavior, but not with hers, she commits suicide.

Kate [Katharina, Katharine; Katharina Minola]. Feisty title character of William SHAKESPEARE's comedy *THE TAMING OF THE SHREW* (c. 1593). Known as "the Shrew," she is "renown'd in Padua for her scolding tongue." Her wealthy father insists that she must be married before her much-courted younger sister Bianca may wed, but she keeps all suitors at bay with her ferocious disposition and acid invective, until PETRUCHIO finds a way to "tame" her temper and (perhaps) win her heart.

Kennicott, Carol. Reform-minded protagonist of SINCLAIR LEWIS's novel *MAIN STREET* (1920). A librarian from St. Paul who marries a doctor from the Minnesota hamlet of Gopher Prairie, she arrives in town planning to "get my hands on one of those prairie towns and make it beautiful," but is stymied by the provincialism and hypocrisy of townspeople devoted to the status quo.

Kinbote, Charles [Vseslav Botkin, Charles Xavier Vseslav]. Delusional scholar in Vladimir NABOKOV's novel *PALE FIRE* (1962). He is presented as the author of an extensive exegesis of the final, autobiographical poem of slain American poet John Shade, the two works together comprising the novel. Kinbote, who claims to be Charles II, exiled king of the obscure country of Zembla, finds the poem replete with (imaginary) references to himself.

Konstantin. *See* **Treplev, Konstantin**

Kowalski, Stanley and **Stella.** Central characters of TENNESSEE WILLIAMS's play *A STREETCAR*

NAMED DESIRE (1947). Stella has left a world of decayed Southern gentility for marriage to the coarse, virile Stanley. Expecting her first child, she is torn between loyalty to her desperate older sister, Blanche DUBOIS, and to her sometimes brutal husband, who wants to be king in his own home.

Kubla Khan [Kublai Khan, Khubilai Khan]. Celebrated Mongol emperor of China (1216?–1294; reigned 1260–94). In Samuel Taylor COLERIDGE's poem "KUBLA KHAN; OR, A VISION IN A DREAM" (written 1797, published 1816), the poet imagines him as the lord of Xanadu (K'ai-p'ing or Shang-tu, in Mongolia), where he orders the construction of "a stately pleasure-dome" in a fantastic landscape: "It was a miracle of rare device, a sunny pleasure-dome with caves of ice."

Kumar, Hari. Indian journalist and central character of PAUL SCOTT's tetralogy of novels, *THE RAJ QUARTET* (1966–75). Educated at an English public school, Kumar falls in love with a young Englishwoman, Daphne Manners. When she is gang-raped during a riot, he is falsely accused of being one of her rapists, and is imprisoned despite her refusal to incriminate him.

Kurtz, Mr. [Mistah]. Notorious ivory trader and central character in Joseph CONRAD's novella *HEART OF DARKNESS* (1902). Once a proponent of "civilizing" Africa, when he is found by MARLOW deep in the Congolese jungle, he has "taken a high seat amongst the devils of the land," and controls an empire of "savages" who raid the countryside for ivory. The character is based on an ivory trader Conrad encountered under similar circumstances, Georges-Antoine Klein.

Ladislaw, Will. Unconventional central character in GEORGE ELIOT's novel *MIDDLEMARCH* (1872). A part-Polish cousin of the middle-aged scholar Edward CASAUBON, husband of Dorothea BROOKE, Ladislaw is his opposite in every way — charming, artistic, and energetic — and he and Dorothea fall in love.

Laertes. 1. Son of POLONIUS and brother of OPHELIA in William SHAKESPEARE's tragedy *HAMLET, PRINCE OF DENMARK* (c. 1601). Bent on avenging his father's slaying and his sister's madness and death by drowning, Laertes plots to kill HAMLET under the guise of a duel.
2. Father of ODYSSEUS, who succeeded him as king of Ithaca. He appears in HOMER's epic poem the *ODYSSEY* (8th century B.C.).

Lancelot of the Lake, Sir [Launcelot, Lancelot du Lac]. Legendary knight of the Round Table. In Thomas MALORY's romance *LE MORTE D'ARTHUR* (c. 1469–70), he is a paragon of chivalry, but his illicit romance with King ARTHUR's wife, Queen GUINEVERE, helps to bring about the downfall of Camelot. He appears in many other works, including CHRÉTIEN DE TROYES's romance *Lancelot (Le Chevalier de la Charrette; ou, Lancelot,* c. 1180); Alfred, Lord TENNYSON's poetic cycle *IDYLLS OF THE KING* (1859–85); and T. H. White's tetralogy of novels, *THE ONCE AND FUTURE KING* (1938–58).

Lara [Lara Guishar, Lara Antipova; Larissa]. Central character of Boris PASTERNAK's novel *DOCTOR ZHIVAGO* (1957). The daughter of a Moscow dressmaker, she marries a revolutionary, then becomes the mistress and great love of the title character, Yuri ZHIVAGO, after they meet during World War I. Based in part on Pasternak's mistress Olga Ivinskaya (1912–1995).

Latour, Jean. French missionary and main character of Willa CATHER's novel *DEATH COMES FOR THE ARCHBISHOP* (1927). At the end of his life, he recalls how he endured many hardships to build a diocese in the territory of New Mexico and erect the cathedral of Santa Fe. Based on Archbishop John Baptist Lamy (1814–1888).

Laura. Beloved of PETRARCH and the idealized central figure in his collection of 366 Italian love lyrics known as the *Canzoniere (Song Book)* or *Rime (Rhymes)* (c. 1336); traditionally identified as Laure de Noves (1308–1348), though the identification is disputed. Petrarch tells us that he first saw "Laura" on Good Friday, 1327, in an Avignon church; it is not clear whether he ever met her. In his verse, she is associated with the myth of Daphne, who was pursued by Apollo and transformed into a laurel tree, symbol of poetic achievement. Petrarch himself was formally crowned with laurel leaves as Poet Laureate of Rome in 1341.

Lear, King. Title character of William SHAKE-SPEARE's tragedy *KING LEAR* (c. 1605–6). Betrayed by his elder daughters, GONERIL and REGAN, to whom he imprudently willed his kingdom during his lifetime, he wanders his realm in madness, served only by his fool and a man he had unjustly banished. Majestic in his adversity ("Every inch a king"), he rages at the elements and his fate: "Blow, winds, and crack your cheeks! rage! blow!" His mind is restored by a reunion with his youngest daughter, CORDELIA, who truly loves him.

Leary, Macon. Alienated travel writer and protagonist of Anne TYLER's novel *The Accidental Tourist* (1985). Increasingly isolated after the death of his son and his separation from his wife, he writes guidebooks for business travelers who, like himself, hate to travel. His life starts to change when he begins a relationship with Muriel Pritchett, a quirky dog obedience trainer.

Lee, Lorelei. Diarist and quintessential flapper in Anita LOOS's comic novel *Gentlemen Prefer Blondes: The Illuminating Diary of a Professional Lady* (1925). Sent on a European tour by her gentleman friend, the "Button King," she is unimpressed by continental manners ("Kissing your hand may make you feel very very good, but a diamond and safire bracelet lasts forever"), but enjoys meeting luminaries like "Dr. Froyd." Eventually, she marries a wealthy New Yorker she met on the Orient Express. The story continues in *But Gentlemen Marry Brunettes* (1928). Loos coauthored stage and musical adaptations; Marilyn Monroe played Lorelei in Howard Hawks's 1953 film version.

Legree, Simon. Drunken Yankee plantation owner who buys the slave Uncle TOM after Little EVA's father dies in Harriet Beecher STOWE's antislavery novel *UNCLE TOM'S CABIN* (1852).

Merciless toward his slaves, he whips Uncle Tom to death. His name has become a synonym for a brutal authority figure.

Lestrade, Inspector. Scotland Yard inspector whose sleuthing abilities are hopelessly outmatched by Sherlock HOLMES's in Arthur Conan DOYLE's *THE ADVENTURES OF SHERLOCK HOLMES* (1892) and other stories and novels about the great private eye. Lestrade is described as "a little sallow, rat-faced, dark-eyed fellow" (A *Study in Scarlet*, 1887) who can be useful to Holmes; although "absolutely devoid of reason, he is as tenacious as a bulldog when he once understands what he has to do" ("The Adventure of the Cardboard Box," 1893). He also appears in *The Sign of Four* (1890) and *The Hound of the Baskervilles* (1902).

Leverkühn, Adrian. *See* **Faust**

Light, Christina. *See* **Casamassima, Princess**

Lippi, Fra Lippo [Filippo]. Florentine painter-monk (c. 1406–1469) and title character of ROBERT BROWNING's dramatic monologue "FRA LIPPO LIPPI" (in *Men and Women*, 1855). While in the service of Renaissance art patron Cosimo de' Medici (1389–1464), the friar is caught leaving a house "where sportive ladies leave their doors ajar." He defends his life and art in a colorful verbal self-portrait.

Little Eva. *See* **Eva**

Little Nell. *See* **Nell**

Lolita [Dolores Haze, Mrs. Richard F. Schiller; Lo, Dolly]. Title character of Vladimir NABOKOV's novel *LOLITA* (1955), whom her stepfather and lover Humbert HUMBERT calls "light of my life, fire of my loins." She is 12 years old when Humbert first sees her, and 14 when he loses her to Clare QUILTY. Humbert coins the word "nymphet" for girls of Lolita's "fey grace," who appear to him as "nymphic (that is, demoniac)" in nature.

Loman, Willy. Traveling salesman whose decline forms the story of ARTHUR MILLER's drama *DEATH OF A SALESMAN* (1949). Fired from his job, he reviews a life of unrealized dreams, including those he had for his two grown sons.

In his wife Linda's words, "He's not the finest character that ever lived. But he's a human being, and a terrible thing is happening to him. So attention must be paid."

Lonigan, "Studs" [William]. Title character in a trilogy of novels by James T. FARRELL, published collectively as *STUDS LONIGAN* (1935). In the years from 1916 to the beginning of the Great Depression, Lonigan, son of a respectable Irish Catholic family on Chicago's South Side, moves from robust youth to dissolute manhood to impoverishment and early death.

Lopakhin, Yermolai Alexeyevich. Pragmatic businessman in Anton CHEKHOV's melancholy drama *THE CHERRY ORCHARD* (1904). The descendant of serfs on the Ranevsky estate, he describes for Madame RANEVSKAYA how the family can escape penury by sacrificing their beloved cherry orchard. When she refuses, he himself buys the entire estate at auction.

Lothario. Notorious libertine, "that haughty gallant, gay Lothario," in a tragedy by Nicholas Rowe (1674–1718), *The Fair Penitent* (1703). After Lothario is found with a married woman, her husband kills him in a duel. His name has become an eponym for a heedless, but courtly, womanizer. See also JUAN, DON.

Lucifer. *See* Satan

Lulu. *Femme fatale* in Frank WEDEKIND's plays *Earth Spirit* (*Erdgeist*, 1898) and *PANDORA'S BOX* (1904). A beautiful, amoral woman whom newspaper tycoon Dr. Ludwig Schön had rescued from the streets as a child, she is pursued by a series of men (and one woman), all of whom die on her account. Her final rendezvous is with Jack the Ripper.

Lyndon, Barry. *See* **Barry Lyndon, Redmond**

Macbeth. King of Scotland (d. 1057; reigned 1040–57). His rise to power and his murderous reign are dramatized in William SHAKESPEARE's tragedy *MACBETH* (c. 1605). Driven by ambition and spurred on by his wife, he slays King DUNCAN and takes the throne.

Macbeth, Lady. Wife of MACBETH in William SHAKESPEARE's tragedy *MACBETH* (c. 1605). She goads her husband to murder, then is overwhelmed by guilt; sleepwalking, she despairs of cleansing her hands of bloodstains: "Out, damned spot! out, I say."

Macomber, Francis. Wealthy American title character of Ernest HEMINGWAY's short story "THE SHORT, HAPPY LIFE OF FRANCIS MACOMBER" (1936). Unable to face down a charging lion while on safari in Africa, he is also unable to thwart his wife Margot's interest in the more "manly" British guide Wilson.

Maggie [Maggie Pollitt; Maggie the Cat]. Tenacious wife of BIG DADDY's favorite son, Brick, in TENNESSEE WILLIAMS's play *CAT ON A HOT TIN ROOF* (1955). The restless "cat" of the title, she tries everything she can think of to reverse her husband's hurtful rejection of her, and give her a chance to produce an heir to the Pollitt plantation.

Mahon, Christy [Christopher]. Title character of J. M. SYNGE's comedy *THE PLAYBOY OF THE WESTERN WORLD* (1907). Believing he has killed his bullying father, he captivates the Irish village where he takes refuge with his boasting about the deed, until his father turns up, very much alive.

Maigret, Inspector Jules. Gifted detective in 75 mystery novels and 28 stories by Georges SIMENON (published 1931–72). Among them are *The Sailor's Rendezvous* (*Au Rendez-vous des Terre-Neuvas*, 1931), *The Crime of Inspector Maigret* (*Le Pendu de Saint-Pholien*, 1931), and *Maigret Returns* (*Maigret*, 1934). The pipe-smoking Maigret uses pragmatism and his knowledge of human psychology to solve cases.

Malaprop, Mrs. Meddlesome, language-mangling aunt of romantic lead Lydia Languish in Richard Brinsley SHERIDAN's comedy *THE RIVALS* (1775). Her name is derived from the French *mal à propos*, meaning "inappropriate"; her infallible sense for the wrong, sound-alike word (usually a polysyllabic near miss: "A progeny of learning") has granted her the immortality of a word in her honor: malapropism.

Malvolio. Supporting character in William SHAKESPEARE's comedy *TWELFTH NIGHT; OR, WHAT YOU WILL* (c. 1600). Obtrusive steward to Olivia, he is tricked into believing he is the one whom Olivia desires, instead of "Cesario" (VIOLA in disguise).

Mannon, Lavinia. *See* **Electra**

Mannon, Orin. *See* **Orestes**

Marchmain, Lord and **Lady** [**Marquis** and **Marchioness of Marchmain**]. In EVELYN WAUGH's novel *BRIDESHEAD REVISITED* (1945), parents of central characters Lord Sebastian FLYTE and Lady Julia, both beloved of the narrator, Charles RYDER. The devout, domineering Lady Marchmain is from an old Catholic family; Lord Marchmain, who converted to Catholicism upon his marriage, has left the Church and his family, and lives in Venice with his mistress.

Mark Antony. *See* **Antony, Mark**

Marley, Jacob. Deceased partner of Ebenezer SCROOGE in Charles DICKENS's Christmas fable *A CHRISTMAS CAROL* (1843). On Christmas Eve, Marley returns as a ghost, to tell Scrooge that he will be visited by other ghosts offering visions of Christmases past, present, and future.

Marlow, Charlie. Partly autobiographical central character of Joseph CONRAD's novella *HEART OF DARKNESS* (1902). He narrates most of the story, which describes his journey into the central African jungle to bring back famed ivory trader KURTZ. The journey becomes a metaphorical excursion into the heart of the darkness in the human soul. Marlow also appears in other novels by Conrad, such as *LORD JIM* (1900).

Marlowe, Philip. Hard-boiled Los Angeles private eye in seven mystery novels by Raymond CHANDLER: *The Big Sleep* (1939), *Farewell, My Lovely* (1940), *The High Window* (1942), *The Lady in the Lake* (1943), *The Little Sister* (1949), *The Long Goodbye* (1954), and *Playback* (1958); an eighth, *Poodle Springs*, was unfinished at Chandler's death. An incorrupt-

ible knight-errant in a corrupt world, Marlowe operates by his own code of chivalry. Humphrey Bogart, in Howard Hawks's *The Big Sleep* (1946), was the most memorable of the many cinematic Marlowes.

Marner, Silas. Embittered linen weaver and title character of GEORGE ELIOT's novel *SILAS MARNER* (1861). Falsely accused of theft, he lives as a friendless miser until his gold is stolen. Shortly afterward, he receives a new treasure in the form of a little girl he finds asleep on his hearth. Naming her Eppie, he comes to love her, and is redeemed as a human being.

Marple, Miss Jane. Spry, lucid elderly spinster and amateur sleuth in 12 detective novels and 20 short stories by Agatha CHRISTIE, including *The Murder at the Vicarage* (1930) and *A Pocket Full of Rye* (1953); last in the series is *Sleeping Murder* (written in the 1940s, published 1976). Miss Marple relies on intuition, unobtrusive powers of observation, and her intimate knowledge of the inhabitants of her village, St. Mary Mead, to ferret out killers.

Masha. *See* **Prozorov sisters**

Mason, Perry. Surefire defense attorney in ERLE STANLEY GARDNER's detective novels *The Case of the Velvet Claws* (1933), *The Case of the Perjured Parrot* (1939), and some 80 others. He is invariably successful in clearing his invariably innocent clients by fingering the real guilty party in court. One of the highest-selling series in crime fiction. As embodied by Raymond Burr, Mason was also among the most durable of TV sleuths.

Masterson, Sky [Obadiah]. Colorful New York schemer and gambler who falls for a Salvation Army lassie in Damon RUNYON's short story "The Idyll of Miss Sarah Brown" (1933; published in the collection *Runyon à la Carte*, 1944), which is the chief source for *Guys and Dolls*, the Broadway musical (1950) and movie (1955).

Matzerath, Oskar. Narrator of Günter GRASS's novel *THE TIN DRUM* (1959). Having contrived to stop growing at age three, mute except for glass-shattering shrieks and the beating of his toy drum, Oskar observes the Third Reich, World War II, and the first years of the new Germany from the point of view of an anarchic child.

McCoy, Sherman. High-flying New York financier and protagonist of TOM WOLFE's satiric first novel, *THE BONFIRE OF THE VANITIES* (1987).

Medea. In Greek mythology, sorceress and wife of Jason. In the epic *Argonautica* (3rd century B.C.) of APOLLONIUS OF RHODES, she helps Jason and the Argonauts to steal the Golden Fleece from her father, King Aeëtes of Colchis. In EURIPIDES' play *MEDEA* (431 B.C.), she murders Jason's new bride (daughter of King Creon of Corinth) and her two children by Jason to punish him for leaving her for another woman.

Meeber, Carrie [Caroline; Carrie Madenda]. Title character of Theodore DREISER's novel *SISTER CARRIE* (1900). Fleeing Midwestern rural life, young Carrie works briefly in a Chicago shoe factory, then lives with and discards two men, eventually rising to Broadway stardom as "Carrie Madenda."

Mellors, Oliver. A main character in D. H. LAWRENCE's *LADY CHATTERLEY'S LOVER* (1928). A disgruntled self-made intellectual from a working-class background who speaks both broad dialect and "standard" English, Mellors served as an officer in World War I. He is working as gamekeeper for Sir Clifford Chatterley when he begins an affair with Sir Clifford's wife, Lady Constance CHATTERLEY.

Menard, Pierre. Title character of Jorge Luis BORGES's short story "Pierre Menard, Author of Don Quixote" ("Pierre Menard, Autor del Quijote," 1939; included in the collection *FIC-TIONS*, 1944). Menard, a brilliant Symbolist writer, had undertaken the task of recreating verbatim (although not copying) CERVANTES's *DON QUIXOTE* (1605–15), but he completed only a couple of chapters.

Menelaus. In Greek mythology, king of Lacedaemon (Sparta), brother of AGAMEMNON, and husband of HELEN OF TROY. The abduction of his wife by the Trojan prince PARIS precipitates the Trojan War. He succeeds in retrieving her at war's end. He appears in HOMER's epics the *ILIAD* and the *ODYSSEY* (8th century B.C.) and in three plays by EURIPIDES: *Andromache* (c. 425 B.C.), *THE TROJAN WOMEN* (415 B.C.), and *Helen* (*Helenē*, 412 B.C.).

Mephistopheles [Mephistophilis, Mephisto]. In versions of the FAUST legend, including Christopher MARLOWE's tragedy *DOCTOR FAUS-TUS* (c. 1588) and J. W. von GOETHE's dramatic poem *FAUST*, Parts I and II (published 1808 and 1832, performed 1829 and 1854), the emissary of SATAN with whom Faust concludes his fatal pact. In Marlowe, he is a "servant to great Lucifer" who appears to Faust drawn by his blasphemies, not his conjuring. In Goethe, he is a witty, urbane gentleman-devil who accompanies Faust on his travels.

Merlin. Magician and adviser to King ARTHUR. In Thomas MALORY's romance *LE MORTE D'ARTHUR* (c. 1469–70), he helps Arthur to gain the throne. He is a major character in most Arthurian works, including Alfred, Lord TEN-NYSON's poetic cycle *IDYLLS OF THE KING* (1859–85), Mark TWAIN's fantasy *A CONNECTI-CUT YANKEE IN KING ARTHUR'S COURT* (1889), and T. H. White's tetralogy of novels, *THE ONCE AND FUTURE KING* (1938–58), and a minor character in many others, such as Ludovico ARIOSTO's *ORLANDO FURIOSO* (1532) and Miguel de CERVANTES's *DON QUIXOTE* (1605–15).

Meursault. Thirty-year-old shipping clerk and dispassionate narrator of Albert CAMUS's novel *THE STRANGER* (1942). For failing to react emotionally to such events as his mother's death and his own killing of another man, he is described at his murder trial as "an inhuman monster wholly without moral sense." He faces death comforted by the thought of the "benign indifference of the universe."

Micawber, Mr. (Wilkins). Chronically debt-ridden but eternally hopeful character in Charles DICKENS's novel *DAVID COPPERFIELD* (1850). Based in part on Dickens's father, he lives in the conviction that something will "turn up." His wife, Emma Micawber, stands by her man, repeatedly avowing, "I never will desert Mr. Micawber."

Minderbinder, Milo. Squadron mess officer and ultimate capitalist in Joseph HELLER's antiwar novel CATCH-22 (1961). Amid the chaos of the Italian campaign in World War II, Lieutenant Minderbinder establishes "M & M Enterprises," a multinational black market "syndicate" that purports to put the war on a "businesslike basis."

Minola, Katherina. *See* **Kate**

Miranda. Daughter of PROSPERO and central character of William SHAKESPEARE's last play, THE TEMPEST (c. 1611). At age three, she was cast away on an island with her father, and has seen no other human beings in the 12 years since except the monstrous CALIBAN. She falls in love with young Ferdinand, son of King Alonso, when Prospero causes the royal party to be shipwrecked.

Mitty, Walter. Middle-aged suburbanite who imagines acts of derring-do on a trip into town in James THURBER's short story "The Secret Life of Walter Mitty" (1939; included in the collection *My World—And Welcome to It,* 1942). After envisioning himself as a Navy pilot, a surgeon, a crack shot, and a bomber squadron leader, he returns to his henpecked mundane existence. "Walter Mittyish" has become an adjective describing a bumbling daydreamer.

Moncrieff, Algernon [Algy]. Quintessential dandy and central character in Oscar WILDE's comedy THE IMPORTANCE OF BEING EARNEST (1895). He embodies Wilde's philosophy "that we should treat all the trivial things of life seriously, and all the serious things of life with sincere and studied triviality." This includes his courtship, under the assumed but desirable name of Ernest, of his best friend Jack WORTHING's ward, Cecily CARDEW.

Montague, Romeo. Title character and one of the "star-cross'd lovers" in William SHAKESPEARE's tragedy ROMEO AND JULIET (1595). Scion of a prominent Verona family, young Romeo falls in love with Juliet CAPULET, daughter of his family's bitter enemies, the Capulets, and marries her in secret. His passion is expressed in such memorable lines as "But, soft! what light through yonder window breaks? / It is the east, and Juliet is the sun!"

Morel, Paul. Sensitive protagonist of D. H. LAWRENCE's autobiographical novel SONS AND LOVERS (1913).The second of three sons, he becomes his mother's favorite child when the eldest son dies. Into adulthood, he is torn between his duty to a possessive mother and his artistic aspirations and sexual desire.

Moriarty, Professor James. Arch-nemesis of Sherlock HOLMES in Sir Arthur Conan DOYLE's short stories "The Final Problem" (1893) and "The Adventure of the Empty House" (1903), and his novel *The Valley of Fear* (1915). A mathematician who uses his "extraordinary mental powers" to organize the London criminal world, he is called "the Napoleon of Crime." He is said to have been modeled on Adam Worth (1844–1902), a noted thief.

Morse, Detective Chief Inspector [E. Morse, Endeavour Morse]. Irascible, beer-drinking, Wagner-loving, crossword puzzle–solving pride of the Thames Valley Constabulary in 13 novels, from *Last Bus to Woodstock* (1975) to *The Remorseful Day* (1999), and a story collection, *Morse's Greatest Mystery* (1993), by Colin Dexter (1930–). Brilliant, if not infallible, Inspector Morse copes with the surprisingly high body count in the placid university town of Oxford with the help of his faithful sidekick, Sergeant Lewis. His first name was revealed only on the last page of the next-to-last novel, *Death Is Now My Neighbour* (1996). In the popular television series, John Thaw embodied Morse and Kevin Whately was Lewis.

Motes, Hazel [Haze]. Protagonist of FLANNERY O'CONNOR's novel WISE BLOOD (1952). Motes comes to the town of Taulkinham, Tennessee, preaching the gospel of the "church without Christ, where the blind stay blind, the lame stay lame, and them that's dead stays that way." His given name comes from the Hebrew for "he who sees God."

Myshkin, Prince [Lev Nikolayevitch]. Guileless title character and protagonist of Fyodor DOSTOYEVSKY's novel *THE IDIOT* (1874). Although his naive frankness and simplicity earn him the nickname "the idiot," he is distinguished by his deep compassion for the suffering of others. Like Dostoyevsky, he suffers from epilepsy.

Nell [Little Nell, Nelly; Nell Trent]. Pathetic young heroine of Charles DICKENS's novel *The Old Curiosity Shop* (1841). When she and her emotionally disturbed grandfather are forced to flee because of his gambling debts to the dwarf Quilp, she is his faithful companion in their wanderings across the bleak English countryside. Her death scene agitated England at the time of the novel's serialization; later, it was often cited as an example of Victorian sentimental excess. Oscar WILDE quipped, "One must have a heart of stone to read the death of little Nell without laughing."

Nemo, Captain. Mysterious, misanthropic captain of the marvelous submarine *Nautilus* in Jules VERNE's novel *TWENTY THOUSAND LEAGUES UNDER THE SEA* (1869–70). His name means "no one"; he has lost family and country, and wages a private naval war against the unidentified "accursed nation" responsible for his loss. His vast erudition and astounding (but scientifically plausible) technological innovations amaze the three men he holds captive during a year's adventures. Nemo also appears in Verne's novel *The Mysterious Island* (*L'Île Mystérieuse*, 1874–75).

Nickleby, Nicholas. Title character of Charles DICKENS's novel *NICHOLAS NICKLEBY* (1839). "A young man of an impetuous temper and of little or no experience" seeking his fortune after his father's death, he is sent to teach at the appalling Dotheboys Hall, run by the odious Squeers. Later, he joins a troupe of traveling actors, then proceeds to other alternately comic and melodramatic adventures in London.

Nina. *See* **Zarechnaya, Nina Mikhailovna**

Oberon. King of the fairies in William SHAKESPEARE's comedy *A MIDSUMMER NIGHT'S DREAM* (c. 1595–96). Quarreling with fairy queen TITANIA over an Indian boy, he has his servant PUCK fetch a magic herb, whose juice will "make or man or woman madly dote / Upon the next live creature that it sees." Titania and two pairs of inadvertently mismatched mortal lovers become the herb's victims before Oberon commands Puck to restore order.

Oblomov, Ilya Ilyich. Chronically idle title character of Ivan GONCHAROV's satirical novel *OBLOMOV* (1859). An extreme example of a 19th-century Russian literary type, the "superfluous man," Oblomov is a landowner who lives in the city and spends much of his time in bed dreaming about what he might do if he got up. He eventually perishes of his "oblomovism" or "oblomovitis," Goncharov's term for the lethargy of the idle aristocracy that his antihero exemplifies.

Odette [de Crécy Swann]. A main character in Marcel PROUST's multipart novel *REMEMBRANCE OF THINGS PAST* (1913–27). A beautiful courtesan, she figures most prominently in the first book, *Swann's Way* (*Du Côté de Chez Swann*, 1913). She marries Paris gentleman Charles SWANN and bears him a daughter, Gilberte.

Odysseus. Resourceful king of Ithaca in Greek mythology and hero of HOMER's epic the *ODYSSEY* (8th century B.C.). In Homer's earlier *ILIAD* (8th century B.C.), he was one of the Greek leaders in the Trojan War; in the *Odyssey*, he struggles to get home to his wife PENELOPE and son Telemachus after the war, surviving by his wits through many adventures. He appears in many other works, including SOPHOCLES' play *Philoctetes* (*Philoktētēs*, 409 B.C.), William SHAKESPEARE's play *TROILUS AND CRESSIDA* (c. 1601–2), Heinrich von KLEIST's tragedy *Penthesilea* (published 1808, performed 1876), and Nikos KAZANTZAKIS's epic poem *The Odyssey* (*Odysseia*, 1938). Known as Ulysses to the Romans, he provided the model for LEOPOLD BLOOM in James JOYCE's novel *ULYSSES* (1922).

Oedipus. In Greek mythology, ill-fated king of Thebes who unwittingly kills his father Laius and marries his mother JOCASTA, fulfilling a prophecy that he was fated to do so. He becomes father of his own half-siblings, including ANTIGONE. Upon discovering the truth, he blinds himself. Earlier, he saved Thebes from the Sphinx by solving its riddle. His story is told most memorably by SOPHOCLES in the plays OEDIPUS THE KING (c. 430 B.C.) and *Oedipus at Colonus* (*Oidipous epi Kolōnōi*, performed posthumously 401 B.C.). Other versions of the legend include SENECA's play *Oedipus* (1st century A.D.) and Jean COCTEAU's play THE INFERNAL MACHINE (1934).

O'Hara, Scarlett. Headstrong heroine of MARGARET MITCHELL's Civil War–era novel GONE WITH THE WIND (1936), introduced in the book's opening line: "Scarlett O'Hara was not beautiful, but men seldom realized it." A spoiled coquette in antebellum days, she is aided by her ruthlessness and solid business sense in rebuilding her family's plantation, Tara, after the war. In love with the married Ashley Wilkes, she weds three other men, including Rhett BUTLER, realizing too late that he is the real love of her life.

Okonkwo. Fiery-tempered Ibo leader and protagonist of Chinua ACHEBE's novel THINGS FALL APART (1958). A powerful man in his village in 1880s Nigeria, he is exiled for seven years when he accidentally kills another villager. Upon returning, he finds that British colonial forces are trying to eradicate the traditions he was raised in.

Olenska, Countess Ellen. Central character in Edith WHARTON's novel of 1870s New York, THE AGE OF INNOCENCE (1920). After separating from her Polish husband, Countess Olenska returns to her native New York, where she disturbs upper-class society with her unconventional, European manners, and kindles love in Newland Archer, her cousin's fiancé.

Olga. *See* **Prozorov sisters**

Ophelia. Daughter of POLONIUS and sister of LAERTES in William SHAKESPEARE's tragedy HAMLET, PRINCE OF DENMARK (c. 1601). Following her father's wishes, she rejects HAMLET's attentions, and endures his rejection of her in his "madness" ("Get thee to a nunnery"). After Hamlet kills Polonius, she goes mad, singing snatches of old songs, and dies by drowning.

Orestes. In Greek mythology, son of AGAMEMNON, brother of IPHIGENIA and ELECTRA. In AESCHYLUS's plays *The Libation Bearers* and *The Eumenides* (part of the ORESTEIA, 458 B.C.), he avenges his father's death by killing his mother, Clytemnestra, and her lover, Aegisthus, then is haunted by the Furies (Eumenides) and vindicated in a trial. He also appears in SOPHOCLES' play ELECTRA (4th century B.C.); in EURIPIDES' plays *Iphigenia in Tauris* (*Iphigeneiaē en Taurois*, c. 414 B.C.), ELECTRA (c. 413 B.C.), and *Orestes* (408 B.C.); in J. W. von GOETHE's play *Iphigenia in Tauris* (*Iphigenie auf Tauris*, published 1787, performed 1800); and in Jean-Paul SARTRE's rewriting of the last two plays of the *Oresteia*, THE FLIES (1943). His modern counterpart is named Orin Mannon in Eugene O'NEILL's dramatic trilogy MOURNING BECOMES ELECTRA (1931).

Orlando. 1. Lover of ROSALIND in William SHAKESPEARE's comedy AS YOU LIKE IT (c. 1599). He meets "Ganymede" (Rosalind disguised as a boy) in the Forest of Arden, and she undertakes to "cure" him of the "madness" of love. 2. Hero/heroine of VIRGINIA WOOLF's novel ORLANDO: A BIOGRAPHY (1928), who begins life as an Elizabethan nobleman but is transformed, over the course of centuries, into a contemporary woman poet. 3. Italian name for ROLAND, knight of Charlemagne.

Orpheus. Peerless musician of Greek mythology, son of Apollo and the Muse Calliope. His music moves the very gods of the underworld, who permit him to retrieve his wife Eurydice from their abode, but he loses her when he violates their order not to look back. Afterward, he spurns women and is torn apart by Maenads, followers of Dionysus. Orpheus appears in numerous works, including VIRGIL's *Georgics* (*Georgica*, 37–30 B.C.), OVID's verse tales METAMORPHOSES (c. A.D. 8), Rainer Maria RILKE's cycle of SONNETS TO ORPHEUS (1923), and Jean COCTEAU's play *Orpheus* (*Orphée*, 1927; author's film version, 1950). William SHAKESPEARE celebrated him in a song in HENRY VIII (c. 1612–13): "Orpheus with his lute made trees, / And the mountain tops that freeze, / Bow themselves, when he did sing."

Othello. Title character of William SHAKESPEARE's tragedy *OTHELLO, THE MOOR OF VENICE* (1604). Misled by his malevolent ensign IAGO, the great general wrongly suspects his wife DESDEMONA of having betrayed him with the equally innocent Cassio.

Palliser family (Lord Plantagenet, Lady Glencora, and **children).** Main characters of six related Anthony TROLLOPE novels with the informal collective title *THE PALLISERS* (1864–80). The series linchpins are Plantagenet Palliser, who chooses a political career over a life of aristocratic idleness, and his vivacious, impulsive wife, the former Glencora M'Cluskie. Plantagenet becomes Duke of Omnium in the fourth novel, and Prime Minister of England in the fifth.

Pandarus. Legendary Trojan warrior. 1. In HOMER's epic the *ILIAD* (8th century B.C.), he breaks a truce by wounding MENELAUS and is slain by Diomedes. 2. In Geoffrey CHAUCER's poem *TROILUS AND CRISEYDE* (c. 1385) and William SHAKESPEARE's play *TROILUS AND CRESSIDA* (c. 1601–2), he is CRISEYDE's uncle and the lascivious go-between for the lovers; the name is the source of the noun and verb "pander."

Pangloss, Dr. Professor of "metaphysico-theologico-cosmolonigology" in VOLTAIRE's satiric novel *CANDIDE* (1759). Tutor to CANDIDE, he steadfastly espouses the doctrine that "all is for the best in this best of all possible worlds," despite repeated confrontations with natural disasters and human depravity. His "optimism" is modeled on the philosophy of Leibniz (1646–1716), as popularized by Alexander POPE ("Whatever is, is right," from *AN ESSAY ON MAN*, 1733–34).

Pantagruel. Giant and son of GARGANTUA; title character of François RABELAIS's satirical work *GARGANTUA AND PANTAGRUEL* (1565). Born "all hairy like a bear" and possessed of the strength of many men, his great size is the death of his mother Badebec. He is educated at universities, befriends the rogue Panurge, fights in a war, and continues to study throughout his life.

Panza, Sancho. Squire and portly companion to the title character in Miguel de CERVANTES's novel *DON QUIXOTE* (1605–15). He offers pithy epigrams and provides practical alternatives to his master's "quixotic" plans.

Paris. 1. In Greek mythology, the handsome son of King Priam of Troy. In a divine beauty contest, he judged that Aphrodite was the fairest, angering her competitors Athena and Hera. As a reward, Aphrodite helped him capture HELEN, wife of MENELAUS, an act that precipitated the Trojan War. HOMER's epic the *ILIAD* (8th century B.C.) portrays him as a cowardly libertine. He also appears in William SHAKESPEARE's play *TROILUS AND CRESSIDA* (c. 1601–2). 2. In Shakespeare's play *ROMEO AND JULIET* (1595), the nobleman to whom Juliet CAPULET is betrothed against her will, and despite her secret marriage to Romeo MONTAGUE.

Patterne, Sir Willoughby. Title character of George MEREDITH's comic novel *THE EGOIST* (1879). The handsome and well-to-do Baronet likes himself very much, and assumes everyone else must be of his opinion. He successively courts three women, but they all reject him, even his "constant admirer" Laetitia Dale.

Pecksniff, Seth. Memorable hypocrite of Charles DICKENS's novel *MARTIN CHUZZLEWIT* (1844). Purporting to be an architect, he is described as "a moral man," although "some people likened him to a direction-post, which is always telling the way to a place, and never goes there." His name, and its derivatives "Pecksniffian" and "Pecksniffery," are applied to sanctimonious dissemblers and their deeds.

Penelope. Faithful wife of ODYSSEUS and mother of Telemachus in HOMER's epic poem the *ODYSSEY* (8th century B.C.). During her husband's absence from his island kingdom of Ithaca, suitors try to win her hand, but she stalls them by claiming she will not marry until she finishes weaving a shroud for Odysseus's aged father, LAERTES, which she secretly unravels every night.

Percy, Sir Henry. *See* **Hotspur**

Petruchio. Central character in William SHAKE-SPEARE's comedy *THE TAMING OF THE SHREW* (c. 1593). In search of a wealthy wife, he courts KATE, the Shrew, "taming" her first by pretending her bad qualities are their opposites, then — after the wedding — by matching her, caprice for caprice, until she accepts him as "master of what is mine own."

Phaedra. In Greek mythology, daughter of King Minos of Crete and wife of King Theseus of Athens. In EURIPIDES' play *Hippolytus* (*Hippolytos*, 428 B.C.), her infatuation with her stepson Hippolytus leads her to commit suicide, leaving behind a message accusing him of trying to violate her. The story is retold in many works, among them SENECA's play *Phaedra* (1st century A.D.), Jean RACINE's play *PHAEDRA* (1677), and Mary RENAULT's novel *The Bull from the Sea* (1962).

Phelan, Francis. Protagonist of William KENNEDY's novel *IRONWEED* (1983). A one-time baseball player, now a skid-row bum, Phelan returns to Albany, New York, where he had abandoned his family 22 years earlier after accidentally killing his infant son, to confront the ghosts of his violent, neglectful past. He is the father of the protagonist of Kennedy's earlier "Albany cycle" novel, *Billy Phelan's Latest Game* (1978).

Pickwick, Samuel. Benignly eccentric title character of Charles DICKENS's first novel, *THE PICKWICK PAPERS* (1837). He and the three other founding members of the Pickwick Club report in the club's "papers" on their various misadventures during excursions across England. "Pickwickian" has come to mean "charmingly idiosyncratic"; specifically, it applies to a word used in an esoteric sense.

Pierrot. Buffoon stock character in French pantomime, a descendant of Pedrolino in the Italian commedia dell'arte. White-faced and white-gowned, usually a young servant, he is a love-struck pursuer of Pierrette or COLUMBINE. He has come to represent the lover hiding emotions behind a mask.

Piggy. One of a group of marooned British schoolboys in William GOLDING's bleak allegorical adventure novel *LORD OF THE FLIES* (1954). Pudgy and unathletic, nearly blind without his glasses, he is taunted and derided, but he is wiser than the other boys and becomes the adviser to the more "civilized" of their leaders, Ralph.

Pilgrim, Billy. Central character of Kurt VONNEGUT's novel *SLAUGHTERHOUSE-FIVE; OR THE CHILDREN'S CRUSADE* (1969). Billy has become "unstuck in time," and travels freely across his present, past, and future lives.

Pip [Philip Pirrip]. Orphaned protagonist and narrator of Charles DICKENS's novel *GREAT EXPECTATIONS* (1861). As a small boy, he helps an escaped convict try to make his getaway. Shortly afterward, he is summoned by the eccentric Miss HAVISHAM to be the playmate of her ward, Estella. When the adolescent Pip comes into a fortune, enabling him to be educated as a gentleman, he assumes his anonymous benefactor to be Miss Havisham, but eventually learns that he is mistaken.

Plurabelle, Anna Livia. *See* **Anna Livia Plurabelle**

Poirot, Hercule. Mustachioed Belgian private detective and protagonist of 42 detective novels and short-story collections by Agatha CHRISTIE, beginning with her first whodunit, *The Mysterious Affair at Styles* (1920); others include *The Murder of Roger Ackroyd* (1926) and *Murder on the Orient Express* (1934). Serving Poirot in his investigations are his years in the Belgian police and "the little grey cells" of his brain. Poirot's death made headlines around the world when *Curtain: Poirot's Last Case* (which Christie had written in the 1940s) was published in 1975. He is also well known to filmgoers and television viewers, in several incarnations.

Pollitt, Big Daddy. *See* Big Daddy

Pollitt, Maggie. *See* Maggie

Polonius. Lord Chamberlain to CLAUDIUS, king of Denmark, and father of OPHELIA and LAERTES in William SHAKESPEARE's tragedy *HAMLET, PRINCE OF DENMARK* (c. 1601). He apprises the king of HAMLET's presumed madness, and gives fatherly advice to his children about the ways of the world, telling Laertes, "This above all: to thine own self be true, / And it must follow, as the night the day, / Thou canst not then be false to any man."

Pontellier, Edna. Restless New Orleans housewife and aspiring artist in Kate CHOPIN's novel *THE AWAKENING* (1899). An outsider in the Creole high society into which she has married, she finds no fulfillment in her expected role as an obedient wife and devoted mother. A close friendship with a man she meets on a summer holiday leads to her intellectual and sensual awakening.

Pontifex family (John, George, Theobald, Ernest). Central characters in Samuel BUTLER's autobiographical novel *THE WAY OF ALL FLESH* (1903). Each of four generations of the family passes on character traits and pent-up resentments to the next, from great-grandfather John, an art-loving carpenter married to a domineering woman, to great-grandson Ernest, who endures a miserable early life at his tyrannical father's hands, before rebelling and breaking with his family. Eventually he becomes a writer.

Porthos. One of the title characters in *THE THREE MUSKETEERS* (1844), the novel by ALEXANDRE DUMAS *PÈRE*. He is noted for his physical stature and prowess.

Portia. 1. Central character in William SHAKESPEARE's comedy *THE MERCHANT OF VENICE* (c. 1596–97). A wealthy heiress, she disguises herself as a "doctor of laws" and appears in court to plead for the merchant Antonio, who faces a cruel retribution from SHYLOCK after defaulting on a loan. Her eloquent plea begins, "The quality of mercy is not strained." 2. Wife of the conspirator BRUTUS in Shakespeare's *JULIUS CAESAR* (c. 1599).

Portnoy, Alexander. Jewish-American title character of PHILIP ROTH's comic novel *PORTNOY'S COMPLAINT* (1969). Portnoy, an Assistant Commissioner of the New York Commission on Human Opportunity, bares his deepest sexual and other anxieties in a monologue addressed to his analyst, in which he complains of living his life as "the son in the Jewish joke — only it ain't no joke!"

Prewitt, Robert E. Lee. Defiant U.S. Army private and central character in James JONES's novel *FROM HERE TO ETERNITY* (1951). Stationed near Honolulu just before Pearl Harbor, Prewitt refuses to box on his company's team because he had once blinded a man in the ring; he is given "the treatment" as punishment. A career soldier who loves the army, he struggles to do his duty, as Jones describes it, "without sacrificing his self-respect and integrity, which he refuses to do."

Primrose, Dr. Charles. Narrator and central character of Oliver GOLDSMITH's sole novel, *THE VICAR OF WAKEFIELD* (1766). Vicar Primrose, "by nature an admirer of happy human faces," endures an array of family and financial disasters that disrupt his idyllic country life, including the abduction of a daughter and a period in prison; but — "To what a fortuitous occurrence do we not owe every pleasure and convenience of our lives?" — all is righted in the end.

Prism, Miss (Laetitia). Governess and companion of Cecily CARDEW in Oscar WILDE's comedy *THE IMPORTANCE OF BEING EARNEST* (1895). Unwittingly, she holds the key to a mystery concerning the origins of one of the main characters.

Prospero. Magician and deposed Duke of Milan in William SHAKESPEARE's last play, *THE TEMPEST* (c. 1611). Cast away with his daughter MIRANDA on an enchanted island, he conjures a tempest that shipwrecks his enemies there. Aided by the island spirits, he engineers reconciliations, his daughter's betrothal, and the restoration of his dukedom. He is sometimes considered Shakespeare's alter ego; his epilogue to a masque within the play may be the playwright's farewell to the stage: "Our revels now are ended.... We are such stuff / As dreams are made on, and our little life / Is rounded with a sleep."

Proudie, The Right Rev. Thomas, and Mrs. Proudie. Prominent citizens of Barchester in Anthony TROLLOPE's six-novel sequence *THE BARSETSHIRE NOVELS* (1855–67). Central characters in the second novel, *Barchester Towers* (1857), in which Thomas Proudie is named Bishop of Barchester, they have smaller roles in the succeeding novels. Throughout, the domineering Mrs. Proudie overshadows her husband, whose prayer is "that God might save him from being glad that his wife was dead." HENRY JAMES remarked, "Mrs. Proudie has become classical; of all Trollope's characters, she is the most referred to."

Prozorov sisters (Olga, Masha, Irina; Olga Sergeyevna Prozorova; Masha [Marya] Sergeyevna Kulygina; Irina Sergeyevna Prozorova). Title characters in Anton CHEKHOV's play *THE THREE SISTERS* (1901). From the confining provincial town to which they had moved more than a decade previously, the sisters dream of returning to Moscow. Olga is unhappy as an overworked schoolteacher, Masha is unhappy in her marriage, and the youngest, Irina, longs to do useful work.

Prufrock, J. Alfred. Title character and narrator of T. S. ELIOT's poem "THE LOVE SONG OF J. ALFRED PRUFROCK" (1915). The middle-aged observer expresses his alienation from his superficial, "civilized" existence: "I should have been a pair of ragged claws / Scuttling across the floors of silent seas."

Prynne, Hester. Wife of Roger CHILLINGWORTH and central character in Nathaniel HAWTHORNE's novel *THE SCARLET LETTER* (1850). In colonial Boston, Hester is forced to wear a scarlet "A" on her clothing, to mark her as an adulterer. Although the illicit union resulted in a child, Pearl, Hester refuses to name her lover.

Puck [Robin Goodfellow]. "Shrewd and knavish sprite" and servant of fairy king OBERON in William SHAKESPEARE's comedy *A MIDSUMMER NIGHT'S DREAM* (c. 1595–96). In charge of doling out a magic love herb, he accidentally mismatches two pairs of mortal lovers, but he carries out Oberon's plan to humiliate fairy queen TITANIA by having her dote on the weaver BOTTOM, whom he has "translated" into a creature with an ass's head.

Pyncheon family (Colonel Pyncheon; Jaffey, Clifford, Hepzibah, Phoebe). Central characters in Nathaniel HAWTHORNE's novel *THE HOUSE OF THE SEVEN GABLES* (1851). In the 1600s, Colonel Pyncheon obtained land for his seven-gabled mansion by falsely accusing Matthew Maule of witchcraft, and he and his descendants were cursed by the victim from the scaffold. In the 1800s, Jaffey Pyncheon falsely accused his cousin Clifford of murder, blighting the lives of Clifford and his sister, Hepzibah. The love of Phoebe, the youngest Pyncheon, for a descendant of Maule finally lifts the power of the curse.

Quasimodo. Deformed, deaf bell ringer for the Parisian cathedral in Victor HUGO's historical novel *THE HUNCHBACK OF NOTRE DAME* (1831). When he is unjustly scourged and pilloried, no one will give him water except the Gypsy dancer Esmeralda, and henceforth he adores her. He shelters her in the church when she is falsely persecuted by the wicked Archdeacon Frollo, who is also obsessed with the beautiful Gypsy.

Queeg, Lieutenant Commander Philip Francis. Neurotic captain of the USS *Caine* in Herman WOUK's World War II novel *THE CAINE MUTINY* (1951). The alternately despotic and cowardly commander of the mine sweeper is relieved of his command by crew members, then cracks up openly while testifying at their court-martial.

Queequeg. Harpooner on the *Pequod* in Herman MELVILLE's whaling epic *MOBY-DICK* (1851). A "pagan" prince from a Polynesian island and a reputed cannibal, he becomes friends with narrator ISHMAEL when they meet in a New Bedford inn, and signs on board Captain AHAB's ship with him.

Quentin. *See* **Compson family**

Quested, Adela. Central character of E. M. FORSTER's novel *A PASSAGE TO INDIA* (1924). A young British visitor to India who wants to get acquainted with the Indian people, she is invited on an excursion to the Marabar Caves by open-hearted Doctor AZIZ. She accuses him of assaulting her in the caves, but drops the charges during his trial.

Quilty, Clare. Sinister playwright in Vladimir NABOKOV's novel *LOLITA* (1955). He absconds with 14-year-old LOLITA (Dolores Haze) while she is engaged in an affair with her stepfather, Humbert HUMBERT. Humbert suggests, and some critics believe, that he is merely a projection of Humbert's own darkest impulses.

Quixote, Don. Title character of Miguel de CERVANTES's novel *DON QUIXOTE* (1605–15). Alonso Quixano, a middle-aged gentleman addled from reading too many chivalric romances, fancies himself a knight-errant and is reborn as "Don Quixote de la Mancha." With his faithful squire Sancho PANZA, who dubs him "Knight of the Woeful Countenance," he embarks on a journey to right the world's wrongs. "Quixotic" has come to mean "impractically idealistic."

Rabbit. *See* **Angstrom, Harry**

Ragged Dick [Richard Hunter]. Archetypal rags-to-riches boy hero of *Ragged Dick; or, Street Life in New York with the Boot-Blacks* (1868), a novel by Horatio Alger, Jr. (1832–1899). Through hard work and native resourcefulness, the street urchin rises from penury to modestly comfortable circumstances (the riches come later), offering an object lesson for youths of the age. His saga continues in *Fame and Fortune; or, The Progress of Richard Hunter* (1868) and *Mark, the Match Boy; or, Richard Hunter's Ward* (1869).

Ramsay, Mr. and **Mrs.** Complex central characters in VIRGINIA WOOLF's novel *TO THE LIGHTHOUSE* (1927). Where Mr. Ramsay, a self-doubting philosopher, conceals his emotional life beneath a stern and aloof exterior, the warm, open Mrs. Ramsay lives for her nurturing relationships with her large family and circle of friends. They are based on the author's parents, Leslie and Julia Stephen.

Ranevskaya [Ranevsky], Madame [Lyubov (Lyuba) Andreyevna]. Central character in Anton CHEKHOV's melancholy comedy *THE CHERRY ORCHARD* (1904). After five years abroad, she returns to her beloved country estate when its celebrated cherry orchard is in bloom, to be told she must sacrifice the orchard or the entire estate will be sold for her debts.

Raskolnikov, Rodion Romanovich. Impoverished law student and protagonist of Fyodor DOSTOYEVSKY's *CRIME AND PUNISHMENT* (1867). Seeing himself as a superior being not subject to human laws, he kills and robs a miserly old woman he considers "useless." Confusion and guilt torment him until he finally confesses, first to the pure-hearted prostitute Sonia and then to the police.

Rastignac, Eugène [afterward Comte Eugène de Rastignac]. Ambitious central character in Honoré de BALZAC's novel *Père Goriot* (*Le Père Goriot*, 1835). An impoverished law student in old GORIOT's boardinghouse, he becomes the lover of Goriot's daughter Delphine de Nucingen, a wealthy banker's wife. He also appears in eight other novels of Balzac's 90-volume work *THE HUMAN COMEDY* (1829–47); in these installments, he becomes rich with the Nucingens' help, breaks with Delphine after a dozen years, and eventually acquires a title, a ministry, and the hand of Delphine's daughter.

Red Cross Knight [George]. Central character in Edmund SPENSER's allegorical poem *THE FAERIE QUEENE* (1590). Standing for St. George, patron saint of England, and for the struggling Christian in quest of holiness, he overcomes an onerous series of obstacles before he can slay the dragon threatening the parents of his beloved Una (who represents Truth, and the Anglican church), winning her hand.

GREAT LINES FROM GREAT PLAYS: A MATCHING QUIZ

Match the quotation to the playwright:

1 ...since an arrow shot towards a target first had to cover half the distance, and then half the remainder, and then half the remainder after that, and so on *ad infinitum*, the result was, as I will now demonstrate, that though an arrow is always approaching its target, it never quite gets there, and Saint Sebastian died of fright.

2 All women become like their mothers. That is their tragedy. No man does. That's his.

3 Attention, attention must be finally paid to such a person.

4 But what matters to me is not whether it's true or not but that I believe it to be true, or rather, not that I *believe* it, but that *I* believe it ...I trust I make myself obscure?

5 Cover her face; mine eyes dazzle; she died young.

6 Faith, sir, we are here today, and gone tomorrow.

7 Good heavens! For more than forty years I have been speaking prose without knowing it.

8 He is the very pineapple of politeness.

9 Hell is other people.

10 I have always depended on the kindness of strangers.

11 If I continue to endure you a little longer, I may by degrees dwindle into a wife.

12 Nothing happens, nobody comes, nobody goes, it's awful!

13 Oh, earth, you're too wonderful for anyone to realize you....Do any human beings ever realize life while they live it? Every, every minute?

14 People don't *do* such things!

15 Second to the right and then straight on till morning.

16 Strange how potent cheap music is.

17 To Moscow, to Moscow, to Moscow!

18 Walk? Not bloody likely! I am going in a taxi.

19 Was this the face that launched a thousand ships / And burnt the topless towers of Ilium?

20 Years from now...when you talk of this... and you will...be kind.

21 You leave me little notes on my pillow. I told you a hundred times, I can't stand little notes on my pillow. "We're all out of Corn Flakes, F.U." It took me three hours to figure out that F.U. was Felix Ungar.

(A) Robert Anderson

(B) James M. Barrie

(C) Samuel Beckett

(D) Aphra Behn

(E) Robert Bolt

(F) Anton Chekhov

(G) William Congreve

(H) Noël Coward

(I) Henrik Ibsen

(J) Christopher Marlowe

(K) Arthur Miller

(L) Molière

(M) Jean-Paul Sartre

(N) George Bernard Shaw

(O) Richard Brinsley Sheridan

(P) Neil Simon

(Q) Tom Stoppard

(R) John Webster

(S) Oscar Wilde

(T) Thornton Wilder

(U) Tennessee Williams

ANSWERS:

1-Q, Tom Stoppard (George in *Jumpers*); 2-S, Oscar Wilde (Algernon in *The Importance of Being Earnest*); 3-K, Arthur Miller (Linda Loman in *Death of a Salesman*); 4-E, Robert Bolt (Thomas More in *A Man for All Seasons*); 5-R, John Webster (Ferdinand in *The Duchess of Malfi*); 6-D, Aphra Behn (Noisey in *The Lucky Chance*); 7-L, Molière (M. Jourdain in *The Bourgeois Gentleman*); 8-O, Richard Brinsley Sheridan (Mrs. Malaprop in *The Rivals*); 9-M, Jean-Paul Sartre (Garcin in *No Exit*); 10-U, Tennessee Williams (Blanche DuBois in *A Streetcar Named Desire*); 11-G, William Congreve (Millamant in *The Way of the World*); 12-C, Samuel Beckett (Estragon in *Waiting for Godot*); 13-T, Thornton Wilder (Emily in *Our Town*); 14-I, Henrik Ibsen (Judge Brack in *Hedda Gabler*); 15-B, J. M. Barrie (Peter Pan in *Peter Pan*); 16-H, Noël Coward (Amanda in *Private Lives*); 17-F, Anton Chekhov (Irina in *The Three Sisters*); 18-N, George Bernard Shaw (Eliza Doolittle in *Pygmalion*); 19-J, Christopher Marlowe (Faustus in *The Tragicall History of Doctor Faustus*); 20-A, Robert Anderson (Laura Reynolds in *Tea and Sympathy*); 21-P, Neil Simon (Oscar Madison in *The Odd Couple*)

Regan. Middle daughter of the title character in William SHAKESPEARE's tragedy *KING LEAR* (c. 1605). She wins half of LEAR's kingdom by falsely professing her love, but her treachery soon leads Lear bitterly to regret his generosity. Like her older sister, GONERIL, she will also prove to be vicious, adulterous, and murderous.

Richard II. King of England (1367–1400; reigned 1377–99) whose reign and overthrow are dramatized in William SHAKESPEARE's history play *RICHARD II* (c. 1595). An inept, if eloquent, monarch ("For God's sake, let us sit upon the ground / And tell sad stories of the death of kings"), he is deposed and imprisoned by Henry Bolingbroke, who becomes King HENRY IV.

Richard III [Duke of Gloucester]. King of England (1452–1485; reigned 1483–85) whose rise to power and brief, violent reign are dramatized in William SHAKESPEARE's history play *RICHARD III* (c. 1594). One of Shakespeare's great villains, the hunchbacked usurper gleefully murders anyone who stands in his way, including his two young nephews, the "Princes in the Tower." His cry "A horse! a horse! my kingdom for a horse!" does not avail him on Bosworth Field, where he is slain by the Earl of Richmond (the future Henry VII). Richard also appears in two earlier Shakespeare history plays, *HENRY VI*, Parts II and III (c. 1590–92).

Roark, Howard. Uncompromising architect in Ayn RAND's novel *THE FOUNTAINHEAD* (1943). He embodies Rand's "objectivist" philosophy of "enlightened self-interest." Although Rand denied basing him on innovative American architect Frank Lloyd Wright (1867–1959), many critics have noted a resemblance.

Robin, Magdeleine. *See* **Roxane**

Rochester, Edward. Brooding master of Thornfield Hall, who hires Jane EYRE as governess in CHARLOTTE BRONTË's novel *JANE EYRE* (1847). He falls in love with her "soul made of fire, and the character that bends but does not break," but an old secret that has darkened his life threatens to separate the couple forever.

Rogozhin, Parfyon Semyonovich. Wealthy central character in Fyodor DOSTOYEVSKY's novel *THE IDIOT* (1874). Obsessively in love with the "fallen woman" Nastasya FILIPPOVNA, he is murderously enraged by the attention shown her by gentle Prince MYSHKIN.

Roland [Orlando]. Legendary knight and nephew of Charlemagne. The *SONG OF ROLAND* (c. 1100) and other *chansons de geste* tell of Roland's ambush by the Saracens at Roncesvalles, his prideful refusal to sound his horn to summon help, and his heroic death. The epitome of French chivalry, he appears also in Italian literature as Orlando, notably in Ludovico ARIOSTO's epic *ORLANDO FURIOSO* (1532), which describes how Orlando is driven mad by his love for the pagan princess Angelica.

Romeo. *See* **Montague, Romeo**

Rosalind. Central character and daughter of a deposed duke in William SHAKESPEARE's comedy *AS YOU LIKE IT* (c. 1599). Banished from the new duke's court, she flees to the Forest of Arden. There, disguised as the shepherd boy "Ganymede," she encounters her would-be lover and fellow exile ORLANDO and teasingly instructs him in how to be cured of lovesickness for the girl he thinks he left behind.

Rosencrantz and **Guildenstern.** 1. Minor characters in William SHAKESPEARE's tragedy *HAMLET, PRINCE OF DENMARK* (c. 1601). HAMLET's former schoolfellows at Wittenberg, they have been summoned to Elsinore by CLAUDIUS, the King of Denmark, to aid in his schemes against Hamlet. 2. Leading characters in Tom STOPPARD's comedy *ROSENCRANTZ AND GUILDENSTERN ARE DEAD* (1966). Here we see the off-stage life of the pair as they attempt to make sense of the tragic events in which they have been unwittingly caught up. Guildenstern is the more intellectual of the two; Rosencrantz is more cunning, but naive.

Rostova, Natasha. A central character in Leo TOLSTOY's epic novel *WAR AND PEACE* (1868–69). Vivacious and spirited, she is loved by Prince Andrey BOLKONSKY and his friend Pierre BEZUKHOV. Oppressed by her long engagement to the serious Andrey, she nearly elopes with another man; as Andrey lies dying of war wounds, she tends him faithfully and is forgiven. After his death, she learns to love Pierre.

Roxane [Magdeleine Robin]. Witty and beautiful beloved of poet-swordsman CYRANO in Edmond Rostand's play CYRANO DE BERGERAC (1897). She is wooed and won by the eloquence that Cyrano lends to a handsome young fellow soldier, Christian, who soon dies in battle. Years later, as Cyrano is dying, she learns of his deception, and laments, "I loved but once, yet twice I lose my love!"

Rubashov, Nicholas Salmanovitch. Former Commissar of the People and protagonist of Arthur KOESTLER's novel DARKNESS AT NOON (1940). A leader of the 1917 Russian Revolution, he is imprisoned during Stalin's purges. Tortured and broken psychologically, he confesses to "crimes" he never committed. The character is a composite based on several Old Bolsheviks, including Nikolai Bukharin (1888–1938) and Leon Trotsky (1879–1940).

Rudkus, Jurgis. Lithuanian immigrant and protagonist of Upton SINCLAIR's novel THE JUNGLE (1906). Working in Chicago's Packingtown, he encounters appalling conditions that shorten workers' lives and deliver tainted food to the public. His family is destroyed and his spirit broken; he turns to socialism in search of answers.

Rumpole, Horace and Hilda. Central characters of John MORTIMER's popular television series *Rumpole of the Bailey* (1975–92), about a cynical "Old Bailey hack," WORDSWORTH-quoting, cigar-puffing Rumpole (Leo McKern), whose motto is "Never plead guilty!" and his harridan wife, whom he refers to as "She-Who-Must-Be-Obeyed," after H. Rider HAGGARD's queen AYESHA in *SHE* (1887). Rumpole also began to appear in a series of short-story collections beginning in 1978 with *Rumpole of the Bailey*.

Ryder, Charles. Architectural artist and narrator of EVELYN WAUGH's novel BRIDESHEAD REVISITED (1945). Looking back from wartime, he relates his "sacred and profane memories" (the book's subtitle) of the wealthy Catholic aristocratic family with which his life was intertwined since his Oxford days, when he befriended Lord Sebastian FLYTE; later, he loved and lost Sebastian's sister, Lady Julia (Mrs. Rex Mottram).

Salome. Daughter of Herodias; stepdaughter of Herod Antipas, tetrarch of Galilee. In the BIBLE (New Testament, Gospels of Matthew and Mark), her stepfather grants her whatever she wishes for her entertaining dancing. At Herodias's prompting, she wishes for the head of the prophet John the Baptist, imprisoned for condemning her stepfather's incestuous marriage. Her dance is described vividly in Gustave FLAUBERT's short story "Herodias" ("Hérodias," in his *Trois Contes*, 1877); in Oscar WILDE's play *Salomé* (1896), she is infatuated with the prophet, who rejects her. The latter work serves as the libretto for Richard Strauss's 1905 opera, with the celebrated "Dance of the Seven Veils."

Samsa, Gregor. Traveling salesman transformed into a gigantic insect in Franz KAFKA's short story "THE METAMORPHOSIS" (1915). Awakening one morning to find himself turned into a "monstrous vermin," Samsa worries at first more about having missed the early train than coping with life in his radically altered form, but encounters with his family and his office manager soon compel him to reassess his situation.

Santiago. Cuban fisherman and title character of Ernest HEMINGWAY's short novel THE OLD MAN AND THE SEA (1953). On his 85th day without a catch, Santiago snares an enormous marlin. After a monumental two-day battle, he harpoons it and lashes it to his boat. On the voyage home, sharks devour all but the skeleton, but the old man's courage and manliness are vindicated.

Sarto, Andrea del. Italian Renaissance painter (1486–1530) whose reflections, addressed to his wife and model Lucrezia, comprise ROBERT BROWNING's dramatic monologue "Andrea del Sarto" (in *Men and Women*, 1855). "The Faultless Painter" considers his attachment to his beautiful but uninspiring wife, and laments that

Raphael and others less technically "faultless" surpass him in artistry: "Ah, but a man's reach should exceed his grasp, / Or what's a heaven for?"

Sartoris family. Aristocratic dynasty in William FAULKNER's fictional Yoknapatawpha County, Mississippi, notably in two novels. In *Sartoris* (1929; published in unexpurgated form under Faulkner's preferred title, *Flags in the Dust*, 1974), Bayard Sartoris, a self-destructive veteran of the Great War in which his twin brother John perished, is the great-grandson of family patriarch and Civil War veteran Colonel John Sartoris, whose brother, the first Bayard, died in that war. His grandfather, bank president Old Bayard or "Colonel" Bayard, often accompanies him on wild automobile rides around the countryside. In *The Unvanquished* (1938), a "blended" series of stories, Faulkner relates the history of the first John Sartoris, planter and railroad entrepreneur (modeled on his own great-grandfather, William Clark Falkner, who spelled his last name without the "u"), and his son, Old Bayard, in the Civil War era. The family is mentioned in many other Faulkner works.

Satan. Spirit of evil and the adversary of God in Judeo-Christian theology. Also known as the Devil, he is a fallen angel (Lucifer) who presides over Hell. He appears in the BIBLE, notably as EVE's tempter in a serpent's guise in the Book of Genesis; as Job's tormentor in the Book of Job; and as JESUS' tempter in the Gospels of Matthew, Mark, and Luke. As head of the host of fallen angels ("Better to reign in Hell, than serve in Heav'n"), he is a central character in John MILTON's epic poem *PARADISE LOST* (1667) and its sequel, *Paradise Regained* (1671). As Dis (Roman god of the underworld) or Lucifer, he is encountered in the bottommost circle of Hell, a three-faced monster half-buried in ice, in DANTE ALIGHIERI's *Inferno*, part of his epic poem *THE DIVINE COMEDY* (c. 1314–21). He appears as Lucifer in Christopher MARLOWE's tragedy *DOCTOR FAUSTUS* (c. 1588). See also MEPHISTOPHELES.

Savage. *See* **John, the Savage**

Sawyer, Tom. Archetypal American boy and title character of Mark TWAIN's novel *TOM SAWYER* (1876). An orphan chafing under the tutelage of his fussy Aunt Polly, Tom seeks adventure in a series of escapades involving characters like the murderous Injun Joe and the beauteous Becky THATCHER. In many, he is accompanied by Huckleberry FINN, outcast son of the town drunk. Tom reappeared in Twain's *HUCKLEBERRY FINN* (1884) and two further boys' books.

Scarlet Pimpernel. Title character of Baroness Orczy's adventure novel *THE SCARLET PIMPERNEL* (1905), also featured in a dozen other novels and short-story collections. Affected English fop Sir Percy Blakeney is secretly the Scarlet Pimpernel, who fearlessly aids persecuted members of the French nobility during the Reign of Terror.

Scheherazade. Central character in the collection of ancient stories *THE THOUSAND AND ONE NIGHTS* (14th or 15th century). In the framing story, she marries the Emperor of Persia, who has vowed to wed a new wife each day and have her killed at dawn, but she spins a tale an hour before her scheduled death. It is a cliffhanger, gaining her a day's respite so she can relate the end; and so she continues for a "thousand nights and a night."

Schlegel sisters (Margaret, Helen). Cultured, unconventional central characters of E. M. FORSTER's novel *HOWARDS END* (1910). Helen is high-spirited and idealistic; Margaret is described by Forster as "not beautiful, not supremely brilliant, but filled with . . . a profound vivacity." Margaret, who marries the widowed head of the Wilcox clan, eventually becomes heir to their estate, Howards End, which her husband's first wife had wanted to bequeath to her.

Scrooge, Ebenezer. Miserly taskmaster whose redemption is the center of Charles DICKENS's short novel *A CHRISTMAS CAROL* (1843). Uncharitable to his clerk Bob CRATCHIT on Christmas Eve, he is visited in his dreams by painful and terrifying visions of Christmases Past, Present, and Future, which induce him to be reborn in spirit.

Sethe. Runaway slave and main character in Toni MORRISON's novel BELOVED (1987). Escaped from Sweet Home Plantation before the Civil War, and now living in Ohio with her family, Sethe is haunted first by the ghost of her baby daughter, "Beloved," whom she killed to save from a life of slavery, and afterward by a strange, adolescent flesh-and-blood "ghost" of Beloved.

Shandy, Tristram. Narrator and title character of Laurence STERNE's novel TRISTRAM SHANDY (1759–67). Beginning with his mother's untimely question at the moment of his conception ("Pray, my dear... have you not forgot to wind up the clock?"), Shandy discourses on his "Life and Opinions," with frequent and far-ranging digressions.

Sharp, Becky. Wily antiheroine of William Makepeace THACKERAY's "novel without a hero," VANITY FAIR (1848). Voraciously ambitious and utterly without scruples, Becky says of herself, "I think I could be a good woman if I had five thousand a year." Lacking that, she gets as much as she can out of a series of increasingly powerful men.

Shelby, Uncle Tom. See **Tom, Uncle**

She-Who-Must-Be-Obeyed. See **Ayesha**; **Rumpole, Horace** and **Hilda**

Shimerda, Ántonia [Tony Shimerda, Ántonia Cuzak]. Stalwart Bohemian immigrant to the Nebraska prairies in Willa CATHER's novel MY ÁNTONIA (1918). As recalled by her childhood friend Jim Burden, Ántonia experiences hardship on the farm and trouble in town as a hired girl before finding happiness in marriage to another immigrant farmer. When Jim last sees her, she appears as "a rich mine of life, like the founders of early races."

Shukhov, Ivan Denisovich. Title character of Aleksandr SOLZHENITSYN's novel ONE DAY IN THE LIFE OF IVAN DENISOVICH (1962). A peasant serving a ten-year sentence in a Stalinist Siber-

ian labor camp on a false charge of espionage, Shukhov struggles to survive through a typical day of miserable conditions and hard labor.

Shylock. Jewish moneylender in William SHAKESPEARE's comedy THE MERCHANT OF VENICE (c. 1596–97). Despised by Christian society for pursuing one of the few professions open to him, he agrees to lend money to the merchant Antonio, who has abused him in the past, but demands "a pound of flesh" as his bond. He defends the harsh bargain in the speech beginning, "Hath not a Jew eyes?... If you prick us, do we not bleed?... if you poison us, do we not die? and if you wrong us, shall we not revenge? If we are like you in the rest, we will resemble you in that."

Sinbad the Sailor. Enterprising merchant of the collection of ancient stories THE THOUSAND AND ONE NIGHTS (14th or 15th century). As he recounts to the poor porter Hindbad and his other guests over seven nights, he acquired his vast wealth on seven voyages, on which he overcame a variety of fantastic challenges, such as monstrous beasts and birds, a cyclops, cannibals, and pirates.

Sloper, Catherine. Protagonist of HENRY JAMES's novel WASHINGTON SQUARE (1881). The uncherished daughter of a wealthy doctor, she is courted by handsome ne'er-do-well Morris Townsend, who jilts her when he learns her father will disinherit her if they wed.

Slothrop, Lt. Tyrone [Rocketman]. World War II lieutenant assigned to the Political Warfare Executive in Thomas PYNCHON's novel GRAVITY'S RAINBOW (1973). He strives to discover why the approach of a rocket makes him have an erection; as another character suggests, he may be "in love, in sexual love, with his, and the race's, death."

Smith, Winston. Rebel against totalitarian control in George ORWELL's anti-utopian novel NINETEEN EIGHTY-FOUR (1949). Small-time party member Smith labors in Oceania's Ministry of Truth, changing the printed word to agree with the latest version of Party history. He attempts to fight BIG BROTHER's mind control by keeping a journal and taking a lover, but is captured, tortured in the Ministry of Love, and broken in spirit.

Snopes family. Prolific clan in William FAULKNER's fictional Yoknapatawpha County, Mississippi, the setting for most of his novels; their rise parallels the decline of the aristocratic Yoknapatawpha families, the COMPSON FAMILY and the SARTORIS FAMILY. Around three dozen Snopeses are mentioned in various Faulkner novels and short stories, notably the "Snopes" trilogy of novels comprising *THE HAMLET* (1940), *THE TOWN* (1957), and *THE MANSION* (1959). The family patriarch is the sharecropper and former horse thief Abner (Ab) Snopes; his son, Flem Snopes, is a major character in the trilogy, as he rises from store clerk to bank president.

Sorel, Julien. Ambitious protagonist of STENDHAL's novel *THE RED AND THE BLACK* (1830). Determined to escape his working-class background, he is helped by friends in the Church to positions with powerful people, and helps himself to a sentimental education in the form of liaisons with two beautiful women: the passionate Mme de Renal, wife of his provincial hometown's mayor, and the haughty Mathilde de la Mole, daughter of a Parisian marquis.

Spade, Sam. Quintessential hard-boiled private eye in Dashiell HAMMETT's novel *THE MALTESE FALCON* (1930); he also appears in three stories in the collection *A Man Named Spade and Other Stories* (1944). Considered the first of his breed, Spade is introduced as looking "rather pleasantly like a blond Satan"; Hammett described him as "able to get the best of anybody he comes in contact with, whether criminal, innocent bystander or client."

Stahr, Monroe. Driven 1930s Hollywood mogul and protagonist of F. SCOTT FITZGERALD's unfinished novel *THE LAST TYCOON* (1941). Stahr strives to maintain high artistic standards despite pressure from corrupt commercial interests; he is said to be based on "boy wonder" producer Irving Thalberg (1899–1936), whose overwork hastened his early death.

Starbuck, Mr. Chief mate on the *Pequod* in Herman MELVILLE's whaling epic *MOBY-DICK* (1851). A "good man, and a pious," the Quaker Starbuck attempts to persuade Captain AHAB that his obsessive quest for "vengeance on a dumb brute" is "blasphemous."

Stark, Willie [Boss]. Demagogic Southern United States politician at the center of Robert Penn WARREN's novel *ALL THE KING'S MEN* (1946). Modeled on Louisiana governor and U.S. senator Huey Long (1893–1935), Stark rises to power as a champion of the poor; once established, he maintains his position by means of a web of corruption, blackmail, and deceit.

St. Clare, Evangeline. *See* **Eva**

Stella. *See* **Kowalski, Stanley** and **Stella**

Strether, Lambert. Middle-aged protagonist of HENRY JAMES's novel *THE AMBASSADORS* (1903). Enlisted by his intended, Mrs. Newsome, to extricate her son Chadwick from his Parisian entanglements, he travels from Woollett, Massachusetts, to Paris, where he finds Chad seemingly much improved by his sojourn abroad. Falling himself under the spell of the Continent, he advises the youth to "Live all you can; it's a mistake not to."

Subtle. Archetypal con man and central character of Ben JONSON's comedy *The Alchemist* (1610). Posing as an alchemist and astrologer, he connives with Doll Common and trickster Jeremy Butler [Face] to amass money by devising miraculous remedies tailored to each of his victims, who represent a variety of contemporary London types.

Sutpen family (Thomas, etc.). Doomed dynasty in William FAULKNER's novel *ABSALOM, ABSALOM!* (1936). Thomas Sutpen repudiates his Haitian first wife and oldest son when he discovers his wife is part black; he moves to Yoknapatawpha County, Mississippi (Faulkner's fictional home territory), and builds a plantation on "Sutpen's Hundred." Henry and Judith, his children by his second wife, meet his son Charles Bon without knowing their relationship, which leads to trouble when Charles and Judith want to marry. Thomas, Charles, and

Henry all fight in the Civil War (Thomas serves with Col. John SARTORIS). Thomas also has a daughter, Clytemnestra (Clytie) Sutpen, by a slave. Thomas Sutpen also appears in several other Faulkner works.

Svengali. Mesmerizing main character in George du Maurier's novel TRILBY (1894). Svengali, a Hungarian musician, discovers the popular artist's model Trilby, who has a powerful voice but is tone deaf, and leads her to fame as a singer, controlling her voice on stage through his powers.

Swann, Charles. A central character in Marcel PROUST's multivolume novel REMEMBRANCE OF THINGS PAST (1913–27); his story is recounted in the first book, *Swann's Way* (*Du Côté de Chez Swann*, 1913). A bourgeois dandy who is working on a never-finished study of Vermeer, he is infatuated with and marries the courtesan ODETTE de Crécy. Their daughter, Gilberte, is loved for a time by the book's narrator.

Tanner, Jack. *See* **Juan, Don**

Tenorio, Don Juan. *See* **Juan, Don**

Tevye, Reb [Tevye the Dairyman]. Central character in eight humorous short stories by SHOLOM ALEICHEM, published in Yiddish, 1895–1914; in English in the collections *The Old Country* (1946) and *Tevye's Daughters* (1949). A milkman in the Russian Pale at the turn of the 20th century, he and his wife, Golde, face life's tribulations, particularly those related to finding suitable husbands for their seven daughters. Several stories were adapted as the musical *Fiddler on the Roof* (1964).

Thatcher, Becky. Tom SAWYER's sweetheart in Mark TWAIN's novel TOM SAWYER (1876). The daughter of a judge, "a lovely little blue-eyed creature with yellow hair," she is the new girl in town with whom Tom is smitten, and joins him on an adventure in a cave.

Thomas, Bigger. Main character of RICHARD WRIGHT's first novel, NATIVE SON (1940). A young black man living in a one-room, rat-infested apartment in a Southside Chicago slum, he accidentally kills the daughter of his wealthy white employer, then panics and kills his own girlfriend. Although he is sentenced to death, he comes to understand the forces that incited him: "I didn't know I was really alive in this world until I felt things hard enough to kill for 'em."

Thomas à Becket, Saint. Archbishop of Canterbury (c. 1118–1170; in office 1162–70; canonized 1173), whose martyrdom is dramatized in T. S. ELIOT's verse play MURDER IN THE CATHEDRAL (1935). He incurs the wrath of King Henry II for opposing the king's efforts to limit the power of the church, and is murdered in Canterbury Cathedral. The story is also told in Alfred, Lord TENNYSON's tragedy *Becket* (published 1884, performed 1893) and Jean ANOUILH's play *Becket; or, The Honor of God* (*Becket; ou, L'Honneur de Dieu*, 1959; filmed in 1963 with Richard Burton and Peter O'Toole).

Thompson, Sadie. Main character of W. Somerset MAUGHAM's best-known short story, "Rain" (in *The Trembling of a Leaf*, 1921; original title "Miss Thompson"). On a South Sea island, Sadie, a prostitute who has been expelled from Hawaii, encounters Rev. Alfred Davidson, a stern Scottish missionary, with disastrous consequences. Her celebrated last line is, "You men! You filthy, dirty pigs! You're all the same, all of you. Pigs! Pigs!" Stage, screen, and television adaptations followed; Gloria Swanson, Joan Crawford, and Rita Hayworth all played Sadie onscreen.

Tiny Tim (Cratchit). Crippled young son of Bob CRATCHIT, clerk to Ebenezer SCROOGE, in Charles DICKENS's short novel A CHRISTMAS CAROL (1843). Tiny Tim's Christmas grace, "God bless us, every one!" is reiterated as the story's final words.

Titania. Queen of the fairies in William SHAKESPEARE's comedy A MIDSUMMER NIGHT'S DREAM (c. 1595–96). When she refuses to give a changeling Indian boy to her consort, fairy king OBERON, he orders PUCK to dose her with a magic herb that makes her dote on the first creature she sees: BOTTOM the weaver, with an ass's head.

Todd, Sweeney. Murderous barber and protagonist of Thomas Peckett Prest's "penny dreadful" *The String of Pearls* (1846), George Dibdin Pitt's melodrama *A String of Pearls; or, The Fiend of Fleet Street* (1847), Stephen Sondheim and Hugh Wheeler's stage musical *Sweeney Todd* (1979), and many others. The demon barber slits his customers' throats; meat pies are made from their flesh.

Tom, Uncle [Tom Shelby]. Virtuous title character in Harriet Beecher STOWE's antislavery novel *UNCLE TOM'S CABIN* (1852). Once the trusted manager of the Shelby plantation, he is purchased by the "good" slave owner Augustine St. Clair, and becomes friends with St. Clair's daughter Little EVA. Later he suffers martyrdom at the hands of Simon LEGREE to cover the escape of other slaves. "Uncle Tom" has become a pejorative term for a black who is too accommodating to the demands of whites.

Topsy. Child slave and friend of Little EVA in Harriet Beecher STOWE's antislavery novel *UNCLE TOM'S CABIN* (1852). Impishly subversive of the world view of whites (asked if she knows who made her, she replies, "Nobody.... I 'spect I grow'd"), she is given by Little Eva's father to his New England–born cousin Ophelia as an educational challenge. "Just growed, like Topsy," has become proverbial.

Torquemada, [Don] Francisco [de]. Madrid moneylender and protagonist of four of Benito PÉREZ GALDÓS's novels of 19th-century Spanish society, published collectively in English as *Torquemada* (*Torquemada en la Hoguera, Torquemada en la Cruz, Torquemada en el Purgatorio, Torquemada y San Pedro,* 1889–95; also translated as *The Cape of Don Francisco Torquemada*). Beginning as a sordid usurer, Torquemada rises to become a member of parliament and a wealthy pseudo-aristocrat. Ironically named for the infamous Inquisitor, Tomás de Torquemada (1420–1498), he had previously appeared in other works by the author, including *FORTUNATA AND JACINTA* (1886–87).

Trask brothers (Caleb [Cal], Aron). Sons of California settler Adam Trask in John STEIN-BECK's novel *EAST OF EDEN* (1952). Based on the BIBLE's Cain and Abel, the twin brothers (one or both of whom may actually be the son of Adam's half-brother) vie for their father's love; Cal, feeling rejected, devastates the pious Aron by telling him that their supposedly dead mother is a notorious Salinas madam.

Trent, Nell. *See* **Nell**

Treplev, Konstantin Gavrilovich. Aspiring author in Anton CHEKHOV's play *THE SEAGULL* (1896). Frustrated by his inability to win success as a writer, the approval of his mother, Irina ARKADINA, or the heart of Nina ZARECHNAYA, he shoots a seagull and presents it to Nina, threatening to do the same to himself.

Trigorin, Boris Alexeyevich. Successful writer in Anton CHEKHOV's play *THE SEAGULL* (1896). The lover of Irina ARKADINA, Konstantin TREPLEV's mother, he seduces, then abandons Nina ZARECHNAYA, the young actress with whom Treplev is in love.

Tristan [Tristram]. In medieval legend, nephew of King Mark [Marke] of Cornwall and lover of Mark's wife, ISEULT [Isolde]. Tristan and Iseult fall helplessly in love when they drink a magic potion on the way to the court of Tristan's uncle and liege lord, whom Iseult is to marry. The tragic story has often been told, notably in Gottfried von Strassburg's unfinished Middle High German epic poem *Tristan and Isolde* (*Tristan und Isolde,* c. 1210; one of the principal sources for Wagner's 1859 opera), and in Sir Thomas MALORY's romance *LE MORTE D'ARTHUR* (c. 1469–70).

Troilus. Trojan prince and lover of Criseyde [Cressida] in Geoffrey CHAUCER's poem *TROILUS AND CRISEYDE* (c. 1385) and William SHAKESPEARE's play *TROILUS AND CRESSIDA* (c. 1601–2). In both, the couple's bond is broken when Greek warrior Diomedes seduces Criseyde/Cressida. In Chaucer's version, the discovery leads to Troilus's death.

Trout, Kilgore. Untalented but visionary science-fiction writer and recurrent character in Kurt VONNEGUT's novels. Introduced in *God*

Bless You, Mr. Rosewater (1965), he is Billy PIL-GRIM's favorite author in *SLAUGHTERHOUSE-FIVE* (1969); in *Breakfast of Champions* (1973), he is invited to a Festival of Arts and wins the Nobel Prize in medicine. He also appears in *Jailbird* (1979) and (as a ghost) in *Galapagos* (1985). Vonnegut based him on several science-fiction authors, including Theodore Sturgeon (1918–1985).

Tulliver, Maggie. Independent-minded miller's daughter and protagonist of GEORGE ELIOT's novel *THE MILL ON THE FLOSS* (1860). Unappreciated by her father in her youth, as an adult she suffers from a strained relationship with her beloved brother, Tom, and cannot reconcile the suits of two young men with her sense of duty to family members, whom either match would wound.

Twist, Oliver. Orphaned title character and hero of Charles DICKENS's novel *OLIVER TWIST* (1838). Starved in a workhouse, he dares ask for "some more" food, and is sent away to be apprenticed to an undertaker. He flees to London and falls in with a criminal band led by FAGIN, who tries to train him for the criminal life.

Tyrone family (James, Mary, Jamie, Edmund). Tormented central characters of Eugene O'NEILL's tragedy *LONG DAY'S JOURNEY INTO NIGHT* (written 1940–41, performed 1956), based on O'Neill's own family: James, the father, an actor who wore himself out in one role; Mary, the mother, a morphine addict; Jamie, the elder son, an alcoholic and a bitter failure; and Edmund, the younger son (O'Neill's alter ego) plagued by ill health, guilt, and shame. Jamie achieves a kind of redemption in O'Neill's final play, *A MOON FOR THE MISBEGOTTEN* (written 1943, performed 1957).

Ulysses. *See* **Odysseus**

Uncle Tom. *See* **Tom, Uncle**

Usher, Roderick. Fatalistic protagonist of Edgar Allan POE's Gothic short story "THE FALL OF THE HOUSE OF USHER" (1840). He and his sister Madeline are the last Ushers, and he morosely anticipates the extinguishing of the family line in a dilapidated mansion that also awaits its fall.

Valjean, Jean. Reformed ex-convict and protagonist of Victor HUGO's novel *LES MISÉRABLES* (1862). Having served 19 years in the galleys for stealing bread for his sister's family, Valjean is inspired to renounce crime when a benevolent bishop forgives him for a new theft. He strives to live an honorable life under an assumed name, but is pursued relentlessly by police inspector JAVERT.

Van Winkle, Rip. Bewitched title character of WASHINGTON IRVING's short story "RIP VAN WINKLE" (1819). An easygoing farmer, Rip wanders into the Catskills to escape his domineering wife. After playing ninepins and drinking ale with some oddly dressed fellows, he falls asleep, and awakens 20 years later. The revelers, it is hinted, were the ghosts of Henry Hudson and his crew.

Vanya, Uncle [Ivan Petrovich Voinitsky]. Title character of Anton CHEKHOV's play *UNCLE VANYA* (1897). Casting aside his own aspirations, he has spent his life managing the affairs of his brother-in-law, the scholar Serebryakov, whom he once esteemed as a genius but now sees as a manipulative fraud.

Viola. Cross-dressing heroine of William SHAKESPEARE's comedy *TWELFTH NIGHT; OR, WHAT YOU WILL* (c. 1600). Shipwrecked in a strange country, she disguises herself as a youth, Cesario, and becomes a page to Duke Orsino, with whom she falls in love, while Orsino's beloved, Countess Olivia, falls for the comely "young man."

Vladimir [Didi]. Central character in Samuel BECKETT's absurdist play *WAITING FOR GODOT* (1953). For two days, he and fellow tramp ESTRAGON (Gogo) vainly await the arrival of the mysterious Mr. Godot, while discoursing on a variety of topics. Vladimir is the more philosophically inclined of the pair.

Voinitsky, Ivan Petrovich. *See* **Vanya, Uncle**

Vronsky, Count Alexey Kirilich. Lover of the title character in Leo TOLSTOY's novel *ANNA KARENINA* (1878). A dashing officer, he falls in love with the beautiful, married Anna KARENINA and induces her to leave her family for him.

Vye, Eustacia. Passionate main character in Thomas HARDY's novel *THE RETURN OF THE NATIVE* (1878). Longing to leave her native Egdon Heath, she spurns her lover Damon Wildeve to marry Clym YEOBRIGHT, newly returned from glamorous Paris, but feels trapped in the marriage when Clym's plans conflict with her aspirations.

Walker, Coalhouse, Jr. Central character of E. L. DOCTOROW's novel of turn-of-the-20th-century America, *Ragtime* (1975). Ragtime musician Walker turns to terrorism when his car is damaged by racists. His experiences are intermingled with appearances by contemporary historical figures, including Henry Ford, Emma Goldman, J. P. Morgan, and Sigmund FREUD. His name and the outline of his story are derived from Heinrich von KLEIST's novella *Michael Kohlhaas* (1810) and its eponymous rebel hero.

Wandrous, Gloria. Lonely New York party girl whose phone number prefix forms the title of JOHN O'HARA's novel *BUtterfield 8* (1935), based on the true case of speakeasy demimondaine Starr Faithfull (1906–1931). Amid her life's tawdry glamour, Gloria seeks love, but two men who might have rescued her let her down, and she dies in a paddle-wheeler accident. Elizabeth Taylor won an Oscar for her updated Gloria in the 1960 film.

Watson, Dr. John. Friend and associate of detective Sherlock HOLMES and the transcriber for posterity of his adventures, in four Arthur Conan DOYLE novels, beginning with *A Study in Scarlet* (1887), and 56 short stories (published in *THE ADVENTURES OF SHERLOCK HOLMES*, 1892, and several other collections).

Werther. Title character of J. W. von GOETHE's novel *THE SORROWS OF YOUNG WERTHER* (1774). The embodiment of the early Romantic era of "sensibility" in the German variant called "Storm and Stress," he falls stormily and stressfully in love with village beauty Lotte, although she is betrothed to — and marries — another man, and can offer Werther only friendship.

Wife of Bath. Bawdy, lusty teller of "The Wife of Bath's Tale" in Geoffrey CHAUCER's collection *THE CANTERBURY TALES* (c. 1387–1400). Five times widowed, and looking for a sixth husband, she recalls her life with her first five mates in the lengthy Prologue to her tale, as she reflects on women's desire for "maistrie," or sovereignty, over men.

Willard, George. Observant recurring character in SHERWOOD ANDERSON's collection of small-town tales, *WINESBURG, OHIO* (1919). An aspiring reporter on the local newspaper, he listens to the stories confided to him by the "grotesques" of the town.

Windermere, Lady (Margaret). Title character of Oscar WILDE's comedy of manners *LADY WINDERMERE'S FAN* (1892). A young wife and mother with "something of the Puritan" in her, she thinks that a woman who has committed a fault should "never be forgiven." She learns to be more tolerant when her fan is found in a bachelor's apartment, and her reputation is saved by the intervention of the scandal-tainted Mrs. ERLYNNE.

Wingfield family (Amanda, Laura, Tom). Main characters of TENNESSEE WILLIAMS's play *THE GLASS MENAGERIE* (1945), based on Williams's own family. Amanda, the mother, is a faded beauty trapped in genteel illusions; Laura, the daughter, is painfully shy and wears a brace on her leg; Tom, the son (also the on-stage narrator of this "memory play"), yearns to escape and devote himself to literature.

Winkle, Rip Van. *See* **Van Winkle, Rip**

Wolfe, Nero. Corpulent sleuth of around 80 novels, novellas, and short stories by Rex STOUT, from *Fer-de-Lance* (1934) to *A Family Affair* (1975). Operating from his brownstone in New York City, Wolfe uses logic and the findings of investigator Archie GOODWIN to solve crimes. In between cases, he indulges his love of orchids and gourmet food. (Several additional adventures were written by Robert Goldsborough in the 1980s.)

Woodhouse, Emma. Title character and protagonist of Jane AUSTEN's novel *EMMA* (1816). "Handsome, clever, and rich, with a comfortable home and happy disposition," her chief flaws are a tendency "to think a little too well of herself," and a serious overestimation of her skill as a matchmaker.

Wooster, Bertie. Quintessential young man about town in a series of P. G. WODEHOUSE comic stories and novels beginning with the collection *MY MAN JEEVES* (1919). Short on brains, long on bonhomie, Bertie requires the infinite resourcefulness of his valet, JEEVES, to extricate him from the clutches of unforgiving aunts, unsuitable fiancées, and truly unfortunate neckties.

Worthing, Jack [John Worthing, J.P., Mr. Ernest Worthing]. Dual-natured dandy in Oscar WILDE's comedy *THE IMPORTANCE OF BEING EARNEST* (1895). He is the frivolous "Ernest in town," under which assumed but desirable name he courts his best friend Algernon MONCRIEFF's cousin Gwendolen FAIRFAX, and the sober "Jack in the country," where he serves as guardian to Cecily CARDEW. Not until the play's end does he realize "the vital Importance of Being Earnest."

Wulf, Anna Freeman. Main character of Doris LESSING's novel *THE GOLDEN NOTEBOOK* (1962). Wulf, a writer in 1950s London, maintains four notebooks, about her youth in colonial Africa, her experiences in the Communist Party, her fictional alter ego, and her actual daily life. Struggling to complete her new novel, "Free Women," she tries to bring her fragmented existence together in a fifth, "golden," notebook.

Yeobright, Clym [Clement]. Title character in Thomas HARDY's novel *THE RETURN OF THE NATIVE* (1878). Leaving a job in the Parisian diamond trade, he returns to his native Egdon Heath and marries the passionate Eustacia VYE. He plans to start a school, but eyestrain obliges him to take work as a furze-cutter, which frustrates Eustacia, who had hoped to escape from the heath.

Yossarian, Captain John. World War II bombardier and protagonist of Joseph HELLER's satirical novel *CATCH-22* (1961). Appalled by the carnage of the war and the stupidity of military bureaucracy, Yossarian tries to opt out of combat by any available means, including pleading insanity, but is thwarted by the army's "Catch-22," which deems such exertions proof of sanity.

Ysoult. *See* Iseult

Zarechnaya, Nina Mikhailovna. Aspiring actress in Anton CHEKHOV's play *THE SEAGULL* (1896). She performs in an experimental play that Konstantin TREPLEV, who loves her, stages for his friends and family. Among the spectators is Treplev's mother's lover, the writer TRIGORIN, and Nina becomes infatuated with him.

Zenobia. 1. Main character in Nathaniel HAWTHORNE's novel *The Blithedale Romance* (1852). A feminist member of the utopian community Blithedale, she and other intellectuals attempt unsuccessfully to live in harmony. Hawthorne called her "passionate, luxurious, lacking simplicity, not deeply defined." 2. Sickly older wife of the title character in Edith WHARTON's novel *ETHAN FROME* (1911); also called Zeena. When she invites her young cousin Mattie to visit the couple at their New England farm, she sets in motion an unanticipated turn of events.

Zeus. King of the gods in Greek mythology; known as Jupiter or Jove to the Romans. His emblem is the eagle, and his weapon the thunderbolt. He is married to Hera (Juno to the Romans), but roves the heavens and earth in many guises in search of others worthy of his divine embrace. He appears in HOMER's epics the *ILIAD* and the *ODYSSEY* (8th century B.C.), and many other works, including comedies entitled *Amphitryon* by MOLIÈRE (1668) and Heinrich von KLEIST (published 1807, performed 1899), in which he deceives the faithful Alcmene by appearing to her as her husband, Amphitryon.

Zhivago, Yuri Andreievich. Title character of Boris PASTERNAK's novel *DOCTOR ZHIVAGO* (1957). A sensitive poet/physician, he works as an army doctor during World War I and is caught up in the chaos of the Russian Revolution and the following civil war. Twenty-five of his poems make up the work's final chapter.

Zuckerman, Nathan. Central character of PHILIP ROTH's self-mockingly autobiographical novels *THE GHOST WRITER* (1979), *ZUCKERMAN UNBOUND* (1981), and *THE ANATOMY LESSON* (1983); the three works were published with the novella *The Prague Orgy* as *Zuckerman Bound: A Trilogy and Epilogue* (1985). The Roth-like novelist is faced with such problems as a search for a literary protector, the public controversy over his bestselling novel, and coping with "overnight" success. He also appears in several other Roth works, including *The Counterlife* (1987) and *American Pastoral* (1997).

Dictionary of Literature

TERMS, STYLES, MOVEMENTS, GENRES

ABSTRACT POEM Poem whose effect derives from its combination of sounds, rather than from the meaning of its words. The term was coined by Edith Sitwell, who was an adept at the form. Some of the poetry of Arthur Rimbaud and Gerard Manley Hopkins is abstract, as is the work of early 20th-century Russian poet Velimir Khlebnikov. Roy Campbell is one of the best-known and most prolific practitioners.

ABSURDISM Movement emphasizing the fundamental meaninglessness of the universe and of human actions. Although it had its origins with the early Church Fathers, the contemporary manifestation emerged as a response to the violence of World War II and the traditional values and culture of Europe that produced that violence. Philosophers such as Martin Heidegger, Karl Jaspers, and Jean-Paul Sartre developed existentialism around the absurdist idea that human freedom requires us to act in an unknowable and irrational world that lacks any guidelines for determining our actions. In literature, writers such as Albert Camus, Samuel Beckett, Eugène Ionesco, and Jean Genet created novels and especially theatrical works that challenged the intelligibility of humans and human society. They employed the comic mode as a way of challenging the serious and high-minded pretensions of the culture; the senselessness of their plots and characters forced readers or spectators to confront the fundamental meaninglessness of the world, or else to engage in the struggle to create new meanings.

ACCENT Vocal prominence of a particular syllable or syllables. Accent, which depends upon the words' sense, is formally distinguished from stress, which depends upon meter. Verse that follows a regular pattern of accented and unaccented syllables is known as accentual poetry. This type of meter forms the basis of English and numerous other poetries, unlike Greek and Latin prosody, which is structured on the alternation of long and short syllables.

ACMEISM (from Greek for "highest point") Russian poetic movement at the beginning of the 20th century that emphasized craft and precise imagery. Acmeism defined itself in opposition to the mysticism and lack of clarity in Symbolism. Founded in St. Petersburg by Sergei Gorodetsky and Nikolai Gumilyov, it was associated with the journal *Apollon*, so called for its rejection of Dionysian tumult. The Soviets disapproved of the Acmeists' stress on language, and silenced its most prominent members, executing Gumilyov, censuring the work of Anna Akhmatova, and sentencing Osip Mandelshtam to a labor camp, where he perished.

AESTHETIC DISTANCE Space established between the work of art and reality. It functions to remind audiences that the work of art is not meant to be confused with some putative reality, nor must verisimilitude be the benchmark for critical assessment of the work. The term was coined by Edward Bullough in 1912 and was notably espoused by Bertolt Brecht, whose dramatic theory of epic theater emphasized the importance of aesthetic distance as a means to

■ 621

alert the audience to the political and social aspects of the play that might be missed if the audience identified too completely with the characters or the world on the stage.

AESTHETICISM Late 19th-century artistic movement that held beauty to be the highest standard for the work of art. It represented a backlash against the utilitarianism that characterized contemporary social and aesthetic theories. Philosophically, it was rooted in the aesthetics of Immanuel Kant, who held that art formed a separate sphere that could not be judged on the basis of utility or morality. Early proponents included Madame de Staël, Goethe, the German Romantics, and the British Pre-Raphaelite Brotherhood, while other practitioners included Walter Pater and Aubrey Beardsley in England and the Parnassians in France. The works of Edgar Allan Poe and Charles Baudelaire inspired the French Symbolists, and Oscar Wilde strove to personify Aestheticism in both his life and work. Critics of Aestheticism, including John Ruskin, Samuel Butler, and Leo Tolstoy rejected as bankrupt art that lacked a moral impulse.

AFFECTIVE FALLACY The error of overemphasizing the importance of a work's emotional impact upon its audience. It was so defined by Monroe Beardsley and W. K. Wimsatt in 1946 and was taken up by the New Critics as a rebuke to earlier impressionistic critics. The idea implies the objectivity of criticism, valued over analyses that attend to factors outside of the work of art. Both Aristotle's claim that the purpose of tragedy is to evoke "terror and pity" and the contemporary reader-response school of criticism oppose this critical impulse.

AGON (Greek, "contest") In a literary work, the conflict or contest between the main character and a rival, from which are derived the terms "protagonist" for the former and "antagonist" for the latter. The word comes from ancient Greek comedy, as in the works of Aristophanes, in which two characters or sections of the audience debated.

AGRARIAN MOVEMENT Conservative movement, holding sway at the beginning of the 20th century in Germany and the United States, that championed a return to the modes and values of agrarian life against the development of industrial capitalism. In the United States, it was centered around a group of Southern writers associated with Vanderbilt University, including John Crowe Ransom, Allen Tate, Donald Davidson, Robert Penn Warren, Merrill Moore, and Laura Riding, although many of those who initially identified with the movement later repudiated it. The movement produced a journal, *The Fugitive*, and a manifesto, *I'll Take My Stand* (1930). The movement's influence could be felt upon Imagism, in the analytical work of New Criticism, and, most significantly, in the literary renaissance of the South.

ALEXANDRINE Line of poetry of 12 syllables with major stresses on the sixth and final syllables, two secondary accents, and a caesura after the sixth syllable. Its name probably derives from the 12th-century *Roman d'Alexandre*, the story of Alexander the Great. The standard French heroic line, rarely used by poets of other languages, it plays a role similar to that of iambic pentameter in English. Generally considered too long and too awkward for the uninflected English language, it is, however, used as the last line of a Spenserian stanza. The alexandrine is flexible enough for use in a wide range of forms, from lyric poetry to the comedies of Molière and the tragedies of Corneille and Racine. In the late 19th century, a modified form known as "vers romantique" appeared.

ALIENATION EFFECT OR **A-EFFECT** (German, "Verfremdungseffekt" or "V-Effekt") Idea associated with the epic theater of Bertolt Brecht that drama should constantly emphasize its own artificiality in order to create a space in which the audience might reflect upon social and political questions. Actors are encouraged to adopt a critical attitude toward their characters, rather than to "become" the character, as in the more naturalistic Stanislavsky method. In addition, various techniques, including the use of captions on a screen and exposing the technical apparatus of the stage, work to prevent the audience from losing itself in the performance.

ALLEGORY (from Greek for "speak in other terms") Narrative whose component parts are meant to be read symbolically as illustrating an abstract idea or situation not explicitly mentioned in the text. A number of types of allegory exist, including the fable, beast fable, parable, apologue, exemplum, and dream vision. Since classical times, such writers as Plato, Cicero, and Apuleius have used allegories to convey complicated ideas; however, the use of the form reached its height in the Middle Ages, with such works as the *Romance of the Rose*, depicting a lover's courtship of a flower. Celebrated later examples include the moral allegory of *The Pilgrim's Progress* and the political allegory of *Peter and the Wolf*.

ALLITERATION OR **HEAD RHYME** The repetition of initial sounds, especially consonants, as with the letter "s" in T. S. Eliot's "Scuttling across the floors of silent seas." With assonance and consonance, it is one of the tools that add texture to language by making associations between words and by drawing attention to the possibilities of sound.

ALLUSION (from Latin for "to play with") An indirect reference to a person, event, or other text, often made to religious traditions, national historical events, or political personalities as well as classical literature, as in Edna St. Vincent Millay's "I dreamed I moved among the Elysian Fields," in which a reference to Greek mythology suggests the speaker's delight in a love affair. Types of allusion include topical, personal (something known only to the author's intimates), imitative (to another work, in parody), or structural (when the structure of one work suggests that of another).

ALTERITY Mikhail Bakhtin's term in *The Dialogical Imagination* (*Voprosy Literatury i Estetiki*, 1958) for the author's ability to see a character as an other and not solely in relation to the self. The author must have compassion for the character, but still be able to see it as separate and external. Bakhtin criticizes authors who do not accomplish this dual movement for using characters merely as their own mouthpieces.

AMBIGUITY Language that implies multiple meanings or understandings; often considered an error, especially in factual prose, although it may add depth in literary language. Ambiguity allows words to convey more than their literal meaning and can draw attention to the flexibility of language as a signifying scheme. William Empson identified distinctions among its usages in the classic *Seven Types of Ambiguity* (1930).

ANGRY YOUNG MEN Group of 1950s British writers who criticized the class consciousness of English society. Their rage at social distinctions and privileges was reflected in a literary preoccupation with avoiding all sorts of mannerism and falsity in literature in favor of working-class language and themes. The name, which comes from the title of Leslie Allen Paul's autobiography, was first applied in print to John Osborne, and soon came to refer to the entire literary phenomenon, and to any young man protesting against the status quo. The group included Kingsley Amis, Bernard Kops, Alan Sillitoe, John Wain, and Arnold Wesker. Osborne's play *Look Back in Anger* is the group's quintessential work. Their dominance of the literary scene had passed by the 1960s.

ANTHOLOGY An edited collection of partial or complete texts. In the classical period, it included a variety of epigrams and other works. Early celebrated exemplars include the collection of Chinese verse known as *The Book of Odes* (*Shi Jing*), selected by Confucius (551–479 B.C.), and the *Greek Anthology* (*Anthologia Hellēnikē*), compiled between the 1st and 11th centuries. The first anthology published in English, *Songes and Sonettes, Written by the Ryght Honorable Lorde Henry Haward Late Earle of Surrey and Other* (1557, usually known as *Tottel's Miscellany*), accomplished one of the main charges of the anthology: making a range of work available to a broad audience.

ANTICLIMAX An abrupt shift from the lofty to the trivial. Dr. Samuel Johnson provided the first definition: "a sentence in which the last part expresses something lower than the first." It lends itself to humor or irony in its implicit linking of the significant and the preposterous. Not every movement away from the climax is anticlimactic; tragedy typically ends not with the climax, but with some comment on the events represented.

ANTIHERO A protagonist deficient in the traits associated with the hero. Not having merely a tragic flaw, the antihero represents a major departure from the idea of the hero as strong, brave, and personifying the best of the culture's ideals. More prevalent in contemporary literature and, indeed, characteristic of a modern distrust of heroism, the antihero nonetheless has existed in all eras. Prominent examples include Cervantes's Don Quixote, Henry Fielding's Tom Jones, and T. S. Eliot's J. Alfred Prufrock.

ANTINOVEL A work of experimental fiction that abandons many of the traditional narrative conventions, such as psychologically coherent characters and the development of the plot in linear time or, indeed, of any obvious plot. Other features may include unorthodox vocabulary and syntax, highly repetitive prose, multiple and differing expositions of the same event, and meticulous attention to the physical characteristics of objects. Initially describing the work of Nathalie Sarraute, Alain Robbe-Grillet, Michel Butor, and other practitioners of the French *nouveau roman* (new novel) of the 1950s, the category later came to include other writers, including Flann O'Brien, Vladimir Nabokov, and Christine Brooks-Rose. Jean-Paul Sartre coined the term in his introduction to Sarraute's *Portrait of a Man Unknown* (*Portrait d'un Inconnu*, 1948).

ANTITHESIS 1. A contrast or opposition. In rhetoric, antithesis signifies an opposition between related phrases or clauses, usually highlighted by parallel syntactical structure, as in Dryden's "Thus wicked but in will, of means bereft, / He left not faction, but of that was left." 2. In philosophy, an argument that counters a previously stated principle, or thesis. In the dialectic, the result of posing the thesis and antithesis will be a third term, synthesis.

APOCALYPTIC LITERATURE Eschatological literature common to ancient Hebrew and early Christian periods predicting the sudden and decisive end of the world and God's final judgment, resulting in the humbling of worldly powers and the triumph of the downtrodden. A prophetic view of history, apocalypticism is found also in other times and places marked by tumult and rapid change. Exemplary texts include the Book of Daniel in the Hebrew Bible and the Revelation of St. John the Divine, also called the Apocalypse, in the New Testament. This literature generally features numerous signs and characters, such as angels, animals, and numbers, which are interpreted symbolically.

APOCRYPHA The 14 books of the Septuagint, the 3rd-century B.C. translation of the Hebrew Scriptures into Greek; they are considered non-canonical by Protestantism. Roman Catholicism includes 11 of these books, using a version of the Bible only slightly revised from the Vulgate of St. Jerome, the original Latin translation from the Greek. The term also refers to various books proposed, but not accepted, for inclusion in the New Testament; these works are not considered to be divinely inspired. By extension, any work or story only dubiously attributed to an author may be considered apocryphal. In the latter sense, a lower-case "a" is used.

APOLOGY (from Greek for "speech in defense") Defense or explanation of actions or ideas. In this sense, an apology does not suggest any admission of fault or regret. The most famous example in Western literature is undoubtedly Plato's account of Socrates' *Apologia*, in which the philosopher answers charges of impiety. Modern instances include Percy Bysshe Shelley's *Defence of Poetry* (1821), refuting Thomas Love Peacock's insistence that poetry was a waste of time better spent engaged in the sciences, and John Henry Newman's *Apologia pro Vita Sua* (1864), which countered Charles

Kingsley's contention that Newman did not value truth as a virtue.

APOSTROPHE (from Greek for "turning away") Figure of speech for the direct address of an absent person or thing. The object of apostrophe might be a celebrity or a real person known to the author, or the personification of an inanimate object, as in Wordsworth's "And O, ye Fountains, Meadows, Hills, and Groves, / Forbode not any severing of our loves!" Its effect of making rhetorically present that which is absent leads to its particular use in the elegy and ode. In classical rhetoric, apostrophe refers to the speaker's direct address of a member of the audience.

APPRENTICESHIP NOVEL A fictional account of the trials a youth faces in the process of becoming an adult. The name comes from Goethe's *Wilhelm Meister's Apprenticeship* (1795–96), which inaugurated the genre and remains its exemplary text. The genre holds an important place in German letters, where it is known as the *Bildungsroman*; in English, Charles Dickens's *David Copperfield* and Thomas Wolfe's *Look Homeward, Angel* may be counted among its numbers.

ARCHETYPE (from Greek for "first molded as a pattern, exemplary") An image or theme said to represent part of the collective heritage of human memory. Drawing from the studies of psychology, myth, and folklore of J. G. Frazer and C. G. Jung, archetypal critics attempt to interpret these images as part of a universal collective unconscious, which reflects itself in themes, such as the quest, rite of passage, feud, and descent to the underworld, and in characters, such as the hero, *femme fatale*, mother, magician, and fool. Popular in the early and middle 20th century, its influence has waned owing to contemporary concerns that its emphasis on seeing similarities across times and cultures leads to reductionism.

ART FOR ART'S SAKE The English version of Victor Cousin's dictum *"l'art pour l'art"* sounded the call to arms of Aestheticism. The idea that art must be separated from any moral or utilitarian purpose was a reaction against the perceived philistinism of the industrial age. The influential aesthetic theory represented by the slogan had roots in the Romantic period, and enjoyed a dominant position from the late 19th century through the beginning of World War II. It was challenged by more didactically inclined critics, such as Samuel Butler, who asked, "What is art that it should have a sake?"

ARTHURIAN LEGEND Body of chivalric literature detailing the exploits of King Arthur and the realm of Camelot. A conflation of a historical Welsh chieftain with ancient Celtic mythological figures, Arthur was the son of Uther Pendragon and Igraine, and the protégé of Merlin the Magician. He proved his right to rule by pulling the sword Excalibur out of a stone, and held court at the Round Table with knights who performed noble and heroic deeds, including Perceval, Gawain, and the strongest and most valiant, Launcelot. The fierce warriors joined in the quest for the Holy Grail, the cup used by Jesus at the Last Supper, as well as amorous adventures, notably the illicit liaison of Launcelot and Queen Guinevere. Arthur was finally defeated in a battle that destroyed Camelot, and the mighty Excalibur returned to the Lady of the Lake.

Arthur first appeared in Welsh literature as early as the 6th century. In 1137, Geoffrey of Monmouth included him in a history of British kings, while various authors added the distinctive features of the legend, such as the Round Table by the Norman poet Wace and the theme of courtly love by the French Chrétien de Troyes, who began the practice of recounting the exploits of individual knights and added the theme of the Grail in *Perceval*. The first English-language version was produced by Layamon (1198–1207). In the 13th century, Robert de Boron's *Merlin* chronicled the king's youth, while the anonymous *Sir Gawain and the Green Knight*, about one of Arthur's knights, is considered one of the finest examples of medieval English poetry. Sir Thomas Malory's influential *Le Morte d'Arthur*, which dates from the late 15th century, collected the various traditions in one comprehensive work. More recent adaptations include Tennyson's moralistic and symbolic *Idylls of the King* and Mark Twain's comic *A Connecticut Yankee in King Arthur's Court* as well as retellings by William Morris, Edwin Arlington Robinson, T. H. White, and Marion Zimmer Bradley.

ASSONANCE (from Latin for "to sound in response") The repetition of vowel sounds, as in "day" and "fail." As with alliteration and consonance, assonance adds richness and color to language. In poetry, assonance may take the place of rhyme; hence, it is also called "vowel rhyme" or "vocalic rhyme." It played an important role in early Celtic, French, and Spanish poetry, but seldom appeared in English until Gerard Manley Hopkins and later Wilfred Owen, W. H. Auden, and Dylan Thomas used it as a substitute for end rhyme.

AUTOBIOGRAPHY A biography of the author's own life. Robert Southey first defined the genre in 1809, differentiating it from the memoir, a record of an era through which the writer lived, and the journal, diary, or travel narrative. Although the first prominent example is *The Confessions of St. Augustine*, autobiography is primarily a modern form. Famed autobiographers include Benjamin Franklin, John Stuart Mill, Adolf Hitler, Golda Meir, Winston Churchill, and Jean-Jacques Rousseau. A related category, autobiographical fiction, includes such works as Marcel Proust's *Remembrance of Things Past* and James Joyce's *A Portrait of the Artist as a Young Man*. While Samuel Johnson opined that the subject is his or her own best biographer, critics point out that any author shapes the story through the selection of the material and personal biases, which may or may not be unconscious.

AVANT-GARDE (French, "advance guard") Literature or art that pushes ahead of or challenges the standards or proprieties of its own era. Originally a military term for the vanguard of an army and later referring to radical political movements, it has come to signify the heroic status of both art and the artist. It implies a fundamentally modern conception of the author as being in continuous strife with philistine conventions and beliefs, and explicitly values novelty and formal innovation in the arts.

BALLAD (from Latin and Italian for "to dance") A short narrative song generally transmitted through the oral tradition. Originally signifying musical accompaniment to a dance and etymologically related to the word "ballet," the ballad is told simply and exists in multiple versions, as the singer customizes the material in each retelling. Some early ballads were the province of minstrels charged with recording the history of a particular court or nobleman, while others are of popular origin. Types include the historical ballad, outlaw ballad, lament ballad or coronach, and broadside ballad. Ballads from the United States are descended from Old English ballads, but add a distinctively American flavor, such as a disregard of rank and a focus on work or popular heroes. The ballad form has also been adopted by poets, as in Oscar Wilde's *The Ballad of Reading Gaol*, and by contemporary folk singers, such as Woody Guthrie and Bob Dylan.

BARD Title awarded to a poet in ancient Gaul and Britain, signifying membership in a privileged caste and the responsibility of commemorating heroic actions and historic events. The formal category survives today in Wales for a poet who has participated in the National Eisteddfod, the annual poetry and arts festival. Informally, any poet may be called a bard. When capitalized, the term refers to Shakespeare.

BAROQUE Flamboyant and highly ornate style characteristic of 16th-, 17th-, and early 18th-century art of Europe, particularly of Catholic Europe. It also refers to this period, when the classical simplicity of the early Renaissance gave way to a more lavish and florid sensibility. The term, which is related to the word for "grotesque or absurd pedantry" rather than from "irregular pearl" as commonly cited, more appropriately refers to art, architecture, and music, although it can be applied to literature following in the tradition of Giambattista Marino in Italy, Luis de Góngora in Spain, and some of the metaphysical poets, including John

Donne and Richard Crashaw in England, who employed elaborate conceits to discuss such issues as religion, temporality, and beauty. When used in a pejorative sense, the term denigrates the excessive and artificial.

BATHOS (Greek, "depth") The movement from a lofty or significant idea to the trivial in the pursuit of pathos, which by failing becomes ridiculous. Denoting an unintentional anticlimax, it may be applied to a figure of speech or of drama that becomes absurd when trivial events are given exaggeratedly weighty treatment or when lofty ideals are handled frivolously. Alexander Pope first defined the term in a parody of Longinus's essay *On the Sublime*, offering as an example "Ye Gods! annihilate both Space and Time, / And make two Lovers happy."

BEAT MOVEMENT OR BEAT GENERATION Group of American writers in the 1950s who rejected prevailing middle-class cultural values and norms in order to seek forms of enlightenment that those values precluded. Anti-intellectual and cool, they sought to distinguish themselves from the trappings of "square" society. Their experiments with expanded states of consciousness through drugs, sex, mysticism, and Buddhism were matched by a literary desire to do away with what they perceived as falsity and mannerism in literature by adopting a freeform, unrevised style that sought to reflect the real life of the streets.

The movement was split between New York City and San Francisco, where City Lights Books, the bookstore and publishing house founded by Lawrence Ferlinghetti, was located. Members included Jack Kerouac, Allen Ginsberg, William S. Burroughs, Gary Snyder, and Gregory Corso, with, at various times, Kenneth Rexroth, Henry Miller, and Norman Mailer serving as mentors. Kerouac's novel *On the Road* (1957) typifies Beat sensibility in the cross-country travels of its hero, while Ginsberg's poem *Howl* (1956) showed him to be a forceful and eloquent elegist.

Many origins have been suggested for the term *Beat*, including beatific (referring to

ecstasy produced by mysticism or drugs), beaten down, beaten up, jazz beat, and weary; the term *beatnik* comes from a combination of "beat" and -*nik*, the Russian noun suffix signifying a representative or one concerned with something. Largely over by the 1960s, the Beat movement did not achieve widespread recognition in the United States until the 1970s, although the Beats' example helped make possible succeeding countercultural movements.

BILDUNGSROMAN (German, "novel of education") A novel that follows the hero's often difficult passage from youth into maturity. Goethe's highly influential *Wilhelm Meister's Apprenticeship* (1795–96), the prototype of the genre, was followed by such works as Novalis's *Heinrich von Ofterdingen* and Thomas Mann's *The Magic Mountain*. Dickens's *David Copperfield* may be considered an English example, and Charlotte Brontë's *Jane Eyre* a prominent female *Bildungsroman*. If the protagonist is an artist, the work may be described by the term *Künstlerroman*; also related are the *Erziehungsroman* (novel of upbringing) and the *Entwicklungsroman* (novel of development). In English, it is also known as an "apprenticeship novel."

BIOGRAPHY (from Greek for "life" + "to write") A written account of an individual's life. Although biography is a relatively modern form, antecedents can be found in antiquity, as in Plutarch's *Parallel Lives*, and in medieval hagiography and chronicles detailing the histories of kings and other nobles. Biography as we understand it today, with an emphasis on exploring the character and motivation of the subject, first appears in the 17th century. Samuel Johnson's *Lives of the English Poets* (1779–81) and James Boswell's *Life of Samuel Johnson* (1791) set the standard for the genre, and Johnson argued for biography's status as the only literary genre to depict the truth. Despite their claims of objectivity, Victorian biographers notoriously sanitized their subjects' lives, while novelists sometimes take historical figures for their topics, to name just a few complications to the genre's boundaries. Psychobiography, which speculates on psychological development, is a popular subgenre.

BLACK HUMOR/COMEDY (from French, "humour noir") Morbid or ironic humor that highlights the absurdity and grotesqueness of life. Cultivated in the Theater of the Absurd and a common feature of modern fiction, its wish to make comedy out of suffering paradoxically suggests both disillusion and the irrepressibility of the human spirit. Prominent examples include the work of Franz Kafka, Samuel Beckett, Günter Grass, Kurt Vonnegut, and Joseph Heller. The Surrealist poet André Breton used "humour noir" in the title of an anthology in 1940, and the term came into wide use in the 1960s. The "sick joke" and "gallows humor" are related concepts.

BLACK MOUNTAIN POETS Innovative group of poets associated with North Carolina's Black Mountain College during the 1950s; their influential and experimental work was presented in the journals *Black Mountain Review* and *Origin*. Member Charles Olson expressed the group's philosophy of poetry through the concept of "projective verse" (derived from the words *projectile*, *percussive*, and *prospective*), which advocated the significance of the creative process and the poem as a vehicle for communicating that experience to readers. The group's focus on oral aspects of poetry included a belief that form should be a reflection of the poet's breath, and a fondness for conversational language and the loose style of William Carlos Williams. Counting among its members such poets as Robert Creeley, Robert Duncan, Ed Dorn, Paul Blackburn, Denise Levertov, and Gary Snyder, the group had dispersed by the mid-1960s.

BLANK VERSE Unrhymed verse, generally in iambic pentameter. One of the closest forms to ordinary speech, it demands that practitioners develop the musicality of language through such devices as variations in expected stress and the placement of caesura, as well as the enthusiastic exploitation of the form's characteristic flexibility.

Blank verse developed in 16th-century Italy as a way of freeing the poet from the constraint of rhyme; it was intended, moreover, to echo the epic quality of classical heroic verse. Along with such other contemporary Italian forms as the sonnet, blank verse was introduced into English poetics by Henry Howard, Earl of Sussex. The form first found a worthy exemplar in Christopher Marlowe, whose *Tamburlaine* and *Edward II* demonstrated its versatility and power. It reached its highest expression in the drama of William Shakespeare, as in these lines from Antony's eulogy in *Julius Caesar*: "The evil that men do lives after them; / The good is oft interrèd with their bones." Blank verse was reclaimed for its original purpose of poetry by John Milton, and later became a favored form of the English Romantics. In the 20th century, William Butler Yeats, Robert Frost, and Wallace Stevens have made extensive use of the form.

BLOOMSBURY GROUP A circle of writers, artists, and intellectuals who converged in the Bloomsbury section of London from 1907 through 1930, and who helped to define English modernism by advocating new aesthetic and intellectual principles, agnosticism, radical politics, and unconventional lifestyles. Counting among its members Vanessa and Clive Bell, Leonard and Virginia Woolf, Lytton Strachey, E. M. Forster, Duncan Grant, and John Maynard Keynes, the group rallied around the philosophy of Cambridge philosopher G. E. Moore. Despite, or perhaps because of, their influence, they developed a reputation for both sophistication and elitism.

BLUESTOCKING A member of a loosely formed society of women led by Elizabeth Vesey and Elizabeth Montague in the mid-18th century to promote discussions of literary interest. Unlike traditional gatherings, bluestocking events prohibited alcohol, swearing, card games, gossip, and politics in favor of intellectual discourse. The group's name comes from Benjamin Stillingfleet's refusal of Vesey's invitation to participate, since he did not own formal white stockings. She advised him to come "in his blue stockings," referring to the worsted, everyday stockings he was then wearing. The term stuck, sometimes going instead by its French translation, "Le Bas Bleu." Women involved in the association include the novelist Fanny Burney, Hester Chapone, Elizabeth Carter, and Hannah More, author of the 1786 poem "Le Bas Bleu, or Conversation." Among the invited guests were such luminaries as Samuel Johnson, James Boswell, Samuel Richardson, and Horace Walpole. The term quickly came to refer to women who ostentatiously display intellectual ability.

BURLESQUE (French, from Italian for "joke, ridicule") Comic imitation of a serious work or genre that derives humor from the gulf between the subject and the way it is treated. Burlesque can refer to the ludicrous presentation of dignified subjects or the exalted handling of trifles. It is related to parody, which usually indicates specific attention to literary styles, and is gentler than satire, whose goal is derision rather than entertainment. Antecedents include the comedies of Aristophanes and Chaucer's send-ups of medieval romance. Paul Scarron's and Nicholas Boileau's late 17th-century mockery of classical conventions consolidated the critical usage of the term, which was also applied to the poetry of Samuel Butler, John Dryden, and Alexander Pope, the prose of Jonathan Swift, Daniel Defoe, and Washington Irving, and the drama of John Gay, Henry Fielding, and Richard Brinsley Sheridan. In the United States, it refers specifically to a theatrical tradition combining ribald comedy and striptease.

CAESURA (from Latin for "a cutting off") In prosody, an extrametrical pause or break in a line of poetry, as in the one following the comma in Pope's line, "Careless of censure, nor too fond of fame..." In classical versification, the result of ending a word within a foot, and thus contrasted with diaeresis. Other bodies of poetry employ caesura more freely, for two opposing purposes: highlighting the formal technique of the poem, and making the diction more colloquial. A break in the middle of a line is called "medial caesura," although breaks may also be "initial" or "terminal." Several types of caesura are distinguished, including masculine (caesura following a stressed syllable), feminine (following an unstressed syllable), epic (feminine caesura preceded by an additional unstressed syllable), and lyric (feminine caesura following an unstressed syllable required by the meter).

CAMBRIDGE APOSTLES A secret society founded at Cambridge University in 1820 for the purpose of fostering intellectual exchange and strong friendships. Formally named "the Cambridge Conversazione Society," it counted among its members Alfred, Lord Tennyson and Arthur Henry Hallam. G. E. Moore greatly influenced the society with his *Principia Ethica* (1903), which held that the pursuit of beauty and friendship underpinned an ethical life. In the early 20th century, many of its members, including E. M. Forster, John Maynard Keynes, Lytton Strachey, and Leonard Woolf, later belonged to the Bloomsbury Group, leading to a close association of the two.

CAMBRIDGE CRITICS Group of critics associated with Cambridge University who collectively established English literature as a legitimate field of study, comparable in scope and importance to classics, in the aftermath of World War I. Key figures such as I. A. Richards, F. R. Leavis, Q. D. Leavis, and William Empson insisted upon the importance of English literature to an understanding of the creative processes that define human existence. They favored close reading of texts over less rigorous, more impressionistic criticism; their work also featured middle-class interests and influences, in contrast to the more patrician field of classics. Cambridge linguistic philosophers G. E. Moore, Ludwig Wittgenstein, and Bertrand Russell were influences, as were the literary theories of Coleridge and T. S. Eliot. Much of their work was published in the journal *Scrutiny*, launched in 1932 by F. R. and Q. D. Leavis.

CANON The term has a number of related meanings that have put it at the center of literary debate since the mid-20th century, each

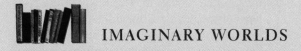

IMAGINARY WORLDS

VANITY FAIR

"Then I saw in my Dream, that when they were got out of the Wilderness, they presently saw a Town before them, and the name of that Town is *Vanity*; and at the Town there is a Fair kept called *Vanity-Fair*, because the Town where it is kept, *is lighter than Vanity*; and also, because all that is there sold, or that cometh thither, is *Vanity*. As is the saying of the wise, *All that cometh is vanity....* And moreover, at this Fair there is at all times to be seen Juglings, Cheats, Games, Plays, Fools, Apes, Knaves, and Rogues, and that of every kind."

John Bunyan, *The Pilgrim's Progress* (Part I, 1678; Part II, 1684)

LILLIPUTIA

"I could only look upwards; the Sun began to grow hot, and the Light offended my Eyes. I heard a confused Noise about me, but in the Posture I lay, could see nothing except the Sky. In a little time I felt something alive moving on my left Leg, which advancing gently forward over my Breast, came almost up to my Chin; when bending my Eyes downwards as much as I could, I perceived it to be a human Creature not six Inches high, with a Bow and Arrow in his Hands, and a Quiver at his Back. In the mean time, I felt at least Forty more of the same Kind (as I conjectured) following the first. I was in the utmost Astonishment, and roared so loud, that they all ran back in a Fright...."

Jonathan Swift, *Gulliver's Travels* (1726)

CAMELOT

"As a rule, the speech and behavior of these people were gracious and courtly; and I noticed that they were good and serious listeners when anybody was telling anything—I mean, in a dog-fightless interval. And plainly, too, they were a childlike and innocent lot; telling lies of the stateliest pattern with a most gentle and winning naivety, and ready and willing to listen to anybody else's lie, and believe it, too. It was hard to associate them with anything cruel or dreadful; and yet they dealt in tales of blood and suffering with a guileless relish that made me almost forget to shudder."

Mark Twain, *A Connecticut Yankee in King Arthur's Court* (1889)

THE ISLAND OF DOCTOR MOREAU

"Then suddenly upon the bank of the stream appeared something—at first I could not distinguish what it was. It bowed its head to the water and began to drink. Then I saw it was a man, going on all-fours like a beast! He was clothed in bluish cloth, and was of a copper-coloured hue, with black hair. It seemed that grotesque ugliness was an invariable character of these islanders. I could hear the suck of the water at his lips as he drank."

H. G. Wells, *The Island of Doctor Moreau* (1896)

THE EMERALD CITY

"Even with her eyes protected by the green spectacles, Dorothy and her friends were at first dazzled by the brilliancy of the wonderful City. The streets were lined with beautiful houses, all built of green marble and studded everywhere with sparkling emeralds. They walked over a pavement of the same green marble, and where the blocks were joined together were rows of emeralds, set closely, and glittering in the brightness of the sun. The windowpanes were of green glass; even the sky above the City had a green tint, and the rays of the sun were green.

"There were many people, men, women and children, walking about, and these were all dressed in green clothes and had greenish skins.... Many shops stood in the street, and Dorothy saw that everything in them was green. Green candy and green popcorn were offered for sale, as well as green shoes, green hats and green clothes of all sorts. At one place a man was selling green lemonade, and when the children bought it Dorothy could see that they paid for it with green pennies."

L. Frank Baum, *The Wonderful Wizard of Oz* (1900)

NEVER LAND

"What you see is the Never Land. You have often half seen it before, or even three-quarters, after the nightlights were lit, and you might then have beached your coracle on it if you had not always at the great moment fallen asleep.... It is an open-air scene, a forest with a beautiful lagoon beyond but not really far away, for the Never Land is very compact, not large and sprawly with tedious distances between one adventure and another, but nicely crammed. It is summer time on the trees and on the lagoon but winter on the river, which is not remarkable on Peter's island where all the four seasons may pass while you are filling a jug at the well."

J. M. Barrie, *Peter Pan, or, The Boy Who Would Not Grow Up* (1928)

SHANGRI-LA

"So far the appointments of Shangri-La had been all that he could have wished, certainly more than he could ever have expected. That a Tibetan monastery should possess a system of central heating was not, perhaps, so very remarkable in an age that supplied even Lhasa with telephones; but that it should combine the mechanics of Western hygiene with so much else that was Eastern and traditional, struck him as exceedingly singular. The bath, for instance, in which he had recently luxuriated, had been of a delicate green porcelain, a product, according to inscription, of Akron, Ohio. Yet the native attendant had valeted him in Chinese fashion, cleansing his ears and nostrils, and passing a thin, silk swab under his lower eyelids."

James Hilton, *Lost Horizon* (1934)

ANIMAL FARM

"The pigs now revealed that during the past three months they had taught themselves to read and write from an old spelling book which had belonged to Mr. Jones's children and which had been thrown on the rubbish

(Imaginary Worlds, continued)

heap.... They explained that by their studies of the past three months the pigs had succeeded in reducing the principles of Animalism to Seven Commandments. These Seven Commandments would now be inscribed on the wall; they would form an unalterable law by which all the animals on Animal Farm must live for ever after. With some difficulty (for it is not easy for a pig to balance himself on a ladder) Snowball climbed up and set to work, with Squealer a few rungs below him holding the paint-pot. The Commandments were written on the tarred wall in great white letters that could be read thirty yards away. They ran thus:

The Seven Commandments

1. Whatever goes upon two legs is an enemy.
2. Whatever goes upon four legs, or has wings, is a friend.
3. No animal shall wear clothes.
4. No animal shall sleep in a bed.
5. No animal shall drink alcohol.
6. No animal shall kill any other animal.
7. All animals are equal."

George Orwell, *Animal Farm* (1945)

related to the idea of an authoritative body of works. First, the books included by the Church in the Bible are canonical and considered to be divinely inspired, as distinct from other testaments, which are deemed to be apocryphal. By extension, the critically accepted works of any author may be considered canonical.

In another sense, the canon refers to a written or unwritten list of books deemed worthy of continued interest and critical study by virtue of some particular merit. As such, the canon has recently become the subject of considerable scrutiny by those critics who ask why its ranks consist largely of the works of white, male authors. These critics have highlighted the ways in which canon formation marginalizes the works of women and people of color.

CANTO (Italian, "song") A unit of an epic or narrative poem, comparable to a chapter in a book. Originally, it referred to a pause in a long epic recitation that allowed the singer to rest. While all long works are divided into smaller sections, the use of the term was established by medieval Italian poets, including Dante and Ludovico Ariosto. Authors such as Voltaire, Pope, Byron, and Ezra Pound have organized works into cantos.

CARICATURE (French, from Italian for "exaggeration") A humorous portrayal that exaggerates and accentuates a recognizable characteristic or trait. The motive behind caricature may be to ridicule or simply to amuse. Lady Bracknell from Oscar Wilde's *The Importance of Being Earnest* is an excellent example of a caricature of a British aristocratic and self-important mother.

CATASTROPHE (Greek, "overturning") In classical tragedy, the resolution of the plot, synonymous with dénouement. The final of the four divisions in Greek drama, following "protasis" (introduction), "epitasis" (continuance), and "catastasis" (heightening). The term gained its negative connotation from its particular applicability to the outcome of classical tragedy.

CATHARSIS (Greek, "purgation") The purgation or purification of emotion that results from the climax in tragedy. Aristotle used the medical

THE MATRIX

"'The matrix has its roots in primitive arcade games,' said the voice-over, 'in early graphics programs and military experimentation with cranial jacks.' On the Sony, a two-dimensional space war faded behind a forest of mathematically generated ferns, demonstrating the spacial possibilities of logarithmic spirals; cold blue military footage burned through, lab animals wired into test systems, helmets feeding into fire control circuits of tanks and war planes. 'Cyberspace. A consensual hallucination experienced daily by billions of legitimate operators, in every nation, by children being taught mathematical concepts....A graphic representation of data abstracted from the banks of every computer in the human system. Unthinkable complexity. Lines of light ranged in the nonspace of the mind, clusters and constellations of data. Like city lights, receding....'"

William Gibson, *Neuromancer* (1984)

term in his *Poetics* to explain why the "terror and pity" that spectators feel is both pleasurable and therapeutic. Although there is critical debate as to his precise meaning, Aristotle seems to claim that by providing a carefully regulated situation in which to arouse and then expunge the passions, tragedy serves a useful purpose in society. His view contradicts Plato's denunciation of art for recklessly engendering dangerous emotions.

CÉNACLE (from Latin for "dining room," particularly referring to the room in which the Last Supper took place) In 19th-century France, a literary and social circle that gathered around a particular figure. Participating in the Romantic cult of personality, it took over the salon's function of providing a forum for discussion and criticism. Famous examples centered around Charles Nodier and Victor Hugo. Balzac incorporates the doings of a *cénacle* into some of the works of *The Human Comedy*.

CHANSON DE GESTE (French, "song of heroic deeds") An Old French epic poem that relates the heroic exploits and courtly romances of the nobility. These narratives, of which some 80 are extant, were popular during the 11th–14th centuries although set considerably earlier, in the 8th and 9th centuries. The major cycle establishes the legend of Charlemagne as a defender of the faith surrounded by 12 noble lords, including Roland and Olivier, while another strand elaborates the history of William of Orange; in addition, other *chansons de geste* featured wars between nobles and against the Saracens, and intrigues among feudal lords. They were composed by *trouvères*, court minstrels in Northern France, and performed by *jongleurs*. The 12th-century *Song of Roland*, one of the earliest and most renowned of the *chansons*, is a defining work of French literature and national identity.

CHARACTER (from Greek for "engraved mark, brand") A person represented in fiction, drama, or other work of art. From this also comes the name of a literary genre entailing the short, clever portrayal of a type of person or of a personality trait. Theophrastus introduced the genre with his collection of 30 personality types, aptly named *Characters*, in the late 3rd century B.C. It enjoyed some vogue in the early 17th century among English and French writers, known as character writers, such as Sir Thomas Overbury, Joseph Hall, John Earle, and Jean de La Bruyère.

CHARACTERIZATION The delineation of a person in drama or narrative through description or indirectly by action and speech. Characters in realistic works are generally expected to be consistent, psychologically and morally comprehensible (according to the standards of the time), and to have clear motivation for their behavior.

CHICAGO CRITICS An influential group of critics, associated with the University of Chicago and founded in the mid-1930s, who undertook an analysis of the nature and object of criticism. Neo-Aristotelian in their belief that a poetics should not apply its own preconceptions to literary works, but rather be derived from those works, they attended to the ways in which authors elected to structure their works. They differed from their contemporaries who espoused New Criticism, which was concerned only with the internal coherence of the text, and with lyric poetry to the exclusion of narrative and drama. The Chicago critics include R. S. Crane, W. R. Keast, Richard McKeon, Norman Maclean, Elder Olson, Bernard Weinberg, and Wayne C. Booth; *Critics and Criticism: Ancient and Modern*, edited by Crane in 1952, presents many of their main ideas.

CHORUS (from Greek for "dance") In classical Greek drama, an ensemble that comments upon the unfolding action of the play, often offering society's view of the action. The term originally referred to a group of masked performers who recited poetry and danced during religious festivals, especially fertility rites. Drama is said to have begun when an actor (by tradition, the tragedian Thespis) first stepped out of the chorus and engaged it in a dialogue. Authors have utilized the chorus in varying ways: Aeschylus allowed it to participate in the plot, Sophocles made it a passive spectator, while Euripides gave it a largely ornamental function. In comedy, musical interludes came to substitute for the chorus, hence that meaning of the term in music. The role of the chorus waned in favor of dramatic interest in the actors. Since the Renaissance, the chorus has been revived in numerous works, including Shakespeare's plays (where a single character may fulfill its role), Milton's *Samson Agonistes*, and T. S. Eliot's *Murder in the Cathedral*.

CLASSICISM Doctrine contending that the ancient Greeks and Romans exemplify the apex of literary and cultural creation, and advocating a return to their emphasis on harmony, simplicity, decorum, logic, and attention to structure, as represented in the Greek ideal of unity. Proponents, sometimes called "Neoclassicists," dismissed disorderly and passionate self-expression in favor of technical mastery, which could be achieved through the imitation of the forms and themes of the ancient masters.

Classicism developed out of the Renaissance's return to the values associated with antiquity. Perhaps most influential in France in the 17th and 18th centuries, where it was espoused by Corneille, La Fontaine, Molière, Racine, and Voltaire, it also attracted such German authors as Goethe, Lessing, Schiller, and Hölderlin. Classicism's prominence extended to England, where it numbered among its supporters Ben Jonson, Dryden, Pope, and Swift, and continued into the 19th century through the impact of such figures as Matthew Arnold and Walter Pater. In the 20th century, its best-known advocates included Ezra Pound and T. S. Eliot as well as the American exponents of New Criticism, who focused upon the formal attributes of poetry. Classicism is often opposed to Romanticism, in which intensity of emotion, the supremacy of individual experience, and a high value on originality rebel against its perceived strictures.

CLIMAX (from Greek for "ladder") 1. In rhetoric, a figure of speech in which a series of clauses are so ordered that they create a crescendo of energy and intensity. 2. The moment of highest tension as perceived by the audience in a drama or work of fiction. Since the end of the 19th century, the climax has tended to occur close to the end of a play, although traditionally it took place at the end of the third act in a five-act piece.

CLOSE READING A critical analysis that pays close attention to the language of a text in order to ferret out the meaning within. Close reading claims to be a rigorous and objective technique, unlike the impressionistic, biographical, and historical criticisms that preceded it. I. A. Richards set forth its principles in *Practical Criticism* (1929), and it was favored by the Cambridge School. In addition, it was championed by the New Critics in the United States, who, believing that a text is a self-contained unit, found it especially useful.

CLOSET DRAMA A dramatic work more successful when read than when produced, also called a dramatic poem. The reasons that a closet drama may be unsuited to performance include its length, minimal use of dialogue, awkward or sometimes impossible stage instructions, and the use of author's notes to convey pertinent information not otherwise elucidated on stage. Closet drama flourished in England during the 19th century, when legitimate theater was pushed off the stage by popular spectacles such as burlesque, melodrama, and operetta. Well-known examples include Milton's *Samson Agonistes*, Shelley's *Prometheus Unbound*, and Hardy's *The Dynasts*.

COMEDY (from Greek for "a singer in the revels") A drama or film designed to amuse and evoke laughter. One of the two original dramatic genres of antiquity, along with tragedy but differentiated from it in form and content: tragedy uses a lofty tone to address situations affecting aristocrats, while comedy deals in an unassuming style with mundane situations and characters. The great number of comedic forms testify to its importance in Western letters: comedy of humors, of ideas, and of manners; black, drawing-room, domestic, high, low, musical, romantic, and sentimental comedy; burlesque; farce; tragicomedy; commedia dell'arte; *commedia erudita*; and *comédie larmoyante*.

Comedy developed from fertility rites associated with Dionysus. The preeminent classical

Greek practitioner of comedy was Aristophanes, whose 5th-century B.C. Old Comedy presented social criticism and satire; at the end of that century, Menander developed New Comedy, which focused upon light and romantic themes and influenced the Roman dramatists, the best known of whom were Plautus and Terence. In the Middle Ages, comedy waned owing to the Church's disfavor, and the term came to denote any narrative with a happy ending, as in Dante's *Divine Comedy*. Renaissance comedies and the example of the commedia dell'arte reinvigorated the form, especially in the hands of Lope de Vega, Ben Jonson, and Shakespeare, and the Restoration in England and the work of Molière in France marked a high point in terms of sophistication and wit. The 20th century's Theater of the Absurd demonstrates the genre's flexibility in response even to the outrages of history.

COMEDY OF MANNERS Witty and refined drama lampooning the codes and customs of the upper classes, known for sparkling conversation, sophisticated characters and situations, and cerebral humor. Its origins can be found in the classical Greek New Comedy of Menander, and it was utilized by both Shakespeare (*Love's Labour's Lost* and *Much Ado About Nothing*) and Molière (*The Affected Young Ladies* and *The Misanthrope*). Restoration comedy in England provides the consummate example in the work of practitioners such as William Wycherly and William Congreve. Later manifestations include Oliver Goldsmith's *She Stoops to Conquer* and Richard Brinsley Sheridan's *The School for Scandal* in the 18th century, a large body of work from Oscar Wilde, such as *The Importance of Being Earnest*, in the 19th century, and the refined 20th-century comedies of W. Somerset Maugham and Noël Coward.

COMMEDIA DELL'ARTE (Italian, "professional comedy") Troupes of wandering masked performers, which developed in 16th-century Italy and became widely popular throughout Europe, especially in France, where they became known as *comédie-italienne*. The name "commedia dell'arte" derives from the Italian term for medieval artisans' guilds, not, as often assumed, for "artistic comedy." Specializing in romantic intrigues and a bevy of masters and mistresses, servants and confidants, lovers and villains, the troupes' largely improvised plots drew from a wide stable of stock characters, including the rich father (Pantaloon), the Inamorato and Inamorata, the captain, the doctor, Harlequin, Scaramouche, Pulcinella, and the Ballerina. The broad comedy achieved through buffoonery and farce had a lasting influence on pantomime, light opera, and ballet; the Punch-and-Judy puppet show was also a descendant.

COMMONPLACE BOOK A collection of literary passages, quotations, ideas, and observations that an author collects for personal use and, occasionally, publication. A commonplace book may be organized around a particular theme. "Commonplace" in this usage refers not to something ordinary, but to a passage of universal application.

CONCEIT (from Middle English, from Latin for "concept, notion") Elaborate figurative device involving an ingenious and fanciful parallel between dissimilar images. Two major types are identified: the Petrarchan conceit, used in the Renaissance by Petrarch and his imitators, involved an extreme metaphor to express the lover's complaint against a disdainful mistress; the metaphysical conceit, named for the 17th-century British metaphysical poets, offered a more intellectual, elaborate metaphor. For example, John Donne used the conceit of a draftsman's compass to express the relationship between lovers. Despite the derogatory connotation of the term in everyday usage, in prosody its usage does not necessarily imply a negative judgment, but rather draws upon its etymological relation to the word "concept."

CONCRETE POETRY (from German "konkrete Dichtung") Poetry in which the words on the page form a pattern, such as an object described in the poem or another meaningful arrangement. For example, E. E. Cummings's poem "r-p-o-p-h-e-s-s-a-g-r" illustrates the erratic movement of a grasshopper, while in Apolli-

naire's "Il Pleut" ("It's Raining"), the words seem to spill down the page like flowing water. Concrete poetry explores the typographical potential of the word and makes connections between poetry and the visual arts. Antecedents can be found in the emblem poems in which Renaissance poets arranged words so that they produced the silhouette of the person portrayed; modern experimentation with the form takes place in the work of Eugen Gomringer, Max Bill, Emmett Williams, Jonathan Williams, and Mary Ellen Solt.

CONFLICT (from Latin for "to clash together, contend") The opposition between or within characters that produces dramatic tension. Conflict may exist between the character and an adversary, society, nature, or fate, or may be purely internalized as a struggle of the character with some aspect of itself.

CONTROLLING IMAGE The dominant metaphor or image of a literary work that organizes and unifies it. As a means of focusing the reader's attention, it often provides clarity and rhetorical force. However, it runs the risk of seeming overdone. The device was frequently used by the metaphysical poets.

CONVENTION Literary device, technique, or form sanctioned by tradition, which the audience accepts without question. In drama, examples include the aside, soliloquy, and dialogue in blank verse, while in poetry, formal structure itself is conventional. Both Romanticism and late 19th-century realism decried the artificiality of conventions, which led to their better disguise.

COUP DE THÉÂTRE (French, "theatrical or dramatic stroke") 1. A sensational or startling twist in a dramatic plot, as when the identity of an orphaned character is disclosed or a character thought to be dead turns out to be alive. It is a stock feature of melodrama, although not exclusive to that genre. 2. From the first meaning, something intended to shock or designed solely for effect. 3. A theatrical success.

COUPLET (from Old French, from diminutive of "couple") Two successive lines of rhyming verse. A highly adaptable form, the couplet has been widely used throughout Western literature. The most common usage in English versification is the heroic couplet, comprised of two lines of iambic pentameter. A couplet may be closed, if it expresses an idea that is complete in both meaning and syntax, or open, if it is part of a larger stanza. The Shakespearean sonnet always concludes with a couplet, and a couplet often marks the end of a scene in his drama.

COURTLY LOVE (from French, "amour courtois") The conventions dictating the form and expression of heterosexual love centered around the court and celebrated by the troubadours. Beginning in the 11th-century courts of Southern France, it married the concept of vassalage to a lord with devotion to the Virgin Mary. The result was the elevation of the earthly lady, for whom the courtier willingly suffered, offering in return obedience and absolute devotion. The lover pledged his allegiance to his lady, whose disdain or distance both tortured and ennobled him.

The roots of courtly love lay in Ovid's *The Art of Love* (*Ars Amatoria*, c. 1 B.C.), which depicted love as a consuming passion. Created by the court poets of Southern France, the highly developed codes of behavior spread to the *trouvères* of Northern France, the German love poets known as *Minnesänger*, and English romance writers through the patronage of Eleanor of Aquitaine as well as to Italian poets who developed the *dolce stil nuovo* (new sweet style). The medieval romance elaborately fused the conventions of courtly love with adventure tales, reaching its apex in such works as the anonymous *Romance of the Rose* and Chrétien de Troyes's *Lancelot*.

CRISIS (from Greek for "turning point") A key moment in a story or play that leads inexorably to the final resolution of the plot. As the point that determines the drama's outcome, it may result from either an action or inaction on the part of the hero. As a structural term, crisis does not necessarily coincide with the climax, which is the moment of the audience's highest interest.

CUBISM Early 20th-century artistic and later literary movement that abandoned standards of realism in favor of stylized and geometric representations. Founded in 1907 by the visual artists Pablo Picasso and Georges Braques, who were influenced by the abstract quality of African art, Cubism became the defining aesthetic of early modernism. In literature, French poets Guillaume Apollinaire and Pierre Reverdy, and American novelist and poet Gertrude Stein, experimented with abstraction, temporality, and repetition. In Russia, a group of poets known as Cubo-futurist, including Vladimir Mayakovsky and Velimir Khlebnikov, published poetry and manifestoes in which they sought to re-create poetic language by smashing literary conventions and privileging sound over sense.

CYBERPUNK School of science fiction addressing the disaffection that results when technological advances force a reconceptualization of the meaning of humanity. The term is a combination of "cybernetics," the study of the flow of information in electronic, mechanical, and biological systems (and associated with robotics), with "punk rock," the alienated and anarchistic music and youth culture that sprang up in the 1970s. The writing is characterized by a violent, nihilistic, and technological virtuosity. William Gibson's Cyberspace Trilogy of novels—*Neuromancer, Count Zero*, and *Mona Lisa Overdrive* (1984–88)—exemplifies the genre, which also includes work from Philip K. Dick, Davis Grubb, Bruce Sterling, John Shirley, and Thomas Pynchon.

CYCLE A cluster or series of poems, plays, or stories that share a central theme. Epics, romances, and sagas are often presented as series. The name "Cyclic Poets" is applied to the writers of Greek epics extending Homer's version of the Trojan War; other famous cycles include the medieval European mystery plays, known as the York Cycle, the Chester Cycle, and the Wakefield Cycle, and the major romance cycles known as the Matter of Britain (the Arthurian legends), the Matter of France (the tales of Charlemagne), and the Matter of

Rome (works based on the Latin classics). Adrienne Rich's "Twenty-one Love Poems" provides a contemporary instance of a poetic cycle.

DADA OR DADAISM (from French for "pet theme, hobbyhorse") Movement founded by the Swiss poet Tristan Tzara in 1916 that sought to protest the destruction of World War I through negation of the art, philosophy, and culture that made violence inevitable. Dadaists wanted to destroy the intellectual underpinnings of European culture and so cultivated irrationality in the face of the senselessness of war; for this reason, they chose their name randomly from the dictionary. Tzara brought Dada to France in 1919, where he associated with André Breton, Louis Aragon, Paul Éluard, and Philippe Soupault; in New York, the artists Francis Picabia and Marcel Duchamp presided over a similar campaign, while in Germany, the movement took a more political turn, supporting communism. The more literary emphasis of the French branch evolved because it was spearheaded by a number of poets. Breton led a group of members away from Dada to form Surrealism in 1921. The movement's influence can be seen in the development of the Theater of the Absurd and the antinovel.

DANDYISM A literary style of the late 19th century marked by excessive refinement and precious language, and associated with the Decadents. The term derives from "dandy," a man who affects extravagant elegance in dress and manner, and suggests a celebration of art not as a reflection of nature, but as inherently superior to it. Its principles are reflected in Oscar Wilde's dictum, "The first duty in life is to be as artificial as possible. What the second duty is no one has yet discovered." Writers such as Baudelaire, Poe, and Disraeli have identified with dandyism's flamboyant style.

DECADENCE (from Latin for "to decay") Literary or artistic style marked by artifice, depravity, and languor, qualities associated with a great culture that has fallen into decline. Modeled upon perceptions of the later Roman Empire and Byzantine-era Greece, decadence implies a high level of cultivation, self-indulgence, and perfection of technique. The Alexandrian period in Greek literature, the Silver Age of Latin literature, and the 19th-century Decadents in France and England are examples.

DECADENTS Group of French and English writers and artists at the end of the 19th century who held a preference for the elegant, unnatural, and perverse in literature and art. Counting among its adherents the French Symbolists Paul Verlaine, Charles Baudelaire, Arthur Rimbaud, and others, including the painter Gustave Moreau and the novelist J. K. Huysmans in France as well as Oscar Wilde, Ernest Dowson, and the illustrator Aubrey Beardsley in England, they luxuriated in style to the exclusion of substance, rebuffed quotidian values, and held art above all else.

DECONSTRUCTION A philosophy that sees language as a disruptive force that cannot provide access to any transcendental truth; as a result, deconstruction challenges no less than the foundations of Western culture. Developed in the late 1960s by the French philosopher Jacques Derrida, deconstruction has its roots in the philosophies of Nietzsche and Heidegger. It attempts to show that language is *not* a transparent medium referring directly to external reality; instead, language always refers to itself. In so doing, the reality that might ground knowledge and meaning is exposed as a product of a particular system. Derrida claims that the text, not the critic, deconstructs itself. Within each text is an *aporia*, an impasse that undoes its own logic, because language always reveals what we intend *not* to say. Texts are based upon dualisms (good/evil, white/black, man/woman) that pretend to neutrality but in fact are hierarchical. Deconstructive criticism does not seek to answer all the questions proposed by a text; instead, it explores the process through which meaning is generated.

DEFAMILIARIZATION The ability of great art to portray the world in a new and startling fashion. The term, a translation of the Russian *"ostranenie,"* was coined in the early 20th century by Viktor Shklovsky and readily adopted by his fellow Russian Formalists. These critics and authors believed that the role of art is precisely *not* to achieve verisimilitude, but rather to produce an estrangement that would arouse human faculties and senses grown dull out of laziness and tedium. Art accomplishes this task by calling attention to its own artifice, thus "laying bare" the process of constructing a work. Readers are shocked into an understanding that they are perceiving not reality but the play of art itself. Shklovsky's favored example of defamiliarization is Laurence Sterne's experimental novel, *Tristram Shandy* (1759–67).

DÉNOUEMENT (French, "unknotting, untying") The final outcome, explanation, or solution of the plot, which follows the climax of a play or work of fiction. The dénouement unravels all the strands that have produced the dramatic conflict. In tragedy, the term is synonymous with catastrophe.

DETECTIVE STORY Popular fiction in which an investigator solves a crime through the logical analysis of evidence. Edgar Allan Poe is considered to have fathered the genre with "The Murders in the Rue Morgue" (1841), the first detective story, and in this and other works established its main conventions. The detective story is distinguished from the mystery story if the detective has privileged access to information not available to the reader or, if there is no detective, if the answer cannot be deduced from the clues, or if the criminal is identified from the beginning of the story.

The best known of all fictional detectives is undoubtedly Arthur Conan Doyle's Sherlock Holmes, who arrived in 1887, providing the model of a brilliant sleuth with keen powers of logic and observation. The detective story reached its apex in the United States with the hard-boiled work of Dashiell Hammett and his successors Mickey Spillane, Raymond Chandler, and Ross Macdonald. British practitioners such as Agatha Christie, John Dickson Carr (also known as Carter Dickson), and Dorothy L. Sayers developed a more genteel, less streetwise style, while French author Georges Simenon and New Zealander Ngaio Marsh achieved considerable fame. Christie, who created the most celebrated female detective with Miss Jane Marple, has been followed more recently in the work of Sara Paretsky and Sue Grafton.

DEUS EX MACHINA (Latin, "god from the machine") An improbable or contrived solution to a vexing dramatic situation. The term derives from the Greek dramatic convention of lowering a god onto the stage on a crane, the "machine" in question. Sophocles at times and Euripides often settled an apparently unresolvable situation by such divine intervention. By extension, it refers to any unlikely conclusion offered at the last moment.

DEVICE (from Old French for "invention, design") Any contrivance or method by which an author produces a desired effect. Some artistic styles seek to naturalize devices, as does the 19th-century realist novel, whereas others, such as Bertolt Brecht's epic theater and postmodern literature, emphasize the need to underscore the use of device in order to draw attention to the workings of ideology in the text.

DIDACTICISM (from Greek for "to teach") Emphasis on literature's role in teaching or guiding its readers, rather than on its ability to delight or entertain. While most, if not all, literature has instructive elements, the term is generally reserved for works in which art is subordinated to the lesson being taught. A number of genres are explicitly instructive, including the didactic novel, referring to both the 18th-century works that exemplified educational principles (e.g., Rousseau's *Émile*) and novels that teach a lesson (e.g., the Horatio Alger novels); didactic poetry, ranging from philosophical disquisitions to rhymes that serve as aide-mémoire; and parables.

DIME NOVEL Cheaply produced novel, which became popular in the United States in the second half of the 19th century for its combination of adventure and melodrama. It featured such topics as the American Revolution, crime investigation, and especially the American frontier, and was the precursor of the western. Among the most successful were the "Deadwood Dick" frontier novels and the "Nick Carter" detective stories. The introduction of pulp magazines damaged its preeminence by stealing its audience. In Britain, its counterpart was the "penny dreadful."

DISCOURSE (from Latin for "a running back and forth, conversation") 1. In linguistics, a unit larger than a single sentence. 2. A dissertation or discussion of a particular topic. 3. The historical use of language in a given community or era (e.g., medical discourse or Romantic discourse). 4. A key concept in contemporary poststructuralism, where it refers to the conviction that language does not merely refer to objects, but creates those objects as meaningful categories.

DOGGEREL (from Middle English for "poor, worthless," perhaps from "dog") Strictly speaking, verse with an irregular meter and loose construction, although the term is often used to denigrate poetry marked by a clumsy execution, uninspired rhymes, plodding rhythm, and banal or trivial content. Poets such as Samuel Butler, Ogden Nash, and Stevie Smith have parodied doggerel for comic effect; the German *Knittelvers* (literally, "badly knit verse") is a comparable category.

DOMESTIC TRAGEDY Tragedy in which the protagonists are members of the middle or lower classes, differentiated from classical tragedy's focus on the affairs of the aristocracy; it portrays a downfall that did not start out from so lofty a position as that of the classical hero's, but is no less tragic in its implications. The form has its origins in Elizabethan drama, and was greatly influenced by George Lillo, whose *The London Merchant* (1732) and *Arden of Feversham* (1759) introduced it into France and Germany. The ascription of dignity and gravity to ordinary people distinguished the work of Henrik Ibsen, G. E. Lessing, Tennessee Williams, Eugene O'Neill, and Arthur Miller.

DOPPELGÄNGER (German, "double") The haunting double of a literary character. The Doppelgänger represents a repressed aspect of the character, appearing as an alter ego, a diabolical bent in the personality, a temptation, or a premonition or warning of impending doom. The concept of the Doppelgänger derives from German folklore, where it is based upon the popular belief in the wraith, an apparition of a living person. The term was coined by Jean Paul in 1796 to name this important symbol, found in the horror genre throughout the 18th and 19th centuries. German novelist and story writer E. T. A. Hoffmann was one of the foremost authors to utilize the Doppelgänger in his uncanny and supernatural tales. Other notable instances include Fyodor Dostoyevsky's *The Double*, Robert Louis Stevenson's *Dr. Jekyll and Mr. Hyde*, and Oscar Wilde's *The Picture of Dorian Gray*. In the literature of the American South, half siblings born alternately to a black and a white mother may appear as doubles, as in Mark Twain's *Pudd'nhead Wilson*.

DOUBLE ENTENDRE (French, "double meaning") A word or phrase having a suggestive or salacious secondary meaning in addition to its literal meaning.

DRAMA (from Greek for "deed, action on the stage") A literary work intended for theatrical production in which a story is conveyed through the action and dialogue of characters played by actors. Drama, in which the characters tell their own stories, is distinguished from the lyric poem, told in the words of the author or narrator, and the epic, which includes both narration and the speech of characters. In addition to the classical genres of tragedy and comedy, drama may be classified as tragicomedy, melodrama, history, mystery play, or pantomime, among others.

DRAMATIC UNITIES The unities of action, time, and place championed by French classical dramatists of the 17th and 18th centuries, based on their reading of Aristotle's *Poetics*. Aristotle suggested the virtue of a single action, which would allow the play to function as a harmonious whole with a beginning, middle, and end in proper relation to each other; his views, however, were derived from a descriptive study of tragedy, and were not meant to be prescriptive. Justifying their aesthetic principles in a return to classical wisdom, the classicists dictated that all drama adhere to the dramatic unities: plays were to represent a unique storyline occurring in one place in the course of a single day, in order to heighten the play's verisimilitude. The unities were never very influential in England, perhaps owing to the legacy of Shakespeare. Even in France, the insistence upon the unities waned with the advent of Romanticism and its rejection of convention.

DRAMATIS PERSONAE (New Latin, "characters of the drama") 1. The characters or actors of a drama or, more rarely, of a poem or novel. 2. A list of the characters and/or actors included in a playbill or printed text of a play. Brief explanations of familial or other types of relationships among the characters may be elucidated for the spectator or reader.

ECLOGUE (from Greek for "selection") A short poem, usually with a pastoral theme, presented in the form of a soliloquy or dialogue. Perhaps the best-known examples are Virgil's *Eclogues* (42–37 B.C.). Renaissance Italian poets, including Dante, Petrarch, and Boccaccio, and Edmund Spenser in England revived the genre. Common types include the dialogue or singing contest between two shepherds, and the love song or lament of a shepherd.

EDITION (from Latin for "a bringing forth, publication") 1. The collective name for all of the copies of a text made from a single typesetting, which may include one or more printings. 2. Any of the various forms in which a given text appears, as in a scholarly edition or a paperback edition. 3. The revised version of a previously published text.

ELEGY (from Greek for "lament") A sorrowful or mournful poem, especially a lament for the dead. In classical versification, the term refers to any poem, regardless of subject matter, written in elegiac distichs (alternating lines of dactylic hexameter and pentameter), while in modern usage, the mood is the defining feature. It typically expresses the poet's grief for the loss of a person or more generally for the sorrows of earthly existence, often bringing consolation in the idea that there is continuity despite the transience of the world. The pastoral elegy, starting with the classical Greek idylls of Theocritus, forms an important subgenre. Well-known examples include Milton's "Lycidas," Thomas Gray's "Elegy Written in a Country Church Yard," Percy Bysshe Shelley's "Adonais," and W. H. Auden's "In Memory of W. B. Yeats."

ELLIPTICAL (from Greek for "defective, to fall short") Writing marked by intentionally difficult language or obscure allusions.

EPIC (from Greek for "song, word") A lengthy narrative poem written in an elevated style celebrating the founding and history of a nation or culture through the exploits of a legendary hero. The epic is the story through which a people defines itself as a community with a shared history and cultural legacy. Despite its widespread use across cultures and time periods, a number of common features mark the epic: an opening statement explaining the purpose of the story; an invocation to the muse whose beneficence testifies to the noble purpose of the narrative; starting *in medias res* and only later going back to explain the story's beginnings; the focus upon a hero of legendary proportions who, in his person, represents the greatness of the society; the use of epic simile (also known as Homeric simile), an extended comparison that may last several lines; and heroic battles and divine intervention into the hero's doings, both of which underscore an idea of the nation's destined grandeur.

Many of the traditional epics are considered "primary," derived from an oral tradition with multiple, anonymous authors, as in the stories of the *Iliad* and the *Odyssey*, attributed to Homer; "secondary" or "literary" epics are those originally written in the style of an epic, as in Virgil's *Aeneid* or Milton's *Paradise Lost*. The earliest surviving epic is the Babylonian *Gilgamesh* (c. 2000 B.C.); also in this tradition are the Sanskrit *Mahābhārata* (4th century), the Anglo-Saxon *Beowulf* (8th century), the French *Song of Roland* (12th century); and the German *Nibelungenlied* (13th century). By extension, the term may also refer to an ambitious novel or film of historical or mythic sweep, such as Tolstoy's *War and Peace*.

EPIGRAM (from Greek for "inscription") A pithy, witty expression in poetry or prose. From its origins as an inscription in stone comes the emphasis on brevity; it generally takes the form of a couplet or quatrain. The Roman poet Martial, following in the footsteps of classical Greek writers and of the Latin poet Catullus, popularized the genre in the 1st century with a collection of more than 1,500 clever and often vulgar verses. Renaissance poets revived the form; in England, Ben Jonson paved the way for numerous imitators. It was especially well suited to the wit and refinement of the 18th century as well as to the acerbic humor of Oscar Wilde and George Bernard Shaw. An example by Samuel Taylor Coleridge defines the genre: "What is an epigram? A dwarfish whole, / Its body brevity, and wit its soul."

EPIGRAPH (from Greek for "written on") 1. An inscription on a statue, monument, or coin. 2. A quotation placed at the beginning of a literary work or section of a work. The epigraph is an economical way for an author to connect the present work with key themes or ideas from another.

EPILOGUE (from Greek for "to say more, to add") The final section of a literary work, which comes after the conclusion of the action proper and may be used to sum up or complete the work; also called an afterword, it is structurally the opposite of the prologue. In fiction, conventional uses include a meditation on the story or a sketching of the characters' future. In English Renaissance and especially Restoration drama, it was used to forestall criticism and encourage applause; an example is Puck's final speech in *A Midsummer Night's Dream*, which begs the audience not to take offense at the preceding work.

EPIPHANY (from Greek for "appearance, manifestation") A manifestation of the essential nature of a person, thing, or scene. James Joyce used the name of the Christian feast celebrating Jesus' presentation to the Magi to describe a sudden insight, an instant when reality seems to shine through an ordinary object, when its "soul, its whatness, leaps to us from the vestment of its appearance." An explanation of the term is found in *Stephen Hero* (1944), an early version of *A Portrait of the Artist as a Young Man*. Joyce used the term to describe a number of his early short works that cultivate revelatory insight, and constructed his later fiction around these insights. Earlier poets, especially Wordsworth, also emphasized such moments, although without using this term.

EPISTOLARY NOVEL A novel told as a series of letters written by one or more of the characters. Samuel Richardson's popular *Pamela* (1740), about a virtuous servant girl, established the genre as a major form throughout the 18th century. One of the earliest types of the novel, it offered readers an immediate entry into the world of the characters through the inherently social medium of correspondence. Among the most influential examples are Fanny Burney's *Evelina* and Pierre Choderlos de Laclos's *Les Liaisons Dangereuses*. Contemporary use is rare, perhaps related to the waning of letter-writing as a social phenomenon.

EPITAPH (from Greek for "over a tomb, funeral oration") Short piece of prose or verse inscribed upon a tombstone or written as if intended for this purpose. Related to the eulogy, it always commemorates a human life, although its tone may vary from laudatory to flippant. The earliest extant examples are found on Egyptian sarcophagi; a number are collected in the *Greek Anthology*, the best known of which is dedicated to the fallen at the Battle of Thermopylae: "Go, tell the Spartans, passer-by, / That here obedient to their laws we lie." Samuel Johnson and Wordsworth composed treatises on the art of epitaph-writing.

EPONYM (from Greek for "to name") An actual or fictional person for whom a place, thing, or work is named or thought to be named. In some cases, a mythical figure may lend his or her name to some other object, as in Europa, a beloved of Zeus, for Europe. Emma Bovary is the eponymous heroine of Flaubert's *Madame Bovary*.

EROTICA (from Greek for "of or caused by love") Literature that deals with desire and sexuality in a provocative and carnal fashion. The erotic theme in literature may be secular, as is largely the case in the Western tradition, or melded with the religious, as in the biblical *Song of Songs* and some Indian and Persian love poetry. A range of tones is found, from the coarse humor of the Middle Ages to the seriousness and lasciviousness of Victorian erotica. Modern practitioners, such as Anaïs Nin and Henry Miller, participate in a tradition that stretches from the Sanskrit *Kāma Sūtra* through the work of Ovid, Chaucer, the Marquis de Sade, Walt Whitman, and D. H. Lawrence. The distinction between pornography and erotica is usually made by noting that pornography's primary goal is sexual arousal, while erotica is part of a larger artistic whole.

ESSAY (from Old French for "trial") A short, often informal prose composition that addresses a particular subject without claiming to exhaust it; it is more limited in scope and pretension than the dissertation, treatise, or study. The term, which signifies an attempt or trial, comes from Montaigne, whose *Essays* (1580) established the modern form of the personal, relaxed, and colloquial inquiry; however, classical antecedents can be found in the writings of Plutarch, Cicero, and Seneca. The rise of the periodical in the early 19th century created a ready forum for the essay, which may be political, philosophical, scientific, critical, or humorous. Great writers of essays include Ralph Waldo Emerson, Mark Twain, Virginia Woolf, Edmund Wilson, James Baldwin, and Susan Sontag.

EULOGY (from Greek for "praise") A formal composition or oration in praise of a person or thing, especially an encomium extolling the virtues and good deeds of a person who has died. The epitaph is the most succinct version.

EXPLICATION DE TEXTE (French, "explanation of text") A method of literary analysis that emphasizes a thorough examination of the language and stylistic features of a given text, and of the relationship between its form and content, especially in terms of the tension between the two; its focus on the inner workings of text avoids scrutiny of the historical, biographical, and political aspects emphasized in some other bodies of criticism. Derived from a French pedagogical technique, it is associated with British practical criticism and particularly with American New Criticism.

EXPRESSIONISM Late 19th- and early 20th-century artistic, literary, and cinematic movement that abandoned verisimilitude, instead seeking to portray inner reality through the things of the objective world. Combining Freudian psychological insights with Marxist political fervor, these writers and artists sought to portray emotion through abstraction, distortion, and symbolism, resulting in moody, nightmarish compositions that reflected the internal struggles of humanity. It is distinguished from impressionism, which seeks to portray the effect on the artist of some external object.

The movement's roots and strongest expression were found in Germany, where the concerns of artists Edvard Munch, Oskar Kokoschka, and Paul Klee were matched in the condensed, richly symbolic lyric poetry of George Trakl, Georg Heym, Ernst Stadler, Gottfried Benn, and Franz Werfel. In the theater, the nonnaturalistic drama of August Strindberg inspired a group of playwrights, including Frank Wedekind, Georg Kaiser, and Ernst Toller to create atmospheric productions marked by symbolic character types and settings designed to reflect inner perceptions. Outside of Germany, their influence could be felt in the work of Federico García Lorca in Spain, Luigi Pirandello in Italy, and Eugene O'Neill and Elmer Rice in the United States. Expressionist cinema includes Robert Wiene's silent classic, *The Cabinet of Dr. Caligari* (1919), which led to such stylized and anguished masterpieces as F. W. Murnau's *Nosferatu* (1922) and Fritz Lang's *Metropolis* (1926); its exemplary use of such cinematic tools as lighting (and especially shadow) and dramatic camera angles to convey feeling had a broad effect upon other filmmakers, including Alfred Hitchcock, and the schools of horror in

Germany and film noir. The practice of Expressionism in Germany was halted by Nazi censorship, which considered the movement decadent and immoral.

FABLE A short allegorical tale in which animals, plants, and things speak and behave like humans, told to illustrate a moral that is generally verbalized at the conclusion. A variety in which all the characters are animals may be further labeled a beast epic. The form has been widely used throughout history to lampoon human nature. The oldest extant fables are those found upon Egyptian papyri dating to the 15th century B.C. and the Indian *Panchatantra* stories, written in the 8th century, but existing in oral form perhaps as early as the 5th century B.C. The earliest classical Greek fable belongs to Hesiod (8th century B.C.), but the collection ascribed to Aesop, according to legend a Greek slave living in the 6th century B.C. and most likely a composite figure, is undoubtedly the most famous in the Western tradition. The 17th-century French fables of La Fontaine have influenced modern writers by their example of sparkling wit and nimble language.

FAIRY TALE Fanciful story about the magical escapades of fairies and their ilk, fantastic creatures such as goblins, elves, and brownies generally associated with a particular place. Since the 17th century, folklorists and writers have compiled collections of national fairy traditions, as in the French *Contes de Ma Mère l'Oye* (*Tales of Mother Goose*); the German *Kinder- und Hausmärchen* (often translated as *Grimm's Fairy Tales*); and the Russian *Russkie Narodnye Skazki* (translated under the titles *Russian Fairy Tales* and *Russian Folk Tales*). Fairy literature generally develops from a culture's oral tradition, although writers since the Romantic era have created original fairy tales; the best known of these writers is undoubtedly Hans Christian Andersen, in whose company are Oscar Wilde, John Ruskin, E. T. A. Hoffmann, and Goethe.

FAMILY SAGA. *See* ICELANDERS' SAGAS

FANTASY Fiction that creates within its narrative a coherent world that does not correspond to the perceived reality of everyday existence. Its pages are filled with magical characters and objects in strange or unreal settings doing things that would not be possible given the physical limitations of quotidian life. Fantasy encompasses fairy tales, fables, ghost stories, and science fiction. J. R. R. Tolkien's renowned trilogy *The Lord of the Rings* is an enduring classic of the genre.

FARCE Broad humor that derives its effect from wildly exaggerated actions, ludicrous situations, crass jokes, and buffoonery; also, dramatic pieces that employ it. Derived from the French word "to stuff," the term originally signified short comic interludes improvised by the actors of liturgical drama, which later came to be written independently. Especially popular in European drama of the 18th and 19th centuries, its broad physical appeal easily lent itself in the early 20th century to the new medium of silent film, best represented in the antics of Charlie Chaplin and the Keystone Kops. A popular subgenre is the bedroom farce, based on amorous confusion among consenting adults.

FEMINIST CRITICISM A school of literary criticism holding that gender is constructed by social systems, including those of language and literature; consequently, literature can and must be interrogated and challenged in order to counteract its inherent patriarchal biases.

FEUILLETON (French, diminutive of "leaf") The section of a newspaper dedicated to entertainment, criticism, and features, rather than news. Taken from the French word *feuillet* (leaf, folio sheet), in the 19th century it denoted the bottom part of the page reserved for such items. In contemporary usage, it may refer to a serialized novel (which would have been published there), a pamphlet, a short and sometimes humorous piece, or, more generally, material intended to amuse.

FICTION (from Latin for "a making, fashioning") An imaginative work that comes from the mind of the author rather than from history or fact, even though it may refer to the latter. The term generally refers to narratives in prose; poems and drama are typically excluded. Philosophically, a significance of fiction derives from its negative relationship to fact, and vice versa.

FIGURE OF SPEECH An expression designed to achieve rhetorical effect by its distance from ordinary construction or literal meaning. In modern usage, the term more generally refers to all figurative language. Although poetry may present a particularly self-conscious utilization of figures of speech, all language relies upon figuration.

FIN-DE-SIÈCLE (French, "end of the century") Characteristic of the last decade of the 19th century, a period marked by decadence, ennui, despair, and a giddiness produced by the receding of social, religious, and aesthetic norms. When used to describe literature, it specifically calls to mind the Decadents in France and Aestheticism in England.

FOIL (from Latin for "thin sheet of metal") A literary character whose actions and traits contrast with and therefore underscore those of another, just as the thin sheet of metal from which it takes its name highlights the sparkle of a jewel. For example, in *Moby-Dick*, the quiet integrity of the first mate, Starbuck, serves as a foil for the monomania of Captain Ahab.

FOLIO (Latin, "leaf") 1. In printing, a standard-sized sheet of paper folded in half to form the leaves of a book. Also, a book made of folio sheets, which may be folded again into four pages; such a book forms the largest regular book size. 2. A special usage relates to the first published collection of Shakespeare's works, which was compiled into a folio edition posthumously in 1623; as a result, the term also refers to this edition and those that followed in 1632, 1663, and 1685, and is distinguished from the unauthorized quarto editions.

FOLK LITERATURE A culture's heritage of stories and belief as created by and for the people as part of their oral tradition. This literature includes folk tales, songs and ballads, riddles and jokes, proverbs and sayings, spells and incantations, and is part of the broader category of folklore (adding rituals, customs, and popular beliefs). It became a popular subject of

scholarly inquiry in the 19th century, leading to the appearance of collections such as Jacob and Wilhelm Grimm's in Germany, A. N. Afanasyev's in Russia, and Douglas Hyde's in Ireland. In the United States, the traditions of Native-American, African-American (most famously in the early 20th-century compilations of Zora Neale Hurston), Appalachian, Ozark, and cowboy folk literature were gathered and studied. Early studies were influenced by Romantic notions of the people and the nation, while at the beginning of the 20th century, formalist analyses of folk material dominated, especially through the example of the Russian critic V. I. Propp.

FOLK TALE A story that deals with popular subject matter and is part of the oral tradition of a particular country, region, or language. The term refers collectively to anonymous narratives that may exist in many variants over time and place, such as fairy tales (also known as *Märchen*), legends, fables, shaggy dog stories, ghost stories, and (particularly in the United States) tall tales. Regional variations and changes in the story over time may occur as a result of the oral mode of transmission. Folk tales frequently provide the source material for formal literature, attested by the endurance of the Cinderella story in both George Bernard Shaw's *Pygmalion* and countless movies.

FOOT In versification, the basic unit of rhythm defined by a patterned relationship between its syllables. In English accentual-syllabic meter (based upon the number of accents and the number of syllables in a foot), it consists of one stressed syllable (´) and one or more unstressed syllables (˘), while in the quantitative meter of classical poetry it is determined by the pattern of long and short syllables. The most common feet in English poetry are the iamb (˘´), trochee (´˘), anapest (˘˘´), dactyl (´˘˘), spondee (´´), and pyrrhic (˘˘). The number of feet per line is also measured; poems with lines of one foot are referred to as "monometer," of five feet as "pentameter," and so forth. The usage of this terminology comes to English from classical prosody, and is not entirely suitable for English poetry because of a greater tendency for irregularity in the latter. The foot may be compared to the bar in music.

FORESHADOWING The strategic imparting of information in a narrative or drama to prepare the reader or spectator for events that develop later. Foreshadowing ranges from the use of a particular event that suggests the dénouement—when Oedipus solves the Sphinx's riddle, it suggests his ultimate comprehension of the riddle of his own past—to a focus on a particular object, such as the repeated references to trains that foreshadow Anna Karenina's suicide. By unifying the plot through this technique, authors subtly condition their audiences to accept and understand an ending.

FORMALISM Attention to aesthetic principles and artistic techniques to the exclusion of content and sociological aspects of a work; the term refers to artistic practice or, more frequently, to criticism that emphasizes such approaches. The most important variety is the Russian formalism of the 1920s, associated with Viktor Shklovsky, which utilized linguistic theory to analyze literary language as a distinct entity unrelated to conversational speech, and therefore outside political and other extratextual elements. The Soviets rejected it as antirevolutionary, forcing its removal to Czechoslovakia, where the work of Roman Jakobson and the Prague Linguistic Circle would come to influence American New Criticism, which, although not interested in the structural linguistics that informed the European variants, shared a conviction of the hermetic nature of the literary work.

FREE VERSE Poetry with no fixed or regular meter, and which derives its rhythms instead from the cadences of everyday speech. In attempting to free poetry from the arbitrary constraints of meter and rhyme, free verse demands that poets develop the sonorous and emotional potential inherent in language itself. Moreover, it claims to be closer to reality than other verse forms. The term is a literal translation of the French *vers libre*, coined in the late 1880s by Gustave Kahn, and has counterparts in German *freie Rhythmen* and Russian *svobodnii stikh*. In the United States, it was popularized by Walt Whitman, whose long, flowing lines of verse in *Leaves of Grass* (1855) represented the author's attempt to create a truly American poetry. Authors who expanded and refined the form include Charles Baudelaire in France; William Carlos Williams and Carl Sandburg in the United States; Pablo Neruda in Chile; Kuo Mo Jo in China; and Gerard Manley Hopkins in England. Much of the contemporary poetry in the United States and elsewhere is written in free verse.

FUTURISM Avant-garde literary and artistic movement of early 20th-century Europe that rejected all manner of tradition in a desire to harness the revolutionary potential of the technological era. Launched in Italy by Filippo Tommaso Marinetti with the 1909 publication of the first of many Futurist manifestoes, it sought to liberate literature from the stultifying conventions of the past. Its most important manifestation occurred in Russia, where the poets Vladimir Mayakovsky and Velimir Khlebnikov called for the complete rejection of the 19th-century masters Pushkin, Dostoyevsky, and Tolstoy, and pushed sense and syntax to their limits in experimental poetry. Russian Futurism was not marked by the fascist undertones of its Italian cousin, instead identifying itself with the revolutionary spirit of the newly created Soviet Union; however, its formal iconoclasm threatened the Soviet literary establishment, which by the 1920s rejected it in favor of Socialist Realism.

GAUCHO LITERATURE Latin American ballads written in imitation of the songs composed by the cowboys of Argentina and Uruguay, and novels extolling the virtues of these representatives of a seemingly simpler and nobler life. Consciously mining the folkloric tradition of the *payadores* (singers of popular poetry), writers of this literature starting in the 19th century contributed to the creation of a romantic Spanish-American identity. Among the greatest works are *Martin Fierro* (1872, 1879) by José Hernández, which used the gaucho as a symbol of the continent in its struggles against a corrupt Europe; Estanislao del Campo's *Fausto* (1866), which retells Gounod's opera in gaucho dialect; and Ricardo Güiraldes's *Shadows in the Pampas* (*Don Segundo Sombra*, 1926), about a dignified ranch hand, which is one of the most important gaucho novels.

GENDER STUDIES School of criticism that examines the ways in which gender identity comes to be constructed and understood by individuals and by society. It forms an interdisciplinary field comprising a number of different methods of analysis that take the social, political, philosophical, and biological implications of gender for its subject. It developed out of the insights and methods of feminist criticism, but it is distinguished by its focus on men as well (although there is obviously considerable overlap between the two fields); other important influences are gay/lesbian studies and queer studies. In literary criticism, it analyzes not merely the work of women artists and images of women in literature, but also studies the role of gender in creating meaning in language for both men and women.

GENRE (from Latin for "race, kind") A category or classification of literature according to form and/or content; the major classical genres are the lyric, epic or narrative, and drama (including the major forms, tragedy and comedy), to which can be added more modern forms, including the novel, short story, and biography. The elasticity of generic boundaries has been celebrated and sometimes exploited in such hybrid forms as the prose poem or autobiographical fiction.

GEORGIAN POETRY Pastoral poetry of the early 20th century in Britain. Inspired by Rupert Brooke, Edward Marsh championed the group of young poets producing this gentle, bucolic poetry; he edited five volumes of poetry that established the movement and that included works by such poets as Lascelles Abercrombie, W. H. Davies, John Drinkwater, James Elroy Flecker, W. W. Gibson, Ralph Hodgson, Harold Munro, J. C. Squire, and W. J. Turner. The work they produced is traditional in form and content, as is suggested by their using the name of the reigning monarch, George V; this poetry often devolves into mere sentimentalism and nostalgia, modeling itself after Wordsworth but failing to attain his depth of vision. Its inability to engage with the demands of modernity in the aftermath of World War I led to a rapid loss of prominence as well as a pejorative use of the term to imply conservatism.

GEORGIC A didactic poem, especially one offering instruction on agriculture, animal husbandry, or rural affairs. Also common is the exaltation of nature and country life, but the genre is distinguished from the pastoral by its primarily prescriptive and educational intent. The exemplary work is Virgil's *Georgics* (37–30 B.C.), which is itself modeled upon Hesiod's *Works and Days* (8th century B.C.).

GLOSS (from Greek for "tongue, language") 1. A translation, definition, or brief interpretation, often inserted into a text or else placed in the margins; a list of these terms may also be presented at the end of a work as a "glossary." Medieval copyists often used glosses to translate obscure Latin words into the vernacular, and in modern editions of Shakespeare they often explain Elizabethan language and customs. Generally added by an editor or copyist, glosses are occasionally provided by the authors themselves, as in T. S. Eliot's *The Waste Land* and in Samuel Taylor Coleridge's "The Rime of the Ancient Mariner." 2. By extension, a detailed commentary or interpretation of a difficult text, which may be published jointly with the text it explicates or on its own.

GOTHIC NOVEL Lurid fiction replete with supernatural and mysterious elements, extremely popular despite its disreputability in Britain at the end of the 18th and beginning of the 19th centuries. The genre derived its name from the dark and eerie medieval castles in which the stories were typically set, resulting in an atmosphere of terror and foreboding. Horace Walpole's *Castle of Otranto* (1765) inaugurated the genre, which reached its acme in Ann Radcliffe's much imitated *The Mysteries of Udolpho* (1794) and *The Italian* (1797). Two strains of the Gothic novel existed, an earlier one that provided rational explanations for all the mysteries raised within the story, and a later trend, emphasizing the violent and supernatural, that flourished in Germany and arrived in English with Matthew Gregory Lewis's *The Monk* (1796). The tradition was easily and quickly parodied, notably in Jane Austen's first novel, *Northanger Abbey* (1817). Gothic elements continued to appear in the works of many writers, especially Mary Shelley, the Brontë sisters, Charles Brockden Brown, Nathaniel Hawthorne, and Edgar Allan Poe. The concept has been revived in the idea of the Southern Gothic to explain the grotesqueries of that regional fiction. Romance novels that utilize such elements are also called Gothic, highlighting the long-standing association of the Gothic with women as both readers and writers.

GRAVEYARD SCHOOL A group of 18th-century British poets whose melancholy and somber reflections on death were often set in graveyards. A loose grouping rather than a formal school, it consisted of such poets as Edward Young, Robert Blair, and Thomas Parnell as well as their followers, whose work expressed the futility and transience of human existence. The finest example of the movement, Thomas Gray's "An Elegy Written in a Country Church Yard" (1751), became unquestionably the most popular poem of its time. In the United States, its influence could be found in the work of William Cullen Bryant. Although only a minor literary school, it made fashionable the despairing mien and woeful sensibility that would later find new expression in Romanticism.

GREEK TRAGEDY. *See* TRAGEDY

GROTESQUE (from Old Italian for "of a grotto") In literature, a style marked by the bizarre, distorted, or abnormal, used since the 18th century to refer to characters who are either physically deformed or evince an alarming and peculiar disposition. It may be used to amuse or unsettle, and is found in the work of Charles Dickens, Edgar Allan Poe, and Flannery O'Connor, among others. The term comes to

literature from a 16th-century Italian art style, modeled after cave painting, that featured disturbing and hybrid human, animal, and plant forms.

GRUB STREET Literary trash, the hack writers who produce it, and the sordid lives they lead. Named for a London street, now renamed Milton Street, where impoverished, second-rate writers lived during the 18th century. Samuel Johnson characterized the locale as "much inhabited by writers of small histories, dictionaries, and temporary poems; whence any mean production is called grubstreet." George Gissing alludes to the phrase in the title of his novel *New Grub Street* (1891).

HAIKU (Japanese, "amusement" + "verse") A Japanese poetic form consisting (in order) of three unrhymed lines of 5, 7, and 5 syllables. Its brief composition expresses a complete emotion or mood through a word picture focused around the natural world and a particular season. The form is difficult to approximate in languages that lack the short, unstressed syllables of Japanese. Originally the opening verse of a longer poem, it eventually became a separate unit and earned distinction in the 17th century in the hands of Matsuo Bashō. The use in haiku of concrete and objective reality to suggest an idea or impression greatly influenced 20th-century imagism.

HAMARTIA. *See* TRAGIC FLAW

HARD-BOILED FICTION A 20th-century American crime genre notable for its gritty realism, sordid settings and situations, graphic violence and sexuality, and vivid language. The magazine *Black Mask*, founded in 1919, provided a vehicle for the new popular form, which achieved prominence through the work of Dashiell Hammett, James M. Cain, Raymond Chandler, and later Mickey Spillane. This fiction offered a new and distinctly American twist to the genre of detective fiction, eschewing European upper-class sophistication for the realism developed by Ernest Hemingway and John Dos Passos. Many of its detectives have become household names—Sam Spade, Ellery Queen, Philip Marlowe—both through this fiction and through its cinematic manifestation, film noir.

HERO In its most general meaning, the protagonist, or main character. In this literary sense, the term does not imply any value judgment of goodness; Faust is the eponymous hero of Goethe's play. In a specific sense, the hero is a legendary or mythological character of epic proportions. With strength and bravery beyond that of mere mortals, the hero lives boldly and violently. Rarely a thoughtful creature, he speaks with his actions. As passed down through tradition, the hero is generally a flat character, offering little room for psychological criticism. The national or cultural hero/heroine establishes the ideal character of a people. A small sample from around the world includes Gilgamesh (Sumerian), Achilles (Greek), Cu Chulainn (Irish), Abraham (Hebrew), Nanaabozho (Chippewa/Ojibway), and Roland (French).

HEROIC COUPLET A rhymed couplet in iambic pentameter. Although of obscure origins in English poetry, it was popularized by Chaucer in the 14th century. The name comes from the heroic drama of the 17th and early 18th centuries, of which it was the consummate form. As mastered in the work of John Dryden and Alexander Pope during the Neoclassical period, it was a "closed" couplet, expressing a complete thought in a contained grammatical unit with no enjambment, or running on of a thought, between couplets. Its usage waned in the 19th century with Romanticism's desire to escape poetic conventions. The following example is from Pope's *An Essay on Man*: "Say first, of God above, or Man below, / What can we reason, but from what we know?"

HEROIC DRAMA A form of tragedy and tragicomedy popular in late 17th-century Restoration England. Drawing from the traditions of French classical tragedy and the still-developing field of opera, it aspired to the epic mode that gives it its name. It generally focused upon love themes, and particularly a struggle between love and duty, set in exotic locales and marked by bombastic dialogue in closed couplets that came to be known as "heroic." John Dryden was the foremost practitioner.

HEXAMETER In versification, a line of six feet. It is little used by English poets, who have tended to find it cumbersome, with notable exceptions such as Spenser in *The Faerie Queene* and Longfellow in *Evangeline*. As the alexandrine, it is, however, the most popular meter in French poetry.

HIGH COMEDY Intellectual comedy in which humor is derived from the audience's awareness of incongruity and its recognition of human nature. The comedy of manners provides the prime instance of high comedy, and can be seen in the work of George Bernard Shaw and Jane Austen. The term was coined by George Meredith in *The Idea of Comedy* (1877), and is distinguished from low comedy, which relies upon farce, buffoonery, and other "inferior" forms of humor; the class bias in these terms is evident.

HOMERIC EPITHET A compound adjective used so frequently that it becomes indelibly associated with the person or thing it names. Homer used the form in the *Iliad* and the *Odyssey* to great effect, as in "rosy-fingered dawn" and "gray-eyed Athena."

HORATIAN ODE A melancholy, reflective lyric written in the manner of the 1st-century B.C. Latin poet Horace, as distinguished from the exalted tone of Pindaric odes. The gentle and private thoughts of a Horatian ode contrast strongly with the fiery verses the 5th-century B.C. Greek poet Pindar wrote in honor of athletic victors, as do its regular stanzas and metrical form. The Horatian ode was adopted by Pierre de Ronsard, Nicolas Boileau, John Keats, and in the eponymous "An Horatian Ode upon Cromwell's Return from Ireland" (1650) of Andrew Marvell.

HORATIAN SATIRE Satire in the mode of the 1st-century B.C. Latin poet Horace, characterized by a tolerant, generous form of correction, rather than the harsh, indignant ridicule of Juvenalian satire. In his collection *Satires*, Horace shows himself as a humane, indulgent viewer of the human condition, standing in contrast to earlier, outraged satirists such as Juvenal, Lucilius, and Hipponax, whose brutality is said to have provoked two of the objects of his wit into hanging themselves. Following Horace's example of aiming to modify human behavior through a gentle prodding were satirists such as Alexander Pope, Voltaire, and Cervantes.

HORROR STORY A story designed to frighten its readers. Fear may be evoked through some combination of supernatural and fantastic elements, the suggestion of violence, the macabre, and psychological torments, the latter particularly important as many writers have exploited the dark and profoundly terrifying reaches of the reader's own mind. Its roots are intertwined with those of the Gothic novel; the two genres emerged in the 18th century as a form of amusement that thrilled through terror, and Horace Walpole's *The Castle of Otranto* (1765) is considered the founding work of both. Early examples have become enduring classics, including E. T. A. Hoffmann's *Tales* and especially Mary Shelley's *Frankenstein*, which combines horror with ethical philosophy. The most important figure in the development of the genre was undoubtedly Edgar Allan Poe, whose arabesque and grotesque tales greatly influenced French letters and later those of his native United States. In the 20th century, the popular writer Stephen King is credited with reinvigorating the narrative genre, while horror has also become a staple of the B movie.

HOWLER The inappropriate use of a word that leads to unintentional and, for the author, often mortifying hilarity. Walt Whitman provided a fine example when he substituted "semitic muscle" for "seminal muscle" in the "Preface" to the 1885 edition of *Leaves of Grass*.

HUBRIS OR HYBRIS The excessive pride or ambition that leads to catastrophe in tragedy, as it challenges the harmony and moderation that to the Greeks characterized the moral order. Owing to this conceit and haughtiness, typically the tragic flaw (or *hamartia*) of classical tragedy, the hero ignores prophecy or breaks moral laws with disastrous consequences.

HYPERBOLE (from Greek for "excess") A figure of speech that uses extreme exaggeration for rhetorical effect. Common examples abound, as in "colder than ice" or "ugly as sin." It functions to emphasize the point of comparison, and is a characteristic feature of love poetry, where moderation is not advised. Such forms of deliberate overstatement may also be used for comic effect, as in burlesque.

ICELANDERS' SAGAS (also called sagas of Icelanders or family sagas, from Old Norse "Íslendinga sögur," "stories about Icelanders") Thirteenth-century prose epics chronicling the families of 10th- and 11th-century Iceland. They stand out among medieval works of literature for their complex characters, realism, and tragic conception of life. Their structural unity and sophistication suggest that they were originally written works, not primarily drawn from oral tradition. The finest example is usually considered to be *Njáls Saga*, which relates the adventures and tragic deaths of its two heroes, Njáll and Gunnar.

IDYLL OR IDYL (from Greek, diminutive of "form, picture") 1. A usually brief poem or part of a poem on a pastoral theme that expresses a scene of rustic beauty or country life and is characterized by a mood of tranquility and contentment. No particular form is called for, making it a descriptive term rather than a genre. Its classical origins can be found in the *Idylls* of Theocritus and, through his example, the *Eclogues* of Virgil. 2. Less frequently, it may also refer to a long narrative poem on an epic or romantic theme, as in Tennyson's *Idylls of the King* and Robert Browning's *Dramatic Idylls*.

IMAGE (from Latin for "making a likeness") The representation in language of a mood, idea, or thing through an appeal to perception, often, but by no means exclusively, visual. Through the use of literal and figurative language, writers attempt to reproduce within the mind of the reader a particular sensation that sheds light upon the subject at hand.

IMAGISM Brief but influential poetic movement inspired by T. E. Hulme and led initially by Ezra Pound in the years before World War I.

It advocated the use of concrete, even harsh, images; the avoidance of cliché; freedom of subject matter; and capturing the rhythms of everyday language. Important figures were H. D., Carl Sandburg, William Carlos Williams, and Richard Aldington. Pound deserted the group in 1914 for Vorticism, at which time Amy Lowell became the de facto leader of the group, which published its work in four anthologies and the journal *Poetry*. Although the group lost momentum after the war, its emphasis on a distinct image, which it borrowed from Japanese haiku, greatly influenced poetry in English through the middle of the century, including the work of T. S. Eliot and Wallace Stevens.

IMITATION 1. A term used by Aristotle in his influential theory of the arts. He defended literature as a reflection of nature, unlike Plato, who denigrated art as twice removed from truth. 2. A work of literature that copies the form of another work.

IMPRESSIONISM A term borrowed from art criticism to denote the 19th-century French technique that focused upon re-creating the feeling an object evokes in an observer, rather than attempting to mirror its objective features in a realistic manner. In literature, it is applied somewhat more loosely to attempts to convey a mood or characterization subjectively, rather than to achieve a concrete representation of the external world. It has been applied to the French Symbolist poets, some German writers of the late 19th and early 20th centuries, including Rainer Maria Rilke and Thomas Mann, and English writers such as Virginia Woolf, James Joyce, and Joseph Conrad. In criticism, it refers to the practice of conveying the critic's personal reactions to a work of art. Reader-response criticism is a contemporary variety.

IN MEDIAS RES (Latin, "into the middle of things") The literary device of starting a work in the middle of the action and later filling in the plot details through the use of flashback. The term comes from Horace, who coined it to describe the technique as used by Homer.

Horace notes that an opening *in medias res* compels the reader's attention, contrasting it with literature that opens *ab ovo* (from the egg), at the beginning. It is a typical feature of the epic.

INTENTIONAL FALLACY Term proposed by Monroe Beardsley and W. K. Wimsatt in 1946 to describe the error of judging or understanding a work based upon what the author meant to say. An important idea in New Criticism, it reflects the view that a work of art is part of the public domain of language; authors do not have privileged access to the meaning of the work, nor do their explicit or implicit goals carry special weight in analyzing it.

INTERIOR MONOLOGUE A representation of a character's inner world through the thoughts, feelings, and sensations that constitute consciousness. Interior monologue is related to dramatic monologue, but is less bound than the latter to the requirements of coherence and logic. Rather, in the specialized case known as stream of consciousness, it often attempts to depict the conflicts and desires that influence internal reality; as such, its importance as a device in the 20th-century novel is connected with the discovery of the unconscious. Interior monologue may be direct, offering a window into a character's mind, or indirect, in a third-person narrative, such as was perfected by Virginia Woolf. Édouard Dujardin is considered an innovator of the technique, while the Molly Bloom chapter of James Joyce's *Ulysses* is a highly celebrated example of direct interior monologue.

INTERTEXTUALITY In literary theory, the concept of a text's interrelatedness with other texts, which affects the constitution of meaning. Tom Stoppard's *Rosencrantz and Guildenstern Are Dead* is an intertext of *Hamlet*, from which it clearly draws and without reference to which it would be difficult to understand. However, Julia Kristeva coined the term in the 1960s (based upon the work of Mikhail Bakhtin and Roland Barthes as well as her own semiotic research) to describe in a broader sense the ways in which meaning in language never stands alone, but is created through the utterance's relationship to all utterances that precede *and* follow it. Thus, all forms of language are connected to one another by virtue of the inherently social nature of language.

INTRUSIVE NARRATOR A narrator who interrupts the flow of the text in order to provide additional information or to reflect and remark upon the events and their significance. Although it appeared in the 18th century, it was the 19th-century realist novel that fully exploited its possibilities for moral and/or social commentary; Leo Tolstoy and George Eliot are its foremost practitioners.

INVOCATION (from Latin for "a calling upon") An appeal to a muse or deity for inspiration. The invocation is an epic convention, and is usually placed at the beginning of a work or new section of a larger work. In the Renaissance, invocations were directed to both pagan and Christian divinities, while the later mock-epic naturally produced mock invocations. Famous examples include the invocations of the *Iliad*, the *Odyssey*, and Milton's *Paradise Lost*.

IRONY (from Greek for "dissembling, feigned ignorance") In rhetoric, an expression that conveys something other than its literal meaning. Also, a literary style characterized by this mode. Among the many types of irony are verbal irony, often conveyed by inflection, as in sarcasm; structural irony, in which an alternate meaning is produced by some narrative feature, such as the unreliable narrator of Swift's "A Modest Proposal"; and dramatic irony, in which the audience has information unavailable to a character, as when Oedipus searches for Laius's murderer without realizing that he himself is the killer (this also being the specialized case of tragic irony). The term derives from Greek comedy, in which the artful Eiron frequently outwitted his rival, Alazon.

JUVENALIAN SATIRE Formal satire marked by its bitter, self-righteous, condemnatory tone. So named for Juvenal, the 1st-century Roman author who furiously denounced the failings of his fellow Romans, particularly those of high social standing and women. Juvenalian is contrasted with Horatian satire, which is offered as a gentle corrective to its recipients, among whom the author may even be included. Samuel Johnson and especially Jonathan Swift continued the Juvenalian tradition in English.

KABUKI (Japanese, "art of singing and dancing") Popular form of Japanese drama established in the 17th century, having roots in the more aristocratic Nō drama and bunraku puppet theater. The all-male casts, who did not wear masks (as in Nō) but were heavily made up, performed on low, often rotating, stages, amid ornate and stylized sets. The dramas often drew from legends, addressing issues of romance and vengeance, although the emphasis was on the actors' technical virtuosity over verisimilitude.

KITCHEN-SINK DRAMA Theater that realistically portrays working-class life, in which the focal point of the drama is the kitchen, rather than the drawing room that set the stage for bourgeois plays. The term has been used somewhat derogatorily and chiefly in Britain since the 1950s to refer to the theater of the Angry Young Men.

KNICKERBOCKER SCHOOL Early 19th-century literary coterie centered in New York City. The name derived from Washington Irving's *A History of New York from the Beginning of the World to the End of the Dutch Dynasty* (1809), written under the pseudonym "Diedrich Knickerbocker," also the narrator of "Rip Van Winkle." The group's prominence helped to establish New York (rather than Boston) as the literary center of the United States. Besides Irving, it counted among its members William Cullen Bryant, James Fenimore Cooper, and John Howard Payne. *The Knickerbocker Magazine* (1833–65) took its name from the group, which had already disbanded.

LAKE POETS OR LAKE SCHOOL Name for the English poets William Wordsworth, Samuel Taylor Coleridge, and Robert Southey, all of whom lived in the Lake District of Cumberland. Francis Jeffrey of the *Edinburgh Review* referred to the three poets disparagingly as "Lake Poets" or "Lakers."

LAMENT (from Latin for "expression of sorrow") Poem expressing grief and sorrow over the loss of a person, place, or thing. The form is used widely, appearing in most national literatures, often as part of the oral tradition. Among the best-known examples are the biblical Lamentations of Jeremiah and the Anglo-Saxon *Deor's Lament*; Federico García Lorca's "Lament for the Death of a Bullfighter" is a moving modern instance.

LAMPOON A caustic, abusive, and often coarse form of satire in prose or verse. The term dates from 17th-century France, possibly from the phrase "let us drink," a common refrain in drinking songs. The form thrived in 17th- and 18th-century England in the work of John Dryden and Alexander Pope, among others, until libel laws reined in its use. In contemporary parlance, it refers to ridicule directed at a person or establishment, such as the work that appeared in the *National Lampoon*.

LAY OR LAI A short verse (usually narrative although occasionally lyric) or song, popular in medieval France and England. The oldest narrative lays were written in the 12th century by Marie de France, among the greatest women writers of the Middle Ages; her lays were written in octosyllabic couplets and based upon Celtic legends and romances. English writers in the 14th century imitated the form, which became known as the "Breton lay," producing such works as the *Lay of Sir Orfeo* and the best known of this variety, Chaucer's "Franklin's Tale." More loosely, the term refers to medieval lyric poetry, with no standard metrical form implied. After the Middle Ages, it came to mean a ballad or historical tale in verse, as in Sir Walter Scott's *Lay of the Last Minstrel*.

LEGEND (from Latin for "things for reading") A popular story, often assumed to be historical, but generally grown beyond any putative truth value through successive retellings as it comes to reflect some aspect of its culture. The story of George Washington and the cherry tree is an exemplary American legend. Legends are gen-

erally focused more specifically upon a single personage than are myths, which also tend to take on larger cosmological and religious themes. By extension, the subject of such a tradition can be called a legend. The term originally signified narratives of the lives of saints as well as collections of such accounts; it also refers to the caption of an illustration or an explication of the symbols used on a map.

LEITMOTIF OR LEITMOTIV (German, "leading motif") A dominant theme, symbol, or phrase that is repeated in order to unify a work. The multiple and various references to water in George Eliot's *The Mill on the Floss* provide an example. The term is borrowed from music criticism, where it originally signified a recurring musical theme in the operas of Richard Wagner.

LIMERICK A humorous, often bawdy, English verse form consisting of five anapestic lines of two feet each in the third and fourth lines and three feet in the others, and with the rhyme scheme *aabba*. The form originated in the early 19th century, and was popularized by Edward Lear's *Book of Nonsense* (1846). Several theories have been offered for the origin of the term, including its popularity among writers of County Limerick, Ireland, and the refrain "Will you come up to Limerick?" from a well-known song.

LIMINALITY (from Latin for "threshold") The quality of being on the threshold. From anthropology comes an attention to the various meanings of the borderline, whether geographical, physical, political, economic, or social. Poststructuralism's interest in decentering Western philosophy makes the threshold an important site in the critique of social structures.

LITERARY CRITICISM The study of literature; literary criticism explores the nature, goals, and values of literary works. Western literary criticism began with Plato's critique of art as doubly removed from truth, and Aristotle's subsequent defense of art as representing nature, both exploring the relationship of art to reality. From the poetics of Horace came a shift to looking at the role of art—in his widely adopted formulation, to entertain and instruct—that remained dominant through the Renaissance. Neoclassicism and the Age of Reason brought a return to Aristotelian principles; this impulse was later violently rejected by Romanticism, which insisted upon literature as the self-expression of individual genius. Throughout the 19th century, various forms of autobiographical and impressionistic criticism attempted to establish what the author intended to say.

The 20th century experienced an explosion in critical fields, most of which share an emphasis on textual analysis. Formalism examines the textual practices that distinguish literature from everyday language. New Criticism isolates the text from the external world to explore its internal coherence. Marxist criticism views literature as a social and material process that must be analyzed in relation to other social practices. Psychoanalytic criticism employs the theories of Freud to manifest the multiple levels of meaning that exist simultaneously in a text. Archetypal criticism, an offshoot of Jungian criticism, searches the text for symbols believed to reflect universal patterns of human existence. New historicism interrogates the dynamic relationship between the text and ideology. Reader-response criticism explores the reader's role in making the text meaningful.

LITOTES. *See* **UNDERSTATEMENT**

LITTÉRATURE ENGAGÉE (French, "engaged literature") Socially committed literature. As a response to World War II, French existentialists insisted that the artist's primary responsibility was to society. Jean-Paul Sartre and others believed that in order to transform the world and thus prevent another Holocaust, art could and should participate in pressing social issues. Technical virtuosity mattered only in terms of the uses of the literature, not in and of itself, as in so-called "bourgeois understandings" of the nature of art.

LITTLE MAGAZINE Any of the small, noncommercial literary journals dedicated to promoting a particular literary theory or to providing a forum for avant-garde work. Beginning in the late 19th century, these periodicals established important creative outlets in the United States and England and, to a lesser extent, France and Germany. The decade after World War I was particularly fertile for the little magazine, as were the 1960s, when radical and iconoclastic sensibilities ran high. Among the most influential can be counted *Poetry: A Magazine of Verse* (1912–), *The Little Review* (1914–29), and *The Dial* (1880–1929) in the United States, and Aubrey Beardsley's *The Yellow Book* (1894–97) and *The Egoist* (1914–19) in England. Many of the most distinguished writers of their times got their start in little magazines. (See Influential Literary Periodicals.)

LOCAL COLOR Writing that is closely tied to a particular geographical region. The interconnection between place and language comes out in the use of dialect, local customs and stories, and descriptions of the physical environment. The exemplary form, the humorous short story, played a prominent role in the American literary scene at the end of the 19th century. Mark Twain is the foremost American practitioner; other writers famously associated with their locales include Sarah Orne Jewett and Harriet Beecher Stowe in New England, Joel Chandler Harris and Kate Chopin in the South, and Bret Harte in the West. Among European writers, Émile Zola and Rudyard Kipling can be counted as local colorists.

LOW COMEDY Comedy whose appeal is base— the humor of a man slipping on a banana peel—rather than intellectual, as in high comedy. Slapstick, buffoonery, clowning, fighting, and bawdy jokes are staples of low comedy. Originating as an improvisation in ancient comedy and later becoming an interlude in medieval morality plays and Renaissance drama, low comedy may also appear on its own, as in farce. The value judgment implicit in the word *low* reflects the elitist belief that this type of comedy is the purview of the uneducated masses.

LYRIC (from Greek for "lyre") A usually short, nonnarrative poem in the voice of a single speaker. In classical poetics, a lyric was a song performed to the accompaniment of a lyre, hence the name. Along with dramatic and narrative verse, it is one of the main types of poetry and, since the early 19th century, has been the dominant of the three. Its musical qualities—a focus on elements such as sound and meter—and its traditional use for expressing emotion have made it the preeminent form of modern poetry. Numerous poetic varieties fall under its heading, including the elegy, ode, pastoral, and sonnet.

MACARONIC VERSE Verse that incorporates two or more languages. The form originated in the 15th century, when Tisi degli Odassi wrote comic poetry composed of vernacular words with Latin endings, but gained popularity through the work of his student, Teofilo Folengo. Poets since have exploited the humorous potential of mixing languages. Less commonly, noncomedic poetry can also be referred to as macaronic, as in the work of Ezra Pound and T. S. Eliot.

MacGuffin A narrative element needed to motivate a plot, but in itself insignificant. The term is often associated with the work of Alfred Hitchcock, whose films frequently turn on such a device. For example, in *Notorious*, the Nazi scheme is not the center of a story exploring its own twists and turns; rather, it provides the pretext for the heroine's dangerous marriage and the suspenseful question of whether she will be able to escape from the house.

MADRIGAL (from Latin for "of the womb") A short, lyrical poem, usually on a romantic or pastoral theme, especially one set to music and arranged in several vocal parts. The form played an important role in two periods: it originated in 14th-century Italy, where it generally consisted of two or three tercets and a rhyming couplet, modeled after Petrarch's example; it was reworked by 16th-century English authors. The only common formal feature between the two periods was the use of the couplet to end the piece. Tudor writers arranged madrigals for five to six voices, and these popular songs were sung without accompaniment. Its vogue spread throughout Europe, as composers explored music's potential to reflect and extend meaning expressed in words.

MAGIC REALISM (from Spanish, "lo real maravilloso") Literature that naturalizes the supernatural, taking for granted magical elements in an otherwise realistic narrative. Cuban writer Alejo Carpentier coined the term to describe its adherents' keen awareness of the fantastic aspects of the political and historical realities of Latin America, which resulted in a fiction both cruel and beautiful. Among its innovators are some of the most important modern Latin American writers, including Nobel Prize winners Jorge Luis Borges and Gabriel García Márquez as well as Isabel Allende, Jorge Amado, and Julio Cortázar.

MALAPROPISM The error of substituting one word for another with a similar sound. In *The Rivals* (1775), Richard Brinsley Sheridan's character Mrs. Malaprop (whence the term, from the French *mal à propos* [out of place, inappropriate]) has the comical habit of misusing words, as when she speaks of "a nice derangement of epitaphs." The gaffe predates the term, however; Shakespeare's Dogberry in *Much Ado About Nothing* is one of many literary characters to have a similar linguistic propensity.

MASQUE OR MASK A form of masked entertainment popular in the Middle Ages and Renaissance. The form likely developed out of pagan religious rites, taking the form in the Middle Ages of masked processions leading to impromptu gatherings. Also known as a "disguising" or "mummery," it was adopted as court entertainment throughout Europe. Actors and musicians, often aristocrats, performed allegories that ended with an unmasking and a dance in which the audience joined. Especially popular in Tudor England, the form reached its apex in the lavish spectacles of poet Ben Jonson and designer Inigo Jones at the court of James I (1603–25). The unparalleled extravagance of their productions led to the form's decline after the establishment of parliamentary government. The masque's progeny include opera and pantomime.

MEDIEVAL ROMANCE. *See* **ROMANCE**

MELODRAMA (from French for "musical drama") A play or movie offering a sensational tale of virtue threatened but ultimately triumphant. It originally signified a musical entertainment because the English Licensing Act of 1737 restricted "legitimate" (i.e., spoken) drama to a monopoly of theaters. Such spectacles combined pantomime, dialogue, and music, and thus focused upon creating a spectacle at the expense of character development and psychological subtlety. Extremely popular in 19th-century theater, melodrama's lurid tales of good and evil were readily adapted to the developing silent cinema.

MEMOIR (from Latin for "memory") An account of the life and times of its subject, who may be the author or an intimate of the author. Strictly speaking, a memoir is distinct from an autobiography, which focuses more upon the individual doings and personal psychology of the subject; however, because the term *autobiography* entered the critical vocabulary only recently, some early examples of such works have been called memoirs. François-René de Chateaubriand wrote a celebrated memoir designed for posthumous publication (1849–50). Political figures such as Charles de Gaulle and Golda Meir have also recollected the circumstances of their public lives in memoirs.

METAPHOR (from Greek for "transference") A figure of speech in which the qualities of one thing are highlighted through a comparison to another, as in E. E. Cummings's "thy hair is one kingdom." In metaphor, the comparison is implied ("my beloved is a beautiful flower"), while in simile, the comparison is stated explicitly ("my beloved is like a beautiful flower"). Metaphor, one of the main figures used in poetry, is also an important feature of nonpoetic language as well as an efficient way of elucidating abstractions. A dead metaphor is one that has been used so long that its metaphorical qualities are overlooked, as in the "leg" of a chair. A mixed metaphor is the often comical result of combining incompatible elements: "a rolling stone bites the dust."

METAPHYSICAL POETS A name chiefly applied to a number of 17th-century English poets. Their work, written in reaction to the highly conventional late-Elizabethan sonnet, is characterized by its intellectual and philosophical bent, striking and elaborate conceits, an appreciation of paradox, use of everyday language and rough meters, and frank discussions of sexuality. The foremost metaphysical poet is unquestionably John Donne; other notables include Andrew Marvell, George Herbert, Richard Crashaw, Abraham Cowley, and John Cleveland. The appellation "metaphysical" comes from Samuel Johnson, who used it pejoratively. Their reputation enjoyed a reappraisal in the early 20th century, thanks in part to a laudatory essay by T. S. Eliot.

METER (from Greek for "measure") In versification, the regular (or fairly regular) rhythmic pattern of a poetic line. There are four standard systems for measuring meter: (1) quantitative, based upon the alternation of long and short syllables and measured by the length of the line, is the classical meter; (2) syllabic, which counts the number of syllables in a line regardless of the number of accents present, is well suited to languages that are not accented, such as French and Japanese; (3) accentual, which allows a varied number of syllables within a line of a fixed number of accents, is the meter of German and Old English poetry as well as popular English verse, such as the nursery rhyme; and (4) accentual-syllabic, the customary form of English poetry, which measures both the number of accents and syllables. The most common meters in English poetry are iambic (˘´), trochaic (´˘), anapestic (˘˘´), dactylic (´˘˘), spondaic (´´), and pyrrhic (˘˘). Based on the number of feet per line, poetry may be monometer (1 foot), dimeter (2), trimeter (3), tetrameter (4), pentameter (5), and so on; the latter two are most often found in English verse. Despite the elaborate rhythmic systems developed for poetry, the effect created when a poet establishes a meter and then purposefully disappoints its expectations can be extremely powerful.

METONYMY (from Greek for "substitute meaning") A figure of speech in which a name is used to refer to something else that is associated with it, as in "the Crown" for royalty. Strictly speaking, it is differentiated from synecdoche, in which a part is used for the whole or a whole for the part, as when a laborer is called "a hand." In contemporary literary theory, emphasis is placed on metonymy's creation of meaning through contiguity, as opposed to metaphor, which in emphasizing similarity necessarily erases difference in a way that metonymy does not.

MIMESIS (Greek, "imitation") The Greek word for imitation or mimicry. Plato and Aristotle held that all art was mimetic, in that it copied nature or truth, although they valued the work of art very differently.

MIRACLE PLAY A medieval drama based on either the miraculous intervention of the Virgin Mary or the lives of the saints, especially St. Nicholas. These plays were written in the vernacular and produced by trade guilds. Some 40 French miracle plays dating from the 14th century are still extant. Few English plays have survived, as they were first banned during the reign of the Protestant king Henry VIII and then became casualties of the Reformation, which burned existing works. They are closely related to morality and mystery plays.

MOCK EPIC OR **MOCK-HEROIC** A satire that subjects an inconsequential subject to the lofty style and conventions of an epic is known as a mock epic. The term *mock-heroic* can be applied to a work that is not as long as a full-fledged epic, but still pokes fun at the genre. The classical *Battle of the Frogs and Mice* is an undated early instance, spoofing the Homeric epic. In English, the form was especially popular in the late 17th and early 18th centuries, Alexander Pope's *The Rape of the Lock*, about a nobleman who ever so courageously snatches a lock of his beloved's hair, being the exemplary work.

MODERN Of or relating to the contemporary era or recent times. Confusion sometimes arises about its meaning because of the two distinct periods to which it is applied. On the one hand, it is used to describe the period characterized by Western liberal values and philosophies that began with the Enlightenment and continues to this day (e.g., modern history). It also pertains to styles of contemporary art, literature, and music participating in aesthetic modernism, a movement active during the period roughly from the beginning of the 20th century through the end of World War II.

MODERNISM The dominant aesthetic movement in the West during the early and mid-20th century, modernism reflects a rupture with traditional knowledges and beliefs, and a desire, in Ezra Pound's famous phrase, to "make it new," the "it" being both literature and society. At the beginning of the century, modernism reflected the energy and utopianism of the dawn of the machine age. However, the devastation of World War I inaugurated the more pessimistic phase of high modernism, characterized by a sense of fragmentation and loss of meaning. In literature, authors rejected realism's pretense to objectivity and naive belief in the transparency of language. Considering themselves an avant-garde opposed to bourgeois norms, they strove for a mode of expression equal to the new era. They experimented with novel ways of representing human consciousness, as in the stream-of-consciousness technique employed by James Joyce and Virginia Woolf; broke with normative understandings of chronology, linearity, and traditional logic, as in the work of Gertrude Stein; and created its effect through the accretion of symbol, evident in the poetry of Pound and T. S. Eliot. Modernist literature demands that its readers engage in the struggle to find meaning in the text as in the world; the difficulty of these works has earned great appreciation from admirers as well as charges of elitism from frustrated audiences. Postmodernism came into being in the aftermath of World War II, but whether it represents a supersession or continuation of modernism is a question of considerable debate.

MODERNISMO (BRAZILIAN) A post–World War I movement devoted to freeing Brazilian literature from the influence of European traditions. Proponents sought to develop the literary potential of the nation by turning for inspiration to indigenous folk themes and the rhythms of conversational language, which led to innovations in syntax and the use of free verse. A progressive movement, it also advocated social reform. Major authors include Manuel Bandeira and Mánuel de Andrade.

MODERNISMO (SPANISH-SPEAKING WORLD) A Spanish-American literary movement conceived by the Nicaraguan poet Rubén Darío as a rejection of Romanticism. Dominant from the end of the 19th century to the beginning of the 20th, the movement was responsible for reinvigorating the Spanish poetic language and later for introducing to it specifically American themes. The French Symbolists greatly influenced Darío and his fellow writers, whose work was marked by exoticism, decadence, a belief in art for art's sake, and a tendency toward melancholia as well as formal innovation. Among its adherents are such well-known figures as José Martí, José Asunción Silva, José Enrique Rodó, Leopoldo Lugones, and Rufino Blanco Fombona.

MONOLOGUE (French, from "mono" + "logue") A lengthy speech given by one person. A monologue is typically addressed to either the audience or other characters who remain silent. If a second party is addressed, the monologue is considered "dramatic." On stage, a speech that reveals the character's thoughts is known as a soliloquy. "Interior monologue" is a fictional device that expresses a character's thoughts.

MOOD The pervasive emotional and intellectual climate that the writer communicates to an audience.

MORALITY PLAY A type of allegorical drama popular in the Middle Ages, along with the miracle play and the mystery play. Morality plays dramatized the Christian sermon, representing the battle between the abstract forces of good and evil in the form of concrete characters such as Death, the Seven Deadly Sins, Truth, and Everyman/Mankind. The most famous English morality play is *Everyman*, in which the hero discovers that Good Deeds, alone of all the other characters, will accompany him when Death summons. Eventually, the strictly didactic form made space for the actors to improvise comic interludes.

MOTIF (Old French, "motive") A basic theme that recurs in literature. Strictly speaking, it is differentiated from the *leitmotif*, a recurrent and/or dominant theme or thematic element that unifies a single work, although in common usage the term *motif* is used for both. Literature abounds in motifs, such as the travails of the orphan in melodrama or the *carpe diem* theme in lyric poetry, which have fascinated writers and audiences alike for centuries.

MUSE One of the nine Greek goddesses of the arts and sciences. The daughters of Zeus and Mnemosyne (Memory), their gifts were regularly invoked by mortals engaged in the creative endeavors they patronized. The individual muses and their respective fields are Calliope, epic poetry and eloquence; Clio, heroic poetry and history; Erato, love poetry; Euterpe, lyric poetry and music; Melpomene, tragedy; Polyhymnia, sacred music and poetry; Terpsichore, choral song and dance; Thalia, comedy; and Urania, astronomy. Since the classical period, the muse can be understood as a personification of artistic inspiration.

MYSTERY PLAY A medieval drama that presented stories from the Bible. Along with miracle and morality plays, the mystery play developed from liturgical drama. By the 13th century, it had become the province of trade guilds, each of which would present a particular biblical scene on a movable wagon, often with elaborate mechanical devices to provide special effects. In some of the larger English towns, during the major feasts (especially Corpus Christi) a pageant consisting of multiple plays could be performed at various sites for the benefit of the entire community; in France, the mysteries were generally enacted at a fixed location. The mystery cycles of York, Coventry, Wakefield, and Chester are the best known of the English plays. The term *mystery* derives from the Latin homophones that signify both "sacred rite" and "handicraft," the latter a reference to the trade guilds.

MYTH (from Greek for "tale, utterance") Any of the traditional stories by which a culture seeks to understand the world and its relation to human life. Myths may explore such fundamental questions as the meaning of life and death, the dimensions of the natural world and the sacred, and the nature of heroism; as such, they represent the deepest beliefs of a particular people.

NARRATOLOGY The study of the ways in which the various elements of a narrative combine in order to create a meaningful whole. A body of criticism indebted to both Russian formalism and French structuralism, narratology looks at such issues as the type of narrator (e.g., omniscient, naive, untrustworthy), the temporal structure of the story (whether it is told chronologically or in flashback), and the style in which a given plot is related. Ultimately, narratology suggests that the way in which a story is told affects the type of story that can be told.

NATURALISM A literary movement of the late 19th century. Naturalism developed out of realism, extending to literature a scientific determinism based on the writings of Charles Darwin, Auguste Comte, and Hippolyte Taine. It sees human existence as driven by forces, such as evolution and mean instinct, beyond any individual's control, and tends to focus upon the victims, favoring the squalid and tawdry. Coming out of realism, naturalists sought to depict the world objectively, without filtering it through the author's subjective reactions. Émile Zola is undoubtedly the most celebrated naturalist, having an American counterpart in Theodore Dreiser.

NEGATIVE CAPABILITY John Keats's phrase for the quality of receptivity needed to produce great literature. In an 1817 letter to his brothers, Keats described it as the capacity "of being in uncertainties, mysteries, doubts, without an irritable reaching after fact and reason." He

takes Shakespeare as his example of an artist so overcome with beauty in the world that he is able to tolerate all the questions it raises; the true artist is content to experience beauty without trying to dominate and delimit it.

NÉGRITUDE (French, "blackness") A literary and cultural movement that began in the 1930s in francophone Africa and the Caribbean. Négritude rejected the colonial European assumption of cultural superiority, and insisted that African beliefs, traditions, and history should provide the basis for literary endeavor as well as a cultural identity, both in Africa and the diaspora. The term was coined by Aimé Césaire, a poet and politician from Martinique; Léopold Sédar Senghor, who became the first president of Senegal in 1960, was its most important writer.

NEOCLASSICISM A belief in the perfection of classical models of literature, as they exemplify harmony, restraint, decorum, order, proportion, and universal truths. Although the term can be applied to adherents of any period, it is especially characteristic of the Age of Reason, when writers embraced the virtues of the ancients as a reaction to the excesses of the Renaissance. Neoclassicists advocate imitation of the rules they believe derive from the masters of antiquity, although it has never been entirely clear that those critics (especially Aristotle) intended their remarks to be prescriptive rather than descriptive. Neoclassicism is not substantively different from classicism.

NEOREALISM (ITALY) Post–World War II Italian literary movement that explored the causes and legacy of fascism, especially in terms of the social issues of contemporary Italy. In fiction, writers such as Alberto Moravia, Italo Calvino, Salvatore Quasimodo, and Carlo Levi drew from prewar Realismo to depict the aftermath of the century's upheavals as they affected daily life. Neorealist cinema achieved worldwide renown for its mixture of drama and documentary toward the goal of an authentic representation of human existence; its characteristic look came from the use of nonprofessional actors and location shooting. Luchino Visconti,

Roberto Rossellini, and Vittorio de Sica are among the most celebrated Neorealist directors.

NEW CRITICISM An American critical movement prominent from the 1910s to the 1960s. The New Critics considered the poem (for them, the literary object par excellence) as a self-contained unit that could be analyzed objectively, that is, with respect only to the way it deployed language. They rejected prior critics' interest in anything that lay beyond the poem itself; history, culture, and the biography of the author were all out of bounds to the critic. Instead, they advocated the technique of "close reading," a detailed textual analysis that attends to the poem's internal coherence. By the 1940s, New Criticism had become the established approach in American classrooms, despite critiques of the political conservatism of its adherents and of their desire to remove the work of art from its social context. Its legacy has been far-reaching, and socially engaged forms of criticism continue to borrow, even while they expand upon, its method of rigorous textual analysis.

NEW FORMALISM OR NEOFORMALISM A term somewhat loosely used to designate contemporary poets who have reclaimed formalist devices, such as meter, rhyme, and stanzaic forms. The term dates to the early 1980s; of course, poetic interest in the formal aspects of language never really disappeared. Despite the widespread impression that *vers libre* has led the 20th century away from traditional forms, poets such as these remind audiences of the visceral quality of sound and rhythm that endure both in traditional poetic modes and even in free verse. Affiliates of the New Formalism include John Berryman, Anthony Hecht, John Hollander, Howard Nemerov, Robert Pinsky, and Richard Wilbur.

NEW HISTORICISM Critical school that developed in the early 1980s around the principle that literature and history are dynamically interrelated. Rejecting formalist approaches that ignore the context of the literary work, it also differs from the "old" historicism that sees literature as merely a reflection of its culture. In contrast, new historicism derives from poststructuralism, especially the work of Michel Foucault, its belief that the text produces ideology while it is also produced by it. New historians therefore complicate their analyses by reading literature along with material from other discourses, such as law, medicine, or politics. The school's principles were largely created by scholars working on the British Elizabethan period, with which new historicism is still largely associated; its most important adherents include Stephen Greenblatt, Marilyn Butler, Jonathan Goldberg, and Jerome McGann.

NEW JOURNALISM A type of journalism that eschews the traditional pose of objectivity. Coming to prominence in the 1960s, and indebted to the subjective accounts of John Dos Passos and Ernest Hemingway, new journalists were often also creative writers whose work blurred the boundaries between fiction and fact. New Journalism is characterized by a personal voice and idiosyncratic style that underscore the author's presence and shaping of the material. Among its most prominent practitioners are Truman Capote, Joan Didion, Norman Mailer, Hunter S. Thompson, and Tom Wolfe.

NEW YORK INTELLECTUALS Irving Howe's name for a coterie of New York literary critics whose liberal views of literature and politics were a dominant influence in the New York media throughout the mid-20th century. Through influential essays and book reviews in a number of respected journals and newspapers, writers such as Lionel Trilling and Alfred Kazin helped to shape the cultural milieu of the city.

NEW YORK SCHOOL OF POETS A mid-1950s school of poetry that captured the creative environment of New York City in personal and conversational verse. Breaking with academic poetry of the early century, members drew inspiration from Abstract Expressionist painting, then making waves in the New York art scene, as well as jazz and the rhythms of urban life. Led by Frank O'Hara, the school included John Ashbery and Kenneth Koch.

Nō DRAMA OR NOH (Japanese, "talent, ability") Japanese classical drama that combines highly stylized gestures, masked actors in elaborate costumes, music, chanting, and dance. The form developed in the 14th century, making it one of the world's oldest dramatic genres; its repertory was set by the 17th century. Nō, which is the aristocratic form of drama in Japan, as opposed to the more popular kabuki, developed from Shinto ritual dance. Contemporary Western writers, such as W. B. Yeats and Ezra Pound, and the dramatists Bertolt Brecht and Thornton Wilder, have shown considerable interest in the form's nonrepresentational storytelling.

NONFICTION NOVEL A narrative representing factual events through the use of novelistic techniques that take it outside the boundaries of history. Truman Capote coined the term to describe *In Cold Blood* (1966), his gripping account of a brutal slaying told as if through the eyes of various people involved. A nonfiction novel may appear seamless or may highlight its own ambiguities, as when Thomas Keneally, author of *Schindler's List*, confronts head-on the difficulties of fully knowing his subject.

NONSENSE VERSE A category of humorous verse in which absurd logic, flawed or incomprehensible grammar, and nonce words (i.e., neologisms) chosen for their amusing sound qualities rather than any purported meaning combine to create a playful whole. Nonsense verse is often written specifically for children, as is the case with the greatest of such works written in English, Edward Lear's *Book of Nonsense* (1846) and the "Jabberwocky" section of Lewis Carroll's *Alice's Adventures in Wonderland*, which famously begins, "Twas brillig and the slithy toves / Did gyre and gimble in the wabe; / All mimsy were the borogroves / And the mome raths outgrabe." Common forms of nonsense verse include limericks and some nursery rhymes.

NORSE SAGA. *See* SAGA

NOUVEAU ROMAN (French, "new novel") An influential 20th-century French form of the antinovel. Beginning with Nathalie Sarraute's *Tropisms* (*Tropismes*, 1938), the *nouveau roman* was established as an important avant-garde form by the mid-1950s in the work of Alain Robbe-Grillet, Michel Butor, Claude Simon, and Marguerite Duras. These writers claimed to be "new" insofar as they challenged traditional notions of the novel by dispensing with such recognizable features as plot, coherent characters, and linear time. The *nouveau roman* was intimately linked with postwar French philosophical trends based upon a profound antihumanism and desire to interrogate the effects of language; it additionally shared some of its preoccupations and techniques with French New Wave cinema, especially through the agency of Robbe-Grillet and Duras, both occasional screenwriters and directors.

NOVEL A work of fiction in prose and of considerable length. Of the major literary genres—novel, poetry, drama, and short story—the novel was the last on the scene; despite some classical and medieval antecedents, most critics consider the appearance of Cervantes's *Don Quixote* (1605–15) to mark the birth of the genre.

The novel became established as a form in England in the early 18th century in the hands of Daniel Defoe, Henry Fielding, and Samuel Richardson, while in France, Madame de Lafayette's *The Princess of Cleves* is its inaugural event. By the beginning of the 19th century, types of novels proliferated wildly. In England, Sir Walter Scott introduced the historical novel, while Jane Austen perfected the novel of manners and Mary Shelley created science fiction with *Frankenstein*; meanwhile, the Gothic novel entertained countless readers. The novel flourished at the end of the century, offering a flexible vehicle for exploring the realist impulse based in modern understandings of science, technology, psychology, and society; thus the great realist novels of Gustave Flaubert, Honoré de Balzac, Leo Tolstoy, Fyodor Dostoyevsky, George Eliot, and Henry James emerged. Modernist writers explored the nature and limitations of language, seeking to capture a different kind of realism, that of interior consciousness rather than of an external world. This questioning of the meanings of knowledge, language, and narrative continued in later 20th-century experiments with the anti-novel, *nouveau roman*, and postmodern novel.

NOVELLE (GERMAN) A German form of short narrative that arose in the late 18th century and was largely responsible for the development of the short story in that language. The *Novelle* centered around a discrete event, presented straightforwardly, often with an unexpected twist at the end. Such writers as Goethe (who introduced the term), Franz Kafka, Heinrich von Kleist, and Thomas Mann have explored the genre.

NOVEL OF MANNERS A fictional work steeped in the mores and behaviors of a particular class. Although not an intrinsic aspect of the genre, the manners in question generally belong to the upper- or upper-middle classes. In this type of fiction, the fortunes of the characters rise and fall upon their ability (or lack thereof) to negotiate the often stifling social codes that define the time and place. Jane Austen's arch satires on the rituals of courtship among the English minor landed gentry epitomize the novel of manners; the novels of Edith Wharton and John P. Marquand also belong in this tradition.

OBJECTIVE CORRELATIVE An external image or action that conveys an internal feeling or state. T. S. Eliot, who first applied the term to literary theory, claimed, "The only way of expressing emotion in the form of art is by finding an 'objective correlative'; in other words, a set of objects, a situation, a chain of events which shall be the formula of that *particular* emotion; such that when the external facts, which must terminate in sensory experience, are given, the emotion is immediately evoked." The concept supports his criticism of 19th-century poetic verbiage as failing by its tendency to *tell* rather than *show*, and explains his preference for the precision and concrete symbols of his own imagism.

OCCASIONAL VERSE Poetry written specifically to commemorate a particular event of some importance, whether public or personal. Poets laureate in their official capacity often celebrate public events, although poetry celebrating more private moments, such as weddings and funerals, also falls into the category of occasional verse. The epithalamion (or poem celebrating a wedding), funeral elegy, and some odes are typical forms. Examples include Tennyson's "Charge of the Light Brigade" and Dylan Thomas's "On a Wedding Anniversary."

ODE (from Greek for "song") A dignified lyric poem written in honor of a moving or inspiring event, object, or person. Two general forms existed in antiquity: the exalted declamatory of the Greek poet Pindar in choral pieces written to celebrate the victors in athletic competitions, and the quieter meditations of his Latin counterpart, Horace. Both forms were rediscovered by English poets in the 17th century and were frequently employed during the 18th century. The Romantic sensibility was well suited to the ode, producing notable work from Samuel Taylor Coleridge, William Wordsworth, Percy Bysshe Shelley, and John Keats. Stirring contemporary odes have been written by Matthew Arnold, W. H. Auden, and Allen Tate.

ONOMATOPOEIA (from Greek for "name making") In the narrow sense, the derivation of a word from its representative sound, such as *buzz*, *ring*, and *crackle*. More broadly, this figure of speech refers to the effect produced when the sound of words evokes their meaning. Tennyson's "murmuring of innumerable bees" is considered an exemplary instance.

ORGANIC FORM The idea that the form of a literary work grows out of the author's conception, having a life of its own. This profoundly Romantic formulation was proposed by Coleridge in opposition to the Enlightenment dictum that art should follow the rules laid down by the ancients. American New Criticism embraced the idea, which implies that content cannot be separated from form, and thus literature is always more than the sum of its parts.

OTTAVA RIMA An eight-line stanza with a rhyme scheme of *abababcc*. It originated in 14th-century Italy and was popularized as a heroic and narrative verse form by Boccaccio,

Ludovico Ariosto, and Torquato Tasso. English writers adapted the form, changing the Italian 11-syllable line to iambic pentameter. Such varied poets as Edmund Spenser, John Milton, John Keats, and William Butler Yeats have employed it; Byron, in particular, exploited its traditional epic connotations for his mock-heroic *Don Juan.*

OuLiPo (France) (French, short for *Ouvroir de Littérature Potentielle,* "Workshop of Potential Literature") A group of experimental French writers of the 1970s. Their chief interest lay in the linguistic possibilities of words, as reflected in their choosing as a mentor the one-time Surrealist author Raymond Queneau, who offered 99 retellings of a single incident in order to illustrate various ways of playing with language in the tour-de-force *Exercises in Style* (*Exercices de Style,* 1947). The group participated in the post–World War II search for new ways of creating meaning.

PAEAN (Greek, from an epithet used for Apollo) A song expressing joy, praise, or triumph. Such hymns originally honored Apollo in his guise as physician to the Olympic gods, who was invoked prior to important military campaigns; later, the term signified any such song celebrating a deity or human whose victories were especially laudable.

PALIMPSEST (from Greek for "rubbed again") A text written upon a surface (generally parchment, vellum, or papyrus) that had previously been used and then erased. Because of the high cost of writing materials through the Middle Ages, economy provided the motive for this practice. Many ancient texts are extant solely by virtue of contemporary technological advances that allow the recovery of the effaced script. By extension, a text that shows traces of other works may be called palimpsestic, a concept that has become important in contemporary feminist criticism and deconstruction.

PANEGYRIC (from Greek for "for a public festival") An elaborate and ceremonious laudatory speech. Celebrating a city and its people, such declamations were part of Greek festivals and games; formal rhetorical rules for the panegyric were established by Menander and Hermogenes. The Romans expanded the tradition to include the praise of great leaders, as in Pliny the Younger's panegyric in honor of the Emperor Trajan. The effusive diction and, at worst, fawning tendency of the panegyric explains the term's current pejorative connotation.

PANTOMIME (from Greek for "all imitator") Originally, a classical Roman dramatic form in which a single actor depicted all the roles in a play without speaking, while a chorus communicated the narrative in song. By the beginning of the 18th century, the pantomime had become a popular form of children's entertainment in England, in which fairy tales or nursery rhymes were performed, traditionally at Christmas. These lavish spectacles involved music, dance, and elaborate costumes, scenery, and special effects, and featured such comic touches as cross-gender casting, particularly the use of a girl to play the lead boy. Broadly, any acting in which gesture, movement, and expression take the place of the spoken word can be considered pantomime.

PARABLE (from Greek for "juxtaposition, comparison") A short allegorical story that illustrates a moral principle. As a rhetorical form, the parable is considered a useful pedagogical tool, capable of bringing home an abstract idea. It is a common feature of classical rhetoric as well as ancient religious traditions; perhaps the most famous parables of Western literature are the 40 attributed to Jesus in the New Testament.

PARADOX (from Greek for "conflicting with expectation") A proposition whose seemingly self-contradictory logic suggests or illustrates a profound, if elusive, truth, as in the commonplace that "you have to spend money to make money." Rhetorically, paradox startles listeners into thinking about its subject in new ways. The metaphysical poets made frequent use of paradox, and such prodigious wits as Oscar Wilde, George Bernard Shaw, and, in particular, G. K. Chesterton have exploited its capacity to entertain. A term in which two words appear to be paradoxical is called an oxymoron: "jumbo shrimp" or "honorable thief."

PARALLELISM (from Greek for "beside one another") In grammar, the arrangement of corresponding ideas in like constructions, in order to balance and emphasize the relationship between various elements. It is commonly used in poetry, particularly in the oral tradition and in Hebrew verse, both of which exploit its sonorous and rhetorical qualities, as in Psalm 103: 2–4: "Bless the Lord, O my soul, and forget not all his benefits: / Who forgiveth all thine iniquities; who healeth all thy diseases; / Who redeemeth thy life from destruction; who crowneth thee with loving kindness and tender mercies."

PARNASSIANS A French school of poets active in the late 19th century. The Parnassians, who took their name from the Greek mountain associated with Apollo and the Muses, reacted against what they perceived as the self-indulgences of Romantic poetry by championing an impersonal and restrained poetry of precise imagery and perfected form. Many of their themes were derived from history, philosophy, and nature. They clustered around Charles Leconte de Lisle, and adhered to Théophile Gautier's dictum of "art for art's sake." Of the approximately 50 members of the school, some of the most prominent were Théodore de Banville, François Coppée, Sully Prudhomme, and Anatole France.

PARODY (from Greek for "mock song") Writing that imitates and exaggerates the style of another work or of an author for comic effect. It is distinguished from satire, which ridicules the content of a work or idea. The tone of parody may vary from disgust and ridicule to a good-natured appreciation of another author's idiosyncracies. Parody has contributed to some of the world's great literature, from Plato's caricatures in the *Symposium* to Cervantes's mocking of the picaresque novel in *Don Quixote* to Jane Austen's send-up of the Gothic novel in *Northanger Abbey*. Max Beerbohm's *A Christmas Garland* (1896), which relates holiday stories in the voices of such writers as Rudyard Kipling, John Galsworthy, and Thomas Hardy, is a more recent example. Periodicals, including *The New Yorker* and *Punch*, have provided a ready forum for contemporary parody.

PASSION PLAY A play depicting the suffering, death, and resurrection of Jesus, usually performed during Holy Week. The tradition of dramatizing the passion began in 13th-century Sienna and spread throughout Europe, sometimes as a precursor to the presentation of miracle plays at the feast of Corpus Christi. Passion plays are still popular, the most famous undoubtedly that of the Bavarian village of Oberammergau, which has been performed every ten years since 1633 to honor a vow made during an outbreak of the plague.

PASTICHE (French, "literary imitation") An imitation of the style of another writer, as an exercise or for a humorous purpose. Also, a work of art that combines a variety of elements (e.g., styles, themes, quotations) from other works.

PASTORAL (from Greek for "of a shepherd") A highly conventional form of literature that celebrates an innocent and idealized rustic life. Interestingly, such sentiments are generally written for urban audiences by authors who have not experienced the simple pleasures they extol. The classical innovator was the Greek poet Theocritus, whose work centered on the lives of shepherds. Virgil brought the pastoral to Rome, influencing innumerable writers throughout Europe with his eclogues. Christian writers added to it the idea of Jesus as the Good Shepherd, and the form was given new life in the Renaissance. In England, Edmund Spenser's poetry and Shakespeare's *As You Like It* are just two examples; other authors who favored the form include Christopher Marlowe, John Milton, John Donne, and Andrew Marvell. By the 19th century, the pastoral was largely relegated to the elegy, famously in the work of Percy Bysshe Shelley and Matthew Arnold. The form continues to provide a forum for the criticism, often conservative in nature, of modern life.

PATHETIC FALLACY The practice of ascribing human emotions to inanimate objects, as in Sylvia Plath's line, "The grasses unload their griefs on my feet as if I were God." The art critic John Ruskin introduced the term in 1856 to register his disapproval of usages such as "dancing" leaves and "angry" storms. Ruskin, who greatly valued realism, considered the personification of nature to be "morbid"; however, this convention is ubiquitous in poetry, and contemporary critics use the term descriptively rather than damningly.

PATHOS (from Greek for "passion, suffering") An aspect of a work of art or literature that evokes in the audience feelings of sorrow, pity, or commiseration. Pathos describes the emotional reaction, in contrast to *ethos*, the intellectual response, to art. Pathos that overreaches descends into bathos.

PATTERN POETRY Poetry in which the lines are arranged on the page in a meaningful configuration, such as the form of an object or a geometric shape. Pattern poetry is most likely of East Asian origin, and classical examples date from the 4th century B.C. Writers who have experimented with the typographical potential of the written word include George Herbert, Guillaume Apollinaire, Vladimir Mayakovsky, E. E. Cummings, and Dylan Thomas. Pattern poetry is a close cousin of concrete poetry, an experimental form that experienced a certain vogue in the 1950s and 1960s; the distinction between the two is that only pattern poetry retains its sense (although with some loss) if read aloud.

PERSONA (Latin, "mask") A speaking voice in a work of literature, the "I" who narrates a novel or enunciates a lyric poem. The persona is important in literary criticism because it allows a reader to distinguish between the speaker, always a fictive character, and the actual author. Thus, while it is perhaps intuitive that Ishmael, the narrator of *Moby-Dick*, is not Herman Melville himself despite their ample similarities, it is equally important to separate the persona who says, "How do I love thee? Let me count the ways…" from the flesh-and-blood Elizabeth Barrett Browning. Otherwise, the artistic aspects of literature are diminished, reducing it to mere autobiography.

PERSONIFICATION A figure of speech in which inanimate objects are imbued with human characteristics, emotions, and desires. Personification is a staple of allegory, in which animals or even abstract concepts are given human form. Personification is also a frequent device in poetry, where human motivation is often ascribed to nature or other objects, as in Edna St. Vincent Millay's "No one but Night, with tears on her dark face, / Watches beside me in this windy place." These lines also illustrate the pathetic fallacy.

PETRARCHAN SONNET A 14-line poem consisting of an octave with a rhyme scheme of *abbaabba* and a sestet of *cdecde*, *cdcdcd*, or *cdcdce*. A creation of 13th-century Italy, the sonnet form was perfected in the 14th century by Petrarch, and so named after him. It has been adapted into many different languages, including English. Formally, its most important feature is that it does not conclude with a final couplet, as in the Shakespearean sonnet.

PHILOLOGY (from Greek for "love of learning or reason") The study of language and literature, especially with an emphasis on the comparative and historical analysis of language. Because the literary criticism and linguistics that it encompasses are today considered separate fields, the term has mostly fallen into disuse in English, although it continues to have currency in Europe and in some corners of the Anglo-American academy.

PICARESQUE NOVEL (from Spanish for "roguish") A novel expounding the adventures of a *pícaro*, a rascally servant whose wanderings from place to place and master to master allow him to expose the foibles of many different aspects of society. One of the earliest forms of the novel, the picaresque is modeled upon the medieval romance, although it exchanges a lowly and rather jaded hero for romance's noble knights, and a realistic tone for the marvels of chivalric tales. It is episodic in structure, made up of a series of incidents without the development that characterizes the later novel. The first picaresque is the anonymous *Lazarillo de Tormes* (1553), which soon became widely imitated. Cervantes's *Don Quixote* fits into the genre broadly understood and indeed caricatures it, while Daniel Defoe's *Moll Flanders* depicts an unusual female servant.

PINDARIC ODE An exalted or decorous ode written in the style of the 5th-century B.C. Greek poet Pindar. Considered the greatest lyric poet of Greek antiquity, Pindar wrote verses of lofty praise in honor of the victors in the athletic games. The form of the Pindaric ode is tripartite, following the movements of the chorus who performed it; the chorus moved across the stage during the first verse, known as the "strophe," traveled to the other side of the stage during the "antistrophe," and returned to address the audience during the "epode." The Pindaric ode is contrasted with the more reflective and somber Horatian ode.

PLAGIARISM (from Latin for "kidnapping") The use of another's words or ideas without appropriate acknowledgment. As everyone who has ever written a college term paper knows, copying material from another author and passing it off as one's own work is plagiarism. The theft of an idea or plot also falls into this category. Of course, the latter crime is more difficult to prove, particularly as only a thin line separates it from the acceptable practices of imitation and pastiche. Generally, dishonesty becomes the determining factor in plagiarism.

PLÉIADE, LA An influential group of 16th-century French writers who established French as a literary language. Clustered around the poet Pierre de Ronsard and named after the constellation associated with the daughters of Atlas, these seven authors introduced into the language such important forms as the ode, sonnet, and alexandrine. To put French on a par with the classical languages, they advocated the creation of neologisms, the recovery of provincial words, and some imitation of ancient models. La Pléiade never had more than seven members, who, at various times, included Ronsard, Jean-Antoine de Baïf, Joachim du Bellay, Rémy Belleau, Jean Dorat, Étienne Jodelle, Jacques Peletier, and Pontus de Tyard.

PLOT (from Old English, of obscure origin) The sequence of events in a work of fiction, poetry, or play. Although in general usage the term is synonymous with "story," contemporary critics specifically refer to plot as the plan or design of incidents, the author's motivated and meaningful arrangement of the raw materials of the story. Aristotle, who initiated the study of plot, calls it "the first principle" of tragedy. He demands that a plot be "whole"—consist of a beginning, middle, and end—and preferably include some reversal or insight. In an influential work, E. M. Forster suggests that plot is a series of incidents linked by causality.

POÈTE MAUDIT (French, "accursed poet") A great and penetrating genius suffering at the hands of a brutal or indifferent society. The term, which exemplifies the Romantic notion of the poet's distance from the world of ordinary men and women, derives from a collection of critical essays written by the French poet Paul Verlaine in 1883. Associated with the French Symbolists Arthur Rimbaud and Stéphane Mallarmé, whose work Verlaine discussed, and especially with the life and work of Charles Baudelaire, the term connotes a destitute, alcoholic, diseased, mercurial, or self-destructive writer.

POETIC JUSTICE A conclusion in which evil is punished in a singularly fitting and satisfying manner, as when a miser is forced to forfeit his fortune. The term was coined in the 17th century by Thomas Rymer to describe the prevailing belief that literature should reward virtue and punish vice in order to instruct audiences in wholesome morals; by the end of the century, such literal didacticism had already begun to wane in popularity.

POETIC LICENSE The liberty commonly granted poets to transgress against the rules of grammar, convention, or verisimilitude. In order to achieve a particular effect, poets may employ such "errors" as irregular constructions, archaisms, elision, hyperbole, or alliteration. Of course, rhyme and meter are instances of poetic license integral to poetry throughout the ages, without which all of literature would be nearly unthinkable.

POETICS A branch of criticism that addresses the nature, forms, and principles of poetry. The field of poetics deals with the practical questions of what are the distinctive features that belong to poetry, how it can be distinguished from other forms, and how to establish its value. By extension, the term may be used for the study of the aesthetics underlying other genres, as in "the poetics of the novel."

POET LAUREATE A great poet, particularly one who officially represents a nation or region. The wreathing of a poet with laurel derives from poetry's association with Apollo in his function as the god of music, who chased the nymph Daphne until the gods pitied her and changed her into the laurel tree. In the United States, the Poet Laureate also serves as a consultant on poetry for the Library of Congress. Individual states may also recognize their own Poets Laureate. In England, John Dryden became the first official Poet Laureate in 1668; until the reign of Queen Victoria, the Poet Laureate regularly produced odes commemorating public occasions, such as the monarch's birthday.

POETRY (from Greek for "to make, create") Language that highlights the role of sound in creating meaning, in particular through the use of meter and rhyme. Poetry is generally distinguished from prose by its compression, higher frequency of tropes, use of the line as a significant unit, elevated diction, and looser syntax; poetry may also be differentiated from verse, which is considered a lesser form. It may be classified as epic, lyric, or narrative; among its many subclassifications are didactic, erotic, religious, political, patriotic, and pastoral. Poetic forms include the ode, sonnet, sestina, and free verse. Poetry is intrinsic to all cultures and eras, although the conventions associated with its imaginative composition vary widely.

POETRY SLAM Popular contests for poetry writing and declaiming. Slams originated in Chicago in the early 1990s, and quickly spread throughout the country. They involve team performances, in which poets are graded by judges holding up scorecards. The poetry produced for slams is oriented toward oral expression rather than written form, and emphasizes the musicality and rhythmic qualities of language. Poetry slams can be credited with helping to erode the elitist associations of poetry by integrating it with street culture and language.

POINT OF VIEW The position from which a story is narrated. Most stories fall into categories of first- or third-person narration. A first-person narrative is told through the voice of a character within the fictional world, and its insights into the scene are limited to those of that character. The opening line of *Moby-Dick*, "Call me Ishmael," is one of the great fictional cues that a first-person narrative follows. A third-person narrative is told by a narrator external to the story. That narrative may be considered "omniscient" if it offers knowledge or thoughts belonging to multiple characters, or "limited" if its awareness is restricted to one character. Contemporary fiction often experiments with multiple points of view as a way of decentering control by the narrator or any one character.

PORNOGRAPHY (from Greek for "writing about prostitutes") Literature designed to arouse sexual excitement, usually through the explicit description of sexual acts. Illustrating Freud's insight that words produce affects in people, amorous writing has been a part of all literatures, including great works such as Ovid's *Ars Amatoria* (c. 1 B.C.) and episodes of Boccaccio's *Decameron*. The modern pornography industry dates from the 18th century, with John Cleland's *Fanny Hill: or, Memoirs of a Woman of Pleasure* (1748–49) being perhaps the first masterpiece of the genre, and has flourished until this day. The Internet has become, among other things, a ubiquitous purveyor of pornography. Although it is notoriously difficult to define, pornography is generally distinguished from erotica as having no larger artistic goal than titillation.

POSTCOLONIALISM The literary, philosophical, and cultural study of the impact of colonialism. In the aftermath of modern colonialism—beginning with Spain's conquest of the Americas in 1492 and including the imperialism of England, France, Belgium, and Portugal—postcolonial writers challenge Western history, science, and art as forming master narratives that allowed for the subjugation of non-Europeans. They often focus upon the particular ways in which cultural criteria serve to define colonized peoples as other, and ask about the ways this process continues to affect subjectivity, politics, and economics even after independence. Among the most influential forays have been Frantz Fanon's inquiry into the psychological effects of racism in Northern Africa, Edward Said's questioning of cultural imperialism and the exoticization of the Middle East in the seminal work *Orientalism* (1978), and Gayatri Chakravorty Spivak's examination of the politics of speaking in the colonizers' language.

POSTMODERNISM A controversial term for the period that succeeded high modernism, implying both a repudiation and continuation of modernism. Its onset dated variously from the end of World War II to the triumph of advanced consumer capitalism in the 1950s and 1960s, postmodernism implies a radical questioning of meaning and knowledge at the end of a millennium. If modernism mourned a lack of coherence and a loss of traditional meanings, postmodernism celebrates the fragmentary nature of contemporary existence. Theorists such as Jean Baudrillard consider it representative of the cultural condition of advanced societies—the age of computers, television, and music video—valuing heterogeneity, superficiality, and sensation over continuity, depth, and coherent narratives; for these reasons, conservative critics often deplore it as a rejection of traditional values and standards. The preeminent postmodern art is architecture that playfully combines elements from radically disparate eras and styles; however, the novel may also be considered postmodern, particularly the antinovel, and works by such contemporary authors as Thomas Pynchon, Don DeLillo, and Kathy Acker. Postmodern literature encompasses a variety of techniques, including pastiche, parody, bricolage, self-reflexivity, and ironic detachment.

POSTSTRUCTURALISM A contemporary critical movement in France and the United States that critiques claims of objectivity in structuralism and in criticism generally. Poststructuralism takes the position that any discourse rests upon unacknowledged and unquestioned assumptions; its procedure is to decenter and displace those assumptions in order to reveal the workings of ideology. As such, poststructuralism differs from most bodies of theory by not offering a general explanation of cultural and literary phenomena, but rather by offering a critique of such explanations. Jacques Derrida, founder of deconstruction, instigated the critique of structuralism and, indeed, of the foundations of Western culture. Other influential poststructural theorists include Jacques Lacan, Michel Foucault, Luce Irigaray, and Julia Kristeva as well as Roland Barthes, who later in his career questioned the structuralism he had helped to instate.

POTBOILER A work of literature written to keep the pot boiling, that is, solely for the money it will bring in. The pejorative term is reserved for works of dubious artistic value; novels by such financially strapped artists as Fyodor Dostoyevsky and D. H. Lawrence are never referred to as potboilers.

PRE-RAPHAELITES A group of artists gathered in 1848 under the leadership of Dante Gabriel Rossetti, William Holman Hunt, and John Millais to resist the contemporary academic painting style. The Pre-Raphaelites—who used Raphael to represent the high-Renaissance artistic tendencies that had dominated European art—advocated a conscious return to medieval imagery and styles. Rossetti, also a poet, linked the movement to literature; among its most important adherents can be included his sister, Christina Rossetti, as well as Algernon Swinburne and William Morris, another artist-writer whose well-known wallpapers based upon medieval design have left a lasting impression on the contemporary art of decor. Combining archaisms, frank themes, and, above all, a sensuous language, these writers were deemed "the fleshly school of poetry" by hostile critics.

PRIMITIVISM The belief that "simple" or "uncivilized" people lived a purer or nobler existence, not having been warped by the pernicious effects of civilization. The idea, which has been prominent at various times since the 18th century, reacts against the positivistic belief in progress, which suggests that human history forms an unceasing trajectory toward the good. Jean-Jacques Rousseau was undoubtedly the most influential primitivist, with his concept of the "noble savage." A second version of primitivism, known as chronological primitivism, refers to nostalgia for a prelapsarian past. Having classical antecedents as well as contemporary manifestations, this is the longing for a lost "Golden Age." Primitivism had considerable impact upon Romanticism, and has been a primary tendency in modern art.

PROLOGUE (from Greek for "spoken before") A preface or foreword to a novel, poem, or play, presenting explanatory material that the author prefers to separate from the story proper. In drama, the prologue is a speech given by one of the characters. The ancient Greeks used such a prologue to establish background material needed to understand the play about to be performed.

PROSE (from Latin for "straightforward, direct") The language found in ordinary speech, as opposed to that which follows the formal rules of poetry. Orally, prose is distinguished from poetry by its comparatively lighter reliance on rhyme and meter; on the page, prose is identified by its use of the sentence, rather than the line, as a formal unit. The term denotes straightforward or unadorned discourse. In fact, all language exploits the devices associated with poetry to some degree; in everyday usage, however, these tropes often go unnoticed in prose.

PROSE POEM Poetry organized into sentences rather than lines. As such, it is distinguished from prose by its use of such other formal features of poetry as internal rhyme, figurative language, and compression. Prose poetry is closely related to free verse, although the latter employs the line as a meaningful unit. Prose poetry is generally considered to have originated in France in the 19th century, perhaps in reaction to the strict rules of versification promulgated by the French Academy in the previous century; such great poets as Charles Baudelaire and Arthur Rimbaud have produced prose poems, as has that country's most important prose writer, Marcel Proust. In English, well-known writers of prose poetry include T. S. Eliot, Amy Lowell, and John Ashbery.

PROSODY (from Greek for "accompanied song, modulation of voice, pronunciation, diacritical mark") The study or science of the formal aspects of poetry. Prosody takes as its subject such features of versification as rhyme, rhythm, meter, and stanzaic forms in order to analyze the use of language in poetry.

PROTAGONIST (from Greek for "first actor") The main character or hero in a play. According to legend, the dramatist Thespis invented tragedy in the 6th century B.C. by stepping out of the chorus and engaging it in dialogue. A second actor (or deuteragonist) was introduced by Aeschylus and a third by Sophocles. The second actor provided conflict in the drama, and hence became more commonly known as the antagonist.

PROVERB (from Latin for "set of words put forth") A pithy saying of anonymous authorship that captures some piece of traditional wisdom, as in "a rolling stone gathers no moss." It differs from the aphorism and the maxim, which can be attributed to an author. Proverbs are part of the oral tradition of a society, often later collected in written form. The most famous such compilation in Western literature is unquestionably the biblical Book of Proverbs.

PSYCHOLOGICAL NOVEL A novel that emphasizes the internal state and development of the protagonist, rather than the external action or plot. The psychological novel exploits the length of the novel as a forum to thoroughly explore characters through their emotions, fears, dreams, and fantasies as they change over time. Originating in the 18th century, the psychological novel has become a major literary strand. It flourished through the second half of the 19th century in the hands of such realist novelists as George Eliot, Henry James, Gustave Flaubert, and Fyodor Dostoyevsky. Interest in Freudian psychoanalysis in the 20th century has led to experimental attempts at representing the unconscious mind by such authors as Virginia Woolf, James Joyce, and Marcel Proust.

PURPLE PASSAGE OR **PURPLE PATCH** A conspicuously ornate or overwrought passage, especially gratuitously inserted in otherwise ordinary prose. The term comes from Horace, whose *Ars Poetica* (c. 19 B.C.?) compared such writing to pieces of purple cloth—traditionally, a princely and extravagant material—sewn into a larger garment. More rarely, the term refers to an author's tour de force without the usual pejorative connotation.

QUATRAIN (from Latin for "four") A stanza of four lines. The quatrain is the most common verse form in Western versification, and is commonly used in hymns, ballads, and longer narrative poems. In addition, the sonnet begins with two quatrains.

QUEER THEORY A body of theory that began to distinguish itself from gay and lesbian studies in the late 1980s and early 1990s. Using the pejorative term "queer," these theorists questioned the assumption fundamental to gay and lesbian studies of a stable identity based upon sexual orientation that needs to be reclaimed from a hostile society. Instead, queer theory interrogates the ways in which given cultures at given times produce varying sexual practices as well as the cultural discourses and practices by which some of those practices come to be defined as unnatural or perverted. Many of the approaches of queer theory were inspired by the work of the French historian Michel Foucault. Its adherents often reject liberalism in both critical and political activity. Queer theory has become increasingly influential in the academy, becoming the subject of numerous critical works, journal articles, and college classes.

RAP A sometimes controversial urban musical form that emerged in the 1970s. Rap consists of highly rhythmic, rhyming, and often improvised verse over music, usually accompanied by a strong drumbeat. Its confrontational attitude and unflinching social critique give voice to African-American youth and street culture.

READER-RESPONSE CRITICISM A critical approach that focuses upon the act of reading as a dynamic process in which the reader is not a passive recipient, but an active producer of meaning. Reader-response criticism rejects New Criticism's claim that a text is a coherent whole; instead, it focuses upon the gaps and inconsistencies in any work (even and especially the great ones) that elicit some reaction from readers. The assumptions and choices that the reader makes in order to transform mere words on a page into a meaningful text can then be analyzed in order to show the workings of psychology and ideology. Reader-response criticism is not a unitary body of theory, but rather a critical tendency that attracts members from various other schools of theory. Some of its major figures are I. A. Richards, Wolfgang Iser, Stanley Fish, and Jonathan Culler.

REALISM The aesthetic principle of verisimilitude—that literature should depict life as it is, without embellishment or idealization—and the late 19th-century movement based upon it. Realism reacted against the falsity of classical and Romantic literary conventions, arguing instead for an objective view into the world, and found its greatest expression in the novel. Realist works generally deal with middle- or lower-class life, include commonplace characters and situations, and attend to physical detail, especially the grime and misery that earlier styles consciously avoided. The greatest realist novelists of the 19th century include Honoré de Balzac and Gustave Flaubert in France; Leo Tolstoy and Fyodor Dostoyevsky in Russia; George Eliot in England; and Henry James in the United States. Naturalism developed out of realism, adding to it a belief in social determinism. In the theater, Henrik Ibsen, August Strindberg, and Anton Chekhov de-emphasized the plot in favor of a loose construction and substituted quotidian language for poetic diction.

RECOGNITION The moment in a literary work when insight or knowledge is gained, generally leading to a change of fortune for the hero. The supreme example is Oedipus's staggering realization that he has killed his father and married his mother. In a more modern example, the narrator of Daphne du Maurier's *Rebecca* experiences such a world-altering instant when she realizes that Maxim never loved his first wife. Detective novels, in particular, turn upon such flashes of recognition, while in melodrama many an orphan has been saved in the nick of time by the recognition of her true parentage. The rhetorical term for recognition is "anagnorisis."

RED HERRING An action, theme, or piece of information meant to lead a character or the reader astray. Mysteries often employ red herrings to complicate the plot and draw the reader's attention away from the real solution, thus prolonging the pleasure of reading. The term derives from hunters' use of the smoked fish to distract their dogs.

REFLEXIVE NOVEL A novel that does not permit its readers to forget that they are reading a novel, rather than a simple reflection of reality. While authors have long played with the conventions of fiction, the reflexive novel is a contemporary phenomenon adopted by authors who reject realism's idea of a transparent language that can objectively portray the world. Abandoning any pretense at verisimilitude, these authors highlight the workings of language and literary conventions. Examples include the fiction of Samuel Beckett and Gertrude Stein.

REVENGE TRAGEDY A macabre play that centers around the desire for and execution of vengeance. Such drama achieved considerable popularity in France and Spain in the work of Corneille, Lope de Vega, and Calderón, and in Elizabethan and Jacobean England. Inspired by Seneca's tragedies, Thomas Kyd initiated the phenomenon in England with the immensely popular and highly imitated *The Spanish Tragedie* (c. 1586), which elicited a slew of imitative melodramas. Shakespeare drew upon *The Spanish Tragedie* in writing the greatest revenge tragedy, *Hamlet,* and Kyd has been suggested as the author of the *Ur-Hamlet,* a play that is no longer extant but is believed to have been Shakespeare's source. Other notable writers of these intrigues include Christopher Marlowe, John Webster, and Cyril Tourneur. Revenge tragedies abound with all things morbid, including ghosts, graveyards, weapons, and, of course, byzantine revenge plots, which conclude in a wash of blood that usually destroys everyone on stage.

RHAPSODY (from Greek for "weaver of songs") An emotional or ecstatic literary work, especially one in verse. The term comes from the ancient Greek itinerant minstrel, who "stitched together" various memorized and improvised portions of epic poetry, especially in the Homeric tradition. More rarely, the term refers to a collection of miscellany.

RHETORIC (from Greek for "public speaker") The art of using language to persuade. Classical Greek orators developed rules for the invention (research on the topic), arrangement, style, memorization, and delivery of a speech. Rhetoric remained an important field throughout the Middle Ages, when it was one of the seven liberal arts taught as part of the university education. The Romantic era's emphasis on unmediated self-expression led to a repudiation of rhetoric, providing its current pejorative connotation of style without substance.

RHYME The correspondence of sound between the final syllables of words or lines of verse. Various types of rhyme are distinguished, including masculine, one identical syllable (fine/wine); feminine, two identical syllables (discover/recover); triple rhyme, three identical syllables (enveloping/developing); end rhyme, occurring at the end of lines; internal rhyme, occurring within the same line; cross rhyme, occurring at the end of one line and the middle of the next;

leonine rhyme, occurring in the middle and at the end of the same line; and initial rhyme, occurring at the start of lines. Near or slant rhyme, characterized by similar but not identical syllables, is not a true rhyme. Rhyme is one means by which poets unify verse and make connections between words. However, rhyme is a relatively recent feature of verse; it first appeared in the West in North African poetry of the 3rd century, and took over alliteration's predominant role in English prosody only in the 14th century. Despite contemporary poetry's tendency to avoid rhyme, it is still one of the most important poetic devices.

RHYME ROYAL A stanza of heroic verse (iambic pentameter) with a rhyme scheme *ababbcc*. The term presumably derives from its use in *The Kingis Quair* (c. 1424), which is attributed to James I of Scotland. Its more important innovator, however, was Chaucer, who used the stanza first in *Troilus and Criseyde* and later in several of *The Canterbury Tales*, as a result of which the stanza is also known as the "Chaucerian" or "Troilus" stanza. Both Shakespeare and Milton also employed rhyme royal, making it the only form in common to the three poets considered to be the greatest in English. Authors of long narrative poems in the 15th and 16th centuries found it extraordinarily pliable. Other practitioners include Edmund Spenser and William Morris.

RHYME SCHEME The organization of rhyming lines that establishes the characteristic structure of a poem or stanza. According to standard notation, each end rhyme is assigned a different letter. Thus, the Shakespearean sonnet would be represented as *abab cdcd efef gg*.

RHYTHM (from Greek for "cycle, flow") The flow of sound generated by the regularly alternating pattern of stressed (or long) and unstressed (or short) syllables, appealing to the ear and the mind. All language is rhythmic, although poetry generally has more consistent rhythmic patterns than prose, which tends to follow the cadences of everyday speech. Rhythm is an element of meter.

ROCOCO (from French for "fancy decoration") A term imported to literature from art history and architecture, rococo style became popular during the 18th century at the end of the Baroque period. It is characterized by a preference for ornamentation suggesting a whimsical or playful sensibility. In literature, rococo refers to works marked by a fanciful or intimate tone, as in Alexander Pope's *The Rape of the Lock* or Voltaire's *Candide*. In English, rococo is often used interchangeably with baroque, and both negatively connote excessive frills and lack of seriousness.

ROMAN À CLEF (French, "novel with a key") A novel in which some or all of the characters stand for real people. Originating in France in the 17th century, the *roman à clef* became something of a fad in the hands of authors such as Madeleine de Scudéry and others, who wrote only slightly disguised stories about and for small groups of their own intimates. Earning numerous enemies for the obvious and often defamatory portraits of their acquaintances are such well-known figures as Thomas Love Peacock, who mocked Coleridge, Shelley, and Byron; Aldous Huxley, whose *Point Counter Point* includes a character based upon D. H. Lawrence; Simone de Beauvoir, many of whose familiars were incorporated into *The Mandarins*; and W. Somerset Maugham, who penned a number of such works.

ROMAN À THÈSE (French, "novel with a thesis") A didactic novel that propounds some thesis or social doctrine dear to the author. For example, Harriet Beecher Stowe's *Uncle Tom's Cabin* advances the author's abolitionist views. Russian Socialist Realist fiction can be seen as an example seeking to prove that happiness lies in adherence to the principles of the Communist Party.

ROMANCE 1. In the Middle Ages, a tale of chivalry, relating the fantastic exploits of a hero or group of heroes. Strength, bravery, and devotion characterize the errant knights, whose quests form the basis of this literature. Originally merely a story of adventure, the important medieval strands of courtly love and religious devotion were later interwoven with the genre to great effect, as in the many versions of the illicit love between Tristan and Isolde. The three great bodies of medieval romance are the stories of King Arthur and the Round Table in England, of Charlemagne and the honorable Roland in France, and of Alexander the Great. Romances derive their name from the vernacular languages in which these popular stories were written. 2. In modern literature, an unabashedly unrealistic story of intrigue and love, set in exotic locales with mysterious and even dangerous characters. The Gothic novel is a form of romance, as is its modern incarnation, the mass-produced romance that has spawned an entire industry. 3. In Spanish, the romance (pronounced *ro-MAHN-thay*) is a popular ballad.

ROMAN-FLEUVE (French, "river novel") A series of novels chronicling the experiences of a central character or group of characters. Marcel Proust's *Remembrance of Things Past* is perhaps the crowning achievement of a category that includes such series as Honoré de Balzac's *The Human Comedy*, Romain Rolland's *Jean-Christophe*, Anthony Trollope's Barsetshire novels, Doris Lessing's *Children of Violence*, and Anthony Powell's *A Dance to the Music of Time*.

ROMANTICISM A broad term describing the reaction to the rationality and restriction of classicism that became the predominant cultural philosophy in Europe and the United States from the end of the 18th century through the early 19th century. Rejecting the Neoclassical ideals of moderation, proportion, imitation, and adherence to classical literary poetics, the Romantics embraced self-expression, emotionalism, political and social revolution, and, above all, individualism. They established the cult of the artist as a prophet and a rebel, who became for the first time a person who *was* a genius, rather than one who *had* a genius for a particular field; the artist was a person who could feel more profoundly than the ordinary type, and thus this literature abounds in passion, sexual desire, suffering, and especially an intense melancholy.

Romanticism was inspired by the philosophy of Jean-Jacques Rousseau, and later influenced by the German idealism of Immanuel Kant, Johann Gottlieb Fichte, and G. W. F. Hegel. Romanticism can be separated into a first and second period. Early Romanticism included the work of Samuel Taylor Coleridge, William Wordsworth, William Godwin, and Mary Wollstonecraft in England, and Goethe, Novalis, and the Schlegel brothers in Germany. The second period witnessed the great poetic tradition of John Keats, Lord Byron, Percy Bysshe Shelley, and the fiction of Sir Walter Scott and Mary Shelley in England, the vastly influential prose and poetry of Aleksandr Pushkin and Mikhail Lermontov in Russia, and the flowering of Romanticism in France after 1820 in the work of Victor Hugo, Stendhal, George Sand, and Alexandre Dumas *père*.

RONDEAU (Old French, "small circle") A French poetic form consisting of 13 or 15 octosyllabic lines divided into three stanzas, in which the first half of the opening line becomes a refrain for the second and third stanzas. The rondeau, which dates to the 14th century, uses only two rhymes besides the refrain; thus its characteristic pattern *aabba aabR aabbaR*, where R is the refrain.

RUNE (from Old Norse for "secret, writing") Any of the 24 characters of the earliest Germanic alphabet, dating from the 2nd century and used in Scandinavia and the British Isles. Runes were based on the Greek and Latin alphabets, modified to facilitate carving into stone or beechwood. Each rune is named for a common object, of which it represents the first letter. As is often the case when preliterate societies begin the transition to a literature culture, the written word garnered magical connotations; the association of runes with incantations and mystical power remains to this day.

SAGA, NORSE SAGA (from Old Norse for "story, what is said, or told") A medieval prose epic recounting historic and legendary exploits in Scandinavia and Iceland. Most were composed c. 1100 to c. 1350; some derive from older oral tradition. Ranging from historical annals to revenge narratives to tales of supernatural exploits, they exhibit great artistry and often a subtlety in characterization that seems to prefigure modern psychology. They can be divided into subcategories, including kings' sagas, about early Scandinavian rulers; legendary sagas, treating mythical themes; contemporary sagas, about living people known to the authors; and, most important, Icelanders' sagas (also known as family sagas), recounting events from the time of the original settling of Iceland (10th–11th centuries). By extension, an extended chronicle or series of novels may be called a saga.

SAGAS OF ICELANDERS. *See* **ICELANDERS' SAGAS**

SAMIZDAT (Russian, "self" + "published or publishing house") A work of literature clandestinely printed and distributed in defiance of the state-controlled publishing organs of the Soviet Union. Because of the official monopoly on the right to publish, most of these novels, poems, and essays were circulated in the form of carbon copies. The work of such major dissident authors as Aleksandr Solzhenitsyn and Natalya Gorbanevskaya existed in the Soviet Union only in samizdat until the fall of the regime.

SATANIC SCHOOL A derogatory epithet for John Keats, Percy Bysshe Shelley, and Lord Byron. Robert Southey originated the term in the preface to *A Vision of Judgment* (1821), a poem that attacked the radical political, religious, and sexual doctrines, and, indeed, the unorthodox lifestyles, of these younger Romantic poets. Byron retaliated with a parody called *The Vision of Judgment* (1822).

SATIRE (from Latin for "full of food, sated") A work in which the follies, faults, and vices of a person or institution are held up to ridicule in order to expose and perhaps rectify them. Numerous types of satire exist. The major trends are the bitter and indignant Juvenalian satire and the gently corrective Horatian satire, both of which are formal (also called direct) satire, in which the speaker addresses the audience or reader; indirect satire, found in novels

and drama, allows the situation to bring forth the satire. From these classical Roman antecedents, satire survived the Middle Ages in the beast epic. The 17th and 18th centuries were the golden age of satire, producing such masterpieces as Voltaire's *Candide* and Jonathan Swift's "A Modest Proposal" and *Gulliver's Travels*.

SATYR PLAY A burlesque performed after a trilogy of Greek tragedies during the dramatic contests that accompanied festivals of Dionysus. The chorus played the mythical creatures that were half man and half goat in these ribald dramas, which provided comic relief after the gravitas of the tragic presentation. Written by the tragedians themselves, these plays were distinct from the classical tradition of comedy. The only complete extant satyr play is the *Cyclops* of Euripides.

SCANSION (from Latin for "a climbing") A system for analyzing the metrical structure of a poem. Scansion translates the poem's rhythm into visual form, which may then be more easily evaluated. Poetry may be scanned according to one of three methods: graphic, musical, and acoustic. The most common of these is graphic, which uses symbols to represent stressed or long syllables (´ or –), unstressed or short syllables (x or ˘), foot divisions (|), and long pauses or caesuras (_). Musical scansion uses musical notes to capture subtler distinctions in stress, while acoustic scansion, used by linguistics, employs such tools as an oscillograph. Scansion also attends to rhyme scheme.

SCIENCE FICTION A popular body of literature that explores the changing nature of human existence in the scientific era. Science fiction is a subgenre of fantasy, but is generally distinguished by its fidelity, if not always to legitimate science, at least to the kind of logic that science implies. Science fiction reflects a fascination with and celebration of the possibilities of science and technological advances, and often a profound uncertainty about their impact on humanity; the latter impulse has produced a distinctly dystopian strand of science fiction. The precursor to science fiction is

Mary Shelley's story of a Faustian scientist, *Frankenstein* (1818), today one of the most widely read books on college campuses. However, science fiction took off only in the latter part of the 19th century, with the work of Jules Verne and H. G. Wells. The term itself was popularized by Hugo Gernsback, founder in 1926 of *Amazing Stories* magazine, thereby consolidating science fiction as a genre. By the 1950s, the genre had gained greater respectability in the hands of serious writers such as Ray Bradbury, Isaac Asimov, and Kurt Vonnegut. Among the most interesting contemporary authors are J. G. Ballard, Ursula K. Le Guin, Samuel R. Delany, Octavia Butler, and William Gibson, whose cyberpunk has developed into a subgenre of science fiction.

SCRIBLERUS CLUB A literary coterie founded in 1714 by Jonathan Swift, Alexander Pope, John Gay, Thomas Parnell, John Arbuthnot, and Robert Haley, earl of Oxford. They created the fictional character Martinus Scriblerus as an icon of the bombastic scholasticism they opposed. After the group ceased meeting in London, they kept their circle alive through correspondence. Among the fruits of this association are the third book of Swift's *Gulliver's Travels* and Gay's *The Beggar's Opera*; Arbuthnot produced a "memoir" in Scriblerus's name.

SEMIOTICS OR **SEMIOLOGY** (from Greek for "observant of signs") The study of signs and sign-systems. The American logician Charles Sanders Pierce and the French linguist Ferdinand de Saussure each independently invented a science to explore the ways in which social events or entities become meaningful. For Saussure, whose work greatly influenced French structuralism, this led to the recognition that in language the relationship between a signifier (the spoken or written word) and its signified (the referent) is arbitrary; thus, language does not reflect any positive relationship between the word and thing, but is rather a system of differences, where meaning is created as a result of the relationships of one signifier to another. The desire to analyze the ways in which such social relations become meaningful

has informed many fields, including the anthropology of Claude Lévi-Strauss, the psychoanalysis of Jacques Lacan, and the history of Michel Foucault. Other influential semioticians include Roland Barthes, Julia Kristeva, and Umberto Eco.

SENECAN TRAGEDY A tragedy in the style of the Stoic philosopher and playwright Lucius Annaeus Seneca, which proved tremendously popular on the Elizabethan stage. Seneca's lurid and violent tales of revenge recounted the tragedies of Euripides for Roman audiences then unfamiliar with the Greeks. His dramas were probably intended for recitation, not performance, and describe rather than show their action in grandiose and long-winded speeches. English dramatists borrowed the sensationalism and casts of ghosts, murderers, and avenging victim, but enlivened the genre by placing the action back on the stage. Thomas Sackville and Thomas Norton's *Gorboduc* (1561) is the first drama modeled after Seneca, but it was Thomas Kyd's *The Spanish Tragedie* that established the genre, which includes as its high point *Hamlet*.

SENSIBILITY (from Latin for "sense, feeling") Aesthetic, moral, and emotional sensitivity, especially the ability to be moved by beauty and pathos. The 18th century embraced such refined feelings as an antidote to the stoicism and Hobbesian self-interest of the 17th century. The cult of sensibility tended toward excess, bleeding into sentimentalism; Jane Austen ridiculed such self-indulgence in *Sense and Sensibility*. By the 19th century, the term had been largely replaced by *sensitivity*, which did not receive the same weight as its predecessor.

SENTIMENTAL COMEDY OR **DRAMA OF SENSIBILITY** A dramatic genre of 18th-century England that reacted against the corruption and cynicism of Restoration comedy. Sentimental comedy rejected the aristocratic values of the earlier age in favor of respectable bourgeois heroes of unquestioning virtue facing trials over which they inevitably triumphed. The flatness of the characterizations and simplicity of the plots speeded the genre's demise, although it left its mark on 19th-century melodrama. Richard Steele is considered the innovator of sentimental comedy. Its French counterpart is *comédie larmoyante* (tearful comedy).

SENTIMENTALISM (from Latin for "feeling") Excessive or trite emotionalism. In literature, it refers to manipulative attempts to enkindle feeling, especially pathos or sorrow. The many tearful deaths of melodrama express sentimentalism, much like the trend in commercial advertising toward using tender appeals to family affection as a way of selling products such as greeting cards or long-distance telephone service. Sentimental literature can be distinguished by its use of clichéd language and images, rather than the exciting and innovative imagery that characterizes greater works.

SENTIMENTAL NOVEL OR **NOVEL OF SENSIBILITY** An early novelistic subgenre of 18th-century England that portrayed assaults on virtue in an excessively emotional fashion. The sentimental novel, like its dramatic counterpart, reacted against the emotional restraint and cynicism of the previous century, offering stories in which a hero or heroine of great sensibility ultimately triumphs. It pulled at the heartstrings of readers, who could then rest assured of their own delicate feelings. Samuel Richardson's *Pamela, or Virtue Rewarded* (1740) is the exemplary sentimental novel.

SESTINA (from Italian for "six") A highly intricate medieval verse form consisting of six unrhymed stanzas and a three-line envoi. The sestina derives its unity not from rhyme, but from the repetition of the final words of each line of the first stanza. A complicated pattern regulates where in the stanza each word must reappear: 123456, 615243, 364125, 532614, 451362, 246531. The envoi has terminal endings of 531, while words 2, 4, and 6 must appear internally in its successive lines. The form is attributed to the Provençal poet Arnaut Daniel, and such tours de force were popular among the troubadours. More recently, Algernon Charles Swinburne, Ezra Pound, W. H. Auden, and James Merrill showed themselves to be up to the sestina's technical challenges.

SET PIECE A literary work or passage clearly intended to produce an effect, usually through dazzling technique that may seem out of proportion with the piece as a whole. The term is generally used pejoratively, for works that have little to offer besides the impression they create.

SHORT STORY Stories that are short have always existed, as the fables of antiquity, the life-saving tales of *The Thousand and One Nights*, and the medieval lays attest. Primarily its length distinguishes the short story from the novel, which has the luxury of time in which to develop its characterization; by contrast, the short story aspires to a brief moment in which character is revealed in what Nadine Gordimer calls "the flash of fireflies." The short story ranges from the one- or two-page short-short story to the long short story, which may be as long as a novella. Some of its most celebrated authors are Edgar Allan Poe, Nathaniel Hawthorne, Mark Twain, and Ernest Hemingway in the United States; Anton Chekhov, Nikolai Gogol, and Aleksandr Pushkin in Russia; Jorge Luis Borges in Argentina; E. T. A. Hoffmann in Germany; Guy de Maupassant and Prosper Mérimée in France; James Joyce, Frank O'Connor, and Liam O'Flaherty in Ireland; and D. H. Lawrence, Katherine Mansfield, and Joseph Conrad in England.

SIMILE (from Latin for "similar") A figure of speech in which two dissimilar objects are compared. In simile, the comparison is explicit, marked by the use of the words "like" or "as," unlike metaphor, in which the comparison is implicit. Byron's line "She walks in beauty like the night" exemplifies the power of simile to create an effect through the juxtaposition of differing terms.

SLAVE NARRATIVE An American form of autobiography in which a former slave recounts personal history in order to document the horrors of slavery. Although the genre was established as early as 1760 with the first such memoir, *A Narrative of the Uncommon Sufferings and Surprising Deliverance of Briton Hammon, a Negro Man*, its most active period was 1830–60, leading up to the Civil War. Abolitionists disseminated these accounts in order to elicit sympathy and influence political views. The best-known example is unquestionably Frederick Douglass's *Narrative of the Life of Frederick Douglass, an American Slave* (1845; revised 1882). Harriet Jacobs's *Incidents in the Life of a Slave Girl*, written under the pseudonym Linda Brent, expresses the typical sexual jeopardy of the female slave.

SOCIALIST REALISM The official artistic policy of the Soviet Union from 1932 until its dissolution, which charged literature with the responsibility of helping to realize the birth of the Communist state and the New Soviet Man. In the eyes of the bureaucrats who administered the Writer's Union, a state organ, and the monopoly on the means of publishing, aesthetic impulses were firmly subordinated to political aims. Literature had to present optimistic and highly didactic portraits of men and women firmly committed to their society, as a result of which Socialist Realism has earned a reputation for false characters and contrived plots. As a form of realism, the socialist variety is distinguished by its proponents from the "bourgeois" realism of the late 19th century and from the "decadent" technical feats of modernism, the latter deemed too intellectual for comprehension by the proletariat. The most important example is F. V. Gladkov's *Cement* (*Tsement*, 1926), whose title alone captures the genre.

SOCIOLOGICAL NOVEL A subgenre of the problem novel or thesis novel, which uses the novel form to advance or explore some viewpoint. The sociological novel examines a particular question of social organization, generally with didactic intent and in order to suggest some extraliterary solution.

SOLILOQUY (from Latin for "to speak" + "alone") A dramatic speech in which a character presents his or her inner thoughts, desires, and motivations. The soliloquy is a dramatic convention in which the character reveals him- or herself directly to the audience. Uncommon on the classical stage (with the notable exception of Medea's indecision about murdering

her children in Euripides' play), it is often used in Elizabethan and Jacobean drama, notably Hamlet's "To be or not to be" speech. It fell into disfavor in the late 19th century with the advent of more naturalistic acting methods.

SONNET (from Old Provençal for "little song, sound") A verse form consisting of 14 lines of iambic pentameter (alexandrines in the French sonnet) with a fixed rhyme scheme. The sonnet developed in Italy in the 13th century as a vehicle for discussing love, particularly in the troubadour tradition. The form known as the Italian sonnet is composed of an octave rhyming *abbaabba* and a sestet, which may be either *cdecde*, *cdcdcd*, or *cdedce*; between the octave and the sestet is a volta (Italian for "turn"), which effects a change in the proposition that began the octave. This sonnet is also known as Petrarchan, after the poet in whose hands it reached its highest expression. The sonnet form was introduced into England in the early 16th century, where its rhyme scheme was altered. The most common version, known as the English or Shakespearean sonnet (again, after its most important practitioner), is divided into three quatrains and a couplet rhyming *abab cdcd efef gg*. A variant is the Spenserian sonnet, in which the quatrains are tighter: *abab babc cdcd ee*.

John Donne expanded the sonnet by using it for religious themes, and it is no longer restricted in terms of content. It is an intricate yet flexible form of exceptional longevity. Some of the great sonneteers are Rainer Maria Rilke in Germany; John Milton, William Wordsworth, John Keats, Elizabeth Barrett Browning, and Gerard Manley Hopkins in England; and Edwin Arlington Robinson, Robert Frost, and Edna St. Vincent Millay in the United States.

SOTIE OR SOTTIE (from French for "fool") A medieval comic drama in which actors in fool's dress made sport of well-known people and political events. The repertory also included acrobatics and other types of broad humor. Originally, *soties* were an opening act for mystery and morality plays, but later came to stand on their own. This form of entertainment was banned in the 16th century.

SOUTHERN GOTHIC A lurid or macabre writing style native to the American South. Since the middle of the 20th century, Southern writers have interpreted and illuminated the history and culture of the region through the conventions of the Gothic narrative (or Gothic novel), which at its best provides insight into the horrors institutionalized in societies and social conventions. Foremost among these authors are William Faulkner, Flannery O'Connor, Tennessee Williams, and Carson McCullers.

SPOONERISM A transposition of the initial letters or syllables of neighboring words, either for effect or as a slip of the tongue, as in the exchange of "bed row" for "red bow." The term honors the Reverend William Archibald Spooner (1844–1930), a dean and warden of New College, Oxford, whose reputation for constantly making such mistakes seems to be overstated; he did, however, once toast "the dear old queen" as "the queer old dean." Spoonerisms were used intentionally for comic purposes and to exploit linguistic possibilities by James Joyce, among others.

STOCK CHARACTER A conventional and stereotypical character that appears repeatedly in a given dramatic genre. The use of these characters allowed the audience to immediately recognize a particular type, sometimes, but not always, at the price of a lack of subtlety in characterization. The characters of the commedia dell'arte are stock characters; other such figures include the evil villain and ingenue in melodrama and the wicked stepmother and prince charming in the fairy tale. Occasionally, an author will work through and against the superficiality of the stock character for artistic purposes, as when T. S. Eliot sharpens our understanding of J. Alfred Prufrock through Elizabethan drama's stock character of the fool.

STREAM OF CONSCIOUSNESS A narrative technique that aims to represent in language the experience of consciousness. Greatly influenced by modern psychology, stream of consciousness technique attempts to reproduce all of the twists and turns of the mind. The term was popularized by William James in *The Principles of Psychology* (1890) to describe the various and simultaneous impressions and associations that comprise consciousness. Thus, in addition to the rational discourse that characterizes the thoughts of characters in realist fiction, it traces the impact on those thoughts of unconscious desires, memories, and fantasies. As a literary technique, stream of consciousness is credited to Edouard Dujardin at the end of the 19th century. It was adopted by modernists seeking a language that might portray internal reality. Virginia Woolf and William Faulkner are considered masters of the technique; the "Molly Bloom" chapter of James Joyce's *Ulysses* may be the greatest example of stream of consciousness.

STROPHE (from Greek for "a turning") Often a synonym for the stanza, the term is used to designate the irregular grouping of lines in free verse. It may also describe the first section of the tripartite Pindaric ode, which developed according to the rules of classical Greek prosody. The strophe was the first part of an ode and was sung by a chorus as it moved across the stage. The chorus then reversed its movement during the antistrophe, and stood still while singing the epode.

STRUCTURALISM A widely influential 20th-century theoretical movement that grew out of the linguistic principles of Ferdinand de Saussure, structuralism is the study of the ways in which self-contained and self-regulated systems produce social phenomena. Structuralism's approach to the literary text is to ask not the typical critical question of *what* it means, but rather *how* a text comes to have meaning at all. To answer that question, structuralists examine the rules and codes that organize relations between signs within a given text or discourse. By abjuring the study of content, structuralism claims a scientific objectivity that eventually elicited skepticism about its positivistic claims to knowledge, and criticism that it insufficiently attended to history. Structuralism transformed a number of fields: Claude Lévi-Strauss proposed that the elements of a culture could be analyzed in such a systematic fashion, creating the field of structural anthropology, while Jacques Lacan explores the topography of the unconscious mind in his extension of Freudian psychoanalysis. Roland Barthes is the most important of a group of prominent structuralist thinkers that includes Julia Kristeva and René Girard.

STRUCTURE (from Latin for "to construct") The configuration of elements that create a work of literature. The structure can be understood as the skeleton of a story, play, or sentence, which may then be stripped down for analysis. What constitutes the structure varies according to genre: the structure of a lyric poem includes its central idea, while that of narrative includes its plot, and of drama its arrangement into acts and scenes.

STURM UND DRANG (German, "storm and stress") A late 18th-century German precursor to Romanticism, the *Sturm und Drang* movement rejected the rigidity of French classicism and the arid rationalism of the Enlightenment in favor of creativity, individuality, and revolution. Its young artists expressed interest in folk traditions as well as the work of the then newly translated Shakespeare. Drawing its name from the title of a play by Maximilian Klinger, its preferred mode was drama, although adherents also produced poetry and fiction. Its well-known leaders were Johann Gottfried von Herder and the young Goethe, whose novel *The Sorrows of Young Werther* epitomized the movement's ethos. Friedrich Schiller also became a prominent adherent.

STYLE (from Latin for "writing instrument, style") A distinctive way of using language. Style answers the question of *how* a writer expresses an idea. Stylistic features may include diction, devices, themes, or a host of other factors that combine to create an author's unique voice. Style may be classified in numerous ways, such as by author (Proustian or Faulknerian), school (Metaphysical or Expressionistic), period (Romantic or Augustan), level (high, middle, or low), or discourse (literary, scientific, or legal).

SUBLIME (from Latin for "threshold, boundary, limit") The grandeur and awe that nature and great art inspire. The concept comes from an anonymous tract misattributed to the 3rd-century Greek philosopher Longinus. It gained importance in the 17th century after an essay by Edmund Burke reclaimed the term. The sublime evoked a sense of infinity, and was the appropriate response to the majesty of mountains and powerful storms, as opposed to the merely beautiful, which is finite, gentle, and, implicitly, effete. The sublime was an important critical category in the 18th and 19th centuries, particularly for Romantic authors who sought to create lofty and powerful works.

SUBPLOT An ancillary plot in a drama or narrative. The subplot may represent a variation on or contrast to the main plot. Jessica's elopement in Shakespeare's *The Merchant of Venice* provides an example. The subplot was a frequent feature of the Elizabethan and Jacobean stage.

SUPERFLUOUS MAN (Russian, "lichnii chelovek") A character type ubiquitous in 19th-century Russian literature. The superfluous man is an idealist who is incapable of effective or decisive action. He remains detached from the world around him owing to inertia, the rigidity of Russian society, and the decadence that results from the system of serfdom. The term derives from Ivan Turgenev's "Diary of a Superfluous Man" (1850), although the type precedes him. Such well-known literary heroes as Pushkin's Eugene Onegin and Tolstoy's Pierre Bezukhov (in *War and Peace*) illustrate the breed, of which Ivan Goncharov's Ilya Oblomov is the ultimate example.

SURREALISM A literary and artistic movement that came out of France between the two world wars with the aim of fusing the realms of the unconscious and conscious minds, thus creating a sphere that would be more real than mere reality, hence "sur-real." After the devastation of World War I, a significant questioning of Western values took place, particularly of the Enlightenment tenets that failed in their promise to prevent such violence. Surrealism grew out of the prewar antirationalism of Dadaism, but rather than seeking to negate logic, as the latter did, attempted to expand it. Freud provided an escape from the repressive force of reason through his concept of the unconscious mind, thus establishing Surrealism's enduring interest in dreams, hallucinations, and a startling juxtaposition of images, through which it aspired to liberate the mind. André Breton inaugurated the movement by issuing "The Surrealist Manifesto" in 1924, and in two further versions. Among the distinguished Surrealist poets are Paul Éluard, Louis Aragon, Philippe Soupault, and Pierre Reverdy. Their influence extended to the drama and film, in the works of Luis Buñuel, Antonin Artaud, and later the Theater of the Absurd.

SUSPENSION OF DISBELIEF The readers' or audience's willingness to accept literary conventions and other deviations from verisimilitude in exchange for the pleasure of visiting an imaginary and artistic world. This suspension is never total—only a disturbed person would confuse Laurence Olivier, the actor, with Hamlet, the character—but it is sufficient to make theatergoing an enjoyable experience. Coleridge introduced the term in the *Biographia Literaria* (1817).

SYMBOL (from Greek for "token for identification") A symbol is commonly understood to be a thing that stands for something else. It alludes to an abstract idea by reference to a concrete object. Thus, a flag is the symbol of a country and the dove a symbol of peace. While symbols such as these are conventional and easily recognizable to the larger public, writers often create new symbols, whose meaning arises from the context and combination of images. The structure of a literary work can also be symbolic; for example, the terza rima that Dante invented for *The Divine Comedy* symbolizes the Christian Trinity in its interlocking tercets. Symbolism can be distinguished from allegory by its greater allusiveness. Where allegory offers a simple correspondence for each element (in *Peter and the Wolf*, Peter clearly and only represents Rus-

sia), symbolism defies easy identification. The highly suggestive whale in *Moby-Dick* cannot be pinned down to any one thing; indeed, a considerable power of the novel lies in the multiplicity of meanings that the white whale evokes.

SYMBOLISM A school of poetry that formed in France in the late 19th century. The Symbolists sought to create a new language that might convey a mood or feeling through the accretion of unusual images. Rejecting expository forms of poetry that say rather than show what the author is feeling, the Symbolists held that the very imprecision of the symbol would allow the reader to sense a deeper and more elastic truth. They also reacted against the rigidity of French metrical forms, adopting and popularizing *vers libre*. Their work accentuated the musicality of language toward the goal of achieving synaesthesia, a melding of the senses. Baudelaire was a forerunner of the movement, which included such luminaries as Paul Verlaine, Arthur Rimbaud, and Stéphane Mallarmé. Symbolism spread throughout Europe, becoming particularly important in Russia through such figures as Aleksandr Blok, Vladimir Solovyov, and V. I. Ivanov, who produced an important body of work and paved the way for the Silver Age of Russian poetry. The legacy of the Symbolists cannot be overstated; their influence on 20th-century literature in English can be seen in the poetry of William Butler Yeats and in Imagism, and extended to the modern novel.

TALL TALE A genre common to the American frontier that depicts wildly exaggerated and extravagant stories of individual strength or ability. These stories are generally told in a matter-of-fact tone that highlights the incongruity of the story. Common folk heroes such as Paul Bunyan frequently figure in the tall tale, which has roots in the oral tradition. They later came to be written by such authors as Mark Twain and O. Henry. R. E. Raspe's *Baron Munchausen's Narratives of His Marvellous Travels and Campaigns in Russia* provides a European example of these tales.

TERZA RIMA (Italian, "third rhyme") An Italian verse form consisting of interlocking tercets in which the second line of one stanza provides the rhyme for the first and third lines of the next. The poem finishes with an extra line that completes the rhyme: *aba bcb cdc...yzy z.* No particular meter is required, although English terza rima generally employs iambic pentameter. Dante is said to have originated the form for *The Divine Comedy*; the connection between terza rima and the Christian Holy Trinity made it highly appropriate for Dante's purpose. The form was introduced to England in the 16th century by Sir Thomas Wyatt, but its difficulty, especially in languages lacking Italian's rich rhymes, has prevented widespread use. Those who have shown themselves up to its demands include Percy Bysshe Shelley, Robert Browning, Elizabeth Barrett Browning, and W. H. Auden.

TEXT (from Latin for "woven thing") From its meaning as the written words of a finished work, the text has come to refer to a linguistic object (written or spoken) that can be distinguished and analyzed.

TEXTUAL CRITICISM A form of scholarship seeking to establish the definitive edition or authorship of a given work. By comparing manuscripts and early editions, textual critics attempt to discern the original form of a work, before censorship or errors in transmission (either in the printing process or in the older practice of hand-copying texts) corrupted it. They may also attempt to use internal clues, such as style, references, or handwriting analysis, to determine the authenticity of an anonymous work or one whose origins are otherwise in question.

TEXTUALITY The quality of being a text. In poststructural criticism, the term implies the inherently linguistic nature of the world, which can be read and analyzed as a text, but cannot be considered to have any reality outside of the social system of language. One of the most misunderstood ideas of popular criticism, textuality does not presuppose that the world does not exist, but rather that humans have no access to that reality except through the social processes by which we create meaning.

TEXTURE (from Latin for "weaving") The concrete, material aspects of language as used in a literary work. Borrowed from the plastic arts, the term refers to the surface quality, and may be opposed to the deep meaning, of a work. It consists of those elements of sound, such as alliteration, assonance, rhythm, and rhyme, that cannot be paraphrased. New Criticism, particularly that of John Crowe Ransom, contrasted the texture of poetry with its structure, its main idea or argument.

THEATER OF CRUELTY An experimental form of theater intended to purge audiences of societal malaise by bringing them into contact with the elemental energies of life. The French actor and theorist Antonin Artaud claimed in a 1932 manifesto that theater must disturb audiences in order to break through the repressions that characterize modern life. He wanted to return the theater to its religious origins, making it a rite that brings spectators into contact with cruelty, the deepest and often violent instinctual drive. Theater would cease to be an imitation of life (what he considered the anemic "theater of psychology"); instead, life would be understood as the double (and product) of this powerful and liberating theater. His method included a de-emphasis of words to focus instead on gesture, lighting, and effects that would shock the spectator out of a comfortable, bourgeois perch. Although he produced only one such play, Artaud's ideas greatly influenced the avant-garde theater, notably the Living Theater and Peter Brook's production of Peter Weiss's *Marat/Sade* in 1964.

THEATER OF FACT OR DOCUMENTARY THEATER A type of political drama appearing in Germany in the 1960s that used documentary techniques to explore the Holocaust. In order to further dialogue about the responsibility for and meanings of Nazi genocide, its proponents incorporated historical and legal documents into drama in order to challenge what they believed were overly comfortable official inter-

THE LITERARY SATELLITES OF URANUS

Uranus, the first planet to be discovered in modern times (1781), is so far the only one whose satellites have been named after literary figures, rather than beings from classical mythology. First came TITANIA and OBERON (1787), from the fairy king and queen in Shakespeare's comedy A *Midsummer Night's Dream* (c. 1595–96). They were followed by ARIEL and UMBRIEL (1851), named for, respectively, a sylph and a gnome in Alexander Pope's mock-epic poem *The Rape of the Lock* (1714); Ariel is also the name of the airy sprite in Shakespeare's drama *The Tempest* (c. 1611). The tradition was continued in 1948, when a fifth satellite was discovered and named MIRANDA, after the young heroine of *The Tempest*. A whole spate of new names was required during 1985–86, when the (man-made) satellite *Voyager 2* passed close enough to Uranus to become the discoverer of no fewer than ten more moons of the remote planet. Except for BELINDA, named for the shorn heroine of *The Rape of the Lock*, they were all named for Shakespearean characters, as follows. From comedies: Bianca, the desirable younger sister of the title character in *The Taming of the Shrew* (c. 1593); PORTIA and ROSALIND, respectively the heroines of *The Merchant of Venice* (c. 1596–97; Portia is also the wife of the conspirator Brutus in the tragedy *Julius Caesar*, c. 1599) and *As You Like It* (c. 1599); and PUCK, the prankish spirit in A *Midsummer Night's Dream*. From tragedies: CORDELIA, the devoted daughter of the title character in *King Lear* (c. 1605–6); OPHELIA, the forlorn daughter of the Lord Chamberlain in *Hamlet* (c. 1601); DESDEMONA, the faithful wife of the title character in *Othello* (1604); the faithless CRESSIDA from *Troilus and Cressida* (c. 1601–2); and the doomed JULIET from *Romeo and Juliet* (1595). Six more tiny satellites were discovered between 1997 and 1999 with the help of powerful telescopes and modern technology; five have so far been named for characters in *The Tempest*: PROSPERO, the wise magician-hero; CALIBAN, his deformed monster-servant; STEPHANO, a "drunken butler"; SYCORAX, Caliban's deceased witch-mother; and SETEBOS, the deity worshiped by Caliban (the last two do not actually appear in the play). The sixth satellite, 1986 U 10, was imaged by *Voyager 2*, although not "discovered" until 1999; it is unnamed as of this writing. Since its founding in 1919, the International Astronomical Union has been responsible for assigning the names of planetary satellites.

pretations of the Nazi era. Its predominant authors were Heinar Kipphardt, Rolf Hochhuth, and Peter Weiss.

THEATER OF THE ABSURD A term proposed in 1961 by Martin Esslin for an avant-garde dramatic movement prominent in Europe in the 1950s and 1960s. The Theater of the Absurd presupposes that human existence is a struggle to make sense of a senseless universe. Its scripts flout the conventional rules of narrative, and instead, through repetition, faults in logic and chronology, and the use of ordinary language in nonsensical ways, plunge audiences into a bewilderment that denies resolution. With roots in Dadaism and Surrealism, it, like other forms of absurdism, challenged the traditional values and assumptions of Western culture. The movement's influence on late 20th-century avant-garde theater cannot be overstated. The foremost dramatists of the absurd were Samuel Beckett and Eugène Ionesco; other important practitioners include Harold Pinter, Jean Genet, Francisco Arrabal, Günter Grass, and Edward Albee.

THEME (from Greek for "thing placed, proposition") The underlying idea of a literary work. Unlike the subject, which details the story's action, the theme reflects its broader meaning. The subject of *Macbeth* is a couple's intrigues toward the throne; its theme is the perils of blind ambition.

THEORY (from Greek for "a viewing") In literature, the self-reflexive inquiry into the nature and implications of literary criticism and literary production. Theory examines the criteria that underlie criticism, in order to discover the assumptions that otherwise go unquestioned in the critical enterprise. Theory refers to a wide range of bodies of knowledge examining language and its relation to culture; it therefore asks about the ways in which literature is involved in larger political, philosophical, and historical discourses. By insisting on the theorist's responsibility to study not merely the literary text but also the social relations from which it arose, theorists have opened themselves up to the charge by other critics of abandoning or politicizing the text.

TOUR DE FORCE (French, "a feat of strength") A work that dazzles with its virtuosity, exemplifying the writer's technical skill. James Joyce's *Finnegans Wake* and T. S. Eliot's *The Waste Land* may be considered pieces that demonstrate their author's mastery of language. The term may also be used pejoratively to imply superficial brilliance without literary substance.

TRAGEDY (from Greek for "goat song") A major genre of Western literature, dealing with the noble response of a character to events that culminate in disaster. The term was originally restricted to drama but is now applicable to other genres. Tragedy originated in the fertility rites associated with the worship of Dionysus. In the works of Aeschylus, Sophocles, and Euripides, tragedy retold mythological stories already familiar to audiences; their interest lay in the original responses characters evinced to familiar events. The hero's own tragic flaw (or *hamartia*) led to the catastrophe, yet these works revealed the dignity of which humanity was capable in response to dire events. Based on this tradition, Aristotle defined tragedy as a work that inspired pity and terror, leading to catharsis.

For the Greeks, tragedy was a "high" genre, dealing with aristocratic characters in an august manner. During the 1st century, Seneca reworked the Greek tragedies for Roman audiences in a more sensationalist vein that would later be taken up by Elizabethan playwrights, beginning with Thomas Kyd and including the era's greatest authors, Christopher Marlowe and William Shakespeare. For the 15 centuries in between, the classical tradition was unknown; liturgical drama related the tragedy of the Crucifixion, out of which secular tragedy developed again. In contrast to the Elizabethan tragedy, French tragedy in the 17th century remained more faithful to the style and mood of the Greeks. Neoclassicism, notably represented by Jean Racine and Pierre Corneille, adhered to the three unities and the lofty tone of antiquity. Another fallow period followed until Henrik Ibsen and August Strindberg transformed the genre at the end of the 19th century, showing human struggles against social, psychological, and emotional forces, rather than fate. Written in prose rather than verse, tragedy was no longer restricted to aristocratic subjects, and by the 20th century, authors such as Arthur Miller and Eugene O'Neill explored the tragic aspects of contemporary life.

TRAGIC FLAW The defect of character that precipitates the downfall of the hero in tragedy. For example, Hamlet's indecisiveness is his tragic flaw, while ambition undoes Macbeth. In Greek tragedy, the flaw was often hubris, the overweening pride of the hero. The Greek term *hamartia* is often used synonymously with tragic flaw; however, in Aristotle's elaboration, *hamartia* may refer to an improper action rather than a moral deficiency on the part of the hero.

TRAGICOMEDY A literary genre that blends aspects of both tragedy and comedy. Simply put, its plot bears the gravity of tragedy, but veers away at the conclusion to the happy ending characteristic of comedy. The term was coined by the Greek dramatist Plautus to describe works in which the status of characters is reversed. Throughout the Renaissance, tragedy was restricted to aristocratic characters and comedy reserved for the lowly; tragicomedy breaks down this barrier, mingling characters of varying social castes. All of these elements reflect the genre's flexibility. Thus, a work such as Shakespeare's *The Merchant of Venice*, which saves Antonio in the nick of time but is otherwise too morbid to be a comedy, falls into the realm of tragicomedy. In the 19th and 20th centuries, comic and tragic elements serve to highlight each other, bringing out the calamity and senselessness of the contemporary world. Some dramas by Anton Chekhov, Samuel Beckett, and Harold Pinter are considered tragicomedies.

TRANSCENDENTALISM An important early 19th-century spiritual, philosophical, and literary movement centered in New England that reacted against the materialism of American culture. Influenced by Unitarianism, the English Romantics' interpretation of German Transcendentalism, the mysticism of Emanuel Swedenborg, and the philosophy of Immanuel Kant, Transcendentalists believed in the need to create an individual relationship to a divine principle. They valued self-reliance, personal conscience, and faith in the individual's connection to an oversoul that transcended mere knowledge derived from the senses. As a progressive movement, Transcendentalism supported abolition and women's suffrage. Ralph Waldo Emerson was Transcendentalism's leading exponent; other well-known and influential members include Henry David Thoreau, Bronson Alcott, and Margaret Fuller. The movement produced the influential little magazine *The Dial* and an early experimental community, Brook Farm, which became the subject of a novel, *The Blithedale Romance* (1852), by one-time member Nathaniel Hawthorne.

TRAVESTY (from Latin for "change of garment") A parodic work that ridicules a serious or dignified subject by presenting it in a low or base manner. Travesty reverses the method of the mock-epic, which treats a trivial subject in an overblown or lofty fashion. Cervantes's *Don Quixote* can be considered a travesty of the picaresque novel, while Jane Austen's *Northanger Abbey* travesties the Gothic novel.

TROPE OR FIGURE OF THOUGHT (from Greek for "a turn, way, manner") 1. A use of language for rhetorical effect achieved by altering the standard meaning of words. Tropes "turn" words around, as the etymology suggests, by using them in unusual ways, as opposed to figures of speech, in which meaning is changed by changing standard word order. Common tropes include simile, metaphor, metonymy, synecdoche, personification, irony, hyperbole, litotes, and periphrasis. 2. In the Middle Ages, the amplification and elaboration of a liturgical text. Liturgical drama developed from this practice.

UNDERSTATEMENT OR LITOTES An utterance whose rhetorical force lies in its deliberate lack of emphasis. Cordelia's response when Lear asks his daughters how much they love him is characterized by understatement, in contrast to the effusions of her sisters. In rhetoric, understatement is known as litotes.

UNITY (from Latin for "one") The structuring of a literary work so that all of its various elements combine into a harmonious whole. In drama, unity refers to the rules Neoclassical playwrights inferred from Aristotle's *Poetics*. From Aristotle's descriptive comment that tragedy generally takes place over the course of a day or so, in opposition to the flexible length of the epic, Renaissance Italian scholars understood a prescription that plays dramatize only the events of one day: a unity of time. They readily expanded this directive to three basic unities that came to govern the Neoclassical stage, adding unity of place and unity of action. The three unities became the guiding principle of French Neoclassical drama, spawning intense and often absurd arguments over their interpretation. English playwrights were less susceptible to the doctrine, perhaps because of the example of Shakespeare, who, of course, had never heard of them and whose drama was not circumscribed by such principles.

UNIVERSITY WITS A group of pioneering young playwrights whose work led the day at the end of the 16th century. They established the genres that would come to characterize the Elizabethan stage, including the Senecan or revenge tragedy, the chronicle, the romantic comedy, and the court comedy. The most important of these university-educated writers was Christopher Marlowe. Other notable wits were Robert Greene, Thomas Lodge, Thomas Nashe, and George Peele; John Lyly is sometimes included in this group.

UNRELIABLE NARRATOR A narrator whose judgment is suspect. Narrators may be untrustworthy for a number of reasons; they may be dishonest, self-serving, or self-deceiving (as in Nabokov's *Lolita*), deranged or of questionable sanity (as in his *Pale Fire*), or naive and unaware of the full significance of the events they relate (as in Twain's *Huckleberry Finn*). Such narration forces readers to bring their own critical capacities to bear on the account in question.

VARIORUM EDITION (from Latin for "edition with the notes of various commentators") An edition of an author's works or of a single work that reflects all possible variants, based upon the evidence provided by manuscripts and early editions, as well as the commentary and notes of editors and critics.

VATIC (from Latin for "prophetic") Derived from the Latin term for a poet or bard who was inspired by the gods, the term refers to poets whose work is prophetic or revelatory. In antiquity, the Sibyl was considered a vatic poet, as was Virgil. William Blake and Walt Whitman have similarly impressed readers with the prescience of their work.

VERISIMILITUDE (from Latin for "true similarity") The appearance of truth. In literature, the principle that the work of art should conform to truth so that the reader perceives it as a reflection of reality. Aristotle believed that art is mimetic, a reflection of nature. Some experimental writers, however, reject this view and instead highlight the workings of convention and ideology in creating the impression of realism.

VERISMO (ITALY) (Italian, "true") An Italian school of literary and musical naturalism that flourished in the late 19th and early 20th centuries. Its members produced minutely detailed realistic works written in an unaffected language and offering characters whose speech conformed to everyday rhythms. They often took the miserable conditions of the poor as their subject matter. The best-known writers of *verismo* include Luigi Capuana, who initiated the movement, Giovanni Verga, and Grazia Deledda, winner of the Nobel Prize in Literature in 1926. *Verismo* receded during the war years, but paved the way for the more influential school of Italian Neorealism in the aftermath of World War II.

VERS DE SOCIÉTÉ (French, "society verse") A light, ironic verse intended to amuse. *Vers de société* tends to be sophisticated, sparkling, and astute, making it perfectly suitable for the drawing room. Serious issues may be treated, but they are handled flippantly and an intimate tone prevails. The 18th century was ripe for this kind of witty verse, in which such luminaries as Alexander Pope and Voltaire partook. In the 20th century, Ogden Nash and Dorothy Parker were American masters of the genre, and John Betjeman amply represented the British tradition.

VERS LIBRE (French, "free verse") Poetry that does not employ any of the standard metrical or rhyme patterns. *Vers libre*, also known as free verse, may have lines of varying length, in which breaks are placed depending upon the sense and the impression the author wishes to create. Many poets believe that *vers libre* as a form allows the author's individual voice to emerge. *Vers libre* originated in France in the late 19th century and was readily adopted by the Symbolists; it quickly spread throughout other Western poetic traditions. Arthur Rimbaud and Paul Verlaine were among the earliest of the major French poets to have adopted the form; Walt Whitman established it in the United States.

VILLANELLE (from Latin for "country house") Originally applied to an Italian pastoral poem, the term came to refer to a fixed metrical form used in France in the 16th century, and later spread to other languages. It consists of five (or occasionally more) tercets and a final quatrain. The first and third lines of the first stanza alternate regularly as the third line of succeeding stanzas, until they appear together as a couplet to end the final quatrain. The rhyme and repetition scheme is *a1ba2 aba1 aba2 aba1 aba2 aba1a2*. Poets such as W. H. Auden and Edmund Gosse experimented with the form, which found its highest expression in Dylan Thomas's "Do Not Go Gentle into That Good Night."

VOLTA (Italian, "turn") The turn or shift in mood or argument that takes place in a sonnet. In the Petrarchan sonnet, the volta takes place at the beginning of the sestet, while in the Shakespearean sonnet, it occurs either at the couplet or after the eighth line.

VORTICISM A short-lived movement in poetry and painting founded by Wyndham Lewis in the years before World War I. Vorticism developed out of Futurism, and sought to capture the power of the vortex or whirlpool, which represented pure energy given concrete form. Ezra Pound, its most eminent member after his abandonment of Imagism, hoped to harness the energy of the machine age in the name of an artistic avant-garde. The Vorticists published modernist manifestoes in the journal *Blast*, which lasted only two issues.

WELL-MADE PLAY (from French, "pièce bien faite") A now pejorative term for a highly conventional dramatic form influential in the 19th century. The French playwright Eugène Scribe is credited with establishing the formula for popular romantic comedy and melodrama, which stipulated the building of suspense, the disclosure of a crucial secret that saves the hero or heroine just in the nick of time, and the tidy resolution of all unanswered questions. Well-made plays achieved great commercial success and dominated the stage in Europe and the United States for most of the century. Critics, particularly George Bernard Shaw, denounced these tightly constructed dramas for their emphasis on mechanical plots at the expense of subtlety in characterization.

WELTANSCHAUUNG (German, "worldview") A term describing both an individual author's characteristic outlook on the world or general philosophy, and also the spirit or mood of a particular era.

WELTSCHMERZ (German, "world pain") A feeling of melancholy, pessimism, or vague discontent with one's way of life. Associated with the Romantic era, it refers to the sorrow and weariness that come from shouldering the weight of the world, which all great artists of the time were believed to do. The term was coined by Jean Paul in the bleak novel *Selina* (1827).

WESTERN An American popular genre of fiction dealing with the frontier experience. Set in the last half of the 19th century, the western mingled adventure and romance in the creation of an American ideal of masculinity as rugged individualism and quiet integrity. Popular subjects of dime novels, westerns told stories of cowboys and settlers struggling against "savage" Indians and of cattlemen in conflict with farmers attempting to fence in the open prairies. Among the best-known authors are James Fenimore Cooper, Zane Grey, and the contemporary writers Louis L'Amour and Larry McMurtry.

WIT (from Old English for "intelligence, knowledge") The term *wit* has gone through numerous shifts in meaning over the centuries. Its root suggests intelligence and knowledge, as in the term "half-wit" or "unwitting." In the 16th and 17th centuries, it signified "fancy," a faculty for literary invention; in this can be found the roots of the current sense of a gift for clever repartee. The Romantics subordinated wit, along with everything else, to imagination and genius.

Later, T. S. Eliot argued for the value and wit of the metaphysical poets, in whom seriousness and ingenuity enhanced one another. This sense of creativity is largely absent from common understandings of wit as deftness in expression, epitomized in the epigram.

YALE SCHOOL A group of literary critics associated with Yale University who were largely responsible for introducing deconstruction to the American academy in the 1970s and 1980s. Led by the Belgian critic Paul de Man and his colleagues J. Hillis Miller and Geoffrey Hartman, the Yale School developed a distinctively American brand of deconstruction, and in so doing became a widely influential and often controversial force in the intellectual life of the country.

Chronology of
World Literature

Readers should bear in mind that some ancient works of literature were lost for centuries after their creation. It is therefore wise to be cautious about tracing lines of influence in this Chronology, which does not usually provide the dates when such works first became known to modern scholarship or when they were first translated into modern languages. For example, William Shakespeare knew nothing of the Old English epic poem *Beowulf* (c. 700–50), which today is the earliest work in the standard canon of English literature.

c. 3500 B.C. The first system of written language is developed by the Sumerians in Mesopotamia.

c. 3000 B.C. The Egyptians develop a hieroglyphic system of writing and initiate the use of papyrus, rather than stone tablets.

c. 2000 B.C. *Gilgamesh*, a Mesopotamian verse epic. The earliest surviving narrative in world literature (the oldest nearly complete text dates to c. 700 B.C.), it relates the mythical, arduous journey of the king Gilgamesh and his confrontation with mortality.

The Chinese system of writing, still in use, is invented.

c. 1500 B.C. The Phoenicians develop the first alphabetic writing, employing letters for individual sounds rather than using signs to represent whole syllables. The foundation of Western writing, the Phoenician alphabet will give rise to Hebrew, Arabic, Sanskrit, and Greek.

c. 1200–100 B.C. The Old Testament. The sacred text of Judaism, written in Hebrew and Aramaic, will later be adopted by Christianity.

c. 800–700 B.C. The *Iliad* (*Ilias*) and the *Odyssey* (*Odysseia*), ancient Greek epic poems attributed to the blind poet Homer. Based on oral legends, these narratives of the Trojan War and the Greek warriors' homecoming explore the nature of heroism.

c. 800–300 B.C. The Chinese classic spiritual text *The Way of Power* (*Tao-Te Ching* or *Dao de Jing*), which elaborates Taoist principles of harmonious living.

c. 700 B.C. Hesiod's *Theogony*, a genealogy in verse of the Greek gods, long a major source of classical mythology in Western cultural history.

c. 600–500 B.C. The earliest known record of the Latin alphabet, adapted from Greek and Etruscan writing, appears in Rome.

c. 610–580 B.C. Sappho's poems. The Greek poet from the island of Lesbos is one of the first known practitioners of the lyric form.

c. 500–479 B.C. *Analects* (*Lun Yu*) and other teachings of the Chinese political philosopher Confucius. Recorded by disciples, his lessons concerning social precepts will play a major role in Chinese culture.

458 B.C. Aeschylus's trilogy, the *Oresteia*, the masterpiece by the first of the great playwrights of ancient Greece. Aeschylus's plays are central to the classical genre of tragedy, formal verse dramas presented at Greek religious festivals.

c. 450–430 B.C. Herodotus's history, the first work of factual, rather than mythical, history in world literature, focusing on the Greek-Persian wars.

c. 442–441 B.C. Sophocles' *Antigone* (*Antigonē*), a tragedy about a woman's loyalty to her family in the face of her king's opposition.

431 B.C. Euripides' *Medea* (*Mēdeia*), a tragedy concerning the mythical Jason's betrayal of his wife Medea, and her vengeful killing of their children.

c. 430 B.C. Sophocles' *Oedipus the King* (*Oidipous Tyrannos*), his greatest work, in which the tragic hero discovers that he has unwittingly killed his father and married his mother.

411 B.C. Aristophanes' *Lysistrata* (*Lysistratē*), a comic masterpiece by the greatest of the Greek comic playwrights, in which women embark on a sexual strike in an attempt to end war.

c. 400 B.C.–A.D. 400 The *Mahābhārata*, the seminal Indian epic orally composed and written in Sanskrit. It includes the famed Hindu text the *Bhagavadgīta*.

c. 380 B.C. Plato's *Republic* (*Politeia*), one of the great founding works of Western philosophy, which elaborates the teachings of Socrates and emphasizes the importance of ideal forms as the basis of philosophical and ethical systems.

c. 335–322 B.C. Aristotle's *Poetics* (*Peri Poiētikēs*), a classic work of early literary criticism, which defines and evaluates forms of poetry and drama. It will serve as a major point of reference throughout the history of Western literary study.

300–200 B.C. Apollonius of Rhodes's *The Voyage of the Argo* (*Argonautica*), a four-book epic recounting Jason's quest for the Golden Fleece and his relationship with Medea.

Theocritus's *Idylls*, short poems portraying bucolic life, considered the earliest surviving work in the pastoral genre.

Vālmīki's *Rāmāyaṇa*, an epic in verse based on oral tradition and, along with the *Mahābhārata*, a mainspring of later Indian literature.

c. 41–37 B.C. Virgil's *Eclogues* (*Bucolica*), a collection of poems in Latin, among the finest examples of the pastoral form.

c. 35–30 B.C. Horace's *Satires* (*Satirae*), ironic commentaries on human folly. Also celebrated for his lyric *Odes*, Horace is an early practitioner of the literary form of verse satire, along with the later Roman poet Juvenal (c. A.D. 100).

c. 29–19 B.C. Virgil's *Aeneid* (*Aeneis*), an epic poem about the founding of the Roman nation, notable for its complex vision of heroism and war.

c. A.D. 1–100 Papermaking is invented in China.

c. A.D. 8 Ovid's *Metamorphoses*, a poetic narrative elaborating Greek and Roman myths, an abundant source of inspiration for later Western literature.

c. 50–100 The New Testament, relating the life, death, and teachings of Jesus Christ, is composed by early Christians, probably in Greek. The oldest known manuscripts date to the 2nd century.

c. 60–70 The *Satyricon*, a Roman work attributed to Petronius, which presents a vivid, satiric portrait of contemporary Roman life.

400–500 Kālidāsa's Sanskrit epics, dramas, and lyrics, including *The Recognition of Śakuntala* (*Abhijñā-naśākuntala*) and *The Cloud Messenger* (*Meghadūta*).

413–26 St. Augustine's *The City of God* (*De Civitate Dei*), one of the most influential texts of the European Middle Ages, and his *Confessions*, a spiritual autobiography, a work seminal to the development of the genre of autobiography.

633 The Koran, the sacred text of Islam, is recorded in Arabic.

c. 700–50 The epic poem *Beowulf*, the earliest extant work of Old English literature. Composed orally, it attained its present written form around 700. The oldest extant manuscript dates to c. 1000. The first translation into Modern English appeared in 1837.

c. 700–900 Old Irish heroic myths are recorded, including the popular tragic love story of Deirdre and Noisi.

A golden age of Chinese poetry, when the great writers of the T'ang dynasty are active, including Li Bo, Du Fu, Han Yu, and Yuan Zhen.

c. 800 *The Thousand and One Nights* (*Alf Laylah wa Laylah*), a classic compilation of Indian and Middle Eastern tales, is probably first recorded in Arabic.

c. 1000 The *Caedmon Manuscript*, the first Old English translation/paraphrase of portions of the Bible.

1010 Ferdowsī's classic epic *Book of Kings* (*Shāh-Nāmeh*), an account of heroism in Persian history.

c. 1020 Lady Murasaki's *The Tale of Genji* (*Genji Monogatari*), a chronicle of court society and romantic love that is one of the finest achievements of Japanese literature.

c. 1045 In China, movable type (utilizing woodblocks) is invented.

c. 1085 In Spain, the first known European papermaking operation is reported.

c. 1100 Old English evolves into Middle English.

In England, the first "miracle play," a vernacular drama recounting the lives of the saints and of the Virgin Mary, is performed. The genre will be popular throughout the Middle Ages.

The Song of Roland (*La Chanson de Roland*), a verse epic and masterpiece of Old French literature depicting the 8th-century battle between Charlemagne and the Saracens.

1135–39 Geoffrey of Monmouth's *History of the Kings of Britain* (*Historia Regum Britanniae*), a legendary history of Britain, and the major source for later stories of King Arthur.

c. 1150–early 1300s *Song of My Cid* (*Cantar de Mio Cid*), the great Spanish epic poem celebrating the heroic achievements of the 11th-century military leader El Cid.

1165–80 Chrétien de Troyes's courtly tales of chivalric adventure and love, including *Lancelot*, *Yvain*, and *Perceval*, all significant contributions to the developing medieval genre of romance.

late 1100s Marie de France's *Lais*, a series of short rhymed verses telling fanciful stories of love and adventure, which will inspire the popular "Breton lai" poems in England. The author is the first known French woman poet.

c. 1200 Gottfried von Strassburg's *Tristan and Isolde* (*Tristan und Isolde*), a classic Middle High German romance elaborating a legendary Celtic love story.

The Brut, the first work of Arthurian literature composed in English.

1200–1300 The popular medieval genre of the "mystery play," loose dramatizations of biblical events that combine spiritual representations with social satire and spectacular scenic effects, develops throughout Europe.

The great Icelandic sagas, historical prose epics about the great families of Iceland, are recorded.

c. 1220 *The Tale of the Heike* (*Heike Monogatari*), a classic Japanese epic chronicling the reign and defeat of the 12th-century Heike family. Marked by Buddhist themes, the work will be a major influence on later Japanese literature.

1225–40 Guillaume de Lorris's *Romance of the Rose* (*Roman de la Rose*), a poetic allegory of courtly love, to which, around 1280, Jean de Meun adds a second part satirizing aristocratic ideals. Widely translated, the work is popular throughout medieval Europe.

c. 1294 Dante's *The New Life* (*La Vita Nuova*), a collection of prose and poetry that immortalizes his beloved Beatrice.

c. 1297 Marco Polo's popular *Travels* (*Il Milione*), a landmark of travel literature, introduces Europeans to Asian culture.

1300–1400 Nō drama—a genre presenting narratives from classical Japanese literature in highly stylized, ceremonial performances—develops in Japan.

c. 1314–21 Dante's *The Divine Comedy* (*La Divina Commedia*), a long narrative poem depicting the poet's journey through the worlds of the afterlife, among the finest achievements of Western literature.

c. 1350–74 Petrarch's *Rimes*, psychologically searching poems about his beloved Laura that represent a movement away from the idealizations of courtly love, which will be an important influence on Renaissance poetry.

1351–53 Giovanni Boccaccio's *Decameron* (*Decamerone*), a collection of tales inspired by Italian folklore and legend.

c. 1362–87 *Piers Plowman*, an allegory by William Langland (or Langley) satirizing corrupt worldly behavior and exploring Christian morality and ethics, and one of the first great Middle English poems.

c. 1375 Woodblock printing, developed in China c. 1045, first appears in Europe.

c. 1375–1400 *Sir Gawain and the Green Knight*, one of the finest Middle English romance poems.

c. 1387–1400 Geoffrey Chaucer's *The Canterbury Tales*, a collection of stories told by pilgrims on their journey to Canterbury, expands medieval literature beyond aristocratic and Christian themes, offering a rich array of characters and narratives.

1405 Christine de Pisan's *The Book of the City of Ladies* (*Le Livre de la Cité des Dames*), an early feminist treatise, presents a learned defense of women, citing examples of female heroism and virtue.

c. 1432–36 *The Book of Margery Kempe*, the spiritual narrative of an English mystic, and one of the earliest known European autobiographies written in the vernacular.

1436 Leon Battista Alberti's *On Painting* (*Della Pittura*), a treatise elaborating the rules for drawing a three-dimensional scene on a two-dimensional surface, which will exert a profound influence on the development of art during the Renaissance. The Italian visual artists prefigure the European Renaissance in literature.

c. 1450 Johannes Gutenberg of Germany devises movable metal type, introducing what will become the modern printing press, and later prints his Bible (c. 1456), now known as the Gutenberg Bible, the first book in Europe printed with movable type.

c. 1469–70 Sir Thomas Malory's *Le Morte d'Arthur*, a compilation of Arthurian romances and a major source of Arthurian legend for later writers. It is one of the finest works of late medieval prose.

c. 1475 William Caxton, an English printer working in Bruges, produces the first printed book in the English language, *The Recuyell of the Historyes of Troye*, his own translation of a French work.

1489 François Villon's autobiographical *Le Testament*, which the notorious poet, who was often in trouble with the law, composed in the form of a will.

1499 *La Celestina*, attributed to Fernando de Rojas, marks the beginning of a golden age in Spanish literature, which will flourish for the next two centuries. The work is the seriocomic tale of a bawd who mediates in the love affairs of noblemen and women.

c. 1500 *Everyman*, a play depicting Everyman's concerns as he faces Death, arguably the finest example of the English "morality play," presenting allegorical representations of Christian moral values.

c. 1511 The satire *The Praise of Folly* (*Moriae Encomium*) by the great humanist scholar Erasmus, a Dutchman living in England, a landmark of early Renaissance literature.

1516 Sir Thomas More's *Utopia*, portraying an imaginary land governed by humanist principles. More coined the word "utopia" (from the Greek roots meaning "no place," with an implied secondary meaning of "good place" [*eu + topos*]), and his work will inspire later writers concerned with the creation of ideal societies.

1517 On the door of a church in Wittenberg, Germany, Martin Luther posts his 95 theses, a critique of corruption in the Catholic Church, marking the beginning of the Protestant Reformation.

1525 William Tyndale prints his translation of the New Testament, the first English-language edition of a section of the Bible.

1528 Baldassare Castiglione's *The Courtier (Il Cortegiano)*, a discourse on the ideal qualities of the "perfect courtier," or gentleman attendant of a sovereign's court, a work that will be widely translated, and hence one of the key texts of the Renaissance.

1532 Niccolò Machiavelli's *The Prince (Il Principe)*, a treatise on obtaining and maintaining political power, controversial because of its pragmatic treatment of politics.

1532–64 François Rabelais's *Gargantua and Pantagruel*, a multivolume satire of religious, political, and social conventions incorporating extravagant fantasy, bawdy realism, scatological humor, and erudite wit.

1543 Polish astronomer Copernicus's *On the Revolutions of Heavenly Bodies (De Revolutionibus Orbium Coelestium)* asserts the existence of a heliocentric universe, displacing man, who has historically been placed at the center of the universe.

1545 The first known work of commedia dell'arte, an Italian dramatic form marked by improvisational comedy and stock figures, which will remain popular in Europe through the 18th century. Its best-known English descendant is *Punch and Judy*.

1557 *Songes and Sonnettes*, a collection of English poetry including work by Sir Thomas Wyatt, who introduces the Italian sonnet form to English literature, and Henry Howard (Earl of Surrey), who develops the English technique of sonnet composition and introduces the form of blank verse.

1558–1603 The reign of Queen Elizabeth I is associated with a golden age of English literature, a highly fertile period of wide-ranging achievements in poetry, drama, and prose. Now known as the English Renaissance, this period will continue to flourish during the reign of James I (1603–25).

1580–88 Michel de Montaigne's *Essays (Essais)*, his series of remarkably candid, skeptical, and profoundly searching personal reflections, introduce a new literary form, the essay (coining the term from *essai*, or "attempt").

1582 Richard Hakluyt's *Divers Voyages Touching the Discovery of America*, the first of his widely read accounts of early English explorations of the New World.

c. 1587 Christopher Marlowe's *Tamburlaine the Great*, a tragedy that introduces blank verse, which will become the major compositional form in Elizabethan drama.

c. 1589–92 William Shakespeare's first plays are produced, including *Henry VI* and *The Comedy of Errors*. The master playwright will produce mainly histories and comedies in the first portion of his career, c. 1589–1600, including *A Midsummer Night's Dream* (c. 1595–96), *The Merchant of Venice* (c. 1596–97), *Much Ado About Nothing* (c. 1598–99), and *Henry V* (1599).

1590 Sir Philip Sidney's *Arcadia*, a major pastoral romance in prose.

1590–1609 Edmund Spenser's *The Faerie Queene*, a long allegorical romance that elaborates knightly virtues and explores the moral, spiritual, and political concerns of the English nation, and one of the finest achievements of Elizabethan poetry.

1591 Sir Philip Sidney's *Astrophel and Stella*, an important Elizabethan sonnet sequence concerning an unfulfilled romantic relationship.

1592 Robert Kyd's *The Spanish Tragedy*, a drama about revenge, one of the most popular plays of Elizabethan England.

In China, Wu Cheng'en's comical allegorical novel *Journey to the West*, or *Monkey* (*Xi you Ji*), a major achievement of the Ming dynasty (1368–1644), a period that will witness the flowering of vernacular Chinese literature.

c. 1601 William Shakespeare's *Hamlet*, the first of his major tragedies and one of the most celebrated works in world literature.

1603–25 In England, masques, court theatrical productions, flourish under King James I. Light entertainments involving music, spectacular sets, and poetry, masques exert an important influence on Elizabethan drama, and are written by such major figures as Ben Jonson.

1604 William Shakespeare's *Othello, the Moor of Venice*, one of his greatest tragedies, dramatizing with acute psychological penetration the story of a heroic — but flawed — general who is maliciously manipulated with disastrous consequences by an aide into believing that his blameless wife has betrayed him.

c. 1605–6 William Shakespeare's *King Lear*, generally considered his greatest work, about the tragic downfall of a willful, aging king who, as one of his treacherous daughters observes accurately, "hath ever but slenderly known himself." In a December 1999 *Times Literary Supplement* survey, an internationally renowned group of writers and scholars were asked to select the "Book of the Millennium"; *King Lear* and Dante's *Divine Comedy* were the titles most frequently mentioned.

1605–15 Miguel de Cervantes's *Don Quixote* (*El Ingenioso Hidalgo Don Quijote de la Mancha*), a satirical chivalric romance recounting the adventures of a gentleman who leads a fantasy life as a knight-errant. An inventive exploration of the nature of reality and illusion, it is one of the monuments of world literature.

1606 Ben Jonson's *Volpone*, a mordant comedy about a wealthy man's greed. Jonson's elegant satirical comedies will be important influences on Restoration drama later in the century.

1609 William Shakespeare's 154 *Sonnets*, 126 of which are addressed to a handsome male friend and all but two of the rest to an enigmatic "Dark Lady." The identities of both continue to inspire much speculation among readers and scholars.

The first regularly published newspaper, *Avisa Relation oder Zeitung*, is printed in Strasbourg. England's first newspaper, the *Weekly News*, will begin publication in London in 1622.

c. 1611 William Shakespeare's final play, *The Tempest*, a drama set on an enchanted island ruled by the magician Prospero, explores themes of retribution and reconciliation.

1611 The King James Bible, authorized by James I, is published. The classic English version of the Bible, it will have a profound and lasting influence on literature in English.

c. 1613 John Webster's *The Duchess of Malfi*, portraying the ill-fated love between a duchess and her steward. The last great Elizabethan tragedy, it is celebrated for its brooding and darkly poetic language.

1616 Ben Jonson is appointed Poet Laureate of England, and an edition of his collected *Works* is published. Jonson's classically balanced, epigrammatic, and formally controlled style will be influential throughout the next century.

c. 1619 Lope de Vega's *The Sheep Well* (*Fuente Ovejuna*), his best-known play, concerning villagers who band together against a lord who has raped a peasant girl.

1625 Francis Bacon's *Essays*, notable for their then unusual concern with actual human experience rather than with abstract ideals, and for their concise, detached prose.

1630 In North America, William Bradford, the English governor of the Plymouth colony, writes his *History of the Plymouth Plantation*, a classic representation of Pilgrims in the New World.

1633 John Donne's posthumously published collected *Poems*.

1635 Pedro Calderón de La Barca's play *Life Is a Dream* (*La Vida es Sueño*), which explores destiny and mortality.

1637 Pierre Corneille's *Le Cid*, a widely popular drama about the 11th-century Spanish national hero.

René Descartes's *Discourse on Method* (*Discours de la Méthode*), a promulgation of rationality and deductive thinking, will be a major intellectual force throughout Europe.

1644 John Milton's classic prose treatise *Areopagitica*, a defense of freedom of the press.

1650 Puritan poet Anne Bradstreet's *The Tenth Muse, Lately Sprung Up in America* is published in England, becoming the first volume of English verse written in North America to appear in print.

1660–1700 The Restoration period in English literature follows the restoration of the monarchy after the fall of the Puritan Commonwealth. Reacting against Puritan asceticism and influenced by French Neoclassicism, the Restoration's literary culture is noted for its elegance, worldly ease, and satiric wit.

1660–69 English politician Samuel Pepys records his *Diary*, a vivid, thoughtful account of upper-class life in Restoration England, which is first published (in part) in 1825.

1662 Molière's first major play, *The School for Wives* (*L'École des Femmes*), a satire of contemporary conventions of courtship and marriage.

1663–78 Samuel Butler's *Hudibras*, a mock-epic poem that wittily satirizes Puritan narrow-mindedness and hypocrisy.

1664 Molière's play *Tartuffe* (*Le Tartuffe*), concerning a deceitful, avaricious man who poses as a pious Christian. This satire of hypocrisy and greed is denounced by the clergy.

1665 Under the authorization of King Louis XIV, *Le Journal des Sçavans*, a pioneering literary journal, is founded in Paris.

1666 Molière's play *The Misanthrope* (*Le Misanthrope*), a complex, sharply observed satire of a pretentious intellectual in a genteel but frivolous society.

1667 John Milton's *Paradise Lost*, a great epic poem in blank verse portraying Satan's fall from heaven and mankind's fall from Eden.

1668 The poet, playwright, and critic John Dryden is named Poet Laureate of England; he will be the dominant figure in Restoration literary culture. Dryden's brilliant use of the heroic couplet meter and his clear, restrained style prefigure later developments in 18th-century Neoclassical literature.

1668–94 Jean de La Fontaine's verse *Fables* (*Fables Choisies Mise en Vers*), renowned for their ironic wit and generous, worldly tone.

1671 John Milton's verse drama *Samson Agonistes*, concerning the biblical figure of Samson and his struggles against the Philistines.

1675 "A Satire Against Mankind," a poem satirizing human affectation and the principles of rationality by the Earl of Rochester (John Wilmot), a Restoration courtier and poet notorious for his libertine behavior.

William Wycherley's play *The Country Wife*, a comedy about a jealous husband and his simple country wife, who travels to London and learns the ways of the town. Wycherley is a major practitioner of the comedy of manners, a popular Restoration genre of witty, sophisticated plays that examine social conventions and human follies.

1677 John Dryden's blank verse tragedy *All for Love*, based on Shakespeare's *Antony and*

Cleopatra, influential because of its careful observance of the classical unities.

Jean Racine's *Phaedra* (*Phèdre*), his best-known play, dramatizing the classical Greek tragic love triangle with an elevated, formal style and an intense psychological acuity.

1678 Madame de La Fayette's *The Princess of Cleves* (*La Princesse de Clèves*), about a princess's struggle to remain faithful to the vows of her conventionally arranged marriage even though she loves another man. Often considered the first French novel, it is notable for its realistic style and psychological characterization.

1678–84 John Bunyan's *The Pilgrim's Progress*, an allegorical narrative recounting Christian's journey through life in vivid, unaffected prose. It will become one of the most popular books ever written in English.

1681 John Dryden's *Absalom and Achitophel*, a satiric poem that adapts a biblical story to criticize anti-Catholic politics.

1682 Ihara Saikaku's *The Life of an Amorous Man* (*Kōshoku Ichidai Otoko*), a popular novel of urbane, merchant-class life in Japan.

1687 Sir Isaac Newton's *Principia*, a work presenting the laws of gravitation, contributes to a new world view of a mechanical, rationally explainable universe.

1688 Aphra Behn's *Oroonoko*—a fictional narrative about an African prince cruelly enslaved by white Christians—enjoys great popularity. Behn will become the first English woman to earn her living by her pen.

1689–1700 The collected writings of Sor Juana Inés de la Cruz, the Mexican poet and nun, are published. Her prose writings defend women's rights to intellectual pursuits and are considered classics of early feminist literature.

1690 John Locke's influential *An Essay Concerning Human Understanding*, which elaborates principles of empiricism and contends that man's knowledge is learned rather than innate.

1694 Matsuo Bashō's *The Narrow Road to the Deep North* (*Oku no Hosomichi*), a celebrated diary of his travels through Japan, interwoven with haikus.

1700 William Congreve's comedy of manners *The Way of the World*, a masterful achievement of Restoration comedy that satirizes the social conventions of love and marriage with acute insight and wit.

c. 1700–50 The Augustan Age in English literature, corresponding with Neoclassicism, which is dominant throughout Europe. Looking to classical Rome, writers such as Alexander Pope seek clarity, balance, and polish in their work, which is marked by satirical wit, economical style, and social and political subject matter.

1702 The first daily newspaper in England, *The Daily Courant*, begins publication. The first regularly published newspaper in the American colonies, *The Boston News Letter*, is launched two years later.

1709 The British Parliament passes the Copyright Act, the first British law to give rights of literary ownership to authors.

1709–11 Richard Steele publishes *The Tatler*, a pioneering English literary periodical that offers commentary on manners and mores for a genteel middle-class audience. *Tatler* essayists, including Joseph Addison, are known for a prose style that is both witty and graceful.

1711–12 Joseph Addison and Richard Steele publish *The Spectator*, a leading English periodical. Slyly presented as a series of essays written by members of the fictional "Spectator's Club," the journal offers critical commentary on contemporary social life.

1714 Alexander Pope's *The Rape of the Lock*, a mock-epic poem satirizing the conventions of drawing-room society by portraying trivial, domestic events in a parodically heroic style.

1715–26 Alexander Pope's popular translations of Homer's *Iliad* and *Odyssey* enable him to become the first major English poet to support himself financially, without depending on aristocratic patronage.

1719 Daniel Defoe's *Robinson Crusoe*, the vivid tale of a man who survives a shipwreck on a deserted island. The work will greatly influence the development of the English novel.

1722 Daniel Defoe's *Moll Flanders*, a landmark of picaresque fiction recounting the life and colorful adventures of a female rogue.

1726 Jonathan Swift's satirical *Gulliver's Travels*, a work chronicling a sea captain's journeys to fantastic lands and a mordant critique of humanity's moral and ethical flaws.

1729 Jonathan Swift's "A Modest Proposal," a mock treatise that scathingly satirizes English exploitation of the Irish peasantry. Swift's ironic, critical writings will influence later Enlightenment thought.

1731 The popular *Gentleman's Magazine*, the first modern English magazine, begins publication, featuring a wide variety of essays, political reports, and poems.

1733–34 Alexander Pope's *An Essay on Man*, a long poem discussing man's place in the harmonious order of the universe, and affirming the values of reason and adherence to tradition.

1735 In the colony of New York, journalist and printer John Peter Zenger is acquitted of seditious libel, a landmark ruling in the development of the principle of the freedom of the press in the English colonies of North America and, later, the United States.

1737 *A Faithful Narrative of the Surprising Work of God* by Puritan theologian Jonathan Edwards, whose intensely emotional sermons and writings are associated with the Great Awakening, a popular American evangelical movement that flourished in the English colonies of North America in the early to middle 18th century.

1740 Samuel Richardson's epistolary novel *Pamela*, the story of a servant girl who virtuously avoids a gentleman's seduction and ultimately convinces him to marry her. The novel's intimate, psychological tenor anticipates the growing importance of emotion in late-18th-century literature.

1747–48 Samuel Richardson's epistolary novel *Clarissa*, concerning the struggles of a heroine who, refusing to acquiesce to the conventional marriage of convenience, suffers at the hands of a libertine.

1749 Henry Fielding's *Tom Jones*, an English novel comically recounting the life journey of the abandoned child Tom Jones while painting a detailed, expansive picture of 18th-century English town and country.

1750–52 *The Rambler*, a significant English periodical written almost entirely by Samuel Johnson, is published. Johnson is prominent in 18th-century English letters because of his learned, considered, and witty essays and conversation.

c. 1750–1800 A Welsh literary renaissance arises with a renewed interest in ancient Welsh compositions. Poets who draw upon ancient Welsh traditions include Thomas Gray, the author of the popular "An Elegy Written in a Country Church Yard" (1751). The movement marks an early shift away from classicism toward a Romantic interest in emotion, local history, and rural life.

1751–80 The French *Encyclopédie*, with articles on science, philosophy, and the fine and applied arts, is issued under the direction of Denis Diderot. A landmark of the 18th-century Enlightenment, this massive work breaks new ground with its secular, liberal, and rational approach to the study of knowledge in all its branches.

1755 Samuel Johnson's *A Dictionary of the English Language*, the first major English dictionary, which he compiled single-handedly.

1759 Voltaire's *Candide*, a novel featuring an extravagant series of calamities that befall the naive protagonist, and a witty critique of

Enlightenment ideals of rationalism and optimism.

1759–67 Laurence Sterne's multivolume experimental novel, *Tristram Shandy*, whose labyrinthine web of complex storytelling, jokes, surreal digressions, and wordplay anticipates the modernist stream-of-consciousness novel.

1762 Two of Jean-Jacques Rousseau's most influential works, *The Social Contract* (*Du Contrat Social*), an essay propounding the political rights of citizens, and *Émile*, a didactic romance concerning childhood education and the innate goodness of human nature.

c. 1763 Cao Zhan's novel *The Dream of the Red Chamber* (*Honglou Meng*), one of the greatest achievements of Chinese literature, chronicling the lives of an upper-class family with a blend of realism and supernatural romance. The novel will not be published until 1791, after its author's death.

1766 Gotthold Ephraim Lessing's *Laocoön* (*Laokoon*), a critical treatise examining the distinctive features that characterize different forms of art and literature.

Oliver Goldsmith's *The Vicar of Wakefield*, a novel depicting rural village life with ironic humor, which will inspire a renewed interest in pastoral literature.

1768–71 The *Encyclopaedia Britannica* is published in Edinburgh. Other notable achievements of the Scottish Enlightenment include the works of the philosopher David Hume and the economist Adam Smith, whose *Wealth of Nations* (1776) expounds laissez-faire economics and the significance of commercial rather than religious values.

1773 Phillis Wheatley's *Poems on Various Subjects*. A slave who had received an exceptional education in the home of her Boston master, Wheatley is renowned for her Neoclassical, religious verse.

Oliver Goldsmith's play *She Stoops to Conquer*, the success of which revives the comedy of manners.

1774 Johann Wolfgang von Goethe's *The Sorrows of Young Werther* (*Die Leiden des Jungen Werthers*), an immensely popular epistolary novel portraying a sensitive hero who is spurned in love. With its intense emotional color, the work is a benchmark of literary Romanticism.

1776 Thomas Jefferson writes the Declaration of Independence, a philosophical manifesto asserting the independence of the American colonies from Britain and the "unalienable rights" of individuals.

1777 Richard Brinsley Sheridan's *The School for Scandal*, a classic comedy of manners satirizing the duplicities surrounding love and fortune in a world of gossip-mongering and hypocrisy.

1779 Gotthold Ephraim Lessing's play *Nathan the Wise* (*Nathan der Weise*), a parable advocating religious tolerance among Christians, Jews, and Muslims, and a pioneering work of the German Enlightenment.

1781 *Critique of Pure Reason* (*Kritik der Reinen Vernunft*) by German philosopher Immanuel Kant, whose inquiries into the operations of subjective knowledge will exert an important influence on modern thought and whose concept of the sublime will play a significant role in Romantic literature.

1782 Pierre Choderlos de Laclos's *Les Liaisons Dangereuses*, an epistolary novel that creates an international sensation because of its coolly detached depiction of moral depravity and licentious sexual relations among the aristocracy.

1782–89 Jean-Jacques Rousseau's posthumously published *Confessions*, a groundbreaking autobiography, controversial for its frank discussion of sexuality, its affirmation of personal morality, and its emphasis on expressing private, interior experiences.

1784–85 The Marquis de Sade's *The 120 Days of Sodom* (*Les 120 Journées de Sodome*), written while the author is imprisoned in the Bastille for debauchery. De Sade's novels, which will not be published legally until the 20th century, portray organized rituals of sexual perversion in Gothic settings, and become underground classics.

1786 Robert Burns's *Poems, Chiefly in the Scottish Dialect*, portraying love, nature, and rural life, make the "Heaven-taught plowman" famous virtually overnight.

1791 James Boswell's *The Life of Samuel Johnson*, an intimate account of the life of the great literary figure, and one of the finest achievements of biographical literature.

American statesman, scientist, and writer Benjamin Franklin's *Autobiography*, a classic of the genre, noted for its simple, humorous prose, clear structure, and themes of industriousness and inventiveness.

1791–92 Thomas Paine's *The Rights of Man*, which argues against aristocratic government and asserts the principles of democracy.

1792 Mary Wollstonecraft's *A Vindication of the Rights of Woman*, a landmark critique of the cultural constraints on women and an argument for their equality with men, extending the radical principles of the French and American revolutions to the position of women in society.

1794 Ann Radcliffe's *The Mysteries of Udolpho*, one of the finest examples of the English Gothic novel, a popular form in the late 18th and early 19th centuries, typically set in an isolated castle and characterized by an atmosphere of mystery and horror.

William Blake's *Songs of Innocence and of Experience*, a collection of lyric poems concerned with the conflict between individual creativity and repressive social and political codes, one of the finest works of early English Romanticism.

1795–96 Johann Wolfgang von Goethe's *Wilhelm Meister's Apprenticeship* (*Wilhelm Meisters Lehrjahre*), the founding, classic Bildungsroman, recounting a young man's education in life as he journeys to adulthood.

1797–99 Friedrich Hölderlin's *Hyperion*, an elegiac novel about a Greek man who fights unsuccessfully for his country's freedom.

1798 William Wordsworth and Samuel Taylor Coleridge's landmark collection *Lyrical Ballads*, which initiates English Romanticism. The collection includes Coleridge's "The Rime of the Ancient Mariner," a narrative ballad about sin and guilt, and Wordsworth's "Tintern Abbey," a meditation on nature and memory.

1800 Wordsworth's famous preface to a new edition of *Lyrical Ballads*, which outlines the central themes of English Romanticism, including individuality, nature, imagination, and a democratic identification with common life.

Anglo-Irish author Maria Edgeworth's *Castle Rackrent*, a satirical novel about Irish landowners.

The French dramatist Guilbert de Pixérécourt's *Coelina, ou l'Enfant de Mystère* (adapted by Thomas Holcroft as *A Tale of Mystery* in 1802), a founding work of the popular genre of melodrama, which emphasizes sensation, emotion, and colorful effects, and typically concerns affairs of the heart and the triumph of virtue over vice.

1802 *The Edinburgh Review* (1802–1929), a major journal of liberal social and literary criticism, is founded in Scotland. Its success inspires a profusion of British critical and literary periodicals, including *The Examiner* (1808–81), *The Quarterly Review* (1809–1967), *The London Magazine* (1820–29), and *The Athenaeum* (1828–1921).

The epistolary novel *Delphine*, an important initiator of Romanticism in France, by Madame de Staël, whose novels are noted for their feminist and psychological concerns.

1805 François René de Chateaubriand's highly popular *René*, an early Romantic French novel, concerning a restless, melancholy hero and his illicit passions and far-flung travels in the New World.

1807 William Wordsworth's "Ode: Intimations of Immortality," a reflection on memory, loss, and the nature of subjective experience.

1808 Johann Wolfgang von Goethe's *Faust* (Part I), a verse drama depicting the legendary scholar who promises his soul to the devil in exchange for the fullest life experience. (Part II will be published posthumously, in 1832.)

1809 Washington Irving's *A History of New York*, a satirical history of Dutch colonial New York, the first book by the first American literary author to gain an international reputation. Published pseudonymously by one Diedrich Knickerbocker, the work will inspire the so-called Knickerbocker school, a group of writers in New York City and its environs, including James Fenimore Cooper and William Cullen Bryant, who work to promote American literature.

1810 Heinrich von Kleist's "The Marquise of O…" ("Die Marquise von O…"), a short story concerning a woman's mysterious pregnancy, notable for its preoccupation with irrationality and the difficulty of discerning truth.

1811–17 Jane Austen's *Sense and Sensibility*, *Pride and Prejudice*, *Emma*, and *Persuasion* — witty and sharply observed novels about the manners and mores of the English middle and upper classes — are published anonymously.

1812–18 Lord Byron's immensely popular *Childe Harold's Pilgrimage*, a long and colorful verse satire that sparks a vogue for the brooding and passionate "Byronic hero."

1812–22 *Grimm's Fairy Tales*, a classic of folklore literature (gleaned by the authors, Jacob and Wilhelm Grimm, from oral folktales) including "Snow White," "Little Red Riding Hood," "Rapunzel," and "Hansel and Gretel," and a landmark of the German Romantic movement.

1814–15 E. T. A. Hoffmann's first collection of stories, *Fantasy-pieces* (*Fantasiestücke*), which are notable for their uncanny depictions of supernatural events within naturalistically rendered settings.

1814–32 Sir Walter Scott's *The Waverley Novels*, a series of 32 historical novels, including *Rob Roy* and *Ivanhoe*, which find a wide popular readership. Scott's romantic narratives burst with great historical events, regional atmosphere, adventure, and broad social conflicts.

1816 Publication of Samuel Taylor Coleridge's dreamlike "Kubla Khan" (which he claimed was composed under the influence of laudanum), a poem suffused with supernatural and mythological motifs.

1817 William Cullen Bryant's "Thanatopsis," a meditation on death and nature, is published in *The North American Review*, bringing the young poet instant fame.

1818 Mary Shelley's *Frankenstein*, a classic Gothic novel about a scientist who creates a living man from the parts of corpses, and a profound exploration of the philosophical and psychological issues surrounding science, ambition, mortality, and the soul.

1819–20 Washington Irving's most celebrated stories, "The Legend of Sleepy Hollow" and "Rip Van Winkle."

1819–24 Lord Byron's *Don Juan*, a long satirical poem narrating the adventures of the legendary Spanish libertine, and a spirited and witty assault on hypocrisy and social convention. It is generally considered Byron's finest work.

1820 Percy Bysshe Shelley's lyric "Ode to the West Wind" and the verse drama *Prometheus Unbound*, the latter based on the Greek myth about the god who defies Zeus by stealing fire from heaven to benefit mankind. Two years later, Shelley, only 30 years old, will drown in the Gulf of Spezia in Italy.

John Keats's finest odes and the ballad "La Belle Dame sans Merci." Keats will die the next year in Rome at the age of 25.

1821 William Cullen Bryant's *Poems*, including his two most famous works, "Thanatopsis" and "To a Waterfowl."

1822 Thomas De Quincey's *Confessions of an English Opium Eater*, a memoir about his drug addiction.

Victor Hugo's first collection of poems, *Odes et Poésies Diverses*.

1823–41 James Fenimore Cooper's *The Leatherstocking Tales*, a series of novels— including *The Last of the Mohicans* (1826) and *The Deerslayer* (1841)—chronicling the adventures of Natty Bumppo (nicknamed Leatherstocking) on the ever-westward-expanding American frontier.

1824 Giacomo Leopardi's *Canzoni*, his first collection of poems.

Lord Byron dies at Missolonghi, Greece, on April 19; on May 17 in London, the manuscript of his *Memoirs* is burned by Byron's publisher, who presumably fears that its publication would irrevocably damage the poet's already dubious reputation.

1827 Alessandro Manzoni's *The Betrothed* (*I Promessi Sposi*), a key work of modern Italian literature, portraying the challenges and adversities faced by two 17th-century peasant lovers.

Heinrich Heine's *Book of Songs* (*Buch der Lieder*).

1828 Noah Webster's *An American Dictionary of the English Language*.

1829–47 Honoré de Balzac's immense cycle of novels, *The Human Comedy* (*La Comédie Humaine*), including *Eugénie Grandet*, *Le Père Goriot*, and *La Cousine Bette*, chronicling a wide range of contemporary French society with vivid, detailed observation.

1830 Stendhal's novel *The Red and the Black* (*Le Rouge et le Noir*), which examines with psychological penetration the character of Julien Sorel, an ambitious young man in post-Napoleonic France.

Harvard law student Oliver Wendell Holmes reads a newspaper article reporting plans to scrap the rotting but historic frigate the USS *Constitution* (launched in Boston in 1797), and responds with a rousing protest poem, "Old Ironsides," which is printed across the nation. As a result of the ensuing public uproar, the *Constitution* is spared destruction.

1830–65 What is now known as the American Renaissance in literature, marked notably by the flowering of Transcendentalism and the achievements of, among others, James Fenimore Cooper, Edgar Allan Poe, Nathaniel Hawthorne, Herman Melville, Walt Whitman, and Emily Dickinson.

1831 Victor Hugo's *The Hunchback of Notre Dame* (*Nôtre-Dame de Paris*), set in medieval Paris, concerning Quasimodo, the deformed bell ringer of the cathedral, and his futile attempts to protect a gypsy woman from harm.

Publication of Aleksandr Pushkin's verse tragedy *Boris Godunov* (written 1824–25), a psychologically acute exploration of the nature of power that depicts the historical Boris Godunov (tsar of Russia, 1598–1605).

1832 George Sand's widely popular French novel *Indiana*, portraying a woman who, flouting social convention, abandons an unhappy marriage for her lover.

1833 Aleksandr Pushkin's verse novel, *Eugene Onegin* (*Evgeniĭ Onegin*), offering a panoramic view of contemporary Russian society and focusing on the experiences of its eponymous hero, a disenchanted "superfluous man."

1833–34 Thomas Carlyle's satirical philosophical novel *Sartor Resartus*, which explores the author's disillusionment with conventional society and the need for new philosophical paradigms.

1835 Alfred de Vigny's French drama *Chatterton*, which depicts the troubled life of 18th-century English poet-prodigy Thomas Chatterton, a precursor of the English Romantics who committed suicide at age 17, in 1770.

Danish author Hans Christian Andersen's first collection of fairy tales, artfully drawn from folklore and notable for their sympathetic treatment of outcasts, including "The Ugly Duckling," "The Snow Queen," "The Red Shoes," and "The Little Match-Seller."

The sole manuscript of volume 1 of Thomas Carlyle's *The French Revolution* is accidentally burned by a servant while the manuscript is in the care of John Stuart Mill. Carlyle must begin the book again from scratch.

1836 Ralph Waldo Emerson's long essay "Nature," a landmark of American literature, which proposes that value be sought not in tradition but in spiritual communion with nature.

The first meeting of the informal Transcendental Club, Concord, Massachusetts.

1837 In a Harvard College commencement speech, Henry David Thoreau startles his audience by suggesting that man work only on Sunday, and designate "the other six his Sabbath of the affections and the soul, — in which to range this widespread garden, and drink in the soft influences and sublime revelations of nature."

Aleksandr Pushkin dies at the age of 39, following a duel fought to defend his wife's honor.

In monthly installments, the first of his extremely successful forays into the serial novel, a form of publishing popular in the 19th century, Charles Dickens issues his first novel, *The Posthumous Papers of the Pickwick Club*, better known as *The Pickwick Papers*.

Nathaniel Hawthorne's short-story collection *Twice-Told Tales*. With their psychological concerns and Romantic symbolism, the *Tales* will significantly influence the genre.

1837–1901 During the reign of Queen Victoria, England witnesses a long, fertile period of literary activity. Victorian literature is marked by such contemporary trends as the rise of both industrialization and the middle class, the entry of women into the ranks of professional writers and editors, and the growing prominence of the novel, especially the immensely popular works of Charles Dickens.

1838–39 Charles Dickens's novels *Oliver Twist* and *Nicholas Nickleby*.

1839 Henry Wadsworth Longfellow's first collection of poems, *Voices of the Night*. Longfellow's later poetry, including "Evangeline," "Hiawatha," and "Paul Revere's Ride," will be very popular in both America and England.

1840 Edgar Allan Poe's *Tales of the Grotesque and Arabesque*, works influential in the development of the modern short story.

1840–44 *The Dial*, the magazine of the American Transcendentalist writers. The philosophical movement of Transcendentalism stresses independent thinking and the innate spiritual goodness of human nature. Writers associated with the group include Ralph Waldo Emerson, Henry David Thoreau, and Margaret Fuller, author of the feminist classic *Woman in the Nineteenth Century* (1845).

1841 Ralph Waldo Emerson's first volume of *Essays*, which includes the famous "Self-Reliance."

Edgar Allan Poe's "The Murders in the Rue Morgue," considered the first detective story, and an influence on the French Symbolist and Surrealist writers.

1842 Alfred, Lord Tennyson's highly popular *Poems*, including "Locksley Hall" and "Ulysses," exploring themes of temporality, mortality, and the progress of civilization.

Nikolai Gogol's *Dead Souls* (*Mertvye Dushi*), a mordantly satirical novel about a social-climbing swindler, and "The Overcoat" ("Shinel'"), a haunting short story about an impoverished clerk.

1842–43 Eugène Sue's *The Mysteries of Paris* (*Les Mystères de Paris*), a popular, sensationalistic novel about the seamy underside of the city, is denounced in the French Chamber of Deputies as a tour through "the sewers of Parisian life."

1844 *The Three Musketeers* (*Les Trois Mousquetaires*) by Alexandre Dumas *père*, one of his best-known historical romances, portraying swashbuckling adventures in 17th-century France.

Ralph Waldo Emerson's second volume of *Essays*, featuring the celebrated essay "Experience."

1845 Edgar Allan Poe's *The Raven and Other Poems* and *Tales*, the latter including the short story "The Fall of the House of Usher."

The Narrative of the Life of Frederick Douglass, recounting Douglass's experiences of slavery and his journey to freedom, a classic work of autobiography and a landmark of the slave narrative.

On July 4, Henry David Thoreau moves from Concord, Massachusetts, to a small cabin beside Walden Pond.

1846 Charlotte, Emily, and Anne Brontë publish, at their own expense, the pseudonymous *Poems, by Currer, Ellis, and Acton Bell*. In July of the next year, Charlotte will send a copy to Thomas De Quincey with a wry note: "[O]ur book is found to be a drug; no man needs it or heeds it; in the space of a year our publisher has disposed but of two copies, and by what painful efforts he succeeded in getting rid of those two, himself only knows."

1847 Two Brontë novels: Charlotte Brontë's *Jane Eyre*, a stirring female Bildungsroman about a restless, orphaned young woman and her love for the mysterious Mr. Rochester; and Emily Brontë's *Wuthering Heights*, a visionary, multilayered narrative, set on the wild English moors, about the tragic love affair of Catherine and Heathcliff.

1848 William Makepeace Thackeray's *Vanity Fair*, a satirical novel of manners centering on the indelible Becky Sharp, a scheming social climber.

Elizabeth Gaskell's *Mary Barton*, a pioneering social-problem novel portraying the struggles of a working-class family in industrial Manchester.

Founding of the Pre-Raphaelite Brotherhood in England, a circle of poets and painters including Dante Gabriel Rossetti and William Morris, who are inspired by early Italian painting and who value directness, sensuousness, and organic forms in art.

The Communist Manifesto (*Manifest der Kommunistischen Partei*)—a treatise calling for the full-scale overthrow of industrial capitalism by a unified working-class revolt—by German socialists Karl Marx and Friedrich Engels.

1849 Fyodor Dostoyevsky is condemned to death for revolutionary activities, a sentence subsequently commuted by the tsar to penal exile in Siberia.

1850s Cheaply sold paperbound novels, called penny dreadfuls in England and dime novels in the United States, grow in popularity. These novels—colorful, melodramatic, and sometimes lurid—recount tales of adventure, mystery, romance, crime, and exploration. During the same period, mechanical mass production helps to make traditional hardcover books less costly.

1850 William Wordsworth's great long poem *The Prelude*, written over the course of 40 years, which explores his development as a poet and his search for spiritual faith.

Alfred, Lord Tennyson's long poem *In Memoriam*, which mourns the death of an intimate friend while exploring issues of time, mortality, and religious faith. The poem is a great critical and popular success; later that year, Tennyson is named Poet Laureate.

Charles Dickens's autobiographical novel *David Copperfield*, his own "favourite child" of his novels.

Nathaniel Hawthorne's *The Scarlet Letter*, a symbolic novel exploring guilt and redemption in Puritan New England, and a masterpiece of American literature.

The influential American periodical *Harper's New Monthly* (later, *Harper's Magazine*) begins publication in New York City.

1851 Herman Melville's masterpiece, *Moby-Dick*, which chronicles Captain Ahab's obsessive pursuit of a great white whale and explores the metaphysical and psychological dimensions of his quest.

The first issue of *The New York Times* (the New York *Daily Times* until 1857) appears on September 18.

1852 On February 24, a mentally unstable Nikolai Gogol burns the (presumably completed) manuscript of *Dead Souls*, Part II; on March 5, Gogol dies.

Harriet Beecher Stowe's antislavery novel *Uncle Tom's Cabin; or, Life among the Lowly* sells 300,000 copies within six months of publication and helps to rally support for the Abolitionist movement.

Peter Mark Roget's *Thesaurus of English Words and Phrases*.

1853 Charles Dickens's *Bleak House*, one of the greatest of his mature novels.

1854 Henry David Thoreau's *Walden*, recording his experiences at Walden Pond, where he lives simply, in a cabin, without material comforts, and closely observes nature.

Coventry Patmore's *Angel in the House*, a widely read, long verse narrative about marriage, which crystallized Victorian ideals of the roles of women in society, emphasizing domesticity, modesty, and subservience.

1855 The first edition, self-published, of Walt Whitman's *Leaves of Grass*, the collection of poems he will continue to enlarge throughout his long life, with its romantic, generous treatment of American life, expressing themes of democracy, individuality, and sexuality.

John Bartlett's *Familiar Quotations*.

1855–67 Anthony Trollope's Barsetshire novels, a popular series portraying life in a fictional cathedral town in the English countryside.

1857 Elizabeth Barrett Browning's *Aurora Leigh*, a popular novel in blank verse portraying the life and career of a fictional woman poet.

First edition of Charles Baudelaire's *Flowers of Evil* (*Les Fleurs du Mal*), dedicated to Théophile Gautier, which provokes a public scandal. In August, after an obscenity trial, six poems in the volume are ordered suppressed. *Les Fleurs du Mal* will strongly influence 20th-century literature because of its open treatment of sensuality and everyday life and its expression of states of spiritual and emotional ambivalence.

The Atlantic Monthly, the distinguished journal of literature and opinion, is founded in Boston, with James Russell Lowell as its first editor.

Gustave Flaubert's novel *Madame Bovary*, a landmark of the genre, notable for its precise style and realistic, objective observation, portraying the life of a romantic, bored housewife, Emma Bovary, and revealing the profound limitations of both its heroine and her provincial society.

1858 In Amherst, Massachusetts, Emily Dickinson begins the practice of binding her poems into small, hand-stitched booklets, or fascicles, which are discovered only after her death in 1886.

1859 Charles Darwin's landmark *On the Origin of Species*, proposing the theory of natural evolution, which conceives of humanity as an animal species, implicitly challenging notions of divine order.

In August, William Makepeace Thackeray assumes editorship (through March 1863) of the new *Cornhill Magazine* (1860–1975).

1860 Wilkie Collins's *The Woman in White*, one of the finest early mystery novels, concerning a plot to steal a woman's inheritance by confining her to a mental asylum.

1861 Harriet Jacobs's *Incidents in the Life of a Slave Girl*, the best-known slave narrative written by an African-American woman, controversial because of its accounts of the sexual abuses connected with slavery.

Charles Dickens's *Great Expectations*, considered by many critics his finest novel.

Francis Turner Palgrave's popular anthology of "all the best original Lyrical pieces and Songs in our language," *The Golden Treasury*.

1862 Victor Hugo's historical novel *Les Misérables*, about Jean Valjean, a peasant convicted of stealing a loaf of bread to feed his family.

Christina Rossetti's *Goblin Market and Other Poems*, one of the finest works associated with the Pre-Raphaelites.

Ivan Turgenev's *Fathers and Sons* (*Ottsy i Deti*), a realist novel portraying the conflicts in Russian society between the traditional aristocracy and a younger generation of nihilists and materialists.

1865 Lewis Carroll's *Alice's Adventures in Wonderland*, describing the illogical, fantastic journey of its young heroine, Alice.

The Nation is founded in New York City.

1867 Fyodor Dostoyevsky's *Crime and Punishment* (*Prestuplenie i Nakazanie*), a darkly intense, psychological novel portraying a poor student who murders a pawnbroker, his struggle with guilt, and his eventual redemption.

Matthew Arnold's "Dover Beach," his elegiac poem about a culture experiencing the ebbing of religious faith.

1867–94 Karl Marx's profoundly influential *Das Kapital*, a critical analysis of the capitalist economic system and an argument that culture is rooted in the historical conditions of economic production.

1868–69 Leo Tolstoy's monumental novel *War and Peace* (*Voĭna i Mir*), set during Napoleon's invasion of Russia, vividly portraying a range of characters who are caught in the sweep of turbulent historical forces.

1868–1935 The San Francisco–based *Overland Monthly*, edited for its first two and a half years by Bret Harte.

1869 Louisa May Alcott's *Little Women*, a perennial classic of girls' literature, combining moral didacticism and resonant depictions of the lives of four young sisters.

1870 The Elementary Education Act in England lays the groundwork for compulsory public education, and will lead to increased literacy in Great Britain. In the United States, compulsory public schooling is instituted state by state during the 19th century, based on the Tenth Amendment to the Constitution.

On March 15 in London, Charles Dickens gives his final public reading with performances of *A Christmas Carol* and *The Trial from Pickwick*.

c. 1870–1914 In America, a period of expansive industrialization, political corruption, and urbanization will take its name from the novel *The Gilded Age* (1873), a satire of rampant materialism by Mark Twain and Charles Dudley Warner. The period witnesses the rise of literary realism, including the increasing prominence of social protest literature.

1871–93 Émile Zola's *Les Rougon-Macquart*, a 20-volume cycle of novels set during the reign of Napoleon III, including *L'Assommoir* (1877), *Nana* (1880), and *Germinal* (1885), and detailing the lives of three branches of the Rougon-Macquart family. The novels, which exemplify literary naturalism, are marked by a careful observation of social environments and their effect on character.

1871–96 English poet W. S. Gilbert and English composer Arthur Sullivan produce their popular comic operettas, noted for their exuberant whimsicality, verbal brilliance, and social satire.

1872 George Eliot's *Middlemarch*, a milestone in the development of the realistic novel.

Publishers Weekly is founded in New York City.

1873 Teenage poet Arthur Rimbaud's *A Season in Hell* (*Une Saison en Enfer*), an autobiographical prose poem.

1874 Paul Verlaine's *Song Without Words* (*Romance sans Paroles*), written during his romantic involvement with Rimbaud.

WRITING THE FUTURE

■ In H. G. Wells's *The Time Machine* (1895), the narrator journeys forward in time and discovers the horrifying evolution of the class system: humanity is now divided into two types of beings, Morlocks and Eloi. The cunning, terrifying Morlocks, descended from the lower classes of factory workers, live in darkness below the earth. The childish, sheeplike Eloi are humans descended from the British aristocracy of Wells's day who make easy meals for the Morlocks. Eventually, Earth is populated only by giant crabs that survive under a guttering sun.

■ In *Brave New World* (1932), Aldous Huxley depicted a united World State more than 600 years in the future, whose motto is "Community, Identity, Stability." The inhabitants revere its founder, Henry Ford, as a god. (Huxley transparently named him after the American industrialist who invented the assembly line.)

Humanity is engineered for maximum usefulness from the moment of conception. Embryos are gestated in test tubes in giant hatcheries, and infants and children are conditioned into five social classes: Alphas, Betas, Gammas, Deltas, and Epsilons. In descending hierarchy, Alphas are raised to rule; Epsilons, to perform simple physical tasks. Soma—a drug that produces a feeling of well-being—is prescribed for anyone suffering from dangerous states of personal frustration or emotion.

■ In George Orwell's *1984* (1949), the world is divided into three superpowers—Oceania, Eurasia, and Eastasia. Orwell's hero, Winston Smith, lives in Oceania, a society controlled by Big Brother, or the Party, whose three slogans are "War is Peace," "Freedom is Slavery," "Ignorance is Strength." Thoughts contrary to Party ideology are "Thoughtcrimes," punishable by

---

1878 Leo Tolstoy's great novel *Anna Karenina*, about a woman who abandons her husband and young son for her lover, a work that investigates marriage and social mores while it raises spiritual questions about a meaningful existence.

1879 Henrik Ibsen's *A Doll's House* (*Et Dukkehjem*), concerning a woman's questioning of her role as a pampered wife. Ibsen's work will have a major impact on Western drama, introducing realistic, analytical treatments of domestic middle-class life.

1880 Fyodor Dostoyevsky's *The Brothers Karamazov* (*Bratya Karamazovy*), a psychological novel focusing on the dynamics of a disturbed

family, a work exploring Dostoyevsky's deepest spiritual and moral concerns.

1881 Henry James's *The Portrait of a Lady*, concerning an American expatriate who is betrayed by her English husband, an examination of the relations between men and women, and the Old World and the New.

1883 Mark Twain has part of his memoir *Life on the Mississippi* transcribed by a professional typist, and becomes the first author to submit typed copy to a publisher. In a later testimonial about the event, Twain wrote, "This experience with a type-writer has been of so high a value to me that not even the type-writer itself can

death. Except for members of the Inner Party, composed of the ruling classes, all members of Oceania have a TV screen in their rooms that observes their every move—hence the expression "Big Brother is watching you."

■ A totalitarian regime also figures in Margaret Atwood's *The Handmaid's Tale* (1985). Atwood describes a world in which a fanatic conservative group seizes power in the mid-1980s and creates the nation of Gilead. The new regime denies women legal protection, financial rights, and education in order to control their reproductive capacity, as nuclear and biological warfare have jeopardized humanity's survival. Fertile women become Handmaids, slaves given to rulers for the sole purpose of procreation. Atwood vividly depicts the enslaved women's resourcefulness and courage, as they begin to escape to Canada through the Underground Femaleroad.

■ In *Looking Backward* (1888), Edward Bellamy created a hero who falls asleep in 1887 and wakes up in the 21st century. He describes Americans as flourishing under a system in which production is both centrally controlled and efficient. With enough food and shelter for everyone, greed and avarice have virtually disappeared.

■ The French author Jules Verne depicted a submarine and an Aqua-Lung, long before such inventions were produced or perfected, in *Twenty Thousand Leagues Under the Sea* (1873). In *For the Flag* (1896), he described a bomb—the Roch Fulgurator—that could destroy all life within a six-mile radius, and in *From the Earth to the Moon* (1865), he imagined space travel. The fascinating *La Journée d'un Journaliste Américain en 2890* (1910; expanded and substantially rewritten by Verne's son Michel after his father's death) depicts another futuristic vision: a world of cities filled with skyscrapers and moving sidewalks, where people watch television programs from Mars, Venus, and Jupiter, and speak to each other via visual telephones.

describe it. It has banished some of the prime sorrows of my life."

1883–85 Friedrich Nietzsche's *Thus Spake Zarathustra* (*Also Sprach Zarathustra*), which investigates the dynamics of power, criticizes Christian ideals, and affirms the "death of God" (or the irrelevance of an absolute authority). Nietzsche's writings will have an enormous influence on 20th-century literature and philosophy.

1884 Mark Twain's masterpiece, *The Adventures of Huckleberry Finn*, a novel depicting a runaway boy's travels on the Mississippi River with an escaped slave, exploring the themes of youthful innocence and the corrupting influence of society.

Two years after his death, a bust of Henry Wadsworth Longfellow is unveiled in Poet's Corner, Westminster Abbey; he is the first American poet to be so honored.

1884–1928 *A New English Dictionary on Historical Principles*, in 10 volumes, which will be revised and updated in 1933 as *The Oxford English Dictionary*, in 13 volumes.

1885 William Dean Howells's realistic novel *The Rise of Silas Lapham*, portraying the moral corruption of a businessman.

1886 Robert Louis Stevenson's *The Strange Case of Dr. Jekyll and Mr. Hyde*, a novella about a scientist who develops a split personality, a terrifying story that resonates with late 19th-century concerns about cultural and psychic disintegration.

1886–87 Benito Pérez Galdós's *Fortunata and Jacinta* (*Fortunata y Jacinta*), concerning a bourgeois wife and her husband's mistress, a novel noted for its realistic social and psychological observation.

1887 Sir Arthur Conan Doyle's novel *A Study in Scarlet*, the first of his famous tales featuring the deductive mastermind Sherlock Holmes.

Stéphane Mallarmé's *Poésies*, a major work of French Symbolism, notable for its evocative, self-conscious language and elliptical instability.

1888 Rubén Darío's collection *Azul*, which marks the beginning of "modernismo," the Latin American and Spanish modernist movement.

1890 Henrik Ibsen's *Hedda Gabler*, a realistic play about an amoral, destructive woman struggling against the constraints of middle-class society.

Poems by Emily Dickinson, edited by Mabel Loomis Todd and Thomas Wentworth Higginson, appears four years after the poet's death, the first collection of her work.

J. G. Frazer's *The Golden Bough*, subtitled "A Study in Magic and Religion," a groundbreaking work that draws parallels between primitive myths and customs and contemporary religions, including Christianity, and will influence such 20th-century writers and thinkers as T. S. Eliot, Robert Graves, and C. G. Jung.

Danish-American immigrant Jacob Riis's *How the Other Half Lives*, an exposé of the squalor and poverty in New York City tenements, shocks the nation.

1891 Thomas Hardy's tragic novel *Tess of the d'Urbervilles*, controversial in its day for its realistic and sympathetic portrayal of an impoverished young rural woman who gives birth to an illegitimate child and who later murders her seducer.

1892 Charlotte Perkins Gilman's feminist classic "The Yellow Wallpaper," a haunting short story exploring female madness, medical science, and social confinement in the lives of women.

1894 *The Yellow Book* is founded in London. With contributions by, among others, Oscar Wilde, W. B. Yeats, and illustrator Aubrey Beardsley, the periodical experiments with French influenced Decadence and Symbolism. An early landmark of the "little magazines," small avant-garde periodicals that will flourish in the early 20th century, it will cease publication in 1897.

1895 On April 5, shortly after the triumphant premiere of his last and greatest play, *The Importance of Being Earnest*, Oscar Wilde is arrested at the Cadogan Hotel in London. The next day, he is denied bail in police court and is ordered held, charged with violations of Section Eleven of the Criminal Law Amendment Act of 1885 (i.e., homosexual offenses).

H. G. Wells's *The Time Machine*, a seminal early science-fiction novel about time travel and a dystopian future characterized by class warfare.

Stephen Crane's *The Red Badge of Courage*, a novel groundbreaking in its realistic, psychologically acute portrayal of a soldier's experience of war.

Founding of The New York Public Library, a landmark in the widespread establishment of public libraries throughout the United States and Great Britain in the late 19th and 20th centuries.

1896 Sarah Orne Jewett's *The Country of the Pointed Firs*, a series of sketches about women's lives in coastal Maine, considered an outstanding achievement of "local color" writing.

Alfred Jarry's *Ubu Roi*, a fantastical comedy that overtly mocks bourgeois values, opens in Paris to great controversy. The play will prove an important influence on later avant-garde literature, particularly that of the Dadaists and Surrealists.

1897 Bram Stoker's Gothic horror novel *Dracula*, a vampire tale drawn from European folktales and medieval history.

1899 Kate Chopin's classic feminist novel *The Awakening*, realistically portraying a Louisiana woman's discovery of her sexual and emotional desires, causes a public scandal.

Austrian founder of psychoanalysis Sigmund Freud's *The Interpretation of Dreams* (*Die Traumdeutung*), an enormously influential exploration of the unconscious forces that, together with the conscious ego, constitute the self.

1900 Theodore Dreiser's novel *Sister Carrie*, a landmark of American realism, which generates controversy because of its sympathetic portrayal of a "fallen woman."

1901 Anton Chekhov's play *The Three Sisters* (*Tri Sestry*), concerning the discontented lives of middle-class sisters stuck in the provinces who dream of going to Moscow.

Rudyard Kipling's classic novel *Kim*, set in India, about the adventures of an Irish orphan who passes with ease as a native Indian.

In Stockholm, the first Nobel Prize in Literature is awarded to French poet Sully Prudhomme (pen name of René François Armand Prudhomme) "in special recognition of his poetic composition, which gives evidence of lofty idealism, artistic perfection, and a rare combination of the qualities of both heart and intellect."

1902 Joseph Conrad's *Heart of Darkness*, an early modernist novel telling of a mariner's mysterious journey up the Congo River to meet the despairing, mad colonist Kurtz.

Henry James's *The Wings of the Dove*, the first of the three novels of James's final, "major" phase, a study of a dying American heiress in Europe written in James's increasingly allusive and dense prose style.

The Times Literary Supplement is founded in London, beginning its distinguished run as an authoritative forum for reviews and essays about literature and scholarship from around the world, with contributions (published anonymously until 1974) from a stellar array of writers, including Virginia Woolf, Henry James, and T. S. Eliot.

1903 Samuel Butler's autobiographical novel *The Way of All Flesh*, a scathing treatment of middle-class family life and Victorian moral codes.

W. E. B. Du Bois's *The Souls of Black Folk*, an examination of the African-American cultural tradition, which articulates and attempts to bridge the gap between the black and white social worlds.

"The New Colossus," a sonnet by American-Jewish poet Emma Lazarus eloquently expressing her hope that America will serve as a haven for the oppressed peoples of the world, is affixed to the Statue of Liberty in New York Harbor.

Jack London's *The Call of the Wild*, a highly popular novel depicting a sled dog's struggle to endure the harsh conditions of the Alaskan wilderness.

In Paris, the Académie Goncourt is founded, with Joris-Karl Huysmans as its first president. The first Prix Goncourt, for an outstanding work of imaginative prose, is awarded to John-Antoine Nau (pen name of Eugène Léon Édouard Torquet) for his novel *Force Ennemie*.

1904 The Abbey Theatre is founded in Dublin, where it will present plays by, among others, John Millington Synge, W. B. Yeats, Sean O'Casey, and Lady Gregory in its first years. The Abbey, which is still in operation today, will be a major center of the Irish Literary Renaissance, a movement passionately concerned with Irish nationalism and Gaelic traditions.

Henry James's final novel, *The Golden Bowl*, a supremely nuanced study of moral corruption, adultery, and betrayal.

1905 Edith Wharton's *The House of Mirth*, her first major novel and a biting examination of upper-class New York society at the turn of the century.

Albert Einstein's epoch-making paper on special relativity, propounding the relational characteristics of time and space.

1906 Upton Sinclair's muckraking novel, *The Jungle*, which depicts corruption and unsanitary conditions in the Chicago meatpacking industry.

In London, the first volumes of the Everyman's Library, edited (and named) by Ernest Rhys, are published. The series' motto is taken from the 15th-century English morality play, *Everyman*: "Everyman, I will go with thee, and be thy guide, / In thy most need to go by thy side."

1907 *The Education of Henry Adams*, one of the great classics of autobiography and a landmark of American literature, reflecting on the search for meaning in the rapidly shifting, fragmented modern era.

John Millington Synge's *The Playboy of the Western World*, a comic portrayal of Irish manhood exploring the conflict between a romantic young man and his domineering father.

1908 August Strindberg's *The Ghost Sonata* (*Spöksonaten*), an important early work of Expressionism, dramatizing sin and revenge, and employing psychological symbolism rather than realistic conventions.

La Nouvelle Revue Française is founded in Paris by André Gide and others.

Ford Madox Ford founds *The English Review* in London, with the purpose of "giving imaginative literature a chance in England." The new periodical goes on to publish writers from Ezra Pound to Ivan Turgenev until its distinguished run ends in the 1930s.

1908–14 The collected works of the Russian-Jewish émigré Sholom Aleichem are published in the United States, including the short stories featuring the character Tevye, who is later immortalized in the musical *Fiddler on the Roof* (1964).

1909 Gertrude Stein's *Three Lives*, her first major novel, notable for its techniques of repetition and abstract simplification.

In Italy, Filippo Tommaso Marinetti's "Futurist Manifesto" marks the birth of Futurism, an avant-garde movement of artists and writers seeking new methods of representing the speed, rapid industrialization, and instability of the era.

1912 Rabindranath Tagore's *Gītāñjali: Song Offerings* (*Gītāñjali*), a collection of poems (with a foreword by W. B. Yeats), characteristic of Tagore's effort to reconcile modernity with traditional Indian culture, and the work that would lead directly to his winning the Nobel Prize the next year.

1912–25 The Chicago Literary Renaissance, noted for the realistic literary treatment of industrialized, urban environments, involves such poets and novelists as Theodore Dreiser, Carl Sandburg, Sherwood Anderson, and Edgar Lee Masters, and the significant "little magazine," *Poetry*.

1913 D. H. Lawrence's *Sons and Lovers*, an autobiographical novel about a working-class family, exploring familial and sexual relationships as well as cultural concerns about industrial society.

George Bernard Shaw's *Pygmalion*, a popular comedy in which the pedantic Henry Higgins attempts to raise the Cockney flower girl Eliza Doolittle above her lowly station by teaching her to speak English with a "proper" accent.

1913–27 Marcel Proust's seven-volume masterpiece *Remembrance of Things Past* (*À la Recherche du Temps Perdu*), tracing the formation of the narrator's identity, and employing associative techniques to explore the shifting realities of time, memory, and consciousness.

1914 *The New Republic*, a weekly journal of opinion and politics, is founded in New York City, and will gain renown for the excellence of its criticism under such literary editors as Malcolm Cowley, Alfred Kazin, and Leon Wieseltier.

1914–19 The English periodical *The Egoist* serves as a major outlet for the Imagists, a modernist movement of poets including Ezra Pound, H. D., and Amy Lowell, who focus on concentrated, concrete imagery.

1914–29 *The Little Review*, a highly influential "little magazine" edited by Margaret Anderson in Chicago and New York, promotes such experimental modernist writers as Ezra Pound, Gertrude Stein, and James Joyce.

1915 T. S. Eliot's "The Love Song of J. Alfred Prufrock," a modernist poem portraying a man's despair with his middle-class life, notable for its fragmented language and allusive symbolism.

Robert Frost's "The Road Not Taken," a poem about a traveler who encounters a fork in the path through the woods, which becomes a metaphor for the choices he has made in his life.

Franz Kafka's "The Metamorphosis" ("Die Verwandlung"), a long short story about a man who is transformed into an insect, characteristic of Kafka's depiction of nightmarish events within otherwise ordinary lives as a means to explore alienation and insecurity.

1915–29 The Provincetown Players (including the young playwright Eugene O'Neill) pioneer in creating a modern American theater, producing experimental plays first in Provincetown, Massachusetts, and then in New York City's Greenwich Village.

1916 James Joyce's *A Portrait of the Artist as a Young Man*, an autobiographical novel recounting the development of a young writer from childhood to early manhood.

1916–20 The avant-garde Dada movement— known for its anarchic mockery of bourgeois values—thrives in Zurich, Paris, and New York, with Tristan Tzara, Hugo Ball, and Marcel Duchamp among its most notable champions.

1917 The Modern Library is founded by the New York publisher Boni and Liveright to provide American readers with inexpensive reprints of European modernist titles. In the 1920s it becomes an imprint of Random House, which casts it as "The Modern Library of the World's Best Books," reflecting an expanded scope that continues to define it today.

Edna St. Vincent Millay's first book, *Renascence and Other Poems*, a collection celebrated for its bohemian tone and its explorations of love and moral liberation.

In March, Leonard and Virginia Woolf order a hand printing press and later that year issue the first publication of the Hogarth Press, their *Two Stories*, containing her "The Mark on the Wall" and his "Three Jews."

1918 The first collected edition of the work of English poet and Jesuit priest Gerard Manley Hopkins (d. 1889), who was little known during his lifetime, but whose work will influence many important 20th-century poets with its compressed syntax, metric innovations, and spiritual concerns.

Willa Cather's *My Ántonia*, a novel about immigrant pioneers on the 19th-century American frontier.

Lu Xun's satirical short story "Kuang ren Riji" ("Diary of a Madman"), an unsettling depiction of traditional Chinese society.

1918–30 The group of American writers Gertrude Stein called the Lost Generation, including Ernest Hemingway, F. Scott Fitzgerald, Sherwood Anderson, and John Dos Passos, reach maturity between the end of World War I and the start of the Depression. The works of this fabled generation of writers (many of whom spent long periods of their lives as expatriates) are characterized by alienation, disillusionment, and rootlessness.

1919–31 The Harlem Renaissance, a fertile period in African-American literature and art, introduces major black American authors, including Langston Hughes, Jean Toomer, Countee Cullen, and Zora Neale Hurston, many of whom first gain notice in the journal *The Crisis* during the literary editorship of novelist Jessie Redmon Fauset.

1920 Wilfred Owen's poems, many expressing his despair at the devastation and waste of war, are published two years after his death in combat during World War I.

The Magnetic Fields (*Les Champs Magnétiques*), by André Breton and Philippe Soupault, the first poetic work of the Surrealists, a group that will play a major role in 20th-century culture through its emphasis on irrationality, chance, and the liberating force of the unconscious.

Katherine Mansfield's short-story collection *Bliss*, tales celebrated for their compression and psychological acuity.

Colette's *Chéri*, a novel portraying the love affair between an aging courtesan and a young man.

Agatha Christie's first book, *The Mysterious Affair at Styles*, which introduces detective Hercule Poirot, as well as the signature elements of her ultimately huge body of work: ingenious plots and upper-class settings.

1921 Margaret Anderson is convicted of obscenity for publishing portions of James Joyce's novel *Ulysses* in *The Little Review*.

Luigi Pirandello's innovative play *Six Characters in Search of an Author* (*Sei Personaggi in Cerca d'Autore*), an unsettling examination of the nature of fiction and reality.

1922 The first publication in book form of Joyce's *Ulysses*, a great modern epic modeled on Homer's *Odyssey*, tracing a day in the life of contemporary Dublin with kaleidoscopically shifting perspectives and stream-of-consciousness interior monologues.

T. S. Eliot's great modernist poem *The Waste Land*, which laments the spiritual barrenness of modern life in dense, fragmented, and allusive language.

1923 E. E. Cummings's *Tulips and Chimneys*, the first collection of his poems, which are noted for their inventive typography, colloquial language, humor, and lyricism.

Rainer Maria Rilke's *Duino Elegies* (*Duineser Elegien*), a famous series of poems reflecting on the nature of art and the elemental search for spiritual harmony and peace.

1924 E. M. Forster's *A Passage to India*, an exploration of racial politics among British and Indian characters in colonial India.

Sean O'Casey's *Juno and the Paycock*, a masterful examination of the struggles of a poor family during the Irish civil war over the terms of independence from Great Britain.

Thomas Mann's *The Magic Mountain* (*Der Zauberberg*), which depicts a young man's sojourn in a Swiss tuberculosis sanitarium, and philosophically reflects on spiritual health and spiritual disintegration in an unstable modern world.

1925 Virginia Woolf's novel *Mrs. Dalloway*, which portrays its characters' interior states with shifting points of view and fluid temporality.

F. Scott Fitzgerald's novel *The Great Gatsby*, a touchstone of the Jazz Age, which sustains a current of tragic desperation in its discerning portrayal of the age's wealth and glamour.

The New Yorker magazine is founded in New York by Harold Ross. Like many of the magazine's early contributors, including Robert Benchley and Dorothy Parker, Ross is a participant in the nearby Algonquin Hotel Round Table, a regular gathering of writers famed for their urbane, sardonic wit.

1922: A VINTAGE YEAR

In the world of literature, the year that opened with the publication of *Ulysses* and closed with that of *The Waste Land* can be regarded only as an extraordinary one. It was of that year that Willa Cather said, "The world broke in two in 1922 or thereabouts." Following is a list of some of 1922's remarkable books and the season in which they appeared.

WINTER

Ulysses, James Joyce

The Forsyte Saga, John Galsworthy

The Beautiful and Damned, F. Scott Fitzgerald

The Garden Party, Katherine Mansfield

SPRING

Late Lyrics and Earlier, Thomas Hardy

The Book of American Negro Poetry, James Weldon Johnson

Harlem Shadows, Claude McKay

The Enormous Room, E. E. Cummings

Aaron's Rod, D. H. Lawrence

SUMMER

Babbitt, Sinclair Lewis

Swann's Way, the first volume of Marcel Proust's *Remembrance of Things Past* to be published in English translation (translated by C. K. Scott Moncrieff)

Jacob's Room, Virginia Woolf

One of Ours, Willa Cather

The Seven Pillars of Wisdom, T. E. Lawrence

My Life and Loves, Frank Harris

The Ballad of the Harp-Weaver, Edna St. Vincent Millay

Men I'm Not Married To, Dorothy Parker

Geography and Plays, Gertrude Stein (source of the famous line "Rose is a rose is a rose is a rose")

The Hairy Ape, Eugene O'Neill

Kristin Lavransdatter, Sigrid Undset

AUTUMN

Tales of the Jazz Age, F. Scott Fitzgerald

Later Poems, W. B. Yeats

The Waste Land, T. S. Eliot

1925–68 Ezra Pound's *The Cantos,* a formally inventive, epic meditation on world cultural transformations, incorporating diverse historical literary sources.

1926 Ernest Hemingway's *The Sun Also Rises,* a novel portraying the disillusionments and personal entanglements of a group of American expatriates in Europe, members of the so-called Lost Generation.

Langston Hughes's volume of poems *The Weary Blues,* which adapts vernacular musical forms to literary verse and establishes Hughes as one of the most celebrated figures of the Harlem Renaissance.

1927 Virginia Woolf's autobiographical novel *To the Lighthouse*, a landmark of literary modernism.

1928 William Butler Yeats's *The Tower*, one of his greatest collections of poetry, which includes "Sailing to Byzantium."

Federico García Lorca's collection *The Gypsy Ballads* (*Romancero Gitano*), combining Andalusian folk forms with a modern preoccupation with sexuality and alienation.

1928–29 Tanizaki Jun'ichirō's novel *Some Prefer Nettles* (*Tade Kuu Mushi*), exploring conflicts in everyday life between Japanese tradition and Western modernity.

1929 William Faulkner's *The Sound and the Fury*, a novel illuminating the decline of an aristocratic Southern family through stream-of-consciousness monologues and shifting points of view, a work whose experimental form will greatly influence other 20th-century novelists.

Virginia Woolf's *A Room of One's Own*, a landmark of feminist criticism that examines the history of women's writing and the social and economic conditions obstructing women's creative work.

Erich Maria Remarque's *All Quiet on the Western Front* (*Im Westen Nichts Neues*), a wrenching portrayal of the experiences of ordinary German soldiers in World War I.

1930 Hart Crane's *The Bridge*, a major modernist poem exploring the American experience.

Dashiell Hammett's detective novel *The Maltese Falcon*, featuring hard-boiled private eye Sam Spade, who will be immortalized by Humphrey Bogart in John Huston's 1941 film adaptation of the novel.

1930–36 John Dos Passos's *U.S.A.*, a trilogy of social-protest novels, combining fiction, journalism, historical sketches, and personal reminiscences to provide a kaleidoscopic portrait of American life from 1900 to the Great Depression.

1932 Aldous Huxley's *Brave New World*, a dystopian novel portraying a scientifically ruled, utilitarian society that is bereft of spiritual, moral, and aesthetic values.

1933 Éditions de la Pléiade, the renowned series of French literary classics founded by Jacques Schiffrin in Paris, is acquired in 1933 by the publisher Gallimard, for whom it remains a successful imprint.

1933–47 Three volumes of verse by Pablo Neruda, known collectively as *Residence on Earth* (*Residencia en la Tierra*), which portray modern Chilean life in an innovative poetic language strongly influenced by Surrealism.

1934 Henry Miller's autobiographical novel of Bohemian life in Paris, *Tropic of Cancer*, pathbreaking in its candid depiction of sexual exploration.

Lillian Hellman's play *The Children's Hour*, concerning two teachers who are maliciously accused of lesbianism.

The left-wing literary magazine *Partisan Review* is founded in New York City. Its early roster of contributors includes Lionel Trilling, Edmund Wilson, Mary McCarthy, Norman Mailer, and Gore Vidal.

1935 The Group Theater in New York produces Clifford Odets's *Waiting for Lefty*, a provocative drama about a labor strike, staging the action both on stage and in the audience. Active throughout the 1930s, the Group Theater will advocate leftist politics as well as Russian director Konstantin Stanislavsky's acting techniques, which stress psychological realism.

The first 20 paperback Penguin Books are issued in England, at sixpence each.

1935–40 Anna Akhmatova's *Requiem* (*Rekviem*), a powerful cycle of poems that mourns and memorializes the death of the poet's husband and the imprisonment of her son during the years of the Stalinist terror.

1935–42 The literary quarterly *The Southern Review* is founded by Robert Penn Warren,

Cleanth Brooks, and Charles Pipkin; its contributors include such prominent writers as T. S. Eliot, Wallace Stevens, Randall Jarrell, Eudora Welty, and John Crowe Ransom. Revived in 1965, it continues to publish distinguished fiction, verse, and criticism.

1936 Walter Benjamin's influential essay "The Work of Art in the Age of Mechanical Reproduction" ("Das Kunstwerk im Zeitalter Seiner Technischen Reproduzierbarkeit"), a meditation on artistic practices in modern industrial society.

Margaret Mitchell's hugely popular historical novel *Gone with the Wind*, portraying the struggles of Southern belle Scarlett O'Hara during the Civil War.

1937 Zora Neale Hurston's novel *Their Eyes Were Watching God*, depicting a young black woman's coming of age in the South, a work noted for its incorporation of vernacular language and folk traditions.

1938 Antonin Artaud's avant-garde *The Theater and Its Double* (*Le Théâtre et Son Double*), a critique of realistic drama that advocates the direct involvement of the audience and the subversion of rational logic.

1939 James Joyce's *Finnegans Wake*, a notoriously complex modernist novel presenting an ordinary man's dream by means of radically experimental language, multilevel puns, fragmentation, and elaborate mythical and historical allusions.

John Steinbeck's novel *The Grapes of Wrath*, an attack on the exploitation of farm workers that portrays the migration of a poor farming family from Oklahoma to California during the Great Depression.

Aimé Césaire's long poem *Return to the Native Land* (*Cahier d'un Retour au Pays Natal*), a work central to Négritude, a movement of French-speaking African and Afro-Caribbean writers living in Paris during the 1930s, 1940s, and 1950s, who affirm their African identities and reject Western cultural and political domination.

Raymond Chandler's first novel, *The Big Sleep*, a hard-boiled crime novel depicting the dark underbelly of Southern California.

1940 Richard Wright's *Native Son*, a novel about a young black man who kills two women, and his victimization by the harsh realities of class and race in America.

Carson McCullers's novel *The Heart Is a Lonely Hunter*, portraying the struggles of alienated outcasts in a small Southern town, one of the most significant works in the emergence of Southern writers during the modernist period.

W. H. Auden's poetry collection *Another Time*, which includes the famous "Musée des Beaux Arts" and other poems exploring the afflictions of the modern age.

1941 Eudora Welty's first book, the short-story collection *A Curtain of Green*, which vividly demonstrates her gift for perceptive observation of character and social relations in the rural South.

Bertolt Brecht's *Mother Courage and Her Children* (*Mutter Courage und Ihre Kinder*), an example of his method of "epic theater," which repudiates naturalism and seeks to provoke the audience to critical inquiry.

1942 Albert Camus's philosophical novel *The Stranger* (*L'Étranger*), an exploration of the lack of coherent meaning in modern culture through its portrayal of a man who is startlingly alienated from society.

1944 Jorge Luis Borges's *Fictions* (*Ficciones*), short stories that playfully explore themes of memory, time, and the relativity of perception and identity, and which, like all of Borges's works, will be a major influence on postmodern fiction.

Jean Genet's poetic novel *Our Lady of the Flowers* (*Notre-Dame des Fleurs*), about a male prostitute in Paris and the criminal underworld of the city.

Jean-Paul Sartre's play *No Exit (Huis Clos)*, portraying the plight of individuals in a world bereft of meaning or identity.

1945 Tennessee Williams's *The Glass Menagerie*, an autobiographical "memory play" focusing on the Wingfield family, and Williams's first play to be produced on Broadway.

Gwendolyn Brooks's first poetry collection, *A Street in Bronzeville*, which delineates the everyday lives of urban blacks in a Chicago neighborhood with precise craft and an intricate incorporation of vernacular language.

1946 *The Portable Faulkner*, a widely read anthology of selections from Faulkner's series of works set in the fictional Yoknapatawpha County (Mississippi) that revives the career of the great modern American novelist.

1946–63 William Carlos Williams's long poem *Paterson*, an exploration and celebration of both daily life in a New Jersey city and the American experience.

1947 Tennessee Williams's play *A Streetcar Named Desire*, depicting the clash between the fragile Blanche DuBois and her pragmatic, carnal brother-in-law, Stanley Kowalski.

Anne Frank's *The Diary of a Young Girl (Het Achterhuis)*, a shattering account of a family's life while hiding from the Nazis in occupied Amsterdam.

Primo Levi's *Survival in Auschwitz (Se Questo è un Uomo)*, a powerful, sensitively crafted memoir about his experiences in a concentration camp.

1948 Ezra Pound's *The Pisan Cantos*, a section of his lifelong poem-in-progress that is noted for its experimental collage technique, and which incites heated controversy about Pound's anti-Semitism and Fascist sympathies when the volume is awarded the first Bollingen Prize for poetry.

Norman Mailer's first novel, *The Naked and the Dead*, which relates, in a journalistic style, the experiences of American soldiers in the Pacific theater during World War II.

Yasunari Kawabata's *Snow Country (Yukiguni)*, which probes the relationship between a wealthy aesthete and a geisha with an oblique, elliptical style.

1949 Arthur Miller's play *Death of a Salesman*, about a salesman, Willy Loman, who discovers the emptiness of the middle-class American dream.

George Orwell's *Nineteen Eighty-four*, a dystopian novel portraying a totalitarian society ruled by Big Brother, monitored by the Thought Police, and awash in propagandistic "newspeak."

Simone de Beauvoir's *The Second Sex (Le Deuxième Sexe)*, analyzing the destructive myths of femininity and arguing for women's freedom.

1950 In New York City, the first National Book Awards are given, for fiction, to Nelson Algren for *The Man with the Golden Arm* and, for poetry, to William Carlos Williams for *Paterson: Book III* and *Selected Poems*.

Charles Olson's seminal essay "Projective Verse," which will inspire a group of innovative poets (many of whom, like Olson, are connected with Black Mountain College in North Carolina), whose advocacy of open, indeterminate poetic forms will have a major impact on postmodern writing.

1951 J. D. Salinger's *The Catcher in the Rye*, a novel offering a vivid portrait of Holden Caulfield, a teenager who is alienated by the hypocrisies and conformism of adult society.

Anthony Powell's *A Question of Upbringing*, the first novel of his 12-volume series, *A Dance to the Music of Time* (1951–75).

Constantine Cavafy's *Poems*, the first collected edition in English translation.

1952 Ralph Ellison's *Invisible Man*, concerning a black man who struggles with the question of his identity in the face of a racist society.

A City in Winter by Frank O'Hara, the first collection from one of the most important of the New York School of poets, writers (including John Ashbery and Kenneth Koch) who will forge artistic and personal ties with painters of the Abstract Expressionist school, and who will work to move American poetry beyond classic European modernism by combining surrealism with an improvisatory urban colloquial style.

Samuel Beckett's *Waiting for Godot* (*En Attendant Godot*), a major work of the Theater of the Absurd.

Dylan Thomas's *Collected Poems*, which appears one year before the poet's early death.

1953 James Baldwin's first novel, *Go Tell It on the Mountain*, a poetic depiction of a young black boy's spiritual, sexual, and moral coming of age.

Saul Bellow's comic novel *The Adventures of Augie March*, about a young Chicago man's attempts to find meaning in the 20th-century world. Bellow, Bernard Malamud, and Philip Roth will all figure prominently in the development of postwar Jewish-American literature.

Ray Bradbury's popular *Fahrenheit 451*, a dystopian novel about a society in which books are banned as part of the social agenda, an example of the burgeoning success of American science-fiction writers, including Isaac Asimov and Robert A. Heinlein, throughout the 1950s.

Doubleday Anchor Books, a new series of quality intellectual and literary paperbacks, is launched in New York City with 12 titles, including Edmund Wilson's *To the Finland Station*, D. H. Lawrence's *Studies in Classic American Literature*, and Stendhal's *The Charterhouse of Parma*, contributing to what will become known as "the paperback revolution." Soon, paperback editions will follow the hardcover publication of most books, making literature accessible to a broader audience.

1954 Wallace Stevens's *Collected Poems*, which brings the modernist American poet the Pulitzer Prize and, for the first time in his long career, widespread public recognition.

1954–56 J. R. R. Tolkien's trilogy of novels *The Lord of the Rings*, a sequel to his celebrated *The Hobbit* (1937), portraying fantastic creatures in the classic struggle between good and evil.

1955 Vladimir Nabokov's novel *Lolita*, an elaborately stylized, darkly satirical narrative tracing an intellectual's sexual obsession with a young girl. Published first in France, the controversial work will cause a furor when it is published in the United States in 1958.

On October 7, Allen Ginsberg gives the first public reading of his long, visionary poem *Howl* ("I saw the best minds of my generation destroyed by madness, starving hysterical naked") at the Six Gallery in San Francisco, where fellow Beat poets Gary Snyder, Michael McClure, and others also perform, the evening in effect launching what would become known as the San Francisco Poetry Renaissance.

1956 Eugene O'Neill's autobiographical play *Long Day's Journey into Night*, a shattering psychological examination of a troubled family. Written in 1940–41, the play is withheld from production until after O'Neill's death.

Nathalie Sarraute's *The Age of Suspicion* (*L'Ère du Soupçon*), a collection of four essays that discuss the novel as a literary form while elaborating the principles of the French "New Novelists," who also include Alain Robbe-Grillet and Marguerite Duras.

New Hampshire novelist Grace Metalious's *Peyton Place* is denounced by the *Manchester Union-Leader* as embodying the "complete debasement of taste and a fascination with the filthy, rotten side of life that are the earmarks of the collapse of civilization." The novel will go on to sell more than 12 million copies.

1956–57 Naguib Mahfouz's *The Cairo Trilogy* (*al-Thulāthīyah*), a landmark of postcolonial Arabic literature that traces three generations of a family in 20th-century Cairo in vivid, realistic detail.

1957 Jack Kerouac's novel *On the Road*, noted for its heady depiction of bohemian antimaterialism and its revitalized use of the American vernacular, the most celebrated example of "spontaneous" prose, the freeflowing, supposedly unedited style of writing that was championed by the Beat movement.

Ayn Rand's *Atlas Shrugged*, a bestselling political allegory about a utopian colony based on free-enterprise capitalism and conservative individualism.

John Osborne's play *Look Back in Anger*, a landmark of the "Angry Young Men" movement in English fiction and theater.

1958 Chinua Achebe's novel *Things Fall Apart*, a classic work of postcolonial African literature that vividly portrays traditional Nigerian culture and the destructiveness wrought on that culture by colonialism.

1959 Robert Lowell's *Life Studies*, a collection of candidly autobiographical poems that will influence later American poets, especially the so-called confessional poets, including John Berryman, Sylvia Plath, and Anne Sexton.

Grace Paley's first short-story collection, *The Little Disturbances of Man*, tales that perceptively portray the lives of urban working people.

The first edition of *The Elements of Style* by E. B. White and William Strunk, Jr.

1960s New York City's Off- and Off-Off-Broadway theaters emerge as among the most important venues for experimental drama. Under less commercial pressure than their Broadway counterparts, they stage works by many important but "uncommercial" dramatists, including Samuel Beckett, Edward Albee, and Sam Shepard. Avant-garde groups like the Living Theater present performance art events that seek direct audience involvement.

The "boom," a major flowering of Latin American literature beginning in the early 1960s, will bring such writers as Carlos Fuentes, Gabriel García Márquez, and Julio Cortázar to worldwide prominence.

1960 Harper Lee's *To Kill a Mockingbird*, a popular novel portraying a young girl's experiences in a small Southern town, including her developing awareness of racism and of the plight of outcasts.

John Updike's novel *Rabbit, Run*, about a man who is dissatisfied with the emptiness of his suburban life.

1961 Joseph Heller's *Catch-22*, a dark satire about a World War II bomber pilot trapped in the insanity of warfare, an early example of the black humor, paranoia, and absurdism that will become increasingly prominent in American literature during the 1960s and 1970s.

Tillie Olsen's novella *Tell Me a Riddle*, portraying the inner experience of a Russian-Jewish immigrant woman at the end of her life.

V. S. Naipaul's *A House for Mr. Biswas*, a darkly comic novel about a poor West Indian man who struggles to buy a home of his own.

1962 Doris Lessing's *The Golden Notebook*, a portrayal of a woman writer struggling with writer's block that interweaves reflections on the fragments of her life.

Anthony Burgess's *A Clockwork Orange*, a dystopian novel about a teenage criminal who is forced by the state to undergo rehabilitative behavioral conditioning.

Carlos Fuentes's *The Death of Artemio Cruz* (*La Muerte de Artemio Cruz*), which presents an aging businessman's fragmented memories and explores the conflicts between revolutionary ideals and modern capitalism.

1963 Betty Friedan's *The Feminine Mystique*, a groundbreaking critique of the limitations of the domestic roles assigned to middle-class women, and an argument that women be given access to expanded opportunities in society.

Founding of *The New York Review of Books*, a liberal journal noted for the depth and seriousness of its books reviews, essays, and opinion pieces.

1964 *The Dead Lecturer*, a collection of poems, and *Dutchman*, a play, by LeRoi Jones [Amiri Baraka], both dealing with issues of racial and class injustice.

Marshall McLuhan's *Understanding Media*, examining the technologies of the electronic and print media and their cultural and psychological implications.

1965 Sylvia Plath's collection *Ariel*, which gathers poems remarkable for their alienation, anger, and confessional intensity, is published two years after her suicide.

The Autobiography of Malcolm X, written with Alex Haley, a story of self-creation and redemption, tracing the African-American leader's journey from prison (for burglary) through his conversion to the Black Muslim movement, and his rise as a political activist. The work will profoundly influence black cultural consciousness throughout the world.

Truman Capote's "nonfiction novel" *In Cold Blood*, a fictional recreation of an actual multiple murder.

1966 Anne Sexton's poetry collection *Live or Die*, expressing intimate emotional conflicts in surrealistic pop imagery and with sardonic humor.

Jean Rhys's novel *Wide Sargasso Sea*, a vividly imagined "prequel" to Charlotte Brontë's *Jane Eyre*, the central characters of which are Mr. Rochester and his Creole first wife, Antoinette Cosway, the "madwoman in the attic" in Brontë's novel.

Tom Stoppard's *Rosencrantz and Guildenstern Are Dead*, a witty play focusing on two minor characters from William Shakespeare's *Hamlet*.

1967 Gabriel García Márquez's novel *One Hundred Years of Solitude* (*Cien Años de Soledad*), a landmark of magic realism.

Jacques Derrida's *Writing and Difference* (*L'Écriture et la Différence*), which challenges notions of inherent truths, and advocates an anti-authoritarian, conditional approach to meaning.

1968 Susan Sontag's *Against Interpretation*, an influential collection of her early critical essays, including the famous "Notes on Camp."

1969 Kurt Vonnegut's novel *Slaughterhouse-Five*, a satire on modern society and war.

Philip Roth's novel *Portnoy's Complaint*, an irreverent, comic exploration of a young Jewish man's struggles with feelings of inadequacy, troubling sexual desires, and a smothering mother.

In London, the first Booker Prize, for the best novel written in English by a citizen of the United Kingdom, the Commonwealth, Ireland, Pakistan, or South Africa, is awarded to P. H. Newby's *Something to Answer For*.

1969–71 Yukio Mishima's *The Sea of Fertility* (*Hojo no Umi*), a series of novels tracing one man's four successive reincarnations, works embodying Mishima's spiritual conflicts with 20th-century Japanese culture and reflecting his profound fascination with ancient samurai and Buddhist traditions.

1970 Joyce Carol Oates's "Where Are You Going, Where Have You Been?," a short story about a girl's coming of age, part of Oates's growing body of fiction centering on the ambiguities and violent forces in everyday life.

1972 Italo Calvino's *Invisible Cities* (*Le Città Invisibili*), in which Marco Polo describes fantastical cities to Kublai Khan.

1973 Thomas Pynchon's *Gravity's Rainbow*, a profusely allusive postmodern novel that juxtaposes heterogeneous characters and events, and revolves around a vision of a vast Nazi conspiracy.

Erica Jong's bestselling novel *Fear of Flying*, a comic, frank account of a woman's sexual adventures.

1973–75 Aleksandr Solzhenitsyn's *The Gulag Archipelago* (*Arkhipelag GULag*), an exposé of the Stalinist labor camps, which rouses public opinion against repressive Soviet policies.

1974 Stephen King's first book, *Carrie*, about a socially outcast girl who uses her supernatural powers to gain vengeance on those who have hurt her.

1975 John Ashbery's poetry collection *Self-Portrait in a Convex Mirror*, whose title poem is a meditation on the Italian Renaissance painter Parmigianino's self-portrait.

Wole Soyinka's play *Death and the King's Horseman*, examining the clash between traditional Yoruban and British colonial values.

Ntozake Shange's play *For Colored Girls Who Have Considered Suicide When the Rainbow Is Enuf*, which explores black women's struggles in life and love in a collage of poems and dance.

1976 Maxine Hong Kingston's *The Woman Warrior*, an autobiographical novel incorporating fantasy and myth that examines the author's female ancestry and Chinese heritage.

Ann Beattie's first novel, *Chilly Scenes of Winter*, which registers the undercurrents of unease in everyday life.

1977 Leslie Marmon Silko's novel *Ceremony*, which combines fantasy, folklore, and realism to explore the resonances of Native American cultural traditions in modern life.

A. B. Yehoshua's *The Lover* (*Ha-me'ahev*), which explores ethnic identity conflicts among Jews and Arabs in contemporary Israel.

1978 Georges Perec's *Life, a User's Manual* (*La Vie, Mode d'Emploi*), a maze-like novel that presents the lives of the residents in each unit of an apartment building, and explores the interpenetration of logic and irrationality.

Sam Shepard's first widely celebrated play, *Buried Child*.

The Virago Modern Classics series is launched in London, "dedicated to the celebration of women writers and to the rediscovery and reprinting of their works."

1979 William Styron's *Sophie's Choice*, portraying a young writer's involvement with a Catholic woman (a concentration camp survivor) and her emotionally unstable Jewish lover.

1980 Anita Desai's novel *Clear Light of Day*, concerning a modern Indian woman's relationship to her traditional family legacy.

Umberto Eco's *The Name of the Rose* (*Il Nome della Rosa*), an erudite, conceptual novel concerning a murder investigation in a medieval monastery.

Marguerite Yourcenar becomes the first woman elected to the Académie Française.

1981 Raymond Carver's *What We Talk About When We Talk About Love*, short stories exploring the tensions of everyday life, which spark renewed interest in literary realism in the short story.

1982 The Library of America, a publishing venture founded in 1979 to preserve American writing in authoritative editions, publishes its first volumes.

Alice Walker's novel *The Color Purple*, a vernacular narrative of the struggles of a Southern black woman.

Murakami Haruki's *A Wild Sheep Chase* (*Hitsuji o Meguru Bōken*), portraying modern Japanese life with mordant humor, dizzying fantasy, and allusions to popular literature and mass media.

1983 David Mamet's *Glengarry Glen Ross*, a scathing portrait of a group of salesmen who work in the ruthless world of real estate.

1984 William Gibson's *Neuromancer*, a landmark of the American cyberpunk novel, written in the style of a hard-boiled thriller, stylishly portraying a high-tech world saturated by electronic information.

Marguerite Duras's *The Lover* (*L'Amant*), her late autobiographical novel about a teenager and her Chinese lover in colonial Indochina.

Milan Kundera's *The Unbearable Lightness of Being* (*Nesnesitelná Lehkost Bytí*), a novel that ironically depicts a young man's sexual exploits, examining issues of power and responsibility in a spiritually arid, modern society.

1985 Don DeLillo's novel *White Noise*, an examination of anxiety and paranoia in an unstable American culture.

Margaret Atwood's *The Handmaid's Tale*, a dystopian novel featuring the rigid subjugation of women in a totalitarian religious society.

Russell Banks's *Continental Drift*, a novel about two migrants—a plumber from New Hampshire and a luckless, desperate woman from Jamaica—whose lives intersect in Florida, offering a gripping portrait of uprootedness and greed in contemporary American life.

1987 Toni Morrison's novel *Beloved*, an exploration of memory and mourning among ex-slaves just after the Civil War.

Paul Auster's first widely popular work, *The New York Trilogy*, a series of conceptual, postmodern detective stories.

Gloria Anzaldúa's *Borderlands/La Frontera*, a seminal work of Chicano literature written in both English and Spanish, which, combining poetry and critical prose, explores the issue of cultural hybridity.

Russian-born American poet Joseph Brodsky wins the Nobel Prize.

1989 Iran's supreme religious authority, the Ayatollah Khomeini, issues a *fatwa*, or order of assassination, against Salman Rushdie for his novel *The Satanic Verses*, claiming that the work blasphemes Islam. Rushdie is forced into hiding until 1998, when the Iranian government announces that it will no longer attempt to enforce the *fatwa*.

Jeanette Winterson's novel *Sexing the Cherry*, a linguistically playful, fantastic narrative exploring sexuality and the ambiguities of identity.

The Remains of the Day, a probing psychological portrait of a self-effacing English butler, by Japanese-born English novelist Kazuo Ishiguro.

Martin Amis's satirical novel *London Fields*, about an end-of-the-millennium London on the brink of destruction.

1990s The World Wide Web via the Internet has an escalating impact on the world of literature: online booksellers deal the last blow to many small independent bookstores, already suffering from competition with large chain booksellers. Some literary and intellectual magazines begin to publish exclusively online; the full texts of out-of-copyright literary works are available on many websites; and literary reference sources of all kinds are present on the Web, free or for a fee. Stephen King tries a much publicized experiment to publish a novel in serial form on the Web, but finds that readers are reluctant to pay.

Performance poetry becomes a significant, popular form in the United States, pioneered by such writer/performers as Miguel Algarín, Wanda Coleman, and Joy Harjo, whose work is marked by musical forms, social concerns, and multicultural inclusiveness.

1990 Derek Walcott's *Omeros*, a long poem in five books that follows the wanderings of a West Indian fisherman, a richly imagined refashioning of the Homeric epics.

1991 South African novelist and anti-apartheid activist Nadine Gordimer wins the Nobel Prize in Literature.

Nina Berberova's *The Tattered Cloak*, a collection of short stories (originally written in Russian) from the 1930s and 1940s, which eloquently portray the lives of Russian émigrés.

1991–93 Tony Kushner's *Angels in America*, a powerful two-part play centering around issues of AIDS, social ethics, and moral responsibility, notable for its fantastic, symbolic imagery.

1991–95 Pat Barker's *Regeneration* trilogy, a series of novels offering an unflinching, compassionate exploration of the human consequences of World War I.

1992 Cormac McCarthy's *All the Pretty Horses*, the first novel of his Border Trilogy, which follows the adventures of three young men as they travel from West Texas to Mexico in the late 1940s and early 1950s, a work acclaimed for its sensuous, Faulkneresque prose.

Michael Ondaatje's Booker Prize–winning novel *The English Patient*, tracing the interwoven lives of four people who come together at a deserted Italian villa at the close of World War II, a spellbinding and poetic meditation on the consequences of love and war; Anthony Minghella's 1996 screen adaptation will win nine Academy Awards, including that for Best Picture.

1995 Penelope Fitzgerald's novel *The Blue Flower*, a haunting portrait of the 18th-century German Romantic poet Novalis and his era.

1996 David Foster Wallace's experimental novel *Infinite Jest*, a vast, comic, and multilevel exploration of addiction and entertainment in contemporary America, detailing—among many other things—the quest for a lost film, titled *Infinite Jest*, that is so dangerously hilarious that it induces catatonia in anyone who watches it; although the novel receives mixed reviews, it becomes a cult favorite with Generation X readers.

1997 Thomas Pynchon's *Mason and Dixon*, a vertiginous, allusive, and inventive novel about the 18th-century surveyors who mapped the American frontier, famously demarcating the line that bears their name, and which historically has stood for the division between North and South.

1998 Nobel Prize–winner Seamus Heaney's *Opened Ground: Selected Poems*, spanning three decades of work by the Irish poet whose vision makes space, in his words, "for the marvelous as well as for the murderous."

1999 The National Book Award–winning novel *Waiting* by Ha Jin, a Chinese-born American author who writes in English. Set during China's Cultural Revolution, it is the story of the enduring love between a nurse and a married doctor.

Günter Grass's *My Century* (*Mein Jahrhundert*), a collection of interlinked stories, one for each year, offering a panoramic and highly personal history of Germany in the 20th century.

Seamus Heaney's acclaimed translation of the Old English epic *Beowulf*, which becomes a surprise bestseller.

2000 An English translation of French author Michel Houellebecq's corrosive and profoundly pessimistic novel, *Les Particules Élémentaires* (1998), is published in New York as *The Elementary Particles* (U.K title, *Atomised*); the work, which created a sensation in France and throughout Europe, squarely places the blame for what the author calls the "suicide of the West" on the destructive influences of the so-called liberation movements of the 1960s.

Chinese-born novelist and playwright Gao Xingjian, who settled in France after being forced to leave his homeland permanently in 1987, wins the Nobel Prize in Literature, the first to be awarded to a Chinese writer. Upset that the Swedish Academy has selected an exiled writer for the prize, China's Foreign Ministry charges the Nobel Committee with having "ulterior political motives."

In January, 24-year-old author Zadie Smith, fresh out of Cambridge University, scores a critical and popular triumph in England with her first novel, *White Teeth*, an exuberant, witty, and inventive narrative following the fortunes of two immigrant families (from Jamaica and Bangladesh) in England during the last half of the 20th century. At the end of the year, Martin Amis's memoir *Experience* tops the London *Independent on Sunday*'s annual survey of the British press's "Books of 2000" lists.

In its April 27 issue, *The New York Review of Books* publishes "Rattle of Pebbles," an essay by the American editor and publisher Jason Epstein (first delivered as a lecture at The New York Public Library), in which he begins to elaborate his vision of the future of publishing as it is radically altered by new electronic technologies and the World Wide Web, a transformation he sees as no less revolutionary than Gutenberg's introduction of movable type more than 500 years ago. He envisages, among much else, a publishing landscape in which by the year 2050 bestselling authors will become their own publishers and bookstores will coexist with a vast, multilingual library of digitized texts that provides instant access to the world's literature to anyone with access to a computer and a modem.

Websites for Literature

Because the World Wide Web is vast and constantly evolving, this annotated roadmap to some of the best literary resources available on the Web is of necessity quite selective, focusing on well-established sites that feature outstanding lists of links. Priority has been given to sites for the general reader, but included too is a representative selection of more academic sites for readers pursuing serious literary research. Information is accurate as of April 2001.

The symbol ** indicates subscription-based websites. These are often available, without a fee, on computers at many public and academic libraries; some may also be available at home to library-card holders through the websites of individual library systems, again without a fee.

1 Navigating: Finding Sites for Books and Literature on the Web

BookSpot

http://www.bookspot.com/

Offers links to book-related sites, with the intention of simplifying "the search for the best book-related content on the Web." Featured sites are organized into categories such as bestseller lists, book awards, online books and e-books, first chapters, reading lists, genres, book reviews, and book news.

The BookWire Directory

http://www.bookwire.com/index.html

R. R. Bowker's *BookWire* site includes a directory page divided into four major categories:

booksellers, publishers, libraries, and "other book resources" (including associations, author indexes and websites, book awards, book-related newsgroups, review sources, wholesalers, and writing resources).

Guardian Unlimited Books: Literary Links

http://books.guardian.co.uk/links/

A guide to the "best literary resources on the net," with subsections covering "sites for enthusiasts" (awards, censorship, graphic fiction, literary theory, buying and collecting, foreign languages, and more), periods and genres, and authors. *Guardian Books Unlimited* is part of the website of the respected British newspaper *The Guardian*.

Literary Resources on the Net

http://andromeda.rutgers.edu/~jlynch/Lit/

A collection of links to sites on the Internet dealing primarily with English and American literature.

Voice of the Shuttle: Web Page for Humanities Research

http://vos.ucsb.edu/

A "structured and briefly annotated guide" to online humanities and humanities-related resources, with more than 70 pages of links.

Yahoo! Arts: Humanities: Literature

http://dir.yahoo.com/Arts/Humanities/Literature/

A popular search engine's literary directory.

2 VIRTUAL REFERENCE DESK FOR LITERATURE

AMERICAN NATIONAL BIOGRAPHY**

http://www.anb.org

This online version of the landmark *American National Biography* (1999) from Oxford University Press offers portraits of more than 17,400 men and women—from all eras and walks of life—whose lives have shaped the nation; the coverage of American writers is both up to date and superb. By subscription; check with your local library.

BARTLEBY.COM

http://www.bartleby.com/

Notable for its access to literary reference books, many of them older editions of enduring reference classics, including:

■ *The American Heritage Dictionary*, 4th ed. (2000)

■ *Bartlett's Familiar Quotations*, 10th ed. (1919)

■ *The Cambridge History of English and American Literature* (18 vols., 1907–21)

■ *The Columbia Encyclopedia*, 6th ed. (2001)

■ Brewer's *Dictionary of Phrase and Fable*, rev. ed. (1898)

■ *Roget's International Thesaurus* (1922) and *Roget's II: The New Thesaurus*, 3rd ed. (1995)

The site also publishes the full texts of specific editions of many works of literature (see **Section 5** below).

ENCYCLOPAEDIA BRITANNICA

http://www.britannica.com

Now available free online, the electronic version of this venerable encyclopedia includes the complete texts, fully updated, of the *Encyclopaedia Britannica*, *Merriam-Webster's Collegiate Dictionary*, and the *Britannica Book of the Year*, as well as current events coverage and other features. The site features more than 72,000 articles and 75,000 definitions, as well as myriad links. Provides outstanding coverage of both world literary history and specific authors.

ENCYCLOPEDIA MYTHICA

http://www.pantheon.org/mythica

Encyclopedia Mythica is an online encyclopedia covering mythology, folklore, legends, and more. It contains more than 5,700 definitions of gods and goddesses, supernatural beings, legendary creatures, and monsters from all over the world.

LITERATURE ONLINE**

http://chadwyck.com

Chadwyck-Healey's *Literature Online* is a full-text, fully searchable library of more than 300,000 works (and growing) of English and American poetry, drama, and prose, plus biographies, bibliographies, and key secondary sources. Criticism and reference works include the *Annual Bibliography of English Language and Literature* (*ABELL*) with links to the full texts of 60 literature journals, the *New Princeton Encyclopedia of Poetry and Poetics*, the *Columbia Dictionary of Modern Literary and Cultural Criticism*, the *Concise Oxford Dictionary of Literary Terms*, the Fitzroy Dearborn *Encyclopedia of the Novel* and *Encyclopedia of American Poetry: The Nineteenth Century*, *Webster's Dictionary*, the *Concise Oxford Dictionary*, the King James Bible, links to other Web resources, bibliographies for over 400 authors, and biographies for over 1,000 of the most-studied authors. By subscription; check with your local library.

LITERATURE RESOURCE CENTER**

http://www.galenet.com/

From the Gale Group, the *Literature Resource Center* offers biographical, critical, and bibliographical coverage of more than 100,000 writers from all time periods and genres, including fiction, nonfiction, poetry, drama, history, and journalism. Provides more than 10,000 biographical and critical scholarly essays, as well as full-text critical essays on major authors via links to 74 prominent literary journals. The *Lit-*

erature Resource Center is designed for students at all levels, as well as for the "sophisticated casual user." By subscription; check with your local library.

THE OXFORD ENGLISH DICTIONARY ONLINE**
http://dictionary.oed.com/

Besides the complete text of the 20-volume *Oxford English Dictionary*, "the principal dictionary of record for the English language," the site includes the three-volume *Additions Series*, and also contains draft material from the current *OED* project, a completely revised and updated Third Edition (at present about half completed). By subscription; check with your local library.

VIRTUAL REFERENCE LIBRARY
http://www.bl.uk/collections/resources/humanities/vrlnew.html

A page of links to "humanities resources for research," selected by the staff of the British Library.

YOURDICTIONARY.COM
http://www.yourdictionary.com

Contains a quick-look-up dictionary based on *Merriam-Webster's Collegiate Dictionary*, 10th edition, and provides links to more than 1,500 freely available, high-quality dictionaries covering more than 230 languages. Also includes specialized subject dictionaries and other language tools, such as thesauri, as well as rhyming, phrase, pronunciation, acronym, synonym, homophone, antonym, and spelling dictionaries.

3 REVIEWS AND CRITICISM

A. Book Reviews and Literary Journalism

ARTS & LETTERS DAILY
http://www.cybereditions.com/aldaily

Seeing the Web as a "typical Australian goldfield, with vast mountains of low-grade ore," this site strives "to pan and select from among the most intellectually stimulating sites on the Internet." Includes daily links to essays, book reviews, interviews, obituaries, and news in a wide range of online publications, as well as a directory of sites for newspapers, news services, journals, magazines, e-zines, radio news, and columnists. Strong coverage of literature, as well as of language, aesthetics, history, philosophy, criticism, and culture.

THE ATLANTIC ONLINE
http://www.theatlantic.com/

The online edition of *The Atlantic Monthly*, the distinguished "journal of literature, politics, science, and the arts," founded in 1857. Includes the online journal "Atlantic Unbound," extending the print magazine's coverage. An online archive includes nearly all articles published in the magazine since November 1995, as well as a growing selection of articles dating back to the *Atlantic*'s earliest issues.

BOOK REVIEW DIGEST**
http://www.hwwilson.com/databases/brdig.cfm

The online version of H. W. Wilson's *Book Review Digest*, a familiar presence in libraries since 1905, "provides excerpts from and citations to reviews of current adult and juvenile fiction and non-fiction." Abstracts of reviews of more than 7,000 English-language books published in more than 100 periodicals are added each year to a database extending back to 1983. By subscription; check with your local library.

BOOKSONLINE
http://www.booksonline.co.uk

"The home of London *Telegraph* book resources—book reviews, articles and information." Contains reviews and other book-related articles published online since August 1996.

THE BOSTON REVIEW
http://www-polisci.mit.edu/BostonReview

A bimonthly "magazine of political, cultural, and literary ideas," with an excellent "Literary Links" page. Full-text online archives extend back to 1993.

THE CENTER FOR BOOK CULTURE

http://www.centerforbookculture.org

The Center for Book Culture is the publisher of the Dalkey Archive Press, which specializes in modern and contemporary fiction, poetry, and literary criticism/theory from around the world, with an emphasis on the sort of subversive writers who are usually ignored by the mainstream media and the academy, while also reprinting modernist masters such as Gertrude Stein, Flann O'Brien, and Raymond Queneau. The Center's website provides access to, among other things, the online edition of the Center's journal *CONTEXT*, which focuses on avantgarde and experimental writing, as well as a large archive of superb author interviews, ranging from Kathy Acker to Marguerite Yourcenar.

THE LONDON REVIEW OF BOOKS

http://www.lrb.co.uk

Founded in 1979, the bimonthly *London Review of Books* is, in its own words, "dedicated to carrying on the tradition of the English essay." Its website features sample articles, a full listing of contents, and the letters column from the current print issue, as well as an extensive full-text archive that can be browsed by subject or by reviewer.

THE NEW REPUBLIC

http://thenewrepublic.com

A distinguished political and cultural weekly journal that has long featured outstanding coverage of literature. The online edition publishes selections from the current print issue, and includes an archive dating back to 1996, as well as a selection of "Classic reviews" from the last 85 years. Also features online-only content.

THE NEW YORKER

http://www.newyorker.com/

The online version of the celebrated weekly of culture and commentary, featuring selections from the current print issue, "On-Line Only" content, and "From the Archive," which reprints articles and cartoons from vintage issues of the magazine.

THE NEW YORK REVIEW OF BOOKS

http://www.nybooks.com/nyrev/

The online version of *The New York Review of Books* offers the full text of selected pieces published in the print edition, with an archive that currently goes back to November 1996. A fully searchable index provides access to full citations of articles going back to the *NYRB*'s founding in 1963.

THE NEW YORK TIMES: BOOKS

http://www.nytimes.com/books/home/

The homepage of the Books section of the online edition of *The New York Times* provides free, full-text access to all reviews and other literary features published in the *Times* since 1980. Registration (free) is required.

PROQUEST DIRECT**

http://www.umi.com:8090/proquest/

ProQuest Direct provides access to a large collection of articles, book reviews, and essays in newspapers, popular magazines, and scholarly journals, with many of the articles available in full-text, full-image versions. This subscription service, which covers more than 8,000 publications, is available to library patrons (at no cost) at many academic and local public libraries.

SALON.COM: BOOKS

http://www.salon.com/books/index.html

Featured in this section of *Salon* are daily book reviews; interviews with writers; the "Book Bag" (a weekly list of must-reads recommended by celebrated authors); and the *Salon.com* Book Awards, an annual event honoring the staff's "favorite books of fiction and nonfiction" published during the year.

THE TIMES LITERARY SUPPLEMENT**

http://www.the-tls.co.uk/

Offers free excerpts from the current issue's reviews and features. The site also features an online archive extending back to 1994, which can be accessed only by subscribers to the paper edition of this authoritative literary weekly; check with your local library.

TLS Centenary Archive**

http://www.tls.psmedia.com/

This fully searchable archive offers facsimile images of all reviews and articles published in the *Times Literary Supplement* between the years 1902 and 1990. By subscription; check with your local library.

B. Scholarly Criticism

Literature Online**

http://chadwyck.com

Literature Online (for complete description, see **Section 2** above) includes the *Annual Bibliography of English Language & Literature* (*ABELL*), containing more than 755,000 records covering periodical articles, critical editions of literary works, book reviews, collections of essays, and doctoral dissertations published anywhere in the world from 1920 on. By subscription; check with your local library

Literature Resource Center**

http://www.galenet.com/

Gale's Literature Resource Center (for a fuller description, see **Section 2** above) contains extensive full-text, excerpted, and commissioned works of literary criticism from the publisher's Literature Criticism Series and other sources. Includes contemporary reviews and criticism of 19th- and early 20th-century authors. By subscription; check with your local library.

MLA International Bibliography**

http://www.mla.org/publications/bibliography.htm

The bibliography of the Modern Language Association provides a classified listing and subject index for books and articles published on modern languages, literatures, folklore, and linguistics, including works on film, radio, television, and theater, and indexes more than 50,000 books and articles a year, selected from more than 4,000 journals. Available by subscription; check with your local library.

Online Literary Criticism Collection

http://www.ipl.org/ref/litcrit

From the Internet Public Library: a collection of more than 4,500 critical and biographical websites about authors and their works that can be browsed by author, by title, or by nationality and literary period. A good starting point; for other sources, see the IPL's Online Literary Criticism Guide: http://www.ipl.org/ref/litcrit/guide.html.

Project MUSE: Scholarly Journals Online**

http://muse.jhu.edu/

Launched in 1995 at Johns Hopkins University, *Project Muse* offers more than a hundred scholarly journals online in full text, covering the fields of "literature and criticism, history, the visual and performing arts, cultural studies, education, political science, gender studies, and many others." Libraries and educational institutions may subscribe to selected journals or the entire package; check with your local library. A list of the journals available on *Project Muse*, with descriptions and a search feature, is freely available online.

C. Trade Journals

BookWire

http://www.bookwire.com/

R. R. Bowker's *BookWire* is "*the* comprehensive online portal into the book industry. Our mission is to provide librarians, publishers, booksellers, authors, and general book enthusiasts with the resources they need." A book-industry website with reviews, literary information, publishing news, and links to a large number of industry-related sites.

Publishers Weekly

http://www.publishersweekly.com/

The online version of the international news magazine for book publishing and bookselling. Features include news (U.S. and international), bestseller lists, interviews, children's books, forecasts, and "authors on the highway" (schedules of author appearances).

4 WEB-BASED MAGAZINES AND E-ZINES

THE ALT-X ONLINE PUBLISHING NETWORK

http://www.altx.com

A webzine "where the digerati meet the literati," founded in 1993. The publishers seek "to challenge both the art and literary publishing establishments by supporting some of the most iconoclastic voices and visions in the international art world." Features include AltX Imprints and the Electronic Book Review, "a review forum on new media art & theory."

ARRAS: NEW POETRY AND POETICS

http://www.arras.net/

This web adjunct of the print 'zine *Arras* presents innovative, electronically active visual poetry, as well as links to cyberpoetry sites and new poetry and criticism.

THE BARCELONA REVIEW: INTERNATIONAL REVIEW OF LITERARY FICTION

http://www.BarcelonaReview.com

Based in Barcelona (Spain), with contributions in English, Spanish, Catalan, and French. Includes fiction, poetry, plays, interviews, and book reviews, all content "unique to the Net." The editors favor "especially authors well known within their own country or region, but not necessarily internationally…everything from cyberpunk to ultra-postmodern." Includes excellent links to other literary reviews.

JACKET MAGAZINE

http://www.jacket.zip.com.au/index.html

A free Internet review of new writing published three or four times a year from Sydney by Australian poet John Tranter as a showcase for "lively" writing. Publishes poetry, prose, interviews, reviews, and articles, including original material and writing excerpted from "hard-to-get books and magazines."

TIMOTHY MCSWEENEY'S INTERNET TENDENCY

http://www.mcsweeneys.net

An online literary journal from the American writer Dave Eggers. "Timothy McSweeney's Internet Tendency is an offshoot of Timothy McSweeney's Quarterly Concern, a journal created by nervous people in relative obscurity, and published four times a year."

WEB DEL SOL

http://webdelsol.com

A site promoting collaboration in new media, hypertext, photography, and the literary arts, *Web Del Sol* is neither simply a literary publication nor an Internet portal, but rather, by its own description, "a literary arts new media complex which pushes the envelope of both definitions." Among its many ventures, *Web Del Sol* publishes original material (site reviews, book reviews, news, essays, and new poetry and fiction), hosts more than 20 literary arts periodicals, and promotes "superlative discoveries" from the World Wide Web, in addition to providing various multimedia and interactive features, including an online poetry workshop.

5 LITERARY WORKS ON THE WEB

AFRICAN AMERICAN WOMEN WRITERS OF THE NINETEENTH CENTURY

http://digital.nypl.org/schomburg/writers_aa19/toc.html

From The New York Public Library's Schomburg Center for Research in Black Culture, a searchable collection of some 52 published works, with biographies of the writers and digital images of the original volumes' title pages, bindings, and illustrations.

THE AMERICAN VERSE PROJECT

http://www.hti.umich.edu/a/amverse/

Includes approximately 170 volumes of American poetry published before 1920, with another 240 announced as forthcoming. A collaborative project between the University of Michigan Humanities Text Initiative (HTI) and the University of Michigan Press.

BARTLEBY.COM

http://www.bartleby.com/

Besides literary reference books (see **Section 2** above), this site offers the full text of thousands of poems and hundreds of other works of literature from a wide range of authors, including the 1914 Oxford edition of the *Complete Works of William Shakespeare* and many volumes of the Harvard Classics and the Harvard Classics Shelf of Fiction.

BIBLIOMANIA

http://www.bibliomania.com/

A popular site offering easily accessible reading editions of around 800 classic works of fiction, drama, and poetry. Also offers study guides, reference works, and an online literary magazine, *Well Red.*

ELECTRONIC POETRY CENTER

http://www.epc.buffalo.edu/

Founded in 1994 at the State University of New York at Buffalo, the EPC aims "to make a wide range of resources centered on contemporary experimental and formally innovative poetries," including new media works and e-poetry, an "immediate actuality." Features a "Library of Author Home Pages at the EPC" (for writers in the "hypertextual electronic media"), extensive links to other sites of interest, and information on the Poetics Program at SUNY–Buffalo.

ELECTRONIC TEXT CENTER, UNIVERSITY OF VIRGINIA LIBRARY

http://etext.lib.virginia.edu

The Electronic Text Center currently holds approximately 51,000 on- and off-line humanities texts in 12 languages, with more than 350,000 related images. Of these, several thousand are freely available over the Internet, or can be downloaded as free e-books.

INTERNET SHAKESPEARE EDITIONS

http://web.uvic.ca/shakespeare/index.html

Internet Shakespeare Editions makes scholarly, fully annotated texts of Shakespeare's plays available in a form "native to the medium of the Internet," capitalizing in particular on the hypertext capabilities of the World Wide Web to create a "new kind of edition."

MAJOR AUTHORS ONLINE**

http://www.majorauthors.psmedia.com/index.html

Covering the Brontës, Miguel de Cervantes (in Spanish and English), Samuel Johnson, Walt Whitman, and Virginia Woolf, this resource provides a comprehensive archive of their complete works, as well as digital images of manuscripts, portraits, and first editions. Includes digital images of important holdings from the rare book and manuscript collections of The New York Public Library. A subscription-based service from Primary Source Media; check with your local library.

THE ON-LINE BOOKS PAGE

http://digital.library.upenn.edu/books/

Provides links to "legitimately available" full-text editions of more than 13,000 books in English, all at no charge. Search or browse by author, title, or subject; literary works are in class P (language and literature).

ONLINE TEXTS COLLECTION FROM THE INTERNET PUBLIC LIBRARY

http://www.ipl.org/reading/books

Contains links to more than 15,000 online texts, which can be browsed by author, title, or Dewey Decimal Classification (select class 800, literature and rhetoric).

THE PERSEUS DIGITAL LIBRARY

http://www.perseus.tufts.edu

An "evolving digital library" containing textual and visual materials illustrating the ancient Greek and Roman worlds. Includes the full texts of many significant works in Greek and

Latin and in English translation, as well as many important secondary works. Established in 1987; recently the site's coverage has expanded into other periods, including the English Renaissance.

POEM FINDER**

http://www.poemfinder.com/

International in scope, covering poetry from antiquity to the present, and continually updated, this database offers 750,000 indexed poems and 70,000 full-text poems. Provides coverage of "all well-known anthologized poems" and the complete works of many poets. By subscription; check with your local library.

POETS' CORNER

http://geocities.com/~spanoudi/poems/index.html

Begun in 1995 and maintained by three poetry enthusiasts, the site currently contains around 6,000 poems by nearly 700 authors, covering public domain English-language poetry of all periods, along with some foreign-language poems in translation. Edition information is seldom provided, but this is a good place to quickly find a reading text of a well-known poem.

PROJECT GUTENBERG

http://promo.net/pg/

Begun in 1972, and thus long predating the Internet, this project now includes more than 3,300 public domain e-texts—mostly classic works of literature and reference books. Originally presented only in "plain vanilla ASCII," without formatting, some texts have now been converted to XHTML and XML.

VICTORIAN WOMEN WRITERS PROJECT

http://www.indiana.edu/%7Eletrs/vwwp/index.html

Indiana University's in-progress full-text library of works by British women writers of the 19th century includes anthologies, novels, political pamphlets, poetry, and verse drama, and currently features nearly 200 works by more than 40 authors. Many of these writers are now little-known, and their works were previously available only at large research and specialized libraries.

6 BOOK BUYING, BROWSING, AND SELECTING

AMAZON.COM

http://www.amazon.com

The well-known online book retailer, which now sells many other types of merchandise. Its Books section includes a "bargain book outlet" and subsections for e-books and rare and used books. For those in search of foreign-language imprints, Amazon has affiliates in the United Kingdom, Germany, Japan, and France.

BARNES&NOBLE.COM

www.barnesandnoble.com

The online wing of the large bricks-and-mortar bookseller.

BOOKFINDER.COM

http://www.bookfinder.com/

"Connects readers to over 20,000 booksellers from around the world." This search engine for new and used books combines searches of the listings of such retailers as amazon.com and barnesandnoble.com (bn.com), with searches of several used and rare books dealers, including Advanced Book Exchange, Alibris, Antiqbook, Bibliofind, Biblion, BookAvenue.com, Half.com, JustBooks, Powell's Books, and TomFolio.com.

BOOKSENSE.COM

http://www.booksense.com

Independent bookstores.

NON-ENGLISH ONLINE BOOKSELLERS

http://www.bookwire.com/booksellers/Non-English-Booksellers.html

An extensive listing, *from BookWire* (see **Section 3C** above).

THE READER'S CATALOG (VIA BARNESANDNOBLE.COM)

http://shop.barnesandnoble.com/rdrscat/index.asp

This online edition of *The Reader's Catalog*, the second print edition of which was published in 1997, includes sections on international literatures. From the "editors and friends" of *The New York Review of Books*, it provides a "guided tour through the collective and continuously updated 'Dream Library' of dozens of noted writers, scholars and critics."

7 ONLINE LIBRARY CATALOGS

RLG UNION CATALOG VIA EUREKA**

http://www.rlg.org/eureka.html

RLG (the Research Libraries Group) is a consortium of more than 160 universities, national libraries, and other research institutions. Its catalog, containing more than 100 million catalog records for books, manuscripts, recordings, films, videotapes, newspapers, magazines, and other materials held by member institutions, is available by subscription through RLG's Eureka search service. Check with your local library.

WORLDCAT DATABASE, THE OCLC ONLINE UNION CATALOG**

http://www.oclc.org/firstsearch/databases/details/dbinformation_WorldCat.html

Contains catalog records for more than 41 million books, newspapers and magazines, and other items held by OCLC member libraries. OCLC (Online Computer Library Center, Inc.) is a global library cooperative serving nearly 40,000 libraries in 76 countries and territories—the world's largest library consortium. Access to WorldCat is available to all OCLC members, and to others by subscription; check with your local library.

8 LITERARY ORGANIZATIONS AND AWARDS

THE ACADEMY OF AMERICAN POETS

http://www.poets.org/index.cfm

Founded in 1934 "to support American poets at all stages of their careers and to foster the appreciation of contemporary poetry." Its website provides extensive links, a directory of members, information on awards and prizes, a New York City and national poetry calendar, a poetry forum, a catalog of the Academy's audio archive (with samples), and the text of around a thousand poems, including many by contemporary poets.

THE AUTHORS GUILD

http://www.authorsguild.org/

The nation's largest society of published authors, The Authors Guild is a leading advocate for fair compensation, free speech, and copyright protection. The Guild's website offers news, press releases, information on membership, and features on contract advice, legal searches, domain name registration, and more, as well as *Backinprint.com*, the Guild's online bookstore featuring copies of out-of-print books made available by its authors.

ELECTRONIC POETRY CENTER

http://www.epc.buffalo.edu/

For a complete description of the EPC, see **Section 5** above.

NATIONAL BOOK AWARDS

http://www.publishersweekly.com/NBF/docs/awards.html

A complete list of winners since the prizes were first awarded in 1950, and the acceptance speeches of selected winners.

THE NOBEL PRIZE IN LITERATURE (FROM THE NOBEL e-MUSEUM)

http://www.nobel.se/literature/index.html

Includes biographies and portraits of the laureates, and, for many of the winners, press releases, interviews, video archives, and texts of their Nobel Lectures.

PEN AMERICAN CENTER

http://www.pen.org

According to its website, "PEN American Center, the largest of nearly 130 centers worldwide that make up International PEN, is a membership association of prominent literary writers and editors that seeks to defend freedom of expression wherever it may be threatened, and works to promote and encourage the recognition and reading of contemporary literature." The website offers information on the PEN American Center's many activities, including its Prison Writing Program, the literary awards it grants, and its Freedom-to-Write project, which works to resist censorship worldwide.

THE POETRY PROJECT AT ST. MARK'S CHURCH

http://www.poetryproject.com/

Founded in New York City's East Village in 1966 as a forum and resource center for experimental and innovative poets, writers, artists, and performers whose work proposes "fresh aesthetic, cultural, philosophical and political approaches to contemporary society." The Project's website includes news and announcements, a calendar of events, excerpts from the Project's publications, archives, and other features, as well as links.

POETS & WRITERS ONLINE

http://www.pw.org

Poets & Writers is an organization that helps authors find "career-related information, outlets for their work, opportunities for professional advancement and community with other writers." The site offers "resources for creative writers," including an abbreviated version of the *Directory of American Poets and Fiction Writers*; selections from the group's journal, *Poets & Writers Magazine*; Poets & Writers Out Loud (audio interviews, readings, and advice); an online forum; and literary news and links.

THE PULITZER PRIZES

http://www.pulitzer.org/index.html

Provides a complete list of all Pulitzer Prize winners from 1917 to the present, and, beginning with the 1995 prizes, the full texts, photographs, and cartoons of all journalism award winners.

SHARP WEB

http://www.indiana.edu/~sharp/

Home page for SHARP (Society of the History of Authorship, Reading and Publishing), with links to sites relating to the history of books and publishing, including publishers' records and histories, online resources and projects, scholarly societies, exhibitions, announcements, and journals.

THE WATCH (WRITERS, ARTISTS, AND THEIR COPYRIGHT HOLDERS) FILE

http://www.hrc.utexas.edu/watch/watch.html

Provides the names and addresses of copyright holders or contact persons for authors and artists whose archives are housed in libraries and archives in North America and the United Kingdom for those seeking to publish text or images that are under copyright protection.

Libraries with Significant Literary Holdings

THE BEINECKE RARE BOOK AND MANUSCRIPT LIBRARY

121 Wall Street
New Haven, CT 06511
http://www.library.yale.edu:80/beinecke/

The Beinecke is Yale University's principal repository for literary papers, manuscripts, and rare books. Important collections are held in American and German literature, Western Americana, and English literary manuscripts (the Osborn Collection). Among the British and American authors represented in depth are Charles Dickens, James Weldon Johnson, Samuel Johnson, James Joyce, Eugene O'Neill, Ezra Pound, Gertrude Stein, Rebecca West, and Thornton Wilder.

BIBLIOTHÈQUE NATIONALE DE FRANCE

Site François-Mitterrand
Quai François-Mauriac
75706 Paris Cedex 13
France
http://www.bnf.fr/site_bnf_eng/index.html

The vast holdings of the Bibliothèque Nationale de France (BNF) include the manuscripts and archives of a large number of important French writers, including Victor Hugo, Gustave Flaubert, Émile Zola, Colette, and Georges Bataille. In addition, the collections include nearly 30,000 volumes of ancient Greek and Latin manuscripts and 10,000 medieval and Renaissance illuminated manuscripts. The website address provided above is for the English-language version of the BNF's website, providing access to the library's online catalogs; to Gallica 2000, a digital library containing multimedia documents from the Middle Ages to the early 20th century; and to many other features, including outstanding online exhibitions.

THE BRITISH LIBRARY (AT ST. PANCRAS)

96 Euston Road
London NW1 2DB
United Kingdom
http://www.bl.uk/

The British Library, the national library of the United Kingdom, has immense rare book and manuscript holdings, including the Early Printed Collections (books in English and Western European languages printed before 1851), publishers' and author archives, and important manuscripts in most European languages, from the 4th century B.C. to modern times, including unique manuscripts of the Anglo-Saxon *Beowulf*, the medieval *Sir Gawain and the Green Knight*, and Thomas Malory's *Le Morte d'Arthur*. Its website provides information about the library's collections and access to its catalogs, its online exhibitions, and its Digital Library Programme, as well as to various other online resources and services.

FOLGER SHAKESPEARE LIBRARY

201 East Capitol Street, SE
Washington, DC 20003-1094

http://www.folger.edu/

The Folger Shakespeare Library is home to the world's largest collection of Shakespeare's printed works, as well as to important collections of rare Renaissance books and manuscripts in all disciplines—history and politics, theology, exploration, law, literature, and the arts. Included in the Folger's holdings are over 280,000 books and manuscripts; 27,000 paintings, drawings, engravings, and prints; and musical instruments, costumes, and films.

THE HOUGHTON LIBRARY

Harvard Yard
Harvard University
Cambridge, MA 02138

http://www-hcl.harvard.edu/houghton/

The Houghton Library, the principal rare book and manuscript library of the Harvard College Library, houses collections that focus on the study of Western civilization, particularly European and American literature and history, with special concentrations in printing, graphic arts, and the theater. Literary highlights of the Houghton's collections include personal effects, manuscripts, rare editions, and other objects of interest from such authors as Emily Dickinson, John Keats, Edward Lear, Dante, Tennessee Williams, Goethe, Cervantes, and Lewis Carroll.

THE HUNTINGTON LIBRARY, ART COLLECTIONS, & BOTANICAL GARDEN

1151 Oxford Road
San Marino, CA 91108

http://www.huntington.org/

Highlights of the library's collections, which focus principally on rare books and manuscripts in the fields of British and American literature and history, include the Ellesmere manuscript of Chaucer's *The Canterbury Tales* (c. 1410)

and a major collection of early editions of Shakespeare's works.

THE LIBRARY OF CONGRESS

101 Independence Avenue, SE
Washington, DC 20540

http://www.loc.gov/

"The nation's oldest federal cultural institution," whose collections number more than 120 million items. Among the authors represented in its many special collections of rare editions and manuscripts are Washington Irving, Walt Whitman, Mark Twain, Rudyard Kipling, and Henry James. Its website provides access to the library's online exhibitions and to several versions of its catalog, to the Copyright Office, and to many other features, including excellent links pages and to *American Memory*, a digital library project documenting the nation's culture and history.

THE LILLY LIBRARY

Indiana University
1200 East Seventh Street
Bloomington, IN 47405-5500

http://www.indiana.edu/~liblilly/lillylibrary.html

The large collections (a half million books and pieces of sheet music, and more than 6.5 million manuscripts) of The Lilly Library, Indiana University's rare book and manuscript library, include important holdings of literary manuscripts and publishers' archives. The website features online exhibitions and other resources, including searchable indexes of the Lilly's manuscript and chapbook collections.

THE PIERPONT MORGAN LIBRARY

29 East 36th Street
New York, NY 10016

http://www.morganlibrary.org

One of the world's greatest collections of illuminated manuscripts, rare books, literary and historical manuscripts, Old Master drawings and prints, and music manuscripts and books.

THE NEWBERRY LIBRARY

60 West Walton Street
Chicago, IL 60610-3305
http://www.newberry.org

An independent research library, focusing on the humanities, with important rare book and manuscript holdings in American, British, French, and Italian history and literature, as well as other subject areas.

THE NEW YORK PUBLIC LIBRARY

Fifth Avenue and 42nd Street
New York, NY 10018-2788
http://www.nypl.org

Comprising four research centers in Manhattan and 85 circulating branch libraries in the Bronx, Manhattan, and Staten Island, The New York Public Library has vast literary holdings. Notable literary collections at its Humanities and Social Sciences Library at Fifth Avenue and 42nd Street include:

■ The Henry W. and Albert A. Berg Collection of English and American Literature, which holds approximately 20,000 printed items and 50,000 manuscripts, including the archives of Vladimir Nabokov, Virginia Woolf, and W. H. Auden

■ The Carl H. Pforzheimer Collection of Shelley and His Circle, a leading repository for the study of English Romanticism, containing some 25,000 books, manuscripts, letters, and other objects

■ The Manuscripts and Archives Division, which holds the papers of many significant authors, organizations, and publishers, including those of Truman Capote, Herman Melville, H. L. Mencken, The Drama League of America, Farrar, Straus & Giroux, Inc., and *The New Yorker*

Important literary holdings in NYPL's other research centers include those in The New York Public Library for the Performing Arts and the Schomburg Center for Research in Black Culture. NYPL's website provides information about its collections, as well as access to its catalogs and online exhibitions, and to the growing NYPL Digital Library collection.

THE HARRY RANSOM HUMANITIES RESEARCH CENTER

The University of Texas at Austin
NE corner of 21st Street and Guadalupe Street
Austin, TX 78713-7219
http://www.hrc.utexas.edu/

The Ransom Center's holdings include more than one million printed volumes, from incunabula to the 20th century, and more than 30 million manuscripts. Some collection strengths are 19th-century English fiction, 20th-century English and American literature, the archives of publishers and literary agents, modern French literature, theater arts, and early English literature (the Pforzheimer Library of Early English Literature).

THE ROSENBACH MUSEUM & LIBRARY

2010 DeLancey Place
Philadelphia, PA 19103
http://www.rosenbach.org

One of America's greatest collections of fine art, antiques, and rare books and manuscripts, whose literary treasures include original manuscripts of Charles Dickens's *The Pickwick Papers*, James Joyce's *Ulysses*, and Joseph Conrad's *Lord Jim*.

Literary Factbooks and Handbooks

1 ALLUSIONS

Allusions: Cultural, Literary, Biblical, and Historical: A Thematic Dictionary. 2nd ed. Laurence Urdang and Frederick G. Ruffner, Jr., eds. Detroit: Gale, 1986.

Bloomsbury Dictionary of Phrase & Allusion. Nigel Rees. London: Bloomsbury, 1991.

Brewer's Dictionary of Phrase & Fable. Revised by Adrian Room. London: Cassell, 1999.

Common Knowledge: A Reader's Guide to Literary Allusions. David Grote. New York: Greenwood Press, 1987.

A Dictionary of Biblical Allusions in English Literature. New York: Holt, Rinehart and Winston, 1965.

Dictionary of Classical Reference in English Poetry. Eric Smith. Totowa, N.J.: Barnes & Noble, 1984.

Dictionary of Historical Allusions & Eponyms. Dorothy Auchter. Santa Barbara, Calif.: ABC-CLIO, 1998.

The Facts on File Dictionary of Classical, Biblical, and Literary Allusions. Abraham Harold Lass, David Kiremidjian, and Ruth M. Goldstein. New York: Facts on File, 1987.

The Facts on File Dictionary of 20th-Century Allusions from 1000 to 2000 A.D. Sylvia Cole and Abraham Harold Lass. New York: Facts on File, 1991.

1500 Literary References Everyone Should Know. Lloyd T. Grosse and Alen Lyster. New York: Arco, 1983.

Grand Allusions: A Lively Guide to Those Expressions, Terms, and References You Ought to Know But Might Not. Elizabeth Webber and Mike Feinsilber. Washington, D.C.: Farragut, 1990.

2 CHARACTERS

Black Plots and Black Characters: A Handbook for Afro-American Literature. Robert L. Southgate. Syracuse, N.Y.: Gaylord Professional Publications, 1979.

Characters in 19th-Century Literature. Kelly King Howes. Detroit: Gale, 1993.

Characters in 20th-Century Literature. Book I: Laurie Lanzen Harris, ed. Detroit: Gale, 1990. Book II: Kelly King Howes. Detroit: Gale, 1995.

Cyclopedia of Literary Characters. Rev. ed.; A. J. Sobczak, ed. 5 vols. Pasadena, Calif.: Salem Press, 1998.

Dictionary of American Literary Characters. Benjamin Franklin V, ed. New York: Facts on File, 1990.

Dictionary of British Literary Characters: 18th- and 19th-Century Novels. John R. Greenfield, ed. New York: Facts on File, 1993.

Dictionary of British Literary Characters: 20th-Century Novels. John R. Greenfield, ed. New York: Facts on File, 1994.

Dictionary of Fictional Characters. Martin Seymour-Smith. Boston: The Writer, 1992.

Dictionary of Real People and Places in Fiction. M. C. Rintoul. New York: Routledge, 1993.

Imaginary People: A Who's Who of Fictional Characters from the Eighteenth Century to the Present Day. David Pringle. Brookfield, Vt.: Ashgate Publishing, 1996.

Larousse Dictionary of Literary Characters. Rosemary Goring, ed. New York: Larousse, 1994.

Major Characters in American Fiction. Jack Salzman and Pamela Wilkinson, eds. New York: Henry Holt, 1994.

The Originals: An A–Z of Fiction's Real-Life Characters. William Amos. Boston: Little, Brown, 1985.

Trouble Is Their Business: Private Eyes in Fiction, Film, and Television, 1927–1988. John Conquest. New York: Garland, 1990.

The Vampire Gallery: A Who's Who of the Undead. J. Gordon Melton. Detroit: Visible Ink, 1998.

Who Was Really Who in Fiction. Alan Norman Bold and Robert Giddings. Burnt Mill, Harlow, Essex, England: Longman, 1987.

3 CHRONOLOGIES

Almanac of British and American Literature. John O. Stark. Littleton, Colo.: Libraries Unlimited, 1979.

Annals of American Literature, 1602–1983. Richard M. Ludwig and Clifford A. Nault, eds. New York: Oxford University Press, 1986.

Annals of English Literature, 1475–1950: The Principal Publications of Each Year Together with an Alphabetical Index of Authors and Their Works. 2nd ed. Oxford: Clarendon Press, 1961.

Calendar of Literary Facts: A Daily and Yearly Guide to Noteworthy Events in World Literature from 1450 to the Present. Samuel J. Rogal. Detroit: Gale, 1991.

A Chronological Outline of American Literature. Samuel J. Rogal. New York: Greenwood Press, 1987.

A Concise Chronology of English Literature. P. J. Smallwood, comp. Totowa, N.J.: Barnes & Noble, 1983.

4 DIRECTORIES

Directory of Literary Magazines. Prepared by the Coordinating Council of Literary Magazines. New York: The Council, 1984–.

Literary Market Place: LMP. New York: R. R. Bowker, 1988–. Annual.

MLA Directory of Scholarly Presses in Language and Literature. New York: Modern Language Association of America, 1991–. Annual.

Writers' and Artists' Yearbook. London: A. & C. Black, 1906–. Annual.

The Writer's Handbook. Boston: The Writer, Inc., 1954–. Annual. "Articles...were, for the most part, originally published in the *Writer*."

The Writer's Market. Cincinnati: F & W Publications, 1922–. Annual.

5 PLACES

American Author Houses, Museums, Memorials, and Libraries: A State-by-State Guide. Shirley Hoover Biggers. Jefferson, N.C.: McFarland, 2000.

An Atlas of English Literature. Clement Tyson Goode and Edgar Finley Shannon. 1925. Reprint, Norwood, Pa.: Norwood Editions, 1976.

The Atlas of Literature. Malcolm Bradbury, general editor. New York: Stewart, Tabori & Chang, 1996.

Atlas of the European Novel, 1800–1900. Franco Moretti. New York: Verso, 1998.

The Booklover's Guide to New Orleans. Susan Larson; with additional research by Kevin McCaffrey. Baton Rouge: Louisiana State University Press, 1999.

The Dictionary of Imaginary Places. Alberto Manguel and Gianni Guadalupi. Illustrated by

Graham Greenfield; with additional illustrations by Eric Beddows; maps and charts by James Cook. New York: Harcourt Brace, 2000.

Florence: A Literary Companion. Francis King. London: J. Murray, 1991.

Greece: A Literary Companion. Martin Garrett. London: J. Murray, 1994.

A Literary Atlas & Gazetteer of the British Isles. Michael Hardwick; cartography by Alan G. Hodgkiss. Detroit: Gale, 1973.

Literary Cafés of Paris. Noël Riley Fitch. Washington, D.C.: Starrhill Press, 1989.

A Literary Gazetteer of England. Lois H. Fisher. New York: McGraw-Hill, 1980.

Literary Landscapes: Walking Tours in Great Britain and Ireland. L. N. Franco. New York: George Braziller Publisher, 1998.

Literary New York: A History and Guide. Susan Edmiston and Linda D. Cirino. Salt Lake City: Peregrine Smith Books, 1991.

Literary Russia: A Guide. Anna Benn and Rosamund Bartlett. London: Picador, 1997.

Mystery Reader's Walking Guide, New York. Alzina Stone Dale. Lincolnwood, Ill.: Passport Books, 1993.

New York Literary Lights. William Corbett. Saint Paul, Minn.: Graywolf Press, 1998.

The Oxford Illustrated Literary Guide to Canada. A. F. Moritz and Theresa Moritz. New York: Oxford University Press, 1987.

The Oxford Illustrated Literary Guide to Great Britain and Ireland. 2nd ed. Dorothy Eagle and Meic Stephens, eds. New York: Oxford University Press, 1992.

The Oxford Illustrated Literary Guide to the United States. Eugene H. Ehrlich and Gorton Carruth. New York: Oxford University Press, 1982.

The Oxford Literary Guide to Australia. Rev. ed. Peter Pierce, general editor. Melbourne; Oxford: Oxford University Press, 1993.

Rome: A Literary Companion. John Varriano. London: J. Murray, 1991.

Scotland: A Literary Guide. Alan Norman Bold. London: Routledge, 1989.

The Smile of Apollo: A Literary Companion to Greek Travel. Patrick Anderson. London: Chatto & Windus, 1964.

Spain: A Literary Companion. Jimmy Burns. London: J. Murray, 1994.

Walks in Hemingway's Paris: A Guide to Paris for the Literary Traveler. Noël Riley Fitch. New York: St. Martin's Press, 1990.

Wordsworth and the Lake District: A Guide to the Poems and Their Places. David McCracken. Oxford: Oxford University Press, 1984.

6 PLOTS

Black Plots and Black Characters: A Handbook for Afro-American Literature. Robert L. Southgate. Syracuse, N.Y.: Gaylord Professional Publications, 1979.

Masterplots: 1,801 Plot Stories and Critical Evaluations of the World's Finest Literature. Rev. 2nd ed. Frank N. Magill, ed. Pasadena, Calif.: Salem Press, 1996. This 12-volume set is only one of a large series of reference books covering plots in world literature published by Salem Press. All provide critical analyses, plot summaries, and details on the forms, periods, principal characters, and themes of the most popular works in the history of literature. Other titles in the *Masterplots* series cover a wide range of genres (fiction, poetry, drama, the short story, etc.), as well as specific areas of study (women's literature, African-American literature, European fiction, etc.).

Masterplots Complete CD-ROM. Frank N. Magill et al., eds. Pasadena, Calif.: Salem Press, 2000. Available at many academic libraries, as well as at larger public libraries systems, this CD-ROM gathers 21 multivolume *Masterplots* reference book sets, the five-volume *Cyclopedia of World Authors*, and more.

Plot Summary Index. 2nd ed., rev. and enl. by Carol Koehmstedt Kolar. Metuchen, N.J.: Scarecrow Press, 1981.

7 PSEUDONYMS, ETC.

Dictionary of Literary Pseudonyms: A Selection of Popular Modern Writers in English. Frank Atkinson. Chicago: American Library Association, 1986.

A Dictionary of Literary Pseudonyms in the English Language. 2nd ed. T. J. Carty. London: Mansell; Chicago: Fitzroy Dearborn, 2000.

Pseudonyms and Nicknames Dictionary: A Guide to 80,000 Aliases, Appellations, Assumed Names.... 3rd ed. Jennifer Mossman, ed. 2 vols. Detroit: Gale, 1987, and *New Pseudonyms and Nicknames: Supplement to the Third Edition of Pseudonyms and Nicknames Dictionary....* Jennifer Mossman, ed. Detroit: Gale, 1988.

8 QUOTATIONS

Bloomsbury Dictionary of Dedications. Adrian Room. London: Bloomsbury, 1990.

Bloomsbury Dictionary of Quotations. 2nd ed. John Daintith et al., eds. London: Bloomsbury, 1991, and its companion volume *Thematic Dictionary of Quotations*. 3rd ed. Fran Alexander, John Daintith, and Anne Stibbs, eds. London: Bloomsbury, 1997.

Cassell Dictionary of Cynical Quotations. Jonathon Green, comp. London: Cassell, 1994.

The Columbia Granger's Dictionary of Poetry Quotations. Edith P. Hazen, ed. New York: Columbia University Press, 1992.

The Concise Dictionary of Foreign Quotations. Anthony Lejeune, ed. London: Stacey London, 1998.

A Dictionary of American Proverbs. Wolfgang Mieder, ed. New York: Oxford University Press, 1992.

The Dictionary of Biographical Quotation of British and American Subjects. Richard Kenin and Justin Wintle, eds. New York: Knopf, 1978.

Dictionary of Foreign Quotations. Robert Lewis Collison and Mary Collison. New York: Facts on File, 1980.

A Dictionary of Literary Quotations. Meic Stephens. New York: Routledge, 1990.

Familiar Quotations: A Collection of Passages, Phrases, and Proverbs Traced to Their Sources in Ancient and Modern Literature. 16th ed., rev. and enl. John Bartlett. Justin Kaplan, general editor. Boston: Little, Brown, 1992.

The Home Book of Quotations, Classical and Modern. 10th ed. Selected and arranged by Burton Stevenson. New York: Greenwich House, 1984.

Leo Rosten's Treasury of Jewish Quotations. New York: McGraw-Hill, 1972.

A New Dictionary of Quotations on Historical Principles from Ancient and Modern Sources. H. L. Mencken. New York: Knopf, 1942.

The New Penguin Dictionary of Quotations. J. M. Cohen and M. J. Cohen. New York: Viking, 1992.

The New Quotable Woman. Completely rev. and updated. Elaine Partnow, comp. and ed. New York: Facts on File, 1992.

The New York Public Library Book of Twentieth-Century American Quotations. Stephen Donadio, et al., eds. New York: Warner Books, 1992.

The Oxford Dictionary of English Proverbs. 3rd ed. Revised by F. P. Wilson. with an introduction by Joanna Wilson. Oxford: Clarendon Press, 1970.

The Oxford Dictionary of Literary Quotations. Peter Kemp, ed. New York: Oxford University Press, 1997.

The Oxford Dictionary of Twentieth Century Quotations. Elizabeth Knowles, ed. New York: Oxford University Press, 1998.

The Prentice-Hall Encyclopedia of World Proverbs: A Treasury of Wit and Wisdom Through the Ages. Wolfgang Mieder, comp. Englewood Cliffs, N.J.: Prentice-Hall, 1986.

Quotations in Black. Anita King, comp. and ed. Westport, Conn.: Greenwood Press, 1981.

The Quote Sleuth: A Manual for the Tracer of Lost Quotations. Anthony W. Shipps. Urbana: University of Illinois Press, 1990.

Random House Webster's Quotationary. Leonard Roy Frank, ed. New York: Random House, 1999.

Respectfully Quoted: A Dictionary of Quotations Requested from the Congressional Research Service. Suzy Platt, ed. Washington, D.C.: Library of Congress, 1989.

They Never Said It: A Book of Fake Quotes, Misquotes, and Misleading Attributions. Paul F. Boller, Jr., and John George. New York: Oxford University Press, 1989.

A Treasury of Jewish Quotations. Rev. ed. Joseph L. Baron, ed. New York: J. Aronson, 1985.

The Wisdom of the Novel: A Dictionary of Quotations. David Powell. New York: Garland, 1985.

9 STYLE MANUALS

The Chicago Manual of Style. 14th ed. Chicago: University of Chicago Press, 1993.

The Elements of Style. William Strunk, Jr. With revisions, an introduction, and a chapter on writing by E. B. White. Boston: Allyn and Bacon, 2000.

MLA Handbook for Writers of Research Papers. 5th ed. Joseph Gibaldi. New York: Modern Language Association of America, 1999.

MLA Style Manual and Guide to Scholarly Publishing. 2nd ed. Joseph Gibaldi. New York: Modern Language Association of America, 1998.

The New Fowler's Modern English Usage. H. W. Fowler. 3rd ed. Revised by R. W. Burchfield. New York: Oxford University Press, 2000.

The New York Public Library Writer's Guide to Style and Usage. New York: HarperCollins, 1994.

10 TERMS

The Book of Literary Terms: The Genres of Fiction, Drama, Nonfiction, Literary Criticism, and Scholarship. Lewis Turco. Hanover, N.H.: University Press of New England, 1999.

The Cassell Dictionary of Literary and Language Terms. Christina Ruse and Marilyn Hopton. London: Cassell, 1992.

Critical Terms for Literary Study. 2nd ed. Frank Lentricchia and Thomas McLaughlin, eds. Chicago: University of Chicago Press, 1995.

Critical Terms for Science Fiction and Fantasy: A Glossary and Guide to Scholarship. Gary K. Wolfe. Westport, Conn.: Greenwood Press, 1986.

A Dictionary of Literary and Thematic Terms. Edward Quinn. New York: Facts on File, 1999.

A Dictionary of Literary Devices: Gradus, A–Z. Bernard Marie Dupriez. Translated and adapted by Albert W. Halsall. Toronto: University of Toronto Press, 1991.

A Dictionary of Literary Terms and Literary Theory. J. A. Cuddon. Revised by C. E. Preston. Malden, Mass.: Blackwell, 1998.

A Dictionary of Modern Critical Terms. Rev. and enl. ed. Roger Fowler, ed. New York: Routledge & Kegan Paul, 1987.

A Glossary of Literary Terms. 6th ed. M. H. Abrams. Fort Worth: Harcourt Brace Jovanovich College Publishers, 1993.

Literary Terms: A Dictionary. Karl E. Beckson. New York: Noonday Press, 1989.

Poetry Handbook: A Dictionary of Terms. 4th ed. Babette Deutsch. New York: Funk & Wagnalls, 1974.

11 THEMES AND MOTIFS

Dictionary of Literary Themes and Motifs. Jean-Charles Seigneuret, ed. 2 vols. New York: Greenwood Press, 1988.

Themes & Motifs in Western Literature: A Handbook. Horst S. Daemmrich and Ingrid Daemmrich. Tübingen, Germany: A. Francke, 1987.

Index

This index lists all main entries in the various sections of the book, including personal names (authors, critics, editors, publishers, thinkers, translators, biographers), titles of works (novels, plays, poems, stories, essays, periodicals), characters, terms, styles, movements, genres, and awards. Also included are the personal names and titles found in two chronologically organized sections, "Landmarks in Literary Censorship" and "Chronology of World Literature," and in the various essays and other diversions, which are listed by title at the end of the index. Page numbers in **boldface type** refer to main entries.

ESSAYS AND OTHER DIVERSIONS